HOW SHAKESPEARE PUT POLITICS ON THE STAGE

HOW
SHAKESPEARE
PUT POLITICS *on the* STAGE
POWER *and* SUCCESSION *in the* HISTORY PLAYS

PETER LAKE

YALE UNIVERSITY PRESS
NEW HAVEN AND LONDON

Published with assistance from the foundation established in memory of Oliver Baty Cunningham of the Class for 1917, Yale College.

For information about this and other Yale University Press publications, please contact:
U.S. Office: sales.press@yale.edu   yalebooks.com
Europe Office: sales@yaleup.co.uk   yalebooks.co.uk

Typeset in Minion Pro by IDSUK (DataConnection) Ltd
Printed in Great Britain by TJ International Ltd, Padstow, Cornwall

Library of Congress Cataloging-in-Publication Data

Names: Lake, Peter, author.
Title: How Shakespeare put politics on the stage : power and succession in
    the history plays / Peter Lake.
Description: New Haven : Yale University Press, 2016.
Identifiers: LCCN 2016017316 | ISBN 9780300222715 (hardback)
Subjects: LCSH: Shakespeare, William, 1564-1616—Histories. | Historical
    drama, English—History and criticism. | Literature and history. |
    Politics in literature. | BISAC: HISTORY / Europe / Great Britain. |
    LITERARY CRITICISM / Shakespeare. | HISTORY / Modern / 16th Century. |
    POLITICAL SCIENCE / History & Theory.
Classification: LCC PR2982 .L35 2016 | DDC 822.3/3—dc23
LC record available at https://lccn.loc.gov/2016017316

A catalogue record for this book is available from the British Library.

10 9 8 7 6 5 4 3 2 1

For San, the first person not to finish this book

Contents

Introduction and acknowledgements

I started to think about the basic questions that lie behind this book during performances of various Shakespeare plays that I saw during the 1990s. Crucial here were a production of *Troilus and Cressida* at the National Theatre and a student production in Cambridge of *King John*. While I was watching *Troilus*, it occurred to me that a play about an interminable war, the rationale for which no one on either side can coherently recall, and the justice of which no one can quite defend, might have had a certain resonance in 1601, when the play was apparently written. I also thought that a play that pits a faction of policy-makers, led by an old and rather dull man, Nestor, and his altogether more ruthless and astute younger protégé, Ulysses, against a faction of soldiers, a rivalry in which the soldiers view the policy wonks with contempt because of their weakness, and the policy wonks view the soldiers with contempt because of their stupidity, might have reminded its first audiences of the late Elizabethan political scene as it first polarised between the Essex faction and the Cecils, and then imploded into the debacle of the Essex rebellion

But what really got my attention was a short exchange from the first scene of Shakespeare's *King John*. As John and the king of France dispute John's claim to the throne of England, John proclaims 'our strong possession is our right for us', only to be corrected by his mother who reminds him, in a remarkable stage whisper, 'your strong possession much more than your right'. These few words seemed to me to have a dramatic impact on the meaning of the play. They show that both John and his mother know that he is a usurper and that his nephew, Arthur, is the true king and that much of the posing about 'right' that follows is empty non-sense. The exchange sets up the bastard's (and indeed the audience's) realisation that the politics of princes are the politics of what the bastard calls 'commodity'; a question of possession and of might, rather than of right. The play shows John struggling first to secure control of his nephew Arthur's person and then trying to have him killed. John is responsible for Arthur's death, but desperate to put the blame for that death on the person he has chosen to do the deed. All of which seemed to me to establish a quite striking parallel between King John and Queen Elizabeth, on the one hand, and Arthur and Mary, queen of Scots, on the other.[1]

That realisation in turn prompted a series of linked questions: if I noticed those parallels, might not members of an Elizabethan audience have noticed them as well? And if they did, where might the consequent chains of association and application of the action on stage to contemporary events and concerns have led them? And what might such processes of interpretation have to tell us about the relationship of the drama to its audience, and indeed to the politics of late Elizabethan England? And what might those sorts of connection tell us, in turn, about the nature of the late Elizabethan political scene, and the ways in which contemporaries actually thought about 'politics'?

These remained relatively idle thoughts of the sort that occur to you while watching a play. However, some years later, reading an entirely different set of texts convinced me that such questions might have real potential and indeed significance, as subjects of historical research and enquiry. I had become interested in a number of Catholic pamphlets that sought to describe the Elizabethan regime as a conspiracy of evil counsel, a functional tyranny, yet one without a tyrannical monarch at its heart. Reading perhaps the greatest of them, *Leicester's commonwealth*, I noticed how frequently and insistently that tract returned to certain incidents in recent and indeed remote English history as guides to what was happening now in England, to what would happen next, if something were not done now about the succession question and the conspiracy of evil counsel now surrounding the queen. The historical figures, incidents and reigns in question – those of Henry VI, Richard III, Richard II and Henry IV, and King John were precisely the ones about which Shakespeare and others were later to write plays. That struck me as interesting and I came to wonder how far we might read both plays and pamphlets as comments upon, indeed as ways to recuperate the contemporary understandings of, essentially the same historical conjuncture or set of issues.

In 2002 I was given a fellowship to work for a year at the Folger Shakespeare Library, on a project centred on the Roman Catholic tracts. A central task that year was to get to grips with Robert Parsons' great book *The conference about the next succession*. In so doing, I discovered how Parsons used the reigns of King John and of Richard II to show the English polity working precisely as he said it could and should; that is to say, as an elective monarchy with a residual power inherent in the commonwealth to resist or depose tyrants and to divert the course of hereditary succession in the name of the common or general good. While I was at the Folger, no doubt intoxicated by the plethora of Shakespeareana with which that wonderful institution surrounds its readers, I decided, more or less as an experiment, to write an account of Shakespeare's plays about King John and Richard II from the perspective provided by Parsons. One thing led to another, and I embarked on an attempt to read other of his history plays in a similar light.

While what I found upon doing this was all news to me, I rapidly discovered that it was news to no one else, and that it was virtually impossible for me at least to say much of anything very novel about Shakespeare. However, I also formed the impression, which I retain, that it might be possible to use some of Shakespeare's plays, read in conjunction with my Catholic texts and other such materials, as a way to something interesting and important about the politics and political culture of the 1590s.

Initially, I envisioned a book that would encompass a full-scale analysis of the tracts and the plays, all integrated into something like a political narrative. Very rapidly, however, I came to realise that such a project could not be coherently encompassed within one volume, however capacious. So what had started out as one book became two, and over the next decade or more, I proceeded to work on the two in tandem. This was not always a conscious choice. In 2006–7 I was on a fellowship at the Huntington, ostensibly to finish a book on Shakespeare's history plays, but found myself spending a good part of the second half of that year working on the Catholic project, diverted thereto by, amongst other things, a lunch time talk on Parsons' *Conference* by Paulina Kewes and a brilliant article by Alex Gajda on *The state of Christendom*.

This meant that neither project got finished as quickly as, at various points, I intended, or indeed as I told a number of grant-giving bodies, the Folger and the Huntington, and indeed the Guggenheim, amongst them, to all of whom I apologise, and whom I thank for their support, which is now (at long last) bearing fruit with the publication of this book. Initially I had intended to finish the Shakespeare book first, but the crucial stimulus to get the Catholic materials in shape came with an invitation to give the Ford lectures in 2011, an expanded version of which has now been published by OUP under the title *Bad Queen Bess? Libels, secret histories and the politics of publicity in the reign of Queen Elizabeth I*. Getting that done brought the Shakespeare material into sharper focus and enables me now to cite that book here rather than to recapitulate at length the materials contained therein.

The other 'delay' proceeded from the need to read my way into the vast body of literary criticism that has been devoted to these plays. Initially I had hoped to integrate the plays into an essentially historical analysis and thus escape the duty of engaging head on with the critical literature. Not because I doubted its value, but because I doubted my ability to come to terms effectively with so vast and sophisticated a body of writing. While I still doubt my capacities in that regard, the more seriously I engaged with the plays the more deeply I had to read in the critical literature. And so I embarked upon what amounted to a series of graduate courses, self-taught by someone who did not know what he was talking about for the benefit of someone else who knew even less. The somewhat inadequate results are distributed throughout the text and notes of this book. As the reader will see, I have read promiscuously across different styles and moments of literary criticism, citing and using often rather antiquated critical books, rather than trying to keep sedulously up to date with the most recent trends. I have at least tried to stay abreast of the torrent of publications on these plays, and some of the most recent writing about them – like Margreta de Grazia's *Hamlet without Hamlet*, David Womersley's magisterial *Divinity and state*, Scott McMillin and Sally-Beth MacClean's and Brian Walsh's books on the Queen's Men, MacClean and Lawrence Manley's on Lord Strange's Men, or Andras Kisery's *Hamlet's moment* – has been of major significance in shaping what follows. But in general I have used and cited materials that speak to the central concerns of the book and thus omitted or passed over in silence some enormously important modes of critical thought and very distinguished works of criticism. The result, I am afraid, is eclectic, episodic and inadequate. Thus, while I have benefited an enormous amount from the exercise, indeed I think it has transformed the book, as an outsider to Shakespeare studies I also know that to people who really know and care about this material my efforts can only appear both amateurish and opinionated.

One of the downsides of taking forever to finish something is that whatever trends or fashions the project might have been riding on or engaging with when it was first conceived are likely to be over and done with by the time it is finished. This book is no exception. I started it at what turned out to be the fag end of the period when historicism was a real force in literary studies. Indeed I was encouraged to take the very considerable risks involved in dealing with literary texts for historical purposes by the example of various essentially literary scholars, talking rather a lot about 'history'. If they could use versions of history for their essentially literary purposes, then surely turnaround was fair play and I could use various literary texts for my own essentially historical ones. And indeed, while different, perhaps the two enterprises might even have something to say to one another.

Since then historicism in literary studies seems to me, if not definitively to have had its day, then certainly to have long passed its zenith. Of the emergent approaches struggling to displace historicism at the forefront of Shakespeare studies, the one to which I might be thought to have the most to say was the religious turn. But of late that has taken an almost comically ahistorical form, with theology replacing high theory as the abstract language of choice in and through which to draw an extremely constricted range of canonical texts into dialogue with a variety of urgently contemporary concerns.

The (until recently) intensely controversial topic of Shakespeare's own religious views, centred on the claim that he might have been some sort of Catholic, has also lost much of its allure, and all of its capacity to shock. Indeed of late a whole slew of scholars seem to have come, by admittedly somewhat different routes, to the conclusion that Shakespeare probably wasn't a Catholic; that even if he was, given the state of the evidence, it is impossible to tell for sure; and that anyway, since we are dealing with literary texts not pamphlets or tracts, and since religious belief itself is an ineffably elusive topic, it does not really matter much either way.[2] Certainly, that is not a question with which this book will be much concerned, the focus here being not so much on the nature of Shakespeare's personal beliefs, for which (outside of the plays) we have almost no evidence, but rather on the ways in which at least some of his plays – in the present instance, those concerned, in the most general sense of the words, with history and therefore with politics – intersected with, fed off and fed into a range of other contemporary concerns and events. I want, in short, to use the plays to reconstruct the political scene, or, if you prefer, the political imaginary, of the Elizabethan *fin de siècle*. At the most general level, I want to treat them as evidence for how contemporaries thought about politics and/or history as process, a series of interactions between individuals bent on realising their particular aims and defending their particular interests in a variety of institutional, cultural and political contexts or settings. More specifically, I want to use them to see how contemporaries thought about the linked (and almost equally forbidden) topics of succession, tyranny and resistance, usurpation and war. At a slightly higher level of abstraction, I want to use the plays in order to watch Shakespeare and his audiences think about (monarchical) legitimacy; about what it was, how it might be lost and, once lost, how it might be recovered again.

In the protracted period during which this book has been written I have accumulated many debts. I have been in receipt of grants from the Folger Shakespeare Library, the Huntington Library and the Guggenheim Foundation. I have benefited from the advice and kindness of a number of Shakespeare scholars whose capacity to listen to, and even to read, some of this stuff without derision, indeed, at times with every appearance of serious interest, has been a great encouragement and relief. I would like to thank Heather James and Rebecca Lemon who, along with Cyndia Clegg, and above all Markuu Peltonen, made my time at the Huntington not merely pleasurable but intellectually stimulating. Heather in particular took a great deal of time and trouble over the ravings of an historian who had wandered into her field. David Kastan and Deborah Shuger's willingness, over a period of years, to give an interloper like me the time of day has always been a great comfort and I have also taken encouragement from the seriousness with which Constance Jordan has always taken my forays into territory that she has made her own. Pat Parker was also very kind during my stay at the Folger. David Loewenstein's comments on a paper on *Julius Caesar* were also very valuable.

At Vanderbilt, despite her very different interests and approach, Lynn Enterline has consistently encouraged me to keep going. Michael Neill's friendship and advice has also been very important, as has that of Jonathan Lamb and Bridget Orr, both at Princeton and Vanderbilt. Finishing, in the summer of 2015, a (long overdue) piece, commissioned by Michael Neill, played a crucial role in resolving various structural issues, and I would like to thank Michael for his good humour and encouragement under what must have been rather trying circumstances. Many of the ideas canvassed in this book were first broached in undergraduate seminars taught at Princeton University, some of them co-taught with Nigel Smith, whose friendship and enthusiasm, not to mention advice and erudition, have been crucial.

I always come away from conversations with Richard McCoy both informed and encouraged, and Joad Raymond has been similarly kind. I am grateful to Jeff Dhoty for asking me to comment on a SAA seminar at Vancouver in 2015. Jeff was also a participant at a SAA seminar that I ran with Andras Kisery on the public sphere and the drama. His interests and mine overlap closely and his book on the public sphere will make an important contribution to many of the topics discussed in this book.

However, amongst literary scholars, my greatest debt is to Andras Kisery. We first met when we had both just arrived at Vanderbilt and ever since he has been a constant source of advice and criticism. We are working on cognate topics, and Andras has been incredibly generous, both in sharing his own work and in reading and talking about mine.

Amongst historians, Paul Hammer has always been extremely generous in sharing his deep knowledge of things Essexian. I have an article on the history plays and the public sphere forthcoming in a collection edited by Malcolm Smuts, and Malcolm's comments on that piece and related topics have had a considerable impact on what follows. I have, of course, also relied on the conversation and friendship of the usual suspects. Ann Hughes, Richard Cust, Nicholas Tyacke and Michael Questier have all listened to me on this subject with more forbearance than I deserve and responded to extraordinarily beneficial effect. Tom Cogswell's interest in the drama as a form of political commentary has had a formative influence. Simon Adams' often caustic scepticism has had a beneficial effect, although, as even the most cursory reader will see, it has not brought me entirely to my senses. While we did not always agree, conversations with (the late) Kevin Sharpe always had a tonic effect. I miss him a great deal. Noah Millstone's forthcoming work on politic history and the circulation of news, and more generally on the narrative templates contemporaries used to think and talk about politics, is of central significance for the argument of this book, and Noah has been very generous in talking about our shared interests and listening to me rant on about the drama. But here my greatest debt is to Alex Gajda whose interests in this topic intersect very closely with mine. Alex has provided extraordinarily astute advice and insight (not to mention, information) over a period of years, when she had much better things to do.

Over the past twelve years or so I have given papers based on the argument of this book at the universities of Syracuse, Miami, Rutgers and Warwick (once each) and at Oxford (three times) and London (more times than I care to remember), at NYU and the Shakespeare Institute, and (four times) at the

Huntington. When you are operating as far out of your comfort zone as I am in this book, you need all the criticism and comment you can get, and I benefited enormously from all of those interactions.

I should particularly like to thank Chris Fitter for inviting me to contribute to a conference on Shakespeare and the social depth of politics at the Huntington in spring 2015 and Lori-Ann Ferrell who has allowed me twice to present material at the early modern seminar at the same venue. Lori-Ann's friendship and, in particular, her sustained interest in this project, have been a considerable source of encouragement over many years.

My wife, Sandy Solomon, shares, and, even when she does not entirely share, is nearly always prepared to indulge, what has become my voracious appetite for performances of early modern drama. Even when I despaired, she remained convinced that I had something to say. Let's hope she is right. Either way, her interest in and enthusiasm for this project has been genuinely sustaining.

Finally, I have to thank Robert Baldock at Yale University Press for his patience, forbearance and advice. Without his encouragement and support neither this book (nor indeed *The Antichrist's lewd hat*) would ever have seen the light of day. The three readers' reports from Yale, mediated by Robert's typically tactful but firm interventions, played a crucial role in helping to shape the final version of the book, which, during the past decade, has gone through more iterations than I care to think about. Robert is a wonderful editor, and I want to acknowledge a very considerable personal, professional and intellectual debt to him.

I have used throughout editions of Shakespeare's plays from the Arden Shakespeare third series, except for *King John* and *2 Henry IV*, where I have used editions from the second series, edited by E.A.J. Honingman and A.R. Humphreys, respectively.

PART I
CONTEXTS AND STRUCTURES

This section has a dual purpose. It is intended to address a set of linked issues, both historical and historiographical. I want to outline some of the ideological, political and institutional structures and contexts within which the plays under discussion here were produced and consumed and, in so doing, relate the current project to a range of recent scholarly writing on the period and these plays. I will outline the ways in which a variety of Catholic tracts, produced from the early 1570s until the mid 1590s, used history to conduct their critique of the Elizabethan regime as a conspiracy of evil counsel and to delineate, and prognosticate about, the succession crisis that they presented as the inevitable result of the policies currently being pursued in the queen's name. This, it will emerge, was a propensity anything but limited to Catholic treatments of this and related topics.

I will then survey the relevant developments in Elizabethan political history, paying particular attention to the notions of 'the monarchical republic', 'the Elizabethan exclusion crisis' and 'the succession crisis' that followed it. I will also address the issue of the notion of 'the post-reformation public sphere', and the various publics called into being by the different public pitches for support made both by the regime and by its Catholic critics and enemies. At stake in these exchanges was first interpretative and then political control over the alternately terrifying and exhilarating prospects conjured by a now inveterately unsettled succession, the war with Spain and what was now, given her relatively advanced age, the increasingly imminent death of the queen. In so doing, I will pay particular attention to recent work on the Queen's Men, and stress the contribution of the public theatre to the process whereby variously political publics were created or enabled by the peculiar, both confessional and dynastic, dynamics of the English post-reformation.

I will outline contemporary notions about the writing and reading of history for use, paying particular attention to the ways in which putting history on stage enabled audiences to feel not only that they were watching history take place before their very eyes, but also that they were being made privy to the ways in which politics really worked. Central here will be an emergent notion of 'politics' as an increasingly coherent and distinct arena or mode of human behaviour, susceptible to analysis and prognostication, very often through the invocation and analysis of various 'histories'. Finally I will discuss the vexed question of censorship in this period and outline what I take to be the impact of all these related factors and forces on the production and consumption of the play texts that form the main subject of this book.

Throughout, both in my own analysis of the period and in my readings of the plays, I will be concerned to demonstrate (and insist upon) the relative autonomy of politics, conceived as the manoeuvres of a variety of political agents or groups in contention for the control of events, of the discursive structures through which events were perceived and, ultimately, of the levers of power in the English monarchical state. Both here, and in the book more generally, the aim is to rescue the plays from views of the political which either see politics thus conceived as epiphenomenal, mere froth atop the wave of deep structural, social or cultural change, or seek to submerge politics, as these plays conceive and stage it, in the (often subterranean) workings of an hypostatised and decentred, and thus, to my mind, thoroughly mystified and occluded, notion of 'Power'.

Back to the future: Catholics and protestants learn the lessons of history

In a series of tracts, stretching from *The treatise of treasons* (1572), through *Leicester's commonwealth* (1584), the group of tracts known collectively as Cecil's commonwealth in the early 1590s, to Robert Parsons' *Conference about the next succession*, a variety of Catholic writers pictured the Elizabethan regime as a conspiracy of evil counsel. These tracts claimed that on the back of paranoid and entirely fantastical talk about a non-existent Catholic conspiracy – a conspiracy that encompassed English Catholics, the king of Spain and Mary Stuart – a group of atheistical, low-born, evil counsellors had persuaded the queen that only they could save her from what they now habitually talked about as a pervasive popish threat. They used this conviction to push aside their rivals for power, the ancient, and largely Catholic, nobility, and then sought to commit the queen to a series of foreign adventures in Scotland, France and the Low Countries. Justified as pre-emptive strikes, necessary to counter a Catholic threat that did not (yet) exist, the tracts explained that these escapades in fact brought into existence the very threat that they were supposed to counter. By allying the queen with a rout of protestant rebels against their lawful sovereigns, in France and the Low Countries, the conspirators had alienated her from the ancient allies of the English crown, the king of Spain being foremost amongst them. Having come to monopolise all the crucial offices under and around the throne, the conspirators and their hangers-on controlled not only the distribution of royal patronage, but who the queen saw and what she knew.

The final sophistication of this conspiracy to seize all power for themselves involved the succession. Having persuaded Elizabeth not to marry, the queen's evil counsellors tried to turn her against her only heir – Mary Stuart – by portraying the queen of Scots as the ultimate threat to the security of both queen and realm. This, these tracts argued, was the very opposite of the truth, for, as her lineal successor, her heir by blood, Mary Stuart was all that stood between Elizabeth and the malign plans of her own counsellors. Once the conspirators had prevailed upon Elizabeth to do away with Mary, the tracts claimed, they would be at liberty to remove Elizabeth herself at their own convenience and replace her with a candidate of their own choosing. According to *Leicester's commonwealth*, the Earl of Huntingdon, the possessor of a Yorkist claim through the female line, and a frequently named protestant claimant for the throne, should Elizabeth die without an heir of her body, was the preferred candidate. This conspiracy was the ultimate treason which *The treatise of treasons*, *Leicester's commonwealth* and the group of texts known collectively as *Cecil's commonwealth* all claimed to unmask.

But, the pamphlets claimed, while the conspirators used the language of confessional conflict and protestant zeal, religion had nothing to do with their schemes. Thus the guilty men were presented not as crazed heretics desperate to preserve the cause of true religion as they misguidedly understood it, but rather as functional atheists, Machiavels, who were using religion as a mask for the pursuit of their own private (and purely secular) interests and ambitions.

The identity of the leading Machiavels and evil counsellors and conspirators varied, depending upon attendant political circumstance. The villains of the piece in *The treatise* were William Cecil and his close ally and kinsman, Lord Keeper Nicholas Bacon, while *Leicester's commonwealth* conferred that role on the earl of Leicester. Then, in the early 1590s, with Leicester dead, the tracts known collectively as *Cecil's commonwealth* shifted attention back to the personal and dynastic ambitions of Burghley and the Cecils.

What first led me to relate the plays to the tracts were the ways in which the Catholic pamphlets deployed history to further their argument. Breaking with the legitimist claims of the Stuarts and, in particular, reverting to the Yorkist claim of Huntingdon, would, the Catholic tracts warned, reopen the dynastic disputes that had caused the Wars of the Roses, only now that old dispute would be greatly exacerbated by the almost certain involvement of foreign princes, overdetermined by the influence of post-reformation confessional conflict. Thus, *Leicester's commonwealth* claimed, if you wanted to know just what sort of disaster would be visited upon England by the machinations of Leicester and his ilk in preventing the queen from marrying, removing the legitimate heir to the throne and diverting the succession, you had merely to go back to the future and refer yourself to the history of England in the previous century. In this relatively recent past various combinations of noble and court faction, dynastic uncertainty and ambition, had plunged the settled monarchical state established by the Lancastrians into civil war, reducing the commonwealth to the sort of chaos through which new men and princes could rise and eventually achieve supreme power.

The treatise of treasons embarked on a long comparison between the usurpation of Richard III and recent events in Elizabethan England, in particular the plots and stratagems being undertaken now by Cecil and Bacon, a pair of evil counsellors. *The treatise* referred to as the two English Catilines.[1] According to the *The treatise*, the first move of the evil counsellor was always to sow division and faction in the midst of the royal family and court. Richard of Gloucester's efforts to spread dissension between 'the two kindreds' of Edward IV 'and his wife' and 'the fine devices and fair set policies used to circumvent king Edward IV in making away his brother the duke of Clarence' not only proved this general insight but were also near-perfect guides to what was happening now, as an extended comparison between Richard's manoeuvres and the recent machinations designed to set Queen Elizabeth against her cousin and heir Mary Stuart showed only too clearly.[2] Richard's purge of the queen's relatives and the summary execution of Hastings were compared to the recent arrest of Norfolk, Arundel, Pembroke and Lumley.[3] The rumours spread against the the queen's family, the Wydvilles, found their modern analogue in the rumours spread against Mary Stuart and Norfolk. The wild tales told about Elizabeth Wydville – that she was a 'sorcerer, a witch and by necromancy' had 'wasted the protector's body and limbs' – were directly comparable to the equally malign and absurd whispering campaign now being directed against Mary Stuart.[4]

Then as now the pamphlet saw no shortage of creatures and catspaws able and willing to do the great ones' dirty work for them. 'Among the clergy there lacked no Shaws, nor now no Sampsons. Among the lawyers there wanted then no Catesbies, nor now no Nortons.'[5] Thus the pamphlet was able triumphantly to conclude that what had happened before was now happening again (having already almost happened during the duke of Northumberland's attempted coup at the end of Edward VI's reign). And thus the past could provide not only a guide to what was happening now, but also a dreadful warning of what was going to happen next, if, that is, the lessons of history, conveniently encapsulated in *The treatise*, were not heeded and preventative action taken immediately.

Such parallels and political lessons, culled from the history of both Edward VI's reign and of fifteenth-century England, represented a relatively minor element in *The treatise*, but they played a rather more prominent role in *Leicester's commonwealth*. Leicester was compared to a whole slew of previous overmighty subjects, ranging from Vortigern, Harold, Henry of Lancaster, Richard of Warwick, Richard of Gloucester, John of Northumberland, and others, who 'by this mean [dominance of the court and patronage of the crown] specially have pulled down their lawful sovereigns'.[6] Particular attention was paid also to 'Richard Duke of York, in the time of King Henry VI'.[7]

The danger presented to stable monarchical rule by such overmighty subjects and favourites was, of course, considerably compounded if the monarch lacked an heir of his or her body, or if the succession was otherwise uncertain; a point the tract drove home by citing the examples of Henry Bolingbroke, duke of Lancaster, under Richard II and Richard, duke of Gloucester, under Edward IV and V.[8] The defenders of the earl of Leicester might argue that so great was his current authority and standing in the realm, so high his favour with the queen, that he had no need to connive for yet further preferment and greater power, but, the tract claimed, history told us otherwise. After all, the Percies under Henry IV had had power enough, as had the

Nevilles under Edward IV.[9] For such aspiring spirits nothing short of supreme power would ever suffice.

Again, confronted by the (alleged) alliance between Leicester and Huntingdon to advance the latter's claim to the throne, the tract used recent history to predict a falling out, and a final struggle for sovereign power, between the two earls, using the fates of Lord Stanley under Henry VII, of the Duke of Buckingham under Richard III and of the Percies under Henry IV, to illustrate what became of kingmakers unless they got their retaliation in first.[10]

While Robert Parsons' great tract of the mid 1590s, *The conference about the next succession*, took much of the analysis of the previous pamphlets for granted, concerning itself with the likely consequences of a succession now left definitively unsettled, its discussion of the rights and wrongs of the succession was drenched throughout with readings from a whole variety of histories; histories culled from the Old Testament, from the ancient world, but also from the annals and chronicles of medieval western Europe and particularly, of course, of England. Such a detailed engagement with the particularities of history, history which he found in and took from the chronicles, was central to various of Parson's purposes.[11] It was central, first, to his drive to muddy the genealogical waters, by casting doubt on the Stuart claim to the English throne as so obviously the best that it could brook no legitimate challenge, but it was also central to his attempt to characterise the English polity as a form of elective monarchy with powers inherent in what he termed the 'commonwealth' to divert the succession from its obvious, hereditary course, and to discipline, control, and even to depose and replace, a peccant monarch, when the demands of the common good seemed to demand it.

As we shall see below, in making that last case, Parsons put particular stress upon the reign of King John and the deposition of Richard II, as textbook examples of how the English commonwealth could indeed depose tyrants and divert the succession according to the demands of the political moment and the common good. He also cited Richard III as a monarch of undoubted dynastic legitimacy, deposed in favour of someone with a far more dubious hereditary claim, by the (violent) action of a commonwealth united in opposition to tyranny, red in tooth and claw. Anyone, he claimed, who accepted the deposition of Richard and the accession of Henry VII as legitimate, must, by implication, also accept his version of England as an elective monarchy and a commonwealth well able to defend itself against tyranny and divert the succession according to the promptings of the common good.

In taking this tack, in using history to guide their thoughts and prognostications about what an unsettled succession might bring to the realm, these Catholic tracts were bending to their own purposes modes of thought and argument used by other (protestant) groups and individuals, over the course of the reign, for their own equally partisan confessional and political purposes.

Let us look first at a remarkable manuscript tract of 1566,[12] written, at least according to *Treatise of treasons*, by the puritan divine Thomas Sampson. Sampson cited various sorts of histories to confirm his warning, directed notionally to the queen herself, that it was 'most certain that, unless the succession after you be, and that in time, appointed and ordered, England runneth to most certain ruin and destruction'.[13] As things stood, the tract argued, at the queen's death without an heir of her body, or a succession 'ordered and stablished', there would be multiple contenders. The result would be a struggle for the crown and, for all that 'God doth (by his provident government) give kingdoms, make and depose kings', if we judged the outcome according to 'men's dealing, by which God bringeth his purpose to pass', it was almost certain that 'this quarrel' would be won by the strongest party, 'and might overcome right'.[14] This, our author claimed, was a recipe for disaster; for since the outcome was sure to be decided 'in the field fighting, not in judgement pleading' the 'new prince' would inevitably come 'into the realm wading in blood up to the neck, continue in blood, whose end is oft also mixed with blood'.[15]

Even if, at the first, violence were to be averted and some attempt made to elect a new prince, Sampson predicted disaster. Who would be the electors? 'The multitude'? They were composed of 'as many minds' as heads and thus 'always distract'. If 'the few', how would they bind the many to accept their final decision? What if the electors could not agree? Would the winner then be decided 'by the greater part?' Under such circumstances, our author asked, who could assure 'the chosen person of the consent and subjection of all?'[16] Inevitably, there would be winners and losers. The chosen monarch would have to favour those who had, in Shakespeare's phrase, 'helped him to the crown' or face their disappointment and disaffection. Conversely, Sampson observed, 'kings themselves do often times wax jealous, not only on the electors, but also on them by whose special aid they have come to their kingdoms and think they, which can do so much to make a king, can do too much to depose a king'.[17]

Frustrated candidates might turn factious,[18] and the monarch not think himself safe while any of his former rivals' descendants remained alive. The result would be dissension, strife and even civil war, transferred down the generations, a point he illustrated from English history by the fates of 'Maud, Arthur, Edmund Mortimer and Edward, the son of Henry VI'.[19] 'See', our author concluded, 'what it is to leave a kingdom uncommitted in the hands of ambitious men. They disinherit, they kill, they divide, they fight, they covet, they lose all.'[20] Once started, such internecine strife could last for years, even for generations, and thus so weaken the polity as to leave it easy prey to that most dreadful of all fates, foreign invasion and rule.[21]

Here then, stated in relatively abstract terms, were the plot outlines and central concerns of many of the plays discussed in this book; of the *Henry VI* plays, of *Richard II* and *Henry IV*, indeed of *Titus Andronicus*, and even of

Hamlet. Moreover, these politique observations and prognostications were everywhere illustrated by, and drawn out of, myriad historical examples taken from Roman, ancient British, and English history, 'since the conquest'.

The reigns of Roman emperors both early and late were cited to show the wisdom and necessity of settling the succession, and the dreadful consequences of failing to do so. From the early history of Britain the fates of King Lucius and of Ferrex and Porrex, famously the subject of the play *Gorboduc* by Thomas Norton and Thomas Sackville which, just like Sampson's tract, pressed the queen both to marry and settle the succession in her lifetime, were also cited at length. All of which drew from our author the observation that 'the fruit of such strifes is civil, and therefore the most cruel and dangerous, war'.[22]

From more recent English history our author noted with approval the efforts of the childless Richard I and Richard II to settle the succession; the first by appointing 'Arthur, son of his brother to be his successor', and the second by holding a parliament at Westminster in which 'Edmund earl of Mortimer was declared next heir to succeed', 'lest, as the history saith, there should be any doubt or contention for the inheritance of the throne'. He also cited the repeated, and rather more successful, efforts of both Henry IV and the queen's own father, Henry VIII, to settle the succession, ensuring that the crown did, in fact, pass in orderly fashion from Edward to Mary, and 'to yourself last of all';[23] an arrangement that the propensity of the modern English to be 'led by known and allowed law' had made stick, even 'against the attempt of the Duke of Northumberland' at the end of Edward's reign.[24]

It was thus easy, our author claimed, just from 'the histories since the conquest' to see the dreadful effects of unsettled or contested successions. But perhaps our author's most daring recourse to English history occurred in the quite remarkable section of the work in which he exhorted the parliament to order the succession, if necessary, in the teeth not only of royal opposition, but even, it seems, of a direct royal command to cease and desist. He first cited examples, drawn from sacred history, of prophets, counsellors and people refusing to obey (or checking) corrupt or unjust royal commands. He then proceeded to claim that 'we do willingly pass over many examples tending to this purpose. We will not take any out of the histories of this land, for if we should either cite' 'Vortigern, before the conquest, or Edward II, or Richard II sithence, it might seem to commend that which hath some foul spot marks of condemnation. For, though faults were found in government worthy of amend-ment and evil counsellors did lead princes in ways meet for their private purposes, . . . yet did corrupt affection not only force men then too far, but ambition, under pretense of reformation, practiced unusual revenge and destruction. To wade too deeply in this matter is odious, but, if it prove needful, it is good to know what may justly be done and also to do it. Kings have to learn their state. The higher it is, the more at liberty, the greater need is of good aid, counsel and advertisement.'[25] This is a remarkable passage, in which, by claiming that he was not going to mention the unmentionable, Sampson managed to mention it in ways that surely lodged the point that he claimed that he was *not* making firmly in the mind of the reader, and he did so by again citing reigns that were to provide the subjects of plays by Marlowe and Shakespeare; plays which, at least in Shakespeare's case, adverted to the explosive matter contained within them with much the same sort of direct indirection displayed by Sampson

If we fast-forward to 1584 when John Leslie, the bishop of Ross's defence of the Stuart claim, first produced in 1569, was once more reprinted as part of a Catholic propaganda offensive that also included both *Leicester's commonwealth* and Cardinal Allen's reply to Burghley's *Execution of justice in England*, we find a manuscript reply to Leslie indulging in very similar uses of historical precedent and interpretation. One of the major arguments against the Stuart claim was the assertion that a maxim of the common law barred from inheriting the throne those born abroad to parents out of allegiance to the English crown. In response, Leslie cited the examples of 'King Stephen, Henry II, Arthur, duke of Brittany, Edgar Aetheling and Lewis, son to the king of France, all the which, notwithstanding that they were strangers, yet were two of them kings of this realm, two were established heirs apparent to the crown and the fifth called in by the barons to inherit the crown in the right of Blanche his wife, being a descendant from the crown yet a stranger born'.[26]

This elicited from Ross' nameless critic a detailed discussion of the relevant chronicle materials, a discussion that concentrated with particular intensity on the events of John's reign. Distinctions were drawn between different writers; Polydore Vergil was all but dismissed because he was 'a stranger, a late writer and therefore of least credit'.[27] Other sources, more nearly contemporary, were rated higher, with one being hailed as, 'by all presumption', 'an eye witness in this matter' and then quoted as proving definitively that Arthur had never been intended or established by Richard as his heir but rather 'both prince and people resolved fully upon king John as undoubted heir apparent to the realm'.[28] It would, our author concluded, be 'tedious to rehearse what all authors write of this matter. It sufficeth to have proved that those that make for Ross are of the least credit because of a later age' and because they disagreed amongst themselves as to the manner and 'time of Arthur's supposed establishment'.[29]

Various assertions and interpretations were weighed against one another, and an historical explanation provided for what out author claimed was the entirely illusory claim that Richard had chosen Arthur as his heir. (It had proceeded from the machinations of the evil bishop of Ely who had invented a letter from the king to that effect in order to keep his enemy John away from the throne and, since Arthur was then a child, in the event of Richard's death on crusade, to prolong his own power as regent.)[30]

Similar attention was lavished on the alleged claim to the throne enjoyed by Lewis, the son of the French king, through his wife Blanche, with our author concluding that none of the sources 'maketh mention that the barons called Lewis into the realm in respect of any right that he had to the crown by his wife but to fortify themselves against the pope, who had excommunicated the said Lewis and all of them, supporting king John against them, because he had made his realm tributary to the church. Neither did Lewis claim the crown, at his coming into England, by colour of his wife's right', but rather thanked the barons for 'their voluntary calling him to the government'.[31] Our author's authority for all this was Polydore who, since he was now on the right side, was instantly transformed into a reliable source.

Ross' providential gloss on the crucial events also came in for a good hiding. Where Leslie claimed that Harold, Stephen and John had all suffered from the providential judgement of God for usurping the throne from the rightful (and foreign born) claimants – Edgar Aetheling, Maud and Arthur respectively – our author replied that 'the stories report these men to have committed other grievous offences for the which they deserved God's punishment, though we should deny that they offended in securing the crown into their hands'. In John's case the relevant lapse was 'an horrible murder in the persons of the said Arthur and Eleanor his sister, for the which God plagued him as well with the loss of his countries abroad as with civil wars at home'.[32]

The crucial point, of course, is that controversial claims and counter-claims about the succession were being canvassed here through detailed historical argument. Disputes about what had actually happened, and about what that meant – conducted here with every appearance of scholarly rigour – thus took on a heightened political significance. Indeed, the point was reached when any discussion or version of the crucial historical events could – I am tempted to say would, or even must – have been taken to contain some sort of covert or coded reference to the controversial matter, the crucial and forbidden issues, assumed to turn upon these highly charged precedents and examples. There could, in short, be no such thing as an entirely innocent depiction or re-enactment of such controverted and controversial historical events. And, of course, as we shall see below, in the face of one version of the key events of John's reign, staged in *The troublesome reign of King John* and performed all round the country by the Queen's Men, Shakespeare produced his own tellingly different account of the selfsame events.

Such uses of history in disputes about politics, the succession and the nature of the English monarchical polity remained a more or less consistent feature throughout the period. Just as there is a quite remarkable degree of overlap between the fears and phobias that Thomas Sampson set before the parliament men of 1566 and those being evoked and exploited by Robert Parsons in

1594, so precisely the same historical events, the same interpretative claims and counter-claims, at issue between Leslie and his anonymous critic of 1584, are to be found at the centre of Parsons' account, in the *Conference*, of the English monarchy as elective. The only real difference was that, in the 1560s, it was the protestants who were appalled by the prospect of the accession of the Stuarts and, by the 1590s, it was a certain sort of Catholic.[33]

Here, then, were contemporaries of very different, indeed of mutually exclusive, ideological perspectives and political interests – Catholics and puritans, no less – using history not only to decide specific disputes about the nature and course of the succession, but also, more generally, to provide templates, exemplary narratives, models of behaviour and patterns of moral probity and political probability that could be brought to bear on present events and future prospects as a ready guide to what was happening now and, more importantly, to what might be about to happen next. History, then, was crucial, not merely to questions of 'right', but also to questions of prudence, to both the 'is' and the 'ought' of contemporary politics.

The tracts known collectively as *Cecil's commonwealth* and indeed Parsons' *Conference* were all being produced at the very moment when Mary Stuart's death, the war with Spain and Elizabeth's advancing age were returning to the very centre of contemporary attention and concern, the question of what would happen once the queen died (as it now seemed certain that she would) with the succession unsettled. At the same moment, the public stage resounded with plays about these very same events: about the reigns of Edmund Ironside, of King John and Henry VI, the rise of Richard III, the depositions of Richard II and Edward II and the tumults of Henry IV's reign.

Not only that, but many of the scenarios conjured by Sampson and Parsons – contested successions, tumultuously conducted elections, the mutual suspicions and emergent jealousies between new rulers and their erstwhile supporters, the destabilising effects of dynastic conflict and change, the downward spiral of civil strife and civil war leading to foreign invasion and the imposition of new rulers from abroad – formed the subject matter of plays like *Richard II* and *Richard III*, of the *Henry IV* and *Henry VI* plays, and of *King John*, not to mention of *Titus Andronicus*, *Julius Caesar* and *Hamlet*. In the process, various dramatists proceeded, on the public stage, to 'wade' very deeply indeed into what Sampson had called the 'odious matter' at the heart of the reigns of Edward II and Richard II.

We have here, then, a transition from the illicit and libellous Catholic pamphlets, and the incendiary and unpublished manuscript tracts of the 1560s, 1570s and early 1580s to the public stage, where, by the early 1590s, topics and notions previously discussed only in the most illicit or constrained of media and circumstances were being publicly canvassed in front of both ideologically and socially heterogenous audiences. That transition and what it has to tell us about the political culture and condition of late Elizabethan England is one of the primary subjects of this book.

Putting the (high) politics back into 'power'

The origins of this book, then, lie in the juxtaposition of two insights or rather commonplaces: the first that contemporaries regularly used recent history to think (and talk) about the here and now, and in particular about the dreadful prospect that might be awaiting Elizabethan England once the old queen died and a struggle for the succession began; and the second, that the plays that dealt with those historical events regularly contained elements that seemed to speak directly to current circumstances and concerns, and did so in ways that invited contemporary audiences to use the events being acted out on stage to think through some of the most controversial, and in the case of the succession, most taboo, questions of the age.

My aim became to examine the relation between history plays and, not so much the history they staged, as the events, if you will, the history, within which they were written and to which, I am arguing, they were very directly – albeit in Shakespeare's case, with typically Shakespearean indirection – addressed. The aim here is historical and the interpretative mode circular; not, I hope, a circle of the futile, self-consuming sort, described by the fabled oozlum bird, but rather one of a far more virtuously hermeneutic type.[34] I want to use the immediate political context to interpret the plays; and the plays, thus contextualised and interpreted, to cast light back upon the politics, the political culture, indeed the political imagination, of the period. My main objective is thus not to talk about Shakespeare *per se*, but rather to use plays – most, but not all, of them by Shakespeare – to say something about the period, and then perhaps to use the resulting picture of the period to say something about the theatre and indeed the plays under discussion in this book.

But if the result is a history book about Elizabethan politics and political culture, it is one whose primary unit of analysis and argument is a series of heavily contextual readings of particular plays. Of course, and perhaps inevitably, it has also, to some extent, become a book about plays and in partic- ular about the history plays of Shakespeare. For as I worked myself into the project, it seemed to me that many, indeed most, of the plays that spoke most directly to the issues in which I was interested turned out to be by Shakespeare. That being the case, a series of juxtapositions seemed to be in order; not only between the plays and the immediate political contexts in which they were written and to which they were addressed, and between the plays and other (more overtly) political texts, but also within and between the plays them- selves. On that basis, it seemed, something might be said, or suggested, about the ideological and political trajectory described by Shakespeare's history plays through the 1590s. And so, despite my own injunctions to myself to write a book about plays (mostly written by Shakespeare), to which 'Shakespeare' was incidental, I have also ended up, in part, writing a book about 'Shakespeare', although I would still insist that that part of the analysis remains, if not incidental, then certainly peripheral – contingent rather than necessary – to the basic thrust and purpose of the book.

While it is true enough that the present exercise in historical research has been conceived, in more or less equal measure, as an homage to, and a reaction against, the 'new historicism' practised by Stephen Greenblatt, Louis Adrian Montrose and a host of their emulators and epigones, it is not intended to represent anything like a return to the (old) historicism practised by the likes of Lily B. Campbell and E.M.W. Tillyard. For the relation envisaged here between text and context is anything but static or one way. To make that point, and to characterise the approach adopted here, I want both to quote and appro-priate a passage from Wayne Rebhorn's seminal essay on 'The crisis of the aristocracy in *Julius Caesar*'. On his account, the relations between the play and the context in which was written and consumed is 'far from simple'. 'The play may be said to reflect its context insofar as it is seen as merely presenting the preoccupations of many of Shakespeare's contemporaries. But at the same time, it also participates in the constitution of that context: it defines the shape of Elizabethans' preoccupations for them, in a sense supplying the very language they needed to articulate their fears and desires. In other words, *Julius Caesar*, like any text, is not a *repetition* of its context, but a *re-presentation* of it; it does not simply reiterate what it already knows but re-forms it, thereby actually helping to constitute the very context of which it is a part. It is not a mirror but a shaping presence. What is more, as a shaping presence, as a re-presentation, the play must be recognised as having an active, rather than a passive, merely reflective, relation to what it represents as well as to the audience viewing the representation: that is the play offers a particular perspective on its context, seeking both to define the shape of what it represents and to shape its audience's response to that representation.'[35]

Amongst recent readings of these plays my approach comes closest to that adopted by Leah Marcus in her *Puzzling Shakespeare*, which tries to produce what Marcus calls 'local' readings of the plays. However, the sort of 'local' read-ings produced below are not, in the obvious sense of the word, local at all, but rather national, that is to say, conditioned and framed by what Howard Erskine-Hill has termed 'the realm of politics'; a realm defined, in his account, by 'the deliberations, decisions, deeds of rulers, debates about their title to rule, change in the forms of government, war and revolution at home and abroad'.[36]

The historicism in play here is thus concerned with events and persons, with history as contemporaries tended to regard it, and as Erskine-Hill has defined it – that is to say, with the doings of great men (and women), of sovereigns and noblemen, and with the fates of kingdoms and dynasties rather than with the workings of an hypostatised notion of power; with shifts and tensions in overarching ideological and social structures, movements in the techtonic plates of society, ideology and culture.[37]

Elizabethans may have been living through a crisis of the aristocracy, or of patriarchy, or of gender relations, or a transition from 'feudalism' to 'capitalism', or indeed the dawn of various sorts or styles of 'modernity'. Or they may not; after all, these remain intensely controversial topics amongst modern historians of the period. What seems more certain is that contemporaries of all classes knew very well that Queen Elizabeth was getting old; that she had no designated heir; that there was a variety of possible claimants to the throne, amongst them James VI and the Infanta; that there was a war on; that the reformation (i.e. the breach with Rome and the return of protestantism) had happened; that religious division and confessional conflict were facts of life; that France was being plunged into a vicious and seemingly interminable both dynastic and religious civil war; that the earl of Essex was the queen's favourite and a coming man, widely identified with the aggressive prosecution of the war with Spain; that there were debates at the centre of power over how to wage that war and, in the later 1590s, about whether to sue for peace or to fight on, with renewed ferocity and determination.

Politics thus conceived was a peculiarly monarchical and aristocratic affair, and as Gary Taylor has observed, Shakespeare's stagings of history were peculiarly intense in their concentration on the doings of kings and princes.[38] In an emergently absolutist personal monarchy – absolutist, that is, at the level of aspiration and ideology, if not anything like always and everywhere in practice[39] – and during a period in which issues of succession and legitimacy were much on people's minds, plays that were so insistently about kings and queens were also quintessentially political plays.

Of course, as a great deal of recent work has shown, such political concerns could well structure and, in their turn, be structured by, parallel sets of concerns and beliefs about, say, the workings of the social order and the gender hierarchy; about the proper relations between God and his creation, between providence and human agency and free will. Gender or the anxieties and instabilities inherent in social relations structured by credit, debt and exchange thus became useful ways to think about politics, and, *pari passu*, political narratives became useful ways to figure and interrogate the dynamics of economic exchange and value determined by the market or the workings of the gender hierarchy, a topic whose ideological significance and emotional freight were considerably heightened by the fact that, virtually for the first time, England was being ruled by a woman.[40]

The notion of 'the political' that animates this book is thus most definitely not intended to preclude the examination of how the experience of religious and political change, compounded, in this instance, by the threat of even more rapid and cataclysmic dynastic and political conflict – conflict that did not, in the event, occur – was interpreted in terms of (and sometimes brought into the most radical question) a whole set of other assumptions and anxieties about the social, gender and cosmic orders. Thus, while the reading of the plays attempted here starts with the somewhat attenuated notion of the political, outlined above, that reading also shows that such inherently political concerns and anxieties were often expressed in terms that were anything but limited to what at least some revisionist historians of the high politics of the period might regard as the properly political domain. Consequently, as we shall see below, my analysis will engage with the ways in which these plays invoke, stage and interrogate many of the structuring assumptions of late Elizabethan religion, society and culture.

But what this book will not do is construe the (in modern parlance 'high') political elements in the plays as epiphenomenal, or regard them as so obvious, even as so boring, as to be worthy of sustained attention only insofar as they can be shown to have been determined by, or to reflect upon, other, deeper structures, more profound social changes and cultural shifts. Still less will it regard the plays as of interest only to the extent that they can be made to speak to the essentially modern, indeed irredeemably present-minded, concerns that have become indelibly attached to certain versions of 'early modernity' or 'the Renaissance'. On the contrary, the plays' concern with wider issues of power and legitimacy, with both the 'is' and the 'ought' of contemporary life and thought, will be shown to be politically constructed, both prompted and profoundly shaped by the immediately political concerns and events (and indeed the non-events) of the day and by the often intense hopes and fears that attended them.

Just as I want to to escape the tendency to construe the political as simply determined by some combination of the economic, the social or the cultural, I also want to contest the assumption that reading the plays in terms of the immediate political circumstances in which they were first written, performed and consumed is in some way methodologically illicit, because irredeemably reductive. It is often asserted that such an approach immediately and inevitably converts the plays into so many *romans-à-clef*, coded accounts of contemporary events. Since any given character or event can be taken to have simply stood for some immediately contemporary correlative, once the necessary correspondences have been worked out, the play can immediately be made to yield a stable 'message' about contemporary politics. While I do want to argue that these plays *sometimes* contained such references and suggested such correlations, I also want to insist that those moments were relatively rare and nearly always fleeting. Rather than turning the play into some straightforward exercise in political message-sending or propaganda, such correlations or references in fact operated to open up the events being staged to contemporary interpretation and application, thus inviting the audience or the reader into an active engagement both with the action of the play and with contemporary events and concerns.

In short, these were plays not pamphlets or tracts. They were stagings of history that opened themselves up to a variety of often actually or potentially contradictory readings or applications, the full extent and nature of which are probably not recoverable, but the general outlines and reach of which can at least be sketched or suggested with (what I want to claim are) important results for our sense of how Elizabethans thought about politics and conceived the events through which they were living and the various outcomes to which immediately contemporary events either were, or might be thought to be, leading. The claims being advanced here are thus relativist and limited, rather than totalising. My aim is not to constrain, still less to rule out of bounds, other (literary, rhetorical, cultural or psychoanalytic) modes of interpretation, but merely to claim that these plays do indeed lend themselves to this sort of political analysis and that this sort of analysis, applied to this sort of text, has a good deal to teach us about the politics and political culture of late Elizabethan England.

That agenda has certain consequences for the ways the plays under discussion here are read. My attention will be concentrated throughout on what we might term the political surface of the plays; on how these texts and performances functioned as political narratives, accounts of the English monarchical polity, of the political process, and as commentary upon a series of political events and issues that were of the highest interest and concern to contemporaries.

The analysis proceeds on the assumption that, at nearly all the crucial moments, the *political* meanings of these plays are to be found within what is happening and being said on the page and indeed on the stage, the explication of which is at the core of the book. The basic unit of analysis is the entirety of each play, conceived as a political narrative. I have been told that this is not, in fact, what modern literary criticism does. That might well be the case and insofar as it is, it is not an accident, since this is not, in fact, a work of literary criticism. I am not a literary critic, and there would be small point in my attempting to replicate what modern literary critics do – in itself a difficult enough task since at present they seem to be doing a good number of rather different, and sometimes mutually incompatible, things, almost none of which I am competent to replicate. Were I to attempt such an exercise in *imitatio*, I would inevitably end up doing it very badly. Rather this is a history book that attempts to use the history play broadly defined as a way to think about the political thought and culture of the Elizabeth *fin de siècle*.

Elizabethan political history, now

In taking this tack, I am responding to a number of developments in the political and religious history of post-reformation England, as it has been written, by a variety of scholars, over the past forty or so years. By calling many of the central features of the received religio-political narrative/s into question, that historiography has rendered the politics of the post-reformation interesting again. Instead of a stable political story in need of deep structural cultural and social explanation, we have a far more open-ended, contingent and multivalent sense of politics; a sense which renders various versions of the political history of the period available for deployment in the interpretation of a whole variety of contemporary texts and scripts. It is, therefore, to what I take to be some of the central features of that historiography that I now, briefly, turn.

(i) The 'Elizabethan exclusion crisis'

The first and most important of these changes in the recent historiography is indelibly associated with two seminal articles by Patrick Collinson,[41] which stressed the anxiety boiling away under the surface of the apparent continuity, peace and unity of the reign. For such were the blessings presented by the Elizabethan regime to its subjects as the fruits of the reign of Gloriana. Subsequently a good deal of historical writing followed suit. Refusing, as he did throughout his career, the sort of Elizabeth worship practised by his mentor, Sir John Neale, Collinson gave pride of place to issues of succession and dynastic security. The political consequences of the queen's motto, *semper eadem*, which took its most controversial form in her refusal either to marry or to settle the succession, or indeed even, for nigh on twenty years, to do anything definitive about Mary Stuart, seemed, to many of her subjects and counsellors, desperately dangerous. Elizabeth's stance represented a gamble on her own longevity and involved risks that many of those whose careers, ideological convictions, and even lives seemed dependent on the queen's continued health were far less willing than Elizabeth herself to take. It sometimes seemed as though the only person not making political calculations about what would happen after the death of the queen was the queen herself, because, of course, she would be dead, and the fate of her kingdom in the hands of providence. Everyone else – Catholics and protestants alike – remained obsessed with what was going to happen if and when the queen died; which explains why questions of marriage, succession and Mary Queen of Scots remained such hot-button issues throughout the reign.

Collinson called the resulting political conjuncture the 'Elizabethan exclusion crisis'. This is something of a misnomer, since we are dealing here not only with a 'crisis' that never happened, but also with a political conjuncture that lasted, in various forms, for virtually the entire reign. (Collinson's own comparison of 'the exclusion crisis' with the Cold War makes the point well enough.)What we have is a crisis in prospect or *in potentia*; based on a structural weakness created by the interaction of the peculiar marital history of Henry VIII with the course of post-reformation confessional and religious change, and on the consequent accident that, after Henry's death, from 1547 to 1603, England was ruled by a boy and two women, one unable to bear a child, the other serially unwilling to marry. Moreover, between 1547 and 1587 the most likely heir to the throne was always of the oppo-site religious persuasion to the current incumbent. The heir of Edward, a protes-tant, was Mary, a Catholic; the heir of Mary, a Catholic, was Elizabeth, a protestant; the heir of Elizabeth, a protestant, was Mary, queen of Scots, a Catholic. The result was that there was always a reversionary interest of the opposite confessional colouring threatening the stability of the current regime. Each successive regime was consequently left entirely dependent on the current incumbent's continued well-being. As Thomas Sampson told the queen in 1566, the welfare of the whole realm hung on the single 'thread of twine' of her own life.

Under Elizabeth the situation was rendered worse by the increasing confes-sional polarisation of the later sixteenth century and the continuing, indeed the worsening, geopolitical tensions between England and the two great Catholic powers, France and, more particularly, Spain. Anxiety was also heightened by the memory of what had happened in 1550s, upon which both Sampson's tract and *Leiceister's commonwealth* harped. Nearly all of the major political players of Elizabeth's reign had lived through a period in which two perfectly viable, one protestant and the other Catholic, regimes had collapsed like the prover-bial house of cards, because of the sudden (unlooked for) death of a monarch who lacked an heir of his or her body, or indeed any viable successor of the same religious persuasion as themselves.

Under Edward, as the boy king sickened, central elements in the regime, led by Leicester's father Northumberland, had hastily assembled a dynastic coup designed to exclude Elizabeth and Mary Tudor and put Lady Jane Grey on the throne. That ploy failed. Mary adopted a different tack; by acting against the advice of some of her counsellors and leaving Elizabeth alive, even after the massive provocation/occasion provided by Wyatt's rebellion, she gambled on her own fertility and longevity and lost. As both John Guy and Steven Alford have emphasised, William Cecil, for one, took these lessons to heart and spent a great deal of his waking life under Elizabeth trying to make sure that the same fate did not befall the (protestant) regime constructed or enabled by the acces-sion of Elizabeth I, which, he feared, might well go the same way as those constructed under Edward and Mary, if Elizabeth died without an heir of her body and with Mary Stuart alive.[42]

Cecil, of course, was far from alone. The situation created by Elizabeth's decision to remain unmarried produced an overriding imperative amongst protestants committed to the regime to do something about the succession. The first preference was to induce the queen to marry and produce an heir.[43] That did not work, and while Elizabeth refused to take that option and while Mary Stuart remained alive, Mary remained the most likely next successor. But Mary was Catholic and, and certainly after the events of the late 1560s and early 1570s, entirely unacceptable to the protestant elite. How could the (for committed protestants) appalling prospect of Mary's accession be avoided? The preferred, because definitive, option was Mary's death. This Elizabeth would not allow precisely because such an act might be construed as regicide.

The second option was a series of legal/constitutional expedients that Collinson has dubbed 'monarchical republicanism'. These proposals took the form of a series of legislative instruments, whereby, if the queen died, the Privy Council, expanded to include the great peers, would continue to govern the realm, recall the last parliament, and settle the succession. By creating an inter-regnum – formally a legal nonsense – these measures promised a 'legal' means to avoid Mary Stuart at all costs by rallying the protestant nation in parliament, while the regime both perpetuated and reconstituted itself.

(ii) Not a factional politics

These proposals failed to get off the drawing board because the queen would not countenance them; an outcome which itself serves to remind us that, for all the recent talk about 'republicanism', Elizabethan England remained a monarchy, not a monarchical republic; a fact of which Shakespeare, if his remorselessly monarchical account of English history is anything to go by, was very well aware. The result was that during the high Elizabeth period, from the early 1570s until the later 1580s, the great political fault lines within the Elizabeth polity – fault lines defined both by disagreements about particular policy options and by wider ideological issues – did not run between a rela-tively united regime and a puritan opposition, nor even between rival courtiers and factions, each contending for the favour of the queen and being played off the one against the other by the exquisite political skills of their royal mistress, but rather between the queen, on the one hand, and a relatively united inner circle of counsellors, on the other. On the issues of marriage, the succession, and Mary Stuart; on the question of further reformation and puritanism; on the issue of the Catholic threat; on foreign policy, over intervention in Scotland, France and in particular the Low Countries, the main story was not factional divisions amongst the queen's counsellors and courtiers – although there were, of course, moments of debate and sharp disagreement, and of considerable personal tensions (between, say, Leicester and Sussex, or later Leicester and Hatton, Burghley and Whitgift, or later still between Essex and Raleigh, and finally and fatally between Essex and Cecil) – but rather a pattern of consistent disagreement between the queen and a central group of her counsellors. On all of the subjects listed above – marriage, a settled succession, a dead Mary Stuart, further reformation, more draconian measures against Catholics, intervention in favour of the protestant interest abroad – a majority of her counsellors tended to want to take action and the queen wanted to delay. On some other issues, however – marriage to the duke of Anjou, the sacking of Archbishop Grindal, more draconian measures against the puritans (rather than the Catholics) – it was the queen who wanted to take action and her counsellors who viewed her inclinations with various degrees of dismay and alarm.[44]

The result was often stalemate, or at least change achieved at a snail-like pace; if the Privy Council took nearly twenty years to kill Mary Stuart, the queen took even longer to get an anti-puritan crackdown of the sort that she had wanted since the 1560s. Grindal died in office, albeit suspended from its exercise and under house arrest. There was a typically Elizabethan mish-mash over the fate of English Catholics, with laws not as draconian as many on the council, or on the bench of bishops, or in parliament wanted, not being enforced with the enthusiasm or consistency that the law seemed to demand.

As a result, the politics of the court, the council and the parliament often became a series of attempts by elements within the inner circle, and their clients, hangers-on and allies, to get the queen to do the right thing, as they conceived it. Where earlier generations of historians have seen either the machinations of court factions or the hand of a puritan opposition in the House of Commons, more recent work has discerned groups of counsellors, their clients and sympathisers anxiously trying to induce the queen to do things that, left to her own devices, she would never have contemplated.

At times these exercises in subtle and not so subtle persuasion got out of hand or were hijacked by freelancing (often puritan) members of the Commons. But often groups of counsellors operated through, or were in tacit alliance with, third parties – their clients and allies – who were ready to take the risks, and sometimes carry the can, for pushing along an agenda that could be extremely unpopular with the very person, the queen, whose interests and person they all claimed to be trying to protect.[45]

(iii) Parliament and 'the post-reformation public sphere'

Parliament thus became a means of expanding the counsel-giving classes, bringing wider (protestant, and even puritan) opinion to bear on the policy-making process; reopening issues closed down, or arguments lost, in court and council. This was far from the entirely top-down process that some of the more enthusiastically revisionist accounts of the period have claimed. At stake were as much questions of ideological affinity, of shared values and aims, as ties of patronage or interest. Many so-called 'council men of business' had views and agendas of their own. Indeed, their value to their patrons in the council turned as much on their reputation for independence, their expertise as parliament men and their godly connections, as it did on personal connection or ambition. Moreover, on occasion, other people, from outside the charmed circle of official patronage, could raise their voices and seek to take over the agenda.

Parliament thus became a pressure point, in Geoffrey Elton's phrase, a point of contact, as well as of friction. But these appeals to wider publics, to the protestant political nation, if you will, were not only launched in and through parliament. At moments of particularly intense crisis, sometimes in order to prepare for a parliament and sometimes not, appeals could be made to broader bodies of opinion via a range of media – print, pulpit, libel, rumour.

Perhaps the best example of such a co-ordinated campaign comes from the early 1570s when, in an effort to get the duke of Norfolk and Mary Stuart executed, that quintessential council man of business, Thomas Norton, wrote a series of anonymous pamphlets. Sanctioned by authority, these tracts presented themselves as the thoughts of an independent commonwealthsman concerned for the safety of his queen and the realm. At the behest of Cecil himself, a scandalous pamphlet attack on Mary Stuart by George Buchanan was translated from Latin into imitation Scots and published in London. Rumours were spread in the capital, security measures put in place designed to disseminate news of a planned rising and invasion; all of which activity and agitation culminated in a campaign in both houses of parliament to have Norfolk and Mary executed. The result was a classically Elizabethan compromise: Norfolk went to the block, but Mary survived.

In that case members of the council and the bench of bishops were working with members of both Houses, and using the privileged sounding board of parliament, to put pressure on the queen; at other times, the mere prospect of a parliament, together with popular agitation, might do the trick. Here the outstanding example is the queen's projected match with the duke of Anjou, which was met with printed propaganda in the shape of John Stubbs' famous tract, A gaping gulf, and by a pulpit campaign; these together with Burghley's claim that a marriage treaty could not be concluded without parliamentary approval, worked, and the match went unmade.[46]

A protestant political nation was being mobilised, indeed called into being, through such agitations. The reasoning behind these manoeuvres becomes clearer in the context of the underlying dynastic situation. Contemporaries of all confessional stripes knew that if Elizabeth died with Mary Stuart alive or the succession unsettled, the reaction of the populace would matter enormously. At the crucial moment of Northumberland's coup, after Edward's death, what had done for the duke and the Greys had been the spontaneous rallying to Mary of the East Anglian gentry and others. This time round, in the event of Elizabeth's sudden death, men at the centre of the regime knew that they would have to mobilise the protestant political nation at every social level against the both loyalist and Catholic impulses backing Mary Stuart or (after 1587) any other Catholic claimant.

Thus in 1584, alarmed by the recent assassination of William of Orange, terrified of a similar attempt on Elizabeth, desperate to bring James VI back under something like English protestant control, and alarmed by a proposal to associate Mary with her son in the government of Scotland, the council also had recourse to the Bond of Association. This was an oath to be signed by any and every willing subject, with each signatory swearing that if the queen were killed, he would hunt down and kill first her murderers and then anyone likely to benefit from her death. Expressly couched in the language of revenge, the bond was an official exercise in something like lynch law, designed to persuade any potential Catholic assassin that an attempt on Elizabeth's life would simply not be worth the candle.[47]

Such activities were predicated on a species of officially disseminated conspiracy theory, a vision of the threat at home and abroad, from Catholics plotting the downfall of the queen and realm. Since the early 1570s elements within the Elizabethan establishment and their clients and supporters had been pumping out versions of that story organised around different dastardly Catholic plots, ranging from the revolt of the northern earls, through the Ridolfi conspiracy, the Throckmorton and Parry plots, to the Babington conspiracy, the machinations of Dr Lopez and beyond. On this account, English Catholics were part of an international conspiracy: to kill the queen, to put Mary on the throne, and thus to undermine the integrity, unity and independence of the kingdom. Spain, the Guise and French Catholics, Catholic missionary priests, indeed English Catholics *tout court*, were all pictured as being in on the conspiracy.

There were religious and secular versions of this theory. In the religious version, the Pope was Antichrist and the real threat was popery, a false idolatrous anti-religion, demonic in its origins and tyrannical in its methods. In the more secular version, Spain was the real threat, and the aim a universal monarchy to be wielded not so much by the papacy as by Philip II. Here religion was not the major motivating factor, and the spread of popish error and papal power not the main aim. Rather religion was being used as a mask or pretext for the oppressive and tyrannical secular ends of the Spanish crown.

(iv) Theatre and the creation of a 'protestant nation'

Thanks to the remarkable researches of Scott McMillin and Sally-Beth MacClean we now know that the theatre was an integral part of these attempts to create, shape, appeal to, and if regicidal push ever came to Marian shove, to mobilise, a protestant political nation. In March 1583, the Queen's Men was

founded. Twelve of the leading actors from the existing acting troupes, which
had hitherto operated under the patronage of the earls of Leicester, Sussex,
Oxford and Derby, were brought together into a company which was now to
operate under the direct patronage of the queen. This amalgamation was
effected by the earl of Leicester and Sir Francis Walsingham for what McMillin
and MacClean argue were largely political reasons. While the company thus
formed dominated court performance until the early 1590s and regularly played
in and around London, they lacked a permanent London base and spent a great
deal of their time on the road, their travels taking them not only into East
Anglia and the south-west but also into the midlands and far into the north.
McMillin and MacClean conclude that 'from the beginning of their career in
1583 to their final year, 1602–3, the Queen's Men were quite simply the best
known and most widely travelled professional company in the kingdom'.[48]

On the one hand, McMillin and MacClean claim, the aim was simply to
extend the reach of royal influence into the provinces. Since the queen did not
go on progress during the 1580s and, once she resumed the practice in 1591
and 1592, did not venture beyond Sudeley Castle, 'it was all the more important', they argue, 'for her performers to concentrate on extending the royal
outreach to Dorset and Devon in the south-west and the north beyond
Coventry where their patron did not go'. In taking on this role, the new company
was emulating Leicester's Men, who, 'carrying their patron's name across the
land', had 'made local contacts of undoubted political use'.[49]

But the new company was doing so at a new level of intensity, a level enabled
by their capacity as a very large troupe to divide into two in order to take
reduced versions of their repertoire into more areas of the country than, as a
unified whole, they otherwise could. This practice maximised both their
income – earning them 'higher rewards than had ever been paid for travelling
players' – and their geographical and social reach. (McMillin and MacClean
argue that the maintenance of what they term 'public relations' may have been
'a key motive for the northern tours, as financial profit could more readily be
had in the south'.) Thus, as McMillin and Maclean conclude, the Queen's Men
were able 'to cover most regions of the kingdom' – 'except perhaps the further
reaches of the south-west and the Scottish borders and the north west' – as
well, of course, as London, to which they returned every October or November,
playing at various venues in and about the city and at the Christmas festivities
at court.[50]

But the intended effect transcended what we might term the medium –
the display of the royal livery and the queen's servants in the provinces – to
include the message, that is to say, the nature and contents of the plays actually
being performed. Thus, McMillin and MacClean identify *Three Lords and
Three Ladies* as 'obviously an anti-Catholic play' but also one with distinctly
anti-puritan overtones. *The true tragedy of Richard III* explicitly asserted the

hereditary right of Queen Elizabeth and the moral mission of the Tudors; *The troublesome reign of King John* placed the current show-down with popery and Spain in a long-term apocalyptic context, picturing Henry VIII and Elizabeth as the successful inheritors of King John's failed attempt to see off the papacy and exhorting the English people and nobility to unite against the foreign and papal threats. *Selimus* celebrated the defeat of the Armada and *The famous victories of Henry V* the achievement of one of the greatest of English military heroes in a war fought against the greatest European power of the day. 'There is no question', claim McMillin and MacClean, 'that these plays' represent 'a campaign to give legitimacy to a protestant drive for substantial truth and plain speech', and that the Queen's Men of 1583 provided the regime with ideal means to bring 'the theatre back into the service of a protestant ideology which could be identified with the "truth" of Tudor history'. 'It requires no great stretch of imagination', they assert, 'to think that Walsingham or others from the Barn Elms literary circle regarded English history as the best field for the company to dramatise', and dramatise it they did, virtually inventing the English history play in the process.[51]

It would, of course, be ludicrous, on this basis, to categorise the theatre as a whole, or even the Queen's Men themselves, as some sort of ideological state apparatus, a mere engine or emanation of state power, especially since the researches of Sally-Beth MacClean and Lawrence Manley have revealed that in Lord Strange's Men, the acting company patronised by Ferdinando, Lord Strange, later the earl of Derby, we have a company whose repertoire was decidedly more conservative, and rabidly anti-puritan, than anything produced by the Queen's Men.[52] Evidently the theatre could be used to broadcast more than one take on the current religio-political conjuncture. Here we find fundamental differences of tone and orientation within the political nation, differences between hot protestant, puritan-friendly supporters of the protestant state and catholic loyalist and rabidly anti-puritan conformist supporters of a rather different version of what the Elizabethan regime either was or ought to become, reflected in the different offerings on the public stage.

However, while the theatre can scarcely be accused of pumping out an ideologically uniform message, thanks to McMillin and MacClean we surely can identify the commercial theatre, and the touring theatre companies, as amongst a number of cultural institutions and practices operating – in this case, designedly – to connect the centre to the localities, to take messages and cultural materials from the centre out into the periphery, to create syntheses between various traditional festive cultural and even perhaps, in one sense of the word, religious forms and some of the most avant-garde and innovatory trends and tendencies of the period. These trends are often organised under the signs of protestantism, humanism and capitalism or, perhaps rather more precisely, of post-reformation confessional conflict, various attempts at further reformation and the creation of godly and loyalist publics, and the sale of different sorts of text and performance to the increasing swathe of contemporaries with disposable income to spend on various leisure activities and forms of conspicuous consumption.[53]

As just such an emergently mixed form, the commercial theatre has long been acknowledged as the cause of considerable contemporary social and political anxiety. What McMillin and MacClean's analysis suggests is that, despite that, elements within the regime could perfectly well see how the theatre and theatrical performance could be made to serve the interests of protestant and monarchical order; and all that at the crisis point of 'the monarchical republic', when the 'Elizabethan exclusion crisis' seemed about, perhaps definitively, to heat up.

According to Andrew Gurr the next great restructuring of the theatre in the early 1590s was also a function of careful planning by central elements in the regime, as the existing repertory and acting talent was reorganised once more. The virtual monopoly enjoyed by the Queen's Men was turned into what into Gurr terms a 'duopoly', with two companies, the Lord Chamberlain's Men and the Admiral's Men, based on two London theatres, the Theatre and the Rose, monopolising performance in the city and largely sharing performances at court.[54]

In many ways the Queen's Men were the victims of changing tastes in dramaturgy, changes driven by the emergence of Marlowe, Shakespeare and Kyd and, in all likelihood, of the shifting sands of court patronage, after the passing of many of the dominant figures of the high Elizabethan age – including both Leicester and Walsingham – in the late 1580s and early 1590s. Certainly they gave their last performance at court in 1594, and lived out the rest of their existence as a touring company. Again, just as with the foundation of the Queen's Men in 1583, we have no direct evidence of the thinking behind these changes, but, Gurr argues, the neatness with which the spoils were divided, with the Admiral's Men getting Marlowe's plays and the Lord Chamberlain's many of the Queen's Men's, suggests a coherent plan emanating from the centre of the regime.

The result was a major shift in the structure of the theatre; as McMillin and MacClean conclude, 'henceforth the purpose built playhouses would be central to the successful companies . . . The peripatetic movement of the Queen's Men was giving way to fixtures near the city and after 1594 there is no doubt that London was the centre of the commercial theatre.'[55] In London, the companies addressed a mass, both socially and ideologically heterogeneous, audience. As Gurr concludes, 'in 1595 the estimates suggest that the two acting companies were visited by 15,000 people weekly'. 'On average', he opines, over the 'seventy years or so of London commercial theatre' there were 'as many as a million visits to the playhouse a year'.[56] The audiences thus assembled encompassed a very wide social spectrum. As Andrew Gurr observes, 'beggars and fishwives, epitomes of Elizabethan penury, were noted presences in the yard as much as the hordes of apprentices'.[57]

It was, therefore, for such inherently mixed mass audiences, assembled both in the metropole and in the localities, and in the context, not of the 'Elizabethan exclusion crisis' nor of a coherently 'monarchically republican' version of the Elizabethan regime, of the sort that had called the Queen's Men into being, but rather during the prospective succession crisis that character-ised the Elizabethan *fin de siècle*, that Shakespeare wrote his history plays.

(v) Putting the Catholics back in

Such efforts to propagandise and mobilise protestant opinion, and the inter-mittent attempts – at moments of actual or perceived or incipient crisis – to put pressure on the queen, almost inevitably provoked a response from Catholics.

Confronted by the efforts of the regime and various of its supporters, hangers-on or hot protestant critics, all of whom, for different reasons, were anxious to make much of the popish threat and to cast Catholicism and Catholics in general, and Mary Stuart in particular, as the ultimate threat to the continued stability of the regime, some English Catholics responded by producing the completely different account of events based on the conspiracy theory outlined in the opening pages of this section. *The treatise of treasons* was written in response to the campaign against Norfolk and Mary Stuart; *Leicester's commonwealth* in response to the failure of the Anjou match and the very same conjuncture that, on the protestant side, called forth the Bond of Association.

What these Catholic authors produced was a generic amalgam of the polit-ical libel and the secret history, which portrayed the politics of the regime as a politics of conspiracy and offered to tear the veil of official lies away from what was really happening in order to reveal the entirely self-serving, corrupt and tyrannical conspiracy that was, in fact, shaping the politics of the realm.

We have here two sets of conspiracy theories; different accounts of the same events, each an inverted mirror image of the other. Where the supporters of the regime saw a monarchical republic, a collection of good counsellors and virtuous commonwealthsmen, dedicated both to the service of queen and country and to the values of true religion in the face of the popish threat, their Catholic victims saw a conspiracy of evil counsellors and Machiavels, practical atheists, dedicated to the service of their own corrupt interests and ambitions rather than to any recognisable version of the common good or of true religion. These mutually exclusive, but in many ways mutually dependent, views of the situation were in play from (at least) the early 1570s until the end of reign.

In the way of conspiracy theories, these two often seemed to confirm one another. Thus while the signatories of the Bond of Association claimed to be protecting the person of the queen and the integrity of the realm, certain Catholics saw in those very expedients the culmination of a plot to do in Mary and to do away with Elizabeth. But, of course, the Council claimed only to be having recourse to such desperate measures because of the duplicity and malice of the Catholics, of which books like *The treatise of treasons* or *Leicester's commonwealth* seemed (to them) the perfect proof.[58]

(vi) The Essexian project

Collinson's notion of the exclusion crisis was organised around the threat of Mary Stuart, and one might be tempted to assume that with Mary's demise the 'crisis' would go away. But that was far from the case. After all, for all that Mary's son, James VI, was a protestant, the succession remained unsettled, and thus a subject for speculation, intrigue and anxiety. Not only that, but the dynamics of 'the exclusion crisis' might be thought to have had a positively integrative effect on the inner workings of the Elizabethan regime, serving to unite the major players against the spectre of a Marian accession. Thus, the removal of the immediate Marian threat freed up the succession issue to operate in far less unifying ways, as different groups and individuals started to jockey for position in advance of what was now taken to be the imminent death of the queen, with the succession still unsettled and the identity of the succeeding monarch, and thus the character of the next regime, both threateningly unclear. The situation was exacerbated by the removal by the Grim Reaper of most of the central pillars of the Elizabethan establishment, who began to die with alarming regularity in the late 1580s. By the early 1590s, with Walsingham, Leicester, Warwick, Mildmay and Hatton all gone, Burghley was almost the last surviving member of the governing clique that had dominated the high Elizabethan period. Indeed with the exception of Hatton, who rose to prominence in the later 1570s, that group had been together since the 1560s, and their dispersal now, almost at a stroke – at a moment when the issue of the succession was rendered increasingly pressing by the advancing years of the queen, and the war with Spain was reaching a crisis point – occasioned a good deal of anxiety and no little conflict.

On this basis, some scholars have written of the 1590s as a distinctively new beginning, even as 'a second reign', while others have spoken of a 'succession crisis'.[59] On this account, the 1590s experienced levels of factional conflict unheard of during the high Elizabethan period, as the looming prospect of the queen's death with the succession still unsettled, together with the conduct of the war and latterly the issue of whether, and on what terms, to conclude a peace with Spain, combined to plunge the regime into something like crisis; a crisis that culminated in the fiasco of the Essex rebellion.

While acknowledging the very considerably heightened tensions of the 1590s, recent work has tended to push the start of unappeasable factional division into the period after 1598; that is to say, after the death of Burghley, when the linked questions of peace with Spain and the succession became integrally connected, at least in the minds of the earl of Essex and James VI, both of whom suspected those in favour of peace of wanting to include the succession amongst the issues in play in any negotiations with the Spanish.

Along with these developments has come a major reappraisal of the role and significance, not to mention of the political and cultural style, of the earl of Essex himself. Work by Paul Hammer and Alexandra Gajda has identified Essex as perhaps the major political and military figure of the decade.[60] Hammer's work places him at the very centre of the Elizabethan war effort. Essex emerged as the leading patron of military men, and thus as the successor to his uncle Leicester. He also made perfervid efforts to establish intelligence networks of his own and thus to take on the mantle of Sir Francis Walsingham as well. Essex's determination to sustain a career as a soldier and a counsellor was matched by his commitment to the prosecution of the war against Spain at the highest levels of intensity. Also, from the early 1590s he was also the only member of the Elizabethan inner circle in close contact with James VI and by 1594/5 at the latest, when Parsons dedicated his *Conference about the next succession* to the earl on precisely those terms, was widely believed to be the most likely architect of the next reign.

Alex Gajda's recent work on the cultural and intellectual milieu of the Essex circle has now revealed what we might term the ideological underpinning of the Essex project. Thanks to the researches of Hammer and Gajda, it is now clear that what was at stake in Essex's career was not merely the overweening ambition of a decidedly unstable young aristocrat on the make, but rather an ambitious ideological and political programme or project, organised around the need to defend the civil and political liberty of Western Europe, and in England the protestant succession, from Hapsburg schemes for universal monarchy.

Essex's determination to personify the political and intellectual legacies of Leicester and Walsingham involved the patronage of the puritan godly. Together with his aggressively anti-Spanish agenda, this won him a very considerable puritan following. But while Essex could talk the appropriately anti-popish talk when he had to, his version of the universal monarchy against which he took the realm to be engaged in a life or death struggle was centred on an essentially secular analysis of Hapsburg ambition rather than on a conventionally anti-Catholic vision of the Pope as Antichrist. In this view, the pope was an agent or adjunct of Hapsburg imperialism and tyranny rather than the king of Spain an instrument or willing dupe of the Antichristian spiritual pretensions of the papacy. While the differences in play here were ones of nuance, they also meant that Essex was quite willing to entertain the notion of Catholic loyalism and accept into his service and circle Catholics of proven anti-Spanish or anti-Hapsburg mettle. Hence his continued insistence that

Henry IV remain England's major ally in the struggle with Spain even after Henry's conversion to Catholicism and his close friendship with Phillip II's former secretary Antonio Pérez, not to mention with Thomas Wright, the renegade Jesuit.

The result was that Essex had both a clientage network and a range of admirers or well-willers that encompassed radical puritans like the divine, Stephen Egerton, more moderate puritans like the Somerset gentleman and parliament man, Sir Francis Hastings, evangelical protestants and rabid anti-Catholics like the Archbishop of York, Matthew Hutton, as well as Pérez, and the renegade Jesuit, Thomas Wright. As Gajda's work shows, this was not an ideologically incoherent mélange, the product of mere opportunism or confusion, but rather of an intellectually consistent ideological agenda, with a version of liberty of conscience somewhere near its heart.[61]

Within Essex's circle a variety of intellectuals, intelligencers and men of business were employed in exercises in politic history, of varying degrees of sophistication and abstraction. In this, too, Essex proved the inheritor of various practices and attitudes prevalent in the circles surrounding Leicester, Walsingham and Sir Philip Sidney. Intelligence was sifted, contemporary events analysed from the perspective provided by the histories of near-contemporary and medieval Europe and the ancient world. While a great deal of the resulting intellectual effort went into unmasking Hapsburg tyranny, decoding Hapsburg plotting and manoeuvre, and framing policy initiatives to counter them, it also produced a general attitude to the dynamics of power and the analysis of court politics that could be applied at home as well as abroad. The result was an increasingly suspicious and polarised view of the moves and machinations of the Elizabethan court and an increasingly contemptuous attitude to the earl's erstwhile colleagues and rivals within the Elizabethan establishment.[62]

For the mode of politic history being practised within the Essex circle recalled nothing so much as the evil counsel narratives of the Catholic tracts. Lent perhaps an extra layer of sophistication through the study of Tacitus and other classical authors, this mode of analysis looked for surreptitious manoeuvre and dissimulation within a court politics conceived as a struggle for advantage, access and power. Not only that, but Essex himself fitted rather well into the category of the ancient aristocracy shoved aside by the low-born Machiavels, identified by the majority of the Catholic tracts with Essex's current rivals, the Cecils.

As the decade progressed, rivalry, tension, animosity, a certain mutual contempt and distrust morphed into an outright conspiracy theory which saw the Cecils and their allies pursuing peace with Spain with every intention of selling the protestant succession of James VI down the river, and all to preserve their own hold on power. It was that vision which prompted, and was intended to legitimise, the Essex rebellion, and which Essex himself articulated at his trial, citing Robert Cecil's conversance with the *Conference about the next succession* to clinch the argument.[63]

On this basis there is a good case to be made that the polarisation and factionalisation of the late Elizabethan political scene began in the perfervid imaginations of the Essex circle. This is not to accept the claim that either Essex himself, or indeed central elements within his circle, were mere paranoid fantasists. On the contrary, given their premises and aims, their view of the contemporary world and of the nature of politics, and their sense of what was at stake in the court politics of the day – nothing short of the fate of Europe and of the Gospel, of the cause of liberty, both civil and spiritual, in its confrontation with Hapsburg tyranny – these were not irrational opinions. Certainly, irrational or not, they were shared by a range of contemporaries, up to and including not merely Jesuit exiles and Catholic *engagés* like Robert Parsons and Joseph Cresswell, but also James VI himself.[64]

As the researches of Paul Hammer have revealed, Essex was also the inheritor of the now long-standing Elizabethan mode of public politics, whereby pitches for public support were made through various media, to unite a range of protestant and politique opinion behind the policies of the regime, often by the dissemination of conspiracy theories concerning the conduct and ambition of the English Catholics, the house of Guise, the Catholic League and Philip II of Spain.

This was a political style of which Burghley and his circle were past masters. But whereas Burghley was always careful not to use such tales to talk about himself – he used other means, most notably the acquisition of vast wealth and an aggressively grandiloquent building programme to promote the glories of the house of Cecil – Essex was almost always the hero of his own story. In court entertainments, circulated manuscripts, leaked memos, tracts and treatises prepared for the press and sometimes even printed, Essex presented himself as the hero of the hour; an aristocrat of ancient lineage, one of the natural counsellors of the queen, anxious to vindicate his honour, and prove his virtue, in the service of the queen and commonwealth as both a soldier and a counsellor.[65]

But the purpose of all this self-promotion was not only mere self-aggrandisement. For just like Burghley before him, Essex was attempting to mobilise various levels of opinion to force certain policies or agendas on the queen; policies and agendas that he took to be crucial for the safety of the queen and state, but which Elizabeth herself was often anything but keen to adopt. The result was that Essex quickly acquired a reputation for 'popularity', a drive to promote himself before the people in ways that, his enemies claimed, were deeply subversive of the monopoly that all monarchs ought to enjoy over the rapt attention and love of their subjects.

By the early to mid-1590s there had emerged to public view the lineaments of what we might term 'the Essexian project'; one designed to prosecute to the uttermost the war against Spain, conceived as a life or death struggle between liberty and tyranny, between true religion and liberty of conscience and persecution; to use that struggle against the foreigner, conceived in largely secular, rather than aggressively confessional terms, to unite all true Englishmen, up to and including a certain stripe of Catholic loyalist, in the defence of the queen and realm, while also ensuring the cause of monarchical legitimacy (not to mention the protestant succession) by securing the accession of the queen's one true heir, James VI. And to achieve all that through a mixture of the politics of aristocratic honour and virtue, of military prowess and of 'popularity', attributes and modes of political action that, it was claimed both by Essex himself and his admirers, all reached their apogee in the person and career of the earl of Essex.

In what follows I read several history plays not so much against various aspects of the career and fate of the earl of Essex – although at crucial points in the argument I do just that – but more broadly against the Essexian melange conceived as a political project and ideological synthesis. Some of Shakespeare's histories can be found buying in hard to that project – here one thinks of *1 Henry VI, King John* and (read one way) *Henry V*; but others – *Richard II, 1 and 2 Henry IV,* and even (read another way) *Henry V* itself – emerge as classic instances of criticism as compliment and compliment as critique, and perhaps even as counsel. Others – *Julius Caesar, Hamlet* and most obviously *Troilus and Cressida* – subject the coherence and consequence of the Essexian project, both the compatibility of its constituent elements and the earl's own temperament and career, to an intense, almost forensic, and sometimes positively withering, critique.

The arts of history

In 1584 the French king's younger brother, Anjou, died. Anjou's death meant that if Henry III of France died childless, as now seemed inevitable, his heir would be the protestant, Henry of Navarre. The situation in France now exactly paralleled that in England, only in reverse. Both countries had a current incumbent of one religious persuasion – in England, protestant, in France, Catholic – and an heir of another – in England, Catholic, and in France, protestant. Anjou's death sparked in certain Catholic circles in France initiatives very similar to those taken by the protestant regime in England. The Catholic League and the Guise pressed Henry III to disinherit Navarre, to settle the succession on a Catholic, and to crush heresy once and for all. Such policies appealed to Henry III about as much as their English equivalents appealed to Elizabeth.

After a series of political stand-offs – the day of the barricades, the murder of Guise (allegedly because he was plotting to murder the king), the assassination of Henry III – France descended into an overt and bloody civil war

between Navarre and the League over who should be king. In France, therefore, Elizabethan onlookers could see precisely the fatal combination of
dynastic and religious civil war that the Catholic pamphlets of the early 1590s
(the so-called Cecil's commonwealth tracts) predicted would overtake England
when Elizabeth died, as now, it appeared, she inevitably must, with the succession unsettled. On this view, if late Elizabethans wanted a glimpse of what
might well be lying in store for them in the near future they could do so, not
only by looking back to English history, but also by merely looking across the
Channel to France.

For a period, France was the military arena in which the balance of power
in Western Europe was being decided. The Armada may have failed, but the
threat of invasion had scarcely gone away, and the severity of that threat now
turned on who controlled the Channel ports of northern France. In France, the
Catholic League was in alliance with Spain; after the death of Guise, Cardinal
Bourbon became the leading Catholic candidate for the French throne and,
after his death, some Catholic zealots began actively pushing the candidacy of
the Infanta or even of Philip II himself. Parma's army entered France to help the
League, while English troops were fighting in France and the Low Countries. If
Spain and the League prevailed in France, they would control the Channel
ports and be able to threaten both the Dutch and the English at will.[66]

Understandably, then, the number of publications about events in France
reached a peak in the period 1588–92. These texts covered the full range of available genres and forms: news-sheets, polemic, extended political treatises, plays,
and libellous secret histories. These last constituted counter-libels, in effect replies
to the Catholic libels about the Elizabethan regime, with essentially the same
narrative structures and claims. Again, these libellous accounts of recent French
politics presented religion as a mere mask for the barefaced pursuit of power.
They depicted the methods to be employed to attain supreme power as essentially
the same: first establishing a monopoly of access and influence, of power and
patronage, at court; then parting the prince from his heir; then doing away with
prince himself in a desperate attempt to divert the succession and usurp the
throne. It was just that in these narratives the villains of the piece were the Guise,
the League, and Spain – and the aim, the usurpation of the French crown, first by
the Guise, and then, after his death, by Philip of Spain or the Infanta, or some
other Spanish surrogate. But, the pamphlets claimed, the real aim was universal
monarchy, a form of world domination by the Hapsburgs and the Spanish, a
secular ambition which paralleled the spiritual ambitions and pretensions of the
papacy, and for which the furtherance of the Catholic faith and the suppression
of heresy was merely a means and a blind.[67]

By the late 1580s and early 1590s there were, therefore, two different sorts
of what we might (somewhat anachronistically) call political history widely
available in England. First, there was the libellous secret histories of court

manoeuvre and faction, of machiavellian calculation, of sedition and assassination, resistance and civil war, usurpation and tyranny, to be found both in the illicit Catholic versions of recent Elizabethan history and in the entirely licit, translated accounts of recent French history; and, second, there were the chronicle histories of England – the most famous Holinshed's *Chronicle*, the first version of which was produced in the 1570s, with a revised and extended second edition coming out in 1587.

These chronicles were famously the sources of a third form of history, that contained in the history plays themselves; plays which brought the events of the relatively recent past to wide audiences both in London and in the provinces. On the current argument, it was no accident that precisely this period – that is to say, the late 1580s and early 1590s – saw the emergence of the genre of the history play. For we are dealing here with a political conjuncture created by the interaction of three 'crises': firstly, the crisis *in potentia* created by an ageing queen and an unsettled English succession; secondly, the very pressing and continuing crisis of the war with Spain, now reaching its climacteric point in the final struggle over the fate of the French crown; and thirdly, the awful warning provided by current events in France of what could happen in England, if and when the first two crises coincided and bled into one another. On this account, the history play was a genre called into being by the availability of relatively new cultural materials, different modes of doing history, and the pressing nature of a range of issues – succession, the war and how the two might interact in the immediate future, the explicit public discussion of which was entirely illicit but could be handled in plain sight on the public stage, when dealt with, as it were, historically.

The plays, then, used history – events in the past – the English past and to a lesser extent the Roman past – to comment upon the history of the day and to stage what were often extremely controversial subjects of immediately contemporary concern and discussion. War against the foreigner, England threatened by invasions and internal seditions, by monarchical weakness, by an excess of enervating and corrupting female influence over the levers of power, by evil counsel – were all staged in Peel's *Edward I*, *Edward III*, and *The troublesome reign of King John*. Disputed successions and civil war were central themes in *Locrine*, *Edmund Ironside*, and Lodge's *Wounds of civil war*. Marlowe introduced central elements of the French civil wars into English settings and to the English stage. The story of Edward II and Gaveston had been used in a famous Catholic League pamphlet written in French by an English Catholic to excoriate the weakness and corruption of Henry III and his mignons. In his play *Edward II* Marlowe returned the favour by using the same events to bring materials and concerns from the French wars of religion directly to the English stage,[68] something Marlowe did more directly still in *The massacre at Paris*. Tyranny and sedition, resistance, usurpation and regicide, all these were staged in *Edward II* (again), in Shakespeare's *Henry VI* plays, *Richard III*, *Richard II* and in the anonymous *Woodstock*.

What some of these plays – certainly those written by Shakespeare – acted out on stage was what the libellous histories also claimed to reveal – that is to say, the inner workings of royal government, the mysteries of state, the workings of the *arcana imperii*, what politics was really about, rather than the smooth-faced official version(s) used to legitimise the policies of the queen and her counsellors, so comprehensively described by Kevin Sharpe in his magisterial study *Selling the Tudor monarchy*.[69] These were topics about which the ordinary subject was not supposed even to think, let alone to talk or speculate. But in the plays such issues were being offered up for discussion in plain sight, before mass audiences who merely had to pay a few pence for the pleasure of seeing the doings of the great and the good stripped bare before their very eyes.[70]

As a number of historians have argued, late humanists were trained to read history (and indeed other classical texts) for 'use', that is to say to extract from various accounts of the past crucial insights and apothegms with which to engage with contemporary concerns and dilemmas. Conventional scholarly wisdom sees the earliest accounts of how to do this dominated by a Ciceronian concern with virtue and prudence; with history conceived (as Cicero put it in his *De oratore*) as *magistra vitae* and *lux veritatis*. This Ciceronian, virtue-centred, mode was then superseded, conventional wisdom has it, by a more politic, Tacitean mode, centred less on the dynamics of virtue than on the demands of reason of state and the description and negotiation of what was perceived as an increasingly corrupt court politics. This transition is often taken to have occurred in England during the 1590s, when the sharpening tone of factional conflict at court coincided with the availability of the central texts by Tacitus, translated with a suitably Machiavellian inflection by Sir Henry Savile,[71] and the writing of the first politic histories in English, developments all associated (although far from exclusively) with the circle around the earl of Essex.[72] Some scholars have read into this transition from a Ciceronian to a Tacitean mode or moment other equally stark contrasts and binary oppositions between a secular, 'modern'-minded politic history and a moralised and providentialised, indeed a positively 'medieval', chronicle tradition. As we shall see below, such contrasts are considerably overdrawn.[73]

Certainly, as Daniel Woolf explains, the central, essentially Ciceronian, contentions of myriad exercises in the *ars historica*[74] had, by the 1580s, become entirely conventional. 'By 1581, such assumptions had grown so prevalent that John Marbeck could define history in a mere two lines: "What an historie is. Tullie calleth an historie the witnesse of times, the light of virtue, the life of memorie, maistres of life." '[75] That is true as far as it goes, but such formulations perhaps underplay the extent to which history was studied not merely to see virtue rewarded and vice punished, but also for reasons of policy and prudence.

We can see how this all worked if we turn to the first English example of the *ars historica* in English, John Blundeville's *True order and method of writing and reading histories*. This was, in fact, a translation of, and compilation out of, two Italian texts, the one written by Francesco Patrizzi and the other by Giacomo Aconcio (Acontius).[76] Blundeville claimed that there were three reasons to read history: 'to acknowledge the providence of God', 'by the examples of the wise', to 'learn ... wisely to behave ourselves in all our actions, as well private as public, both in time of peace and war' and to be 'stirred by example of the good to follow the good, and by example of the evil to flee the evil'. Similarly, in his dedication to the earl of Leicester, Blundeville commended as exemplary the earl's reading of histories 'not as many do, to pass away the time, but to gather thereby such judgement and knowledge as you may thereby be the more able as well to direct your private actions as to give counsel, like a most prudent counsellor in public causes, be it matters of war or peace'.[77]

That Aconcio had been Leicester's client and that Blundeville dedicated his tract to Leicester were no accidents. As Anthony Grafton and Lisa Jardine have shown, from the 1570s onwards scholars and counsellors about the court, and particularly members of the earl of Leicester's circle, had been engaged in critical readings of historical texts, readings often intensely focused on topics of immediate contemporary concern. In so doing, they had employed university-educated humanists and scholars, men anxious to make their way in the world, to do the initial legwork for them, by epitomising or abstracting the passages or texts deemed crucial to whatever the problem or topic of concern might be. In this way, large quantities of historical knowledge could be reduced into usable packages of precedent or apothegm.

Grafton and Jardine have identified spates of such intensive reading, involving Gabriel Harvey and various luminaries of the Elizabethan political elite. One such occurred in and around 1580, immediately after the intense discussions within the regime, in general, and within the Leicester circle in particular, of the wisdom or otherwise of the Anjou match.[78] At one point, all of the inner circle of the regime had been called upon to respond to an initial position paper by the earl of Sussex, which praised to the skies the advantages of the match. The result was a number of extended politic disquisitions on the options with which the regime was now confronted. Here was a crucial question of policy being subjected to various sorts of politique, historical and prudential, as well, of course, as moral and religious, argument. Nor were such exercises in politic analysis limited to the inner reaches of the regime. In John Stubbs' notorious tract, *The gaping gulf*, versions of many of the central arguments – some of them overtly apocalyptic and drenched in anti-popery, but others almost entirely politique in both form and content – were laid before the reading public

It may not be an accident that Sir Philip Sidney produced his *Defence of poetry* immediately after these exchanges, just as, as Blair Worden has argued, in the *Arcadia*, he turned to 'poetry' to discuss what he saw as the most pressing issues of the day and to process what Worden's researches have revealed as the trauma of the Anjou debacle. *The defence of poetry* claimed to subsist in a Ciceronian world of virtue, a world in which the poet far exceeded either the historian or the philosopher in his capacity to discover, depict, and disseminate what could and what ought to be, as opposed to what is or what had been. As Blair Worden puts it, 'Sidney's *Defence of poetry* ... pleads a case which its author' only 'half believes'; even as it proclaims 'the superiority of poetry to other forms of instruction, particularly philosophy and history,' it [*The defence*] mocks them in terms which are at odds with what he [Sidney] writes in other places'.[79]

Certainly, we know that Sidney had been, and continued to be, committed to the reading of histories for intensely practical, politic as well as morally improving purposes. Indeed, Gabriel Harvey even went so far as to identify Sidney as one of those who had 'won my heart to Livy'. On this basis, Worden describes Sidney as having been 'in at the birth' of 'the "politic" or "civil" history which, in the late sixteenth and early seventeenth centuries ... invented, or reinvented, the science of politics'. Waxing epigrammatic, Worden observes that just as 'ethical Humanism was inherited by his [Sidney's] generation', so 'political history was discovered by it'.

Admittedly, 'in at the birth' and 'discovered' might be taken somewhat to overstate the case, for Kathy Shrank finds the reading practices and habits of mind identified by Worden, Grafton and Jardine as distinctive of the 1570s and 1580s 'representative of humanist reading practices throughout the sixteenth century'. Certainly, she finds them already alive and well in Edward VI's reign, in the circles of university-educated humanists and bureaucrats clustered around the centre of the regime. That group encompassed the likes of Sir John Cheke, William Cecil, Sir Thomas Wilson, Sir Thomas Smith and William Thomas, who, as Shrank points out, was employed by Northumberland to send the young Edward VI weekly essays on political topics, essays suffused with the influence of Machiavelli. Thomas' *History of Italy* of 1549 was, Shrank observes, quite as 'geared to political analysis' and practice as any of Gabriel Harvey's later readings of Livy.[80] First identified nearly thirty years ago by Winthrop Hudson as 'the Cambridge connection', the same circle is to be found at the centre of Mary Partridge's seminal account of the English appropriation (and translation) of Castiglione's *Book of the courtier*. As a number of historians have observed, the Elizabethan political (and ecclesiastical) establishments were in many ways returning Edwardian establishments and they clearly brought their fundamental reading practices and habits of mind back into office with them from various (either real or internal) states of Marian exile.[81]

However, whatever the precise chronology, Worden's basic point surely still stands; the 'tension' he finds in Sidney – 'between his ethical Humanism, which says how men ought to be, and his embrace of politic history, which says how they are' – was indeed a central feature of the engagement with history of the English humanists, courtiers and counsellors of the second half of the sixteenth century and beyond. Thus, when Worden concludes that 'the insights Sidney derived from Machiavelli were not always compatible with the philosophy of public virtue,'[82] he is remarking on precisely the same sorts of tensions, even contradictions, that Daniel Woolf discerns in later (early Stuart) historical writing, which he finds 'fraught with tensions, ambiguities, and uncertainties', all of them centred on 'Machiavelli and his teachings'.[83]

On this account, then, the line between a Ciceronian, virtue-obsessed, 'before', and a cynical, Tacitean and Machiavellian, reason-of-state-centred, 'after' becomes ever harder to draw, and certainly the date of the alleged transition between the two modes of analysis keeps getting pushed ever earlier. The point emerges more strongly still when Catholic texts like the *Treatise of treasons* or *Leicester's commonwealth* are factored into the equation. For the attraction of 'politic' or 'civil' history resided precisely in its capacity to strip away the carapace of pretended virtue from the official version of events and thus to reveal the realities of both ancient and contemporary politics, and in these (Catholic) texts, the official version – a Ciceronian, virtue-centred account of good and loyal protestant counsellors and a godly prince, united in the defence of the commonweal and of true religion against the linked spectres of popish idolatry and sedition, and foreign invasion and rule – was inverted, indeed laid bare as a pack of lies, designed to hide what was really going on. And what was really going on was a court-centred conspiracy of atheists and low-born evil counsellors, a conspiracy that constituted the real threat to, and the ultimate treason against, the crown and commonweal. These texts were expressly designed to reveal that fact to a shocked public. And, as we have seen, in order to do so, they applied the lessons of history, using parallel sets of circumstance and outcome taken from both the recent and more distant history of England, and indeed from the classical past, to address both current events and circumstances and future prospects and contingencies.

On this account, therefore, the writings and doings of insiders like Thomas Norton, Sir Thomas Smith, Thomas Wilson, and Lord Burghley himself, not to mention the likes of Leicester, Sidney and their intellectual facilitator Gabriel Harvey (so brilliantly illuminated by Blair Worden, Anthony Grafton, Lisa Jardine, Kathy Shrank, Mary Partridge and others) need to be set beside the activities of their papist *bêtes noires* in those other early exercises in contemporary politic history, *The treatise of treasons* and *Leicester's commonwealth*. Only when such Catholic texts are put front and centre can we see that the reading of history 'for use' did not only take place in the closets of Elizabethan insiders – amidst the

cliques and coteries of the actual or wannabe courtiers, counsellors and politicians and their humanist clients and hangers-on, described by Grafton and
Jardine. Those same techniques could be mobilised by out-groups, albeit ones
anxious to become in-groups as quickly as possible, for overtly oppositionist
purposes. Nor was a politique, positively 'Tacitean' reading of the secret history of
an increasingly corrupt court and tyrannical regime an innovation of the 1590s.
Rather, that mode of analysis, and the deployment of historical examples, parallels and analyses that went with it, had been being presented by a number of
Catholic authors to various publics from at least the early 1570s on.[84] When the
Essex circle and their enemies started to import that style of analysis into their
accounts of and calculations about domestic court politics they were in fact introducing, into establishment protestant circles, insights and hermeneutic habits of
mind that our Catholic authors had been using to analyse the politics of the
Elizabethan regime for decades.

Putting history on the stage

It should, therefore, come as small surprise that, by the late 1580s and early
1590s, in the emergent (sub) genre of the history play, we find history being read
and applied for use in plain sight, on the public stage and, when the plays were
printed, in the pamphlet press. Taking Blundeville's work of 1574 as something
of an epitome of the assumptions underlying contemporary humanist historiography, it might be worth comparing the central strictures laid out in his text with
the plays analysed in this book. When we do so, we find the plays performing
precisely the same educative or hermeneutic functions that Blundeville had
imputed to the works of the true historian.

Like the ideal historical writers and readers evoked by Blundeville, the plays
were almost entirely concerned with politics, that is to say with what Blundeville
described as 'deeds done by a public weal or against a public weal' and with
'changes of government'. Of necessity, these were deeds done by public persons,
as 'princes and lords of states, as kings and tyrants and also the magistrates of
commonweals'.[85] The plays were just as intent as Blundeville's ideal historian on
investigating 'for what cause' such 'changes in government' had been effected
and with 'how the same was done and what good or evil ensued therefrom'.[86]

While the moral status of the deeds and outcomes being staged or studied
remained crucial – as Blundeville explained, 'excellency in virtue' was 'to be
followed' and 'excellency in vice' was 'to be fled'[87] and the operations of 'the
providence of God' duly noted and acknowledged[88] – the aims of the plays, in
this again just like Blundeville's notional histories, were more analytical than
such nostrums might lead us to assume. The 'three principal points to which all
public actions do appertain' were, Blundeville maintained, 'peace, sedition and
war',[89] and the aim of true histories was to analyse how those outcomes had

been attained or averted, by particular political agents operating in specific historical and political circumstances.

The aim of the historian, Blundeville argued, was to isolate a principal 'deed' and 'to show the very moment, as well of the beginning, as of the ending of the deed, to the intent that the reader may know the continuance of the principal deed and also of the inferior deeds' constituent of that larger event and thus necessary to effect (and retrospectively properly to understand) the outcome or outcomes in question.[90] In other words, by a process of selection and omission, of compression and analysis, the historian was to delineate a coherent sequence of events and their outcomes, and then to recount them in a way that showed how the actions of the various historical agents in play had produced the outcome in question. (The *Henry VI* plays, or indeed *Richard II* or *Julius Caesar*, were surely all sustained, and increasingly coherent and sophisticated, attempts to do just that.)

Just as the historian was to identify a principal deed, so he had to discover what Blundeville termed 'the chief doer' of that deed, a figure to be identified 'by his power, skill and industry'.[91] In all this, particular attention was to be paid to attendant circumstance. Thus, 'in speaking of conspiracies he [the historian] must tell how the conspirators came together, how they got fautors [followers or supporters] and how they ended their enterprise, how they were chastised or how perhaps they escaped free, and such like.'[92] (It is difficult here not to think of *Julius Caesar* and of *Richard II*, not to mention the *Henry IV* plays and *Henry V*, and indeed *Titus Andronicus*.)

Having identified the 'chief doer', the historian was to identify the key attributes or virtues that had enabled his protagonist to achieve his (or her) purposes and shape the 'deed' or event in question. These included 'his nature, affections and election, proceeding either of wisdom, passion or custom, his education, exercises, deeds and speeches and also the age and time wherein every notable act was done and the qualities of his body, whether they were signs and tokens of his mind or else helps to his actions. And as the writer is bound to show the education of the person chronicled and those exercises and studies whereby he hath formed his manners, so also is he bound to tell every deed, word, sign or token that may signify either his manners, nature, his affections, thoughts or any manner of motion of his mind.'[93] (Such concerns played a central shaping role not only in *Richard III* but also in the depiction of Hal in both the *Henry IV* plays and *Henry V*.)

Thus, Blundeville explained, the reader and writer of history would be 'taught not only to note the taking and leaving of all occasions and opportunities, whereby any good hath been procured, but also the dangers of evils that either in time have been very wisely foreseen and fled, or into which, through lack of foresight, men have headlong fallen, having therein regard to every man's state, condition, faculty, profession and other such like circumstances, to the intent that we ourselves may learn thereby to do nothing unadvisedly.'[94] (Again one thinks of *Richard II* or *Julius Caesar* as exemplifying precisely such concerns.)

Through a timely invocation of God's providence, Blundeville was able to reassure his readers that the results of such analysis would be entirely conducive to good morals, as well as to prudent or successful action. 'The examples of prosperous successes, which God hath given as just rewards to those that undertook work according to virtue', not to mention the 'fame, glory and praise, sounding in all men's mouths', and the consequent 'immortality' conferred on 'their noble acts', all served 'to stir us to virtuous, honest and commendable doings'. *Pari passu*, the 'evil successes' given by God 'to the wicked', and the 'shame and infamy, the hatred and enmity that they procure to themselves, not only whilst they live, but also after their death', would all serve to turn us away from evil courses. And all this was to be 'laid open to the world by written history, in such sort that men will not for shame once name those persons which, in their life time, would be honoured as Gods.'[95] (Again, *Richard III* and *Henry V*, not to mention *Julius Caesar* and *Hamlet*, spring to mind.)

It would be hard to find a more accurate summary of the subject matter and organising concerns of the plays under discussion in this book. Just as Blundeville prescribed, the plays were indeed concerned to study the dynamics of 'peace, war and sedition', of 'changes of states' and conspiracies, both doomed and successful. Just like Blundeville's ideal writers and readers of history, the plays applied themselves to discerning and delineating causally, thematically and morally coherent concatenations of events – what Blundeville termed 'principal deeds'. The plays were as concerned as Blundeville said they should be, precisely to delineate the role in shaping events of what Blundeville termed 'chief doers'. The question of how far great men might indeed make events and determine outcomes was central to many of the plays – here one thinks particularly of *Henry V*, *Caesar* and *Hamlet* – as was the analysis of the formative influences, the education, self-fashioning and external forces that went into the making of a 'chief doer', be he lauded by posterity as the epitome of the good ruler, like Henry V, or universally reviled as the archetypal Machiavel and tyrant, like Richard III. The plays were quite as interested as Blundeville's historian in the interactions of prudence, justice and fortitude in the personality and practice of the successful ruler. They, too, were concerned with the interaction of human prudence and calculation (of the sort studied by the historian and staged by the playwright) and the operations of divine providence.

On this account, then, if we accept Blundeville's exercise in the *ars historica* as representing some sort of contemporary norm of humanist historiographical best practice, then the plays can be seen as actualising that style of historiographical theory into a whole series of exercises in first theatrical and then textual, politic, and sometimes frankly political, practice. This is the conduct of public history and the public discussion of politics through history with a vengeance.

We should thus conceive of the popular stage performing, in the 1590s, a similar service for its variegated, both elite and plebeian, metropolitan and provincial, publics as that performed, in the 1570s and 1580s, by the likes of Gabriel Harvey, for their noble and courtly patrons.[96] The plays too reduced vast quantities of material – culled either from chronicle histories of England or from other, classical Roman sources – into compressed, portable and schematic narrative form. The overall plot structures of these plays might thus be taken to epitomise certain crucial political or moral lessons, of direct and compelling relevance to some of the central dilemmas of the age. As Andras Kisery has argued, the resulting texts came to be both marketed and consumed as containing all sorts of moral and political wisdom – saws, sayings and *sententiae* that could be commonplaced away, to be recycled later to elucidate either future plays or current or future events.[97] The plays thus made 'history' available to their audiences as an interpretative key both to the present and the future, as both moral and politic templates relevant to current concerns and future contingencies. In this way, the plays might be taken to have created their own historically and politically educated audiences; a public or publics whose expectations and attitudes had been formed, in part at least, by the drama itself. Thus the popular stage helped to inculcate, in its various audiences, a set of sensibilities, interpretative modes and expectations, which could then be appealed to and exploited, gratified and provoked by subsequent plays and performances.[98]

Unlike Sir Philip Sidney, Blundeville had ranked poets decisively below both historiographers and philosophers. While he agreed with Sidney that, much like God at the creation, poets 'make much of nothing' when 'they frame' 'their fables', 'poesies and poetical histories', Blundeville also maintained that it was 'the office' of 'true philosophers and historiographers' 'to tell things as they were done, without augmenting or diminishing them, or swerving one jot from the truth'. This meant that it was the job of the true historian, amongst other things, 'not to feign any orations, nor any other thing, but truly to report every such speech and deed, even as it was spoken or done'.[99]

Sidney, of course, had reversed those priorities, ranking the poet far above the historian, as someone not restrained to the study of what was or had been but, rather, free to talk, in the most exalted, compelling and alluring terms, about what might and ought to be. However, in downgrading the historian, Sidney had also, as Fritz Levy (amongst others), has remarked, associated the literary or rhetorical practices of the historian with those of the poet.

As Sidney slightingly observed, 'many times', the historian 'must tell of events whereof he can yield no cause; or, if he do, it must be poetical'. The result was that even 'historiographers (although their lips sound of things done and verity be written in their foreheads) have been glad to borrow both fashion and perchance weight of poets'. Ever since the time of Herodotus, Sidney claimed, 'both he and all the rest that followed him either stole or usurped of Poetry their passionate describing of passions, the many particularities of battles, which no man could affirm, or, if that be denied me, long orations put in the mouths of great kings and captains, which it is certain that they never pronounced.'[100] In Levy's words, 'the conclusion of Sidney's argument was that the historian's craft and the poet's overlapped: not only did the historian poeticize when he invented fictional speeches, but, more critically, the causes which those speeches elucidated were themselves the result of poetical thinking'[101]

Just as the likes of Blundeville might repine at such practices, so the modern commentator, hot in pursuit of the origins of identifiably modern attitudes to historical research and historical truth might assume that, in this regard at least, Blundeville's was the voice of the future. However, as Fritz Levy has pointed out, amongst even the most advanced politic historians of the day, there was nothing like consensus on some key issues about the nature and use of 'history'. Thus at the start of his *First part of the life and raigne of King Henry IIII* John Hayward addressed, as questions to be answered rather than as matters already decided, the following concerns: in the writing of history 'what things are to be suppressed, what lightly touched and what to be treated at large; how credit may be won, and suspicion avoided; what is to be observed in the order of times and description of places . . .; what liberty an author may use in framing speeches and in declaring the causes of, councils and events of things done; how far he must bend himself to profit; when and how he may play upon pleasure'.[102] Of course, these very issues – the invention of speeches, the conflation of different events and even persons, and the rearrangement of chronology in the interests of moral and narrative coherence, the balance between 'pleasure' and 'profit', entertainment and 'use' – were all central to the processes whereby history plays were produced and consumed. And yet, as Levy points out, on this evidence none of the questions raised by Hayward had been resolved in ways that would definitively expel the history play from the category of 'history' or the playwright, as poet, from the realm of the 'true historiographer'.[103]

Adopting the terms of reference and evaluation set by Sidney's *Defence of poetry*, we might conclude that as a mixed genre of the sort that Sidney had himself explicitly endorsed, the history play could claim to speak to its audience or readers with the authority and voice not only of the historian but also of the poet. That is to say, as a genre, the history play could combine the capacity, claimed by Sidney for the poet, to conjure heroic or tragic figures from the mythic, or indeed from the historical, past for the emulation and admiration of the audience (or reader), with the historian's fidelity to events that had actually happened and with history's implicit claim to be able to speak to issues of prudence and policy, grounded in the way things had been and were rather than in the somewhat high-flown world of Ciceronian virtue, to which Sidney consigned the poet.

History and the 'now' of performance

On occasion, these plays put a great deal of effort into evoking a particular time and place – sometimes a very remote time and place: in *Julius Caesar*, late republican Rome, in *Troilus and Cressida*, the siege of Troy, and in *Titus Andronicus*, the indeterminately antique, entirely fictional, but also very carefully delineated, Romanitas evoked by that play. But then, at a stroke – with the chiming of the clock in *Caesar*, with Aaron's denunciation of Lucius as 'popish' in *Titus*, with the direct address of the audience by Pandarus at the close of *Troilus* – Shakespeare could at times collapse to nothing the spatial and temporal distance between the action on stage and the here and now of late Elizabethan London. These moments of conflation draw the history being played out on stage into the current experience and concerns of his audience, and vice versa. Nowhere, perhaps, does he pull this trick off so consistently as in the *Henry IV* plays where, as many commentators have observed, the low-life scenes set in Eastcheap and elsewhere involving Falstaff and his mates are immediately contemporary in their ambience and feel, in marked contrast to the 'historical' nature of the scenes of high politics that drive the action of these plays.[104] This created what Brian Walsh terms a 'dialectic between "the pastness of the past" and the presentness of performance',[105] something he describes elsewhere as 'a perhaps irresolvable tension between the past and present that is endemic to historical revival'.[106] It was that dialectic, that tension, that, I would argue (and Walsh denies), enabled these plays to operate *both* as works of history, attempts to revive the past, to bring the dead to life before the audience's very eyes *and* as political and moral commentaries of immediately contemporary resonance.

According to Walsh, the evocation of the past, through what he calls 'theatrical time', 'invites spectators to understand the idea of history' to be as 'transient' as the theatre itself, and thus, 'in order to be intelligible', to be entirely 'dependent on the type of willful engagement evident in the work of theatrical production'.[107] In other words, the recreation of the past on the stage offered by these plays was peculiarly dependent on the active collaboration, indeed on the very considerable imaginative work, of the audience, something to which, through the chorus, Shakespeare directly adverts in *Henry V* where he insisted, in Walsh's words, 'that the power to raise the dead is not within the scope of the dramatic historian's capabilities. His own take on the job of performing the past is that he writes words that Elizabethan players speak, for Elizabethan audiences to make something of in their minds.'[108]

For the audience, the very considerable work involved in creating and sustaining the experience of having conjured the past on stage had its own reward, since it conferred on them what Walsh describes as 'the illusion of a preternatural viewpoint'. The plays offered 'the illusion', not only that 'spectators' could 'see the past',[109] but that they could actually watch 'the making of history as a process'.[110]

But, as we have seen, 'history' here also meant 'politics', the doing of deeds and the making of policy by the great and the good in ways that decided the fate of kingdoms and the shape and destiny of states. And so, the audience of history plays like these was also being given a privileged insight into politics as 'process'; what really happened behind the closed doors of the court and the council chamber. Here were the real springs of action in a monarchical state; here was what really animated events, what really determined precisely who was up and who was down; here was a way to judge who was doing what to whom and why and what the likely outcomes might be.

Indeed one might go further and say that history plays conferred on spectators the illusion not only of being able to see the past but also of being able to see the present from the perspective provided by the past, or at least by the particular vision or version of the past being conjured for them by the play they were watching. That privileged perspective necessarily involved a capacity to watch the operation of the forces that drove the process of history along; observing (and weighing in relation to one another, if not simply choosing between) the different visions of history canvassed in these plays as a product of the inexorable workings of divine providence and/or as the outcome of the politique manoeuvres, the choices, errors and insights, the virtues and vices, the skills and incapacities, of particular human actors, strutting, for a brief two or three hours, on the stage of history.[111]

The result, both on the stage and indeed on the page, and thus, we might imagine, also between the ears of the viewer or reader, was not so much a species of 'Political Thought' as a sustained outbreak of thinking about politics. This is not to say that the plays did not raise and address the sorts of formal issue at the centre of the modern study of Political Thought; issues also crucial to much early modern thought and writing about politics. As Andrew Hadfield, amongst many others, has observed, they most certainly did. It was just that, as Martin Dzelzainis has recently noted,[112] on those topics, Shakespeare's plays have nothing very novel to say. Indeed, as Dzelzainis maintains, as exercises in 'Political Thought', conventionally defined, the plays are something of a bust, either so bland or so indeterminate as scarcely to bother the scorers in the great struggle to identify the genuinely novel thinkers of really significant Political Thoughts.

But as sustained exercises in thinking about politics as process, in staging the sorts of interactions between political agents that actually made 'history' and determined the fate of nations and states, the plays had far greater claims to make on the attention of contemporaries, and, I would add, on that of modern scholars, interested, not so much in 'Political Thought', as in the ways in which contemporaries actually thought about politics; that is to say, about how power had been and was still being claimed and attained, contested and legitimised, distributed and deployed, in monarchical states like Elizabethan England. All this, many contemporaries agreed, history could reveal, and these plays brought such revelations to promiscuously (both ideologically and socially) mixed audiences all over the England of the 1590s.

The actively interpretative role played by, and the apparent epistemological privileges conferred upon, the audiences of these plays lies somewhere near the centre of the argument of this book and its account of the transactions between past, present and future that, I want to argue, these plays enabled their audiences to effect. For, on this view, the audience of a history play was placed, for the brief duration of the performance, in what Walsh calls 'theatrical time', that is to say, in a place above and beyond the course of history, and certainly outside the temporal and epistemological limits of their own time. Thus positioned, they could see the past in relation to the present, the present in relation to the past and both in relation to the future. Standing on the Bankside, on any given day in the 1590s, they could survey past events, brought, through the now of performance, into the present, and by applying the past events being acted out on stage to present concerns, and vice versa, they could see things and think thoughts that might otherwise have been entirely unavailable to them.

Not that these plays merely constructed a position of epistemological or interpretative privilege for their audiences. As something like the voice of history itself, they also constructed a position of very considerable authority for themselves. As Walsh observes, at least 'in the case of the sequential history plays' 'historical recall' became synonymous with 'recall of an earlier play as much as of historical events'. Thus 'the events of the past' became 'inextricably tied to their historical embodiments' on the stage.[113] In *Richard III* the perceptions and actions of all of the major characters are framed by the memory of past events, that is to say, of events portrayed in previous plays, which are continually evoked throughout the play. 'The persistence of those events in the language of *Richard III*,' Walsh concludes, 'makes this play's own historical sensibility peculiarly theatrical.' Indeed, Walsh argues, 'by citing *3 Henry VI* as the historical past, and bringing it to mind for the many playgoers who doubtless recalled those scenes, *Richard III* transforms its predecessor from the status of a past play to *the status of the past itself*.[114] 'Through this motif, *Richard III* aligns history with a memory of theatre and, often, the visual memory of events acted in theatre, a conception which is heightened in a later scene depicting the King, his successor, and a series of ghosts on the night before Bosworth.'[115]

Nor was all this lost on contemporary observers. When in his apology for actors of 1612 Thomas Heywood sought to defend the stage from its detractors he made the claim that 'plays' 'have made the ignorant more apprehensive, taught the unlearned the knowledge of many famous histories, instructed such as cannot read in the discovery of our English Chronicles'.[116]

But if history spoke in and through these plays, it did not speak with anything like one voice. Even within Shakespeare's own *oeuvre* one play might not merely cite or feed off another but also seek to modify or challenge it. Thus when, in *Richard II*, the bishop of Carlisle makes his prophecy about the fell consequences of Bolingbroke's usurpation, he is, of course, referring to events that in historical time have not yet happened but about which the audience know a good deal, because, in theatrical time, they have already taken place in the *Henry VI* plays. Not only that, but, as we shall see below, in casting those events in a providential frame almost entirely absent from the *Henry VI* plays themselves, Carlisle, or rather Shakespeare through Carlisle, is inviting the audience to locate those events in a very different causal framework, to see them in a very different light, than that cast upon them by the original plays themselves.

Not only Shakespeare's plays but the entire repertoire of the public theatre was in constant dialogue with itself, to such an extent that certain plays would have proved virtually unintelligible if they could not have presumed upon the audience's knowledge of previous versions of the same material. Recent productions of some of the plays illustrate vividly how this worked. Thus whereas Shakespeare's version of *King John* starts, as it were, *in medias res*, a recent production at the Globe spliced the opening scene from *The troublesome reign* on to the beginning of Shakespeare's play to bring the audience up to speed about the circumstances of John's accession. Again, the audience's comprehension of central passages and incidents in *Richard II* – the nature of the financial depredations of his regime, indeed, the death of Gloucester itself – seems to turn on prior knowledge, perhaps derived from performances of *Woodstock*, an earlier play about preceding events in Richard's reign. And so, in a recent BBC production of *Richard II*, all the scenes in which mention was made of the murder of the duke of Gloucester were cut, almost certainly because a modern television audience could not be assumed to have any sense of who Gloucester was, of who had had him killed or of what his murder might have meant or signified. In contrast to modern television and theatre directors, Shakespeare could rely on the fact that his audience did know all those things and could thus allow himself the entirely allusive and ambiguous treatment of Gloucester's death that is so central to *Richard II*. As that production very usefully demonstrated, without this material the play loses much of its political point and moral depth, and becomes instead an alternately winsome and bathetic tragedy about the fatal flaws and final apotheosis of Richard himself.

In *2 Henry IV* Falstaff's Hal's casual references to Hal's having boxed the ear of the Lord Chief Justice and then been imprisoned for his pains only make sense if the audience already knows that story, as many, if not most, of an Elizabethan audience surely would have done from their prior exposure to the *Famous victories*. In a recent production of *2 Henry IV* at the National Theatre a slide projected at the back of the stage explained the incident in order to render Shakespeare's version of the story intelligible to spectators entirely unfamiliar with the earlier play. An Elizabethan audience would have needed no such prompting.

In thus playing off established parts of the existing repertoire Elizabethan dramatists and acting companies were seeking to pique the interest of an audience already familiar with, or hooked on, not merely existing genres, but, as often as not, existing versions of the very same stories or events. This is particularly true in the case of Shakespeare who spent a good deal of his early career reworking the plots of previous plays, many of them culled from the repertoire of the Queen's Men. As McMillin and MacClean observe, 'no fewer than six of Shakespeare's' history plays, those on King John, Richard II, Henry IV, Henry V, Henry VI and Richard III, were all 'closely related to the plots of plays performed by the Queen's men'.[117] 'The Chamberlain's Men made their career in large part on the basis of the connected series of English history plays which Shakespeare wrote for them by the turn of the century . . . Shakespeare did not lift the comedies of the Queen's Men, he lifted their history plays. And it was the history plays which along with Marlowe's tragedies made the 1590s a revolutionary decade in English theatre.'[118] This serial rewriting could not help but advert to, and thus invite the audience to notice, the differences between the new and the old versions. Since the second version represents a sort of comment upon the first, watching the way one play appropriated or changed its predecessor provides us with perhaps our best sense of how these plays were consumed and interpreted by contemporaries. In this way, read against one another, the plays themselves provide us with our best evidence for their own reception.

As David Womersley has observed, such opportunities reach their height in the case of the direct 'dramatic riposte' of one play to another. Perhaps the best example here is provided by *Sir John Oldcastle*, which is a direct response to Shakespeare's rendition of Oldcastle as the character subsequently known as Falstaff in the *Henry IV* plays. As such, the Oldcastle play separated and radically rewrote both the Oldcastle and the Falstaff character functions in order to refute (indeed, in some ways, simply to invert) the ideological valences set up within Shakespeare's version of Oldcastle as Falstaff. All of which is proof positive of how sharply immediate contemporary recognition of the polemical and personal points being made in those plays could be.

Thus, at least some of the imaginative and hermeneutic effort required of the audience, if the events of the past were successfully to be summoned on stage, involved comparing and contrasting the different versions of the same events, in effect the different readings of history, and its moral and political meanings, being provided for them by Shakespeare and his contemporaries, and, as we shall see below, that effort could involve the exercise of political as well as historical and aesthetic judgement. Walsh, however, writes of 'the pleasure' to be derived from such fleeting spectatorial privilege in almost exclusively 'aesthetic' terms. Thus he talks of the audience's 'fantasy of access to the past as an imaginative triumph over the tyranny of time and space, similar perhaps to the pleasures afforded later audiences and readers of time travel narratives; a desire for an experience of the past driven by the acknowledgement of its inalienable absence'.[119]

Walsh does concede 'the genre's topical relevance for Elizabethan and Jacobean questions of national identity, kingly authority and the interpellation of subjects',[120] and observes that 'these plays are, almost without exception, centred in some way on contested kingship and crises of succession'. However, he then insists that such concerns can have had nothing to do with contemporary anxieties about the succession and the linked spectres of dynastic discontinuity, civil war and foreign rule. Rather, he attributes such resonances to something he calls 'the historical culture of rupture', which, he claims, animates the plays and thus prevents them from having much of anything to do with 'the specifics of partisan Elizabethan politics'. So, on Walsh's account, the plays are either about a history entirely separated off from contemporary political concern and reality, or they are about 'the specifics of Elizabethan politics'; a possibility which Walsh uses the plays' undoubted 'ideological ambivalence' to rule entirely out of court.[121]

But these mutually exclusive polarities do not, in fact, exhaust the available interpretative options. For, as Walsh's own analysis of the complexities of historical and theatrical temporality shows, we do not need to make so hard and fast a division between what we might (somewhat anachronistically) call the aesthetic and the historical, on the one hand, and the political and even the polemical, on the other. As, amongst others, John Hayward admitted, in both historiographic and dramatic texts concerned with past events the balance between 'pleasure' and 'profit', between reading or watching for 'use' and application, or for mere entertainment or diversion, was far from clear cut. These were issues that had to be worked out in each and every (either literary or dramatic) attempt to write 'history'. They were certainly at stake during each and every performance of 'history' upon the public stage. As this book is an extended attempt to argue, if the original and abiding appeal of these plays is to be understood, and their significance for the political and cultural worlds of late Elizabethan England to be effectively recuperated, we need an analysis that brings the aesthetic, the historical and the political together, rather than, with Walsh and other critics, one that sees them as mutually exclusive or radically incompatible.

Getting the audience to do the work

As a site of communication, of social and cultural interaction, the theatre was caught between the court and the street. The companies all enjoyed aristocratic patronage and many plays were staged at court. Yet players were of a singularly low status; devoid of their claim to be servants of the peerage they were jurally cast as mere 'vagabonds', and the theatre was intermittently condemned in pulpit and press as both depraved and depraving. Moreover, for all their aristocratic patronage, the companies were thoroughly commercial enterprises. Their need to attract paying customers in large numbers created a voracious demand for new material and a pressing need to pander to, as well as to shape, popular taste and interest. Thus once a genre or sub-genre – like the history play – had emerged and proved popular the impulse was to run with it for as long as possible. Hence there was a strong commercial impulse behind Shakespeare's serial rewriting of the history plays of the Queen's Men.

As a variety of theatre historians have shown, theatre audiences were socially mixed, stretching from the earls of Essex or Southampton to London apprentices, and encompassing most of the social groups in between. Historians of the theatre have rightly stressed the mass scale and social heterogeneity of the audience. An almost equally wide range of ideological opinions is likely to have been present amongst the audience at any given theatrical performance. We can, I think, imagine Catholics – both the most stubborn – 'recusants' – and varieties of Catholic loyalist and church papist – through the full gamut of protestant opinion, up to and including some puritans, attending the theatre. After all, although the theatre was an object of intermittent vituperation by hot protestants, there is evidence – if only from the complaint literature that set out to dissuade such people from going to plays – that some godly persons did indeed attend the theatre and read plays.

The point, then, is that in front of mass, economically, socially and ideologically, mixed, audiences, history plays were staging some of the central issues and concerns of the day. To quote Walter Cohen, 'any drama of state performed in the public theatre automatically converted a heterogeneous and, it seems, largely popular audience into judges of national issues, a position from which most of its members were excluded in the world of political affairs'.[122] Both presenting and calling into question the major metanarratives in and through which contemporaries made sense of their political experience – of what was happening now and what was about to happen in the near future – the plays addressed the great what ifs and what nexts of the day.

Moreover, they were doing all this in a period when, it mattered a great deal which version of the narrative of contemporary politics you believed, and when a variety of structurally similar, but polemically opposed and mutually exclusive, conspiracy theories were both available and subject to the manipulation

for their own purposes by a variety of groups or factions; Catholic and protestant, amongst the Catholics, Hispanophile and Jesuited or loyalist, amongst the
protestants, puritan, anti-puritan and politique, and latterly perhaps even
Cecilian or Essexian.

Open espousal of some of those views and some of these versions of
events could get you into very serious trouble indeed – Peter Wentworth died
in the Tower for trying to talk about the succession in parliament and in print
and John Stubbs, the author of the *Gaping gulf*, famously lost his right hand
for seditious libel. Here, then, is at least one source of the notorious ambiguity,
the multivocality or perspectivism, of Shakespeare's work; his capacity to
contain, both in tension and in balance, a number of different perspectives
and viewpoints; to stage, while refusing finally to resolve, any number of
ideological, emotional, epistemological or spiritual dilemmas or contradictions.[123] This is why the same play can be staged in such completely different
ways. It is also why so many of Shakespeare's plays have been (and continue
to be) subjected to so many mutually contradictory interpretations. Here is
the enabling ground for the whole academic sub-field of Shakespeare studies
dedicated to the explication of the ambivalences and ambiguities at the
centre of the plays according to the interests and insights of different ages,
generations,and ideologies.

My point is that, over and over again – sometimes by the addition of just
a few lines, a mere aside, a passing reference, and here the exchange in *King
John* with which we started is an excellent example – Shakespeare's plays do
indeed open themselves up to a variety of readings.[124] Rather than closing off
certain interpretations, rather than preventing certain possible applications of
the action on stage to current concerns and events, the plays instead move,
more often than not, to open themselves up to such interpretations and applications. They do this repeatedly and, it seems to me, quite deliberately.

In a period when, as I have argued, politics was in large part about which
narrative, which conspiracy theory, which story, you believed about what
had just happened, was happening and was about to happen next, and in
which telling certain versions of those stories, at certain times and in certain
places, was likely to get you thrown into gaol, your right hand cut off or worse,
Shakespeare's serial multivocality, his entirely self-conscious and repeated
determination to open up the stories being staged in his plays to multiple
interpretations or applications was in itself intensely political.

It seems to me that what was involved here was a series of self-conscious
decisions to exploit what Annabel Patterson has termed 'the historical conditions of an era of censorship'; a censorship regime that established a 'common
interest' between 'writers and readers' in establishing a shared sense 'as to how
interpretation in fact worked'. The result, she concludes, was, in effect, a 'theory
of functional ambiguity in which the indeterminacy inveterate to language was

fully and knowingly exploited by authors and readers alike'; a process at which Shakespeare emerged as something of a master.[125]

Now, much turns here on precisely what is meant by 'censorship'. Since Patterson wrote these words in 1984 a great deal of work has been done on the topic of censorship, in relation both to the drama and more generally, and considerable doubt has been cast on the existence of anything like a systematic or consistent censorship regime in early modern England. Each example of censorship has been shown to have had very particular political roots. Indeed, it has even been argued that opinions were almost never censored. Thus Richard Dutton feels able to asssert that 'within our period, there is no clear evidence of any Master of the Revels objecting to the opinions, attitudes or doctrines (as such) expressed within a play'. Since 'a high proportion of the interventions made by Tilney and his successors seem to relate to matters of immediate moment, to the over-specific shadowing of specific people and current events, rather than to considerations of doctrine', Dutton concludes that the role of the Master of the Revels seems to have been more one of 'preserving public order than of promoting ideological orthodoxy'.[126]

All this has allowed Deborah Shuger to argue that it was libellous speech, a form of ad hominem attack identified by Shuger as the equivalent of 'hate speech', which most frequently attracted the opprobrium and action of the authorities.[127] Such claims have a good deal to recommend them. Just as with other aspects of early modern English government, there was indeed an episodic, ad hominem, case by case, aspect to the mechanisms whereby books were approved for the press and plays allowed access to the public stage. A great many texts appear to have gone through more or less on the nod, and the extent, and, in particular, the consistency, of official surveillance of either print or performance can be (and indeed has been) called into the most serious question.

What we appear to be watching here is not what a modern observer would recognise as the routine operation of a bureaucratic system, but rather the working out of a series of trade-offs and bargains between various interests and individuals, resulting in the intermittent enforcement of a system of rules and embargoes that were perhaps more often left in various states of abeyance than systematically applied. Given the nature (and what, to a modern eye, can too often seem, somewhat anachronistically, to be the mere 'weakness') of the early modern English state, this should not surprise us.

Richard Dutton quite rightly exhorts us to eschew what he terms 'twentieth century notions of efficiency' in order the better to appreciate 'the extent to which the authority of the office [of Master of the Revels] derived from a consensual agreement', a balance achieved between and amongst 'the coalition of forces that ran the country'. Thus Dutton insists that 'whatever Tilney's patent might say, his powers were always restricted by the existence of other sources of authority and vested interests', and, one might add, by the vicissitudes of particular political situations and the course of events. What was at stake, Dutton concludes, was 'the complex accretion of power by process of consent, mutual convenience, habit and longevity, rather than by direct fiat'. 'Successive masters, who eventually acquired some wider authority, seem to have done so while looking for more ways to make money rather than out of zeal for greater efficiency.'[128]

Thus Dutton writes of Edmond Tilney in the 1590s that 'he must by now have been making a steady income out of the licensing of plays and playhouses' and can therefore conclude that, what 'with his court perspective and financial involvement', Tilney must have appeared to the inveterately anti-theatrical 'city authorities' as more of a poacher than a gamekeeper, more of an enabler than an enforcer, 'a confederate to the actors [rather] than their disciplinarian'.[129] Indeed, Dutton sees what he terms 'the symbiotic relationship between the Master and the actors' as 'the heart of the system' and, as such, 'the first line of defence against truly offensive material ever reaching the stage'.[130] Thus, insofar as the use of the term censorship by modern historians carries with it connotations more appropriate to post-war East Germany than to early modern England,[131] there remains the temptation to deny that anything that modern observers would recognise as 'censorship' was in operation in Elizabethan or early Stuart England.[132]

Of course, the surviving source base is exiguous. Janet Clare laments the 'patchiness of the evidence',[133] evidence which, in his turn, Richard Dutton describes as 'thin enough'. Dutton's attitude to these limitations represents a sort of regretful acceptance, a stoical determination to work determinedly within the limits set by the decidedly exiguous source materials, whereas Clare adopts a rather more aggressively interventionist approach. Thus, where Dutton opines that 'we can only talk, of course, about what we know – about plays that have survived or where some record exists either of their licensing or of contentious performance', Clare reads many of the discrepancies between the various printings of certain plays as sure signs of censorship.

To take an (in)famous example, where Clare is in no doubt that the omission of the so-called 'parliament scene' from the early printed versions of Shakespeare's *Richard II* was, or must have been, a result of 'censorship', Dutton's account is altogether more cautious. After reviewing a number of options he declares that 'the plethora of possibilities – no censorship at all but revision, censorship for the press but not for the stage (although later rescinded), censorship for both stage and press, though both were later rescinded – make rational discussion of the subject almost impossible'.[134] But even if, as his own treatment of the issue shows, 'rational discussion' does indeed remain an option, the paucity of the sources renders unattainable the final resolution of many of the questions we would most like answered.

It is, of course, entirely understandable (indeed arguably both necessary and inevitable) that scholars of 'censorship' should have concentrated their attention on the relatively sparse and discrete instances when 'censorship' indubitably occurred; that is to say, when we can either detect the alteration or suppression of texts intended for print or performance or observe the punishment of peccant printers, authors or acting companies, when certain texts or performances either escaped the initial attention of the censor or subsequently caused unexpected levels of offence. But such a concentration of scholarly attention has also produced a situation in which there is a danger of the baby being thrown out with the bathwater. This becomes immediately apparent if we expand our sense of the range of opinions seeking free expression in post-reformation England to include the views of a whole variety of English Catholics (let alone presbyterian or separatist critics of the national church).

We know that there was no shortage of either English Catholic readers or authors in Elizabethan England. We also know that Catholics wrote rather a lot of plays and that there was, in this society, both a considerable demand for, and an equally considerable, both actual and potential, supply of, Catholic books. And yet it was, if not impossible, then certainly very difficult (in England) to print such books or indeed to perform such plays, without really rather dire consequences. The same applied to certain styles of puritan critique of the national church. Of course, such books were printed, but only either abroad or on underground presses in England, the owners and operators of which took serious risks and often suffered very severe consequences.

We might try to organise all such writings under the sign of 'sedition', but as soon as we do so, we start to take sides in, rather than merely to describe or analyse, contemporary theological and ecclesiastical, political and polemical, dispute, which is always an uncomfortable position for the historian to find him- or herself in.[135] Of course, some texts were genuinely libellous; that is to say, they did indeed constitute overt, outrageous and, in contemporary terms, seditious attacks on the honour and reputation of central figures in the regime, up to and including the queen herself. One thinks here, on the Catholic side, of *The treatise of treasons*, of *Leicester's Commonwealth*, of Nicholas Sanders' *De origine ac progressu schismatis Anglicani*, and, on the puritan side, of John Stubbs' *Gaping gulf* or the Marprelate tracts.

It is less clear that, say, the printed works produced in the course of the Campion/Parsons mission can be so described. Certainly, it was of the essence of the two Jesuits' both spiritual and political purposes to claim that their mission was all about religion, not politics, about the promptings of conscience and not the pursuit of power, and the books they published, concerned, as they were, with the demands of conscience and the nature of right doctrine, reflected that claim.[136] It is even less clear that the full range of Catholic theological and pietistic writing produced in this period can usefully be described as libellous. And yet such texts were very effectively banned; that is to say, all but impossible to produce in England. While Campion ended up dead, having been strangled to death and then eviscerated by the state, Parsons was chased into exile, the presses upon which their tracts had been printed were seized and those involved in their production and circulation imprisoned.

Even when official restraint was lifted, it could be reimposed suddenly and with awful violence. During the Archpriest controversy, when elements in the Elizabethan regime did not merely wink at, but positively enabled the appellant group of Catholics to sustain a vigorous pamphlet war against the Jesuits, the printer James Duckett produced, amongst other things, reprints of earlier tracts written by Robert Southwell and Robert Parsons as part of an attempt to embarrass the appellant's Jesuit opponents. However, at a certain point, alarmed at rumours that they might really be considering conceding toleration to Catholics, the regime decided to reassert its anti-popish credentials. Poor Ducket found himself amongst the collateral damage created by that decision, for the Council used the fact that the Southwell tract in question had asserted that the Babington conspiracy was a put-up job, concocted by Walsingham to incriminate the Catholics and execute Mary Stuart, as an excuse to try and execute Duckett for treason. This, we might conclude, was censorship with a vengeance.

The suppression of the puritan movement between 1589 and 1592/3 shares many characteristics with such outbreaks of anti-Catholic repression. Provoked by the genuinely libellous activities of Martin Marprelate, the eventual crackdown encompassed leading Presbyterian divines, like Thomas Cartwright, who had gone out of their way to distance themselves from Martin, and culminated in a judicial, and then a propaganda, campaign against the spectre of puritan 'reformation'. On their view of the matter, the proponents of 'the discipline' were calling for no more than the completion of the process of reformation started by Henry VIII and then only half realised by his daughter, who had indeed reformed the realm of doctrine but left that of discipline sadly lacking the scripturally informed rigour that the exigencies of the times and the will of God both demanded. Their opponents, however, were determined to equate the activities of the puritan movement with disloyalty and popularity, sedition and even treason.[137] While the likes of Thomas Cartwright, the intellectual leader and figure head of the movement, escaped relatively unscathed, ending up in the Channel Islands, the puritan printer William Waldegrave was chased into exile in Scotland, John Udal died in prison and a couple of separatists, not to mention John Penry, went to the gallows.[138] Of course, neither Campion and Parsons, nor indeed John Penry and William Waldegrave, let alone poor Duckett, were, in any meaningful sense of the word, 'typical', but they were arguably representative. Certainly, it is entirely unclear how many times the regime had to perform this sort of viscerally disgusting state violence before the penny dropped.

It was not within the Elizabethan state's power to suppress entirely the expression of Catholic, or for that matter of radical puritan, opinions through the press. No doubt they would have liked to have done so, but, given the access of certain English Catholics (and certain English puritans) to foreign presses and support, that task was quite beyond them. Rather the intention, or perhaps we should say the anticipated effect, was to render it all but impossible to produce such tracts in England and in the process to put the public expression of such opinions, if not the private possession of such books, quite beyond the pale. The aim was to mark the boundary between the licit and the illicit, the acceptable and unacceptable, the normal and the deviant; we might even say, the orthodox and the heterodox. Thus, if we want to achieve an accurate sense of just how opinion was controlled and certain topics put out of bounds for overt, public discussion on either page or stage – in effect, how 'censorship' operated in Elizabethan England – such 'extreme' and 'untypical' events as the official response to Campion and Parsons, or the final assault on the puritan movement, have to be factored into our account. We cannot restrict our attention to the extremely patchy evidence for the quotidian mechanisms through which individual books were licensed for the press, or particular plays approved for performance, and then pronounce the system surprisingly benign and (by modern standards) winningly inefficient.

Similar constraints applied to the expression of opinion on topics like the succession, or indeed to any public discussion of the high politics of the day. Since the early 1570s it had been illegal to discuss the succession. As Mortimer Levine has shown, we have a range of manuscript tracts on the subject dating from the 1560s, none of which were libellous in any very obvious sense of the word. Far from constituting any variety of 'hate speech', they were very often rather tediously detailed legalistic evaluations of one claim or another.[139] And yet talk about the succession was banned and the result of that ban was an almost complete silence on this subject, sustained, in public and in print, over decades. When the likes of Peter Wentworth tried to break that silence they paid a very heavy price for their temerity. None of which prevented people speculating on the subject in private, but that, of course, was another matter.[140]

Nor was the theatre altogether insulated from such draconian punishments and dire outcomes. We do not know precisely what got the Privy Council so exercised about The Isle of Dogs in 1597, but we do know that when they went after the actors and authors of that play they did not deal with Tilney but rather worked directly through the Middlesex JPs, Richard Topcliffe amongst them. One author, Ben Jonson, and some of the actors, were committed to prison. Thomas Nashe fled to Yarmouth. The Council issued an order for the total suppression of playing and the demolition of the London theatres. That did not happen, but a message had undoubtedly been sent.[141]

The result of all this was something that we can surely call a form of 'censorship', although, as Jason Peacey has recently suggested, 'control and constraint' might better reflect the realities of the situation.[142] The relative scarcity of instances in which we can actually watch the institutions of the state controlling, editing or suppressing a book or play should not be taken only as a function of the paucity of the sources, still less as evidence for the absence or lightness of control or 'censorship'. Rather it was a testament to the relative success of the regime in laying down clear parameters outside of which people would stray only in the most extreme of circumstances and only then by risking the most serious of consequences, as, amongst others, John Stubbes, Edmund Campion, Thomas Cartwright, John Penry, Peter Wentworth, James Duckett and, to a lesser extent, Ben Jonson and Thomas Nashe, could all testify.

Too overt guying, or mention, of specific individuals – as seems to have happened in the case of *The Isle of Dogs* – or the staging of incendiary actions or speeches at moments of maximum tension – as seems to have happened with the popular insurrection in *Sir Thomas More* – undoubtedly attracted the (hostile or admonitory) attention of the authorities.[143] But, as Dutton explains, the ordinary course of 'censorship' seems to have involved the removal or mitigation of such moments from the plays, so that they could then be performed without difficulty. In the early Stuart period, the same cosy relationship seems to have pertained between various episcopal licensers like Daniel Featley and a series of godly authors, whose works Featley did not seek to suppress, but rather to prune, so that they could achieve the apotheosis of print, thus acting more as an editor, indeed as a facilitator, than as a 'censor'; a syndrome which Featley's Laudian critics and enemies, Richard Montague and John Cosin, decried as a form of puritan fellow-travelling.[144]

Even if we abandon Professor Dutton's relative passivity before the very considerable limitations of, and lacunae in, the evidence, and adopt the rather more activist approach taken by Janet Clare, many of the changes that she sees as the result of 'censorship' can be construed, not as attempts to suppress the political resonances of the history play – as Clare herself admits, given the nature of the genre, that would scarcely have been possible – but rather to enable (often only slightly) modified versions of the plays as written to be presented on the public stage without attracting the hostile attentions of authority. In short, the censoring party – presumably the Master of the Revels – emerges, even from her account, as (at the very least) a mediator between the playwrights and theatre companies and various sorts of authority, or, better yet, as precisely the sort of collusive enabler or facilitator envisaged by Richard Dutton, except, as he observes, on the few occasions when peculiarly pressing circumstances or particularly daring or offensive plays dictated otherwise.[145] Such a view of the question of 'censorship' accords rather well with recent work by McMillin, MacClean and Gurr, who see various sorts of official or court patronage of the drama as much as forms of control, constraint and indeed appropriation as of straightforward protection of the theatre against the hostile attentions of the city authorities.[146]

All of this created a situation in which, if such hotspots, such moments of direct allusion or derision, were avoided, the theatre appears to have been able to get away with a very great deal, particularly under the rubric of the history play, which, although intensely political, was, as Brian Walsh quite properly insists, by definition, not about the present but about the past, and also, since they were plays and not pamphlets, susceptible to a wide range of different readings and applications. I take this to be the situation which prompted Professor Patterson to talk, in 1984, of self-censorship and 'functional ambiguity' as central features of what she termed an 'era of censorship'.

Certainly, these are the realities and constraints under which, in the late Elizabethan period, certain authors and acting companies sought to titillate and inform various publics, and perhaps even to counsel various statesmen, by using history to comment upon both events and immediately contemporary concerns and anxieties. It was that situation, and the sometimes contradictory pressures and opportunities it produced, that framed, prompted, and even enabled, the plays under discussion in this book; that, in fact, made Shakespeare's history plays the complex and contested, the deeply ambiguous and almost infinitely glossable, texts that they are.

On this account, since meaning had to be imputed to or extracted out of the play by its audience or readership, all of the really subversive thoughts or associations or applications took place, not on the stage or the printed page, but rather between the ears of the reader or spectator, who had to pick up the significance of an aside, an allusion, an association of images and ideas, and then run with it. Nothing explicit happened, or at least had to happen, in either the performed or the printed play.

In order to formulate a coherent accusation, the would-be accuser himself would have to read a libellous, subversive or even treasonous message into the play; a message that the play itself did not formally contain. Consequently, in the very act of framing his accusation, the accuser might be taken to be casting rather more doubt on his own loyalty and discretion than on those of the play, playwright or acting company about whom he was complaining.

All of which might explain why it was that, as Richard Dutton suggests, and Annabel Patterson's position requires, 'the authorities and their censors normally became "strong readers" ', bent on the divination of 'subversion, only when the circumstances or the provocation made the matter unignorable and especially if there were some suspicion that the licensing provisions had been circumvented.'[147] And just how much it took to render a situation unignorable, and just how far this syndrome might allow a playwright to go, can be seen in Shakespeare's nerveless assault on Lord Cobham, in *The merry wives of Windsor*, analysed below in Part 6. And of course, precisely the same logic applied, if anything even more strongly, when it came to making accusations about other, rather more political, and less ad hominem, chains of association and thought, of the sort at stake in the other plays under discussion here.

A great deal of the argument being pursued in this book thus turns on the ways in which Shakespeare deliberately opened these plays up to multiple readings; enabling a range of applications of the events and sentiments being acted out on stage to current concerns and realities. He did so in the full knowledge of the multifarious, both socially and ideologically heterogeneous, nature of his audience and it is the interaction between those two forces or factors that drives the argument of this book.[148]

Plays and pamphlets, pamphlets and plays

These, then, are some of the central premises upon which this book is based and some of the crucial structural, political and ideological contexts within which the plays that form its subject were written, produced and consumed. The basic procedures of the book are very simple. I read the plays in the order in which they were written, against the political circumstances of the day, and, as the analysis proceeds, against both one another and other dramatic texts against which they were reacting or that, at the very least, they were seeking to adapt and appropriate, or which, in their turn, were reacting to them.

One difficulty here is that, because the precise dates of many of these plays are doubtful, or even, in terms of direct evidence, unknown, reading them in the order in which they were written is not anywhere near as straightforward as it sounds. I have tried therefore, with a couple of exceptions, to hew as close as possible to the current scholarly consensus on the dating of the plays. Only in a couple of places does the interpretation turn on what might be thought to be uncertain or controversial dating. Perhaps the most obvious case involves the *Henry VI* plays where I accept the case that *1 Henry VI* was written in late 1591/2 as a prequel to parts II and III, which were in turn written in the very early 1590s. I therefore take *1 Henry VI* to be a retrospective gloss on the action of the two former plays, and argue that when they are read or thought about with the action of part I in mind, they mean something rather different than when they are viewed on their own.[149]

On the vexed question of the date of *Titus Andronicus* I take the line most recently outlined by Manley and MacClean that, although it was described by Henslowe in 1594 as a 'new play', a version of it was first written around the time of *2* and *3 Henry VI*. It seems to me to have been addressed to the same sort of extreme moral and political meltdown as that conjured in the Henry VI plays,[150] only in *Titus* a way out is offered in the form of the conspiracy, assassination and foreign invasion used by the Andronici to unseat Saturninus and bring Tamora and Aaron to justice. On the equally vexed question of the authorship of the play, I accept the claim that Shakespeare co-wrote *Titus* with George Peele, who seems to have written at least the first act. But, following Michael Neill, I contend that since 'Shakespeare was clearly the principal partner in this enterprise' 'it seems reasonable to grant him responsibility for the overall design', which, for the purposes of this book, provides the prime focus of attention.[151]

On the date of *Richard III*, I follow the line laid out in the recent Arden edition that it was probably being written in 1592, 'while the *Henry VI* plays were still being performed', but was not performed in London until 1594.[152] I similarly accept the close association established there between Shakespeare's *Richard III* and both *1 Henry VI* and *Titus Andronicus*, and by Manley and MacClean between Lord Strange's Men and the same three plays,[153] all of which are discussed together below as proffering alternative ways out of the political and moral meltdown delineated with such precision and ferocity in *2 and 3 Henry VI*.

I also accept the case made, most recently, by Beatrice Groves, Brian Vickers and Charles Forker, that Shakespeare's *King John* comes after *The troublesome reign* and not vice versa, and the conventional view that *King John* and *Richard II* were written very close together in 1595–6; that, in Forker's words, *Richard II* was 'a companion piece to *King John* on the theme of royal legitimacy'.[154] This dating is important for my analysis since it helps to legitimise my reading of these plays against Parsons' *Conference*, which started to circulate in England in the autumn of 1595. I follow conventional opinion in taking *1 and 2 Henry IV* to have been written in 1596/7.

On the controversial dating of *The merry wives of Windsor*, I remain agnostic, but tend toward a version of the revised dating produced by Professor Melchiori.[155] *Henry V*, *The Oldcastle play* and *Julius Caesar* can all be more or less precisely dated to various points in 1599. On the vexed question of the precise date of *Hamlet* in its various versions, I hedge my bets, taking the play as it has come down to us to be a product of the period between 1599 and 1601. I take *Troilus and Cressida* to have been written after *Hamlet* and tend to accept the very cogent case for a date in late 1601 advanced by David Bevington in his Arden edition of the play.[156]

My definition of what constitutes a history play includes not merely English history plays but also Roman ones and indeed *Troilus and Cressida*, which I take to be about an event – the siege of Troy – that contemporaries would have regarded as historical. The same rationale underlies the inclusion of *Hamlet*, which is based on an account of what contemporaries took to be early Danish history.

I include *The merry wives of Windsor* because of the presence therein of a character– Falstaff – formed in a history play and because of the ways in which I take *The merry wives* to have been a vehicle for the continuation of an argument, even something of a feud, occasioned by the identification, in the first versions of the *Henry IV* plays, of the character subsequently known as Falstaff as Sir John Oldcastle. This material is particularly valuable because the fuss over Oldcastle represents almost uniquely direct evidence for immediately contemporary responses to the resonances and meaning of some of Shakespeare's history plays.

The one exception here – what I would like to think of as the exception that proves the rule – is *Titus Andronicus* which, since it lacks any historical sources and in fact makes much of its origins in various entirely fictional ancient texts, is not a history play at all. I have included it here because of its elaborate attempts to look and sound like a history play; to evoke and sustain an impression or aura of a pagan Romanitas, that is, in fact, also entirely made up. I take it to be a pretend history play which, having established its (completely spurious) claims to historicity, then proceeds to deal, in quite extraordinarily daring ways, with precisely the sorts of directly contemporary and entirely political issues that other of the history plays – in this case particularly *Richard III* and later *Hamlet* – also address.

The book is framed both chronologically and thematically by the contours of the succession crisis *in potentia* that stretched from the late 1580s until 1603, and generically by the relatively generous notion of the history play outlined above. I take the connection between those two framing categories to have been not merely accidentally correlative but causal; the rise of the history play being, in large part, a function of the pervasive anxiety and concern prompted by the succession crisis. On this view, it was anything but an accident that, after the accession of James I took the issue of the succession off the agenda, the genre of the history play lost a great deal of its popularity and allure.

In what follows particular attention is paid to the earl of Essex, since it was in and through the persona of Essex, and the ideological and political agenda that cohered around him – referred to below as the Essexian project – that many of the tensions and contradictions inherent in the succession crisis came together. In consequence, to many contemporaries, the author of these plays amongst them, Essex, or rather the Essexian project, came to represent the solution to the dominant religio-political dilemmas of the age.

Almost as great prominence is given to the strand of catholic religio-political commentary outlined above and analysed at some considerable length in *Bad Queen Bess*? This reached its culminating point in Parsons' great tract *The conference about the next succession*, which plays a central role in the analysis. This is not because I want to claim that the author of these plays was a Catholic, intent on sending secret and subversive Catholic messages to an underground audience. Such a case has been made[157] and I have no wish to remake or indeed to endorse anything like it here. I do not even want to claim that the author of these plays *must have* read these particular tracts. That remains a distinct (but entirely unprovable) possibility.

But luckily the case being made here does not in the least rest on that having happened. For what is at stake here is not so much influence as confluence. The argument runs that both the plays and the tracts were not only addressing the same political conjuncture, the same set of issues and anxieties, they were also using a very similar range of historical materials and cultural practices and assumptions to do so. But they were not doing so because the one (necessarily) influenced the other or even because they shared the same sources, but rather because they were both reacting, albeit from widely different subject positions, and for widely divergent purposes, to essentially the same political and ideological conjuncture. And, of course, that point emerges with far greater force if Shakespeare had never laid eyes on *Leicester's commonwealth*. For then both the plays and the pamphlets – the one totally illicit, printed abroad by exiles and catholic *engagés*, the other marginal and for the most part ephemeral, comprising fictive and festive, albeit also historical, elements, brought together in texts and performances designed to entertain and titillate largely popular audiences – would have come, pretty much independently of each other, to be talking about essentially the same set of issues, anxieties and contingencies, before precisely the same sort of ideologically mixed audience.

After all, even the Catholic tracts were not designed simply to preach to the choir, to appeal solely to disaffected Catholics. On the contrary, they often affected an entirely a-confessional tone, and were clearly set up both to exacerbate and to exploit, albeit for their own narrowly confessional and Hispanophile purposes, what their authors clearly took to be a very widespread body of malcontent opinion, a melange of fears and fantasies, of grievances and antipathies, rumours and urban legends, experienced or espoused by a range of persons not anything like all of whom were, in any meaningful sense of the word, 'Catholic'.[158] What the evidence of the plays tells us is that in so doing the authors of the pamphlets were not merely whistling in the dark. On the contrary, there was a large body of (perhaps only partially acknowledged or half-articulated) discontent, unease and foreboding, on which many of the history plays under discussion in this book were also playing for quite other, largely pragmatic and commercial, purposes; at its most reductive, in order to put bums on seats and turn an honest penny.

Now I certainly do not want to argue that the plays (and tracts) give us access to an underground torrent of discontent and criticism otherwise suppressed by a draconian censorship regime. Such claims would massively exceed what the admittedly marginal, elusive and vagrant nature of the sources under discussion here would bear, or indeed anything that the both episodic and collusive censorship mechanisms of the Elizabethan state could have achieved.

Rather I want to suggest that, taken together, these sources allow us access to something that, if they were analysed apart, would remain almost completely closed to us; that is, they allow us a fleeting glimpse, or rather a series of fleeting glimpses, of the underside of the relentlessly upbeat celebration of the queen, the easy official triumphalism of Gloriana, the 'official version' that in later generations morphed into the legend of 'good Queen Bess', that is summarised so well in Kevin Sharpe's aptly titled monograph on *Selling the Tudor monarchy*. In these plays all the unwanted side effects, the hostile and negative reactions, the fears and grievances, the rumours, urban legends and misogynistic fantasies, generated by the Elizabethan protestant state – everything in short that the propaganda efforts analysed in such detail by Professor Sharpe were designed to efface and suppress, and which could otherwise only be coherently voiced in the outpourings of the exile Catholic press – found something like public expression. And thus it is that the texts being discussed in this book can take us to parts of the Elizabethan political imaginary that other sources cannot reach; they give us access to something we might want to regard as the political unconscious of the Elizabethan *fin de siècle*.

Hence, we might imagine, the almost obsessive recurrence of the rhetoric of 'subversion' and 'containment' in new historicist accounts of these issues and materials. Where new historicist analysis was conducted in what we might broadly call cultural terms, with 'Power' summoning the subversive or dissident elements within the ideological and cultural system in order the more effectively to dispel or contain them, this book seeks to examine some of the same topics through a more self-consciously political frame of reference. On the view being pushed here, it is the purposive (political) actions of, and the resulting contentions and disagreements between, various individuals, factions and ideologically defined or constituted groups, rather than Foucauldian abstractions like the 'micro-physics of power' or some ensemble of 'ideological state apparatuses' that were framing the range of cultural expression, driving the political narrative and indeed determining the political and cultural outcome.

Such an approach is not merely a function of methodological preference or prejudice, it is also a response to substantive difficulties intrinsic to the period itself. For the subversion/containment dyad implies that it is relatively easy to distinguish between that which is being subverted and that which is being contained, between, that is, a stable status quo and opinions and impulses taken to be self- evidently opposed thereto, when, in fact, such hard and fast distinctions, such binary oppositions, are hard to come-by, and almost impossible to sustain, in the Elizabethan *fin de siècle*.

Throughout the reign the public politics of appeal to various bodies of opinion, through the press, various forms of public performance, circulating manuscript and rumour, had been pioneered, not only or mainly by the regime's Catholic and puritan critics, but by central elements within the regime itself. Normal but anything but normative, indeed not even formally licit, by the 1590s, the politics of popularity had become part of the settled modus operandi, not only of dissident groups but of central figures in the regime. Not merely a mode of political operation or communication, 'popularity' had also become a boo-word, an accusation to be flung at groups or persons whose appeals to, or promotion of themselves before, the people, were deemed, or could be construed as, threatening to the status quo.

By the 1590s a newly minted anti-puritan push had rendered not merely oppositional but – on some, hyper-conformist, views of the matter – entirely seditious a range of opinions and practices that, in certain parts of the country, indeed in certain parts of the ecclesiastical establishment, had been, and indeed still remained, hegemonic, if not normative. The effects of this shift applied not merely to the realm of religious belief and practice – that is to say to the domain of activity, self-description and polemical contention organised (then and now) under the sign of puritanism – but also to secular ideology. The death of the Catholic Mary Stuart and the consequent emergence of her protestant son, James VI, as the leading candidate for the throne had thrown the ideological dynamics and polarities of the high Elizabethan period into reverse. Before it had been certain protestants, desperate to avert the accession of Mary Stuart, who had embraced the cause of elective monarchy. But now that it would lead to the accession of Mary's protestant son, James VI, those same protestants had as strong a vested interest in the doctrine of indefeasible hereditary right as the Catholics had had when they had been desperate to ensure the succession of the Catholic Mary. *Pari passu*, now that hereditary succession led straight to the protestant James, at least some Catholics were as anxious to embrace the principle of elective monarchy as they had been earlier to champion that of hereditary right.

The results of this *renversement d' alliances* were compounded by the anti-puritan push of the early 1590s, so that now, in (some) official circles, the notions of mixed and elective monarchy, which had been central to the so-called 'monarchical republic' of the high Elizabethan period, were giving place to increasingly absolutist readings of the English monarchical state and an increasingly stringent insistence that England was a free *hereditary* monarchy. The paradoxical outcome was that, by the mid-1590s, the most coherently 'monarchically republican' reading of the English polity was to be found in the work of that Hispanophile Jesuit exile, Robert Parsons.

Given the queen's stubborn refusal not merely to settle the succession, but to allow it to be publicly discussed, expressions of dynastic legitimism, and support for the next hereditary successor (James VI) constituted, in the here and now, not a form of loyalty, but rather of disobedience, disaffection and subversion. Moreover, by the mid 1590s, a variety of dissident or disaffected groups, with mutually exclusive visions of how the ecclesiastical and secular state should be ordered – crudely put, both puritans and Catholic loyalists – along, of course, with central elements within the Elizabethan establishment, were all looking to the most likely next successor (James VI) as their best hope. And James, desperate to maximise his support in the face of what he feared might well turn out to be a contested succession, was busily encouraging all of above to put their (often entirely incompatible) hopes in him.

By 1598 at least, even expressions of enthusiasm for a fight to the finish with the Spanish and popish enemy were coming to represent an intervention into an increasingly fractious and semi-public debate about the virtues of peace or war, and indeed about what sort of war to fight; a debate that, along with increasing tensions about the succession, was starting to divide the inner counsels of the regime into warring factions. Both Essex and James VI became convinced that those in favour of peace with Spain were more than prepared to negotiate with the Spanish about the succession. At a stroke, the (seemingly fanciful) suggestion, conjured by Parsons in the *Conference*, that the Infanta might become a viable claimant to the English throne, became an imminently threatening prospect. Consequently James became desperate that his ally Essex not be removed from the centre of power in England and that peace with Spain not be concluded before he came to the throne.[159]

From 1598 onwards, a dissident clique of professedly loyalist Catholics, the so-called appellant party, were receiving covert support from within the regime, in their campaign against a Jesuited and Hispanophile Catholic group, led and personified by Robert Parsons, who was now being outed by his Catholic enemies, as well as the by the protestant authorities, as the personification of a quintessentially duplicitous and seditious Jesuit threat; a threat equated, both by the appellants and elements in the regime, with that represented by the puritans. Not only did elements within the regime protect the appellants from the toils of the law, allow them to raise funds, and to stage two appeals to Rome, but, after 1601, the appellants were enabled to mount a virulent pamphlet war against their Jesuited enemies and in favour of toleration for at least a certain sort of Catholic and (by implication, albeit not explicitly) in support of the Stuart succession. Unsurprisingly, these developments went down rather badly with the more traditionally anti-popish members of the Elizabethan establishment and still worse with hot protestant and puritan supporters of the high Elizabethan status quo, who entertained a very different vision of what the accession of James VI and I would bring.[160]

In this situation, with the queen and central elements of her regime the virtual leaders of an opposition to what had been in many areas – and, for many people, remained – the organising concerns and underpinning assumptions of the Elizabethan protestant state, it is virtually impossible to speak in coherent terms of government and opposition, of subversion and containment.

The resulting confusions, paradoxes and tensions came to be epitomised by, to centre on or circle around, the figure of the earl of Essex, in and through whose person and personae many of these seeming contradictions were at least notionally – in prospect, if not in fact – 'resolved'. Essex patronised both military men and the godly, and maintained a clientage network that contained both puritans and Catholic loyalists, united in support for a total war to be fought, not so much against the papal Antichrist as against Hapsburg pretensions to universal monarchy. He combined the politics of honour (that is to say of ancient lineage and military aggression and glory, pursued in the personal service of the queen) with commitment to the cause of 'liberty' and its protection against the threat of Spanish tyranny. He simultaneously espoused a cult of personal loyalty and service to the queen and a very public commitment to what Francis Bacon called 'commonwealth causes'. He cultivated a popular following for himself, and maintained a covert, but by no means unknown, connection with the cause of James VI. In all these ways, Essex seemed both to personify, and to reconcile, many of the most glaring political and ideological contradictions and tensions of the age in one compelling, intensely personal, but also ideologically aggressive and culturally avant-garde, both monarchical and commonwealth-centred, political project.[161] When these tensions and contradictions boiled over in what became the final disgrace of Essex, the debacle of the so-called Essex rebellion, and the execution for treason of the earl himself, 'containment' of a sort had no doubt been achieved, but not of the (merely) cultural or ideological variety.

Notoriously, there is an almost total absence of direct evidence for how these plays were received by their first audiences. In consequence, the arguments pursued below about the contemporary resonances of many of the plays turn on the construction of what we might term virtual reception histories: elaborated accounts of how a variety of contemporaries might or could have used any given play to think about the events and concerns of the moment. The anlysis turns on how the various ideological materials, the matrices of reference and resonance, contained, or implied, in any given play could have been combined with the interpretative frameworks, the political and religious opinions, the knowledge and prejudice, brought to the play by various members of the audience. The aim is to recover a sense of the range of available or possible readings both of the play and of the current political/ideological conjuncture.[162]

At the very least, if we introduce the central insights and contentions of the Catholic tracts into the interpretative matrix within which these plays are read, we gain an at once expanded and more precise sense of the range of thoughts and associations that these plays might have set off in their first audiences. To take one example, for many Catholics the execution of Mary Stuart had been, at best, an act of judicial murder, and at worst one of regicide. Either way, far from helping to settle the succession, for many Catholics Mary's death had merely confirmed the illegitimacy of the Elizabethan regime and identified Elizabeth as, if not a usurper, then as something of a tyrant and certainly as the only successful regicide in England. As the relevant parliamentary debates show, even some of the most vociferous proponents of Mary's death knew that what they were doing was dangerous in the extreme. And, of course, up until the very last, Elizabeth herself remained desperate to avoid personal responsibility for what she clearly regarded as a thoroughly illegitimate, albeit politically necessary, act. When those perspectives are recalled, plays like *King John* or *Richard II* in which reigning kings or legitimate heirs are killed by usurping monarchs, or others, like the *Henry IV* plays, in which a monarch, guilty of usurpation and regicide, struggles to reimpose order, restore legitimacy and stave off despair, take on a new range of resonances and meanings.

On this view, in the 1590s, things were being done and said on the public stage that could not be (publicly) done and said anywhere else in Elizabethan England – except, that is, in entirely illicit political pamphlets written and published abroad by Catholic exiles. Even if we accept the existence of the sort of unwritten rules, the nexus of tacit assumption and self-limitation, described by Annabel Patterson, and even if we emphasise the elements of plausible deniability, of interpretative flexibility and multivocality, built into both text and performance, it surely remains the case that there were very considerable risks involved here. But they were risks that, I would argue, these plays took consistently and, just as consistently, got away with.

PART II

Past into present and future: 2 and 3 *Henry VI* and the politics of lost legitimacy

CHAPTER 1

Losing legitimacy: monarchical weakness and the descent into disorder

In the Catholic tracts it was claimed that, with the succession definitively unsettled, the queen's death would inevitably lead to a struggle for the crown between contending factions, organised around different claimants and characterised by different religious colourings and confessional allegiances. Since England had (for years) been embroiled in an unjust war with Spain, and since the king of Spain not only had certain dynastic claims on the English throne but also a major stake in ensuring that England – portrayed by these Catholic authors, at least, as the rogue state of the age – returned to the path of true religion and legitimate authority and, of course, to the lawful conduct of her relations with the other monarchies of western Europe, there was every likelihood of foreign intervention into a situation that seemed to be descending very rapidly indeed into the sort of bitter dynastic and confessional civil war that was even then raging just across the Channel in France.

The calmingly orthodox version of the comparison between England and France emphasised the contrast between the two states, playing up the blessings of God conferred on his faithful handmaiden, Queen Elizabeth, who not only received providential help in defeating the assaults of her foreign popish enemies but was able to intervene effectively in a number of foreign theatres, while preserving her own realm from the ravages of war. But the French example could also be used for other, considerably less reassuring, purposes. Here the fate of France served as a warning of what lay in store for England. As a general rule, God might protect his people from their enemies, but if they fell into serious sin, or refused to reform, he might well stop, using even idolators and tyrants as sticks with which to beat his people for their recalcitrance and sin, just as he had employed the Assyrians or Babylonians to admonish and punish the people of Israel.

Such arguments were, of course, available to a range of contemporary authors and preachers; puritans using them to urge England to hurry on down the path of further reformation, and papists to urge her to forsake heresy and return to the fold of the true church (of Rome). In a more politique mode, the fate of France might be used to illustrate the result of a contested succession and religious division and thus to warn the English of the fate that awaited them if the queen did indeed die with the succession unsettled. Such fears were not, of course, limited to Catholics; they provided a range of protestants with central arguments as to just why the succession needed to be settled sooner rather than later, or not at all, and it was precisely the prevalence of such anxieties in other than Catholic quarters that rendered Catholic harping on these concerns such effective propaganda.

But if the French wars of religion provided a pressing contemporary example of what dynastic and religious civil war looked like, the recent history of England itself contained other awful warnings of what a genuinely unsettled and then actively contested succession might bring in its wake. Those examples were, of course, to be found in the Wars of the Roses and the descent of England into civil strife and then civil war under the impact of the struggle between the houses of Lancaster and York. As we have seen, as long ago as *The treatise of treasons* and *Leicester's commonwealth* Catholic polemicists had pointed their readers to precisely those events, if they wanted a guide to what lay in store for England if the malign conspiracy of the queen's favourite to unsettle and then to divert the succession were not foiled. In *Leicester's commonwealth*, Mary Stuart was presented as the great bulwark against the descent of Tudor England into just such a crisis. For, it was argued, with Mary dead, the last legitimist obstacle standing between the queen and the conspirators would have been removed. In such circumstances, Elizabeth's fate would be sealed; it would be merely a question of time before Leicester and his mates made their move for the crown and thus plunged the nation into certain civil war, foreign invasion and confessional conflict.

Those warnings had been written in the early 1580s. But now Mary was dead, the succession remained unsettled and Elizabeth was getting old. As a number of tracts by Catholic authors like Parsons and his sidekick Richard Verstegan were about to argue, having spent years ensuring that the queen remained unmarried and that the succession remained unsettled, the better to advance their power and plans, the clique of politique atheists around the queen were about to reap the whirlwind. Now when the queen died, as she soon must, there was no way to avert the cataclysm of a contested succession and religious war that had been looming for so long.

The very fact that at almost the same moment that those threats were being made by a variety of Catholic authors the events of the Wars of the Roses were being staged in the London theatres suggests that such fears were not merely a figment of the perfervid imagination of a few Catholic exiles and polemicists desperate to destabilise an otherwise secure Elizabethan regime, nor even the preserve of Catholics. Rather, we might conclude, such anxieties enjoyed a far more general provenance; constituting a body of opinion that the authors of the Catholic tracts were seeking to bend to their own intensely partisan purposes.[1]

The events of Henry VI's reign spoke, of course, to current English anxiety and experience in myriad ways. Here was a nation engaged in a long-standing war with a major continental monarchy, plunged by defeat abroad and internal factional conflict at home into dynastic civil war, an all or nothing struggle for supreme power between two factions organised around mutually exclusive claims to the throne. Here was an historical narrative that could link current realities and worries to a luridly threatening image both of the past and of the immediate future; a future prefigured not merely by the recent English past but by the current state of France. And that, I want to argue, is precisely what the Henry VI plays offered their first audiences.[2]

In *Edward III*, Peele's *Edward I* or *The troublesome reign of king John*, English monarchs were depicted being tried, sometimes almost to breaking point, by their own sins – often of the flesh – and by the blandishments, duplicities and threats of women, foreigners and papists. But, at the end of the day, sin and temptation were overcome, and unity and then victory over the foreigner were secured. There was, however, no such happy resolution to be extracted either from *The contention betwixt the two famous houses of Lancaster and York* or from *The true tragedy of Richard duke of York*.

The politics of faction anatomised

The first scenes of *2 Henry VI*, or *The contention*, delineate a political and moral landscape dominated by the corrosive effects of noble faction, by feuds and conflicts between rival claimants to power and influence under the crown. The play opens with the announcement of Henry's marriage to Margaret and of the fatal marriage settlement that the king has made with the French to bring that match about. As that epitome of good rule and English valour, the duke of Gloucester, along with Warwick, York and Salisbury, recoils in horror at what the king has done, Henry himself expresses himself well pleased with the exchange, and he creates his agent in the negotiations, William de la Pole, duke of Suffolk for his pains. There follows a scene in which the underlying tensions at the court are swiftly laid bare. Outspoken in his criticism of the marriage terms, Gloucester is upbraided for his temerity by Cardinal Beaufort, who is swiftly revealed as Gloucester's arch-rival and enemy. Gloucester then exits, leaving the cardinal to denounce him not only as 'my enemy' but 'an enemy unto you all,/And no great friend I fear me to the King'. As 'the next of blood' to the king, Gloucester has, Beaufort explains, good reason to repine at the king's marriage, 'even had Henry got an empire' by it. A man with a dangerously popular following – 'the common people favour him,/Calling him "Humphrey, the good duke of Gloucester" ' – for all his 'flattering gloss', he would prove 'a dangerous Protector' [Pt. II, I, i, 145–61] Buckingham agrees with the cardinal, proposing an alliance with the newly ennobled Suffolk to 'hoist Duke Humphrey from his seat' [Pt. II, I, i, 162–66].

Beaufort having left the stage, Somerset puts his 'cousin of Buckingham' straight about the cardinal who, although an enemy of their enemy, the

Protector, is in fact just as haughty and dangerous as Gloucester himself [Pt. II, I, i, 173–74]. Having enlisted each other into a pact against both Gloucester and the Cardinal, the better to enhance their own power in the state – 'Or thou or I, Somerset, will be Protectors,/Despite Duke Humphrey, or the Cardinal' – [Pt. II, I, i, 175–76] Somerset and Buckingham storm off, leaving Salisbury to observe to his son, Warwick, and to York that 'Pride went before; Ambition follows him'. Noting the virtue of Gloucester and the viciousness of his enemies, Salisbury appeals to Warwick and York, as proven servants of the commonweal, trusted by the people for their loyal service to the crown in Ireland and France, to stand with him 'together for the public good,/In what we can to bridle and suppress/The pride of Suffolk and the Cardinal,/With Somerset's and Buckingham's ambition;/And, as we may, cherish Duke Humphrey's deeds,/While they do tend the profit of the land' [Pt. II, I, i, 177, 196–201].

Almost immediately York dispels this (paradoxical) impression of a faction determined to divide and rule in the interests of the 'common profit of his country' [Pt. II, I, i, 202]. Once the others have left the stage, he reveals his plan to claim the throne for himself and his determination to use the mutual suspicions, the loathings and machinations, of the others to do so [Pt. II, I, i, 246–54].

The tensions and divisions exposed in these opening exchanges are compounded and completed by later conversations between the queen and Suffolk in which Margaret expresses herself appalled at the political condition of the realm and, in particular, at the weakness of the king. The first object of her wrath is, of course, the protector Gloucester. 'What, shall King Henry be a pupil still/Under the surly Gloucester's governance?/Am I a queen in title and style/And must be made a subject to a duke?' [Pt. II, I, iii, 43–50]. But not far behind him, in the queen's estimation, come the rest of the Council [Pt. II, I, iii, 69–75]. To redress this imbalance Suffolk enlists the malcontent Margaret to his scheme, 'although we fancy not the Cardinal' yet to 'join with him and with the lords/Till we have brought Duke Humphrey in disgrace'. That project completed, 'one by one we'll weed them at last,/And you yourself shall steer the happy helm' [Pt. II, I, iii, 95–101].

In these opening exchanges we can see, being peeled back like the layers of an onion, the mutual suspicions and factional animosities at the heart of the court of Henry VI. Despite York's monologue, the basic political problem besetting the realm is not presented here as an unsettled or contested succession. For, as Beaufort's denunciation of the untrustworthiness of Gloucester shows (York aside), issues of succession are operating less as motivating factors, driving the action than as contributory elements to an escalating process of mutual denunciation and distrust. The sole exception here is York. As for the other characters, they are revealed, at the outset at least, to be entirely oblivious to the existence and nature both of his claim to the throne and of his monarchical ambitions.

Out of this situation York emerges as a sort of Leicester or Huntingdon figure – as Leicester or Huntingdon had been portrayed in *Leicester's commonwealth* – that is to say, as a Machiavel, plotting darkly behind the scenes to divert the succession in order to seize power for himself. Certainly, it is York who, possessed of and animated by the *damnosa hereditas* of a (viable) claim to the throne, operates as the ultimate solvent on the party of 'public good', as it has been assembled in the opening scenes. What diverts Salisbury and Warwick from the course of political virtue is York's explanation of his claim to the throne, proffered as a further excuse to prosecute their feud against their enemies, the cardinal, Suffolk, Somerset and the queen. Confronted by a wonderfully confounding and confusing explication of York's claim, derived, as it is, through two female heirs, from Edward III's third son, the duke of Clarence, rather than (like that of the Lancastrians) from his fourth, John of Gaunt, Salisbury replies with a remark that can certainly be played for laughs rather more easily than it can be taken straight. 'What plain proceeding is more plain than this' [Pt. II, II, ii, 1–53]. Miraculously converted on the spot to the righteousness of York's case, both Salisbury and Warwick instantly give over their commitment to the defence of the blameless Gloucester and immediately embrace York's plan to 'wink at the Duke of Suffolk's insolence,/At Beaufort's pride, at Somerset's ambition,/At Buckingham, and all the crew of them,/Till they have snared the shepherd of the flock,/That virtuous prince, the good Duke Humphrey./'Tis that they seek; and they, in seeking that,/Shall find their deaths, if York can prophesy' [Pt. II, II, ii, 70–76].

Thus have the ambitions and rivalries of the good and the great reduced the nobility to a series of warring factions, each determined to do down the other and achieve some version of dominance for themselves. Now, through the open canvassing of York's claim to be king – which is converted in this scene from its previous role as the object of York's private plans and secret fantasies into the organising principle of a faction – the final, fatally destabilising, factor has been introduced into the mix. And, of course, the fact that it has been thus introduced by York, who emerges from the subsequent action of the play as far from the most obviously corrupt or vicious of the political agents on view, serves only to highlight the elements of systemic breakdown consequent upon the interactions between weak kingship, unbridled noble faction, an unsettled succession and, as we shall see below, excessive female influence over the exercise of monarchical authority.

The 'good duke' (of Gloucester)

With the defection of the Nevilles from the party of the commonwealth to the Yorkist camp, Humphrey, duke of Gloucester now remains the one character who stands for the common good and the common weal. As Berry observes,

Gloucester plays 'an emblematic role' in the play 'as an epitome of the good governor'; alone amongst the counsellors and nobles on display, he is just, yet merciful.[3] While he is beloved of the commons for his fairness, he also knows how to enforce order and to maintain justice and his only aim is to do just that in the king's name. The play goes out of its way to establish Gloucester's bona fides in this regard, setting up a series of piquant contrasts, not only between the duke and his fellow magistrates and counsellors, but also between Gloucester and the king himself. In one scene a series of petitioners approach a man they take to be 'my lord Protector' only to find out too late that they are addressing his arch-enemy and evil twin, the evil counsellor par excellence, Suffolk. One appeals against oppression at the hands of 'my Lord Cardinal's man', while another petitions against the depredations of Suffolk himself in 'enclosing the commons of Melford'. Predictably, both receive short shrift, only a third, Peter, the apprentice, who seeks to report his master, Horner, for high treason for having told him that York is the true king, receives a hearing [Pt. II, I, iii, 1–36] – and only then because the furtherance of this complaint will serve Suffolk and the queen's wider factional purposes in their campaign against York [Pt. II, I, iii, 98–99].

Such behaviour is in marked contrast to that of the Protector himself, whose sagacity and justice as a governor are established beyond doubt in two scenes. The first involves his hearing of the case, brought by Peter the apprentice (and by Suffolk) against his master Horner and, behind him, the duke of York. Called upon by the king to judge the affair, and unable on the face of it to determine who is telling the truth, Gloucester allows the case to be decided by trial by combat, deferring the verdict to divine providence. Ostentatiously refusing to play politics, Gloucester uses the case to end a festering dispute between Somerset and York over who should command the royal forces in France [Pt. II, I, iii, 206–11].

Despite his protestations about his utter unfitness for the fight, Peter overcomes his master, Horner, who, as he expires, confesses 'treason'. 'O God! Have I overcome mine enemies in this presence? O Peter, thou hast prevailed in right!' is Peter's comment on his own triumph; one confirmed by the king's verdict on events: he proclaims the result a triumph for God's – in effect the Protector's – justice [Part II, II, iii, 99–100]. Thus does Henry recognise and laud the complete congruence between human and divine justice, between the workings of human government and the operations of divine providence, that a properly forceful exercise of magisterial or royal power can produce. It is just that Henry himself remains entirely incapable of the toughness, either of mind or of will,that would bring such a happy confluence about.

That point is driven home by Gloucester's handling of an alleged miracle experienced by one Simpcox and his wife. Simpcox claims to have been blind since birth. Having been 'called/A hundred times and oft'ner, in my sleep,/By good St Alban', Simpcox has finally made the pilgrimage to St Albans and his devotion is rewarded with the restoration of his sight. King Henry is thrown into paroxysms of pious excitement at this news. Endorsing the popular cry that this is indeed 'a miracle', something that 'the Lord hath done', he calls on the man to 'tell us here the circumstance/That we for thee may glorify the Lord' [Pt. II, II, i, 73–74, 81–83].

Gloucester, however, smells a rat. The man claims to be lame as well as to have been born blind and when he explains that, despite this, he came by his injury falling out of a tree which he had scaled to pick plums, the Lord Protector sets a trap for him, asking him what colours the attendant lords are dressed in. When Simpcox answers not merely by distinguishing between the various hues but by giving them their correct names, Gloucester pounces [Pt II, II, i, 122–29]. He calls for the town beadle to whip him. After the first blow, the supposedly lame Simpcox cuts and runs, leading Gloucester to decree his and his wife's fate. 'Let them be whipped through every market town/Till they come to Berwick, from whence they came' [Pt. II, II, i, 150–51]. Having established Gloucester's sagacity and cunning as a magistrate, the play then sets up two contrasts; the first between his tough-minded doing of genuine justice and the credulity and simple-minded piety of the king; the second between Gloucester's virtue and the self-serving corruption of Suffolk.

If these two scenes establish Gloucester's bona fides as a genuinely good magistrate and ruler, other exchanges in private establish his freedom from the ambition and the disloyalty that afflicts all the other major characters. Beaufort has already claimed that since, as things stand, if the king dies without an heir of his body, the duke would succeed to the throne, he represents a source of danger to the royal person. It is thus that Gloucester's own wife urges him to wrest the crown from the weakling king and establish both of them on the throne of England. But Gloucester will have none of it [Pt. II, 1, ii, 5– 21]. When his wife persists, telling him of a dream that, she claims, prefigures their elevation to the crown, Gloucester responds in righteous anger [Pt. II, I, ii, 5–50].

Just as his dealings with Simpcox and his wife, and with Horner and his apprentice, have left us in no doubt as to his wisdom and incorruptibility as a source of public justice, so these entirely private exchanges with his wife leave us similarly convinced not only of Gloucester's virtue and loyalty to the king, but also of his complete lack of the 'ambitious thoughts' and 'presumption' for which he rebukes his wife. Similarly, his willingness – without prejudging the issue but in light of Horner's allegations about York's aspirations to the throne – to block York's appointment to high command in France reveals a readiness to defend the king's interest at the merest hint of danger, without malice, but also with no concern for his own personal political fortunes or popularity.

Finally, when his wife is convicted for compassing the king's death by witch-craft, Gloucester makes no attempt to protect her, casting her off from bed and

board if the accusations made against her prove true [Pt. II, II, i, 181–90].
Again, Gloucester's public professions of virtue are confirmed by entirely
private exchanges with his wife; intercepting her as she makes her way into
exile, he takes essentially the same tack, counselling her to 'forget this grief';
'thy greatest help is quiet, gentle Nell' [Pt. II, II iv, 26, 67]. Here, of course,
Gloucester's capacity not merely to identify and withstand, but also to reprove
and repudiate, his own wife's prideful and corrupt impulses stands in marked
contrast both to King Henry's and the corrupt Suffolk's treatment of that other
proud and ambitious woman, Queen Margaret.

Good counsellor/evil counsellor

The play thus goes out if its way to establish Gloucester's bona fides as a loyal
subject, even-handed and, if necessary, stern magistrate (and husband), wise
judge and good counsellor.[4] But even as it does so, it makes available a very
different estimation of him through the allegations of his enemies, who identify Gloucester as a traitor and usurper waiting to happen, a source of clear and
present danger to the king, whose safety can be ensured only by Gloucester's
immediate removal, not only from office but from the royal presence *tout
court*. As they urge this course upon a reluctant king, Suffolk, the Cardinal,
Somerset, the queen and Buckingham gang up to blackguard the duke as the
quintessential evil counsellor, corrupt judge and self-serving magistrate, out to
line his own pockets and pursue his own private interests at the expense of both
king and subject, to the extent of selling out the kingdom to the French enemy
[Pt. II, I, iii, 124–36].

The scene is repeated with a new list of accusations in a final confrontation
before the king between Gloucester and his accusers. The queen starts off.
Gloucester's demeanour, formally so 'mild and affable' – 'all the court admired
him for submission' – has suddenly been transformed. 'How insolent of late he
is become, how proud,/How peremptory, and unlike himself'. In a man of his
stature and birth this is not something to be ignored. 'Mesemeth then it is no
policy,/Respecting what a rancorous mind he bears/And his advantage
following your decease,/That he should come about your royal person/Or be
admitted to your highness' Council./By flattery hath he won the commons'
hearts;/And when he please to make commotion/'Tis to be feared they all
will follow him' [Pt. II, III, i, 4–33]. Suffolk concurs, claiming that even if
Gloucester were technically ignorant of his wife's dabbling in prophecy and
witchcraft, 'yet by reputing of his high descent,/As next the king he was successive heir –/And such high vaunts of his nobility –/Did instigate the bedlam
brainsick Duchess/By wicked means to frame our sovereign's fall' [Pt. II, III, i,
47–63]. The earlier litany of complaints is then repeated. Abroad defeat
in France is laid at his door, while at home, he has devised 'strange tortures

for offenders, never heard of,/That England was defamed by tyranny' [Pt. II, III, i, 104–6, 121–23].

To all this Gloucester offers a blunt denial. 'So help me God, as I have watched the night,/Ay, night by night, in studying good for England!' [Pt. II, III, i, 107–18]. Not one penny of the crown's revenues has stuck to his hands; on the contrary, he has spent his own money in the kingdom's defence. As a judge 'pity was all the fault that was in me . . . Unless it were a bloody murderer,/ Or foul felonious thief that fleeced poor passengers,/I never gave them condign punishment' [Pt. II, III, i, 125–30].

It is worth remarking here that the charges of ambition, corruption and pride in his lineage, of profiting from the war and war finance, of devising new tortures and torments that have dragged England's name through the mud, of dominating the monarch, arrogating the exercise of royal power to himself and even of harbouring aspirations to a regal power, all echo charges already made or about to be made in various Catholic tracts against Lord Burghley, just as Gloucester's reply that all he has ever done is 'study good for England' replicate perfectly the Lord Treasurer's pose of injured innocence, struck in response to such charges.[5]

We are entering here the nightmare world conjured by *Leicester's commonwealth*, and later by *Cecil's*, a world where one person's good counsellor was another's Machiavel; one man's godly magistrate and honest broker another's self-serving hypocrite and corrupt courtier. But the play does not (yet) take this opportunity to plunge us into a world of perspectival relativism, of moral ambivalence and ambiguity, making us view events through the fog of misinformation created by the rumours and false accounts, the accusations and counter-accusations, spread by the major players (and interested third parties) against and about one another. Still less does it endorse the charge sheet compiled against good Duke Humphrey (and indeed against Lord Burghley).[6] On the contrary, as we have seen, by this point the play has gone out of its way to establish the moral standing of Gloucester as a genuine servant of his king and the commonwealth. His character and fate have been established as a touchstone, an Archimedean point of moral certainty, from which to view (and judge) the moral condition and prospects of the other major players and indeed of the polity itself.

True tragedy: the fall of Gloucester

The point is, of course, driven home by Gloucester's fate, which represents both a symptom and a further development of the moral decline, the descent into chaos and violence, set off by the un-rule of Henry VI. For despite the virtually unanimous claims of his other counsellors and queen, Henry himself remains entirely unconvinced by the charges laid against the duke. Thanking his counsellors for their assiduousness in protecting his interests, Henry yet persists in his belief in the duke's innocence [Pt. II, III, i, 68–73]. Despite this royal vote of confidence, which, under another monarch, would surely have been the end of the matter, at his next appearance at court Gloucester is arrested by Suffolk to answer not only the charges already made against him, which, in the face of Gloucester's robust rebuttals, Suffolk admits to be 'quickly answered', but also for 'mightier crimes', yet to be specified [Pt. II, III, i, 133–34].

In response, all Henry feels able to do is express his 'special hope/That you will clear yourself from all suspense./My conscience tells me you are innocent' [Pt. II, III, i, 139–41] and then to wash his hands of the matter. 'My Lords, what to your wisdoms seemeth best/Do, or undo, as if ourself were here'. To his wife's despairing question, 'what, will your highness leave the parliament?', Henry replies by citing his deep misery, even despair, at the turn events have taken. Convinced of his uncle's innocence – 'Ah, uncle Humphrey, in thy face I see/ The map of honour, truth and loyalty', 'thou never didst them wrong, nor no man wrong' – all he can do is lament the fate that awaits him at the hands of 'these great lords and Margaret our Queen/' who 'do seek subversion of thy harmless life' [Pt. II, III, i, 218–22].

This is, of course, a quite extraordinary speech for a regnant monarch to make. In delivering it Henry becomes a lamenting chorus, commenting on the tragedy of his own reign; in effect, abdicating from his role as ruler in the face of the pressure from his queen and counsellors. In a remarkable image, Henry gives up not only his office but his masculinity, placing himself in the role of the impotent, grieving mother of the calf being led off to death at the slaughterman's hands. By thus absenting himself from the scene he repudiates responsibility for a tragic outcome that he foresees all too well. It is a moment that crystallises all that is amiss with his rule.

The play thus shows Henry precisely not to be a classic victim of evil counsel. Rather, barraged by the accusations of a united court, he simply refuses to believe that Gloucester is what they claim he is. But he then does absolutely nothing about it. On this view, while there is nothing wrong with Henry's conscience, he suffers from a chronic debility of will, and without the robust exercise of royal will, the whole system of monarchical government, over which Henry presides and which he personifies, must break down. More particularly, without the backing of a just and merciful prince, the position of even the best of royal servants (like Gloucester) is rendered impossible. For, absent a strong monarch, the exercise of political virtue, like Gloucester's, ceases to be a source of strength and becomes instead a source of positive weakness. The problem here is thus not the absence of good counsel, or the presence of evil counsellors, nor the failure of the monarch to recognise good counsel when he hears it, but rather his refusal, indeed his incapacity, to act upon that counsel. Put another way, the scene stages the dependence of even the best of counsellors on the active exercise of royal rule.

When Gloucester meets his wife on her way to exile, he counsels her to patience, and she reviles him for his failure to come to her aid. This, of course, could be taken as but more of the same from the turbulent, ambitious duchess, but now her case has a further twist to it. While the audience knows that she is guilty as charged, they also know that her fall is part of a set-up or sting whereby Suffolk and the queen have provoked her into a boiling resentment and anger – the queen has boxed her ears in open court, 'mistaking' her for a serving woman, and then put her in harm's way by introducing her to a suborned cunning man. Aware that she has been first set up and then done in by her enemies, the duchess warns her husband that he is next on the list. [Pt. II, II, iv, 43–57]

As the audience is well aware, having been shown the machinations of Gloucester's enemies, all this is true enough, but Gloucester will have none of it. He excoriates his wife's advice as a recipe for disaster. For him to come to her aid, as she suggests, would be absurdly dangerous. 'Wouldst have me rescue thee from this reproach? Why yet thy scandal were not wiped away,/But I in danger for the breach of the law.' As for his own case, he is innocent, and therefore has nothing to fear, 'So long as I am loyal, true and crimeless' [Pt. II, II, iv, 59–68]. It is a confidence that Gloucester continues to feel in the face of the accusations of his enemies. As he tells Suffolk, even as he is being arrested, 'A heart unspotted is not easily daunted./The purest spring is not so free from mud/As I am clear from treason to my sovereign./Who can accuse me? Wherein am I guilty?' [Pt. II, III, i, 99–103].

What is at stake here is not simply Gloucester's political naivety or obliviousness. As he later tells his tormentors and accusers, he has long been aware of their machinations and manoeuvres against him [Pt. II, III, i, 165–67]. Rather, what we are seeing here is a set of operating assumptions appropriate to a monarchical normality in which the king maintains control of his own affairs and counsellors and is prepared to act upon what he knows to be the truth. It is the essence of Gloucester's loyalty to his prince, a central, indeed defining characteristic of his political virtue, that he will not descend to the underhand factional manoeuvrings, the determination to do down his rivals, before they can do for him, that his wife urges upon him as she passes into exile. Moreover, there is real sense to his claim that to pervert the course of justice, to free his wife from royal custody or to undo his rivals would render him guilty of precisely the sort of offence of which he was currently being accused and thus play into the hands of his enemies. And yet all of this is only true if the king remains a source of independent, justice-doing authority, operating above, and maintaining control over, the manoeuvrings and rivalries of his counsellors and subjects. And this Henry VI simply will not – indeed apparently cannot – either be or do. The terminally weak Henry is thus instigating, against his will but through the irreversible logic of his own actions, a situation in which virtue can be denounced as vice, and charges of treason simply be made up to aid the personal or factional interests and ends of nobles whose mutual antipathies and ambitions the king himself has not merely failed to control but in fact enabled, even called into being, through his own refusal to exercise the office that he has held, as he repeatedly tells us, since he was nine months old.

Henry's absent presence on the throne has thus created a world turned upside down to which Gloucester's operating assumptions, the very instincts and principles that make him a good rather than an evil counsellor, a godly rather than a corrupt and self-serving magistrate, are no longer an adequate response. Indeed, it is no small irony that it is his proud, ambitious, disobedient and, in the end, treasonous, wife who understands the ground rules of the new political game better than the virtuous, experienced and utterly loyal duke himself. For, in this moral and political environment, far from virtue being its own reward or innocence the best defence, in order merely to survive, let alone to thrive, it is now *necessary*, in the immortal words of Carwyn James, to get your retaliation in first; to do down your enemies – and this is now a world in which nearly everyone is at least a potential enemy or rival – before they can do you down. At the end even Gloucester himself comes to realise the truth of these propositions, warning the king, as he is carted off to prison, 'these days are dangerous./Virtue is choked with foul ambition,/And charity chased hence by rancour's hand;/Foul subornation is predominant,/And equity exiled your highness' land' [Pt. II, III, i, 42–46].

The play stages the demise of the good duke as the fag end of a golden age of good government, the exclusion from the governance of the realm of a whole series of both personal and political virtues. In so doing it was taking its place alongside other almost exactly contemporary texts, which might be taken to be both reflecting and playing off anxieties about what was clearly perceived to be a crucial point of generational transition in Elizabethan England. At the end of the 1580s and early 1590s a whole raft of central figures from the high Elizabethan regime – Leicester, Walsingham, Mildmay, Warwick, Bedford, Hatton – were dying off, leaving behind the ageing queen and Lord Burghley as the central representatives of the Elizabethan 'golden age'. In their place was a new generation of younger men, favourites and would-be counsellors – fractious in their relations with one another and intensely ambitious to make their way at court, in the counsels of the queen and in the conduct of the war. Central here were the figures of Sir Walter Raleigh and of the young earl of Essex, whose feud was a matter of public knowledge at precisely the time these plays were being written and performed.[7]

Monarchical rule as the enabling condition of good counsel

We can see how anxieties and tensions resultant upon this changing of the guard were being given expression on the stage in the almost immediately contemporary play, *Thomas of Woodstock*. There another good duke, another epitome of political virtue and sagacity, of loyalty to the prince and service to the commonwealth, falls victim to the conspiracies of a group of young favourites and courtiers and their corrupt men of business. In that play nearly all the emphasis falls on the corruption and ambition of the young king and his courtiers, and on the fiscal exactions and informer-fed oppressions needed to finance them. In other words the play uses the fate of Thomas of Woodstock to examine and stage a range of immediately contemporary grievances and concerns about the conduct and financing of government in the early 1590s. In *2 Henry VI*, the passing of the 'good duke' of Gloucester is connected, through the linked issues of noble faction, foreign war and the succession, to a vision less about the present than the immediate future.

Thus as he confronts his accusers, Gloucester himself waxes prophetic. Not only will his exclusion from the counsels of the king deprive Henry of 'his crutch' which is now being thrown away 'before his legs be firm to bear his body' [Pt. II, III, I, 190–92], but Gloucester foresees his own death at the hands of his enemies – a death that, he claims, will not be the end of the current turmoil, but rather the start of something worse [Pt. II, III, i, 151–60].

All of which, of course, proves to be case. Gloucester's death, arranged by them all but carried out by Beaufort, with Suffolk's connivance and the queen's express approval, is but the start of the final descent of the realm into chaos, revolt and bloody civil war. Gloucester's murder is the occasion of popular turmoil, and then revolt, of the exile and death of Suffolk, and of the return, in armed rebellion from Ireland, of York, ostensibly to put down Cade's rebellion (at which, from the start, he has connived) and to exclude his arch-enemy Somerset from the counsels of the king, but in fact to claim the throne for himself. The outbreak of open violence opens the way to civil war between two factions; factions now organised around openly canvassed and mutually exclusive claims to the throne. This is a situation that beckons to the world of unappeasable blood feuds and power struggles, a veritable war of all against all, staged in part III.

CHAPTER 2

Disorder dissected (i): the inversion
of the gender order

The plays show a good deal of this disorder stemming from women either aspiring to get or else successfully climbing 'on top'.[1] This process can be seen quite clearly, in the first half of part II, in the pairing of the duchess of Gloucester with Queen Margaret, and throughout both plays in the progression of Queen Margaret from ambitious and unfaithful wife and subject to faction leader, warrior and ruler, until finally she becomes the virtual personification of violent revenge pursued for its own sake.[2]

Disorderly wives and witches

From the outset the play portrays both duchess and queen as disobedient, proud and ambitious women, aspiring to a degree of power and influence first over their husbands, and then over the wider political system, far greater than anything a properly obedient and ordered woman and wife ought to aspire to, let alone exercise. As always, Gloucester is the personification of orderly normality. He attempts not only to put his own wife in her place but also to contain the ambition of the queen. At one point, Margaret argues that Somerset rather than York should be given the command in France 'because the king, forsooth, will have it so', only to be rebuked by Gloucester: 'Madam, the king is old enough himself/To give his censure. These are no woman's matters.' That, of course, is the right answer, except that Henry's serial weakness leaves Gloucester open to the riposte that 'if he be old enough, what needs your grace/ To be Protector of his excellence?' [Pt. II, I, iii, 116–20]. Here, as so often, it is Henry's failure to act his part as king that opens the way for female power-grabbing and aspirational intrigue. Nevertheless, for all that its origins are to be found in an initial breakdown of patriarchal power, the nature and extent of the resulting disorder are figured in terms of overbearing and ambitious women breaking through the constraints of the gender order and occupying what ought to be the strongholds of patriarchal power.

On the feminine side of the equation, the play locates the origins of this breakdown in the traditionally female vice of pride. Thus, even as he claims the throne, Edward IV tells Queen Margaret that her advent as Henry's wife has 'heaped sedition on his crown at home./For what hath broached this tumult but thy pride?/Hadst thou been meek, our title had still slept,/And we, in pity of our gentle King,/Had slipped our claim until another age' [Pt. III, II, ii, 158–62]. As for the duchess of Gloucester, Margaret rages against 'that proud dame, the Lord Protector's wife./She sweeps it through the court with troops of ladies,/More like an empress than Duke Humphrey's wife./Strangers in court do take her for the queen.' As ever with 'deviant' women, sartorial excess is taken to be a marker of moral fallibility. 'She bears a duke's revenues on her back/And in her heart she scorns our poverty' [Pt. II, I, iii, 77–88]. When the duchess is disgraced, it is her pride that Suffolk remarks upon [Pt. II, II, iii, 45–46]. But the duchess' pride is not something we learn about only from her enemies. It is a vice for which her own husband rebukes her as she tries to ensnare him in her plot to seize the crown: 'presumptuous dame, ill nurtured Eleanour' [Pt. II, I, ii, 42–49]. Eleanour herself confirms this picture. As she passes into exile for conjuring the king's death, she expresses sorrow, not for her sins or crimes, but rather for her disgrace. In exile, she exclaims, 'to think upon my pomp shall be my hell' [Pt. II, II, iv, 30–33].

It is surely by no means an accident that the duchess' rebellion against both familial and royal patriarchal authority is tinged with the demonic. Her offence has been to dabble in what turns out to be witchcraft, consulting with a cunning man, seeking to further her plans to succeed to the throne by ascertaining, through magical means, the fate of the king and his leading counsellors. Initially, the play sets up the duchess' encounter with the devil as a fraudulent sting. The cunning man she consults has been suborned by her enemies, and the duchess herself provoked into action by a physical assault by that 'proud Frenchwoman' [Pt. II, I, iii, 141], the queen. Her very encounter with the cunning woman 'mother Jourdain' and her accomplices, Hume and Bolingbroke, starts out as a piece of theatre – Bolingbroke at one point instructing Jourdain: 'be you prostrate and grovel on the earth' [Pt. II, I, iv, 10–11] – only suddenly to turn very real indeed, with the appearance of a genuine devil, Adnath, who proceeds to deliver himself of various cryptic prophecies about the fates of Henry, York, Suffolk and Somerset, all of which, in a paradoxical, roundabout (and typically demonic) way, are shown subsequently to be 'true'. The duchess, then, through her indulgence of the typically female sin of pride, has been led, if not to become a witch herself, then certainly to do more than dabble in witchcraft and it is her fall into witchcraft and then treason that provides the grounds for the ruin of her entirely virtuous husband. Her rivalry with the queen – which culminates in a physical confrontation at court, during which she threatens 'could I come near your beauty with my nails/I'd set my ten commandments in your face' [Pt. II, I, iii, 143–44] – encapsulates the vicious personal rivalry and feuding that is undermining the kingdom.

In the course of the altercation between the two women, the duchess provides a prophetic warning to the king. 'Good King look to't in time;/She'll pamper thee, and dandle thee like a baby./Though in this place most master wear no breeches,/She shall not strike Dame Eleanor unrevenged' [Pt. II, I, iii, 145–48]. The duchess here has recourse to a proverbial saying, and that image of a household in which not the master but his wife wears the breeches was, of course, an image of social, moral and political disorder that ran throughout the culture of early modern England. Amongst 'the people' such households were subject to the spontaneous communal discipline dished out through the 'rough music' of the charivari.[3]

When such disorder spread to the highest levels of the social and political order, disaster could not be far away. And the play, of course, stages systematically the process whereby Queen Margaret does indeed come to wear the breeches, dominating and finally displacing her husband from the centre first of the regime and later of the Lancastrian party. She does so initially as an adulteress, disgusted with the failures of Henry as a man and a ruler and enamoured of the qualities of his emergent favourite, the duke of Suffolk. Appalled at Henry's piety, meekness and continued tutelage under the rule of the protector, she rails at Suffolk, 'Am I a queen in title and in style/And must be made a subject to a duke?/I tell thee, Pole, when in the city Tours/Thou ran'st a-tilt in honour of my love/And stol'st away the ladies' hearts of France/I thought King Henry had resembled thee/In courage, courtship and proportion.' But in this she had been sadly mistaken, since Henry's 'mind is bent to holiness', not the exercise of power or martial prowess [Pt. II, I, iii, 49–65].

There could scarcely be a clearer juxtaposition between the conventional traits of noble masculinity, the central characteristics of royal rule, personified in Margaret's eyes by Suffolk – and the attributes of the king. Confronted by what she perceives to be Henry's unmanly weakness, and appalled by its consequences for her own standing as his queen, she looks to Suffolk, forming a liaison with him that is amorous as well as political, whereby they will purge the regime first of Gloucester and then of the rival factions so that, as Suffolk puts it, at the last, 'you yourself shall steer the happy realm' [Pt. II, I, iii, 101]. Margaret's adultery confirms Henry's weakness by establishing him as that epitome of failed or ineffectual masculinity, a cuckold, and establishes Margaret as not merely an adulteress but, in effect, as a traitor twice over; for not only did adultery to the prince constitute treason in itself, in this case the queen's adultery is part of a greater plan to seize power for herself and her lover.

Women on top: the resistible rise of Queen Margaret

These plays trace, through a series of set pieces, the queen's increasing dominance over, and final marginalisation of, her husband. As we have seen, she attempts to ventriloquise her husband in having Somerset appointed over York as the commander in France. In later scenes she simply seizes control of events from the king, in the process usurping the traditional masculine roles of, in the domestic sphere, head of the household and lineage, and, in the domain of royal rule and political dominion, of political and military strategist and leader. The progression here is from covert manipulation to overt bullying in part II, to a simple assertion of command, a straightforward seizing of the reins of power, in part III.

The transfer of power from king to queen becomes overt as the realm descends into civil war. After the Lancastrian defeat at St Albans, with a typically pious fatalism, Henry accepts defeat as the judgement of God (just as he had earlier accepted the news of English defeat in France – 'Cold news, Lord Somerset, but God's will be done') [Pt. II, III, i, 86]. At this Margaret rounds on him: 'What are you made of? You'll nor fight nor fly.' That question is, of course, entirely rhetorical and is followed by a mini-lecture on the exigencies of their current politico-military position and what 'policy' dictates should be their best course of action [Pt. II, V, ii, 72–83]. Here, then, we have the queen telling the king precisely what the dictates of 'manhood, wisdom and defence' are, in an exchange that directly calls his manhood – 'what are you made of?' – into question.

The same process is seen in its next stage early in part III, after Henry has bargained away his son's right to the throne. Coming upon her wretched husband trying to creep from the stage and escape her wrath, the queen tells him that had she been in his place she would have left her 'dearest heart-blood there' rather than 'have disinherited thine only son' [Pt. III, I, i, 223–25]. Henry's limp excuse, that 'the Earl of Warwick and the Duke enforced me', elicits a contemptuously dismissive response. 'Enforced thee? Art thou king, and wilt be enforced?/I shame to hear thee speak. Ah, timorous wretch,/Thou hast undone thyself, thy son and me,/And give unto the House of York such head/As thou shalt reign but by their sufferance./To entail him and his heirs the crown,/What is it, but to make thy sepulchre/And creep into it far before thy time?' The play thus leaves it to the wife and subject to explain to her husband and king the realities of power, the current disposition of which leaves him at the mercy of his enemies. Again, she places herself in her husband's shoes, explaining in detail how he should, and she would, have acted if their roles had been reversed. 'Had I been there, which am a silly woman,/The soldiers should have tossed me on their pikes/Before I would have granted to that act./But thou preferr'st thy life before thine honour./And seeing thou dost, I here divorce myself/Both from thy table, Henry, and thy bed,/Until that act of Parliament be repealed/Whereby my son is disinherited./The northern lords, that have foresworn thy colours,/Will follow mine if once they see them spread:/And spread they shall be, to thy foul disgrace,/And utter ruin of the house of York' [Pt. III, I, i, 229–54]. As Howard and Rackin observe, Prince

Edward has now become *her* son, and as his mother, in the face of Henry's refusal to protect the hereditary claims of the lineage, she in effect becomes 'the family's patriarch in the sense that she not only assumes authority in the family and in the state, but also takes upon herself the burden of guaranteeing Prince Edward's succession to the English throne'.[4]

In this passage Margaret has gone from telling the king what she would have done, if she had been in his place, to literally taking his place, not only at the centre of the Lancastrian party, but also at the head of the Lancastrian army. As she takes 'my son' away from the 'unnatural father' who has sold his 'birth-right', Henry asks the prince to stay with him – 'to be murdered by his enemies', as Margaret bitterly interjects. The young prince's reply is crushing: 'when I return with victory from the field/I'll see your grace; till then, I'll follow her' [Pt. III, I, i, 259–62].

The play stages the culmination of Margaret's usurpation of her husband's powers and position in a series of exchanges before the battle of Towton in which the two sides spit defiance and loathing at one another as a series of blood feuds accumulated from earlier encounters come to a head. While to most of the participants these exchanges are a ritualised preparation for a further and final round of score-settling and bloodletting, Henry treats them as a sort of parley. Twice trying to enter into the conversation as some sort of mediator, he is twice told to shut up by members of his own faction. 'Have done with words my lords, and hear me speak,' he demands only to be told by his wife to 'defy them, then, or else hold close thy lips'. This is too much even for Henry and he claims a royal prerogative to speak; 'I prithee, give no limits to my tongue:/I am a king and privileged to speak.' But this ploy only elicits from Clifford the damning put-down 'my liege, the wound that bred this meeting here/Cannot be cured by words; therefore, be still' [Pt. III, II, ii, 117–22]. Edward's further query, addressed to the king 'say, Henry, shall I have my right or no' [Pt. III, II, ii, 126], is the excuse for a further round of threats and insults, in which Margaret and Prince Edward carry the Lancastrian side, accompanied by complete silence from the king. By now Henry has been reduced to the status of a mere cypher and the process of marginalisation by which that outcome has been effected has been the work not only (or perhaps not even mainly) of the Yorkists, but rather of the queen herself.

The 'Amazonian trull'

As we have seen, Margaret's usurpation is almost as much a function of her husband's incapacity or refusal to discharge his functions as husband and monarch as it is of any pride and ambition inherent in her character. Henry's weakness, if it does not simply cause, certainly enables Margaret's emergence from under the legitimising exercise of royal and patriarchal authority. But

whoever's fault the resulting exchange of functions and attributes between king
and queen may be, the result is 'unnatural'. That is the epithet applied both by the
northern lords and the queen to Henry when he disinherits his son as part of his
deal with the Yorkists. But equally there is something unnatural about a household and kingdom run by the wife of the ruling monarch, and an heir whose
hereditary rights have to be asserted by his mother rather than his father. Under
the pressure to protect her progeny and defend the honour of the lineage,
Margaret's motherly instincts – the very impulses that lead her to act in this way,
in the first place – turn feral; indeed become perverted into their polar opposite.
The play figures the resulting inversion of the natural order of things in the
increasing viciousness of Margaret's character and conduct. From the outset the
depravity of a feminine nature unconstrained by the legitimising and controlling
exercise of patriarchal power has been apparent in Margaret's behaviour and
affect. Thus the play shows her conspiring with Suffolk almost as much against
her husband and monarch as against the other nobles. Her adultery leads naturally to murder – she is, after all, a willing, indeed an enthusiastic, participant in
the death of Gloucester. When Suffolk is exiled for that act, as she curses Salisbury
and the king, Suffolk pleads with her to stop. She, however, will have none of it
'Fie, coward woman and soft-hearted wretch!/Hast thou not spirit to curse thine
enemies?' [Pt II, III, ii, 300–8]. Here again is Margaret teaching her man how to
be manly; accusing him of womanish weakness, she herself assumes the traits
and prerogatives of what she takes to be a properly masculine toughness and
defiance. After Suffolk's death, she vows vengeance, again steeling herself against
the encroaching effects of feminine softness [Pt. II, IV, iv, 1–3].

Just how effectively she has taught herself that lesson emerges in part III in
the dreadful death of York, whose last agonies she choreographs with exquisite
care in order both to maximise his anguish and to increase her own pleasure in
his agony. It is Margaret who manages the scene as she directs the two noblemen
Northumberland and Clifford to place York upon a molehill in a mock coronation, necessary because 'York cannot speak unless he wear a crown' and Margaret
wants to hear 'the orisons he makes', under the lash of her tongue, his current
humiliation and in the face of death. It is a torment pushed to its peak by her
deployment of a 'napkin' stained with the blood of York's son Rutland 'that valiant
Clifford with his rapier's point made issue from the bosom of the boy'. It may
have been Clifford who had slaughtered the boy, but it is now Margaret who
produces the napkin. 'If thine eyes can water for his death,/I give thee this to dry
thy cheeks withal'. 'I prithee grieve to make me merry, York./What, hath thy fiery
heart so parched thine entrails/That not a tear can fall for Rutland's death?/Why
art thou patient, man? Thou should'st be mad;/And I to make thee mad do taunt
thee thus./Stamp, rave and fret, that I may sing and dance' [Pt. III, I, iv, 66–108].

When York's ensuing speech brings tears to the eyes of the watching
Northumberland [Pt. III, I, iv, 150–51, 169–71] Margaret mocks him: 'What

weeping-ripe, my Lord Northumberland?/Think but upon the wrong he did us all,/And that will quickly dry thy melting tears' [Pt. III, I, iv, 173–76], once again upbraiding a man for his lack of toughness. Here it is worth remembering that both Northumberland and Clifford are motivated by a drive to revenge the death of their closest kin. York's slaughter of Clifford's father on the field of battle is the particular motive for his bloodlust against the Yorkists, a homicidal urge that has already led him to kill young Rutland in cold blood and that will move him, at the end of this mock coronation, to cut down the helpless York. Margaret, on the other hand, is avenging no one's death (except perhaps that of her paramour Suffolk). And yet, as the orchestrator of this savage scene, she proves herself to be the most implacable, the most aggressively and imaginatively vengeful, of all the participants. Admittedly, at the scene's end, as she stabs York's wounded body, she claims to be acting on behalf of 'our gentle-hearted king' [Pt. III, I, iv, 176], but that very remark itself merely serves to underscore the extent to which she is acting here in and for herself.

Just what Margaret has become is revealed in a long speech of denunciation and rebuke delivered by York. [Pt. III, I, iv, 111–55]. Starting out as a proud and ambitious wife, she has slipped into a number of connected sins; first, adultery, then treason and murder. This is the conventional trope of the chain of sins leading from initial temptation, grounded in some garden variety sin (in Margaret's case the commonplace feminine fault of pride), into greater and greater misdemeanours and crimes. Such a progression was familiar enough to any contemporary playgoer or reader of murder pamphlets.[5] The play shows that Margaret's increasingly habitual sinning has hardened her. As York says, she is a woman 'made impudent with use of evil deeds'. She is also one, by this point, entirely unconstrained by what should be her subordinate position within the structures of patriarchal power. It is the want of 'government' (both in the sense of self-control and the exercise of external patriarchal authority) that, York claims, has made Margaret 'abominable'. Having effectively displaced her husband and monarch from his position as head of his household, lineage and realm, her character has undergone a gradual metamorphosis as she takes on more and more masculine roles, traits and attributes. The result is a monstrous creature – an 'Amazonian trull'. This process of transformation is rendered both complete and completely patent by this scene with York, in which Margaret emerges as a banning, cursing principle of violence and revenge, bent only on the pursuit of power and the death of her enemies. Unlike the duchess of Gloucester, Margaret is untainted by direct contact with the demonic, but she has something of the witch about her as she literally teaches Suffolk to curse his enemies to perdition; demonic propensities which reach their height in the scene in which she taunts and torments the dying, and – in this last scene at least – Christ-like, York. As Emrys Jones and Beatrice Groves have remarked, in the death of York Shakespeare was evoking scenes from the mystery plays that staged the passion of Christ. This echoes Donald Watson's insight that 'Margaret's revenge grotesquely parodies the basic structure of the Passion and mutilates as well familiar images of monarchy, humanity, knighthood and fatherhood' and, we might add, femininity.[6] For the effect of this Christological imagery is not so much to confer a Christ-like innocence on York as to align Margaret with Christ's tormentors and thus to confirm her, by this point, positively demonic malignity and cruelty.

On York's account of her, Margaret is best regarded as a sort of monster; neither woman nor man, she is a composite, combining the cursing verbal violence of the woman out of control with the real physical violence of a masculine honour culture at the end of its tether. The result, for him, is a creature so depraved, so sunk in sin, as to be best described through analogies with savage beasts: with French wolves and 'Hyrcanian tigers'. Certainly, for York, Margaret has become the very opposite of what a woman should be. Nature designed women to be 'soft, mild, pitiful and flexible' but Margaret is 'stern, obdurate, flinty, rough, remorseless'; worse even than the most appallingly savage of human kind ('hungry cannibals'), she is a 'ruthless queen', 'more inhuman, more inexorable' than the most savage of beasts. In York's view, Margaret is the principle of inversion personified – 'as opposite to every good/As the Antipodes are unto us'. In this scene, and in York's commentary upon it, and indeed throughout these plays, we see Margaret featured as a deeply misogynist personification (and, in many ways, cause) of the world turned upside down, the war of all against all, the seemingly unappeasable outbreak of violence, disorder and dishonour, that the weakness of Henry VI has produced.[7]

For Henry's weakness reveals itself in its most patent and disastrous forms in his basic incapacity to control his wife. In this masterless woman, escaped from patriarchal control, the play depicts the depths to which human nature can sink, once the constraining structures of (patriarchal, political and religious) authority have been removed. It is not just that in the person of Margaret, and the duchess of Gloucester, many of the sinful impulses that, left uncontrolled by authority, will produce bloody chaos and disorder are being typed female. More precisely, such dreadful outcomes are being presented as the result of women getting above themselves and either (like the duchess) seeking to get, or (more disastrously still, with the queen) actually getting, on top. This is a trope to which, in the character of another 'Amazonian trull', Joan Puzel, 1 Henry VI will return, with, if anything, renewed force.

Not clerical but lay: the cross-dressing Henry VI

There is, then, a sort of 'gender bending' going on here. The attributes given to women by York in his speech denaturing Margaret – 'soft, mild, pitiful, flexible' – are, of course, the very attributes displayed throughout these plays by

Henry VI. He is continually accused by other characters of being too charitable, too pitiful; his mildness does indeed prevent him from seizing control of
his wife and counsellors, let alone of events. His scruples of conscience and
desire to avoid civil strife, to compose differences and to avoid violence are,
throughout, the causes of the very violence, disorder and conflict he is trying,
so sedulously, to avert. (The contrast here with Gloucester's readiness to inflict
sometimes savage punishments on malefactors is surely quite deliberate and
very telling.) These very characteristics lead him, time and again, to slide away
from the centre of events. Refusing to acknowledge that, as king, he is entirely
responsible for what is happening under his rule and being done in his name,
he seeks to observe and to lament, rather than to dominate and control, the
doings of his wife and counsellors. Throughout these plays Henry can be found
regretting that he was born a king and hankering after the role of subject rather
than that of ruler, of passive observer rather than of active participant. As we
have seen, this is a role that Henry himself, on one occasion at least, genders as
female, figuring himself, as he abandons the innocent Gloucester, as the
grieving (and, of course, entirely innocent and impotent) mother of a young
calf, watching helplessly as her offspring is led off to the slaughter. Here, at
least, is Henry's passivity being cast (by himself) as feminine.

Of course, such directly gendered comments or images applied to the king
either by himself or others are relatively few and far between. Henry *is* accused
of a form of cross-dressing, of representing, in his basic nature, a form of category mistake, but the play represents this mismatch not so much in terms of his
being too much like a woman and not enough like a man as in terms of his
being too much like a clergyman and not enough like a prince. So says the
queen, as she denounces her new husband to Suffolk: 'All his mind is bent to
holiness,/To number Ave-Maries on his beads./His champions are the prophets
and apostles,/His weapons, holy saws of sacred writ;/His study is his tilt-yard,
and his loves/Are brazen images of canonised saints./I would the college of the
cardinals/Would choose him Pope, and carry him to Rome/And set the triple
crown upon his head:/That were a state fit for his Holiness' [Pt. II, I, iii, 56–65].
So too says York, who tells the king to his face that 'that head of thine doth not
become a crown;/Thy hand is made to grasp a palmer's staff/And not to grace
an awful princely sceptre' [Pt. II, V, i, 96–98].

The play makes this point most clearly through another of its neat inversions. There is, of course, one prominent clergyman in the play – Cardinal
Beaufort – and he is perhaps the most overtly corrupt and malevolent figure on
display. Beaufort is the great enemy of the good Duke Humphrey. Almost all
the other characters are united in their apprehension of Beaufort as a thoroughly corrupt and secular-minded man. To Gloucester he is an 'ambitious
churchman' [Pt. II, II, i, 173] or 'proud prelate' [Pt. II, I, i, 139]. To Somerset he
is 'the haughty Cardinal' whose 'insolence is more intolerable/Than all the

princes' in the land beside' [Pt. II, I, i, 171–73]. So thoroughly is Beaufort embedded in the mores of the court that he almost fights a duel with Gloucester, a man in whose murder he is not merely a ready participant but of which he is the main instigator and agent. 'That he should die is worthy policy' [Pt. II, III, i, 235] is Beaufort's conclusion on the matter. And once it has been decided to do away with Gloucester behind closed doors, rather than risk a public trial, it is the cardinal who pushes himself forward to deliver the means: 'ere you can take due orders for a priest./Say you consent and censure well the deed/And I'll provide his executioner' [Pt. II, III, i, 273–76].

Here, then, we have the man who should be the keeper of the king's conscience, the counsellor with the clearest duty and capacity to care for the king's spiritual well-being, not merely talking the language of 'policy' but citing his zeal to protect the safety of the king – 'I tender so the safety of my liege' [Pt. II, III, i, 277] – to justify murder; a murder that both represents the culmination of a long-standing private feud and furthers his immediate political ambitions. The death of Gloucester, however, proves a crime too far. As soon as the deed is done, the cardinal collapses, as it were, under the weight of his own sins. As Vaux informs the queen the 'Cardinal Beaufort is at point of death;/For suddenly a grievous sickness took him,/That makes him gasp, and stare, and catch the air,/Blaspheming God and cursing men on earth./Sometime he talks as if Duke Humphrey's ghost/Were by his side; sometime he calls the King/And whispers to his pillow, as to him,/The secrets of his overcharged soul./And I am sent to tell his majesty/That even now he cries aloud for him' [Pt. II, III, ii, 369–78]. Here is a perfect reversal of roles, as the prince, the secular ruler, is called to the deathbed of a churchman to give spiritual counsel and comfort to a soul overcharged, indeed rendered desperate, by a lifetime of sins committed in the pursuit of political power and personal advantage.

Henry arrives to find the cardinal delirious, his conscience unable to suppress the enormity of Gloucester's murder, but so burdened by that sin, and so terrified by the prospect of damnation, as to be unable to acknowledge his need for divine grace in any genuinely repentant and thus potentially saving way. Broken by the weight of his sins, the cardinal is being tempted by the devil to despair in the face of death. Mistaking the king for death, with a reflex resort to the same methods of corrupt subornation that had characterised his entire career, the cardinal offers 'Death' a deal, offering him 'England's treasure,/Enough to purchase such another island,/So thou wilt let me live and feel no pain'. His protestations of innocence are followed by all the telltale signs of guilt. 'Bring me unto my trial when you will./Died he not in his bed? Where should he die?/Can I make men live whe'er they will or no?/O, torture me no more! I will confess./Alive again? Then show me where he is./I'll give a thousand pound to look upon him' [Pt. II, III, iii, 2–13]. Murder will out, it seems, in spite of the best efforts of even the most corrupted of consciences to suppress it.

Confronted by this awful scene, Henry takes on the role of a doctor of the soul, commenting 'what a sign it is of evil life/Where death's approach is seen so terrible', before praying to God to 'look with a gentle eye upon this wretch./O beat away the busy meddling fiend/That lays strong siege unto this wretch's soul,/And from his bosom purge his black despair'.[8] Then, addressing himself to the dying man, he intones, 'Peace to his soul, if God's good pleasure be./Lord Cardinal, if thou thinkst on heaven's bliss,/Hold up thy hand, make signal of thy hope.' But all is hopeless. 'He dies and makes no sign. O God forgive him.' When this draws from Warwick the judgement that 'so bad a death argues a monstrous life', Henry typically counsels charity. 'Forbear to judge, for we are sinners all' [Pt. II, III, iii, 5–6, 19–23, 26–31].[9]

Here, then, is Henry's natural métier and mode. He is far more comfortable dispensing Christian charity and grace, imploring God for mercy and justice, commenting, more in sorrow than in anger, upon the sins of his subjects, than he is when seeking to control those sins by dispensing a forceful (albeit necessarily imperfect) human justice himself. The active engagement of his conduct here is in marked contrast to the passivity of his response to the news of Gloucester's death and the very considerable evidence of foul play that attends it. When Henry sends Warwick off to view the scene of the crime, instead of vowing to do justice, Henry begs God to 'stay' his suspicions that 'some violent hands were laid on Humphrey's life./If my suspect be false, forgive me, God,/For judgement only doth belong to thee' [Pt. II, III, ii, 136–40]. Viewed *sub specie aeternitatis*, from the long-term perspective of the ultimate justice of the next world, that claim is true enough. But when viewed from the short- to medium-term perspective provided by the urgent need to do justice and maintain order in this life – which, after all, is the sphere of operations in which Henry must fulfil his divinely ordained calling as king – that claim is also patently false, indeed absurd. In the here and now, judgement belongs to the king and by continually refusing to do (an admittedly proximate and imperfect) justice, Henry succeeds only in plunging his realm into chaos and disorder.

Thus it is that those polar opposites, deadly enemies and evil twins, Margaret and York, come to the same verdict about Henry's unfitness to be king; both denounce him as not man enough, indeed as too much of a clergyman, to do the job effectively and both set out to displace him: York by usurping his place upon the throne, Margaret by taking on the exercise of more and more of his powers and prerogatives, and more and more of the masculine traits and attributes necessary to rule. As we have seen, in the process she reduces her husband to a pathetic, impotent figure, unable even to speak, let alone to affect the course of events or determine the actions being taken in his name. She renders him, in short, a cuckold, indeed a wittold, squared. Thus his weakness enables and prompts her usurpation, which in turn increases his weakness, which in turn enables York's usurpation and thus drives on the descent of the kingdom into chaos. But as Margaret assumes more and more power she also transforms herself into the monstrous figure, neither male nor female but beastly and strange, denounced by the dying York.

Beyond evil counsel: the Christian prince as oxymoron

But while Henry and Margaret might be equally responsible for her unnatural usurpation of his male and monarchical prerogatives, the moral blame to be distributed between them is anything but equal. Henry's weakness, his unfitness to rule, may be congenital, and, judged in terms of its effects on his capacity to fulfil his divinely ordained function as king, both utterly debilitating and delinquent, but it is not presented as simply sinful. For all the dreadful consequences of his actions, Henry emerges as anything but a sinner. Characteristics that the play reveals to be political vices are also presented as but the obverse side of his spiritual (Christian) virtues. Henry appears as a model of Christian piety, indeed even of sanctity. As his ministrations at the deathbed of Cardinal Beaufort reveal, Henry's is an almost entirely pious, even saintly, incapacity. Throughout, whenever he encounters some reverse of his fortunes, he shows a pious acceptance of God's will and, in consequence, a fatal propensity to withdraw into himself. Of Cade's rebels he laments, Christ-like, 'Oh, graceless men! They know not what they do' [II, IV, iv, 37]. As he tells Margaret in the face of the first armed challenge to his rule, they should 'learn to govern better;/For yet may England curse my wretched reign'. When confronted by the alleged miracle at St Albans, unlike that archetypically good magistrate, Gloucester, Henry shows himself only too willing to accept that what he is being shown is indeed a miracle. Taunted to his face by York's claims to be the true king, Henry sees the issue in terms of the inherent justice of his and York's claims, hesitating at the crucial moment because he comes suddenly to see that 'my title's weak' [Pt III, I, i, 134]. Although the successful discharge of his role as king called for the forceful assertion, rather than the conscientious interrogation, of his 'right' to the throne, Henry follows his conscience, with predictably disastrous results. Later in the same scene, he tries to thrash out a compromise between what remain incompatible claims to rule, partly at least to save his realm from civil war. Still later, he persists in his utterly impractical attempts to settle by negotiation the issues dividing the two sides.

Observing the consequences of civil war in the death of a son at the hands of his father and of a father at the hands of his son, he asks 'was ever king so grieved for subjects' woe?/Much is your sorrow; mine, ten times so much' [Pt. III, II, v, 111–12]. Presented by a triumphant Margaret with 'the head of [York] that arch enemy that sought to be encompassed with your crown', impaled upon the walls of York, Henry takes no pleasure in the sight, but rather expresses sorrow and concern that God will hold him responsible for having broken his oath to let York or his heir succeed him [Pt. III, II, ii, 1–8].

Arrested, 'in God's name and the king's', by two huntsmen, after he has been deposed by Edward IV, Henry first remonstrates gently with the men for the fickleness of their allegiance before (typically) giving himself up without a struggle. 'In God's name lead; your King's name be obeyed,/And what God will, that let your King perform:/And what he will, I humbly will yield unto' [Pt. III, III, i, 96–100]. Restored to the crown by the efforts of his wife and the defecting Warwick and Clarence, he appoints both men lords protector 'while I myself will yield a private life/And in devotion spend my latter days/To sins' rebuke and my Creator's praise' [Pt. III, IV, vi, 41–44]. Challenged once more by Edward, Henry puts all his faith in the mildness of his rule. He simply cannot conceive how any of his subjects could turn against him. 'I have not stopped mine ears to their demands,/Nor posted off their suits with slow delays./My pity hath been balm to heal their wounds./My mildness hath allayed their swelling griefs./My mercy dried their water-flowing tears./I have not been desirous of their wealth./Nor much oppressed them with great subsidies,/Nor forward of revenge, though they much erred . . . These graces challenge grace,/ And when the lion fawns upon the lamb,/The lamb will never cease to follow him' [Pt. III, IV, viii, 38–50].

Alone amongst the protagonists of these plays, indeed one is tempted to observe alone amongst Shakespeare's kings, Henry dies an unequivocally good, Christian death. Slaughtered in cold blood in the Tower by Richard of Gloucester he dies begging God to 'forgive my sins and pardon thee' [Pt. III, V, vi, 60]. Indeed, as Donald Watson observes, at the end, 'Henry is associated with the crucified Christ, mocked by his executioners and dying with forgiveness on his lips', while Richard of Gloucester, his murderer, is associated 'with those who scourged, mocked and killed Him'.[10] While all this leaves us in little doubt that Henry is going to heaven, due in no small part to his own (political) incapacities, many of his leading subjects, not to mention his wife, are heading for the other place. Meanwhile, his kingdom has gone to hell in a handbasket.

As we have seen, a variety of characters, both Yorkist and Lancastrian in allegiance, blame Henry's abject failure as a ruler on what Clifford, being polite, at one point calls the king's 'too much lenity/And harmful pity' [Pt. III, II, ii, 9–10]. And while the play makes it crystal clear that such verdicts are true, it also seems to assure us that Henry's spectacular failures in his public role as king are a direct function of his private virtues as an individual professor of Christianity. The polarities here are stark: the central paradox so clearly stated that we might almost conclude that these plays are positing a basic incompatibility between the characteristics necessary successfully to discharge the duties and functions of secular rule and the moral qualities necessary to be a good Christian.

These two plays present us with an account of misrule founded upon a complex series of transactions and reversals of role and attribute acted out between a good, but calamitously ineffective, increasingly passive, even femi-nised, king and his ambitious, overbearing and increasingly vicious, because increasingly 'masculine', wife. One might conclude that the resultant picture of the consequences of a combination of monarchical weakness and an excess of female influence for the exercise of royal power was about as close as any publicly staged or published text could get, in late Elizabethan England, to a direct critique of female rule.

The dystopian vision conjured in these plays was certainly much more direct than anything attempted in the Catholic pamphlets known collectively as *Cecil's commonwealth* where the weakness of the crown was coded female and the access of evil counsel to the centres of royal power was coded male. The resulting misrule, indeed tyranny, was attributed to the influence of male evil counsellors over an innocent (because weak, suggestible and sequestered) female ruler. In the plays the central monarchical weakness (that of Henry VI) is coded male, and the usurping influence of evil counsel (an influence that by the end has reduced the role of the monarch to that of less than a mere cypher and entirely taken over the direction of the Lancastrian cause) is coded (increas-ingly) female.

Henry starts off surrounded by a plethora of (male) evil counsellors, with Margaret figuring both as his queen and as the adulterous other half of perhaps the worst of those counsellors, Suffolk. At the outset, then, hers is but one factious voice amongst many. By the end, however, Henry's role as leader of the Lancastrian cause has been usurped by the increasingly monstrous, and, it must be said, for long stretches of the action, frighteningly effective, virago-figure of Queen Margaret. Here is an altogether more sinister and malign version of a monarch with 'the weak and feeble body of a woman but with the heart and stomach of a man' than that used to celebrate the famous victory of Queen Elizabeth's forces over the Armada.[11]

Viewed in terms of gender politics, Queen Margaret might be seen, at certain moments, as evoking a sinister version of Queen Elizabeth, spitting defiance at her foreign and popish enemies. Thus, the situation staged in these plays represents an almost perfect inversion of the Catholic critiques of the Elizabethan regime. Here the origins of dysfunction (both political and moral) are entirely monarchical in origin, and the quintessence of disorder, of moral and political chaos, presented in these plays is located in a fatal mixture of monarchical weakness and female rule. Might we, then, conclude that the indeterminacy of reference and resonance allowed by the stage, and inherent in the history play, enabled these plays to stage contemporary anxieties about female rule and weak and wilful monarchy in far more daring and direct ways than anything attempted even in the (entirely illicit) Catholic critiques of the regime as a conspiracy of evil counsel?

CHAPTER 3

Disorder dissected (ii): the inversion of the social order

The connection between the action staged in the play and contemporary concerns and events is made even more strongly through the play's treatment of the Cade rebellion, and the resonances of puritan popularity with which the play surrounds that revolt. On the one hand, the play presents Cade's rebellion as a straightforward consequence of Henry's non-rule and of the noble faction-alism and succession disputes that that non-rule enabled. Certainly, in one of the soliloquies that mark York out as the play's leading Machiavel, he expounds his double-sided plan to seize the political initiative and the crown. Placed in charge of royal forces to suppress a revolt in Ireland, York commends the nobles, who have just conferred this command upon him, for furthering his plans. ''Tis politicly done,/To send me packing with an host of men . . . Twas men I lacked, and you will give them me;/I take it kindly, yet be well assured/ You put sharp weapons in a mad man's hands.' York then explains his plan to stir revolt in England using as his catspaw 'a headstrong Kentishman,/Jack Cade of Ashford'. Cade is to personate the earl of Mortimer and claim the throne as his own. 'By this I shall perceive the commons' mind,/How they affect the house and claim of York' [Pt II, III, i, 340–82].

Cade is suited to the role not merely because of his physical resemblance to Mortimer but also because of his madcap desperate natures, established by various feats of courage and endurance performed in the Irish wars. 'Say he be taken, racked and tortured,/I know no pain they can inflict upon him/Will make him say I moved him to those arms' [Pt. II, III, I, 375–77]. The play, there-fore, leaves us in doubt that elite political manoeuvres lay behind Cade's insur-rection. On this view, the roots of popular revolt, as of female disorder, must lie not in the agency of subaltern political actors, be they plebeian or female, but rather in the dereliction of duty of their social superiors and natural rulers, and thus in the machinations of court politics. But just as with women 'on top', so with the lower orders, once released from elite control, the subaltern would look to seize control of events for themselves. So, once Cade and his rebellious supporters appear on stage it is immediately clear that we are dealing here not merely or even mainly with some sort of Yorkist rent-a-mob, an entirely manip-ulated, elite-scripted dry run for York's later attempt on the throne. Rather, having once risen in revolt, the commons set their own agenda and the results are presented by the play as an example of genuine popular agency.

Cade himself makes this clear. After he has recited his claim to be the long-lost son of the earl of Mortimer, he is told by Stafford's brother that 'the Duke of York hath taught you this'. Cade, however, will have none of it, responding, shamelessly enough, that 'he lies, for I invented it myself'. Thus Cade tells Stafford that for the sake of the king's father, Henry V, he, Cade, is content to let Henry VI continue to 'reign, but I'll be Protector over him' [Pt. II, IV, ii, 144–49]. This, of course, is the role that York is planning and later (albeit briefly) assumes for himself, but it is clearly a role that Cade, here usurping the would-be usurper, has now adopted in his own right.

'We are in order when we are most out of order'

As a number of commentators have observed, throughout these scenes, the world, as the rebels would remake it, is presented as a sort of plebeian utopia, a carnivalesque world of social and political inversion, of material plenty and perpetual festivity.[1] Having started out as an elite manoeuvre, prompted by divisions within the aristocracy and court, and having been first set in motion, for his own purposes, by the duke of York, the rebellion becomes a genuinely popular affair, taken over by, and directly appealing to, 'such as go in clouted shoon', or 'leather aprons', 'handcraftsmen' [Pt. I, IV, iv, 11]. The revolt's guiding principle is the claim that 'there's no better sign of a brave mind than a hard hand' [Pt. II, IV, ii, 17–18]. The participants proudly identify themselves, and one another, by their callings as 'a butcher', as 'the tanner of Wingham', or 'Smith the weaver' [Pt.II, IV, ii, 20, 22, 26]. Cade himself is variously identified as a 'shearman' and 'the son of a plasterer' [Pt. II, IV, ii, 123–24] or, in the quarto, as 'Jack Cade the dyer of Ashford' [sig. F3r.]. It is their status as working men, artisans, that qualifies them, in their own minds, to reform and remake 'the commonwealth'. Thus, one rebel observes to another that 'Jack Cade the clothier means to dress the commonwealth, and turn it, and set a new nap upon it', only for Nick to reply that 'so he had need, for tis threadbare'. [Pt. I, IV, ii, 4–6]. The reference to turning inside out old clothes, worn threadbare, thus associates the re/dress of the grievances of the commonwealth with a peculiarly plebeian form of inversion and improvement.

No one – not even Cade himself – believes his entirely fictitious claim to be the son of Mortimer, with a legitimate claim to the throne. Not that the admission does him any harm in the eyes of his followers, who regard his made-up pedigree with both derision and delight. Confronted with his claim that his father was a Mortimer, one rebel observes that 'he was an honest man, and a bricklayer' and his mother not a 'Plantagenet', but 'a midwife'. His boast that his wife was 'descended of the Lacies' elicits the response that 'she was indeed a pedlar's daughter and sold many laces' [Pt. II, IV, ii, 35–42]. And yet the plebeian rebels follow Cade anyway, which, of course, is a good part of the point, for this is a genuinely popular uprising, whose participants follow Cade precisely because he is, like them, a horny-handed son of toil, and not any sort of gentleman.

Social and political hierarchy is presented as the enemy of the people. 'It was never merry world in England since gentlemen came up,' claims one rebel [Pt. II, IV, ii, 6–7]. Commenting on the current discord and misrule afflicting the commonwealth, one rebel complains that 'the King's Council are no good workmen'. Inverting the nostrums of social order and political hierarchy, pumped out from pulpit and press to legitimise the status quo, another rebel concurs; 'yet it is said "labour in thy vocation"; which is as much as to say, "Let the magistrates be labouring men"; and therefore should we be magistrates' [Pt. II, IV, ii, 12–16]. Cade himself appeals to 'you that love the commons . . . 'tis our liberty./We will not leave one lord, one gentleman:/Spare none but such as go in clouted shoon,/ For they are thrifty honest men, and such/As would, but that they dare not, take our parts' [Pt. II, IV, ii, 171–76].

But it is not only the gentry who are targeted as the enemy. Famously, the butcher proposes 'that the first thing we do, let's kill all the lawyers'. Cade immediately agrees. This exchange is followed by the encounter with the clerk of Chartham, who because 'he can read and cast account', 'make obligations and write court hand' and has been apprehended 'setting of boys' copies' with a 'book in his pocket with red letters in't', immediately becomes subject to the crowd's ire. Examined by Cade, the unfortunate pleads benefit of clergy, not realising that, in the world turned upside down of Cade's commonwealth, that capacity has itself sealed his fate 'He hath confessed,' cry the multitude, 'away with him! He's a villain and a traitor.' Cade concurs, pronouncing the man's doom: 'Hang him with his pen and inkhorn about his neck' [Pt. II, IV, ii, 71–101].

The rebels, then, are the enemies not only of social hierarchy, of the gentry and nobility, but also of all learning and of the learned professions. Again, one of the accusations against Lord Saye and Sele is that he has 'most traitorously corrupted the youth of the realm in erecting a grammar school; and, whereas before our forefathers had no other books but the score and the tally, thou hast caused printing to be used and, contrary to the King his crown and dignity, thou hast built a paper-mill. It will be proved to thy face that thou hast men about you that usually talk of a noun and a verb, such abominable words as no Christian ear can endure to hear' [Pt. II, IV, vii, 29–37]. Earlier Saye's capacity to speak French is cited as proof positive that 'he is a traitor'. On this basis, Saye is blamed by the rebels for 'selling the dukedom of Maine'. Observing that 'the Frenchmen are our enemies', Cade asks the crowd, 'can he that speaks with the tongue of an enemy be a good counsellor or no?' 'No, no, and therefore we'll have his head' is the entirely predictable reply [Pt. II, IV, ii, 150–62]. The same logic pervades Saye's later confrontation with the rebels. Starting his speech of self-defence with a Latin tag, Saye is greeted with Cade's cry 'away with him, away with him! He speaks Latin' [Pt. II, IV, vii, 52–53].

Against the old world of hierarchical relations between rulers and ruled, the landed classes and the people, the learned and the unlearned, Cade's common-wealth offers a radical egalitarianism. Thus Cade tells his followers that under his rule 'there shall be in England seven half-penny loaves sold for a penny; the three hooped pot shall have ten hoops, and I will make it a felony to drink small beer. All the realm shall be in common, and in Cheapside shall my palfrey go to grass. And when I am king, as king I will be . . . There shall be no money, all shall eat and drink on my score, and I will apparel them all in one livery, that they may agree like brothers and worship me their lord' [Pt. II, IV, ii, 59–70]. Having taken London, Cade commands 'that, at the city's cost, the Pissing Conduit run nothing but claret wine this first year of our reign. And now henceforward it shall be treason for any that calls me other than Lord Mortimer' [Pt. II, IV, vi, 1–6]. Here the overturning of all order in state and society is directly connected with the establishment of a plebeian utopia, a perpetual holiday of festive plenty and feasting guaranteed by the arbitrary rule of Cade himself.[2] Thus Cade tells Dick, the butcher of Ashford, that 'thus will I reward thee: the Lent shall be as long again as it is, and thou shalt have a licence to kill for a hundred lacking one' [Pt. II, IV, iii, 5–7]. Here gestures towards carni-valesque festivity, prolonged through the exercise of Cade's absolute authority turn sinister, as Dick the butcher's patent to continue killing throughout an arbitrarily prolonged Lent gestures at the killing fields that the rebellion is threatening to create.

The inversionary principles in play throughout these scenes are intermit-tently rendered completely explicit. The rebellion is 'inspired with the spirit of putting down kings and princes', claims Cade [Pt. I, IV, ii, 31–32]. 'Henceforward,' Cade announces at one point, 'all things shall be in common' [Pt. II, IV, vii, 16]. Told at one point by the butcher that the loyalist forces are 'all in order and march toward us', Cade replies with the memorable axiom, 'we are in order when we are most out of order' [Pt. II, IV, ii, 177–79]. When, Stafford alleges that 'thy father was a plasterer,/And thou thyself a shearman, art thou not', Cade responds, 'And Adam was a gardener.' 'What of that?' is Stafford's baffled reply [Pt. II, IV, ii, 123–25]. But what to Stafford is an absurd non sequitur is in fact a statement of the animating assumptions, indeed the ideological core, of the rebellion, which is an attempt to recapture a sort of pre-lapsarian paradise, an ancient state of equality and plenty, that the people had enjoyed in some dim and distant past, before 'gentlemen came up' [Pt. II. IV, viii, 8]. The struggle Cade claims at one point is for 'liberty', or later for 'your ancient freedom' [Pt. II, IV, viii, 26]. We are dealing here with a lack of hierarchy and constraint that is in itself a form of utopian order, which, once lost, can now, through the inversionary fury of the rebellion, finally be restored.[3]

In a brilliant paper delivered at a recent conference at the Huntington Library, Stephen Longstaffe[4] pointed out that in the quarto edition the lines quoted above read "'Twas never merry world since *these* gentlemen came up'. Similarly, Nick's claim that 'the nobility think scorn to go in leather aprons' [Pt. II, IV, viii, 11] becomes, in the quarto, 'thou shalt never see a lord wear a leather apron nowadays' [sig. F3r].[5] These subtle shifts, Longstaffe argued, render the text less a generic conjuration of age-old class tensions and hatreds and more a pointed reference to immediately contemporary social reality, and in particular to certain processes of social differentiation and upward social mobility, which had seen various groups – 'these gentlemen' rather than 'gentlemen' in general – profit from the course of economic change, prompted by population increase and price inflation, and, thus distancing themselves from their erstwhile neighours amongst the commons, establish themselves as gentry. The golden age to be restored by the rebellion may, then, have two referents, one in a genuinely plebeian utopia, a vision of endless festivity and plenty, of ancient pedigree, the other, more prosaically, in a somewhat idealised vision of the recent past, before 'these gentlemen came up'. As Richard Wilson has argued, all this serves to tie these scenes into immediately contemporary social tensions and indeed to recent events in London. Once again the history being staged in the play is speaking directly to immediately current concerns.[6]

Except, of course, that there is a very distinct hierarchy present in these scenes; one based on the absolute, indeed arbitrary, rule of Cade himself. Indeed Laroque speaks of Cade 'founding his own despotism upon a leveling uniformity'.[7] Cade's pronouncement, quoted above, that henceforward it shall be treason to call him anything other than Lord Mortimer, is followed by the summary execution by the crowd of a messenger unfortunate enough to call him by his real name. Both the clerk of Chartham and Lord Saye are executed after personal hearings of terrifying brevity and levity before Cade himself, who, in these scenes, plays out his authority as king and judge in a series of call and response exchanges with his followers. The radical equality of the new dispensation is to be established amongst 'brothers', all of whom will wear Cade's livery and are thus equal in, and united by, their subjection to him.

Cade does indeed want the records of the realm burnt: not only to free his followers from the binding shackles of the current dispensation of property and authority, but also so that 'the laws of England may come out of' his 'mouth'. 'My mouth shall be the parliament of England' [Pt. II, IV, vii, 5, 11–13]. If all things will be held in common, they will also all be at Cade's personal disposal. 'The proudest peer in the realm shall not wear a head on his shoulders, unless he pay me tribute; there shall not a maid be married, but she shall pay to me her maidenhead ere they have it; men shall hold of me *in capite*, and we charge and command that their wives be free as heart can wish or tongue can tell' [Pt. II, IV, vii, 113–17].

The plebeian utopia of Cade's commonwealth is thus also a dystopia of tyranny, violence and fear; a place in which the mob is free to loot and pillage whomsoever and wheresoever it wants. At various points Cade exhorts his followers to 'pull down the Savoy' and 'the Inns of Court', to 'set London Bridge on fire and, if you can, burn down the Tower too' [Pt. II, IV, vi, 14–15; vii, 1–2]. Later he sends them 'up Fish street! Down Saint Magnus' Corner! Kill and knock down! Throw them into Thames!' [Pt. II, IV, viii, 1–2].

At times all this both festive and deadly serious mayhem is legitimised by Cade's pretensions to be 'Lord Mortimer' the legitimate king or at least Protector of the realm; claims that he advances both to his own followers and to the representatives of the crown. However, as all of the comic asides quoted above show, neither he nor his followers believe a word of it. Similarly, the grandiloquence of Cade's claim that 'the laws of England shall come out of my mouth', is met with the dismissive comment that 'Mass, twill be a sore law then, for he was thrust in the mouth with a spear and 'tis not whole yet.' 'Nay, Nick, it will be a stinking law, for his breath stinks with eating toasted cheese.' A third adds, 'Then are we like to have biting statutes, unless his teeth be pulled out' [Pt. II, IV, vii, 5–10, 14–15]. All of this comically expressed scepticism goes a long way to explaining why, when they are offered a free pardon, and with the name and fame of Henry V bandied about before them, the populace abandon Cade and revert to loyalty to the king.

Puritan popularity personified

But the rebellion receives legitimation from sources other than the multitude's impulse towards class war, festive inversion and equal opportunity rampage and pillage, on the one hand, and Cade's political ambition to be king, embodied in his simultaneously absurd and deadly serious claims to be a Mortimer and thus the rightful heir to the throne, on the other. Throughout, Cade (and others) describe his rebellion in the language of 'reformation', of the purging of the commonwealth of the peccant humours and corrupt elements that have led to defeat by the French and to the present parlous and divided condition of the kingdom. At the outset, Cade himself vows 'reformation' [Pt. II, IV, ii, 60] and prophesies that 'our enemies shall fall before us, inspired by the spirit of putting down kings and princes' [Pt. II, IV, ii, 31–32]. Later he tells Saye and Sele that he is 'the besom that must sweep the court clean of such filth as thou art' [Pt. II, IV, vii, 27–28]. Earlier a messenger has reported to the king that 'all scholars, lawyers, courtiers, gentlemen,/They call false caterpillars and intend their death' [Pt. II, IV, iv, 35–36].

Here, then, is the language of 'commonwealth' reform, of puritan 'reformation' (and, indeed, of Catholic critique); of the moral imperative to work 'reformation' in church and state by removing from the court and counsels of the crown the 'caterpillars of the commonwealth', those evil counsellors and corrupt courtiers who together stood between the monarch and an accurate apprehension of the true condition of the realm and the grievances of the subject. In Cade's mouth that language is being appropriated to prompt and legitimise an inversionary popular revolt, the aims of which do not constitute the reformation of the social and political orders but rather their utter sub- indeed their in-version.

It has been plausibly argued that in the Cade scenes the play is in fact referring to, and playing off immediately contemporary polemical stereotypes of puritan radicalism developed during the reaction against Martin Marprelate by such writers as Thomas Nashe (who has even been credited by some critics as the author of the Cade scenes themselves). Cade's festive and inversionary tactics, his violence both of language and of deed, replicate certain central features of Martin's style. His regime of violent discipline – for instance, making it 'felony to drink small beer' – can be read as a dark parody of the draconian and disorderly nature of puritan discipline, as a variety of anti-puritan polemicists and satirists mis/represented it. In the Cade scenes the inversionary impact of puritan reformation is here guyed by representing the puritan reformation of morals as leading to the sort of carnivalesque excess which the godly claimed to want to repress and expunge. As we shall see below, this was a mode of anti-puritan satire to which Shakespeare would return in the figure of Falstaff.[8]

In the summer of 1591, with the leaders of the presbyterian movement still trapped in the toils of the law, a self-styled prophet named William Hacket, and his two followers, Coppinger and Arthington, launched what was, in effect, an attempt at populist puritan revolution. Arguably Hacket really was inspired by what he took to be the 'the spirit of pulling down kings and princes'. Calling on England to repent, he proclaimed that the queen deserved to be deprived and that she had, in fact, forfeited her crown. Like Cade, Hacket promised great rewards to his followers, or rather in his case to those who would repent, while threatening terrible judgements against those who would not. In a newsletter of 19 July 1591 it was reported that Hacket's conspiracy was in everyone's mouth. Some likened him to John of Leyden who took on himself the kingdom of the Anabaptists, and, while others took Hacket and his mates to be mere fanatics, the enemies of the puritans were already making hay, as the *soi disant* prophets were known to have been great followers of the puritan preachers and to have solicited all those they knew to be well-affected to the puritan cause, including the Lord Treasurer, Essex, the countess of Warwick and Mr Davison. Even the queen was reported to be greatly alarmed by the affair.[9] As Chris Fitter has argued, the Cade scenes seem to play off the Hacket affair, thus aligning the play's portrayal of plebeian revolt not merely with recent popular tumults in London and elsewhere but also with the spectre of a rabidly puritan mode of popularity and commonwealth reform.[10]

Subsequent works of anti-puritan polemic by Richard Cosin, Matthew Sutcliffe and Richard Bancroft used Hacket's activities to tar mainstream presbyterian schemes to reform the English church, with the brush of populist rebellion and Anabaptist frenzy. It was one of the central tenets of the anti-puritan propaganda of the 1590s that the puritans were the moral equivalents of the Anabaptists and that, once given their head, they would institute a tyrannical world turned upside down of the sort produced by Thomas Munzer and John of Leyden. The rampant popularity of the Presbyterian discipline was demonstrated by the fact that it would have ceded central offices in the church and some of the most exalted spiritual functions of the clergy – ordination and excommunication amongst them – to the dregs of the people; that is to say to precisely the same social groups that, in the play, made up Cade's rebel host: 'men of occupation', mustard sellers and chandlers, 'tailors, butchers, carpenters, shoemakers, thatchers, daubers and such', 'the base sort of people, leaving the shuttle, the plough and the spade and the shop board' to run the church, and ultimately the state, and this to overthrow all order in church, state and society.[11]

Leading anti-puritan polemicists like Matthew Sutcliffe and Richard Bancroft were to warn how, through its assault on property rights – most obviously those of the church – and its disruptive effect on the workings of the legal system in church and state, the presbyterian platform would offer the lower orders the opportunity to work precisely the same sort of inversionary change that the play shows Cade and his followers pursuing.

Not that Cade is portrayed as acting alone in this regard. On the contrary, the play makes it clear that, initially at least, he had been prompted and sponsored by the duke of York. But that relationship, too, had its parallels with contemporary strands of anti-puritan polemic and Catholic political comment. Since the *Treatise of treasons,* and through *Leicester's commonwealth,* Catholic commentators had stressed the links of patronage and protection that tied the puritan godly to great court patrons like Leicester. Leicester they portrayed as a man of no religion; his espousal and protection of the puritan cause, like York's patronage of Cade, was an alliance of convenience, based on the narrow pursuit of Leicester's personal political advantage and upon his need to build up a faction and popular following in the state. Conformist critics of presbyterianism made similar claims about the alliance of convenience that held together the clerical, aristocratic and plebeian supporters of the discipline. These diverse groups, it was alleged, supported the cause of further reformation for reasons of their own, each hoping to extract different, and, indeed, mutually incompatible, benefits from the process of puritan reformation. The protestant anti-puritan authors also muttered darkly – without, of course, naming names – about the sinister motives that led some prominent members of the regime to provide sanction and support to so subversive, popular, anti-monarchical and inversionary a programme as the presbyterian platform.[12]

A mirror for (dysfunctional) magistrates?

However, even when it is presented as an autonomously popular incident, Cade's revolt does not operate only or even mainly in the play as a commentary on the beastliness and disorder of the 'many headed monster'. Throughout, the actions of Cade and the rebels parallel, parody and indeed provide a bitter running commentary on the doings of their social betters. As Paola Pugliatti puts it, 'the deformity of the rebels' 'holds a mirror up to the deformity of the party in power'. In this instance at least, she observes, 'disorder' was being 'generated' quite as much 'from the top down' as 'from the bottom up'.[13]

Thus, Cade's entirely arbitrary and totally unjust condemnation of Lord Saye and Sele closely parallels the treatment of the equally innocent Gloucester at the hands of his noble adversaries. In the minds of the rebels Saye is the quintessential evil counsellor and thus a marked man [Pt. II, IV, ii, 150–62] but, as the rebels enter London, rather than flee, he decides (heroically) to stay in hiding in the city, so as not to further endanger the king by his presence in the royal entourage. Like Gloucester, facing down the accusations of his enemies, Saye claims that 'The trust I have is in mine innocence,/And therefore am I bold and resolute' [Pt. II, IV, iv, 58–59]. However, as with Gloucester, such confidence proves entirely misplaced. Once he has been captured, the accusations ranged against Saye are remarkably similar to those levelled against Gloucester. Abroad, corrupted by the French, he has been instrumental in the loss of the English possessions in France; at home, corrupted by sinister interests, he has oppressed the poor subjects through the unjust doing of justice and the visitation upon them of cruel and unusual punishments, often just because they were poor. Like Gloucester before him, Saye dismisses these claims as the very opposite of the truth, claiming, again just like Gloucester, that his efforts have been ceaseless, 'Kent to maintain, the king, the realm and you'. 'These cheeks are pale with watching for your good' [Pt. II, IV, vii, 60–96].

Even Cade is moved by the patent sincerity and truth of these claims, admitting, albeit in an aside, that 'I feel remorse in myself with these words'. However, faced with a choice between conscience and convenience, Cade decides to follow the political logic that the revolt, and indeed his own demagoguery, has set in motion, by consigning Saye to an entirely undeserved death. 'He shall die, an it be but for pleading so well for his life'. Then, turning once more to address his followers, he proclaims Saye's fate. 'Strike off his head presently; and then break into his son-in-law's house, Sir James Crowmer, and strike off his head, and bring them both upon two poles hither' [Pt. II, IV, vii, 98–105]. Here, then, is Cade, just like Gloucester's noble adversaries before him, sending an entirely innocent, indeed entirely well-deserving, servant of the king and commonweal to his death, just to serve his own immediate political interests and projects.

Again Cade's spurious dynastic claims, advanced as a series of mere assertions, in the course of the 'oh yes you did, oh no you didn't' exchange with Sir

Humphrey Stafford, provide both a foretaste of, and a satirical comment upon, what will become the increasingly debatable and arbitrary assertions of indefeasible hereditary right made later in part II and throughout part III by a number of Cade's Lancastrian and Yorkist betters. The fickleness of his following, as they shift from murderous support of Cade to loyalty to King Henry, mirrors the impact on the political allegiance of the people and realm of a contested succession.

Again, the arbitrary cruelty that characterises the revolt parallels the increasingly merciless violence that comes to characterise the feuds of the nobility as they struggle for the crown. Cade's carnivalesque byplay with the severed heads of Saye and Crowmer, which he orders to be borne before him through the London streets on poles 'and at every corner have them kiss' [Pt. II, IV, vii, 126–28], prefigures the gruesome game played later by the Yorkists and Lancastrians when they celebrate the shifting fortunes of their increasingly merciless struggles over the succession by placing and replacing the severed heads of York and Clifford on the walls of York.

Suffolk's desperately defiant and unrepentant death, which concludes the opening scene of Act IV, is remarkably similar to Cade's demise, with which that act closes. Thus Suffolk addresses his would-be slaughterer as an 'obscure and lousy swain', 'a jaded groom', someone so base as to be entirely incapable of shedding 'the honourable blood of Lancaster' [Pt. II, IV, I, 50–52]. Moved by an onlooker to sue for favour, Suffolk refuses. He would 'sooner dance upon a bloody pole/Than stand uncovered to the vulgar groom./True nobility is exempt from fear;/More can I bear than you dare execute.' 'Great men oft die by vile Bezonians./A Roman sworder and banditto slave/Murdered sweet Tully; Brutus' bastard hand/Stabbed Julius Caesar; savage islanders/Pompey the Great; and Suffolk dies by pirates' [Pt. II, IV, i, 123–40].

Cade dies with just the same mixture of proud desperation and defiance. Cut down by that epitome of English virtue and moderation, Alexander Iden, he exclaims, 'Oh I am slain! A famine and no other hath slain me. Let ten thousand devils come against me, and give me but the ten meals I have lost, and I'd defy them all. Wither, garden, and be henceforth a burying place to all that do dwell in this house, because the unconquered soul of Cade is fled' [Pt. II, IV, x, 59–64]. In terms of their birth, their claims to noble or hereditary honour, Cade and Suffolk, the bricklayer's son and the Plantagenet prince, could hardly be more different. And yet the play presents them as twinned epitomes of misrule and disorder; persons who, although they may have risen to power from opposite ends of the social order, have visited equally disordered and disastrous consequences upon the commonwealth. And, of course, both men meet comparably desperate and defiant ends, in the light of which the differences between the corrupt Suffolk's vainglorious boasts of 'true nobility' and Cade's plebeian braggadocio fade almost to nothing.

But of course, of all the play's elite characters, Cade's career parallels and parodies most closely that of his erstwhile patron York, whose roles as 'true claimant', 'protector' and usurper Cade tries to usurp for himself. Here, as Berry has pointed out, the issue is not inversion but something more like parody; 'Cade is neither York's equivalent nor his opposite, but *his reductio ad absurdum*.'[14]

******

The Cade scenes serve to connect the action of the play to directly contemporary issues and events. As Richard Wilson and more recently Andy Wood have argued, they also evoke authentically popular strains of critique of, revulsion at and revolt against the current social order, which, given the social crisis being experienced in various parts of England in the 1590s and the very recent riots of the summer of 1591 in London, carried a pressingly contemporary resonance and threat. Again Cade's use of the language of 'reformation' serves to establish parallels between Cade's commonwealth and, on the one hand, the very recent Hacket and Coppinger debacle and, on the other, the plebeian, puritan utopia planned (according to their enemies, at least) by the godly reformers of the puritan movement. The connections of connivance and patronage that, in the play, link York and Cade, parallel and evoke those that, in the Catholic and conformist rumour and polemic of the period, linked the likes of Leicester and latterly of his stepson Essex to the puritans.

Here then is another evocation of contemporary events and present concerns. This can be added to these plays' evocation (and dismissal) of the (Catholic but not only catholic) charges against Burghley of corruption, overweening ambition and tyranny; the lament for the passing of an older generation of good counsellors – epitomised by Gloucester/Burghley – who are being supplanted by a younger generation of factious and ambitious nobles and prelates, all of them about to fall out both over the conduct of foreign war and the increasingly contested issue of the succession, in a political scene presided over by a queen who epitomises the disorder inherent in women trying to play the inherently masculine roles of ruler and soldier. These plays, in short, gave their first audiences ample reason to conclude that they were not only watching a staging of the past but also being vouchsafed considerable insight both into the present and into a distinctly dystopian vision of the immediate future.

Taken together as a sign both of the threat of genuinely plebeian disorder and as a further indictment of aristocratic dysfunction and faction, these scenes underscore the complete inability of 'the commonwealth', or to put the matter slightly differently, of Michael Bush's society of orders, or indeed of Patrick Collinson's acephalous 'monarchical republic', to set the world to rights, still less to reconstitute itself, in the absence of the effective exercise of the royal will. Absent that, in the face of noble faction, a contested succession, an excess of female influence on the exercise of royal power and the popular (and puritan) impulse to disorder and inversion evoked in the Cade scenes, it was entirely unclear how any semblance of order might be re-established, or any variety of legitimate rule reconstituted.

CHAPTER 4

Hereditary 'right' and political legitimacy anatomised

These plays thus located the problems faced by the England of Henry VI, and indeed of Elizabeth I, not simply in an unsettled or contestable succession. Rather they identified a combination of other factors and forces – monarchical weakness, noble faction, foreign defeat, a surfeit of female influence over the levers of power, the resort of the people to open revolt, in the face of political breakdown and social crisis – which, taken together, threatened to render a currently unsettled and potentially contested succession a source of unappeasable political and moral crisis. In this, the plays echoed the view of various Catholic pamphlets – of *The treatise of treasons* and *Leicester's commonwealth* certainly, but also of a group of pamphlets known collectively as *Cecil's commonwealth* that were being produced at precisely the same time that the Henry VI plays were being written and performed.

But if neither the tracts nor the plays saw the succession as the simple cause of the problem, dynastic issues remained a crucial part of the crisis that both the Catholic pamphlets and the plays saw coming. Accordingly, these plays did indeed treat, in some detail, issues of succession; that is to say, both *de jure* questions of what constituted a legitimate claim and of how such claims might be adjudicated, and also *de facto* issues about how a dynastic claim, formal legitimacy, if you like, could be turned into practical legitimacy; that is to say, established as the basis of a stable, functioning regime whose rule was accepted more or less by all, as, if not fully legitimate, then at least as an established fact. In that sense, the plays anticipated the formal treatment of these issues in Parsons' *Conference about the next succession* by some three or four years.

The right to rule unravelled

At the close of the Cade rebellion, when Buckingham and Old Clifford are seeking to outbid Cade for the allegiance of the commons, their clinching argument is the memory of Henry V and his martial exploits against the common enemy, the French [Pt. II, IV, viii]: 'Is Cade the son of Henry the Fifth/That thus you do exclaim you'll go with him?/Will he conduct you through the heart of France/And make the meanest of you earls and dukes? . . . Were't not a shame that whilst you live at jar/The fearful French, whom you late vanquished,/ Should make a start o'er seas and vanquish you?/Methinks already in this civil broil/I see them lording it in London streets,/Crying "Villiago!" unto all they meet./Better ten thousand base-born Cades miscarry/Than you should stoop unto a Frenchman's mercy' [Pt. II, IV, viii, 14–18, 34–50]. Such appeals surely recall another monarch whose claims to rule rested on her descent from a gloriously warlike father and whose rule was legitimised, and whose hold on popular allegiance was sustained, by the threat posed to the realm by a foreign power; not now from France, but from Spain – a fact surely registered in the play by the cry of 'villiago', put here into the mouth of the invading foreigner as he violates the streets of London itself.

If the play establishes one basis of Henry VI's legitimacy (at least in the eyes of the people and of those who want to rally the people to his defence) in the martial glory and charisma attached to the exploits of his father, there are other, less glamorous, wellsprings of popular support for, or acceptance of, his rule. In a particularly telling scene, Henry himself confronts the *de factoist* instincts of the people. Having lost the throne to Edward IV, he returns from exile in Scotland 'to greet mine own land with my wishful sight' [Pt. III, III, i, 14]. He is almost immediately recognised by two huntsmen as 'the king King Edward hath deposed;/And we his subjects sworn in all allegiance/Will apprehend you as his enemy'. Henry responds to these claims with a series of simple questions: 'but did you never swear and break an oath?' 'Where did you dwell when I was King of England?' The two men admit that they lived in England when Henry reigned as king but deny that they are breaking any oaths. To Henry such claims make no sense. 'I was anointed king at nine months old./My father and grandfather were kings,/And you were sworn true subjects under me:/And tell me, then, have you not broke your oaths?' 'No,' comes the reply, 'for we were subjects but while you were king' and now 'we are true subjects to the King, King Edward'. In response to these claims Henry upbraids them as 'simple men' who 'know not what you sware'; prime examples of 'the lightness of you common men', 'commanded always by the greater gust'. Henry, however, is decrying what had been one of the greatest sources of his own power when king; that is to say, the power of what Warwick calls at one point 'prescription', the habitual, reflex loyalty of the common people, and indeed of the nobility, to the current incumbent. By the end of the conversation Henry himself implicitly concedes as much, accepting the present power of the current king and throwing himself (as ever) on God's will [Pt. III, III, I, 69–100].

In passages such as this, both Henry and his supporters harp on the fact that he was anointed as king while a babe in arms; that both his father and grandfather were kings; and that his father, Henry V, was the great conqueror of France. When, in an exchange at the French court, Warwick calls Henry a usurper, Oxford, a Lancastrian loyalist, replies that in so doing Warwick 'disannuls great John of Gaunt . . . And after Gaunt, Henry the Fourth . . . and after that wise prince, Henry the Fifth,/Who by his prowess conquered all France:/From these our Henry lineally descends'. But, Warwick replies, this appeal to the past glories of Henry V omits the sorry failures of his son 'who hath lost/All that which Henry the Fifth had gotten'. Besides, in the prescription stakes, how long is long enough? 'You tell a pedigree of three score and two years, a silly time/To make prescription for a kingdom's worth' [Pt. III, III, iii, 79–94]. But by the same token, Oxford can make the same reply to Warwick that Henry VI himself had made to his two plebeian captors. 'Why, Warwick, canst thou speak against thy liege/Whom thou obeyed'st six and thirty years/ And not bewray thy treason with a blush?' [Pt. III, III, iii, 95–97]. Again the experience of 'common men' echoes and parodies that of the good and the great.

These exchanges recall another conversation about the rights and wrongs of the succession, involving both Henry VI and his challenger, York, who has just, for the first time in the play, made a pitch for the crown itself. With unwonted force, Henry starts on about his royal ancestry: 'think'st thou that I will leave my kingly throne,/Wherein my grandsire and my father sat?/No, first shall war unpeople this my realm.' Seeing the attendant lords hesitate to rush to his defence, Henry rounds on them: 'why faint you lords?/My title's good, and better far than his.' Told by Warwick to 'prove it, Henry, and thou shalt be king', Henry resorts this time, not to an argument from prescription, that is to say from continuous possession, over a number of generations, accepted as legitimate by the mass of the nobility and people, but rather to right of conquest. 'Henry the Fourth by conquest got the crown,' he claims, only to have that assertion met with the counter-assertion from York that ''twas by rebellion 'gainst his King'. At this Henry folds – 'I know not what to say. My title's weak' – only then immediately to shift the grounds on which he claims the crown, reverting from an argument from conquest to one involving the right of the reigning king to divert the succession by 'adopting an heir'. If such an act is lawful, then, Henry claims, 'am I lawful king:/For Richard, in the view of many lords,/Resigned the crown to Henry the Fourth,/Whose heir my father was, and I am his.' But this claim, too, is refuted. According to York, Richard's was a constrained resignation; 'he rose against him, being his sovereign,/And made him to resign his crown perforce'. Besides, asks Warwick, even if Richard had resigned willingly, could such an act be 'prejudicial to the crown'? 'No,' comes the answer from Exeter, 'for he could not so resign his crown,/But that the next heir should succeed and reign'. In making that reply Exeter changes sides from Lancaster to York. 'Art thou against us, Duke of Exeter,' asks Henry, only to receive the crushing reply that 'his is the right, and therefore pardon me' [Pt. III, I, i, 124–48].

Confronted by a newly vertiginous sense of the fragility of his claims to dynastic right and by this fresh evidence of his shrinking support amongst even the previously loyal aristocracy and now by a show of force by Warwick's soldiers, Henry snatches at a compromise, one founded upon that same right of the reigning monarch to adopt an heir, upon which he has just based his own claim to the throne. If York will allow him 'for this my lifetime [to] reign as king', he will 'confirm the crown to' York and his heirs. This proves to be an offer the Yorkists cannot refuse [Pt. III, I, i, 170–75].

While such a solution might serve Henry's immediate purposes – it acts both to perpetuate his personal possession of the throne and, as he puts it, 'to cease this civil war' [Pt. III, I, i, 197] – it remains both a political and a dynastic non-sense. Intended as a compromise with the Yorkists, it is an act based on the very principle – the right of the incumbent monarch to will or bequeath the crown where he or she will – upon which Henry himself has based his own claim to the throne, and which the Yorkists – the projected beneficiaries of his latest expedient to avert conflict – have just rejected by pointing out that even if Richard could be deemed willingly to have resigned the throne, he could not, by a mere act of his private will, have diverted the succession from the course dictated by natural, indefeasible hereditary right. But this was precisely what Henry himself was now proposing to do by diverting the succession from his own natural son to the duke of York and his heirs.

Henry's act in willing the crown away to York and his heirs thus either makes no sense or calls into radical question the Yorkists' dynastic right to the throne. For, if York is king by right, the crown is already his. And in that case, what is Henry doing giving York and his heirs something that already belongs to them? And by what right, then, is he retaining the crown until his death? And why on earth should the Yorkists allow him to retain it? But if, on the other hand, they have no right to the crown save through the exercise of Henry's mere will in ceding it to them, what is there to prevent Henry's son and his supporters waging a war against them, on the basis of precisely the same theories of indefeasible hereditary right upon which the Yorkists themselves are basing their claims to rule in Henry's stead?

Nor are these merely theoretical flaws; there remain a number of characters, of whom the king's wife and son are only the most obvious examples, who are more committed, for a variety of often intensely personal, rather than formally legitimist reasons, to the Lancastrian cause than Henry himself. And their response to Henry's latest lapse from proper kingly conduct, in disowning his own son, is predictable in the extreme. Like the Yorkists before them, they deny that the current incumbent can, by the mere exercise of his will, 'prejudice' the future descent of the crown. Certainly, the king can abdicate, but, in so doing, he cannot divert the throne from the line of descent dictated by the hereditary principle. In the current circumstances, of course, this means that Henry cannot legitimately disinherit his own son, Prince Edward, who expostulates to Henry that 'you cannot disinherit me./If you be king, why should not

I succeed?' [Pt. III, I, i, 226–27]. On this basis, Queen Margaret's conclusion that Henry is 'so unnatural a father' [Pt. III, I, i, 218] is itself natural enough. According to precisely the same principles upon which Henry has just claimed the throne for himself, his son should, indeed must, succeed him. On Henry's own arguments, the conclusion reached by Clifford, who exclaims 'what wrong is this to the Prince, your son?' [Pt. III, I, i, 176], is inescapable.

In these scenes, the play stages something like the full range of arguments available to contemporaries to decide questions of contested dynastic right. (The one exception, which, as we shall see below, was a matter of no small significance, is a version of the succession as overtly or genuinely elective, which, in these plays at least, simply does not figure as an option.) The play's staging of these various arguments for the legitimacy of a ruling dynasty is calculated to show that they are very far from mutually consistent, still less mutually rein-forcing. In the event of a political crisis or of a genuinely contested succession, or rather in the event of both – the second being a natural product or effect of the first – none of these criteria – not prescription, not conquest, not indefea-sible hereditary right, not even the (Henry-VIII-like) exercise of the testamen-tary rights of some previous or regnant monarch – will, in and of themselves, carry the day, and any attempt to combine them is likely simply to collapse under the weight of its own internal contradictions. As the vertiginous shifts of allegiance and conviction experienced both by Henry VI and his previously stalwart supporter, Exeter, show, when the case for obedience, the assertion of the right to rule, comes down to the fine print of lineal succession and dynastic legitimacy, there is always room for doubt, indecisiveness, fatal hesitation and change of mind.

A monarchical republic (not)

In 1594–5, in the *Conference about the next succession*, Robert Parsons would use similar observations to argue that, judged by the criteria of pure dynastic right, there was no monarch in the world whose claims to rule could not be challenged. Parsons, therefore, sought to ground the right to rule in even the most ancient of monarchies on the power residing within the commonwealth to elect and remove princes and, if necessary, to divert the succession from the lines of descent dictated by mere hereditary right. In this Parsons was rendering coherent and explicit the principles underlying a view of the monarchical state in England as some sort of 'monarchical republic'; a view which, as Patrick Collinson has famously observed, underlay protestant and establishment schemes of the 1560s and 1580s to divert the succession from Mary Stuart.[1] In asserting the right of the crown in parliament – indeed in some cases the right of the parliament acting in the absence of royal authority – to determine or divert the succession, some tracts of the 1580s had made much of York's assertion of his dynastic right in parliament, which act they interpreted as 'Richard, duke of York' pleading 'his title to the crown in open parliament, where, after long debating, he was declared successor after King Henry VI's death.'[2] 'In the 28 of Henry VI . . . Richard duke of York made his claim, setting himself in the chair within the parliament chamber, after the course of the common law, as cousin and heir to King Richard II . . . and, by authority of parliament, an agreement was made that Henry VI, for term of his life, should abide king and the duke should be protector, and, if Henry VI should infringe any covenant, then the crown should descend to the duke of York, if he then lived, and else to the next heir of his lineage.' This settlement having been undone by the 'ambition of the queen and the dukes of Exeter and Somerset', armed conflict broke out. 'After the fortunes of battle, off and on tried', Edward IV had 'opened his title at London . . . and in Westminster Hall, before all the people, made his claim two ways, the first by title of inheritance, the second by the act of parliament, in respect of forefeiture, a story well known and never called in question.'[3]

Of such a view of York's efforts in parliament to secure the crown, or indeed of the wider vision of the workings of the English monarchical state that under-pinned it, there is no trace in these plays, which portray England as a monarchy pure and simple. As we have seen, in Shakespeare's version, York is not appealing, nor Henry responding, to the authority of parliament. The dynamics of the situation are dynastic and political, backed up by the main force of Warwick's soldiers. In these plays, neither in the collective wisdom of the nobility nor in the people can any source of authority or counsel be found by which, in the event of breakdown, the fabric of monarchical rule or legitimacy might be repaired, sustained or remade. In these plays, the interventions of the nobility serve not to protect the commonweal but rather to fuel its descent into disorder, conflict and ultimately civil war, and the sole contribution of the people is Cade's rebellion, which however accurately it may have staged a genuinely popular response to the inequities of late Tudor England, or the dynamics of the social crisis of the 1590s, can scarcely be said, in Shakespeare's rendition of it, to have produced anything like a viable version of social order or political stability. Gloucester is the only force for good on display and his influence is rendered entirely inoperative, not so much by Henry's failure to heed the duke's advice, as by his inability to act upon it. The play pictures an entirely monarchical political system; a system that can be made functional only by the effective exercise of royal authority and which, in the absence of a monarch capable of doing that, has no means to save or right itself, either by legitimately removing one king and replacing him with another, or by diverting the succession in order to decide a contested succession. These, then, at the level of both constitutional theory and political practice, are decidedly monarchical plays.

By leaving the issue of formal dynastic legitimacy hanging, the play opens the way for an altogether more pragmatic, *de facto* as well as *de jure*, approach to the question of 'legitimacy'. The play shows the construction of the house of Lancaster's position to have been achieved by a combination of not always formally compatible arguments and methods: the assertion of right of conquest; (coerced) abdication and (royal, but not popular or parliamentary) election; 'prescription', that is to say, by popular and elite acquiescence, both active and passive; the martial prowess of the ruler, exercised in wars fought against the foreigner; and, of course, the vigorous, even ruthless, prosecution and defence of what were always already plausible but imperfect, and therefore inherently challengeable, arguments from hereditary right. Crucial here was as much the prowess, the political will, of the present incumbent as the rightness or legitimacy of his or her claims to power.

Thus when York finally makes his pretensions to the throne public he does so not at the end of some elaborate process of political or prudential calculation, nor on the grounds of his superior dynastic claims, but rather because he can no longer stand to watch someone so inept, so fundamentally unsuited to kingship, as Henry VI continue in office while someone as eminently qualified as himself stands idly by. When he sees his enemy Somerset at large, rather than, as promised by the king, imprisoned in the Tower, York rounds on Henry in a speech that contrasts his own fitness to rule with Henry's complete incapacity. Henry, York claims, is a 'false king', twice over; that is to say one who had broken his word to York and who is 'not fit to govern and rule multitudes,/ Which dar'st not, no, nor canst not rule a traitor./That head of thine doth not become a crown . . . That gold must round engirt these brows of mine,/Whose smile and frown, like to Achilles' spear,/Is able with the change to kill and cure./Here is hand to hold a sceptre up/And with the same to act controlling laws./Give place! By heaven thou shalt rule no more/O'er him whom heaven hath created for thy ruler' [Pt. II, V, i, 91–105]. Here, then, is a theory of legitimacy, of the right to rule, based not on descent but on something like true nobility, aptitude or virtue. While, given York's fate, the play can hardly be said to endorse this positively Marlovian theory of a right to rule inherent in the prowess, the martial virtue and political skill, of some providentially provided Achilles lookalike, it does surely endorse York's verdict on Henry as sadly incapable of bearing rule and confirms York's emphasis on certain qualities or virtues as necessary for the successful discharge of monarchical rule and thus as essential components of 'legitimacy'. In so doing, given the intensely masculine nature of those attributes or virtues, the play might also be taken to be (again) reflecting back (negatively) upon the dangers and perhaps even the 'legitimacy' of female rule.

We can, I think, conclude from all this that the plays under discussion here stage the creation and maintenance of 'legitimacy' as a complex process: a mixture of the formal and the informal, the theoretical and the practical, of *de facto* and *de jure* factors and forces. The two plays show that legitimacy is constructed out of a range of ideological materials; produced by mixing and matching a number of claims and arguments, many of which are not, on the face of it, obviously mutually reinforcing or even, in the final analysis, logically compatible and any one of which, taken alone, is unlikely to prove sufficient. Thus, what undermines the seemingly invulnerable position achieved, over two and a bit generations, by the Lancastrians is not some fatal flaw, inherent in what had always been an imperfect hereditary claim. As these plays go out of their way to remind us, such flaws had been all but forgotten, even by those with an intense personal and political interest in remembering them. (Only York enters the action with any doubts about the legitimacy of Henry VI's claim.) Rather, what renders the Lancastrian grasp on power suddenly questionable are the personal failings, the serial weaknesses, the repeated refusals to do what is necessary to maintain his, and his heir's, claim to the throne, of Henry VI.

When honour becomes revenge

But once a dubious or disputed succession is added to the heady brew of defeat abroad and disunity, division and popular revolt at home, factional and personal rivalry rapidly become armed conflict, which morphs soon enough into open civil war between factions now organised around mutually exclusive claims to the throne. But for all that the resulting conflict claims to be about issues of dynastic right, the processes of political polarisation and moral decay now set in motion develop a logic of their own; a logic entirely separate from, indeed antipathetic to, the resolution, or even the serious discussion, of such formal questions of 'right'.[4] Once the war has started and people have been killed, factional rivalry and dynastic competition become blood feud. Now the issue is not who should be king but rather how quickly and effectively one side can revenge itself upon the other.

In these plays the *locus classicus* for this attitude is, of course, the speech, during a parley with the Yorkists, by young Clifford in defence of Henry's claim. Exeter has just expressed his newfound sense that 'my conscience tells me he [York] is lawful king' and Henry has responded with the fear that 'all will revolt from me and turn to him'. To these developments Clifford, whose father has been killed in battle by York, responds, 'King Henry, be thy title right or wrong,/Lord Clifford vows to fight in thy defence./May that ground gape and swallow me alive/Where I shall kneel to him that slew my father' [Pt. III, I, i, 150–62]. When, later in the same scene, Henry suggests that he 'reign as king' 'for this my lifetime', to be succeeded by York and his heirs, rather than by his own son, Edward, it is Clifford (and the other northern lords) who angrily reject the proposal.

Of course, in doing so they might be thought to be acting on dynastic principle. Distinguishing between 'the king's two bodies', they are remaining loyal to the principle of hereditary succession and to the Lancastrian line, even as they oppose the fallible workings of Henry VI's private will. That seems to be the principle underlying Clifford's first response – 'what wrong is this unto the Prince, your son'; and even Northumberland's more dismissive comment – 'base, fearful and despairing Henry!' But, as we have seen, Clifford's earlier commitment to defend Henry's claim, right or wrong, had not been based on any developed sense of the legal or genealogical niceties of the case, but rather on his atavistic drive, at all costs, to revenge himself on York, the killer of his father, and indeed on as many of York's kin as he can get his hands on. We might conclude, therefore, that Clifford's second response to Henry's proposed settlement of the dynastic issue – 'how hast thou injured both thyself and us' – gets us closer to the complex mixture of his motives and feelings on the subject of the succession [Pt. III, I, i, 176–79].

The same point is driven home during the second extended debate about the succession in the play, that held at the French court between Warwick and the Lancastrian party. Warwick has urged Oxford and the others to respect 'the right' and 'for shame, leave Henry and call Edward king'. Oxford replies with a more extended version of what had been Clifford's case for his espousal of the Lancastrian cause. 'Call him my king by whose injurious doom/My elder brother, the lord Aubrey Vere,/Was done to death? And more than so, my father . . . No, Warwick, no: while life upholds this arm,/This arm upholds the house of Lancaster' [Pt. III, III, iii, 101–7]. So, the pursuit of personal revenge – or, to put the best possible face on it, the vindication of the honour of the lineage, loyalty to the most basic ties of family solidarity, linking fathers, or indeed in Margaret's case, mothers to sons and sons to fathers – trumps not only the niceties of dynastic legitimacy but also obedience to the person of the king and (on some versions of what Henry VI is trying to do in coming to an accommodation with York) the interests of the kingdom or commonwealth. After all, (the admittedly self-interested) Warwick greets Henry's proposal with the expostulation 'what good is this to England', presumably referring to Henry's expressed intent in settling with York, to 'cease this civil war' [Pt. III, I, i, 177, 197]. But, then, the last thing that the likes of Clifford and Oxford want is an end to civil war before they have destroyed their enemies and won what amounts to total victory, through what Clifford's subsequent career reveals to be campaigns of merciless violence.[5]

In the case of Oxford, or Clifford (or indeed, in their turn, of Clifford's victims), the vindication of honour becomes synonymous with the pursuit of revenge. In the absence of a stable monarchical authority, the legitimacy of which is accepted by everyone, that is what 'honour' comes to mean. Absent a stable source of monarchical authority and legitimacy, questions about what constitutes honourable conduct and about the role of honour in constraining the bare pursuit of self-interest, power and revenge are all called into radical question. Thus when Warwick, sent to France to negotiate a match between Edward IV and the Lady Bona, hears the news of Edward's sudden marriage to Lady Grey it is to his honour that he has recourse in justifying his sudden change of sides. Up until now, Warwick has been making a case for Edward's legitimacy in terms of 'right'. Now he repudiates Edward's claim and offers his services to the Lancastrian cause. Edward, he argues, is 'no more my King, for he dishonours me –/But most himself if he could see his shame.' Having expended his credit, fortune and blood to make Edward king, Warwick asks, 'am I guerdoned at the last with shame?/Shame on himself, for my desert is honour!/And to repair my honour lost for him,/I here renounce him and return to Henry' [Pt. III, III, iii, 185–94]. In these circumstances, then, 'honour' trumps 'right'; it can prompt and legitimise sudden changes of side, *renversements d'alliances* so complete as to unite sworn enemies, like Margaret and Warwick or indeed Warwick and Oxford, on the basis of what appears to be nothing much more than the principle that my enemy's enemy is my friend.

The corrosive effects of this lack of legitimacy work not only at the visceral level of honour as it morphs into revenge but also at more exalted levels of political calculation and casuistry. Immediately after the deal has been struck between Henry VI and York, whereby Henry will rule during his lifetime and be succeeded by York or his heirs, both sides start to back out of the bargain. While Henry does so under the influence of Margaret and his son [Pt. III, II, ii, 92], York does so under the influence of his sons, who claim that the crown is his by right, and by delaying taking possession thereof until Henry's death he is merely laying himself open to the plots of his enemies. But York will have none of it: 'I took an oath that he may quietly reign'. For Edward this is not a consideration; when playing for stakes as high as these, mere oaths, questions of right or conscience, are simply beside the point. 'I would break a thousand oaths to reign one year'. Amoral rant like this is not, however, going to persuade a residually honourable man like York.

At this point brother Richard steps in, claiming to be able to explain how it is that his father can claim the throne without being 'forsworn'. 'An oath', he explains, 'is of no moment, being not took/Before a true and lawful magistrate/That hath authority over him that swears./Henry had none, but did usurp the place./Then, seeing 'twas he that made you to depose,/Your oath, my lord, is vain and frivolous./Therefore, to arms. And, father, do but think/How sweet a thing it is to wear a crown,/Within whose circuit is Elysium' [Pt. III, I, ii, 21–29]. York is now persuaded and proceeds to launch the violent power play for the throne that costs him his life.

It is not only that, through the process of political conflict, the social and political order is being broken down into its most basic, familial and biological, units and connections, but also that, under the pressure of civil war, the integrity of even the most basic kinship relations starts to give out. Safely ensconced as king, Edward IV almost immediately undermines the integrity of his own family through his entirely wilful decision to marry Elizabeth Wydville. It is a decision based on 'lust', that is to say on the gratification not merely of his sexual desires but also of his private will. Just like Henry VI's marriage to Margaret, so Edward's to Elizabeth Wydville completely screws up crucial diplomatic negotiations with France and in so doing puts both his own right to rule and the interests of the commonweal into the most serious jeopardy. As Coppelia Kahn has pointed out, in the early histories 'liaisons with women are invariably disastrous because they subvert or destroy more valued alliances between men'.[6] In the case of these two disastrous royal marriages, the kings' determination to marry entirely unsuitable women simply because they want to represents, in the clearest possible (gendered) terms, an entirely un-kingly propensity to follow the promptings of private (in this case, sexual) desire rather than the dictates of policy.

In Edward's case, at least, this lapse prompted an even more serious descent into genuinely tyrannical attitudinising and, indeed, behaviour. Thus Edward tells his brother Clarence that 'it was my will and grant,/And for this once my will shall stand as law'. And when Clarence declares in response that 'I shortly mind to leave you', Edward replies peremptorily that 'leave me, or tarry, Edward will be king/And not be tied unto his brother's will' [Pt. III, IV, i, 49–50, 64–66]. 'I am Edward, your king and Warwick's, and must have my will' [Pt III, IV, i, 15–16]. This is to mistake the basic political obligation to take (and give) counsel with a mere clash of wills, and to confuse the gratification of the king's private desires with the exercise of his public will in the defence of the common- wealth and crown. These are basic moral lapses and they prompt disastrous political mistakes. As his new wife seeks to calm the resulting distempers amongst the Yorkist lords, Edward tells her not to bother. 'What danger or sorrow can befall thee/So long as Edward is thy constant friend/And their true sovereign, whom they must obey?/Nay, whom they shall obey, and love thee too,/Unless they seek for hatred at my hands;/Which if they do, yet will I keep thee safe,/And they shall feel the vengeance of my wrath' [Pt. III, IV, i, 75–82].

It is clearly not only the upstart Cade, that totally spurious claimant to royal authority, who mistakes his own will for the law and his own person for the commonwealth or realm. Just as Cade's outbursts were followed in short order by the collapse of the revolt, so here Edward's little display of royal wilfulness is followed by a rupture of relations with France, the defection of Warwick and of Clarence to the Lancastrian party and his (admittedly temporary) loss of the crown to Henry VI.

It is thus surely no accident that it is in response to these exchanges that Edward's brother Richard first announces himself as a Machiavel.[7] If in 3 Henry VI we see the 'gradual dissolution' of the political and social order until only the most basic unit of the family remains as a focus of allegiance and a source of constraint on the pursuit of purely personal advantage, by the end of that play, at the very centre of the family romance of the Yorkist regime, we see even 'the single bond of kinship' starting to come apart in the delinquency and self-indulgence of Edward IV, the defection of Clarence and, most importantly, in the sudden emergence of Richard of Gloucester as a Machiavel, bound and determined to achieve the crown by any means necessary.[8]

As a number of critics have remarked, there has been little or nothing in the previous depiction of Richard to prepare us for this sudden change, which is much less a product of the development of Richard's 'character' – what Berry terms 'the inner workings of individual psychology' – and far more a function of the demands of the general vision of political and moral decline in time of civil war being staged in the play.[9] As David Riggs puts it, 'emerging from an environment in which the *lex talionis* enjoins men to violate all moral and political obligations, the youngest son of York determines to disregard the very fraternal ties that hold together his own house to act as "myself alone".[10] Since they know who Richard of Gloucester is and what he will become, the immediate effect of all this is to deny the audience of *this* play any real sense of closure. Despite all appearances to the contrary, and despite the treatment of Edward IV's reign in the chronicles, there is no final resting place to be found in Yorkist rule. Indeed, things would have to get a great deal worse before they got better.[11]

From Lancaster to Tudor

Such conclusions had of course direct contemporary relevance and resonance. Arguably the Tudors, and more particularly the current incumbent, Elizabeth Tudor, themselves ruled in part by right of conquest (Henry VII's conquest of Richard III); in part by virtue of the power and prestige of Henry VIII and Elizabeth's claim to be his (legitimate) daughter; in part because of the nature of Henry's will, which, of course, excluded the Stuart line, just as Richard II's was taken to have excluded the Yorkists; and in part by prescription. Elizabeth too had established herself on the throne at the expense of another claimant – Mary Stuart – who, like York, derived what some people thought was a better claim to the throne through the female line. Whatever the precise rights and wrongs of the matter, by this point, just like the Lancastrians, the Tudors ruled because they ruled; their possession of the crown and hold on their subjects' reflex loyalty being more than nine-tenths of the law.[12]

But just as, under certain circumstances, and through the right mixture of monarchical weakness, excessive female influence, uncontrolled noble faction and foreign defeat, Lancastrian rule had collapsed into delegitimised chaos, disputed succession and civil war, so, in similar circumstances, for all its apparent solidity, might the Tudor regime suffer a parallel, if not an identical, collapse.

We know that many of Elizabeth's subjects, up to and including some of the regime's most enthusiastically loyal supporters, and indeed of her own counsellors, felt that, in her dealings with Mary Stuart and with the succession more generally, and in her conduct of the war with Spain, and in particular in her wavering commitment to the current campaigns in France, Elizabeth, too, had been anything but decisive. Many within the regime feared that, overly obsessed with questions of dynastic or hereditary right and overly attracted by the lure of peace, the queen had precisely not taken and was not, even now, at the time that these plays were being written and performed, taking, decisive enough action. After all, the succession remained unsettled and the war in France, and thus the fate of Henry IV and the entire balance of power in western Europe, seemed balanced on a knife edge. Much was at stake, then, and these plays might be thought to be staging one version of what might well happen next if the queen did not act, and if, delinquently or weakly run, the war went badly, and if the succession became a subject of (renewed) contest. In that event, the outcome would or could be the outbreak of precisely the same sort of dynastic civil war that had torn apart the England of Henry VI. Only now, compounded by the confessional conflicts of the post-reformation period, the situation would be if anything worse, as the crisis currently tearing apart the French monarchy showed all too clearly.

There was a parallel here with what, in certain circles, the regime, and perhaps even the queen herself, had been suspected of doing in excluding the Stuarts – the nearest thing to direct lineal descendants with genuinely Tudor blood in their veins. The exclusion of the Stuarts opened up a route to the throne for the earl of Huntingdon, the bearer of a Yorkist claim, traced through the female line from the duke of Clarence. In the play the demands of political stability and monarchical order require from Henry VI an active assertion, not only of his own right – however faulty its origins in the now dim and distant past may have been – but also of that of his direct lineal successor. A direct application of that lesson to the present conjuncture might lead to a form of Stuart legitimism. On this view, present circumstances required that the queen not only actively assert her own right, but also just as actively defend that of her own lineal heir – James Stuart. But if, at the crucial moment, with Henry VI, Elizabeth hesitated or havered, then England might once again be propelled down the slippery slope that led to dynastic civil war. Here, of course, is a direct parallel with the situation of Elizabethan England, a country in which all discussion of the succession had been banned since the beginning of the 1570s. Now, as the queen neared the end of her mortal span, speculation and anxiety about an unsettled (and therefore contestable) succession might well start to interact with weak monarchy, an excess of female influence over the exercise of power, defeat in foreign war and, as a generation of good counsellors faded from the scene to be replaced by more factious and ambitious younger men, the emergence of noble factionalism, to produce, in the present and immediate future, the same sort of downward spiral into civil war, moral chaos and ruthless violence depicted in these plays, and currently being enacted in earnest in France.

Thus these plays can be seen as occupying the same sort of mental universe as both *Leicester's commonwealth* and *Cecil's*. Clearly, the point here is not to argue for simple influence; to see the tracts, in any conventional sense, as 'sources' for the plays. After all, the author(s) of the Henry VI plays could scarcely have been 'influenced' by the *Cecil's commonwealth* tracts since they had not been produced when the plays were being written and performed. Nor is it to attribute to the plays polemical purposes identical or even similar to those displayed by the tracts. The Catholic pamphlets were intended to bring about precisely the sort of political and dynastic meltdown that they affected to be warning their countrymen against, the better to effect the authors' Hispanophile, Catholic purposes. That was most decidedly not what the plays were doing. By staging these events in this way on the popular stage in London the plays show not that their author(s) were Catholics, or even that they had read the Catholic tracts but merely that contemporaries of all stripes were reacting to the same set of circumstances and using some of the same historical events to make sense of those circumstances. The question, then, is one not of influence but of confluence; the concerns and themes shared by the two (very different) sorts of text providing proof positive of the existence of bodies of opinion and concern which both plays and pamphlets were seeking to articulate and exploit; in the case of the pamphlets, for political and, of the plays, for commercial, advantage

To put it another way, the plays show that the Catholic tracts were not merely whistling in the dark; that there were, in late Elizabethan England, anxieties – about the war, about the succession, about the moral condition of both the commonweal and the court, indeed about the queen herself – of precisely the sort that the Catholic tracts were attempting to manipulate for their own partisan purposes. Indeed, those concerns were so prevalent that it was worth the while of the contemporary public stage to try to turn an honest penny by staging them in London at almost precisely the same time that the authors of the tracts known collectively as *Cecil's commonwealth* were putting pen to paper.

In Elizabethan England, open discussion of the issues and the fears broached in both the pamphlets and the plays was pretty much impossible in other arenas or media. That we find such matters discussed both in illegal pamphlets written and published abroad by Catholic exiles, who were entirely ill affected to the current regime, and on the London stage, should not, therefore, surprise us. The former were entirely outside the reach of the legal and political, the social and cultural, constraints that prevented such material being openly canvassed in England, and the latter enjoyed the licence conferred not merely by the stage, but also by the purely historical nature of the material being performed. On this basis, we might well expect these to be precisely the two places in which to find such material being presented, if not for overtly public discussion, then certainly for intense private reflection. Differently marginal locales, the illicit (in this case, the Catholic exile) pamphlet press and the theatre have a great deal to tell us about the period that other more conventional sources cannot reveal. That they confirm one another might then be taken as an argument that historians of the period need to pay more attention to these sources than they have done in the past.

PART III
Happy endings and alternative outcomes: *1 Henry VI* and *Richard III*

CHAPTER 5

How not to go there: *1 Henry VI* as prequel and alternative ending

There is a debate about the dating of *1 Henry VI*. Some critics see it as the first part of a trilogy, a trilogy written in the same order as the events portrayed on the page and stage. Others have identified it as a sort of prequel, written after the success of the plays that have become known as *2* and *3 Henry VI* had rendered a return to the same subject a profitable prospect.[1] While scholarly consensus on this question seems a long way off, I find the second of the two positions the more compelling. Either way, it might be worth conducting a thought experiment that, accepting the later dating for part I, seeks to determine just how that play might have made the action and portent of its two predecessors look different, when viewed retrospectively from the perspective provided by part I. What follows is an attempt to argue that *1 Henry VI* subtly changes or adjusts the polemical resonance and purport of the earlier plays, and recruits all three of them for a coherently aggressive view of the current political conjuncture and what to do about it.

1 Henry VI reshuffles the pack of narrative tropes and ideological materials it inherited from parts II and III. It relocates the threat of female political agency outside England and organises it under the sign not merely of witchcraft but of popery. It similarly displaces the locus of ancient political virtue from civil to military affairs, and downgrades the role of the king. Still central is the topos of noble faction, but that faction is centred not on the succession but rather on the conduct of the war.

Faction politics

In a scene that neatly parallels, even as it subtly diverges from, the opening of *2 Henry VI*, the play establishes, from the outset, that the realm is riven with the most serious personal and factional rivalries amongst the elite. On this account, far from being above the fray Gloucester is redescribed as just another aristocratic bully boy and his feud with Cardinal Beaufort is placed front and centre as one of the prime sites of dissension. The two enter the play squabbling at Henry V's funeral, of all places. Gloucester is the aggressor here, but Beaufort gives as good as he gets [Pt. I, I, i, 44–45]. Their feud is fuelled by

Beaufort's jealousy of Gloucester's role as protector and by his own ambition [Pt. I, I, i, 173–77]. The two men's followers come to blows on the streets of London. Threatened with force by Gloucester, Beaufort replies 'I beard thee to thy face' and Gloucester responds in kind [Pt. I, iii, 44–46]. Later, as the two principals meet to have their differences mediated in parliament, they again fly at each other, this time in the royal presence.

Confronted by this outbreak of overt hostility between two of his leading counsellors, the king begs both men not only to desist, but 'to join your hearts in love and amity'. For, as even one of his tender years can tell, 'civil dissension is a viperous worm,/That knaws the bowels of the commonwealth' [Pt. I, III, i, 68, 71–74]. A later attempt to make peace between the two draws from the king the bitter plaint, – 'O, how this discord doth afflict my soul' – and a desperate request to Winchester to give over, which the bishop spurns; 'he shall submit, or I will never yield'. It is only under pressure from the king, Warwick and Gloucester that Beaufort finally agrees to make up [Pt. I, III, i, 107–36].

Later in the play, we find Beaufort paying off a papal legate for his appointment to a cardinal's hat. 'Now Winchester will not submit, I trow,/Or be inferior to the proudest peer;/Humphrey of Gloucester, thou shalt well perceive/That neither in birth or for authority/The Bishop shall be overborne by thee./I'll either make thee stoop and bend thy knee,/Or sack this country with a mutiny' [Pt. I, V, i, 51–62].

Not that Gloucester and Beaufort's is the only feud between royal counsellors on display. Just as bitter is the contention between York and Somerset. The outbreak of hostilities between these two is shown clearly and explicitly to predate any concern with King Henry's title or the succession. It takes place in the famous (and entirely fictive) scene in the Temple garden, to which a number of nobles have repaired after their discussions have become too loud to be contained 'within the Temple Hall'. The point at stake seems to be a legal one, although its precise nature is left obscure. Somerset and York are both appealing to a group of lords, including Suffolk and Warwick, to have their case arbitrated. Suffolk and Warwick express themselves quite unable to judge the legal issues [Pt. I, II, iv, 8–9, 11–18], but Somerset and York will not take no for an answer and insist that the attending lords choose sides by each plucking either a white or a red rose [Pt I, II, iv, 26–33]. Having thus chosen their colours and assembled their supporters, the two sides proceed to threaten one another [Pt. I, II, iv, 72–76]. By the end of the scene both Somerset and York are having recourse to the full-blown language of faction and feud [Pt. I, II, iv, 105–13].

Just as with the Beaufort/Gloucester altercation, the next time we see the parties at each other's throats is in the royal presence, their feud taken there by an outbreak of violence between their followers, Vernon and Bassett. As in the earlier altercation between Beaufort and Gloucester, when confronted by the feuds and factions of his peers Henry begs for peace and unity. But both peers respond by simply standing by their men. As the two clients demand to be allowed to settle their dispute in violent combat, so their two good lords square up to each another. At this point, Gloucester weighs in, admonishing both Vernon and Bassett and their noble patrons to back off. Only now does the king join in, reminding the assembled company that there is a war on and that the French cannot but take great encouragement 'if they perceive dissension in our looks'. 'Beside, what infamy will there arise/When foreign princes shall be certi-fied/That for a toy, a thing of no regard,/King Henry's peers and chief nobility/ Destroyed themselves and lost the realm of France!/O think upon the conquest of my father,/My tender years, and let us not forgo/That for a trifle that was bought with blood./Let me be umpire in this doubtful strife' [Pt. I, IV, i, 111–51]. With that, the king proceeds to divide up the command of the royal forces in France between Somerset and York, leaving them to prosecute the war there while the king, 'my lord protector and the rest', return to England. The results, of course, are disastrous, as the English suffer a calamitous defeat because Somerset and York cannot co-ordinate their movements to relieve the beleaguered forces of the noble Talbot.

Thus, throughout the play, the internal dissensions, the rivalries, factions and feuds of the nobility remain unappeased and uncontrolled, and, because they are unappeased and uncontrolled, they get worse. By the play's end a third factor has been introduced into the mix: the determination of a Machiavel, an archetypal evil counsellor, to exploit these jars, and the increasingly apparent weakness of the young king, in order to seize control of the state for himself. That figure is Suffolk, who, having arranged the marriage of Henry to Margaret, and fallen for Margaret in the process, ends the play determined to use his influence over Margaret, and hers over Henry, to dominate the state. 'Margaret shall now be queen, and rule the King:/But I will rule both her, the King and realm' [Pt. I, V, iv, 107–8]. The effect of all of this is to establish that the roots of the dissensions, the feuds and rivalries of the nobility predate any real concern with the issue of the succession. What is at stake are personal rivalries and dislikes, the mutually exclusive ambitions, the claims to influence and honour, of the great and the good, and the emergent factions and parties amongst both the gentry and indeed the commons that those rivalries and conflicts are starting to spread throughout the polity.

Succession politics

Insofar as the issue of the succession raises its head at all it does so in ways expressly designed to deny it any causal role in the broils and contentions being played out on stage. Thus the crucial side-taking scene in the Temple garden [Pt. I, II, iv] takes place directly before another between York and his uncle Mortimer [Pt, I, II, v], in which the dying Mortimer explains to York the reasons why he has spent his life in prison; an account which amounts to a direct challenge to the legitimacy of Lancastrian rule and a justification of why York and not Henry should, in fact, be king. Again, as with Warwick and Salisbury in part II, York is portrayed as knowing nothing of these things before Mortimer explains them to him. He had come to his dying uncle to find out 'the cause my father, Earl of Cambridge, lost his head' [Pt. I, II, v, 53–54]. Only once the intricacies of the dynastic situation consequent upon the deposition of Richard II have been explained to him does York exclaim that 'methinks, my father's execution/Was nothing less than bloody tyranny' [Pt. I, II, v, 99–100].

Having explained that it was because he was the true king that he has spent his days in prison, Mortimer spells out the consequences for York [Pt. I, II, v, 92–103]. York, Mortimer informs him, is in effect the rightful king, and the current incumbent and his immediate ancestors have been guilty of something like 'tyranny' in 'suppressing' the Mortimers in whom the true title rested and from whom it has now passed to York.

Mortimer then tells his nephew that 'the rest, I wish thee gather'. Quite what this means is unclear; it could mean that Mortimer wants York to 'gather' 'the rest' of the story from elsewhere, from other witnesses and sources, or it could mean that what he wants him to 'gather' is 'the rest' of his birthright, i.e. the crown itself. Either way, he counsels caution; 'with silence, nephew, be thou politic'. As things stand 'the house of Lancaster' is 'like a mountain', 'not to be removed' [Pt. I, II, v, 102–3]. In other words, the hold on power of the present incumbent is firm, the stability of his regime clear and his legitimacy as king beyond challenge. The fate of York's father and uncle serves as a warning about what knowledge of the dynastic rights and wrongs of the situation, let alone actions based upon that knowledge, can lead to.

Certainly, Mortimer's final dying wish to his nephew 'that fair be all thy hopes,/And prosperous be thy life in peace and war' [Pt. I, II, v, 113–14] falls a long way short of a clarion call for York to assert his claim to the throne. Rather, Mortimer's words seem to express an acceptance of the brute fact of Lancastrian rule and the hope that, despite his newfound (and extremely dangerous) dynastic knowledge, forewarned will be forearmed, and York will somehow manage to manoeuvre his way to a glorious and successful career under Lancastrian rule.

Quite what York makes of all this is not here revealed. He is certainly not transformed, on the spot, into the figure who enters the action in part II; that is to say, a Machiavel, plotting to realise his claim to be king by exacerbating and exploiting the divisions amongst his fellow nobles and counsellors. 'Well, I will lock his counsel in my breast,/And what I do imagine – let that rest', is his only comment. From making hurried arrangements for his uncle's funeral, York then turns back to the major business in hand – his feud with Somerset. 'I doubt not but with honour to redress./And therefore haste I to the parliament

-/Either to be restored to my blood,/Or make my will th'advantage of my good'
[Pt. I, II, v, 118–29].

What this scenes does, of course, is gloss, indeed explain, York's determination, patent almost from the outset of part II, to set his cap at the throne. But it also makes clear that the origins of the divide between Lancaster and York predated his knowledge of his claim to the throne, lying instead in a feud between himself and Somerset over an unexplicated legal issue. This only serves to emphasise the completeness of the triumph of the house of Lancaster. When even a potential claimant to the crown, the heir of two men, the first of whom (his uncle) has been imprisoned and the second (his father) executed by the current regime, does not know the true state of affairs, the legitimacy of the ruling house must be said to have been well and truly established. Indeed, York has, as he boasts on more than one occasion in these plays, expended his treasure, his credit and his blood in serving the Lancastrian crown in France.

In these exchanges, despite the dynastic facts of the matter – facts that, of course, he has just expounded, at some length, to his nephew – Mortimer has been articulating what amounts to a *de factoist* theory of legitimacy. Armed with what was at best a faulty, indeed, on Mortimer's account, an openly false, claim to the throne, the Lancastrians have nevertheless managed to establish themselves in an unchallengeable position, a position from which, for all the legitimacy of his formal claims, York would be very ill advised to try to remove them. All of this, of course, serves to emphasise, even more firmly than the action of parts II and III already has, that the origins of the jars and stirs being depicted not merely in this play but also in its predecessors were not located in a doubtful or contested succession, but rather in the conjunction of noble faction, weak monarchical oversight and foreign war; a conjunction which might, of course, be thought to have had rather obvious and immediate contemporary relevance and resonance.[2] Only later, further along in the processes of political polarisation and moral decline set off by the events being depicted in this play, will a contested succession take an active role in events, creating, by the end, the perfect storm of political and moral breakdown (already) staged in parts II and III.

The politics of virtue

Just as in part II, so in this play, there is one figure of what we might term antique virtue; someone who stands apart from and above the bickering contentions of the nobility. In part II that figure had been Gloucester, the very epitome of the good magistrate. But in this play the epitome of virtue, true loyalty and honour is Talbot, who is, of course, not a figure from civil government but from martial affairs. His virtues are those of the soldier rather than of the magistrate, the judge or the counsellor.

Indeed, Talbot is portrayed throughout as the perfect epitome of martial honour. The action virtually opens with the news that Talbot has been taken by the French. Surrounded, he had sold himself dearly, only at the end to be overcome by superior odds. Indeed so great had been Talbot's prowess that, given the appropriate reinforcements from Sir John Fastolfe, victory could still have been snatched from the jaws of defeat. Fastolfe, however, preferred the safety of flight to the risks of battle and left Talbot to his fate [Pt. I, I, i, 118–40]. Once captured, Talbot had been treated with a mixture of cruelty and fear by the French. But however great the torments and humiliations visited upon him by his captors, Talbot scorned to be ransomed in exchange for one he deemed to be his inferior [Pt. I, I, iv, 26–33].

Talbot, then, is the epitome of martial honour. He is proud, too proud to have his honour demeaned by a humiliating exchange for a man who is not his equal, but not so proud as to be unable to accept that such equals exist. He has a strong sense of his own worth and prowess and is quite prepared to fight to the death to preserve his name, but he is also quite happy to admit that his prowess also relies on that of his troops. In a remarkable, and purely invented scene for which there are no historical sources, Talbot is invited to visit a French noblewoman, the countess of Auvergne, and accepts the invitation to 'try her courtesy'. It is, of course, a trap. When he first arrives, the countess remarks on his unimposing appearance. Expecting 'some Hercules', or 'a second Hector', she insultingly concludes that 'it cannot be this weak and writhled shrimp/Should strike such terror to his enemies' [Pt. I, II, iii, 14–23]. When she attempts to lay hands upon him, Talbot tells her that she has captured but 'Talbot's shadow/Whereon to practise your severity . . . my substance is not here'. To her riposte that ' . . . he will be here, and yet he is not here:/How can these contrarieties agree?' Talbot answers by sounding his horn and at once the room is filled with his soldiers, whom he describes as 'his substance, sinews, arms and strength,/With which he yoketh your rebellious necks,/Razeth your cities and subverts your towns,/And in a moment makes them desolate'. With that Talbot accepts the countess' apology for her deception and sits down to dinner [Pt. I, II, iii, 14–79]. In short, the scene reveals Talbot to be crafty – he sees through the countess' stratagem; humble, in that he knows that his 'substance, sinews, arms and strength' reside not (only) in his own person but (also) in his troops; and magnanimous, in that, having avoided the countess' plot, he readily accepts her hospitality. Moreover, unlike his hostess and indeed the French more generally, with their superstitiously idolatrous adoration of Puzel (i.e. Joan of Arc), he knows the difference between sign and substance, between his mere physical presence and the real roots of his power as a military leader.[3]

The only objects of the honourable Talbot's scorn are the dishonourable. When his troops flee before Joan and the dauphin's forces he rounds on them and, when his first appeal falls on deaf ears, tells them to 'either renew the fight/ Or tear the lions out of England's coat./Renounce your soil, give sheep in lion's stead;/Sheep not run not half so treacherous from the wolf,/Or horse or oxen from the leopard,/As you fly from your oft subdued slaves' [Pt. I, I, v, 27–35]. But his greatest contempt is reserved for the miscreant coward Fastolfe who is depicted in the play as not once, but twice, fleeing the scene of battle to save his own skin. As the English lords assemble in Paris for the coronation of Henry VI, Fastolfe and Talbot come face to face and Talbot immediately tears the garter from Fastolfe's leg. Fastolfe's conduct has (twice) shown that he 'doth but usurp the sacred name of knight,/Profaning this most honourable order,/And should (if I were worthy to be judge)/Be quite degraded, like a hedge-born swain/That doth presume to boast of gentle blood'. A verdict immediately confirmed by the king who sends Fastolfe – 'thou that wast a knight' – 'packing', banished 'on pain of death'[Pt. I, IV, i, 14–47].

Here Talbot establishes the equivalence between true honour, noble blood and martial prowess and gathers all those attributes around the Order of the Garter as the highest acknowledgement of, and reward for, true nobility and loyal (military) service to the crown; qualities that Talbot personifies.

Honour and its enemies: women on top – again

As we have seen, in parts II and III, Gloucester's virtues were juxtaposed against, defined, and finally overthrown or defeated by, on the one hand, the personal ambitions and increasingly factious rivalries of the nobility and, on the other, the excessive influence on affairs of state of an increasingly mannish and demonic woman. So, too, in part I, Talbot's virtues are juxtaposed against, defined, and finally defeated by those same forces. Only now the resulting conflicts are configured and located somewhat differently; not to be found solely within the English camp, clustered around an increasingly vicious faction politics and an emergent struggle for the crown, but rather around and within the prosecution of the war in France.

Let us turn first (and again) to the issue of women on top. This features just as prominently in part I as it does in parts II and III, but whereas there the corrupting, indeed inversionary, power of female agency and power operated from within the English polity, albeit in and through the activities of a French woman, Queen Margaret, now it is to be found operating only on the French side of the equation, through the extraordinary figure of Joan Puzel. Rather than, like Queen Margaret, growing into an increasingly violent, overreaching, mannish version of womanhood, Joan enters the action in precisely that condition. Unlike the duchess of Gloucester, she does not need to enlist the supernatural powers of others. She can lay claim to spirits and familiars of her own. Like Jack Cade, she emerges from 'the people' to claim a position of rule in the commonwealth, but she does so by laying entirely spurious claim not to noble or royal birth, but to supernatural sanction.

Introduced to the dauphin for the first time, she reveals a seemingly miraculous ability to tell who's who amongst the French nobility. She also challenges the dauphin to single combat, a challenge he accepts; and, in the ensuing combat, Joan displays an un- or rather a super-natural – and, of course, an entirely un-womanlike – strength. 'Stay, stay thy hands,' gasps the dauphin. 'Thou art an Amazon/And fightest with the sword of Deborah.' 'Christ's mother helps me, else I were too weak,' comes the reply. The dauphin is bowled over. 'Who'er helps me, 'tis thou that must help me./Impatiently I burn with thy desire./My heart and hands thou hast at once subdued./Excellent Puzel, if thy name be so,/Let me thy servant and not sovereign be.' To this proposal Joan makes the right answer once again: 'I must not yield to any rights of love,/For my profession's sacred from above./When I have chased all thy foes from hence,/Then will I think upon a recompense' [Pt. I, I, ii, 72–116]. Joan, she tells him, has been 'assigned' by God 'to be the English scourge' [Pt. I, I, ii, 129].

Joan's claims to divine sanction and supernatural powers are confirmed by the response to those claims of the French. 'Bright star of Venus, fallen down on earth,/How may I reverently worship thee enough?' is the dauphin's first response to her claims [Pt I, I, ii, 140–45]. Later, after she has expelled the English from Orleans, he hails her as 'divinest creature, Astraea's daughter' [Part I, I, v, 43]. 'No longer on Saint Denis will we cry,/But Joan de Puzel shall be France's saint' [Pt. I, I, v, 62–68]. Elsewhere she is described as a 'glorious prophetess' [Pt. I, I, v, 47], a 'holy maid' [Pt. I, I, ii, 52), 'ordained', 'by a vision sent from heaven' 'to drive the English forth the bounds of France' [Pt. I, I, ii, 53–54].

Joan comes to personify the French cause just as Talbot does the English. Just as the French compare Talbot to 'a fiend of hell', 'or if not of hell, the heavens favour him' [Pt. I, II, i, 46–47], so the English demonise Joan. When he first encounters Joan on the field of battle, Talbot denounces her as a witch. They fight, and neither wins, causing Talbot to exclaim 'heavens, can you suffer hell so to prevail?' [Pt. I, I, v, 5–9]. In seeking her aid, Bedford claims that the dauphin has joined forces 'with witches and the help of hell'. The success of the French, Talbot concurs, has been 'contrived by art and baleful sorcery' [Pt. I, II, i, 17–18, 15]. Later, Talbot is yet more explicit: Puzel is 'that witch, that damned sorceress', or again that 'foul fiend of France and hag of all despite,/Encompassed with thy lustful paramours' or again that 'railing Hecate'. Burgundy concurs: she is 'a vile fiend and shameless courtesan' [Pt. I, III, ii, 44, 63, 51–52]. Talbot exclaims, 'let them practise and converse with spirits./God is our fortress, in whose conquering name/Let us resolve to scale their flinty bulwarks' [Pt. I, II, i, 25–27].

In the Christian universe inhabited both by the (Catholic) characters in the play and by the play's Elizabethan audiences, extraordinary, superhuman powers like those claimed by Joan must come either from the devil or from God. Given that the play repeatedly shows Joan to be genuinely possessed of real supernatural powers the audience is, therefore, confronted with a simple choice: she enjoys such powers either because she is a saint indeed, or because she is an agent of the devil; a choice exemplified, of course, in the very different French and English responses to her exploits. In choosing between those alternatives the audience are also, perforce, compelled to make a confessional choice between Catholic and protestant, and between English and French, views of the matter.

While at the outset, and for a good deal of the play, Joan's precise status is left deliberately ambiguous, the audience is given a series of clues to her real spiritual identity. Thus, even when her supernatural powers are at their most effective, Joan's manner is not exactly saint-like. Throughout, she is accused of sexual incontinence. At one point, Burgundy outs her as 'the dolphin's trull' [Pt. I, II, ii, 28]. She consistently rails against the English, taunting them in defeat and triumphing over their misfortunes.

Through manoeuvres like this, the play hints at what she really is, while leaving her precise status wrapped in uncertainty until the scene in Act V when, as the fortunes of war turn against the French, Joan unsuccessfully importunes her 'choice spirits' to 'appear, and aid me in this enterprise'. Hitherto, as she explains both to them and to us, like any regular witch, Joan has fed her familiar spirits 'with my blood'. Now she offers to lop off an entire member and 'give it you/In earnest of a further benefit'. Finding this an offer her demons can only too easily refuse, she then offers them 'my body, soul and all'. This bargain too is turned down and Joan is abandoned to her fate at the hands of the English [Pt. I, V, ii, 1–50]. *Pace* the claims of Gillian Woods, there is nothing 'equivocal' about this scene. Nor is it true 'that the devils refuse to perform'. Having responded to Joan's summons, they merely refuse to speak, which refusal is, of course, in itself a form of performance.[4]

Captured by York, Puzel is denounced as a 'fell banning hag', to which accusation she replies 'I prithee, give me leave to curse awhile' and then proceeds to perform her status as a both witch and a whore at some length. Confronted with her father, a shepherd, she repudiates him, claiming for herself (just as had Cade before her) an entirely spurious noble birth. Initially, condemned to death, she sticks to her story. When these appeals and claims fall on deaf ears, Puzel changes her tune. She now protests that she cannot be executed because she is pregnant. Asked to name the father of the child she first fingers the dauphin, then switches to that 'notorious machiavel', Alençon, before finally settling on Reignier, king of Naples.

These desperate pleas and contradictory claims merely serve to confirm the English (and presumably the audience) in their conviction that Joan is indeed both a witch and a strumpet. 'Why, here's a girl! I think she knows not well –/There were so many – whom she may accuse', concludes York. 'It's a sign she hath been liberal and free', concurs Warwick. 'And yet, forsooth, she is a virgin pure./Strumpet, thy words condemn thy brat and thee.' 'Break thou in pieces, and consume to ashes,/ Thou foul accursed minister of hell' [Pt. I, V, iii, 21–93].

Joan's powers consisted of a mixture of the sort of magical legerdemain and feats of 'policy' of which contemporary witchcraft belief held that the devil and his instruments were more than capable. However, Joan's deeds have never risen to the level of the truly miraculous. By the end of the play an audience that, unlike most modern critics, actually believes in witches and the agency of the devil has been left in no doubt that Joan is both the witch and the whore that the English have throughlout denounced her as being. It is, therefore, precisely not the case that, as Gillian Woods claims, Joan is 'dragged off cursing, defeated but not resolved'. On the contrary, by the end both her status as a witch and the stark contrast between a French cause, led by that banning fiend, the 'dolphin's trull' and 'minister of hell', Puzel, and an English one, led by that epitome of true nobility, martial prowess and honour, Talbot, have both been established beyond doubt.

Anti-popery

There are, of course, very strong parallels being established between Puzel, as the play portrays her, and popery as it was analysed and excoriated in myriad sermons and tracts as a false religion of satanic origins, a series of quintessentially *Anti*christian claims, performances and powers, all tricked out as (entirely spurious) proof of direct divine inspiration, spiritual sanctity and power. In Joan we have a person who claims direct divine inspiration and supernatural powers from the Virgin; someone of alleged sexual and spiritual purity, whose more than feminine, indeed more than human, strength and prescience, whose feats of arms and policy, achieved by a mere shepherdess, represent a sustained, walking and talking, prodigy, indeed an apparent miracle, or rather a series of apparent miracles.

Joan's claims to sanctity lead the French to hail her as a saint and the English immediately to recognise her as a witch. And, of course, as the play takes great delight in showing, over the entire course of the action, it is the English who are right. Her powers are real but their source is demonic, not divine; her claims to sanctity are false, not merely delusional but deliberate, part of a satanic plot to take over the world through professions of a fraudulent sanctity and the performance of what amount to false miracles, strokes of policy passing themselves off as wonders of God.

The figure of Puzel thus introduces into the play anti-popery in some of its crudest and most demotic forms. Through her, the foreign French enemy stand condemned not merely because of their foreignness and Frenchness, as they are, for instance, in the roughly contemporaneous *Edward III*, but also as popishly inclined and demonically led. Thus the opposition between Talbot and Puzel outlined above takes on the aspect of a struggle, not just between good and evil, between God and the devil, but between Christ and Antichrist. If it is indeed the case that '*1 Henry VI* realizes and dissolves binaries' – as common wisdom would have it that nearly all of Shakespeare's plays do – then it is safe to say that the binary opposition between Joan and Talbot, that is to say, between English protestant virtue and foreign popish vice, between true and false religion, is not one of them. Rather by play's end, it seems clear that whatever else the play is, it is most definitely a piece of rather crude anti-popish polemic.[5]

However, anti-popery being the slippery ideological quantity that it was,[6] this still left more than enough room for a subtly subversive and threatening ambiguity in the play's handling of these very themes. For the gradual course of the play's revelation to its audience of Joan's true nature, and of the utterly demonic source of her powers and claims, might be thought to stage not only the gradual revelation of the pope's status as Antichrist achieved over the course of the reformation, but also the ongoing process of enlightenment still to be undergone by those English people – some of them no doubt to be found in the play's first audiences – who were still in thrall to Antichrist's charms. The play uses Puzel not merely to locate popery safely abroad but to advert to the residual presence within England, indeed within its own audiences, of both papists and popery, a presence it tries to expunge through its own gradual revelation of Joan's ultimately demonic and wholly popish malignity.

Not only that, but precisely because of all the talk of her as another 'Deborah', or 'Astraea's daughter', or 'Venus', a miraculously empowered, virginal, female leader in time of war, the figure of Joan also stands as a stark reminder of the entirely unnatural, indeed entirely corrupt, unchaste and demonic, nature of such female aspirations to military authority and national leadership in time of war. As Leah Marcus has argued,[7] as with the figure of Queen Margaret in parts II and III, we may be getting just about as close to a critique of female rule in wartime as it was possible to get in late Elizabethan England. And here the gradual revelation and final confirmation of Joan's unequivocally demonic status serves merely to underline that, however compelling, virginal, saint- and Deborah-like a wartime female ruler might appear, over the long haul the dreadful truth would out.

So the real ambiguity surrounding Puzel stems not from any doubt, by the play's end, surrounding what she was or represented, but rather from the question of whether the malign forces she personified – demonic enchantment, popery, the exorbitancies and inversions that clung to female rule – could be safely relegated to 'the other', the foreign, the un-English, or whether fatally destabilising traces thereof were still at work within England herself. Crucial here was the figure of the bishop of Winchester, Cardinal Beaufort. Throughout,

Beaufort clothes himself in the mantle of ecclesiastical power and Roman jurisdiction. Praising Henry V, in the play's opening scene, Winchester claims that
'the battles of the lord of hosts he fought;/The Church's prayers made him so
prosperous'. Gloucester, however, responds to that claim with one of *the* basic
reformation questions. 'The Church? Where is it? Had not churchmen prayed,/
His thread of life had not been so decayed./None do you like but an effeminate
prince,/Whom like a schoolboy you may overawe' [Pt. I, I, i, 31–43].

The exchanges at the Tower between Gloucester and Winchester are
onducted in scabrously anti-clerical and haughtily prelatical, indeed sometimes frankly Romanist, terms. Gloucester starts in, accusing Winchester of
having conspired to kill Henry V. 'Stand back thou manifest conspirator,/Thou
that contrived'st to murder our dead lord,/Thou that giv'st whores indulgences
to sin;/I'll canvas thee in thy broad cardinal's hat/If thou proceed in this thy
insolence' [Pt. I, I, iii, 33–37]. 'Under my feet I stamp thy cardinal's hat./In spite
of Pope or dignities of Church,/Here by the cheeks I'll drag you up and down'
[Pt I, I, iii, 33–51].

Despite the violence of Gloucester's language here, of the two, Beaufort is by
far the more ruthless and determined prosecutor of their feud. In their stand-off
at the Tower it is the cardinal who wins from the Lord Mayor the comment 'this
cardinal's more haughty than the devil' [Pt. I, I, iii, 83]. Along with that quintessential Machiavel, Suffolk, the cardinal shares the ambition to 'sit at chiefest
stern of public weal' [Pt. I, I, i, 173–77]. Denounced by Gloucester as 'a saucy
priest', Beaufort stands on his clerical dignity. 'Am I not a prelate of the church?'
he asks, only to be told 'Yes, as an outlaw in a castle keeps/And useth it to
patronage his theft'. 'Unreverent Gloucester!' 'Thou art reverend/Touching thy
spiritual function, not thy life', to which last sally Winchester replies with the
ultimate popish put-down, 'Rome shall remedy this' [Pt. I, III, i, 45–52].

We have here central elements in the contemporary protestant stereotype of
popery being organised around the cardinal. Greed, ambition, corruption,
both sexual and financial, a remarkably un-Christian drive towards secular
power and status and a willingness to get down and dirty in their pursuit – all
these pervade Winchester's speeches. To them can be added, if Gloucester is to
be believed, a willingness to kill kings, if they get in the way.

Here then is the play's real claim to ambiguity, the place where it does
indeed undermine the conventional binary oppositions and equivalences
between true religion and popery, England and abroad. For we have here the
full gamut of anti-clerical and anti-prelatical stereotypes and characteristics, so
central to contemporary notions of popery, being embodied in an English
prelate and politician. Given the notorious tensions between Burghley and
Whitgift over the latter's crackdown on the Elizabethan puritan movement,
tensions that had reached their height at precisely the time this play was being
written and first performed, the play might well have been taken, at least by

some puritanically inclined contemporaries, to have been gesturing at the more than residual presence of popery, operating not only amongst the alien, demonised French but also, here at home, amongst the more corrupt and ambitious members of the clerical hierarchy, undermining the peace and unity of England from within.[8]

1 Henry VI evokes and handles many of the central themes of parts II and III – the concern with the impact of weak monarchy, of noble rivalries and faction and of excessive and unnatural female influence on matters of estate and of war. But it then attaches them to the prosecution of a war waged against an enemy now unequivocally identified, not merely as foreign and French, but also as demonic, Antichristian and popish. And it does so in ways that render Womersley's invocation of the 'mode of the apocalypse' to describe this play more than just.

In this, the play moves away from the universe of action and argument occupied by *2* and *3 Henry VI* and into that occupied by plays like *Edward I*, *Edward III*, *The famous victories of Henry V* or *The troublesome reign of King John*, all of which invoked glorious instances of English victory over a threatening foreign (French) rival or invader to address the present struggle against Spain, being fought at sea, in the Low Countries and in France. In those plays, however, we see royal weakness and corruption being overcome – in the cases of Edward III and Henry V, by the prince himself, in the case of King John, by the bastard, conjoined, at the last, with Henry III. And all those plays end in victory over the foreigner. That, however, is not the case in *1 Henry VI*. Puzel is indeed unmasked and burnt, but the play scarcely ends on an unequivocally victorious note.

Certainly, the English are shown triumphing over the forces of darkness represented by Joan, who, after all, is burnt at the stake by York and Warwick, with the audience left in no doubt as to her identity not only as a witch, but also as a synecdoche for all things popish. For all her demonic powers and considerable, albeit temporary, success, Joan never personally overcomes Talbot or even his son. At their moment of personal combat both come off unscathed, Joan conceding to Talbot that 'thy hour is not yet come' [Pt. I, I, v, 13]. Later, her attempts to draw young Talbot into combat are equally fruitless [Pt. I, IV, iv, 149–55]. Indeed, even when Joan is at the height of her powers and military success, Talbot manages to recapture Orleans from the French, overcoming all Joan's cunning (and supernatural powers) with his military skill and personal prowess. To turn the tide in favour of the French, Joan has to resort not to military but to political means, or rather to a sexually charged attempt to 'enchant' Burgundy 'with thy words'[Pt. I, III, iii, 40]. Although, typically, the play leaves it unclear whether what was at work here was witchcraft or policy, enchantment or persuasion. As Burgundy exclaims after his change of sides, 'either she hath bewitched me with her words,/Or nature makes me suddenly relent' [Pt. I, III, iii, 58–9, 78–80].

Divided we fall: the politics of faction in time of war

But if Joan is unmasked and defeated, Talbot, too, ends up dead. However, what kills him is not the force or superior skill of the French, but rather the internal divisions amongst the English nobility that prevent York and Somerset from co-operating to come to the relief of the two Talbots. To return to the scene with the countess of Auverne, Talbot's 'substance' is indeed to be found in the forces at his command. Denied that substance, however noble his death may have been, Talbot is inevitably reduced not merely to the 'weak and writhled shrimp', derided by the countess, but to the 'stinking and fly blown' carcass lying at Puzel's feet in Act IV, sc. iv (187–89). Talbot dies because he has been denied sufficient force to overcome his enemies, but he has been denied that, not by the efforts of those enemies, still less by the supernatural machinations, the charms and tricks, of Puzel's 'policy', but by the internal divisions and personal rivalries of the English.[9]

York, apprised of the dire straits in which the Talbots find themselves, responds by blaming Somerset. Pressed by Lucy to do something, York responds by blaming Somerset once again. 'O God, that Somerset, who in proud heart/Doth stop my cornets, were in Talbot's place;/So should we save a valiant gentleman/By forfeiting a traitor and a coward./Mad ire and wrathful fury makes me weep,/That thus we die while remiss traitors sleep.'

York, at least, knows the consequences of his own failure or refusal (or perhaps of his incapacity?) to act. 'He dies, we lose, I break my warlike word./We mourn, France smiles; we lose, they daily get,/All long of this vile traitor Somerset' [Pt. I, IV, iii, 9–33]. Somerset, on the other hand, denies all responsibility. 'It is too late, I cannot send them now.' Disaster may be staring the English in the face, but it is everybody's fault but his. 'This expedition was by York and Talbot/Too rashly plotted. All our general force/Might with a sally of the very town/Be buckled with: the over-daring Talbot/Hath sullied all his gloss of former honour/By this unheedful, desperate, wild adventure./York set him on to fight and die in shame,/That, Talbot dead, great York might bear the name' [Pt. I, IV, iii, 54–63].

It is Lucy who provides the crucial commentary on these events and excuses. 'Thus, the vulture of sedition/Feeds in the bosom of such great commanders,/Sleeping neglection doth betray to loss/The conquest of our scarce-cold conqueror,/That ever living man of memory,/Henry the fifth. Whiles they each other cross,/Lives, honours, lands and all hurry to loss.' 'The fraud of England, not the force of France,/Hath now entrapped the noble-minded Talbot./Never to England shall he bear his life,/But dies betrayed to fortune by your strife' [Pt. I, IV, iii, 47–53, 89–92].

Whatever the precise rights and wrongs of their dispute – and the play clearly presents Somerset as more culpable than York – because of their joint failure to come to Talbot's aid, both York and Somerset are presented as the functional, indeed as the moral, equivalents of that arrant coward Fastolfe, a man who, in full view of the court, has had his garter stripped from his leg by a righteously indignant Talbot, before being banished for ever by the king himself. That was the moral condition to which that viper in the bosom of the commonweal, faction, could, indeed (unchecked) would, lay low even the greatest of peers, while fatally undermining the English war effort.

These comments pick up earlier remarks made by a nameless messenger at the play's outset when he had announced the loss of 'Guyenne, Champagne, Reims, Rouen, Orleans,/Paris, Gisors, Poitiers'. Asked by Exeter 'how were they lost? What treachery was used?' the messenger replies that the cause was 'no treachery but want of men and money./Amongst the soldiers this is muttered:/ That here you maintain several factions,/And whilst a field should be dispatched and fought/You are disputing of your generals./One would have lingering wars, with little cost./Another would fly swift, but wanteth wings./Another thinks, without expense at all,/By guileful fair words fair peace may be obtained./ Awake, awake, English nobility,/Let not sloth dim your honours new begot;/ Cropped are the flower de luces in your arms;/Of England's arms one half is cut away' [Pt. I, I, i, 60–61, 69–81]. These comments are followed in rapid succession by news from a second messenger and then a third, who brings word of Talbot's capture. Thus is the circle of the play's argument closed; the same forces that, at the outset, had wrought the great man's defeat and capture, have, by the play's close, brought about his death.

To get a further handle on just what is happening here we need to set the play against the immediate political context in which it was written and indeed into which, I shall argue, it was intended to intervene. As we have seen, the play is dominated by the theme of internal division, personal rivalry and factional conflict amongst the counsellors and military commanders of Henry VI. There is a direct contemporary resonance to such depictions of foreign campaigns broken on the wheel of aristocratic rivalries and fundamental differences about the nature of the mission at hand. Not only had Leicester's command in the Low Countries been characterised by bitter personal and military disagreements between Leicester and Sir Henry Norris, it had culminated in recriminations at court featuring Leicester, Buckhurst and Cobham. Later, in the Lisbon expedition of 1589, the attempt to exploit the defeat of the Armada by reinstating the pretender to the Portuguese throne, Don Antonio, had been fatally disrupted by the breakdown in relations between the naval and military commanders, Sir Francis Drake and Sir Henry Norris, who had been intent on pursuing mutually exclusive versions of the enterprise. The extent of that failure would have been widely known and well remembered in London because of the mutinous demonstrations for redress conducted in the London streets, only a few months earlier, by the unpaid soldiers and sailors from the expedition.

In addition, the period of the early 1590s saw an upsurge of bitter interpersonal tensions amongst certain members of the Elizabethan elite. Here the big story was not any sort of rift between Essex and the Cecils; at this period, as Paul Hammer has pointed out, relations between Essex and Burghley were quite close, with Burghley helping the earl secure command of the Rouen expedition and seeking to protect him throughout that campaign from the queen's ire. Rather the eye of the storm was provided by the intense rivalry between Essex and Raleigh, two young men vying both for the role of the ageing queen's favourite and for military command and glory.

On occasion, this relationship came close to boiling over into violence, with Essex at one point actually challenging Raleigh to a duel. This was a rivalry that took other than political forms, with the two men writing poems to the queen and against one another; poems which circulated in court circles and made quite clear the nature and extent of the breach between them. Not that Essex's relations were fractious only with Raleigh. Once, he nearly came to blows with the earl of Kildare in the presence chamber, again over the favour shown towards the Irish peer by the queen.[10]

Nor were these the only or most obvious parallels or resonances between the events described in the play and contemporary circumstances. Some of the most spectacular military action staged in the play takes place during a siege of Rouen. At precisely the same time that this play was being written and performed (that is to say, late 1591 and early 1592), a real siege of Rouen was under way, under the command of the young earl of Essex. At that siege Essex's brother was killed, ambushed as he pursued a group of fleeing French. We know that the conduct and course of the siege were of very considerable public interest back in England. The one newsbook printed on the subject goes on at length about the penumbra of largely false rumours then circulating in London about the expedition, rumours which the pamphlet in question then sets itself to correct. It was not true, the author contended, that the soldiers were dying like flies, picked off by hunger and disease. Supplies, on the contrary, were plentiful and things were going splendidly under the command of the earl.

If this is anything to go by, the expedition was an object of both popular and elite interest and there were a number of different accounts of what was happening, and of whose fault it all was, in circulation. We also know that during the autumn the issue of the need to reinforce Essex's army was a pressing one. Recalled to England, the earl had to make that case to the queen in person.[11]

Those who argue that *1 Henry VI* was a prequel to parts II and III see it as an attempt to exploit the box office success of those plays. On the argument being pursued here, it was doing so at least in part by recasting central thematic and narrative materials from the earlier plays around the intensely current issues of war in France and noble and conciliar politics at home. It was thus an attempt to cash in not only on the success of *2 and 3 Henry VI* but also on the

buzz of popular interest surrounding the current politico-military conjuncture, in general, and the earl of Essex and the siege of Rouen, in particular.

But we can perhaps go further even than this. As Paul Hammer has explained,
the Rouen campaign was of crucial importance to Essex. His first major
command, it was the means by which he hoped to establish his bona fides as
a great commander and effect his transition from the status of royal favourite
to that of a man of war and of affairs, a major player on the European scene
like his stepfather, Leicester, or his newfound friend and ally, Henry IV. 'In
political terms, Essex hoped to win conspicuous honour on the battlefield, to
commit Elizabeth to new and greater efforts in France – and also to boost his
own career. . . . Along with Essex's "ambition in war", therefore, went a belief in
the political efficacy of "military renown".'[12] The campaign, however, was not a
success. Dogged throughout by the criticism and cold feet of the queen, it ended
with Rouen un-taken and Essex back in England. We know from a remarkable
series of letters written to the earl throughout the early stages of the siege that
the queen was furious about the conduct of the campaign, regarding it as an
almost total waste of time and money. We also know from that newsbook
account of autumn 1591 that a series of rumours were circulating about the
supposedly disastrous course of events at Rouen. After it was all over, even Essex
was forced to admit to Henry IV that 'I am very ashamed that we English have
so soon quitted your Majesty's service'.[13]

An account of other military campaigns in France which concentrated on
the military heroism, the martial prowess and true nobility of the commander
and blamed his failure on the failings and fallings-out of others had an obvious
value here. In the play, as we have seen, Talbot failed because York and Somerset
refused to come to his aid, and they did so because they personally loathed one
another. Earlier in the play, Talbot's first capture by the enemy had been blamed
on the perennial debates and disputes amongst the counsellors about what sort
of war this was and how best to fight it. Of course, we know that a major proponent of cautious war-making on the cheap, of the sort derided in the play, and,
indeed, the major cause of the lack of support and reinforcement for Essex at
Rouen, was the queen herself. In the play the disastrous effects of such pusillanimous doubts and disagreements were expressed, as so often, through the
deep code of evil counsel. But either way, to provide such an analysis of what
had gone wrong was also, by implication at least, to provide – in the suppression of the feuds and factious disputes of the council and nobility and an end
to futile debate about the nature and ends of the war – a recipe for future
success.

On this account, then, the play might be taken not merely as a commentary
on recent events and the seemingly disastrous course of the war effort over the
past few months, but also as something of an exercise in Essexian propaganda,
designed to validate the earl's view of himself, and of the war, and, by vindicating

Essex's conduct at Rouen and placing the blame for the ultimate failure of that enterprise elsewhere, to issue a warning about what was likely to happen, if the counsel proffered in the play went unheeded and divisions within the regime about the nature, conduct and aims of the war went unaddressed.

But perhaps one can go further still. It is true that Essex's brother Walter had died during the siege and that the queen, for one, had been worried about Essex's safety, but there was another recent event in the war against Spain that bore a much closer resemblance to the depiction of the death of Talbot and his son staged in the play, and that was the death of Sir Richard Grenville on the *Revenge*. That event had been the subject of a recent pamphlet by none other than Sir Walter Raleigh himself, published late in 1591. Again, it seems, we have an event of some notoriety, again concerned with the conduct of the war against Spain.

Like Talbot in the play, Grenville found himself confronted by impossible odds and 'utterly refused to turn from the enemy, alleging that he would rather choose to die than dishonour himself, his country and her majesty's ship, persuading his company that he would pass through the two squadrons in despite of them and enforce those of the Seville to give him way'. Even Raleigh was forced to concede that 'the other course had been the better ... notwithstanding out of the greatness of his mind, he [Grenville] could not be persuaded'.[14] Not only that, but after a savage combat against overwhelming odds, when it became obvious 'that himself and the ship must needs be possessed by the enemy, who were now cast in a ring round about him', Grenville decided to 'split and sink the ship that thereby nothing might remain of glory or victory to the Spaniards'. There ensued a debate with the master gunner and the surviving members of the crew about the rights and wrongs of resistance to the death. Grenville, Talbot-like, tried to 'persuade the company, or as many as he could induce, to yield themselves unto God and to the mercy of none else, but as they had, like valiant resolute men, repulsed so many enemies, they should not now shorten the honour of their nation, by prolonging their own lives for a few hours, or a few days'. The master gunner readily concurred, but the captain and the master refused. Grenville stuck to his guns, maintaining 'that the Spaniards should never glory to have taken one ship of her majesty's, seeing they had so long and so notably defended themselves'. His position, however, was undercut by the captain and master. The latter went off to negotiate terms with the Spanish, while the captain remained behind to win over 'the greater party' of the crew. A deal was struck and, in the face of Grenville's continued protests, and the threatened suicide of the master gunner, what was left of the *Revenge* and her crew, the mortally wounded Grenville amongst them, surrendered to the Spanish.[15]

Here, then, is another example of desperate courage in the face of insurmountable odds; featuring appeals to honour and reputation and a series of debates about the relative merits of flight rather than of hopeless resistance, and of resistance to the death rather than surrender in the face of certain defeat. The parallels between Raleigh's account of Grenville's fate on the *Revenge* and the play's account of the death of Talbot and his son are patent. Raleigh's pamphlet, just like the newsbook account of events at Rouen of September/October 1591, legitimised itself as a response to 'rumours diversely spread, as well in England as in the Low Countries'.[16] What we have here, then, is another instance of the way in which the play is seeking to pick up on, reflect and comment upon recent events of great popular interest, investing the action on stage with a currency, an intensely contemporary set of resonances and associations, of precisely the sort to maximise the interest of the paying public. The play, on this view, was seeking to feed off and exploit a penumbra of rumour, a buzz of interest surrounding spectacular recent incidents in the war against Spain and the Catholic League.

Raleigh's account of the fate of Grenville and the *Revenge* was designed, of course, to turn a defeat, indeed something of a mini-disaster, into a triumph. To do so, it uses precisely the same rhetorical means – the acknowledgement of a glorious death against insuperable odds as the final proof of martial honour, true nobility and service to queen and country – that the play deploys to trans-form the death of Talbot into a fit topic for celebration rather than for regret, recrimination or embarrassment. In so doing, Raleigh sets the engagement that cost Grenville his life and the queen's navy the *Revenge* in the context of recent English martial exploits against the Spanish. Predictably enough, Raleigh starts with the Armada, an event that, just like their engagement with the *Revenge*, the Spaniards had trumpeted throughout Europe as a victory rather than the crushing defeat it, in fact, turned out to be. Next comes Drake's ravaging of New Spain with just 800 men. Raleigh ends with the expedition of Sir John Norris 'to the gates of Lisbon'.[17] That little list opens the pamphlet. It closes with a long defence of 'the justice of our cause against the ambitious and bloody pretenses of the Spaniard, who, seeking to devour all nations, are themselves devoured. A manifest testimony how unjust and displeasing their attempts are in the sight of God, who hath pleased to witness, by the success of their affairs, his mislike of their bloody and injurious designs, purposed and practised against all Christian princes, over whom they seek unlawful and ungodly rule and empirey'.[18] But, Raleigh concluded, the Spanish bid for world domination and universal monarchy was doomed to fail, foiled in large part by the English, who had 'discovered to the world' the 'weakness' of the Spanish by the 'overthrows and dishonours' of their 'forces at home, abroad, in Europe, in India, by sea and land'.[19]

The tract ends with a passage of patriotic rant and of veiled counsel to the queen. 'It hath ever to this day pleased God to prosper and defend her majesty, to break the purposes of malicious enemies, of forsworn traitors and of unjust practices and invasion. She hath ever been honoured of the worthiest kings, served by faithful subjects and shall, by the favour of God, resist, repel and confound all whatsoever attempts against her sacred person or kingdom.'[20]

This, of course, is precisely not how the play ends. Talbot's death is a triumph of sorts; certainly it is a vindication of his true nobility, martial prowess and honour and, as such, proof positive of his (and Essex's) view of the integral relationship between, indeed of the moral equivalence of, service to the crown in war, virtue and honour. But at the play's end the canker of internal division and personal rivalry remains and, Queen Margaret and her soon to be paramour, Suffolk, are shown, to anyone familiar with the action of 2 and 3, poised to plunge the kingdom further into chaos, disorder and defeat. And, of course, the most notorious contemporary example of the sort of rancorous personal rivalry and internal dissension portrayed in the play was the continuing feud between Raleigh and Essex.

Remarkably, the litany of English martial exploits against Spain with which Raleigh opened his account of the fate of Grenville and the *Revenge* contained a favourable mention of Raleigh's arch-rival Essex, for his part in the Portugal expedition; 'where the earl of Essex himself and other valiant gentlemen braved the city of Lisbon, encamped at the very gates'.[21] More than a mere aside, this passage may well have presaged what Hammer describes as 'an extraordinary rapprochement between the two men, who were once such bitter rivals'.[22] Raleigh needed to end his feud with Essex because he was suddenly vulnerable at court, due to his secret marriage to Elizabeth Throckmorton in November 1591. Essex needed to end his feud with Raleigh because only by doing so could he convince the queen that he had turned over a new leaf and was now fit to start a career as more than a mere favourite; rather as a soldier, statesman and Privy Counsellor. (Essex was finally admitted to the Council in February 1593.)[23] On 10 April 1592 Essex served as the godfather to Raleigh's daughter. A fortnight later, at the St George's Day celebration, in a public demonstration that their feud was well and truly over, Essex nominated Raleigh as a knight of the Garter.

It is perhaps worth recalling here the speech in praise of the Order of the Garter delivered by Talbot in *I Henry VI*. Talbot presents the order as giving vivid expression to the 'intimate association of martial honour with nobility and virtue' that Paul Hammer identifies at the heart of Essex's political and moral credo.[24] Stripping the Garter from the leg of the coward Fastolfe, Talbot explains to the assembled company, 'when first this order was ordained, my lords,/Knights of the Garter were of noble birth,/Valiant and virtuous, full of haughty courage,/Such as were grown to credit in the wars' [Pt. I, IV, i, 33–38]. Such a one was Talbot, his status as such sealed by his conduct and death in France; such a one Essex himself claimed to be, his status sealed by his conduct at Lisbon and now at Rouen. Such a one, too, was Raleigh, his status as such asserted in and through his praise for (and appropriation of) the heroic death of Grenville and sealed by Essex's nomination of him as a member of the very Order of the Garter praised in such extravagant terms by Talbot.

But Raleigh was not the only youngish courtier/aristocrat up for the Order of the Garter in that year. Actually elected was none other than Gilbert Talbot, seventh earl of Shrewsbury, a descendant of, and natural referent for, the Talbot depicted in the play, upon whose elaborate (and erroneous) concatenation of titles Lucy places such stress in the play. At this point, as Paul Hammer points out, Talbot was a trusted (both local and national) associate of the earl of Essex.[25] As Alexander Leggatt observes, when Lucy hails the death of the Talbots with the prediction that 'from their ashes shall be rear'd/A Phoenix that shall make all France afeard' [Pt. I, IV, vii, 92–93], within the world of the play, 'the prophecy comes to nothing'.[26] Instead, it reaches out across the decades, from the past being staged in the world of the play, into the present, to be fulfilled by Talbot's natural successors, the current champions of English martial valour – like, we might surmise, the earl of Essex or Sir Walter Raleigh or indeed Gilbert Talbot and the knot of young aristocrats gathered around Essex. For, as Hammer observes, in the early 1590s Essex found himself at the head of 'as impressive a group of noblemen as any seen in the sixteenth century . . . Many of these peers were young men who shared Essex's desire for martial glory and looked to him as the realm's military leader'. Amongst them was Gilbert Talbot, seventh earl of Shrewsbury, whose ancestor's martial virtue and tragic end was, of course, being so memorably evoked in the play.[27]

In the light of all this it is tempting to argue that the play represents a part of a political strategy; a justification for actions past and a preparation of opinion for alignments and actions to come, most particularly for the emergent alliance between Raleigh and Essex. For all their previously rancorous relations, both men now had a claim to what Talbot termed the 'sacred name of knights' [Pt. I, IV, i, 40] (of the Garter); both were men 'grown to credit in the wars' and in the service of the crown; and both were dedicated to the vigorous prosecution of the war against an implacable Spanish foe, in all theatres and by all available means. In their union lay the answer to the problems posed by the play, which, as we have seen, posited the factional and personal rivalries of the counsellors and soldiers, and disagreements about what sort of war this was and how best to fight it, as the major threats to the successful prosecution of the war, the integrity of the regime, and the safety of the realm.

In this regard it is worth remembering that at this point in his career Essex was still posing as the champion of the godly. The portrait of the corrupt, ambitious and overbearing prelate, Winchester, and of his feud with that experienced governor Gloucester, had anti-Whitgiftian resonances that any clued-up member of the audience would have been bound to pick up. In addition, the threat of female rule, which in 2 and 3 *Henry VI* had been located somewhere near the centre of the regime, had here been associated unequivocally with popery, in ways entirely absent from the earlier plays. Expelled from England, in this play these peccant humours were fairly sytematically assimilated to the great national enemy, the French. Central thematic and ideological elements from the earlier Henry VI plays were hence being rearranged to create here a pitch for a puritan-friendly, anti-popish war party, with the hero-figures Raleigh and Essex somewhere near its head. These of course were elements entirely missing from 2 and 3 Henry VI.

There, the transition from an older generation of peers and counsellors, personified by Gloucester as the epitome of virtue, loyalty and good counsel, to a younger generation of ambitious young aristocrats, personified by the likes of Suffolk, Somerset and York, was portrayed as a moment of maximum danger, as the virtue of a passing generation was displaced by the factious ambition and corruption of an emergent claque of younger men. When this change was compounded by an emergent dispute over the succession, the result was the descent into moral and political chaos and dynastic civil war delineated in the later stages of part II and throughout part III. All of which spoke pretty directly to that moment in the late 1580s and very early 1590s when so many of the dominant figures of the high Elizabethan regime – such as Leicester, Walsingham, Mildmay, Warwick and Bedford – started to drop like flies, and fractious young men like Essex and Raleigh jostled to replace them. In 1 Henry VI, however, at least some of the older generation – Gloucester again and, of course, Beaufort – were painted in an altogether darker hue and the transition to a younger generation emerged as a moment, not only of danger, but also, potentially at least, if not of opportunity, then certainly of choice. Either those assuming command in court, council and camp could (with Talbot) come together, bury their personal rivalries and feuds and embrace an aggressive prosecution of the war, or else (with Suffolk, Somerset and York) they could continue both to bicker amongst themselves and to disagree about how to fight the war. In the former event all might yet be well. In the latter, the world would (continue to) go to hell, if not in a handbasket, then certainly in a welter of defeat abroad, and factional conflict, and finally (dynastic) civil war, at home.

As Hammer points out, the political moment encapsulated here was of very brief duration. By May, news of Raleigh's marriage had broken and he found himself first in prison and then banned for years from court. Rapidly thereafter, under the influence of the queen, and as part of his rebranding of himself as a sober counsellor rather than as a headstrong firebrand and favourite, Essex came to a rapprochement with Whitgift.[28] But on the current argument, the play remains as testimony to, and, at least in part, a product of, a crucial political conjuncture in the career of the earl of Essex and the course of English policy and politics in the early 1590s. If there is anything to the reading essayed above, it also stands as testimony to the very close links between a variety of media – the pamphlet press, the popular stage, news and rumour, disseminated by word of mouth and in manuscript as well as in print – and court politics, diplomacy and the conduct of the war. After all, the history play had an inherent capacity, while seemingly dealing exclusively with the past, to evoke, parallel and comment upon topics of enormous current interest; topics that, like the career of Essex, the tenor of court politics, the feuds between Burghley and Whitgift, or Raleigh and Essex, the likely course of the succession and the conduct of the war, were located at the very centre both of the *arcana imperii* and of the interests of the populace. As such, the history play provided the perfect vehicle to get certain political messages across, while attracting some very large audiences and thus turning a handy profit. The result was not only a win–win situation for all those involved in the production of the play, but also the very complex interplay between contemporary politics and 'history,' between the stage and the conduct of court and popular politics, between rumour, the pamphlet press and dramatic performance, described above.

On the current reading, the often very close correspondences and reso-nances of at least some of the events staged in the play with immediately contemporary happenings and concerns served to locate the action of the play on the cusp between the immediate past, the present and the future. As we have seen, central elements in parts II and III had similarly placed the action of those plays within that same liminal space. Just where, on that continuum, the action of the plays was located was, of course, left up to the individual viewer, but whereas in parts II and III, wherever the action of the play was temporally positioned, the perspective offered, both on the current conjuncture and on the immediate future, was unremittingly dark, in part I the audience (and indeed the queen and her counsellors) were given a sort of choice.

For whether the current conjuncture ended in the moral and political melt-down depicted in parts II and II or in an altogether happier outcome – presaged by the defeat and death of Puzel, rather than by that of Talbot – depended on how central figures in the regime reacted to their current circumstances and to the message of this play. If the English elite, the crown and its counsellors, heeded the warning of the play, and indeed of 'history,' forgot old enmities, definitively rejected popery, both at home and abroad, and united around a vigorous prosecution of the war against a demonic foreign enemy, then all might yet be well. The sacrifices of Talbot (of Grenville, or indeed of Essex's brother) might not be in vain, and the demonically inspired enemies of the English crown – here the Spanish and the Catholic League – might yet be sent the way of Puzel. But for that to happen, unlike Henry VI, the queen would have to cease listening to the siren song of a peace to be concluded with a more or less overtly demonic (popish) enemy, and stop allowing, enabling, indeed perpetuating, the personal and factional rivalries of her commanders and advisors; unlike Puzel, she would have to put an end to a thoroughly unnatural female meddling in military affairs, and, unlike Henry VI, commit unequivocally to as aggressive a prosecution of the war as possible, in the process ceding control of the war effort to her most steadfast, honourable and virtuous commanders. If that happened all of the corrupting, satanic, Antichristian and popish elements surrounding not merely Puzel and the French but also Cardinal Beaufort, Suffolk and, as an audience familiar with the action of parts II and III would know, Queen Margaret, could be kept successfully at bay; left to operate on the other side of the binary divide that (still, just) separated an honourable, virtuous and godly England from her foreign, popish enemies. If not, as anyone who could recall the action of parts II and III would have been only too well aware, all hell would break loose again. Just as a series of Catholic tracts had warned, and indeed as the likes of Parsons and his close ally and translator Richard Verstegan were about to warn again, what had happened to England under Henry VI could happen again, as the house of Tudor followed the house of Lancaster into the dustbin of history, ending with neither a bang nor a whimper, but rather with another descent into protracted and bloody dynastic and, this time around, confessional, civil war.

CHAPTER 6

Richard III: political ends, providential means

1 Henry VI showed how the dreadful outcomes both depicted and predicted in parts II and III might be avoided in the here and now. In other words, the way of escaping the political meltdown, the complete collapse of political order and loss of legitimacy, staged in *2 and 3 Henry VI*, was not to go there in the first place but rather to avoid such outcomes in the future through the adoption of certain political courses in the present. But if *1 Henry VI* imposed a sort of closure on the two earlier plays by suggesting how the outcomes depicted therein might have been avoided, *Richard III* imposed a rather more conventional sense of an ending, by depicting what actually happened next. In so doing it departed from the modes of exposition and explanation adopted in the *Henry VI* plays, which had told a largely political, indeed a politique, story, about how weak monarchy, excessive female influence over the levers of power, noble faction, defeat in foreign war and an increasingly disputed succession, had driven a process of moral and political decline until all claims to monarchical legitimacy, honour or nobility had been called into the most radical question, and politics had become a desperate struggle for self-preservation, power and revenge, to be pursued by any and every available means. Insofar as the intervention of providence in human affairs had been staged in those plays, it had not been shown shaping the overall structure of events; certainly not bringing the story to any sort of stable or just conclusion, but rather intervening occasionally to shape the fates of particular malefactors, bringing to light peculiarly egregious crimes and criminals – like the murder of Gloucester by Cardinal Beaufort. Similarly, while the devil had been an intermittently active presence, his role had been a distinctly limited one – leading the reprobate Winchester into a damning deathbed desperation and embroiling unruly women like the duchess of Suffolk or Puzel in the sin of witchcraft. As for the role of portents or prophecy, that had been extremely minor; the vision of the three suns in *3 Henry VI* while indubitably a wonder, served only to highlight the self-delusion of the sons of York, as they rushed off to meet their fate.

That all changed in *Richard III*, where providence, portents and prophecy take on a central role in the workings of the plot and the shaping of events. Not that *Richard III* altogether abandons the politique mode of analysis of politics as process, as the sum total of the interactions of various political agents all pursuing their various ends in and through the modes and methods of manoeuvre appropriate to a personal monarchy. Far from it. As Donald Watson observes, 'the play provides us with essentially two approaches to explaining Richard's triumph, [and, one might add, his fall] one on the level of providential ritual and the other through the making and unmaking of political factions'. 'Usually regarded as a brilliantly lurid melodrama', as Watson reminds us, the play is also about politics, indeed about tyranny, providing a vision of 'how power might work', and of how a tyrant might emerge, 'within a monarchy not totally unlike' that of late Elizabethan England.[1]

Working, as it were, from both the inside and the outside, the play privileges neither of these modes of explanation but rather seeks to fit the one within the other. It does that from the outside through the overarching structures of the plot, and the providential and prophetic framework into which the play induces its audience to fit the action and, from the inside, through the interior monologue, maintained throughout by Richard III himself, which constitutes a running commentary upon his career both as a Machiavel and as a reprobate soul doomed, first to discharge the purposes of a just and merciful God, and then to suffer the pangs of hell for his pains. Over the course of the play, Richard's tyranny thus emerges not only as the problem – the natural consequence of the processes of political conflict, of moral and political decline, staged in the *Henry VI* plays – but also as the solution; that is to say, as the enabling, both practical and providential, grounds for the re-emergence (in the rule of the future Henry VII) of political and moral legitimacy.

The making of a Machiavel

In a series of soliloquies towards the end of *3 Henry VI*, and at the outset of *Richard III*, Richard announces himself as the atheistical Machiavel whose machinations will dominate the latter play and he does so in ways that make it clear that the roots of his emergence as such a monstrous creature are both political, that is to say, entirely explicable in terms of the effects of the moral and political meltdown depicted in *2* and *3 Henry VI*, and also providential, his status as a monster announced, and indeed in some sense caused, by his monstrous birth and prodigiously deformed body.

The process starts with a long soliloquy in *3 Henry VI* made just after Edward has announced his intention to marry the widow Grey and the news of Henry VI's final capture has arrived. At the end of that speech Richard famously declares that 'I can smile and murder whiles I smile,/And cry "Content!" to that which grieves my heart,/And wet my cheeks with artificial tears,/And frame my face to all occasions./I'll drown more sailors than the mermaid shall,/I'll slay more gazers than the basilisk,/I'll play the orator as well as Nestor,/Deceive more slyly than Ulysses could,/And, like a Sinon, take another Troy./I can add colours to the chameleon,/Change shapes with Proteus for advantages,/And set the murderous Machiavel to school./Can I do this, and cannot get a crown?/ Tut, were it farther off, I'll pluck it down' [Pt. III, III, ii, 181–95]. As a number of commentators have noted, we are being plunged here into the moral and political universe of *The treatise of treasons* and of *Leicester's commonwealth* and *Cecil's*. The characters by which Richard determines to shape his own behaviour – Catiline, Ulysses, Sinon, Machiavel – are, of course, precisely the same as those used in *The treatise* to characterise the conduct of Cecil and Bacon and later in *Leicester's commonwealth* that of Leicester himself.[2]

On the face of it civil war has taught Richard the dark arts of factional struggle and violent political intrigue. Richard, having learned what he takes to be the rules of that game, now vows to continue to play by them, even after the civil war has ended. In Richard we see a pared-down will to power, uninformed and unconstrained by any considerations of right or justice or honour. Richard's depravity is, then, a logical *terminus ad quem* for the political and moral declension delineated throughout 2 and 3 *Henry VI*. As Howard and Rackin observe, alone of the other protagonists, Richard extracts a rounded philosophy of life, a completed self-image, from the dissolution of all the basic bonds of human society that the civil war has produced.[3] To quote John Danby, 'it is only in Richard – the great wearer of masks – that the corruption of his time is made aware of itself. This is the ambiguity of his role: to be the logical outcome of his society, and yet a pariah rejected by that society.'[4]

Monstrous bodies and providential signs

However, as the middle portions of Richard's speech at the end of 3 *Henry VI*, show, Richard's emergence as an entirely amoral Machiavel is presented not only as a function of the political circumstances that have formed him, but also of his physical deformity. Gingerly, towards the end of 3 *Henry VI,* and then more and more explicitly throughout *Richard III*, a providential interpretation is being imposed on, or rather extracted out of, Richard's deformed body. When Richard dispatches Henry VI in the Tower the saintly king cites Richard's monstrous birth and the prodigies that had attended it as marking him off as an agent of darkness. This tirade elicits from Richard the desperate response 'I'll hear no more! Die prophet in thy speech'– at which he stabs Henry to death. As Robert G. Hunter observes, it is as though 'Richard kills Henry in order to make him stop talking – stop telling Richard that he is indeed predestined to evil, a creature without freedom.'[5] Indeed, since Richard persistently 'boasts of choosing to be what he is', there is an element of free will being suggested here, but only, Hunter points out, 'in a context that limits' that 'freedom almost to the point of making it disappear.'[6] Thus Richard's very next

line – 'for this among the rest was I ordained' [3 *Henry VI*, V, vi, 44–57] – seems
to accept precisely the fate that Henry has just prophesied for him. A point he
drives home by returning again to the topic of his own prodigious, indeed
monstrous, birth. 'For I have often heard my mother say/I came into the world
with my legs forward./Had I not reason, think ye, to make haste,/And seek
their ruin that usurped our right?/The midwife wondered and the women
cried,/"O, Jesus bless us, he is born with teeth!"/And so I was, which plainly
signified/That I should snarl, and bite and play the dog.' As if to make good that
claim, he then proceeds to outline, for himself and for us, his plan to rid himself
of his brother Clarence, the next obstacle on his path to the throne [Pt. III, V,
vi, 67–93].

Here, then, Richard's physical deformity is certainly being used, along with
the deformed condition of the kingdom, to provide an explanation of the
deformation of his character and of his final emergence as an atheistical
Machiavel. As Womersley puts it, Richard 'is created by these times, and in his
deformity, he is proper to them.'[7] But his deformity is also being used to mark
that emergence as a providentially charged, prophetically loaded or significant,
event; something that might be taken to link the quotidian contingencies, the
happenstance of sublunary political manoeuvre in a fallen world depicted
throughout 2 and 3 *Henry VI*, to the higher purposes of unseen powers; the
interaction between 'heaven' and 'hell' that had first shaped Richard's body and
then 'made crook'd his mind in answer to it.'

As the action of *Richard III* unfolds, Richard is increasingly seen as a
demonic figure. For the Lady Anne he is a 'fiend' conjured by a 'black magi-
cian'; 'a dreadful minister of hell'; a 'foul devil'. It is, she claims, 'wonderful
when devils tell the truth'. He is a 'diffus'd infection of a man'; 'cursed' [I, ii, 34,
46, 50, 72–73, 78, 80]. This is a status also marked by the language of the bestial
and the monstrous. Again, Anne calls him a 'foul toad', a 'hedgehog'; he is
worse than a 'beast' [I, ii, 150, 104, 71]. This pattern of denunciation, started
by Henry VI's daughter-in-law is carried on by his widow, Queen Margaret.
For her Richard is a 'devil' 'a cacodemon' [I, iii, 117, 143], 'hell's black intelli-
gencer' [IV. iv, 71], a 'dog', upon whom 'sin, death and hell have set their
marks' and 'all their ministers attend' [I, iii, 288–93]. Later, Margaret tells the
duchess of York that 'from forth the kennel of thy womb hath crept/A hell-
hound that doth hunt us all to death . . . That foul defacer of God's handiwork/
Thy womb let loose to chase us to our graves' [IV, iv, 47–54]. Even Richard's
mother shares Margaret's vision of her own 'accursed womb' as 'the bed of
death' which had 'hatch'd' a 'cockatrice' 'whose unavoided eye is murderous'
[IV, i, 53–55].

On this account, Richard is both less and more than human; he is prodigious, albeit prodigiously evil, indeed genuinely satanic, and thus a creature
best described as the product of an unnatural combination of the human and

the bestial. As such, his rise to power operates as the means whereby the prophetic and the providential enters, and comes to dominate, the account of politics being offered to us in the play. That is to say, precisely at the same point that the delegitimation of politics has reached its nadir, in the character of Richard, the atheistical Machiavel, providence, in the person of Richard, the monstrous prodigy, re-enters to put things back together again.

Signs and prophecies

From the moment he is picked out by the dying Henry VI, Richard's career is attended and marked by a series of providential signs and prophecies, which in fact structure the action of *Richard III*, to an extent unparalleled in the *Henry VI* plays. These range from the corpse of Henry bleeding afresh in the presence of the man who had killed it, through Clarence's premonitory nightmare immediately before his murder, Stanley's dream in which 'a boar had razed off his helm' and indeed Richard's own nightmare on the night before Bosworth. At this point it is also worth noting that, just like freshly bleeding corpses,[8] dreams and even the reported testimony of ghosts could play a role in the contemporary judicial process if they were deemed to have helped uncover previously hidden crimes or identify previously unknown felons. Thus the play is enlisting here a series of contemporary beliefs about the role of providence, miracles, dreams, ghosts and even the dead, in bringing previously unknown crimes to light and previously unidentified murderers to book.[9] As Emrys Jones observes, through Clarence's dream, and we might add through Margaret's prophecies, the audience, if not the characters in the play, is reminded 'of the outermost circle of spiritual reality – the supernatural order of the four last things, death, judgement, heaven and hell'.[10]

But if dreams tend to operate though the men, prophecies and curses emanate from the women, indeed, for the most part, from that most tainted of sources, Queen Margaret. Starting with King Edward, she outlines the fates awaiting all the central figures in the regime. The objects of these ravings take them, understandably, to be just that, the 'frantic' curses of a 'lunatic' woman, driven to despair and beyond by grief and the desire for revenge. But, in fact, all these prophecies turn out to be true, as each of their victims or subjects comes, in their turn, to admit.

Rivers, Grey and Vaughan, confronting death at Pomfret, are the first to do so. Thus Grey tells Rivers that 'now Margaret's curse is fall'n upon our heads,/ When she exclaimed on Hastings, you and I,/For standing by when Richard stabb'd her son'. Rivers replies by recalling: 'Then cursed she Richard; then cursed she Buckingham;/Then cursed she Hastings. Oh, remember, God,/To hear her prayer for them, as now for us' [III, iii, 15–20]. The next to feel the full force of Margaret's powers as a seer is Hastings. At the last he blames himself for heedlessly ignoring the warnings provided by Stanley's dream and other recent portents, before concluding 'O Margaret, Margaret, now thy heavy curse/Is lighted on poor Hastings' wretched head' [III, iv, 80–92].

By Act IV it is Edward's widow Elizabeth who is being forced to concede that Margaret had been right all along. Next to go, in Act V, is Buckingham, who meets his end with Margaret's prophecy on his mind and lips [V, i, 25–29]. But Buckingham's end is rendered doubly piquant since it takes place on All Souls' Day, the very 'day which, in King Edward's time,/I wished might fall on me when I was found/False to his children and his wife's allies./This is the day wherein I wish'd to fall.' No mere accident, this fatal coincidence proves, Buckingham laments, that 'That high All-seer which I dallied with/Hath turned my feigned prayer on my head,/And given in earnest what I begged in jest./Thus doth He force the swords of wicked men/To turn their own points in their masters' bosoms' [V, i, 11–24]. While Buckingham falls victim to a hypocritical prayer intended to mask his real intentions from his enemies, so the Lady Anne falls victim to a curse of her own, directed against Richard, but retroactively enforced upon herself [IV, i, 70–84].

There is a certain symmetry or balance being established here; one rendered explicit in the semi-liturgical exchanges between Margaret, the duchess of York, and Queen Elizabeth in Act IV, scene iv. 'Plantagenet doth quit Plantagenet;/Edward for Edward pays a dying debt.' 'I had an Edward, till a Richard killed him;/I had a husband, till a Richard killed him./Thou hadst an Edward, till a Richard killed him;/Thou hadst a Richard, till a Richard killed him.' Behind the symmetry of these deaths, and throughout these incantatory, prayer-like lines, lies, of course, the figure of Richard. It is his depredations, wrought upon Yorkist and Lancastrian alike, that have produced these perfectly symmetrical equivalences of misery and death [IV, iv, 20–21, 40–45].

Now at the end, the houses of Lancaster and York, personified by these three grieving, cursing women, have indeed come together to curse Richard to hell. The scene ends with the duchess of York and Elizabeth hurrying off, as the duchess puts it, 'to smother my damned son' 'in the breath of bitter words' [IV, iv, 116–17, 133–34].

On the one hand, for all the intense religiosity of Margaret's imagery – 'Earth gapes, hell burns, fiends roar, saints pray,/To have him suddenly convey'd from hence' [IV. iv, 75–76] – there is nothing very Christian about all this. The figure of Margaret is based on the allegorical (and wholly pagan) figure of Revenge.[11] Set in Christian terms, Margaret's account of how to curse represents a sort of inversion, a (demonic?) parody of the forms and functions of intercessory prayer. In answer to Elizabeth's request to 'teach me how to curse mine enemies' Margaret replies 'Forbear to sleep at night, and fast the day;/Compare dead happiness with living woe;/Think that thy babes were sweeter than they were,/And he that slew them fouler than he is./Bettering thy loss makes the bad causer worse./Revolving this will teach thee how to curse' [IV, iv, 118–23].

Here is Margaret as anti-nun; a person separated from the world, fasting, mortifying the flesh, engaging in constant contemplation and fervent prayer, but all of this dedicated to the destruction of her enemies and designed to consign human souls not to heaven, but to hell, and all in order to feed her own unappeasable thirst for revenge. If these plays do indeed consign Henry VI to heaven it would seem unlikely that, even in retreat from the vanities of the world and the pursuit of power, his wife will be joining him there any time soon.[12] However, as Harold Brooks observes, while 'the old type of vengeance, itself a new crime, perpetuating the Senecan chain of wrong and curse on royal houses, is embodied in her', in the overall argument of the play, 'when Richmond is made the minister of chastisement', 'it is superseded by vengeance which is God's, is just and calls for no further vengeance'.[13]

The audience as 'high all-seer'

But if Margaret's black devotions are unlikely to do her any great spiritual good, they provide the main means through which the play reintroduces providence into the action, and indeed the consciousness of the audience, as a shaping force in events.

It is notorious that the play's prime interest, its major claim on the attention of at least modern audiences, has not in fact resided so much in its status as a theatre of God's judgements as in its staging of Richard's Machiavellian style of political manoeuvre. This dominates the early stages of the play. Here, as we have seen, we are back in the mental and moral universe of *The treatise of treasons* or *Leicester's commonwealth* with the play showing us Richard's modus operandi as an atheistical Machiavel and emergent tyrant, both from the inside and the outside, from both his perspective and from that of his victims.

Throughout, Richard announces his intentions to the audience, explaining his purposes and the course and nature of his plans, while the action of the play shows him putting those plans into action. 'I do the wrong, and first begin the brawl./The secret mischiefs that I set abroach/I lay unto the grievous charge of others . . . But then I sigh, and with a piece of scripture,/Tell them that God bids us do good for evil:/And thus I clothe my naked villainy/With odd old ends, stol'n forth of Holy Writ,/And seem a saint when I most play the devil' [I, iii, 323–37]. The fun, then, is to see through him, while at the same time watching him bend the other characters to his will.

Here is *Leicester's commonwealth* rendered, as it were, three-dimensional and transparent, as we get to watch both the inner workings of the Machiavel's mind, and the outward effects of his machinations on others. Or to put it another way, here is politics rendered, as Womersley puts it, 'as itself a kind of drama'. Here is Richard as the supreme political dramatist, writing his own script and, through the skill and magnetism of his performance, inducing the other characters to play the parts he has devised for them to the letter.[14]

Let into Richard's secrets, the audience gets to share his sense of superiority over the other characters, while marvelling at his political skill and moral depravity, at the sheer energy and attack, of his performance of his various selves or personae. But at the same time they know that the (guilty) pleasure they are taking in all this is ultimately licit, because moral and political closure is at hand. Precisely because the character they are watching is Richard III, and because, as Emrys Jones observes, for an Elizabethan audience 'the real significance of Richard III was his destined role as antagonist to Richmond/Henry VII',[15] the audience also knows that not only is Richard himself going to come to a very bad end indeed, but that this time we are dealing not with just another villain meeting his just deserts at the hand of providence; this time, Richard's end will usher in a real end to the moral and political chaos staged in this and the preceding plays.

The audience is thus placed both within and above the action. They are able to see what is happening both between the characters and within them. The effect here is at once to draw the audience into the inner workings of the plot and to distance them from it. The insights the play offers into Richard's purposes and plans heightens the epistemological privileges of spectatorship, conferring on the audience what Harry Berger Jr has memorably termed 'the voyeuristic power of divine judgement'.[16] Thus placed in the position of providence, of Buckingham's 'high All-seer', the audience are rendered the more susceptible to the providential reading of the action inscribed in the play and made available to them through the prophetic commentary provided both by the chorus of grieving and cursing woman and by the dream lives of some of the men. If the audience's insight into Richard's inner purposes gives them an advantage over the other characters, so their capacity to view the action from these providential and prophetic perspectives gives them an advantage over that ultimate master of ceremonies, Richard himself. Their total, indeed, at least potentially, totalising, view of the action, gives them a similar advantage over the seers and prophets in the play, even the most perceptive of whom can achieve only a partial view of proceedings.[17]

Viewing the puny attempts of the characters on stage to work their wills, achieve their ends, or protect their interests in the everyday world of political reality, competition and conflict, as it were from above, the audience can construct, out of the materials, the admittedly rather heavy-handed hints and prompts, provided by the play, a metanarrative that transcends the purposes and ends of any of the characters on view; a metanarrative that they can then link to the achievement of some (previously unseen or unrealised) higher moral purpose or greater good. In short, they can produce an account of what they are watching, or have just watched, that is genuinely providential; one, moreover, that is all the more convincing and compelling for having been their own creation.

Such an outcome is, of course, further encouraged or enabled by the beliefs about providence, murder and retribution (both human and divine) which many members of the audience are likely to have brought with them to the play. Here, of course, the tropes of the bleeding corpse or of the premonitory dream spring immediately to mind, if only because of the care with which the play enlists them to confirm its essentially providential reading of the events it is staging. In this way, the commonplace assumptions of the audience about the moral structure of the world, about right and wrong, about sin, providence, divine justice and retribution, are inserted into the amoral world conjured by the play, and its immediate predecessors. Thus, after the political and moral upheavals of the Wars of the Roses, is normal service to be resumed, and a world of political and moral inversion to be turned the right way up. But, in theatrical terms, this transformation is effected not so much by 'providence' as through the 'spontaneous' reactions of the audience, as the play elicits and constructs those reactions. And thus, too, are the play's two major levels or layers of action and interpretation, the political and the providential, brought together.

Ambiguities of 'evil counsel'

What the play shows Richard doing in history is remarkably similar to what the Catholic tracts had shown Cecil and Bacon, Leicester and then Burghley again doing in the present. What Leicester was presented as planning to do, and Burghley successfully did, to Mary, queen of Scots, Richard is shown doing to Clarence: inducing the current incumbent to remove the major obstacle on his own path to the crown [I, i, 32–40].

Like that of Leicester or Cecil, Richard's plan revolves around the exploitation of existing divisions within the realm and regime. By setting the aristocracy against one another he removes political as well as dynastic obstacles, in the process building a faction and eliminating his enemies. Again, just as in the Catholic tracts, the divide between the old aristocracy and new men and low-born favourites is central. Here the crucial figures are the queen and her recently ennobled relatives.

Richard harps, too, upon the corrupting effects of too much feminine influence on the centre of power. Thus he tells Clarence on his way to the Tower that 'this it is, when men are ruled by women:/'Tis not the King that sends you to the Tower;/My lady Grey, his wife, Clarence, 'tis she/That tempers him to this extremity./Was it not she, and that good man of worship,/Anthony Woodeville, her brother there,/That made him send Lord Hastings to the Tower,/From whence this present day he is delivered?/We are not safe, Clarence; we are not safe.' Hastings, Clarence concurs, has only gained his liberty by playing the 'humble suppliant' to the king's mistress, Mistress Shore. 'I'll tell you what', replies Richard, 'I think it is our way,/If we will keep him in favour with the King,/To be her men, and wear her livery./The jealous o'erworn widow and herself,/Since that our brother dubbed them gentlewomen,/Are mighty gossips in our monarchy' [I, i, 62–83]. Later Richard assures his brother that, however distasteful he might find such an act of self-abasement, he will defer even to the queen to effect Clarence's release [I, i, 107–10].

Richard continues to harp on the evil influence exerted on the king by the queen and about the low-born origins and dangerous aspirations to place and power of her relatives. It is they, he tells anybody who is willing to listen, who lie behind the disgrace, imprisonment and, ultimately, the death of Clarence. In this way he manages to portray himself to the world as the bluff opponent of evil counsel, a plain-speaking old aristocrat and loyal subject, whose only real fault is his inability to dissimulate. Unlike his subtle, shifty opponents, whose natural métier is the privacy of the court and, he implies, of the bedroom, he always operates in public, calling a spade a spade, denouncing enemies of the crown or of the realm to their faces. 'They love his grace but lightly/That fill his ears with such dissentious rumours./Because I cannot flatter, and look fair,/Smile in men's faces, smooth, deceive and cog,/Duck with French nods and apish courtesy,/I must be held a rancorous enemy./Cannot a plain man live and think no harm,/But thus his simple truth must be abused/With silken, sly, insinuating Jacks?' [I, iii, 45–53].

Accused by the queen of a consistent enmity towards her and hers, Richard returns to this theme of the corrupting effect on political life of low-born coun-sellors and newly minted noblemen. 'Since every Jack became a gentleman/There's many a gentle person made a jack' [I, iii, 71–72]. 'Our brother is impris-oned by your means,/Myself disgraced, and the nobility/Held in contempt, while great promotions/Are daily given to ennoble those/That scarce some two days since were worth a noble' [I, iii, 77–81]. To hear Richard tell it, the king's own kindred, the very people who had helped him to the throne in the first place, were being displaced from his favour by upstarts who had fought for the house of Lancaster during the civil wars [I, iii, 120–32]. The result of all this, as Richard explains to Clarence, is that both Clarence and Gloucester, and, by implication, any of the rest of the ancient nobility who get in the way, 'are not safe'. In thus playing the evil counsel card, allied here to the trope of the rise of ill-deserving and ambitious new men at the expense of the ancient nobility, all worked through an excess of female influence over royal policy and patronage, Richard is echoing some of the central themes of both *The treatise* and *Leicester's commonwealth*. This, of course, represents the final sophistication of evil counsellor speak – the warning against evil counsel as the ultimate weapon of the successful evil counsellor.

The success of this strategy shows most spectacularly in the scene at the opening of Act II in which Edward attempts to compose the differences afflicting his court and regime, compounding the feuds between Hastings and Rivers, and between Buckingham and 'my wife's allies', and indeed between them and Gloucester. Coming late to the proceedings, Richard enters expressing his intent 'to reconcile me to this friendly peace:/'Tis death for me to be at enmity;/I hate it, and desire all good men's love.' Starting with the queen and running through 'my noble cousin Buckingham' and the lords Rivers and Grey, Richard makes his peace with all the attendant lords. He then concludes with the pious exclamation that 'I do not know that Englishman alive/With whom my soul is at any jot at odds,/More than the infant that is born tonight –/I thank my God for my humility' [II, i, 54–73].

This, of course, is a consummate performance. In his earlier scene with the queen and her relatives, a scene acted out before an audience of lords, Richard had played the outspoken enemy of evil counsel and the bluff defender of the ancient nobility and Yorkist establishment against the insinuating influence of low-born new men (and women). Now, before the king, he plays out his role as a man more sinned against than sinning. Rough-tongued and outspoken he may be, but he seeks enmity with no man and is prepared to compose any differences his manner, or indeed the 'false intelligence or wrong surmise' of his enemies, may have created.

But having established the effect, Richard then suddenly shifts gears, using the queen's pious wish that Clarence might be included in the general hatchet-burying and peace-making, to announce his brother's death. 'Why, madam, have I offered love for this,/To be so flouted in this royal presence?/Who knows not that the gentle Duke is dead?' [II, i, 78–80]. This is a brilliant *coup de théâtre* because, of course, no one in the room (except Richard, whom we have seen at the end of the last act overseeing his brother's murder) *does* know that Clarence is dead. By pretending that it is common knowledge, Richard achieves a number of effects. He emphasises the extraordinary charity of his own willing-ness to make peace even with his brother's murderers. He shows up the heart-less dissimulation of the queen, who, in his version of the scene, is trying to cover up her complicity in the duke's death by pretending to know nothing about it. He also manages to establish that he has had nothing to do with his brother's death, which was carried out on royal orders. Such, certainly, is the interpretation of these events that Richard imparts to Buckingham and the attendant lords after a distressed Edward has departed the scene lamenting his brother's death [II, i, 135–40].

One consistent strand running throughout these scenes is Richard's perfor-mance of the outward forms of Christian piety. Throughout his rise to power, he plays the saint; trusting in God's will for revenge on, or protection against, his 'enemies'; seeking peace with all and expressing repentance for past wrongs.

Forever quoting scripture, he thanks 'God for my humility', rebukes Buckingham for swearing and generally clothes his 'naked villainy with old ends stol'n forth of holy writ', seeming 'a saint when most I play the devil'. The scripture-citing, saint-seeming, hypocrite was, by this point, an established feature of anti-puritan satire and stereotyping and on this basis it may not be going too far to add the depiction of Richard III to the list of anti-puritan gestures and stereotypes that can be found throughout these plays.

In both *The treatise* and *Leicester's commonwealth*, issues of religion and professions of protestant, indeed in Leicester's case, of puritan, religious zeal were shown providing mere cover for the pursuit of personal and factional political advantage. This, of course, was a standard feature of the behaviour of the functionally atheist Machiavel, a type of which the Leicester of *Leicester's commonwealth*, the Cecil of *Cecil's commonwealth* and the Richard of *Richard III* were all presented as perfect specimens. Here it is perhaps worth reminding ourselves that in the former work Leicester's espousal of the puritan cause and patronage of the godly was presented as a relatively late addition to his political repertoire; one adopted merely to help build himself a following and hide the real aims and methods underpinning his career.

But if there is something distinctly Leicestrian in Richard's hypocritical performances of 'puritan' godliness, then his deployment of the rhetoric of evil counsel, defence of the ancient nobility against upstart new men and his denunciation of female influence on monarchical power all point elsewhere. In adopting that particular repertoire of complaint and analysis Richard is reminiscent not of Leicester but rather of the authors of *The treatise* or of *Leicester's commonwealth* themselves. For these are precisely the claims and categories used by a succession of Catholic critics to type the Elizabethan regime as a conspiracy and a tyranny. Richard, then, encapsulates the methods and discourses of a whole range of contemporary malcontents and insurgents. We cannot, on this basis, identify Richard with any one historical figure or tendency, or with any one side in the religious and dynastic politics of the period. What we can do is observe that the play is inhabiting precisely the same narrative and discursive world as the tracts, and using precisely the same sort of materials as those deployed there to describe events of a very similar, indeed a functionally identical, nature.

From providence to predestination: the return of legitimacy

The play, then, operates on two levels. On the one hand, it gives us a largely this-worldly, thoroughly 'secular' and 'political', explanation of events; one comprised almost entirely of the interplay of the different interests, intentions and perspectives of the major players, as they encounter one another in a political world still disrupted and delegitimised by the recent civil wars. On the other, in an altogether distinct, prophetic register, one restricted for the most part either to the dreams of men (Stanley, Clarence, Richard himself) or to the waking curses, prophecies and incantations of women (a chorus of vengeful anti-nuns – queens Margaret, Elizabeth and the duchess of York)[18] the play subjects those same events to an altogether different prophetic and providential interpretation.

The two modes of analysis or presentation come together over the course of the last two acts in and through the character and fate of Richard himself. Almost from the moment he achieves the throne, Richard undergoes a fundamental change. No longer the plotting Machiavel, always under and in control, forever explaining to himself and to us just how his plans will go and are going, Richard becomes much more the irrational tyrant; a man always close to running out of control; threatened by his own fears and passions, unable even to control himself, let alone others and still less events. The two types had, of course, always been closely linked, the one representing the obverse side of the other. Thus in *Leicester's comonwealth* Leicester is described throughout as both a 'machavel' and a 'tyrant'.

Having attained the crown, Richard immediately plunges into a series of increasingly desperate actions to ensure that he keeps it. Chief amongst these is the murder of his nephews. Putting the matter to Buckingham, he gets a decidedly cold response; 'your grace may do your pleasure'. Thus rebuffed – 'high-reaching Buckingham grows circumspect' – Richard takes the matter into his own hands [IV, ii, 8–45]. But if Buckingham has failed the test of his loyalty put to him by Richard, he returns with a test of his own for the king, asking him to make good on a promise, made as they plotted together to seize the crown, to confer on Buckingham 'th'earldom of Hereford and the moveables' thereof; a request that Richard proceeds to ignore.

Preoccupied with the threat to his security presented by Richmond, Richard dwells obsessively on a series of prophecies. Throughout these musings, Buckingham persists with his request, only to be told finally and definitively that 'I am not in the giving vein today'. With that refusal, the political link between Richard and Buckingham is broken, and Buckingham leaves the court determined to get his retaliation in first before Richard can visit upon him the same fate that he had already visited upon Hastings [IV, ii, 94–122].

For the first time someone has seen through Richard's intentions and taken action against him, before he has been able to take action against them. And what enables Buckingham to do that is Richard's musings upon omens and prophecies of his own doom. Once Richard, the Machiavel, had derided such 'drunken prophecies, libels and dreams', as mere trifles to be disseminated and manipulated for purely political purposes [I, i, 33]. Now, however, for Richard the tyrant, such things have become not merely objects of fear and fascination, but still worse, distractions that divert him from the central tasks of political management and dissimulation, in ways that previously would have been unthinkable, and now prove to be disastrous.

Not that Richard ceases to plot the course of his own survival, as ever explaining both to himself and to us the intricacies of his schemes to remove potential rivals and close down various challenges to his rule through a variety of murders and marriages. But he does so now with a desperation and in a language unlike anything to be found in the first half of the play. 'I must be married to my brother's daughter,/Or else my kingdom stands on brittle glass./ Murder her brothers, and then marry her –/Uncertain way of gain! But I am in/ So far in blood that sin will pluck on sin;/Tear-falling pity dwells not in this eye' [IV, ii, 53–65]. Encapsulated here is the notion – central to both providentialised pamphlets and plays – of the chain of sins; the belief that sin, once entered into, will indeed pluck on sin, and that the soul, once plunged deep enough in evil, can neither relent nor repent, but must, in a desperate and doomed search for security, plunge on through a welter of sin upon sin, crime upon crime, towards an inevitable death and damnation. As we have seen, throughout the play others have spoken of Richard as a devil, a minister of hell, in effect, as a reprobate; now, for the first time, he is beginning to register, within his own consciousness and mode of speech and through his own actions, the affective signs and fatal consequences of such a status. The last two acts of the play show him hurtling down the chain of sins to a desperate death, urged on by the curses and prophecies of a chorus of avenging women.

Richard's spiritual decline is mirrored, of course, by the decline of his political fortunes. His tyranny now patent, the dissimulating skills of the Machiavel by which he has ascended to power are now useless to him. We are shown that process starting at the very moment that he moves to usurp the throne – in the sullen silence with which the Londoners greet his claim to be king. It continues through his failure to keep Buckingham on side and reaches its culminating point in his attempt to persuade Queen Elizabeth to help him win over her daughter to his proposal of marriage. Their conversation parallels his earlier exchange with the Lady Anne in Act I. In the reprise of that exchange, Richard's rhetorical skills, his powers of persuasion, remain undiminished, but this time they have no effect. Desperately searching for a means to persuade Elizabeth, Richard starts to swear by 'my George, my Garter and my crown', only to be told that each has been in turn 'profaned, dishonoured and the third usurped'. He tries next to swear by 'the world' – ''tis full of thy foul wrongs', comes the unrelenting reply; by 'my father's death – 'thy life hath it dishonoured'; 'Then by myself – thy self is self-misused.' He turns at last, in desperation, to God, only to have that proposal go down in a shower of bitter scepticism. From there he turns to what has always been his one and only guiding principle – his own future, worldly good fortune and felicity, what he terms 'the time to come', 'as I intend to prosper and repent/So thrive I in my dangerous affairs/Of hostile arms' [IV, iv, 366–99].

At the outset, the fact that the pursuit of immediate political and personal advantage, of this worldly power and felicity, is his one article of faith had been his own dirty little secret; a fact effectively hidden from the world by the godly pretence and honest, bluff-sounding bluster with which Richard had habitually concealed his true nature and intentions. But now that secret is out. His evil nature and hypocrisy have been rendered not merely patent but transparent by his deeds, and he has literally nothing left to swear by; no means of obtaining the consent of those he needs to bend to his plans. Again as Emrys Jones observes, given the audience's knowledge of just what 'the time to come' holds for Richard, the moment is doubly ironic.[19] Here, of course the prophetic and political aspects of the play's plotting of events are starting to come together.

Richard is now 'surrounded not only by a divinely controlled universe', a train of events the nature of which is equally well known to God and to the audience, but also by a political situation slipping inexorably out of his control.[20] The audience ceases to gasp at what Womersley has described as 'the exuberance, the energy, and the improvised self-invention of the earlier, free Richard' and is now merely watching 'an actor in a play scripted', not by himself, but 'by providence'.[21]

No longer an aspiring Machiavel, working in the shadows on the vulnerabilities and blind spots of others, Richard now confronts the world as a tyrant, his rule based on sheer force and fear. As Blunt tells Richmond and the others as they march to meet Richard at Bosworth, 'he hath no friends but what are friends for fear,/Which in his dearest need will fly from him' [V, ii, 20–21]. At the end of their interview, Elizabeth makes as though to agree to Richard's plan and is rewarded, to her face, with 'my true love's kiss' and, behind her back, with a contemptuous verdict very similar to that with which Richard had met Anne's similar acquiescence to his proposal of marriage in Act I. 'Relenting fool, and shallow, changing woman!' [IV, iv, 431]. Except that, later, we hear that Elizabeth has, in fact, assented to her daughter's marriage to Richmond. By now the only person deceived by Richard the Machiavel is Richard himself.

The two processes working Richard's decline and ruin, what we might term the political and the providential, meet, of course, at Bosworth Field. There Richard and Richmond are visited in their sleep by the ghosts of Richard's victims. In succession Prince Edward, Henry VI, Clarence, Rivers, Grey, Vaughan, Hastings, Anne and Buckingham parade across the stage, wishing comfort and victory to Richmond and death and despair to Richard. In unison the ghosts address both parties. While Richard is bidden to 'despair and die' [V, iii, 146–48] Richmond is enjoined to 'sleep in peace and wake in joy;/Good angels guard thee from the boar's annoy./Live, and beget a happy race of kings;/Edward's unhappy sons do bid thee flourish' [V, iii, 149–53].

Richard wakes sweating as if from a nightmare, a victim of the promptings of a conscience that can only operate when his conscious self is asleep. There is, of course, a stark contrast being drawn here between Richard and other murderers who, earlier in the play, have been shown experiencing the pangs of conscience during their waking lives, indeed even as they performed the dreadful deeds upon which Richard has sent them. To this point, however, Richard has not experienced the merest twinge of conscience. Indeed, the very notion of sin has only once crossed his lips. Now, however, assaulted in his sleep by the shades of those he has slaughtered, even he succumbs [V, iii, 179–207].

The speech which ensues plays off and echoes the soliloquies in 3 Henry VI, in which Richard had announced, indeed, on one view of the matter, chosen,[22] his indentity as a self-willed Machiavel, a principle of evil and malignity, a stripped-down will to power. The chain of reasoning there had concluded in his proclamation of his own singularity-in-evil: 'I have no brother; I am no brother./ And this word "love" which grey beards call divine,/Be resident in men like one another/And not in me: I am myself alone' [3 Henry VI, V, vii, 80–84]. Here that self, the 'I' in effect created in that speech, confronts the consequences of its own singularity, its complete isolation from human society, and of the entirely unqualified and unmitigated nature of its own evil. Here, then, the play finally connects the political with the providential; showing precisely how the collapse of Richard's political cause is mirrored by an inner collapse, even an identity crisis, as his whole sense of self as an amoral Machiavel, someone marked off from human society by his ruthlessness and political skill, is called into radical question by the sudden emergence of a sense of himself as not merely a sinner but as a perjurer and a murderer in 'the direst degree'.

As Robert Hunter observes, 'conscience', which to contemporaries consti-tuted 'the voice of God within', is 'the origin of Richard's fear', but even conscience can 'exercise its power over him only in sleep'. This is anything but a good sign; indeed it is a direct result, and a sure indication, of Richard's condition as a reprobate. The whole scene provides us with a densely compressed image of the awful paradox of reprobation, of the relation between evil and God's sover-eignty, in a universe presided over by an omnipotent, both perfectly just and perfectly merciful, God. Here, then, is the terrifying underside of the doctrine of providence, the upside of which the play shows returning England to some-thing like moral and political normality after the chaos and disorder of the Wars of the Roses. The two are, of course, integrally related. As Hunter observes, Richard can play the role assigned to him by God's providence in both punishing the sins of the surviving participants of the Wars of the Roses and in returning England to a state of monarchical legitimacy and moral health, 'only by being absolutely horrible' to everyone; for it is only the extremities of Richard's tyranny that 'forces his society to unite in hatred against him'.[23] Richard's tyranny thus serves as a scourge to punish the sins committed during the Wars of the Roses, to purge the political scene of potential rival claimants to the throne and to unite a political society split apart into warring factions by civil war, not only into opposition to him but into support for his successor.

Similarly, it is also only the appalling nature of his sins that (in this speech) has finally provoked in him some sense of his desperate spiritual condition; and, we might think, provided him with one final chance to repent and save his soul, if not his life. But then again, it is the weight of those very same sins, and the condition of a heart now congenitally hardened by continual sinning – a moral and spiritual condition that, in those two crucial speeches in *3 Henry VI* and at the opening of this play, we have watched Richard himself not merely choose but enthusiastically embrace – that now prevents him from taking, in his waking life, the final chance to repent and be saved, offered to him, in his dreams, by the operation of conscience.

Hunter lays out what he takes to be the theological or interpretative issues raised by Richard's fate, asking 'does Richard avoid grace or does grace refuse to bless him? Or, to focus on the final moment of the failure of grace, when Richard says "Have mercy, Jesu," and then continues "Soft, I did but dream," is the failure to complete the impulse toward contrition the result of Richard's freely willed avoidance of grace, or of God's refusal to bless the appeal? The play does not tell us, but it certainly asks us.' The big point, however, is surely that, whether through his own serial persistence in sin, or through the operation of God's hardening of his heart, or of some combination of the two – and the play does indeed leave the precise nature of that mixture an open question – Richard is now demonstrably incapable of repentance. Even if, as Hunter puts it, Richard's 'pangs of conscience' are viewed as the operation 'of grace itself, battering Richard's heart, attempting to bring contrition', rather than as 'a deserved and divinely inflicted punishment upon a reprobate sinner', far from being an offer that Richard can't refuse, by now it is one that he is unable to accept.[24]

Here we are getting a glimpse of the interiority of reprobation; or rather, the play is enabling its audience to view reprobation both from the outside in and from the inside out; from the perspectives provided, on the one hand, by prophecy and providential judgement, and, on the other, by the operations of the human will and psyche, as the play shows Richard actively refusing the offer of divine grace, proffered to him through the workings of his conscience, and (once more, even at the last) positively choosing to embrace and play out to the bitter end the persona and role that both providence and prophecy, his own (un)natural deformity and the times, have conferred upon him.

Thus at the end of this speech Ratcliffe comes in and Richard returns to the waking world of the tyrant, the world of terror and war, in which the need to creep from tent to tent 'to see if any mean to shrink from me' drives out all thoughts of moral culpability and still less of repentance [V, iii, 222]. Later in the same scene the play underlines just how far behind him Richard has put the terrifying promptings of conscience, as he exhorts his troops and himself to 'let not our babbling dreams affright our souls' and asserts that 'conscience is but a word that cowards use,/Devised at first to keep the strong in awe./Our strong arms be our conscience, swords our law./March on, join bravely, let us to it pell-mell,/If not in heaven, then hand in hand to hell' [V, iii, 307–11].

Richmond, on the other hand, sleeps soundly and rises to deliver a rousing speech to his troops, drenched in God-speak [V, iii, 240–54]. In stark contrast, in his speech to his soldiers, Richard makes no mention of God, justice or legitimacy. Rather, he bases his appeal on the base and foreign nature of their adversaries, 'a sort of vagabonds, rascals and runaways,/A scum of Bretons and base lackey peasants,/Whom their o'ercloyed country vomits forth/To desperate adventures and assured destruction'. 'And who doth lead them but a paltry fellow?/Long kept in Bretagne at our mother's cost,/A milksop'. 'If we be conquer'd, let men conquer us!/And not these bastard Bretons, whom our fathers/Have in their own land beaten, bobbed and thumped,/And in record left them the heirs of shame./Shall these enjoy our lands? Lie with our wives? Ravish our daughters?' [V, iii, 315–37].

In the play's final speech Richmond famously announces his intention to 'unite the white rose and red'. 'England hath long been mad, and scarred herself:/The brother blindly shed the brother's blood;/The father rashly slaughtered his own son;/The son, compelled, been butcher to the sire./All this divided York and Lancaster,/Divided in their dire division./O, now let Richmond and Elizabeth,/The true successors of each royal house,/By God's fair ordinance conjoin together;/And let their heirs, God, if Thy will be so,/Enrich the time to come in smooth-faced peace,/With smiling plenty, and fair prosperous days'. With that Richmond lapses into prayerful mode. 'Abate the edge of traitors, gracious Lord,/That would reduce these bloody days again,/And make poor England weep in streams of blood./Let them not live to taste this land's increase,/That would with reason wound this fair land's peace./Now civil wounds are stopped; peace lives again./That she may long live here, God say amen' [V, v, 19–41].

Richard III as a guide to the past, present and future

It is worth noting here how little mention is made in this speech, and indeed in the play in general, of issues of dynastic legitimacy or right. There is one mention, in an aside, of Richard II's death at Pomfret. That apart, there is almost no discussion of the rights and wrongs of the dynastic struggles that have just torn England apart and consequently no real sense that England is being punished for having revolted against or removed a legitimate monarch. Rather, as one murder or betrayal punishes another, the sins that we are shown being punished by Richard in his role of (demonic) instrument of divine justice are far more immediate and visceral than that.

Again no great emphasis is placed upon Richmond's dynastic right. His claim to the throne is established through supernatural means – the prophecy of Henry VI and the unanimous election of the ghosts of Richard's victims, a group which comprises both Lancastrians and Yorkists and which together places great emphasis on the role of Richard's slaughtered nephews in bringing Richmond victory. When Richmond himself makes his pitch to his troops all his emphasis is placed on the support of God for the removal of such a dreadful tyrant as Richard III. There is one passing reference to Richard's status as a usurper, but the discourse of tyranny rather than of usurpation or dynastic right predominates. Indeed, the unequivocal evil of Richard's character and rule renders issues of dynastic legitimacy almost nugatory. As Barbara Hodgdon observes, 'no other Shakespearean play so rigorously schematizes the claims of a royal successor, constructing its close as though to mask their absence. In *Richard III*, it is not proofs of dynastic legitimacy but design that endorses Richmond's kingship.'[25]

The point, then, is less the strength of Richmond's hereditary claim than the undeniable tyranny of Richard. The play thus stages not the triumph of dynastic right over usurpation but the just judgement of God visited upon a tyrant of unimpeachable evil. That judgement is effected through a number of overtly, and by no means uncontroversially, political means – by, in fact, a combination of home-bred rebellion, conspiracy and foreign invasion. But while these actions are staged in the play their true nature is obfuscated, if not entirely elided, by the intensely providential reading of the events being staged upon which the whole structure of the play insists.[26] The mechanisms whereby Richard's fall is finally brought about are thus figured less as a political process than as the ineluctable working out of a moral design.

Thus is a combination of politics and providence made to solve the conundrum of legitimacy, its nature, origins and how to recover it, once lost; thus is a Gordian knot of questions about the nature of legitimacy – questions posed and examined from almost every angle, but never resolved, throughout the *Henry VI* plays – simply cut through by the decisive intervention of providence.[27] The result is not to render any clearer the questions of tyranny and resistance, and the practical (as well as theoretical or jural) issues involved in restoring legitimacy to a polity stripped thereof by a mixture of monarchical dysfunction, usurpation and tyranny. Rather those questions are simply avoided, by an appeal to heaven.

Richmond, of course, was none other than Henry VII. Traditionally his triumph at Bosworth, and promise to reunite the two royal houses of Lancaster and York in order to produce a line of successors fit and able to bring peace and plenty to the land, has been construed as a powerful piece of official propaganda, indeed of Tudor myth-making. And, on one level, so it is, or rather the play leaves itself open to precisely such a reading, although it is remarkable how relatively little Shakespeare does to render such an interpretation necessary or normative. Rather, the play leaves the exemplum provided by Richard and his fate open to a variety of equally plausible, telling and immediately contemporary interpretations and applications.

At this point it is worth asking how the presentation of such historical events in the early 1590s might have been interpreted by the audiences of the early 1590s. What if, instead of taking the play as simply an account of what had happened in the past, they also took it as a guide to or comment upon either what was happening now or what might be about to happen in the near future? Here we have a prince, introduced into England from abroad, with foreign backing, indeed with foreign troops, who promises, by ending a period of intense internal dissension and tyranny, to bring peace and unity to the land. While Richmond makes his pitch for support almost entirely in universalist terms, banging on about the cause and support of God, it is Richard who relies on crude (and transparently false) sectional, as we might say, narrowly 'nationalist', appeals about the need to protect the realm from the foreigner. Just like Richard, the Elizabethan government was certainly not above making appeals for national unity in the face of a foreign (popish) threat, and, as the Catholic tracts that made up *Cecil's commonwealth* were only too happy to explain, in the 1590s England was not characterised by too much 'smooth-fac'd peace', 'smiling plenty and fair prosperous days'.

Barbara Hodgdon has noted how 'at its very edge *Richard III* opens up and then bridges a gap between time past and time present'; 'the most securely enclosed of Shakespeare's histories, *Richard III* also folds out, in its closing gestures, to embrace the present'. She goes on to observe that what she terms the 'ancestors' of Shakespeare's play, 'Legge's *Richardus Tertius* and the anonymous *True tragedy of Richard III* close with a genealogical review of Elizabeth's line'. *The true tragedy* is particularly fulsome. 'She is that lamp that keeps fair England's light,/And through her faith her country lives in peace:/And she hath put proud Antichrist to flight,/And been the means that civil wars did cease./Then England kneel upon thy hairy knee,/And thank that God that still provides for thee.'[28]

As a number of critics point out, Shakespeare's play does not follow suit, but rather concludes with a paean of praise to peace. Hodgdon notes that in the last two lines of the play – 'Now civil wounds are stopp'd; peace lives again/That she may long live here, God say amen' – 'the syntactic antecedent of "she" is obviously 'peace'. But 'on another level', Hodgdon claims 'that "she" alludes to Elizabeth I, the "true succeeder" who reigns over the present of *Richard III's* first audiences'. Hodgdon's conclusion is that 'bettering its ancestors ... Shakespeare's play pays homage to a real Queen as an absent, though complicit, witness to closure'. This is to gloss the conclusion of the play in the orthodox sense but to do so while adverting to the way in which the actual words of the play do anything but insist on such a reading or meaning.

Indeed, for all her rather strenuous efforts to avoid the obvious consequences of her own argument, Hodgdon's analysis makes it clear that, despite its recycling of the Tudor myth at its most providentially insistent, at the close the play teasingly refuses any direct reference to Elizabeth herself, satisfying itself with a prayer for peace at a time when England was still at war with the greatest power in Europe.[29] If the audience want to construe Richmond's final speech as a prayer for Elizabeth, then that 'she' certainly enables them to do so, but it is most definitely something that the play does not do for them.

All of which leaves us with the question: just who, in the early 1590s, might have been thought likely, by arriving from abroad, to confer the benefits of a God-satisfying legitimacy, and of peace and plenty, upon a land racked by internal (both religious and political) divisions, and by the effects of war? If we set aside the Infanta (and, of course, we do not *have* to set aside the Infanta) the obvious candidate seems to be James VI of Scotland. After all, if salvation and legitimacy were to be found in the Tudor line, represented here by its founder Henry VII, then the only available candidate with Tudor blood flowing in his veins is James Stuart.

The play ends with a dire warning against traitors 'that would reduce these bloody wars again'. In the context of the early 1590s we might interpret or rather surmise that many protestant contemporaries would have interpreted this as a reference to Catholics, and in particular to certain sorts of Hispanophile Catholics, traitors indeed, anxious, as were the authors of *Cecil's commonwealth*, to talk up a succession crisis and build up a party for the Infanta. Other, Catholic, onlookers might have taken that reference to traitors 'that would reduce these bloody wars again' as a reference to the clique of Machiavels currently in control of the regime and to their own potentially destabilising and tyrannical designs on power. Still others might have identified the most likely cause of dynastic civil war as an unsettled succession, and, of course, there was only one person widely deemed to be the cause of that. Pursuing that line of thought, the play could be construed as a delineation of the sort of crisis into which the current policies of the regime and condition of the realm, combined with a chronically unsettled succession, might well be about to pitch the English, once the old queen finally died. And here the presence at the centre of the action of a hypocritical, seemingly pious, but entirely villainous, Machiavel and younger son with a hump may well have served, for at least some observers, to tie the play very tightly indeed to immediately contemporary events. For at precisely the point at which this play was being written and produced, Robert Cecil, a seemingly godly younger son, disfigured with a hump, was emerging into prominence as the political heir of his father, Lord Burghley.[30]

Given the nature of the political aims and methods, not to mention the atheistical amorality attributed to the Cecils in *Cecil's commonwealth*, this is a parallel that may well have struck at least some contemporaries as ominously telling. Read in this way the play represents the future imputed to England by such tracts as *Leicester's or Cecil's commonwealth*, given frighteningly realistic historical form on the public stage, with the audience being invited or enabled to go back into history in order to glimpse at least one version of the future in store for England and the English if present trends continued unabated.

In short, a great deal turns upon whether the audience took the action of the play to be dealing solely with the past, or applied it directly to the present, or situated it on the cusp between the present and the future. However, one thing that both the present and future applications of the play had in common was a strong sense that salvation from the (either current or future) conjuncture being staged in the play would only be forthcoming from a new ruler, brought to the realm from outside, and, again, the in the early 1590s, there were only two leading candidates available to play that role, James VI and the Infanta.

In conclusion, it might be salutary to emphasise once again that the claim being made here is not that the play demands or demanded any one of these readings or interpretations either from contemporaries or from us. It is rather that it enables, or, to put the case at its strongest, invites, a range of such readings and applications, leaving it up to the reader or playgoer to choose between them. Certainly, in marked contrast to *The true tragedy of Richard III*, this play did not clearly identify Elizabeth as the heroine of the hour or saviour of the country. This, of course, ensured that all the really dubious or dangerous ideological work took place between the reader's or viewer's ears, leaving the play to stand as a mere history, a morally improving and thoroughly entertaining account of shocking and spectacular events from the English past, so different from the reign of our own dear queen.

CHAPTER 7

Going Roman: *Richard III* and *Titus Andronicus* compared

What is obscured and obfuscated through the resort to providential, indeed to predestinarian, explanation in *Richard III* is rendered crystal clear in *Titus Andronicus,* a play, probably written at around the same time as *2* and *3 Henry VI,* in the early 1590s, but produced as 'a new play' in 1594. Not any sort of history play, as T.J.B. Spencer famously observed, *Titus* 'does not assume a political situation known to Roman history, it is rather a summary of Roman politics. It is not so much that any particular set of Roman institutions is assumed in Titus, but rather that it includes all the political institutions that Rome ever had. The author seems anxious, not to get it all right, but to get it all in.' The result, as Spencer argues, was that the play 'would easily be recognised as a typical Roman history by a sixteenth century audience'. Indeed, Spencer points out, it appears in the Stationers' Register, albeit not on the title page of the first printed quarto, as 'a noble Roman history'.[1] All of which served to locate the action being staged in the play safely in a sort of temporal and historical limbo, a never-never land, a very long way away from Roman, let alone from English, history, and consequently, it might be thought, an equally long way away from Elizabethan England. And yet while the play is set in a carefully established and sustained version of pagan Romanitas, it also evokes a polity and a series of political situations that spoke directly to pressingly contemporary Elizabethan concerns.

If we compare *Richard III* with *Titus,* we can see if not the same then very similar political and moral problematics being worked through in *Richard III,* in a recognisably English, Christian context, and in *Titus,* in a pagan and Roman one. While both polities are monarchical, the English version is hereditary and the Roman, elective. On the one hand, this might be thought to have had a distancing effect, since the ideological and institutional locale provided by an elective monarchy, set in a version of pagan Rome that did not in fact exist, might very well allow ideas to be tried out that would have been far more controversial in a version of monarchical and Christian England. On the other, we know that many Elizabethans were only too eager to characterise England itself as an elective monarchy. During the 1580s that had been a position canvassed by protestants anxious to avoid, at almost any cost, the accession of the Catholic Mary Stuart. By the 1590s that same position was becoming the natural ideological terrain of those, mostly Catholics, who wanted, equally badly, to avoid the accession of Mary's protestant son, James VI. Indeed such a vision of the English monarchical polity was about to receive its most coherent statement in Robert Parsons' great tract *The conference about the next succession*, a text in gestation during 1593–4, and finally published in 1595.

Both *Titus* and *Richard III* have at their centre an elaborated picture of (admittedly differently constituted sorts of) tyranny. While *Titus* comes off as a revenge tragedy, as Coppelia Kahn has pointed out, it also features a political under-plot, in which, as well as revenge being achieved by the Andronici, through a combination of domestic plot, foreign invasion and regicide, legitimacy is restored to a Rome ravaged by the tyranny of Saturninus and the Machiavellian atheism and evil counsel of Tamora and her lover Aaron, the Moor.

While the radical purport of what actually happens in *Richard III* – that is to say, the insertion on the throne of a successor whose hereditary claims were not of the strongest, through a combination of sedition and conspiracy, foreign invasion and regicide – is obscured rather than highlighted by the heavily providential mix of prophecy and prodigy that suffuses the action, none of that is true of *Titus Andronicus*.

There events, which in other texts and plays would have cried out for a providential gloss, are presented as the result of human planning and ingenuity. The conventional murder pamphlet narrative, animated by the dictum 'murder will out', is reproduced in the play complete with the providential discovery of clues and the dramatic unmasking of the culprits, but only as a plotted frame-up devised by Aaron to incriminate the Andronici.

The revelation of the real guilty parties is realised through means – such as the testimony of the tongueless Lavinia – that in any other context would be presented not only as providential but as genuinely miraculous. But in *Titus* there is nothing miraculous about it. Lavinia is enabled to speak through the device of the stick guided by her mouth and stumps, and her recourse to Ovid. The revelation of another key element in the plot is made through a monstrous birth – that of Aaron's bastard son – but the child's monstrousness resides in its blackness, which in turn is a function of the entirely natural circumstance that its father is a Moor. The figure of Revenge appears on stage; not as some preternaturally providential commentary on the action of the play but rather as part of a ludicrous spoof designed to deceive the supposedly mad Titus – a ruse that goes predictably and disastrously wrong. The dénouement of the play, which serves to punish each of the central characters in ways entirely appropriate to their master sins and evil deeds, is not the result of a concatenation of accidents or coincidences, wrought by providence to bring closure to the action. Rather it is minutely choreographed by Titus himself. Indeed the play presents the revelation and punishment of the tyranny of Saturninus, Tamora and Aaron as the result of a carefully calibrated campaign of internal sedition and conspiracy co-ordinated with an invasion by an army of Rome's ancient enemies, the Goths, led by Titus' son, Lucius.

As not merely a revenger, but also a murderer, not only of Tamora and her sons, but also of a number of his own progeny, up to and including the blameless Lavinia, Titus must die the death. That leaves Lucius, the man who has just killed the emperor, Saturninus, to be elected by the Roman people to the imperial throne. There could scarcely be a clearer acknowledgement of the legitimacy, as well as the justice, of that regicidal act. Moreover, since Lucius was the name of the mythic king said to have first introduced Christianity into Britain, Lucius might be thought not to be any old new ruler, but rather the initiator of a new golden age of peace and unity. In this, of course, he plays an even more exalted version of the role given to Richmond in *Richard III*. Thus, what had been presented in *Richard III* as the work of providence, an outcome whose legitimacy reposed in the absolute evil of the ruler being displaced, and in the unanimity of the living and the dead that his tyranny had produced, is presented in *Titus* as the outcome of the cunning, virtue and the (admittedly 'cruel and irreligious') piety of the Andronici. What is occluded in the heavily providentialised history play, set in the Christian monarchy of England, is very deliberately laid bare in the explicitly un-providential play set in the invented, pagan and elective, monarchy of Rome.

As with *Richard III*, so with *Titus*, just what political meanings or contemporary resonances were to be extracted from the play depended on whether the action being performed on stage was related to the past, present or future. As Spencer and a good many other critics have explained, the play puts a good deal of time and effort into evoking its ancient Roman, pagan setting. But there are moments when the gap between the play's version of a very archaic ancient Rome and the Elizabethan, post-reformation present is collapsed almost to nothing. There is the 'ruined monastery', where Aaron and his bastard child are discovered. There is the moment during his ensuing interview with Lucius, when Aaron accuses Lucius of 'popery'. There is the scene when the entirely superfluous figure of the clown not only introduces the vibrantly Christianised street speech of Elizabethan London into the version of pagan Rome otherwise so painstakingly conjured by the play, but also makes reference to (what Jonathan Bate has identified as) the execution of two London separatists in 1593.[2]

But perhaps the most obvious elision of the Roman past with the Elizabethan present occurs in the scene in which Titus declares that Astraea has left the earth. As Jonathan Bate has suggested, since Elizabeth was very frequently figured as Astraea, that claim might be taken to imply that the action of the play refers to a period after the death of Queen Elizabeth and thus conjures up the sort of civil strife, disputed succession and vengeful religious war that it was widely feared would follow Elizabeth's death. On this view, as Bate observes, 'the descent into imperial tyranny could well have looked like a warning as to what might happen once Astraea, the virgin queen, had left the earth'. Moreover, the fact that 'one of the writers who said that "the Christian faith" was received into Britain "in the time of Lucius their king" was none other than John Foxe' might well prompt a Foxeian reading of the play in which 'the Goths who accompany Lucius . . . are there to secure the Protestant succession.'[3]

That certainly is one possible reading. But there is nothing in the text to require it. After all, if Titus' claim that Astraea had left the earth were applied to the present and not to the future, in other words if it were taken to be a comment on the patent absence of justice from a world ruled by a persecuting tyrant like Saturninus or, on certain Catholic views of the matter, like Elizabeth, then it became available as an ironic comment on the lack of justice to be found under the rule of 'Astraea' herself.

And if that line were taken, then a whole series of other parallels between the action of the play and certain versions of Elizabethan political reality might well kick in. The form of revenge-based persecution visited by Tamora and Saturninus on the Andronici turns on a trumped-up crime or conspiracy and an entirely summary punishment imposed on Titus' two sons, with no recourse to anything resembling due process. These were proceedings that any Elizabethan audience would have recognised as entirely illegal, indeed as altogether tyrannical.[4] Not only that, but this style of oppression rather accurately reflected what certain Catholic critics described as the persecution visited upon its Catholic subjects by the Elizabethan state. Robert Southwell, in a 'supplication' directed both to the queen and the reading public, just as Titus' 'supplications' for justice and redress had been directed both to Saturninus and the populace, maintained that the state routinely used trumped-up charges to condemn some of its Catholic subjects to a traitor's death, and employed criminal proceedings utterly subverted by the sinister operations of royal power and the influence of great men to oppress and impoverish others.[5]

Similarly, the Andronici consistently refer to the mutilations visited upon the entirely innocent Lavinia as a form of 'martyrdom', her wounds described as so many 'martyred signs', whose meaning is to be 'interpreted', both by the other characters and the audience [II, ii, 36–45; III, i, 82, 108, 132; III, ii, 36–45].[6] In one famous scene her uncle Marcus employs the same sort of exalted Petrarchan language to describe her mutilated body [II, iii, 11–57][7] as English Catholics employed to describe the eviscerated bodies and quartered remains of their martyred co-religionists.

Again, the style of tyranny imputed to Saturninus and Tamora in the play can usefully be compared both to that imputed to the Elizabethan regime by the Catholic tracts and to that described in the *Henry VI* plays. Where the pamphlets had left the person of the queen untouched by the tyrannical and persecutory policies being pursued in her name, *Titus* put the blame squarely on the prince himself, presenting his relation with his atheistical evil counsellors of choice as a mutually enabling co-dependency, figured in the love triangle described between Saturninus, Tamora and Aaron. If a comparison is made between the relations pertaining, in *2 Henry VI*, between Henry VI, Margaret of Anjou and her paramour, Suffolk, and those linking Saturninus, Tamora and her lover Aaron, the main difference is the active participation of Saturninus in the malign purposes of his queen and her lover. Here the problem is not the absence of the royal will, but rather the malign and misguided nature of its exercise.

Again, just like the *Henry VI* plays, and unlike the pamphlets, a great deal of emphasis is put on excessive female influence on the levers of power. Here the depiction of Tamora as a woman whose maternal, feminine nature has been warped into its tigerish, almost bestial, opposite by the drive to be revenged on her enemies almost exactly parallels the *Henry VI* plays' depiction of Queen Margaret. There is a quite remarkable resemblance between the scene in which Margaret torments York, and the one in which Tamora torments Lavinia. Just as Margaret taunts York with the handkerchief dipped in his son's blood, so Saturninus, Tamora and Aaron taunt Titus, not only with the mutilated body of Lavinia, but with the severed heads of his two executed sons and his own amputated hand.

Again, just as in the Catholic pamphlets, for all that Saturninus, Tamora and Aaron are described as inflicting 'martyrdom' on their victims, there is nothing religious about their own motivation. Rather their cruelty is prompted by a purely secular, entirely this-worldly mixture of Tamora's atavistic drive to be revenged on the Adronici and all their works, Saturninus' petulant mistrust and hatred of Titus and Aaron the Moor's pure malignity.

Just as in *The treatise of treasons* or *Leicester's commonwealth*, there is atheism here aplenty, in Aaron's case, of the theoretical, self-consciously God-denying, rather than the merely practical, sort. When we recall that Elizabeth used to call Sir Francis Walsingham her 'Moor'[8] and that Walsingham was identified by Southwell as the *éminence grise* behind what Southwell maintained was the essentially fabricated Babington conspiracy – a device designed to send not only the conspirators themselves, but also Mary Stuart to their deaths – the daring and range of the resonances and applications at least potentially set off by the play emerges rather clearly. Certainly, if such lines of reasoning and association were to be followed, the 'light' restored by Lucius at play's end might be thought not to be so very protestant after all.

Not, of course, that any of these partial, fleeting identifications or resonances are in any sense necessary. On the contrary they are neither inherent to the structure of the play nor essential to its interpretation. It was, and is, quite possible to experience the play without noticing any of them. As with Bate's interpretation of the Astraea reference, there is nothing in the play to compel such readings or applications, but neither is there anything to rule them out; and the materials that allow them, while anything but integral to the plot, have been quite deliberately distributed throughout the text.

As with *Richard III*, it is left up to the viewer or reader whether to locate the action of the play safely in what was, in this case, a distinctly distant, mythic Roman never-never land, the moral territory of the revenge tragedy rather than of the history play, or, more riskily, to place it in, or rather to apply it to, the immediate past, present and future of Elizabethan and post-Elizabethan England. This would be to deploy the play as an interpretative tool, a moral and political template, in and through which to interpret the current religio-political conjuncture. But, as we have seen, anyone who started to do that might be led, rather quickly, to some distinctly alarming conclusions. Unless, of course, he or she merely viewed the play, with pleasure tinged with horror, as a rather bloody drama about revenge, based heavily on recent box-office successes by Kyd and Marlowe.

Read as plays about politics, *Titus,* and even *Richard III,* can be seen as having anticipated many of the central claims of Robert Parsons' great book, *The conference about the next succession.* There elective monarchy, a residual right to limit, oppose and, finally, to resist tyranny and depose tyrants was taken to inhere not only within the commonwealth of England but within any and every polity, no matter how monarchical in form it might otherwise appear to be. Combined with that was a robust defence of the right of all such monarchical polities to divert the succession from the next hereditary claimant whenever the interests of the 'commonweal' were deemed to require it. Parsons' tract was being planned in 1593, was extant in 1594, but not known in England until the second half of 1595. Depending upon when we date the play, *Titus* had anticipated many of the Jesuit's key claims and contentions, quite possibly a good many years before the *Conference* appeared. As for *Richard III,* Parsons himself used the deposition of the tyrant Richard to confirm his own view of the English polity, claiming that anyone who held Richard's deposition to have been justified must, in effect, agree with him that, under the right circumstances, the commonwealth of England did indeed retain the capacity legitimately to depose a tyrannical prince and to divert the succession from the claimant or incumbent with the strongest hereditary claim, something which, after the death of his brother and his nephews, Richard III undoubtedly enjoyed.[9]

Where Parsons' tract became a *cause célèbre,* proscribed, denounced as seditious, but also much answered and responded to, *Titus* provoked no such reaction or response. Appearing in print first in 1594, it was printed a total of three times during Shakespeare's lifetime. It would seem that such was the liminal status of the drama in relation both to 'power' and to 'history' that things could be said or implied, and notions canvassed, in this format that, in any other venue or medium, would have had the most serious consequences for all concerned. Not so for the drama, for here, in *Titus,* we can see some of the most subversive of doctrines, the most seditious and incendiary of images, being staged and ventriloquised in that most promiscuously public of all venues, the popular theatre; indeed being canvassed and disseminated twice over, first in performance and then in print.

All this could, of course, be taken as testimony to the liminality, the marginality, indeed, to the unimportance, of the drama. The commercial theatre was a low cultural form, ephemeral, its plays written for a (socially mixed, but also) irredeemably popular audience. If it was accused by its enemies of being seditious, that was not because of anything it had to say about serious issues, but rather because of the morally debasing effects on its audience exerted by its disgusting form and content. On this basis, it could be argued that historians interested in Elizabethan politics and political culture should take as little notice of the theatre as did the authorities at the time.

On the other hand, of course, all this might be taken to be a testament to the power and importance of this medium. For here was a place where, as long as the canons of plausible deniability, the appropriate gestures towards either historicity – it's just about history – or fictionality – it's just a story, based on Roman poetry – were made, topics and issues, images and fantasies, of the most dangerous, indeed, when expressed in other venues and genres, of the most illegal, seditious and even treasonous, sort, could be canvassed and staged in plain sight. That, in turn, might have a good deal to tell us about why the theatre was quite so popular a medium and about why playwrights might have wanted to sail as close to the wind as they sometimes did – whatever else it did, it put bums on seats – and why historians of the period might want to take rather more notice of just what was going on, on the popular stage, than they traditionally have.

For plays, on this account, reached parts of the political imaginary that other sources and genres simply could not, or did not, reach; and, if we read them aright, they have a great deal to tell us about the sophistication and intensity of contemporary comment on, and debate about, a range of (forbidden) topics which in theory, at least, remained of the essence of the *arcana imperii*; the sole concern of the queen and her counsellors. But here, the study of the popular stage provides us with an altogether different account of the matter. And it is an account, I want to argue, to which historians of the period should pay some attention.

PART IV
How (not) to depose a tyrant: *King John* and *Richard II*

CHAPTER 8

The Elizabethan resonances of the reign of King John

Plays, of course, are not pamphlets or tracts. Inherently dialogic and glossable, they do not so much make arguments themselves as, by eliciting certain responses from their audiences, enable other people to do so. Telling stories, they provide materials through which those stories can be both interpreted and applied by the audience to their own experience and concerns. On one level, in *Titus Andronicus*, elective monarchy and the right relations between tyranny and evil counsel, resistance and regicide, were all staged and canvassed, indeed, on one reading, vindicated in plain sight, albeit under the rubric, or perhaps under the guise, of revenge tragedy. But the really controversial bits, the particular applications of those general positions to contemporary circumstances, were not communicated through anything like explicit argument or exposition. Rather, through a series of images and tableaux, a complex set of exchanges between expectations elicited by the play from its audience and the actual course of the action being played out on stage, a range of responses were being enabled, chains of association or thought set up or set off. At most, certain interpretative choices, certain associational opportunities, were being laid before the audience. If any 'subversive' conclusions were going to be drawn, any dangerous connections made, or potentially seditious chains of thought initiated, that would happen, certainly not on stage or on the printed page, but between the ears of the viewer or the reader. And if not, not.

What was *not* being made was a case; rather, a narrative template, or a series of narrative templates, a nexus of sometimes loosely connected images, tropes and associations, were being provided, through which elements in the audience could or might interpret both the play and the times.

It was, therefore, one thing to explore the sorts of issues outlined in the previous chapter through the secret fantasies, fleeting associations, dark suspicions, forbidden thoughts and violent imaginings animated by a play like *Titus Andronicus*, which after all was not (quite) a history play but rather a tragedy, very loosely based on narrative materials taken not from Roman history but from Roman poetry. But it was quite another for a pamphlet or tract to set out a formal case for the legitimacy of many of the actions staged in the play.

In the theatre the audience might well have felt or experienced the righteousness and legitimacy of the (both shocking and dreadful) acts with which the play concludes. But to do that there was no need for them to view the actions that close the play as a template for formally legitimate political actions (and thus as directly applicable to the political world of late Elizabethan England). They could do that, of course, but they certainly did not have to. (After all, this was just the way that revenge tragedies ended; with a pile of bodies and both the revenger and his victims dead.)

It was surely entirely possible to leave the theatre after a performance of *Titus Andronicus* with a general sense that justice had been done, a conventional moral and narrative closure achieved, without also feeling that one had been converted to the legitimacy or utility either of elective monarchy or of resistance and regicide. One could also leave the theatre entirely convinced that mutilating and massacring people was wrong, and that summarily executing others on trumped-up charges for crimes they had not, in fact, committed was indeed a mark of tyranny, without having come to the conclusion, or indeed without ever having entertained the notion, that this was also the way in which the Elizabethan state was treating its Catholic victims.

The same, of course, was not true for a tract or pamphlet seeking to claim that (in the face of tyranny and persecution, heresy and evil counsel) conspiracy, regicide, collusion with the foreign enemy and the diversion of the succession were not merely licit, but entirely legitimate, indeed salutary acts. But those were certainly amongst the tasks that Parsons' famous tract, *The conference about the next succession*, set itself. And, for all its infamous indirection, its claims not to be taking sides but merely informing the English public about a subject – the succession – about which, for decades, they had been criminally kept in the dark, Parsons' screed proceeded by making arguments – what it presented as logically necessary and historically valid claims – that its readers were forced to consider as such and either accept or reject.

I have already argued that there was a sense in which the action of *Titus Andronicus* anticipated many of the central claims and contentions contained in Parsons' tract. But precisely because the one was a play and the other a work of political theory and polemic, there is only a limited sense in which such a claim could be true. But, insofar as it was true, insofar as the play did indeed explore some of the same ideological terrain as that mapped out in the tract, the existence of Parsons' book surely rendered the risks taken in the play that much greater. That a Jesuit, in the pay of the king of Spain, was explicitly making such claims in a tract clearly designed to destabilise the Elizabethan state by bringing closer precisely the sort of succession crisis that Parsons claimed to be trying to avert, could only increase the stakes. Moreover, we know that between 1593 and 1594 Shakespeare had entered into some kind of patronage relationship with the earl of Southampton. Southampton came from an intensely Catholic milieu and enjoyed extensive Catholic connections in west Sussex and Hampshire. But, as Michael Questier has shown,[1] those connections were virtually all of the loyalist persuasion. Southampton was also an intimate of the earl of Essex. That Parsons' tract also seemed intended to discomfort Essex, to whom it was dedicated as the most the powerful man in England under the crown, and hence as the person who would almost certainly, when the time came, determine the course of the next succession, could only have made matters worse.[2]

In *Titus* issues of elective monarchy, resistance and regicide were canvassed through a made-up version of Roman history. Parsons, however, made his case through the analysis of real history; history taken, not only from the Old Testament and the histories of Rome and other pagan commonwealths, but also from the polities of the Christian west and, in particular, from the history of Christian England. Precisely the same events as those being portrayed on the contemporary stage were grist to Parsons' mill, providing proof positive that the monarchical polity of England really was elective and that the commonwealth really did possess a residual right to limit, actively restrain and, if need be, to remove tyrannical or unsatisfactory rulers, diverting the succession as they did so, if such an act seemed in the best interests of the common weal. As we have seen, amongst the reigns that Parsons used to clinch that case was that of Richard III. This was to render explicit, and very, very close to home, claims and positions that were certainly implied or enabled by *Titus Andronicus* (and indeed by *Richard III*), but which the particular generic, and un- or ahistorical forms, taken by the former play, and the heavily providentialised nature of the latter, served to occlude.

The move from the *Henry VI* plays to *Richard III* and thence to *Titus Andronicus* can be read as process of radicalisation. The account, in the former plays, of misrule and incipient tyranny, centred on evil counsel, feminine influence over a cypher-like (male) monarch and an increasingly disputed succession was replaced in *Titus* by a vision of out and out royal tyranny, centred upon both evil counsellors and monarchs of the most double-dyed malignity. If the radical political implications of *Richard III* remained masked or qualified by the intense providentialism of that play, in *Titus* many of the same moves and claims about tyranny, resistance and regicide, merely suggested in *Richard III*, were rendered far more starkly. Stripped bare of their providential gloss, and associated with a definition of tyranny with religious violence and persecution at or near its heart, in *Titus* elective monarchy, resistance theory and regicide were acted out on stage pretty much without qualification or apology. But what we will be watching in this section is not a continuation of the ideological path that led from the *Henry VI* plays to *Richard III* and thence to *Titus*, but rather a distinct drawing back from the positions implied in or enabled by that last play.

That process of ideological retrenchment and withdrawal took place in two plays – *King John* and *Richard II* – both of which dealt with reigns and events central to Parsons' purposes. If we accept the conventional dating for both plays, and the links between them – links that for instance led the editor of the Arden edition of *King John* to refer to that play as the 'twin' of *Richard II* – then Shakespeare chose to write versions of these two key reigns which, as we shall see below, diverged fundamentally from Parsons' account, rather close together and immediately after Parsons' book became a *cause célèbre* in England.

The dates of these two plays, and particularly that of Shakespeare's *King John*, remain uncertain and controversial. The balance of scholarly opinion, and recent research by Beatrice Groves,[3] favours a date somewhere around 1595 and a close link between *King John* and *Richard II*. But whenever we date them, it remains the case that the political meanings of the two reigns in Shakespeare's version are very different from that contained in Parsons' tract. Not only that, but the account given in these two plays of what it was both legitimate and prudent to do in the face of tyranny and usurpation (at least in a Christian and monarchical England) was very different from that implied by *Titus*. In and between all these plays, we can see something of a debate being conducted. Various moves and manoeuvres, arguments and claims, about the nature of monarchical legitimacy and tyranny, about resistance and regicide, about the elective or hereditary nature of monarchy, and about how, through a combination of tyranny and the equal and opposite reaction of usurpation, legitimacy might be lost and, once lost, how it might best be regained, are being staged and juxtaposed, tried on and tried out, in ways that directly engage with what the tract literature reveals were immediately contemporary concerns and debates.

Catholic and protestant appropriations of King John

John's reign was at the epicentre of the ideological and religious conflicts of post-reformation England. As we have seen, it was crucial to the debates about the succession that had punctuated Elizabeth's reign from the 1560s down to the publication of Parsons' *Conference* and beyond. One of the principal arguments against Mary Stuart's claim to the English throne was that no matter how good her hereditary right might appear to be, she could not inherit the English throne because she was foreign born; there being, her opponents claimed, a bar against those born outside the realm, of parents not in allegiance to the English throne.

To both make and refute that case a number of historical precedents and parallels were cited, one of which featured King John and his young nephew, Arthur. In a 1569 tract designed to argue that, in the event of Elizabeth's death without an heir of her body, Mary was in fact the natural and legitimate successor,[4] John Leslie, bishop of Ross claimed that Richard I had 'declared by consent of his nobility and commons, Arthur son of his brother Duke of

Brittany, his next heir in succession of the crown'. Not only was this a sign of Richard's 'care and foresight' in settling the succession – and here, of course, a heavy hint was being dropped to Elizabeth – it was a sure sign that, despite his foreign birth, Arthur could indeed succeed. It was true that John had subsequently seized the throne from his nephew, but since he had 'usurped also upon the said King Richard the first, his eldest brother', that was 'no proof that he [Arthur] was rejected because he was born out of the realm'. On the contrary, at the time, Arthur had been accepted as the heir apparent by 'all the world' and subsequently taken 'for such a one in all our stories'. Far from Arthur having been 'justly excluded by King John his uncle because he was a foreigner born', for 'this outrageous deed' John had been widely taken 'for an usurper . . . and afterward for a murderer, for imprisoning him and privily making him away'; 'which most foul and shameful act the said John needed not to have committed, if by foreign birth the said Arthur had been barred to inherit the crown of England'.

Moreover, when later, in their extreme alienation from the tyrant, John, the English barons had been casting around for an alternative they had lit upon 'Lewis, the eldest son of Philip the French king . . . through the right of Blanche his wife, which was a stranger born'. All of which proved, Leslie triumphantly concluded, that 'foreign birth was then thought no bar to the title of the crown'.[5] Such claims put the events of John's reign and, in particular, the question of Arthur's (and of John's) legitimacy slap bang in the middle of contemporary disputes about the succession in general and the Stuart claim in particular.

Leslie's tract went through many editions. The one produced in 1584 explicitly defended not merely the rights of Mary but also of her son James[6] and elicited a (manuscript) response which devoted several pages to an elaborate discussion of the various chronicle accounts of Arthur's claim and fate in order to conclude, *contra* Leslie, that Richard I had never adopted his nephew; or that, if he had, he had never intended that he should succeed; that Richard's action in adopting his nephew, if it had ever happened, rather than strengthening Arthur's case, implied that, before that act of adoption, Arthur had enjoyed no clear blood right, for 'where there is an undoubted right, what needeth such establishment?'; that at the time no one had regarded Arthur as the heir apparent; and that King John had been acknowledged as the legitimate king, chosen by his brother, elected and acclaimed by his subjects and initially accepted even by the kings of Scotland and of France.[7]

But John's reign was significant not only for its role in essentially secular debates about the law of the succession. John's conflict with the papacy, his deposition by Innocent III, and the multiple revolts against his rule, all ensured his reign a prominent place in other debates about the power of the papacy and the relation of the English crown to that power. The complex and contested course of John's reign meant that it provided ample material for both protestants and Catholics anxious to give historical heft to their particular take on these and related questions

There were at least two distinct Catholic approaches to the reign. The first and most radical is relatively easily summarised. We find it succinctly stated by Cardinal Allen. Twice in his reply to Cecil's *Execution of justice in England* Allen cited the example of John's reign to illustrate the pope's authority not only over Christian princes but more particularly over the crown of England.[8]

Allen explained that the same disciplinary and admonitory functions now being fulfilled by the pope in his relations with peccant Christian princes had been fulfilled, under the Old Testament, by the prophets in their dealings with the errant kings of Israel. 'Samuel denounced and executed God's sentence against Saul, Elijah against Jezebel and other prophets and priests against other kings without all malice and with much love.' Writing in 1584, Allen claimed that this was precisely what the pope, and indeed English Catholics, were doing now to Queen Elizabeth, lovingly subjecting her to the discipline of the church in order to bring her back to the fold, just as Henry II and King John had been, who, 'as mighty princes as they were', had yet 'yielded and reconciled themselves to the See Apostolic', a move that, Allen concluded, was 'in fine the only sure and honourable way before God and the world to keep themselves and their realms from perdition'.[9] Writing in 1588, in a tract designed to accompany the Armada, Allen made rather less irenic use of the same examples.[10]

The protestant versions of the reign were, in part, negative functions of the Catholic use of the same events and, in part, a function of a larger polemical effort to find (often eschatologically charged) precursors in the history of England for the breach with Rome and the rise of the reformation. Thus, King John featured prominently in the 'homily against disobedience and rebellion', where his reign was used to illustrate the propensity of 'these ambitious usurpers, the bishops of Rome', to incite 'the rebellions of ignorant subjects against their natural lords'; efforts which have 'overflowed all Italy and Germany with streams of Christian blood'. The pope's quarrel with King John 'about the election of Stephen Langton to the bishopric of Canterbury' is represented as a typically popish intrusion on the 'ancient right' enjoyed by all John's 'progenitors, all Christian kings of England before him'. That it ended with King John being cursed by the papacy and his subjects being discharged from 'their oath of fidelity to their sovereign lord' was presented both as all too typical of popish tyranny and as the *fons et origo* of all the subsequent trials and tribulations of John's reign.

For, on this account, John had literally been driven into the arms of the papacy by the disobedience and rebellion of the English, both nobility and people, whose natural allegiance to their prince had been undermined by their popish superstition and slavish subservience to the authority of the pope.

Throughout the homily, an insistent opposition between what was described as the 'natural' allegiance owed by all Englishmen to their 'natural lord' and 'country', and the 'usurped' and 'foreign' authority of the papacy, was used to drive home a basic, xenophobically anti-popish message. The clear implication was that what the prince, or rather a series of godly princes, had achieved could be preserved only if, now, unlike in John's reign, the people apprised themselves of the scriptural truths of right religion, resisted the blandishments of the pope and united behind their native prince against the foreign popish threat.

Not that the pope's help had come cheap. He had only supported John 'upon that condition' that John and his successors would all 'hold the crown and kingdom of England . . . , as the vassals of the said bishops of Rome forever'. And so not until the reigns of Henry VIII, Edward VI and 'our own gracious sovereign's days' had there been any real push back against the foul usurpations of the popish Antichrist.[11] On this account, John had been the precursor of current attempts to take back powers inherent in the English crown long usurped by the pope, and then to use said powers for the reformation of the church; a procees John had started, but which was only now being completed by his Tudor successors. In the account of John's reign in Foxe's *Acts and Monuments* – which was written by John Bale, the author of the virulently anti-papal play *King Johan*[12] – popery was more elaborately evoked as an Antichristian nexus of error, idolatry and superstition against which King John was pictured as having manfully struggled, only eventually to succumb because the time for the final revelation of, and breach with, Antichrist had yet to come. The result was an eschatologically charged view of the reign which set it within the framework of a prophetic history organised around the rise, reign, revelation and eventual fall of Antichrist; a view of history in which England had a special role to play in the working out of God's providential purposes and in which John represented an important precursor for, and figure of, Henry VIII, Edward VI and now Queen Elizabeth herself, all three of whom were presented, once again, as completing the programme of reform of which John's reign had been the harbinger.

Just like John (both at home and abroad), they were meeting with the furious opposition of Antichrist. But while John had been fighting against Innocent III, who represented Antichrist at the very zenith of his power and pretensions, these later monarchs were confronting Antichrist in the last days, when, unmasked, he was fighting for his very life. Where John's subjects had been mired in popish error, theirs now enjoyed the light of the gospel, and thus should be able to understand the difference between true religion and false, between obedience and rebellion, between the machinations of foreign princes and the usurped authority of foreign powers and the authentic exercise of his (or her) just rights by an English prince. On this view, although he had struggled manfully, precisely because of his position in sacred history, John had had to fail. But where he had failed, his Tudor heirs, precisely because they were operating at a different point in the divine plan, had not only succeeded to this point but might continue to succeed, both in throwing off the usurped claims of the Roman Antichrist from England and perhaps in presiding over his final fall.

Parsons' account of John's reign was designed to sit athwart the conventional protestant/Catholic divide represented by the book of homilies, on the one hand, and the works of William Allen, on the other. John's reign mattered to Parsons for a number of reasons. For one thing, he derived one of the Infanta's claims to the English throne through John's niece, Blanche. For another, the complex palimpsest of coups and counter-coups, of depositions and readeptions, that made up the high politics of the reign provided Parsons with one of his prime sites for proving that the conventions whereby the English throne could be inherited or transferred from one incumbent to the next were not set in stone, but in fact left ample room for manoeuvre according to the interests, actions and elections of the commonwealth. At the very outset of his reign, John's nephew Arthur 'was against the ordinary course of succession excluded'[13] and John chosen as king. While Parsons was happy to condemn John's later murder of his nephew as a foul crime for which he justly forfeited his throne, he accepted as entirely legitimate the process whereby the claims of Arthur had been set aside and those of John preferred. Indeed Parsons presented that move as a perfect example of the right of the commonwealth of England, here represented by the 'nobles and barons of the realm', confirmed in this instance 'by the will and testament of Richard his brother', to divert the throne to the most effective of the available candidates.[14]

Here, Arthur's status as a child, rather than his foreign birth, was taken to be reason enough to disqualify him from the succession. But no less legitimate, for Parsons, was John's later deposition by the barons and his replacement by Lewis (son of Philip) of France, an act the cancellation of which, on the occasion of John's unexpected death, was itself also, on Parsons' account, entirely legitimate, as the subsequent and highly successful reign of Henry III showed. Here, then, was the ultimate proof, within the short chronological compass of one admittedly tumultuous reign, of Parsons' account of the power of the English commonwealth to ensure its own interests and safety by diverting the succession and deposing tyrants.

The Holinshed account

In the version of the reign contained in Holinshed's *Chronicles* we have an amalgam of elements taken from all of these accounts (with the exception, of course, of the papalist Catholicism of Allen and, in certain moods, of Parsons).

Holinshed's analysis was largely political. For all its (relatively weak and peripheral) gestures towards the prophetic and the providential, in this rendition of
the reign, providence had pretty much nothing to do with shaping the outcome.
Nor, with Bale and Foxe, did the Holinshed account make any sustained
attempt to set John's reign in some wider prophetic, eschatologically charged,
narrative of church or English history.

The account in Holinshed opens with speeches by the Archbishop of
Canterbury and John's mother addressed to the lords temporal and spiritual,
pressing John's claim to the throne over those of his nephew Arthur. Those
arguments are by no means dominated by the superiority of John's hereditary
right or title but by his superior qualities as a ruler.[15] Here 'the difference of
government between a king that is a man and a king that is but a child' was
portrayed as crucial.[16] All of which seems to endorse some notion of elective
monarchy.

Thereafter the account spends no time at all discussing, still less casting
doubt on, the legitimacy of John's subsequent claim or tenure. In this version,
John is the legitimate king of England. Any subsequent doubts about his kingship stem not from the nature of his title, or the means by which he came to the
throne, but rather from his conduct once safely ensconced upon it.

As for Arthur, his supporters are shown to be motivated by self-interest
rather than by any sincere espousal of legitimist principle. Having done a deal
with John, sealed by the marriage between his son Lewis and John's niece
Blanche, the French King Philip is shown reactivating Arthur's claim for political advantage. Arthur himself is pictured suddenly turning on his uncle with a
full-scale claim to be the real king only when his capture by John has left him
with no choice.[17] Later still, the French king is described as making 'the revenge
of his [Arthur's] death' 'his chief quarrel' merely because such a claim would
greatly enlarge his party in England.[18]

As for the death of Arthur itself, this receives a remarkably ambiguous, even
open-ended, treatment. It was an event, we are told, about which 'writers make
sundry reports'. Some claimed that Arthur died trying to escape, others that he
wasted away in prison and still others 'that king John secretly caused him to be
murdered and made away, so as it is not throughly [sic] agreed upon in what
sort he finished his days; but verily king John was had in great suspicion,
whether worthily or not, the lord knoweth'.[19]

With the homilies, the Holinshed account condemns the rebellious tendencies of the nobility and the people as both misguided and counterproductive –
forcing John into concessions both to foreign power and to the exorbitant
demands on his subjects, which in their turn became grounds for further rebellion. But unlike both Foxe and the homily, the Holinshed version explicitly
convicts John of a serial lack of 'prudence', 'prowess' and 'policy'.[20] Throughout,
he is shown oscillating between fits of rage, wilfulness and cruelty, and a series

of entirely ill-judged and insincere concessions, all designed to allow him ultimately to work his will and wreak revenge on his serially disloyal subjects.

Terrified by the 'the general apostasy of his peers and people' that had followed his excommunication by the pope,[21] John had immediately submitted to the papacy. While the account emphasises that that submission had been complete and abject, it is also careful to maintain that 'those kings that succeeded King John have not observed any such laws of reconciliation'. The account insists that, whatever later popish authors might subsequently have claimed, what it calls 'the authentic chronicles of this realm' make no 'mention of any' physical 'surrender' of the crown to the pope or his representatives and make it clear that the terms imposed by the papacy 'pertained' only to John himself, 'and not to his successors'.[22] But the account does insist that, after his submission to the papal legate, Pandulph, the papacy became John's great ally,[23] and that, for the rest of the reign, John's alliance with the pope remained a cornerstone of his kingcraft. The result was that, having 'resigned the superiority of his kingdom ... unto the pope' and 'done to him homage', 'he was no absolute king indeed'.[24]

Nor was this an aberrant or isolated decision. Rather John is presented continuing in the same mode for the rest of the reign, giving away, in Magna Carta, even more than was demanded, in order to 'win him further credit' with the people, while he plotted his revenge, when a firm stance on the just rights of the crown might have stood him in better stead.[25] At a number of crucial junctures, he is described as having sufficient forces at his disposal to have seen off the threat of the moment, if only he had possessed the fortitude to stand his ground and act as a proper monarch should.[26] On several occasions the figure pushing him in the wrong direction is revealed to be Stephen Langton, the pope's choice as Archbishop of Canterbury and the quintessential evil counsellor and ambitious and overmighty cleric. Certainly, it is this political modus operandi, and John's concomitant determination to work 'his revenge and heart grudge' against his own subjects, that, the account maintains, rendered John more and more reliant on the pope and on foreign forces.

Thus the account strongly suggests, without ever quite actually saying so explicitly, that John was, or rather – confronted by first the recalcitrance and then the open rebellion of his own subjects – had become, something of a tyrant. Just before his death, so great had his hatred of his own people become that he is presented as wishing 'all misery to light upon them' and determining to push up the price of grain as high as possible, in order to starve them into submission.[27] By the end, his death, at the hands of the monk of Swineshead Abbey, is presented almost as a blessed release, about which the Holinshed account strikes a not merely neutral but positively approving note. In stark contrast to the account in Foxe, which makes great play with the regicidal propensities of popery and illustrates the king's murder at the hands of the monk with no fewer than six woodcuts, in Holinshed, John's assassin is presented, not as some popish zealot, but rather as 'being moved with zeal for the oppression of his country'.[28]

Popery certainly figured in this account, but the popery in Holinshed was a largely political affair, centred on subjection to the usurped claims of a foreign power rather than on any elaborated account of an Antichristian anti-religion. Admittedly, a couple of gestures are made in the latter direction. Peter of Pomfret, a false prophet, is described as 'a deluder of the people and an instrument of Satan, raised up for the enlargement of his kingdom', since it was fear, brought on by Peter's prophecy that John would lose his throne by the next Ascension Day, that prompted the king 'the sooner to agree with the pope'.[29] One Alexander Cementarius, a preacher active in the defence of the king's cause against the pope, is described as suffering at the hands of the pope because he told 'the truth against the beast, whose horns were pricking at every Christian prince, that he might set himself in a seat of supremacy above all principalities'. But, certainly when compared either to Foxe or to the homily, such gestures are few and far between and, for the most part, do little to disrupt the otherwise relentlessly 'political', even politique, tenor of the analysis.

On this score, it is surely no accident that the two great set-piece statements of anti-papal principle in the Holinshed narrative emanate, respectively, from the mouths of a Catholic king of France[30] and of a group of rebellious English nobles,[31] both of whom are intent, at that very moment, on establishing a foreigner on the English throne. On each occasion it is made clear that the motivation for the espousal of these principles is entirely self-serving and hypocritical, since each group either has, or will, on other occasions, just as enthusiastically claimed the support of the papacy. Indeed, the very same rebellious lords had earlier used the fact that John was under papal interdict as an excuse not to help him in his foreign wars against the Scots and the French.[32]

The point, therefore, seems to be that it is not so much the nature of the sentiments being expressed as the purposes for which they are being used that really matter and what emerges from the Holinshed account as the right end towards which all true subjects and loyal English people ought to be bending their best efforts is the defence of England from foreign invasion and rule. But that is something which, by the conclusion of the account, all the major players have pretty much abandoned. Not only are the barons and people fighting against their native prince, in alliance with a foreigner whom they are trying to establish on the English throne, but John himself, having subjected the English throne to that ultimate foreign power, the papacy, is now waging a ferocious war on his own subjects, using troops, raised largely in Poitou and Gascony, 'the only sight' of whom 'stroke the hearts of all the beholders with great fear and terror'.[33] John's cruelty and 'tyranny' are only matched by those of the French. 'Forgetting all former promises (such is the nature of strangers and men of mean estate . . .) they did many excessive outrages, in spoiling and robbing the people of the country, without pity or mercy. Moreover they did not only break into men's houses, but also into churches, and took out of the same such vessels and ornaments of gold and silver as they could lay hands upon'.[34] Here John's sacrilege in robbing the church is exactly paralleled by that of his enemies.

The result is an image of complete moral and political meltdown, of extreme dysfunction, which, while it might serve simply as a reminder of just how much had gone right under the rule of the Virgin Queen, could just as well operate as a warning of what could happen again, if certain trends in court and country were allowed to continue unchecked. For Holinshed's account presents the reader with a monarch whose hereditary right to rule has been contested for much of his (or her) reign. We have a nation beset by foreign threats. Military campaigns have to be fought in Ireland, Scotland and in France. We have an English monarch locked in conflict with the papacy and a great foreign power and a nation threatened with the spectre of foreign (then French, now Spanish) invasion and rule. We have a people heavily taxed and a (recalcitrant) nobility and church called on to support a monarch with all their substance in time of war. We have subjects whose loyalty to their prince is tested by anathemas, indeed by an act of deposition, cast against that prince, by the pope. We have a prince sorely tempted to do a deal, if not with the devil, then at least with the pope, in order to secure his political future. In John's reign, as recounted here, every part of the commonwealth, every element in the social and political order – the prince, the people, the nobility, and the clergy – fail in the discharge of their basic obligations both to one another and to 'England'. Unlike in the homily, or in Bale or Foxe, then, the parallels between John's reign, as the Holinshed account describes it, and the reign of Elizabeth operate, for the most part, to establish John less as a type than as an antitype, not as a prefiguration or harbinger of the virgin queen, but as a dreadful warning to both Queen Elizabeth and her subjects.

Of course, in Elizabethan England, one of the main ways of building the requisite unity was the sort of virulent anti-popery that animated the accounts of John's reign written by Bale and included in Foxe, where popery figures as a a demonic anti-religion. Of that there was small supply in the Holinshed account, which instead told a story, not of a country groaning under the sway of a popish superstition, idolatry and clerical tyranny, but rather of one 'over-swayed with foreign and profane power'.

Indeed, on the issue of religious error the account was suffused with a certain relativism; while admitting that his had indeed been a superstitious age, the account produced a remarkably generous estimation of John's religion, even while excoriating the political and moral faults that led him to subject both himself and his realm to the sovereign claims of the pope. So little to the point were the religious errors of popery that John's generosity in founding monasteries and in building abbeys[35] was cited as proof positive that he was not as irreligious as his clerical critics claimed, just as his church-robbing activities were excoriated as sacrilegious and seen as all too likely to bring down upon him 'a punishment appointed by God', namely the loss in the Wash, 'together with the spoilers', of all 'the spoil which had been gotten and taken out of churches, abbies and other religious houses'.[36]

The loss of John's treasure in the Wash is the one and only time that providence is pictured intervening actively to shape events. Not that the account is innocent of references to portents and signs of all sorts. There are mentions of the appearance of five moons, and of a man-sized fish, which together with various climatic prodigies are hailed as portentously providential. Indeed, at one point a notionally sceptical reader is roundly taken to task for denying any wider providential significance or moral meaning to such 'wonders'.[37] It is just that, with the exception of that single reference to the loss of John's treasure in the Wash, the account makes no attempt to use such providential signs in order to discern the hand of God shaping these events to some higher moral, spiritual or, still less, eschatological purpose. Thus, having been careful to assert his own orthodoxy on the providence front, the Holinshed author produces an account of the central events of John's reign not only largely devoid of providential framing or comment but also (and consequently) almost entirely 'secular' or 'political' in its terms of reference and causal explanation. What emerges is a version of popery centred on the political claims of the papacy, with all the elements in the social and political order – prince, people, nobility and clergy – being exhorted to unite now against the linked spectres of foreign rule and internal dissension.

If the Holinshed account has a hero, that role is filled neither by King John nor by any of his many opponents, but rather by an entirely marginal figure, a walk-on character in the struggle between princes and popes, prelates and peers, that constitutes the main storyline. While the foreign invader, the dauphin Lewis, was sacking his way through Sussex, 'subduing that county unto his obeisance, there was a young gentleman of those parts named William de Collingham', who 'loathing foreign subjection', 'would in no wise do fealty to Lewis', but instead took to 'the woods and desert places, whereof that country is full', in order to wage a guerrilla war against the French, thus displaying himself as a 'worthy gentleman of English blood'.[38]

In de Collingham's case, English is as English does, and true loyalty and true Englishness a function of the defiant defence of England against the foreigner. All of which is, of course, in marked contrast to King John who, as we have seen, was, by this point, using largely foreign forces to lay waste to his own kingdom, egged on by that most foreign of potentates, the pope. The account thus conjures not a confessionalised, inherently protestant, version of national identity, but rather something much more like a secular Englishness; an Englishness, be it noted, not centred, or even ultimately dependent, on the personal characteristics or conduct of the monarch, who, in the Holinshed account of John's reign has morphed into the decidedly tyrannical figure dispatched by the monk of Swineshead Abbey. On this basis, we might conclude that the Holinshed account effectively transcended the highly confessionalised versions of John's reign produced by Foxe and Bale, on the one side, and by Allen and Parsons, on the other. In so doing, it was at least as likely to appeal to certain sorts of Catholic loyalist – who might, after all, be no keener on Queen Elizabeth than many of his subjects had been on King John – as it was to the puritan godly.

*****

By the late 1580s and early 1590s, then, the confessional and polemical issues raised in interpreting and appropriating John's reign had been rendered both crystal clear and intensely contested. Not only were there established protestant accounts available in Foxe's *Acts and Monuments* and indeed in the book of homilies, but Catholic propaganda, written both before and at the time of the Armada, made considerable play with the pope's rightful deposition of the king, and with his reinstatement of John as a vassal of Rome. An extended account of the reign, of a decidedly ambivalent ideological hue, had been included in Holinshed's *Chronicles* of 1587, and, as we shall see below, a version of the protestant interpretation had been staged in *The troublesome reign of King John* a text of which had been printed in 1591. Finally, in the *Conference,* Parsons had put his own distinctive spin on the reign and in so doing rendered the topic newly controversial and contentious.

The point, then, is that writing a play about King John in the early or middle 1590s was not an ideologically neutral act. The subject-matter was so contested that no politically sentient contemporary was likely to produce an account of the reign, as it were, in a fit of absence of mind. That in such circumstances Shakespeare chose to write a play about King John is of some significance. For, by the very act of writing such a play, he could not help but position himself within a set of ideological co-ordinates laid down by the other available interpretations and stagings of the reign, and thus by the prior knowledge and expectations of his audience. Taken together, these different versions and appropriations of the reign constitute a sort of ideological grid or map, in terms of which the ideological and confessional co-ordinates and claims of Shakespeare's reworking of these events can be established and evaluated.

The first time as polemic, the second time as play: Shakespeare's *King John* and *The troublesome reign*

The stakes were further raised by the existence of a play prominent in the repertoire of the Queen's Men on *The troublesome reign of King John*.[1] There has, of course, been considerable scholarly debate about the relationship between the two texts; a debate centred on the issue of which came first and therefore of which provided the source for the other. The balance of scholarly opinion favours an earlier date for *The troublesome reign,* with *King John* dating from the mid 1590s, but this is clearly a question upon which certainty is not possible. Similarly, building on the researches of Brian Vicars, Charles Forker has recently attributed the *The troublesome reign* to George Peele, who many scholars, again following the researches of Vicars, now take to have co-authored *Titus Andronicus*. Given the existence, at least for a time, of a close collaborative relationship between the two men – if Shakespeare's *King John* does indeed post-date *The troublesome reign* – might we not take Shakespeare's subsequent decision to rework (while also sticking remarkably closely to) Peele's earlier version of John's reign as another form of collaboration, if not, in effect, a form of co-authorship? All of this certainly means the resulting differences in tone and content between the two plays have to be seen as the product of a series of highly self-conscious ideological as well as aesthetic and dramatic choices.

Either way, *The troublesome reign* represents a hot protestant take on the reign, written in effect as a piece of proto-nationalist propaganda in the period immediately following the Armada, and the current discussion takes place on the assumption that whichever came first a triangulation between the two plays and the use made of John's reign in Parsons' *Conference* (and, of course, Holinshed's *Chronicle*) has much to tell us about both the ideological resonance of Shakespeare's play and the political culture of the 1590s.

Legitimacy problematised

Both plays open not with John's dealings with Rome or popery but with a challenge to John's claim to the throne delivered by the king of France in the name of John's nephew, Arthur. Arthur is John's elder brother Geoffrey's son and thus, it is claimed, the real heir to the childless Richard Coeur de Lion. Again in both plays, as if to foreground issues of legitimacy and loyalty still more, the opening scene in which the French king's challenge to John is delivered is followed by another in which the king is called upon to arbitrate a disputed succession to the lands and title of the Faulconbridge family. Sir Robert Faulconbridge, who had been knighted while on crusade with Richard, has died and left two sons and there is a dispute between them as to who is the true heir. The elder brother Philip's title is being challenged by his younger sibling, on the grounds that Philip is, in fact, a bastard: 'base born, and base begot, no Faulconbridge' [TR, Pt. I, 120] and hence no true heir to his father's lands. It is true, the brother concedes, that the world, his father and now his mother all repute Philip to be the true heir, but this is false, since he is in fact the bastard son of Richard Coeur de Lion. In *The troublesome reign,* John refuses to accept that such claims – unsubstantiated as they are, and indeed flatly denied by the widow Faulconbridge – can provide any grounds for overturning Philip Faulconbridge's inheritance. Turning to Philip, he asks him who his father was. All Philip has to do is assert that he is the son of Sir Robert Faulconbridge and the lands are his. The life of a comfortably off Northamptonshire gentleman awaits. And yet he cannot do it. He is tormented by the thought that he is, in fact, the son of a king [TR, Pt. I, 253–62]. Philip, in short, cannot bring himself to deny that he is King Richard's son and so the words will just not come [TR, Pt. I, 270–79] and, in the end, he chooses honour over advantage. Royal blood will out, and the search for honour and renown in the loyal service of the crown stir the blood of any true-hearted Englishman far more than an easy life at home. Philip's touching display of loyalty to his royal blood is rewarded immediately by his new grandmother, Queen Eleanor, who embraces him as her 'son' [TR, Pt. I, 294–98]. King John knights him on the spot as 'Sir Richard Plantagenet, King Richard's son' [TR, Pt. I, 301]. As the others leave the stage, Philip confronts his destiny as a Plantagenet, pledging to 'act some wonders now I know my name./By blessed Marie I'll not sell that pride/For England's wealth, or all the world beside./Sit fast the proudest of my father's foes,/ Away good mother, there the comfort goes' [TR, Pt. I, 412–21].

Shakespeare's version follows the same structure but differs in highly significant ways. Early on in the opening exchanges with Chatillon the French envoy John cites 'our strong possession and our right for us' [KJ, I, i, 39] only to have his mother interject, in his ear, 'your strong possession much more than your right,/Or else it must go wrong with you and me:/So much my conscience whispers in your ear,/Which none but heaven, and you, and I, shall hear' [KJ, I, i, 40–43].

When placed in the context of the recent debates about Mary Stuart's claim to the throne of England outlined above, this brief exchange, which tells the audience that both John and his mother acknowledge that Arthur is the rightful king, takes on a very considerable significance. In effect, it places the play unequivocally on the Marian side of those debates and shows Shakespeare's version of the reign both playing off, and choosing between, a variety of parallels between the events of John's reign and pressingly controversial current concerns about the legitimacy of the Stuart claim; concerns no longer clustered around the Catholic Mary, queen of Scots, who was, of course, now dead, but rather around her protestant son, James VI. This was intended deliberately to locate the play in the midst of a contemporary fuss about the succession, a fuss delineated, on the one side, by the activities and fate of Peter Wentworth, recently imprisoned in the Tower for his attempts publicly to discuss the succession[2] and, on the other, by the publication of Parsons' *Conference about the next succession.*

Just in case anyone in the audience missed the point about Arthur's legitimacy, it was driven home later in the play by the bastard, who, as he watches Hubert carry Arthur's dead body from the stage, remarks, 'How easy dost thou take all England up/From forth this morsel of dead royalty!/The life, the right and truth of all this realm/Is fled to heaven' [*KJ*, IV, iii, 140–45]. It is thus no exaggeration to claim that the brief exchange between Eleanor and King John (compounded by the bastard's lament over Arthur's corpse) transforms the ensuing narrative, placing the issue of legitimacy at the very centre of the play in ways that are simply not true of the accounts in Foxe, Holinshed or *The troublesome reign.*

That shift of emphasis is underlined by Shakespeare's treatment of the succeeding scene in which John is called upon to arbitrate the dispute over the Faulconbridge inheritance.[3] As we have seen, in *The troublesome reign*, the issue is simply whether or not Philip is a bastard. If he is, he has no right to succeed to his father's lands. In Shakespeare's play the case turns on the status of his father's will; a will in which he had tried to disinherit his elder son because he was a bastard. In Shakespeare's play, King John decides the case according to law, pointing out that, whoever Philip's biological father may have been, as the child of Sir Robert's wife, born in wedlock, he must be accepted by his mother's husband as his child. This is an infrangible legal tie, the king explains; a bond so strong that it could withstand even the will of a king. For even if Coeur de Lion himself had subsequently tried to claim Philip as his own, Sir Robert could quite legitimately have refused him [*KJ*, I, i, 116–29].

John's verdict serves to tie the Faulconbridge inheritance to the Plantagenet inheritance, for later in the play (as in *The troublesome reign*), confronted with Arthur's claim (as the elder brother Geoffrey's son) to the English throne, Eleanor tells Constance that 'I can produce/A will that bars the title of thy son'; a claim that Constance contemptuously dismisses [*KJ*, II, i, 191–94]. Here, then, is John's claim to the English throne shown resting, in part at least, on the same sort of testamentary basis as the younger Faulconbridge's claim to his father's estate; a claim that had cut precisely no ice when advanced to King John himself in the dispute over the Faulconbridge estate. There could scarcely be a clearer exemplification of the deeply compromised nature of John's kingship, as his legally correct judgement of the Faulconbridge cases throws into high relief the contradictions and difficulties inherent in his own claim to the throne.

Nor were the subversive resonances of this scene limited to the world of the play. For, as Robert Lane points out, the role of royal wills in determining the course of the succession was a question of very considerable contemporary import. For not only did Queen Elizabeth's claim to the throne turn on Henry VIII's will, so too did the validity of the Stuart claim in general and thus, in particular, of the right of James Stuart to succeed to the English throne after Elizabeth's death.[4] In Shakespeare's account the weakness of John's claim is shown as having direct effects on his decisions. Thus it is John and Eleanor's knowledge of the weakness of John's claim to be king that makes the offer of a marriage alliance between the dauphin and Blanche one that they cannot refuse. The political calculations at work here are made quite explicit by Queen Eleanor, who, as soon as the proposal is made by the people of Angiers, advises John to adopt it as his own. 'Son, list to this conjunction, make this match:/Give with our niece a dowry large enough:/For by this know thou shalt so surely tie/Thy now unsur'd assurance to the crown,/That yon green boy shall have no sun to ripe/The bloom that promiseth a mighty fruit' [KJ, II, i, 468–73]. Such are his political circumstances, so, if not tenuous, then at least contestable, his claim to the throne, that it is more than worth John's while to part with all of the English possessions in France to separate the French king from Arthur.

The bastard

In both *The troublesome reign* and *King John*, the bastard goes on to play a central role; indeed he emerges as something like the hero of both plays. In *The troublesome reign* he first proves his mettle by repeatedly braving to his face, pursuing into single combat and finally killing the duke of Austria, the murderer of his newfound father, King Richard. Just as the first mention in the royal presence of his father's name had rendered him unable to deny his true ancestry, so the mere sight of Limoges, clad in the lion's skin he had taken from King Richard's dead body, moves him to the height of passion [TR, Pt. I, 555–79]. At their first meeting in battle the bastard worsts Limoges, driving him from the stage and seizing the lion's skin taken from Richard's corpse, hailing it as 'the first freehold that Richard left his son;/With which I will surprise his foes,/As Hector's statue did the fainting Greeks' [TR, Pt. I, 667–69]. Even as, at Blanche's wedding with the dauphin, peace is concluded between the various parties, Philip tries to challenge Limoges to single combat and has to be restrained by John and Eleanor [TR, Pt. I, 961–63]. In the next battle Philip pursues Limoges and kills him. It is an action that proves Philip's claims to be Richard's 'base-begotten son', his heir in blood, and in deed, if not in law [TR, Pt. I, 1044–50].

Philip also opposes the foreign match arranged for the king's niece Blanche with the dauphin. Philip had wanted Blanche for himself, offering to win his father's lion skin back from Limoges in return for her favour [*TR*, Pt. I, 583–84]. Having secured said skin in combat with Limoges, Philip lays it at Blanche's feet, 'being the first adventure I achieved,/And first exploit your grace did enjoin:/Yet many more I long to be enjoined' [*TR*, Pt. I, 710–13].What appears to be the natural course of all this chivalric foreplay is, however, disrupted by the match arranged at breakneck speed between the dauphin and Blanche. In the midst of the negotiations for this union Philip seeks to prevent the marriage and press his own suit, only to be put in his place by Eleanor: 'peace Philip, I will look thee out a wife/We must with policy compound this strife' [*TR*, Pt. I, 790–96]. But as the action of the play reveals, England and John would have been far better off had they followed the bastard's bluff English instincts rather than the dictates of Queen Elinor's 'policy' and avoided this match with a foreigner. For not only is the accord which the marriage is designed to cement almost immediately disrupted by the intervention of the papal legate and the perfidy of the French king, but after the death of Arthur it is his marriage to Blanche that gives the dauphin a claim to the English throne and thus makes him the preferred candidate of the dissident English lords, the French and the papacy.

Philip is no less central to Shakespeare's play than to the *The troublesome reign*. However, unlike the character in *The troublesome reign*, in the early acts of *King John* Philip shows no sign of the inherent nobility, of the spontaneously chivalric and honourable characteristics, that mark the bastard in *The troublesome reign* as the son of Richard Coeur de Lion. In *The troublesome reign*, Philip's royal blood, his true identity, is shown simply taking over his conscious mind and forcing him to accept his destiny as a Plantagenet.[5] In Shakespeare's version, however, as Edward Gieskes has pointed out, things are very different; Philip is portrayed as choosing to forsake his inheritance and accept Queen Eleanor's offer of royal patronage. Given the opportunity, he will seize his chance of adventure and advancement in the service of the king. 'Well won is still well shot/And I am I, howe'er I was begot' [*KJ*, I, i, 174–75].[6]

Certainly, there is no hint in Shakespeare's version of a chivalric courtship between Blanche and Philip. Nor, in his ridicule and pursuit of Limoges, is there any explicit mention of the need or desire to avenge the death of his father.[7] Rather he picks a fight with Austria as a yob on a street corner might: returning to the stage with Limoges' head, he sets it down casually to take a breath. There is violence and energy aplenty here, but no gesture towards any notion of chivalric honour or of ancient lineage; no talk of owing a tribute of valorous or glorious deeds to the Plantagenet name. Throughout the first half of Shakespeare's play the bastard keeps up a coarse and direct commentary on the actions of his betters. When the dauphin woos Blanche, on cue, it is the bastard who mocks both the insincerity of his protestations of love and the stilted courtly terms in which they are couched [*KJ*, II, i, 504–9]. In short, while to Limoges the bastard is 'a cracker', to King John he is 'a good blunt fellow' [*KJ*, I, i, 71].

Philip, then, emerges in the early acts of Shakespeare's version as a plebeian man on the make, the quintessential outsider, anxious to learn the ways of his betters and to make his way in their world as best he can. That certainly is how many critics have typed him. As Gieskes puts it, 'his is a "mounting spirit", willing and eager to trade financial security and stability for a sixteenth-century version of upward mobility'. [8] For Michael Mannheim the bastard is a 'soldier of fortune', even something of a Machiavel. [9]

But this is not quite right, or rather, while it is an accurate enough description of how, in the earlier parts of the play, the bastard wants to sound, it does not adequately characterise what he subsequently goes on to do. While he confidently presents his suggestion that the kings unite their forces against the town of Angiers as smacking 'of the policy' [*KJ*, II, i, 395–96], the bastard is shocked to the core by the subsequent deal struck between the English and French kings. On this basis he is still a neophytre in the policy stakes. Entirely at home with the frank violence and aggression of the battlefield, happy enough to threaten death and destruction to Angiers, the bastard is first staggered and then baffled, indeed morally appalled, by the duplicity that underlies the peace.

But that bafflement is momentary. Almost immediately, he collects himself, trying again to assume the mantle of the hard-boiled new man, maintaining that he is only railing 'on this commodity' 'for because he hath not woo'd me yet'. Comparing himself to 'a poor beggar' that 'raileth on the rich', he resolves that 'whiles I am a beggar, I will rail/And say there is no sin but to be rich;/And being rich, my virtue then shall be/To say there is no vice but beggary./Since kings break faith upon commodity,/Gain, be my lord, for I shall worship thee!' [*KJ*, II, i, 587–98]. This, of course, recalls his earlier promise, made to himself, not to be 'a bastard to the time' but rather, through a process of 'observation' of the doings of 'worshipful society', to 'extract/Sweet, sweet, sweet poison for the age's tooth:/Which, though I will not practise to deceive,/Yet, to avoid deceit, I mean to learn;/For it shall strew the footsteps of my rising' [*KJ*, I, i, 205–16]. But despite these repeated resolutions to take on the persona of the new man on the make, as subsequent events prove, that is a role that the bastard can never quite bring himself to play with any real conviction. [10]

However, in the early acts his efforts to do so, and his satiric, boisterous commentary both on those efforts and on the actions of the major players, constitute a central feature of the play's exposure of the amoral, commodity-centred politics of a world devoid of dynastic and moral legitimacy. Indeed, as someone who has actually chosen illegitimacy, the bastard provides the ideal commentator for this moral and political scene. To quote Michael Neill, 'in a world tainted with illegitimacy' the bastard's status as ' "a sort of moral oxymoron ... a true bastard to the time" ' lends his both mordant and jokey analysis of contemporary mores 'a paradoxical quality of "authenticity" '.[11] As Womersley observes, his comment – 'legitimation, name and all is gone' [*KJ*, I, i, 248] – while intended to describe his own situation after he has repudiated his Faulconbridge inheritance, could serve just as well as an epigraph for the entire political world staged by the play, 'a world in which absolute standards of value do not exist'.[12]

Commodity

In Shakespeare's version, that world is evoked most starkly in the scene before Angiers. This is designed to rip away the facade of high-sounding legitimist principle with which all the participants in the war between John and Philip have sought to justify their actions. In confronting the French, John casts himself as 'God's wrathful agent' called 'to correct/Their proud contempt that beats His peace to heaven' [*KJ*, II, i, 87–88]. Earlier Philip has greeted Arthur with the words 'Ah noble boy, who would not do thee right?' [*KJ*, II, i, 18]. Limoges has sworn never to return home until Arthur is ensconced on the English throne, concluding his harangue with the claim that 'the peace of heaven is theirs that lift their swords/In such a just and charitable war' [*KJ*, II, i, 19–36, quote at 35–36]. Later, in conference with John, King Philip claims to be drawing his authority to intervene in the English succession 'from that supernal judge that .... hath made me guardian to this boy:/Under whose warrant I impeach thy wrong/And by whose help I mean to chastise it'. 'Alack, thou dost usurp authority', counters John; 'excuse it is to beat usurping down' comes the inevitable reply [*KJ*, II, i, 106–19]. It is an exchange that shows the ways in which competing claims to legitimacy render the appeal to legitimist principle and divine aid – so fundamental to the ideology of kingship in the play and indeed in Elizabethan England – immediately problematic, turning the world into a nightmare of claim and counter-claim in which there is no way to establish the rights and wrongs of the situation. As the citizens of Angiers put it, 'he that proves the king/To him will we prove loyal' [*KJ*, II, i, 270–71].

Such a view echoes Parsons' critique of all theories of indefeasible hereditary right. Trace any hereditary claim back far enough and it becomes deeply problematic. For Parsons the existence of such dynastic skeletons in the closets of all major monarchical polities meant that mere hereditary right could never be the sole or even the main basis for monarchical legitimacy. Here Shakespeare's play seems to agree with the first half of that analysis, but not, as we shall see, with the second, which proceeded to argue that all such monarchies must therefore be, at bottom, elective.

The world of incommensurate claim and counter-claim conjured by the play, and the pursuit of immediate self-interest and preservation to which it inevitably leads, is almost immediately illustrated by the behaviour of the citizens of Angiers. This city is a possession of the English crown, recently invested by the besieging French forces that are seeking to claim it in Arthur's name. It is to relieve this siege that John has rushed with breakneck speed into France. Both he and Philip the French king then compete rhetorically for the allegiance of the city, appealing, in the most exalted terms, to the natural loyalty and allegiance felt by the citizens for their true prince. 'You men of Angiers, and my loving subjects' John starts, only to be interrupted by Philip's counter-plea to 'you loving men of Angiers, Arthur's subjects' [KJ, II, i, 203–4]. In response to the two kings' pleadings the citizens reply that 'in brief, we are the king of England's subjects;/For him, and in his right, we hold this town'. 'Acknowledge then the king, and let me in,' comes John's response, only for him to be told that until they can be sure who is the real king of England they will bar their city's gates against all comers [KJ, II, i, 266–72]. The citizens want, in fact, the kings to duke it out in front of them and then they will submit to the victor.

This, of course, is a craven attempt to avoid taking sides until they can with certainty side with the winner. The bastard gets it typically right when he describes their conduct: 'by heaven, these scroyles of Angiers flout at you, kings,/And stand securely on their battlements,/As in a theatre, whence they gape and point/At your industrious themes and acts of death' [KJ, II, i, 373–76]. But the citizens do not present it that way; theirs, they claim, is a conscience-based appeal to providence. 'A greater power than we denies all this,' they claim. 'And till it be undoubted, we do lock/Our former scruple in our strong-barr'd gates:/Kings of our fear, until our fears, resolv'd,/Be by some certain king purg'd and depos'd' [KJ, II, i, 368–72]. On this account, their fears are not merely for their temporal safety but also concern conscientious scruples about the ultimate object of their political loyalty and trust. Until they can be sure of the identity of their true king – a decision which providence will make for them, they claim, by deciding the issue of the battle between the two kings – they must reserve their judgement and allegiance. Here the play adds the appeal to providence to the long list of ways of establishing or asserting the legitimacy of any given claim or right to rule.

The exchanges before Angiers also constitute a very effective demonstration of the fallacies, the practical inadequacies, of any elective theory of monarchy. For the scene stages the incapacity of 'the people' to act effectively in deciding issues of hereditary right and succession, once the succession has been called into real question and become the object of overt military contest between the rival claimants. In such circumstances, faced by the violent force mobilised by the contending parties, all hot in pursuit of their own advantage, far from being able to arbitrate and decide such disputes, the people would (naturally enough) seek their own security, by saving their own skins, rather than standing up, either for the cause of hereditary right or the interests of the commonweal, as Parsons' theory suggested that they could, would and must.

The citizens of Angiers are only disturbed from their position of self-serving and -preserving neutrality by the bastard's suggestion that the two kings unite their forces to sack the town before returning to their former internecine struggle for the English crown. Suitably enough, therefore, it is the citizens of Angiers who come up with the compromise settlement, turning on the marriage between Lewis the dauphin and Blanche that will restore peace between England and France and save their own bacon into the bargain. Both sides eagerly embrace this outcome, leaving only poor Arthur, who is, after all, only the legitimate heir to the English throne, and his volubly protesting mother, Constance, in the lurch. When the French king reminds King John of that inconvenient fact, John brushes his scruples aside. 'We will heal up all,' he claims, by making Arthur duke of Britain and earl of Richmond and giving him the lordship of Angiers[KJ, II, i, 545–52]. Here, then, from the inside, as it were, is laid bare the pursuit of personal and dynastic interest, or, in Philip's word, of 'vantage', that lies behind this sudden reversal of political stances and fortunes.

The same point is made in still more forcible terms by certain outsiders. The most voluble commentary comes (predictably) from the ultimate loser in these transactions, Arthur's mother, Constance, who rails against the deal, struck at her son's expense, between these two 'perjured kings'. When Limoges responds to this outburst with the ejaculation 'Lady Constance, peace!', she flies at him. 'War! War! No peace! Peace is to me a war' before launching into an extended denunciation of his disgraced honour and perjured faith [KJ, III, i, 107–29]. When first confronted by this sudden *renversement d'alliances*, Constance had pictured the political world as an arena ruled over not by a just God, a divine providence bent on the preservation of true sovereignty and legitimate authority, not to mention the defence of widows and orphans like Arthur and herself, but by the fickle Goddess Fortune, a deity who favoured the strong and victimised the weak, while intermittently overturning the just claims and structures of legitimate authority for the sheer joy in her own power. 'That strumpet fortune', has, Constance laments, been 'corrupted, chang'd and won from' her son Arthur. 'Sh'adulterates hourly with thy uncle John,/And with her golden hand hath pluck'd on France/To tread down fair respect of sovereignty,/And made his majesty the bawd to theirs./France is a bawd to fortune and King John' [KJ, II, ii, 54–62].

While Constance rails on fortune the bastard marvels at the influence in the counsels of kings of what he terms 'commodity'. Thus, by the end of Act II, we have a distinctly dark vision of the political world. It is one in which questions of political and therefore moral legitimacy, of dynastic right and political allegiance, are always already, if not contested, then certainly capable of contest. And, once they have become contested, all claims to higher divine sanction or moral purpose, all claims on the allegiance and honour, the loyalty and obedience, of the subject become deeply problematic. In such circumstances there is something farcical about the sort of principled appeals to divine sanction and the claims to political allegiance and moral obligation, advanced against each other by John and the French king or by both of them to the inhabitants of Angiers. Just as suspect is the resort to religion; made first by the citizens of Angiers in their recourse to 'conscience' and 'providence' to legitimise their own self-serving neutrality and then by Pandolph in his deployment of the spiritual authority of Mother Church in defence of the political authority of the papacy.

On this view, relations between princes become an endless struggle for 'vantage'. This is a war of all against all, a struggle for self-interest and self-preservation, which, when played out between kings, kills thousands. Wars begin and end according to the dictates of royal self-interest. Appeals to peace are mere tactics in a struggle for rhetorical and hence political advantage. The kings of France and England conclude a peace not to preserve the lives of their subjects but to enhance their own political interests. When that alliance breaks down, both resort to force, with undiminished rage and intensity. Even the widow Constance, in her appeals to heaven for justice, calls not for peace but war. The ruling deity here is not providence but 'fortune', which means, when translated from Constance's into the bastard's terms, a political and social world governed by the imperatives of 'commodity', a term which, as Emrys Jones points out, was a synonym for the narrow pursuit of material self-interest, usually deployed in direct contrast to the defence of the common good, and, couched, as it was, in the language of commerce, completely antithetical to the values of aristocratic or royal honour.[13]

Shakespeare's play, at least in its first three acts or so, thus occupies a very different moral universe to that sketched not only in *The troublesome reign*, but in all the other protestant accounts of these events, and it does so, I am arguing here, because of the deliberate and explicit undermining of King John's claims to the throne with which the play opens. Once that has been called into radical question, all the relativising rhetoric of Constance and the bastard falls instantly into place.

Popery in *The troublesome reign*

Perhaps the most basic reason for the difference of tone between the two plays lies in their very different treatments of popery. While in *The troublesome reign* John's reign is dominated by the struggle against popery and John's and the bastard's status as, respectively, flawed and triumphantly heroic characters is defined by their relation to the popish threat, in Shakespeare's version that is decidedly not the case.

(i) The bastard

In *The troublesome reign* the most strident elements of anti-popery are associated with the bastard, and that association serves to underwrite his emergence
in the second half of the play as the play's real hero. As hostilities break out
against the now papally sponsored French, Philip echoes the most inflated of
the eschatologically inflamed prophecies and prognostications that attended
the defeat of the Armada, as he crows 'Pandulph thyself shalt see/How France
will fight for Rome and Romish rites./Nobles, to arms, let him not pass the
seas./Let's take him captive, and in triumph lead/The king of England to the
gates of Rome' [*TR*, Pt. I., 1031–36]. Once the war in France has been won,
Philip is sent back to England to begin the process of expropriating the church's
property to help pay the costs of the king's (in part anti-papal) wars; a task
which he views with unconcealed glee [*TR*, Pt. I, 1129–32] and discharges with
considerable gusto and threatened violence.

At one point Philip enters demanding that a friar in his custody show him
'where the abbot's treasure lies or die'. These threats are greeted with a barrage
of rhyming gibberish, a crude version of protestant satires on the superstitiously incantatory and magical nature of Catholic piety. Philip answers with a
sing-song parody of his own, which concludes 'now, bald and barefoot Bungay
birds when up the gallows climbing,/Say Philip he had words enough to put
you down with rhyming'. This is followed by another burst of popish, Latin-
spangled, gobbledygook. 'A pardon, O parce, Saint Francis for mercy,/Shall
shield thee from nightspells and dreaming of devils,/If thou wilt forgive me,
and never more grieve me./With fasting and praying, and hail Mary saying./
From black purgatory a penance right sorry,/Friar Thomas will warm you,/It
shall never harm you.' Philip however proves completely impervious to these
blandishments. 'Come leave off your rabble,/Sirs hang up this lozell.'

Having failed to buy Philip off with intercessory prayers, the monks turn to
money and a second friar offers to lead him to the prior's chest which, he
claims, has a thousand pounds of silver and gold in it, if he will just spare the
life of the friar, 'the good old man, my hostess' oldest guest'. The chest is duly
produced and opened, only to contain not money but a nun. Of course, it falls
to Philip to draw the appropriately anti-popish conclusion. 'Is this the nunneries
chastity? Beshrew but I think/They go as oft to venery, as niggards to their
drink./Why paltry friar and pandar too, yee shameless shaven crown,/Is this
the chest that held a hoard, at least a thousand pound?/And is the hoard a holy
whore? Well be the hangman nimble,/He'll take the pain to pay you home, and
teach you to dissemble' [*TR*, Pt. I, 1181–233] We are here slap bang in the
middle of John Bale's hyper-protestant version of these events; with the stage
filled with the basic rhythms and tropes of a popular anti-popery founded
upon such texts as Bale's *King Johan*; a nexus of references and images long
since reduced, by myriad pamphlets, ballads and interludes, to the status of

popular commonplace, of instantly recognisable jokes, caricatures and stereotypes, a nexus of meanings and associations upon which Philip's diatribes are
here effortlessly drawing.

The scene concludes with Philip arresting a spurious prophet named Peter,
who enters the action as a downmarket fortune teller and con man. Asked, by
Philip, who he is and whence he comes Peter replies, 'I am of the world and in
the world, but live not as others by the world: what I am I know, and what thou
wilt be I know. If thou knowest me now be answered: if not, enquire no more
what I am.' To this farrago Philip replies 'Sir, I know you will be a dissembling
knave, that deludes the people with blind prophecies: you are him I look for,
you shall away with me: bring away all the rabble, and you friar Laurence
remember your ransom – a hundred pound and a pardon for your self, and the
rest come on. Sir Prophet, you shall with me, to receive a Prophet's reward' [*TR*,
Pt. I, 1294–313] – which, of course, turns out to be hanging.

Later in the play, as John, threatened by the French and deserted by his
barons, prepares to submit to the pope, it is Philip whom he sends to recall his
subjects to obedience. As he goes, Philip observes that 'This is the cursed priest
of Italy/Hath heapt these mischiefs on this hapless land./Now Philip, had thou
Tully's eloquence,/Then mightest thou hope to plead with good success' [*TR*,
Pt. II, 254–57]. Confronted with the barons' defence that they are merely about
to remove a tyrant, replace him with the rightful heir and do the bidding of the
pope, the bastard demolishes their case, point by point. 'For any private causes
that you have,/Methink they should not mount to such a height,/As to depose a
king in their revenge.' As for 'Arthur's death, King John was innocent' of it. And
even if he had not been, that was still no grounds for subjects to rebel against
'against a king anointed by the Lord'. Such revenge belonged only to God. 'And
doth a pope, a priest, a man of pride/Give charters for the lives of lawful kings?/
What can he bless, or who regards his curse,/But such as give to man, and takes
from God?' There was no one who dies in such 'belief', Philip claimed but 'sells
his soul perpetually to pain./Aid Lewis, leave God, kill John, please hell,/Make
havoc of the welfare of your souls,/For here I leave you in the sight of heaven,/A
troup of traitors, food for hellish fiends' [*TR*, Pt. II, 453–78]. Here then, clearly
enunciated, is the claim, central to the self-image of the Elizabethan protestant
state at bay, that Catholics, as devotees of the papacy and believers in various
sorts of resistance theory, were all actual or potential traitors.

(ii) King John

John's relation to popery is however presented as far more ambivalent and, in *The
troublesome reign* at least, it is that ambivalence that is the cause of his eventual
slide into tyranny, impotence and failure. At the outset of both *The troublesome
reign* and *King John* the king is presented by himself, and perceived, even by his

enemies, as a man of force, vigour and virtue. In the former play young Arthur opines that 'I rather think the menace of the world/Sounds in his ears as threats of no esteem,/And sooner would he scorn Europa's power,/Than loose the smallest title he enjoys;/For questionless he is an Englishman' [TR, Pt. I, 447–51]. In *King John*, Chatillon reports to his royal master that John's initial descent on France has been carried off with staggering speed. [KJ, II, i, 56–61]. When the peace concluded between the two monarchs breaks down, John rounds on the French with violent anger and terrible force [KJ, III, i, 249, 266–69]. After he has won the ensuing battle, the French again describe the speed and efficiency of his manoeuvres with awed admiration [KJ, III, iii, 10–14].

From the outset of *The troublesome reign*, John's vigorous assertion of Englishness is given a decidedly anti-popish inflection. 'I will not be commanded/ By any power or prince in Christendom,/To yield an instance how I hold mine own,/More than to answer, that mine own is mine' [TR, Pt. I, 604–7].

He shows a similar (anti-popish) spunk in his first confrontation with the papal legate, Pandulph. 'I scorn to be subject to the greatest prelate in the world. Tell thy master so from me, and say, John of England said it, that never an Italian priest of them all, shall either have tithe, toll, or polling penny out of England, but, as I am king, so will reign, next under God, supreme head both over spiritual and temporal: and he that contradicts me in this, I'll make him hop headless' [TR, Pt.1, 978–84]. Then turning his attention to the king of France, John continues: 'though thou and all the princes of Christendom suffer themselves to be abused by a prelate's slavery, my mind is not of such base temper. If the pope will be king in England, let him win it with the sword, I know no other title he can allege to mine inheritance' [TR, Pt.1, 986–91].

Later, John spits defiance at the French king and the pope's legate. Because 'thou giv'st thy sword into a prelate's hands', Philip was an 'unworthy man to be accounted king'. As for Pandulph, John tells him that 'where I of abbots, monks and friars/Have taken somewhat to maintain my wars,/Now I will take no more but all they have./I'll rouse the lazy lubbers from their cells,/And in despite I'll send them to the pope' [TR, Pt. I, 1018–26]. The war triumphantly concluded, with young Arthur captured and the French dispersed, John proclaims he will 'Ransack the abbeys, cloisters, priories,/Convert their coin unto my soldiers use:/And whatso'ere he be within my land,/That goes to Rome for justice and for law,/While he may have his right within the realm,/Let him be judged a traitor to the state,/And suffer as an enemy to England' [TR, Pt. I, 1103–13]. As for his nobles, he exhorts them to 'each look unto your charge,/And arm your-selves against the Roman pride' [TR, Pt. I, 1133–34]. Here, then, is John as spokesman for and vigorous defender of the independence of England against both the formal claims of the papacy and clergy and the duplicitous, both superstitious and self-serving, efforts of foreign princes, in alliance with the pope, to invade the country and seize the crown. So long as he persists in that

mode John does famously. But in victory he starts to depart from the path of
virtue.

Throughout, *The troublesome reign* endorses the legitimacy of John's title to
be king. The only characters who challenge it are Arthur himself and his
mother Constance [*TR*, Pt. 1, 510–14, 519–20, 525–27, 1057–59, 1097–98].
Even the rebellious barons denounce John as a tyrant not as a usurper, basing
their right to resist on John's tyranny and their own popery: 'who upholds a
tyrant in his course/Is culpable of all his damned guilt' and incurs 'the pope's
most dreadful curse' [*TR*, Pt. II, 390–419, quotes at 410–11, 415]. However,
despite what the play presents as the strength of his dynastic position, even at
the zenith of his power and success, having defeated the French and secured
control of Arthur's person, John continues to worry that Arthur presents a
threat to his continued rule. The play presents this not, as Shakespeare's version
does, as a rationally explicable, perhaps even inevitable, response to John's
always already tenuous claims to dynastic right, but rather as something altogether more irrational, deeply connected not merely to the external threat of
popery, but to the spiritual thrall that popery continues to exert over the king
himself, let alone his people.

Having prevailed upon his nobility to allow him to be crowned a second
time, to reaffirm his right to rule in the face of the pope's anathema, and having
promised in return to release his nephew from prison, John reverses himself
because of Peter of Pomfret's prophecy that he will not last as king past
Ascension Day. As we have seen, Peter had been discovered, by the bastard, to
be the merest phoney, but John is badly shaken by the prophet's claims. His
response reveals the paradoxical extent to which he has, and has not, emanci-
pated himself from popish superstition, for the prophet is both dismissed as a
witch – 'hell's damned secretary' – and his prophecy believed [*TR*, Pt. I, 1641–
47]. Or rather, while claiming to disregard Peter's prophecy, John takes steps to
avert its fruition. Such a reaction is, of course, both illogical and pointless. If
the prophecy is genuine, nothing that John can do will prevent its coming true.
If it is false, there is, by definition, no need for remedial action of any sort.
Moreover, the steps John does take are of the most serious and morally appalling
nature. For, so shaken is the king by the claims of this false prophet that, despite
his promise, just given to his nobles, to free young Arthur, he now resolves
to have the innocent boy killed. 'The brat shall die that terrifies me thus./
Pembroke and Essex I recall my grant,/I will not buy your favours with my
fear;/Nay murmur not, my will is law enough,/I love you well, but if I loved you
better,/I would not buy it with my discontent' [*TR*, Pt. I, 1648–59].

Having himself crowned again, breaking his word to his nobles, equating
his will with law and finally vowing to murder his nephew, on the say-so of a
mere cunning man and fortune teller who has previously made his living
selling lies to a credulous populace, John is now turning from some sort of

proto-protestant hero into a figure John himself eventually describes as 'a tragic tyrant, stern and pitiless'. 'Not a title follows after John,/But butcher, blood-sucker and murderer' [*TR*, Pt. I, 1702–3]. Not only is this John's first act of genuine tyranny, it is also the course of action that, by alienating the affections of the English lords, leaves the realm open to foreign invasion and ultimately forces John to make his fateful peace with the pope.

John had been proffered two prophecies by Peter of which his claim that the king would not survive Ascension Day had been only the second. The first had been the interpretation of an external event, a genuine portent seen by all. At the moment the crown had been placed on John's head at his second corona-tion five moons had appeared in the sky. Desperate to know what this might mean, John had sent for the 'wizard', Peter, to interpret it for him. Peter's reading had been that 'the sky wherein these moons have residence,/Presenteth Rome, the great metropolis,/Where sits the pope in all his holy pomp./Four of the moons present four provinces,/To wit, Spain, Denmark, Germany and France,/That bear the yoke of proud commanding Rome,/And stand in fear to tempt the prelate's curse./The smallest moon, that whirls about the rest,/Impatient of the place he holds with them,/Doth figure forth this island Albion,/Who 'gins to scorn the see and state of Rome,/And seeks to shun the edicts of the pope' [*TR*, Pt. I, 1616–27]. John comments, 'why then it seems the heavens smile on us,/Giving applause for leaving of the pope' [*TR*, Pt. I, 1630–31]. But this is not the prophecy to which he attends. Instead, he listens to Peter's second predic-tion, one based, as even Peter himself admits, not on some vision vouchsafed to all, but merely on 'some other knowledge that I have/By my prescience' [*TR*, Pt. I, 1635–40].

However flimsy its basis, this prediction fits all too closely with John's own fantasies and fears. Peter, like all papists and witches, is from the devil, and his prophecies, even when they are in some sense 'true', are spiritual snares. Deliberately enigmatic, the prognostications of such people represent screens upon which the intended victims can project their own worst fears and fanta-sies. The purpose of such delusory prophecies and visions is thus to serve as traps to lure sinful humans into greater and greater depravity, so that, in the end, they (in effect), consign themselves to hell. John recognises this fact, calling Peter wizard and witch, even as he, in effect, believes him and in so doing seals his own (temporal, if not spiritual) fate.

The appearance of the five moons, which is merely noted in Holinshed and remains unglossed there, either by Peter or by the author of that account, here receives an explicitly anti-Catholic, eschatolgically charged, interpretation which serves both to align the play with the prophetic vision of the Foxeian or Baleian accounts of the reign and to throw into far higher relief the extent of John's spiritual blindness in the face of popery. For in choosing to heed the second rather than the first of Peter's prophecies, John is allowing his own residual implication in popish superstition – personified here by the entirely spurious Peter of Pomfret – to lead him on into actions that will doom his reign to failure and himself to infamy.

At this moment Hubert comes in to tell the king that Arthur is dead. This is a lie, concocted to protect the boy from the king's continuing malice. In an earlier scene, Hubert has told Arthur of the king's order that he be blinded, only to be dissuaded therefrom by the boy's moving exposition of the subject's obligation to obey the commands of God rather than of man and his argument that John's order to have him blinded was so flagrantly unjust that Hubert had to disobey it, on pain of eternal damnation [*TR*, Pt.1, 1366–438].

Hubert's scruples, his careful observation of the proper limits of obedience to royal command, thus save John from the worst effects of his own sinful tyranny. In the long run, that act redounds to the king's greater (spiritual) good. In the short term, however, it works out to his very considerable political detriment. For to save both his own and Arthur's skin, Hubert determines to lie to the king, telling him that, in the course of being blinded, Arthur has died. When he arrives at court with these glad tidings, they serve merely to confirm the suspicions of the lords, who have long suspected John of plotting to make away with Arthur. The dissident barons had, indeed, produced their own reading of the appearance of the five moons as a confirmation of just such an event [*TR*, Pt. 1,1598–603]. Convinced of John's villainy, the lords rush off to find Arthur dead in a ditch. For in an attempt to escape from imprisonment, Arthur has succeeded only in killing himself. Confirmed twice over in their opinion of John's tyranny, the barons seize on the dauphin who, because of his marriage to Blanche, they now take to be the next heir. They ally with the French and the pope in proclaiming the dauphin king.

John's fortunes are now at their lowest ebb. He has been 'interdicted by the pope', all the churches have been 'cursed' and 'sealed up'. 'For the pleasure of the Romish priest,/The service of the highest is neglected;/The multitude (a beast of many heads)/Do wish confusion to their sovereign:/The nobles blinded with ambitious fumes,/Assemble powers to beat mine empire down,/And more than this, elect a foreign king' [*TR*, Pt. II, 229–37]. John sees the cause of his troubles clearly enough, locating them first in his own sins and secondly in the pope. 'The pope of Rome, tis he that is the cause,/He curseth thee, he sets thy subjects free/From due obedience to their sovereign;/He animates the nobles in their wars,/He gives away the crown to Philip's son/And pardons all that seek to murder thee' [*TR*, Pt. II, 267–72].

John's answer to this predicament is not, however, to renew his efforts against popish tyranny but rather to compound his sins by making his submission to Rome. This, he makes clear, is an entirely insincere act, done in pursuit of short-term political gain. To keep his crown he must 'dissemble with the pope'. In this he has no choice because, he tells himself, 'Thy sins are far too great to be the man/T'abolish pope and popery from thy realm:/But in thy seat, if I may guess at all,/A king shall reign that shall repress them all' [*TR*, Pt. II, 274–81].

To make peace with Rome the papal legate exacts the final humiliation: John must give up his crown to the pope, before receiving it back again as the 'true liegeman', or, as John puts it, the grateful 'tenant to the pope'. It falls, of course, to Philip the bastard to observe that this represents 'a proper jest, when kings must stoop to friars,/Need hath no law, when friars must be kings' [*TR*, Pt. II, 635–40]. John, too, comes to share this perspective; regarding his situation with despair and his conduct in yielding to the pope with disgust [*TR*, Pt. II, 704–7].

Even though from this point on, Pandolph (the papal legate) becomes John's fast friend, the king's fortunes do not improve. The French having arrived in force, Lewis the dauphin arranges to meet the rebellious English lords at Bury St Edmunds at the shrine of St Edmund. They meet in the guise of pilgrims, characterising their colloquy as 'a holy troop', whose unity they confirm with a religious oath of allegiance to Lewis, thus constituting themselves into what Lewis calls 'this religious league,/A holy knot of Catholic consent' and what Salisbury, in reply, affirms to be 'this holy league' [*TR*, Pt. II, 544–45, 562].

But while theirs is a typically seditious popish cause, it soon becomes subject to the condemnation of the pope and his legate, who have now, of course, switched over to John's side. Lewis, however, will have none of that. He will keep his own, 'let pope and popelings curse their belly's full' [*TR*, Pt. 1, 682]. The English lords agree: 'Lord Lewis is our king,/And we will follow him unto the death' [*TR*, Pt. II, 696–7]. In the ensuing battle, for all the bastard Philip's vigour and valour, the English troops give up the ghost, dispirited by a rumour that John has fled the field. (He has in fact been stricken with a fever.) All seems lost. What saves the day is, first, the defection back to the king's cause of the rebellious English lords, who have been alerted at the last to the dauphin's plan to make away with them as untrustworthy traitors once their help has given him the victory. Forewarned of Lewis' plan, they rediscover their loyalty to John. Almost at the same time news arrives that the reinforcements sent to the dauphin's host from France have been shipwrecked on the Goodwin Sands.

But what really enables the play's resolution is John's death. As in the account in Foxe and Bale, this is presented as the work of a monk of Swineshead Abbey anxious to do away with a king 'that never loved a friar'. By murdering a monarch 'that doth contemn the pope', 'robbed the holy church' and 'aims at abbies' lands' [*TR*, Pt. II, 869–73], the monk hopes to 'free my country and the church from foes/And merit heaven by killing a king' [*TR*, Pt. II, 921–22]. Having opened his plan to the abbot, he is confirmed in his belief that John's murder would be a holy act, is absolved and sent on his way.

Having taken the poison and lying on his deathbed, sinking under the weight of his sins, John flirts with desperation. 'I must be damned for Arthur's sudden death./I see, I see a thousand thousand men/Come to accuse me for my wrong on earth/And there is none so merciful a God/That will forgive the number of my sins' [TR, Pt. II, 1051–53]. But ultimately he dies 'well', flinging himself, with David, 'whose hands, as mine, with murder were attaint'[Pt. II, 1080], on the mercy of God and dying 'in the faith of Jesu' [TR, Pt. II, 1090]. But John is like David in another respect too. 'I am not he shall build the Lord a house,/Or root these locusts from the face of earth:/But if my dying heart deceive me not,/From out these loins shall spring a kingly branch,/Whose arms shall reach unto the gates of Rome,/And with his feet tread down the strumpet's pride,/That sits upon the chair of Babylon' [TR, Pt. II, 1081–87].

In this final speech, delivered, inevitably, to the bastard, John acknowledges that his master sin, the act that has doomed his reign and rule, is his residual popery and the submission to the pope that that popery had prompted. 'I tell thee man,/Since John did yield unto the priest of Rome,/Nor he nor his have prospered on the earth;/Cursed are his blessings, and his curse is bliss' [TR, Pt. II, 1074–77].

In a providentially ironic comment upon John's conduct and predicament, John gives up his crown to the pope on Ascension Day, thus formally fulfilling Peter of Pomfret's prophecy, but not, of course, in the way in which John had initially assumed or feared. The king's experience is paralleled by that of the rebellious lords, who see in the vision of the five moons divine encouragement for their 'pilgrimage' to St Edmund's shrine and the nearly fatal 'holy league' they conclude there with Antichrist and France. In theirs, as, indeed, in John's case, popery reveals its satanic capacity to appeal to and play on the peculiar proclivities and weaknesses, the master sins and susceptibilities, of even the most apparently robust, noble and virtuous of persons.

Popery and the descent into tyranny in King John

While Shakespeare's play follows precisely the same narrative course as The troublesome reign its treatment of popery and therefore its account of John's decline into tyranny, and the realm's collapse into chaos, civil war and foreign invasion, is very different. Let us turn first to the play's account of John's descent into tyranny and then examine in more detail its rendition of popery.

Shakespeare's decision to disclose John's claim to the throne as genuinely problematic not only rendered entirely explicable the alacrity with which John and Eleanor embraced a settlement with the French that gave away almost all the English possessions beyond the English Channel, it also gave added force to John's subsequent desire to rid himself of Arthur. Far from the seemingly irrational, popishly induced fantasy of The troublesome reign, it is clear in Shakespeare's play that John's fear of Arthur is entirely rational. As the legitimate heir, so long as he remains alive, Arthur will always be a source of danger.

His death, therefore, becomes, if not a question of political necessity, then a prospect with which John will always be tortured.[14] In Shakespeare's version, John's panic in the face of both the internal and external challenges to his rule long predates his altercation with the papacy. It is not a function either of his or his people's popery or of his subjects' propensity to rebel, but rather of the fragility of his claim to the throne. This feature of Shakespeare's account can be found in none of the other narratives of the reign and serves to mark out his version as very different in its ideological tone, even from the relatively politique version to be found in Holinshed.

The political logic of the situation in which John finds himself, having secured control of Arthur's person, is expounded precisely by Pandulph the papal legate, in his role as evil political genius and *éminence grise*. Here he is trying to persuade the dauphin that the loss of the battle before Angiers has been a good thing after all. 'Now hear me speak in a prophetic spirit . . . John hath seiz'd Arthur: and it cannot be/That, whiles warm life plays in that infant's veins,/The misplac'd John should entertain an hour,/One minute, nay, one quiet breath of rest./A sceptre snatch'd with an unruly hand/Must be as boister-ously maintain'd as gain'd;/ . . . That John may stand, then, Arthur needs must fall;/So be it, for it cannot but be so.' Thus do princes of the Roman church know the rules and necessities of the political game. But what good, asks the dauphin, does that do me? 'How green you are and fresh in this old world!' God's priest replies. 'John lays you plots; the times conspire with you; . . . This act so evilly borne shall cool the hearts/Of all his people, freeze up their zeal,/That none so small advantage shall step forth/To check his reign, but they will cherish it;/No natural exhalation in the sky,/No scope of nature, no distemper'd day,/No common wind, no customed event,/But they will pluck away his natural cause/And call them meteors, prodigies and signs,/Abortives, presages, and tongues of heaven,/Plainly denouncing vengeance against John' [*KJ*, III, iii, 126–59]. And so it proves. Here is Hubert reporting on the political condition of the populace. 'Old men and beldams in the streets/Do prophesy upon it dangerously:/Young Arthur's death is common in their mouths:/And when they talk of him, they shake their heads/And whisper one another in the ear;/And he that speaks doth gripe the hearer's wrist,/Whilst he that hears makes fearful action,/With wrinkled brows, with nods, with rolling eyes./I saw a smith stand with a hammer, thus,/The whilst his iron did on the anvil cool,/With open mouth swallowing a tailor's news;/Who, with his shears and measure in his hand,/Standing on slippers, which his nimble haste/Had falsely thrust upon contrary feet,/Told of a many thousand warlike French/That were embattailed and rank'd in Kent:/Another lean unwash'd artificer/Cuts off his tale and talks of Arthur's death' [*KJ*, IV, ii, 185–202].

At this point John rounds on the unfortunate Hubert, blaming him for what has turned into the political disaster of Arthur's death. Shown the hand and seal that warranted the evil deed, John responds by blaming Hubert again. 'The murther had not come into my mind:/But taking note of thy abhorr'd aspect,/ Finding thee fit for bloody villainy,/Apt, liable to be employ'd in danger,/I faintly broke with thee of Arthur's death;/And thou, to be endeared to a king,/ Made it no conscience to destroy a prince' [KJ, IV, ii, 208–29]. This, of course, was how John had wanted the previous scenes between himself and Hubert to play out. For there he had tried to induce Hubert to dispatch the boy without ever quite issuing a direct royal command to do so. Plausible deniability may be a phrase of Nixonian provenance, but, on this evidence, it was also an early modern reality or, at least, in this case, aspiration.

At this point it is worth standing back from the action of the play for a moment to consider just what the contemporary resonance of such scenes might have been. We have here a monarch whose claim to the throne is, at best, contested, and, at worst, flimsily illegitimate. All that stands between the present incumbent (John/Elizabeth) and the true claimant (Arthur/Mary Stuart) is a (possibly spurious) will (of dubious legal force). Desperate to cement his/her hold on power, the usurping monarch goes to great lengths to secure control of the rival claimant's person. That control having been secured, he/she is incarcerated. An inexorable political logic now pushes the ruling monarch/usurper towards the dispatch of the legitimate claimant/heir. Unable to rest easy until the rival has been killed, the present incumbent also realises the political costs inherent in being seen to connive at the death of an innocent (and royal) prisoner. Desperately, they cast about for a means to make away with said person while escaping the blame for having them killed. Having failed to seduce their prisoner's (Arthur/Mary's) keeper into doing away with their royal charge in secret, that is to say at the mere suggestion, rather than on the explicit and direct command, of the crown, they are reduced to giving formal orders to effect their malign purpose, only immediately, after the fell deed has been done, to repudiate and blame the persons who have done it. The parallels between John's treatment of both Arthur and Hubert and Elizabeth Tudor's of Mary Stuart and poor William Davison are so patent as scarcely to require further explication or emphasis. Of course, such parallels had been present in The troublesome reign, but they are heightened by Shakespeare's depiction of John as a usurper and of Arthur as the true and innocent claimant/ heir/victim and by the extended exchanges between the king and his (unwilling) instrument Hubert, in which John is shown trying to put the blame for a deed he so desperately wanted done, on poor Hubert.

Pandulph's analysis of what would eventuate if John had Arthur killed represented what many English Catholics hoped would happen after the death of Mary Stuart. In endorsing that view of what might happen in Elizabethan England, through its retrospective account of what had happened in John's reign, Shakespeare's play comes very close to adopting a 'Catholic' perspective on the recent past, present and likely future of the Elizabethan regime. That certainly is the purport of the bastard's speech over Arthur's corpse cited above. With the true heir/monarch dead, 'England now is left/To tug and scamble, and to part by th'teeth/The unow'd interest of proud swelling state'. 'Now powers from home and discontents at home/Meet in one line; and vast confusion waits' [KJ, IV, iii, 140–54]. If we take this to be a statement of the likely consequences of the death of Mary Stuart, then it becomes for the audiences of the 1590s a comment on their current war-torn state, surrounded by enemies, subject to the threat of invasion from abroad and of sedition, division and rebellion at home. When we add in the further fact of John's (and, of course, Elizabeth's) excommunication and deposition by the pope and their confrontation by the threat of a (papally sponsored) foreign invasion and foreign claimant to the English throne, the case for a very close parallel indeed between the conduct and predicament of John and of Elizabeth is all but clinched. It is surely not going too far to claim that no politically sentient or aware member of the audience at a performance of this play in the 1590s could have failed to note such parallels. We are surely dealing here with something rather more intense than the 'atmosphere of contemporary pertinence' imputed to the play by David Womersley.[15]

As one might surmise from the previous account, there is no trace in Shakespeare's play of the protestant providentialist version of John's reign; no attempt to read these events typologically in order to present John as some sort of precursor of the Tudors, no emphasis on prophecy or providential intervention to give the reign a special significance in sacred history, an eschatologically charged role in the world historical struggle between Christ and Antichrist. Indeed, there are only two prophecies of any sort in the play. The first is that of Peter of Pomfret, that John will give up his throne by Ascension Day. The second, the political prognostication, ironically termed a 'prophecy' by Pandulph, as he explains to the dauphin that John will feel compelled to kill Arthur and that that act will cause his regime to unravel. Both these 'prophecies', are, in their different ways, proved true. As for the vision of the five moons, that does indeed feature in Shakespeare's play but it is attributed no specific meaning, but rather associated, as some sort of cloudy, indeterminately providential portent, with the death of Arthur. Indeed, it is recounted in the same report of popular speculation and anxiety attendant upon the death of Arthur and the arrival of the French, cited above [KJ, IV, ii, 182–84]. This outbreak of popular agitation, of superstitious prognostication and excitement, had been foreseen by that archetypal papist, Pandulph, and it is he who characterises such speculations as illusions and fantasies, false interpretations of events with patently natural causes, to which the populace, especially when in a state of political excitation or moral distress, are particularly prone. On this account, then, there is nothing distinctively or characteristically 'popish' about popular

superstition and, unlike *The troublesome reign*, Shakespeare's play is devoid of
any critique or expose of popish superstition or priestcraft.

Nor is there anything either heroic or comic about John's, or the bastard's,
assault on the wealth of the church or the monasteries. At the outset of his
military expedition to France, John observes in an aside that 'our abbeys and
our priories shall pay/This expeditious charge' [*KJ*, I, i, 48–49]. Later, engaged
in France, John instructs the bastard to 'away for England! Haste before:/And,
ere our coming, see thou shake the bags/Of hoarding abbots; imprison'd angels/
Set at liberty: the fat ribs of peace/Must by the hungry now be fed upon:/Use
our commission in his utmost force.' To this injunction the bastard replies with
relish that 'bell, book and candle shall not drive me back/When gold and silver
becks me to come on' [*KJ*, III, ii, 16–23]. In short, John's designs on the wealth
of the church and monasteries are presented as purely financial in their motivation and violent in their realisation.

Unlike in *The troublesome reign*, the bastard's depredations on the clergy all
take place offstage and there is no attempt to portray the sort of priestly or
monastic superstition, duplicity, corruption or greed that might legitimise such
arbitrary, confiscatory action. When the bastard reports back on the success of
his efforts they are immediately associated with the outbreak of popular
discontent at and resistance to John's rule. 'As I have travaill'd through the
land/I find the people strangely fantasied;/Possess'd with rumours, full of idle
dreams,/Not knowing what they fear, but full of fear', at which point he introduces his prisoner Peter of Pomfret and what turns out to be his true prediction
that John 'should deliver up your crown ... 'ere the next Ascension-day at
noon' [*KJ*, IV, ii, 141–52]. This association of popular disaffection (and divine
displeasure?) with John and the bastard's assault on the church is confirmed by
Pandulph's report to the dauphin; 'The bastard Faulconbridge/Is now in
England ransacking the church,/Offending charity: but if a dozen French/Were
there in arms, they would be as a call/To train ten thousand English to their
side' [*KJ*, III, iii, 171–75]. None of this throws John's confiscation of the wealth
of the church into a very positive light. There is nothing here to justify such a
course except royal greed, and the hostile popular response thereto is all but
endorsed by the play, which refuses virtually all the opportunities offered by
the story of John's reign, and the conventional Tudor rendition thereof, for
anti-popish rant directed against the nature or content of Catholic religion or
piety.[16]

Thus the journey of the rebel lords to meet the French at St Edmundsbury
is stripped of the popish trappings or connotations conferred on it by *The troublesome reign* or indeed even in Holinshed. It is never described as a pilgrimage,
nor is the subsequent alliance described as a holy or Catholic league. Both
rebels and dauphin swear allegiance to one another and take the sacrament to
seal the bond. But this act is not pictured as superstitious or popish in either

form or content. It merely serves to emphasise the perfidy of the French as they plan, having won the throne, to turn on the rebellious English lords. John's handing over of his crown to Pandulph and receiving of it back again from the pope happen offstage, as, even more remarkably, does the king's murder by the monk of Swineshead. There is no dwelling upon the inwardness of this act, no attempt to use it to identify popery with treason or king-killing. In fact, it is reported to the bastard in rather matter of fact tones by Hubert. 'The king, I fear, is poison'd by a monk', 'a resolved villain –/Whose bowels suddenly broke out' [KJ, V, vi, 23–30]. Nor is there any hint of Antichrist in even the play's most intense moments of anti-popery.

The one locus for anti-Catholic polemical positioning and posing which the play does exploit centres on John's political relations with the papal legate Pandulph. For Pandulph figures as perhaps the central villain of the piece and in so doing gives John virtually his last chance to act the hero. It is Pandulph who destroys the recent peace between England and France. Just as the marriage has been concluded between Blanche and Lewis, he bursts in to demand from John an explanation for his decision to block the appointment of Stephen Langton as Archbishop of Canterbury [KJ, III, I, 69–72]. John responds to this question with an explosive statement of the imperial powers and independence of the English crown. Here, as in *The troublesome reign*, the distance between King John and the Tudors shrinks almost to nothing. 'What earthly name to interrogatories/Can taste the free breath of a sacred king?/Thou canst not, cardinal, devise a name/So slight, unworthy and ridiculous,/To charge me to an answer, as the pope./Tell him this tale; and from the mouth of England/Add thus much more, that no Italian priest/Shall tithe or toll in our dominions;/But as we, under God, are supreme head,/So under him that great supremacy/Where we do reign, we will alone uphold/Without th'assistance of a mortal hand:/So tell the pope, all reverence set apart/To him and his usurp'd authority'[KJ, III, i, 73–86].[17] It may well be significant that, in Shakespeare's formulation, the entity of which John asserts he is the 'supreme head' is not identified precisely. Certainly, he does not claim to be supreme head of the church. Moreover, this version of his claim to supremacy lacks any mention of the control of both 'temporals *and* spirituals' that the John of *The troublesome reign* had advanced. The result is a decidedly 'Gallican' version of the Royal Supremacy, that even certain sorts of Catholic loyalist might accept.[18]

Told by an appalled French king that 'brother of England, you blaspheme in this', John launches into a tirade against the servility shown by other rulers to the pope's tyranny. However great, their pusillanimous weakness and superstition will not stop him, standing alone, from asserting his rights as a Christian prince and English king. 'Though you and all the kings of Christendom/Are led so grossly by this meddling priest,/Dreading the curse that money may buy out;/And by the merit of vild gold, dross, dust,/Purchase corrupted pardon of a man,/Who in that sale sells pardon from himself;/Though you and all the rest so grossly led/This juggling witchcraft with revenue cherish,/Yet I alone, alone do me oppose/Against the pope, and count his friends my foes' [*KJ*, III, i, 74–97]. In response to these statements of Tudor orthodoxy Pandulph makes the inevitable popish response, excommunicating John and pronouncing 'blessed' anyone 'that doth revolt/From his allegiance to an heretic' and 'meritorious' the 'hand' that makes away with the king. Moreover, Pandulph promises, the perpetrator will be 'canonised and worshipp'd as a saint' [*KJ*, III, i, 98–104]. He then demands that, 'on peril of a curse', the French king break his recently contracted alliance with England, 'and raise the power of France upon his head,/Unless he do submit himself to Rome' [*KJ*, III, i, 117–20].

There follows a passage entirely absent from *The troublesome reign* and equally foreign to the deeply xenophobic tenor of the Holinshed version. In both those accounts the duplicitous French snatch at this opportunity to break their faith with England and to play once more, this time with papal backing, for all the marbles. In Shakespeare's version the French king vacillates. Desperate to preserve his faith so recently pledged to England and the peace so recently snatched from the very jaws of war, he begs Pandulph to find him a way out of this predicament with his honour and the peace of Christendom intact [*KJ*, III, i, 152–78].

We have here a striking role reversal, indeed inversion. For here is a secular prince, and Catholic king, someone typed earlier by the bastard as a dedicated disciple of 'commodity', making a desperate plea about the horrors of war, about the sacredness of vows publicly pledged and for the maintenance of peace between Christian princes. On the other side, we have a prince of the church making the case for war and the breaking of faith. 'All form is formless, order orderless,/Save what is opposite to England's love./Therefore to arms! be champion of our church,/Or let the church, our mother breathe her curse,/A mother's curse on her revolting son./France thou mayst hold a serpent by the tongue,/A cased lion by the mortal paw,/A fasting tiger safer by the tooth,/Than keep in peace that hand which thou dost hold' [*KJ*, III, i, 179–87].

As for Philip's scruples about breaking his oath publicly given to John, Pandulph produces a long exercise in casuistical reasoning. In a speech of quite outstanding and quite deliberate opacity and indirection, the legate tries to explain why, in this instance, breaking faith was in fact keeping faith [*KJ*, III, i, 189–223]. Hard to decipher on the printed page, when delivered as a speech, Pandulph's disquisition is pretty much unintelligible. The audience is presented with a palimpsest of paradoxes and apparent contradictions that, in their convoluted syntax and logic, constitute a parody of the worst sort of self-serving and obscure popish casuistry.

While the syntax is tortured and the meaning at any given juncture anything but clear, the general drift of the speech emerges plainly enough and is not, in and of itself, obviously objectionable or wrong; since religion is that which underpins all vows – that which makes them binding in the first place – a vow made unknowingly or by mistake against religion cannot bind. In that case, to be true to one's original oath to protect religion involves breaking subsequent undertakings, however solemnly made, that undercut or contradict that initial commitment. While that point might be clear enough, however, the real question is whether Philip's vow to John and the peace it has concluded really are against religion. Or to put the matter another way, could the cause of religion be so easily, even automatically, equated with the secular interests and commands of the Roman church? For Pandulph that equation was axiomatic and all the persiflage of his elaborate justification of perjury and perfidy to Philip cannot hide the fact. What that justification does reveal is the capacity of certain styles of popish casuistical argument, combined with the usurped, both spiritual and political, authority claimed by the popish clergy, to undermine even the clearest, the most publicly acknowledged and deeply felt, ties of political or moral obligation when the interests or authority of the papacy were deemed to be at stake. In a period when the political allegiance of English Catholics was much in doubt and Catholic priests were thought to be agents of a foreign power, both able and willing to free their English flock from their political allegiance to queen and country, and indeed at a time, in the late 1580s and early 1590s, when the persecution of such priests had reached new heights, these were highly charged scenes, with a very direct political and polemical register.

The systematically parodic obfuscation of Pandulph's treatment of the moral issue stands in stark contrast to the pellucid clarity and directness of his analysis of the political situation, as he advises first Lewis and then his father Philip about how to exploit John's capture, and the likely murder, of young Arthur. On this evidence, Pandulph is better at Machiavellian realpolitik than he is at moral theology; or rather, a practised Machiavel, he is rhetorically skilled enough to know when his purposes are best suited by clarity and when by obfuscation. But what does emerge from these exchanges is the resolutely secular, this-worldly, wholly 'political' nature of those purposes. What is at stake here are the power and interests, the perpetuation and exercise of the usurped jurisdiction of the Roman church, rather than the cause of true religion or the moral or spiritual good of John or Philip, or indeed of England or of France, still less the peace of Christendom or the demands of conscience.

The resolutely political nature of Pandulph's conception of the cause of the church or religion receives final confirmation once John submits himself to the papacy. Immediately John calls in his political debts and Pandulph just as immediately complies, making it clear, the while, that for him war and peace between nations, the deposition or setting up of princes, are mere means to the papacy's ultimate end: the establishment and maintenance of its power [KJ, V, i, 5–7, 17–21].

Pandulph, however, proves unable to keep his side of the bargain, since, having raised Lewis' hopes for the English throne and provoked a French invasion of England, an invasion now seemingly about to achieve final victory, he finds the dauphin unwilling to stand down merely on the pope's say-so. Here Pandulph's pellucid lessons in realpolitik, delivered to young Lewis, trump the always already mystified and mystifying claims to spiritual power advanced by the papacy. 'You taught me how to know the face of right,/Acquainted me with interest to this land, . . . And, now it is half-conquered, must I back/Because that John hath made his peace with Rome?/Am I Rome's slave? What penny hath Rome borne,/What men provided, what munition sent,/To underprop this action? Is't not I/That undergo this charge? Who else but I,/And such as to my claim are liable,/Sweat in this business and maintain this war?' [KJ, V, ii, 88–102].

It is not without irony that the speaker of these lines is not only a Catholic prince, but the very same dauphin who had earlier been only too eager to urge his father to obey the spiritual authority of the pope by breaking his word and turning on England. Now, having been educated in the darks arts of Machiavellian realpolitik by Pandulph himself, here he is defying the spiritual authority of the pope because his own immediate political interests conflict directly with the instructions and interests of the papacy. We are back here in the world of commodity, the ceaseless pursuit of power and interest, which these passages make clear is just as much Pandolph's world as it is John or Philip's and by extension, of course, just as much the present pope's as it is that of Philip of Spain, the Catholic League or indeed of Elizabeth herself.

Thus, while the play is far from devoid of anti-papal attitudinising and polemic it produces a remarkably attenuated vision of the nature of popery and the popish threat. Even more so than in the Holinshed account, popery is perceived and presented as a largely political phenomenon, its distinctive characteristics the claims to jurisdiction over national churches and secular rulers that drive Pandulph's confrontations with John. John's anti-popery consists similarly of a robust assertion of (a notably 'secular' version of) the royal supremacy. Apart from his glancing reference to the use of bought indulgences to perpetuate the power of the papacy over certain superstitious princes, there is no account of popish religious error, superstition, priestcraft or idolatry to be found anywhere in the play. In direct contrast with The troublesome reign, Shakespeare's play deals not so much in anti-popery, the denunciation of Catholicism as a nexus of error, a satanically derived false religion, but rather more in anti-papalism, a rejection of the pope's claims to temporal authority and a laying bare of his status as just another secular power in duplicitous, self-serving pursuit of commodity, rather than as any sort of guarantor of Christian peace or the demands of 'charity', 'conscience' or 'the right'.

As for John himself, as we have seen, in The troublesome reign the break point in his career and fortunes, the beginning of his decline into tyranny and

THE FIRST TIME AS POLEMIC, THE SECOND TIME AS PLAY 221

weakness, failure and death, is provided by his attempt to have Arthur killed and his submission to the pope. On his deathbed, John insistently returns to these sins, but it is his submission to the pope that represents his most heinous fault. Unlike the death of Arthur, over which the moral scruples and refusals of Hubert have saved him from the worst consequences of his own malign intentions, John is unambiguously guilty of that. It is his entirely insincere, both servile and self-serving, deal with the papacy for which, more than anything, he is barred from building the Temple, i.e. from finally expelling the pope and popery from the land. As we have seen, it is his deep repentance for this lapse that provokes his prophecy of a line of English monarchs who will one day rise and s break with the pope and popery for good and all.

This is not the case in Shakespeare's version, where it is John's treatment of Arthur that takes centre stage. It is true that, as in *The troublesome reign*, the bastard bitterly criticises John for his dealings with Pandulph. But in Shakespeare's play his lamentations do not take what we might term the overtly anti-popish form that they do in *The troublesome reign*. On the contrary, they are firmly set in the context of John's seeming passivity and panic in the face of the French invader. Philip exhorts the king to pull himself together and seize the military initiative [*KJ*, V, i, 45–55]. 'Be great in act, as you have been in thought;/Let not the world see fear and sad distrust/Govern the motion of a kingly eye!/Be stirring as the time, be fire with fire,/Threaten the threat'ner, and outface the brow/Of bragging horror: so shall inferior eyes,/That borrow their behaviours from the great,/Grow great by your example and put on/The dauntless spirit of resolution./Away, and glister like the god of war,/When he intendeth to become the field' [*KJ*, V, i, 45–55].

To this inspiring tirade, John replies passively that there is no need for such activism, he has squared away Pandulph 'And he hath promis'd to dismiss the powers/Led by the Dolphin' [*KJ*, V, i, 62–65]. Disgusted with this limp response, the bastard denounces this 'inglorious league', but the rest of the ensuing speech does not concern the evils of popery and the humiliation involved in making submission to the pope. Rather it turns into a tirade against the French and a call to arms to assert and defend English honour against the invading foreigner. 'Let us, my liege, to arms!/Perchance the cardinal cannot make your peace;/Or if he do, let it at least be said/They saw we have a purpose of defence'[*KJ*, V, i, 65–76].

The apotheosis of the bastard

The bastard is, of course, an entirely fictional character inserted into the narrative of John's reign by the author of *The troublesome reign*.

But he almost certainly had some basis in the Holinshed account, which contains one brief mention of 'Philip, king Richard's bastard son' who 'slew the viscount of Limoges' 'in revenge for his father's death'[19] Here then is the origin of the character, but the persona and role that Philip takes on in the play is not that of this Philip, who thereafter disappears from the Holinshed account, but rather of that 'worthy gentleman of English blood', William de Collingham, who, unlike many of his countrymen, had led a staunch English resistance against the French. Whereas, in both Holinshed and the Homily of Obedience, the majority of the English people had been pictured succumbing to popery and rebellion, in Philip we have the epitome of an always already staunch, loyal, violent and foreigner-hating Englishness, which, despite John's weakness and vacillation, responds, at every turn, with zeal and courage in the defence of England against the foreigner and the pope. In his violence, his plebeian frankness, his royal blood and his anti-popish zeal we see central elements in the Holinshed account – crudely the appeal for English unity and loyalty against the foreign threat – being combined with central elements from the overtly anti-popish accounts of Bale and Foxe.

That certainly is the role that the bastard plays in *The troublesome reign*, but not quite in Shakespeare's play. Throughout the later stages of both plays Philip emerges as more decisive, brave and authoritative by far than the increasingly erratic, panicky and depressive John. As John declines, the initiative now passes definitively to the bastard, a moment marked almost formally in Shakespeare's version by John's command 'have thou the ordering of this present time' [*KJ*, V, i, 77]. However, in Shakespeare's play, but most definitely not in *The troublesome reign*, the bastard undergoes a transformation of his own. As John suffers a vertiginous moral and psychological decline, the bastard casts off his persona as an outsider, a bemused, amused and amusing, spectator of, and commentator upon, the doings of his elders and betters, a sort of comic chorus or vice,[20] and instead emerges as a figure of heroic force and vigour, inheriting all John's verbal and martial violence, elan and decisiveness, his reflexive desire and ability to defend the realm and crown from foreign invasion. As David Womersley observes, 'just as it is clear that the Bastard is, in the first half of the play, a descendant of the Vice, it is also clear that in the second half of *King John* his vice like qualities are muted',[21] indeed they all but disappear, transmuted into the vital energies that the bastard goes on to display in the defence of the realm or, as Weimann puts it, of 'the nation state'.[22]

In the opening acts of the play he consistently deploys a plebeian, colloquial, indeed derisive tone; making sexual jokes about his mother and frequent allusions to his own status as a bastard, he interrupts the negotiations between the two kings and seeks to disrupt the peace by picking a fight with Limoges. But that is a linguistic mode he must give up; as Michael Neill observes, he must give over 'this dialect of liberty before he can offer his "true subjection" to the "lineal state" of King Henry and become the choric spokesman of the legitimate and the "true" '.[23]

He remains still a mixed and miscegenated figure. Illegitimate, yet the epitome of legitimacy; 'royal', yet base born; both noble and plebeian; a new man, and yet the saviour of the old order, he is the personification of English vigour and independence and as such he emerges as the organiser, vigorous centre and presiding spirit of native English resistance to both domestic rebellion and foreign invasion. If he usurps the role of the king, moving seamlessly into the power vacuum, the practical and symbolic, rhetorical and military void, created by the moral and physical collapse of King John, he remains a loyal subject and servant of the crown. In the bastard, then, we are being presented with the natural (illegitimate) legitimacy, the inherent Englishness of England and her people – personified by this scion of the mythical Richard Coeur de Lion and the provincial gentry – bursting into spontaneous and revivifying life.[24]

In both plays, seeking to rouse John from his lethargy, he spits defiance at the French and the rebel English lords, while trying to organise the English military effort against the invaders. Both plays make it clear that, Pandulph having failed to get Lewis to back off, all would have been lost without the bastard's military prowess and vigour. Shakespeare has Salisbury report 'that misbegotten devil, Faulconbridge/In spite of spite, alone upholds the day'. John meanwhile has been struck 'sore sick' and forced to leave the field [*KJ*, V, iv, 4–6]. It is thus the patriotic valour of the bastard that creates the space within which the English lords can discover the intended treachery of the French and return to obedience 'to our great king John' [*KJ*, V, iv, 55–57] and Lewis can learn of the destruction of his reinforcements on the Goodwin Sands.

In Shakespeare's play the bastard is shown making the decision to stick with King John at the very moment that he discovers the dead body of young Arthur, concluding his speech over the corpse with the determination 'I'll to the king/A thousand businesses are brief in hand,/And heaven itself doth frown upon the land' [*KJ*, IV, iii, 157–59]. This is a moment of greatly heightened significance precisely because Shakespeare has been so explicit about both the weakness of John's claims to dynastic legitimacy and about the bastard's acknowledgment thereof. In Shakespeare's version John is both an emergent tyrant and a usurper, and the bastard knows it.

As Womersley points out, at this point in Shakespeare's play, but not in *The troublesome reign*, which has after all consistently endorsed John's legitimacy as king, the bastard has a political choice to make; apprised of the appalling consequences of John's actions, and with the succession under active contest, he can either join the rebels and support a foreign claimant to the crown of England or he can rally to the king. With Mary Stuart dead, the succession unsettled and contested by, amongst others, Philip II's daughter, the Infanta and by James Stuart, and with Spanish invasion still a real threat, this was, of course, a choice with which potentially every subject of Queen Elizabeth might very shortly be confronted.[25] But, as Robert Jones points out, at the crucial moment, when he determines to support the king, despite his full acknowledgement of what the death of Arthur means, 'the bastard does not explain his meaning here, and I don't think he can – which is the point'.[26] His is a visceral decision; not so much a product of considered political judgement, still less of a calculated pursuit of commodity or gain, the bastard's commitment to the king is presented as a spontaneous or reflexive expression of his native Englishness; an almost automatic response to the need to defend the realm from foreign invasion and rule.

If, as Calderwood puts it, we are indeed to construe the bastard as here choosing 'honour' over 'commodity', the 'honour' being chosen is devoid of any conventional concern for the rights and wrongs of monarchical legitimacy, or for the virtue or otherwise of the current ruler, but is defined solely by the necessity to defend England from foreign invasion and from the spectre of foreign rule.[27] In a play that, as David Kastan has observed, lacks any 'absolute standards of value and conduct',[28] this visceral drive to defend England from the foreigner becomes the sole source of such value and it is his dedication to that task that transforms the bastard from the 'cracker', the new man on the make, the wannabe disciple of commodity and gain, of the first part of the play, into the heroic figure of the concluding acts.

But even a reformed bastard is still a bastard and as such he cannot provide, but merely personify and perform, monarchical legitimacy, speaking in the place of 'our English king', and seeking to supply, through the force of his rhetoric and martial prowess, the role that the real king should be playing. *Pace* the claims of some critics, who see him as entertaining and then rejecting aspirations to the throne for himself, the bastard's very illegitimacy protects him from such thoughts.[29] Saved from the ambition, the drive to supreme power, that was the chief characteristic of the Machiavel, the bastard can, therefore, at least for a time, supplant the king without trying to replace him.[30] 'Now hear our English king,/For thus his royalty doth speak in me' [*KJ*, V, ii, 128–30, 148–58]. Here, in Jones' terms, is the bastard 'as the impassioned spokesman for what ought to be', using his own rhetorical skill to fill the void created by the moral collapse and physical absence of King John himself. [31] Thus it is precisely because he is illegitimate that the bastard can supply the effects of monarchical legitimacy that the usurpation and consequent misdeeds of King John has stripped from the political system, without seeming to undermine for a moment the principles of monarchical legitimacy and hereditary succession upon which the state is about to be refounded, after the unfortunate detour into illegitimacy represented by John's reign has been concluded.

Here the bastard's primary role is to rally the English to the defence of the realm from foreign invasion and foreign rule. The invasion to be repelled has, by this point, pretty much lost whatever popish colouring it may once have had. Pandulph, in search of papal commodity, has now changed sides and the French are proceeding against papal instructions. We are left, then, in Shakespeare's version, with a foreign invasion, pursued for reasons of political gain and dynastic ambition, and a rebellion against at least the appearance of tyranny. Both are entirely devoid of religious motivations or connotations. It is thus the foreignness (and not, as in *The troublesome reign*, the foreignness *and* the popery) of the invaders that finally confers legitimacy on the reign, if not the person, of that usurping sinner, King John. For legitimate or not, John is still an English king, and king of England, and as such the leader of the nation against the forces of foreign invasion and the threat of foreign rule. Not that this visceral patriotism, this instinctive secular nationalism, in the face of the foreign invader, is limited to the bastard. Even the English rebels feel it. Thus Salisbury laments 'That we, the sons and children of this isle,/Were born to see so sad an hour as this;/Wherein we step after a stranger, march/Upon her gentle bosom, and fill up/Her enemies' ranks' [*KJ*, V, ii, 24–39].[32] Such sentiments make the rebels' discovery of the dauphin's treacherous intentions toward them a source of positive relief. Indeed Salisbury describes it as a 'most fair occasion, by the which/We will untread the steps of damned flight,/ . . . And calmly run on in obedience/Even to our ocean, to our great king John' [*KJ*, V, iv, 51–58].

Returning to serve King John, the nobles find him dying, and unite instead around the person of his son Henry. As the bastard, typically, busies himself with military preparations, it emerges that, their ranks depleted by the defection of the English lords and the destruction of their fleet on the Goodwin Sands, the French have given up the ghost and are preparing to return home, the dauphin having 'put his cause and quarrel/To the disposing of the cardinal' [*KJ*, V, vii, 91–92]. As Pandulph turns peacemaker, English thoughts turn to the next reign. 'At Worcester must his body be interr'd;/For so he will'd it', intones the new king. 'Thither shall it then,' chimes in the bastard. 'And happily may your sweet self put on/The lineal state and glory of the land!/To whom, with all submission, on my knee/I do bequeath my faithful services/And true subjection everlastingly.' Salisbury, the leader of the rebels, takes his cue from the bastard. 'And the like tender of our love we make,/To rest without a spot for evermore.' It is left, inevitably, to the bastard to draw the political moral of all this. 'O let us pay the time but needful woe,/Since it hath been beforehand with our griefs./This England never did, nor never shall,/Lie at the proud foot of a conqueror,/But when it first did help to wound itself./Now these her princes are come home again/Come the three corners of the world in arms/And we shall shock them! Naught shall make us rue/If England to itself do rest but true!' [*KJ*, V, vii, 99–118].

England and providence

According to *The troublesome reign*, John and England were saved by two things. On the one hand, we have the native virtue and vigour of Hubert and the bastard, and, on the other, the workings of providence. It was Hubert's careful observation of the limits of true obedience that saved John from the worst consequences of his own incipient tyranny, leaving him formally innocent of, albeit deeply morally implicated in, the death of Arthur. Similarly, in the second half of both plays, it is the martial vigour and loyalty of Philip, the bastard, that repeatedly saves John from his own fears and fantasies and, in the end, saves the English aristocracy (and England itself) from the worst consequences of their own folly and treason.

Here moral virtue and true prowess trump monarchical right. It is the prince himself who stumbles into sin and tyranny and the ancient nobility who fall into open treason and rebellion. It is left to that epitome of English virtue, martial vigour and (in *The troublesome reign*, of simple anti-popish zeal), the base-born Philip, to save the day. In the bastard's relations with John at play's end may we not be being shown a version of the queen's relations with her council, or at least with the more militarily aggressive, rabidly anti-Spanish members of that council? We re-enter here, perhaps, the world of the 'monarchical republic', except, of course, that there is nothing remotely 'republican' about the intensely monarchical, blood-centred, political world conjured by the play, just as there is nothing particularly civic or citizen-like about the bastard's viscerally monarchical decision, taken over the corpse of young Arthur, to stick with King John.[33]

In *The troublesome reign*, albeit not in Shakespeare's play, almost alone of the play's characters, Philip is totally immune to the threats and seductions of popery. He is the repository of all the reflexive violence, the anti-foreigner, anti-clerical, anti-popish impulses and prejudices that were common enough in the lower reaches of London (indeed of English) society under Elizabeth. But through Philip's descent from a mythical English king, these decidedly plebeian attributes and attitudes are not merely ennobled, they are rendered (pseudo) royal, associated with the symbols and claims of the monarchy, indeed with the very person of the prince.

Thus, in the fantasy world evoked by *The troublesome reign* was the circle squared; a regime notable for the novelty of many of its religious claims and institutional arrangements, a regime in which new men and their creatures played a central part, was associated with a mythical English past and defended by someone in whose person was united the true nobility of active virtue, martial prowess and protestant principle and noble, indeed royal, blood. An increasingly erratic, fearful, panic-stricken, superstitious and indecisive monarch has been saved from the consequences of his (or her?) own actions and inactions not only by the counsel but by the active intervention, the martial deeds, of that personification of mere English loyalty, zeal and virtue, the bastard. Thus did the new become old, the plebeian become noble and even royal, and the divisive novelty of protestantism and the breach with Rome become an expression of loyalty to and continuity with an ancient English heritage of independence, martial prowess, and loyalty to crown and country.

But, at least in *The troublesome reign,* even Philip cannot, unaided, save John or England from their sins or the invasive force of the foreigner and the operations of providence have to play a decisive part. Working, as often as not, through the actions and plots of the wicked themselves, providence wrenches John away from his potentially damning alliance with the pope and, through his death at the hands of the poisoning monk of Swineshead, delivers him up for the saving repentance of his good death. Almost simultaneously, by the destruction of the French fleet on the Goodwin Sands, England is saved from foreign rule. The salvation of prince and realm come together at Swineshead Abbey where John's death allows for the coronation, by the now repentant English lords, of his son Henry, 'that by succession is our lawful king'.

This providential view of the matter was, of course, based on the play's typological reading of the reign, with John featured as David to Queen Elizabeth's Solomon, a precursor whose heart had been in the right, anti-popish place, but whose sins, indeed whose residual popery, had been too great to allow him the honour of rebuilding the temple; a task even now being undertaken by Queen Elizabeth herself.

John's and England's achievement had however not been inconsiderable. Even as popery was reaching its highest and most virulent form in the pontificate of Innocent III and the Lateran Council, England, alone amongst the kingdoms of Christian Europe, has put up a fight. At that point, popery was too strong and her own sins too great for England to win through. Even so, providence had protected John and England from foreign rule. Moreover John's prophetic words (confirmed by the miraculous portent of the five moons) about a race of kings to come who will pursue the Antichrist even to the very gates of Rome, reveal the special role of England in the process of Antichrist's fall. The story of the reign is thus set within an essentially eschatological vision that locates England within a version of sacred history dominated by the rise and fall of the papal Antichrist. Indeed, England and her monarchy are placed at the forefront of a struggle between the forces of good and evil, the true and false churches, a struggle that will ultimately bring human history to a close and usher in the second coming of Christ.

But the play's message is scarcely a straightforwardly triumphalist one. Indeed, it shares, with certain contemporary modes of anti-papal thought and feeling, a distinctive combination of hope with fear, of promise with threat. While victory in the struggle against Antichrist was certain, the timing of that victory was anything but. Similarly, while popery was an easily identifiable external enemy – quintessentially foreign, outside, other – it was also the most elusive of opponents; its supporters covertly ubiquitous, constantly at work, undermining from within. More serious and insidious still, the sinful urges and impulses that rendered popery the corruptly natural religion for a corrupt, because fallen, humanity were all to be found boiling away within each and every one of us. This, of course, was the source of popery's superhuman, indeed supernatural and demonic, power. And it was because of this power that popery could be overthrown only with the aid of divine grace and providence. Thus, while, from God's perspective, Antichrist's defeat was inevitable, its timing and date certain, from the viewpoint of fallen humanity no such certitude was possible. All humankind could know was that Antichrist would fall and that in order to bring that about they would have to struggle mightily against the sins and corrupt impulses within themselves and their own society.[34] There was, on this view, something conditional, reciprocal, even covenantal, governing the relations between God and his people, the English and their God. Only if the English, both rulers and ruled, kept their part of the bargain, waging constant war on the sin and popery in their midst, without giving in to the carnal fears, the calculations and manoeuvres for temporal (and therefore temporary) personal and political advantage that had done for King John, would God come to their rescue and vouchsafe them final victory over their popish enemies. Only if all true Englishmen rallied, with the bastard, to their true English sovereign, refusing, in the process, to examine too closely the peccadilloes and shortcomings of their rulers, throwing themselves the while into the struggle against popery and the foreigner, could England be saved.

All this shows how things will turn out in the future, how indeed they could turn out in the present, if only the English – crown, nobility and commons – do the right thing: avoid the sins and failings of King John and follow the (both bloody and bloody-minded) example of the bastard's instinctively anti-popish mere Englishness. In the words of the bastard in the closing lines of the play, '*if* England's peers and people join in one,/Nor pope, nor France, nor Spain can do them wrong' [*TR*, Pt. II, 1195–96].

Thus for all the seemingly platitudinous orthodoxy of the play's political doctrine – entirely orthodox renditions of the doctrines of (passive) obedience, and the royal supremacy, standard denunciations of popish superstition, hypocrisy, sedition and treason – when read in terms of its immediate political and polemical context the play's overall message emerges as anything but anodyne. On this view, the story of King John was at once a warning, an exhortation and a promise, directed to a ruler, and a nation, engaged on the same anti-papal course, hedged around by the same dangers and threats and subject to the same fatal fears and weaknesses, as John.

After all, when the play was written and printed, Elizabeth's regime had just dispatched Mary Stuart. Mary, like Arthur, had been, in the eyes of some, the rightful queen, and, in the eyes of a lot more, the rightful heir. Her execution/murder was, on some (largely Catholic) views, a crime quite as dreadful as the death of Arthur, and Elizabeth's role in Mary's end at least as murky, ambiguous and sinful as John's involvement in the demise of his nephew. Moreover, the realm was under papal condemnation and confronting foreign (Spanish, not French) invasion and the prospect of foreign (popish) claimants (the Infanta ?) to the English throne. In such circumstances might not some English nobles be contemplating revolt or a deal with foreign, popish powers to divert the succession elsewhere? Might not the danger threatened to the realm from without prompt some sort of compromise with the forces of Antichrist? Indeed, on some (radical) puritan views of the situation, through its failure fully to reform the English church and people, the regime had already done such a deal, striking an entirely unworthy bargain with the forces of Satan and Antichrist for the sake of an illusory political stability. After all, at almost precisely this point, the regime was being excoriated, by Martin Marprelate, even as it was being denounced by a series of foreign and domestic Catholic observers.

Of course, those most likely to criticise the regime on the grounds of its insufficient zeal, both at home and abroad, in the struggle with Antichrist, were precisely not the same people likely to have been disgusted or repelled by its treatment of Mary Stuart. The play evokes godly criticism of the reign in much the same way and for much the same purposes as it evokes a certain sort of Marian or legitimist unease: not to endorse either, but rather to exhort both sides to shut up and rally around queen and country in order to repel the foreign, popish forces currently threatening ruin to the entire realm.

Shakespeare's version took on much of the same admonitory energies as *The troublesome reign*, but, as we have seen, it made three major changes that subtly transformed the purport of the play. Firstly it added real doubts about the legitimacy of John's claim; in effect redescribing him as a usurper as well as an incipient tyrant. It stripped the tale of all of the eschatological scaffolding erected around it by the Foxe/Bale account and by *The troublesome reign*, reducing almost to nothing the role of providence. And it took out all of the anti-popery that suffused the earlier play, leaving only a virulent anti-papalism that conceived the papacy as just another peculiarly duplicitous and voracious player of the game of commodity politics. For absent a sense that what was at stake here was a struggle between the absolute good of true religion and the absolute evil of popery, the political conflicts being depicted in the play emerged as a mere struggle for what the French king calls 'vantage' and the bastard 'commodity'. The action of Shakespeare's play thus takes place in a world stripped by John's usurpation of any source of absolute value or legitimacy, and the result is a bare-knuckle power struggle; a politics of commodity indeed.

Shakespeare's play, just like *The troublesome reign*, ends with a patriotic appeal to English unity in the face of the foreign threat; a paean to the invincibility of what, near the play's outset, Austria calls 'that white fac'd shore,/Whose foot spurns back the ocean's roaring tides/And coops from other lands her islanders'. 'That water-wall'd bulwark' [*KJ*, II, I, 23–27] will remain, the bastard promises, 'still secure and confident from foreign purposes', only if her inhabitants – prince, nobility and people – eschew internal division and come together to oppose the threat of foreign invasion and rule. But, of course, the action of the play, here agreeing with the Catholic pamphlets that made up *Cecil's commonwealth*, suggested that, in the post-reformation world of late Elizabethan England, such unity could not be assumed. As David Kastan observes, just as, through his own rhetoric and action, the bastard had earlier created 'a king worthy of loyalty', so now, in the concluding speech of the play 'he creates a country capable of it'.[35] For all its seeming finality, the vision of English strength and unity conjured by the bastard is conditional; prefixed by an 'if', his speech merely offers the prospect of such unity and power *if* the various constituent parts of the commonwealth of England remain true to themselves and to England. That had been precisely the same note upon which both the Holinshed account and *The troublesome reign* had ended. But by removing the providentially and eschatologically charged framework in which *The troublesome reign* had set the events of the reign, and, in this quite unlike the Holinshed account, by emphasising John's status as a usurper, Shakespeare's version gave the audience even more reason to think that such an outcome was anything but inevitable. Indeed, one might go further and argue that the nature of the 'England' being rallied to here was deeply problematic, not merely contested or up for grabs, but teetering on the edge of dissolution if, that is, the right choices were not now, at the last, made, and made to stick. The 'England' to which loyalty is being urged is, in short, being constituted in and through the very action of Shakespeare's play, and, by implication, through the course of the immediately contemporary (Elizabethan) events and political choices to which the play is addressed and which, through its staging of history, it is presenting to its audience.[36]

But these plays, and particularly Shakespeare's play, show the English uniting not so much behind the monarch as behind the regime; indeed between the most aggressively militarist elements within the regime, represented by the bastard. For another consequence of Shakespeare's questioning of the legitimacy of John's claim – and his removal of any sense that John was an eschatologically charged precursor of Elizabeth, and thus a major player in the sacred drama of English, and indeed, of world history – is a further shift of emphasis away from John and towards the bastard as the only source of legitimacy on offer, at least in the second half of the play.

For while the spontaneous activism in the face of foreign invasion and succession evinced by the bastard is enough to save the nation from foreign conquest and rule, it cannot save the fatally flawed figure of John. Not only is his death necessary in order for full legitimacy to return, but Shakespeare, unlike the author of *The troublesome reign*, strongly suggests that the sins into which John's status as a usurper have led him are so great as to consign him, in all likelihood, to hell. As we have seen, in *The troublesome reign*, having been tormented by his former sins, John repents, denounces popery and dies well. In *King John*, befuddled by the poison eating away at him, the king dies unrepentant and desperate. 'Within me is a hell; and there the poison/Is as a fiend confin'd to tyrannise/On unreprievable condemned blood' [*KJ*, V, vii, 46–48]. He dies, indeed, denied even the prospect of temporal salvation for his kingdom, expiring at the very moment when the bastard is telling him that his own forces have been destroyed in the Wash and that the dauphin 'is preparing hitherward' [*KJ*, V, vii, 59].

The play provides us with a sharply divergent version of a good death, that of the Frenchman Melun, who, confronted by the certainty of his own death reveals to the English nobility the truth about the dauphin's duplicity, and then, having discharged his conscience, withdraws to meet his maker in peace. As Emrys Jones comments, 'his good end . . . affects the way we view the death of John', which 'agitated, distracted, self-preoccupied, "a module of confounded royalty" ' – is anything but a "good" one.'[37]

By stripping the play of its elements of anti-popery and replacing it with the anti-papalism organised around the figure of Pandulph, Shakespeare rendered the style of xenophobic foreigner-hating nationalism present in both versions, if not, in any straightforward sense of the word, 'secular', then decidedly a-confessional. Indeed, in his speech lamenting his part in a rebellion waged in favour of a foreign ruler, Salisbury had fantasised about a future in which 'these two Christian armies', might be whisked magically 'unto a pagan shore', where they 'might combine/The blood of malice in a vein of league,/And not to spend it so unneighbourly!' [*KJ*, V, ii, 24–39]. His speech thus combines a vision of an England reunited in opposition to foreign rule with one of a Christendon united in defiance of the common enemy, the Turk. This is about as far away from a heavily confessionalised, exclusively protestant, vision of Englishness as it was possible to get, on the public stage, in the mid 1590s. The result is an appeal to national unity in the face of the foreign threat to which a range of different sorts of loyalist Catholic could sign on with relative ease.[38] The same could hardly be said of the rabidly anti-popish *Troublesome reign*.

That point emerges with even greater force when we remember just what sort of regime the bastard and then the English nobility are shown rallying around. As we have seen, Shakespeare's John is a usurper, a wannabe murderer, even, if Arthur is the true prince, a regicide, morphing, in the latter stages of the play, into that worst of all worlds, a thoroughly ineffectual tyrant, entirely incapable of defending his realm from the depredations of the pope and the French. Transposed into contemporary terms this is anything but a flattering portrait of the condition of England under Elizabeth. Indeed, with its location of the real fault not in the counsellors but in the monarch, Shakespeare's play exceeds in the severity of its critique that offered in the Catholic pamphlets of the early 1590s. But, the play argues, even a regime as bad as this is still better than the spectre of foreign rule. That is to say, even if virtually everything certain Catholic critics said about the Elizabeth and her regime were true, faced with the threat of foreign rule the only thing to do is to emulate the bastard and rally to the defence of the realm. Shakespeare's play is, therefore, a defence of the Elizabethan regime but it is an extraordinarily downbeat one, and as such calculated to appeal even to some of that regime's most (Catholic) jaundiced critics, as well as to its most committed (protestant) supporters.

With John recast as a usurper and a tyrant, and, on that basis, consigned to hell, the returning sense of legitimacy and Englishness that floods the stage at play's end derives from two distinct sources. On the one hand, in the person of the bastard, it rises up, as it were spontaneously, from the body of the English people (impregnated, it must be said, with the royal sperm and spunk of Coeur de Lion himself). On the other, it proceeds – in the person of John's son Henry, the future Henry III – from the accession to the crown of a claimant of unimpeachable hereditary credentials. With both the problematic true heir (Arthur) and the usurping *de facto* monarch (John) now dead, Henry emerges as the only, unchallenged and unchallengeable, legitimate claimant to the throne. At once Richard Coeur de Lion's natural son, the bastard, moves aside, his illegitimate legitimacy trumped by the just claims and prowess of the legitimate heir. Royal blood will, it seems, always in the end, out.

Again to translate the terms of the play into the immediately contemporary circumstances of the mid 1590s this means that while a holding operation needs to be conducted in the face of the threat of foreign rule, real salvation can only come from a next successor whose dynastic legitimacy everyone can accept, and that means – with both that Arthur look-alike, Mary Stuart and that John analogue, Elizabeth Tudor, both dead – from the only claimant with Tudor blood in his veins, James VI.

Shakespeare's play thus emerges as something like a virulently nationalist, a-confessional, but also anti-papalist and anti-Spanish, legitimist defence of the Stuart succession. As such it represents a view of the reign diametrically opposed to that of Robert Parsons.

Unlike Parsons' tract, in Shakespeare's play succession to the English throne is lineal, determined by strict rules of hereditary right. The play has no truck whatsoever with the elective principle and in the scene before the walls of Angiers stages the impotence of any principle of popular election to assuage the rush towards civil war consequent upon an openly contested succession. When reality diverges from those rules, as when John pushes aside young Arthur to rule as a usurper, bad things happen to both king and realm. In Shakespeare's account, far from representing 'the commonwealth', the nobles are never anything other than rebels and the dauphin never king of England. John's deposition by the pope is thus neither a confirmation of the prior exercise of the English commonwealth's right to remove a tyrant nor, in and of itself, a legitimate act, removing an old and creating a new monarch. More broadly still, the whole play is a denunciation of both the legitimacy and the desirability of foreign invasion and rule. Indeed, it is the reflexive unity of the English created by that threat that creates, or rather recreates, the legitimacy of even a usurper and sinner like John, and clears the way for the succession of the one true heir and future king, his son Henry; a role to be played in the current context by none other than Mary Stuart's son, James VI and subsequently I.[39]

Unlike *Richard III* or *Titus*, there is no trace here of resistance theory or of elective monarchy; no looking abroad to the ancient enemies of the realm for salvation or legitimacy; no conviction that, in the face of usurpation and tyranny, conspiracy, rebellion, collusion with the enemy and regicide might be necessary, even lawful, means to restore monarchical legitimacy. On the contrary, the play condemns all such expedients, typing them, with the homily of obedience, as sinful, and, with Holinshed, as imprudent.[40]

In taking that line – in effect exhorting his audience to unite not so much around the person of the present incumbent as around the most activist and aggressive, the most virtuous and valorous, of her counsellors, and the prospect of the next successor – Shakespeare was both signing on to, and glossing, in his own sense, at least a version of the political project of the earl of Essex and his supporters. In making such a move, Shakespeare was returning to a position that he had already occupied in 1591–92 with his part in the writing of *1 Henry VI*. I have argued above that through a subtle interplay between the events staged in that play and immediately contemporary circumstance, news and rumour, *1 Henry VI* had suggested ways in which the prospect of disputed succession, civil war and confessional conflict – in other words of the sort of political and moral meltdown already staged in *2* and *3 Henry VI*, and predicted with some degree of glee by the Catholic tracts – could be averted. The root of the problem was identified not as a disputed or uncertain succession, or even as foreign war, but rather as a combination of foreign war with noble faction-alism and monarchical weakness. The crucial problems stemmed from the interplay of disputes within the regime about what sort of war this was and about how best to fight it, disputes and divisions compounded by a series of entirely personal and factional rivalries that set the nobility at one another's throats, despite the best (and almost entirely ineffectual) efforts of the monarch to compose their disputes and instil unity against the common enemy. The answer to this situation was presented as renewed unity in the face of the foreign threat and a prosecution of the war with full vigour and violence. Only thus could the promise of success held before the audience by the ignominious defeat and death of the witch-like Puzel be realised and the threat placed before them by the defeat and death of the valiant Talbot be averted.

I argued above that this message was very likely closely tied to the recent exploits and future plans of the earl of Essex, whose vision of what was wrong and of what to do about it the play reflected. For Essex was the proponent of a vigorous prosecution of the war, particularly in France in alliance with Henry IV. His vision of the immediate future of the war featured himself in a starring role as a second Talbot, leading the queen's military forces to victory abroad and ensuring unity at home. This, the play implied, was the only way to avoid the sort of paralysing rivalries and dissensions that would otherwise push the realm down the slippery slope to foreign defeat, domestic dissension, a contested succession and then civil war.

King John in many ways repeated that recipe for political and military success. Again unity at home was to be ensured by vigorous prosecution of the war against the foreigner. On the one hand, *King John* is the more optimistic of the two plays. It certainly has the more upbeat ending. In *1 Henry VI* the hero figure, the epitome of military virtue, loyalty and honour, is Talbot. But not only does he end up dead, he is only intermittently central to the action, which is dominated by other, more sinister figures and forces. In *King John* Talbot's role as the epitome of English vigour and virtue is played by the bastard, who, in this quite unlike Talbot, becomes more and more central as the action proceeds and ends up not only alive but victorious. On the other hand, the analysis of what is wrong with the regime that the bastard ends up saving – usurpation and incipient tyranny – is far more damningly profound than anything to be found in *1 Henry VI*. For in that play Henry VI is an intermittent and ineffectual, rather than a malign, presence. Again in *King John* the issue of the succession is put front and centre in ways that it was not in *1 Henry VI*. The result is, in many ways, a far more radically critical vision of the current conjuncture – of what might well be happening, or be about to happen next and what needs to be done about it – than that contained in *1 Henry VI*. It represents a shift in political circumstances to a world in which the succession has become yet more central; a world, as we have seen, both reflected in, and now increasingly shaped by, Parsons' *Conference*.

There are other differences of emphasis and nuance between the two plays. In *1 Henry VI*, the figure of Puzel, the foe against whom England should unite, had been typed not merely as foreign but also as popish. In *King John* a similar function had been served by Pandulph. But there are significant differences between the popery personified by the two characters. Puzel evokes the full range of anti-popish stereotypes and fantasies about popery as an anti-religion, a genuinely demonic, simply Antichristian nexus of error and illusion, a conspiracy by corrupt clergymen, foreign powers and the devil and his agents to undermine true religion and the integrity and independence of an England always already disposed to oppose such plans. Such certainly had been the purport of the hyper-protestant versions of John's reign put out by Bale and confirmed by Foxe, and indeed by the Book of Homilies and subsequently performed on the popular stage in *The troublesome reign*. But if many of the standard contemporary renditions of John's reign were drenched in such anti-popery, Shakespeare's was not. Thus, where *1 Henry VI* put forward an aggressively protestant nationalism, *King John* did not; the version of Englishness canvassed in the latter play might thus appeal to or encompass certain strands of Catholic loyalist sentiment far more easily than that conjured in the former.

All of which accorded rather well with the circumstances of the mid 1590s and with Essex's position within those circumstances. While much admired by the godly, Essex had long abandoned a partisan commitment to the puritan cause and his vision of the pan-European and cross-confessional alliance necessary to defeat Spain turned on the willingness of politique Catholics abroad, like Henry IV of France, or the Spanish renegade, Antonio Pérez and of Catholic loyalists at home, to unite against the threat posed to the political and religious liberties of Europe by Hapsburg universal monarchy.[41] His platform, by this point, thus amounted to an aggressive prosecution of the war against Spain on all fronts, in alliance with politique Catholics as well as with hot protestants, together with a *sotto voce* espousal of the Stuart claim; a situation adverted to with typical acumen and malice by Parsons, who had famously dedicated *The Conference* to Essex as the queen's greatest favourite and, as such, the man most likely to preside over the course of the next succession.

I have argued above that, amongst other things, *1 Henry VI* was a highly topical piece of Essexian propaganda, dedicated to the claim that the prospect of moral and political meltdown and civil war, conjured in *2* and *3 Henry VI* and threatened by the (imminent) death of the queen with the succession unsettled, could be averted by renewed unity in the face of the foreign and popish enemy and by the consequent prosecution of the war against Spain and the Catholic League with a vigour, virtue and intensity worthy of the great Talbot (or indeed of Essex) himself. In *King John* Shakespeare returned to that vision of national redemption and all under the rubric of a quintessentially loyal, rabble-rousing piece of wartime propaganda aimed to incite popular audiences to new heights of foreigner-hating loyalty and zeal in the defence of queen and country. And who, in the 1590s, could object to that?

CHAPTER 10

Richard II, or the rights and wrongs of resistance

The other reign of an English medieval king that had been central to Parsons' wider purposes in the *Conference* was that of Richard II. For Parsons, Richard's deposition represented a textbook example of how these things had been done in the past, and could, and indeed should, be done in the future. It provided him with a paradigmatic instance of the smoothly managed, consensual and bloodless deposition of a tyrant and the election of his successor. Here was proof positive that the English monarchy was precisely as Parsons described it, that is to say both elective and with a residual right, inherent in the commonwealth, to control, resist and, if need be, to remove a tyrant and elect his successor.

On Parsons' account, there had been, and indeed could be, no doubt as to Richard's status as a tyrant, pure and simple; 'suffering himself to be carried away with evil counsel of his favourites and then the perverting of all laws generally under his government' and 'joining with his minions for oppressing the nobility'. His removal had therefore represented no hole-in-corner conspiracy, no illegitimate court coup, or violent popular or aristocratic revolt, but rather 'the reformation of the realm against so potent a tyrant as king Richard was then accounted'. The event's status as such was clear, Parsons argued, both from its course and its consequences. When Bolingbroke had first arrived in England he had come with but 'three score men in all' and yet by the end Richard's removal had been effected with the support, and through the efforts, of what amounted to the whole realm. For all that Richard's removal had had to be effected, as these things nearly always had to be, through the use or at least the threat of force, the transition had been made 'without slaughter'. And lastly the king was deposed by Act of parliament. All of which prompted Parsons to conclude that 'neither can there be any more circumstances required . . . for any lawful deposition by a prince'.

It is then at least interesting that, having dealt with the nexus of events, precedents and strands of lineal descent and dynastic connection located in John's reign, Shakespeare should also, very probably at around the same time, have produced a dramatic treatment of the deposition of Richard II. The dates more or less fit. Parson's *Conference* was known in England – how widely remains unclear, but certainly in the circles around the court – from autumn 1595 and the composition of the play is conventionally ascribed to the period between 1595 and its first publication in 1597. It is, then, at least possible that Shakespeare was responding to Parsons' text, or perhaps more likely to a penumbra of rumour and argument surrounding it.

Either way, given the centrality of Richard's deposition and replacement by Bolingbroke, for Parsons' purposes it is certainly worth reading the one text against the other to see how Shakespeare's treatment of the event squares up against that of the Jesuit. It is also worth reading *Richard II*, as it were, against *King John*. For the two plays were very likely written close together and with a similar problematic in mind. Certainly, both deal with the same issues of legitimacy, succession and rebellion, albeit in very different ways.

Thus to situate the play, to triangulate between *John*, *Richard* and the nexus of issues and arguments surrounding the succession, particularly as that question had been framed by Parsons, is to depart from the more conventional ways in which *Richard II* has been contextualised or read in terms either of Shakespeare's *oeuvre* as a whole or of contemporary political concerns. Criticism in that latter mode has tended to concentrate on the alleged involvement of the play on the edges of the Essex revolt, when a revival of a play on Richard's deposition – a play assumed, on what Blair Worden has argued are somewhat questionable grounds, to be Shakespeare's – was put on at the behest of many of the men about to be centrally involved in that ill-starred event. But this, of course, was not the context in which the play was written or first performed. Here we will be trying to set the play in the immediate context provided by other plays and texts of the early and mid 1590s, texts concerned with tyranny, resistance and succession, texts emanating, as we have seen, from the pen of Robert Parsons and of other people in his circle. The impulse to do this is not an original one. As long ago as 1874 Richard Simpson attempted such an exercise in contextualisation and as recently as 1997 Cyndia Clegg juxtaposed the deposition scene in the play to Parsons' book, seeking in the political conjuncture thus created between the two texts an explanation for what she took to be the 'censorship' of what the 1608 edition (rather misleadingly) calls 'the parliament scene'.[1]

Similarly, when viewed in terms of Shakespeare's other works, the play is most often seen as the start of the second tetralogy of history plays, the so-called Henriad. But might it not, in fact, just as well be conceived not so much as the starting point of the second tetralogy, a series of plays that can have been no more than a glimmer in the author's eye as he sat down to write *Richard II*, but rather as the culminating point of the ideological development sketched in the previous chapters of this book, and as such a companion piece to *King John*? For, as we shall see, *Richard II* casts a retrospectively providential gloss over the three parts of *Henry VI*, a gloss which quite alters their meaning, by enlisting them as central portions of a version of fifteenth-century English dynastic and political history that was entirely absent from the *Henry VI* plays but which certainly makes sense as a response to, indeed even as a refutation of, not only Parsons' very different gloss on those same events but also of the ideological positions implied by *Titus Andronicus*.

As for *King John* and *Richard II,* they complement one another through their differences, each one approaching a similar set of issues, indeed we might even say the same basic problematic, from radically different starting points. In *King John* we are confronted with a situation in which legitimacy has been lost through the reign of a usurper, a monarch whose right to rule is actively contested throughout the play. In *Richard II,* on the other hand, political legitimacy is lost through the actions of a ruler whose dynastic legitimacy is above reproach. In *King John,* everyone, including the king himself and his own mother, seems to be aware of the fragility of his claim to the throne. In *Richard II* no one is in any doubt as to the legitimacy of this scion of that dominating, even mythic, figure in the pantheon of English military heroes, the Black Prince, himself the eldest son of the even more fearsome Edward III. What drains Richard's reign of legitimacy is his own conduct, which, by the time the action of the play starts, is degenerating into something like open tyranny.

Tyranny anatomised

The play is very careful to demonstrate with almost forensic clarity just how and why Richard is guilty of tyranny.[2] The first evidence of this is his direct responsibility for the death of Gloucester. This act is the original political sin that lurks behind the action of the play, curdling the moral and political atmosphere in which all the major players act and react to one another and to events. Richard's responsibility for this primal political and moral crime is clearly common knowledge and is revealed as such by Gaunt's conversation with Gloucester's widow. As the countess demands that Gaunt take action to revenge the slaughter of his brother, Gaunt responds by simply assuming her knowledge of Richard's direct involvement in her husband's death, citing his higher duty to obey the Lord's anointed, as the reason why he cannot act. 'Alas, the part I had in Woodstock's blood/Doth more solicit me than your exclaims/To stir against the butchers of his life./But since correction lieth in those hands/Which made the fault that we cannot correct/Put we our quarrel in the will of heaven,/Who, when they see the hours ripe on earth,/Will reign hot vengeance on offenders' heads' [I, ii, 1–8]. 'God's is the quarrel, for God's substitute,/His deputy anointed in His sight,/Hath caused his death, the which if wrongfully,/Let heaven revenge, for I may never lift/An angry arm against his minister' [I, ii, 37–41].

This exchange puts into an entirely new light the opening scenes of the play in which Hereford challenges Mowbray to trial by combat for treason.

Confronted by this outbreak of noble feud and faction, Richard attempts to mediate the dispute. As both men insist that their honour dictates that they decide the rights and wrongs of the affair on the field of battle, Richard concedes. Now, however, Gaunt's remarks reveal his son Hereford's challenge to Mowbray to be an attempt to wreak the revenge for Gloucester's death that his widow is demanding of Gaunt, while preserving what Gaunt claims is his (and Hereford's) ultimate obligation to obey, and certainly not overtly to defy or resist, the authority of the king, who is the real culprit in the affair. In the succeeding scene Richard interrupts the intended trial by combat by banishing both parties – Hereford, his cousin, for six years and Mowbray in perpetuity. What is staged by the king as a statesmanlike attempt to preserve the peace of the realm from an outbreak of what could have become an uncontrollable noble blood feud, now appears to the audience as something altogether more sinister, as Richard, the real cause of Gloucester's death, uses a dispute occasioned by that crime permanently to remove (in Mowbray) the main instrument that he has used to do the deed, and (in Hereford) a major source of potential resentment and even opposition to his rule, while all the while presenting himself as the impersonal voice of even-handed royal rule. Once we know the inwardness of these events, what is clearly intended to appear to be the exercise of a positively Solomonic royal justice, emerges as a further example of Richard's tyrannous substitution of his own will for the laws and customs of the realm, an arbitrary interruption of what should have been the natural course of justice; an intervention prompted by Richard's pursuit of personal, political and factional advantage. Here, in short, is the quintessence of tyranny.

To confirm this point, from the king's own mouth as it were, there is a later scene between Richard and Aumerle in which the extent of the malice and distrust directed towards Hereford by the king's inner circle is rendered explicit. Asked by the king 'how far brought you high Hereford on his way?' Aumerle replies with a slighting account of their parting, in which he goes out of his way to emphasise to the king how glad he was to see the back of Hereford. 'Marry, would the word "farewell" have lengthened hours/And added years to his short banishment/He should have had a volume of farewells,/But since it would not, he would have none of me.' Richard's reply to this is even more chilling: 'he is our cousin, cousin, but 'tis doubt,/When our time shall call him home from banishment,/Whether our kinsman come to see his friends' [I, iv, 16–22].

The extent to which Richard's tyranny has started to invade other spheres apart from his relations with and management of the peerage, is revealed from a similar variety of perspectives. Richard himself is the first to broach this subject as, turning from Hereford's banishment to the subject of war in Ireland, he admits to Green and his other intimates that 'for our coffers with too great a court/And liberal largesse are grown somewhat light,/We are enforced to farm our royal realm,/The revenue whereof shall furnish us/For our affairs in hand. If that come short,/Our substitutes at home shall have blank charters/ Whereto, when they shall know what men are rich,/They shall subscribe them for large sums of gold,/And send them after to supply our wants;/For we will make for Ireland presently' [I, iv, 42–52]. Informed, at the end of these exchanges, of Gaunt's approaching death, Richard seizes on this opportunity to augment the strained royal finances. 'Now put it, God, in the physicians' mind/ To help him to his grave immediately!/The lining of his coffers shall make coats/To deck our soldiers for these Irish wars./Come gentlemen, let's all go visit him./Pray God we may make haste and come too late!' [I, iv, 59–64].

Richard's deeply unflattering portrait of his own rule and regime is, then, almost immediately confirmed in rather less morally neutral language by the dying Gaunt. England, he claims 'is now leased out – I die pronouncing it –/ Like to a tenement or pelting farm./England, bound in with the triumphant sea,/Whose rocky shore beats back the envious siege/Of wat'ry Neptune, is now bound in with shame,/With inky blots and rotten parchment bonds./The England that was wont to conquer others/Hath made a conquest of itself' [II, i, 59–66]. These words, delivered in private to York, are then repeated in, if anything, even more heightened language to Richard himself, as Gaunt exploits the privilege and, as he hopes, the special efficacy, of the words of the dying to bring the king to his senses. After a bantering exchange about which of them is the sicker, Gaunt launches into a tirade against the king's rule and regime. 'Thy death-bed is no lesser than thy land,/Wherein thou liest in reputation sick;/ And thou, too careless patient as thou art,/Commit'st thy anointed body to the cure/Of those physicians that first wounded thee./A thousand flatterers sit within thy crown,/Whose compass is no bigger than thy head;/And yet, encaged in so small a verge,/The waste is no whit lesser than thy land./ . . . Why, cousin, wert thou regent of the world,/It were a shame to let this land by lease;/ But for thy world enjoying but this land/Is it not more than shame to shame it so?' [II, i, 95–112].

The tyrannical and oppressive character of Richard's policies is further confirmed by a group of dissident nobles, who whip themselves up into open resistance. 'The commons hath he pilled with grievous taxes,/And quite lost their hearts,' claims Ross. Willoughby agrees: 'And daily new exactions are devised,/As blanks, benevolences, and I wot not what.' Moreover, his current financial straits are entirely his own fault. 'Wars hath not wasted it, for warred he hath not,/But basely yielded upon compromise/That which his ancestors achieved with blows./More hath he spent in peace than they in wars.' Thus Northumberland. Ross concurs: 'The earl of Wiltshire hath the realm in farm.' 'The King's grown bankrupt like a broken man,' adds Willoughby. 'He hath not money for these Irish wars,/His burdenous taxations notwithstanding' (II, i, 246–60).

According to a set of contemporary conventions, quite as pertinent to the Tudor period as to the late Middle Ages (as, amongst others, Gerald Harris has shown),[3] kings were quite at liberty to resort to extraordinary ways of raising supply, to forced loans, benevolences and other exactions, *if* they had first exhausted other conventional means, or asked for and been refused normal forms of revenue, and were confronted with a national crisis, a foreign war, a domestic rebellion, or some other exigency that required the marshalling of the nation's resources in defence of the common good. These exchanges are designed, of course, to show with crystal clarity that such considerations do not apply to Richard. His financial exigencies are not a question of necessity, of dire need and national emergency requiring extreme measures and arbitrary exactions, all other conventional means and requests having been exhausted. On the contrary, his current financial situation is entirely his own fault; the consequence of riotous peacetime spending rather than of the demands of war or national defence. It is this royal misrule that has left his coffers empty; his own misconduct, rather than the demands of war, that is causing his current extremities. The point here, of course, is, once again, to render Richard's tyranny patent.

Finally, lest this testimony of would- or about-to-be rebels be distrusted, the play allows us to eavesdrop on the conversations of several of Richard's intimates, the men blamed for these policies and who had profited from the promiscuous distribution of royal patronage that had brought the king's finances to their present parlous condition. As the rebellion starts, Bushy, Bagot and Green cabal together and discuss their options. Their almost chorus-like, call-and-response, conversation neatly parallels the structure of the earlier exchanges between the rebel lords, and the purport of their exchanges serves to confirm the lords' estimation of the nature of the king's policies, the state of the realm and the political affections of the people, albeit the opinions are arrived at from an entirely different political position and couched in very different evaluative terms. 'Our nearness to the King in love/Is near the hate of those that love not the King,' observes Green. 'And that's the wavering commons,' concurs Bagot, 'for their love/Lies in their purses; and whoso empties them,/By so much fills their hearts with deadly hate'. 'Wherein the king stands generally condemned,' concludes Bushy. 'If judgement lie in them, then so do we,/Because we ever have been near the king' [2, ii, 126–31].[4]

Here, then, is the voice of the evil counsel to which the king has been subjected, indeed which he has elicited from his inner circle, those 'thousand flatterers' that 'sit within thy crown' denounced by Gaunt, by whom, according to Northumberland, the king is 'basely led'. To demonstrate the difference between such evil and good counsel and to show that the king has been amply exposed to both, the play shows us Richard receiving an earful from Gaunt, a man whose loyalty to Richard and the principle of monarchical legitimacy the

play has gone out of its way to establish. As a counsellor, too, he knows inti-
mately what his obligations are, and has been able, under even the most extreme
of pressures, to distinguish between the public interests of the realm and his
own private interests as a magnate, the head of a noble house and a father. This
is made crystal clear in a series of exchanges with Richard after the king has
announced Hereford's fate. As Gaunt repines at his son's banishment, the king
rounds on him. 'Thy son is banished upon good advice,/Whereto thy tongue a
party-verdict gave./Why at our justice seem'st thou then to lour?' [I, iii, 233–35].
Richard, in other words, in deciding the Mowbray/Hereford feud, has been
careful to take the prior advice of his council and thus while he can stage his
interruption of the trial by combat as an irruption of an arbitrary royal will,
determining the rights and wrongs of the case and imposing a settlement
despite the preferences and aims of the two participants, he has also been
careful to cover his back. He is now able to reap the benefit, as he upbraids
Gaunt for seeming to repine at the banishment of his son, an outcome about
which he was consulted, to which he, in his role as counsellor, has consented
and in which he is thus now deeply implicated. In response, Gaunt cites the
precision and punctiliousness with which (he claims) he has observed the
distinction between his public duties as a royal counsellor and his private interests as a noble and a father. Richard had consulted him in his public role 'as a
judge' and thus he had felt unable 'to argue like a father'. 'Had it been a stranger,
not my child', Gaunt would have felt free to argue for clemency, but constrained
by his public role of counsellor to avoid 'the partial slander' of favouritism,
Gaunt had 'in the sentence my own life destroyed' [I, iii, 236–42]. It is an
account that reveals just how much he has been manipulated and entrapped by
the king, who, perhaps sensing a plot between father and son to discomfort
him and reopen the issue of Gloucester's death,[5] has moved to disrupt this
Lancastrian stratagem by using Gaunt's status as a counsellor to get him to sign
off, not only on the frustration of his and his son's plan to do something about
Gloucester, but also on the banishment of his own flesh and blood.

The result is that Gaunt has become impossibly implicated in his nephew's
tyrannical misrule, except that now, on his deathbed, confronting his Maker,
Gaunt is given one last opportunity to strike back, to reclaim his moral standing
from the complicities inflicted upon him by his own commitment to the divine
right of kings, his nephew's political cunning and, perhaps, as his sister-in-law,
the duchess of Gloucester, more than implies, his own moral cowardice. As
Berger memorably puts it, now at the last, Gaunt 'tries to squeeze himself into
his words as into his name, so that there will be nothing left outside of the
iconic death mask, no unruly surplus of ambivalence, guilt, desire, or unmeant
meaning'.[6] Gaunt's, then, may not be a purely disinterested telling of truth to
power; nevertheless the moral authenticity, the both personal and political
virtue, that he is here trying to recuperate, demands that he tell the king some-

thing that he and the likes of York, and his sister-in-law (not to mention his son, Bolingbroke) can all recognise as the truth of the matter.

For the political logic of the play, the main significance of this is that the audience get to watch Richard receive, from an unimpeachable (because dying and previously uber-loyal) source, the quintessence of good counsel, that is to say the unvarnished truth about his past conduct and current moral and political condition. That this exchange is immediately followed by Richard's seizure of Hereford's inheritance, what Richard terms 'the plate, coin, revenues and moveables/Whereof our uncle Gaunt did stand possessed' [II, i, 161–62], provides final and clinching evidence of Richard's tyranny.

But if Richard's seizure of Hereford's Lancastrian inheritance is all of a piece with his previous tyrannical behaviour, it also moves beyond the limits that, up to this point, Richard has been shown setting to his own depredations. Hitherto, Richard has been scrupulous to observe the outward legal forms that are supposed to govern the conduct of kings. He may have been behind Gloucester's death, but the deed was clearly done by third parties and Richard has been able to distance himself from it, in the process forcing his subjects, even those most integrally and personally involved, who wish to take revenge for the duke's death, and indeed know perfectly well that the king was behind the murder, to act as though that were not the case. Hereford comes closest to breaking the taboo, including in his indictment of Mowbray as a 'traitor coward' the allegation that he had 'sluic'd out his innocent soul through streams of blood –/ Which blood, like sacrificing Abel's, cries/Even from the tongueless caverns of the earth/To me for justice and rough chastisement;/And by the glorious worth of my descent,/This arm shall do it, or this my life be spent' [I, i, 102–8]. But even this claim had been contained within a wider characterisation of Mowbray, not as the murderer of Gloucester, but rather as a traitor to the king; a treason comprised not only of Gloucester's death but also of his having diverted money intended for the payment of the king's troops to his own 'lewd employments' and, in a portmanteau claim rendered nugatory and even absurd by its generality, having 'complotted and contrived in this land' all the major conspiracies against the crown for some 'eighteen years' [I, i, 87–96]. There is, therefore, an explicit act of deference towards royal authority encoded even in the terms in which Hereford makes his challenge against Mowbray. Mowbray replies by accusing Hereford in his turn of being 'a recreant and most degenerate traitor' [I, i, 144]. Admittedly both Mowbray and Hereford use the defence of their honour as justification for their joint refusal of Richard's initial attempt to make peace between them, but as their mutual accusations of treason show, the whole dispute is taking place within an overarching deference to, and indeed being conducted in terms of, an imputed defence of Richard's authority as king. And so when at Coventry Richard cites his supervening responsibility to defend the peace of the realm against the threat represented by noble feud to enforce his initial desire that their combat not take place, both parties are left without either practical or theoretical recourse. The fact that, in the interim, Richard has consulted his council, and that Hereford's own father has been numbered amongst those consulted, renders the king's behaviour, at least on the surface, a punctiliously correct use of royal powers, the legitimacy of which all the parties to the dispute are forced to concede.[7]

If, in A.D. Nuttall's phrase, in the opening scenes 'it is easy to think that we are watching a politician of genius,'[8] it is because, within the limited terms in which Richard has always operated, we are. In Harry Berger Jr's phrase, 'this is political, not merely poetic, mastery'.[9] Thus, while politics is being played within the legal fiction, the outward forms, of legitimate rule, Richard reveals himself a past master at the manipulation of those forms as a legitimising and enabling screen for his own tyrannical policies.

Tyranny outed

What the seizure of Hereford's inheritance does is move Richard's actions definitively outside the realm of the legally justifiable. There is now no more hiding tyrannical action behind the plausible deniability conferred by the actions of third parties or the punctilious observance of legal or customary forms or arguments. This is a clearly arbitrary act, undertaken entirely outside, indeed against, the law. Richard is overreaching himself, creating a dangerous precedent and calling down all sorts of political difficulties upon his own head. While the murder of Gloucester might be thought of as the greater sin or crime, Richard had maintained a certain distance, a crucial space for (im)plausible deniability between himself and that act. This was not the case with the seizure of Hereford's lands, something that is immediately recognised by a number of onlookers. Here the key figure is York, who hitherto has acted as a restraining influence even on Gaunt, trying to talk him out of his dying tirade to Richard and thereafter explaining the result to the king as but the effect of 'wayward sickliness and age in him' [II, i, 142]. But now even York has to speak out. 'How long shall I be patient? Ah, how long/Shall tender duty make me suffer wrong?/ Not Gloucester's death, nor Hereford's banishment,/Nor Gaunt's rebukes, nor England's private wrongs,/Nor the prevention of poor Bolingbroke/About his marriage, nor my own disgrace/Have ever made me sour my patient cheek,/Or bend one wrinkle on my sovereign's face.' But this last is the final straw. 'Take Hereford's rights away, and take from Time/His charters and his customary rights;/Let not tomorrow then ensue to-day;/Be not thy self, for how art thou a king/But by fair sequence and succession?/Now, afore God – God forbid I say true –/If you do wrongfully seize Hereford's rights,/Call in the letters patent that he hath/By his attorneys-general to sue/His livery and deny his offered homage,/You pluck a thousand dangers on your head,/You loose a thousand well-disposed hearts/And prick my tender patience to those thoughts/Which honour and allegiance cannot think' [II, i, 195–208]. In short, by thus seizing Hereford's inheritance Richard is calling into question the very principles of right succession and inheritance by which he holds his own throne and thus inviting rebellion. For if York cannot bring himself to utter or consider, still less to undertake, that course of action, there are others who both can and will.

Immediately after these exchanges, as Richard and York quit the stage, they leave behind them the knot of lords – Northumberland, Willoughby and Ross – whose conversations have been quoted above. They too see the likely implications of Richard's actions. For them the issue is not theoretical – a calling into question of the principle of right inheritance – but more pressingly personal. The king, Northumberland claims, is 'not himself, but basely led/By flatterers and what they will inform/Merely in hate, 'gainst any of us all,/That will the King severely prosecute/'Gainst us, our lives, our children and our heirs'. 'But, lords,' declaims Northumberland, 'we hear this fearful tempest sing,/Yet seek no shelter to avoid the storm./We see the wind sit sore upon our sails,/And yet we strike not, but securely perish' [II, i, 241–45, 263–66]. In other words, if Hereford goes down what is to stop the same happening to any of us? It is that terrifying prospect, combined with the objective weakness of the king's current political position – as they all agree, Richard, through his harsh rule, has 'quite lost the hearts' of both 'the commons' and 'the nobles', 'and now reproach and dissolution hangeth over him' [II, i, 246–48, 258] – rather than the wider condition of the realm or moral outrage at the king's misgovernment, that moves these lords to rebellion, stirred by the news, delivered at the strategic moment by Northumberland, that Hereford has just landed from France at Ravenspur, along with some other English lords, to reclaim his just inheritance.

At this point we move from the world of legitimacy, of a politics conditioned and constrained, even in the face of Richard's misgovernment and incipient tyranny, by the legally and socially enforced and, as Gaunt's case shows, also the fully internalised, limits of legitimacy, into the world of 'commodity', the pursuit of immediate political and personal advantage, in a political universe stripped of the fixed points of settled allegiance to divinely ordained monarchical rule. *King John* had started in that condition, a condition created by the fact of John's displacement of the just claimant, Arthur, and consequent usurpation of the throne. In *Richard II* we have been thrust into it by the serial misgovernment, and increasingly open tyranny, of Richard himself. In *King John* legitimacy is always already lost, and the play is about what to do and how to act in its absence in order to get it back again. In *Richard II* the issue is what to do if the ultimate repository of legitimacy, the monarch, systematically destroys it. What will happen, what should happen and how can legitimacy be reconstituted once the ruler has turned tyrant?

It is this that explains the very different stylistic and theatrical forms taken by the two plays. Where *King John* is antic, violent, full of action, conflict and noise, *Richard II* is stately, the verse formal and the action highly ritualised, at almost every stage adopting the forms of the secularised liturgy that surrounds court life and kingly authority. From the opening scenes involving the challenge and then trial by combat between Mowbray and Hereford, through Richard's return from Ireland, his confrontation with Bolingbroke at Flint Castle, until his deposition and death, the action of the play is ceremonious in tone and often ceremonial in outward form. The editor of the recent Arden edition counts 'elements of ritual and formality' occurring in thirteen of the play's nineteen scenes. As he further points out, 'the magniloquent speeches, the stately balances and symmetries, the courtly etiquette and mannered formalities of speech and movement assist this effect, as does the absence of low comedy'.[10]

The same, of course, could not be said of *King John*, which, almost from the start, serves to rip the mask of formality from the exercise of kingship, revealing the outward poses, the claims to principle, to be serving God and receiving divine aid, made by all the principal characters, on both sides of the dynastic conflict, to be entirely hollow. The reality principle of the play lies in the bastard, and nearly all his scenes in the first half of the play are typified by elements of 'low comedy'. In short, *King John* starts where *Richard II* ends, in the world of commodity, and the verse and action of both plays reflects that fact.

It is thus only in its later stages, in the outbreak of gage-slinging centred on Aumerle, which immediately precedes the deposition scene, and in the exchanges between York, his son and his wife, and then between all three of them and the king, which immediately follow it, that *Richard II* enters a similar world of semi-farce. This is a change of tone and rhythm which is surely designed to signal or reflect the decline of the realm into the anarchy of commodity politics, a rip tide of manoeuvre and counter-manoeuvre, of conspiracy and counter-conspiracy. The suddenly staccato, farce-like movement of the action, is surely intended to stage the extemporised, improvisational nature of Bolingbroke's increasingly frantic efforts to respond to, and bend to his own advantage, events that, if they are not quite slipping beyond his control, are certainly diverging from the carefully choreographed script through which he had intended to establish himself in power.

But if the two plays are separated by their language and forms, they are united by a remarkably similar structure. Both feature kings transformed from the first to the second half of the plays named after them. Just as John turns from the heroic martial figure of the first two acts into the increasingly desperate and impotent failed tyrant of the second half, so Richard turns from the clearly tyrannical figure of the first two acts into something altogether different after his return from Ireland, the collapse of his cause, the capture of his person and his deposition from the throne. Similarly, in both plays the two kings' alter egos undergo parallel transformations from one half of the play to the other. As the bastard sheds his antic, vice-like characteristics to epitomise Englishness and seize control of the action in *King John*, so, in *Richard II*, Hereford is transformed from the straightforwardly honourable and English, the innocent and loyal, victim of royal duplicity and tyranny, into Bolingbroke, the altogether more ambiguous, and quite possibly Machiavellian, rebel and usurper of the play's second half.

In both plays, too, the action is driven by what one might term an iron law of political necessity, that, almost in spite of the best or better intentions of the major players, forces them to take actions that undermine the cause of legitimacy and thrust the world into a ceaseless struggle between individuals and factions for security and advantage; in the bastard's terms, for 'commodity'. In *King John* the person subject to this iron rule of self-preservation is the king himself. Since the political logic of his role as usurper dictates that he can enjoy no security while Arthur lives, he feels himself almost bound to make away with the boy, in this subject to rules of political probability and prudence that Pandulph the legate understands and expounds only too well. Once that fatal step has been taken, once John has started to act like a tyrant, events follow precisely the scenario sketched by Pandulph. Tyranny leads to resistance, resistance to deposition and usurpation.

In *Richard II*, the same laws of political probability apply. While in *John* usurpation leads to tyranny and tyranny to revolt, in *Richard II*, tyranny leads to revolt and usurpation, which leads again, if not to tyranny, then to what looks like the first stages of a John-like descent into violence and political turmoil, into the world of commodity that is consequent upon the loss of legitimacy. The resulting political force field is initially set in motion by Richard's seizure of Gaunt's lands, and the wider tyranny it epitomises; a tyranny that then proceeds to invert what ought to be the natural political relationships, reactions and expectations that regulate and characterise a legitimately constituted and lawfully governed polity.

The fallacies of sacred kingship

Richard espouses what we might term a divine right view of sacred kingship. It is a view that has often been presented as normative, or at the very least straightforwardly hegemonic, for this period, one in which the authority of the prince in his kingdom is a direct creation of God, in its major characteristics and operations reproducing almost exactly the sovereignty of God over his creation. Royal authority is a natural authority, to which people are naturally bound and which, other things being equal, they naturally obey. Royal authority is the coping stone of a hierarchy of beings and ends, the final guarantee and ordering principle of a natural social and political hierarchy, a hierarchy created by God and presided over by his anointed deputy, the king. On this view, there is something sacred about both the office and person of an anointed king; the royal person and will are embodiments of divine authority on earth.

As any number of critics and historians have noted, there is something inherently performative, para-liturgical, even theatrical, about the resulting style of rule. The display and deployment of the person and will of the monarch in a number of ritually defined and symbolically charged arenas of power is a crucial means of establishing political legitimacy and control. It is, of course, the evocation and depiction of this style of rule, and of the modes of being and forms of subjectivity that go with it, that produce the formalities of much of the verse in which the play is written and the ceremonial gravitas of many of its great set pieces – the trial scenes with which it opens, the meeting between Richard and Bolingbroke at Flint, the deposition scene.

Throughout Richard is shown to be both a past master at, and the prisoner of, this sort of monarchical performance. As we have seen, his (ultimately tyrannical) rule is established and maintained precisely through his manipulation of the outward forms, the shaping assumptions and symbol systems, underpinning this monarchical style. But Richard is shown not merely as a masterful performer in this mode, innately capable of playing the part of the prince and thus able expertly to manipulate the forms and appearances of legitimate monarchical authority to his own (partisan) advantage. Of course, he does so manipulate those forms, but he is also revealed to be a true believer in this particular vision of kingship. At times, it is not so much that he speaks the language of sacred monarchy, as that that language speaks him.[11] Richard really does believe, that since 'he is the Lord's anointed', 'not all the water in the rough rude sea/Can wash the balm off from an anointed king;/The breath of worldly men cannot depose/The deputy elected by the Lord./ . . . for heaven still guards the right' [III, ii, 54–62]. He really does 'know' that 'no hand of blood and bone/Can gripe the sacred handle of our sceptre,/Unless he do profane, steal or usurp'. These were political sins which 'my Master, God omnipotent' was even then preparing 'armies of pestilence' to punish down the generations [III, iii, 72–90]. He really does believe that the physical substance, the flora and fauna, the rocks and earth, of his kingdom will resist the very tread of the rebel Bolingbroke and his host [III, ii, 4–26]. Viewed from within Richard's version of divine right kingship, this is not a mere conceit but something altogether more substantial, a fantastic rendition of a number of linked beliefs about the naturalness of divine right monarchy and the infrangible nature of the bond between, indeed the literal identity of, the king and his kingdom. In this view of the world, rebellion *was* unnatural and therefore nature herself would rebel against it; the link between the authority and person of the king and his kingdom was so intimate and so unbreakable that an assault upon the one would provoke the natural resistance of the other.

In short, rebellion simply is not possible in the face of the royal presence. Employing the image of the king as the sun, an image which, of course, recurs throughout the play, Richard proclaims that 'when the searching eye of heaven is hid/Behind the globe and lights the lower world,/Then thieves and robbers range abroad unseen/In murders and in outrage boldly here;/But when from this terrestrial ball/He fires the proud tops of the eastern pines/And darts his light through every guilty hole,/Then murders, treasons and detested sins,/The cloak of night being plucked from off their backs,/Stand bare and naked, trembling at themselves' [III, ii, 37–46]. So too, he prophesies, will Bolingbroke's rebellion fold when faced down by the king. Such assumptions continue, subtly changed but not essentially altered, even after his fall, when Richard's insistent references to himself as an analogue for Christ reveal his stubborn adherence to the belief in the divine status of kings that has all along animated his performance as monarch.

Bolingbroke himself uses very similar imagery when, at Flint Castle, he compares Richard to 'the blushing discontented sun' emerging 'from out the fiery portal of the east,/to dispel' 'the envious clouds' gathering 'To dim his glory and to stain the track/Of his bright passage to the Occident' [III, iii, 62–67]. However, the fact that Bolingbroke can talk like this even as he is initiating the chain of events that will end with Richard's deposition and death shows with crystal clarity that, by this point, the prevalence of such language is no longer constraining action or framing reality in the ways that Richard has come to believe it must. What for Richard had always been facts of political life have become or are becoming for Bolingbroke and others mere persiflage, with which, for a time at least, they can conceal from others (and perhaps even from themselves) what is really happening to Richard, and indeed the realm.

Once the bubble of Richard's divine right reverie has been pricked, reality does not merely refuse to accord with this vision, it positively inverts it. Not only do Richard's Welsh troops desert him and York, the deputy he has appointed to rule England in his absence, and defect to the rebels, but the whole social order flocks to support Bolingbroke [III, ii, 110–20].

The description of that act of collective desertion is strongly reminiscent of Hubert's account in *King John* of the effect worked on the allegiance of the populace by the news of Arthur's death. 'Whitebeards have armed their thin and hairless scalps/Against thy majesty; boys with women's voices/Strive to speak big and clap their female joints/In stiff unwieldy arms against thy crown;/The very beadsmen learn to bend their bows/Of double fatal yew against thy state;/Yea distaff women manage rusty bills/Against thy seat. Both young and old rebel,/And all goes worse than I have power to tell' [III, ii, 110–20]. This, of course, is the effect of tyranny on the political, social and moral relations that should bind the ruler to the ruled, the prince to his people and realm, and the people to their prince. If the natural response to the legitimate rule of a legitimate prince is obedience, harmony and order, so the equally natural response to such a rule, not merely gone bad but turned tyrant, is rebellion, and the dissolution of all the bonds of mutuality, of obedience and protection, that should bind the ruled to their rulers, the prince to his subjects.

Those links and obligations between rulers and ruled are in some sense natural; they have been hard-wired into the nature of reality; there is a predisposition to order and obedience in human society as God has created it. But this is also a fallen world and such natural connections and propensities need the positive intervention, the skilful and well judged management of a practised, controlling human hand, if they are indeed to produce order. That, of course, is the purport of the garden scene, which uses the organic imagery of natural growth and fecundity to display both what true kingcraft means and what Richard's misrule has wrought. The gardeners' careful husbandry in the king's garden is contrasted with Richard's performance in the state, which has produced a realm 'full of weeds, her fairest flowers choked up,/Her fruit trees all unpruned, her hedges ruined,/Her knots disordered and her wholesome herbs/Swarming with caterpillars [III, iv, 40–47]. (Presumably those same 'caterpillars of the commonwealth' that Bolingbroke, using the same organic, husbandry-centred imagery, had vowed to uproot?) The results are described in telling language. 'He that hath suffered this disordered spring/Hath now himself met with the fall of leaf./The weeds which his broad-spreading leaves did shelter,/That seemed in eating him to hold him up,/Are plucked up, root and all, by Bolingbroke –/I mean the earl of Wiltshire, Bushy, Green'. 'Bolingbroke/Hath seized the wasteful king . . .' 'Depressed he is already, and deposed/'Tis doubt he will be' [III, iv, 48–55, 68–69].

Interestingly, in this version of events, the decline, indeed the incipient deposition and replacement, of the king is described as an impersonal, even a natural event. Having allowed 'a disordered spring', Richard has met with a compensating 'fall of leaf'. Such are the self-righting mechanisms of the natural order of political society; thus are disordered polities restored to a posture of natural balance; except that, of course, such recalibrations and adjustments do not, in practice, take place without human agency and intervention. Significantly, in this version of events, it is Bolingbroke who is cast in the role of skilful gardener, giving the otherwise disordered garden of the realm a much-needed prune and general tidy-up. There is, of course, a considerable irony at work here. For the very naturalising images and metaphors used to render monarchical rule itself natural, a central part of the God-given order of the both natural and human worlds, is here being used to cast acts like resistance and usurpation, conventionally regarded as the greatest of political crimes and moral sins, not merely as natural consequences of tyranny, but as much needed palliatives for a polity thrown into disorder by tyranny.

These are points that Richard at no stage seems to apprehend. He never sees his political circumstances as a result of his own mistakes, let alone tyrannies.

This is as true after his deposition as it was before it. As we have seen, throughout the play, Richard is shown as enamoured of, indeed as almost entirely defined by, his image of himself as God's anointed. The consequent analogies and correspondences between his powers and prerogatives and those of God himself dangerously contaminate his political judgement, rendering him all but unable to perceive the very real limits placed on his power by his status as a mere mortal; just another player, albeit a major one, in the drama of sublunary and post-lapsarian human politics. This characteristic is on display throughout the play. It represents Richard's fatal weakness as a practitioner of politics.

Richard's greatest political skill resided in his capacity to manipulate the forms of monarchical legitimacy and power. As long as others remain in some sense constrained by their adherence to legitimist assumptions and the protocols of sacred monarchy, that facility remains his greatest source of political strength. It is what enables him to get away with the murder of Gloucester and to disrupt, with such apparent ease, the threat posed to his regime by Hereford's (and Gaunt's) challenge to Mowbray. But once the spell has been broken and his fatal mistake in seizing Hereford's lands and title has been made, the case is altered. Having virtually forced Hereford and others into open resistance, Richard has created a situation in which the political game is no longer simply defined by the outward forms and inward constraints of monarchical legitimacy and authority. He can no longer rely on the operation of the deeply internalised scuples that had led the likes of Gaunt and York, and even (although perhaps to a lesser extent) Hereford, to swallow the death of their kinsman, Gloucester. In such a situation Richard's political instincts and skills, which have been honed within precisely such a state of affairs, desert him, or rather, remaining stubbornly the same, even as circumstances change radically around him, they become no longer a source of strength but of debilitating weakness, as his belief in the almost magical efficacy of the forms of sacred monarchy and divine right strip him of any capacity to act effectually on the situation with which he is now confronted.

Nuttall, then, is precisely right when he observes that 'Richard is therefore both a fantasist and a realist'.[12] The two capacities or potentials are integrally connected, for not only does Richard's brilliant capacity to inhabit and manipulate to his own advantage the norms of divine right absolutism enable the political mastery that he displays in the opening scenes, it also prompts his deep understanding of what is at stake in the acts of rebellion and then of usurpation that remove him from power. It is this insight that enables him to analyse with such unrelenting realism what must happen to him once he has fallen into Bolingbroke's hands and, perhaps more importantly, what is going to happen to Bolingbroke as he attempts to exercise the powers of a king without the aura of legitimacy that attends 'God's anointed'. But in the interim, while things are still in some sense in the balance, it is also precisely his commitment to this belief system that prevents Richard from taking effectual action in a world in which his own status as king is no longer the fundament, the both theoretical and practical bottom line, of all political life and decision-making.

And even his closest supporters know it. The bishop of Carlisle emerges in the course of the play as a proponent of the ideology of sacred monarchy and divine right second in intensity and enthusiasm only to Richard himself. But even he feels called upon to rouse the king from the divine right reverie into which he has lapsed immediately upon his return from Ireland, reminding him that while 'That Power that made you king/Hath power to keep you king in spite of all./The means that heavens yield must be embraced/And not neglected; else heaven would/And we will not. Heaven's offer we refuse –/The proffered means of succour and redress.' 'He means, my lord,' adds Aumerle, lest the king has still not understood, 'that we are too remiss,/Whilst Bolingbroke, through our security,/Grows strong and great in substance and in power' [III, ii, 27–35].

The play thus offers us a picture of an ideology of divine right kingship, that in Richard's case has curdled and turned back on itself. Believed and applied too literally, it has hardened into certain habits of mind and styles of rule, certain modes of subjectivity and of action, that lead eventually, but also directly, not only to tyranny but also to the complete political incompetence, indeed incapacity, displayed by Richard in the central sections of the play.

The tyranny thus produced necessarily – even, to adopt the terms set by the garden scene, naturally – produces resistance. Just as the final step into overt tyranny was the disinheritance of Hereford, so the ensuing resistance is led by Hereford himself, whom Richard has left with no choice other than to accept the extinction of his line or to resist. But once set on that path, Hereford, now in his new persona as Bolingbroke, is subject to laws of political probability, indeed of necessity, no less strong than those that had pushed the usurper John into the enormity of seeking young Arthur's death. For, however just his initial cause may have been, once launched on the path of direct challenge to royal authority, Bolingbroke has even less hope of personal, political or dynastic security until he has replaced Richard on the throne, than John had while Arthur lived. This, of course, is not something that Bolingbroke ever admits; certainly not publicly or, the pregnant silences of the play might be taken to suggest, perhaps even to himself.

From the reformation of the kingdom to rebellion, usurpation and regicide

Throughout the initial stages of their revolt neither Bolingbroke nor his supporters espouse the removal of Richard as their aim. As we have seen, the noble conspirators cite the condition of the realm, the injustice done to Hereford, the disaffection of both the commons and nobility and their own political danger as their reasons for joining Hereford, a course they seek to justify positively through their desire to free the king from evil counsel and the commonwealth from oppression. Their aim, Northumberland claims, is 'to shake off our slavish yoke,/Imp out our drooping country's broken wing,/Redeem from broking pawn the blemished crown,/Wipe off the dust that hides our sceptre's gilt/And make high majesty look like itself' [II, i 291–95]. There is, of course, nothing here about the deposition of the king, but a great deal about the vindication of the glory and rights of the crown and the reformation of the commonwealth. The king, on this view, is to be saved, certainly from his evil counsellors, and perhaps even from himself, but he is not to be removed or replaced.

Hereford makes a similar pitch. Challenged by York as a traitor, a status proved by his presence, as a banished man, in arms, in England, Bolingbroke denies any seditious intent or royal aspirations. Indeed he takes refuge in a sort of legalism. 'As I was banished, I was banished Hereford;/But as I come, I come for Lancaster. . . . Wherefore was I born?/If that my cousin king be King of England? It must be granted I am Duke of Lancaster. . . . I am denied to sue my livery here,/And yet my letters patent give me leave./My father's goods are all distrained and sold,/And these, and all, are all amiss employed./What would you have me do? I am a subject,/And I challenge law. Attorneys are denied me,/And therefore personally I lay my claim/To my inheritance of free descent'. Northumberland concurs: 'The noble duke hath been too much abused'. On this account both Bolingbroke and his supporters merely want his lands and title to be restored to him [II, iii, 113–37].

Beyond that, Bolingbroke commits himself to some element of reform of the commonwealth, pushing on to 'Bristol Castle, which, they say, is held/By Bushy, Bagot, and their complices,/The caterpillars of the commonwealth,/Which I have sworn to weed and pluck away' [II, iii, 164–67]. When, in the next act, Bolingbroke is shown in physical possession of said caterpillars he has them summarily executed for offences committed not only or even mainly against himself but rather against King Richard and the realm. 'To wash your blood/From off my hands, here in the view of men/I will unfold some causes of your deaths:/You have misled a prince, a royal king,/A happy gentleman in blood and lineaments,/By you unhappied and disfigured clean./You have in manner with your sinful hours/Made a divorce betwixt his queen and him,/Broke the possession of a royal bed/And stained the beauty of a fair queen's cheeks/With tears drawn from her eyes by your foul wrongs./Myself, a prince by fortune of my birth,/Near to the King in blood, and near in love,/Till you did make him misinterpret me,/Have stooped my neck unto your injuries/And sighed my English breath in foreign clouds,/Eating the bitter bread of banishment,/Whilst you have fed upon my signories,/Disparked my woods and felled my forest woods,/From my own windows torn my household coat,/Raised out my imprese, leaving me no sign/Save men's opinion and my living blood/To show the world I am a gentleman./This and much more, much more than twice all this,/Condemns you to the death' [III, i, 5–30]. Here still is the rhetoric of evil counsel, of a king misled by low-born favourites and minions. The references to these men's having 'broke the possession of a royal bed' and reduced the queen to tears suggest a physical as well as an emotional or political seduction or enthralment of the king.

There is, of course, no warrant within Shakespeare's play to confirm this view, for in his version of the reign the evil counsellors of the king play almost no role in defining or framing his tyranny. As Paul Gaudet observes, 'we have not seen the favourites misleading and disfiguring the king. On the contrary, Shakespeare has gone to great pains to dramatise Richard as wilfully insulated against all counsel.' The implication is there to be drawn that Bolingbroke is here emphasising the role of the hated Bushy, Bagot and Green in order to protect himself from the charge of directly challenging the king, even as his summary execution of them as traitors to king and commonwealth usurps one of the central prerogative powers of the crown.[13]

Notably, in the speech quoted above, Bolingbroke leaves his own grievances until last, and, while he takes care to mention his own royal blood, makes no (even passing) allusion to a claim to the throne. He continues in the same mode on his first meeting with Richard, telling Northumberland to tell Richard that 'Henry Bolingbroke/On both knees doth kiss King Richard's hand/And sends allegiance and true faith of heart/To his most royal person, hither come/Even at his feet to lay my arms and power/Provided that my banishment repealed/And lands restored again be freely granted' [III, iii, 35–41], which is the same message that Northumberland delivers to the king, adding,'This swears he, as he is a prince and just;/And, as I am gentleman, I credit him' [III, iii, 112–20].

Richard, of course, does not believe a word of this. Here, despite, or rather precisely because of, his high view of sacred kingship, Richard betrays a certain grasp of the dynamics of the situation in which he now finds himself. He exploits that understanding throughout his exchanges with Bolingbroke, both at their first meeting at Flint Castle and later, using it to taunt his nemesis with the absurd hypocrisy of his continued pretence that Richard is still really king and Bolingbroke merely a suppliant subject. When, at their first meeting, Bolingbroke kneels before the king, Richard replies, 'Up cousin, up. Your heart is up, I know,/This high at least', indicating, as the stage direction explains, his crown. Despite this opening provocation, Bolingbroke ploughs on with the charade. 'My gracious Lord, I come but for mine own.' 'Your own is yours, and I am yours and all,' replies the contemptuous Richard. 'So far be mine, my most redoubted lord,/As my true service shall deserve your love.' 'Well you deserve. They well deserve to have/That know the strong'st and surest way to get! . . . Cousin, I am too young to be your father,/Though you are old enough to be my heir./What you will have, I will give, and willing too;/For do we must what force will have us do' [III, iii, 194–207].

But if Richard ridicules Bolingbroke's outward show of loyalty, in their behaviour towards Bolingbroke many of the rebels, in effect, falsify his public claim only to be asking for his own. From the outset, Northumberland and the others treat Bolingbroke with rather more respect than a returning duke of Lancaster might expect. In return Bolingbroke is both elaborately courteous and knowingly coy [II, ii, 59–62, 65–67]. But if they start to treat Bolingbroke like a king, the rebels also start to refer to Richard as something less than their sovereign. York immediately jumps on a reference by Northumberland to the king merely as Richard. 'It would beseem the Lord Northumberland/To say "King Richard". Alack the heavy day/When such a sacred king should hide his head.' 'Your grace mistakes; only to be brief/Left I his title out,' responds Northumberland, which reply sparks a tirade by York that is only stopped by the brusque instruction from Bolingbroke: 'mistake not, uncle, further than you should'. 'Take not, good cousin, further than you should,/Lest you mistake: the heavens are o'er our heads.' 'I know it, uncle, and oppose not myself/ Against their will,' comes the heavily ambiguous reply [III, iii, 7–19].

That exchange shows the political need to maintain the mask or appearance of acting only against the king's evil counsellors and past courses rather than against his person or claim to authority. For it is only by maintaining that, as it were, legal fiction that Bolingbroke can hope to attach the likes of York to his cause. Confronted by Bolingbroke's preponderant force, York had first launched a volley of legitimist bluster at his nephew. 'Grace me no grace, nor uncle me no uncle./I am no traitor's uncle, and that word "grace"/In an ungracious mouth is but profane' [II, iii, 87–89]. Having established his legitimist principles, however, York immediately turned his attention to the realities of the situation. Seeing 'the issue of these arms' and seeing that he lacks the means to resist, having once more reminded them all that, if he could, 'I would attach you all and make you stoop/Unto the sovereign mercy of the King', he gives up the ghost, proclaiming that 'I do remain as neuter', before asking them all home for dinner [II, iii, 152–61].

York, then, was co-optable, but not if it was made clear to him that he was, from the outset, signing on to an attempt to depose Richard and replace him with Bolingbroke. Similarly, after having first remained loyal to the king, the earl of Worcester is reported to have broken his staff, dissolved the royal household and joined the rebels, not because he wanted to see Bolingbroke king, but because he was disgusted to find Bolingbroke declared a traitor merely for returning to England to defend his legal rights. A certain functional ambiguity about the nature of his intentions was, therefore, absolutely essential if the support for Bolingbroke was to be maximised and support for Richard minimised.

As for Bolingbroke himself, while he gradually starts to act as though he is, or is about to become, king – using the royal 'we', for instance, as he presides over the disputes between various lords about who was really to blame for

Gloucester's death [IV, i, 107] – he does not expressly mention any designs on, or intention to claim, the throne until the very point of Richard's deposition/ abdication. As the garden scene shows, popular opinion and the rumour mill have him crowned and Richard deposed well in advance of these events [III, iv, 68–71]. But it is not until York publicly announces Richard's intention to give up the throne to Henry 'of that name the fourth', that Bolingbroke acknowl-edges or owns his designs on the throne, replying with alacrity, 'in God's name I'll ascend the regal throne' [IV, i, 113–14]. The extent to which this move is still shocking to some contemporaries is shown by the bishop of Carlisle, who greets the remark with a long speech denouncing such an assault on the divinely ordained power of the Lord's anointed. We will return to the contents and significance of that speech below. For now suffice it to say that as soon as he is finished Northumberland tells the bishop:'Well have you argued, sir; and for your pains/Of capital treason we arrest you here' [IV, i, 151–52].

By this point, of course, we are watching a carefully planned and scripted *coup de théâtre*, designed to effect, legitimise and, if necessary, enforce a smooth transfer of power from Richard to Henry. What the play leaves open is the ques-tion of when precisely in his progress from aggrieved subject, to armed peti-tioner, to rebel, to rival claimant to the throne, Bolingbroke had first formulated his intention to depose Richard and claim the throne for himself. The transition from one persona, one set of aims and intentions, to another was, the play seems to suggest, incremental, the precise moment of decision imperceptible, perhaps even to Bolingbroke himself. The progression itself however is presented as all but certain, indeed as inevitable, a function of the underlying logic of the situa-tion with which Bolingbroke and his supporters were confronted and had them-selves done so much to create. As we have seen, Bolingbroke's reply to York's warning that the 'heavens are o'er our heads' is that he knows it only too well and has no intention of opposing heaven's will. There is a fundamental ambiguity to that form of words that gets to the heart of the matter. On the one hand, Bolingbroke's reply might be taken as an endorsement of York's conventionally pious warning against even contemplating usurpation; on the other, it might betoken a willingness to follow wherever the logic of events might lead, even if that meant eventually seizing or 'accepting' the crown, while construing that outcome as itself the will of heaven.

There is, of course, a further irony at work here, for if that is the course taken by Bolingbroke, it is also adopted by his uncle York, who, for all his volubly expressed scruples, is the first man publicly to proclaim Richard's desire to resign the crown in Bolingbroke's favour and also the first publicly to hail King 'Henry, the fourth of that name'. Later justifying his change of alle-giance to his wife, York resorts to precisely the same providentialist argument used earlier by Bolingbroke to imply his own loyalty to King Richard. York concludes an emotional account of the humiliation of King Richard by the

London crowd as he rode in the procession to the new king's coronation, with the claim that 'heaven hath a hand in these events,/To whose high will we bound our calm contents./To Bolingbroke are we sworn subjects now,/Whose state and honour I for aye allow' [V, ii, 37–40].

Clearly delay and obfuscation were central in allowing others to reconcile themselves to what nearly all perceived were the realities of the situation. Appeals to 'providence' were equally essential as the means whereby 'loyalists' like York could square the circle and reconcile their consciences with their interests in accepting the deposition of one king and the accession of another as somehow an expression of the 'will of heaven' and thus as entirely legitimate. And, in enabling that situation to play out as it did, it may well be that Bolingbroke had been acting all along as a Machiavellian plotter, whose eyes had been set on the prize of the crown long before he landed at Ravenspur.

On one level, of course, the nature of Bolingbroke's motives are beside the point. What counts is the logic of the political situation created by his (and indeed Richard's) initial breach of the principles of legitimacy in a monarchical state.[14] And here, the parallels between the situations of John the usurper and Bolingbroke the rebel go deeper yet. For just as John, having taken the decision to usurp the throne, almost has to, if not kill, then at least connive at the death of Arthur, so Bolingbroke, having taken up arms against his king, almost has to seize the throne and, having seized the throne, if not kill, then certainly connive at the death of Richard.

But just as the result of John's attempted murder and actual removal of Arthur is not the political security and dynastic legitimacy that he craves, so Bolingbroke's murder of Richard does not lead to any sort of return to monarchical normality. On the contrary, Bolingbroke's deposition of Richard merely serves to compound the relativising, delegitimising impact of Richard's initial decision to disinherit him. And those destabilising effects are by no means brought to a close by Richard's death. This point is made in the last two acts of the play in a number of scenes and described and experienced from a number of perspectives.

The political theatre of usurpation and the paradoxes of loyalism

It shows first even before the formal transfer of power has been effected. As Bolingbroke and a group of lords process towards parliament, for the final denouement of Richard's deposition and Bolingbroke's proclamation as king, they pause to call the last surviving member of Richard's inner circle before them. Bolingbroke instructs him to 'Freely speak thy mind,/What thou dost know of noble Gloucester's death,/Who wrought it with the king, and who performed/The bloody office of his timeless end' [IV, i, 2–5]. Presumably this final revelation of the king's involvement in the play's primal political sin is to

be part of the political theatre that attends his deposition; a public relations
coup designed to ease and legitimise the peccant king's removal from the
throne. Unfortunately, Bagot then accuses Aumerle, York's son and Bolingbroke's
nephew. Guilt for the sins of the old regime is now threatening to reach within
the inner circles of the new. Aumerle, affecting contempt for 'this base man',
vigorously denies the charges and throws down his gage in challenge to his
accuser. Bagot is now in the position occupied at the play's start by Hereford/
Bolingbroke, and Aumerle in that occupied by Mowbray. Things are clearly not
going according to plan and Bolingbroke attempts to reassert his control over
the proceedings, telling Bagot to 'forbear. Thou shalt not take it up' [IV, i, 31].
At this point a whole series of lords jump in, trying to win favour with the new
dispensation by turning on Aumerle. First Fitzwater accuses Aumerle and in
response to Aumerle's reply that 'Fitzwater, thou art damned to hell for this', is
seconded by none other than Harry Percy, the son of Bolingbroke's right-hand
man, Northumberland. Percy throws down his gage in challenge to Aumerle
who immediately snatches it up again. Another lord seconds Percy's challenge.
Surrey now enters the conversation and proceeds to back Aumerle and to challenge Fitzwater to combat. Fitzwater rises to this second challenge, maintaining
that 'I heard the banished Norfolk say/That thou, Aumerle, didst send two of
thy men/To execute the noble duke at Calais' [IV, i, 75–83]. At this point
Aumerle re-enters the fray and, borrowing a gage, flings it to the floor in a challenge to the absent and exiled Norfolk. Things have now degenerated into
farce; the stage is littered with gages and the theatrical demonstration of
Richard's and the old regime's culpability that was presumably intended by the
usurper and his advisors has turned into a renewed outbreak of feud and
factionalism that threatens to undermine the stability of the new regime,
almost before it has formally started.

In a desperate attempt to regain control of the situation, Bolingbroke
intervenes to say that, 'though mine enemy', Mowbray will be 'repealed' and
'restored again to all his lands and seignories. When he is returned,/Against
Aumerle we will enforce his trial'. This, of course, is an extraordinarily deft
move; it will ensure the death of one potential enemy to the regime, and in that
death seal up for good the murky question of Gloucester's death. A nifty plan,
it fails because Mowbray has just died in exile in Venice. At this point
Bolingbroke is reduced to postponing – indefinitely, as his later treatment of
Aumerle shows – the resolution of the affair.

What we are seeing here, of course, is the challenge and intended combat
between Mowbray and Hereford, with which the play opened in deadly earnest,
being repeated as farce. The key to this second outbreak of honour-based
factionalism, of challenge and denial, was, however, anything but honourable.
In the first instance Hereford had been trying, as far as his supervening obedience and loyalty to Richard would allow, to revenge his uncle's death, and

Mowbray, through combat, to redeem his own honour. Now, however, Hereford, in his new persona as Bolingbroke, the usurper, is seeking not so much to revenge and resolve the issue of his uncle's death as to exploit it, through a piece of political theatre designed to legitimise his own seizure of power.

Not that Bolingbroke is alone in thus seeking to turn the issue of Gloucester's murder to his own personal and political advantage. The scene described above shows several attendant lords jumping on that particular bandwagon, seeking both to clear themselves and to curry favour with the new regime by denouncing poor Aumerle. The crucial, give-away line here is Fitzwater's. In the midst of his altercation with Surrey, he remarks that 'as I intend to thrive in this new world/Aumerle is guilty of my true appeal' [IV, i, 79–80]. This is how far things have declined since the play's opening scenes; a peer of the realm challenging another to mortal combat in effect swears in public on his own political ambition that he is telling the 'truth'. In the absence of legitimate monarchical authority, which, of course, has been removed, first, by Richard's tyranny and, second, by Bolingbroke's incipient usurpation, honour has become a commodity and people are not above admitting it in public. For all his attempts to use this scene to establish his own political and moral authority as king, presiding over and resolving the feuds and tensions within his nobility and putting to rest the crimes and passions of the previous reign, Bolingbroke is revealed as just another of the seekers after political advantage in this new world of 'commodity'. No more than Richard had, has Bolingbroke been able to allow the normal mechanisms and procedures of royally sponsored justice and honour politics to run their course, thus sealing with the sacrifice of noble blood, spilt on the field of combat, the festering sore and foul offence of Gloucester's death. Once again, the pursuit of royal commodity and the imposition of royal will has disrupted the course of justice and the pursuit of social and political peace; in short, of honour and legitimacy traditionally defined.

Unresolved and unrevenged, Gloucester's death remains a continuing source of disagreement and feud, and in that a powerful symbol for the effects of the even more calamitous deposition and murder of Richard himself. The presumptive moral judgements established at the opening of the play, the moral superiority of Hereford, the challenger, and the guilt of Mowbray, the alleged murderer, have been overturned. For, as the bishop of Carlisle informs Bolingbroke, Mowbray, Richard's presumed or alleged instrument in the murder of Gloucester, having spent years making a traditional Christian satisfaction for his sins on the field of battle against the Turk, has retired to Italy and met a Christian death at Venice [IV, i, 92–101]. Bolingbroke has morphed from his earlier incarnations as the honour-obsessed Hereford, loyal son of old Gaunt, cousin of King Richard, and wannabe revenger of Gloucester, into his new persona as Bolingbroke the usurper, seeking (unsuccessfully) to milk Gloucester's death for all it is worth in his pursuit of worldly power and political advantage. That the action of the play now moves immediately to the deposition of Richard and the proclamation of Bolingbroke as king, by none other than Aumerle's father, York, tells its own story.

If this scene reveals the nature of the commodity politics incident upon the evacuation of legitimacy from the political system, others reveal the intensity of the contradictions that surround any notions of loyalty or obedience once a legitimate prince (however personally corrupt or malign) has been displaced. Again the central figure is Aumerle, who throughout the play has been revealed as an intimate of Richard's but who, unlike Green or Bushy or Bagot, has remained active in the king's cause, even in the face of what rapidly turned into impossible odds. For his pains he has been called out as the murderer of Gloucester by men anxious to curry favour with the new regime by denouncing the supporters of the old. Having escaped from that predicament, he is subsequently demoted in the peerage. York his father introduces him to his own mother as 'Aumerle that was/But that is lost for being Richard's friend;/And, madam, you must call him Rutland now'[V, ii, 41–43].

Presumably protected by his kinship both with the king himself but, perhaps more importantly, with his father York, who, for all his freely expressed legitimist principles, has now emerged as a bulwark of the new order, Aumerle has survived, and has the opportunity now, if he keeps his nose clean and co-operates, to make his way in what Fitzwater terms 'this new world'. Instead, as an inveterate Ricardian loyalist, he becomes involved in a plot to kill the new king, Henry, at a tournament to be held at Oxford, and then to restore the old king, Richard, to the throne. This plot is discovered by his father York, who immediately denounces his son as a traitor [V, ii, 72]. As York makes haste to out his son to the king, his wife begs him to conceal the plot.

This and the ensuing scene between the duke and duchess, Aumerle and the king have considerable comic potential and they are very often played (successfully) for laughs. But what we are being shown here is not merely funny. Or rather, the ways in which the scene is funny are intended to make a serious political and moral point. York's political survival is at stake. Having made a display of his legitimist principles before making his peace with the new regime, he cannot afford to be tainted with his son's treason, and he certainly cannot afford to be implicated in any attempt to cover up the plot. He has, therefore, no choice but to denounce his son to the king. Faced with a clear-cut choice, put to him by his wife, to protect his son or himself, York chooses himself, as ever, justifying the protection of his own interest through the rhetoric of legitimacy and loyalty to the king, only this time that loyalty is directed towards the usurper, Henry, rather than towards the old king, Richard. The enormous risks being taken by Aumerle to preserve and express his loyalty to the old king by conspiring against the new stand in marked contrast to the complete congruence between York's loyalty to the new order and the preservation of his own interests, even if that compatibility expresses itself in an unseemly rush to save his own skin by denouncing his son to the authorities.

Just who is being 'loyal' here and to what, exactly, is the question being posed, and, perhaps inevitably, it is left entirely unresolved. In this 'new world' created by Richard's tyranny and Bolingbroke's usurpation, terms like treason, loyalty and obedience – rendered unstable by Richard's tyranny – have now become so deeply problematic as to be almost meaningless; or, at the very least, their meaning has become a function of the prior commitments and loyalties, the present perspectives and interests, of the particular political actors or observers in question.[15] This is a world in which some expressions of loyalty (like Aumerle's) are treason and others (like York's) all but indistinguishable from the servile and self-seeking pursuit of self-interest and 'commodity'. But then the providentialism evinced first by Bolingbroke to York to cover/legitimise his own pursuit of the throne and later by York to his wife to justify his own attachment to the new order was always a flexible enough instrument to cover, with a pious facade of principle, a multitude of such shifts and accommodations.

These ironies are pushed still further in the subsequent scene between the duke and duchess of York and the king. Realising that his father is going to reveal the conspiracy and denounce him as a traitor, Aumerle beats him to the royal presence and extracts a pardon from the king before York can arrive. There ensues a series of increasingly bizarre and comic exchanges which parallel and parody arguments about honour, treason and loyalty made in earnest in the first half of the play. York makes two arguments to the king in favour of his son's execution. The first is that his honour is at stake and would be tainted for ever if his traitor son were to be pardoned for his sake. 'Mine honour lives when his dishonour dies/Or my shamed life in his dishonour lies./Thou kill'st me in his life, giving him breath,/The traitor lives, the true man's put to death' [V, iii, 66–72]. This echoes arguments made by both Mowbray and Hereford in the opening scene when Richard had tried to mend their feud and prevent them vindicating their honour on the field of battle. Then honour had been dearer than their own lives; here York's honour is dearer to him than his son's life, as he makes a demonstration of political loyalty to the new order that happily combines the defence of his honour with the preservation of his life and interests. His second argument concerns the impact of the political precedent of pardoning Aumerle, as, of course, the king has already promised to do. 'If thou pardon whosoever pray,/More sins for this forgiveness prosper may./This festered joint cut off, the rest rest sound;/This let alone will all the rest confound' [V, iii, 82–85]. Here, then, is an argument couched in terms of commodity, or political expediency, as the new regime needs to make examples of its enemies *pour encourager les autres*.

Of course, all these protestations take place at a time when the king has already granted Aumerle a pardon and in the face of the counter-arguments of the duchess, who insists that York's arguments are in fact insincere [V, iii, 99–109]. The result of these exchanges is that Henry manages to square the circle by confirming Aumerle's pardon while vowing to take swift and summary revenge on the other conspirators. Certainly, the contrast between Aumerle's fate and that of his fellow plotters points up the fact that the hypocrisy and calculation of interest at work here have not only been York's. Clearly, once again, arguments from commodity have won out over arguments about honour or justice, as the king cements his alliance with York, makes a political debtor out of the now thoroughly terrified Aumerle, and walks away having again staged a both moving and terrifying demonstration of the power of the monarch, of the semi-divine, unfathomable, apparently arbitrary and irresistible, workings of royal justice and mercy; a demonstration remarkably similar to that staged by Richard's banishment of Mowbray and Hereford at the play's start. As for York, he has been rewarded for the elaborate political theatre of his (perhaps servile and perhaps genuine, Gaunt-like) pleadings for the death of his son, by the best of all outcomes: his son has been pardoned and his own status as a diehard loyalist of the new regime confirmed and rewarded in the most public way possible. However morally absurd the consequences – and the increasingly comic, indeed farcical, form these scenes take is, as we have seen, no accident – as Dermot Cavanagh concludes, 'clearly, it is fundamental to Bolingbroke's success that he has transcended existing obligations and impressed on his new subjects the necessity of conformity to his will and maintenance of his favour'.[16]

But at some cost. Henry's demonstration of the awful finality and essentially arbitrary operation of royal justice and mercy wins from the duchess of York the claim that 'a God on earth thou art' [V, iii, 135], which, of course, is precisely the sort of response that Henry's careful balancing act had been designed to elicit, but, as the scene reveals, there has been nothing God-like or even particularly monarchical about the ways in which, and the purposes for which, that pardon had been granted. As Berger puts it, the 'amused contempt playing over his [Henry's] reference to "the beggar and the king" ' to characterise the farcical proceeding also lays bear 'the style of political theatre he is trapped in, the moral poverty of the kind of pardon he is empowered to give, and the irony of receiving that power only by wounding himself with' the sin of usurpation and therefore with a 'much deeper version of the need for pardon'.[17] Thus, Henry's apparently lordly claim that 'I pardon him as God shall pardon me' [V, iii, 130] might well be thought to reveal something other than the kingly confidence it is trying so hard to project. As Berger points out, Henry 'concludes his instruction to York to mop up the Oxford conspiracy with one rhymed couplet (signal of the desire for closure) and devotes another to proclaiming the Duchess's suit happily ended: "Uncle farewell; and cousin too, adieu:/Your mother hath well prayed, and prove you true". (V, iii, 142–43). But the duchess foils the attempt by making it a triplet, and the line she adds is charged with an echo of the desire for another kind of closure, the possibility of redeeming grace, a grace beyond the earthly God's competence to bestow on another, much less on himself . . . : Come, my old son, I pray God make thee new" '(V, iii, 144).[18]

Prophecy or prognostication?

These scenes thus reveal the dynamics of the delegitimised politics of this new world as it were from the inside, but the observer who notes them most clearly from without is, of course, Richard himself. From the moment he meets Bolingbroke at Flint Castle, Richard taunts the usurper and his rebel supporters with the fraudulence and contradiction of their position as apostles of legitimacy caught between the desertion of their previous prince and the erection of his successor; as supporters of the latter they are committed to the rhetoric of legitimacy, royal authority, obedience and loyalty that underpins the authority of all kings, but as rebels against the former, their actions call all such claims and commitments into the most radical doubt. At this point in the play Harry Berger's insight that Richard's 'political' 'project' has now become a deeply passive-aggressive game played to the death with Bolingbroke comes into its own.[19] Called to effect the transfer of the crown to Bolingbroke, Richard cries 'Alack, why am I sent for to a king/Before I have shook off the regal thoughts/Wherewith I reigned? I hardly yet have learned/To insinuate, flatter, bow and bend my knee./Give Sorrow leave awhile to tutor me/To this submission. Yet I well remember/The favours of these men. Were they not I mine?/Did they sometime not cry "All hail" to me?/So Judas did to Christ, but He in twelve/Found truth in all but one; I, in twelve thousand none./God save the King! Will no man say "Amen"?/Am I both priest and clerk? Well then, Amen./God save the king, although I be not he,/And yet Amen, if heaven think him me' [IV, i, 164–77]. Later, asked by the ever-present Northumberland to sign off on a list of crimes 'committed by your person and your followers/Against the state and profit of this land', Richard is more direct in making much the same point. 'Gentle Northumberland,/If thy offences were upon record,/Would it not shame thee in so fair a troop/To read a lecture of them? If thou wouldst,/There shouldst thou find one heinous article/Containing the deposing of a king/And cracking the strong warrant of an oath,/Marked with a blot, damned in the book of heaven./Nay, all of you that stand and look upon me,/Whilst that my wretchedness doth bait myself,/Though some of you, with Pilate, wash your hands' – a thrust here surely at the likes of York – 'Showing an outward pity, yet you Pilates/Have here delivered me to my sour cross,/And water cannot wash away your sin' [IV, i, 229–42].

This exposure of the contradictions in the ideological and emotional position occupied by his enemies culminates in an analysis of the internal dynamics of the politics of usurpation delivered by Richard to Northumberland, a man whom the play has cumulatively revealed not only as Bolingbroke's chief supporter, but also as the chief architect and instrument of Richard's fall and Henry's rise. 'Northumberland, thou ladder wherewithal/The mounting Bolingbroke ascends my throne,/The time shall not be many hours of age/ More than it is ere foul sin, gathering head,/Shall break into corruption. Thou shalt think/Though he divide the realm and give thee half/It is too little, helping him to all./He shall think that thou, which knowst the way/To plant unrightful kings, wilt know again,/Being ne'er so little urged, another way/To pluck him headlong from the usurped throne./The love of wicked men converts to fear,/ That fear to hate, and hate turns one or both/To worthy danger and deserved death' [V, i, 55–68].

This speech performs several tasks and combines several modes of analysis and discourse. It is at once a curse, a prophecy and a piece of political prognosis. As a prognosis, it is grounded in an entirely secular, this-worldly, even Machiavellian, account of the political and factional forces, the internal dynamics, at work in a state in which the sacred bonds of loyalty and legitimacy, of trust and obedience, have been severed. As a prophecy, it foretells the ways in which divine judgement is going to punish, through their own internal dissensions and mutual suspicions, the crying sins of the usurper and his supporters. As a curse, it calls on heaven to deliver this judgement on the heads of his enemies sooner rather than later. As both history had shown, and history plays yet to be written will show again, Northumberland's brusque response – 'my guilt be on my head, and there an end' [V, i, 69] – is more pregnant than he realises.

The prophetic elements in Richard's diatribe to Northumberland are confirmed by the famous speech with which the bishop of Carlisle had greeted Bolingbroke's first public avowal of his intention to take the throne. 'What subject can give sentence on his king?/And who sits here who is not Richard's subject?' Carlisle asks. Calling the king 'the figure of God's majesty,/His captain, steward, deputy elect,/Anointed, crowned, planted many years', Carlisle proclaims that 'I speak to subjects, and a subject speaks,/Stirred up by God, thus boldly for his king./My Lord of Hereford here, whom you call king,/Is a foul traitor to proud Hereford's king.' He follows this denunciation with a prophecy that 'The blood of England shall manure the ground,/And future ages groan for this foul act./Peace shall go sleep with Turks and infidels,/And in this seat of peace tumultuous wars/Shall kin with kin and kind with kind confound./Disorder, horror, fear and mutiny/Shall here inhabit, and this land be called/The field of Golgotha and dead men's skulls./O, if you raise this house against this house,/It will the woefullest division prove/That ever fell upon the cursed earth./Prevent it, resist it, let it not be so,/Lest child, child's children, cry against you, Woe!' [IV, i, 122–50].

In these two speeches the discourses of divine justice and providential judgement and of politique secular political analysis and calculation meet. Richard's (and indeed the play's) larger analysis of the dynamics of a polity delegitimised twice over, the first time by tyranny, the second by usurpation, provides the causal motor, the explanation in terms of second-order causes, whereby the supervening authority of God and his providence can enlist the sins and dissensions of the rebels to punish not only them but an entire nation or populace that has both enabled and supported rebellion against the Lord's anointed.

Nor is the fulfilment of these prophecies left entirely in the future. Various chickens start to come home to roost at the play's end, when Richard's analysis of the political instability and moral vacuum caused by the loss of legitimacy is confirmed by the nature and circumstances of his own death at the hands of Sir Piers Exton. There is an irony and a poetic justice at work here typical, not merely of the plots of certain plays, but also, on some contemporary readings, of the workings of divine providence itself. Exton, of course, plays the role for Bolingbroke that John had wanted Hubert to play for him. A suitor for royal favour and close observer of the royal mood and disposition, Exton has detected in Henry IV a strong desire to be rid of Richard. As Aumerle's conspiracy has shown, Henry, in this just like John, cannot sit easily on his throne while the legitimate claimant still lives. Henry both wants Richard dead and not to be involved in his death. Exton resolves to do the king and himself a favour by killing Richard, thus freeing Henry from a persistent source of danger and anxiety and winning himself royal favour, into the bargain [V, iv, 1–11]. Having done the deed, and immediately sensed its fell consequences – 'now the devil that told me I did well/Says that this deed is chronicled in hell'– Exton determines that 'this dead King to a living King I'll bear' [V, v, 115–17]. He comes upon Henry disposing of the body parts of recently slaughtered participants in a still raging rebellion that has just 'consumed with fire our town of Ci'cester in Gloucestershire'. On to this busy scene comes Exton, lugging the coffin of King Richard. King Henry is no more pleased to see him than John was to see Hubert bearing the news of Arthur's 'death'. 'Exton, I thank thee not, for thou hast wrought/A deed of slander with thy fatal hand/Upon my head and all this fatal land.' When Exton remonstrates, 'From your own mouth, my lord, I did this deed', Henry explains that 'They love not poison that do poison need./Nor do I thee. Though I did wish him dead,/I hate the murderer, love him murdered./The guilt of conscience take thou for thy labour,/But neither my good word nor princely favour./With Cain go wander through the shades of night,/And never show thy head by day nor light./Lords, I protest, my soul is full of woe/That blood should sprinkle me to make me grow./Come, mourn with me for what I do lament/And put on solemn black incontinent./I'll make a voyage to the Holy Land/To wash this blood from off my guilty hand' [V, vi, 34–50].

Thus is Hereford/Bolingbroke reduced to espousing the same mode of satisfying or expiating his sins as that adopted by his enemy from the opening scenes of the play, that other shedder of royal blood, Mowbray. But, by the play's end, the prime moral referent or point of comparison for Henry is no longer Mowbray but Richard himself. The great unnameable crime is no longer the murder of Gloucester but that of Richard. For Henry ends the play guilty of nearly all the political mistakes and personal sins that Richard himself had committed. He has connived at, indeed arguably caused, the death of a near and royal relative. (There is, of course, nothing in *this* play to confirm that Richard's role in the death of Gloucester was any more direct or culpable than Henry's role in Richard's murder.) He has left the death of Gloucester unresolved, unexpiated and unrevenged, pardoning Aumerle, who is arguably the major culprit still living, for his own partisan political purposes. And, of course, on top of that, he has deposed a reigning and entirely legitimate monarch and usurped a throne. In that respect, his sins are perhaps even greater than those of either Richard himself or indeed of that other usurper and king killer, King John. Either way, at play's end, Henry confronts a future that looks not much more promising than that which confronted John after the death of Arthur; a future, in fact, of conflict, instability and revolt. On this account, the divine judgement and revenge prophesied by both Richard and the bishop of Carlisle have already started to arrive.

Beyond evil counsel

On the view being advanced here, readings that impute to the play some form of 'nostalgia' for a lost medieval world of monarchical legitimacy, an Eden of stately outward forms, a medieval or feudal 'before' against which a 'modern' or early modern 'after' of political manoeuvre and realpolitik can be set, seem entirely misplaced. To begin with, the ideology of divine right and absolute monarchy with which the play suffuses the kingship and persona of Richard II himself was a distinctly late Tudor phenomenon.[20] Moreover, from the outset the play shows us the ideology of divine right and the external forms of sacred monarchy being used as a stalking horse for a recognisably sixteenth-century, indeed distinctively Elizabethan, version of tyranny. As Nuttall observes, 'Richard's blazing claim to be, as God's anointed, above the petty rules and regulations that restrain his subjects ought to sound as "modern" as his queasy financial dealing.' For Richard is both an 'unpleasingly modern figure, tainted by dodgy financial schemes, and a sacral king, anointed by God, above the laws which bind his subjects, bearing the mystique of a hallowed past.'[21] Thus, rather than some epitome of a lost medieval golden age of monarchical legitimacy, Richard is a recognisably Tudor figure, using an emergent tradition of royal absolutism to legitimise novel claims and exactions. Whether or not Elizabeth ever said 'know you not I am Richard the II' – and, as Cyndia Clegg has shown, despite the prevalence of that anecdote in the modern scholarship the balance of probability seems to be that she did not – one knows what she (would have) meant (had she said it).[22] For, given the, if anything, increasingly stylised cult of the queen, and the emerging divine right absolutist tone of the 1590s, far from being vestiges of some lost medieval past, Richard's vision of kingship and style of rule must have looked worryingly avant-garde; as might his sinister combination of a sedulous observance of the outward forms of monarchical legitimacy with the pursuit of his own private will and the ruthless deployment of the dark arts of political manoeuvre. On this view, just as the ideological questions at the centre of the play were immediately contemporary,[23] so, for an Elizabethan audience, there was nothing distinctively 'medieval' about either Richard's notion of kingship or his (tyrannical) political style.

As in the case of *King John*, it is worth reminding ourselves just how dark the picture of the monarch whose name the play bears has become by the end of the action. I have already suggested that, in Shakespeare's version of the tale, John is consigned to hell. The same might also be said of Richard. As we have seen, it is only when it is too late, only after Richard's power has collapsed and Bolingbroke triumphed, that Richard is able to free himself from the hall of mirrors, the illusions and fantasies about his semi-divine attributes and powers, in which has hitherto been living and which have produced both his tyranny and then his downfall. Only once his cause is lost, and, indeed, as he is being, and after he has been, stripped of the crown, can Richard come to recognise himself as both human and mortal. In other words, that recognition can only come when the dissolution of his image of himself as king brings him – literally, in the mirror scene – face to face with the certain prospect of deposition, imprisonment and death. As any number of critics have argued, the pathos of the consequent dissolution of Richard's self-image, indeed of his identity, provides the latter stages of the play with a great deal of their poetic and emotional energy.

However, it is far from clear that the modicum of self-knowledge that Richard has achieved by the play's end is enough to save his soul. After all, unlike John, Richard is never tormented by his past crimes, never comes even properly to acknowledge, let alone repent for, his sins. Nor, entirely unlike the saintly Henry VI, does he even approach the forgiveness of his enemies. Rather than seeing himself as a sinner desperately in need of divine grace and mercy, he repeatedly casts himself as an innocent Christ-figure, betrayed to his enemies by twelve thousand Judases, and a multitude of Pilates, all of whom conspire to 'deliver me to my sad cross'[V, i, 241]. Called in public to recognise his faults, he refuses, and responds by calling to mind those of his enemies who, he assures them, are all 'damned in the book of heaven' [V, i, 236] for the soul-destroying sin of rebellion. In these exchanges the closest Richard comes to an acknowledgement of any personal fault is in his heavily ironic, entirely passive-aggressive, admission that 'I find myself a traitor with the rest;/For I have given here my soul's consent/ T'undeck the pompous body of a king,/Made Glory base and Sovereignty a slave,/Proud Majesty a subject, State a peasant' [IV, i, 248–52].

Alone at last in prison, he tries to populate his cell with his own thoughts and conceits, desperately searching, even here, for another audience before whom he can perform. In these last speeches there is still little or no trace of repentance. He plays with seeking solace from his current miseries in the oblivion of death and tries to calculate his chances of salvation by 'setting the word against itself', as he juxtaposes the seemingly general offer of salvation to all in the text 'come little ones' against the seemingly stricter terms laid down in the equally scriptural claim 'it is as hard to come as for a camel/To thread the postern of a small needle's eye'. To the end, he is tormented by thoughts of his former glory, of 'Bolingbroke's proud joy', and of his own present humiliated state [V, v, 14–17, 59]. Indeed, his last conversation is with a groom of the royal stables who has come to visit his former master in jail. His contribution to their exchange consists of an extended riff upon Bolingbroke's use, on his coronation day, of Richard's favourite horse, 'roan Barbary', a meditation which ends again with another self-pitying image of himself, 'spurred, galled and tired by jauncing Bolingbroke' [V, v, 72–94].

He dies violently, resisting the efforts of Exton to kill him. This is not a good death, as either contemporary convention or the play itself, in its description of the end of Mowbray, defined it. Having 'many a time' 'fought/For Jesu Christ in glorious Christian field,/Streaming the ensign of the Christian cross,/Against black pagans, Turks and Saracens', 'toiled with works of war', Mowbray had retired to Venice, where he 'gave/His body to that pleasant country's earth/And his pure soul unto his captain Christ,/Under whose colours he had fought so long' [IV, i, 92–101]. Whatever his involvement in the death of Gloucester, Mowbray has made a traditional Christian satisfaction for his sins and (presumably) achieved salvation. The fact that this judgement comes from that epitome of piety and legitimism, the bishop of Carlisle, renders this verdict, in the world of the play, something like definitive.[24] Mowbray's is a very different response to the weight of his own sins to that evinced by Richard.

Typically, as he expires, Richard is in no doubt as to the destination of his soul. Having repeatedly damned the souls of his enemies to hell, he now, just as confidently, recruits himself for heaven. 'Mount, Mount my soul! Thy seat is up on high,/Whilst my gross flesh sinks downward here to die' [V, v, 111–12]. Whether the play intends us to take so generous a view of Richard's destination in the next life remains, of course, a very different question.[25] As Deborah Shuger puts it Richard may have died 'nobly' but it is far from clear that 'an Elizabethan protestant (or Catholic, for that matter) would have allowed this to count as dying well'; a distinction that, she goes on to note, matters rather a lot to the politics of the play.[26]

Many of the Catholic pamphlets in the evil counsellor tradition had been only too happy to speculate on the desperate deaths and destination in hell of the leading lights of the Elizabethan regime; men like Walsingham, Leicester and, in prospect, Burghley himself. On this evidence, in both *King John* and *Richard II* Shakespeare extends that argument to include the person of the monarch him (or her) self. In this version of events, the mask of evil counsellor theory has been stripped away to reveal a doomed and damned monarch at the core of the regime's corruption and tyranny.

CHAPTER 11

Shakespeare and Parsons – again

Are we to read Shakespeare as having outdone even the Jesuit Parsons in his loathing and excoriation of Elizabeth? Certainly, if we were to take the line that the picture of Richard's tyranny and fate did indeed refer to or conjure at least aspects of the rule of the Virgin Queen then we would end up with a version of her (mis)rule closer to that espoused by Nicholas Sander, or by the Allen of the *Admonition,* than to any of the evil-counsellor-centred accounts produced by Parsons and his circle in the early 1590s. But Shakespeare had produced no more sympathetic an account of the monarch and his end in *King John,* and that play, it has been argued above, is best seen as defence of the regime and in effect a refutation of the views and projects not only of the Allen of the *Admonition* but also of the Parsons of the Philopater tract or *The conference.* How, then, might the current reading of *Richard II* be rendered compatible with such a view? To answer that question we need now, finally, to read the play against the central arguments of *The conference.*

Here, there are three main comparisons that might be fruitful: firstly, that between Shakespeare's and Parsons' account of the nature, course and significance of the deposition of Richard II; secondly, that between Parsons' and Shakespeare's account of the long-term political and dynastic consequences of that event; and thirdly, that between the very different answers to the question of what should happen about the succession, once Elizabeth was dead, given by Parsons and (implicitly) by Shakespeare, in his account of Richard's reign and of Bolingbroke's usurpation.

(Not) a parliament scene

Let us turn first to the accounts proffered by the Jesuit and the playwright of the course, nature and significance of Richard's deposition. According to Parsons, Richard's deposition was the epitome of what the legitimate removal of a peccant monarch should look like. Richard was a self-evident, and, by the end, self-confessed tyrant. His removal was effected by 'the choice and invitation of all the realm and the greater and better part thereof'. He had been deposed 'by act of parliament and himself convinced of unworthy government and brought to confess that he was worthily deprived and that he willingly and freely resigned the same'. For Parsons Richard's removal had the clear backing or endorsement of providence; not only was the king's overthrow almost miraculously accomplished by an invading force that started with 'but three score men in all' but providence had then ensured the evil and incompetent Richard was succeeded, in Henry IV and Henry V, by two of the greatest of English kings.

Shakespeare's depiction of these same events served to refute or to call into radical question nearly all of these assertions. The two accounts agree fully on only one point – Richard's status as a tyrant, and the consequent need for 'the reformation of the realm'. Other than that they have virtually nothing in common. Bolingbroke is depicted by Shakespeare as powerfully backed by members of the political elite. He arrives at Ravenspur, Northumberland reports, accompanied by 'Rainold, Lord Cobham,/Thomas, son and heir of th'Earl of Arundel,/That late broke from the Duke of Exeter,/His brother, Archbishop late of Canterbury,/Sir Thomas Erpingham, Sir Thomas Ramston, Sir John Norberry, Sir Robert Waterton and Francis Coint,/All these well furnished by the Duke of Brittany/With eight tall ships, three thousand men of war' [II, i, 279–86]. What follows is not 'the choice and invitation of all the realm' for Bolingbroke to depose Richard and assume the throne, but rather a series of duplicitous political manoeuvres compounded of claims to be doing one thing while moving rapidly to do another. Shakespeare reveals the maintenance of this legal fiction to have been crucial to the process whereby Bolingbroke seized control and then the crown.

In the deposition scene Shakespeare describes the final movement in what has by now become (even if it did not start out as) a scripted plot to depose Richard and install Bolingbroke in his place. For Parsons what this amounted to was the final validation of the transition from one reign to the next by the whole commonwealth represented in and through the parliament. What the play shows, however, is not the smooth working of such a scheme but its breakdown into something like complete disarray.

Here the so-called 'parliament scene' is crucial. As is notorious, this was omitted from the first printed version of the play in 1597. The scene first appeared in another quarto edition of 1608, which announced itself on the title page as containing the 'new addition of the parliament scene and the deposing of king Richard'.[1] This, however, is something of a misnomer; for the scene, as the actual text of the play, rather than the title page of the 1608 quarto, describes it, does not, in fact, take place in parliament at all but in time of, and on the way to, rather than in, parliament. The stage directions in the various editions make this plain. At the start of the crucial scenes at the beginning of Act IV, the 1608 quarto merely has 'enter Bullingbrok, Aumerle and others'. The next quarto edition is more forthcoming: it states 'enter as to the parliament, Bullingbroke, Aumerle,

Northumberland, Percie, Fitzwater, Surrey, Carlisle, Abbot of Westminster. Herauld, Officers and Bagot'. The folio is more laconic but says much the same thing in its instruction 'enter Bullingbroke with the Lords to parliament'. Clearly, then, Bolingbroke and his clique are on the way to parliament. En route they have certain staged events to go through. Of these the first is the calling forth of Bagot and the attempt to reopen the murder of Gloucester. This scene is to be followed by the actual transfer of power from Richard to Bolingbroke, a transfer which, as we shall see, is to be effected by a combination of abdication and deposition.[2]

As we saw earlier, the first scene of this extended exercise in political theatre dissolves rapidly into factionalism, chaos, even farce, and has to be brought to a summary close by Bolingbroke. Reverting to the script, Bolingbroke and his friends hurry on to the next scene in what is clearly a prearranged political pageant or series of tableaux. There is, however, no literal change of scene; no move to the parliament house. York merely enters and proclaims Richard's intention to step down in favour of Bolingbroke. Before the next stage of the scene can be acted, Carlisle delivers his impassioned providential rant about the dreadful crime they are about to commit and its awful consequences for England. This too is scarcely part of the official script, but is turned to a certain advantage by Northumberland's brusque arrest of the bishop for treason. Here, at least, is an opportunity publicly to demonstrate the price of dissent or opposition to the intended shift of power.

Richard is then called in. He is clearly intended to abdicate willingly in favour of Henry, while acknowledging his past faults and current incapacity/ unwillingness to rule. But even this scene does not go smoothly. Given one more chance to be centre stage Richard milks it for all it is worth, effectively disrupting, indeed subverting entirely, the ideological message that these interactions are supposed or intended to convey. Evincing surprise at this sudden call on to the public stage, Richard plays dumb. He enters, asking 'why am I sent for to a king/Before I have yet shook off the regal thoughts/ . . . to do what service am I sent hither?' For all its apparent brevity and simplicity, that first line is in fact incredibly ideologically aggressive. By calling Bolingbroke king already, Richard is adverting to the violent and illegitimate nature of a seizure of power that has already taken place and that he is now being forced, through the public performance of abdication and contrition, to legitimise. That challenge is compounded by the speech that separates those two questions, in which, as we have seen, Richard adverts to the previous loyalty of the assembled company to himself as king, comparing them the while to a mixture of Judases and Pilates. York is thus forced to *tell* him what he is here for. 'To do that office of thine own good will/Which tired majesty did make thee offer –/The resignation of thy state and crown/To Henry Bolingbroke' [IV, i, 178–80]. This tells us that Richard had privately agreed to step down and that his current public performance of nonplussed ignorance and surprise is quite calculated. There follows what Harry Berger Jr calls Richard's 'wicked little game in 4.i'. 'Give me the crown,' replies Richard and then addressing Bolingbroke tells him, 'here, cousin, seize the crown' [IV, i, 181–89]. As Berger summarises the scene ' "here cousin" offers a gift and dangles the bait, while "seize the crown" retracts the offer, publishes the act as a usurpation and transfers both blame and guilt along with the crown to the usurper'.[3]

In these exchanges Richard is, therefore, threatening to undercut entirely the legitimising fictions that this scene is supposed to be establishing about the transfer of power. With extraordinary economy of language and gesture he has demonstrated that, for all the pretence that the crown is still his until he freely gives it up, in fact, for all intents and purposes, Bolingbroke is already king; something that Bolingbroke's entirely kingly bearing during the previous scene in which Bushy, Aumerle and the others wrangle over who killed Gloucester has already demonstrated. Now, Richard's actions serve to re-emphasise that, since Bolingbroke has already in effect assumed monarchical power, the usurper must now publicly acknowledge his usurpation by 'seizing' the crown, thus being seen to effect his own rise through Richard's forced descent.

Confronted by this subtle undercutting of all the meanings that this exchange was supposed to embody and disseminate, Bolingbroke stands his ground. He needs a more explicit statement of abdication from Richard if this is not to turn into a complete disaster. 'I thought you had been willing to resign,' Bolingbroke responds. Richard then immediately backs off. 'My crown I am, but still my griefs are mine./You may my glories and my state depose,/But not my griefs; still I am king of those.' 'Are you contented to give up the crown,' Bolingbroke persists, now desperate to drag from Richard the required state-ment, which Richard now proceeds to give him, although even now, at this late stage, he still prefaces it with a piece of wordplay designed to show how coerced and unwilling this 'abdication' really is: 'Ay, no. No, ay; for I must nothing be./ Therefore no "no", for I resign to thee. Now mark we how I will undo myself' [IV, i, 199–203]. In other words, already un-kinged, i.e. reduced to nothing, Richard literally cannot say no; no longer a king, he can deny Bolingbroke nothing. But if he is no longer a king, and therefore is 'nothing', this raises the inevitable question of what possible legal or moral force the assent of such a non-being could have.

There then follows – at last – the required form of words. 'I give this heavy weight from off my head,/And this unwieldy sceptre from my hand,/The pride of kingly sway from out my heart;/With mine own tears I wash away my balm,/ With mine own hands I give away my crown,/With mine own tongue deny my sacred state,/With mine own breath release all duteous oaths./All pomp and majesty I do forswear;/All manors, rents and revenues I forgo;/My acts, decrees and statutes I deny./God pardon all oaths that are broke to me;/God keep all oaths unbroke that are made to thee./Make me, that nothing have, with nothing grieved,/And thou with all pleased that hast all achieved./Long maist thou live in Richard's seat to sit,/And soon lie Richard in an earthy pit!/"God save king Henry", unkinged Richard says,/"And send him many years of sunshine days!"/ What more remains?' [IV, i, 204–21].

Here, then, is the crucial moment of the transfer of power, and it is effected entirely through the exercise of the royal will. Richard quite literally un-kings himself, the repetition of 'mine own' throughout the early part of the speech emphasising that it is his authority alone that is effecting the transformation in himself, before he gives the crown, again through the exercise of his own authority and will, to his successor. Until the very moment of transfer it is still his crown, his sceptre, his fisc ('rents, manors revenues'), indeed his law '(acts, decrees, statutes)', to dispose of as he pleases. Even in the act of divesting himself of the crown Richard asserts once again his own vision of divine right monarchy and sacred kingship. It is a vision in which the distinction between the king's two bodies, between his person and his office, between the common-wealth or kingdom and the crown, on the one hand, and the person of the prince on the other, has almost disappeared. Here, even as he destroys himself as king, in this act of self-immolation, are inscribed and instantiated the very principles that have animated his rule. To quote Barbara Hodgdon, Richard effectively turns the occasion of his surrender to Bolingbroke 'upside down', asserting the 'hegemony' of his view of kingship 'as the paradoxical process of its destruction'.[4]

Except that, *pace* Hodgdon and others, it is by no means clear that Richard's divine right view of free hereditary monarchy is 'destroyed'; it is certainly not displaced by any coherent alternative. In these exchanges there is no trace of Parsons' vision of elective kingship, of the residual right of the commonwealth to remove one ruler and appoint another, in the process creating, modifying and distributing political office and power as its own needs and interests dictate.

Not that a Parsons-style, parliament-centred view of the polity is entirely absent from Shakespeare's play. At a late stage in the scene the subject of parliament is raised – albeit tangentially. The question with which Richard ends the speech just quoted above – 'What more remains?' – is answered by Northumberland. 'No more, but that you read/These accusations, and these grievous crimes/Committed by your person and your followers/Against the state and profit of this land,/That, by confessing them, the souls of men,/May deem that you are worthily deposed' [IV, i, 223–27]. Such an admission by Richard would, of course, at the very least complicate and on some readings transform these proceedings, from an abdication, a sovereign act of kingship (albeit a coerced and arguably an illegitimate one) into something much more like a deposition, indeed something much more like a judicial proceeding, in which the king has been tried by some greater political entity or authority – in Parsons' terms by the 'commonwealth' or its representatives – and, having been found guilty, removed. Richard appears immediately to realise this and proceeds in effect to refuse to have anything to do with Northumberland or his articles and accusations. His initial reply is the assault on the sin of rebellion of which his enemies are guilty, quoted above. When Northumberland persists, Richard resorts to the extended hissy fit of politicised self-pity and existential despair that is the mirror scene, claiming when told once more to 'read o'er these articles' that 'mine eyes are full of tears; I cannot see' [IV, i, 243–45]. So intense and protracted is Richard's resistance that Bolingbroke decides to cut his losses. He has got Richard to abdicate and transfer the crown to him as his designated successor and that will have to do. Northumberland, however, is not so easily put off. Told by Bolingbroke, to 'urge it no more, my lord Northumberland', he grumbles that 'the commons then will not be satisfied' [IV, i, 271–72].

That remark is sometimes used to argue that what we are seeing here is a list of articles of impeachment, as it were an indictment of Richard, drawn up by the House of Commons and here being put to the accused by the lords of Parliament, who are sitting in judgment on the king. On this view, what we are being shown here is a parliamentary impeachment, or, if you prefer, the deposition by parliament, of King Richard – a parliament scene indeed. It is, further-more, often claimed that the presentation of such events on the public stage, was so subversive that the crucial passage had to be omitted – 'censored', it is often said – from the first printed versions of the play in 1597 and 1598. That may be the case. It is certainly true that the publication of Parsons' book may well have rendered people newly sensitive to the explosive connotations of (at least certain versions) of the deposition of Richard II. There is, however, almost no textual warrant for such a view. The events take place not in, but on the way to, parliament. At no point are Northumberland's articles described as having come from the House of Commons and the 'commons' who 'will not then be satisfied' if Richard does not acknowledge his guilt might just as well be the commons, i.e. the common people, the political nation or opinion beneath the nobility – an entity for which Bolingbroke has been shown throughout the play to have a careful eye – as the Commons, as in the House of Commons. Clearly, these events are taking place in time of parliament, but it looks from the text as though at most that body is being used as an adjunct to, a legitimising audience for, the political theatre being performed by and before Bolingbroke and the lords, before they arrive in parliament.[5]

The parliament men, it seems, are to be presented with a fait accompli. Richard, they will be told, has abdicated in favour of Bolingbroke and admitted his crimes, into the bargain. Parliament is thus not central but peripheral to these events, providing, at most, an *ex post facto* audience, and a legitimising stamp of approval, for things that have happened elsewhere. Moreover, in Shakespeare's version of these events Richard never gets close even to acknowledging his faults as a ruler, let alone acceding to a formal list of charges drawn up either by Northumberland or by the House of Commons. In all this Shakespeare's account differs significantly from Holinshed's, in which parliament's role is clear and Richard is shown actually reading the articles of impeachment.[6]

In sum, at every turn Shakespeare's version represents a falsification or refutation not only of Parsons' account of these events but of his vision of the English monarchy as elective, with the commonwealth retaining a residual right to discipline, constrain and, if necessary, remove and replace a peccant monarch. Here is no call to assume the throne addressed to Bolingbroke by the commonwealth, no providentially underwritten and miraculously effected transformation from lone invader to national leader. Rather Bolingbroke's course to the crown is either an incrementally realised plot to usurp the throne, a plot carried out while pretending to all and sundry to be doing something else entirely, and backed by any number of powerful men intent on protecting their own interests and by a fickle and suggestible populace, or a series of 'I've started, so I'll have to finish' accidents and expedients.

As for the events designed to remove Richard from the throne and replace him with Bolingbroke, they are a bust. From the moment Bagot is called upon to spill the beans about Gloucester's death until Richard is finally shuffled off into the Tower, almost everything goes wrong that could go wrong. To quote Harry Berger Jr again, 'Bolingbroke's reign is inaugurated by a series of ceremonial misfires that, whether accidental or mischievous, compromise the solemnity of state and contribute to the embarrassment of a king whose haplessness increases with his power. Thus in 4.i, the epidemic of gage-throwing builds to a thudding crisis when Aumerle runs out of gages and the news of Mowbray's death frustrates Bolingbroke's attempt at closure. Richard begins his domination of the deposition scene by subjecting Bolingbroke to the tug-of-war over the physical crown and ends it by staging the tantrum with the mirror.'[7] The contrast with the effectiveness of Richard's manipulation of the outward forms and rituals of sacred kingship with which the play opens is, of course, marked and surely quite deliberate.

Here, then, is no act of the commonwealth, no autonomous exercise of parliamentary judgement, but rather a *coup de main* and *coup de théàtre* played out before, but certainly not enacted by, a parliamentary audience. There is no trace in this version of events of the formal exercise, by anybody – peers, parliament or commonwealth – of legitimate, or widely recognised, powers of deposition or, still less, of election. What we have here is a transaction between kings, or rather between a rightful king and a usurper. Even in defeat, therefore, Richard might be said to have won, using the moment of his removal from the throne to assert his view of the English monarchical state and of monarchical power.[8]

Thus I do not think that it is true, at any stage, that, as Womersley claims, 'the de-sacralising of the language of monarchy in *Richard II* is accompanied by an implicit rehabilitation of the language of rebellion'. What the play stages are acts of resistance, usurpation and regicide that are successful only insofar as they eschew the overt 'language of resistance', election or deposition. Indeed, Northumberland aside, the only person anxious to foist such a language on to these proceedings is Richard II himself – most obviously in his wickedly playful injunction to Bolingbroke to 'seize the crown' – and then only because he wants to impose the *damnosa hereditas* of usurpation on his successor, while greedily appropriating the innocent, Christ-like victimhood that he spends the latter stages of the play energetically arrogating to himself.[9]

What we are watching in these scenes is not some once and for all 'desacralising of the language of monarchy' but rather the deleterious effects of the barefaced politics of commodity that had both produced and attended Bolingbroke's act of usurpation. The result is that the capacity of the monarch to use what Berger terms the 'trappings and shows' of monarchical ritual to hide and control the 'hidden impostumes', the guilty secrets and peccant humours, created by Richard's tyranny and Henry's usurpation, has been called into the most radical question.[10] What, in the opening scenes of the play, even that emergent tyrant Richard II had been able to do almost without effort or second thought now proves almost entirely beyond his usurping successor, Bolingbroke. How, and how far, the genie could be put back into the bottle; the outward (and inward) forms, the acts of oblivion and assertion, the assumptions, suppressions and pretences necessary to sustain the illusion (and, therefore, of course, the fact) of legitimate monarchical rule, indeed, of a monarchy deemed to be, in some sense, 'sacred', could be reconstituted out of the ruins created by Richard's tyranny and Bolingbroke's usurpation and regicide is left an open question at the end of the play. Certainly that was to be *the* question that Shakespeare's next three history plays would attempt to answer.

The dynastic consequences of the politics of prophecy

Carlisle's speech also provides a bridge between what we might term the 'political thought' aspects of Parsons' argument and his dynastic case, dependent as that latter case was on a very particular reading of the political and dynastic history of late medieval and Tudor England. The status of both Henry IV and Henry V as great kings had been central to Parsons' claim that providence smiled on nations that deposed tyrants by providing monarchs of outstanding virtue and prowess as replacements. More importantly, it was central to his dynastic case that the Lancastrians themselves were the epitome of kingly virtue and legitimacy. On this view, the real villains of the piece were the Yorkists, whose continual resort to sedition and rebellion had been providentially punished by their own internecine strife, in and through which, under Edward IV, Richard III and finally Henry VIII, bizarrely recruited (presumably because of his father's marriage to Elizabeth of York) to the Yorkist cause, nearly all the families active on the Yorkist side during the Wars of the Roses had been wiped out. Accordingly, Parsons went on to argue that, in general, dynastic claims to the throne that were Lancastrian in origin or line of descent were inherently superior to those which originated in or were transferred through the house of York. In this way he was able to build up the Infanta's claim against those of the Stuarts.

The effect of Carlisle's prophecy and the providential framework in which it places the course of English fifteenth-century dynastic politics is to turn Parsons' view of the matter on its head. Now the original political sin for which the Wars of the Roses were an extended judgement or punishment was the deposition of Richard II by the Lancastrians. The subsequent history of those struggles becomes transformed at a stroke into a form of the so-called Tudor myth, a story of the trials and punishments visited upon the English because of the sins of rebellion and usurpation, until, in the person of Henry VII, legitimacy can triumph once again.

This form of providentialism had not, in fact, been present in the Henry VI plays or even in *Richard III*. As we have seen, even in the latter play, which is drenched in the prophetic and the providential, providence is shown operating within an altogether shorter time frame and on a smaller scale. Present as it might be in a murder pamphlet, in the *Henry VI* plays providence can be seen meting out justice, through both prophetically foretold and then numinously fulfilled means, to the likes of Suffolk or Cardinal Beaufort, or, in *Richard III*, of Hastings, Clarence or Richard himself. Thus, even when the hand of providence was at its most explicit, the result was not to recruit those plays to an overarching providential or prophetic view of English history, featuring the deposition of Richard II as some sort of original political sin which ejected England from a pre-lapsarian paradise of naturally beneficent and automatically legitimate monarchical rule into a fallen chaos of Machiavellian manoeuvre and providential judgement. Richard of Gloucester is guilty – twice over – of king-killing, but, in the dynastic right stakes, he is an equal opportunity regicide, having offed both a Lancastrian and a Yorkist monarch, both of whose rights to rule were, judged by the highest standards of dynastic right, to say the least, contestable. Moreover, as Parsons loved to point out, once his nephews were removed from the scene Richard himself had a very strong dynastic claim. He is guilty of crimes certainly – of cold-blooded murder, of regicide and usurpation – but his crimes have absolutely nothing to do with Richard II and do not constitute an ur-sin against some ultimate symbol of monarchical legitimacy and dynastic right. In fact, rather the reverse.

The perspective provided by Carlisle's speech changes all this. What had been, in the Henry VI plays themselves, stories of noble factionalism, of political ambition and distrust, of feud and violence, of disastrously weak monarchy and excessive female power, played out against a background of foreign war and disputed succession, were now retrospectively recruited for just such a panoptically providential vision of recent English dynastic history; a vision which was, of course, the polar opposite of Parsons' account of precisely the same events.

On the one hand, all this was eminently loyal and, indeed, conventional. But when set in the context of the mid 1590s, and in particular of contemporary debates and anxieties about the succession and what to do about it, what might at first sight pass for garden variety Tudor myth-making could morph into something subtly different and altogether more contentious: a form of Stuart legitimism. For if the return of order and legitimacy were taken to reside in the accession of a claimant of unimpeachable dynastic right, and if Tudor (rather than, as on Parsons' account, Plantagenet and Lancastrian) blood was what counted in the dynastic right stakes, then salvation must lie in the accession of James Stuart. Thus *Richard II* – in this just like *King John* – could not only be read as a defence of the Stuart claim (against Parsons' assault upon it) but, through the providential gloss imposed by Carlisle's speech on events to come and on plays already written and performed, it can also be seen as retrospectively recruiting the *Henry VI* plays and *Richard III* for that very same purpose; a purpose for which, as we have seen, the *Henry VI* plays, at least, had patently not been written.

On the present account, then, both *King John* and *Richard II* effectively undermined both Parsons' version of the English monarchical polity as essentially elective, with a residual right to resist, and, if need be, to remove, tyrants and his providentially charged account of the dynastic issues raised and resolved in the course of fifteenth-century English history. As such they can perhaps plausibly be read not only as a reaction against the positions adopted by the Jesuit but also as a significant retreat from the positions if not taken by, then certainly implied in, both *Richard III* and *Titus*. Having pushed the envelope as far as those plays had, some sort of retreat was, of course, always likely, and after the polemical and political stakes had been raised by *The conference*, probably necessary.

A politique politics?

But what else, besides a refutation of Parsons' central claims, did these plays have to say on the central issues of monarchical legitimacy, hereditary right, tyranny, resistance and regicide? We need to start with what it was that these plays did not do. They did not reply to elective theories of monarchy and resistance theory with a simple endorsement of divine right monarchy and indefeasible hereditary right. *Richard II* may make it clear that, within the structures of the English monarchical state, deposing a king and usurping the throne are both crimes and sins. But it makes it equally clear that, for all the naturalness of royal rule, for all the divinely ordained order created by the rule of a legitimate prince, tyranny, once it became a settled, overt, as it were, publicly recognised, style of rule, must and would bring about an equal and opposite reaction; a reaction that, however much it might be both a crime and sin, was also in some sense a natural and necessary, and, perhaps over the long haul, even a salutary, corrective. (Such certainly seems to be the implication of the naturalising rhetoric of the garden scene.) It is surely to this complex verdict on events that Sanders refers when he speaks of the 'political agnosticism' of the play.[11]

Having thus projected the condemnation of these events on to providence and pushed the effects of that judgement (forwards) on to the (historical) future, and (backwards) on to the recent (theatrical) past – on to plays from which, in fact, such a providential structure or interpretation had been almost entirely absent – *Richard II* leaves the way clear for a largely 'secular', *de facto* analysis of the political dynamics unleashed by the tyranny of Richard II and by the resistance, usurpation and regicide of Bolingbroke. Through Carlisle's gesture towards a providentially configured future, the play both establishes its moral and political orthodoxy on the subjects of resistance, usurpation and king-killing and creates space for itself to engage in a dissection of the political process, if not untainted, then certainly undetermined, by such absolute moral judgements. Certainly, for all the absolute moral certainty evinced by both Richard and Carlisle about the divine right of kings, and Richard's unchallengeable status as God's deputy, the play shows providence assiduously holding its hand when his right to rule is challenged by Bolingbroke and his supporters.

Thus, considerations of absolute moral value and political legitimacy come into play, not as self-evident truths, the structuring assumptions which frame the events staged in the play, but rather as beliefs held by certain participants in that action and thus as political factors in the overall workings of the plot. And, of course, the play does not show all the characters who give voice to such legitimist sentiments taking the same political course, as the contrasts between York and Carlisle, or indeed between York and his son Aumerle, show only too clearly. *Pace* the strident providentialism articulated by Carlisle, the play itself constructs a space in which royal politics, the politics of tyranny and resistance, of usurpation and regicide, can be analysed in largely this-worldly, secular terms, as the politics of commodity. Here is a realm of activity with rhythms and trajectories of its own, largely unaffected by the interventions of providence. This was the level of reality, and of analysis, in which much of the action of the preceding history plays had taken place and by projecting the verdict of providence into the distant future Carlisle's speech opened up the possibility for what we might term a prudential, as well as a moral, discussion of just how, out of the delegitimised political scene, the moral and political chaos, created by (Richard's) tyranny and (Bolingbroke's) rebellion and usurpation, something like monarchical normality might be restored. These, of course, were to be some of the organising concerns of the *Henry IV* plays and of *Henry V.*

But the crisis addressed in both parts of *Henry IV* and in *Henry V* is not that foretold by Carlisle, which, of course, is to take place long after the deaths of both Henry IV and his son and thus has nothing to do with them at all. Rather, the moral and political crisis addressed in the Henry plays is that foretold, not by Carlisle, but by King Richard himself. Just like Pandulph's similar 'prophecy' in *King John*, which outlined for the dauphin the probable consequences of John's capture of Arthur, judged by the standards of prophetic utterance set by Carlisle, Richard's speech, foretelling the imminent implosion of the Lancastrian cause into a set of warring factions, is scarcely a prophecy at all, but rather a prediction, a political prognostication setting out the lines of force, the moral and political logic of events unleashed by Richard's deposition and by Bolingbroke's usurpation. For what Richard foretells is not so much a providential judgement, an irruptive intervention from on high, that will cut across the normal course of events, shaping the interplay of human intentions and ends to the overarching moral purposes of God, but rather a political situation or dilemma, with specific origins and causes in the current conjuncture, and predictable tendencies or effects in the future. As such, it is a product of human political choice and action and, if it is not subject to the complete control or mastery of the men who have made it or even of future political agents, it is certainly susceptible to change and containment through the exercise of the political judgement, the political and moral virtu(e) of human actors.

By the end of *Richard II* we have been plunged headlong into the politics of commodity – the same moral universe in which the action of *King John* had itself taken place. In other words, *Richard II* ends where *King John* starts, and the next three history plays represent an extended working out, or rather an elaborated reworking, of the basic problem of how to get back from a delegitimised politics of commodity, if not to moral and political order, simply stated, then at least to a sort of political normality, with a source of monarchical authority at its heart whose legitimacy was accepted by all; a state, these plays imply, that was the only sort of moral and political order on offer in a fallen world.

Of course, an answer to that question had already been sketched in *King John*, in the character of the bastard, whose combination of royal blood and plebeian vigour, of martial valour, natural loyalty and spontaneous, foreigner-hating Englishness, had been enough to save the state and stave off the threat of civil war, political breakdown and foreign rule just long enough to see the throne successfully transferred to a claimant of unimpeachable dynastic legitimacy.

In that sense, *King John* looks forward to the *Henry IV* plays and to *Henry V* just as much as does *Richard II*. For it is possible to see *King John* as in many ways an early experimental version, a dry run, for the *Henry IV* plays, with the bastard a prototype Hal and King John a prototype Henry IV. As Berry observes, the bastard 'represents Shakespeare's first attempt to explore the means by which political legitimacy may emerge in a fallen world'. 'Like Hal, Faulconbridge is a composite creation, a character who on occasion threatens to split apart into the lesser roles he contained within him', roles which Berry astutely assimilates to those later played by Falstaff and Hotspur.[12] John Danby makes much the same case when he observes that Faulconbridge's emergence as something of a hero represents a 'preliminary sketch for Henry V'. Indeed he goes so far as to claim that in Hal's 'person . . . the Bastard ascends the legitimate throne'.[13] In both *King John* and the *Henry IV* plays we confront a political scene stripped of legitimacy and plunged into the politics of commodity by different combinations of tyranny and usurpation. In both, the integrity of the realm is at stake; in both, a king enters the action as a figure of considerable martial prowess and political effectiveness, only to be broken, in the second half of the play, by the (political and psychological, spiritual and secular) pressures exerted upon him by his role as a usurper. In both, the state is saved and legitimacy restored by a figure half royal and half plebeian; a figure in whose person the spontaneous violence and vigour of the people is combined with the natural virtue and honour inherent in the possession of genuinely royal blood.[14]

In *King John* that figure is the bastard, someone to whom a certain provincial, even plebeian, Englishness comes naturally, but who, despite his parentage, has to learn, if not quite how to be royal, then certainly how to play an effective role in the politics of kings. In the *Henry IV* plays it is Hal, someone who has the royal thing down pat but must learn how to be a bastard in the backstreets of Eastcheap. As the bastard sheds his role of the first half of the play as a 'vice' figure and his persona as a 'cracker' to emerge, in the second, as a prince indeed, so, too, does Hal emerge from the plebeian persona acquired, with so much effort in Eastcheap, in part I, to become, by the end of part II, truly 'himself'. In both Hal and the bastard's cases, the full vigour and effectiveness of the emergent persona is based on the possession of royal blood brought into an enabling contact with a native Englishness that springs from the body of the people.

At the end of both plays truly monarchical order is restored as a king of dubious legitimacy dies, to be succeeded by an heir of whose dynastic claims and, in Henry V's case, of whose personal virtue and prowess, there can now be no doubt. While in *King John* the roles of saviour of the state and of the next successor are split between the bastard and the *deus ex machina* of Henry III, in *Henry IV* those two roles are seamlessly combined in the person and personae of Henry/Hal. In *King John* – which was in this much like both *Richard III* and *Titus* – the return of normality and order is merely gestured at through the figure of a returning prince, newly ensconced on the throne, with Henry III playing the same role in *King John* as Richmond and Lucius play in *Richard III* and *Titus* respectively. In *Henry V*, for the first and only time in these plays, we are vouchsafed what is, amongst other things, an extended disquisition on the entirely successful exercise of emergently legitimate monarchical authority.

The bastard and Bolingbroke compared

But this, of course, is to get somewhat ahead of ourselves. According to the methodological assumptions underpinning this book, using the content and conclusions of plays yet to be written to interpret the plays that preceded them is scarcely a licit procedure. I want to end, therefore, with a final comparison between *Richard II* and *King John*. For all the disorder and warfare that dominates the action of *King John*, that play ends with legitimacy re-established, while for all the seeming ease of the defeat of Richard's tyranny and the apparent success of Bolingbroke's coup, *Richard II* ends with England on the edge of something like moral and political chaos. In *Richard II* the functional equivalent of Hal/Henry, and indeed of the bastard, is, of course, Bolingbroke. That is to say, he is the man who comes to save the state; moving from the periphery of the action to the centre, in the second half of the play he displaces a king who is shown, in the opening acts, dominating events, only to decline into impotence and irrelevance by play's end.

The two plays examine very different responses to the fact and experience of tyranny; where the bastard responds by rallying to the prince and defending the realm from the foreign invasion, Bolingbroke invades the kingdom, to confront and displace the king. In both instances what is at stake is the defence of 'England'. In *King John* 'England' is defined negatively by its opposition to foreign claims and force, represented, of course, by the French, the French-backed Arthur and intermittently by the papacy. In that play, we have the paradoxical situation whereby the necessity to defend 'England', thus defined, sets up the political and moral imperative to defend a usurper against the lawful claimant and, that worst of all worlds, an increasingly ineffectual tyrant, against the rebellion of his own nobility.

In *King John* the epitome of the resulting foreigner-hating Englishness, of the reflex patriotism and loyalism in the face of the foreign threat, is, of course, the bastard. In *Richard II* a similar strand of nationalist panegyric is given expression by the dying Gaunt, whose paean to 'this royal throne of kings, this sceptred isle,/This earth of majesty, this seat of Mars,/This other

Eden, demi-paradise,/ . . . this blessed plot, this earth, this realm, this England'
[II, i, 40–50] has come to represent the acme of English patriotic sentiment,
and been a crucial site for the identification of Shakespeare as the national
poet. In Gaunt's case, the defence of 'England' is anything but coterminous
with approval of or support for the present occupant of the throne. Indeed, as
Dermot Cavanagh has pointed out, Gaunt's speech amounts to an accusation
of treason against the king for his betrayal of England, the treasonous nature of
which accusation is, in turn, immediately registered by the king. But this is a
chain of argument that, even on his deathbed, Gaunt does not, indeed one
might even say, given his prior commitment to the doctrine of divine right
kingship, cannot, pursue. But then, even when in open revolt against his prince,
neither does his son, Bolingbroke, go anywhere near such arguments. Gaunt's
remains an essentially loyalist deployment of the distinction between the king's
two bodies, between the interests of England and the private person, policies
and predilections of the monarch. While in resorting to rebellion Hereford
takes a radically different course from his father, he precisely does not make a
case against Richard as a traitor against 'England', but limits himself to the
claim that he is seeking, admittedly by main force rather than by counsel, to
free both Richard and England from the predations of the 'caterpillars of the
commonwealth', who have seduced the king and are now bankrupting the state
and oppressing both nobility and people.[15]

But the play makes it quite clear that in moving against Richard both
Bolingbroke and the other rebels are motivated not so much by their dedication to 'England' as by the defence and furtherance of their own present private
interests and future security. Thus Bolingbroke's progression from the first to
the second half of the play is directly opposite to that of the bastard. Where the
latter ends the first half of the play an express devotee of the pursuit of
commodity, by the latter stages of King John he has come to epitomise a selfless
devotion to both king and country. Bolingbroke, on the other hand, enters the
action as Hereford, a model of loyalism under pressure, but by the second half
of the play he has morphed into 'that vile politician' Bolingbroke and, having
successfully pursued the crown, ends up subjecting both himself and England
to the devastatingly deleterious, both moral and political, effects of the politics
of commodity. Moreover, however much, at the outset of his rebellion, he may
protest, and perhaps even believe, that he has come only to claim his own
and to reform the realm, the play makes it clear that, from the moment he first
set foot ashore at Ravenspur, Bolingbroke was engaged on a course of action, or
rather had subjected himself to an iron political logic, that could only end,
not merely in the usurpation and regicide that conclude the action of this play,
but in the internecine strife and civil war that King Richard (quite rightly) projects into the next reign and which, of course, the succeeding history plays
depict.

Thus was the whole thrust of the argument from evil counsel refuted; even if its proponents could be taken to be sincere, they were still, always already, sadly mistaken or misguided; as Bolingbroke's ascent to the crown and descent into rebellion and murder showed all too clearly, once committed to the path of forcible reformation there was no security to be had, no resting place to be found, short of usurpation and regicide. To talk, or, still worse, to act, as though there were, was either delusory or delusional or a mixture of the two, as Bolingbroke's career again showed all too clearly.

Thus, *pace* Parsons' account of the same events, for all his apparently seamless progress to the crown and the apparent success of his reformation of the tyranny of Richard II, Bolingbroke ends *Richard II* about to plunge England into moral and political chaos, while at the end of *King John* the bastard's selfless loyalty to a monarch at least Richard's equal in the tyranny stakes is about to return England to legitimacy and unity. The lesson here might be taken to be that even in the face of tyranny, or even, as in the case of King John, in the face of tyranny and usurpation, that is to say, even if everything that the likes of Parsons, Allen and indeed Nicholas Sander had ever said about Queen Elizabeth and her regime were true, the loyalist course taken by the bastard remained by far the best option. Not only were the cures and palliatives being proffered by Parsons and his ilk worse than the disease itself, but (as the central scenes of *Richard II* demonstrate) Parsons' analysis of the polity he claimed to be trying to save was wholly misguided. So much so, that anyone hoping to reform the English monarchical state on the basis of the arguments adduced by critics such as Parsons and Verstegan was likely to end up not only comprehensively failing to save, but actively ruining, his country, while putting his own soul in the gravest danger.

I have argued here that there were Essexian overtones to the account of the bastard in *King John*. Jonathan Bate has recently argued that there were similarly Essexian associations attached to the character of Bolingbroke in *Richard II*.[16] They are to be found in the famous passage in which King Richard denounces his cousin Hereford's 'courtship of the common people'. 'How he did seem to dive into their hearts/With humble and familiar courtesy,/What reverence he did throw away on slaves,/Wooing poor craftsmen with the craft of smiles/And patient underbearing of his fortune,/As 'twere to banish their affects with him./Off goes his bonnet to an oyster-wench./A brace of draymen bid God speed him well,/And had the tribute of his supple knee/With "Thanks my countrymen, my loving friends",/As were our England in reversion his,/And he our subjects next degree in hope' [I, iv, 24–36]. This, of course, is a brilliantly hostile evocation of the politics of 'popularity', that style of self-presentation and address, of mock deference and condescension, which was designed to win over the common people to the support of some person or programme. By the mid 1590s Essex was both acknowledged and feared, noted and excoriated, as the past master of this particular mode of self-presentation and pitch-making. The passage serves, therefore, multiple purposes. It both encapsulates a certain version of the practice of popularity and sums up the contemporary critique of that practice as seditious and subversive – designed to seduce the love of the people away from their natural rulers and, in particular, from their monarch. Not only, therefore, does the passage identify Hereford as popular, it attaches such behaviour to aspirations to the crown, and helps to establish Hereford, in the minds not only of the king and his courtiers but also of the audience, in the role of a Machiavellian plotter, a wannabe usurper. When those suspicions are first voiced by Richard and his intimates, they seem to provide further evidence of Richard's malice, his paranoid willingness to use royal authority and justice to crush all potential threats and rivals. They appear, in short, to enhance Richard's identity as a tyrant. But when viewed from the perspective provided by Bolingbroke's behaviour in the second half of the play, they appear positively prescient, as Bolingbroke comes to play precisely the role of the Machiavellian practitioner of the dark arts of popularity that these remarks attribute to him, and his popularity with the people does indeed prove crucial in draining power away from Richard and giving Bolingbroke the crown. Carlisle's account of the people's flocking to support the invading Bolingbroke and York's later report of the crowd's adulation of the new king and reviling of the old during Henry IV's entry into London serve to drive the point home.

If Professor Bate is right, through the association of this sort of popular playing to the crowd with Essex, the passage might also be taken to be associating, however fleetingly, the character of Hereford/Bolingbroke with the earl. (Contemporary warrant for such an association is provided, albeit from later in the decade, by John Hayward's notorious dedication of his *The life and raigne of king Henry IIII*, to the earl of Essex, who he, in effect, equated with 'our Bolingbroke', observing that so great was Essex's 'name', that, should it 'shine on our Henry's [Bolingbroke's] forehead, he would more happily and safely go forth among the people'. This enthusiastic embrace of an all too subversive-sounding 'popularity' could only compound the offense implicit in the original identification of Essex with the usurper Bolingbroke. Given what turned out to be the circumstances in which his book appeared, Hayward could scarcely have stuck his foot in his mouth with more conviction and force.)[17] On this basis, might we not see the bastard and Bolingbroke as personifying two very different responses to the current conjuncture, if not to the present then certainly to the immediate future of Elizabethan England; alternative responses between which the likes of Essex might some day have to choose? If so, there seems little doubt which of the two was preferable.

Thus, although resistance could be seen (as the garden scene presented it) as the 'natural' response to tyranny, and although the lines of political and moral force and probability unleashed by tyranny, resistance and usurpation might seem to take on the appearance of inevitability, the comparison between the bastard and Bolingbroke (and the very different consequences of their actions) showed that there remained an important sense in which the really crucial political and moral outcomes could still depend upon the choices of key political players. Moreover, as the Essexian associations hanging around both the bastard and Bolingbroke – not to mention that dedication of Parsons' *Conference* to the earl – all showed, by 1595, if not before, the earl of Essex must have seemed to many to be the political actor most likely, in the immediate future, to be presented with the really crucial political (and moral) choices.[18]

On that basis, if Shakespeare's *Richard II* really was the play performed by the Lord Chamberlain's Men, at the behest of two of the Essex plotters, on the eve of the Essex rising, then what was being performed on stage was a genuinely tragic version of the political scenario acted out the next day, by the plotters themselves, as a form of farce.[19]

Part V

THE ESSEXIAN CIRCLE SQUARED, OR A USER'S GUIDE TO THE POLITICS OF POPULARITY, HONOUR AND LEGITIMACY

CHAPTER 12

The loss of legitimacy and the politics of commodity dissected

The attachment to a version of the Essexian and Stuart loyalist projects imputed, in the last section, to both *King John* and *Richard II* continued to animate the *Henry IV* plays and *Henry V*, which returned to the question of how, through the political and personal virtu(e) and prowess of particular human agents, a polity plunged, by tyranny and usurpation, into the moral and political chaos of commodity politics might be returned to legitimate monarchical rule. They did so, through both a chronological continuation of the events staged in *Richard II* and a reworking of themes and tropes, questions and, indeed, answers, central to *King John*.

The claim here is not so much that these plays were in any simple sense about Essex, any more than *King John* or *Richard II* were, but rather that the whole discussion of just how the logic of events might be controlled, the genie of commodity politics forced back into the bottle of monarchical control, is conducted through a staging of ideological materials, modes of political thought and action, of analysis and argument, that were crucial (and widely known to be crucial) to the whole Essexian project.

In particular the central problematic addressed by these plays, and allegedly resolved in the persona of Hal/Henry, involved the ways in which the politics of honour, of martial virtue and prowess, could be combined both with the politics of (puritan) popularity and of monarchical legitimacy. In a famous letter of advice addressed to the earl in October 1596 Francis Bacon summed up the queen's current impression of Essex's career and demeanour. 'A man of a nature not to be ruled ... of an estate not grounded to his greatness; of a popular reputation; of a military dependence: I demand whether there can be any more dangerous image than this represented to any monarch living, much more to a lady, and of her majesty's apprehension?' While such impressions remained, Bacon warned, Essex could only expect the worst and he proceeded to advise Essex how best to dissipate that unfortunate 'impression'. He should make a point of deferring to the royal will; deliberately adopting courses that the queen would not like and then making an elaborate show of giving them up in the face of her displeasure. He should stop making mention of past disappointments which 'cannot be revoked' and seek to emulate and openly admire the examples of those earlier, more flexible, royal favourites, Leicester and Hatton. As for his 'military dependence' and career, he should keep it in substance, but 'abolish it in shows to the queen'. The same applied to Essex's 'popular reputation', which, Bacon conceded, was a good thing in itself, 'being obtained as your lordship obtaineth it, that is *bonis artibus*; and besides well governed, is one of the best flowers of your greatness, both present and to come'. However, in the current circumstances, 'it would be handled tenderly. The only way is to quench it *in verbis* and not *in rebus*.' The earl was therefore advised to 'take all occasions, to the queen to speak against popularity and popular courses vehemently; and to tax it in all others; but nevertheless to go on in your honourable commonwealth courses as you do. And therefore I will not advise you to cure this by dealing in monopolies or any oppressions'. His best recourse was 'in parliament' to 'be forward for treasure in respect of the wars' and then if Her Majesty were to 'object popularity to you at any time I would say to her, a parliament will show that; and so feed her with expectation.'

In Essex's immediate circle, then, the question of how his prickly, honour-obsessed, demeanour, his sense of 'the wars' as his natural 'occupation' and his 'popular courses' could all be combined and continued in ways that did not alienate the queen was the subject of self-conscious debate and analysis. Bacon did not mention succession politics or Essex's connections with James VI in this letter but we know, if only from Parsons' dedication of the *Conference* to Essex and the queen's adverse reaction thereto, that that issue, too, was very much on the Essexian agenda and in the air. And all these issues – honour, martial prowess, popularity and the politics of succession and royal legitimacy – were to be found at the centre of the *Henry IV* plays and indeed of *Henry V*.

Usurpation and its consequences

1 Henry IV plunges us back into the politics of commodity. It opens with the king planning the crusade that he has promised at the close of *Richard II* to atone for Richard's death. But, just as Richard had predicted, that plan is disrupted by the onset of domestic sedition and war. Initially, the threat comes from without, not as in *King John* from France, but this time from within the British Isles, from Wales and Scotland. Bad news from Wales, where the earl of Mortimer has been defeated by Owen Glendower [Pt. I, I, i, 39–46], is counter-balanced by good news from Scotland, where English forces, led by 'young Harry Percy', have destroyed a Scottish host led by the earl of Douglas. Ten thousand Scots have been killed and Douglas himself and a number of other Scottish nobles taken prisoner. We have reverted here to the start of *King John* where a king of dubious legitimacy – in some versions of the very recent past, a usurper – is being threatened by foreign invasion. The result, however, is not English unity in the face of the foreign threat but, as the play hastens to show, a

full-scale breakdown of England into warring factions and civil strife, as dissident English rebels unite with the insurgent foreigner to divide the realm
between them. The rebels' intentions are revealed in considerable detail in the
scene in Act III in which the Percies, now in league with Douglas, Mortimer
and Glendower, puzzle over a map the better to divide the realm between them
[Pt. I, III, i, 66–75].

The reasons for this outbreak of civil dissension in the face of foreign invasion are located clearly in the events of the previous reign and the very weak
claims to legitimacy possessed by Henry IV. What we are seeing here is, of
course, the fulfilment of the political prophecy delivered by Richard to
Northumberland towards the close of *Richard II*, when the deposed king had
foretold that the usurping coalition would split apart, the one side dissatisfied
with their reward for having established Bolingbroke on the throne, the other
deeply suspicious of the loyalty of subjects so overmighty that they have been
able to depose one king and might now decide to do the same to his successor.
The *casus belli* is Hotspur's refusal to hand over some of his Scottish prisoners
to the king. Called to court and upbraided for his refusal, Hotspur initially
excuses himself by claiming mitigating circumstances. He has been misre-
ported; he never actually refused. As Northumberland explains it, 'either envy,
therefore, or misprision,/Is guilty of this fault, and not my son' [Pt. I, I, iii,
25–27].

But, as Henry observes, for all these initial cross-purposes, Hotspur had yet
to deliver his prisoners to the king. He has not done so, the king complains,
because the Percies want to make that transfer conditional on the king's ransom
of the captured Mortimer from Glendower. This Henry refuses to do. For, he
claims, Mortimer had not been captured defending the realm against
Glendower's revolt but had changed sides and married Glendower's daughter
[Pt. I, I, iii, 79–92].

This accusation is met by a blunt contradiction by Hotspur, who replies to
the characterisation of his brother-in-law March as 'revolted' with an elaborate
account of a bitter personal combat between Mortimer and Glendower fought
'on the gentle Severn's sedgy bank'. For all of its rhetorical flourish and gory
detail, Hotspur's account meets with a flat rejection from the king and the blunt
command 'to send me your prisoners with the speediest means,/Or you shall
hear in such a kind from me/As will displease you. – My Lord of Northumberland,
we license your departure with your son./Send us your prisoners, or you will
hear of it' [I, iii, 113–23].

This brusque dismissal had been preceded by an even blunter banishment
of Worcester from both the presence and the council. Worcester had been just
about to mention the unmentionable, that is to say, the political debt owed by
Henry to the Percy interest for their help in deposing Richard and getting him
the crown, at which point Henry cuts him off: 'Worcester, get thee gone, for I

do see/Danger and disobedience in thine eye:/O sir, your presence is too bold and peremptory,/And majesty might never yet endure/The moody frontier of a servant brow./You have good leave to leave us. When we need/Your use and counsel we shall send for you' [Pt. I, I, iii, 10–20].

In short, whatever you do, don't mention the last reign. Henry's role as king cannot withstand the sort of calling in of political debts, the overt horse trading, that Worcester is about to enter into here and in which the Percies are implicitly engaging throughout the scene. Such bargains take place between equals; but Henry is no longer the Percies' equal and to behave, or to even be caught thinking or calculating as though he were, represents an infringement on the authority, a diminution of the charisma, an encroachment on the divinely ordained and anointed apartness, and hence a reduction in the power, of the crown. For as King Henry, rather than as mere Bolingbroke, Henry is no longer *primus inter pares*; he is now, as his son Lancaster later calls him, 'God's substitute'[Pt. II, IV, ii, 28]; his person, in Sir Walter Blunt's phrase, coined, like Lancaster's, as he confronts overt rebellion, 'anointed majesty' [Pt. I, IV, iii, 40].

Smelling potential treason in the shady (side-changing?) activities of Mortimer, the man with arguably a better claim than himself, Henry has to act as he does; he has to establish political distance between himself and all his subjects if he is to be king in more than name. But what looks, from Henry's perspective, to be the entirely justified, politically salutary, even necessary, use of the accepted powers and prerogatives of the crown, appears, from that of the Percies, to be not merely rampant political and personal ingratitude, but something rather more like tyranny.

As we shall see below, in terms of the political conventions, what we might term the public political rhetoric, of the day, the Percies both perceive and present Henry's behaviour as a threatening infringement on their just rights and interests as great lords, counsellors and former intimates of the king. Challenged by the loyalist Westmoreland at Gaultree forest with their status as rebels, the Archbishop of York explains that they have been *driven* to their current recourse to arms. 'I have in equal balance justly weigh'd/What wrongs our arms may do, what wrongs we suffer,/And find our griefs heavier than our offences./We see which way the stream of time doth run,/And are enforc'd from our most quiet there/By the rough torrent of occasion,/And have the summary of all our griefs,/When time shall serve, to show in articles,/Which long ere this we offer'd to the King/And might by no suit gain our audience./When we were wrong'd, and would unfold our griefs,/We are denied access unto his person/Even by those men that most have done us wrong.' This is the rhetoric of evil counsel; cut off from access to the royal person, unable to make their case themselves, they have been blocked and blackguarded by nameless persons 'that most have done us wrong'. This, of course, was the same complaint that Percy and Northumberland had made at their first interview with the king, claiming that Hotspur's reply to the king's demand for his prisoners had been misconstrued either though 'envy or misprision'. Westmoreland, of course, contests this version of events. 'Whenever yet was your appeal denied?/ Wherein have you been galled by the King?/What peer hath been suborn'd to grate on you,/That you should seal this lawless bloody book/Of forg'd rebellion with a seal divine'. In answer to this challenge to his good faith, the archbishop appeals for 'redress' to 'the commonwealth' [Pt. II, IV, i, 67–94].

In an earlier scene in Part I, immediately before the battle of Shrewsbury, both Hotspur and Worcester had made an all but identical case, only here shorn of the fig leaf of evil counsellor speak. Challenged by Sir Walter Blunt as a rebel and asked to outline the nature of his griefs, Hotspur replies that almost immediately after Bolingbroke had (duplicitously) seized the throne, in his new persona as Henry IV he had 'suffered his kinsman March/ (Who is, if every owner be well placed,/Indeed his king) to be engaged in Wales,/There without ransom to be forfeited;/Disgraced me in my happy victories,/Sought to entrap me by intelligence,/Rated mine uncle from the Council board,/In rage dismissed my father from the court,/Broke oath on oath, committed wrong on wrong,/And, in conclusion, drove us to seek out/This head of safety and withal to pry/Into his title, the which we find/Too indirect for long continuance'[Pt. I, IV, iii, 90–105]. This last claim was, however, an opening bid; asked 'shall I return this answer to the king' even Hotspur temporises, replying that the rebels would consider the king's offer and give him their terms 'the next day'.

At that conference Worcester gives the king an almost identical, albeit more temperately stated, account of their grievances; except that this version omits all mention of the tenuousness, indeed the illegitimacy, of Henry's claim to the crown. His conclusion, however, is identical to Archbishop Scroop's; their treatment at Henry's hand means that 'We were enforced for safety sake to fly/ Out of your sight and raise this present head/Whereby we stand opposed by such means/As you yourself have forged against your self,/By unkind usage, dangerous countenance,/And violation of all faith and troth/Sworn to us in our younger enterprise' [Pt. II, V, i, 59–71].

The public politics of insurrection

As the king's reply makes clear, the rebels have sought to legitimise their actions, making a pitch for public support – in the archbishop's language, an appeal for redress to 'the commonwealth' – in precisely these terms, posing before the people as victims both of evil counsel and of royal ingratitude and oppression. 'These things indeed you have articulate,/Proclaim'd at market crosses, read in churches,/To face the garment of rebellion/With some fine colour that may please the eye/Of fickle changelings and poor discontents,/Which gape and rub the elbow of the news/Of hurly burly innovation' [Pt I., V, i, 59–78].

On this account, in its initial stages the rebellion has sought to legitimise itself in public in terms of the king's misgovernment, a critique sometimes based on evil counsel and sometimes not, and one centred on his alleged mistreatment of and ingratitude towards the ancient nobility, particularly that part of the ancient nobility which had helped him to the throne in the first place. As Hotspur's speech to Blunt shows, there was, lurking behind all this, also the issue of the legitimacy of Henry's claim to the throne and at least the hint of a campaign in favour of the 'true heir', Mortimer. Pushed too hard such claims would have made a negotiated settlement impossible to achieve and, as a number of scenes in the play show, when their military and political circumstances seemed to dictate it, both sides were interested in at least considering some sort of negotiated settlement.

Both before Shrewsbury and at Gaultree forest the rebels are offered terms and on both occasions they consider the offer very seriously. Clearly, Mortimer's claim to the throne is never anywhere near the centre of their public manifestos or stated aims. Rather it had been always held in reserve, mentioned, but never quite asserted, and thus available when the ambition consequent upon success or indeed the desperation consequent upon failure either allowed or demanded its deployment. Here, of course, the Percies' tactics mirror perfectly those used by Bolingbroke himself against Richard II. For Bolingbroke had started out merely claiming his own, then moved on to the rescue of the king and commonwealth from evil counsel and oppression, not broaching the issue of the crown until very late in the day.

Thus it was only after their initial defeat at Shrewsbury had rendered the remaining rebels' situation desperate that they had direct recourse to the issue of legitimacy, citing the fate of the now 'fair king Richard' in a last desperate attempt to rouse the people in their cause. Indeed, Richard figures as a sort of royal martyr in what becomes an attempt by the archbishop of York to cloak the rebels' cause in religious rhetoric, and to appeal, on that basis, to the populace. Early in part II [I, i, 189–209], Mortimer gives Northumberland an enthusiastic account of the effects of a religiously charged appeal for popular support, fired with the blood of the martyr-king Richard, 'scrap'd from Pomfret stones', and self-consciously designed to remove the taint from the rebels' cause of 'this word "rebellion" ' that, on Mortimer's account, had quite 'froze up' the spirits of Hotspur's soldiers, 'as fish are in a pond'. Now that the archbishop 'Derives from heaven his quarrel and his cause;/Tells them he doth bestride a bleeding land,/Gasping for life under great Bolingbroke', 'more and less do flock to follow him'.

What is recognisably the same manoeuvre is described, albeit from an altogether more critical perspective, by John of Lancaster who, in a later parley with the rebels, rounds on the archbishop: 'who hath not heard it spoken/How deep you were within the books of God,/To us the speaker in his parliament,/

To us th'imagin'd voice of God himself,/The very opener and intelligencer/ Between the grace, the sanctities of heaven,/And our dull workings? O who shall believe/But you misuse the reverence of your place,/Employ the countenance and grace of heav'n/As a false favourite doth his prince's name,/In deeds dishonourable? You have ta'en up,/Under the counterfeited zeal of God,/The subjects of his substitute, my father,/And both against the peace of heaven and of him/Have here up-swarm'd them' [Pt. II, IV, ii, 16–30].

Not only is this use of religion and invocation of the name of Richard to mobilise the masses successful, the play reveals it to be quite self-conscious on the archbishop's part. 'Let us on,/And publish the occasion of our arms,' he urges his confederates. 'The commonwealth is sick of their own choice;/Their over greedy love hath surfeited./An habitation giddy and unsure/Hath he that buildeth on the vulgar heart./O thou fond many, with what loud applause/ Didst thou beat heaven with blessing Bolingbroke,/Before he was what thou wouldst have him be!/And being now trimm'd in thine own desires,/Thou, beastly feeder, art so full of him/That thou provok'st thyself to cast him up./So, so, thou common dog, didst thou disgorge/Thy glutton bosom of the royal Richard;/And now thou wouldst eat thy dead vomit up,/And howl'st to find it. What trust is in these times?/They that, when Richard liv'd, would have him die/Are now become enamour'd on his grave./Thou that threw'st dust upon his goodly head,/When through proud London he came sighing on/After th'admired heels of Bolingbroke,/Cry'st now, "O earth, yield us that King again,/ And take thou this!" O thoughts of men accurs'd! Past and to come seems best; things present, worst' [Pt. II, I, iii, 85–108].

Just as with the Cade scenes, in 2 Henry VI, so here, for all the archbishop's contempt for the mob, the behaviour, as he describes it, of the 'fond many' doubles as a comment upon that of their betters. After all, the object of Scroop's disgust is the fickleness of the populace in turning on King Henry. But in this their inconstancy is scarcely greater than that of the Percies, who, having put Bolingbroke on the throne in the first place, are now determined to turn him off again, through equally rebellious, violent and populist means. For all his disgust at the fickleness of the people and the changeability of the times, the archbishop himself is quite happy to use his own reputation for sanctity and the blood of martyred King Richard to exploit that 'fickleness' and raise a popular following in his own interest. Evidently the 'sickness' of the 'commonwealth' has infected not merely the 'fond many' but even those, like Scroop, who lament that sickness most vociferously.

Rebellion from the inside out

But if the play exposes the contradictory public plays for legal and moral justification and popular support made by the rebels to the wider world, it also shows us their internal political manoeuvres and calculations, their debates, self-justifications and more general lucubrations upon their own situation and the times. For all their talk of honour and legitimacy, of the commonwealth and religion, these conversations reveal their revolt to be, at bottom, a bastard feudal affair, the raising of a noble affinity or connection against royal authority and, as such, subject to all the self-interested calculation of advantage, the jockeying for position, the waiting on events, while pledging undying support the while, that always attended such manoeuvres. The political dynamics involved in raising what Northumberland at one point calls 'his friends' in rebellion against the crown are very clearly revealed at the opening of Act II scene iii. Hotspur enters reading aloud a letter from a Percy client, who is in the process of declining an offer to join the revolt he was not supposed to refuse [Pt. I, II, iii, 1–12]. Later, Northumberland reveals the difficulties inherent in the manipulation of such political and personal relationships, explaining to Hotspur why, having fallen ill, he has declined to raise his own followers. Unable to act in person, he found 'his friends by deputation could not/So soon be drawn; nor did he think it meet/To lay so dangerous and so dear a trust/On any soul removed but on his own' [Pt. I, IV, i 32–35]. We are here inside the intensely personal politics of the noble affinity or connection. Feelers have to be put out, arms have to be twisted, old debts called in, friends and clients talked round, and all without raising the alarm. After all, Hotspur's immediate thought, upon finishing the letter from his unnamed client, is that 'the pagan rascal' will not limit his activities to simply declining the Percies' invitation to risk his neck in open revolt on their behalf but will also try to save his own skin by reporting the intended rising to the king [Pt. I, II, iii, 27–29]. It was, of course, to avoid precisely such an outcome that Northumberland claimed to have held off from raising his own affinity. It was on the very same grounds that he urged Hotspur and the others, now that they were in arms and their plans known to the king, to go ahead without him [Pt. I, IV, i, 35–41].

On this account, rebellions had a momentum of their own. Conceived in secret, amongst the inner circles of aristocratic households and connections, they had to be broached to a widening circle of clients or friends and then prosecuted with vigour, lest the crown be alerted and act before the rebellion had really had a chance to start, and waverers, fair-weather friends, indeed, would-be supporters, come to see the conspirators themselves as doubtful and divided and their cause as doomed. Hence, the ever politic Worcester sees Northumberland's absence from the rebel host at Shrewsbury as a source of more than military weakness and disadvantage. 'It will be thought/By some that know not why he is away,/That wisdom, loyalty and mere dislike/Of our proceedings kept the Earl from hence;/And think how such an apprehension/May turn the tide of fearful faction,/And breed a kind of question in our cause./For, well you know, we of the off'ring side/Must keep aloof from strict arbitrement,/And stop all sight-holes, every loop from whence/The eye of reason may pry in upon us' [Pt. I, IV, i, 61–71].

What are being revealed here are the cold-blooded calculations at the heart of the intensely personal politics of noble faction and affinity. And yet, even in private, the rebels did not always or only talk of their enterprise in such calculating politique, and highly personalised, terms. Quite frequently, in fact, their private bouts of self-justification are centred on considerations of honour. Recalling the events that put Bolingbroke on the throne the Percies lament their role therein and the subsequent impact of their actions then on their repute and honour now. In Act I of part I Northumberland and Worcester explain to Hotspur just why it is that the king is determined not to ransom Mortimer. Hotspur recounts that his interview with the king ended with Henry 'trembling at the name of Mortimer'. In the ensuing discussion [Pt. I, I, iii, 144–85] the Percies reveal a belated and self-serving recognition of the reality of the crimes committed against King Richard. These are acknowledged first by Northumberland in the passive voice; the king had returned from Ireland 'to be deposed and shortly murdered'. Worcester chimes in, pointing out that they are (unjustly) held to blame for that outcome by 'the world's wide mouth'. Hotspur however cuts to the quick, pointing out that it was the Percies who set the crown 'upon the head of this forgetful man' and who are now widely blamed for the old king's murder. The resulting moral responsibilty, the sin, is sloughed off by both Hotspur and Northumberland in pious asides – 'God pardon it'. What really rankles, at least to the honour-obsessed Hotspur, is the dishonour involved in having done all this and then to have been so disrespected and disregarded by the very king that they have set up on the throne. The prospect of revenge for this slight famously provokes in Hotspur a paroxysm of honour talk [Pt I, I, iii, 199–206]. It is, of course, at this point that Worcester starts to broach to the others the nature of his plan to establish alliances with Glendower, Mortimer and Douglas to undo the king.

While Hotspur rants about honour, it is left to Worcester to reveal the real calculations lying behind his scheme. ' 'Tis no little reason bids us speed,/To save our heads by raising of a head;/For, bear ourselves as even as we can,/The King will always think him in our debt,/And think we think ourselves unsatisfied,/Till he hath found a time to pay us home./And we see already how he doth begin/To make us strangers to his looks of love' [Pt. I, I, iii, 278–85].

For all the talk of honour, and Scrope's later invocations of 'the commonwealth' and religion, here are the real origins of the rebellion in the inexorable political logic of the situation in which the king's former accomplices and supporters now find themselves. Just as the usurping king has no choice but to distance himself from the Percies, in the process, if not creating, then certainly exacerbating, the grounds both of his own fear and distrust of them and of their fear and distrust of him, so they, in turn, have no choice but to observe what Archbishop Scroop calls 'the way the stream of time doth run' and to get their retaliation in first. This is the search for commodity, the protection and advancement of political self-interest, and all the honour and commonwealth talk in the world cannot disguise that fact. For honour, as it emerges in these discussions amongst the rebels, is to be vindicated by rebellion, a rebellion in alliance with foreign princes and aimed not even at the full vindication of Mortimer's just claims to the throne of England against Henry's usurpation but rather at a division and dissolution of the kingdom between the victors.[1]

This is a point to which the play returns again and again. Before the battle of Shrewsbury, as we have seen, the king offers the rebels a settlement and a return to favour. Worcester is to take this offer to 'your cousin, and bring me word/What he will do'[Pt. I, V, i, 109–10]. This, Worcester concedes to Vernon, is a 'liberal and kind offer of the king'. Vernon expresses enthusiasm for it, only to be told by Worcester that if the rebels take it, 'then are we all undone'; a claim he justifies with a repeat of the political logic that had underpinned his initial plan to rebel. 'It is not possible, it cannot be,/The King should keep his word in loving us./He will suspect us still and find a time/To punish this offence in other faults./Supposition all our lives shall be stuck full of eyes,/For treason is but trusted like the fox,/Who never so tame, so cherished and locked up,/Will have a wild trick of his ancestors./Look how we can, or sad or merrily,/Interpretation will misquote our looks/And we shall feed like oxen at a stall,/The better cherished still the nearer death.'

That much of Worcester's analysis was general to the rebel cause; it presents us with a clear view of their common political condition and relationship to the king. But at this point his calculations take another more pointedly self-interested turn. 'My nephew's trespass may be well forgot;/It hath the excuse of youth and heat of blood,/And an adopted name of privilege:/A hare-brained hotspur, governed by a spleen./All his offences live upon my head/And on his father's. We did train him on,/And, his corruption being ta'en from us,/We as the spring of all shall pay for all./Therefore, good cousin, let not Harry know/In any case the offer of the King'[Pt. I, V, ii, 3–25]. Here the reasoning gets personal and does so in a way that, in fact, serves to undermine the rebel cause from within. The undermanned rebel host, and indeed Worcester's own nephew, Hotspur, are to be risked to protect the political and personal interests of Worcester and Northumberland.

Thus Worcester deceitfully precipitates a battle in which the rebels are outnumbered and which they, predictably, lose. But they are outnumbered in large part because Northumberland has failed, either in person or through surrogates, to reinforce their host. The reason given for this is a sudden illness, but in a later scene between Northumberland and his daughter-in-law serious doubt is cast upon this version of events. There Lady Percy is trying desperately to persuade Northumberland not to join the archbishop's forces but instead to flee to Scotland to wait upon events. He claims that he cannot, for 'my honour is at pawn/And, but my going, nothing can redeem it'. She gives this argument short shrift, citing his earlier failure to keep his word, given to 'your own Percy', at which point 'there were two honours lost, yours and your son's'. Since Northumberland had been content then to leave his son, the very 'miracle of men', in the lurch, he has no reason now 'to hold your honour more precise and nice/With others than with him!' Thus exhorted, admonished and tempted, Northumberland gives way to his own better judgement and instinct for self-preservation [Pt. II, II, iii, 9–68]. This duplicitously Machiavellian reading of Northumberland's conduct is 'confirmed', insofar as anything can be confirmed by so unreliable a witness, by Rumour's report, at the start of Part II, where the earl's indisposition is described as old Northumberland lying 'crafty-sick' at home [Pt. II, Induction, 37].

Thus, with the exception of Hotspur, each participant in the rebellion seeks his own commodity, making political calculations in terms of his own imme-diate interests and chances of self-preservation; thus father sells out son and uncle nephew, and thus, at every turn, are the forces of the rebels divided and picked off, one after another, by those of the king. A rebellion, conceived in terms of political interest and commodity, is thus defeated by the corrosive effects of those same impulses upon the internal workings of the rebel cause. And 'honour' has had little or nothing to do with it – except, of course, in the case of the honour-obsessed Hotspur, who, alone of the leading rebels, seems oblivious to the imperatives of commodity and self-preservation. His reward is an honourable death on the field of battle at Shrewsbury, killed by the prince of Wales but also sacrificed to the cause of commodity by his uncle's duplicity and his father's self-interested caution.

Honour

The initial offer of terms to the rebels by the king described above is made towards the end of part I, V, i. The subsequent exchange between Worcester and Vernon takes place at the opening of scene ii. They are separated by a meditation of Falstaff's on honour. 'What is honour? A word. What is in that word "honour"? What is that "honour"? Air. A trim reckoning! Who hath it? He that died o' Wednesday. Doth he feel it? No. Doth he hear it? No. 'Tis insen-sible then? Yea, to the dead. But will it not live with the living? No. Why? Detraction will not suffer it. Therefore I'll none of it. Honour is a mere scutcheon – and so ends my catechism' [Pt. I, V, i, 126–40]. Juxtaposed, as it is, so precisely with Worcester's entirely political calculations and deceits over the king's proffered terms, this meditation on the emptiness of honour accords rather well with the role 'honour' has been shown actually playing in the framing, conduct and legitimation of the rebellion.

Except, of course, that the immediate object of Falstaff's assault is honour won through combat and courage on the field of battle. And that is the one form of 'honour' left to the rebels, or rather left to Hotspur, and, we might add, at this point to Hal as well. As we have seen, Hotspur is duped by his father and his uncle Worcester into fighting a battle he is all but doomed to lose. Defeated, almost as much by the duplicity and self-interest of his relations and allies as by the prowess of his enemies, Hotspur still manages to vindicate his honour through a glorious death in single combat with the prince. His is the only sort of honour managed by the rebels, and it is of a peculiarly amoral, apolitical sort; something to be achieved – no matter the justice or otherwise of the cause being espoused or the course of action being undertaken – simply through the exercise of military prowess, the search for military glory prized for its own sake.

The prince, too, achieves this sort of honour. And it might be tempting to argue that, since he does so in a good cause – the defence of monarchy against rebellion, and of the realm against the foreign invasion and partition planned by the rebels – in him martial honour is reset within an overarching framework of moral and political legitimacy. Except that the conduct of the war on the king's side is shown to be even less 'honourable' than that of the rebels. I refer here, of course, to the negotiations at Gaultree forest between, on the one hand, Scroop and Mowbray and, on the other, John of Lancaster and Westmoreland. Westmoreland and Lancaster offer to consider the rebels' grievances. The rebels, both in public and in private, greet this offer with a certain suspicion and circumspection. Charged by Mowbray that the offer 'proceeds from policy, not love', Westmoreland is shocked and dismayed. It comes, he claims, 'from mercy, not from fear'. Hastings anxiously enquires, 'hath the Prince John a full commission' to make a deal of this magnitude. Again Westmoreland is shocked and stunned that he can ask such a question. 'That is intended in the general's name:/I muse you make so slight a question' [Pt. II, IV, i, 141–67]. The rebels agree to draw up their grievances, but again Worcester-style fears of the impossibility of any true peace being established between the parties return to trouble the inner counsels of the rebels. Here it is Mowbray who is the sceptic. 'There is a thing within my bosom tells me/That no conditions of our peace can stand'. But Hastings will have none of it; they will make 'such large terms, and so absolute', he claims, that 'our peace shall stand as firm as rocky mountains'. But, Mowbray replies, the king will never trust them. The archbishop, however, is not convinced. On his view, the political circumstances will not allow such revenge-taking. 'The king is weary/Of dainty and such picking grievances;/For he hath found, to end one doubt by death/Revives two greater in the heirs of life:/And therefore will he wipe his tables clean,/And keep no tell-tale to his memory/That may repeat and history his loss/To new remembrance. For well he knows/He cannot so precisely weed this land/As his misdoubts present occasion./His foes are so enrooted with his friends/That plucking to unfix an enemy/He doth unfasten so and shake a friend./So that this land, like an offensive wife/That hath enrag'd him on to offer strokes,/As he is striking, holds his infant up,/And hangs resolv'd correction in the arm/That was uprear'd to execution.' 'Besides,' adds Hastings, 'the King hath wasted all his rods/On late offenders, that he now doth lack/The very instruments of chastisement;/So that his power, like to a fangless lion,/May offer, but not hold' [Pt. II, IV, i, 183–219].

We have here, described by the rebels themselves, the results of the loss of legitimacy. Richard's tyranny, Bolingbroke's usurpation, and the lines of polit-ical force unleashed thereby, have combined to create a political scene racked by faction and feud, by civil dissension, rebellion and civil war. No longer the arbiter of his nobility's disputes and affairs, the ultimate source of authority, justice and legitimacy in the state, the monarch has been reduced to making his own political calculations and dispositions in a situation that has reduced him to the status of just another political player, amongst many. And it is precisely because of that, rather than because they trust either him or his professions of love and mercy towards his subjects or, still less, view the crown as the ultimate object of allegiance and obedience, that the rebels persuade themselves that they can do a deal with Henry IV.

And indeed a deal is apparently done.[Pt. II, IV, ii, 55–65]. Having, in his first encounters with the rebels, had recourse to the rhetoric of divinely ordained kingship, of the king as 'God's substitute' and of rebellion as the ulti-mate sin against the 'peace of heaven' [Pt. II, IV, ii, 28–29], Lancaster has now adopted the rebels' own rhetoric of evil counsel to cloak the fact of their rebel-lion against royal authority. The king's 'purposes have been mistook' and his authority abused by those close to him. The prince pledges the 'honour' of his 'blood', indeed his very soul, to re-establish not merely peace 'but love and amity' between the king and his subjects. This again is the language of (moral) legitimacy, of peace and honour, of restored love between ruler and ruled, all confirmed by the overarching claims and sanctions of religion but used now, not to condemn rebellion, but rather to achieve a settlement with former rebels returning to the fold of loyalty and obedience.

As the deal is sealed and the rebel host dismissed, Lancaster's first remark is addressed to the rebels – 'I trust, lords, we shall lie tonight together' – and his second to Westmoreland. 'Now, cousin, wherefore stands our army still?' 'The leaders, having charge from you to stand,/Will not go off until they hear you speak,' comes the reply [Pt. II, IV, ii, 97–100]. This exchange establishes what happens next as a premeditated plot. The rebel host having been dispersed, the royal army is left in possession of the field and Scroop, Mowbray and Hastings are all arrested as traitors.

Having pledged his honour and his soul, Lancaster escapes from the resulting supervening moral obligation to keep his word publicly given with a positively Jesuitical piece of equivocation; 'I promised you redress of these same grievances/Whereof you did complain; which, by mine honour,/I will perform with a most Christian care./But, for you rebels, look to taste the due/ Meet for rebellion and such acts as yours./Most shallowly did you these arms commence,/Fondly brought here, and foolishly sent hence.' Insofar as there is any larger moral justification claimed for these actions it is to be found in Lancaster's almost offhand invocation of divine authority – 'God not we have safely fought today' – and in the concomitant (albeit implicit) claim that, since the preservation of the prince's state is the highest political and moral value, and since consequently treason is the greatest possible sin or crime against both God and man, any deceit or deception is lawful in bringing it to book. There could scarcely be a clearer vindication of Worcester's doubts and scruples before Shrewsbury. What appeared at the time to be his entirely discreditable and duplicitous treatment of his nephew, on this evidence appears to have been political sagacity of a very high order, with his decision to fight, however poor the odds, representing an entirely justifiable military risk taken, and political calculation made, in the face of the implacable enmity and entirely untrustworthy nature of the regime with which the rebels were dealing.

What we are being shown here are the moral and political consequences of a political system that has been drained of legitimacy. On the rebels' side we have a rebellion that, in terms of its ostensible public aims, uses the rhetoric of evil counsel and the grievances of the ancient nobility to make an appeal to the 'commonwealth' against a king misled into something like tyranny, to justify rebellion as a form of armed demonstration. Behind that relatively conciliatory stance lies the option of an aggressively legitimist claim to be opposing usurped authority in the name of the legitimate heir. That last is accompanied by a further claim to religious sanction, justified by the murdered Richard's blood 'scraped from Pomfret stones' and put about by the archbishop of York. As he himself admits, he is using his own reputation for sanctity to place a religious gloss on a rebellion that is in fact motivated by rather more personal aims and ambitions. Scroop's involvement, the play reveals, is predicated on his desire for revenge on the murderers of his own brother during the events that deposed Richard. More generally, the rebels are activated by their own sense of political insecurity in the face of a usurped authority that they helped to create and which is now viewing them with increasing distrust. It had, after all, been precisely Archbishop Scroop who had, before the people, couched the rebels' cause in the most exalted terms, as God's cause, a religious crusade to revenge the death of the martyred King Richard. But at Gaultree it was the same churchman, Scroop, who had most effectively voiced an entirely political, commodity-centred, rationale for selling out what he had previously described, for public consumption, as God's and King Richard's cause, if not for a mess of pottage, then certainly for a laundry list of purely political concessions;

concessions prised from a prince who has now no choice but to give in because of the inherent weakness of his position as a usurper; a usurper created in large part by those now in rebellion against him. Thus, while they sometimes talk amongst themselves the language of honour and legitimacy, the rebels' real motivation is the pursuit of commodity and security, and behind their revolt is an alliance with foreign powers (the Welsh and the Scots) to partition the realm into three provinces, one each for the leading rebels (Glendower, Mortimer and the Percies).

Moreover, whatever the moderation (and piety) of their claims when trawling for popular support or confronted by or negotiating with the forces of the king, amongst themselves they admit the radicalism of their real intentions or perhaps of their best- (or worst-) case scenarios. One rebel describes their project as nothing less than to 'pluck a kingdom down/And set another up' [Pt. II, I, iii, 48–49], while Hotspur declares his aim 'to push against a kingdom' and 'o'erturn it topsy-turvy down' [Pt. I, IV, i, 80–81].

Prompted, as it is, by the impulse towards political self-preservation and commodity, the rebellion is conducted by its various participants in precisely that spirit. Each one seeks commodity as they see it, in the process double-crossing or betraying their fellows. As Worcester observes, as he confronts a traitor's death after his defeat at Shrewsbury, 'what I have done my safety urg'd me to' [Pt. I, V, v, 11]. As a consequence, at no point are the forces at the disposal of the rebellion united, thereby all but ensuring the defeat of the whole enterprise. On the other side, Scroop's estimate of the king's political (and moral) condition, used by him as a reason to come to terms, provides the political justification or rationale for Lancaster's ruthlessness. Reduced, as it has been, by recent events, royal authority must be re-established by whatever means are necessary. Only thus can true order be restored and the kingdom really settled, and, in the short term at least, neither the demands of conscience nor those of honour can be allowed to hinder or delay that process.

The politics of commodity and the language of the market

As a number of critics have noted, the commodification of politics consequent on the reign of a usurper is reflected in the language of the play. All of the characters use terms taken from commercial exchange, trade and investment to describe the political process and their own political projects.[2] This serves to play up the extent to which politics, on both the king's and the rebels' side of the issue, has become a question of the pursuit of self-interest and security; a situation in which risks have to be taken, deals made and ventures launched in circumstances of extreme instability and uncertainty. For questions of value have become entirely relative, determined, in large part, by opinion and rumour. Trust is in short supply and the value of even the basic medium of exchange – in politics, of men's words and vows, in the economic realm, of the very coin of the realm itself – has become radically uncertain.[3] Thus, in the interview with his father, when he is desperate to convince him of his trustworthiness and honour, Hal has recourse to the language of trade, calling Hotspur his 'factor', a mere agent used 'to engross up glorious deeds on my behalf/And I will call him to so strict account/That he shall render every glory up/Yea, even the slightest worship of his time,/Or I will tear the reckoning from his heart' [Pt. I, III, ii, 147–52]. In response, the king starts to talk of the campaign against the rebels as a 'business' full of 'advantage'; 'our hands are full of business. Let's away./Advantage feeds him fat while men delay' [Pt. I, III, ii, 163, 177, 179–80]. Ornstein's comment is instructive: 'like a clever speculator, he [Hal] will not labour in the vineyards of glory, but by using Hotspur as his factor, he expects to win a commodity of good names – to make a killing at Shrewsbury.'[4]

On their side, the rebels too envisage their enterprise in commercial terms; as Mortimer tells the others, 'our indentures tripartite are drawn,/Which, being sealed interchangeably' their enterprise can go forward [Pt. I, III, I, 78–80]. The language of contract and debt suffuses the play. When, before Shrewsbury, Sir Walter Blunt tells the rebels that the king will agree to meet their demands, he bids them 'name your griefs, and with all speed/You shall have your desires with interest' [Pt. I, IV, iii, 48–49]. But no one is taking the king's word or accepting his credit. Hotspur replies contemptuously that 'the King is kind, and well we know the King/Knows at what time to promise, when to pay' [Pt. I, IV, iii, 52–53]. It is with a mind to increase, not merely his own credit rating, but also that of the house of Lancaster that Hal enters the fray at Shrewsbury. When he encounters the Douglas he tells him that 'it is the Prince of Wales that threatens thee/Who never promiseth but he means to pay' [Pt. I, V, iv, 41–42]. Earlier, of course, Hal had talked of his purpose 'to pay the debt I never promised' and thus to 'redeem the time', apparently wasted in his seemingly wild youth.

But more often than not debts in these plays are left unredeemed. Or rather, in Part I they are nearly always fobbed off or left unpaid, but in Part II they come due with a vengeance.[5] There is much punning on debt and death, with Hal's claim that 'we owe God a death' met by Falstaff's typical refusal to even contemplate paying up; ' 'tis not due yet, I would be loath to pay him before his day' [Pt.I, V, i, 26–28]. Indeed, as Sandra Fischer points out, 'by counterfeiting death, Falstaff is able to forstall payment'.[6]

As a number of critics have observed, the plays are also suffused with the language of coinage and counterfeiting. The coin of the realm was often referred to as 'crowns' – as in Poins' invitation 'if you will go, I will stuff your purses full of crowns' [Pt. I, I, ii, 124–25] – because of the king's image stamped upon it. At Gadshill the robbers are informed that 'there's money of the King's coming down the hill; 'tis going to the King's exchequer'. 'You lie, ye rogue: 'tis going to the King's tavern' is Falstaff's response [Pt. I, II, ii, 52–55]. As any number of critics have observed, the robbery, which takes place in the play's festive tavern world, parallels events in the world of politics and war, where first Bolingbroke and then the rebels have tried to rob the king of his crown. Thus Henry IV, no less than Falstaff, could be thought of as a counterfeit king and the play uses the notion of counterfeiting repeatedly to problematise the relation between the real and the fabricated, between true and false value and claim. At Shrewsbury Hotspur tells the Douglas, who has determined to kill the king, that Henry 'hath many marching in his coats' [Pt. I, V, iii, 25] to avoid precisely that fate. Douglas undertakes to 'kill all his coats/I'll murder all his wardrobe, piece by piece,/Until I meet the King' [Pt. I, V, iii, 26–28]. After he has killed the first of Henry's doubles, the Douglas comes upon another, Sir Walter Blunt, who tells him that this time he faces the true king and pays for that lie with his life. In disgust Douglas exclaims that 'a borrowed title hast thou bought too dear./Why didst thou tell me that thou wert a king?' [Pt. I, V, iii, 23–24]. Thus when the Douglas does meet the real King Henry, he can scarcely believe it; 'what art thou/that counterfeit'st the person of a king?' When he is told that it is 'the king himself', his reply – 'I fear thou art another counterfeit,/And yet, in faith, thou bearest thee like a king' [Pt. I, V, iv, 26–35] – speaks volumes about the counterfeit nature of the usurper Bolingbroke's kingship. As David Kastan has observed, under the circumstances created by his own usurpation and the rebels' revolt, the best that Henry can do is bear himself *like* a king.[7]

On one view, then, Henry's kingship forced all his subjects to accept false for true coin; a point that parallels the historical fact that, in Holinshed's account, Henry did indeed debase the coinage. In anticipation of the battle of Shrewsbury, Hotspur tells his wife that 'we must have bloody noses and crack'd crowns,/And pass them current too' [Pt. I, II, iii, 89–90]; it is an image that quite remarkably casts as much doubt on the soundness of the authority that, if the rebels prevail, will replace that of the usurper Henry IV, as on that of Henry himself. To drive the point home, it is also at Shrewsbury that Falstaff delivers his own account of the dynamics of counterfeiting. Having feigned his death to avoid the onrush of the Douglas, Falstaff observes to no one in particular that ' 'twas time to coun- terfeit, or that hot termagant Scot had paid me, scot and lot too. Counterfeit? I lie; I am no counterfeit. To die is to be a counterfeit, for he is but a counterfeit of a man who hath not the life of a man. But to counterfeit dying when a man thereby liveth is to be no counterfeit but the true and perfect image of life indeed' [Pt. I, V, iv, 112–18]. Falstaff, of course, is the ultimate counterfeit; adept at using the coinage both of everyday language and of puritan cant to pass himself off as something that he is not, he deceives no one and yet still manages to debase the truth value of the very language that he is using to do it.

But if Falstaff (and Henry IV) are counterfeits, so, too, in his own way, is Hal. After all, he spends nearly all of part I and much of part II pretending to be the prodigal and rake that he is not. Moreover, in so doing he is using Falstaff at least as much as Falstaff is using him. Just as much as Falstaff, Hal is lying;

indeed he is using Falstaff to spin a yarn about himself that in the end will redound to his advantage just as it will ruin Falstaff. But if Henry IV and Falstaff (Hal's real and surrogate fathers) are both genuine counterfeits, Hal claims that in the long run he is only pretending to be one; something that starts to emerge towards the end of part I. In a world of counterfeits perhaps only a counterfeit counterfeit can be the real thing. Once the Douglas has finally identified the true counterfeit king in Henry IV and is on the point of dispatching him, he is downed and driven off in turn by the true prince, Hal. Indeed, as Dessen observes, 'everyone else in the play readily finds reasons not to pay their debts or keep their vows'. But, in striking contrast, Prince Hal pays all his debts, even those 'he never promised' – except, as we shall see, that made in the depths of his counterfeiting phase to Francis the drawer.

In saving Henry's life at Shrewsbury and killing Hotspur he fulfils his prom-ises and debts to his father.[8] He even keeps his contract with Falstaff, albeit not the one the old counterfeit thinks they have made but the one sealed by the prince's fatal words 'I do; I will', delivered in the midst of the play extempore in II, iv, *1 Henry IV*. It is therefore only through his betrayal of the genuine coun-terfeit, Falstaff, that Hal, the false counterfeit, can show his true mettle. The irony is, of course, that, at one level, Falstaff had always put his hopes in, indeed bet the farm on, Hal's 'true mettle', that is to say his status as the king's son and heir. As the play extempore in part I is broken up when the sheriff's men knock on the door, Falstaff calls on Hal to 'never call a true piece of gold a counterfeit. Thou art essentially made without seeming so' [Pt. I, II, iv, 478–80]. It is an exhortation to Hal to give over counterfeiting and to assert his status as true coin; that is, both to remain true to Falstaff and to use his rank as the prince of Wales to save the old reprobate from the gallows. In the short term, this is an appeal that works entirely to Falstaff's advantage, but, of course, in the end, Hal's emergence as 'more myself' can only work to Falstaff's detriment, indeed to his ruin. It might be thought, therefore, that it is the emergence of Hal as the true prince that pulls the kingdom out of the moral relativism and dubiety, the calculation and uncertainty, the speculation and suspicion, that characterise the politics of commodity. But not only is that emergence itself achieved only through a considerable amount of counterfeiting and deceit, the only character in the play certain that that will happen is Hal himself; everyone else is forced to make their calculations and place their bets in an uncertain world seemingly about to be rendered more uncertain when Hal becomes Henry. And even Henry does not entirely escape from the politics of commodity; at best he ships its most corrosive consequences abroad. Thus in Act V scene ii of *Henry V* he responds to Burgundy's moving description of the effects of war on the French countryside with the entirely mercenary response that the French 'must buy that peace/With full accord to all our just demands;/Whose tenures and partic-ular effects you have/Enschedul'd briefly, in your hands' [V, ii, 70–73].

These references continue and generalise the critique, or rather the analysis, of the politics of commodity started in *King John*. In *King John* that terminology had remained concentrated in the bastard's commodity speech, although arguably the purport of that speech had been exemplified throughout the entire action of the play. In both parts of *Henry IV,* on the other hand, the language of commodity, of credit and debt, of factors and interest, of counterfeit and true coin, is utterly pervasive. Some critics argued that this amounts to a critique of the moral consequences of market relations and commercial exchange. Others have seen it as amounting to a form of 'economic determinism', or a commentary on a ' "critical turning point in British social and political history," one in which a changing social structure affects the language men use in dealing with one another and in which a profit-motivated economy in part defines their interactions.'[9] This, of course, is to elide the political meanings of these passages, to reduce them to a mere commentary upon or reflection of socio-economic change. But arguably the 'economic determinism' in operation here belongs entirely to the critic and not at all to the play. One might just as well see the *Henry IV* plays as using an established language of economic deal making, of credit and debt, of debasement and counterfeiting, the meaning of which was utterly familiar to the audience from their own experience of current economic and social life,[10] in order to evoke the entirely deleterious, both destabilising and relativising, effects of the 'politics of commodity' initiated by the reign of that counterfeit king, the usurper Henry IV.

A range of standard economic terms, practices and realities were thus being used to describe the nature and corrosive effects of political change, with notions of relative value, credit and debt, based in market relations, invading the supposedly stable and morally transparent world of royal legitimacy and divine right, of noble honour and political allegiance, in which kings and their counsellors were at least supposed to subsist. At the very least, we might see the language of the market and the practices of commodity politics as being used to reflect back upon each other, with utterly corrosive effects on any notions of intrinsic value or true mettle.

If the economic terms and conditions being used to evoke the politics of commodity were entirely familiar to Elizabethan audiences, in London certainly, but also in the provinces – after all, Craig Muldrew's seminal study of the social and cultural relations created by credit and debt was based on King's Lynn – so, we might assume, were the political conditions and behaviours that those terms were being used to evoke and describe. Or at least they were when the audience left the theatre, even if they had not been when they entered it.

Lancastrians and Tudors

As Tom McAlindon has observed, in terms of the immediate political experience or memory of Elizabethan audiences the Percy-led northern rebellion staged in the play could not have helped but recall the revolt of the northern earls.[11] That, too, had centred on the bastard feudal affinity of discontented northern lords. Its justification had been provided by the tyrannous treatment of the ancient nobility by evil counsellors around the monarch and by religion, with the prospect of a rival claimant to the throne – in this instance, Mary Stuart – lurking in the background. That rebellion, too, had involved cross-border machinations with dissident Scottish lords and, indeed, intrigues with foreign powers. Dogged by internal dissension and the indecision and back-sliding of the major players, that rebellion, too, had gone off at half cock, as a consequence collapsing in serial disarray before the forces of the crown. The result was defeat, death and exile for all the major players. If we set the play's account of the nature and fate of this Percy rebellion against the accounts of Elizabethan politics proffered by the Catholic texts analysed in the Introduction, the results are striking. After all, *The treatise of treasons* had been occasioned by pseudo-official assaults on the bona fides of the northern earls and, behind them, on the duke of Norfolk and Mary Stuart. Subsequent renditions of the same style of argument had always featured the exclusion of the ancient nobility from the counsels of the crown, in general, and the fate of Norfolk, in partic-ular, as central examples of the tyrannical courses pursued by the Elizabethan regime, if not by Elizabeth herself. By positioning itself, through its thoroughly disenchanted picture of an earlier Percy-led northern rebellion, in this sort of highly critical relation to the revolt of the northern earls, the play was also engaging with, while simultaneously distancing itself from, the strand of Catholic political analysis that ran from *The treatise*, through *Leicester's commonwealth* of 1584 and the tracts of the early 1590s known collectively as *Cecil's commonwealth*.

Of course, behind that northern revolt lay another religiously legitimised rebellion, if not led, then at least fronted by, disaffected northern peers and Percies – the Pilgrimage of Grace. This last had been put down with the same mixture of royal duplicity and violence displayed at Gaultree by Lancaster and Westmoreland.[12] Indeed, we know that in the course of his dealings with the pilgrims the duke of Norfolk, in this just like John of Lancaster, had assured Henry VIII that, as far as he was concerned, terms and undertakings given to rebels and traitors in pursuit of the political advantage of the crown did not bind. For Norfolk, his overriding duty to obey and defend the prince freed him from his otherwise binding obligation as a peer to keep his word once publicly given. In his seminal essay *English politics and the concept of honour*, Mervyn James juxtaposed Norfolk's expressed attitude to honour as something almost totally defined by the relation between the individual and the divinely ordained authority and will of the prince and state, with that espoused by Lord Darcy. Darcy emerged as one of the leaders of the Pilgrimage and after its collapse sought (unsuccessfully) to justify his collaboration with the pilgrims through his oath, given in public, after his capture by the rebels, not to betray their purposes. James sees in the contrast between those stances a vivid illustration of the opposition between two very different codes or theories of honour. On the one hand, we have a prince- and state-centred notion of honour, almost entirely defined by obedience and service to the state and commonwealth. On the other, we have a rather more free floating notion of honour, as something to be defined not by one's relations with the prince, still less with the 'state', but rather to be achieved through the display of military prowess and virtue, in the defence of one's standing and word as a nobleman, and validated by the spontaneous recognition of honourable conduct by a variety of what James calls 'honour communities', groups composed of one's peers and certainly not coterminous with, indeed in many ways entirely separate from, the workings and structures of the state.[13]

In the play, the state-centred version of honour is, of course, espoused and personified by Lancaster and Westmoreland, who see nothing dishonourable in the duplicity and treachery of their conduct towards the rebels at Gaultree. (Whether the audience is intended to agree, or indeed would have agreed with them is, of course, another matter.)[14] Everything is justified by their overarching obligation to both God and man, to protect order and the state from rebellion, a cause which, happily for them, is entirely coterminous with their own hold on power. The perfect epitome of the opposing view of honour is, of course, Hotspur. James argues that the defence of 'honour', defined in that second sense, could legitimise resistance to, indeed even rebellion against, the crown. Hotspur's career and pronouncements on that subject serve as a vivid evocation of precisely such a view of the matter. James tends to see the sixteenth century as the period during which that first, state- and prince-centred, notion of honour (a notion he associates with the 'modernising' trends and tendencies inherent in 'humanism' and 'protestantism' and with versions of history dominated by providence rather than by fortune) displaced what we might term a 'medieval', or even 'feudal', Hotspur-style, notion of honour (centred on the operations of honour communities independent of the exercise of royal authority and on views of the world organised more around fortune than providence).

On some readings the play could be recruited to back up such a view of the matter. It certainly shows the rebels failing before the new model honour system propagated by Lancaster at Gaultree. For all his martial virtue and prowess, for all his honour talk, it is Hotspur who dies at Shrewsbury, and the king, 'who hath many marching in his coats' [Pt. I, V, iii, 25], who wins. But just as (as I will argue below) the play cannot be used to consign Hotspur's sense of honour to a discredited medieval past, neither does it simply endorse Lancaster's state-centred redefinition of honour as duplicity in the cause of order and the defence of the current power structure. On the contrary, in Hal's words over his dead rival's corpse, Hotspur's claims to (and thereby also his view of) honour are reaffirmed as attributes that even his status as a rebel cannot altogether destroy. 'This earth that bears thee dead/Bears not alive so stout a gentleman . . . Adieu, and take thy praise with thee to heaven!/Thy ignominy sleep with thee in the grave,/But not remembered in thy epitaph' [Pt. I, V, iv, 91–100].

Just as the rebellion of the Percies and their allies against Henry IV, as described by Shakespeare, could not help but recall the Pilgrimage of Grace and revolt of the northern earls, so too the opposing royal regime could not help but recall that of the Tudors.[15] Indeed, the stronger the former set of associations became, the more irresistible the second set would become. But the regime thus identified did not emerge from these events in a particularly positive light. The exchanges at Gaultree provided the culmination of the play's composite picture of the regime of a usurper, desperately trying to establish a critical distance from its erstwhile creators, and lurching, as it did so, into increasingly erratic, peremptory and oppressive actions, actions that, in fact, were all too likely to provoke precisely the sort of challenge that they were, in principle and intent, designed to avert. This was a regime that, while it talked the talk of divine right legitimacy, walked the walk of commodity and the ruthless and duplicitous pursuit of political self-interest and self-preservation. Archbishop's Scroop's analysis of the fickleness of popular opinion, combined, as it was, with his own enthusiastic, religiously based appeals to the very same populace that he had just denounced, find their almost exact parallel in a speech delivered by the king to his peccant son. On Henry's own admission what he calls 'opinion' 'did help me to the throne' [Pt.1, III, ii, 42] and it did so because, as he explains to Hal, he knew how to cultivate it. In the popularity stakes, Henry explains, as things stand, Hal is where Richard was when 'I from France set foot at Ravenspur/And even as I then was is Percy now' [Pt I, III, ii, 95–96]. This, he makes it clear, is a very dangerous position to be in. But in instructing his ne'er-do-well son in his own dark political arts, Henry comes very close to admitting the concerted political planning that had gone into his own capture of the crown; a capture that has, of course, itself produced the present circumstance, with rival factions and claimants desperately making their pitch to an inherently fickle people for support; the circumstance, in short, analysed and lamented by Scroop, even as he, in turn, played the popular card by invoking Richard's shade to win popular support for his own cause.

The contradictions at the heart of the 'loyalist' cause between the legitimism of its rhetoric and the commodity-centred ruthlessness of its actions were seen at their starkest in the exchanges at Gaultree. As in *King John*, we are being confronted here with a world in which everyone is seeking political advantage and security according to the iron logic of their own political circumstances. Again, as in *King John*, the political lines of force by which all the major players are constrained have been set in motion by an original political sin, an act of usurpation. In the former play, John's seizure of the throne from the legitimate heir Arthur was the root of the problem; here, of course, it stems from the deposition of Richard II and the usurpation of the man Hotspur describes, at one point, as 'this vile politician Bolingbroke' [Pt. I, I, iii, 239]. Again, as in *King John*, we are being shown the consequences of the loss of legitimacy. Asked how he dare rise in revolt against the crown, Archbishop Scroop replies by shifting responsibility for his current actions away from himself to a more general political condition, a condition he describes as a form of disease. 'Wherefore do I this? So the question stands./Briefly, to this end: we are all diseas'd,/And with our surfeiting, and wanton hours,/Have brought ourselves into a burning fever,/And we must bleed for it; of which disease/Our late King Richard being infected died' [Pt. II, IV, i, 53–58].

The politics of memory

The events of the previous reign hang over the action of these plays; they are constantly recalled by all the major players at the greatest or most intense moments of conflict or tension; when they need most urgently to justify their present conduct, vilify that of their enemies or ease their own consciences about the recent past by heaping blame on others. When first confronted by the representatives of royal authority it is to their version of these events that a variety of the rebels turn. As we have seen, Hotspur replies to Blunt's accusation that he stands 'out of limit and true rule' 'against anointed majesty' [Pt. I, IV, iii, 39–49] with a long tirade about recent history [Pt. I, IV, iii, 54–92]. Worcester tells the king himself a version of what is essentially the same story before the battle of Shrewsbury [Pt. I, V, i, 33–58]. On these accounts, the Percies were but the dupes, indeed the victims, both of circumstance and of Bolingbroke. On their account, the wanton times, the accident of the king's delay in Ireland, all these conspired to give the initiative, and then the crown, to Bolingbroke, who, in Hotspur's phrase, is presented as a 'vile politician' pursuing a gradual and premeditated path to the crown. In Worcester's version it is Bolingbroke's oath to them at Doncaster that had been the great barrier defending King Richard and the cause of legitimacy. By breaking that oath Bolingbroke broke those bounds, and his crime against Richard was but a presage of the massive ingratitude to his former friends that was now provoking them, belated apostles of a legitimist cause they had always, in fact, espoused, into open revolt.

These, of course, are all self-serving, bowdlerised, distinctly mealy-mouthed accounts of these events, as any member of the audience who could recall a performance of *Richard II* would have known. The speeches analysed above are all made in public as justifications of the rebels' conduct. But, as we have seen, they are echoed by very similar remarks made in private, as the Percies talk amongst themselves about their situation and intentions. As for the king, in public he can, of course, give no ground to such claims, but in private he is shown doing precisely that. At one point he tells Warwick that, even as Richard approached abdication, even 'then, God knows, I had no such intent/But that necessity so bow'd the state/That I and greatness were compell'd to kiss' [Pt. II, III, i, 72–74]. Here Northumberland's passive voice, Worcester's wanton times and contrarious winds, are paralleled by a 'necessity' of the state which 'compelled' Henry to take the crown. Clearly, this is an event which none of the people who made it wishes to own; it is something that just happened; either perpetrated by others or brought about by circumstance, 'the times' or even by 'necessity'.

In such passages the play shows us each of the major makers of Richard's deposition and Bolingbroke's ascent to the throne in denial; aware of the enormity of the act and now being made more aware, with every passing day, of its terrible consequences – the diseases in the state described by Scroop in another naturalising metaphor that gets the human agents involved off the hook – they cannot bring themselves to accept responsibility for it. In part, what is involved here is political cunning, and political necessity, the necessary shifting of the blame on to others to legitimise and justify one's own past, present and future. But we are also surely being shown something else here too: genuine acts of self-deception, as it were, real denial, as each and every party to these events shows himself unable to own and accept his part in them. What is made crystal clear here is that none of the parties to Richard's deposition or Henry's rise – not even Henry IV himself – regard either event as simply a defensible or legitimate exercise of powers inherent in the commonwealth either to discipline or depose kings, or to divert the succession and elect their successor.[16]

There is, moreover, a greater truth to both the Percies' and Henry's claims to have been the victims of forces outside themselves; Richard's tyranny, compounded by their resistance and Henry's usurpation, have between them unleashed political forces and interactions that were indeed beyond the power of any of the individual participants in these events to control. Together they may have made events, but events have also made them. Reacting to the iron logic of the political circumstances in which their own and others' actions – in which, indeed, events themselves – have set them, none of these men has been entirely the master of his own fate. In the delegitimised world of commodity, the ceaseless search for political advantage and security, that is to say for power and (both political and moral) legitimacy into which they have all been plunged, all of the normal fixed points of loyalty and legitimacy have either been moved around or removed altogether; the habits of political and personal trust and obedience, consequent upon the legitimate rule of a legitimate monarch, have all broken down. As the play makes clear, this condition is as typical of, and even more fatally deleterious in its effects on, the rebel cause than the king's.

All the political players have been forced to make their determinations, to calculate their advantages and make their decisions in terms of the actions and

intentions of others, the nature and motivation of which they can only imperfectly comprehend, and of which – if the basic dictates and promptings of
political prudence and self-preservation are to be observed – they must think
the worst and therefore remain mightily afraid.

Throughout *Richard II*, and in both parts of *Henry IV*, all the major players,
and the audience, operate in something like a fog of unclarity, sometimes almost
of disinformation. At very turn there are major events that remain shrouded in
mystery, so cloaked in the claims and counter-claims of the participants that it is
impossible either for us, or indeed for the participants themselves, finally to
know what actually happened. Thus in *Richard II* we never find out just who
killed Gloucester. The question of Bolingbroke's character and motivation
remains unresolved throughout all three plays. Was he a usurper plotting to gain
the crown from the outset? If not, when, how and why did he decide to seize the
throne? Did Mortimer change sides and join with Glendower in rebellion, as
Henry claims, or was he the loyal subject defeated in the service of his prince
and then left to rot in captivity, because Henry knew he had a better claim to the
throne, described by Hotspur? Whose idea was it to depose Richard? Were the
Percies the victims of the ambition and deceit of Bolingbroke, of their own
ambition or of events? Did Northumberland betray his son or was he really ill?
None of this is rendered clear to the audience because, of course, none of it is
clear to the participants. That, in part II, a chorus-like role is accorded to a character named 'Rumour' can only serve to drive this point home the more firmly.
In the scene between Hotspur and Henry IV in which they produce diametrically opposed versions of Mortimer's conduct in his campaigns against
Glendower, Harry Berger Jr sees both of them interpreting, with equal certainty,
reports of Mortimer's subsequent marriage to Glendower's daughter in ways
that make sense of their current interests and suspicions.[17] This, then, is how the
fog of rumour, the cloud of unclarity, the fatal lack of precise information about
the nature of events and, in particular, about the nature of the motivations,
intentions and actions, not only of others but even of oneself, come to dominate
the delegitimised world created by usurpation, tyranny and rebellion and the
calculations, the half-truths, the rewritings of the recent past, the acts of both
self- and other-directed deception that such actions inevitably set in train. This
was a major symptom of the 'disease' that Archbishop Scroop pictured afflicting
the commonwealth, the common condition of (fallen) political man in a world
stripped of legitimacy.

However, for all that, none of the circumlocutions, the passive verbs, naturalising metaphors and images, the partial explanations, denials and shiftings of
the blame, used by these men to talk about their pasts and the present are
adequate to what the play reveals actually to have happened, and, amongst the
culprits, it is King Henry who comes closest to recognising that fact. As he gives
his dying advice to his son he blurts out, almost as an aside, 'God knows, my

son,/By what by-paths and indirect crook'd ways/I met this crown, and I myself know well/How troublesome it sat upon my head . . . it seem'd in me/But as an honour snatch'd with boisterous hand' [Pt. II, IV, v, 183–85]. The almost unconscious progress from denial to something like acknowledgement represented by the transition in that passage from 'met' to 'snatch'd' reveals the depth of the denial, the practised surface of pretence, that has prevented all of these men from coming to terms with their actions. But even now that remark is not the start of an elaborated statement of responsibility, still less of repentance, but rather of a stream of essentially political advice from father to son on how the son might best keep the throne that the father has 'met' or rather 'snatched' for him. Henry gets closest to genuine acceptance and repentance at the very end of the speech with the simple exhalation 'how came I by the crown, O God forgive,/And grant it may with thee in true peace live' [Pt. II, IV, v, 218–19]. This is the functional equivalent of the 'God pardon its' with which, at the start of Part I, the Percies had peppered their own deeply indirect and distanced accounts of their role in Richard's end and Henry's rise. While Henry's statement is clearly far more deeply felt than their perfunctory gestures towards their own sins, this is as close as even Henry can get to acknowledging or naming, let alone owning and still less repenting for, his role in the deposition and murder of Richard and usurpation of the throne. And indeed, given the political necessities that prompted his initial rebellion and usurpation, and the fact that even on his deathbed, that same necessity is leading him to cling to the crown with all the cunning and force at his disposal, it is not at all clear that Henry can, in any genuinely effectual way, repent his actions, even as, in the face of death and judgement, he acknowledges their potentially damning nature.[18] As we shall see, in *Henry V* essentially the same constraints – the fact that whatever repentance he can muster comes 'after all', that is to say, after the rush of deceptions, coups, murders and deceits that have given his father and then him the crown – apply almost as much to the son as to the father; rendering Henry's attempts to repent for the sins of his father, in effect, nugatory.

The politics of religion and prophecy

Henry IV had ended *Richard II* promising to go on crusade to expiate the sin of Richard's death and entered the action of *1 Henry IV* planning that same crusade, only to have his plans shattered by the outbreak of foreign broils and civil war at home. Now on his deathbed his thoughts turn to the crusading project again, not as some Mowbray-like act of repentance or expiation for his sins, but rather as an entirely secular, politique way to mend the internal political divisions in the kingdom occasioned by the manner of his own rise to power. As he explains to his son, 'All my friends, which thou must make thy friends,/Have but their stings and teeth newly ta'en out;/By whose fell working

I was first advanc'd,/And by whose power I well might lodge a fear/To be again displac'd; which to avoid,/I cut them off, and had a purpose now/To lead out many to the Holy Land,/Lest rest and lying still might make them look/Too near unto my state. Therefore, my Harry,/Be it thy course to busy giddy minds/ With foreign quarrels, that action hence borne out/May waste the memory of the former days' [Pt. II, IV, v, 192–215]. This amounts to the conversion of what had entered Henry's consciousness in *Richard II* as an intensely religious act, into a mere act of state. In *Richard II* the crusade had been presented as the means whereby Mowbray, whose hands had been stained by the blood of Gloucester, had expiated his sins and prepared him for what is reported as his unequivocally good death in Venice. Now going on crusade has morphed into the conduct of any old 'foreign quarrel' as a diversionary means to cement first Bolingbroke's and then his son's hold on power. On this evidence, Henry's dying concerns are not (only or even mainly) spiritual but intensely this-worldly. Even on his deathbed, what preoccupies him (as in the popularity scene cited above from part I) is the transfer to his hitherto wayward son of the political lessons, the techniques and manoeuvres, the tricks of the trade, that first acquired the crown for 'that vile politician Bolingbroke', and will now (as he thinks) – properly learnt and applied – allow his son and heir to keep it.

Unlike Richard II and John, we do not see Henry IV die. That event is reserved, in what may be either a consolatory or an ironic gesture, to the privacy of 'the Jerusalem chamber'. 'It hath been prophesied to me,' explains Henry, 'many years/I should not die but in Jerusalem,/Which vainly I suppos'd the Holy Land./But bear me to that chamber; there I'll lie;/In that Jerusalem shall Harry die' [Pt. II, IV, v, 236–40]. So Henry does get to Jerusalem in the end, but unlike his old adversary Mowbray, who got both to the real one and to heaven, the precise nature of Henry's ultimate destination is left hanging.[19]

The overwhelmingly secular, this-worldly focus of Henry's all but deathbed scene (and certainly of what is his last interview with his son) is entirely typical of the overall tenor of these plays, in which the prodigious and the supernatural, the prophetic and the providential and, indeed, the religious, are pushed to the very margins both of the action and, indeed, of the consciousness of the major players. There is no equivalent of the pious and prophetic Carlisle; the only churchman on view is Scroop, who it is reported was 'suppos'd sincere and holy in his thoughts' but who is shown throughout as a politician, playing to the people, appealing to 'the commonwealth', 'turning insurrection to religion' and then insurrection into what he takes to be political advantage [Pt. II, I, i, 201–2]. The world of prophecy and providential signs and prognostications is associated with the absurd superstitions and fancies of Glendower [Pt. I, III, i, 145–46, 153], who spends hours recounting the miraculous harbingers of a special destiny that had attended his birth and, we are told, is eventually prevented by a prophecy from joining the rebel forces at Shrewsbury, thus (with the equally but differently delinquent Northumberland) ensuring their defeat.

In these plays, even more than in *King John*, the delegitimised world of commodity, of political manoeuvre and struggle, unleashed by usurpation, tyranny and resistance, is shown in almost entirely secular terms. Once loosed upon the world, 'the disease', as Scroop describes it, of factionalism, political calculation and the ceaseless search for vantage and security comes to obsess those involved in it, plunging them into a world of manoeuvre and counter-manoeuvre in which (even on their deathbeds) religion itself becomes a tactic with which to legitimise or raise support for actions rendered necessary by attendant political circumstance; in short, just another means to further the immediate needs and interests of the political actors involved.

In one crucial scene the play shows us this mentality, this settled propensity, at work in an exchange between King Henry and the earl of Warwick. Ill and laid up at court, the king is receiving news of the various rebellions besetting his kingdom and has recourse to the same (standard) medical metaphor or image used by Scroop [Pt. II, III, i, 38–44]. At this point Henry waxes reflective, even philosophical. 'O God, that one might read the book of fate,/And see the revolution of the times/Make mountains level, and the continent,/Weary of solid firmness, melt itself . . . How chance's mocks/And changes fill the cup of alteration/With divers liquors! O, if this were seen,/The happiest youth, viewing this progress through,/What perils past, what crosses to ensue,/Would shut the book and sit him down and die./'Tis not ten years gone,/Since Richard and Northumberland, great friends,/Did feast together, and in two years after/Were they at wars. It is but eight years since,/This Percy was the man nearest my soul;/Who like a brother toil'd in my affairs,/And laid his love and life under my foot;/Yea, for my sake, even to the eyes of Richard/Gave him defiance.' But Bolingbroke has, of course, been vouchsafed just such a view of the future and he had been given it by none other than Richard himself. 'Which of you was by –/You, cousin Neville, as I may remember –/When Richard, with his eye brimful of tears,/Then check'd and rated by Northumberland,/Did speak these words, now prov'd a prophecy?/"Northumberland, thou ladder by the which/My cousin Bolingbroke ascends my throne . . . The time shall come" – and thus did he follow it –/ "The time will come, that foul sin, gathering head,/Shall break into corruption" – so went on,/Foretelling this same time's condition,/And the division of our amity'[Pt. II, III, i, 65–79]. For the sickening king, Richard's words appear to be a very prophecy, foretelling his and the realm's doom, but Warwick glosses it differently. This was no prophecy but a mere prediction, a piece of political prognostication, based on a close observation of the laws of political probability, applying the lessons of past and current behaviour to the near future. There was no trick to that, Warwick argued; we all knew that score and could react accordingly. 'There is a history in all men's lives/

Figuring the nature of the times deceas'd;/The which observ'd, a man may prophesy/Which near aim, of the main chance of things/As yet not come to life, who in their seeds/And weak beginnings lie intreasured./Such things become the hatch and brood of time;/And by the necessary form of this/King Richard might create a perfect guess/That great Northumberland, then false to him,/Would of that seed grow to a greater falseness,/Which should not find a ground to root upon/Unless on you' [Pt. II, III, I, 80–92].

On this basis, therefore, Richard's prophecy is a prophecy precisely like that of Pandulph proffered to the dauphin in *King John*; that is to say it is no prophecy at all. Coming with no supernatural authority or aura, its predictions were precisely that, predictions, political prognostications, based upon a superior knowledge of, or insight into, the rules of policy and statecraft. As such, the outcomes Richard had foretold were neither certain nor inevitable, but merely likely. Indeed, the outcomes foretold by Richard were the more subject to change, the more readily averted, the more his 'prophecy', and the presuppositions and maxims that underpinned it, were taken to heart and factored into their own calculations by those at the centre of events. Doom-laden, the king still harks on the notion that the fatal outcomes that Richard has foretold are inevitable. 'Are these things then necessities?/Then let us meet them like necessities,' he moans, only to be told, in effect, to pull himself together. He should go to bed and let 'the powers that you already have sent forth' mop up the remaining rebel forces. 'I will take your counsel' [Pt. II, III, I, 92–93, 100–1, 106], Henry replies, before returning to his sickbed.

CHAPTER 13

Learning to be a bastard: Hal's second (plebeian) nature

Just as John's slide into moral and then physical decline, physical and moral lassitude and death, begins from the moment he starts to compass Arthur's death, so in *Henry IV* the king's moral and physical decline starts from the moment that Hal saves him at Shrewsbury from the savage assault of the Douglas. And Henry's slide into illness, impotence and panic is paralleled by the transformation of Hal from the princely ne'er-do-well, who enters the action of part I, into the chivalric hero and model prince who ends the action of part II. Base-born and brought up in the provinces as he is, the bastard has no trouble epitomising a certain plebeian Englishness, the boisterous violence and energy, the spontaneous loyalty and loathing of foreign invasion and rule, which provides *King John* with one of its central themes and major sources of legitimacy. As a bastard, what he cannot do is provide the dynastic bit of legitimacy; in *King John* that has to come from elsewhere – from the *deus ex machina* of Henry III, in fact.

As the legitimate son of the reigning monarch Hal has no problem with the dynastic bit of legitimacy; the capacity that he has to acquire is something that the bastard can do quite naturally: that is, represent in his person and character, instinctively understand and manipulate in favour of his own rule, the spontaneous, festive, violent Englishness that oozes out of the bastard's every pore. Or to put the matter another way, just as the bastard, precisely because he is a bastard, has to be remade as a member of the royal family in order to emerge, as he does in the second half of the play, as a genuinely princely presence, so Hal, precisely because he is the legitimate issue of a reigning monarch, has to retrain as a bastard before he can emerge, as he does at the end of part II and throughout *Henry V*, as the true prince, able to elicit and mobilise the spontaneous valour and prowess of the English in the war against the foreigner and in the interests of royal power.

The play is quite clear that Hal performs this task of bastardisation effectively enough to prompt a series of quite remarkable comments on or queries about his legitimacy. If the bastard's career shows that royal blood will out, Hal's shows that the reverse is also true: royal is as royal does. Early on in part I, Henry is told of the martial exploits of Hotspur. He replies with an extraordinary flight of fancy, a fantasy that his Harry is supposititious, swapped at birth with young Harry Percy, who, unlike Hal, has all the outward marks and characteristics of honour [Pt. I, I, i, 77–89]. When, in the cold light of day, Henry is forced to acknowledge the prince as his own, he configures him as a judgement sent by God, 'marked/For the hot vengeance and the rod of heaven,/ To punish my mistreadings' [Pt. I, III, ii, 8–17]. So unnatural a son has Hal's behaviour made him appear that his father again fantasises that he will 'fight against me under Percy's pay,/To dog his heels and curtsy at his frowns,/To show how much thou art degenerate' [Pt. I, III, ii, 124–28]. Indeed, it appears later that Henry has come to suspect that Hal wants him dead, the quicker to inherit the crown. On this account, then, Hal's behaviour, his carryings-on in Eastcheap, the low company he has kept there with Falstaff and his mates, have all rendered him 'degenerate', an unnatural traitor to 'the greatness of his blood' and thus to his father the king. He has, in effect, delegitimised himself by taking on an acquired second nature at variance with the 'greatness' and honour inherent in his (royal) 'blood'.

As for Falstaff, at one point he simply greets Hal as 'a bastard son of the King's' [Pt. II, II, iv, 280]. Later, as Hal admits that he is ashamed to show how sad he is about his father's apparently fatal illness he asks Poins 'What wouldst thou think of me if I should weep?' 'I would think thee a most princely hypocrite,' replies Poins. 'It would be everyman's thought,' agrees the prince. 'And thou art a blessed fellow, to think as every man thinks. Never a man's thought in the world keeps the roadway better than thine: every man would think me a hypocrite indeed. And what accites your most worshipful thought to think so?' 'Why, because you have been so lewd, and so much engraffed to Falstaff,' comes the inevitable reply [Pt. II, II, ii, 50–59].

Nor was the conceit of Harry's supposititious illegitimacy limited to his irate father and his boon companions; some version of it creeps even into Harry's account of himself. He has not been 'himself', he admits, in the course of an interview during which his ranting and railing father again taunts him with the reproachful example of Hotspur's excellence and his own ruin. 'I shall hereafter, my thrice gracious lord,/be more myself,' claims the prince [Pt. I, III, ii, 92–93]. And 'being more myself' means killing his alter ego Hotspur [Pt. I, III, ii, 132–37]. On this account, in his current debased condition, he cannot as yet tell his father 'I am your son'. In order to do so, he must relegitimise himself, and he can only do that by washing himself clean of the dishonour of his recent conduct by the shedding of Hotspur's blood, through which act he will also add the lustre of Percy's deeds to his own.

While Henry had been afraid of the dissolute Hal, it is the reformed prince, now cleansed by the blood sacrifice of Percy's death, his filial honour vindicated by his rescue of his father on the field of battle, who proves fatal to the king. For from the moment that he comes to the aid of his father at Shrewsbury the balance of power between the two starts to shift. Henry immediately starts the decline into the illness, doubt, infirmity and even, at times, despair, which, throughout part II, removes him from the centre of events and culminates in his death. There is, then, a series of distinctly odd transactions taking place here between the three Henrys, that is to say between the king, Hotspur and Hal.

The pleasures and perils of 'popularity'

But before we can turn to that subject we need to deal with the fourth party to these transactions, Hal's, as it were, other, surrogate father, Falstaff, and with that second, acquired, plebeian, 'bastard', nature which Hal has gone to such lengths to take on in the stews and taverns of Eastcheap. The play provides us with a number of accounts of why Hal repairs so often to the low company to be found at the Boar's Head. The first comes from the horse's mouth as Hal, having been left alone on the stage by Poins, explains to no one in particular that 'I know you all, and will uphold/The unyoked humour of your idleness./ Yet herein will I imitate the sun,/Who doth permit the base contagious clouds/ To smother up his beauty from the world,/That, when he please again to be himself,/Being wanted, he may more be wondered at/By breaking through the foul and ugly mists/Of vapours that did seem to strangle him./If all the year were playing holidays,/To sport would be as tedious as to work;/But when they seldom come, they wished-for come,/And nothing pleaseth but rare accidents./ So when this loose behaviour I throw off,/And pay the debt I never promised,/ By how much better than my word I am,/By so much shall I falsify men's hopes;/And, like the bright metal on a sullen ground,/My reformation, glittering o'er my fault,/Shall show more goodly and attract more eyes/Than that which hath no foil to set it off./I'll so offend to make offence a skill,/Redeeming time when men think least I will' [Pt I, I, ii, 190–212]. This version of the prince's motives, of his real relationship to – in but not of – the society of the Boar's Head, comes early in part I. It is echoed and confirmed by a later remark from the prince to his father, made as he assures Henry (again) that he does not want him dead. 'If I do feign,/O, let me in my present wildness die,/And never live to show th'incredulous world/The noble change that I have purposed!' [Pt. II, IV, v, 151–54].

If, therefore, we simply accept what Hal says about himself here, and indeed what Warwick says about him elsewhere, it would appear that he does not need his father's lectures on the image management necessary to carry off a successful royal politics of popularity. Indeed, not only does he not need his father's advice, that advice is arguably inappropriate, consisting, as it does, of the claim that Hal should merely emulate what his father had done when, as Bolingbroke, he had been an aspirant; a rival of king Richard's, first for public applause and, then, finally, for the crown itself. But Hal is precisely not in that position, but rather the heir of 'anointed', if also deeply tainted, 'majesty'.

The king, of course, is in no position to see his son's planned double act of self-fashioning, the first time as rake, the second time as 'true prince', as a strategy for taking advantage of his status as the hereditary heir to a usurper. But the audience know full well that Hal is about to become not any old king but Henry V, and the passages cited above, the most extended of which comes very early in part I, seem designed to confirm to them that Hal's sojourn in the stews of Eastcheap is a carefully constructed 'before' that was always going to be followed by a spectacularly reformed 'after'; part, in fact, of strategy designed to maximise the political advantage, the popular attention and wonderment, to be gleaned from the transition from the reign of an old king, tainted by usurpation and civil strife, to that of his son, coming to the throne through an unchallenged hereditary right, untainted by his father's 'crimes' and, in Hal's case, newly converted from a spectacularly misspent youth to the path of princely virtue and honour. As Robert Ornstein puts it, Hal intended to be 'a self made prince, he would have the future without the past, the crown without its attendant guilt'. 'Making a scapegoat of Henry IV, who, he declares, has gone "wild into his grave" with Hal's affections, he contrives to be born again with a new mythic paternity – the son of Justice and Good Government.'[1]

As any number of critics have pointed out, Hal is playing the starring role in his own version of the return of the prodigal. But there are other, even more exalted, religious scripts taken from the scriptures and the mystery plays that Hal is acting out in his various metamorphoses. As Beatrice Groves has argued, in Hal's interview with his father in 1 Henry IV, III, ii, 'Hal's emphatic "I am your son" [III, ii, 134] arrogates to himself the proud kinship of Gethsemane rather than the humility of the prodigal who tells his father: ' "I am no more worthie to be called thy sonne." ' In the same exchange, Hal's reworks Isaiah, telling his father that he will 'wear a garment all of blood' and answers 'the question "who is this?" with a triumphal "I am your son" ' As Groves observes, 'Hal, like the authors of Revelation and the mystery plays, recalls Isaiah 63 as he looks forward to the time when a battle has been won and father and son will be reunited.'[2] Perhaps more remarkably still, when he rejects Falstaff at the end of the play, his words – 'I know thee not, old man. Fall to thy prayers' [V, v. 47] – recall, as Edward Berry points out, Christ's response to the foolish virgins.[3]

To this material can be added recent readings of Hal's first soliloquy in which he promises 'to imitate the sun'. Michael Davies and Phebe Jensen have both discerned what they call 'standard Calvinist puns on the "sun" and the "Son" ' operating in this passage, which they also read as reverberating with contemporary hot protestant talk about 'the sun of the gospel' dissipating the clouds of popish error and superstition of the sort beloved of Elizabethan anti-papal preachers and polemicists.[4] The explicitly Christian – it is by no means clear why it is distinctively 'Calvinist' – play on words involved here revolves around the 'sun' and the 'Son of God', i.e. Jesus Christ. Many critics have also seen Hal punning, in this speech, on the association between the 'sun' and himself as the 'son of the king'. If he were taken also to be playing on the secondary, explicitly Christological, set of associations, laid out by Davies and Jensen, then something remarkable would be happening, since Hal would then be comparing himself more or less directly to Christ, while solemnly explaining how, on a timetable entirely of his own making, he will stage his own 'reformation'; a process which he describes as 'pleasing again to be himself', in other words entirely as a function of his own design and choice. And all this the more effectively to attract the admiring eyes 'of men' to the prodigious nature of an apparently sudden, semi-miraculous, but, in fact, long plotted, personal 'reformation'. Real Calvinists, of course, attributed the achievement of true reformation and the experience of conversion to the workings of divine, rather than of human, will and sovereignty.

In these passages Shakespeare is showing us Hal/Henry using such scripture phrases, types and tropes to build up his own legend and image. The play thus gives us ample warrant to see the whole performance as an entirely self-conscious and calculated attempt to appropriate phrases and images, culled from scripture and previously staged in and through sacred drama and liturgical performance, all of them closely associated with Christ, in order to legitimise, indeed to remystify, or, better yet, to resacralise, the power and person of an earthly prince, after the tyranny of Richard II and the usurpation and regicide of his father have threatened to reduce 'the divinity that doth hedge a king' almost to nothing.[5]

The central example of all this is provided, of course, by Henry's 'reformation', or conversion, which, in contemporary Christian, let alone 'Calvinist', terms, is nothing of the sort. As Michael Davies points out, 'Shakespeare's principal historical sources reported (in distinctly Reformed terms too) how Henry V underwent a miraculous change upon becoming king', as too, of course, did the *Famous victories*, which has Hal, coming upon his father with a drawn dagger, intending to kill him, only to be struck with remorse – 'my conscience accuseth me'[6] – and then beg his father's forgiveness in the most spontaneous and passionate of terms. What Davies fails to note is that far from having had 'very little choice in the matter',[7] and simply reproducing this version, Shakespeare, in fact, refused to have anything to do with it, omitting any such miraculous change or conversion in the prince and instead presenting Hal's reformation as the culmination of a long-settled plan. Since the *Famous victories* almost certainly provided considerable sections of the play's first audiences with their basic point of reference for Henry V's reign none of this is likely to have escaped their notice.

Moreover, if Henry's consequent amendment of life – his rejection of Falstaff and turning away from the ways of his youth – is definitive and complete, it is so (at least in part) because his earlier attachment to Falstaff and his wanton ways had been (at the very least, in part) feigned. What we are confronted with, then, is a performance calculated for effect, from which (throughout the play) Hal has been able, seemingly at will, to distance himself and comment upon, as though in the third person. As we shall see below, this is, at best, only a partial account of the nature and intensity of Hal's attachment to Falstaff and the milieu of the Boar's Head, but it is one which the play itself goes out of its way, on a number of occasions, to establish. Indeed, all of the soliloquies allowed to Hal before his final encounter with the crown and his father in Act IV scene v of part 2 are designed to reinforce precisely this version of his behaviour.

If we take this material seriously, we must conclude that the play is showing us Hal using some of the central themes of Christianity as mere outward forms, means to play with and play on the beliefs and expectations of a Christian audience or populace. The play shows us Hal planning a *coup de théâtre* which will look just like the sudden and complete change – the genuinely miraculous conversion – undergone by Hal in the *Famous victories* but which will, in fact, be no such thing.[8] We are very close here to watching a prince use Christianity as a form of civil religion; adopting sacred narrative forms and types to effect entirely secular, political ends and outcomes. For the play shows us Hal carefully scripting, and then performing, his own emergence, not only as the epitome of the Christian prince but as a sort of Christ-figure, and doing so with a degree of self-consciousness, indeed of calculation, entirely incompatible with post-reformation – either Catholic or protestant – notions of true conversion or, indeed, of true religion.

Davies is thus quite right to note the parallels between contemporary Calvinist and even puritan norms of speech and behaviour and Hal's attitude towards both Falstaff's and his own 'repentance' and 'amendment of life', but he misses the entirely strategic and performative nature of Hal's recourse to those forms. In both cases, while the forms might be recognisably Calvinist, there is absolutely nothing 'reformed', distinctively 'godly' or 'Calvinist' – although, according to the canons of contemporary anti-puritanism, there might well be something typically 'puritan' – about the self-conscious contrivance, indeed the hypocrisy, of the resulting performance, for entirely political purposes, of the mere outward forms of personal godliness, repentance and conversion.

The contrast being established here is, of course, between Falstaff and Hal; but it is not one between the godly and the profane, the elect saint and the reprobate sinner but rather between two different sorts of political *actor*; between someone – Falstaff – who mimics puritan forms of speech and affect as a joking way to get away with what remain wholly corrupt private purposes, and someone else – Hal – who uses those same outward forms to further a genuinely virtuous, entirely public, but still quintessentially political, agenda.

That Hal/Henry's adoption of those forms is empty is shown by the fact that he never displays any doubt about the virtue or righteousness of his own purposes or character. The eventual *coup de théâtre*, the definitive performance of his 'reformation', the final revelation of his true 'self', will come only when *he* is 'pleased again to be myself'. The inherent virtue of the 'self' being reclaimed here is simply assumed and the timing of that act of 'reformation' has everything to do with Hal/Henry and nothing to do with God. That was in itself a remarkable enough claim in a religious culture which saw the impulse to defer repentance and the assumption that it lay within the capacity of fallen humanity to decide when and how to repent as defining characteristics, at best, of the unregenerate, and, at worst, if repeated or serially indulged, of the reprobate. At no point does Hal betray any sense of the extent or seriousness of his own sins or any need for some sort of soul-shattering or life-altering repentance or amendment of life.[9] To call this, with Davies, an 'orthodox, Calvinist conversion' or, with Womersley, to cite it as an example of an assertively protestant 'justified monarch' seems to me to be devoid of textual warrant, either in the play itself, or in the surrounding religious and cultural materials of which the play was constructed and to which it spoke.[10] Moreover, if we imagine, as we surely should, that many Elizabethans were a good deal more attuned to the scriptural and theological resonances set off by the play than many modern critics have been,[11] we must conclude that these implications were extremely unlikely to have been lost on at least some of the play's first audiences.

But there was more going on here than a staged return of the prodigal, or indeed of Hal as the risen Christ. In a long excursus on the reasons for the prince's conduct, Warwick tries to comfort the ailing king as he lies tormented by what he sees as his son's irredeemable wildness and corruption. 'My gracious lord, you look beyond him quite./The Prince but studies his companions/Like a strange tongue, wherein, to gain the language,/'Tis needful that the most immodest word/Be look'd upon and learnt; which once attain'd,/Your Highness knows, comes to no further use/But to be known and hated. So, like gross terms,/The Prince will, in the perfectness of time,/Cast off his followers, and their memory/Shall as a pattern or a measure live/By which his Grace must mete the lives of other,/Turning past evils to advantages' [Pt. II, IV, iv, 67–78]. On Warwick's account of Hal, as on Hal's account of himself, his purpose in hanging out in the stews, rather than an exercise in youthful wildness, a holiday of royal juvenile delinquency, is quite deliberate. He is trying to learn, 'like a strange tongue', the nature and mores of his people, the better to be able, later, to appeal to and manipulate, to govern and control, the emotions and allegiance of his subjects, benefiting the while from his repudiation of the very vices he now only seems to be indulging. Each of these rationales for Hal's (mis)behaviour has the prince always clear in his intentions, fully in control of his emotions, identity and actions, and both are confirmed by the later change in the prince's nature; a change which any members of the audience who have seen *The famous victories* know only too well is coming.

It is, however, far from clear that this is all that is going on in Eastcheap; the confusions and shapings of identity, the emotional and ideological attachments and transformations that we are shown taking place there insistently call into question so straightforwardly instrumental a view of the prince's purposes and experience. While these materials do not falsify or refute the instrumentalist view, outlined above, they certainly complicate and qualify it.

In a crucial scene, the prince tells Poins that 'I am sworn brother to a leash of drawers, and can call them all by their Christian names, as Tom, Dick and Francis. They take it already, upon their salvation, that, though I be but Prince of Wales, yet I am the king of courtesy, and tell me flatly I am no proud jack, like Falstaff, but a Corinthian, a lad of mettle, a good boy – by the lord, so they call me – and when I am King of England I shall command all the good lads in Eastcheap. They call drinking deep "dyeing scarlet", and, when you breathe in your watering, they cry "Hem!" and bid you "Play it off!" To conclude, I am so good a proficient in one quarter of an hour that I can drink with any tinker in his own language during my life' [Pt. I, II, iv, 3–20]. Hal, then, can pass amongst the lowest elements even in Eastcheap society. Here is the fantasy figure of a prince immersing himself in his people, becoming one of them, passing amongst them in more than the obvious sense. There are transformations taking place here of an almost magical, mythical quality and Hal delights in them seemingly for their own sake. In part II, as he and Poins are again about to disguise themselves as drawers to take Falstaff by surprise in the Boar's Head, Hal compares his metamorphosis from the hero of Shrewsbury into a mere drawer to that of Jupiter who, for love of Europa, turned himself into a bull. 'From a God to a bull? A heavy descension! It was Jove's case. From a prince to a prentice? A low transformation, that shall be mine, for in everything the purpose must weigh with the folly' [Pt. II, II, ii, 166–69].

But Hal's exultant conversation with Poins is immediately followed by a series of decidedly odd exchanges with both Poins and Francis. First, Hal recounts the whole affair in mock-heroic terms – 'thou hast lost much honour that thou wert not with me in this action'. Then he stages as 'a jest' what amounts to a humiliation ritual for his erstwhile drinking companion, Francis. He stations Poins in the next room, to keep calling the poor lad away from his conversation with the prince. Then Hal sets about taunting Francis with the terms and conditions of his apprenticeship, dandling the prospect of liberty and of fantastic rewards in front of him, before dismissing him with the words 'away, you rogue, dost thou not hear them call' [Pt. I, II, iv, 25–77].

Significantly, the point of this so-called 'jest of the drawer' is entirely lost on Poins. 'Come, what's the issue?' he asks, and it is a good question. On the one hand, the issue seems to be the proof of the prince's difference from Francis. The scene represents a carefully staged demonstration of what the prince sees as the poor boy's gormless stupidity. 'That ever this fellow should have fewer words than a parrot, and yet the son of a woman! His industry is upstairs and down stairs, his eloquence the parcel of a reckoning' [Pt. I, II, iv, 96–99]. On this evidence, Hal finds the whole experience of shedding his identity as the prince, of immersing himself in the milieu of the Boar's Head, of taking on social personae and identities other than his own, immensely enjoyable and exhilarating. But having, with such evident pleasure and abandon, lost himself in the company of the apprentices and drawers, he needs immediately to distance himself from the experience; to demonstrate or reassert his complete difference from and superiority over his erstwhile drinking companions. It is as though the experience of shedding his skin as the prince, of denaturing and losing himself in the lowest ranks of the social order, of becoming, albeit for a transient moment, all but fully integrated into the body of the people, has been so seductively pleasurable, so alternately exhilarating and frightening, that he needs to stage an immediate withdrawal, a carefully choreographed demonstration of Francis' bestial stupidity ('fewer words than a parrot') and of his own ineffable superiority.

At stake here is the whole issue of royalness. The storyline of the royal personage in disguise amongst the people operated around the self-evident royalness, the inherent difference or apartness of the royal person; the proximity of disguised ruler and ruled was not meant to efface, or even to question, the separate status of the ruler, but rather to bring into magically close proximity entities or natures that remained entirely distinct. What Hal has experienced here, and indeed experiences elsewhere in the play, is rather the opposite; his disguise, his shift of identity, has worked all too well; so well, in fact, that he is no longer instantly recognisable, certainly to others and perhaps even to himself, as different.

If these dynamics of changed identity and transference explain this staged scene with Francis they can also be discerned in what happened during and after the Gadshill robbery. The prince and Poins had managed to part the robbers from their swag by merely threatening violence. Falstaff comes back to the Boar's Head, accusing Hal of cowardice for leaving the robbers in the lurch and swearing that they have been robbed by overwhelming numbers and that only after a protracted fight, in which he has killed at least a couple of his assailants. The joke is, of course, that they have been parted from their ill-gotten gains by two men without a blow being struck and that Poins and Hal know it because they were the two men involved. Confronted and momentarily confounded by this ruse, Falstaff claims that he only ran away from the prince because he knew, 'by instinct' who he was and could not allow himself to fight against the heir to the throne. 'The lion will not touch the true prince; instinct is a great matter. I was now a coward on instinct. I shall think the better of myself, and thee, during my life – I for a valiant lion and thou for a true prince' [Pt. I, II, iv, 259–66]. The ironies here are deep and multiple. For Falstaff did not, of course, recognise the prince. The only instinct in play had been his own cowardice. On this view, then, far from enhancing the mystique of royal differ-ence, Hal's sojourn in disguise amongst his people is having precisely the oppo-site effect; it is calling into radical question precisely what it meant to be royal and the consequent loss of identity and charisma was clearly something that Hal himself found alternately intoxicating and threatening, as his treatment of poor Francis the drawer shows. On this view of the matter, Hal might be taken to stand in greater need of his father's lectures on the demystifying, even dele-gitimising, effects of too much 'popularity' than at first sight might appear. For on this evidence, Hal is less in control of himself and of what is happening to him in Eastcheap than his own and others' accounts of his sojourn there might lead us to believe.

But we can go further than this. Let us remind ourselves just what the pros-pect was with which Hal was taunting young Francis. He started by challenging him to leave his apprenticeship: 'Francis, darest thou be so valiant as to play the coward with thy indenture, and show it a fair pair of heels, and run from it?' [Pt. II, II, iv, 45–47]. He ended by inciting him not merely to desert but to rob his master; 'wilt thou rob this leather-jerkin, crystal button, not-pated, agate-ring, puke-stocking, caddis-garter, smooth-tongue, Spanish-pouch?' [Pt. II, II, iv, 67–70]. In between those jeering questions he had offered Francis a reward of 'a thousand pound'. The prince, then, is offering Francis the prospect of a utopian desertion of, or liberation from, social destiny and identity. He can, on Hal's account, simply leave his apprenticeship, rob his master and be rewarded for it into the bargain. In a stroke, Francis can be liberated from all the social and psychological constraints that went with working in the calling in which God had placed him. But this, of course, was a transcendence to which the likes of Francis could not aspire – except that it was the prince of Wales who was offering that prospect to him and if there was anyone who could remove him, as if by magic, from his current circumstances, not merely licensing but rewarding with unimaginable sums, the dereliction of social and legal duty, it was indeed the prince of Wales.

But in hanging out in Eastcheap Hal himself had been playing with the pros-pect of just such a cost-and-consequence-free transcendence of or escape from his own ascribed social role and identity. He, too, at least in play, has been running away from his indentures as prince of Wales, robbing his master/father, the king, and rewarding himself into the bargain with a thousand pounds. The identification with Francis staged by this scene is thus much more intense than that established by the binge of drunken play-acting so jocularly described by Hal to Poins. Even as he torments Francis, using the public demonstration of what he takes to be the young drawer's bestial stupidity to distance himself from his previous identification with the lad and his mates, Hal is in fact identifying yet more intensely with the poor lad's predicament. As Hal ridicules Francis, it is his own illusions and aspirations, his own escape fantasies and identity shifts, his own confusion about which call to answer, that he is both playing out and ridiculing, inhabiting and distancing himself from. The viciousness of his contempt for Francis, the intensity of his determination to re-establish social and intellectual distance between them, is, therefore, a function of the intensity of the mixed and merged identities, the half-acknowledged aspirations and anxieties, that are still, in fact, binding them together.

On this view of the matter, it is perhaps unsurprising that Poins cannot see the point of the 'joke'. But in answer to his bemused question 'what's the issue', Hal gives us another clue to the real intensity that has underlain these exchanges. 'I am now of all humours that have showed themselves humours since the old days of Goodman Adam to the pupil age of this present twelve o'clock at midnight', he claims [Pt. I, II, iv, 90–93]. This is a triumphant, indeed a transcendent, claim. As a future king and current prince, the epitome of God-given order and authority, Hal is descending from his royal apartness to identify himself with, indeed to immerse or incorporate himself in, the body of his people. As we shall see below, with Falstaff, Hal is embracing and acting out the norms and forms of misrule and with the likes of Francis seeking to inhabit the subject position of persons whose experience would otherwise be entirely closed to him. It is on the basis of such experiences that he makes his claim to be the heir to what amounts to all human experience.

But what follows next shows that claim to be, at best and as yet, imperfectly realised. For Hal's speech on Francis's subhuman stupidity continues, without a break, into a mocking description of the young Percy's obsession with martial prowess and honour. As we saw earlier, Hotspur was continually held up by the king both to Hal himself, and, indeed, to others, as a model of what the prince should be. But if he can't and won't fully immerse himself in Francis' world, Hal won't immerse himself in Hotspur's either, or at least not yet. Poised, undecided, between these different, rival versions or projections of himself and his future, the prince calls for Falstaff and another round of festive play-acting. 'I prithee, call in Falstaff. I'll play Percy, and that damned brawn shall play Dame Mortimer his wife. "Rivo!" Says the drunkard; call in Ribs; call in Tallow' [Pt. I, II, iv, 99–108]. Here, then, is Hal caught between his ludic engagement with the world of the Boar's Head, and the world of princely honour and military prowess, between the world not merely of Francis the drawer (who is easily put in his place) but also of Falstaff (who is not) and that of Hotspur. Caught in a sort of limbo, in a genuinely and dangerously liminal space, between those worlds, a space both entirely festive and deadly serious, Hal plays with and hesitates between two completely different versions of what it is to be a young man in the world. Not ready to decide, he reverts to the world of festive play, calling in Falstaff to play-act his way out of the impasse.

CHAPTER 14

Festive Falstaff: of popularity, puritans and princes

Early on, the prince compares his dalliance with Falstaff and his cronies to a holiday. That reference has prompted a variety of what we might term carnivalesque readings of the Falstaffian elements in the play.[1] The insistent joking about Falstaff's girth – he 'sweats to death/And lards the lean earth as he walks along' [Pt. I, II, ii, 103–4]; his status as a man of many names and attributes, as 'Sir John Sack and Sugar' [Pt. I, i, 108], 'Sir John Paunch'; as someone the prince describes to his brother Lancaster as 'the strangest fellow' [Pt I, II, ii, 64] – all these have been taken to establish him as some sort of lord of misrule, a principle of inversion and mocking laughter, the epitome of certain styles of popular mirth. 'Men of all sorts take a pride to gird a me,' Falstaff tells his page. 'The brain of this foolish-compounded clay, man, is not able to invent anything that intends to laughter more than I invent, or is invented on me; I am not only witty in myself, but the cause that wit is in other men' [Pt. II, I, ii, 5–9].

In a famous scene Falstaff is actually installed on a mock throne, playing the angry king to Hal's miscreant prince [Pt. I, II, iv, 368–72]. In the ensuing exchanges they swap different versions of Falstaff's character and attributes. The result is an association of Falstaff and his world with a variety of aspects of popular festivity and the ritualised (dis)order of the carnivalesque mode. He is, as the prince describes him, 'that trunk of humours, that bolting-hutch of beastliness, that swollen parcel of dropsies, that huge bombard of sack, that stuffed cloak-bag of guts, that roasted Manningtree ox with the pudding in his belly, that reverend Vice, that grey Iniquity, that father Ruffian, that Vanity in years. Wherein is he good, but to taste sack and drink it? Wherein neat and cleanly, but to carve a capon and eat it? Wherein cunning, but in craft? Wherein crafty, but in villainy? Wherein villainous, but in all things? Wherein worthy, but in nothing?' [Pt. I, II, iv, 437–47].

Falstaff however sees himself as but old and merry. 'If sack and sugar be a fault, God help the wicked. If to be old and merry be a sin, then many an old host that I know is damned. If to be fat be to be hated, then Pharoah's lean kine are to be loved. No, my good lord, banish Peto, banish Bardolph, banish Poins, but for sweet Jack Falstaff, kind Jack Falstaff, true Jack Falstaff, valiant Jack Falstaff, and therefore more valiant, being as he is old Jack Falstaff, banish not him thy Harry's company, banish not him thy Harry's company. Banish plump Jack, and banish all the world' [Pt. I, II, iv, 458–67]. There is here a claim to a certain universality, a claim to speak for aspects of human experience that are ubiquitous, that cannot ever entirely be banished or suppressed.

It is not, perhaps, without significance here that at one point, at the battle of Shrewsbury, Falstaff actually rises from the dead. Hal emerges from his fight with Hotspur flanked by what he takes to be two corpses; epitomes of the opposed extremes against and in terms of which he has to define his own (middle?) way: on the one hand, the monovocally honour-obsessed Hotspur and, on the other, the shape-changing, honour-despising Falstaff. There is something perfunctory, perhaps even relieved, in the prince's farewell to his erstwhile friend. 'Poor Jack, farewell./I could have better spared a better man:/O, I should have a heavy miss of thee/If I were much in love with vanity./Death hath not struck so fat a deer today,/Though many dearer in this bloody fray./Embowelled will I see thee by and by;/Till then, in blood by noble Percy lie.' Falstaff, however, has been counterfeiting death to escape from the bloody assault of the Douglas and he gets up as soon as the prince has left the stage. 'Embowelled? If thou embowel me today, I'll give you leave to powder me, and eat me too, tomorrow' [Pt. I, V, iv, 102–11]. Falstaff, and all he represents, cannot be got rid of that easily, it seems.

Such claims to indestructibility are repeated elsewhere in Falstaff's self-descriptions. Falstaff later replies to the Lord Chief Justice's reproaches with the claim that 'you that are old consider not the capacities of us that are young; you do measure the heat of our livers with the bitterness of your galls: and we that are in the vaward of our youth, I must confess, are wags too.' To this the Lord Chief Justice replies, with all the outraged logic of the workaday world, that Falstaff is demonstrably old. To this Falstaff responds 'my lord, I was born about three o'clock of the afternoon, with a white head, and something a round belly. For my voice, I have lost it with hallooing, and singing of anthems. To approve my youth further, I will not: the truth is, I am only old in judgement and understanding; and he that will caper with me for a thousand marks, let him lend me the money, and have at him!' [Pt. II, I, ii, 172–93]. In reply to the Chief Justice's comparison of him to 'a candle, the better part burnt out', Falstaff responds that rather he is 'a wassail candle, my lord, all tallow', that is to say one built to last through the night during the popular festive practice of wassailing. Pursuing the candle metaphor Falstaff concludes that if he is taken to be made 'of wax, my growth would approve the truth' in other words, his very bulk should be taken to prove not that he is old and near death but that he is built to last [Pt. II, I, ii, 157–58]. Young and old, not so much a person as a principle of nature, Falstaff both personifies and transcends the life cycle, and thus defeats the puny efforts of quotidian logic and constraint, personified here by the Chief Justice, to define or contain him – or at least he does while the prince continues to protect him, a point to which we shall return below.

The world presided over by this lord of misrule is something like a world turned upside down; it is a place where the constraints of law and order, of worldly calling, status and degree, are in suspension. In reply to Falstaff's first line, 'Hal, what time of day is it lad?' the prince answers with a tirade designed to show just how little such questions matter in a world defined by the basic appetites and imperatives of Falstaff's nature [Pt. I, I, ii, 1–11]. Later in the same exchange Falstaff invokes the duty to labour in the calling into which God has placed one – a doctrine central to contemporary notions of the social and political order – but he does so the better to justify his calling as a thief. In reply to the prince's claim that 'I see good amendment of life in thee, from praying to purse-taking', Falstaff replies 'why, Hal, 'tis my vocation, Hal; 'tis no sin for a man to labour in his vocation' [Pt. I, I, ii, 98–101]. In Falstaff's world turned upside down, then, purse-taking is a lawful calling. This is a state of affairs he hopes the prince will formalise when he is king, suggesting that in that new world 'us that are squires of the night's body', i.e. thieves, should be renamed and henceforward called 'thieves of the day's beauty. Let us be Diana's foresters, gentlemen of the shade, ministers of the moon, and let men say we be men of good government, being governed, as the sea is, by our noble and chaste mistress the moon, under whose countenance we steal' [Pt. I, I, ii, 23–28]. Pursuing the same conceit Falstaff asks the prince, 'I prithee, sweet wag, shall there be gallows standing in England when thou art king? And resolution thus fubbed as it is with the rusty curb of old Father Antic the law? Do not thou, when thou art a king, hang a thief.' 'No, thou shalt,' comes the reply. 'Shall I, O rare! By the Lord, I'll be a brave judge!' 'Thou judgest false already,' replies the prince. 'I mean thou shalt have the hanging of the thieves and so become a rare hangman' [Pt. I, I, ii, 55–65].

The vision of a world without hangmen is a sort of utopia, a land of cockayne, devoid of the normal constraints and repressions that created and kept order in the quotidian world. For the gallows was, in many ways, the ultimate symbol of royal justice, the events that took place there a central site for the acting out of the dreadful power at the disposal of the prince, a public theatre for the operation of both royal and divine justice and mercy. But there was also a carnivalseque element to the choreographies of retribution and repentance, of punishment, putrescence and dissolution, played out at the gallows, and that element centred on the figure of the hangman, to whom a variety of attributes, involving certain sorts of ritual impurity and curative powers, attached. While Falstaff sees himself in the reign of Prince Hal as a judge, in what would be a real world turned upside down, Hal forces his friend back, where he belongs, into the liminal space between holiday and work-day, by figuring him, if not as an incipient victim of the gallows, then as that equally marginal figure, the hangman.

This, then, is a world without work and without time, at least as time is conventionally defined and delineated by the rhyms and constraints of the work-a-day world and the life cycle. It is also a world devoid of constraint, without law or punishment, in which the usual divisions of labour, the hierarchies of social and economic function, of status and social and political power, have all been either dissolved or inverted. In this world Hal is not only the prince of Wales but also 'sweet wag', 'lad', 'the most comparative, rascalliest, sweet young prince' [Pt. I, I, ii, 77–78] or, less flatteringly, 'the bastard son of the king's'. Not even the king himself escapes the linguistic levelling at the heart of Falstaff's circle. At one point the hostess reminisces about a time when 'the Prince broke thy [Falstaff's] head for liking his father to a singing-man of Windsor' [Pt. II, II, i, 87–88]. In part II Hal returns to London and asks Bardolph where Falstaff is to be found. 'At the old place', comes the reply, 'in Eastcheap'. 'What company', asks the prince; 'Ephesians, my lord, of the old church', Bardolph replies [Pt. II, II, ii, 140–42]. This is, then, a world without social division, a place where all the old boundaries of status and degree have been removed or reversed, a gathered church of backsliders. It is a place of radical equality, one in which the prince is, or can at least play at being, the equal of an apprentice, a cutpurse or a fraudster. Falstaff can be the king and Hal his son, the prince of Wales.

In this world the conventional rhetoric of evil counsel is itself inverted. Throughout both plays Falstaff continually claims to have been corrupted by the prince. 'Hal', he begs him 'trouble me no more with vanity. I would to God thou and I knew where a commodity of good names were to be bought. An old lord of the Council rated me the other day in the street about you, sir, but I marked him not; and yet he talked very wisely, but I regarded him not; and yet he talked wisely and in the street too'. 'Thou didst well', replies the prince, 'for wisdom cries out in the streets and no man regards it'. 'O, thou hast damnable iteration and art able to corrupt a saint. Thou hast done much harm upon me, Hal; God forgive thee for it. Before I knew thee, Hal, I knew nothing, and now I am, if a man should speak truly, little better than one of the wicked. I must give over this life, and I will give it over. By the Lord, an I do not, I am a villain. I'll be damned for never a king's son in Christendom' [Pt. I, I, ii, 78–94]. The same conceit is pursued throughout part II. Accused by the Lord Chief Justice that 'you follow the young Prince up and down, like his ill angel' [Pt. II, I, ii, 162–63], 'you have misled the youthful Prince', Falstaff replies (with wonderful unknowing irony) that 'the young Prince hath misled me. I am the fellow with the great belly, and he my dog' [Pt. II, I, ii, 143–45]. To the justice's pious wish that 'Well, God send the Prince a better companion!' Falstaff replies, 'God send the companion a better prince! I cannot rid my hands of him' [Pt. II, I, ii, 199–201]. 'For the box of the ear that the Prince gave you, he gave it like a rude prince, and you took it like a sensible lord. I have checked him for it, and the young lion repents' [Pt. II, I, ii, 193–96].

Antipuritanism – again

In ways that wonderfully undercut modern assumptions about the relationship between puritanism and order, this world turned upside down is persistently associated with the puritan godly. In many of the passages just cited above – in Falstaff's invocation of the doctrine of callings to justify his career as a cutpurse and thief; in Bardolph's use of the church of the Ephesians to refer to the gathered church of misrule and inversion that Falstaff is running in Eastcheap; in Falstaff and the prince's frequent references to the need for repentance and amendment of life; in Falstaff's description of his relationship with the prince as 'the corruption of a saint' – the discourse of this world is drenched in the scriptural language, speech patterns and imagery of 'the godly'. Thus, when Hal seems unwilling to join in the theft on Gadshill, Falstaff tells Poins to talk him round. 'God give thee the spirit of persuasion and him the ears of profiting, that what thou speakest may move and what he hears may be believed, that the true prince may, for recreation sake, prove a false thief, for the poor abuses of the time want countenance' (Pt. I, I, ii, 144–48]. Again, having been overheard insulting the prince by the prince himself (who has disguised himself again as a drawer for precisely such a purpose), Falstaff has recourse to the intensely scriptural language of godly paradox to excuse himself. There was, he claimed, no 'abuse' in his words 'no abuse i' th' world, honest Ned, none. I dispraised him before the wicked that the wicked might not fall in love with thee: in which doing, I have done the part of a careful friend and a true subject, and thy father is to give me thanks for it. No abuse, Hal; none, Ned, none; no, faith, boys, none' [Pt. II, II, ii, 315–21].[2]

Again and again, therefore, we have the discourse and cadences of puritan godliness employed by Falstaff to realise ends the precise opposite of those for which that discourse was conventionally or ostensibly employed by the godly themselves. The language of callings is used to legitimise thieving; the rhetoric of profitable hearing and the spirit of persuasion is used to effect, not the spiritual edification of the godly, but rather the persuasion of the prince into highway robbery; scriptural injunctions and apothegms are used to justify ignoring rebukes from some of the highest authorities in the land. Repentance is repeatedly espoused and always deferred. And, finally, the habitual puritan division between the godly and the wicked is used to tell the most egregious and patent lies and yet to justify the most abusive language directed at both a friend and the heir to the throne, an offence, as the prince observes, that would usually lead to the culprit having his ears cropped.

In part, such parodic appropriation of the norms of puritan speech by the forces of disorder and festivity is merely part of the festive inversionary fun. Here we have the terms and assumptions that were habitually used by the godly to condemn and excoriate the 'common abuses' of the time, being used instead to 'countenance' and constitute those same abuses. Here are the denizens of a festive world of carnival excess – a world which the godly would repress – using the language of puritan godliness to justify their behaviour.

But there was more going on here than that. By putting these terms and allusions in the mouth of the unconstrained, festive figure of Falstaff the play is staging the hypocrisy that was regularly imputed to puritans by their opponents. That is to say, in precisely this period, the claim was coming regularly to be made that, in fact, the godly were no better than the common run of fallen humanity; they were just as subject to the sins of covetousness, avarice and gluttony as everyone else. The only difference was that they used a veneer of surface piety, a series of behavioural and linguistic tics, of acquired characteristics and affected mannerisms – what we might term the performative discourses of outward piety and puritan godliness – to disguise and justify sins that were very often a good deal worse than anything perpetrated by their less demonstratively 'godly' neighbours and contemporaries.[3] Here, as Kristen Poole has pointed out, the very fatness of the 'fat knight' made the point perfectly.[4]

And, finally, there was a more serious and sinister point. As we have seen, Falstaff's was a world in which the usual constraints and divisions that maintained social and political order in the waking world were dissolved or inverted. But that was precisely the charge raised by leading polemicists of the day against the puritans themselves. A central strand in contemporary anti-puritan polemic held that the puritan platform for further reformation in church and state would, if implemented, in fact, turn the world upside down. By subjecting the power of the prince to the power of the church, and by removing all hierarchy and degree from the church, the puritans would reduce both the church and the state to a populist, democratical anarchy. In this view of the puritan project, all social and political hierarchy, all legal authority and order, would fall before the radical spiritual equality established amongst the godly. Equal amongst themselves in their role as elect saints, the godly would then proceed to lord it over everybody else. On this view, the basic division between the godly and the wicked, that in Falstaff's hands, as well as in those of many a puritan preacher, was used hypocritically to justify the sins of the godly, would now also be used to establish something like a rule of the saints. The result would be a tyrannical godly oligarchy, in which all power, status and wealth would be redistributed into the hands of a self-selecting godly elite. This was the vision of puritan disorder that contemporary conformist polemicists like Richard Bancroft, Matthew Sutcliffe, Richard Cosin and, in certain moods, Richard Hooker attributed to the presbyterian movement, as they sought to assimilate Elizabethan puritan schemes for further reformation in church and state to the Anabaptist lunacy of Thomas Munzer or John of Leiden. This was to give an altogether more serious and sinister edge to the vision of inversionary (both festive and puritan) disorder evoked in the gathered church of the old Ephesians being run in Eastcheap by Falstaff and his friends.[5] It also, of course, picks up and renders, in a more subtle, insinuating sense, many of the central anti-puritan elements in the equally plebeian and carnivalesque Cade scenes of *2 Henry VI*.

Of course, as Beatrice Groves has pointed out, it is not the case that Falstaff is simply presented in the play as a puritan, but rather that he is shown appropriating distinctively puritan modes of discourse for his own corrupt purposes. As Groves observes, while 'Falstaff's language can be read as a parody of Puritanism', 'it is also something more engaging – the parodic Puritan's hypocritical inversion of biblical phraseology becomes innocent in Falstaff who does not intend to be misunderstood'.[6] But this, of course, only increases the anti-puritan register of these scenes since it means that, for all his faults, the overt and self-professed villainy and corruption of Falstaff is greatly to be preferred to the inherently hypocritical (and no less sinful because covert) pursuit of material self-interest and enjoyment of the pleasures of the flesh by the godly. Moreover, Falstaff's parody of puritan-speak serves precisely the same function, for him, as the scripturally inflected, incantatory cadence of the godly serves for them; that is, it covers up, renders if not invisible, then (in Falstaff's case) seemingly harmless, indeed in Groves' rather bloodless phrase 'engaging', what emerges from the later stages of part I onwards, as a viciously antisocial pursuit of self-interest, status and material advantage. Not only that, but, in this just like the (equally carnivalesque) Cade scenes in *2 Henry VI*, the anti-puritanism attached to Falstaff is given a directly political, and distinctly subversive, edge. In the *Henry IV* plays that edge is added through the figure of the prince, whose addiction to the fat knight's company provides for puritan popularity and Falstaffian evil counsel a potential point of access to the very centre of power; an access and influence that, if unchecked, could, as Henry IV fears, plunge the reign of Henry V into both moral and political chaos. Thus, however 'innocent' or 'engaging' Falstaff may be or appear, he also represents a threateningly sinister figure for a popular, hypocritical and entirely corrupt puritan threat, located at least potentially at, or uncomfortably close to, the very centre of monarchical power. That, as Michael Davies has observed, Falstaff's continuing addiction to the sins of the flesh, figured so memorably by his girth, and his equally rooted propensity to defer an oft-promised repentance to another day, all brought him close to the contemporary 'type for the Calvinist reprobate', only served to deepen the irony and improve the joke.[7]

As a number of commentators have pointed out, to espouse the anti-puritan cause was scarcely a daring move by the later 1590s; on the contrary, it was to jump on what was by now a rather well established and successful bandwagon. But to make these sorts of anti-puritan gestures by an attack on the Lollard hero Oldcastle – the original name for the Falstaff figure in the first versions of the play – went beyond what we might term the call of conventional anti-puritan duty. For Oldcastle and the Lollards, whose cause he personified, featured prominently in the writings of John Foxe, as precursors not of puritans but of the entire cause of English Protestantism. Lollardy was one of the underground heretical movements that Foxe enlisted to answer the insistent Catholic question: where was your church before Luther? For Foxe there was a true church tradition hidden within and beneath the Antichristian popery that had come to dominate the Roman church and delude the people at the height of Antichrist's power. The Lollards were particularly significant here because they established that England had its own native form of true religion, developed and espoused long before Luther and others started to proclaim the protestant message on the continent. Lollardy thus played a parallel religious role in the Foxeian account to the political role played by King John; taken together, they proved that Antichrist had never triumphed fully over the true church and that England had always been at the forefront of the struggles against the forces of popish darkness. Moreover, the Lollards had been persecuted for their faith by the false church of Antichrist, and some had died as martyrs, which was precisely the role attributed in Foxe's account to Sir John Oldcastle. Thus, even if Shakespeare merely took the name Oldcastle over from *The famous victories of Henry V*, his subsequent use of a character called Sir John Oldcastle as a vehicle for yet another exercise in vicious anti-puritan satire was by no means an ideologically innocent act. For in so doing Shakespeare was not merely kicking the godly while they were down, adverting to the dangerously subversive tendencies of some of Essex's puritan followers and playing to a series of established anti-puritan stereotypes and jokes well known to, and well loved by, many members of his audience, he was also subverting or calling into radical question a central element in what in the later 1590s remained (for all the best efforts of Richard Hooker) the hegemonic protestant account of the nature of the true church in England and of the relations between the Christian (protestant) present and (Catholic and Lollard) past.[8]

In a brilliant article, Tom McAlindon has shown that Falstaff's verbal duel with the Lord Chancellor echoes very closely Oldcastle's exchanges with his interrogators in the Tower as recounted by John Bale.[9] Where Oldcastle's command of the scriptures, verbal dexterity and quick-wittedness is used by Bale as a sign of grace, of Oldcastle's status as a true Christian professor and martyr, Falstaff/Oldcastle's similarly 'quicksilver mind and tongue' are revealed by Shakespeare as anything but signs of 'grace'; rather they are qualities put to completely corrupt, this-worldly purposes by an old miscreant and hypocrite bent on avoiding the shackles of the law. The result is funny, compelling, utterly profane, but also deadly serious in its potential impact not only on the claims of the puritan godly to a superior sanctity, but also on the dominant Foxeian account of the origins of the protestant church of England in a series of underground groups of heretics and deviants, who had kept the cause of true religion and the true church alive in the midst of popish corruption, idolatry and persecution. In Catholic critiques of the Foxeian account these same groups were, of course, relabelled as heretics and rebels, hypocrites and reprobates; just like Shakespeare's Oldcastle/Falstaff, in fact.

This is a move remarkably similar to Shakespeare's earlier reworking of the hot protestant, Foxeian version of King John, where again he had taken a figure central to the protestant version of the English past and radically recast him.[10] The effects are roughly parallel; where, in Shakespeare's play, King John loses virtually all trace of his role as a proto-protestant, anti-popish hero, so here, through the casting of Oldcastle as a corrupt, potentially subversive, hypocrite, Henry's rejection of the Lollards emerges as yet another sign of his political sagacity and Christian virtue. In the opening scenes of Henry V Henry is shown rejecting Lollard proposals to strip the church of its temporal holdings in order to accept the bishops' offer of record levels of clerical taxation to fund his invasion of France; a decision that is presented as providing at least one foundation for the glorious military action upon which Henry's repute as a great English king and Christian prince is based. (Since schemes to fund the war effort by simply expropriating, rather than taxing, the church were associated by contemporaries first with Leicester and later with Essex, and indeed used by antipuritan polemicists to explain noble and indeed gentry patronage of the puritan movement, a major plank in whose platform was the expropriation of the landed estates of the bishops and cathedral churches, this renders such references doubly significant and resonant for the more clued up members of Shakespeare's audience.)[11]

Admittedly, if the prince's sojourn with Falstaff in the stews of Eastcheap could be construed as some variant of holiday mirth, a bout of ritualised inversion and misrule, of carvivalesque laughter and indulgence and therefore of strictly limited duration, then the prince's claims to be fully in control both of his surroundings and himself, even as he submerged himself in the milieu of the Boar's Head, would remain plausible enough. For one strand of both contemporary and indeed more recent scholarly comment upon the world of popular festivity holds, and held, that such bouts of inversionary laughter and misrule served not to undermine or call into question but to bolster the social and political order.[12] But there were also other, both contemporary and more recent (scholarly), evaluations of this milieu which see it as altogether more subversive of the dominant, or perhaps, on some views, emergent, notions of order in Elizabethan England.[13] The godly – and here, of course, the ironies involved in Falstaff's propensity for puritan-speak are peculiarly sharp and deep – certainly saw the world of popular festivity, and indeed its commercial analogues and extensions on the popular stage,[14] as deeply subversive. And some modern commentators have seen the world of popular festivity, however conservative the vision of the social order inscribed within it, as bearing the potential to both legitimise and express popular discontent with exorbitant or innovatory or corrupt exercises of power by those in authority. On this view, as genuinely liminal states or occasions, certain sorts of festive activity contained at least the potential to create, as well as to contain, disorder and disruption.[15] And that, I would argue, is what we are being shown in the play. Falstaff's at once festive, inversionary and puritan world is a genuinely liminal space, a place of danger as well as of delight. To adopt C.L. Barber's terms, but not his line of argument, the functions fulfilled by, and the potentials contained within, Falstaff's version of the festive world of carnival were not merely saturnalian, nor were they only satiric, but at times, at least potentially, they were genuinely subversive.

Misrule stops being festive

The festive energies of Falstaff's world are subversive because they are not, in fact, securely contained – socially, spatially, temporally or indeed emotionally – in a safely cordoned off sphere of holiday mirth. On the contrary, they invade the 'real' world at a number of increasingly threatening junctures. Almost from the outset, what C.L. Barber terms the 'anarchic potentialities' of Falstaffian misrule are not limited to 'holiday extravagance' but seek to establish themselves as 'an everyday racket'.[16] Falstaff and his mates do not operate only in Eastcheap, they threaten, if they do not at first invade, the world of the court.

At first Hal had supported Falstaff directly by protecting him from the attentions of the law and by consistently picking up the tab at the Boar's Head [Pt. I, I, ii, 52–53]. When the robbery at Gadshill is over and the joke has been played on Falstaff, Hal protects 'the gross fat man' from the investigations of the watch and then makes sure that the stolen 'money shall be paid back again with advantage' [Pt. I, II, iv, 533–34]. Thus far, no real harm has been done. The money has been more than paid back and Falstaff festively shamed. But, as the progress of the rebellion draws Hal back into what is for him the real world of war, politics and his father's anger, so he takes elements of Falstaffian disorder with him.

The whole point of the Gadshill jape was, of course, to reveal Falstaff, on his own account as valiant as Hercules, to be the complete coward and incompetent that he is. But immediately after his first reconciliation with the king, Hal tells Falstaff that, having cleared up the small matter of the Gadshill robbery, 'I am good friends with my father and may do anything'; a renewed favour he has used to 'procure' Falstaff 'a charge of foot' [Pt. I, III, iii, 180–81, 185]. This, as the Lord Chief Justice later tells both him and us, obtains Falstaff short-term immunity from prosecution for his exploits at Gadshill. But it also gives him a military command and an authority he can use to batten on to those less fortunate than himself in order to line his own pockets.

Falstaff's promotion then provides Hal with further evidence of Falstaff's uselessness for any practical, and certainly for any military purpose. First, he inspects with incredulity and disgust the scarecrow army that Falstaff has corruptly recruited for service at Shrewsbury and then, on the battlefield itself, attempting to borrow Falstaff's sword, Hal is offered instead the fat knight's pistol, only to discover a bottle of sack in the holster where the pistol should be. He reacts with the disgusted words 'what, is it a time to jest and dally now?' [Pt. I, V, iii, 56]. And yet, despite that, after Falstaff's resurrection at Shrewsbury at the end of part I, Hal not only endorses his lie about having killed Hotspur but, at the beginning of part 2, secures him another command.

On one view, of course, Hal's offer at Shrewsbury – 'for my part, if a lie may do thee grace,/I'll gild it with the happiest terms I have' [Pt. I, V, iv, 158–59] – is a grand gesture; it shows that for all his admiration for Hotspur and his drive to vindicate himself through glorious deeds of arms, Hal is not obsessed, as Hotspur was, with the desire for martial honour and reputation. If there was something basely commercial about Hal's view of Hotspur as 'his factor' and his determination to crop 'all the budding honours on thy crest . . . to make a garland for my head' [Pt. I, V, iv, 71–72], he now distances himself definitively from any such taint, by giving away all credit for the deed to Falstaff. The magnanimity of the gesture bleeds over into Hal's treatment of the Douglas, the disposal of whom he first begs from his father and then immediately cedes to his brother John, whom he instructs to give up the captured Scot 'ransomless and free', in tribute to his 'valours' and 'high deeds'. As his brother Lancaster exclaims, this is 'high courtesy' indeed [Pt. I, V, v, 32–33] – a reflection both of Hal's generosity and of his determination not to appear, Hotspur-like, to be hoarding up and proclaiming his own virtues, while still, in effect, doing precisely that. On this account, Hal has supplanted Hotspur as the true 'king of honour'.[17] But the very same refusal to glory in Hotspur's overthrow also serves to endorse Falstaff as a military hero and thus to perpetuate and empower the fat knight's rogue's progress through the Lancastrian state, the almost entirely deleterious course of which will be set before us in part II.

As Falstaff follows Hal into the world, seeking to exploit for personal gain the new reputation as a soldier conferred on him by the prince's flagrant lie at Shrewsbury and the military office conferred on him by the prince's subsequent patronage, we are being shown festive inversion and misrule starting to invade 'reality'. We see the political clout and patronage of the prince being used to shield the activities of Falstaff as thief, fraudster and entirely cowardly and corrupt military commander. The change is signalled by a shift in Falstaff's mode of discourse; as C.L. Barber has observed, 'in the early portion of Part One he never spoke in asides, but now', 'confident of setting up his holiday license on an everyday basis', 'he constantly confides his schemes and his sense of himself to the audience . . . Instead of warm amplifications centred on himself, his talk now consists chiefly of bland impudence or dry, denigrating comments on the ways of the world.'[18] Indeed, John Danby has gone so far as to claim that Falstaff emerges as 'the most pitiless creature in the play', 'deceiving Shallow, recruiting his Gloucestershire yokels, ruining mistress Quickly, despising Hal'.

In part II, in Danby's words, we see the emergence of a 'predatory Falstaff about to swoop on the body politic and make it a new prey'.[19] Falstaff's pursuit of self-interest and material advantage becomes sharper and meaner, typified by his espousal, as he prepares to take Justice Shallow for everything he is worth, of 'the law of nature' that renders 'the young dace' 'bait for the old pike' [Pt. II, III, ii, 325–26].[20] As Calderwood points out, 'in part I Falstaff was the constant victim – of Hal, Poins, Douglas, his own weight and bulk'. His wit was largely exercised in extricating himself from the various 'tight spots' in which the play put him. In the latter stages of part I and throughout part II, however, Falstaff, starts to make 'victims of others – mistress Quickly, the Gloucestershire conscripts, Justice Shallow, Colevile of the Dale'.[21] Again in part I Falstaff had lived almost entirely in the eternal now of holiday; 'as an inveterate improviser ... he has no plans or programs ... he cannot plot, he can only extemporise to evade the plots of others'.[22] As, in the wake of the prince, in the later scenes of part I, he enters the real world, all that starts to change, and throughout part II Falstaff's wit is used to plan his own rise in the world, and to fleece and exploit others.

We are shown the consequences of this, as, in Falstaff's rogue's progress through the war-torn commonwealth, festive misrule starts to turn into actual misgovernment. This process starts in part I but gains velocity in part II. Military command for Falstaff represents merely an opportunity to mend his finances and it is the rebels he has to thank. 'I am heinously unprovided. Well, God be thanked for these rebels; they offend none but the virtuous. I laud them, I praise them' [Pt. I, III, iii, 188–191]. As a denizen of the inversionary world of carnival Falstaff, of course, has a natural affinity with rebels who, in Percy's phrase, want to 'o'er turn the kingdom topsy-turvy down', an affinity which is here becoming serious.

Falstaff greets Hal's rousing parting words – 'the land is burning, Percy stands on high,/And either we or they must lower lie' – with the retort 'Rare words! Brave world! Hostess, my breakfast, come!/O, I could wish this tavern were my drum!' [Pt. I, III, iii, 202–5]. As one might expect from this, his efforts as a recruiting officer become the epitome of the corrupt use of royal authority for private gain. He re-enters the action at Coventry on the way to the battle of Shrewsbury admitting that 'I have misused the King's press damnably', and explaining in detail how he has turned the process of raising troops into a way to line his own pockets at the expense of the effectiveness of the royal army [Pt. I, IV, ii, 11–38]. In response to the prince's complaint, on seeing his contingent, that 'I did never see such pitiful rascals', Falstaff replies chillingly that they are 'good enough to toss; food for powder, food for powder. They'll fill a pit as well as better. Tush man, mortal men, mortal men' [Pt. I, IV, ii, 63–66]. And Falstaff proves as good as his word; when we encounter him on the battlefield at Shrewsbury he exclaims that 'I have led my ragamuffins where they are peppered; there's not three of my hundred and fifty left alive, and they are for the town's end to beg during life' [Pt. I, V, iii, 35–38].

With his second command under his belt, Falstaff laments both his poverty – 'I can get no remedy against this consumption of the purse' – and his health – 'a pox of this gout! Or a gout of this pox! For the one or the other plays the rogue with my great toe. 'Tis no matter if I do halt; I have the wars for my colour, and my pension shall seem the more reasonable. A good wit will make use of anything; I will turn diseases to commodity' [Pt. II, I, ii, 237–50]. As he is hanging around London, Mistress Quickly tries to have him arrested for debt and he is found violently resisting the officers, Fang and Snare, by his old nemesis, the Lord Chief Justice, against whom Falstaff pleads the prerogatives of military service under the crown [Pt. II, II, i, 121–27].

When finally Falstaff does leave London, he repeats his earlier recruiting practices, enlisting the halt and the lame, despite the protests even of Justice Shallow, as part of precisely the same scam that he had operated in the Shrewsbury campaign. This time he manages to arrive so late at Gaultree that the rebel cause has already collapsed. His only contribution to the royal cause is the capture of the rebel Sir John Colevile of the Dale; a deed of arms achieved solely on the basis of his reputation as a soldier gained at Shrewsbury, as Calderwood emphasises. Having bought a 'commodity of good names' at Shrewsbury, Falstaff is now determined to profit by them. As he tells Colevile, 'I have a whole school of tongues in this belly of mine, and not a tongue of them all speaks any other word but my name' [Pt. II, IV, iii, 18–20]. But if Falstaff's newly formidable (and marketable) name is based on a lie, it is the prince's lie rather than his own that has given it real validity in the eyes of the world.[23]

Returning to London, Falstaff hears of the king's death and Hal's accession while staying with Justice Shallow. As Danby notes, his reaction reveals something 'really sinister . . . in Falstaff's make-up'[24] and confirms in spades what has already been apparent in his conduct in office under the crown. 'Master Shallow, my Lord Shallow – be what thou wilt; I am Fortune's steward! . . . I know the young King is sick for me. Let us take any man's horses – the laws of England are at my commandment. Blessed are they that have been my friends, and woe to my Lord Chief Justice!' [Pt. II, V, iii, 125–34]. We see here the firm intention to do, on an heroic scale, as the intimate of the new king, what he has already begun to do as the friend of the prince; that is, to exploit office under and influence with the crown for his own private gain, doing harm to his enemies and favours for his friends and profiting from the bribes and douceurs he takes along the way. En route to London he has already borrowed a thousand pounds from Shallow on the basis of the influence he will wield in the new regime.

Immediately before Falstaff's return to London, we are shown a scene in which Mistess Quickly and Doll Tearsheet are being led off by beadles. 'She shall have whipping-cheer enough, I warrant her,' one of the beadles observes: 'the man is dead that you and Pistol beat amongst you'. In reply, Mistress Quickly redoubles Doll's threat of awful consequences if the child she is carrying miscarries, with the pious wish that 'I pray God the fruit of her womb miscarry'. She also prays that 'Sir John were come! He would make this a bloody day to somebody' [Pt. II, V, iv, 1–18]. There is, of course, nothing very festive about either of these exchanges, or about what is going to happen to Doll and Mistress Quickly next, or, indeed, about the events that have provoked their detention and incipient punishment in the first place. We have returned here from the world of festive misrule, of ritualised disorder, inversion and mirth, to something like the real world of brothels and bawdy houses, of illicit bought sex and violence, of theft, infanticide and murder, in which the likes of Pistol, Bardolph, Mistress Quickly and Falstaff himself actually lived in the real Eastcheap. On Falstaff's arrival in the capital, Pistol tells him the news that 'thy Doll, and Helen of thy noble thoughts,/Is in base durance and contagious prison,/Hal'd thither/ By most mechanical and dirty hand'. 'I will deliver her,' Falstaff responds [Pt. II, V, v, 33–39]. Again, for all the mock-heroic persiflage of these exchanges, we are back in the real world, where the influence of clients and favourites with the great could be used to divert the course of royal justice.

It is the same world in which Falstaff's current mark Justice Shallow and his man Davy live. In an earlier scene Davy had petitioned Shallow 'to countenance William Visor of Woncot against Clement Perkes a' th' Hill'. To this request Shallow had objected that 'there is many complaints, Davy, against that Visor; that Visor is an arrant knave, on my knowledge'. To this comes the devastating response: 'I grant your worship that he is a knave, sir; but yet God forbid, sir, but a knave should have some countenance at his friend's request. An honest man, sir, is able to speak for himself, when a knave is not. I have served your worship truly, sir, these eight years; and if I cannot once or twice in a quarter bear out a knave against an honest man, I have but a very little credit with your worship. The knave is mine honest friend, sir, therefore I beseech your worship let him be countenanced'; a request to which Shallow willingly accedes – 'Go to; I say he shall have no wrong' [Pt. II, V, I, 34–49].

This, then, is the way the world works and as Davy is to Shallow, so Falstaff intends to be to Hal, and Shallow to Falstaff. 'I will use him well,' Shallow tells Davy of Falstaff. 'A friend i' th' court is better than a penny in the purse' [Pt. II, V, I, 28–29] – hence the loan of a thousand pounds made en route to London to Falstaff as, he supposes, the new king's great favourite. Observing Davy's relations with Shallow, Falstaff discourses on the same theme, demonstrating, as he does so, his mastery of the dark arts of court manipulation and manoeuvre and explaining both how one should play the master off against his servants and the servants off against their master and how he intends to use his capacity to make the prince laugh in order to work his way with him [Pt. II, V, i, 61–82]. We can now see all the evil humours of the commonwealth, the court corruption, the tendencies to evil counsel and flattery, inherent in any personal monarchy, the consequent distorting effect on the course of royal government and justice, coming to centre on the figure of Falstaff, who is ceasing to be a lord of misrule in some licensed, festive, liminal space and emerging, in C.L. Barber's phrase, as 'a favourite for a king' and a 'leader of an interest at court',[25] and as such the focus for real corruption and misgovernment.

Falstaff's capacity to make Hal laugh, to keep him amused and thus to balance what he sees as the cold-blooded propensities of his stock with the balm of alcohol-warmed festivity is but a different version of the capacity of Bushy, Bagot and Green to flatter and insinuate their way into Richard II's favour. And, of course, it was precisely such a prospect that King Henry had feared when he launched into a vision of the world turned upside down that would eventuate from his son's accession that was anything but festive [Pt. II, IV, v, 119–37].

The nature of threat represented by Falstaffian misrule and evil counsel attached to an incoming monarch was, of course, greatly heightened by the associations which stretch throughout both Parts I and II between Falstaff and puritanism. For puritanism, however much its opponents might try, at the level of polemic, to restrict it to a lunatic and laughable fringe of Munzer-like radicalism, plebeian ignorance and transparent (gluttonous, sensual and/or avaricious) hypocrisy, retained friends in high places. Should some of those powerful backers attain real influence at court, all sorts of (to anti-puritans) deeply threatening and subversive possibilities for further reformation in church, state and society might open up. In short, in certain circles, the rise in the counsels of a new monarch of a puritanically tinged, but entirely corrupt and hypocritical, Falstaff figure or favourite was a very threatening prospect indeed. The earl of Essex retained a considerable following amongst the godly and there was a good deal of speculation that the likely next heir to the throne, James VI, who was, after all, the king of a presbyterian country and had of late had a semi-public spat with Richard Bancroft over the excesses of the latter's anti-puritan polemic, might well prove a patron of puritan reformation. These, then, were not concerns without directly contemporary purchase.

Legitimising the bastard: Hal becomes Henry

Clearly, neither Henry IV nor Falstaff is alone in his expectations of what the accession of Hal to the throne of England will mean. As Warwick informs the Lord Chief Justice, he is certain that 'the young King loves you not'. Similarly, Clarence tells the Lord Chief Justice that 'you must now speak Sir John Falstaff

fair,/Which swims against your stream of quality' [Pt. II, V, ii, 9, 33–34]. What
prevents this sort of calamitous palace revolution is, of course, the final public
emergence, out of the chrysalis of the bastardised Prince Hal, of the fully legitimate and virtuous King Henry. At the very start of part I we have, of course,
been primed to expect such a revelation and have been allowed to watch the
preparatory stages of this final denouement in Hal's private interviews with his
father and in his developing, and increasingly distanced, relationship with
Falstaff and his milieu. But what does not come as exactly a shock to the audience does precisely that to the other characters assembled on the stage, as
Henry now stars (as he claimed he had long planned) in his own production of
the return of the prodigal, or rather of the metamorphosis of Hal into Henry,
on the very public stage of English personal monarchy. It is, of course, a transformation that parallels, indeed dramatises, that of the Lancastrian monarchy
itself, as the usurper and regicide Bolingbroke is replaced on the throne by a
son untainted by the sins of his father and possessed of an unchallengeable
claim to the throne.

In what we shall see in *Henry V* is but the first of many such set-ups, whereby
Henry manipulates the expectations of his intimates and interlocutors to
provide an occasion for the public demonstration, the performance, of his own
virtue, he asks the Lord Chief Justice why he looks so apprehensive in the new
king's presence. 'You are, I think, assur'd I love you not'. The Lord Chief Justice
has already admitted to Warwick that he is dreading this moment – 'I ... do
arm myself/To welcome the condition of the time,/Which cannot look more
hideously upon me/Than I have drawn it in my fantasy' [Pt. II, V, ii, 10–13].
However, he rises to the occasion, responding, with what amounts to courtly
defiance, to what he clearly expects will be public ruin and disgrace. 'I am
assur'd, if I be measur'd rightly,/Your Majesty hath no just cause to hate me.'
'No?/How might a prince of my great hopes forget/So great indignities you laid
upon me?/What! Rate, rebuke, and roughly send to prison/Th'immediate heir
of England? Was this easy?/May this be wash'd in Lethe and forgotten?' To this
diatribe the Lord Chief Justice replies with an extended discourse on what
amounts to the theory of the king's two bodies. 'I then did use the person of
your father;/The image of his power lay then in me;/In th'administration of his
law,/Whiles I was busy for the commonwealth,/Your highness pleased to forget
my place,/The majesty and power of law and justice,/The image of the King
whom I presented,/And struck me in my very seat of judgement;/Whereon, as
an offender to your father,/I gave bold way to my authority/And did commit
you./If the deed were ill,/Be you contented, wearing now the garland,/To have
a son set your decrees at naught?/To pluck down justice from your awful
bench?/To trip the course of law, and blunt the sword/That guards the peace
and safety of your person?/Nay more, to spurn at your most royal image,/And
mock your workings in a second body?'

That, of course, was the 'right' answer, and the Lord Chief Justice's having made it provides the king with the perfect opportunity to demonstrate his own virtue, and in particular his new-found commitment to order, justice and the legitimate English monarchical way; an opportunity which he seizes by reappointing the Lord Chief Justice to the post in which he had served under his father. With that Henry immediately proclaims: 'My father is gone wild into his grave,/For in his tomb lie my affections;/And with his spirit sadly I survive/To mock the expectation of the world,/To frustrate prophecies, and to raze out/ Rotten opinion, who hath writ me down/After my seeming' [Pt. II, V, 64–129].

All that remains is the public repudiation of any continuing connection with Falstaff. With wonderful irony, it is the Lord Chief Justice whom Henry sends to deal with 'that vain man', before himself dismissing the fat knight from the royal presence for good and all [Pt. II, V, v, 43, 47–69]. Having, with Hal/ Henry, emerged from the world of holiday mirth and misrule into the real world, Falstaff has come to represent all the evil humours, the corrupting elements that afflict the commonwealth. But Falstaff can exist only as the spirit of holiday, a festive lord of misrule, or as a threateningly corrupt and corrupting evil counsellor and favourite, because of Hal/Henry's support. With that support removed, Falstaff shrinks from being either an eternal principle of festive mirth and disorder, both young and old, ubiquitous and irrepressible, or the epitome of puritan hypocrisy, corruption and misrule, the quintessentially corrupt courtier and evil counsellor about to invade the workings of the monarchical state, and becomes instead an indigent and pathetic old man, waiting for death in the stews of London. From being dangerously liminal he is reduced to an impotent marginality, shrunk almost to nothing by the removal of the royal favour and protection that alone had enabled his rake's progress through the commonwealth. Simply by banishing Falstaff from the royal presence Henry is able, as it were, at a stroke, with almost miraculous efficacy and force, to expel from the commonwealth the evil humours of corruption, the abuse of office and royal favour for private gain, and indeed the threat represented by puritan reformation – all of which have, as we have seen, been gathering around the figure of the fat knight.

There is more than a little irony surrounding the fact that 'reformation' Henry-V-style involves the complete marginalisation and suppression of the 'puritan', at least as that ideal type was personified by Falstaff.[26] But that anti-puritan reaction, does not, as a great deal of contemporary puritan, and later historiographical, comment has tended to assume that it must, entail the embrace of an unreformed, 'traditional' or even crypto-Catholic,[27] version of the social order; an ideal animated, at the popular level, by the conventions and connections of good fellowship, the ale bench and the maypole, and, at the level of the social elite, by those of the noble affinity and of 'honour'. If the first is dismissed with Falstaff, the second has already gone south with Hotspur.

What remained was a decidedly (early) 'modern', distinctively post-reformation, version of what a properly new-modelled monarchy and commonwealth both could and should do to England

If, as Professor Womersley asserts, all this amounts to 'the reformation restaged', the reformation in question is not one based on the church or indeed on any of the central insights or claims of a recognisably protestant religion; still less one administered by the godly, whose dismissal (with Falstaff) into the margins allows (as Womersley puts it), 'spiritual authority' to 'migrate else-where'. It migrates, of course, to the prince, from whose person and actions this (anti-puritan) 'reformation' is seen solely to emanate. The result is an intensely 'erastian', king-centred, version of 'reformation' and a vision of a social and political order suddenly purged, by the action of the prince, of all its evil humours; a vision of a remodelled Tudor erastianism, figured in the triumph of Lancastrian kingship, emerging, remade, from the murk created by usurpation, regicide and tyranny.[28]

Through the rejection of Falstaff, Henry performs and affirms his status as a virtuous prince, between whose private person and whose public authority there can be no chink of daylight. We are seeing here, in the final metamorphosis of Hal into Henry and the adoption by Henry of full public monarchical power, the reconstitution of dynastic, moral and political legitimacy, and the return to the apex of the English monarchical state of true monarchical order. The king's two bodies meet in Henry in a perfect match; the just exercise of his public authority and his private virtues will from henceforth fit exactly the one with the other; in England under his rule there will no room for the influence of favourites or evil counsellors. He will be advised, as by a father, by the Lord Chief Justice, and choose 'such limbs of noble counsel/That the great body of our state may go/In equal rank with the best govern'd nation' [Pt. II, V, ii, 135–37].[29]

CHAPTER 15

Henry V and the fruits of legitimacy

By the end of *2 Henry IV,* the result of the transactions between Hal and Hostpur and between the prince and his two father figures, Henry IV and Falstaff, was something like a complete congruence, if not exactly between the king's two bodies, then certainly between the private virtues of the prince and the effective exercise of his public authority. The effects of those transformations and that congruence are displayed throughout *Henry V*, which, alone amongst the plays under discussion in this book, gives us a fully worked out portrait of successful monarchical rule.

Back to 'normal'?

From the outset of the play the transformation of both the king and the polity consequent upon Henry's accession is figured as almost complete. As we have seen, in the *Henry IV* plays Shakespeare had put a great deal of energy into showing that the miracle of the king's two bodies portrayed in the *Famous victories* had been no such thing; not a sudden transformation, a Saul-on-the-road-to-Damascus conversion, but a long-planned, and entirely calculated, performance or facsimile of such a transformation. However, at the start of *Henry V* Shakespeare went out of his way to show both that that was precisely how the transformation of Hal into Henry was perceived by even the most learned and eminent of his new subjects and that that perception had worked an almost miraculous transformation on the condition of the body politic. 'The breath no sooner left his father's body/But that his wildness, mortified in him,/Seemed to die too; yea, at that very moment,/Consideration like an angel came/And whipped th'offending Adam out of him,/Leaving his body as a paradise/T'envelop and contain celestial spirits./Never was such a sudden scholar made,/Never came reformation in a flood/With such a heady currence scouring faults,/Nor never Hydra-headed wilfulness/So soon did loose his seat, and all at once,/As in this king.' [I, i, 25–37]. 'Hear him but reason in divinity/ And, all admiring, with an inward wish/You would desire the King were made a prelate./Hear him debate of commonwealth affairs,/You should say it hath been in all his study./List his discourse of war, and you shall hear/A fearful battle rendered you in music./Turn him to any cause of policy,/The Gordian knot of it he will unloose,/Familiar as his garter, that when he speaks,/The air, a chartered libertine, is still,/And the mute wonder lurketh in men's ears/To steal his sweet and honeyed sentences./So that the art and practice part of life/ Must be the mistress to this theoric:/Which is a wonder how his grace should glean it,/Since his addiction was to courses vain,/His companies unlettered, rude and shallow,/His hours filled up with riots, banquets, sports,/And never noted in him any study,/Any retirement, any sequestration/From open haunts and popularity' [I, i, 38–59].

This personal transformation has had immediate public, both political and moral, consequences. As the invasion of France approaches, Westmoreland gives the following estimate of the political temperature of England under Henry's reign. 'Never king of England/Had nobles richer and more loyal subjects,/Whose hearts have left their bodies here in England/And lie pavil-ioned in the fields of France' [I, ii, 126–29]. Other commentators give an equally rosy account of the effects of the king's rule. 'Never was monarch better feared and loved/Than is your majesty, there's not, I think, a subject/That sits in heart-grief and uneasiness/Under the sweet shade of your government'. 'Those that were your father's enemies/Have steeped their galls in honey and do serve you/ With hearts create of duty and of zeal' [II, ii, 25–31]. Here, then, is a picture of a virtuous prince who has, at a stroke, quieted the distempers of the common-wealth, altogether removing and suppressing the internal dissensions, the jeal-ousies, factional rivalries and revolts, that had plagued his father's reign.

Later, debating how great a threat the Scots will prove while Henry is campaigning in France, the archbishop of Canterbury hymns the sweetly tempered harmony of the realm in terms that precisely mirror his account of the king's own character and performance as monarch, echoing Exeter's claim that 'government, though high and low and lower/Put into parts, doth keep in one consent,/Congreeing in a full and natural close/Like music' [I, ii, 180–83]. In so doing the archbishop has recourse to the standard trope of the kingdom of 'the honey-bees' [I, ii, 180–214].[1] We have not heard this sort of naturalising discourse about the nature and course of human government since it came spewing out of the mouth of Richard II. Then, of course, it had presaged, indeed, in some ways, it had caused, political disaster. And here it is again, now being applied to the effects of the good government of a virtuous prince on the internal operations of the English polity. Now, and once again, the God-given division of both the social and political orders into hierarchically arranged, interdependent and mutually reinforcing functions or callings is pictured producing order, through an entirely frictionless series of interactions and exchanges. Here the workings of the human social and political orders are depicted working as 'naturally' as nature herself. On this basis, Canterbury feels able to urge the king on 'to France', where he can campaign, safe in the knowledge that his own realm will be able to govern and protect itself with all the spontaneous efficacy and industry of the beehive. The action of the play will, of course, serve (at least ostensibly) to confirm this vision of a realm and regime almost magically transformed from the sick and ailing, corrupt and divided, country presided over by Henry IV, to the very different, perfectly integrated, both virtuous and efficient, political organism (and military machine) that is the England, indeed the 'Britain', of Henry V.

Not that even Henry's regime is devoid of internal difficulties. The church is under the threat of 'reform' – in reality, expropriation – by a Lollard-influenced parliament. Before Act II the chorus identifies the threat of internal dissension. But Henry is shown dispelling such threats with almost absurd ease. As David Kastan has observed, Shakespeare heightens this impression by ignoring the early years of the reign, with their anti-Lancastrian rebellions and Lollard subversion, 'replacing . . . the divided and distrustful country' visible in his sources with a vision of a 'unified England unquestioningly committed to the will of its king'.[2] In Shakespeare's version, while under Henry IV the internal threat to England had been rooted in deep lines of division, envy and emulation that owed their origins to the fall of Richard II and the course of his usurpation, under Henry V the only source of such internal threats is presented as the 'pale policy' of the French, who, terrified of the onset of Henry's invasion, have bribed three English nobles to assassinate him at Southampton before he can take ship for France. The motivations of the traitors are presented as entirely mercenary; they are 'three corrupted men', 'hollow bottoms' which have been filled 'with treacherous crowns' [II, Chorus, 12–30]. Whereas under Henry IV the defeat of treason had taken years of armed struggle, now, under Henry V, the threat to the king from his own subjects is easily dispelled.

Indeed, it provides yet another opportunity for Henry to script and stage a display of royal virtue, here played off against the treason and hypocrisy of the conspirators. Having learned of the conspiracy, Henry leaves the conspirators alone until the very last minute and then consults them about the exercise of royal mercy. Henry has decided 'to enlarge the man committed yesterday/That railed against our person. We consider/It was excess of wine that set him on,/ And on his more advice we pardon him' [II, ii, 39–43]. This decision is vehemently opposed by the conspirators, who, desperate to demonstrate their loyalty to the king, vie with one another in urging Henry to 'severity'. This little scene is followed by the discovery to the conspirators of their own conspiracy and sets up the king's reply to their pleas for mercy. 'The mercy that was quick in us but late/By your own counsel is suppressed and killed:/You must not dare, for shame, to talk of mercy,/For your own reasons turn into your bosoms/As dogs upon their masters, worrying you' [II, ii, 79–83]. As he had in his interview with the Lord Chief Justice at the end of Henry IV, Henry has again enlisted other characters in an exchange calculated to display royal virtue in its best light. The contrast between his treatment of the railing soldier and the noble conspirators shows the power of royal mercy as well as of justice. Henry is not a vengeful but a genuinely just monarch, and the conspirators' own hypocrisy provides the best demonstration of that fact, giving him the perfect occasion for his pursuit of the extremity of the law against 'treason and murder'.

Not only that, once their nefarious schemes have been unmasked, all of the traitors admit and repent their fault. This, of course, is in marked contrast to the rebels in Henry IV, all of whom had consistently proclaimed the justice of their cause and, when defeated, had gone to entirely unrepentant, indeed even defiant, deaths. As we have seen, at Gaultree forest Mowbray and Archbishop Scroop had challenged the equity and honour of their treatment. Worcester submits to his fate, not to the authority of the king or the justice of his cause. 'What I have done my safety urg'd me to;/And I embrace this fortune patiently,/Since not to be avoided it falls on me' [Pt. I, V, v, 11–13]. As for Hotspur, his death on the field of battle confers on him an honour that even the prince acknowledges. The response of these rebels to their defeat at the hands of the crown is very different. Scroop goes first. 'Our purposes God justly hath discovered,/And I repent my fault more than my death,/Which I beseech your highness to forgive,/Although my body pay the price of it.' In the first of the play's two references to the fact that Henry's claim to the throne might be as questionable as his father's, Cambridge insists that 'for me the gold of France did not seduce,/Although I did admit it as a motive/The sooner to effect what I intended'. However, that gesture to the existence of other, alternative claims to the throne does not lead to any sustained challenge to Henry's right but presages an even deeper and more profound genuflection not merely before divine but also before royal authority. 'But God be thanked for prevention,/Which I in sufferance heartily will rejoice,/Beseeching God and you to pardon me.' Grey goes last: 'never did subject more rejoice/At the discovery of most dangerous treason/Than I do at this hour joy o'er myself,/Prevented from a damned enterprise./My fault, but not my body, pardon, sovereign' [II, ii, 151–65]. This, of course, is the right and proper response of rebels to their discovery or defeat by legitimate authority. Here is no search for honour in continued resistance or defiance, no plea for the legitimacy of rebellion against a usurped authority, no stoic embrace of necessity or 'fortune', but rather a measured, indeed a relieved, admission of guilt as, prevented by God and his anointed instrument on earth from committing the soul-destroying sins of treason and murder, into which, as Henry says, they had surely been lured by the devil himself, the conspirators embrace their fate, happy in the knowledge that their discovery has saved the life of the prince and, while it may lead to the destruction of their temporal bodies, can yet, if they properly repent, lead to the salvation of their immortal souls.

The king's response to these speeches confirms these very points. Again, there is no chink of light to be discerned between the king's two bodies, between

Henry's private impulses or will and the demands of his public office; he acts not in private 'revenge' for offences committed against 'our person', but rather to defend the realm, which the conspirators have 'sold' to various fates worse than death: 'your king to slaughter,/His princes and his peers to servitude,/His subjects to oppression and contempt,/And his whole kingdom into desolation'. Henry gives the traitors over to the laws and to God, in the pious hope that, through the deaths of their bodies, they might be brought, via 'true repentance', to salvation [II, ii, 66–182].

There could scarcely be a clearer public demonstration of the claim, made at the end of 2 Henry IV, that 'this is the English not the Turkish court;/Not Amurath an Amurath succeeds,/But Harry Harry' [Pt. II, V, ii, 47–49]. As Henry later tells the French ambassador, 'we are no tyrant but a Christian king' [Pt. II, I, ii, 242]. The point of these scenes with the traitors Cambridge, Scroop and Grey, then, is that even Henry's greatest enemies, his would-be betrayers and murderers, indeed – as Cambridge's brief aside implies – potential supporters of rival claimants to his throne, all recognise that fact and are forced to acknowledge the legitimacy of his rule, even as he sends them to their death.

Under Henry IV, of course, the internal treacheries and dissensions that had threatened the integrity of the English state had stemmed as much from Scotland and Wales as from within the English nobility. But Henry is portrayed as able to leave for his invasion of France with England safe from the threat of Scottish incursions or Welsh revolts. Indeed, Henry V famously features, in Fluellen, an image of Wales brought into staunch loyalty and military service to the English crown, a crown now worn by a Welshman, Harry of Monmouth. Indeed, all of Britain is shown as in some sense united in support of Henry's French ambitions. In the persons of Captain Jamy the Scotsman, Fluellen the Welshman, and MacMorris the Irishman, all active in the service of the king against the French, we have an image of British unity, as the three kingdoms, plus Wales, unite, under the authority of the king of England, to fight the foreigner. Relations between the three are notoriously fractious, but the source of the friction between them comes most obviously from the Irishman MacMorris, which in light of the rebellion that was currently raging in Ireland is surely no surprise.

As a number of critics have observed, there is a certain untamed wildness, an almost pagan exoticism, attributed to Wales in 1 Henry IV. When the defeat of Mortimer by the Welsh is first announced to the king he is informed that 'a thousand of his people' have been 'butchered', 'upon whose dead corpses there was such misuse,/Such beastly shameless transformation,/By those Welshwomen done, as may not be/Without much shame retold or spoken of' [Pt. I, I, i, 42–46]. In Holinshed the nature of these atrocities is spelt out; it involved cutting off the penises and noses of slain Englishmen and stuffing the former in their mouths and the latter into their rectums. Mortimer, captured by

Glendower, goes native and marries the Welsh rebel's daughter, and is shown later in the play in thrall to his new wife. As Howard and Rackin observe, this is to associate Wales with 'emasculation and female power'. They find an immediate Elizabethan context for these scenes in 'anxieties about English colonists who married native women and became assimilated to the culture of the savage places they had been sent to domesticate'. In the 1590s such worries no longer applied to Wales but they certainly did to Ireland, where, as Christopher Highley points out, 'going native' in this way was described by Spenser as a process of 'degendering'. Indeed, Spenser cited as a prime example the fate of the 'great Mortimer, who forgetting how great he once was in England, or English at all, is now become the most barbarous of them all'.[3] If we follow Highley's entirely plausible argument that the threat to the Lancastrian state represented in *1 Henry IV* by the wild, unassimilated Welsh evokes or stands in for the similar threat represented, in the 1590s, by the equally wild, unassimilated and rebellious Irish, then the presence, in *Henry V,* of the faintly ludicrous, but staunch, brave and entirely loyal, Fluellen represents a gesture towards a future in which the Irish will follow the Welsh into the loyal service of the Tudor monarchy and English state. As Terence Hawkes points out, Fluellen's name is an Anglicisation of Llewellyn, the name of the last Welsh prince of Wales, a proud and independent title now 'brutally reduced' to an insultingly inept English mispronunciation.[4] Mispronouncing his name, the play adds insult to injury by continually insisting on Fluellen's failure correctly to pronounce English. Thus in Fluellen, whose service and virtue are consistently recognised, honoured and exploited by his 'kinsman', the king, we have a presage of the sort of integration into a genuinely 'British' monarchy that, under the right circumstances, could incorporate both the Irish and Scots, once the rebels were defeated in Ireland and James VI had come into his own not only in Scotland but in England too. We shall return to that point later; what matters most for our current purpose is the way in which tasks – the putting down of internal rebellion, the maintenance of the integrity of the realm in the face of Welsh revolt and Scots invasion – that had nearly destroyed Henry IV's monarchy, and certainly brought the king himself to his grave, are all being achieved with effortless ease by his son.

Similarly, the threats of misrule, festive or otherwise, that had gathered around the figure of Falstaff and his associates have all but dissolved. Falstaff's death happens offstage and is reported to us through the account provided by Mistress Quickly to Nym and Bardolph. Cut off from the oxygen of princely favour that had hitherto sustained him, Falstaff has sickened and died; the king, Mistress Quickly reports, 'has killed his heart' [II, i, 88]. This claim is corroborated in the same scene by Nym, who claims that 'the King hath run bad humours on the knight,/That's the even of it.' 'Thou hast spoke right,' Pistol concurs, 'his heart is fracted and corroborate' [II, i, 121–24]. Later, Fluellen gives a similar account of Falstaff's passing. Seeking to draw parallels between

Henry V and Alexander the Great, he compares Alexander's killing of his best friend, with Henry's dealings with Falstaff. 'As Alexander killed his friend Clytus, being in his ales and his cups, so also Harry Monmouth, being in his right wits and his good judgements, turned away the fat knight with the great-belly doublet: he was full of jests, and gipes, and knaveries, and mocks; I have forgot his name.' 'Sir John Falstaff,' replies Gower [IV, vii, 44–50]. But if the play wants to insist that there is a real sense in which Henry has killed Falstaff, not even his former intimates and dependants want to contest the justice of that action. 'The King is a good king, but it must be as it may. He passes some humours and careers,' is all that Nym has to say on the subject [II, ii, 125–26]. And, after all, despite the apparent absurdity of Fluellen's comparison, a deadly serious point is being made here; for, while Alexander had killed his friend, Clytus, in a fit of drunken brutality, Henry had dismissed his when stone cold sober, and he had done so, moreover, for the good of the commonweal rather than for the gratification of some transitory and entirely private passion.[5]

Deprived of their lord of misrule, and their link to the power and patronage of the crown, Falstaff's circle revert to type, sinking back into their former lives and milieux as thieves about town, camp followers and pretended soldiers in France.

Subjected to the appropriate disciplinary structures and punishments, some (Bardolph and Nym) die on the gallows, others die racked by disease in prison or in a paupers' hospital (Nell) and others still (Falstaff) in disgrace and debt. The lone survivivor, Pistol, sinks back into the underworld of petty crime, bought sex, disease and beggary whence they all came. As Nym had himself admitted with respect to Falstaff's fate, Henry V was 'a good king' and 'good kings' did indeed have to pass over 'some humours and careers'.

Such, it seems, are the fruits of legitimacy. The chorus before Act II addresses England on her potential as a rightly governed and properly united kingdom and people. 'O England, model to thy inward greatness,/Like little body with a mighty heart,/What mightst thou do, that honour would thee do,/Were all thy children kind and natural' [II, Chorus, 16–19]. And yet the rule and reign of that entirely legitimate, properly Christian prince, Henry V, has reduced the English to precisely that state and the wonders that follow at Agincourt are presented both as a necessary, indeed even as a 'natural', consequence of that rule and as a more or less miraculous demonstration or vindication of it.

Exeter's verdict on the battle, after he has heard the casualties on both sides read out, is more or less endorsed by the play. ' 'Tis wonderful', is all he can say. But, the king is swift to add, this is a divine and not a natural wonder, more like a miracle than a mere feat of arms. 'Be it death proclaimed through our host/ To boast of this, or take that praise from God/Which is his only,' is his response to Exeter's ejaculation. Asked by Fluellen 'is it not lawful, an't please your majesty, to tell how many is killed?' Henry responds again, 'Yes, Captain, but with this acknowledgement,/That God fought for us.' The scene ends with Henry ordering that 'do we all holy rites./Let there be sung Non nobis and te deum' [IV, viii, 113–24]. As Moody Prior points out, at each of these turns Henry is shown as having acted 'correctly according to the best authorities'. His execution of Bardolph was, according to the rules of war, perfectly correct. The attribution of victory to God alone was a gesture approved not only by Erasmus but by 'the best military manuals'.[6]

There is, indeed, a major return of God talk in *Henry V*. Robert Ornstein observes that 'the thought of God is again and again the final resting place of his speeches', which often start boasting of his 'intended accomplishments' only then to recall God's will.[7] From the outset Henry has been anxious to associate his cause with God's; to see God's hands in his preservation from the plotters and in all his victories. After all, the play all but opens with the king demanding to be told by that arbiter of God's justice and word, the Archbishop of Canterbury, whether his claim to the French throne is just. He attributes the revelation of the plot against him at Southampton to God and proceeds thence to the assertion of certain divine aid for his efforts in France. 'Since God so graciously hath brought to light/This dangerous treason lurking in our way/To hinder our beginnings. We doubt not now/But every rub is smoothed on our way./Then forth, dear countrymen. Let us deliver/Our puissance into the hand of God,/Putting it straight in expedition./Cheerly to sea; the signs of war advance./No king of England, if not king of France!' [II, ii, 186–94]. Before Agincourt, he tells Gloucester, 'we are in God's hands, brother, not in theirs' [III, vi, 168]. Told by Mountjoy that 'the day is yours', his first response is: 'praised be God, and not our strength, for it' [IV, vii, 86].

The most obvious and extended deployment of God talk by the king occurs in the Act IV when in prayerful conversation with his God, Henry offers the deity a bargain whereby, in return for Henry's good works in setting up chantries and having prayers and masses said for the murdered Richard II, God will forget his father's sin in usurping the throne and vouchsafe Henry the victory. For the audience, if not for Henry himself – who, as Prior points out, displays no doubt of his *own* rectitude and right, as opposed to that of his father – this renders the outcome of the coming battle a test of the legitimacy of Henry's rule and of the righteousness of his war. As Henry himself proclaims, 'no king of England, if not king of France'. If we accept the terms of this bargain, or, rather, if we accept that God accepts them – and that, of course, is a big 'if' – then the result of the battle represents a massive divine endorsement of Henry's rule.

Nor is the final triumph of the reign pictured as solely or even mainly military. Rather the play concludes with that ultimate Tudor (and, as it would turn out, also early Stuart) fantasy of national redemption and power; a match made by an English monarch, indeed by an English king, with one of the great continental monarchies on terms set by the English. This was the stuff of which English dreams were made, and here was Henry V just doing it.

Legitimacy as an achieved effect

And yet for all its recourse to God talk, for all its consistent Richard-II-like insistence on the naturalness of monarchical rule and of the obedience and loyalty of subjects, both noble and plebeian, to legitimate authority; for all its invocation of divine providence as the natural back-up, the ultimate guarantor and protector, of legitimate monarchical authority legitimately wielded, the play does not end on what we might term a transcendently absolutist, divine right note. On the contrary, it ends by invoking the chaos, civil strife and slaughter to come in the reign of Henry's son, Henry VI. 'Henry the Sixth, in infant bands crowned King/Of France and England, did this king succeed,/ Whose state so many had the managing/That they lost France and made his England bleed,/Which oft our stage hath shown' [Epilogue, 9–13]. The effect of this reference to future events and past plays, was, of course, to emphasise the entirely human, this-worldly, indeed frankly contingent, nature of the sort of political stability and military success achieved by Henry V. What one man's prowess and skill had achieved could just as easily be lost by the malice or incompetence of others. Such a framing device, placed at the very end of the play serves, therefore, to refocus our attention on the constructed, the humanly achieved, rather than the naturally or providentially produced, nature of Henry V's achievements.

And indeed throughout the play all the emphasis is placed on the role of Henry's own prowess in achieving his ends. Moreover, for all Henry's spectacular success on the battlefield, for all his self-presentation, particularly in his wooing of the French princess, as a bluff and simple soldier, a man devoid of the artifice, the subtle and deceitful skills of the courtier, the suitor or the politician, the nature of that prowess is not presented as solely, or even as predominantly military but rather as what we might term 'political', indeed as rhetorical. Throughout Henry is presented as a soldier and the play's defining event is a battle, and yet, for all the fuss made by the chorus about the inadequacy of the wooden O of the Globe to contain the full grandeur of Agincourt, the play makes almost no attempt to stage actual combat. In marked contrast to some of his earlier history plays, as Andrew Gurr observes, the only fighting that takes place on stage is that between Pistol and his wretched French prisoner,[8] and the only violence the beating inflicted on Pistol himself by Fluellen and the killing, pretty much in cold blood, and on the direct orders of the king, of the French prisoners. Again, as a number of commentators have stressed, unlike his sources, Shakespeare makes no attempt to explain Henry's victory in terms of his superior military tactics. To quote Wayne Rebhorn on the same subject, although 'Agincourt constitutes a genuine military victory, Shakespeare shapes his play to make it seem due to Hal's rhetorical masterpiece, the Saint Crispin's Day speech, as much as to battlefield heroics. For after the speech what we see is a French soldier surrendering to Pistol: French commanders lamenting that all is lost; Hal's instruction to his troops to kill their prisoners; and finally, Hal learning from Mountjoy that the English have in fact been victorious. What the audience does not see . . . is any sort of battle.'[9] As Gurr puts it, the key to the English victory is the superior morale of the English host,[10] and that morale is presented as a result of the rhetorical skill of the king.

At every turn, crucial to Henry's success is his capacity perfectly to match his mode of discourse, both his medium and his message, to the immediate political and polemical circumstances with which he is confronted. It is this quintessentially political skill which underlies Henry's rule, but Henry has become so practised in its exercise that he appears not, as his father had, 'a vile politician', but rather a virtuous prince, a figure whose legitimacy and virtue seem to be so obvious, so transparently and transcendently self-validating, that they brook no challenge or denial. These plays dramatise the resulting style of rule. Repeatedly we are shown both the outward appearances and effects for which Henry is always striving and the very considerable rhetorical and theatrical efforts, the successive acts of political self-fashioning, self-representation and manoeuvre, that go into producing those outward appearances and effects. From the scenes at the end of 2 Henry IV with the Lord Chief Justice, through the dismissal of Falstaff, to the staged discovery of the traitorous Cambridge plot at Southampton, and his public consultation of the archbishop of Canterbury about the validity of his claim to the throne of France, we are consistently shown the ways in which Henry manipulates those around him to produce occasions that allow him to enact his own political virtue. Henry's skill as a political dramaturg is shown transcending his own finely controlled performance to encompass the performances of others, as he elicits from the Lord Chief Justice a fine statement of the theory of the king's two bodies, which he is then able to appropriate for himself, and extracts from the stunned traitors expressions of their own guilt and of his justice that serve, in their turn, to strengthen the very authority that their plot was designed to overthrow. Here at least a Greenblattian analysis of the ways in which subversion can be not merely frustrated or suppressed but turned to the advantage of power, through the theatrical enactment of its own operations, seems entirely apposite.

Henry's claims to virtue and honour are thus intensely performative and situational. Henry is the past master of saying what his immediate situation demands in order to effect his own immediate purposes, while looking virtuous and honourable as he does so. As G.K. Hunter puts it, 'the King is given a spectrum of modes of persuasion: peremptory to ambassadors, exhortatory to the army, contemplative in soliloquy, bantering to Katherine, pious when appropriate, earnestly prosaic to the soldiers. . . . Each of these rhetorical modes works as a personal dialect and by this means achieves political power over the person addressed, whether that be Bedford or Gloucester, Fluellen, Katherine, or Scroop, or the Dauphin'.[11] As Rebhorn observes, this marks out Hal 'as a version of the ideal orator as the Renaissance conceived the figure; someone capable of handling any audience by adapting his performance to the circumstances involved, the master of figures and tropes and of all styles, high, middle and low'. In *Henry V* his 'speeches vary in style from regal, ironic, and angry, through martial and uplifting, to the simplicity and directness of the "plain soldier" '. Rebhorn concludes that 'what Hal accomplishes with his rhetoric is precisely what Renaissance rhetors all wanted to accomplish with theirs: by using persuasion as a kind of force superior to actual force, he brings his auditor to subject herself to him of her own free will, to believe in his arguments and in him, ultimately to love the one who commands her destiny'.[12]

The play adverts to this aspect of his kingship through the striking inconsistency, the often considerable tensions within, and often striking contradictions between, the different aspects of his performance of kingly virtue. Thus, before Harfleur, Henry is all too ready to threaten the townspeople with an army loosed from all moral constraint or military discipline, evoking what horrors 'heady murder, spoil and villainy' will visit upon the town if it refuses to surrender in due time. 'If not, why, in a moment look to see/The blind and bloody soldier with foul hand/Defile the locks of your shrill-shrieking daughters,/Your fathers taken by the silver beards,/And their most reverend heads dashed to the walls,/Your naked infants spitted upon pikes,/Whiles the mad mothers with their howls confused/Do break the clouds, as did the wives of Jewry/At Herod's bloody-hunting slaughtermen./What say you? Will you yield and this avoid?/Or, guilty in defence, be thus destroyed?' [III, iii, 8–43]. This, of course, is a remarkable passage. In language of almost Marlovian relish, Henry manages at once to threaten the town with rape, pillage and slaughter at the hands of an army let slip utterly out of control, while yet disclaiming all responsibility for such an outcome. The troops, he claims, will not be acting on his instructions; rather they will have run amok. Theirs will be a 'licentious wickedness', the consequences of their actions best likened to the torments of hell. But if the soldiers will be guilty, the prince will be blameless, since their actions will not be on his instructions but a function of the extent to which they have escaped from his control. Moreover, if things reach this pass, the real blame will rest entirely on the townsmen who, having been warned of the inevitable outcome of further resistance, will have brought this fate upon themselves. Throughout, Henry manages to maintain a position of peerless virtue for himself, by threatening the direst acts while sedulously refusing to accept any responsibility for them. The result is a rhetorical tour de force, through which, of course, Henry attains his end – the fall of Harfleur – without another shot being fired. And here the play improves on its sources, which show Henry sacking Harfleur, while Shakespeare has him doing so only rhetorically, which display of purely verbal power then allows him to spare the town after its surrender.[13]

All of this is in stark contrast to his attitude to even relatively minor breaches of military discipline, when such breaches do not accord with his political needs of the moment. He blithely signs off on the hanging of his old crony Bardolph for an act of petty theft, for essentially political purposes. His soldiers must eschew theft and oppression of the French because, as he says, 'when lenity and cruelty play for a kingdom, the gentler gamester is the soonest winner' [III, vi, 110–12]. 'Lenity,' then, is not a moral principle or commitment but a political good, a propaganda weapon in a wider military and political struggle, and sometimes the military exigencies of Henry's situation supervene, rendering 'lenity' a luxury he cannot afford. As Gurr observes, for all that Erasmus made clemency or lenity the highest attribute of a Christian king and opposed it as such to military glory, 'Henry refuses mercy to the rebels at Southampton . . .; he threatens to deny it to the citizens at Harfleur; and most tellingly of all he denies it absolutely to the prisoners at Agincourt. Lenity stops near the frontier', or rather its absolute prerogatives as the queen of royal virtues bend before the sovereign demands of 'policy'.[14]

Thus, towards the end of the battle, Henry becomes afraid that the French resistance has not been finally crushed and immediately orders that 'every soldier kill his prisoners', the better to be able to meet this new threat [IV, vi, 37]. Given the overwhelming numerical advantage of the French, this may be an entirely sensible military expedient. But whatever it is, it is not exactly 'lenity'. It is followed immediately by the news that the French have slaughtered the boys in the baggage train. This, according to Fluellen, is 'expressly against the laws of war' and it leads Gower to assume that the king's order to kill the French prisoners was an act of revenge for this enormity – 'O 'tis a gallant king!' But that, of course, had not been the case. [IV, vii, 5–10].

We are seeing here the cumulative effect of the king's greedily accumulated reputation as a man of honour and prowess on his admiring audience of subjects and soldiers. It is an impression that Henry is careful to reinforce through his public demeanour, announcing, when he hears the news of the slaughter at the baggage train, that 'I was not angry since I came to France/ Until this instant' [IV, vii, 54–55] thus, by the public display of royal emotion, enhancing his reputation for honour and virtue even as he threatens the French with further slaughter.[15]

At each of these points a case could be made for Henry's conduct in terms of the laws of war and of the informal norms of early modern (or indeed late medieval) military conduct. There is always a legal case to be made in Henry's favour. But the play seems to go out of its way not only to problematise the legal basis for his actions, but also to raise what we might term wider moral questions about just how Christian this model Christian king really is. Or, to put it slightly differently, would a genuinely Christain conscience have been rendered as secure as Henry's evidently is by the formal legalism with which he meets all of the great moral cruxes placed before him by the play? The same sorts of tensions, or even contradictions can be seen in his relationship to martial glory and honour. Before Agincourt, when he needs to psych up his heavily outnumbered army for the coming battle, Henry harks on the theme of honour, won through martial prowess and exercised in the defence of England against the foreigner. In reply to Westmoreland's wish that 'we now had here/But one ten thousand of those men in England/That do no work today', Henry famously repudiates that thought. 'If we are marked to die, we are enough/To do our country loss, and if to live,/The fewer men, the greater share of honour./God's will, I pray thee wish not one man more./By Jove, I am not covetous for gold,/Nor care I who doth feed upon my cost;/It earns me not if men my garments wear:/Such outward things dwell not in my desires./But if it be a sin to covet honour/I am the most offending soul alive./No, faith, my coz, wish not a man from England./God's peace, I would not lose so great an honour/As one man more, methinks, would share from me,/For the best hope I have' [IV, iii, 16–33].

This is Henry as the true heir of Hotspur, 'the king of honour', except that here honour is a category suddenly opened, through military service with and under the king, to all. 'For he today that sheds his blood with me/Shall be my brother; be he ne'er so vile,/This day shall gentle his condition./And gentlemen in England now abed/Shall think themselves accursed they were not here,/And hold their manhoods cheap whiles any speaks/That fought with us upon St Crispin's day' [IV, iii, 41–67].

There was, of course, a stark contrast between this stance, adopted before the battle, and that adopted after victory has been secured. While before the battle he may have opened up the category of gentle status to all who fought with him, afterwards, when the casualties are counted, it has shrunk again to include only the nobility. When Henry asks 'where is the number of our English dead', the paper given him lists only 'Edward the duke of York; the earl of Suffolk; Sir Richard Keighley; Davy Gam, esquire;/None else of name' [IV, viii, 103–6].[16]

Before the battle, Henry proclaimed himself 'the most offending soul alive', if it was a sin 'to covet honour', picturing the survivors of his host bragging to the grave about their role in this great victory. However, afterwards he puts a strict interdict on any such bragging rights. All praise for the victory was to be given to God and none arrogated to themselves by the victors. The chorus at the beginning of Act V pictures the king approaching London in triumph. 'You may imagine him upon Blackheath,/Where that his lords desire him to have borne/His bruised helmet and his bended sword/Before him through the city.

He forbids it,/Being free from vainness and self-glorious pride,/Giving full trophy, signal and ostent/Quite from himself to God. But now behold, in the quick forge and working house of thought,/How London doth pour out her citizens./The Mayor and all his brethren in best sort,/Like to the senators of th'antique Rome,/With the plebeians swarming at their heels,/Go forth and fetch their conquering Caesar in' [V, 0, 16–28]. Henry, then, knows when to blow hot and when to blow cold; when to promote himself and his cause by opening the prospect of honour, won in battle, to all who had fought with him, and when to hang back, denying, even to himself, the praise due for this most famous of victories. But as the play's evocation of his triumphant entry into London shows, while he gives the credit to God, he is quite happy to allow others to lavish all of that same credit upon him. It is the same tact, the same artful appearance of modest artlessness, that he displays in his wooing of the French princess Katherine. There it is the very intensity and style of his disavowals of rhetorical skill and flourish that demonstrate the depth of his rhetorical artifice and skill. Similarly, it is the ardent 'sincerity' of his patently false pretence that his suit to the princess is not an offer that neither she nor her father can refuse, but rather an act of love, that is the final testament to his finely honed political skills; providing proof positive that, whoever we are dealing with here, it is not the bluff and simple soldier framed by Henry's protestations to his Kate.

In fact, by stressing the tensions within and between the king's various pitches for the emotional support of his soldiers, his efforts, through the power of his rhetoric, to construct, out of a host made up of commoners and noblemen, a unified whole, the play is calling attention to the sheer rhetorical (and of course also the political) skill of the king. And, insofar as the theatre audience responds to Henry's rhetoric, even as they note the very considerable tensions and contradictions within it – tensions to which the play itself so insistently adverts – the play is itself repeating, and presenting itself as repeating, the success of Henry's appeal to his troops in its own (equally successful) appeal to its audience; an audience which, as Alison Thorne and Joel Altman have both pointed out,[17] was likely to have been at least as socially heterogeneous and ideologically divided, as sceptical, war-weary and jaded, as Henry's host.

Quoting Michael Goldman's observation that there is a marked similarity between 'the figure of the chorus rousing the audience to co-operation and excitement' and 'the figure of Henry addressing his men',[18] Lawrence Danson points out that if 'the King is like an actor', 'that special actor, Shakespeare's chorus, is like the King'. Just as Henry needs his troops to respond to his rhetoric, so the chorus needs the audience to respond to his. In its relations with the audience, the play attempts to enact in the theatre the same sorts of theatrical effects that it shows Henry working on his men. Lamenting the inadequacy of theatrical performance to evoke the grandeur of the play's matter, theme and hero, the chorus, and indeed the play more generally conceived, proceeds to demonstrate the capacity of its own language, of its own rhetorical skill and theatrical effect, to do the very thing that it claims mere dramatic performance cannot do.[19]

In so doing it stacks the deck against itself. It has become a critical common-place that the exalted language, the agitprop enthusiasm, of the chorus is inces-santly juxtaposed with scenes that call the resulting version of reality into the sharpest question. Thus in Act I, the initial uplift of the play's opening is imme-diately followed by the dubious politicking of the bishops; in Act II, the claim that 'all the youth of England are on fire' to join the war effort is followed by the bickering between Bardolph, Nym and Pistol and the decidedly downbeat news of Falstaff's death; in Act III, the chorus' evocation of the derring-do of the siege of Harfleur and Henry's 'once more into the breach' speech is imme-diately juxtaposed with another scene between Nym and Bardolph which sees them heading in precisely the opposite direction from the breach; the evoca-tion of the miraculous effect on his troops of 'a little touch of Harry in the night' that opens Act IV is followed by a farcical scene between the king and Pistol and then by the altogether more seriously downbeat exchange between Henry, Bates and Williams. Moreover, many of the ecstatic estimations of the miraculous effect of Henry's accession on the moral and political condition of the reign, quoted above, come from the most dubious of sources; from the archbishop of Canterbury, with his vested interest in packing the king safely off to war in France and, still more worryingly, from men who are plotting treason, even as they laud to the skies the rule of the king they are planning to kill.[20]

We might conclude that these juxtapositions and contrasts are designed to advert to the gap between rhetoric and reality, between official ideology and aspiration, on the one hand, and the condition of the real world, on the other. But what the play is also revealing in such passages and scenes is the sort of human material with which Henry has actually to work. Insofar as the official ideology is false, insofar as Henry's accession has not miraculously transformed England into a living exemplar of the great chain of being operating at the very top of its game, of the Elizabethan world picture on speed, the extraordinary military and political success that Henry does manage to conjure out of such dubious and corrupt human materials emerges as all the more remarkable. As with the 'reformation', staged at the end of 2 Henry IV and marvelled at at the start of Henry V, what is at stake here is precisely not some 'miracle of the body politic', a moral and political transformation worked through the divinity that really does hedge a (legitimate) king, but rather a political effect or series of effects, perhaps even (in part at least) a series of illusions, worked by this-worldly political means, and in particular through Henry's manipulation of what we might, somewhat anachronistically, call ideology, or, rather more historically, rhetoric.

For the self-interested lies or half-truths, spouted by the chorus, and indeed by various of Henry's instruments, followers, and even enemies, prove to be crucial to his success, since it is precisely his capacity to get people to believe at least some of this stuff that enables Henry to bend the decidedly imperfect human materials at his disposal to his purposes and thus to succeed as a ruler. And all this despite the fact that a good deal of the audience's actual experience, not to mention a great deal of what is happening on stage, is telling them that none of this is true at all. The play draws attention to this fact by replicating in its own relationship with the audience precisely the same relation that, in the play, Henry's rhetorical artifice enables him to establish with his subjects and soldiers.

It is as though the play wants, in spite of everything, and against adverse odds of its own devising, to overcome what Joel Altman (amongst others) has posited as the deep scepticism and potential division to be found in its first audiences, and to do so not merely through the magnitude of Henry's victory at Agincourt, but also through the theatrical and rhetorical power of its own theatrical and rhetorical effects. As Steven Marx puts it, in Henry V, 'Shakespeare aims the full blast of his rhetorical power at the audience ... The choruses inflame us to collaborate with the author in producing a spectacle to sweep away thought in a flood of patriotic passion.'[21]

On this account, the play is both a depiction of the theatrical power of kingly politics, when the role of prince is being played by a master of the requisite rhetorical and emotional registers, and an extraordinarily daring and confident wager on the power of the theatre – and specifically on the power of this particular playwright's language – to create an affective unity within, or rather out of, an extraordinarily heterogeneous audience and a distinctly unpromising political situation.[22]

According to Leonard Barkan, in a talk on Henry V, while commenting on the opening chorus, Harry Berger Jr turned to the audience and asked, 'what's this guy trying to do? He's trying to get us to join the army!'[23] Of course, the extent to which the play succeeded in persuading its first audiences, if not to join the army (which, at the time, was composed of largely unwilling conscripts), then at least to buy into the sort of sentiments that might have made that an appealing thing to think of doing, must remain a matter of conjecture – and much recent criticism has concentrated on analysing the ideological tensions and contradictions revealed by the play[24] – but there can surely be no doubting the daring and self-confidence of the attempt.

A just war and a Christian prince?

Perhaps the most serious tensions and contradictions between and amongst Henry's various definitions of, and claims to, honour or virtue involve the issue of the justice, or otherwise, of his pursuit of the French crown, and thus of the justice of his wars in France. This is an issue upon which, remarkably, Henry never commits himself, relying rather on the opinions of others to legitimise his enterprise.

Famously, the play opens with a discussion between the archbishop and the bishop of Ely in which it rapidly emerges that there is an attempt pending in parliament to expropriate the wealth of the church. This is a measure which 'was like, and had indeed against us passed' during the previous reign, had not 'the scambling and unquiet time' postponed it. Now it was back again; at stake were huge sums of money. 'If it pass against us/We lose the better half of our possession:/For all the temporal lands which men devout/By testament have given to the Church/Would they strip from us, being valued thus:/As much as would maintain, to the King's honour,/Full fifteen earls and fifteen hundred knights,/Six thousand and two hundred good esquires,/And to the relief of lazars and weak age,/Of indigent faint souls past corporal toil,/A hundred almshouses right well supplied,/And to the coffers of the King beside,/A thousand pounds by th'year. Thus runs the bill' [I, i, 1–19]. As David Kastan and Hugh Grady both observe, the references here to almshouses and relief to lepers and the aged seem calculated to set up an opposition between the demands of Christian charity and the protection of the material interests of the clerical estate and thus to advert directly to the corruption and venality of the bishops,[25] who are obviously keen to know how the king stands effected to the proposal. 'He seems indifferent' [I, i, 72] is the archbishop's estimate. To get Henry fully onside, the archbishop purposes to use the king's intended French enterprise as a douceur. He has promised the king 'a greater sum/Than ever at one time the clergy yet/Did to his predecessors part withal'; an 'offer' which has met 'with good acceptance of his majesty' [I, i, 79–83]. On this account, the clergy have a very strong vested interested in the king's French adventure. All this takes place before the public consultation of the archbishop about the legitimacy of the king's claim to the French throne. Not only that, but, as the French ambassador later reveals, Henry has already sent 'into France for certain dukedoms in the right/Of your great predecessor King Edward the Third' [I, ii, 247–49]. All of which, of course, throws into the most serious question the objectivity of the archbishop's verdict that the Salic Law does not apply and that therefore Henry has a perfectly good claim to the French crown.

The terms upon which Henry asks the archbishop's opinion repay attention. Demanding that the archbishop rule on whether 'the law Salic that they have in France/Or should or should not bar us in our claim', Henry enjoins him not to 'fashion, wrest or bow your reading' in order to 'miscreate' a title 'whose right/Suits not in native colours with the truth'. The stakes, the king reminds him and us, are very high, for the fate of thousands likely to be killed in the ensuing war turned on the archbishop's verdict, or, as Henry put it, on 'what your reverence shall incite us to' [I, ii, 9–32]. This is another remarkable passage, up there with the speech before Harfleur in the intricacy of the logic through which it seeks to exculpate an ever virtuous and honourable Christian prince from the moral consequences of his own actions. All the emphasis, all the responsibility for determining the justice of the king's cause is here placed on the archbishop. It is the archbishop who will 'incite' the king to war. If that war is unjust, all the guilt for the innocent blood shed during its course will fall not on the king's but on the archbishop's head. It is the archbishop's conscience, not the king's, that is on trial here; and it is the operation of that conscience that will wash 'as pure as sin with baptism' whatever course of action the archbishop pronounces just.

This is not to suggest that the play portrays Henry as simply indifferent to the justice of his cause. There is something going on here far more complicated than mere pretence. Thus Robert Ornstein comments on this scene that 'Harry would like to believe that in every war there is a right on the one side and a wrong on the other, because he intends to be certain of his "right".'[26] Foreign war is central to Henry's entire project as king, and the question of right is crucial if the war is successfully to project and confirm Henry's status as a truly legitimate Christian king and warrior. Nuttall ascribes considerable tension to the moment when Henry asks 'may I with right and conscience make this claim?' But for all that, as Nuttall observes, ' "right" and "conscience" are serious words', and for all that the king, while 'straining at the leash to go to war', 'cannot move if he does not receive an affirmative answer', by this point neither the audience nor Henry have any reason to doubt what the archbishop is going to say.[27] No mere Machiavel, Henry is, however, quite Machiavellian enough to know how crucial the appearance of being in the right is likely to prove and also perhaps to realise the need not to look too closely at the fine print if he is to be able to assert the justice of his cause with anything like the necessary conviction.

And the print, of course, turns out to be very fine indeed. For the archbishop's statement of the king's case is so complex and convoluted as to be entirely unintelligible in performance and extremely difficult to follow on the printed page. As Grady comments, 'the solemn tones of King Harry seem to brook no equivocation in their insistence on an absolute moral truth' – and yet they elicit from the archbishop an account which is far from clear-cut, but rather open to all sorts of 'questions, contestation, alternative interpretation, and legal wrangling'.[28] Its closest analogues are to be found in York's explication of his claim to the throne to Warwick and Salisbury in 2 Henry VI and in Pandolph's serpentine account in King John of precisely why it is just and right for the French king to break his oath and terminate the recently concluded peace with England. As these resemblances should remind us, it did not take Parsons's great tract, A conference about the next succession to remind Shakespeare (and his audiences) both that when the succession to the throne came into question any number of eminently plausible and contestable legal cases could be made for a variety of claimants and that the resulting conflicts were far more likely to be settled on the battlefield than in the courts either of law or of opinion.

So complex is the archbishop's exposition of Henry's right that after some 60 lines even the king himself does not understand it, greeting the conclusion of the archbishop's speech with the simple question 'may I with right and conscience make this claim?' only to be answered triumphantly in the affirmative with an evocation of the exploits of his glorious ancestors Edward III and the Black Prince [I, ii, 96, 97–114]. As Kastan comments, 'if an audience loses the thread of the labyrinthine speech, the archbishop's assurance that the complex proof is "as clear as is the summer's sun" (I, ii, 86] is unlikely to undo the damage or do anything other than provoke either suspicion or perhaps even laughter.'[29] Nuttall argues that what is crucial here is not so much the inherent justice of the king's cause but rather the fact that 'there is a legal case' to be made for Henry's preferred course of action. But that is not quite true; for this is a legal case stated by that ultimate spiritual authority, the archbishop of Canterbury, an authority who has been explicitly charged by the king not to provide him with a legal brief but rather to resolve his conscience on the issue of peace or war. And what the play is doing here, quite deliberately,[30] is to ask whether the existence of such a complex and inherently contestable legal case, stated by a figure as compromised in the eyes of the audience as the archbishop of Canterbury now is, can really answer the question of the justice of the king's cause or resolve anyone's conscience. For all the precise legalism, the refined casuistry, with which Henry always tries to surround his decisions and actions, it is by no means clear that the more morally acute members of the audience will share either Henry's conviction that the justice of his cause can be collapsed into the serpentine arguments marshalled on his behalf by the archbishop or his belief that it is only the archbishop's soul that will be in jeopardy should that claim prove faulty and the war prove mistaken or 'unjust'.

This is an issue to which the play returns in Henry's famous impromptu debate with the soldiers Bates and Williams. Bates opines that they would all be better off if the king were there alone, for then he could be ransomed and the rest of them could escape with their lives. To this pious wish, the disguised king responds 'methinks I could not die anywhere so contented as in the King's company, his cause being just and his quarrel honourable'. 'That's more than we know,' replies Williams, and Bates adds, showing an estimably orthodox grasp of the doctrine of the *arcana imperii*, 'ay, or more than we should seek after, for we know enough if we know we are the King's subject. If his cause be wrong, our obedience to the King wipes the crime of it out of us' [IV, i, 126–33]. This, of course, returns us to the issue of the justice of the cause and places the moral burden, not where Henry had put it in that opening scene, on the archbishop of Canterbury, but squarely on the shoulders of the king himself. In itself, this was not a claim to which the king could object, since it put the soldiers in precisely the same relation to the king's conscience as he had placed himself in relation to that of the archbishop of Canterbury.

However, Williams then gives the point at issue a rather eccentric, even heterodox, theological twist. 'But if the cause be not good, the King himself hath a heavy reckoning to make when all those legs and arms and heads chopped off in a battle shall join together at the latter day and cry all "We died at such a place", some swearing, some crying for a surgeon, some upon their wives left poor behind them, some upon the debts they owe, some upon their children rawly left. I am afeard there are few die well that die in a battle, for how can they charitably dispose of anything when blood is their argument? Now if these men do not die well it will be a black matter for the King, that led them to it, who to disobey were against all proportion of subjection' [IV, i, 134–46].

Williams' argument thus moves from placing the responsibility for the deaths of those killed in an unjust war on the head of the person in whose name, or at whose command, that war was fought, to another, far more dubious, both theologically and morally convoluted, not to mention quintessentially popish, claim. Since no one can die well in a battle, the purgatorial pains or worse imposed on such persons must all, in some sense, redound back on to the king who has led them to their death in such an unjust cause in the first place. This is to render the king responsible for the sins, the bad deaths, and thus for the eternal damnation, of many of his soldiers, if his cause is not just.

The premises of this argument are, of course, entirely popish and thus perhaps unlikely to have won the sympathy of London audiences in the 1590s. But even judged within the parameters of Catholic theology, Williams' proposition is a theological nonsense and Henry has no difficulty in disposing of it as such. 'So if a son that is by his father sent about merchandise do sinfully miscarry upon the sea, the imputation of his wickedness, by your rule, should be imposed upon his father that sent him; of, if a servant, under the master's command transporting a sum of money, be assailed by robbers and die in many irreconciled iniquities, you may call the business of the master the author of the servant's damnation. But this is not so: the King is not bound to answer the particular endings of his soldiers, the father of his son, nor the master of his servant; for they purpose not their death when they purpose their services. Besides, there is no king, be his cause never so spotless, if it come to the arbitrement of swords, can try it out with all unspotted soldiers. Some, peradventure, have on them the guilt of premeditated and contrived murder, some of beguiling virgins with the broken seals of perjury, some, making the wars their bulwark, that have before gored the gentle bosom of peace with pillage and robbery. Now if these men have defeated the law and outrun native punishment, though they can outstrip men, they have no wings to fly from God. War is his beadle, war is his vengeance; so that here men are punished for before breach of the King's laws in now the King's quarrel. Where they feared the death they have borne life away, and where they would be safe they perish. Then if they die unprovided, no more is the King guilty of their damnation than he was before guilty of those impieties for the which they are now visited. Every subject's duty is the King's, but every subject's soul is his own' [IV, i, 147–77]. This, of course, is theologically quite right; Henry has made mince-meat of Williams' little foray into Christian doctrine and once again turned an unpromising situation into another occasion for the display of yet another aspect of his astonishingly complete virtue, in this instance, of his exemplary Christian orthodoxy and theological acuity. One is reminded, indeed, of the paean to the king's all-round intellectual and linguistic virtuosity with which the archbishop of Canterbury had opened the play. Indeed so compelling is the king's reasoning that Williams immediately grants him the point; ' 'tis certain, every man that dies ill, the ill upon his own head; the King is not to answer it'. Bates goes further: 'I do not desire he should answer for me, and yet determine to fight lustily for him' [IV, i, 185–88].

But what Henry has not done, of course, is answer the question with which this little disputation started: is this a just war and, if it is not, will the deaths of his soldiers weigh on the king's conscience or affect his chances of salvation? For the eccentricities of Williams' theological chain of argument have allowed Henry altogether to avoid the subject of the king's responsibility for the deaths of his soldiers, if his cause is not just. And, in fact, as we have seen, the text gives us good reason to doubt that it is just. Or rather, it gives us good reason to doubt the moral transparency, the objectivity, of the means whereby, and of the terms in which, the justice of his cause has been ascertained and asserted in the first place.

These doubts are, of course, compounded by the memory of Henry IV's advice to his son in 2 Henry IV when he told the prince to use some form of foreign adventure as a means to distract the nobility from the internal dissen-sion and rivalries that have disrupted both his own and Richard II's reigns and thus build support for his own rule through a common effort against the foreigner. Both Henry's and the clerical estate's secular self-interest thus meet in the French expedition, leaving little room for doubt about the result of Henry's elaborately pious, and very public, act of deference to that most subtle and politically sensitive of instruments, the conscience of the archbishop of Canterbury. Henry's attempt to place the moral onus on the archbishop takes its place alongside a long line of sometimes rapidly extemporised or, as in this case, more elaborately choreographed, public performances of political virtue and Christian kingship; another example of Henry's serial recourse to what Bradley Greenberg has memorably termed 'plotted self-exculpation'.[31] It was yet another piece of political theatre, but, on this evidence, as an attempt to get the archbishop to carry the moral and spiritual can, should the war prove unjust, it is, in the eyes of at least some of his own soldiers, and perhaps in the eyes of God, too, not to mention at least some of the audience, a complete and utter bust.

In a fascinating semi-aside, Harry Berger Jr suggests that Henry's reference, in his speech to Bates, to a son sent out on business by his father represents Henry's sole gesture at an admission of personal responsibility for the war and its consequences. 'It is as if,' Berger writes, 'he has to remind himself that although he is carrying out his father's order to busy giddy minds with foreign quarrels, the guilt and the responsibility are his, not Bolingbroke's. And to remind himself of that is of course to adopt his father's perspective, as indeed he does when his speech on ceremony echoes – and in places replicates – Bolingbroke's insomnia soliloquy in 2 Henry IV. He manages to fight off that perspective, to clear himself and displace the imputation of wickedness, [one might add, yet again] when he speaks of "the fault/My father made".'[32]

Indeed, it may be that, for all his mastery of the relevant theological arguments, for all his repeated God-talk, and for all his (and indeed the chorus') repeated insistence that he is a Christian king, Henry still has not quite got the hang of this Christianity thing. The only occasion on which we see him in (prayerful) conversation with his God occurs in Act IV, scene i. 'O God of battles, steel my soldiers' hearts;/Possess them not with fear. Take from them now/The sense of reckoning, if th'opposed numbers/Pluck their hearts from them. Not today, O Lord, O not today, think not upon the fault/My father made in compassing the crown./I Richard's body have interred new,/And on it have bestowed more contrite tears/Than from it issued forced drops of blood./Five hundred poor I have in yearly pay,/Who twice a day their withered hands hold up/Toward heaven to pardon blood; and I have built/Two chantries, where the sad and solemn priests/Sing still for Richard's soul. More will I do,/Though all that I can do is nothing worth,/Since that my penitence comes after all,/ Imploring pardon' [IV, i, 286–302].

In this speech Henry is, to quote Una Ellis Fermor, seeking to 'bargain with his God like a pedlar'.[33] If we translate the Anglo-Irish social prejudices of the 1940s into the religious prejudices of the 1590s, that is about right, for the terms in which the bargain is being struck are entirely popish. While this renders them historically appropriate to the pre-reformation setting of the play, it is by no means clear that a London audience in 1599 would have regarded a transaction between God and believer framed in these terms as likely to prove effectual. Moreover, while his petition is framed in religious terms, what concerns Henry is an entirely secular outcome; for it is the threat to his immediate military and political fortunes represented by his father's sins that is causing him concern. To meet that threat to his prospects in tomorrow's battle Henry adverts to his own efforts to expiate, via prayers and masses said for the souls of the dead, the sins of his two royal predecessors and kinsmen. The purpose of such acts of expiation should be to benefit the souls of the deceased rather than to further the secular purposes of the living. But here the deal being offered to the deity is an entirely instrumental exchange of outward religious performance – of good works performed by Henry himself, or rather by others at Henry's behest and expense – in return for immediate secular reward. Henry shows no sense of, or concern with, his own sins or salvation and none at all for the spiritual fate of his father.[34]

It is a source of very considerable irony that the only sign that Henry might understand the central truths of Christianity is contained in his admission, at the end of this speech, that, 'since my penitence comes after all', it can be 'nothing worth'; an admission which, as we have seen, and as Henry himself appears here fleetingly to realise, calls the validity of all the previous bargaining with God into the most serious question, and renders absurd, indeed almost blasphemous, the view that his victory at Agincourt should be read as some sort of divine endorsement of the righteousness or legitimacy of his rule.[35]

We might well conclude that all of that goes with the territory of being a king, Christian or otherwise; the whole point of Henry's various performances of Christian kingship, of political virtue and 'honour', being not that they are self-consistent, 'true', in any ultimate or final, objectively God-satisfying sense, but rather that they work, as G.K. Hunter has observed, as pieces of polit-ical theatre, that is to say, as means to effect his immediate political ends. They do so, moreover, while not merely maintaining, but by actually enhancing Henry's reputation as a Christian king, a model of political virtue and chivalric honour. And, in the world of sublunary political ends and ambitions in which all secular rulers have, perforce, to operate, Henry's ends – the maintenance of order, i.e. of his own rule and regime, in England, indeed (recalling Captain Jamy, MacMorris and Fluellen) in 'Britain', through the prosecution of war against the foreigner – are, given the events of the two preceding reigns, more or less unqualified goods. And those ends have been achieved, the play makes clear, almost entirely through the rhetorical and political (rather more than the merely military) skills of Henry V.

Perils of popularity tamed and enticements of honour resisted

Seen in the terms set by Henry's prehistory as Hal, those skills incorporate all the defining attributes and characteristics of the persons upon whose deaths the emergence of the hero/monster, that is Henry V, has been shown to depend. For Henry is the residual legatee of the grandstanding honour politics, the martial prowess and, when appropriate and politically advantageous (but not when it is not), the personal prickliness of Hotspur; of the political cunning and calculation of his father; and of the native wit, the almost infinite rhetorical flexibility, the capacity to shed one persona for another, to turn almost any situation, however apparently unpromising, to immediate personal and political advantage, of Falstaff. He also retains a 'common touch', that is to say a familiarity with the political and emotional instincts, with the stock reactions and responses, of 'the people'; a capacity acquired, as Warwick had claimed to Henry IV that it would be, almost as a 'foreign language' during his sojourn at the Boar's Head. As we have seen, Prince Hal had claimed to Poins that such was the expanded range of social experience and human contact that he achieved at the Boar's Head that it had given him access to 'all humours that have showed themselves humours since the old days of goodman Adam'. The actions of King Henry V show that experience being used to produce neither a genuinely inclusive sense of human sympathy or solidarity, nor even a sense of Englishness that might transcend the divide between king and subject. Rather what Hal has learned from Falstaff and his sojourns in Eastcheap is not some mystic capacity to sympathise with and represent or personify the social body of the people, but rather a rhetorical flexibility that enables him to combine a number of different appeals for popular support and admiration in one (apparently) seamless (but far from ideologically, and still less morally, coherent) performance of royalness.

In the terms of the codes and norms of contemporary political action and discourse, Henry is shown to be the master of the politics both of popularity and of honour. He is able, effortlessly, to combine the two into a seamless web of political manipulation and manoeuvre. Unlike Hotspur, he is no little Johnny-one-note, unable to stop himself from pursuing the imperatives of honour way past the point of enlightened political or military self-interest or -preservation. Nor is he so enamoured of the people that he courts them past the point of royal self-respect or self-interest. On the contrary, he knows precisely when to answer the insolence of the dauphin with a perfectly calculated display of 'scorn, defiance, slight regard, contempt' [II, iv, 117]; when to pass without ceremony amongst his troops, distributing 'a little touch of Harry in the night'; when to stand on his dignity and authority as king, insisting on the disciplines of the wars; when, even in the act of broadening the category of honour and Englishness to include the most 'vile' of his troops, to do so in ways which, in fact, insist on the huge gulf that still separates king from commoner. What we see in Henry V, therefore, is a series of perfectly modulated rhetorical performances, designed to extract the last iota of political advantage from the situation at hand. His is a pitch-perfect performance of almost total self-control, in which, invested totally in the values neither of honour nor of popularity, nor indeed in the simple assertion of his powers and prerogatives as king, nor even in the demands of genuinely *Christian* kingship, he displays and deploys all of those attributes and skills, as circumstances dictate, to get what he wants.

The one occasion on which the mask slips, on which Henry's total control of his emotions fails him, – the only occasion since he first came to France when he really does get angry – also turns into yet another illustration of this basic truth. Having persuaded Williams and Bates of the theological incoherence of their attempt to blame the king (if his cause is not just) for their own bad deaths on the battlefield and thus for their consequent damnation, Henry tries to push home his rhetorical advantage by asserting that the king has sworn not to be ransomed. This is clearly a morale-raising exercise, an attempt to persuade the soldiery that their leader will be risking his life in the coming conflict just as much as they will be risking theirs. Williams again expresses a bracing scepticism at this suggestion: 'Ay, he said so to make us fight cheerfully; but when our throats are cut he may be ransomed and we ne'er the wiser.' This is too much for Henry and the mask begins to slip. 'If I live to see it, I will never trust his word after', is his response and, of course, it is an absurd phrase for a mere subject, a common soldier – which, after all, is the persona that Henry is currently inhabiting – to use about his sovereign and Williams lets him know it in no uncertain terms. 'You pay him then! That's a perilous shot out of an elder-gun that a poor and private displeasure can do against a monarch. You may as well go about to turn the sun to ice with fanning in his face with a peacock's feather. You'll never trust his word after! Come, 'tis a foolish saying.' This is too much for Henry, who even in disguise takes offence. 'Your reproof is something too round', he tells Williams. 'Let it be a quarrel between us, if you live', replies Williams, and they exchange gages so that after the battle they might recognise one another and settle their differences [IV, i, 191–215]. This little outbreak of internal dissension in the ranks is, of course, the opposite effect to that intended by Henry's wanderings amongst his soldiers just before the battle. Not only that, but Henry is now engaged to fight on a matter of honour with a common soldier, something, of course, which his honour as king cannot allow him, under any circumstances, to do. Meeting Williams after the battle, Henry, now *in propria persona*, asks him why he is wearing that gage in his hat and is told that it is the result of a challenge exchanged with 'a rascal that swaggered with me last night'. Henry asks the watching Fluellen – that self-appointed arbiter of the discipline of the wars – whether he thinks the man should keep his oath and fight with Williams or not. Fluellen replies, in no uncertain terms, that he should, indeed, 'keep his vow and his oath. If he be perjured, see you now, his reputation is as arrant a villain and jack-sauce as ever his black shoe trod upon God's ground and his earth, in my conscience, la.' Either way, Henry sends Williams on his way with the injunction 'then keep thy vow, sirrah, when thou meet'st the fellow'. He then hands Fluellen his gage with some cock and bull story that it belongs to a friend of Alençon and 'an enemy to our person', whom Fluellen is to 'apprehend' [IV, vii, 123–56]. An altercation between Fluellen and Williams ensues, and they are brought before the king, whereupon Henry discovers himself to Williams. When Williams replies that he never intended to say anything 'that might offend your majesty', Henry is implacable; 'it was ourself thou didst abuse'. At this point Williams stands his ground. 'Your majesty came not like yourself: you appeared to me but as a common man – witness the night, your garments, your lowliness; and what your highness suffered under that shape, I beseech you take it for your own fault and not mine, for had you been as I took you for, I made no offence; therefore I beseech your highness pardon me', which, of course, Henry duly does. 'Here uncle Exeter fill his glove with crowns and give it to this fellow. – Keep it fellow,/And wear it for an honour in thy cap/Till I do challenge it' [IV, viii, 41–61].

This, of course, is another of those little extemporised scenes, those exercises in 'plotted self-exculpation', set up by the king to display some winning monarchical attribute, here an amalgam of royal wisdom, mercy and magnificence. It is, in the comic mode, the equivalent of the scene from the end of *2 Henry IV* in which Henry had appeared to threaten the Lord Chief Justice with royal displeasure for earlier offences done against the (private) royal person. Now as Williams – just like the Lord Chief Justice before him – makes the right answer, distinguishing between the king's two bodies, Henry is able, not to punish, but rather to reward him, thus publicly demonstrating his own virtue and wisdom, burnishing the royal legend and, in the case of Williams, attaching a naturally bolshy and sceptical subject to the person of the king. Except, of course, that there are undertones here that, for the audience, call many of the operating assumptions behind this little scene into the most radical question, not merely by laying bare the now serial theatricality of Henry's kingship, but also by problematising Henry's relationship, indeed the relationship of any king, to 'honour'. For Fluellen's diatribe on the necessity of any man – 'though he be as a good a gentleman as the devil is' – keeping his oath once given, highlights Henry's own failure to do so. Moreover, Williams' reply to the king's claim that he is guilty of something like *lèse-majesté* and is therefore liable to hang, as Fluellen puts it, under 'any martial law in the world', shows that, in their initial altercation of the night before, Williams had been entirely right. It *was* absurd for a subject to challenge the moral bona fides of his king. Kings simply were not subject to the normal moral constraints that bound ordinary mortals, as Henry's conduct the next day, despite Fluellen's diatribe on the ethics and politics of honour, shows all too well.

And yet, even here, on the surface, where Henry's style of rule, the inherently theatrical and rhetorical mode of kingship that he has now mastered, always operates to its own best advantage, Henry manages to turn even this happenstance to account. The initial altercation with Williams had produced the only loss of self-control suffered by Henry in the entire play. For the first time since he came to France he had allowed himself to get genuinely angry;

first at Williams' refusal to take the king at his own valuation of himself and secondly at his direct rebuke of the stupidity of Henry's remark about never trusting the king again. The result was that Henry lumbered himself with a challenge delivered by a king to a common soldier. There could scarcely be a more overt illustration of the dangers of popularity, of excessive familiarity with the common sort in pursuit of the common touch. As we have seen, in the scene with Francis the drawer and on Gadshill, such encounters of the plebeian or popular kind always involved the risk that the mask of royal difference might slip so that the king became mistaken for, or, to put it the matter more accurately and subversively still, was recognised as, just another mere mortal.

Henry had started the scene with Williams and Bate by trying to exploit that fact to his own polemical advantage by reminding the two soldiers that 'the King is but a man, as I am: the violet smells to him as it doth to me; the element shows to him as it doth to me; all his senses have but human conditions; his ceremonies laid by, in his nakedness he appears but a man; and though his affections be higher mounted than ours, yet when they stoop they stoop with the like wing' [IV, i, 101–8]. On one account, this is a heartfelt plea for understanding from a king about to face the greatest test of his reign. But on another, it is a manipulative and even duplicitous bid for morale-boosting sympathy for the king and his cause. Either way, the situation rapidly spins out of the disguised king's control as the soldiers take his cue and go on to impute altogether too generous a measure of human frailty to their prince, using his common humanity to call into radical question just how much 'higher' his 'affections' really are than theirs. However, the resolution of the affair shows just how skilled Henry has become at a carefully modulated monarchical version of the politics of popularity; for he is now more than capable of using even his own mistakes and mischances to enhance the charisma (and hence, in the straightforward, modern-day sense of the word, the popularity) of the royal person.

And so it proves here, where, acting entirely unlike his earlier incarnation as Hal might have done, Henry does not pursue the matter incognito, thus following the dictates of personal honour but fatally cheapening the honour of the crown. Nor does he seek revenge by punishing Williams for his temerity, but rather, rapidly regaining control of his emotions and withdrawing again into his public persona as king, he turns Williams' 'little touch of Harry in the night' into something magical, even mythical, a brush with an order of being or reality entirely different from that in which Williams and his like ordinarily moved. Williams, of course, had never doubted that kings were different; that was the trouble – he knew only too well that they get ransomed while the rest of us get slaughtered, in wars about the justice of which we have no idea or say. Henry's treatment of him is designed to confirm, but also to transform, that sense of difference. Kings are indeed different; they have the power of life and death over us, but while that power rests in the just but merciful hands of

Christian kings like Henry V, all will be well with the world. That, presumably, is the tale that Williams, his pockets now filled with Exeter's crowns, is sent off to tell the world.[36]

As P.K. Ayers points out, 'neither apologising for his actions nor thanking the king for his largesse', Williams' only response is 'I will none of your money.' Admittedly, these words are directed at Fluellen rather than at the king, but they cannot help but call into the most serious question what Alison Oatland affirms to be Williams' 'willing participation in the respect of authority and the coherence of the community surrounding it.'[37] But Williams is only one man, and a private soldier to boot, and, as Ayers observes, what matters here, as always with Henry's style of rule, is the wider effect of the public performance that, back *in propria persona* as the king, Henry has staged in this scene, with the coerced help of the unfortunate Williams and the entirely uncomprehending co-operation of that willing dupe, Fluellen.[38]

If we compare this close encounter of the plebeian kind with the earlier scene between Hal, Poins and Francis the drawer, it would appear that for all of Henry's new-found capacity, with the quick-wittedness of a Falstaff, to produce a not so much 'plotted' as extemporised 'self-exculpation' out of even a bodged interaction with 'slaves' and 'lackeys' like Williams and Bates, such encounters remain highly charged, liminal and potentially dangerous. Since there is very little of the slave – or lackey – in either Bates' or Williams' conduct in these scenes, the enthusiasm with which Henry thrusts them back into such demeaning categories betrays something of the same impulse to distance himself from his subjects that he had exhibited with such unbecoming intensity in his earlier scenes with Francis and Poins. Nor is it an accident that his initial encounter with the two soldiers is immediately followed by the only occasion in the entire play when Henry's mask slips and we are shown some disjunction, some chink of light, between the glittering surfaces of Henry's performance as king, and what we might somewhat anachronistically call a residual sense of self.

Henry emerges from his discussions with the soldiery disgusted with what he takes to be the propensity of his subjects to lay everything – their 'lives' and 'souls', their 'debts', and 'children', not to mention their 'sins' – 'on the King'. This prompts an extended exercise in monarchical self-exculpation and self-pity. All that separates princes from what he terms 'privates' is that 'idol ceremony', which, while it serves to induce 'awe and fear in other men', does the king himself no good at all. It leads at best to 'poisoned flattery' from his intimates and confers no benefits, either physical or affective, upon the king himself. ' 'Tis not the balm, the sceptre and the ball,/The sword, the mace, the crown imperial,/The interissued robe of gold and pearl,/The farced title running 'fore the king,/The throne he sits on, nor the tide of pomp/That beats upon the high shore of this world,/No, not all of these, thrice-gorgeous ceremony,/Not all these, laid in bed majestical,/Can sleep so soundly as the wretched slave,/Who with a body filled and vacant mind/Gets him to rest, crammed with distressful bread.' 'The slave, a member of the country's peace,/Enjoys it, but in gross brain little wots/What watch the King keeps to maintain the peace,/Whose hours the peasant best advantages' [IV, i, 226–81].

We have heard variations on this theme come spewing out of the mouths of both Henry VI and Henry IV. But what we have not heard before is the elaborate deconstruction of royalness, the condemnation as 'idolatry' of the outward forms which constitute the authority and power of the prince, which precedes these entirely conventional closing sentiments. As Louis Montrose has observed, Henry's analysis combines the demystifying effects of contemporary anti-popish critiques of 'images, vestments and plays' with 'politic Machiavellian' strictures on 'the utility of state spectacles' and, we might add, of certain public professions of religious principle.[39] Thus, *pace* Womersley and others, the effects of Henry's analysis are precisely the opposite of protestant critiques of popish ceremony, for 'ceremony', as Henry here defines it, emerges, not merely from this speech, but from the play more broadly considered, as anything but merely hollow or delusory, a series of malign illusions to be seen through and discarded as obstacles to the triumph of truth, beauty and the protestant way. On the contrary, hollow and delusory as they are, 'ceremony' and its effects are absolutely central to the successful exercise of royal authority and power. (Until the rise of the Laudians, that is decidedly not how English protestants viewed the question of 'ceremony'.)

After all, if the chorus is to be believed – and, as always, that is a very big if – when Henry had passed amongst his troops as his royal self, that is to say, attended with all the charisma that his public persona as king could impart to him, the effects had been just as he hoped. *In propria persona* he could even play against type, downplaying his royal apartness, calling 'them brothers, friends and countrymen', and, in so doing, maximise the tonic effect of his presence: 'every wretch, pining and pale before,/Beholding him plucks comfort from his looks./A largesse universal, like the sun,/His liberal eye doth give to every one,/Thawing cold fear, that mean and gentle all/Behold, as may unworthiness define,/A little touch of Harry in the night' [IV, chorus, 32–47].

However, as soon as he tried to turn the same trick without the trappings of royal office, the results were disastrous. As P. K. Ayers puts it, in a brilliant formulation, 'without the power of his kingship to bridge the gulf he has himself created, he falls into it.'[40] Ceremony, the carefully staged and maintained illusion of royal apartness, while in some sense illusory, is thus also absolutely crucial. Indeed it is crucial precisely because it is an illusion that masks a reality that, left to its own devices, might have an entirely solvent effect on any and every pretension to royal apartness.

We might recall here Stephen Greenblatt's famous comment that Henry's soliloquy represents both a 'testing and a confirming [of] an extremely dark hypothesis about the nature of monarchical power in England: that its moral authority rests upon an hypocrisy so deep that the hypocrites themselves believe it'. While it is clear what Greenblatt means, there is something amiss in this formulation. For starters, as Graham Bradshaw has observed, 'if they believe it, they are *not* "hypocrites" '.[41] And indeed, given what this speech shows Henry to believe about the outward forms and performances of royalty ('ceremony'), his entirely instrumental deployment of those very forms emerges as anything but simply hypocritical. For the play reveals 'ceremony' to be both a set of empty forms *and* absolutely crucial to the maintenance and deployment of royal power, and Henry is shown using such outward forms, and the various moral poses and personae that he adopts in the course of the play, in precisely that spirit.

Herein lies the difference between Henry V's style of kingship and that of Richard II. It is not that while the latter's style was theatrical or performative, the former's was not, but rather that, unlike Richard, Henry never allows himself to get lost in the performance, simply becoming any one of the parts that he is playing. Certainly, Henry V never assumes, as Richard II habitually does, that, as C.L. Barber put it many years ago, 'the names of legitimate power should be transcendently effective regardless of social forces', or indeed political contingencies.[42] But nor is Henry ever shown to be in any doubt of the central importance of such symbols and ceremonies in the successful discharge of monarchical rule.

Not that there is anything fake about the various virtues that Henry displays as king. As many critics have observed, judged in terms of the immediate situations that call them forth, what Henry is displaying, in each of the tableaux in which he performs various aspects of the ideal Christian king and warrior prince, are real expressions of virtue and virtu, as contemporary convention would have recognised them. All of Henry's disparate performances constitute both morally appropriate and politically effective interventions in the circumstances to which they represent an immediate response.[43]

We have, therefore, in the immediate circumstances upon which they are intended to act, no need to doubt the reality either of Henry's honour or virtue or indeed of his sincerity. In each of these situations there is indeed a sense in which, as McAlindon claims, his 'words and deeds are one'.[44] Certainly, the play gives us no textual warrant to regard Henry as, in any simple sense of the word, a hypocrite.[45]

In consequence a number of critics have maintained that there is, at the centre of the play, a certain hollowness, a vacuum or hole, where earlier critics had expected or wanted Henry's 'character' to be. Thus Moody Prior has observed that 'the character' of Henry V 'is a composite', and claimed that the play itself represents 'a sequence of episodes', designed 'to illustrate a number of distinctive qualities which together constitute' the monarchical ideal that Henry exemplifies.[46] Henry is shown in council, acting as a judge, in negotiations with foreign ambassadors, in prayer, in courtship 'and above all in the varied postures of war'. In each scene, Prior concludes, what we are watching is 'some particular manifestation of an exemplum' being played out by the king.[47] In the same vein, Una Ellis-Fermor has declared that 'there is no Henry, only a king' and pronounced it 'vain' to 'look for the personality of Henry behind the king; there is nothing else there ... the character has been converted whole to the uses of his function, the individual utterly eliminated, sublimated, if you will'.[48] Thus P. K. Ayers can observe that so adept is Hal/Henry in responding to the demands of his immediate situation and the expectations of his various interlocutors and audiences that he 'disappears into his roles ... the chameleon linguist reflects in his speech not himself, but the expectation of those to whom he speaks. He himself becomes in the process largely invisible; the Hal, Harry or Henry on display is the one those around him want or need to see', or, we might add, the one that Henry himself wants or needs them to see. The consequence, Ayers contends, is a sort of characterological vacuum, a situation in which 'the would-be observer, frustrated in the search for a palpable core of "identity" or "character" through the traditional analysis of speech acts, is obliged to create whatever kind of protagonist seems appropriate to the circumstances'.[49]

Since Henry's are intensely situational virtues, the product of a chameleon-like capacity to suit his responses to the political and military, the moral and rhetorical, demands of his immediate circumstances, it should be no surprise that his various responses to those circumstances cannot and do not amount to anything like the expression of a unitary moral virtue or of a recognisably Christian (still less, an expressly protestant) faith.[50] But where previous critics like Prior have noted these characteristics of the play as weaknesses, on the reading being advanced here, these supposed aesthetic or dramatic faults are in fact central features of the play's analysis of the workings of monarchical power. For, pace the likes of Prior and McAlindon, the play is doing rather more than merely reproducing the conventional ideal of the heroic king and Christian prince. Rather, it is adverting to the serious contradictions within, and the tensions between, the constituent parts of those ideals and locating successful kingship in the capacity of the king, as a self-consciously theatrical and rhetorically skilled political operator, to apply the different parts of those images to differing circumstances so as, in Prior's wonderfully economical phrase, 'to insure both success and approbation'.[51] If, in consequence, as Prior observes, 'the big scenes seem staged, and the effect is therefore sometimes one of calculation',[52] that is surely because many of the big scenes are staged by Henry and, even when they are not, he is shown calculating how to turn even the most unforeseen or unwelcome encounter or outcome into yet another outbreak, if not of 'plotted', then of rapidly extemporised, 'self-exculpation'. As Ornstein comments, 'very conscious of the way that men respond to the image of royalty, and no less instinctive a politician than his father, Hal is the creator as well as the creature of political mythology, the author as well as the hero of his legend'.[53]

Thus, in *Henry V* Shakespeare did not merely commit himself 'to dramatising a national myth of heroic kingship'[54] but also to dramatising how that myth was initially scripted and performed by its original author, the prince himself. In that sense the play might be thought to be laying bare, and thus demystifying, what it presents as the various illusions and performances necessary to (re-)establish and maintain the largely beneficent effects of rule by a king whose virtue and legitimacy is accepted by all.

As Marie Axton argued years ago, this aspect of the play is perhaps best illustrated by its treatment of the legal doctrine or conceit of the king's two bodies. In *The famous victories of Henry V*, the prince is shown as a genuine thug, and his transition from thuggery to princely virtue presented as a genuine, road-to-Damascus conversion, a sudden change visited upon him as he visits his dying father – something Axton has aptly described as 'a miracle of the body politic', a miracle worked on a genuinely debased private body or nature by the incipient imposition thereupon of the politic body of monarchy.[55] Shakespeare's plays, of course, stage no such thing; rather, throughout both parts of *Henry IV*, Hal is shown acquiring the skills and insights that, once he becomes king, will enable his emergence as a virtuous prince. These plays have gone out of their way to show the audience that what evidently looks to many of the other characters like a miraculous change in the royal character or person consequent upon his succession to the throne – a view of the situation given the clearest articulation by that otherwise dubious witness the archbishop of Canterbury – is, in fact, nothing of the sort, but rather a *coup de théâtre* long planned and prepared for by the prince. There are no miracles on show here; no mystical transformations or sudden conversions effected through the transfer of royal power, office or charisma, or still less through the interventions of divine grace, but merely the exercise of political skills and monarchical virtues, painfully acquired as much in the stews of Eastcheap as on the field of battle or at his father's court.

The irony, of course, is that if what is going on here is, in part, a demystification of monarchical power, a deconstruction of the whole notion of the king's two bodies and of the 'miracles of the body politic' that went with it, the result of that process is itself another sort of mystification. But, since the purpose of the play is to depict the reconstitution of legitimacy out of the entirely delegitimised politics of commodity, some sort of mystification is precisely both what we should expect and what is required.

And that is precisely what we get. For if the creature that emerges from these complex transactions and metamorposes is something of a hero, he is also something of a monster and most definitely something of a fantasy-figure. As C.L. Barber puts it, there is something 'magical' about Henry. In the terms set by *King John*, he is a miraculous meld of the bastard and of Henry III; in those set by the *Henry IV* plays, a synthesis of the characteristics and attributes of Hotspur, Henry IV and Falstaff. Of these, the bastard is a an almost entirely fictive and decidedly folkloric figure and, as for Falstaff, criticism has long associated him with the shape-changing, role-playing, festive aspects of the carnivalesque. And, as Ann Barton has pointed out, the basic narrative structure of the *Henry IV* plays, not to mention the scene in *Henry V* with Williams and Bates, recalls a long tradition of comic folk tales and plays about princes moving disguised amongst the people, there to learn the truth of their subjects' lives. The move in all these plays is from the folkloric to the political, the mythical to the real. Just as the bastard, in the second half of *King John*, sheds his initial vice-like quality, so increasingly, Falstaff sheds his festive character, to emerge as the recognisably corrupt evil counsellor of *2 Henry IV*. Similarly, as Ann Barton has observed, once ensconced as king, Henry's communings with the body of his people are of anything but the festive kind. However, it remains the case that the exchanges staged between the three Henrys – Henry IV, Harry Hotspur and Harry Plantagenet – not to mention those between Hal/Henry and his other surrogate father figure, Falstaff, exceed what Barber terms the 'conscious control' of the prince. Thus 'at the close of Part Two' Barber sees Shakespeare himself using 'ritual, not ironically transformed into drama, but magically'. Barber discerns here 'a retreat into magic by the dramatist, as distinct from his characters'. At stake is what he terms 'the non-logical process of purification by sacrifice – the sacrifice of Falstaff' and, we might add, of Henry IV as well. Transactions that Barber treats, as it were, anthropologically, Harry Berger Jr. redistributes to the realm of something that we might term the 'psychoanalytic', which, of course, may (or may not) be considered an advance in the demystification stakes. But whichever register one prefers, it remains the case that both critics are referring to essentially the same affective and symbolic transactions; transactions that operate some way beneath the level of conscious self-fashioning and political manoeuvre, although in *Henry V*, that, for the most part, is what we get to watch.[56]

And yet even in *Henry V* there remains something of the fantasy figure about Henry. For from the first, Henry is able to achieve, seemingly without effort, ends and effects that had been quite beyond the best efforts of his father (or, for that matter, of Queen Elizabeth). The play offers us a vision not merely of a newly purged and united England but of an emergent British unity, forged in the crucible of foreign war and underpinned by marriage alliances contracted, almost entirely on English terms, with the great continental monarchies. In short, Henry represents a personified resolution of all the (political, ideological and structural) contradictions and constraints currently afflicting the late Elizabethan state.[57] Henry can do all this because of his almost magical ability to combine the energies and capacities of all three of his progenitors or alter egos;

that is to say, he brings together in one person or political project the cold blooded political calculation of his father, that 'vile politican Bolingbroke', the honour-driven martial prowess of Hotspur and the shape-shifting opportunism and rhetorical skills of Falstaff. In him the politics of popularity, military prowess, monarchical legitimacy, and, indeed, of (a decidedly un-, indeed anti-puritan) 'reformation', all meet in a perfectly balanced synthesis. Viewed thus, the play operates almost as much as a critique of current circumstance and achievement, as it does as a propaganda piece in defence of the Elizabethan state as it really was. That such an (admittedly implicit) critique is identified at a crucial point with the figure of Essex might be thought to have a certain significance in the highly charged circumstances of 1599. Of which, more below.

A Machiavel for good: can even the best of princes get to heaven?

In the figure of Henry V, Shakespeare was trying to square the circle; to reconcile virtue with virtu, by showing how, pursuing a version of genuinely royal commodity, Henry could create unity, order and legitimacy. Henry has been saved by his status as the son of a regnant monarch from the archetypal Machiavel's quest to achieve supreme power for himself. His task is neither to seize power, still less to found or refound a state, but merely to restore a going monarchical concern to something like working order. In fulfilling this task, here echoing the verdict of John Danby who sees Henry as 'a Machiavel of good-ness',[58] A.D. Nuttall describes Henry as 'a white Machiavel', a practitioner of 'a strangely ethical realpolitik, a white Machiavellianism'. As what Nuttall terms 'the player king', Shakespeare shows Hal/Henry producing 'major effects by design'. Hal/Henry is presented as the 'central unified cause' of events. 'He, not a fortuitous combination of circumstances, recovers England's greatness.'[59]

Put another way, alone of the history plays, *Henry V* suggests that, under the right circumstances, human effort and planning, the prowess and cunning of a single political actor or agent, deploying a careful combination of virtue and virtu, combining, in his person and practice, the politics of popularity, honour and monarchical legitimacy, and appropriating the language of 'refor-mation' (shorn of its seditious, 'puritan' baggage) could control events, restore both legitimacy and greatness to England, and, in so doing, not merely unite one nation – England – but found another – 'Britain'.

On this view, even if Henry's claims to the French throne were deeply flawed, and his war, therefore, formally unjust, his overall project was, judged in terms of its entirely beneficent results (on the victorious English, if not on the defeated French), a good thing. With someone like this in control, the play seems to be saying, the genie of commodity politics might indeed be forced back into the bottle of legitimate rule and deliverances and victories on the scale of Agincourt could once again be ours. Indeed, if Henry's claims to divine aid and others' estimation of the victory at Agincourt as a 'wonder' are first to be taken literally and then simply believed – and that is a big 'if' – we might even suppose that God and providence would then come back on side.

Such, we might well conclude, are the full effects of the victorious prosecution of a genuinely just war. Except that, as we have seen, the play goes out of its way, on more than one occasion, to raise (but not to answer) the question of just how 'just' Henry's initial *casus belli* really was. Taken together these plays certainly leave us in no doubt that his motivation in going to war in the first place was not simply to vindicate dynastic right or justice, but instead to play a far deeper and more Machiavellian game: attaching the loyalties of his subjects to their new king in and through the crucible of war.

On that account, if Henry's dynastic claim is technically just, and even more so if it is not, Henry's decision to go to war might well be taken to be uncomfortably close his father's to resist, depose and replace King Richard. Both acts are, if not crimes, then certainly sins, but they are also politically necessary, indeed, ultimately salutary in their this-worldly effects. In the fallen world of sublunary political manoeuvre, Henry's actions might well be justifiable in terms of their beneficent political effects in conferring unity and legitimacy on a polity to this point, to all appearances, indelibly stained with usurpation and fatally undermined by division and distrust, rebellion and conspiracy. But such arguments pale before the justice of God. In the fallen world of commodity politics, in which all rulers, however legitimate and virtuous, have perforce to live, certain ends might well justify the sinful means used to effect them, but that could scarcely render sin any less sinful in the sight of God. The beneficent purposes of an omnipotent providence, in punishing sin and creating and sustaining order in a fallen world, might well be being served here, but only through the actions of inherently sinful agents and instruments; persons whose politically necessary, but still sinful, acts could well be sending them to hell, even as they served both the interests of the common good and the beneficently inscrutable purposes of divine providence.

We have here, then, the outlines of something like a tragic view of kingship, in which, in order to perform the functions for which their office has been divinely ordained, and to the exercise of which they have been called by God, that is to say, in order to produce and maintain order in a fallen world, princes have inevitably to commit sin; sin so great as to condemn the perpetrator to hell, even as those same (sinful) acts save the commonwealth, preserving or creating order and legitimacy, where there had been none before.

To this point, in the plays under discussion here, the only king who has definitely not been consigned to hell for his pains is Henry VI and he, of course, is the exception that proves this particular rule. For Henry is a man whose saintliness, whose addiction to the values and practices of true Christian piety, render him entirely unfit to rule. By resolutely preferring peace to war, consistently taking, if not the line of least resistance, then certainly the path of Christian charity, by making his peace with God and with his enemies, by forgiving even his own murderer, Henry may well have managed to secure his own passage to heaven, but at the same time, and precisely because of those same propensities and actions, his kingdom has been sent to hell in a handbasket. This is decidedly not what kings are for.

Henry V is the only one of the monarchs whose reigns are staged in these plays, who we do not get to see die. However, the doubts raised throughout the play about the justice of the war which saves his kingdom and establishes both his rule and his eternal fame, together with his refusal ever directly to address that issue, and his serial legalism, his repeated attempts to defuse genuine issues of conscience through adherence to the relevant legal forms and his consequent failure ever, either to understand the true meaning of repentance or to even notice, still less properly acknowledge, the existence of his own sins, leave the niggling suspicion that, for all his voluble outward professions of Christian belief, and for all his virtues and achievements as a soldier and a politician – indeed perhaps because of those achievements – he too may be going, not to heaven, but to the other place. We might recall here C.L. Barber's remark that 'in the last scenes' [of 2 Henry IV] Henry IV becomes 'almost a sacrificial figure, a king who sins for the sake of society, suffers for society in suffering for his sin, and carries his sin off into death'; the argument being that, for all his claims to legitimacy and Christian principle, the same tragic view of kingship might very well apply to Henry V as well as to his father.[60]

However, even if such a sacrifice might be taken to be implicit in the moral argument of the play, there is certainly no hint that such a burden is being self-consciously taken up by Henry himself, who, as Moody Prior observes, allows himself no doubts about the rectitude of his claim to either the English or the French throne, the justice of his war or the righteousness of his own conduct.[61] It is not the least of the play's ironies that it suggests that for Shakespeare's ideal prince, if not for Machiavelli's, rather than clear-eyed cunning and a frank espousal of the will to power, a certain moral obliquity, even obtuseness, might well be a crucial element in achieving political success. As David Kastan remarks, if Henry 'is Shakespeare's most successful king, he is so precisely because his uncritical moral intelligence forges the unambiguous moral environment that heroic action demands'.[62]

Henry, in short, can so effectively perform 'virtu(e)' in all its myriad, but by no means always morally coherent or compatible, forms, in part, because he believes himself to be virtuous. In these plays the performance, with complete conviction, of a certain both moral and dynastic legitimacy was crucial for the achievement of that 'legitimacy effect' upon which the welfare and safety of the realm is taken to depend. This is the ultimate good that Henry delivers, and as the fate of Bolingbroke shows, it is something that, no matter how great his skills as a politician, no new prince, devoid of claims to dynastic legitimacy and therefore to moral authority, could ever hope to achieve. While the play clearly acknowledges all this, it is also entirely frank about the central role of war in achieving Henry's wider political and ideological ends and entirely clear-eyed about the awful costs of that war. These are figured in quite dreadful terms at a number of points in the play: in the king's speech before Harfleur; in William's evocation of the battlefield, in Act IV scene i; and in Burgundy's description of the ravages of war on 'the best garden of the world, our fertile France', in Act 5 scene ii. They are also played out on stage in the play's one performance of real violence, the slaughter of the French prisoners. That the play is prepared to go to such lengths to reveal what war means and then to present all this as a price well worth paying for Henry's success and its wider political, ideological and moral effects is yet another sign of its confidence in the sheer force both of Henry's achievement and of its own rhetorical and dramatic powers.[63]

As a great deal of recent and not so recent criticism has shown, it is perfectly possible to use such material to argue that the play sets up Henry only to undercut him and that, far from glorifying war, the play sets out to denounce it. However, such a verdict, while it can clearly claim considerable textual warrant, leaves too much of the play's moral argument and rhetorical and theatrical effects out of account. Nor do I think entirely satisfactory Rabkin's brilliantly lucid solution to this dilemma – that since the play contains two radically different versions of the same events, which of the two versions is discerned depends entirely upon the angle of vision of the viewer.[64] Rather, I think the case for Henry is intended to be stronger precisely because of the materials contained in the play that might seem to qualify, or even undercut, a conventionally favourable verdict on his character and conduct. (Another way of putting this is to observe that the play is at least as aware of its own contradictions as are the likes of Dollimore and Sinfield or Thorne and Greenblatt.) What the play is demonstrating is the incompatibility of admiration for Henry, of a frank acknowledgement of both the necessity of his actions and of their beneficent effects, and continued belief in the contemporary moral nostrums, the clichés and sententiae, that conventionally defined the ideal of the Christian prince. To put the case in the terms set by 'pro-Henry' critics like Walter or Moody Prior, on the one side of the argument, and by 'anti-Henry critics', like Roy Battenhouse, on the other, the play's juxtaposition of Henry's conduct with contemporary, and particularly Erasmian, ideals of Christian kingship cuts both ways.[65]

That is to say, while it might call Henry's chances of salvation into radical question, it also trashes the likes of Erasmus as guides to successful kingship. There is, therefore, on this view of the matter, nothing Erasmian about the play's vision of politics and kingship. Or rather, claims to certain types of Erasmian virtue emerge as only one of the ways in which monarchical rule might, indeed, must, seek to legitimise, and thus to establish, itself. *Pace* his more strident modern advocates, if Shakespeare's Henry is indeed intended in some sense to represent the ideal prince, he does so precisely because of, rather than despite, the distinctly 'Machiavellian' elements in his style of rule.

Not that the play represents anything like an endorsement of Machiavellian manipulation and the will to power. For all its claims to a clear-eyed political realism, as we have seen, there remains more than an element of escapist fantasy about *Henry V*. While, in their treatment of high politics, the world of the Percies and of Henry IV, of John of Lancaster and of Westmoreland, both parts of *Henry IV* contain an entirely clear-eyed, un-, if not dis-illusioned, account of how the politics of commodity actually work, in the shape-changing, identity-shifting world of carnival and play in which Hal and Falstaff subsist they also contain entirely unhistorical elements of folklore and fantasy, not to mention entirely anachronistic evocations of contemporary Elizabethan social life. In the meeting and matching of those two worlds, in and through the extraordinary transactions between Hotspur, Falstaff and that other Henry, Hal's father the king, Prince Hal is shaped into Henry V, a figure capable of transcending, that is to say of understanding, operating upon, indeed dominating, without ever quite becoming contained within or reduced to, the world that the politics of commodity has produced.

Having looked into the abyss of commodity politics, of the delegitimised, utterly unprovidential, vision of politics as process, outlined not only in *2* and *3 Henry VI*, but also in much of *Richard II* and indeed of both parts of *Henry IV*, it is as though Shakespeare could only escape by looking, through the fantasy figure of Hal/Henry V, back to the future. For while Henry was an almost impossibly heroic figure from England's glorious past, he was also someone for whom immediately contemporary referents and analogues could be found, perhaps – hilariously enough, as it turned out – in some sort of combination of the earl of Essex and James Stuart. But then again, in 1599, before Essex crashed and burned in Ireland, as virtually all observers of the contemporary political scene would surely have agreed, those were indeed two men with a future.

Peace, war and the politics of the succession

As is notorious, *Henry V* associates the figure of Henry with the earl of Essex. In a passage in the chorus at the start of Act V Henry's triumphal entry into London after the Agincourt campaign is evoked and connection made to some future entry by Essex, returning in triumph from his Irish campaigns [V, 0, 22–34]. On the one hand, this fleeting association between Essex and Henry serves to affirm the loyalty and patriotism of both the play and the playwright. After all, Essex is being praised and blessed as the 'general of our gracious empress', and the campaign in which he is being enjoined to triumph one conducted by English troops against Irish rebels. On the other hand, however, the gesture through Henry towards Essex remains a decidedly daring move. Not only is Henry a king and Essex a subject, the returning hero to whom Essex is being compared is not any old victorious Roman general, but an emperor, perhaps even Julius Caesar himself. Moreover, almost all of the royal and martial virtues conferred on Henry V by the play were quintessentially male and thus precisely not available to a female ruler. In the triumphant combination of the politics of popularity and of martial honour attributed to Henry, contemporaries were being offered an image of a distinctly Essexian modus operandi; not perhaps as the earl himself had ever quite managed to perfect it, but certainly as many of his advisors and admirers hoped that he would be operating, if not in the present, then certainly in the near future.

But it would, of course, be absurd to push the connection between Henry and Essex too hard. Henry was, after all, quintessentially royal and Essex was not. If England was ever to enjoy a return to the sort of moral, political and dynastic legitimacy envisaged in this play it would have to come via someone like Henry V, that is to say someone who not only had unequivocally royal blood in his veins – after all, the bastard, Catherine Grey and later Arbella Stuart all had that – but was also the entirely legitimate heir of a regnant monarch. For all its deconstruction of the mystique of kingship, its clear-eyed presentation of the political methods and rhetorical manoeuvres that underpinned Henry V's style of rule, the play did anything but undermine or subvert traditional notions of hereditary succession and personal monarchy. After all, despite his carefully acquired and cunningly deployed rhetorical and political skills, in the end Henry V could only be Henry V because he was the eldest son of Henry IV. His was a political role and advantage conferred by circumstance and by birth, as that 'vile politician' his father had explained from his deathbed with such typical and illusionless clarity. And, of course, in 1599 the one person who enjoyed that sort of close dynastic relation to Elizabeth I was none other than James Stuart.

As Marie Axton pointed out some years ago, the case made by the archbishop of Canterbury for the legality of Henry's claim to the throne of France, through its repudiation of the Salic Law, echoed a case that had been made at least since the 1560s in defence of the Stuart claim to the English crown.[66] For one of the major arguments against the Stuarts was that they were barred by a maxim of the common law which excluded those born abroad from the English succession. To this, first the Catholic lawyer Edmund Plowden and then, echoing Plowden, John Leslie, the bishop of Ross, had replied that if one were to allow such local municipal laws to infringe the rights of hereditary succession, which were universally applicable to all truly monarchical polities, then the Salic Law would have to be accepted as a legitimate limitation on the French succession and, on that basis, the English claim to the French throne, which had, of course, been asserted for centuries with the expenditure of much blood and treasure, would stand as entirely spurious. Thus, the play offered its audience a choice. If they were to accept Henry V as a hero – as, given his emblematic status as a personification of England at war and at bay, they were surely under an all but irresistible temptation to do – then they almost had to accept that his cause was just. But if they did that, they would, by extension, also be accepting the legitimacy of the Stuart claim to the English throne. Hence Henry's ejaculation, 'no king of England, if not king of France', was, on the current reading, more than a typically Henrician combination of passionate English nationalism, chivalric derring-do and political calculation; it might also be taken to be a statement of legitimist principle and of political fact; one moreover, that would give the English throne to James Stuart just as surely as it had given that of France to Henry V.

But the argument could be pushed further. Even if Henry's claim to the French throne were faulty or spurious, the play showed Henry's vigorous and violent assertion of that claim leading to what were, from an English point of view, undeniably desirable, even, in the terms set by the fallen world of sublunary political affairs, unequivocally good, ends. In short, the message here was clear: all the effects of a return to legitimate monarchical rule could be had, indeed legitimacy itself could be reconstituted, through the aggressive and successful prosecution of foreign war, even in the absence of an irrefutably just or lawful *casus belli*.

Here we need to set the play within the immediate context of debates about making peace with Spain then currently raging not only at court and on the Council but, as Alex Gajda has shown, in the wider political nation, where arguments for peace and for war were being canvassed both through a range of circulating manuscript position papers and through printed news pamphlets and squibs translated from the Dutch and printed in English in London. By far the most famous of the former was, of course, Essex's *Apology*, a manuscript tract that took the form of a letter to the earl's intimate, Anthony Bacon, in which Essex justified himself in the face of accusations that he was a warmonger and a man of blood, someone whose love of military conflict was driven by an egotistical search for personal honour rather than concern for the common good.

As Gadja points out, Essex's apology survives in far more manuscript copies than any of the other position papers on the subject of peace or war and is the only one that is not anonymous.[67] Essex denied that the piece had been intended for circulation. It was, he claimed, a private document, and had been removed without his knowledge from his chamber. But as Paul Hammer has shown, the release of such leaked documents followed by claims of injured innocence, was, by this point, a settled part of the earl's modus operandi.[68] We can, then, add the *Apology* to the end of quite a long list of such manoeuvres through which Essex had sought to take his case to publics beyond the inner circles of the court and council, where discussion of issues like war and peace – the quintessence of the *arcana imperii* – was most definitely supposed to remain. What this means, of course, is that by the time *Henry V* was being performed, in 1599, it would have been a well-known fact amongst the more well-informed denizens of the news culture and gossip networks certainly of the capital, if not of the wider political nation, that the regime was divided on the merits of making peace or war with Spain and that Essex had identified himself (again) as the leading proponent of aggressively pushing the war against the Spanish tyrant to final victory.

By vigorously defending himself against the accusations that he was a warmonger, by deriding the possibility of a settled peace with a tyrant like Philip II, Essex was also adverting to the presence of others at the centre of power who did indeed think that he was warmonger and who were actively urging a policy of appeasement on the queen. On this account, then, in writing a play in which the security of the realm and the legitimacy of the crown are shown to depend directly upon the vigorous, indeed the aggressive, prosecution of a war against the great continental power of the age, Shakespeare was doing a great deal more than writing a piece of loyalist, foreigner-bashing propaganda. He was, in effect, intervening in a directly contemporary debate about the war and what to do about it. And he was doing so, of course, quite overtly on the Essexian side. For while Essex is hailed as the general of our empress as he marches off to campaign in Ireland, the play itself glorifies a land campaign fought on the continent against the great power of the day; precisely the sort of military commitment that Essex himself wanted to pursue against the Spanish, rather than the side-show of the Irish campaign.

In the printed pamphlets translated from the Dutch in which the case for continued war against Spain had been canvassed the legitimacy of the Dutch revolt had been defended through a version of resistance theory in which the power of princes was presented as contractual in nature and in which the proper response to tyranny, certainly on the scale practised by the Spanish in the Low Countries, was resistance. This set up something of a tension, not to say a contradiction, between the absolutist theories of power and the absolute aversion to any notion of right resistance that had characterised English political thought and polemic, certainly since the early 1590s, when the authoritarian, anti-puritan, turn that opened the decade had been compounded by the reaction against the defence of elective monarchy, contract and resistance theory contained in Parsons' *Conference*. Many of the manuscript tracts that argued for peace with Spain adverted to these tensions by emphasising the popular, republican and disorderly character of the government of the United Provinces and the deleterious effects on England herself that continuing support of such disreputable allies against the greatest power in Europe was likely to have. Such claims were compounded by Essex's own widespread reputation for 'popularity' – a reputation which the circulation of his *Apology* could, of course, only have served to confirm. We return here, in 1598–9, to the dilemma outlined so clearly for the earl by Francis Bacon in 1596; we have a man with a reputation for popularity and a large military following; someone obsessed with the pursuit of personal honour and martial glory; someone who has recently been labelled a warmonger, by (if Camden is to believed) Burghley himself, agitating (again) for war, not merely at court and in council, but publicly, through the *Apology*, the pendant rumours that that document had sparked and now, it seems, on the public stage, in *Henry V*.

On the one hand, in taking this line, the play itself might be thought to be compounding the problem. After all, it was placing issues and arguments, made through the relatively discreet and restricted means of circulating manuscript, before the promiscuously heterogeneous audiences of the popular stage. But, in fact, the way the play presented these issues went a good way towards squaring this particular circle. For the war being portrayed and pushed in the play was an inherently monarchical project: undertaken by a great English prince, in defence of his hereditary dynastic rights and the interests of England. As we have seen, the play goes out of its way to place a question mark against Henry's ostensible *casus belli*. But while the issue of the legality of the war is left hanging, so, as the action proceeds, the justification, perhaps even the 'justice', of the war is shown to reside in its wholly beneficent effects on England and the English, and, in particular, in the legitimacy and glory that victory confers on Henry and his regime. If such a rationale for war were to be applied to the current conjuncture, it would not be necessary to embrace the fine print of the Dutch case for their revolt against Philip II in order to argue that the aggressive prosecution of the war against Spain was the right thing to do for the cause of monarchy in England, indeed in 'Britain'. In other words, a war undertaken for these ends, and in such a spirit, would allow *de jure* issues, otherwise central to the debates about peace and war being conducted at precisely this time – issues like the legitimacy or otherwise of resistance, the popularity of the Dutch style of government and, indeed, the tyranny (or otherwise) of Spain – to be sidelined. This is an English (monarchical) war, waged for English reasons and in pursuit of English, and even of 'British' interests, which, if waged in the right places and in the right ways, with the right combination of royal and martial virtu(e), will lead to the most beneficent of results not only for England and her monarch but for a Britain about to be newly unified under Stuart rule. After all, as Richard Simpson first pointed out over a hundred years ago, the gestures at British unity made by the play were, by definition, gestures towards something that could only happen once James had come into his own in England, and once the Irish rebellion had been put down (presumably, as it appeared in 1599, by James' great supporter and Elizabeth's great general, the earl of Essex).

But such considerations applied not only to the issue of peace and war; they also had consequences for that other pressing issue of the late 1590s – the succession. In the minds of Essex and his immediate circle the two issues were integrally linked. For we know that the earl had come to associate the willingness, indeed the enthusiasm, of his rivals at court to pursue a negotiated peace with Spain with a concomitant willingness to transfer the succession from James to the Infanta. As we have seen, through Henry's rejection of the Salic Law and assertion of his basic hereditary right to the throne of France, a right untrammelled by the local, municipal laws of particular kingdoms, the play had gestured hard at the legitimist argument for the Stuart succession. What Henry was doing in the play – forcibly defending, by war, his hereditary right (in this case, to the throne of France) against the local legal limitations placed upon that right by the French – was arguably what Elizabeth was doing, or perhaps rather ought to be doing, in her war with Spain; that is to say, defending, by force, the dynastic rights of her legitimate hereditary successor – James Stuart – against the spurious claims of the Infanta.

But, as we have seen, the play could hardly be said to have unequivocally endorsed or asserted the justice of Henry's claim, and can thus be taken to have refused to put all its eggs in a straightforwardly legitimist basket. By leaving the question of the justice of Henry's claim to the French crown, if not open, then at least questionable, the play also left the way clear for a prudential argument in favour both of Henry's claim to the French throne and of James' to that of England; an argument couched in terms of the benefits that had accrued to England under Henry V and would now accrue to an England, indeed to a 'Britain', newly united by the rule of James Stuart over all three kingdoms.

This, of course, was to have your cake and to eat it, deploying indefeasible hereditary right as a maximum claim while also engaging with Parsons' tract on its own chosen ground of prudential political calculation. Again, by not making the case for the justice (and prudence) of the war turn on the legal niceties of Henry's claim to the French crown, the play was able to address strands of (largely, but not only Catholic) opinion that had never accepted either the justice of the Elizabethan state's war with Spain or the legality of the Dutch revolt.[69] However, in an argument about consequences not rights, about the desirability and necessity of certain political outcomes and ends rather than about the legitimacy, the legal or moral niceties, of various means, an appeal to national unity in a war against the foreigner, laced by the prospect of a return to full monarchical legitimacy at the accession of the next successor, could trump any and all such concerns.

Essex – again

On this account, therefore, as well as being a piece of patriotic agitprop designed to stir up support for the war in Ireland, not to mention a paean to the earl of Essex, the play might also be viewed as a political fantasy about what could be achieved, not merely in England, but in Britain, once full monarchical legitimacy had been returned to all three kingdoms by the accession of James Stuart, an accession to be worked in and through the military and political skill and initiative of Essex. Here it is surely of considerable significance that the relationship to the earl established in the *Henry IV* plays and in *Henry V* was by no means as straightforwardly adulatory as that one, admittedly very telling, reference to him in the chorus of Act V of *Henry V* might lead us to assume. For Henry was very far from being the only character in these plays with associations with Essex.

There are, as David Bevington amongst others has pointed out, if anything, at least as many parallels between Essex and Henry's would-be nemesis and alter ego, Hotspur, as there are between the earl and Henry V. Hotspur's addiction to the politics and poses of honour; his tendency to drift into ranting fits of self-aggrandisement and honour-drenched fantasy, to push points of honour too far, not to know when to stop provoking even his allies, and to lose the political plot as he did all of these things, are all reminiscent of Essex. Indeed, it may not be an accident that the *casus belli* that opens the breach between the Percies and Henry involves Hotspur's refusal to hand over to the king prisoners taken in his campaign against the Scots and is fuelled by his continuing sense that Henry has 'disgraced me in my happy victories'.[70] Essex, of course, had entered into a similar dispute with the queen over his right to ransom prisoners taken at Cadiz and nursed a similar sense of grievance about the ways in which his military services to the crown had been regarded and rewarded. He, too, felt that he had been 'disgraced in my happy victories'.[71] On this account, we might add, there is nothing archaic or medieval about the febrile honour politics of Harry Percy, any more than there was about the divine right absolutism of Richard II. On the contrary, in the 1590s, given the absolutist turn in much royal rhetoric and imagery, and the fervent honour talk being indulged in by Essex, both were entirely contemporary, almost avant-garde, phenomena.

As we have seen, throughout *1 Henry IV* there is an intense and peculiar relationship established between Hotspur and Hal. On the one hand, Hotspur is frequently held up to the dissolute prince as an example of chivalric prowess and military virtue. On the other, Hotspur's conduct and fate mark him down as a signal example of honour politics gone wrong, of what happened when the concern with military glory and personal prowess became an obsession unmoored in any wider framework of political prudence or circumspection.[72] And, of course, just as Hotspur is held up (both by his father and by Hal himself) as both a model and a reproach to the prince, it is only by killing his doppelgänger, Harry Percy, that Harry Plantagenet can start to shed his acquired identity as 'a bastard son of the king's', and effect his return from Eastcheap to the court, from the holiday of the Boar's Head to the work discipline of princely duty, from dream-like play to quotidian political reality and personal destiny.

On the current view, then, the associations established in these plays between Essex and Hal/Henry and Essex and Hotspur do not work to contradict or undercut one another but rather form part of a coherent pattern of political commentary and prognostication (and perhaps even counsel, directed, amongst others, at the earl). For in killing Hotspur, while acknowledging (and appropriating) his real virtues and achievements, Hal is able to take on all that is admirable, both personally and politically useful, in the politics of honour, while sending the residue of infantile, politically counter-productive, Hostpurian (and Essexian?) excess to the grave with Percy. Put crudely, when Hal kills Hostpur, good Essex, a vision of Essex as he could and should be, kills bad Essex, leaving behind him the counter-productive elements in his too hot addiction to the culture and politics of honour and martial glory.

But if Essex was known for his intense (and sometimes deleterious) addiction to the politics of martial honour, he was also, as we have seen, accused by both his friends and enemies of a similarly excessive attachment to the politics of popularity. The two tendencies were, of course, linked as the earl polished his reputation as a soldier, a military hero on a horse, the epitome of vigorous, foreigner- and papist-hating English nationalism, in order to play to the popular gallery. On this basis it might be thought significant that these plays contain two pieces of political counsel, indeed rebuke, the one directed to Hotspur by Worcester and the other directed to Hal by his father Henry IV, that encapsulate the dangers inherent in too enthusiastic and unreflective a pursuit of the politics of honour and of popularity. The first occurs at the end of the scene in *1 Henry IV* in which Hotspur has been provoking Glendower, through his refusal to take seriously the latter's providence- and prophecy-drenched account of the miraculous events that had attended his birth. This display of pride and pique reveals not only Hotspur's lack of self-control but also his lack of political judgement, since it threatens to split the rebel party asunder even before the rebellion itself has begun. Hotspur's behaviour elicits a stern lecture from his uncle, Worcester. 'In faith, my lord, you are too wilful-blame/And, since your coming hither, have done enough/To put him quite beside his patience./You must needs learn, lord, to amend this fault./Though sometimes it show greatness, courage, blood,/(And that's the dearest grace it renders you),/Yet oftentimes it doth present harsh rage,/Defect of manners, want of government,/ Pride, haughtiness, opinion, and disdain,/The least of which haunting a nobleman/Loseth men's hearts and leaves behind a stain/Upon the beauty of all parts besides,/Beguiling them of commendation' [Pt. I, III, i, 173–85]. These, of course, were characteristics that many contemporaries attributed to Essex but which both the *Henry IV* plays and *Henry V* revealed to be the polar opposite of the icy self-control and calculation exercised throughout by Hal/Henry himself.

In the very next scene, Hal receives a remarkably similar lecture from his father, this time on the dangers of popularity. As we saw in the last chapter, in that speech Henry attributed the role that 'opinion' had played in winning him the crown in large part to his own skill in managing his relations with the people. He then proceeded to give his son a lecture on how to manage the politics of popularity. 'By being seldom seen, I could not stir/But, like a comet, I was wondered at,/That men would tell their children, "This is he!"/Others would say, "Where, which is Bolingbroke?"/And then I stole all courtesy from heaven,/And dressed myself in such humility/That I did pluck allegiance from men's hearts,/Loud shouts and salutations from their mouths,/Even in the presence of the crowned King./Thus did I keep my person fresh and new,/My presence like a robe pontifical,/Ne'er seen but wondered at; and so my state/Seldom but sumptuous, showed like a feast/And won by rareness such solemnity.' It was a performance that Henry contrasted deliberately and directly with that of Richard, 'the skipping King' who 'ambled up and down,/With shallow jesters, and rash bavin wits,/Soon kindled and soon burnt'. He 'grew a companion to the common streets,/Enfeoffed himself to popularity,/That, being daily swallowed by men's eyes,/They surfeited with honey, and began/To loath the taste of sweetness' [Part I, III, ii, 46–72]. This passage picks up and refers back to Richard's both contemptuous and fearful description of Hereford's courtship of the people in *Richard II*. What to Richard had there seemed a both contemptible and seditious playing to the multitude appeared now, in retrospect, to the perpetrator himself, to have been a carefully modulated performance that had succeeded in winning him the favour of the people; a favourable 'opinion' which, when the final crisis arrived, had indeed helped him to the crown, just as Richard had feared that it might. On this view, far from 'popularity' being simply a bad thing, done well (as it had been by Henry IV in his personae of Hereford and Bolingbroke) it could well prove crucial to political success. It was just that done badly – with too much craven pandering to, and promiscuous association with, the people – that is to say, practised as it had been by Richard II and, as his father now claimed, as Hal himself was currently practising it – the politics of 'popularity' could also have entirely disastrous effects.

Just like the Cade scenes in *2 Henry VI*, these plays display a thoroughgoing contempt for the political instincts and loyalties of the mass of the people; at least when they have been unleashed from the legitimising structures of elite, indeed of royal, control. Here we might recall Archbishop Scroop's contemptuous description of that 'beastly feeder', the 'fond many'. Scroop's verdict might seem to confirm Henry IV's warning to Hal against the dangers of too great an addiction to 'popularity'. But, as we have seen, Scroop's dismissive, indeed disgusted, remarks come in the midst of a speech that reveals him making his own populist pitch for popular support. Thus Scroop's speech echoes not merely these plays' (entirely conventional) distaste for the moral and political capacities and proclivities of the people, it also confirms the king's sense that, distasteful and indeed dangerous as it might be, at certain times and for certain purposes, the politics of popularity was an absolutely essential weapon in the armoury of any successful political agent.

These plays can, therefore, scarcely be said to deride or dismiss altogether the role of the popular arts in the successful conduct of noble or monarchical politics, since Richard II, York and later Henry IV himself all agree on the central role that Henry's popularity had played in his rise to power. And without Scroop's populist appeal to the people, the rebellion of the Percies would have collapsed almost before it had begun. Thus, while appearing to be denunciations of popularity, Henry's and Scroop's speeches can both be taken as subtle disquisitions on the centrality of 'opinion', and thus on the value of the dark popular arts necessary to cultivate opinion. Indeed Henry IV's speech to Hal can be read as an exposition of those same arts, a how-to-do-it-properly guide to the politics of popularity. For the point being made here is precisely not that the people or popular opinion do not matter, but rather that, while they do indeed matter a great deal, they need to be manipulated by a careful husbanding and control of the image and presence of aristocratic or royal persons; a control that his father believes that, at least at present, Hal sadly lacks, but of which, in *Henry V,* the king shows himself to be a past master.

Moreover, it turns out that Hal/Henry's subsequent mastery of these skills – a mastery not only displayed throughout *Henry V,* but placed by Shakespeare at the centre of Henry's kingcraft – was itself a product, not so much of lessons taught him by his royal father, as of other skills and capacities learned from, and acquired in the company of, amongst others, that old reprobate Falstaff. What is being warned against, then, is not popularity itself, but rather the dangers inherent in too undisciplined or promiscuous a pursuit or practice thereof. Indeed, the total effect is reminiscent of nothing so much as Bacon's advice to Essex of 1596, when he had told the earl to distance himself from the practice of popularity, indeed to deride and condemn it in others, while all the while continuing himself in what Bacon euphemistically called his 'commonwealth courses'.

But Essex's practice of the politics of popularity also had other aspects to it. Central to these was his patronage of the godly, his association of himself not merely with the military legacy and clientele of his step-father, the earl of Leicester, but also with Leicester's status as a patron of puritans. For the military cause which Essex espoused was also famously construed by many contemporaries as the protestant cause; that is to say, the cause of international protestant solidarity in the final struggle against the papal Antichrist and the universal monarchy of Hapsburg Spain. As the great proponent of that cause, Essex retained the admiration of the godly until his disastrous fall from grace in 1601, and indeed beyond. As we have seen, in the polemical literature of the day, puritanism was associated with popularity, with a deliberate attempt to stir up the people in the cause of further reformation, using ignorant, rabble-rousing, popular sermons to alienate the populace from the status quo in church and state, in order to institute a new form of church government that would give to the dregs of the people effective power over not merely the church but large areas of the legal and political systems. Mere tradesmen would be empowered by their roles as lay elders, central figures in the consistorian discipline, to lord it over their social and political betters. Associated, too, with puritanism were schemes to despoil the church – the bishops and the deans and chapters – of their remaining landed wealth; schemes that were associated in some quarters with certain shadowy elements at court – with Leicester and later with his political and ideological legatee, Essex – men who were presented as wanting to use these untapped resources to enrich the crown and themselves and to fund the war effort, and consequently men whose patronage of the godly emerged as entirely hypocritical and self-interested.

Thus, just as, through the figure of Hotspur and his ultimately fatal relationship with Hal, these plays were commenting on the dangers inherent in too intense a pursuit of the politics of honour, so too, in their account of the prince's (differently fatal) relationship with Falstaff, they were commenting on the parallel dangers of too enthusiastic, and in particular of too puritan, an espousal of the politics of popularity. But if there is anything to the analysis conducted above, if Essex was being warned off the deployment of a certain sort of godly rhetoric by those – 'puritans' – bent on a populist pursuit of their own private interests, he was precisely not being warned off the deployment of just such a rhetoric to cloak and further his own (entirely beneficent) political and martial projects. On the contrary, just like Hal/Henry, he was surely being exhorted to deploy the language of 'reformation', repentance and 'amendment of life', and indeed the discourses of martial honour and ancient nobility, when, and insofar as, they suited his wider political purposes, but not when they did not, and certainly not in ways that might play into the populist and subversive hands of the puritans.

On this account, then, we might read certain central aspects of the play as a commentary on a recognisably contemporary, indeed a recognisably Essexian, mélange of political methods and modes. By providing an account of how the politics of honour, of martial prowess and renown, and, indeed, of (puritan) popularity, could be combined with the establishment of legitimacy and order, the play addressed certain immediately contemporary issues and dilemmas. On this basis, it might be read not as a simple piece of panegyrical celebration, but rather as an example of compliment as criticism, an exercise in political commentary, perhaps even in counsel, which mapped out a political course whereby Essex could avoid the pitfalls inherent in his current modus operandi, and, with Hal rather than with Hotspur, 'out of this nettle, danger, pluck this flower, safety'.

Not that the play posits mere safety as the proper end of this process. On the contrary, in the apotheosis of Henry V, it provides an account of the restorative, indeed of the potentially utopian, effects that, if not a return to real legitimacy, then at least a complete achievement of what we might term the legitimacy effect, could produce. Such effects could not be realised by Essex, or, indeed, by any subject, but only by a ruler of unchallengeable dynastic right and, in the current context, that meant by an alliance between the military and political prowess and prudence of a reformed Essex and the accession of James Stuart. Together, these disparate elements could confer a return to something like monarchical normality on a polity currently, or (depending on your religio-political outlook) about to be, plunged into commodity politics by tyranny and usurpation, regicide and rebellion.

PART VI

USING PLAYS TO READ PLAYS: THE COURT POLITICS OF THE DRAMATIC RIPOSTE

CHAPTER 16

Contemporary readings: Oldcastle/Falstaff, Cobham/Essex

In this section I want to use certain scraps of evidence about the ways in which these plays were read and received by contemporaries in order to test and, I hope, confirm, aspects of the analysis conducted thus far. I will start with an analysis of the fuss attendant upon the identification of the first version of the character subsequently known as Falstaff with Sir John Oldcastle, then read central elements in *The merry wives of Windsor* as a quite remarkably daring response to that fuss, before moving on to an analysis of the Oldcastle play as a response to, and a gloss upon, the *Henry IV* plays. In making this move I will be using contemporary dramatic responses to other plays as perhaps our best evidence for the ways in which contemporaries interpreted the plays thus replied to. As David Womersley puts it, 'dramatic ripostes – that is to say, plays written in response to an earlier play or group of plays – carry within themselves encoded readings of the earlier works to which they reply. Once a work has been identified as a dramatic riposte, it can be used as a lens to focus at least the outline of a contemporary reading of the work to which it responds. Moreover, since these ripostes were written for the commercial theatre, this would be not an idiosyncratic or eccentric reading, but rather a reading which would have been acknowledged as being at least plausible by a contemporary play-going audience.'[1]

True in general, these insights are true in spades for the relationship pertaining not merely between Shakespeare's *Henry IV* plays and *The Oldcastle play* but, as I will argue below, between *The merry wives of Windsor* and the initial Cobham-induced fuss over the character formerly known as Oldcastle in Shakespeare's *Henry IV* plays. As G.K Hunter has explained, here is as clear an instance of what he terms 'inter theatre rivalry and political involvement' as we are ever likely to get and it enables us to use the intertextual relations between at least three plays to show with what intensity and acuity the drama could play off matters of immediately contemporary interest and be read as doing precisely that by a variety of audiences.[2]

Oldcastle/Falstaff, Cobham/Essex

As so often, the dating of the crucial texts is less than clear and accordingly the argument will not turn on the adoption of any one of the still controversial attempts to date (precisely) either the *Henry IV* plays or indeed *The merry wives of Windsor*. In the first version of *1 Henry IV* and indeed very likely of *2 Henry IV* as well, the character subsequently known as Falstaff had been called Sir John Oldcastle. We learn, admittedly from far later sources of the 1630s, that 'personages descended from his [title]' i.e. the Brookes, Lord Cobham, had complained about this and insisted that the character be renamed, at first in print and subsequently in performance. This was effected in the first printed version of *1 Henry IV* in 1598, where Oldcastle's name was changed to Falstaff. That choice was in itself interesting, given the prominence of a cowardly knight named Falstofe as the defining alter ego of the hero Talbot in that other densely Essexian text, *1 Henry VI*. Indeed, for anyone conversant with Shakespeare's *oeuvre*, such a renaming might be thought to have removed the obvious or formal cause of offence, but only in a way that served to compound the insult; much to the hilarity or offence of those in on the joke.[3]

And this was, or became, a rather extensive group, which appears to have included Essex, Southampton and his wife, not to mention Sir Robert Cecil and Cobham himself. In a letter written to Robert Cecil of February 1598 Essex referred slightingly to Cobham's supposed affair with Margaret Ratcliffe, one of Elizabeth's maids of honour and the daughter of Sir Alexander Ratcliffe of Ordsall: 'Commend me also to Alex Ratcliffe, and tell him for news his sister is married to Sir John Falstaff.' By this point, therefore, the identification of Cobham with Falstaff via Oldcastle was common knowledge at court, and Essex was here using it to poke fun, not only at Cobham, but also perhaps at Cecil, who was Cobham's brother-in-law. The joke/insult was rendered the more stinging if, as seems likely, Oldcastle had been renamed Falstaff at Cobham's own insistence in order to suppress an association that was now being reaffirmed by this easy reference to Cobham as (the renamed) Falstaff.

Later in July 1599 the countess of Southampton wrote to her husband, then serving with Essex in Ireland, that 'all the news I can send you I think will make you merry is that I read in a letter from London that Sir John Falstaff is by his mistress dame Pintpot made father of a milers thumb, a boy that is all head and very little body, but this is a secret'. To quote James Bednarz' detailed unpacking of this passage 'part of the wit of the countess' allusion depends on the fact that a "miller's thumb" was a small fish with a big head, which was called a cottus gobio in latin and a "cob" in English. More fish than flesh, Cobham's offspring – his bastard cob – is both illegitimate and monstrously disproportioned. Her soubriquet for Cobham's secret lover, "Dame Pintpot", recalls Falstaff's name for Mistress Quickly in *I Henry IV* (2. 4. 397), and her piscatorial conceit might have been similarly suggestive of Falstaff's jest that the hostess was "neither fish nor flesh" (3. 3. 127).[4] In court circles, then, the terms set by the play became the grounds for a series of private jokes and references of very considerable density and compression, all of which centre on the identity of Falstaff as Oldcastle/Cobham, and the use of that identification as a means of insulting and ridiculing Essex's enemy of that name. As late as 1600 the epilogue of the quarto edition of *2 Henry IV* contained the disclaimer that 'for anything I know Falstaff shall die of a sweat, unless already' ' 'a be killed with your hard opinions; for Oldcastle died a martyr, and this is not the man'. . Again, this was a denial of the connection between Oldcastle/Cobham and Falstaff that could only serve to remind the audience that such a connection had once existed and continued, in fact, to be made.

A considerable scholarly debate has grown up around this incident, with different critics affirming or denying that Shakespeare intended to make fun of Cobham. The alternative explanation is that, in the charged atmosphere of the day, Cobham merely took offence at an innocent or accidental reference, thus pitching the playwright and his company into the factional and personal rivalries of the late 1590s by accident. The issue of intention is obviously unprovable one way or another – although the high stakes involved in typing the Lollard martyr a thief and a hypocrite, the tense relations between Henry Brooke, Lord Cobham and Essex, and the contest later surrounding what would become of the ailing Lord Cobham's many offices – amongst them the posts of Lord Chamberlain and Lord Warden of the Cinque Ports – all combine to make a series of acts of inadvertence seem rather unlikely. Certainly, accident or not, the initial affront having been delivered, the subsequent attempts to 'make amends' seem calculated to worsen rather than to mitigate the insult.

But for the current purpose what is interesting and undeniable is the fact, that, at a time of high political tension, Shakespeare (perhaps by accident, perhaps not) can be found insulting on the public stage the one great publicly acknowledged and unappeasable enemy and rival of the earl of Essex, much to the subsequent delight of central members of the earl's circle. And what is not subject to any doubt at all is the close attention paid by members of the court to the political and personal resonances of the drama, and in particular the intimate knowledge and easy reference to these plays made by members of the Essex circle as a means of sending (rather insulting) messages to their rivals at court and making private jokes amongst themselves.[5]

Getting him coming and going (i): *The merry wives of Windsor*

It has long been acknowledged that *The merry wives of Windsor* contains a reference back to the dispute about Oldcastle's identity as Falstaff and to the Cobhams' objections thereto. At an integral point in the main plotline of the play an insanely jealous character named Ford adopts the pseudonym Brook as part of his plot, in effect, to cuckold himself by bribing Falstaff to seduce his own wife. As a number of commentators have suggested, this was almost certainly designed to recall the recent fuss made by the Brookes, Lords Cobham about the Oldcastle/Falstaff identification. But if that reference succeeded in reminding at least a courtly audience of that fracas, it must also have served simultaneously to remind them of the whole Falstaff/Oldcastle/Cobham connection, and thus have invited them to interpret the whole action of the play in the light of those associations and identifications. It created, within the audience, certainly at court and perhaps elsewhere as well, an informed cadre entirely alive to the fact(s) that Ford was Brook, Brook was Cobham, Cobham was Oldcastle and Oldcastle was Falstaff. What follows is a reading of the play predicated on that knowledge. The results turn a good deal of the action into a farcical inside joke, as the twinned characters of Ford/Brook and Falstaff/Oldcastle are held up, in fact hold each other up, to increasingly public ridicule, indeed to various forms of ritual humiliation, as cuckolds, wittolds, witches, frauds and dupes of various sorts.

The basic identifications or associations are driven home in the insistence on the name of Brook in the first exchange between Ford and Falstaff. They are thereafter picked up again and again throughout the play. Every time there is wordplay on the nexus linking Ford with Brook, the audience is being reminded of the fuss over Oldcastle/Falstaff/Cobham.

Ford/Brook and Falstaff/Oldcastle are associated throughout by their equally delusory opinions of, and plans for, Ford's wife. Falstaff is convinced that mistress Ford fancies him madly and that he can seduce her at will. Ford is equally convinced that his wife is unfaithful and is having an affair with Falstaff. Their fantasies thus fit perfectly together, each confirming the other, as both characters set about their entirely delusional purposes. To prove his point, Ford assumes the identity of Brook and bribes Falstaff to seduce his own wife to prove that she is as unfaithful to him as he thinks she is, while Falstaff's conviction that he is in the process of seducing the, in fact entirely faithful, Mistress Ford merely serves to feed Ford/Brook's obsession.

Ford takes his own mad jealousy to be a form of prudence. 'Who says this is improvident jealousy? . . . See the hell of having a false woman: my bed shall be abused, my coffers ransacked, my reputation gnawn at; and I shall not only receive this villainous wrong, but stand under the adoption of abominable terms, and by him that does me this wrong. Terms! Names! Amaimon sounds well; Lucifer, well; Barbason, well; yet they are devils' additions, the names of fiends. But cuckold? Wittol? Cuckold! The devil himself hath not such a name! Page is an ass, a secure ass; he will trust his wife, he will not be jealous. I will rather trust a Fleming with my butter, Parson Hugh the Welshman with my cheese, an Irishman with my acqua-vitae bottle, or a thief to walking my ambling gelding, than my wife with herself. Then she plots, then she ruminates, then she devises; and what they think in their hearts they may effect – they will break their hearts but they will effect. God be praised for my jealousy!' [II, ii, 273–93].

Just as Brook is convinced that his wife is unfaithful to him, Falstaff is equally convinced that both she and Mistress Page are enamoured of him. As he tells Pistol, 'I do mean to make love to Ford's wife. I spy entertainment in her: she discourses, she carves, she gives the leer of invitation. I can construe the action of her familiar style, and the hardest voice of her behaviour – to be Englished rightly – is: "I am Sir John Falstaff's" ' [I, iii, 40–45]. He is no less sure of Mrs Page: 'sometimes the beam of her view gilded my foot, sometimes my portly belly ... O, she did course o'er my exteriors, with such a greedy intention, that the appetite of her eye did seem to scorch me up like a burning glass' [I, iii, 58–64].

Because, in the persona of Brook, Ford bribes Falstaff to seduce his own wife, he is forced to hear both her and himself slandered in the most insulting of tones, while paying for the privilege. Asked by Brook 'do you know Ford, Sir?', Falstaff exclaims 'hang him poor cuckoldy knave, I know him not. Yet I wrong him to call him poor: they say the jealous wittolly knave hath masses of money, for the which his wife seems to me well-favoured. I will use her as the key of the cuckoldy rogue's coffer, and there's my harvest home.' 'Hang him, mechanical salt-butter rogue! I will stare him out of his wits, I will awe him with my cudgel: it shall hang like a meteor o'er the cuckold's horns. Master Brook, thou shalt know I will predominate over the peasant, and thou shalt lie with his wife. Come to me soon at night' [II, ii, 256–61, 264–69]. Later, after the failure of his first attempt to unmask Falstaff in his wife's company, Ford/Brook returns to ask Falstaff for an explanation, only again to have to listen to yet another version of the same insulting rant. Describing his sufferings in the laundry basket Falstaff complains, in his usual grandiloquent terms, that 'I quaked for fear lest the lunatic knave would have searched it; but Fate, ordaining he should be a cuckold, held his hand' [III, v, 95–97]. Their exchange ends with Falstaff reassuring Brook that he will have his evil way with Ford's wife and that the way will then be clear for Brook as well. 'You shall have her, Master Brook. Master Brook, you shall cuckold Ford' [III, v, 126–27]. For an audience, especially a court audience, alerted, to the Ford/Brook/Cobham, and the Cobham/Oldcastle/Falstaff associations, the humour of these scenes would have been very considerably heightened, as well as being given a pointedly satiric edge. What was being staged here was Brook/Oldcastle/Cobham in effect insulting himself; carefully setting up a situation in which both Brook /Ford and Oldcastle/Falstaff would be held up, indeed would hold each other up, to systematic ridicule and humiliation, by constructing a tightly choreographed intrigue, for which Ford/Brook himself was paying.

Nor are the humiliations visited by Ford/Brook upon himself limited to these private interviews with Falstaff. They go public, twice over. Ford carefully assembles an audience for his own folly and humiliation by bringing a group of his neighbours and peers along with him to witness his wife's infidelity and thus attest to his status as a cuckold. Bursting into his own home, certain that Falstaff is there alone with his wife, he sends his friends all over the house to search out the fat knight. They, for their part, try to restrain him. Chastened when the search proves fruitless, Ford invites his companions to dinner, and Page's comment draws the moral from the scene: 'let's go in, gentlemen; but trust me, we'll mock him' [III, iii, 148–51, 151–52, 156–57,199–202, 192–93, 213–15].

The second time Ford is so sure of himself that with manic energy he falls on the laundry basket in which he is now certain that Falstaff is hiding [IV, ii, 110–14]. At this point his companions have immediate recourse to the language of madness. 'Why this passes, Master Ford! You are not to go loose any longer, you must be pinioned.' 'Why, this is lunatics, this is mad as a mad dog.' 'Indeed, Master Ford, this is not well indeed' [IV, ii, 116–19]. Ford, however, persists, frantically unpacking the basket of dirty laundry.

What Ford/Brook is doing here is precisely the opposite of what the conventional values and expectations of the day would have had him do. If he were really being cuckolded, the conventional course would have been to keep that fact a secret, in order to avoid precisely the sort public knowledge, the ridicule and humiliation, that is now being visited upon him; to then reassert control over his own household and wife, before, perhaps, seeking to be revenged on the cuckolder. Rather than do any of these things, Ford not merely loses, he resigns, control over his household. In a peculiarly resonant gesture, he gives up his keys and sends all and sundry to search out his wife's infidelity. So certain is he that she is unfaithful that he thinks he will be vindicated not so much by revenging himself on his wife's lover as through the public revelation of his own condition as a cuckold and of his wife's as an adulteress.

Ford meets the incredulity of his neighbours as they try to restrain him from turning his own house upside down for a second time with a challenge and a promise. 'Help to search my house this one time. If I find not what I seek, show no colour for my extremity, let me be for ever your table-sport. Let them say of me "As jealous as Ford, that searched a hollow walnut for his wife's leman". Satisfy me once more, once more search with me' [IV, ii, 151–56]. In short, Ford/Brook ends by positively inviting upon himself the response which his own jealousy and folly inevitably elicits both from the other characters and, of course, from the audience. Ford/Brook was here shaming himself; in effect arranging (and, of course, paying for) his own charivari, through which to broadcast his failings and foibles as a husband and householder to all and sundry.

This is, we might add, a wonderfully compressed and pointed, both overt and subtle, version of what Cobham had done over the Oldcastle business, making a public fuss which adverted to, indeed perhaps even created where none had previously existed, an association (between Oldcastle, Falstaff and the Brookes, Lords Cobham) that could only operate to Cobham's shame, even as Cobham himself remained blithely confident that, in asserting that connection, he was in some bizarre way vindicating his family's honour. Moreover, plausible deniability was built into the very structure of the occasion. For it would only be by repeating in open court, as it were, the folly for which he was being held up to such ridicule on stage – that is, by making a public fuss about a mere play – that Brook/Cobham could complain about what was being done to him in the *Merry Wives*. Indeed, in order even to frame such a complaint, Cobham would have had to admit publicly that he recognised himself in the play's portrait of the absurdly jealous Windsor tradesman, Ford/Brook. Not only that, he would also have had to have embraced as a recognisable portrait of his noble ancestor, the martyr, Sir John Oldcastle, this play's hapless and absurd, and so even more insulting, version of Falstaff. On this account, then, the play was a brilliantly wrought and effective revenge for the earlier fuss made about the *Henry IV* plays. That at some point later Ford's pseudonym 'Brook' was changed to Brome is further evidence that these references were not lost on contemporaries.[6] But, as the quarto shows, in its first iteration, both in performance and in print, the play did the business on Brook/Cobham in plain sight. There could scarcely be a better illustration of the very tight fit between the inside knowledge, the gossip, the concerns and anxieties of the audience – and in this case, on at least one occasion, of a court audience – and the workings of the drama.

Getting him going and coming (ii): Falstaff/Oldcastle as Cobham

But it is not only the Ford/Brook character whose frailties and follies are outed and who is ritually humiliated in the play. If Ford's insane jealousy and folly are revealed and mercilessly mocked, so, too, is Falstaff's cupidity, lust and credulity. Thus, just as the stratagems of Ford/Brook backfire, so too do those of Falstaff/Oldcastle, with Ford/Brook's costly intrigue revealing both himself and the fat knight to be fantasists, fools and frauds. Threatened with discovery and a good beating by the delusionally jealous Ford, Falstaff's cowardice overcomes his famous wit and he is forced to adopt two stratagems devised by his intended female dupes; stratagems calculated to effect not merely his escape but also his humiliation. Falstaff's fate in these two episodes adverts subtly to, and indeed casts both doubt and derision upon, Oldcastle's status as a martyr.

After Falstaff has been beaten as a witch, Mistress Page comments that she will 'have the cudgel hallowed and hung o'er the altar: it hath done meritorious service' [IV, ii, 193–94]. Here it is the object used to scourge the erstwhile heretic Oldcastle/Falstaff that attains the status of a relic rather than any remnant of his battered body or credit. Later, when all is explained to him, Ford admits the error of his ways, telling his wife, 'Now doth thy honour stand,/In him that was of late an heretic,/As firm as faith' [IV, iv, 7–9]. Here, then, is 'heresy' being defined as belief in Falstaff/Oldcastle's claims about himself, and true 'faith' as the conviction that those who have unmasked the fat knight to the world as a fraud, a lecher and a thief have been right all along; an admission put here into the mouth of Ford, i.e. of Cobham's alter ego, Brook.

Near the end of Act IV Falstaff laments the effect on his reputation at court of his having been 'cozened and beaten' by the merry wives. 'If it should come to the ear of the court how I have been transformed, and how my transformation hath been washed and cudgelled, they would melt me out of my fat drop by drop, and liquor fishermen's boots with me. I warrant they would whip me with their fine wits till I were as crestfallen as a dried pear' [IV, v, 87–94]. Given the Brook/Ford/Oldcastle/Falstaff/Cobham connections that the play sets up with such wonderful economy, the wider resonances of that lament are unlikely to have been lost on a court audience. There was, of course, a threat here, as well as a joke and a lesson. The lesson was: see what a fool you can make of yourself when you start making a fuss about plays. The concomitant threat ran something like this: make a fuss about this play, and think what an even bigger fool you will make of yourself in the eyes, if not of the world, then certainly of the court. In the play, the joke, of course, was on Ford and on Falstaff, but Ford was also Brook and Falstaff was also Oldcastle, a character with whom Cobham, by making such a fuss in the first place, had (at least in court circles) indelibly associated himself, and thus, in reality, the joke was also on Cobham, and if he complained about it, the bigger and better the joke would become.

Shaming rituals and court masques

Falstaff's first two ridings or outings had been largely private affairs, the joke known only to the two merry wives who had contrived it. Now, with everyone in on the joke, they plan a third, and fully public, outing of 'the poor unvirtuous fat knight' [IV, ii, 206]. 'I'll warrant they'll have him publicly shamed, and methinks there would be no period to the jest should he not be publicly shamed' [IV, ii, 209–11]. The husbands enthusiastically agree to their wives' proposal [IV, iv, 12–15], which involves a midnight assignation with Falstaff in the woods, where he will appear disguised like Herne the hunter with antlers on his head. He will there be surprised by children dressed as fairies who 'till he tell the truth' 'pinch him sound/And burn him with their tapers' [IV, iv, 59–61].

At this point, the play takes on the form of a masque, drenched in the language and imagery of the Order of the Garter [V, v, 56–73]. It is this material, together with a number of topical references to events of 1597, that has led many critics to conclude that the play was written for a Garter feast, in April 1597 (or perhaps 1598) and designed to celebrate both the order itself and the 'radiant queen' who 'hates sluts and sluttery' [V, v, 46], evoked in Act V, as 'the queen of fairies'. And, just as in a masque, a magical world of fairy is conjured and, in and through that conjuration, many of the tensions and conflicts, the corrupt impulses and sins, depicted in the body of the action, are unmasked, resolved and reconciled.

The role of the queen of the fairies in this forest festivity is to be played by none other than Ann Page, who in the play's other major plotline has been the object of the attentions of four rival suitors. The confusion created by the outing of Falstaff is to be the occasion upon which three separate plots to marry her in secret will be consumated. She is to be married, with her father's conniv-ance, to the idiot Slender, with her mother's, to the court doctor Caius, and, on her own and Fenton's initiative, and with the connivance of 'mine host of the Garter Inn', to young Fenton. Fenton has personal accomplishments that the other suitors lack; in the words of the host of the Garter Inn, 'he capers, he dances, he has eyes of youth, he writes verses, he speaks holiday, he smells April and May' [III, ii, 60–62]. But Master Page will have none of him. 'The gentleman is of no having, he kept company with the wild Prince and Poins. He is of too high a region, he knows too much – no, he shall not knit a knot in his fortunes with the finger of my substance. If he take her, let him take her simply: the wealth I have waits on my consent, and my consent goes not that way' [III, ii, 64–70].

In a later scene with Ann, Fenton himself admits the truth of these accusa-tions. There is no further point, he claims, in seeking her father's goodwill. 'He doth object I am too great of birth,/And that, my state being galled with my expense,/I seek to heal it only by his wealth./Besides these, other bars he lays before me:/My riots past, my wild societies – And tells me 'tis a thing impossible/I should love thee, but as a property'. To the retort that 'maybe he tells you true', Fenton replies, 'No, God so speed me in my time to come!/Albeit I will confess thy father's wealth/Was the first motive that I wooed thee, Anne,/ Yet, wooing thee, I found thee of more value/Than stamps in gold or sums in sealed bags./And 'tis the very riches of thyself/That now I aim at'. A point he proves by undertaking to marry her anyway [III, iv, 4–18].

At this point in the play, the figure of Ford, shorn of his persona as Brook, the accomplice of Falstaff and alter ego of a man driven almost mad with jealous concern for his reputation, has moved into the background. The main business is now the fate of Falstaff and the marriage of Ann Page, who, as we have seen, has taken on (albeit fleetingly) the distinctly royal persona of 'the queen of fairy'. The action now turns on the contrast between that false, perjured,and wholly mercenary suitor – Falstaff – and his equally pure and honourable anti-type – the reformed Fenton. From the outset, Falstaff's motives in attempting to seduce both Mistress Page and Mistress Ford have been revealed as entirely corrupt; motivated not so much by lust as by cupidity; on his uppers, Falstaff was pursuing both women for gain. The report of Mistress Ford, he tells Bardolph, is that she has 'all the rule of her husband's purse: he hath a legion of angels' [I, iii, 49–50]. As for Mistress Page, 'she bears the purse too: she is a region in Guiana, all gold and bounty. I will be cheaters to them both, and they shall be exchequers to me. They shall be my East and West Indies, and I will trade to them both' [I, iii, 65–69].

In short, Falstaff and Fenton have both ruined themselves in attendance on the wild young Prince Hal and both have been guilty of wooing women for money rather than for love. Fenton, however, has reformed, and the purity of his affections for Ann Page, always a piece of 'pretty virginity' and now typed as the queen of the fairy, is rewarded with marriage. Falstaff, however, has not reformed and he is outed in the woods, 'as full of lecheries and iniquity' [A phrase found only in the quarto edition at sig. G3r]. Here the masque doubles as a sort of charivari, in which the elements of popular shaming ritual – cross-dressing, ducking in the Thames, being beaten as a witch – inherent in his two previous comeuppances are rendered explicit and public. Forced to wear the horns, not only of cuckoldry but also of lust, Falstaff is tormented, if not into repentance, then at least into submission, by the fairies, who dance around him singing 'Fie on sinful fantasy,/Fie on lust and luxury!/Lust is but a bloody fire/ Kindled with unchaste desire,/Fed in heart, whose flames aspire,/As thoughts do blow them, higher and higher' [V, v, 93–97].

Reviled and renounced by his old partner in cuckoldry and fraud, Brook, Falstaff is then schooled by the idiot Welsh schoolmaster, Evans [V, v, 141–44]. At this point the others all pile on, recounting Falstaff's multifarious faults. In the face of this onslaught even Falstaff has nothing to say. 'Well, I am your theme: you have the start of me. I am dejected, I am not able to answer the Welsh flannel, ignorance itself is a plummet o'er me. Use me as you will' [V, v, 150–62]. As he had earlier observed about his failure to see through the fairies, 'see now how wit may be made a Jack-a-Lent when 'tis upon ill employment!' [V, v, 126–27].

We have here something like a comic version of the rejection of Falstaff at the end of 2 Henry IV. For here again is Falstaff, just like the witch for whom at one point he is mistaken, first being identified as the personification of all the evil humours besetting the play, the society of Windsor, and indeed the realm – and then being publicly outed and excluded, here through the simultaneously festive and disciplinary mechanisms of both popular and court culture, as the rough music of the charivari meets the queen of fairy sophistication and whimsy of court pastoral and masque in the woods of Windsor Great Park.

If order and harmony are being restored at play's end by the exclusion and public shaming of the principle of misrule, the entirely false and corrupt suitor that is Falstaff, then to persist in asserting fellowship with, indeed descent from, Falstaff/Oldcastle – as, of course, Cobham has done – was to resist, indeed to exclude oneself from, the amity, order and unity being reconstituted at play's end. Master Ford takes the point and is careful to put as much distance as he can between himself and his former accomplice, and, in the minds of the audience, his alter ego, Falstaff/Oldcastle. In a remarkable tirade, directed as much at his other self, 'Mr Brook', as at Falstaff, Ford demands 'now, sir, who's a cuckold now? Master Brook, Falstaff's a knave, a cuckoldy knave. Here are his horns, Master Brook. And, Master Brook, he hath enjoyed nothing of Ford's but his buck basket, his cudgel and twenty pounds of money which, must be paid to Master Brook' [V, v, 109–14]. Here is Ford, addressing one of his personae, Brook/Cobham, with a denunciation of another, Falstaff/Oldcastle. Again, we might add, the point is being driven home that for Ford/Brook/ Cobham the route back to respectability, to reintegration within the community of the honourable and the virtuous, that is being reconstituted by the masque-like shaming ritual with which the play concludes, is through the complete repudiation, rather than the further patronage or protection, of Falstaff/Oldcastle.

A happy ending

What is going on in these scenes is quite remarkable: a peer of the realm and major courtier is not merely being ridiculed, he is being roasted, before what was, on at least one occasion, a court audience. Committed anywhere else by someone of the social status of a player, such an action could only have led to the direst of consequences. We have here, then, an object lesson in the licence, the plausible deniability, conferred by the drama. That inherent licence had, of course, been further stretched in this instance by the decision to cast the play as a broad comedy replete with silly foreigners, funny accents and slapstick byplay, and to set the action in the decidedly plebeian setting of Windsor. So great was the social distance of the action from its courtly objects or points of reference that to assert any direct correspondences or to make any explicit identifications would in itself have been an insult as great as anything being acted out on stage. Indeed, subsequent commentary has been so convinced that the play is a form of 'citizen comedy' that it has quite failed to note the extent to which it was also a commentary on court politics.[7]

Not only that, but since the play is a comedy, it had to have a happy ending; an ending wrought, in this case, entirely through the exercise of female sagacity and wit in exposing and schooling male folly. As Mistress Page remarks, outraged by Falstaff's presumption, lust and greed, 'why, I'll exhibit a bill in the parliament for the putting down of men' [II, i, 23–24]. It is Mistress Page and Mistress Ford who have inveigled both Falstaff and Ford into situations in which their absurdity and corruption is rendered patent and who devise the mechanisms whereby the fat knight is further publicly outed and punished. And it is they who script and choreograph the final denouement in the woods which brings the play to its happy ending.

Only in one respect do the merry wives of Windsor not get their way, and that is over the marriage of Ann Page, who, as we have seen, is intended by her mother for the absurd Dr Caius. Here Mistress Page's reasoning is as corrupt as Falstaff's; she favours Caius because he has money and powerful friends at court. Ann Page, however, ends up in the arms of Fenton. But even this is not the result of superior masculine cunning or control, still less of the imposition of conventional patriarchal forms of authority or norms of behaviour. Ann's father, after all, favours the even more unsuitable Slender. On the contrary, in the elopement of Ann Page and Fenton both the patriarchal authority of Mr Page and the female cunning and wisdom of his wife are overthrown by the triumph of true love, embodied in this instance in Ann Page's conviction that young Fenton is just what he says he is. True love triumphs here not only through Fenton's display of virtue and fidelity, but also through Ann's exercise of true female wisdom and insight in discerning his virtues for what they are. Here, then, the final arbiter is not merry wives but rather the 'queen of fairy' herself, Ann Page, the woman for whose favour the farcical duel between Caius and Evans had (not) been fought; the woman elected to play the queen of fairies in the play's last scene, the great catch at whose favour, indeed at whose hand, a whole variety of male characters have set their caps.

Thus, while the silliness of the duel between Caius and Evans is avoided by the host of the Garter Inn and Justice Shallow, the real business of sorting out Falstaff and Ford, of trying and choosing Fenton, falls to women. Just as Ford is reintegrated into Windsor society in large part through his repudiation both of Falstaff and of his own insane jealousies – a repudiation scripted and set up by his wife – so, under the influence of Ann Page, Fenton repents his wild youth and repudiates his initially mercenary motives. He thus distinguishes himself definitively from that other companion of the wild young prince, Falstaff, who has been revealed, again through the machinations of women, to be the polar opposite of Fenton; that is to say, an inveterately and (until very late in the day) an unrepentantly mercenary and lustful suitor.[8] With true love, honour and obedience thus identified through the exercise of female wit and judgement, the young couple are then forgiven their deceit and disobedience in eloping and everyone goes off happily to dinner. Even Falstaff, having finally submitted to the shaming discipline of the masque/ charivari staged in the Windsor woods gets to attend the wedding feast. The corrupt impulses and peccant humours, the feuds and animosities, staged in the play and personified most obviously in Falstaff, but also in Ford/Brook, Dr Caius and Pastor Evans, and indeed even in Fenton himself, have all been exposed and expelled, reformed and reconciled, by women; a variety of male characters have been tried, tested and reformed, and the integrity of that society of true honour and nobility – and of service to the queen – the Order of the Garter – to which, of course, both Essex and Cobham belonged – has been reaffirmed.

This then was a happy ending in which the queen's beneficent control over the often fractious and corrupt rivalries of her courtiers and counsellors was reaffirmed and vindicated. Masculine folly has been schooled and tamed by female sagacity.[9] Desert, and the course of true love, have triumphed. Fenton's virtuous devotion to his mistress, the queen of fairy, has been tested, found true and rewarded, and the peccant humours surrounding the Ford/Brook/Falstaff/Oldcastle nexus have been disaggregated; Falstaff/Oldcastle has been repudiated by Brook/Ford and order has been restored. In that way, the quite extraordinarily explicit and developed comic revenge exacted on Cobham was both justified and glossed over.

Political contingencies

Taken together with the evidence that certain central figures at court – Southampton, his wife and Essex certainly, but also Cecil and his brother-in-law Cobham – associated Falstaff with Oldcastle and Oldcastle with Cobham, what we have here is a devastating reply to the Cobham-sponsored attempt to get Oldcastle relabelled as Falstaff. There could be no clearer evidence of the involvement of Shakespeare in the factional and personal rivalries of the late Elizabethan court nor of his popularity with the Essex group, nor indeed of his daring in guying the enemies of the earl of Essex on the public stage. That much is certain, but the precise political meaning or resonance of all this is very hard to determine, given the difficulty in dating with any precision the plays in question.

The merry wives is conventionally dated to 1597 or sometimes to 1598. That conclusion is based on what appear to be certain immediately contemporary references to the conferral of the Order of the Garter on the duke of Württemberg and to the duke's non-appearance at the ceremonies at which he was to have been admitted to the Order. Given that Shakespeare's patron Lord Hunsdon was admitted to the Garter in 1597 and that Hunsdon had just succeeded the deceased William Brooke, Lord Cobham as Lord Chamberlain, this might make some sense, with Shakespeare wreaking his revenge on the new Lord Cobham, safe in the knowledge that Hunsdon was now the Lord Chamberlain. Not only that, but the elder Cobham's decease had provoked a bitter confrontation between Essex and Brooke over who should acquire his offices. Involved here was not only the Lord Chamberlainship but also the post of Lord Warden of the Cinque Ports which Essex had sought unsuccessfully for his friend and client Sir Robert Sidney. When it became clear that Elizabeth would not appoint Sidney, Essex pushed his own candidacy for the post, thus making Cobham's appointment an intensely personal issue about the extent of Essex's own favour with the queen.[10] To produce an assault on Cobham as pointed and sustained as that contained in *The merry wives*, at this point would thus have been a far from politically innocent gesture; one that Shakespeare would surely only have dared to make because of the protection afforded him both by Hunsdon as Lord Chamberlain and by the influence at court of Cobham's bitter rival, Essex.

There remains, however, another possibility. The most recent, extended and, in many ways, rigorous, analysis of the date of *The merry wives of Windsor* has been produced by Professor Melchiori. Melchiori sees the play as a complex text, an amalgam of diverse narrative elements, some of them culled from an entertainment written to celebrate a Garter festival, in 1597 or 1598, but others taken from different storylines and genres. On Melchiori's account, the version(s) which have come down to us date from the period after *2 Henry IV* and *Henry V*. The presence of characters from the second *Henry IV* play – Justice Shallow, Bardolph, Pistol – and of Nym from *Henry V* – introduced into the action with an assurance that the audience will know precisely who they are, together with the Fluellen-like stage Welshman, Pastor Evans, and the absurdly proud and obtuse French Doctor Caius, both of whom recall central comic elements in *Henry V*, signals the audience's presumed conversance with those earlier plays.[11] The date of the first printed quarto of the play was 1602, which, Melchiori argues, puts the date at which the extant version(s) must have been written between late 1599 and 1602. The play, as the title page of the 1602 printing informs us, had been 'divers times acted by the right honourable my Lord Chamberlain's servants both before her majesty and elsewhere'.[12]

If we allow ourselves to entertain the possibility that the final version of *The merry wives* does indeed date from the period after Essex's return in disgrace from Ireland then a whole series of other potential contexts and resonances immediately come into play. Here the figure of Fenton, a once wild young man, who had ruined himself in the service of the young prince and was now seeking to mend his fortunes through an entirely mercenary pursuit of the 'queen of fairy', becomes a type for Essex as many of his enemies were describing him. Essex's loss of the queen's favour was certainly threatening to ruin his always chaotic finances once and for all and while his repeated petitions to the queen to be readmitted into the royal presence (and favour) were couched in precisely the terms of undying personal devotion and thwarted love that we might expect – one letter featuring a plaintive enquiry whether as a knight of the Garter he should wear his robes alone in the Tower on the day that the Garter celebrations were conventionally held[13] – the earl was also not above reminding the queen that his farm of the French wines was about to lapse, leaving him at the mercy of his creditors; a lapse into mercenary self-interest for which he was forced almost immediately to issue a grovelling apology.[14]

On this scenario, the rivalries at court, glanced at in the absurd contentions between the rival suitors for Ann Page's hand, become deadly serious. The attempted duel between Caius and Evans remains absurd, but acquires direct contemporary resonance through the protracted attempt of Lord Grey and the earl of Southampton to meet and fight a duel, first in Ireland and then in the Low Countries. That affair, itself an expression of the extreme animosities dividing the earl's friends and supporters from his enemies, lasted throughout the summer and into the autumn of 1600. As John Chamberlain's newsletters attest, as well as being known to the queen and Council, who did their utmost to stop it, the escapades of the two would-be duellists were widely reported in the gossip and newsletter networks of the capital, where, despite any number of rumours to the contrary, it was known by October 1600 that the pair had failed to meet, just as Caius and Pastor Evans do in the play.[15]

Along with the subplot of the duel, the play's evocation, through the Oldcastle/Falstaff business, of the long-standing feud between Essex and Cobham, who was still widely known to be the earl's sworn enemy, served to connect the action of the play to the pressing political crisis facing Essex and the court. Viewed in this context, the play's happy ending, with the absurd jealousies and rivalries of various men being schooled and shamed, tempered and contained, through the exercise of feminine sagacity and insight, with the virtue of the wild young Fenton tested, vindicated and rewarded and the corruption of his fellow suitor (and companion of the wild young prince) Falstaff outed, became a comic rendition of the Essex affair as the more optimistic of the earl's supporters hoped it would end. As late as the autumn of 1600 Chamberlain was reporting that some of the earl's friends were talking up his prospects of returning to court in time to take part in the Accession Day celebrations of early November.[16] On this reading in The merry wives as the text has come down to us, Shakespeare would have been reworking material initially written for a happier, though still fraught, occasion in 1597 or 1598, in order to comment upon the rather more serious tensions of 1599–1601.

But all this, of course, must remain surmise, based, as it is, on what remain uncertain, indeed controversial, datings and re-datings of the play. What remains certain, however, is that whether or not the initial affront to the Cobhams was indeed inadvertent – as David Kastan and Paul Whitfield White amongst others have insisted that it *must* have been, since the 'pragmatic' Shakespeare would simply not take such a risk[17] – Shakespeare's provocative decision to rename the Lollard martyr, Oldcastle, Falstaff, followed by the incessant reminding of his readers of that association through his elaborate denials thereof[18] and the later roasting of Cobham in The merry wives of Windsor were all anything but accidents. Taken together with the byplay at court over the identity of Cobham with Oldcastle and therefore with Falstaff, there could scarcely be a clearer confirmation of precisely the sort of associations and references that the preceding analysis has identified running through these plays or of Shakespeare's willingness to make hay with them when the occasion seemed to call for it.

CHAPTER 17

Oldcastle *redivivus*

The fuss over Oldcastle broke out when *1 Henry IV* was first performed, prompting the substitution of the name Falstaff for that of Oldcastle in the first printed version of the play in 1598. But in 1599 the issue was reopened by another play. While the politics at stake in the previous chapter were intensely personal, all but devoid of real ideological content, the same cannot be said of the initial identification of the character subsequently known as Falstaff with the Lollard martyr, Oldcastle. It has been suggested above that this represented a really rather daring move: far more than a gesture toward or appropriation of the routine anti-puritanism of the later 1590s, it was rather an attempt to use the anti-puritan atmosphere of the day in order to launch a far more thorough-going assault on the entire Foxeian tradition. Confirmation that that was precisely how at least some contemporaries took it can be found in *Sir John Oldcastle, part I*, a play that was clearly written to respond to, indeed, in some sense, to refute, Shakespeare's version of Falstaff in his original persona as Sir John Oldcastle. Written by Michael Drayton, Richard Hathaway, Anthony Munday and Robert Wilson, this play is (for a change) precisely dateable to the autumn of 1599 when in October Henslowe paid the authors over the odds for a 'new play' about Sir John Oldcastle.[1]

Both in the prologue and the text, Oldcastle or Cobham is unequivocally distinguished from Falstaff. Given the conflation of the two effected by Shakespeare's plays, the prologue explains that the 'doubtful title' of this play may 'breed suspense and wrongfully disturb/The peaceful quiet of your settled thoughts'; loyal and orthodox thoughts presumably, not only about the virtue and piety of Oldcastle/Cobham himself but also about the integrity and veracity of the account of church history in which the heroic version of Oldcastle's char-acter and career played such a starring role. There was, however, no need to worry, since 'it is no pampered glutton that we present,/Nor aged counsellor to youthful sins;/But one whose virtues shone above the rest,/A valiant martyr and a virtuous peer,/In whose true faith and loyalty expressed/To his true sovereign and his country's weal/We strive to pay that tribute of our love/Your favours merit' [Prologue, 1–14]. Later, when (in disguise) King Henry meets the corrupt hedge-priest, this play's Falstaff-figure, Sir John of Wrotham,

Sir John refers to the king's misspent youth and to that 'foul, villainous guts, that led him to all that roguery', 'that Falstaff' [sc. x, 81–83]. Here, then, is Shakespeare's rendition of Cobham/Oldcastle/Falstaff being clearly distinguished, by this play's Falstaff lookalike, from the same play's version of Oldcastle/Cobham.

A clerical Falstaff

In the Oldcastle play Sir John of Wrotham is given Falstaff's role as the epitome of drunken good cheer, of fleshly and sexual exorbitance, of carnivalesque disorder and criminal impunity. But instead of a corrupt and impecunious layman, this figure is here recast as a Catholic priest; a priest who is also a thief and a cutpurse, robbing and dicing his way around Kent with his concubine, one Doll [sc. ii, 149–68]. Explaining to Doll where the proceeds of their latest heist have gone, he admits that 'the devil, drink and the dice, has devoured all' [sc. xvi, 5–6]. On another occasion, Sir John delivers himself of a still more succinct self-description: 'I am a singer, a drinker, a bencher, a wencher. I can say a mass and kiss a lass.' Faith I have a parsonage, and because I would not be at too much charges, this wench serves me as a sexton' [sc. v, 182–85].

Like Falstaff, Sir John is, or at least claims to be, protean in his capacity to shift shape. He is able to break all the conventions and constraints of everyday life, to flout the dictates and sanctions of the law, and all with complete impunity. Viewed from the perspective of the ordered and everyday, he is, as the king describes him, 'this lewd priest, this devilish hypocrite/That is a thief, a gamester and what not'. At bay, just like Falstaff, he can talk his way out of any scrape – in part, by reminding the king of his own time as a thief in Falstaff's company. [sc. xi, 132–33, 146–50]. As for Sir John, he says of himself, 'I confess I am a frail man, flesh and blood as other are; but, set my imperfections aside, by this light, ye have not a taller man, nor a truer subject to the crown and state than Sir John of Wrotham' [sc. xi, 135–38].

But where, in Shakespeare's play, Falstaff is identified with a distinctively puritan style of discourse, here the Falstaff figure is assimilated to a very different set of (equally standard) anticlerical stereotypes. Thus, as he prepares to play at dice with the disguised king, Sir John is asked where he 'has come upon so much gold' and replies, on behalf of the clergy, that 'we have every day tithes, christenings, weddings, burials; and you, poor snakes, come seldom to a booty. I'll speak a proud word: I have but one parsonage – Wrotham; 'tis better than all the Bishopric of Rochester. There's ne'er a hill, heath, nor down in all Kent, but 'tis in my parish: Barham Down, Cobham Down, Gad's Hill, Wrotham Hill, Black Heath, Cock's Heath, Birchen Wood – all pay me tithe. Gold, quoth 'a? Ye pass not for that' [sc. xi, 57–65]. In this passage the traditional the sources of revenue, the fees and perquisites, enjoyed by the parochial clergy in their quotidian dealings with the laity, are equated with highway robbery, and Sir John's enjoyment of what are shown here to be a number of equivalently dishonest and underhand sources of revenue is equated with the clerical pluralism so excoriated by puritan critics of the ecclesiastical status quo. Meanwhile, his career as a highway robber is evoked through the list of sites in and about Kent where innocent travellers were habitually stripped of their belongings by thieves and vagabonds, a list that, through the charged name of Gadshill, connects Sir John's criminal career to that of the other Sir John, Falstaff. This, of course, is entirely to reverse the polemical thrust of Shakespeare's play by turning an anti-puritan figure into an anti-popish and anticlerical one.

A clerical conspiracy

But this Falstaff look-alike is far from the only clerical villain in the play; the distinctively plebeian and comic figure cut by Sir John has a distinctly sinister elite analogue, in the bishop of Rochester, who is a major player in the high political narrative of the play. If Sir John stands for the easy corruption and hypocrisy, the utterly self-serving and this-worldly superstition and fraud of the ordinary popish clergy, Rochester stands for the oppressive, usurping claims to power and jurisdiction in church and state of the pope and the bishops. Both Sir John and his bishop are pictured in passionate opposition to the forces of religious 'reformation'. Rochester enters the action denouncing the fact that 'grievous complaints have passed between the lips/Of envious persons to upbraid the clergy,/Some carping at the livings which we have,/And others spurning at the ceremonies/That are of ancient custom in the Church.' [sc. ii, 5–9] Such persons 'give themselves the name of Protestants,/And meet in fields and solitary groves' [sc. ii, 20–21]. At this news Sir John himself explodes with righteous indignation. 'Was ever heard, my lord, the like till now?/That thieves and rebels –'sblood heretics!/Plain heretics, I'll stand to't to their teeth –/Should have to colour their vile practices/A title of such worth as Protestants.' Reprimanded by Suffolk – 'Oh, but you must not swear. It ill becomes/One of your coat to rap out bloody oaths' – Sir John is defended by Rochester. 'Pardon him, my good lord, it is his zeal;/An honest country prelate who laments/To see such foul disorder in the Church' [sc. ii, 22–31].

Sir John is, of course, no 'honest country prelate', but that is of no matter to Rochester, who will accept any degree of hypocrisy, corruption or worldliness as a sign of 'zeal', so long as it is accompanied by a show of animus against 'heretics', 'schismatics' aka 'protestants', and the supporters of 'reformation'. Again, when Oldcastle's man Harpoole is accused by Rochester of being a 'grizzled heretic' he replies, as he later admits, in jest, that ' 'sblood, my Lord Bishop, you do me wrong. I am neither heretic nor puritan, but of the old church. I'll swear, drink ale, kiss a wench, go to mass, eat fish all Lent, and fast Fridays with cakes and wine, fruit and spicery, shrive me of all my old sins afore Easter, and begin anew afore Whitsuntide.' The bishop's response is telling: 'well, God forgive him and I pardon him' [sc. xiii, 129–36]. Here, then, is the episcopal hierarchy's functional definition of true piety and it is, of course, extremely close to the ethos espoused by Sir John of Wrotham and epitomised in his dual career as both hedge-priest and thief. Any degree of hypocrisy, carnality and corruption is acceptable as long as it is contained within the outward forms of traditional religion and expressed in terms of opposition to what the authorities describe throughout as 'heresy', 'schism' or, in this instance, 'puritanism'.

Thus, when a search is made of Lord Cobham's books, the summoner reports back to the bishop that 'here's not a Latin book, no, not so much as Our Lady's Psalter. Here's the Bible, the Testament, the Psalms in metre, *The sick man's salve*, *The treasure of gladness*, and all in English, not so much but the almanac's English.' Again, the bishop's response is instructive. 'To th' fire with them Clun./Now, fie upon these miserable heretics!/All English! Burn, burn them quickly, Clun.' To this Harpoole interjects, again ventriloquising the part of the traditional believer desperate to curry favour with the bishop: 'but do not, Sumner, as you'll answer it, for I have there English books, my lord, that I'll not part with for your bishopric: *Bevis of Hampton*, *Owlglass*, *The Friar and the Boy*, *Ellen of Rumming*, *Robin Hood*, and other such godly stories, which if ye burn, by this flesh I'll make ye drink their ashes in St Marg'et's ale' [sc. xiii, 145–56]. Here we have a reference to the suspicion of all books in English that allegedly characterised the Catholic persecutors of Lollardy. The Lollards were, of course, a group marked out by their devotion to reading the scriptures in the vernacular. This reference to Lollard reading practices is paired here with a list of sixteenth-century books. Those found in Cobham's chamber, while distinctively and decidedly protestant, were tinged with no puritan sedition or criticism of the established church. However, the titles listed would have served to any contemporary audience as certain markers that their owner was a godly protestant of impeccable piety and orthodoxy.

The books owned by Cobham's man Harpoole identified him, just as clearly, as a profane lover of silly stories and lewd jokes. The polarities being drawn here are those that divided, on the one hand, the proto-protestantism of the Lollards from the repressive tendencies of a persecuting Catholic authority and, on the other, the godly from the profane in late Elizabethan England. The bishop is shown persecuting the mere possession of godly, improving books in English, indeed equating the possession of such books with heresy and schism, while accepting an addiction to the pulp literature of the period as a sure sign of religious orthodoxy. Again anything – no matter how profane – which smacked of opposition to 'reformation' was acceptable as true piety to the episcopal authorities. Thus was the fifteenth-century past collapsed into the late

Elizabethan present and the persecution by the Catholic authorities of Lollardy equated with the distrust and persecution by the Elizabethan episcopate of all puritan and perfect protestant forms of piety.

Later, when the king has refused to proceed against Oldcastle on the basis of the charges of heresy and sedition brought against him by the bishop of Rochester, it is Sir John of Wrotham who reminds the bishop that he has a jurisdiction of his own, which he can use 'To make him answer't, howsoe'er it fall' [sc. ii, 141–45]. Where Shakespeare's Falstaff figure had been revealed as a potentially serious threat to order because of his closeness to the prince, this play's principle of misrule is shown to be a threat to order primarily because of his role as the instrument of an episcopal conspiracy to undermine the work-ings of royal justice, subvert the state and persecute the denizens of true reli-gion, and all in the interests of the clerical estate and the church of Rome.

Episcopal tyranny

Certainly, throughout the play Rochester is portrayed waging a vicious war against those he routinely excoriates as 'heretics' and 'schismatics', upholders of 'this upstart new religion' [sc. ii, 86], a 'strange religion' [sc. ii, 108] which prevents its adherents from 'attending mass' and leads them to 'detract from the power of Rome' and affirm 'Wycliffe's doctrine to be true/And Rome's erro-neous' [sc. i, 87–90]. As we have seen, Rochester identifies the denizens of this new religion as 'protestants', a group who now 'meet in fields and solitary groves' [sc.ii, 20–1]. The result was a set of 'malicious errors as begin/To spot their calling and disturb the Church' [sc. ii, 75–77]. To Rochester, Oldcastle is simply 'a dangerous schismastic,/Traitor to God, the King, and commonwealth' [sc. xiii, 13–14] and he continually denounces him as such to the king, even after the king has given express instructions to the contrary.

Early on, Rochester tries to get the king to allow him to cite Cobham for his errant religious beliefs before the Court of Arches. 'How if he appeal?' asks the king, only to be told peremptorily by the bishop that he cannot, 'not where religion is the plea, my Lord'. Henry demurs at this claim to legal sovereignty on the part of the church – 'I took it always that ourself stood on't/As a suffi-cient refuge, unto whom/Not any but might lawfully appeal' [sc. ii, 113–21]. However, he does not press the point, but reserves the case to his own private intercession with Oldcastle. The bishop is not satisfied with this and acts on Sir John of Wrotham's suggestion to activate his own jurisdiction against Cobham. Throughout, the bishop's enmity towards Cobham is shown to be implacable.

In a later scene Rochester denounces Oldcastle as 'this heretic,/This jew, this traitor to your Majesty' [sc. vi, 49–50] because Cobham's man, Harpoole, has assaulted an episcopal messenger sent to attach Cobham and make him appear before the church courts. At this the king flies into a rage, reprimanding the bishop for filling 'our ears with frivolous complaints./Is this the duty you bear to us?/Was't not sufficient we did pass our word/To send for him, but you misdoubting it,/Or, which is worse, intending to forestall/Our regal power, must you likewise summon him?/This savours of ambition, not of zeal,/And rather proves you malice his estate/Than any way that he offends the law' [sc. vi, 74–82]. Here, then, we have precisely the tensions between ecclesiastical and royal power, between the pretensions to power and jurisdiction in the state of the bishops and the sovereignty of the prince, that were such a feature both of the standard Elizabethan critique of popery and of the puritan critique of the Elizabethan episcopate.[2]

Typically the bishop, rather than being chastened by this stinging royal rebuke, repeats the same trick in the second half of the play, when, despite the fact that Oldcastle has completely cleared himself of all charges of sedition and treason, he continues to pursue a warrant for Cobham's arrest 'for treason'. The warrant has long since been countermanded by word of mouth by the king, but, as Cobham explains, since it is antedated, it provides the bishop with the grounds for his further persecution of the innocent lord during the king's absence in France. Encountering Lady Cobham in his search for her husband, the bishop denounces her as a 'heretic' and threatens her with 'torture to confess/If fair means will not serve to make ye tell' [sc. xiii, 6–8]. Challenged by Oldcastle, the bishop first bases his action on the letter of the law and on the king's warrant [sc. xiii, 64–67]. When, later in the scene, Oldcastle appeals again to the king, the bishop again refuses him. 'Wherein have I incurred your hate so far/That my appeal unto the King's denied?' demands Oldcastle. 'No hate of mine, but power of Holy Church/Forbids all favour to false heretics,' comes the reply [sc. xiii, 112–15]. In reply to Lady Cobham's pleas on her husband's behalf, the bishop replies, 'urge it no more; for if an angel spake,/I swear by sweet St Peter's blessed keys/First goes he to the Tower, then to the stake' [sc. xiii, 103–5]. Here, then, is the authority of 'Holy Church', 'of sweet St Peter's blessed keys', wielded by the church of Rome, and its local episcopal representatives and agents, explicitly opposing itself to the authority of the king of England and the right of all true Englishmen to appeal to royal justice and mercy in the face of the accusations of their enemies. Oldcastle's response stands as a verdict on the moral and legal status of these proceedings. 'Your private malice more than public power/Strikes most at me' [sc. xiii, 116–17].

Oldcastle as the epitome of perfect protestant loyalty

If the clergy, both at the popular level, personified by Sir John of Wrotham, and at the episcopal and courtly level, personified by the bishop of Rochester, are shown to be corrupt and tyrannical, willing to pursue their own interests at the expense of even their loyalty and obedience to the prince, their prime victim,

Oldcastle, is presented throughout as the epitome of both Christian piety and political loyalty. As he tells Rochester 'I am free from treason's very thought./ Only my conscience for the Gospel's sake/Is cause of all the troubles I sustain' [sc. xiii, 94–96]. 'I am as true a loyal gentleman/Unto his Highness as my proudest enemy' [sc. xiii, 49–50]. As for his religion, the play makes it clear that he is known for the practice of a simple and sincere Christian piety. At one point, he is hailed as 'the Lord Cobham, Sir John Oldcastle, that noble alms-giver, housekeeper, virtuous religious gentleman' [sc. v, 35–36]. These are the words of an erstwhile rebel against the king, but they serve to establish the nature of Cobham's popular reputation; a reputation confirmed by the testi-mony of the poor themselves who in scene iii are shown flocking to his door, while his man Harpoole jokingly remonstrates with Cobham for having ruined himself with his charity towards the indigent. Cobham replies by referring to the poor gathered at his gates as 'alms knights', and the mock altercation ends with Cobham instructing the 'poor men' to 'go in . . . into the inner court and take such alms as there is to be had' [sc. iii, 24–83]. Later still, Harpoole vindi-cates the reputation of his master as the epitome of Christian charity and tradi-tional good lordship, describing Cobham as 'a brave lord that keeps good beef and good beer in his house, and every day feeds a hundred poor people at's gate, and keeps a hundred tall fellows' [sc. iv, 34–36].

This estimation of Oldcastle as the epitome of political loyalty and noble virtue is shared by none other than the king himself. Told of Cobham's involve-ment in Lollard sedition, the king refuses to believe it. [sc. ii, 126–29]. Later, when confronted with seemingly irrefutable proof that Cobham has indeed been involved in rebellion, still the king evinces surprise [sc. xii, 60–62]. Finally, when Cobham is cleared of the charges of treason and rebellion, both by the testimony of the real rebels and by his own exemplary conduct, the king's good opinion of him is vindicated and it is with relief that Henry can say 'Go, take these rebels hence;/Let them have martial law. But as for thee [Cobham]/Friend to thy King and country, still be free' [sc. xii, 134–36].

Oldcastle falls under such persistent suspicion and wins the undying hatred of the clergy not because of any of his political activities or opinions, which are quintessentially steadfast and loyal, but rather because of his religious beliefs. The play presents us with an England radically divided between the proponents of 'reformation', the followers of Wycliffe, and the defenders of the old religion and the church of Rome. Indeed, the action opens with an affray at the assizes at Hereford about precisely this issue, between the Lord Powis and the Lord Herbert, in the course of which Herbert is killed. [sc. i, 87–98]. We have, here, then a division about religion; a division that to a late Elizabethan audience would have been instantly recognisable as a local emanation of the meta-struggle between, on the one hand, popish error, tyranny and conspiracy – manifested in Rochester's continual efforts to do Cobham down – and, on the other, protestant truth, monarchical authority and loyal Englishness. In this initial altercation, certain religious opinions, about the 'papacy' and 'the religion catholic' are equated by the defenders of the status quo not merely with schism and heresy – inherently religious offences – but also with treason. For those unwilling to accept that claim, the fact that the quintessentially loyal Cobham was an adherent of this new religion was a clinching argument against any equation of support for 'reformation' with treason. Thus had Oldcastle's name come to be bandied about in the altercation between Powis and Herbert. On the other side, for the likes of Rochester, the fact that Cobham was a follower of Wycliffe and an enemy of Rome meant that he must be a traitor. It is this that explains both the (wholly erroneous) assumption of the Lollard rebels that, when the time comes, Cobham will in fact side with them and the intensity of Rochester and the other clergy's determination to establish that Cobham is not only a heretic and a schismatic, that is to say, in the Elizabethan audience's terms, a proponent of true religion, but also a traitor; not the 'friend to king and country' hailed by the king, but an enemy to both.

Getting it right

Both Cobham and the king know what is going on. As Cobham explains it, 'I know the clergy hate me to the death,/And my religion gets me many foes' [sc. iii, 88–89]. As Rochester attaches him for treason, Cobham maintains that 'only my conscience for the gospel's sake/ Is cause of all the trouble I sustain.' [sc.xiii, 95–6] Henry, too, is entirely sure of Oldcastle's personal and political loyalty, 'but for his conscience'. By this Henry seems to mean that Cobham does indeed hold certain heterodox religious opinions, and scruples of conscience, which have led to his loyalty being questioned by the clergy. But Henry is quite capable of distinguishing, between Cobham's religious opinions and his political affinities and allegiances. Protecting Cobham from the hostile attentions of 'holy church', Henry reserves to himself the examination of Cobham's conscience and its consequences for his loyalty to the crown [sc. ii, 130–33].

Subsequently, we are shown Oldcastle being schooled about his religion by the king. Henry professes himself well pleased. It is just that the bishops are worried by his religious opinions and 'will not so soon be satisfied'. Oldcastle immediately takes up the distinction between politics and religion, between conscience and political allegiance. 'My gracious Lord, unto your Majesty,/ Next unto God, I owe my life,/And what is mine either by nature's gift/Or fortune's bounty, all is at your service;/But for obedience to the Pope of Rome,/I owe him none, nor shall his shaveling priests/That are in England alter my belief./If out of Holy Scripture they can prove/That I am in error, I will yield,/ And gladly take instruction at their hands./But otherwise, I do beseech your Grace,/My conscience may not be encroached upon' [sc. vi, 7–18]. Here, then, is both a classic protestant distinction between the legitimate claims on the allegiance of its subjects of the English crown and the entirely spurious and usurped claims to jurisdiction and allegiance of 'the pope of Rome'. For a late Elizabethan audience, in both his rejection of papal authority and his appeal from the church and clergy to scripture, Oldcastle marks himself out as a prot-estant indeed; someone who is decidedly on the side of the angels in that great struggle between Christ and Antichrist that had reached a new stage of inten-sity with the advent of Wycliffe's ideas, and was still raging with ever greater violence in later sixteenth-century Europe and indeed in Elizabethan England.

Henry responds not by agreeing with Oldcastle about the papacy and popery, but rather by respecting the integrity of his conscience, in particular, and the proper limits of the power of secular princes over the consciences of their subjects, in general. 'We would be loath to press our subjects' bodies/ Much less their souls, the dear redeemed part/Of Him that is the ruler of us all;/Yet let me counsel you that might command:/Do not presume to tempt them with ill words,/Nor suffer any meetings to be had/Within your house but, to the uttermost,/Disperse the flocks of this new gathering sect' [sc. vi, 19–26]. This is to read on to the division between politics and religion, between conscience and political allegiance, something like a division between the public and the private, with Cobham's religious beliefs and scruples kept in the private domain of his own conscience and consciousness, and no use made of his considerable public power and influence as a nobleman to protect or foster the religious (and still less the political) activities of 'this new gathering sect'.

In late Elizabethan terms such a set of distinctions had consequences not only for the more radical 'puritans' but rather more for a certain sort of Catholic loyalist; a group that had long protested its political reliability, and made a case for a certain sort of toleration, in precisely these terms; terms to which Oldcastle gladly accedes, only to follow that act of submission with a request to the king for what he describes as 'a deed of clemency' – the pardon, for the death of Lord Herbert, of his fellow Lollard, Lord Powis. It is a request which the king, in his turn, happily grants [sc. vi, 33–43]. Here, then, was an object lesson in how, by properly observing the lines dividing the realms of conscience and of allegiance, of religion and of politics, of secular power and of religious scruple or belief, of public and private, both king and subject could successfully nego-tiate and contain the existence, within a settled polity, of even the sharpest sorts of religious conflict and disagreement; in the process ensuring that justice was done, order maintained, the guilty punished, the innocent vindicated, and the integrity of the realm protected, by a prince loyally served by subjects of a variety of religious opinions.

Of course, the popish pretensions and episcopal tyranny, the clerical corruption and hypocrisy, of those erstwhile defenders of the church and of 'order', the bishop of Rochester and Sir John of Wrotham, put them way beyond this particular pale. But they are not alone in thus excluding themselves from the category of loyal subject through their misunderstanding of the proper relationships between conscience and allegiance. On the contrary, the play shows the sort of accommodation worked out between Oldcastle and his king being disrupted from a 'puritan' as well as from a 'popish' or conformist direction. For while Oldcastle/Cobham might know precisely where to draw the line between the defence of religious truth and conscientious scruple, on the one hand, and loyalty and obedience to crown and country, on the other, there were other Lollards, other adherents of this 'new gathering sect', this 'strange religion' of 'protestants', or indeed of 'puritans' who palpably did not.

Getting it wrong

The play depicts the famous Lollard rising of 1414, but on this account Oldcastle has absolutely nothing to do with it. To be sure, his name is bandied about by the rebels as they try to attach supporters to their cause. The play shows one William Murley, 'the brewer of Dunstable, your honest neighbour and your friend' [sc. v, 7–8] being recruited by the leaders of the rebellion, Sir Roger Acton and his mates by the promise that Cobham will lead the rebel host and that, in that capacity, he will make Murley a knight.

The rebels claim that the motivation of their rebellion had been entirely religious. All the conspirators are 'professed friends to Wycliffe and foes to Rome' [sc. v, 9]. 'You know our faction', Acton tells the others, 'is grown so great/Throughout the realm that it begins to smoke,/Into the clergy's eyes, and the King's ears;/High time it is that we were drawn to head' [sc. v, 12–15]. Later, after the revolt has failed, when the leading rebels are confronted by the king and asked to justify themselves, they base their actions on the promptings of conscience. 'Pardon, my Lord,' says Acton, 'my conscience urged me to it.' His accomplice Beverley adds 'we meant no hurt unto your Majesty,/But reformation of religion' [sc. xii, 9,15–16].

But the play shows the rebels' motives to have been always already mixed. The plan had been to stage a rising of some forty thousand men at Ficket's Field, near the city, and for that they needed money. The conspirators are shown corrupting Murley the brewer into providing them with ten thousand pounds to equip the rebel host. Murley's religious principles are shown to be shaky at best. He at first refuses to countenance a rebellion on a Friday, since 'Childermass Day this year was Friday' and thus Friday was a 'dismal day' to choose. Beverley has to rebuke him for this popish superstition. 'Nay, Mr Murley, if you observe such days,/We make a question of your constancy./All days are like to men resolved in right' [sc. v, 58–63]. Nor are Murley's political principles any firmer. Later, as he leads his men, Tom and Dick, reluctant and grumbling, into the rebellion, he meets, with derisive contempt, their objections that their enemies are mighty and that they might even have to fight against the king himself. 'Fie, paltry, paltry! In and out, to and fro, upon occasion; if the King be so unwise to come here, we'll fight with him too.' This meets with the question 'what if ye should kill the King?' to which Murley replies blithely 'then we'll make another'. 'Do ye not speak treason?' comes the appalled reply, to which Murley responds 'if we do, who dare trip us? We come to fight for our conscience and for honour. Little know you what is in my bosom; look here, mad knaves a pair of gilt spurs.' Murley, then, does indeed intend to fight and, if need be, to kill and replace the king, but his thoughts are not solely centred on reformation. That reference to the gilt spurs concealed in his bosom reveals his real aim — the knighthood that the rebels have promised him for bankrolling the whole enterprise. 'Was it ever read in the church book of Dunstable that ever malt-man was made knight?' he asks, proudly [sc. viii, 27–43]. Here Acton's comment is more than apt, 'see what ambition may persuade men to!' [sc. v, 97].

Unlike Shakespeare's equally anti-puritan representation of the Cade rebellion, this is no upsurge of plebeian violence, but rather a mishmash of factional intrigue, religious principle and corrupted ambition. The most plebeian members of the plot, poor Dick and Tom, are shown being led uncomprehendingly and unwillingly into the fray by their master Murley, himself the dupe of the elite leadership of the rebellion, whose motivation may indeed be based on conscience and a desire for reformation, but whose base actions belie that claim. As the king later explains to them, theirs are utterly debased and sadly garbled versions of the promptings of 'conscience' and the cause of 'reformation'. When Acton cites his conscience as the basis for his rebellion, King Henry rounds on him. 'Thy conscience? Then thy conscience is corrupt,/For in thy conscience thou art bound to us,/And in thy conscience thou shouldst love thy country;/Else what's the difference' twixt a Christian/And the uncivil manners of the Turk?' Again, told that they meant no harm to him but only to achieve 'reformation', Henry responds 'reform religion? What is that ye sought?/I pray who gave you that authority?/Belike then, we do hold the sceptre up/And sit within the throne but for a cipher./Time was, good subjects would make known their grief,/And pray amendment, not enforce the same,/Unless their king were tyrant, which I hope,/You cannot justly say that Harry is'. [sc. xii, 10–23].

Through the exemplary justice and fairness of his treatment of that other 'heretic', Oldcastle, Harry has indeed shown that he is no tyrant. And in this speech he completes the other half of his warning to Oldcastle to keep his religious opinions to himself, avoiding both polemical attacks on the clergy and the encouragement of public acts of dissent or division on behalf of this 'new gathering sect' or, as Acton calls it, of this 'faction'. For the one public action that subjects are allowed in pursuit of the redress of grievances or of 'reformation' is to petition the prince. These miscreants have completely misunderstood the proper relationship between conscience and allegiance, reformation and loyalty, religion and politics, the public and the private, and the results have been, or rather would have been, disastrous, had the realm not been saved from the consequences of their violent revolt by the political sagacity and military prowess of Henry V himself.

Loyal Lollards and moderate puritans

But if some Lollards, some members of the 'new gathering sect', adherents of this 'new' and 'strange religion', have been led into error, rebellion, treason and death by the siren songs of 'conscience', 'reformation' and 'ambition', another adherent of that same religion, Oldcastle, has not. Thus, while there might well be a popular puritan threat to order, not all puritans were a part of that threat. Indeed some of them (like the figure of Oldcastle/Cobham) were bulwarks against the twin threats to true order and obedience represented, on the one hand, by a populist puritanism and, on the other, by a tyrannical and usurping popery and prelacy. Here, then, was a protestant *via media* but of a distinctly puritan hue.

Quite unlike Shakespeare's picture of plebeian and puritan rebellion, in Cade's rebellion, and indeed quite unlike his depiction of puritan hypocrisy and disorder in the *Henry IV* plays, here the outstanding example of loyalty and virtue, at the very centre of the action, is also a 'puritan'. As we have seen, the play went out of its way to identify Oldcastle as a follower of Wycliffe, an opponent of Rome and of the 'shaveling priests' of the popish church. But his political loyalty is affirmed throughout. Not only is he entirely innocent of any knowledge of, or involvement in, the rebellion of Ficket's Field, but the only basis for that charge was rumour. Cross-questioned by Oldcastle and the king, the real rebels all concede that Cobham's involvement has merely been a matter of hearsay, spread, as the play shows, to encourage others to join an enterprise led by a man of such exemplary piety, virtue and prowess. As Murley admits, 'I did say so, but in what respect?/Because I heard it was reported so.' Acton agrees: 'to clear my conscience ere I die, my Lord,/I must confess we have no other ground/But only rumour to accuse this lord,/Which now I see was merely fabulous' [sc. xii, 109–15]. In that same scene Oldcastle further displays his loyalty by revealing to the king a far more dangerous conspiracy against his life by Cambridge, Scroop and Gray. Cobham had been approached by the conspirators and feigns interest only in order to obtain definitive proof of their intentions and guilt; which proof he now shows to the king. It is this signal service that prompts King Henry's definitive judgement that, for all the singularity of his religious opinions, Oldcastle/Cobham is indeed 'a friend to thy king and country'.

The godly and their episcopal enemies

It is only after this final and complete vindication of Oldcastle, after he has saved the king from certain death at the hands of the Cambridge conspirators, that Rochester finally succeeds, through his essentially fraudulent, indeed seditious, use of an old warrant, in committing Cobham to the Tower. The play shows us that there is a fundamental distinction to be drawn amongst the proponents of reformation – in contemporary terms 'puritans', people that the play's fifteenth-century setting reveals to an Elizabethan audience to be adherents of true protestant religion. That distinction is between those who understand the real nature of conscience and allegiance, the true relation between politics and religion, and thus remain steadfastly loyal, and those who do not, and therefore lapse into treasonous revolt. However, the bishops and their clerical hangers-on – Rochester and John of Wrotham – are shown to be incapable of recognising or accepting this fact. Rather than seeing the loyalty and virtue of the likes of Cobham for what it is, they use the sedition and rebellion of the Actons and Murleys of this world to tar even Oldcastle with the brush not only of schism and heresy but also of disloyalty and treason. This, of course, mirrors perfectly the polemical tactics of myriad anti-puritan polemicists, from Richard Bancroft to Richard Hooker, from Matthew Sutcliffe to Thomas Nashe, who persistently sought to associate men who saw themselves as respectable and moderate proponents of further reformation and loyal servants of the queen with populist sedition and rebellion; conflating the likes of Thomas Cartwright with Martin Marprelate or, still worse, with those plebeian incendiaries and wannabe prophets, Hacket and Coppinger.

In so doing, in the play at least, the bishops and their hangers-on themselves become guilty of something like treason. They subvert the operation of royal justice, prefer the interests and laws of 'Holy Church' to the supervening authority of an English king, and ignore, indeed defy, clear expressions of the royal will, in order to pursue what is in many ways their own private vendetta against those who have seen through their false claims to sanctity and power. Unable to meet Oldcastle's challenge to refute him with scripture, they have recourse to deceit, force and sedition; misleading and defying the prince in order to defend their own material and political interests against the truths of right religion, they oppress the most loyal and reliable of subjects with what are underhand and tyrannical legal shifts.

On the one hand, we have here some of the standard tropes and claims of protestant anti-Catholic argument and stereotype. Viewed from the perspective of the protestant confrontation with Rome, and the defence of the Elizabethan church and state from the Catholic threat, nothing could be either more conventional or more loyal than this. But there was far more going on here than the conduct of a bog standard piece of anti-popery. Rather, under the guise, or rather through such standard anti-popish moves and manoeuvres, the play was conducting a defence of at least a certain sort of (moderate) puritan from the undiscriminating condemnation being handed out to the godly not only by Shakespeare in his portrayal of Falstaff/Oldcastle (in the *Henry IV* plays) and in the Cade scenes of *2 Henry VI*, but also by the bishops and their hangers-on and agents in myriad works of both scurrilous and ephemeral, as well as intensely scholarly, anti-puritan polemic. And that campaign was not limited to the level of representation and stereotype, of verbal violence and satiric assault, but had been carried on in the High Commission, the Star Chamber and indeed on the gallows, with all the legal force and the real, officially sanctioned, violence at the disposal of both the church and the state.

In distinguishing between Oldcastle/Cobham and the other corrupt and seditious Lollards of the rebellion of Ficket's Field the play was asserting the existence of moderate and loyal puritans. But then through the further opposition established between Oldcastle/Cobham and his malign enemies amongst the clergy, and in particular amongst the bishops, the play was also identifying such moderate puritan figures not merely as a good deal more loyal and reliable than their detractors and enemies on the episcopal bench claimed, but as the *most* virtuous, trustworthy and steadfast of all the crown's subjects. Oldcastle emerges from the action of the play as the epitome of loyalism; dedicated to the service of king and country but also opposed to the forces of clerical tyranny and popish conspiracy that are seeking not just the ruin of loyal subjects and good Christians like himself, but the subversion of the authority of the crown as well. Here were persons who, because they understood the true relation between conscience and allegiance, because they had also seen through the pretences and corruptions of the clergy and the bishops, could be *really* loyal, both to the crown and to the commonwealth, to their prince and to their country, to God and to the king, in ways that neither their misguided co-religionists nor their episcopal or clerical enemies could ever hope to be. Precisely because they understood the nature of true religion and of real political loyalty or allegiance, the loyalism of such persons created order of an intensity and stability quite beyond the capacity of persons endowed with less solidly grounded consciences. And, in the terms set by the play, that included even that paragon of kingly prowess and bluff English virtue, Henry V himself, and presumably, by analogy, Queen Elizabeth as well.

The play thus inverted the anti-puritan polemical message of Shakespeare's play(s); recast the figure of misrule as a self-serving popish priest rather than as a puritan; distinguished between radical and moderate puritans, and equated a malign clericalist conspiracy of evil counsel, sedition and tyranny with the denizens of Ficket's Field as equivalent threats to the power and autonomy of the crown and the order and interests of the country. This last was a particularly daring move, and changing the identity of Oldcastle's chief clerical tormentor from the archbishop of Canterbury to the bishop of Rochester a mere fig leaf, which scarcely concealed, and was presumably not intended to obscure but rather to enable or license, what was a clear assault on the anti-puritan policies and repressive methods of Archbishop Whitgift and his henchman Richard Bancroft. There could, therefore, scarcely be more explicit evidence that contemporaries did indeed read Shakespeare's anti-puritanism in precisely the spirit of the current analysis. Nor could there be a clearer example of the discussion on the public stage of polemical and political issues of immediately current interest and import.

Essex – again

We do not, of course, have to assume that the impulses at play here were only or even mainly ideological or factional. For this analysis to be right we do not need to read *Sir John Oldcastle* as a straightforward expression of deeply held pro-puritan sentiment. It could just as well be an attempt by certain play-wrights and impresarios – in this case Henslowe again – to cash in on the popularity of Shakespeare's *Henry IV* plays and of *Henry V*; on the notoriety and popularity of Falstaff himself and in particular on the public interest and fuss occasioned by the identification of Falstaff with Oldcastle and by the objections recently lodged against that identification presumably by the Brookes, Lords Cobham; and finally on the frisson, perhaps even outrage, occasioned by Shakespeare's polemically daring attack not only on the puritan godly – in the later 1590s doing that was like shooting fish in a barrel – but also on the entire perfect protestant, Foxeian, account of the origins and nature of true religion in England.

But there is another, more explicitly Essexian reason why a return to this subject may have seemed particularly apposite in the autumn of 1599. For by that time Essex had returned from Ireland in disgrace. The capital was echoing with claims and counter-claims about what had gone wrong in Ireland and about who was to blame for it; about Essex's likely next course of action and fate at the hands of an angry queen and a hostile court. Where *Henry V* had ended by envisaging Essex's triumph over the Irish rebels, in the figure of the stage Irishman MacChane, *Sir John Oldcastle* brings the disruptive presence of Irish rebellion, treachery and violence back into the heart of England. Accompanying Sir Richard Lee back from two years' service in Ireland, MacChane treacher-ously kills his master and almost gets the entirely innocent Cobham and his wife hanged for the crime. Here is a subtle reminder not only of Essex's failure to repress the Irish rebels, but of the newly pressing nature of the threat presented to English rule and order by Irish treachery and violence, a threat now height-ened by the earl's flight back to England. That, in the end, MacChane is easily brought to justice by this play's Falstaff figure, the erstwhile thief and corrupt priest Sir John of Wrotham, might be thought only to add insult to injury.

Where the *Henry IV* plays might be taken to have been warning against the dangers of an excessive addiction to 'puritan' popularity, and certainly show Hal/Henry triumphantly ridding himself of such puritan and popular humours, *Sir John Oldcastle* contained at its heart the picture of a popular puritan revolt; a rebellion justified by the need for reformation, centred on London, and in the course of which elite leaders duped certain of their plebeian followers into treason, through the lure of knighthoods to be conferred by their general on the field of battle. One of the things that had brought Essex into such opprobrium with the queen was precisely the promiscuous conferral of knighthoods on his followers in Ireland. In the play, that was a tactic adopted by (Lollard) members of the social elite to recruit a (popular) faction or following for their rebellion. As Henry V tells 'Sir Roger Acton, thou retain'st the name/Of knight and shouldst be more discretely temper'd'/Than join with peasants. Gentry is divine,/But thou hast made it more than popular' [sc. xii, 5–8]. If Essex was being associated here with a certain sort of populist appeal to the godly and the people, he was being held up as an example of precisely the sort of behaviour, that, in the play, Oldcastle, the ancestor of Essex's deadly rival, Lord Cobham, had sedulously and loyally avoided. When Henslowe paid Munday and his co-authors for the script of *Sir John Oldcastle* and its sequel, he gave them an extra ten shillings, and, as Paul White observes, 'there is reason to believe this gift came from an outside party', presumably someone connected to the Cobhams. If we accept Melchiori's dating for *The merry wives* this allows us to see that play as a response to the Oldcastle play; returning to an old sore reopened by the return of Sir John Oldcastle to the public stage, Shakespeare's play replied in kind to an assault from Cobham. And if Cobham did indeed help fund the Oldcastle play for his own private and political purposes, then the scenes in *The merry wives* in which Ford/Brook actually pays Falstaff, to humiliate him by proving his wife unfaithful and himself a cuckold, take on a new significance and edge.

Thus *Sir John Oldcastle* confirms as entirely contemporary the reading essayed above of the extreme anti-puritanism of the *Henry IV* plays. It also confirms the connection between those plays and the course of immediately contemporary court and factional politics and indeed, in a more oblique way, the association made there between puritanism, popularity and Essex. And, finally, it provides us with a splendid example of the ways in which the popular theatre sought to play off, exploit and indeed to insert itself into, the immediately contemporary concerns, issues and events of the day.

The play can thus be construed as using the interest generated by the Oldcastle affair, Cobham's upset with Shakespeare's plays, together with the wider perception of those plays as extremely, indeed offensively, anti-puritan, to intervene in a number of overlapping areas of current controversy, scandal and concern. It did so at a point when Essex's fortunes were at an all-time low, and when any attack directed either towards him or towards things or persons associated with him might well be expected to meet with the complaisance, indeed perhaps even the encouragement, of people in high places. But it also did so in order to make some extraordinarily daring and intemperate remarks about the current anti-puritan climate in general, and about the nature and actions of the contemporary episcopate in particular. The play constituted, then, an extremely astute and skilful intervention in, or rather exploitation of, a set of entirely evanescent political and ideological circumstances; an intervention designed, if for no other purpose, then to turn an honest penny by putting bums on seats and, later, by selling pamphlets. The play's success in this regard can be gleaned both from the large sums that Henslowe paid the authors for this play and the sequel and the fact that it was printed in 1600.

The play and its relation both to *Henry V* and indeed to the current political conjuncture thus illustrates perfectly why the products of the popular stage have so much to tell us about the political and ideological timbre of this period. It does so, too, at a moment when the dramatic collapse of the entire Essexian project was about to raise the level of popular interest in immediately contemporary politics, and the political stakes involved in slaking that interest, to unprecedented heights. None of this was lost on the authorities. In June 1599, in the so-called Bishops' Ban, Whitgift and Bancroft, respectively the archbishop of Canterbury and the bishop of London, directed that various sorts of satire – with many titles called in by name and some publicly burnt – be banned and that 'no English histories be printed, except they shall be allowed by some of her majesty's Privy Council' and 'that no plays be printed, except they be allowed by such as have authority'. If the ban was ever put into operation this means that *The Oldcastle play* must have been approved by at least some of the Privy Council when it was printed in 1600.

The association being made here between satire, history and plays as potential sources of subversive comment was in itself telling,[3] as, too, was Shakespeare's response to the ban. He abandoned English history and wrote instead, in short order, three plays about Roman, Danish and Trojan history respectively, all of which – *Julius Caesar*, *Hamlet* and *Troilus and Cressida* – were at least as directly concerned with immediately current concerns and events as any of his previous retellings of the English past had been.[4]

Contemporaries were certainly well aware of what such a change of setting from England to other countries and other histories might mean. In Ben Jonson's play *Poetaster*, performed in 1601, the character Envy lays claim to the choric role of the Prologue. Even as he does so, he is immediately revealed as a typically predatory informer, come to report on the seditious undertones and applications of the play. But he is forced to confess his malign intentions utterly frustrated when he learns of the locale in which the play's action is set. 'Rome? Rome? and Rome? Crack ye strings, and your balls/Drop into earth; let me be ever blind./I am prevented; all my hopes are crosst,/Checht, and abated; . . ./ What should I do? Rome? Rome? O my vext soul,/How might I force this to the present state?' Then the real Prologue enters, armed, a condition rendered necessary, he explains, by this 'dangerous age:/Wherein, who writes had need present his scenes/Forty-fold proof against the conjuring means/Of base detractors, and illiterate apes/That fill up rooms in fair and formal shapes.'

Typically, what Jonson felt compelled to talk about – in the process almost daring his audience (and the authorities) to make the very sorts of connection between his play and 'the present age' that he was here disavowing – Shakespeare merely did, three times, between 1599 and 1602 and it is to the dynamics of that highly charged political moment, and of Shakespeare's engagement therewith, that we must turn in the final sections of the book.

PART VII
Julius Caesar: THE DANGERS OF PLAYING PAGAN AND REPUBLICAN POLITICS IN A CHRISTIAN MONARCHY

CHAPTER 18

The state we're in

Henry V was not the only history play that Shakespeare wrote in 1599. Also date-able to that year is *Julius Caesar*. There the politics of popularity, honour and legitimacy are again in play, in a political scene in which men of the highest virtu(e) are struggling to impose their will on events and, in this case, restore legitimacy to the state by refounding it. Over the *Henry IV* plays, and triumphantly in *Henry V*, Shakespeare had shown what A.D. Nuttall terms 'a player king' 'fash-ioning first himself and then his times'. Producing 'major effects by design not accident', Henry is the 'central, unified cause' of everything that happens in a play that emphasises the capacity of human political agents to impose themselves on events and shape outcomes according to their will. The result is what Nuttall calls a 'centrist causality, located in a single figure who can, alone, modify history'.[1]

It is a point that the play drives home with wonderful irony in its reminder that what Henry has achieved will be systematically undone through the inca-pacity of other, very different political agents during the reign of his son. In *Henry V* providence is shown as having virtually no role in the outcomes achieved by Henry. While Henry certainly gives all the credit to God and the victory he achieves is hailed as 'wonderful', whether and how far to attribute his success to the providential intervention of God is left almost entirely up to the audience to decide. Certainly the play makes no move towards the prophetic or the prodigious of the sort that Shakespeare usually deploys when he wants unequivocally to signal the presence of the providential. Even more tellingly, at play's end, no mention is made of the role of providence in the decline into illegitimacy and chaos that will take place under his son.

Things are very different in the Roman play. For all his world-dominating achievements and well nigh universal fame, Caesar's efforts to transform the Roman state end not only in his own assassination but also with the descent of the Roman world into chaos and civil war. Of course, Caesar's task was infi-nitely the greater. Henry V was attempting to restore a monarchical state to something like 'normality', and thus working with the grain of established notions of legitimacy and order. In marked contrast, Caesar was attempting almost literally to refound the Roman state, transforming it from the (corrupt) republic it had become into something far more like a monarchy.

Viewed in this way, the two plays might almost be seen as lives paired on the Plutarchian model to constitute a comparative meditation on the capacity of even the greatest of men – past masters of both the political and the military arts – to impose their will on events, divert the course of history and – in Caesar's case, if not in Henry's – refound the state. The plays can thus be read against one another as two parts of an extended rumination on the possibilities and limits of human political action, twinned meditations upon the capacity of even the greatest of great men to shape history and control events.

Henry V had been written as Essex was about to take off as the queen's general on a massive military expedition to Ireland. Projecting Henry V's triumph in France on to Essex's campaign in Ireland, the play predicted an entirely happy outcome for that enterprise, associating Essex's triumph with something like the salvation of the state. In Shakespeare's account, acting entirely with the grain of monarchical legitimacy, Henry had been able, almost seamlessly, to combine the politics of honour, popularity and monarchical legitimacy into a coherent strategy to restore order and balance to an England (indeed, to an emerging Britain) otherwise threatened – as it most definitely had been in *1* and *2 Henry IV* – with dissolution and disaster.

Julius Caesar was written and performed while Essex was in Ireland. As his campaigns there fell apart, the earl himself fell under increasing suspicion and disrepute at court and with the queen. Rumours spread that the defensive measures taken to resist what would turn out to be a phantom Spanish Armada were in fact intended by the Council as a show of strength to an increasingly erratic and desperate Essex, who, it was feared, might be tempted to turn his forces in Ireland back on his enemies in England, in a desperate attempt, as he thought, to save the state, the queen and the protestant succession, not to mention his own honour and career, from the machinations of his enemies at court. For, if you took the view of the current conjuncture held, from at least 1598, by the earl and some of his circle, not to mention by James VI, Essex's defeat at the hands of his enemies would open the way for an ignoble peace with Spain and the diversion of the succession from the protestant James, perhaps even to the Infanta. On that view, the England of Elizabeth, just like the Rome of Caesar and Brutus, was poised at a crucial turning point between two rival versions of the future.

From an Essexian perspective it was either about to be refounded by the earl's enemies in an entirely illegitimate act of usurpation, or else to be saved from such a fate by the political action of men of peerless virtue and dedication to the linked causes of their own honour, 'liberty' and the common good – that is by Essex and his mates. From the perspective of Essex's critics and rivals, the state was threatened by some sort of Essexian coup, designed to establish Essex himself, if not as king, then at the very least as the only real power in the land, and the sole arbiter of the next succession.

As a number of commentators have observed, in *Julius Caesar* Shakespeare is very careful to locate the action of the play in a Rome trapped in the throes of political change, indeed in a transition from one sort of state to another. Since this is a history play about one of the most famous men in world history, from the start the audience are in no doubt that Caesar is doomed to die, his murderers doomed to fail and the Roman republic doomed to morph into that most absolute of monarchies, the Roman empire. Despite the many providential warnings and prodigies with which the play is strewn, such foreknowledge is not a luxury enjoyed by the characters in the play, who are all not only entirely unsure of what is going to happen next but also in deep disagreement about both the *de jure* question of just what sort of polity Rome is, or ought to become, and the equally pressing *de facto* question of the current moral and political condition of the Roman state. For Calphurnia, Caesar is already a prince, for Cassius, he is already a tyrant and for Brutus he is both a man of the highest desert and virtue and a wannabe usurper and king, someone whose ambition must be stopped from destroying the liberty that defines the Roman state as a republic and consequently reducing the Romans to a state of subjection not much better than that enjoyed by slaves or bondmen.

The play thus conjures some of the perennial questions of late sixteenth-century political thought about the rights and wrongs of resistance, the nature and control of political change, and about the best form of government, but it does so by locating those questions within a very particular set of historical circumstances; circumstances that were themselves anything but devoid of immediately contemporary relevance and resonance.

The central question might be taken to be that of resistance. However, that question is not posed in its usual conventionally generalised form, but in a far more particular and pointed manner, as in 'how far, in the midst of the sort of complex political and moral transitions being undergone by the Rome of the play, is extreme, indeed violent, political action (undertaken even by men of the best intentions and highest virtue, in order to maintain what they see as the status quo) either morally justifiable or politically prudent?' Or, to put the matter somewhat differently, in a state and society as far gone in corruption as late republican Rome (or indeed as late Elizabethan England), can the linked processes of moral decline and political change be reversed by direct political action?[2] In such circumstances can even men of the greatest virtu(e), like Caesar or Brutus, hope either to save or to refound the state? Viewed thus, the crucial issue is less prescriptive than prudential; not so much a matter of moral principle, and more one of the political or prudential judgement that needs to be brought to bear on the specificities and contingencies of a particular time and place.

Of course, in *Julius Caesar* those issues are examined in a Roman, republican and pagan context[3] and that, too, was not without direct contemporary resonance. For, as a great deal of recent scholarship has shown, many contemporaries, and particularly, but very far from exclusively, the circle around the earl of Essex, were much exercised by the application to the conduct of sixteenth-century politics of the political and moral wisdom to be extracted from pagan, and often republican, works of Roman history and philosophy.[4] And in that regard, the play might be thought to represent a closely argued examination (and indeed critique) of the use of such pagan and republican authorities and insights for the analysis of the politics of an inherently monarchical and Christian polity, like that of late Elizabethan England.

As we shall see below, the play represents an extraordinarily acute recuperation of the set of political attitudes and expectations, the moral values and aspirations, that Quentin Skinner has (almost) dubbed neo-Roman republicanism. (I say 'almost' since Skinner has adopted the moniker 'neo-Roman' precisely to avoid the baggage attaching to the word 'Republican'.) But the play extracts that vision from an account of the crisis point of the republic, that is to say from the very moment when (the play implies) those values were collapsing under the weight of their internal contradictions, and it does so as part of a thought experiment seemingly designed to test the more overtly 'republican' elements in much early modern 'neo-Roman'[5] thought to breaking point.

What is at stake in *Julius Caesar* is not the seizure of power within a stable polity by one party as opposed to another, but rather a far more fundamental process of transformation whereby the locus and nature of power, and thus the very nature of the polity itself, is up for grabs, indeed is in the process of being transformed. For the quasi-regal status that, as the play opens, Caesar appears to be assuming/usurping has no place within the traditional disposition of powers, offices and functions that constitute Rome as a republic. If he is in the process of setting himself up as a king, indeed, given his preponderant power in the state, perhaps even if he is not, the powers that Caesar is arrogating to himself are such that, permanently concentrated in the hands of one man, they would quite subvert the republican nature of the state. The play poses, but does not definitively answer, the question of whether that renders Caesar a tyrant or not. As the failure of generations of critics to agree on the answer to that question demonstrates, there is ample material in the play to warrant either affirmative or negative responses. In that, as Robert Miola amongst others has shown, the play was faithfully reflecting the range of early modern opinion on the subject of Caesar.[6]

Both *Henry V* and *Caesar* are set, therefore, on the very cusp between illegitimacy and legitimacy; it is just that events are moving in entirely different directions. In *Henry V* the action is concentrated upon the moment of triumph. We are shown the prowess and virtu(e) of the central protagonist imposing itself on men and on events, arresting (albeit, as the chorus reminds us at the end, temporarily) the processes of political and moral decline set off by the original political sins of Richard II's tyrannical misrule and the counter- (but also fatally un-) balancing reaction of Henry IV's usurpation. In *Julius Caesar*, however, the process of political change is at an altogether different point; the point, in fact, at which the efforts of the man who gives the play its name are not only failing to achieve legitimacy but threatening to throw the state into moral and political chaos.

Not that Caesar manages to do this all by himself; he is greatly helped by the efforts of Brutus and Cassius, whose attempts to save the state from Caesar only succeed in plunging the Roman world into popular insurrection and civil war, states which then themselves become the enabling conditions for the rise of a form of tyranny far worse than anything visited upon the polity by Caesar himself.

If we set this material in the context of the politics of 1599, Henry's project might correlate to the most exalted version of the task that lay before Essex, on his way to Ireland in the spring; a composite of Caesar's and Brutus' projects might correlate rather more closely to at least the more alarmist versions of what lay before the earl as he contemplated his return from Ireland in something like disgrace, in the late summer and autumn of the same year.

CHAPTER 19

The politics of honour (in a popular state)

'Honour' is at least as ubiquitous in *Julius Caesar* as it is in the Henry plays, but the notions of honour to be found in the Roman play are very different from those in the *Henriad*. Set in a monarchy, the honour on display in the *Henry* plays is recognisably 'chivalric' and military, obsessed with noble lineage and monarchical right, while precisely because *Caesar* is set in a republic, albeit one morphing before our very eyes into something else, the honour code in operation there is just as overtly 'republican' and 'civic'. 'Honour' features equally prominently both on the monarchical, Caesarean and on the conspiratorial and republican sides of the equation. Caesar's very sense of himself as 'Caesar' – he consistently refers to himself in the third person – and the obligations and constraints that being seen to act as 'Caesar' place upon him, all centre on 'honour', the demands of which are just as prominent in Brutus' account of why it is that, despite, indeed in many ways against, his own best interests and desires, he must kill his erstwhile friend and patron.

The play takes its name from that great soldier, Julius Caesar, and is set not only in a society – republican Rome – where military values and service to the state were of the essence, but also in the midst of a civil war. However, the honour at stake in *Julius Caesar* is almost never discussed or described in military terms. This is an almost wholly political play and the honour claimed and performed by all the central protagonists has to be won and vindicated through essentially political, self-consciously rhetorical rather than military, means. It might be worth noting that this again speaks to present circumstance. For while, at the moment when Essex set off for Ireland, the immediate tasks before England and the earl had been military, the crisis to which he was returning in autumn of 1599 was an intensely political one, which required the skills not so much of the soldier as of the politician.

Republican honour

In this section I want to try to reconstruct from a variety of scenes and speeches just what the characters seem to mean by honour. The aim is to see what the central figures in the play do with the word, to observe what ideological work it performs and what legitimising functions it fulfils. In the scene in which Cassius is attempting to broach the subject of Caesar's assassination to Brutus [I, ii, 79–89], Brutus first equates 'honour' with service of 'the general good' and then locates the essence of the honourable man in his capacity to risk his life in that service, and, if necessary, to choose death rather than dishonour.

Cassius immediately takes his cue from these remarks and produces his own disquisition on 'honour' [I, ii, 90–97], associating it with 'virtue' and 'freedom' and again with the willingness of the man of honour to choose death rather dishonour. 'Freedom' here seems to mean the capacity not to be 'in awe' of any other mortal. To be reduced to such a state of dependence or subordination, and certainly to acquiesce freely in such a condition, is, for Cassius, the classic instance of the sort of dishonour to which, for an honourable man, death is to be preferred.

Later soliloquising on the strengths and weaknesses of Brutus' character, and on the ways in which those traits will allow Cassius to bend him to his purposes, Cassius adds a third crucial term to the list. 'Well, Brutus, thou art noble: yet I see/Thy honourable mettle may be wrought/From that it is disposed' [I, ii, 307–9]. Here then we have 'honour' and 'nobility' being associated together and linked with the service of the 'general good' and with 'freedom', to form a nexus, if not of equivalent, then certainly of intensely interrelated, perhaps even mutually dependent, terms.

At another point in their dialogue, Cassius explains to Brutus that, despite the fact that he is a mere mortal, as subject to the weaknesses of the flesh as any other man, Caesar 'is now become a God'; indeed, having got 'the start of the majestic world', he now 'bears the palm alone' and his countrymen must always 'mark him, and write his speeches in their books'. So great has Caesar's dominance grown that 'Cassius is/A wretched creature, and must bend his body/If Caesar carelessly but nod on him' [I, ii, 116–18, 126, 130–1]. In a later exchange with Casca, Cassius expands on this point, by explaining that Caesar's greatness, his preponderant power in the state, has, in effect, rendered Rome 'a monstrous state' and reduced to the status of 'a willing bondman' all those Romans who are prepared passively to acquiesce in his dominance [I, iii, 71–78, 113]. Caesar's greatness – the fact that he 'doth bestride the narrow world/Like a colossus' – has reduced his countrymen to the status of 'petty men', walking 'under his huge legs' 'to find ourselves dishonourable graves' [I, ii, 134–37].

In Cassius' view, therefore, Caesar's dominance has reduced the Romans to 'bondage', which, of course, is the polar opposite of 'freedom'. Acceptance of that condition is the ultimate source of dishonour and we have already noted that it was an essential mark of the man of true honour to risk death rather than to suffer that sort of dishonour. On this view, Rome is already a tyranny and freedom has already been lost. Moreoever, on Cassius' account, the graves of those Romans who have submitted passively to this new dispensation will be dishonourable not merely because their subjection to Caesar has rendered them bond and not free, but also because, by allowing one man such power, they have connived at, indeed, in effect, acquiesced in, the loss of their own freedom – and nothing could be more dishonourable than that.

Thus for Cassius the blame for the loss of their freedom rests primarily not on Caesar's but on the Romans' own heads. For Cassius, then, it is not Caesar's superabundance of virtue that has won him preponderant power in the state, but rather the Romans' lack of same, indeed their corruption, that has ceded such a wholly unnatural dominance to him. 'Poor man, I know he would not be a wolf/ But that he sees the Romans are but sheep./He were no lion, were not the Romans hinds . . . What trash is Rome? What rubbish, and what offal? When it serves/For the base matter to illuminate/So vile a thing as Caesar?' [I, iii, 103–11].

Earlier Cassius had taken a similar tack to Brutus. 'The fault, dear Brutus, is not in our stars/But in ourselves, that we are underlings.' The current 'age' should be 'ashamed' for Rome 'has lost the breed of noble bloods! . . . When could they say, till now, that talked of Rome,/That her wide walks encompassed but one man?/Now is it Rome indeed, and room enough,/When there is in it but one only man./O, you and I have heard our fathers say/There was a Brutus once that would have brooked/Th'eternal devil to keep his state in Rome/As easily as a king' [I, ii, 139–60]. In his later exchange with Casca, Cassius makes the same point more generally, and in overtly gendered terms: 'Romans now/ Have thews and limbs like to their ancestors:/But woe the while, our fathers' minds are dead,/And we are governed with our mothers' spirits:/Our yoke and sufferance show us womanish' [I, iii, 80–84].

The intensity of Cassius' language in these passages speaks to the extent to which, as Marvin Vawter has pointed out, the conspirators themselves are complicit in the process of Caesar's metamorphosis into a demigod, the 'only man in Rome'. 'One of the central ironies of *Caesar*,' he writes, 'is that the men who avow their hatred of the thing that flattery creates are the men who flatter Caesar most.' The point is made as part of Vawter's oddly intense assault on the moral standing of the conspirators, and as such stands as a prime example of the sort of bizarre side-taking that the ironic balance of the play can provoke in some critics. But, of course, it also provides a rather sharp insight into just why the likes of Cassius hate Caesar so much; rather than simple 'envy', it is because the tenor of their relations with him render them despicable, because – that key word again – 'dishonourable', in their own eyes. During their confrontation at Sardis what hurts Cassius most is Brutus' contemptuous dismissal of his claim that 'when Caesar lived he durst not thus have moved me' [IV, iii, 58–62]. Brutus is, of course, quite right and the put-down all the more devastating because of it.[1]

On this account, then, it is lost virtue that has led to lost liberty, and the loss of liberty that is now leading to a further loss of honour and, indeed, of virtue.

Cassius' evocation of this cycle of decline allows us to reconstruct the relations within the Roman republic between honour, nobility, freedom and virtue. The republican honour whose loss is being lamented here comes from the zealous service of the general good, pursued within a polity composed of other autonomous, honour-bearing individuals. This is a version of honour that does not stress hereditary right or rank, but rather service to the 'general' or common good. In the speeches cited in the previous paragraph the notion of 'noble blood' is associated, indeed in effect equated, with virtuous action in the service of the state.

The result is a distinctly aristocratic notion of honour, nobility and virtue; the equation of virtuous action with 'noble bloods', and the obsession with the honour of one's ancestors implies as much. But even when the rhetoric of noble blood is deployed most enthusiastically it does not refer only or even mainly to issues of lineage but rather more to the possession of virtue. When Cassius is ranting on about the honour of the current generation's forebears, he is doing so not in order to emphasise issues of hereditary right or the prerogatives of aristocratic descent, but rather to recall to mind the masculine Romanness and constancy of the current generation's ancestors, in general, and of Brutus' king-killing forebears, in particular, in order to exhort his contemporaries to emulate the zeal of the ancient Romans, who had risked their lives to defend Rome from the tyranny of monarchy. When, speaking over Caesar's corpse, Antony calls Caesar's 'the most noblest blood of all this world' [III, i, 156] he is surely not referring primarily to Caesar's ancestry. Thus when both Caesareans and conspirators are describing the nature of true nobility and honour all their emphasis is placed, not on inherited right or status, but on the service of the 'general' good and, on the republican side at least, on the defence of 'freedom' or 'liberty'. It is worth noting here that Cassius is doing with examples from the Roman past precisely what Elizabethan readers and commentators were trained to do: that is to say, extracting certain exemplars of moral or political virtue not merely for the moral instruction or improvement, but for the active emulation of contemporaries.

The resulting ideal of honourable action is masculine and associated with the mind, while the Romans' current passivity is associated with women and 'the spirit'. Thus the only person to lay great emphasis on issues of heredity or kinship in staking a claim for inclusion in the honour community, and, in this case, in the conspiracy to kill Caesar, is Portia, who makes great play with her status as 'Cato's daughter' and 'a woman that Lord Brutus took to wife'. 'Being so fathered and so husbanded', it would, therefore, be a mistake to regard her as 'no stronger than my sex' [II, I, 291–96]. This is a claim that she seeks to make good by wounding herself in the thigh in order to demonstrate that she is as capable of stoic virtue and constancy in the face of suffering as any man.[2] But, in fact, she proves to be no stronger than her sex; first, left at home, impotent to influence events, she dissolves into anxiety over the outcome of the conspiracy, nearly giving the game away in the process [II, iv, 6–9]. Later, as Brutus reports, her 'woman's might' wins its unequal struggle with 'her man's mind', and, buckling under the pressure of events, she commits suicide by swallowing fire [IV, iii, 150–54]. On this account, then, honour, nobility and virtue are possessions of men of 'noble bloods' and 'constant mind', men active, indeed willing to suffer death, in the service of the general good.

The result is an inherently emulous, competitive system, in which citizens compete for honour through their freely given service to the state. For Cassius, it is precisely Caesar's dominance, indeed his virtual monopoly, of the resulting honour system – as Cassius bitterly complains at one point, 'he alone bears the palm' – that irks him most. Caesar's dominance has ended the free competition between notional equals for nobility and honour in service of the common or general good that is the essence of the republican honour system. Seeking to persuade Brutus to join the conspiracy, it is on this point that Cassius harks, asking Brutus 'Why should that name be sounded more than yours?' [I, ii, 141–46].

Caesar himself subscribes to precisely the same value system as Cassius. (In an important sense, as Coppelia Kahn points out, he is as much a product of republican Romanitas as either Brutus or Cassius.) He understands the inherently competitive nature of the honour system and sees Cassius himself as a danger to him precisely because Cassius is the sort of man incapable of being 'at heart's ease/Whiles they behold a greater than themselves,/And therefore are they very dangerous' [I, ii, 207–9]. It is just that for Caesar his own predominance in the state seems entirely natural, since it is a function of his clearly superior virtue and honour. There is thus a good deal of truth in Kahn's observation that 'when Caesar sounds most republican' is also when he 'sounds most egotistical and arrogant', claiming a both political and moral 'superiority' over his fellows precisely because he so far exceeds them in his espousal of the basic Roman (and indeed republica) virtues.[3]

Throughout, Caesar's behaviour and decisions are dominated by the need to stay true to his claim that 'always I am Caesar' [I, ii, 211], a man free from fear, utterly constant in his devotion to the general good and the principles of justice and virtue that always animate his conduct. When Artemidorus bids him to read his petition first 'for mine's a suit/That touches Caesar nearer', Caesar responds that 'what touches us ourself shall be last served' [III, i, 6–8]. Again, as Calphurnia and others urge the dreadful warning provided by the previous night's prodigy-filled tempest to dissuade him from going to the Senate, Caesar performs his own constancy in the face of fate and danger. 'Caesar shall forth. The things that threatened me/Ne'er looked but on my back: when they shall see/The face of Caesar, they are vanished' [II, ii, 10–12]. 'What can be avoided/Whose end is purposed by the mighty gods? . . . Cowards die many times before their deaths;/The valiant never taste of death but once./Of all the wonders that I yet have heard,/It seems to me most strange that men should fear,/Seeing that death, a necessary end,/Will come when it will come' [II, ii, 32–37]. Told of yet another bad omen discovered by the augurs, Caesar again insists that 'Danger knows full well/That Caesar is more dangerous than he./We are two lions littered in one day,/And I the elder and more terrible,/And Caesar shall go forth' [II, ii, 41–48]. Thus it is Caesar's imperative always to be 'Caesar', at all times, to embody and display, or at least to appear to embody and display, republican honour and Roman virtue, that at the last consigns him to his death.

Caesar's claim here to be the master of his own fate through his acceptance of, and indifference before, the inevitability of death parallels remarks made elsewhere by Cassius on the subject of suicide. Confronted by the virtual certainty that, as Casca explains, 'the senators tomorrow/Mean to establish Caesar as a king,/And he shall wear his crown by sea and land/In every place save here in Italy', Cassius takes this as a sign of the certain arrival of tyranny and servitude to the Roman state. But this, he claims, is a form of 'bondage' that cannot contain the likes of Cassius. 'I know where I will wear this dagger then:/Cassius from bondage will deliver Cassius./Therein, ye gods, you tyrants do defeat./Nor stony tower, nor walls of beaten brass,/No airless dungeon, nor strong links of iron,/Can be retentive to the strength of spirit:/But life being weary of these worldly bars/Never lacks power to dismiss himself./If I know this, know all the world besides,/That part of tyranny that I do bear/I can shake off at pleasure.' To which Casca replies 'so can I/So every bondman in his own hands bears/The power to cancel his captivity' [I, iii, 85–102]. Here, then, is an acceptance of death's inevitability and of the immutability of fate very similar to that which underlies Caesar's sense of his own extraordinary virtue, nobility and honour, reaching its apogee, its logical end point, in the willingness of the genuinely free man to cheat the tyrant by ending a life that had, through the loss of freedom, become the utterly dishonourable lot of a bondman and a subject, rather than that of a free Roman.

Here Cassius' sentiments prefigure those of Brutus expressed later in the play when, in another exchange with Cassius about the appropriateness of suicide as a response to final defeat and disgrace, he censures Cato 'for the death/Which he did give himself – I know not how'. For, he explains, 'I do find it cowardly and vile,/For fear of what might fall, so to prevent the time of life'. Until all else fails, it is incumbent on the man of honour to 'arm himself' with 'patience' and 'to stay the providence of some high powers/That govern us below'. But that condemnation of the cowardice of a suicide undertaken prematurely, as a sign of 'fear of what might fall', itself comes in a speech in which Brutus declares his intention to die by his own hand if he is defeated by Antony and Octavius. Moreover, he justifies that decision as having been informed 'by the rule of that philosophy by which I did blame Cato' for his suicide. 'Think not, thou noble Roman,/That ever Brutus will go bound to Rome./He bears too great a mind. But this same day/Must end that work the Ides of March begun' [V, i, 100–13].

In all this, Caesar, Cassius and Brutus are repeating and claiming as their own what Miles calls 'orthodox stoic wisdom'. For Seneca, suicide 'is the last defence of the sapiens against fortune'. The wise man knows that 'life itself is an "indifferent" thing' and is thus able, 'if it comes to a choice between life and virtue', to choose virtue, honour and, it is to be hoped, an immortal Cato-like fame, by taking his own life.[4]

Thus, while the capacity to contemplate one's own death with equanimity, up to the point of being prepared to end it oneself, is indeed a central characteristic of the man of honour, such readiness to die should, in the truly honourable, be neither a cause nor a sign of an unmanly passivity before events. For an enervating fatalism, a womanish 'fear of what might fall' was the polar opposite of the active virtue that characterised the Roman man of honour. Thus, as the tragic fate of Portia showed, premature suicide was the woman's part. Genuine equanimity before the inevitability of death and the immutability of fate should enable the honourable man to risk all for the general good and, only in extremity, prompt him to choose death rather than dishonour; an option that should be taken only after all other available avenues for the exercise of an active virtue, up to and including desperately dangerous expedients – like those that start on the Ides of March and are culminating now at Philippi – have been exhausted. Only then, when confronted by inevitable defeat and dishonour – represented here by the prospect of being 'led in triumph/Through the streets of Rome' [V, i, 108–9] – can the 'noble Roman' of genuinely 'great mind' contemplate ending his own life.

Again, such values are hardly the exclusive property of the republican and conspiratorial party. It is Caesar who, in the scene immediately before his death, gives an account of an almost megalomaniac intensity, of the constancy that underlies the Roman honour code and of his own claims to a more than human virtue. Asked by Metellus Cimber to return his brother from exile, Caesar protests that he is beyond 'these couchings and these lowly courtesies', the 'sweet words,/Low-crooked curtsies', the 'base spaniel fawning' of the flatterer. These 'might fire the blood of ordinary men', or 'fools', but they will have no effect on Caesar. 'Thy brother by decree is banished./If thou dost bend and pray and fawn for him/I spurn thee like a cur out of my way./Know, Caesar doth not wrong, nor without cause/Will he be satisfied' [III, i, 35–48]. When the request is seconded by Brutus himself, Caesar famously compares his own constancy to that of 'the northern star'. Alone of men there is 'but one/That unassailable holds on his rank/Unshaked of motion. And that I am he/Let me a little show it even in this,/That I was constant Cimber should be banished/

And constant do remain to keep him so' [III, i, 58–73]. In these words claims to Romanness, constancy and honour are pitched at such a height that they have become claims to something else altogether – to an immutability and justice that are more than human, indeed semi-divine. So, when Brutus persists, Caesar rounds on him: 'hence! Wilt thou lift up Olympus?' [III, I, 74].

Here Cassius' complaints that Caesar, a man as susceptible to the frailties of the flesh as any other, has been made into a god receive confirmation from Caesar's own mouth and the figure of Caesar is revealed to the audience as – in this just like Richard II – another bearer of monarchical authority entirely trapped within his own rhetoric of semi-divine majesty and more than human greatness. And, of course, the consequences of this royal solipsism are to prove just as fatal for Caesar as they had for Richard.[5]

Such scenes show Caesar, Cassius and indeed Brutus all occupying much the same ideological and moral space, assenting to and competing for the same pagan, Roman and (for all Caesar's monarchical pretensions) in origin, republican notions of honour, nobility and virtue. Thus it is that Brutus, the most virtuous and honourable character in the play, accedes to Caesar's status as the most honourable of all the Romans. For Brutus does not share Cassius' view that Caesar's claim 'to bear the palm alone', to enjoy a virtual monopoly of all the honour, nobility and virtue in the Roman state, has already reduced Rome to a *de facto* tyranny and all other Romans to the status of 'willing bondmen'. As Cassius rants against the deleterious effects on Roman freedom of Caesar's standing in the state, Brutus uses only the future tense.

Thus, Brutus never endorses Cassius' account of the current condition of Romans living under Caesar's shadow as servitude. On the contrary, his attention remains firmly fixed on the future; on Caesar's desire to be a king and on the deleterious moral and political effects that such an outcome will have both on Caesar himself and on the state that he will then be ruling, not as a Roman of pre-eminent virtue and honour, presiding over fellow citizens, in the service of the general good, but as a prince ruling over subjects. Brutus' parting shot to Cassius betrays their very different take on the current situation. Putting off further discussion of a topic that neither man has yet quite managed to bring himself to mention, Brutus tells Cassius 'Till then, my noble friend, chew upon this:/Brutus had rather be a villager/Than to repute himself a son of Rome/Under these hard conditions as this time/Is like to lay upon us' [I, ii, 170–74].

When we next meet Brutus at the start of Act II, he is summarising (in soliloquy) the terms in which, during the anxiety-filled period since his first discussion with Cassius, he has been considering the subject of Caesar's ambition and the political and moral change that it seems about to impose on the state [II, i, 10–34].

This speech has attracted the attention of a good many critics, most of whom read it as an extended exercise in self-deception, as Brutus logic-chops his way to a conclusion that he has already reached – 'it must be by his death'.[6] On this account, the argument is patently self-deluding and incoherent, based as it is on a series of hypothetical speculations and generalisations about what is likely to happen in the future and what Caesar might become, rather than on what Brutus admits is his directly personal knowledge of what Caesar is. In Anne Barton's estimation, Brutus 'extracts purpose and resolve, not from the facts of the situation, but from a collection of verbal nothings: from words like "may" and "would"'. 'There is, in her view, 'no tangible basis for Brutus' fear of Caesar ... he is driven as a result, to do the thing for which he secretly longs – kill Caesar – purely on the basis of a grammatical construction: a verbal emptiness which pretends to the status of a fact.'[7]

For others it is not merely the hypothetical reasoning of the speech, but his use of terms like 'colour' and 'fashion' which give the game away. The result, it has been claimed, is a 'rationalisation' of something that Brutus wants to do anyway, because, as Gordon Ross Smith puts it, 'he could not bear the thought of anyone's being able to rule over him', or, more subtly, in the words of Anne Barton, because of 'a deeply buried jealousy of Caesar, lurking behind all of Brutus' avowed republican principles', a jealousy no less intense because 'less conscious' than that of Cassius.[8]

Much of this exegesis seems to me, if not simply mistaken, then very considerably over-argued. For in this speech Brutus could just as well be construed as trying to talk himself out of, rather than into, the murder of Caesar. The speech starts *in medias res*; we meet Brutus in the midst of a thought process not yet complete. He has, however, already reached a (provisional?) conclusion – 'it must be by his death' – and is now examining that conclusion to see if it holds water. The issue at stake is whether, to deserve death as a tyrant, Caesar has to be personally malign, composed of the morally degenerate stuff of which tyrants are traditionally made, or whether his desire to introduce a simply monarchical power into Rome is itself enough to render him tyrannical. As Quentin Skinner has pointed out, the classic, neo-Roman (indeed republican) position held that a ruler did not have to be personally vicious to qualify as a tyrant. Both paraphrasing and quoting Livy, Skinner observes that a state can only be defined as a 'self governing community' when ' "the *imperium* of the laws is greater than that of any men". It follows not merely that tyranny but all forms of monarchical government must be incompatible with the maintenance of public liberty.' In consequence, a monarch does not have to act like a tyrant or display any of the ethical marks of the classical tyrant-figure in order to be a tyrant. As Skinner puts it, 'it may be that the community is not in matter of fact governed tyrannically: its rulers may choose to follow the dictates of the law, so that the body politic may not in practice be deprived of any of its constitutional rights. Such a state will nevertheless be counted as living in slavery if its capacity for action is in any way dependent on the will of anyone other than the body of its own citizens.'[9]

On this account, Caesar's present predominance in the state, let alone his future coronation as a king, would be reason enough to treat him as a tyrant. This is the classically republican position; it is the position adumbrated by Cassius and the one ultimately adopted by Brutus. But it is a peculiarly bloodless, theoretical reason to kill your friend and patron and in this speech Brutus is looking for more viscerally personal and compelling grounds in Caesar's character and record and he altogether fails to find them. For Brutus knows nothing about Caesar's past or present conduct that would render him, as someone who lets his 'affections sway more than his reason', liable to tyranny. Of course, if the Caesar whom Brutus has known for years bears any resemblance to the Caesar revealed by the play to its audience, then he can't have been paying much attention. If the speech reveals self-deception it is surely on this point that Brutus is deceiving himself.

Almost in desperation, Brutus imagines what kingly power would do to Caesar's (to this point, in his view, entirely virtuous) character. If his death is to be justified – 'coloured', as Brutus puts it – in terms of the malignities of Caesar's character, the argument will have to be 'fashioned' in the speculative, indeed the frankly hypothetical, terms outlined in the speech. Against his own better judgement, Brutus seems to be trying to talk himself into such a view, perhaps, as Nuttall suggests, with an eye on how the murder might be legitimised or sold to the people once the deed has been done, when the actions of the conspirators will indeed have to be 'coloured' one way or another and arguments in their favour 'fashioned' in rather a hurry.[10] Moreover, as Velz points out, there was nothing unconventional or unlikely about the chain of reasoning itself. 'In the context of Renaissance political thought,' he concludes, 'Brutus is neither hypocrite nor self-deceiver when he reasons that to make Caesar a tyrant "in the entrance" is almost certainly to make him a wilful tyrant "in the execution".'[11]

If Velz is right about that, then what is really remarkable here is not Brutus' recourse to such reasoning but rather what the play subsequently reveals to be his almost total failure to be convinced by it. For later in the same scene we find him reverting to the theoretical case for tyrannicide, to the formal republican analysis, that would render Caesar, however great his personal virtues, a tyrant because he wants to become king. On this account, Caesar's coronation must be stopped not because of what his coronation might or very likely would do to Caesar himself but rather because of what monarchical authority would definitely do to Rome: 'shall Rome stand under one man's awe? What Rome?/My ancestors did from the streets of Rome/The Tarquin drive, when he was called a king./"Speak, strike, redress." Am I entreated/To speak and strike? O Rome, I make thee promise,/If the redress will follow, thou receivest/Thy full petition at the hand of Brutus' [II, i, 52–58].[12]

Brutus makes essentially the same point when, later in the same scene, he commits the conspirators to violence not against the person so much as the 'spirit of Caesar': 'we all stand up against the spirit of Caesar,/And in the spirit of men there is no blood./O that then we could come by Caesar's spirit/And not dismember Caesar!/But, alas, Caesar must bleed for it' [II, i, 166–70]. This is to make the conspiracy a matter of principles not of persons, and shows Brutus abandoning for good and all the line of argument by which the conspirators' act could be justified through reference to personal defects to be found in Caesar's character either now or in the future.

Indeed, that distinction between principle and person becomes so crucial to Brutus' sense of what the conspiracy is all about that he comes to claim that the difference between, as it were, the tyrant's two bodies can, indeed must, be rendered patent in the very act of annihilating violence against Caesar's person which, one might have thought, was about to conflate the two for good and all. Even if he has to be killed, Caesar must be dispatched in the right way; Brutus wants the conspirators to award themselves style points for the way in which they kill Caesar. 'Let's kill him boldly, but not wrathfully:/Let's carve him as a dish fit for the gods,/Not hew him as a carcass fit for hounds./And let our hearts, as subtle masters do,/Stir up their servants to an act of rage/And after seem to chide 'em. This shall make/Our purpose necessary and not envious,/Which so appearing to the common eyes,/We shall be called purgers, not murderers' [II, i, 171–79]. But Brutus does not merely want the conspirators to be called 'purgers, not murderers'; that passage also reveals that he himself conceives of their relation both with Rome and with Caesar in precisely those terms.

The clinching evidence for this view is provided by the fact that when the chips really are down and Brutus has to 'colour' his act in killing Caesar and 'fashion' arguments to justify the conspiracy, he remains true to the conclusions that he had reached when communing with himself in the orchard. He does not resort to a vilification of Caesar's character, but rather cedes to Caesar all the claims to Roman virtue in the world. He talks instead about Caesar's 'ambition' to become king. In other words, he talks in the future tense about what Caesar wanted to do and would have done, had Brutus and the others not removed him from the scene, and in so doing, all his emphasis goes, not on the evils of Caesar's character, but on the malign consequences of his rise to power – the inevitable reduction of Rome from the status of a free state to subjection to one man's will and of the Romans themselves from the status of free men to that of slaves or bondmen – if Caesar had been allowed to become king. Critics who complain that the choices he places before the people are false ones, that the speech is based on specious or undemonstrated premises, thus miss the point that, viewed from within the republican ideology that Brutus thinks – as we shall see erroneously – he shares with his audience, these are close to being simply self-evident claims.[13]

But if there still remains, as there surely does, a sense in which, in his orchard soliloquy, Brutus *is* deceiving himself, the question arises, just what is

Brutus deceiving himself about? The answer is surely not his own motivations; the play does not show him glossing or eliding the pride, envy or ambition to which Cassius has been trying subliminally to appeal in previous exchanges. Rather it shows him deceiving himself about the current moral and political condition of Caesar's character and of the Roman state, about both of which he is taking what the play will shortly reveal to be an unjustifiably, indeed a fatally, sanguine view.

For as John Velz has pointed out, even as he chops and changes his mind over whether to go to the Senate or stay at home, Caesar is shown insisting upon both the constancy and the self-sufficiency of his mere will.[14] The play presents us with a republican political scene in which nearly everyone, at one point or another, uses highly wrought rhetorical speech in an effort to persuade someone else. This happens not only in the public but also in the most private scenes. Thus Cassius uses formal rhetoric to persuade Brutus and then Casca to join the conspiracy; Portia adopts a similarly formal approach in her appeals to Brutus to be let in on the secret. Almost alone of the major characters, Caesar is not shown playing 'the orator's role'; we do not see him seeking to persuade others, but others trying to persuade him. Even his attempt to win the people over to the idea of him as their king does not involve him directly seeking to persuade anyone, but rather performing Roman virtue in a carefully choreographed scene staged before the people. To lapse into terminology devised by Jürgen Habermas, Caesar is operating through the representative publicness typical of a monarch, not through the rhetorically framed appeal to an inherently republican public sphere. Velz, I think quite rightly, sees this as central to what he terms the 'moral', and we might term the political, 'symbolism of the play'.

Thus Velz notes that 'of the eighteen sentences Caesar speaks in his first appearance in Act I Scene ii, eleven (including all of the first six) are impera-tives'. Antony responds to one such command by succinctly outlining the entirely monarchical implications of Caesar's linguistic style: 'I shall remember:/ When Caesar says "Do this", it is performed' [I, ii, 9–10]. And Velz adds, 'when Caesar is not being imperative, he is likely to be declarative, even emphatically so: ". . . I was constant Cimber should be banish'd,/And constant do remain to keep him so" [III, i, 72–73]. And, even more tellingly, ' "the cause is in my will: I will not come;/That is enough to satisfy the Senate [II, ii, 71–72]" '.[15]

While rhetoric, the attempt through language to move or persuade others, might be taken to be a peculiarly republican form[16] – necessary both to win over one's notional equals amongst the governing class and to persuade the people to endorse whatever persons or policies are being canvassed – the imperative or declarative mode adopted by Caesar might be taken to be inher-ently monarchical. Certainly the play works hard to show us that Caesar has already adopted the arbitrary, will-based linguistic style of the monarch. In terms of the values relevant to the monarchical polity of Elizabethan England, this may (or may not) make Caesar a tyrant, but it certainly implies that he has already moved far closer to kingship, and Rome far closer to subjection to one's man's will, than Brutus seems prepared to admit.

We can see what is stake here if we examine more closely the scene between Caesar and the conspirators immediately before Caesar's assassination. This turns on a petition made by Metellus Cimber for the revocation of his brother Publius' exile. On the one hand, this is a mere ruse staged by the conspirators so that they can surround Caesar without arousing his suspicions. On the other, it enables Shakespeare (through Mark Antony) to comment ironically upon the hypocrisy and deceit of the conspirators as they crave Caesar's favour just moments before they cut him down. But it also plays a third function, allowing Shakespeare to reveal the circles around Caesar, and indeed the inner workings of the Roman state under his dominance, to be, in essence, a royal court. Metellus Cimber starts out addressing Caesar as 'most high, most mighty and most puissant Caesar'. Brutus seconds him: 'I kiss thy hand, but not in flat-tery, Caesar', while Cassius abases himself still further: 'pardon, Caesar; Caesar, pardon./As low as to thy foot doth Cassius fall/To beg enfranchisement for Publius Cimber' [III, i, 32, 51–53, 55–58]. This, of course, is the language of monarchy and, as we have seen, its use by those around him allows Caesar to respond to what he terms their 'couchings' and 'lowly courtesies' with yet another performance of his own Roman virtue and constancy of mind.

Here, on one view of the matter, is Caesar displaying in spades precisely the transcendent Roman virtue that (Brutus had been forced to admit) continued to distinguish his putative victim from all the other Romans of the age. Except that Caesar's display of constancy of mind, his performance of what he describes as his own semi-divine virtue, is being used here to justify an entirely will-based dismissal of a legal petition, on no other grounds than that Caesar himself has already determined the case and (like another authoritarian politi-cian obsessed with her own consistency and strength of character) Caesar's not for turning.

Nor does this scene represent, as Velz would have it, and as it would have been in any properly republican polity, 'the legislative body of the state', i.e. the Roman Senate, 'seeking just cause', in the pursuit of justice for Metellus Cimber. On the contrary, this is a clique of Caesar's creatures petitioning him to exercise a quintessentially monarchical, and quite arbitrary, right of pardon. In response, Caesar having started out by asking in quite blatantly monarchical style 'What is now amiss/That Caesar and his Senate must redress?' [III, i, 31–32]. The reference here to 'his' rather than to 'the Senate' is devastating in the brevity and power with which it evokes the political transformation that has taken place. What follows is a series of essentially 'private' exchanges between Caesar and his courtiers; exchanges which, in a certain sort of monarchy, would have constituted nothing more than business as usual, but which, in any sort of republic, did indeed represent barefaced tyranny. For Caesar refuses the suit on no basis other than the arbitrary exercise of his own sovereign will, the justice of which is, at least to him, axiomatic. Here is the fate of a Roman citizen turning, not on the application of the law, nor on the deliberations of the Senate, but rather on the operations of a will that can only be termed royal; a will that all involved in the scene concede could overturn Publius Cimber's sentence in an instant, and which, these exchanges seem to imply, had already determined Cimber's fate for reasons essentially known only to itself. Velz' conclusion – 'small wonder if Decius and the other conspirators regard Caesar as a tyrant' – seems entirely apposite.[17] On this basis, the play seems to be insisting, whether Caesar enjoyed the formal title of king or no, Rome had long since ceased to be any sort of republic.

It is, therefore, hard to recognise, in the play's depiction of Caesar, the noble Roman incapable of allowing emotion or interest to pervert his judgement of Brutus' imaginings. Why therefore, does Brutus cling to such an idealised version of Caesar, even as he is trying to persuade himself that it is right to kill him? He does so because an upbeat view of the moral and political condition both of Caesar and of Rome is crucial to Brutus for a number of linked, both personal and political, reasons. On the personal level, if Caesar has already ceased, or is ceasing, to be the epitome of Roman virtue that Brutus has always taken him to be, then the very closeness of Brutus' relationship with him, not to mention his continuing scruples about killing him, becomes a sign not of honour but of dishonour, and in order to act at all Brutus must at all times remain, in his own eyes, as well as in those of others, 'an honourable man'. After all, his earlier exchanges with Cassius have revealed that Brutus is free from Cassius' envy, resentment and self-loathing precisely because he regards Caesar as the epitome of Roman virtue and honour. Thus Brutus' capacity to pay such transcendent virtue its just due of deference becomes a sign of his own honour, virtue and Romanitas, rather than (as Cassius experiences it) something servile and dishonourable, forced on and out of him by political necessity and fear.

As ever in this play, such apparently personal concerns with the dynamics of honour, virtue and friendship are shown to have directly political consequences. For, if Brutus' vision of the purposes, means and ends of the conspiracy is to remain viable, he cannot allow himself to think that either Rome or Caesar has slipped definitively from the republican ideals of his imaginings into the dystopia of monarchical corruption and servility of his nightmares. For then the mere removal of Caesar could not be expected to restore liberty to the Roman state and any attempt to reverse so deep a process of moral decline and political change would either be doomed to failure or, perhaps still worse, would become a mere coup, designed to displace one clique with another, a power grab, the success of which would depend on precisely the sort of political ruthlessness and deception – the compromises and repressions, the exactions and prescriptions – that (in this entirely unlike Cassius) Brutus finds completely incompatible with his sense of himself as man of true Roman virtue and republican honour.

But that, as the play goes on to show us, turns out to be precisely the case. The resulting contradictions come to determine Brutus' relations with the other conspirators, to prompt a series of disagreements between Brutus and Cassius and to lead Brutus himself into a number of fatal political miscalculations; mistakes which will be passively accepted by his colleagues, not because they are convinced by his reasoning, but rather because, as self-consciously 'true Romans', they remain as obsessed as Brutus himself with his superior virtue. On this view, therefore, Brutus' disagreement with Cassius about what Caesar already is and what his rise to power has already done to Rome is not merely of academic or theoretical significance. Rather, it will render the both moral and political failure of the conspirators' political project all but inevitable.

Emulation and the production and maintenance of republican virtue

If we want to understand how all this works, we need to gain a clearer appreciation of the play's picture of the republican honour system as a self-correcting mechanism for the production of virtue and thus as a means of co-ordinating a series of autonomous and emulous, honour-bearing individuals into a ruling caste capable of guiding the Roman state. This was to be achieved through the construction of stable political alliances or 'friendships' between men who were often not friends in the sense that Brutus and Cassius were friends, but who were almost always rivals, and, in some cases, even enemies.

Central here was the notion of emulation, the workings of which Cassius expounds when, at the conclusion of their first political discussion, he remarks that although he sees that Brutus was 'noble' yet 'thy honourable nature may be wrought/From what it is disposed. Therefore it is meet/That noble minds keep ever with their likes' [I, ii, 307–10]. Cassius is afraid that Brutus will be diverted from the honourable path of conspiracy against Caesar by his love for Caesar and by Caesar's favour towards him. As we shall see below, to avert that Cassius resorts to means of persuasion that are in themselves anything but noble. However, he has, in this passage, also articulated one of the central mechanisms whereby the republican honour community was supposed to police itself. For it was only by competing (in the service of the common good) against men as honourable as themselves that the unworthy instincts, the drive towards the personal and the private, of even the noblest Romans, could be controlled.

Given that it is Cassius who gives this principle such clear expression, in relation to the corruptibility of the noble Brutus, it is wonderfully ironic that the best example of this process in action involves a bitter altercation between Brutus and Cassius about Cassius' signal failure to act as honourably as he might.

Just before Philippi, Brutus accuses Cassius of patronising corrupt underlings, taking bribes and allowing money corruptly collected for the common purpose to stick to his own fingers. Unable to deny the charges, Cassius seeks to exculpate himself through a mixture of bluster and excuses about there being a war on. Brutus, however, will not back down and finally Cassius has recourse to the argument that if Brutus were truly his friend he would overlook or mitigate his faults rather than repeat and exaggerate them. 'A friend should bear his friend's infirmities/But Brutus makes mine greater than they are.' 'I do not, till you practise them on me', comes the reply. 'You love me not', Cassius concludes. 'I do not like your faults', replies Brutus, giving the right answer again. 'A friendly eye could never see such faults', replies Cassius. 'A flatterer's would not, though they do appear/As huge as high Olympus', comes the crushing response [IV, iii, 85–91].

Here is the essence of the honour system as a self-correcting mechanism for the production and maintenance of virtue. Faced with Cassius' appeal to the private connection between them, Brutus puts the demands of the general good, and indeed of Cassius' own honour, above those of private friendship and the gratification of Cassius' own worst instincts and private interests. Here, of course, public and private meet, for, as Cassius' true friend, he must force him to acknowledge his faults. To do less would be to become a flatterer – the worst of all moral conditions, for both the flattered and the flatterer, and a situation, of course, endemic to the asymmetrical power relations engendered by the courts of princes, but entirely foreign to the emulous, but intensely egalitarian, world of genuinely republican honour and friendship. That, then, was how the honour system was supposed to work as a machine for the creation and maintenance of Roman virtue, working, through even the most private of exchanges between friends, to keep otherwise honourable men, seduced by the pursuit of wealth or power or some other private interest, up to the standards of service to the general good set by their own claims to honour and by the conduct and expectations of the most honourable of their peers.

However, these mechanisms only work when both sides of the transaction, indeed the entire honour community within which, and in terms of which, such exchanges are taking place, are in fundamental agreement about the meaning of the key words, the core values, to which appeal is being made. What happens when only one side of the exchange accepts the terms within which the discussion is being conducted is shown in the negotiations between the conspirators and Antony immediately after Caesar's death. Having fled from the scene of the murder, Antony, through a servant, expresses his willingness to come to terms [III, i, 126–37]. The phrasing of this opening gambit is fascinating. It starts by acknowledging, in what we might term classically 'republican' terms, both the 'honour' of Brutus and Antony's equally honourable regard thereof. Brutus is 'noble, wise, valiant and honest' and Antony 'honours' him. Of course, in doing so, Antony also asserts his equal member-ship of the republican honour community. These are the attributes of virtuous service to the commonweal and of true nobility to which any member of the senatorial elite should aspire. However, the achievement or possession of such qualities by any one individual does not imply or necessitate their lack in any other, nor does it bring with it any hint of an inherently or permanently hierar-chical relationship between the honour-bearing party and his fellows.

Caesar, on the other hand, 'was mighty, bold, royal and loving'. These are all rather more monarchical words and attributes, the possession of which did indeed bring with it the implication of permanent differences of worth and hence of equally permanent hierarchical relations. While Antony only accords Brutus the respect due an equal – he honours him for his virtues and nobility – he also 'feared' and 'loved' Caesar, which implies relations of clear inferiority and superi-ority quite unlike anything to be found in the inherently egalitarian and compet-itive world of republican honour. In drawing this implicit contrast between a monarchical, Caesar-dominated world and one from which that dominating presence has been removed, Antony is acknowledging both his peculiar connec-tion to Caesar and that, with Caesar's death, something very significant has happened. For he is, in effect, applying for readmission to the republican honour community of rivalrous equals that Brutus and the others have just killed Caesar in order to recreate. And in doing that he is identifying himself as at least a poten-tial ally, or so he wants Brutus – deeply committed to the continuing political efficacy and moral force of the republican mode, as he is – to believe.

Brutus immediately picks up the conciliatory tone and replies in kind. At this point he clearly hopes to recruit Antony as an active member of the repub-lican honour community that will rule Rome now that Caesar is dead. As he observes to Cassius, 'I know that we shall have him well to friend'. Cassius, ever the politician, replies with scepticism. 'I wish we may; but yet I have a mind/ That fears him much, and my misgiving still/Falls shrewdly to the purpose' [III, i, 138–46].

When Antony takes up Brutus' offer, he finds himself in a quandary. As he tells the assembled conspirators, even as he re-enters the honour community of the republic by coming to terms with them, 'my credit now stands on such slip-pery ground/That one of two bad ways you must conceit me,/Either a coward or a flatterer' [III, i, 191–93]. It is a circle that he tries to square, in classically 'Roman' fashion by offering the conspirators first his life and then his hand. 'There is no hour so fit/As Caesar's death hour, nor no instrument/Of half that worth as those your swords, made rich/With the most noble blood of all this world . . . Live a thousand years,/I shall not find myself so apt to die./No place shall please me so, no mean of death,/As here by Caesar, and by you cut off,/ The choice and master spirits of this age' [III, i, 153–63]. This is, of course, to affirm his nobility as the loyal friend of Caesar, a nobility sealed by his readiness to accept death at the hands of Caesar's murderers, while acknowledging their nobility as 'the master spirits of this age', a status, of course, sealed in turn by their murder of Caesar.

Antony is here talking precisely the same language as the conspirators and, for a second time, Brutus takes the hint and replies in kind. The murder of Caesar, while it cannot but appear 'bloody and cruel' when viewed from the perspective of a friend and admirer of Caesar, will appear very differently when viewed from the perspective of a friend and admirer of Rome. As ever, private interests and perspectives must give place to the public or general good. For, Brutus claims, their seemingly cruel act had been prompted not by spite, by private interest or resentment but by 'pity' – 'pity to the general wrong of Rome'. If Antony can accept such a view of the matter, Brutus claims, he will be received amongst them 'as a brother' 'with all kind love, good thoughts and reverence'. Again, ever the politician, Cassius augments the high-flown republican rhetoric of his co-conspirator with the language of political self-interest. Cutting to the chase, he tells Antony that if he goes along with them 'your voice shall be as strong as any man's/In the disposing of new dignities' [III, i, 164–78].

Antony appears to accede to these terms, but even as he takes the bloody hands of each of the conspirators in turn, he returns to the subject of Caesar's bleeding corpse, imagining Caesar's response to his pact, if not with the devil, then at least with his murderers. Recalled by Cassius from this reverie to the political imperatives of the moment – 'But what compact mean you to have with us?/Will you be pricked in number of our friends,/Or shall we on, and not depend on you?' – Antony answers (provisionally) in the affirmative. 'Therefore I took your hands, but was indeed/Swayed from the point by looking down on Caesar./Friends I am with you all, and love you all,/Upon this hope, that you shall give me reasons/Why and wherein Caesar was dangerous' [III, i, 215–22].

What appears to be happening in these exchanges is the reconstitution of the republican honour community, as political power passes from the monarchical primacy of Caesar to rule through groups of 'friends', sustained by agreements made between equals, each intensely conscious of his own honour and autonomy, anxious to demonstrate and defend his nobility and virtue before his peers (and indeed, as we shall see below, before 'the people' too). Brutus is offering Antony readmission to a version of this group, now reconstituted by the violent removal of Caesar from the scene. Antony confronts this offer, caught between his claim to be an independent bearer of republican honour and his role as a client and friend of Caesar, and is thus called upon to negotiate a situation in which, as he puts it, his 'credit' is at stake. In such circumstances, honour, which, after all, is the only thing that renders him a trustworthy participant in these negotiations, positively requires no less than his bitter speeches of sorrow and praise over Caesar's corpse; speeches made even in the act of becoming reconciled with Caesar's murderers. Even Cassius, much as he distrusts Antony, recognises the logic of the situation: 'I blame you not for praising Caesar so' [III, i, 214].

Typically, Brutus goes further. Taking Antony's espousal of the ideals and constraints of republican honour at face value, he seeks to bind him to the public performance of his new role as a 'friend' of the conspirators by allowing him to deliver Caesar's funeral oration. In terms of the dynamics of the republican honour community, this is a far from stupid thing to do. On the contrary, if Caesar's greatest friend, the man who delivers his funeral oration, with the kind permission of Caesar's assassins, is seen to be reconciled with those assassins, fully integrated into the group of 'honourable men' of 'constant mind' and Roman virtue which is about to replace Caesar at the head of the Roman state, the genuinely 'republican', i.e. public, rather than private, purposes of the conspirators will be confirmed, the political base of the new regime considerably broadened and the people satisfied that Caesar's death was indeed necessary to preserve 'liberty'.

It was, after all, this same line of reasoning that had prompted Brutus to oppose Cassius' insistence that Antony should go the way of Caesar. Being seen to avoid such factious courses by limiting their attentions to one man would, Brutus claimed, 'make our purpose necessary and not envious, which so appearing to the common eyes,/We shall be called purgers, not murderers'. Nor was this a decision taken without political calculation on Brutus' part. For Brutus, Antony was 'but a limb of Caesar'. After the latter's death, 'he can do no more than Caesar's arm/When Caesar's head is cut off' [II, i, 164, 181–82]. Confronted by the new political realities created by Caesar's removal from the scene, Antony would have no choice but to come to terms.

As Simmons observes, Brutus is operating on the assumption that 'when Caesar is rooted out, so localised is the state's corruption that even Antony will either be regenerated or die'.[18] Cassius' repeated attempts to cut to the chase are intended to remind Antony of the realities of his new position. Indeed, on this account, in the negotiations with Antony after Caesar's death we can see Brutus and Cassius as in effect playing good cop and bad cop, with Brutus offering full reintegration into the community of republican honour that Caesar's death has – as he imagines – restored, and Cassius reminding him both of the benefits of such membership – 'a voice', as he puts it, 'in the disposing of dignities' [III, i, 177–78] – and of the downside of refusal – 'shall we on, and not depend on you?' [III, i, 217].

None of this works, of course, but that is not our current concern. For present purposes the value of the exchanges between Antony and the conspirators is the extent to which they reveal how the Roman republican honour community that Brutus and the others killed Caesar to restore is *supposed* to work. And on the basis of the preceding analysis, we can come to some general conclusions about the distinctively Roman and republican versions of those moral quantities and categories that the play presents to its audience. Honour and nobility are a function of freedom and virtue; that is to say, true nobility is displayed and honour acquired through the exercise of virtue in the defence or prosecution of the general or public good, in a state that is not dominated by the power or authority of any one man. 'Freedom' consists in the absence of such domination and in the free competition for honour between a variety of autonomously noble and virtuous servants of the general good. The resulting honour system is intensely emulous and rivalrous, but *pace* Wayne Rebhorn, the result is not 'a zero sum game'.[19] It is the combination of competition and collaboration, of mutual respect and self-regard, that defines this honour code and community as republican. Men compete for honour, but however great the achievements and virtues of any given individual, permanent dominance, still less institutionalised power, is never to be ceded to any; the competition for honour must remain free and in recognising the genuine honour of, and indeed in ceding moral primacy and even a form of political authority to, another bearer of true Romanitas, the true man of honour does not deplete his own store of honour but rather displays and thus augments it. That is why Brutus is able to combine the greatest respect for Caesar with a mortal fear of his pretensions to a genuinely monarchical power, rather than a merely republican primacy, within the Roman state. This is why it matters so much to Brutus that Caesar should not be crowned. His is anything but a 'pedantic' aversion to the mere word 'king' or a 'superstitious' horror at the notional effects of coronation, as some critics have argued.[20] While, unlike Cassius, he is prepared to cede to Caesar the predominance that he believes his superior virtue deserves, he cannot countenance a situation in which that predominance is rendered permanent. And it is, of course, for these very reasons that, for Casssius at least, even without the title of king, the emerging monopoly of Caesar has effectively destroyed Roman republican liberty.

Thus, while Coppelia Kahn is quite right to claim that Caesar's pretensions to a transcendent, god-like virtue have been generated within, and are framed in terms of, the existing canons of republican, and indeed of Stoic, virtue to which all the other characters subscribe, the play goes out of its way to show that those pretensions are more than just 'seemingly unrepublican'. However 'republican' Caesar's attitudes and attributes may have been in origin, they have now taken on a distinctively monarchical, indeed, when viewed from within the republican world-view that spawned them, a decidedly tyrannical, form.[21]

The ideals of honour, virtue and nobility at stake here are intensely aristocratic; they are the preserve of an educated senatorial elite, comprising actions, attributes and prerogatives simply unavailable to the mass of ordinary citizens. And yet while many of the characters make frequent reference to their Roman ancestors, either generally or sometimes more personally conceived – as in Cassius' and Brutus' invocations of Brutus' Tarquin-slaying ancestor – the stress in defining this mode of nobility or honour is not on lineage or blood but on conduct, on the virtuous service of the general, rather than of the private, good.

Also constitutive of the Roman ideals of personal and political virtue and honour being staged in the play is what Portia calls a 'constant mind', one formed not only by the service of the general good but also by the dictates of what Brutus and Cassius both refer to as 'philosophy'. The result is a Stoic or Stoicising constancy of temper in the face of the vicissitudes of fortune and even of the prospect, indeed the certainty, of death. At its most extreme, this constancy of mind will enable the virtuous man to choose death rather than dishonour or bondage, suicide providing the ultimate escape from tyranny and servitude. But, according to the dictates of the same philosophy that validates suicide as a last resort, a good death must never become an end in itself, self-murder a cowardly means of avoiding danger or fear. If there is a form of fatalism in this version of philosophically informed Roman virtue – a sense expressed by Caesar, Casca, Brutus and others that 'that we shall die we know; 'tis but the time/And drawing days out, that men stand upon' [III, i, 99–100] – it is a fatalism designed to lead to an active pursuit of virtue and the defence of liberty and of the general good, rather than a servile acceptance of bondage and defeat or a cowardly avoidance of danger or difficulty. As Miles observes, depending on attendant circumstances, 'being constant . . . can be held to require either a Senecan suicide, or . . . a steadfast sticking to one's post', and Shakespeare reveals Brutus to be entirely cognisant of that fact. Or to put the matter differently, with considerable historical insight, in this play Shakespeare imagines a 'Ciceronian' and republican version of Stoic virtue, based on an active engagement in public affairs, rather than a 'Senecan' and imperial one, based on the defence of personal integrity and constancy in passivity before and withdrawal from the all-embracing fact of tyranny.[22]

The republican honour on display here is, then, a function of 'blood', of gender, of commitment to the common good and of a philosophically grounded constancy of mind, displayed in the active service of the general good. 'Freedom' or 'liberty' is valued precisely because it is the enabling condition for the pursuit, acquisition and display of such honour or nobility, characteristics which must be incessantly performed before, and validated by, a series of audiences. And it is surely the restoration of such a mode of government to which the various conspirators are referring when, immediately after the death of Caesar, they rush 'even to the market place', 'waving our red weapons o'er our heads' and proclaiming, with Cassius, 'Liberty, freedom and enfranchisement!' [III, i, 81], with Cinna, 'Liberty! Freedom! Tyranny is dead' [III, i, 78–79] or, with Brutus, 'Peace, Freedom and Liberty' [III, i, 109–10].

CHAPTER 20

Performing honour and the politics of popularity (in a popular state)

To be honourable one must be accepted as such by other men of honour. In nearly all the scenes and speeches analysed above honour is being performed by one or other of the characters before an audience of his peers and that is because, in the absence of a single source of honour or title, of the sort provided in a monarchy by the prince, honour must be continually asserted and conferred on the members of the honour community by that community itself. On this account, opinion becomes the final court of appeal in deciding just who and what is honourable in republican Rome. This goes a good way to explaining why the play's versions of Roman republican honour and virtue are so performative, indeed theatrical.

For, as Miles puts it, how else 'can honour be defined except as that which others regard as honourable?' However intrinsic its relations with virtue, and however much one might regard virtue as its own reward, honour is an intensely social thing, an attribute entirely within the power of one's peers and, in a republic like Rome, even of the people, to either confer or deny. And because of that it has continually to be performed before a variety of audiences, for it was only through the response of such audiences that the honour-bearing subject could come to know whether or not he had achieved, or indeed still possessed, honour.

Moreover, one of the central characteristics of Stoic virtue was the great premium it placed on the public performance of 'constancy' in the face of life's vicissitudes and of death. To quote Miles again; 'the stoic must "retayne one and the same countenance [faciem]"; he is told to "maintaine thyself such, as thou hast resolved to shew [praestare] thy self". He is a performer who, like a wounded gladiator, must keep a poker face and refuse to acknowledge pain or emotion.' Such constancy is a virtue central to the concept of honour being depicted in the play and Caesar, Cassius and Brutus all remain committed to the maintenance (and, of course, to the performance) of constancy, even to the point of suicide.[1]

What the play shows us again and again is the honourable man's highly self-conscious relationship, to, on the one hand, his own performance of his true self and, on the other, to the response to that performance of his audience. This result is the propensity to refer to themselves in the third person, termed by

John Velz 'illeism'.[2] This reaches its apogee in Caesar but is, in fact, adopted by several of the major characters in the play. As Miles explains it, 'names such as "Brutus" and "Caesar" become the labels of a *persona*, a publicly defined role, which the bearer of the name must play . . . Its effect is to suggest the speaker looking at himself or herself from the outside', accommodating his or her behaviour to the anticipated response of the audience and thus always framing the performance of virtue and honour to the expectations of the audience'.[3] This is an aspect of stoic constancy and republican virtue upon which the play harps insistently, one of its 'recurring images' being 'the theatre, where characters' performances are judged by an audience'.[4] The result is a tense, not to say potentially unstable, relationship between the pretensions of the Roman political actor to an immoveable constancy, a characteristic often defined, as Miles points out, in opposition to what were presented as the fickle and inherently irrational dictates of 'opinion', and the need constantly to perform before an audience, in order to find one's honour, and indeed one's constancy, confirmed and instantiated in their reactions to the performance.[5] This is precisely how and why Brutus expects to be able to constrain the behaviour of Antony after the murder of Caesar by publicly welcoming him back, before both his peers and the people, into the honour-bearing community of true Romanness.

Thus, during Cassius' extended 'seduction' of Brutus, Cassius explains to Brutus that he much regrets that Brutus cannot see himself as others see him, because, if he could, he would realise both the extent of his own virtue and honour and, with Rome 'groaning under this age's yoke', what the possession of such qualities meant or rather ought to mean, for a man of true virtue like himself. 'Since', as he tells him, 'you know you cannot see yourself/So well as by reflection', Cassius offers to play the role of his 'glass' and thus 'modestly [to] discover/That of yourself which you yet know not of' [I, ii, 56–70].

In other words, Cassius is claiming to Brutus that if he really is as honourable as they both take him to be, he ought to act according to the expectations of his most honourable admirers – and that meant joining the conspiracy to assassinate Caesar. Pre-empted by Brutus, who knows only too well what Cassius is getting at – 'into what dangers would you lead me, Cassius?' [I, ii, 63] – Cassius makes no move to close the deal in this exchange. But he continues to pursue the same basic strategy, as he bombards Brutus with entirely fabricated letters from the people imploring him to come to the aid of his country in the hour of its direst need. This proves decisive; Brutus accepts 'the great opinion/That Rome holds of his name' (I, ii, 318–19] and comes to be governed, as Cassius had claimed, as a truly honourable Roman, he should be, by 'that opinion of yourself/Which every noble Roman bears of you.' [II, i, 92–93].[6]

Here, we might think, is the tail wagging the dog, 'opinion' determining the content of virtue and honour and leading Brutus to his doom. Put another way, and cast in terms provided by the late Elizabethan political scene, here is a searing insight into the internal dynamics of the politics of popularity, as even Brutus, the most honourable and virtuous of men, is shown to be susceptible to the corrupting influence of his public, or rather, in this case, to the corrupting influence of what one of his intimates, intent on bending him to his own (malign?) purposes, can induce him to believe that his public wants. Again, in 1599, this is an insight not entirely irrelevant to the career and current condition of the earl of Essex, whose persona, actions and fate were the subject of perfervid popular speculation and whose pursuit of honour and performance of virtue were intensely theatrical.

The politics of honour and the people

Precisely because the Rome of the play is a republic, the honour politics that we have been describing here could not be played out solely before an aristocratic audience. On the contrary, in Rome the achievement of honour, its public performance, recognition and reward, was a function not merely of aristocratic but also of popular approval and acclaim; that was why Cassius sought to manipulate Brutus not merely through expressions of the good opinion of his peers (and fellow conspirators) but also through the fabricated petitions and appeals of the people; entirely spurious messages which Brutus, by this point an increasingly willing dupe, hypostatised as messages sent to him from 'Rome' herself. As ever, there is more at stake here than the moral foibles, the vices or virtues, of any one character, in this case the 'vanity' or 'pride' of Brutus and the Machiavellian cunning of Cassius. Rather we are watching the exigencies of an entire political system, of Roman republican ideology and the politics of popularity, being played out before us. Because of the sort of republic it was, in Rome the politics of popularity was an absolute necessity; a basic feature of the functioning of the polity, it was a game everyone had to be able to play and the play acknowledges, indeed it emphasises, that fact in a number of crucial scenes.

Not, of course, that the play takes anything like a benign or sanguine view of the political or moral capacities of the people or of their role in the polity. After all, in the opening scene Flavius and Murellus provide a running commentary on the conduct of the populace as they rush to applaud the return of Caesar, come home in triumph after his final victory over Pompey's sons. What reason, they ask, have the people thus to celebrate Caesar's 'triumph over Pompey's blood', since Pompey is a man whose triumphs, 'many a time and oft', the people had rushed from their houses to celebrate in exactly the same way that today they were celebrating his death and defeat at the hands of another Roman. According to the two tribunes such ingratitude renders the people worse than 'blocks' or 'stones' or other 'senseless things', and they order them 'home to your houses' there 'upon your knees', to 'Pray to the gods to intermit the plague/That needs must light on this ingratitude' [I, i, 33–56].

But however base the people's nature, and however fickle their favour, precisely because Rome is a republic, it is essential for any man of honour and virtue to win their approval, if he is to enjoy the rewards of moral attributes and political achievements the true nature of which the people can never properly understand or appreciate. Moreover, the Rome in which the action of the play takes place is not merely a republic, with a popular element central to its workings, it is a state in the throes of political change, and anyone hoping to shape and benefit from that change had better be able to win the support of the people. For this very reason the past masters of the arts of popular politics are shown not to be the group most anxious to preserve republican rule, but rather those who want to alter the Roman state from a republic to a monarchy and, in so doing, enhance their own honour and power. Here the central figures are, of course, first Caesar, and then Mark Antony.

To start with Caesar, he is presented as seeking to achieve his ambition to become a king through an elaborate series of exchanges with the people. The scene with which the play opens establishes that from the outset. As Flavius explains, 'let no images/Be hung with Caesar's trophies. I'll about,/And drive away the vulgar from the streets./So do you too, where you perceive them thick./ These growing feathers plucked from Caesar's wing/Will make him fly an ordinary pitch,/Who else would soar above the view of men,/And keep us all in servile fearfulness' [I, i, 69–76]. The seriousness of the issues at stake here explains the fate suffered by Murellus and Flavius who, Casca later tells Cassius and Brutus, 'for pulling scarves off Caesar's images, are put to silence' [I, ii, 284–85].

This information is imparted towards the end of Casca's account of an elaborate acting out before the people of the issue of whether Caesar should be crowned king of Rome or not. Casca describes the whole exchange as a carefully contrived piece of play-acting, with Caesar currying favour with the people and testing the waters of popular opinion on the subject of the monarchy. Three times, Casca explains, Antony had offered Caesar a crown and three times he had turned it down. Each occasion had been greeted with howls of approval from the mob. Hearing the cheers from afar, Brutus had each time taken them to be a sign that new honours, perhaps even the crown itself, were being heaped upon Caesar by the people [I, ii, 79–80, 131–33]. But, in fact, as Casca subsequently informs them, the people had been cheering Caesar's refusal of the crown [I, ii, 242–49], which response had caused Caesar hastily to modify his performance. Perceiving 'the common herd was glad he refused the crown, he plucked me ope his doublet and offered them his throat to cut. An had I been a man of any occupation, if I would not have taken him at a word, I would I might go to hell among the rogues.' At this point in the proceedings Caesar, who, Brutus explains, 'hath the falling sickness', 'fell down in the market place, and foamed at the mouth, and was speechless'. Coming to, he continued the performance, saying to the crowd that 'if he had done or said anything amiss, he desired their worships to think it was his infirmity. Three or four wenches where I stood cried, "alas, good soul", and forgave him with all their hearts. But there's no heed to be taken of them: if Caesar had stabbed their mothers, they would have done no less' [I, ii, 262–74].

We have here, through the bitter commentary of Casca – 'what a blunt fellow he is grown to be' is Brutus' comment on this cameo performance as a political reporter – a vision of Roman politics as popular political theatre. Caesar is described playing to the crowd just as an actor in the theatre would, carefully calculating his performance to appeal to the sympathies of his audience. His is a quintessentially monarchical mode of political communication, in which Caesar does not present the people with anything like a case that he should be made king, still less with a formal account of the need for political change or of the superiority of monarchy over republicanism. Rather he enacts the offer of the crown, proffered to him by Antony before, and in terms of his personal relation with, the people.

Throughout his account of this 'foolery' [I, ii, 286] Casca's contempt for Caesar, the player, is matched only by his disdain for the watching 'rabblement', 'men of occupation' and 'wenches', with their 'stinking breath', 'sweaty nightcaps' and entirely credulous reactions to the crude performance being put on for their benefit by the most powerful man in Rome, the all but divine Caesar. To men of true honour and judgement, to Casca or indeed to Cicero, who is reported commenting snidely on these proceedings in Greek to the considerable amusement of the more discerning souls within earshot, all this might appear ridiculous enough. But it is, in fact, deadly serious; at stake in the relations between Caesar and his popular audience is the very future form of the Roman state. This ensures that while the likes of Casca, Brutus, Cassius and Cicero view the crude theatricality of popular politics with a properly republican and patrician amusement and contempt, they cannot avoid playing the game themselves.

Indeed, the need to do so shapes the nature, composition and outcome of the conspiracy itself. The fatal decision to recruit Brutus is taken only because of the effect his involvement will have on the people. The plan to kill Caesar, the whys and the wherefores of it, has already been worked out. The conspirators' plans are coming to fruition and they are approaching the point of action, and all this without Brutus [I, iii, 121–26].They need Brutus to join them not for his counsel or cunning, but solely because 'he sits high in all the people's hearts:/And that which would appear offence in us/His countenance, like richest alchemy,/Will change to virtue and to worthiness' [I, iii, 157–60]. Later, another of the conspirators suggests recruiting Cicero on precisely the same grounds [II, i, 143–48].

In this polity, then, 'popularity' was a game that everyone had to play, and the reputation for and performance of honour and constancy of mind before the people were crucial means of building support and gaining power. Anxious to get Brutus on board for precisely these reasons, Cassius reveals himself to be a past master in the arts of popular politics. He does so in this case not by appealing directly to the people themselves, but by simulating the effects of popular feeling and support as part of his attempts to induce Brutus to join the conspiracy. 'I will this night/In several hands in at his windows throw,/As if they came from several citizens,/Writings all tending to the great opinion/That Rome holds of his name – wherein obscurely/Caesar's ambition shall be glanced at' [I, ii, 314–19]. To this end he dispatches Cinna to plant a 'paper' 'in the praetor's chair/Where Brutus may but find it. And throw this/In at his window. Set this up with wax/Upon old Brutus' statue' [I, iii, 142–46]. What Cassius is doing here is planting fake popular libels, supposed messages from the people to Brutus, to prompt him to take up the cause of popular liberty, by saving Rome from the 'ambition' of Caesar.

Later, as he wallows in paroxysms of doubt about what to do about Caesar, we are shown Brutus being given such a letter, found in the window by his servant. Opening it, he finds himself being urged ' "to awake and see thyself./ Shall Rome, et cetera. Speak, strike redress."/"Brutus, thou sleep'st, awake."/ Such instigations have been often dropped/Where I have took them up,' Brutus observes. We are seeing here the other side of Cassius' ruse and get to watch Brutus duly receive and process the precise message that Cassius had intended to send, taking the missives to be autonomous expressions of the popular will, messages from 'Rome' to 'Brutus', urging him to emulate his famous ancestor and save the state from the tyranny of Caesar's projected kingship [II, i, 35–58]. Insofar as these missives confirm Brutus in his belief that the people essentially share his own view of the republic, they will have a fatal effect on the fortunes of the conspiracy.

For just what is at stake here is revealed when the fatal moment arrives, Caesar has been killed, and the success or failure of the conspiracy now depends on the conspirators' capacity to rally the people and keep control of the city. For having been manipulated by Cassius into the belief that the people share his own view of the matter, at the hour of his (and the republic's) greatest political need, Brutus makes his pitch for popular support on what he erroneously believes to be a shared set of quintessentially republican beliefs and assumptions. He does so through entirely traditional 'republican' means, in his speech to the people from the public pulpit. Unlike Caesar, Brutus does make a case to the people, a case which, starting out personal ends up being cast in the highly abstract terms of republican theory.

As we might have come to expect, Brutus starts with his own 'honour'. 'Believe me for mine honour, and have respect to mine honour, that you may believe. Censure me in your wisdom and awake your sense, that you may the better judge.' From there he moves, again predictably enough, to the distinction between public and private interests and goods. No man, he claims, loved Caesar more than he. Why then did he raise his hand against Caesar? The answer is obvious: because 'I loved Caesar less and Rome more'. From the stark distinction between the public and the private, between one's allegiance to private interests and men and to the general or public good, Brutus then moves to the other binary opposition at the heart of republican honour, that between 'bondage' and 'freedom'. The argument of the speech at this point is thus based on two premises absolutely central to Brutus' view of what the republic was and, as he thinks, still is. The first is that Caesar's 'ambition' was such that he would indeed have made himself king, and the second that his elevation to the monarchy would have reduced the Romans from the condition of free citizens to that of slaves. That is what the subjection to one man's will means and that is why Caesar's ambition was so capital an offence. We have already watched Brutus in private debate with himself reach this conclusion. His tortured attempts, alone in the orchard, to persuade himself that Caesar was a bad man who deserved to die having failed so comprehensively, he was left with this – to any genuine republican– formally compelling, but also chillingly theoretical, argument as his only rationale for the assassination. This was why there had been only one choice before the conspirators and why the people were now to be faced with exactly the same choice: either, by endorsing the assassination and its consequences, to remain free Romans, or to become 'willing bondmen'.

And so Brutus now puts before the people the same analysis of the situation that he had reached alone in the orchard. 'Had you rather Caesar were living, and die all slaves, than that Caesar were dead, to live all freemen?' If that is indeed the issue then there is only one side for any true Roman to be on. 'Who is here so base, that would be a bondman? If any, speak, for him have I offended. Who is here so rude, that would not be a Roman? If any, speak, for him have I offended. Who is here so vile, that will not love his country? If any, speak, for him have I offended.'

As an honourable man, Brutus seeks to vindicate his own honour in giving Caesar his due. 'As Caesar loved me, I weep for him; as he was fortunate, I rejoice at it; as he was valiant, I honour him; but as he was ambitious, I slew him.' With that, Brutus throws himself on the mercy of his countrymen. 'I have done no more to Caesar, than you shall do to Brutus. The question of his death is enrolled in the Capitol: his glory not extenuated, wherein he was worthy, nor his offences enforced, for which he suffered death' [III, ii, 14–40].[7] Brutus is here being entirely consistent with his previously stated beliefs, commitments and conduct. In particular, in refusing to vilify Caesar from the public pulpit, he is remaining true to his own earlier conclusions about Caesar's character. While pulling out all the rhetorical stops, even with the stakes this high, and the future of Rome (not to mention of the conspirators themselves) in the balance, Brutus is displaying a remarkable emotional and intellectual constancy.

For all its calculated attempts to appeal to the people's emotions as well as to their 'reason', Brutus' argument is not framed in cravenly populist, but in austerely republican, terms. Rather than appeal to the people's private interests, Brutus appeals to them as his 'countrymen', as 'Romans' and free men, as lovers of 'liberty' and enemies to 'bondage'. On this view, therefore, there is nothing 'shallow' – the epithet is Chernaik's – about 'Brutus' appeal to shared republican sentiments'.[8] Rather he is treating the people as full participants in the republican honour system and as bearers of republican virtue. Given the contempt shown by other of the conspirators and their allies towards the populace, this represents a remarkably sanguine view of the people's moral and political capacities, one based in part on Brutus' (erroneous, Cassius-induced) belief that in killing Caesar he was responding to the will of the people.

And, of course, in the very short term, the speech works.[9] The people hail Brutus as a hero; 'bring him with triumph home unto his house'. 'Give him a statue with his ancestors.' 'We'll bring him to his house with shouts and clamours.' 'Caesar's better parts/Shall be crowned in Brutus.' And, rather missing the point, perhaps, 'Let him be Caesar' [III, ii, 49–53]. But once Brutus is replaced in the pulpit by Antony, it appears almost immediately that the republicanism of the people is as paper-thin as that last remark seems to imply. As Velz points out, while the speech 'forms the hearers into a Brutan political party',[10] that party is constituted by the immediate emotional effects of Brutus' oratory upon his audience and by their consequent admiration for Brutus as the 'honourable man' he has presented himself as being, rather than upon any deep understanding of, or commitment to, the republican principles upon which Brutus himself takes his claims to honour to depend. However great the initial impact of his speech, Brutus and his audience thus remain at fundamentally cross-purposes. As Sigurd Burckhardt puts it, while Brutus thinks he is directing his speech to 'an audience of noble, sturdy republicans, capable of moral discrimination and public spirit', 'the actual audience is very different: eager to be led, easily tricked, crude in their responses. The people insist on having their good guy and their bad guy: they are perfectly happy to accept Brutus as their good guy, provided he lets them have Caesar for their bad guy',[11] but this Brutus will not do. Indeed, we can go further and say that, given his vision of himself as an honourable man of constant mind, and given the view of Caesar as a Roman of the highest virtue, to which this self-image has committed him, this is something that he simply cannot do.

Provoked to a pitch of political passion, with all sorts of emotions stirred in them both by events and by Brutus' rhetoric, the people remain fatally susceptible to other, equally emotional but less austerely republican, appeals not only to their affections but also to their interests. And that is precisely what Antony proceeds to give them. His speech to the people is full of emotionalism and pathos, dwelling on the sight of Caesar's bleeding corpse, recalling Caesar's past benefits to Rome and her people [III, ii, 89–92], and hinting, through a series of references to his will, at greater benefits to come. He recalls, too, the people's recent love for Caesar. 'You all did love him once, not without cause:/What cause withholds you then to mourn for him?' [III, ii, 103–4]. As for the will, if he should read it, its generosity to the people would lead them to 'go and kiss dead Caesar's wounds,/And dip their napkins in his sacred blood,/Yea, beg a hair of him for memory,/And, dying, mention it within their wills,/Bequeathing it as a rich legacy/Unto their issue' [III, ii, 133–38].

This, of course, is to make a martyr of Caesar. His dead body is being described here in precisely the terms in which Catholics described and treated the bodies of their executed fellows. But, if Caesar is a martyr, what does that make the men who have killed him? Putting off, for the moment, the issue of the will, that is the question to which Antony turns, taking the people on a guided tour of the wounds in Caesar's body and ascribing each one in turn to a different conspirator [III, ii, 172–84]. His final flourish reveals what he takes to be the real political and moral condition of contemporary Rome, and there is precious little republican about it. 'O what a fall was there, my countrymen!/ Then I, and you, and all of us fell down,/Whilst bloody treason flourished over us' [III, ii, 188–90]. Caesar is now not only a martyr and a saint, but in his death the whole body of the state has been wounded; his murder is no longer a pernicious act undertaken against an individual, but an act of 'treason' against the state. Having stirred the people to the point of 'mutiny', Antony returns at the end to the will, and to the bequests contained therein to the people; seventy-five drachmas to every citizen; his walks, gardens and orchards 'on this side Tiber' left in perpetuity to the people [III, ii, 233–42].

There is, of course, nothing remotely 'republican' about this speech. Brutus had called on the people to act as judges, using their reason ('censure me in your wisdom') to decide the rights and wrongs of the case, and submitting himself to punishment at their hands, if the verdict should go against him. By contrast, Antony's presence in his own speech and relation to his audience is much less direct; indeed it is almost entirely duplicitous. He never comes clean about his intentions, or about his own role in events, or about the relationship he is trying to establish with his audience. All the central claims of his speech are not only false, they are self-conscious lies, or rather, as Gayle Greene somewhat decorously puts it, exercises 'in paralipsis, a mode of irony which works by disclaiming the very things the speaker wishes to emphasise'.[12] He comes 'to bury Caesar, not to praise him'. He has no intention of turning the people against Brutus and Cassius, who are 'honourable men'. He will not read the will [III, ii, 75, 122–26, 130–32]. Above all, in a speech dripping with rhetorical artifice, he claims that 'I am no orator, as Brutus is,/But, as you know me all, a plain blunt man/That love my friend, and that they know full well/That gave me public leave to speak of him./For I have neither wit, nor words, nor worth,/Action, nor utterance, nor the power of speech/To stir men's blood. I only speak right on:/I tell you that which you yourselves do know,/Show you sweet Caesar's wounds, poor dumb mouths/And bid them speak for me' [III, ii, 210–18].

Accomplished rhetoricians, both Brutus and Antony sought to excite and exploit the emotions of the people. It was just that, while the emotional ties to which Brutus appealed were centred upon both his and the people's dedication to Rome, and were thus inherently public, the emotional connections from which Antony's speech drew much of its affective force – ties of friendship, of benefit and gratitude, of mutual dependence and patronage – were, in the 'republican' terms set up by the play, quintessentially 'private'; that is to say, unmediated by any consideration of the general or public good, or of the freedom of the state. Antony was thus free, as Greene puts it, to 'appeal to a whole range of feelings, from grief for the loss of a leader and friend, desire to honour the dead, to curiosity, greed, fury and revenge'.[13] At the centre of the speech is Caesar's goodness to the people and their love for him, often expressed in crass material terms. Caesar has brought home captives to Rome, swelled the general coffers, been good to the poor and left vast sums of money and property to the people in his will. As for Brutus, he cannot be an honourable man because he has treacherously killed his friend. Antony, on the other hand, is honourable because he expresses almost unutterable grief for his fallen mentor and benefactor.

Just as in many a murder pamphlet and play, where the corpse of the victim was believed to bleed afresh in the presence of the murderer, so here Antony speaks through Caesar's wounds to the people. In so doing he at times gets close to something we might recognise as the language of sacred kingship, in effect equating Caesar's body with the social or political body of Rome itself, and conferring something like sanctity and power on his corpse by deploying the discourse of martyrdom. Antony is shown, in effect, performing a counter-ritual to that performed by the conspirators in their heavily stylised murder of Caesar. Their ritual had been designed to present themselves not as revengers or malcontents, moved by private anger or resentment, but rather, as Brutus puts it, as 'purgers' of the body politic, intent on sacrificing Caesar to Rome, and in that act distinguishing definitively between the two and thus restoring liberty to the Roman state and people. Antony's counter-ritual, extemporised in the forum, works to sacralise Caesar's body, indeed to all but identify it with Rome herself, and, in making Caesar a martyr for Rome, to type his killers not as the selfless servants of their country, the honourable men moved, more in sorrow than in anger, to save the state from Caesar's 'ambition', pictured in Brutus' speech, but rather as conspirators, motivated entirely by private grievances and ambitions, and as such enemies to both the Roman state and the people; in short, to cast them not merely as murderers but as 'traitors'.

In making these claims, Antony signals that, whether Caesar has been crowned or not, Rome has already ceased to be a republic and become something else. Or rather, the people's response to Antony's speech establishes that fact. From hailing Brutus as a hero, and damning Caesar as a 'tyrant', the people rapidly come to the conclusion, first, that, since, as Antony reminds them, he had turned down the crown three times, Caesar could not have been 'ambitious' after all, and second that 'there's not a nobler man in Rome than Antony'. By the end they are denouncing Caesar's killers as 'traitors', 'villains, murderers' and baying for 'Revenge! About! Seek! Burn! Fire! Kill! Slay!' [III, ii, 69, 113–14, 117, 154, 156, 199–200].

The picture conjured here of the fickleness and credulity of the people, their support easily bought and their emotions played upon, picks up and confirms the impressions made by the opening scenes of the play. The case against the people is clinched, of course, in the famous scene in Act III when, meeting a man called Cinna, the mob takes him to be Cinna the conspirator only to be told that he is, in fact, Cinna the poet and then kill him anyway [III, iii, 30–38]. We are back here to the world of the Cade scenes in 2 Henry VI, with a mob of mechanicals, rude artisans, the dregs of the people, unleashed upon the world, bent on destruction for destruction's sake and all at the behest of a demagogue – in this instance Antony – bent, as he says himself, on entirely private purposes.

For Antony is unleashing the fury of the people in order to let loose what he terms 'mischief' upon the world. 'Now let it work. Mischief, thou art afoot:/Take what course thou wilt' [III, ii, 251]. The spread of 'mischief' – by which he means violence and mob rule – in turn opens up the world to the destabilising effects of fortune, at her most capricious and inversionary. 'Fortune is merry/And in this mood will give us anything' [III, ii, 256–57]. With all the structures and constraints of normal moral and political life now in suspension, Antony can impose his will on events. He is bent first on revenge, a revenge to be wreaked not only on Caesar's murderers but on the entire Roman world. Speaking alone over Caesar's corpse, in a mixture of 'curse' and 'prophecy', Antony pronounces that 'domestic fury and fierce civil strife/Shall cumber all the parts of Italy'. 'Mothers shall but smile when they behold/Their infants quartered with the hands of war:/All pity choked with custom of fell deeds,/And Caesar's spirit, ranging for revenge,/With Até by his side come hot from hell,/Shall in these confines, with a monarch's voice,/Cry havoc and let slip the dogs of war,/That this foul deed shall smell above the earth/With carrion men, groaning for burial' [III, i, 258–75].

Even if (initially) Antony's sole purpose in unleashing the 'mischief' and 'mutiny' of the people was mere revenge, later chilling exchanges (first with Lepidus and Octavius, and then alone with Octavius demonstrate that his subsequent intentions have come to transcend that initial, entirely atavistic urge. [IV, i, 1–40]. Now, for Antony, the aim is personal power or dominance, the three- or rather two-fold division of the world, an outcome to be achieved through the ruthless deployment of violence and deceit. We are as far here as it is possible to get from the world of republican virtue, honour and true nobility. What had started as a struggle over the nature, future and freedom of the Roman state, has now become a barefaced pursuit of total dominance to be achieved through any and every available means.

If we return to the disagreement between Cassius and Brutus about whether republican freedom had been extinguished by the dominance achieved by Caesar, even without the formal title of king, or was only going to be so extinguished by Caesar's coronation, the events that follow the assassination show that Cassius had been right. The complete failure of Brutus' essentially republican appeal to his 'countrymen', coupled with the personalised, pseudo-monarchical terms of Antony's all too successful pitch for the favour of a venal and credulous people, show just how far gone the republic is, even without the formal elevation of Caesar to the role of king. On this account, the politics of republican honour, at least as Brutus understood and practised it, is just no longer compatible with the politics of popularity as perfected and practised by Caesar and Antony. The realities of late Roman republican politics can no longer be contained within or effectively interpreted by the austerely republican categories and assumptions through which Brutus views both the world and himself and in terms of which he seeks to control events. If, as Schanzer has argued, the play can indeed be interpreted as a tragedy about Brutus, Brutus' tragedy is that of a man out of his time and therefore out of his element; someone unable to impose himself on events through the use of conventional, indeed cherished, categories and practices that no longer answer to the political realities of the age.[14]

For the play shows Brutus to have been operating throughout on the assumption that the removal of Caesar will restore the workings of republican government. It was only this relative optimism that rendered the murder of Caesar a rational act, for the whole scheme (certainly as Brutus conceived it and as the conspirators actually carried it out) turned on the assumption that, with Caesar removed, the republican honour system would immediately snap back into something like full working order. But that could only happen if there were massive latent reserves of the right republican stuff still to be found within the Roman body politic.

After all, it was one of the necessary operating assumptions of the entire republican system that the people, even if not capable of it themselves, could and would both recognise and embrace true Roman virtue when they saw it. Brutus clearly expects them to apprehend, appreciate and endorse the 'honour' of both himself and his act at the very moment that he displays it to them. If the republic, for which he has risked all, is to be saved, this is how the people *must* react. If they do not, all is lost, not only in the superficial political sense that, if Brutus fails to convince the people, the republican faction will have suffered a very severe setback, but in the far deeper sense that, in the absence of the capacity in the people to recognise and respond to republican virtue, the republic itself can no longer survive, indeed has already ceased to exist. Thus I think Schanzer is simply wrong when he claims that 'nor are we made to feel anywhere ... that the Roman Republic has sunk into a state of disorder and corruption which only the establishment of one's rule can cure'. Not only are we shown precisely that, but we are also shown that the efforts of the conspirators to arrest these linked processes of political change and moral decline have merely made matters worse.[15]

The Rome in which the action of the play is set is a republic, but it is a republic in its death throes, at the very least a state experiencing the dangerous and destabilising effects of political change. In playing on the people so skilfully and carefully over the issue of the kingship, Caesar had been seeking to negotiate his way through that moment of transition. Testing the state of popular opinion at every stage, he had been cautiously taking two steps forward and one step back, on the road towards monarchical power. The conspirators' decision to disrupt that process by killing Caesar collapses the death throes of the republic into a single climactic moment of breakdown and crisis; a moment in which everything, not merely power within the state, but the very nature of the state itself, is up for grabs. In that situation the capacity to appeal to and mobilise the people becomes absolutely critical and accordingly the structural and moral tensions and contradictions between the politics of honour and the politics of popularity are now ramped up to breaking-point. For in the ensuing popularity stakes someone as committed to, and therefore as hampered by, the moral constraints of the old republican honour system as Brutus undoubtedly is, is placed at a massive disadvantage. Alternatively, anyone (like Antony) prepared to pull out all the rhetorical stops, to do and say whatever it takes to win the people over to his side, is likely to carry the day.

As Brutus and Cassius are chased by the enraged mob from the city – 'rid like madmen through the gates of Rome' [III, ii, 259], as Antony is told – their flight signals not only the complete incompatibility of the politics of popularity with the politics of republican honour, but also the complete victory of the former over the latter. In Antony's terms, 'mischief' has indeed been loosed upon the world, 'fortune' is predominant in the affairs of men, and therefore control over events can be seised by those – like Antony – of the right temper of mind and ambition.

CHAPTER 21

The politics of popularity and faction (in a popular state)

But the play is about more than the incompatibility of the politics of honour and of popularity. It also reveals the incompatibility of honour with the political process *per se*, when, that is, that process is conceived and evaluated instrumentally, as the pursuit of personal and factional advantage and power. For, however great their personal claims to honour and virtue, the means deployed by all the major characters in the pursuit of their immediate political ends are shown to be incompatible with the demands of honour and virtue, as those same characters themselves define, espouse and at least claim to personify them.

The most obvious case of this is, of course, Caesar himself. Throughout, Caesar's own political practice and behaviour, indeed, his physical condition, the health of the very body upon whose sacral qualities and equivalence with Rome itself Antony insists after Caesar's death, are shown to be at radical variance with his self-proclaimed constancy, justice and virtue. While Caesar proclaims himself as constant as the North Star, the play presents him as a ageing man, deaf in one ear [I, ii, 211–13], subject to fits and seizures. The echoes of another ageing ruler utterly committed – as her motto *Semper eadem* proclaims – to a vision of her own constancy, are readily apparent.

The contrast between his self-image and the realities of his emotional and physical condition, shows most clearly in the exchange with Antony in which he famously marks out the 'lean and hungry' Cassius as 'dangerous'. Caesar then immediately adds that 'I fear him not . . . I rather tell thee what is to be feared/Than what I fear: for always I am Caesar./Come take my right hand, for this ear is deaf,/And tell me truly what thou think'st of him' [I, ii, 197–213]. Here is Caesar making political calculations, noting potential sources of political threat, plotting away with his intimates, while all the while trumpeting his freedom from fear and utter constancy in the face of danger and fate.

We see a similar inconstancy in the elaborate tergiversations, the game-playing to and fro between Caesar and his popular audience, over the issue of the kingship. Where Caesar presents himself as the epitome of Roman constancy and stoic virtue, his enemies at least see his relations with the people as political theatre, his antics those of a popular actor willing to do almost anything to gain the favour of the crowd [I, ii, 234–74]. Admittedly, we only hear of these events through Casca, whose account, studded with parenthetical asides ('to my thinking') [I, ii, 238, 240] leaves us in no doubt that it is anything but 'fair and balanced'.

But we do get to see for ourselves Caesar's vacillations on the day of his death, as he havers about whether to attend the Senate or not. At stake is the prodigious storm that has raged the previous night, glossed by a dream of his wife, Calphurnia, who 'thrice . . . in her sleep cried out,/ "Help ho: they murder Caesar" ' [II, i, 335–36]. Caesar's response is to seek the advice of the augurers. But asked if he intends to 'walk forth', Caesar first says that he does, making in the process a series of pronouncements about his constancy in the face of fate and death and indifference to prodigies. At this point he is told that the results of the augurers' researches are less than optimistic. This, too, Caesar glosses as a test, sent by the gods to try his courage, and responds with another account of 'Caesar's' imperviousness to fear and danger. But when Calphurnia renews her request that Caesar not go forth today, he accedes, telling Antony to inform the Senate that 'I am not well,/And for thy humour I will stay at home' [II, ii, 55–56]. At this point Decius, one of the conspirators, comes in 'to fetch you to the Senate House' and Caesar tells him that he is not going, but changes his mind as to the reason. 'Tell them that I will not come today./Cannot is false; and that I dare not, falser./I will not come today.' Calphurnia insists that Decius say 'he is sick' and Caesar responds with the imperious question, 'shall Caesar send a lie? . . . go tell them Caesar will not come' [II, ii, 64–68].

What we have been shown here is anything but a display of constancy. On the contrary, the scene shows us that Caesar has indeed, as Cassius claims, 'superstitious grown of late', and that, while performing his own stoic indifference and imperviousness to danger and fate, is in fact very carefully calculating the odds. His choice not to go is first blamed on his wife – 'for thy humour I will stay at home' [II, ii, 56] – and then covered up as an exercise of mere will. For Caesar's imperious refusal to 'send a lie' serves, in fact, to do precisely that, in that it covers up the truth of the matter which is either that Caesar will not go because he is afraid, alarmed by the last night's prodigies and his wife's dream, or that he is refusing to go out today merely to allay his wife's fears. That certainly is what he tells Decius when, for his 'private satisfaction' – for public purposes 'the cause is in my will' – he explains that 'Calphurnia here, my wife, stays me at home./She dreamt tonight she saw my statue,/Which, like a fountain with an hundred spouts,/Did run pure blood; and many lusty Romans/ Came smiling and did bathe their hands in it./And these she does apply for warnings and portents/And evils imminent, and on her knee/Hath begged that I will stay at home today' [II, ii, 75–82]. Decius replies to this, neither with a dismissal of such auguries and portents as mere superstitions, nor with an appeal to Caesar's constancy of mind, but simply with a different interpretation of the dream as a good rather than as an evil portent [II, ii, 83–90]. But the clincher Decius saves for last. 'The Senate have concluded/To give this day a crown to mighty Caesar./If you shall send them word you will not come,/Their minds may change' [II, ii, 93–96]. In other words, Caesar is about to be given what all his recent political manoeuvrings and posings before the people have been designed to obtain, and a refusal to go to the Senate might put that at risk. Besides, Decius adds, if you do not come it will look bad, people will talk and your carefully constructed reputation for stoic virtue and Roman constancy will suffer [II, ii, 96–101].

What we are being shown in this scene in effect confirms the view of Caesar's character and actions given by Casca. We have a man desperate for power, racked by fears of potential enemies and plots, and just as anxiously trying to control those fears and events by recourse to augurers and the interpretation of dreams and omens. But he is also keen to maintain both his performance of, and reputation for, a form of virtue and constancy that is increasingly at variance with his real behaviour and attitudes. The result is not constancy but vacillation. In this scene Caesar does not only change his mind twice about whether or not to go to the Senate, he cannot even remain constant about what excuse to give for his decision not to go. Moreover, his final fatal decision to go is made in order to achieve and maintain the two things he cares most about – the crown and his reputation with the people and Senate, the loss of which could, of course, prove fatal both to his present dominance and to his future plans to make himself king. There could scarcely be a better demonstration of the utter incompatibility of the politics of honour and of popularity, of the blatant contradictions between the maintenance of true nobility and Roman constancy of mind, on the one hand, and the barefaced pursuit of private interests and (monarchical) power, on the other.

Of course, the pseudo-monarchical nature of the power which Caesar is shown exercising throughout the play may be significant here. So much, certainly, is suggested in an earlier speech by Decius, who replies to Cassius' fears that Caesar might not go to the Senate today with a detailed account of how Caesar can be persuaded to do so. 'Never fear that. If he be so resolved/I can o'ersway him: for he loves to hear/That unicorns may be betrayed with trees,/And bears with glasses, elephants with holes,/Lions with toils and men with flatterers./But when I tell him he hates flatterers,/He says he does, being then most flattered./Let me work./For I can give his humour the true bent,/And I will bring him to the Capitol' [II, i, 201–10]. The scene with Caesar outlined above is, of course, a fulfilment of this prophecy; a textbook example of how a great man could be worked on by one of his creatures, his susceptibilities exploited to bring him, in this case at least, to his ruin. Such a condition might be thought to be a necessary effect of the dynamics of court life; of the isolations and dangers attendant upon all truly monarchical rule. If we take such a view of the matter, then the incompatibility of Caesar's proto-monarchical political practice with any form of republican virtue or honour is scarcely to be wondered at.

But if the dark arts of the courtier and the (evil) counsellor are most prevalent at the courts of princes, like Caesar, that does not render them a Caesarean monopoly. On the contrary, the play shows them alive and well on the conspiratorial and republican side of the equation. We have already seen Cassius working on Brutus through his orchestration of the appearance of popular pressure or support; seeking to create an impression that 'Rome' wants Brutus to take action against Caesar and save the state. In their first encounter, he had tried a more directly personal approach, by playing on Brutus' sense of himself as a bearer of honour equal to any other Roman, Caesar included.

In a soliloquy delivered at the end of the scene, Cassius describes to himself and us just what he is about [I, ii, 307–14].

The passage starts with the premise both of Brutus' nobility and of his mutability. Brutus' noble mind can be deflected from the course of action to which its nobility would otherwise dispose it by the influence of others. Hence the necessity that 'noble minds keep ever with their likes'. But it is precisely the beneficial effects of that virtuous circle of competition for honour within the republican honour community that the preponderant power of Caesar has undermined. And it is precisely by his relationship with Caesar that Cassius sees Brutus being 'seduced'; that is to say, diverted from the path of virtue that would otherwise lead him, with Cassius and the others, to take violent action against the tyranny of Caesar. Indeed, so close is Brutus to Caesar that, Cassius opines, if their places were changed, if Cassius were Brutus, and Brutus, Cassius, he (that is to say Cassius) would not 'humour' me (that is to say Brutus), and lead me into a conspiracy against my friend and benefactor, Caesar. It is to counteract this seduction of Brutus by Caesar – on the most optimistic view, to restore the natural workings, the beneficial moral effects, of a republican honour system, now fatally disrupted by Caesar's greatness and Brutus' closeness to Caesar – that Cassius determines to have recourse to his ruse of the counterfeited messages from the people, in order to recall Brutus to the path of virtue that his nobility would otherwise have led him to adopt, had he not been seduced by Caesar.

That, at least, is the orthodox, 'republican', version of what Cassius is doing here. But, as many critics have noted, both Cassius' behaviour and this speech are susceptible to an altogether different, and more sinister, reading. The course that Brutus' inherent nobility might be leading him down might well be construed as continued personal loyalty to his friend Caesar and resistance to the temptations and blandishments being offered to him by Cassius. Here the seducer in the passage becomes Cassius, not Caesar. Certainly, in the scene which this speech concludes, we see Cassius working on Brutus in exactly the same way that Decius will later work on Caesar. By appealing to his vanity, and, in the stratagem with the anonymous letters, playing up to his sense of his standing in the eyes of the people, Cassius is trying to work Brutus to his will. Depending on your view of the situation, he is either trying to recall Brutus to his own better nature and away from the seduction of Caesar, or he is calling Brutus away from the path of true nobility, in effect, seducing him through an entirely self-conscious, both corrupt and corrupting, exercise of the dark arts of the courtier and of the popular politician, to kill his great friend and patron, Caesar.

There is a great deal to be said for – and the speech will certainly sustain – both readings, and that, of course, is the point. For, however honourable or noble their purposes, in acting covertly against Caesar the putative defenders of republican virtue and liberty have been reduced to the politics of faction and conspiracy. This is the basic structural contradiction that the doubleness of Cassius' speech reveals.

If, as the complex and compressed syntax of that speech implies, this is a contradiction that even Cassius can only half acknowledge, Brutus takes it head on. At the start of the second act, as the conspirators congregate at Brutus' house, they are described to him by his servant: 'their hats are plucked about their ears/And half their faces buried in their cloaks,/That by no means I may discover them/By any mark of favour' [II, i, 73–76]. Here is the classic group of conspirators – men forced, by the dark and nefarious deeds they are plotting, to creep about disguised, even in the dark. Here is what ought to be, according to the dictates of republican honour, the most public of public business – the preservation of the general or public good and the defence of liberty from tyranny – being conducted through the most private and surreptitious of forms. Brutus acknowledges as much in the term with which he describes his new associates; 'they are the faction', and having identified them as such he goes on to address them under the sign of 'conspiracy' [II, i, 78–85].

In late sixteenth-century England the word faction was, almost always, a term of opprobrium. It signified a group or party, separated off from the main social or political body, united in the pursuit of inherently private and divisive ends or interests, almost always inimical to the public or common good. In using that word, and addressing his colleagues under the title of 'conspiracy', Brutus was adverting to a paradox, the existence of a faction for the general good, whose members, however beneficently public their purposes, still had to pursue those purposes in secret, using the entirely covert and duplicitous means of conspiracy and assassination.

Brutus is here echoing an earlier speech by Casca. When Cassius is trying to recruit Casca into the conspiracy, Casca replies 'hold, my hand./Be factious for redress of all these griefs/And I will set this foot of mine as far/As who goes farthest' [I, iii, 113–19]. The implication, of course, is that faction for the 'redress of the griefs' of the commonwealth, for the salvation of the state from 'tyranny', for the preservation of 'liberty', is no faction at all, but rather the most public and honourable of acts, the most daring of sacrifices for the common good, the most overt of displays of Roman virtue and constancy of mind in the face of tyranny and death. And yet here is Brutus enjoining the most complete secrecy, the deepest-dyed hypocrisy and pretence, in order to effect the designs of what was indeed, as his own choice of words signals, both a 'faction' and a 'conspiracy'.

Later in the scene at Brutus' house, we find Brutus trying desperately to square the moral circle that his own opening speech has delineated with such precision. Cassius suggests that the conspirators bind themselves together by swearing an oath. Brutus, however, demurs [II, i, 113–39].To swear an oath would, Brutus claims, be to enter into a private world, a world populated by 'priests' and 'cowards', 'men cautelous' and 'women', all private spirits, who needed the extra force of an oath to separate them off from the common run of their countrymen and make them keep their word. The members of this conspiracy, however, did not need such private means and agreements; for while they were indubitably members of a faction and a conspiracy, they were not acting in pursuit of private ends, but as what Cassius later calls 'true Romans' [II, i, 222], men of noble blood, active in the defence of the general good. As such they were to be taken at their word, without the aid of an oath. To swear an oath would be to imply otherwise and hence cast the 'even virtue', the 'true Romanness', the inherently public nature, of the whole enterprise into doubt. Brutus' speech is, therefore, a desperate attempt to recast the private factious means forced upon them as conspirators and assassins into the language of 'republican virtue', the public duty owed by each Roman of noble 'blood', 'valour', 'spirit' and 'insuppressive mettle' to defend the state from 'high sighted tyranny' through the active service of the common or general good.

But for all Brutus' best rhetorical efforts, the paradox of 'faction' for the public good, of the 'honourable' 'conspiracy' and 'noble' murder plot will not go away. Later in the same meeting, having just rejected Cicero as a potential member of the faction because he is unlikely to toe the line, Brutus enthusiastically embraces the idea of approaching Caius Ligarius because he 'doth bear Caesar hard,/Who rated him for speaking well of Pompey' [II, i, 214–19]. We are then shown Ligarius literally rising from a bed of sickness to follow Brutus, the 'Soul of Rome,/Brave son, derived from honourable loins' who, 'like an exorcist hast conjured up/My mortified spirit' for an 'exploit worthy the name of honour' [II, i, 320–23, 316]. All of which only goes to show the doubleness of motive that underlies the actions of nearly all the conspirators as even the virtuous Brutus has recourse to the language of personal connection and faction – 'he loves me well' and 'I will fashion him' – while Ligarius, the man with the personal grudge against Caesar, adopts the most exalted notions of honour and Romanitas to justify himself.

As the conspirators prepare to go to the Capitol and do the deed, Cassius exhorts them to 'all remember/What you have said, and show yourselves true

Romans'. On the face of it this is an injunction to the sort of moral transparency upon which the republican honour code fed, so much so that Brutus, of all people, feels compelled to add 'let not our looks put on our purposes,/But bear it as our Roman actors do,/With untired spirits and formal constancy' [II, i, 221–26]. In other words, the conspirators can show themselves 'true Romans' only by concealing their true purposes; by playing a part as any actor might do upon the public stage, where 'constancy' was merely 'formal' i.e. outward, and constancy in the actor's role meant adopting a persona entirely different from one's own for as long as the play lasted.[1] The result, as Alexander Leggatt observes, is a remarkable inversion: 'Brutus and Cassius have virtually exchanged roles; the cynical manipulator now speaks for Roman integrity, and the man who began the scene remarking sourly on the concealment that conspiracy makes necessary . . . now takes to that concealment with relish.'[2] Brutus has now become a conspirator indeed and even his own awesome commitment to Roman virtue cannot save him from the moral consequences.

It is, of course, upon the contradictions inherent in the notion of a republican conspiracy, a faction for the public good, that Mark Antony plays in his speech to the people over Caesar's corpse. For there famously he harks upon Brutus and the others' claim to be 'honourable men'. As we have seen, Antony's is a skilfully constructed piece of demagoguery, designed to play upon the emotions of what will soon become a howling mob, but its central contention, the enormous moral contradiction between what Caesar's killers claim to be, that is 'honourable men', instruments of justice and saviours of Rome and the general good, and what they have actually done, that is conspire secretly to murder brutally and treacherously a man to whom many of them owe a very great deal, is also a simple statement of fact. Indeed as Simmons has pointed out, while Brutus' speech in the market-place dealt in abstract principles, Antony's dealt in facts: the brute fact of Caesar's death; of the identity of his killers; of his great service and generosity to Rome; that he had in fact three times renounced the crown, and so could not be guilty of ambition.[3] Similarly, Antony's bitter account of the behaviour of the conspirators, delivered to their faces on the field before Philippi, is accurate enough. 'When your vile daggers/Hacked one another in the sides of Caesar./You showed your teeth like apes, and fawned like hounds,/And bowed like bondsmen, kissing Caesar's' feet;/Whilst damned Casca, like a cur, behind/Struck Caesar in the neck. O you flatterers!' [V, i, 39–44]. Here, then, are the would-be saviours of the republic, the public servants of the public good, being redescribed (accurately enough) as hypocrites, fawning flatterers and treacherous courtiers; reduced, by the nature of their own act, to the very moral status that they had killed Caesar to avoid. Antony's speeches here and in the forum then represent an essentially accurate, albeit politically motivated and intensely *parti pris*, restatement of the central moral paradox or conundrum at the heart of the very notion of a virtuous faction and an honourable conspiracy.

The conspirators are, of course, in an intensely difficult situation. Operating in a state in flux, a polity morphing from one form into another, with the location and nature of power and legitimacy fundamentally at stake and in question, they are desperate to take action to defend a version of the status quo that no longer (quite) exists. It is the structural logic of this position – the fact that, *pace* Brutus' upbeat estimation of the nature of the times, republican rule in Rome has already ceased to pertain – that forces what should be the most public and honourable of acts, the active defence of freedom and the general good, into the byways of secrecy and conspiracy.

The resulting tensions and contradictions are analysed with almost forensic intensity in and through the relationship between Brutus and Cassius. Throughout, Cassius is portrayed as the more effective politician. Brutus, on the other hand, continually makes mistakes precisely because his calculations of political advantage are fatally contaminated by his commitment to notions of honour, nobility and virtue that no longer accord with the way his contemporaries actually behave. This both constrains his own actions and impedes his capacity to judge how others will act. Famously, at a series of crucial junctures, Cassius and Brutus disagree, Brutus prevails and is proven to be disastrously wrong. Cassius wants Antony to be killed with Caesar, but, as we have seen, Brutus demurs. Later, anxious to integrate Antony into the post-Caesar establishment, and again acting against Cassius' best advice and better judgement, Brutus allows Antony to deliver Caesar's funeral oration, after the conspirators have left the scene. He also refuses to allow Cicero to be approached as a potential conspirator. Finally, at the end of the play, Cassius and Brutus disagree on military tactics. Cassius wants to let Antony and Octavius come to them, and Brutus wants to descend from the hills to meet their adversaries at Philippi. Again, Brutus prevails and, as a subsequent conversation between Octavius and Antony makes clear, he is again at fault, with the clear implication that the conspirators' final defeat is to be laid in large part at Brutus' door.

In each case, save the last, Brutus' judgement is fatally affected by what he deems to be the demands of honour and nobility, what we might term the politics of properly republican appearance, while Cassius retains a sense of the political realities of the situation, unclouded by such considerations. It is not that in any of these cases Brutus' response is in any simple sense more virtuous than Cassius'; that is to say, Brutus' preferences and choices are not framed by purely ethical considerations, a simple product of his commitment to the republican honour code. Rather each case represents Brutus' exercise of a basically political judgement, a calculation of what will happen next and of the balance of political forces. It is just that in each instance Brutus has a tendency to judge others by his own standards and expectations of himself. Not that Brutus is simply assuming that he is only dealing with honourable men. For all the elaborate persiflage of their public exchanges, Brutus had earlier made his slighting opinion of Antony – 'given/To sports, to wildness and much company' [II, i 187–88] – quite clear. The point is that, with Caesar removed, honourable or not, even the likes of Antony will feel the need to conform their outward behaviour to the dictates of republican honour. It is on this basis that Brutus makes his calculations about how others will act. As he explains of Antony, if he is really loyal and virtuous, that is to say, 'if he love Caesar', after Caesar's death 'all that he can do/Is to himself – take thought, and die for Caesar' [II, i, 185–86]. This is what Brutus, being loyal and virtuous, would do in the circumstances and any failure to act in this way is thus a sign of a fundamental lack of serious-ness and honour, a lack which will make Antony relatively easy to manipulate and co-opt. Either way, Antony does not represent much of a threat. Cassius, of course, sees in Antony 'a shrewd contriver'; someone who retained the 'means', if he used them aright, 'to annoy us all' [II, I, 156–58]. What this amounts to, on Brutus' part, is a failure to appreciate the extent of the moral and political changes undergone by the Roman polity. It goes back to the basic difference between him and Cassius over whether tyranny is already in place before Caesar achieves the kingship, or will not come into being until after that event.

Thus Brutus does not refuse to kill Antony because he thinks killing is wrong – after all, they are all going to kill Caesar – but rather because he thinks that, judged according to the notions of republican nobility, honour and virtue that have prompted, and will legitimise, the assassination, killing Antony will firstly look bad and secondly not be necessary. Again, he lets Antony deliver Caesar's funeral oration not because he is a trusting fool, but because he hopes to legitimise the coup, and broaden the support base of the emergent repub-lican regime, by including Antony, whose extremely skilful deployment of the language of republican honour he has just swallowed hook, line and sinker.

Cassius, of course, is in many ways no less committed to the ideals of repub-lican honour than Brutus, but he takes a far less sanguine view of the political and moral state of Rome. His estimation of Antony's character and likely reac-tion to Caesar's death is far more accurate than that of Brutus, and throughout the negotiations with Antony his pitch is couched in the blunt language of political advantage and disadvantage. He wants to include Cicero for the same reasons that he has included Brutus: he is a man of repute whose participation will make the conspiracy look good in the eyes of the people and he 'will stand very strong with us' [II, i, 141].

These serial failures of political judgement on Brutus' part advert again to the incompatibility of the politics of honour with the new political realities of a republic in the throes of political change; realities, of course, which Cassius understands a great deal better than Brutus. Why, then, does Brutus' view always prevail? It does so, of course, because of the thrall in which the politics of honour continues to hold all the conspirators – even, indeed perhaps espe-cially, Cassius. Brutus may well have been recruited largely for public relations purposes; because his reputation for honour and nobility will make the others look good in the eyes of the people, but, having been recruited on those grounds, those very qualities proceed to give him a fatal primacy in the counsels of the conspirators.

As Cassius introduces Brutus to the others for the first time he explains that there is 'no man here/But honours you, and every one doth wish/You had but that opinion of yourself/Which every noble Roman bears of you' [II, i, 90–93]. On the one hand, this is mere persiflage, the same sort of flattery that Cassius has been using since their first meeting to seduce Brutus into the conspiracy. On the other, it is also true, as the reactions of the other conspirators during the ensuing conversation and the subsequent course of Cassius' and Brutus' own relationship both demonstrate. Brutus' nobility, the honour he bears and that his fellow conspirators instantly recognise in him, gives him a certain moral primacy and, at moments of decision and crisis, that moral primacy makes Brutus' the decisive voice in the counsels of the conspirators – with disastrous results for them all.

Just how this works is shown best in the angry exchange between the two men in Act IV. Cassius upbraids Brutus for having 'condemned and noted Lucius Pella/For taking bribes here of the Sardians;/Wherein my letters, praying on his side/Because I knew the man, was slighted off.' To this Brutus replies that, in effect, Pella was guilty as charged and that therefore 'you wronged yourself to write in such a case'. Shifting his ground, Cassius replies that 'in such a time as this it is not meet/That every nice offence should bear his comment.' Brutus then ups the ante by claiming that such corruption is a fault from which Cassius himself is not free [IV, iii, 2–16]. For Cassius, the fact that there is a war on means that such moral niceties are really beside the point, but, for Brutus, such corruption represents a betrayal of the conspirators' whole project. 'Did not great Julius bleed for justice' sake?/What villain touched his body, that did stab/And not for justice? What, shall one of us,/That struck the foremost man of all this world/But for supporting robbers: shall we now/Contaminate our fingers with base bribes,/And sell the mighty space of our large honours/For so much trash as may be grasped thus?/I had rather be a dog and bay the moon/Than such a Roman' [IV, iii, 19–28].

This drives Cassius into a great rage. In the course of the following alterca- tion the real point at issue emerges. As Brutus explains it to Cassius, Brutus has asked Cassius for money with which to pay his troops and Cassius has refused. In response Brutus accuses him of corruption and avarice. For the first time in the play, the contrasts and tensions between Brutus and Cassius are presented as a clear-cut clash between the politically enervating virtue of Brutus and the morally corrupting political pragmatism of Cassius. For Brutus the high moral purpose that lay behind the conspiracy and assassination is indivisible from the way in which the conspirators must prosecute their cause in the political and military power struggle that their failed coup has set in motion. Viewed from the pinnacle of Brutus' virtue, the compromises with the way the world works habitually made by Cassius are unacceptable. And yet Brutus' virtue – in this case, his incapacity to 'raise money by vile means' – 'By heaven, I had rather coin my heart/And drop my blood for drachmas, than to wring/From the hard hands of peasants their vile trash/By any indirection' – means that he has been unable to pay his legions. He has left the messy business of raising revenue to Cassius, to such an extent that although he rails against his friend's corruption, he is reduced to dependence on him for the money he needs [IV, iii, 69–82]. It is only Cassius' refusal to provide him with the necessary funds – a failure that Brutus attributes to covetousness and which Cassius denies – 'he was but a fool that brought my answer back' [IV, iii, 83] – that has precipitated this showdown.

Reduced by his own 'virtue' to reliance on Cassius' 'corruption' in order to pay his troops, even as he taunts Cassius with the virtue that has reduced him to this dependence Brutus also rails against the 'corruption' that has in fact raised the money that they both desperately need to fight the war; a war, be it remembered, upon the result of which the cause of liberty and virtue entirely depends. Certainly, at this point we are being shown Brutus' addiction to his own virtue and honour at its narcissistic height. But we are also being shown the inherent incompatibility of the cult of republican honour, nobility and virtue with the successful prosecution of the desperate struggle for survival and power that the assassination of Caesar has started.

Brutus' taunts reduce Cassius to an impotent fury. At stake, of course, is Cassius' claim to true Romanitas. His standing as a virtuous, autonomous bearer of republican honour is being denied by the ultimate personification and arbiter of such matters, the ever honourable Brutus. His honour called into question in the most fundamental of ways, Cassius even claims at one point that 'when Caesar lived he durst not thus have moved me'. When Brutus persists, Cassius threatens violence. 'Do not presume too much upon my love:/I may do that I shall be sorry for' [IV, iii, 63–64]. However, with the exception of the rather weak disclaimer about his refusal of Brutus' request for funds having been mistaken, at no point does Cassius actually deny any of the major accusations against him. On the issue of Pella he merely claims that now is not the time to be quite so scrupulous over such matters. In response to the accusation about his own 'corruption' he effectively says nothing; choosing instead to stand on his honour as a 'soldier' [IV, iii, 30]. Finally he is reduced to, in effect, ceding the accuracy of Brutus' accusations, only claiming that if Brutus were his friend he would 'bear his friend's infirmities/But Brutus makes mine greater than they are' [IV, iii, 85–86]. The argument ends as Cassius, in true Roman style, wishes himself dead, baring his chest and offering Brutus his dagger [IV, iii, 94–98]. This is, in effect, to admit to the accuracy of Brutus' charges – indeed Cassius concedes that 'I that denied thee gold will give my heart' [IV, iii,

102] – and we might, on this basis, conclude that Cassius' fury reaches the pitch that it does precisely because he knows that Brutus is in the right.

At this point the two men are reconciled, but the exchange has served once more to establish that moral primacy – but not, of course, superior political insight or military skill – belongs to the virtuous Brutus. Cassius has stood on his honour, ranted and raved, but he has been stared down by Brutus – 'fret till your proud heart break./Go show your slaves how choleric you are,/And make your bondmen tremble' [IV, iii, 42–44] – and in that last exchange in effect admitted the justice and accuracy of his friend's charges.

The effect of this performance of Brutus' superior Roman virtue and stoic constancy of mind is then compounded by his almost insouciant announcement to Cassius of the death of Portia. Appalled – 'How scaped I killing when I crossed you so?/O insupportable and touching loss!', 'O ye immortal Gods' [IV, iii, 147–48, 155] – Cassius is quietly told to 'speak no more of her: give me a bowl of wine./In this I bury all unkindness, Cassius' [IV, iii, 156–57]. Brutus then gets to demonstrate the extent of his almost inhuman self-control all over again when Messala enters to tell him of events in Rome and of the death of his wife. As a number of critics have observed, there is an element of art, perhaps even of deceit, in this second display of constancy, since Brutus does not let on to Messala that he already knows that Portia is dead.[4] But this is scarcely the point; after all, Cassius knows full well that Brutus knows and he is still impressed: 'I have as much of this in art as you,/But yet my nature could not bear it so' [IV, iii, 192–93]. The point, of course, is that Cassius quite acknowledges that what he has just seen is a performance, but he takes it as a performance of real virtue, a performance of the sort that distinguishes the truly constant Roman from his contemporaries. For while he is as schooled in the dictates of Stoic philosophy as Brutus, and thus knows precisely what one is supposed to say, and how one is supposed to act, he is forced to admit that, were he in Brutus' shoes, such a consummate performance of virtue and constancy would have been quite beyond him.

The effects of all this are immediate and disastrous. For, when, later in the same scene, the two generals come to discuss where to give battle to Octavius and Antony, it is again Brutus who wins the argument, with fatal results. One of the claims that Cassius had made during his altercation with Brutus had been that he was a 'soldier' 'older in practice, abler than yourself/To make conditions' [IV, iii, 30–32]. As the play's outcome makes clear, that is indeed the case, but again Cassius gives in to Brutus over an issue of pressing (in this case, military rather than political) urgency because of both men's sense of Brutus' greater 'virtue'.

Gordon Ross Smith has discerned in such exchanges, on Brutus' part, the exercise of 'will', and on the part of his colleagues a willing subordination to that exercise. Of the fourteen occasions in the play that Smith has identified as showing the triumph of Brutus' 'will', only about half, he claims, have even 'a nominal source' in Plutarch. The rest are added by Shakespeare, as Smith believes, to show Brutus using his virtue as a cloak for a relentless 'wilfulness'.[5] Shakespeare does indeed shape these materials to make a point about Brutus not to be found in his source, but it is not a point about Brutus' will, or even simply or mainly about Brutus' character, but rather about the dynamics of the republican cult of Roman virtue that animates the conspiracy and more partic- ularly of the contradictions inherent in the pursuit of republican virtue in a changing political world.

For in none of the scenes in question does Brutus have recourse to the language of will but rather to that of virtue, honour and reason. Having heard Cassius claim that ' 'tis better that the enemy seek us', Brutus responds that 'good reasons must, of force give place to better' [IV, iii, 196, 203]. Recourse to 'reason' is a central feature of Brutus' stoic virtue. Immediately after the killing of Caesar he puts all his faith in the capacity of 'our reasons' [III, i, 224] or of 'reason' [III, i, 237] to win over not only the people but even Antony to their cause. Admittedly, as he concedes the point, Cassius does use the word 'will' – 'then with your will go on,/We'll along ourselves, and meet them at Philippi' [IV, iii, 223–24] – but what he is acceding to here is an exercise neither of will, nor (still less) of rational argument. As events prove, Cassius is right and Brutus is wrong, and Cassius, who is the better soldier, knows it, later lamenting that he has been 'compelled to set/Upon one battle all our liberties' [V, i, 74–75]. For all his greater military experience and skill, as Moody Prior has argued, what Cassius is conceding to Brutus in this scene is an emotional and moral primacy based on Brutus' superior virtue; a primacy established over the other conspir- ators throughout the course of play and finally brought home even to Cassius in the immediately preceding quarrel scene.

If we want to see a mere clash of wills it is to the Caesarean side of the lines that we have to go, where, immediately before the battle, Antony and Octavius discuss the disposition of their forces. Antony assumes a Caesar-like note of command: 'Octavius, lead your battle softly on,/Upon the left hand of the field.' But Octavius is not having any of that and replies, using exactly the same peremptory, pseudo-monarchical tone, 'upon the right side. Keep thou the left.' When Antony, bemused and offended, asks 'why do you cross me in this exigent?' Octavius replies, simply and gnomically, 'I do not cross you: but I will do so' [V, i, 16–20]. In his source this debate occurs between Brutus and Cassius but Shakespeare deliberately transposes it from the republican to the Caesarean side in order to show (again) that the language of will and the brute performance of wilfulness remains a monopoly of the pseudo-monarchical Caesareans rather than of the republicans.

According to the republican and stoic values and assumptions to which, for all their faults, all the conspirators subscribe, Brutus is the most virtuous man amongst them. Indeed, judged in their terms, he (not Caesar) *is* the noblest Roman of them all. Moody Prior speaks of 'the studied cultivation of nobility of mind and conduct which sets Brutus apart from the other characters and commands their reverence,'[6] and Coppelia Kahn observes that Brutus wins out so repeatedly in the counsels of the conspirators because he 'finds the most resonant and compelling rhetoric by which to represent the conspiracy as a noble enterprise for the general good of Rome. Republican principle has become the stake in a contest of emulation in which Brutus competes to distinguish himself as the Roman most devoted to the republic.'[7]

Thus, when Brutus asserts his authority, his colleagues do not experience themselves as being subjected to his will so much as to the influence of his superior virtue. Thus I take Simmons to be precisely wrong when he concludes that 'as several commentators have observed, the Caesarean principle of authority has been established within the frame of the conspiracy.'[8] A frame of authority has indeed been established, but that frame is not Caesarean. For all the parallels that the play draws between Caesar and Brutus, it also makes it quite clear that Caesar is both a pseudo- and a wannabe monarch and Brutus is not. Unlike Caesar's, Brutus' remains an essentially republican moral authority; he operates, amongst other autonomous bearers of Roman virtue, as *primus inter pares*, in ways that Caesar simply does not. Thus, *pace* Kahn and others, the play continues to assert a difference between the republican values and forms of the conspirators and the emergently monarchical values and forms to be found amongst the Caesareans.

This is not to say that the play simply underwrites Brutus' view of himself, or indeed the other characters' view of him, as the epitome of human virtue, or anything like it. As Moody Prior drily observes, the play shows us Brutus exercising his moral primacy over his fellow conspirators in ways often 'less than admirable.'[9] But perhaps most important, in so determinedly political a play as this, is the fact that, as well as being morally flawed, Brutus' virtue turns out to be calamitous in its political consequences. In the fallen, post-republican, rapidly monarchising, political world conjured by the play, possession of Roman, republican, Stoic 'virtue', of the sort epitomised by Brutus, is no longer an asset but rather a positive hindrance to the perception of political and moral reality and therefore to the achievement of one's political goals.

Learning to tell the time: universalising scepticism versus historicising relativism

As any number of critics have observed, the play consistently problematises the capacity of any of the characters to distinguish between their own preferred view of themselves and of events and what is really happening. Both Caesar and Brutus suffer from this incapacity and, as Gayle Greene points out, coming from

Cicero, 'the representative of rhetoric for the renaissance', the observation that 'men may construe things, after their fashion,/Clean from the purpose of the things themselves' [I, iii, 34–35] might well be taken as rather more than a comment on the various (mutually exclusive) responses to, and interpretations of, the prodigious storm that precedes Caesar's assassination. So too, Greene avers, 'Titinius' comment on Cassius' suicide, "Alas, thou hast misconstrued everything" [V, iii, 84), and Messala's apostrophe to "error" as the perception of "things that are not" (l. 69)' might well 'have resonances beyond their immediate contexts'.[10] All of which has led many scholars to read the play as an exercise in what is often taken to be a positively Montaignean scepticism;[11] a comment on 'the human condition', no less, and thus on the basic terms, both the possibilities and the limitations, inherent in all human knowledge. On the other hand, we could construe the play, in line with the consequences of its own scepticism, as eschewing all such claims to universal truth. On this view, the play is under-taking a narrower, far more temporally and context-specific, as we might say, politically and historically contingent, analysis. Here the incapacity of any of the main characters, with the possible exception of the utterly opportunistic and ruthlessly ambitious Mark Antony, to see the times aright, might be seen, as a function not of 'the human condition' but rather of the specific, highly volatile, processes of political and moral change through which they are all living.

In staging such a moment of intense change, as Rome morphs from one sort of state and moral system into another, but has as yet to complete that transition in either direction, Shakespeare shows us a situation in which none of the moral and political categories, the conventional norms and expectations which the major characters habitually use to frame their sense of self, to forge their social identities and alliances, to make sense of their own experience and of events, quite work.[12] The seemingly natural fit between identity, expectation and social and political reality that ideology, operating within more stable times and states, can often confer, is just not available, and the result is the serial mistakes and mistakings, the misapprehensions and misapplications of crucial terms and assumptions, that characterise both the action of the play and the actions of nearly all of the major players within it.

A central question posed by the play is thus one of timing.[13] In a crucial line Cassius reassures Brutus that 'men at some time are masters of their fates' [I, ii, 138]. The basic political questions the play poses are, firstly, is this true? And, secondly, even if it is true, how can we tell the time? By what criteria might men decide whether and when the time, their time, is ripe? These questions in their turn raise the wider political issues at stake in the play; about the capacity of political actors, of even the highest virtue and prowess, to control events, impose their will on the course of political change, and either found or refound states; about the utility, in so doing in the here and now, of apothegms and examples culled from the classical Roman, both pagan and republican, past;

and, more generally, about the best way to use history as a guide to current political thought and practice, a means both to decode what is happening now and to decide what to do next. The central question here concerns the prudence of violent attempts to arrest political change and impose political form on the flux of events, even at the height of such moments of change or transition. Put crudely, might not an extended staging of an occasion upon which men of the highest virtue and prowess – world historical figures like Caesar, Brutus and Cassius – had failed signally to tell the times aright, help Shakespeare's contemporaries to do rather better in their own time?

Read in this light, for all its staging of epistemological doubt or incapacity, its insistent concern with the inability of political actors, in the midst of events, to read aright the signs of the times, for all its studied refusal finally to endorse either republicanism or monarchy, resistance or non-resistance, there is nothing ambiguous or equivocal, undecided or even guarded about the play's own response to what I take to be the central moral, prudential, essentially political, questions around which it is organised.

CHAPTER 22

The politics of prodigy, prophecy and providence (in a pagan state)

We might imagine such quintessentially political considerations – the internal contradictions within Brutus' version of republican virtue, the ill fit between his antique moral and political categories and calculations and the nature of the times – to be quite enough to explain the failure of the republican cause, but the play refuses to leave things there. On the contrary, it repeatedly raises the question of whether it is these secular forces and tensions or the workings of a higher power (operating in and through such contradictions) that dooms the conspirators to failure. And it is to its account of that higher power and its workings that we must now turn.

Julius Caesar is a play notoriously suffused with the supernatural. A plethora of prodigies and prophecies, of omens and curses, recur throughout the action. Perhaps the most overtly prophetic of the prophecies is the pronouncement of the soothsayer about the Ides of March. Not far behind comes Calphurnia's dream foretelling the death of Caesar. This, of course, is seconded by the results of the augurers' sacrifice. Antony's vision of a Roman world torn asunder by the devastations of civil war is part prognostication, part curse and part prophecy. Artemidorus' warning to Caesar [II, iii, 1–6] – is not so much a prophecy as a tip-off. However, even here, Artemidorus makes the outcome of his efforts to forewarn Caesar a test of the role of the fates in deciding the course of human affairs. ('If thou read'st this, O Caesar, thou mayst live;/If not, the Fates with traitors do contrive' [II, iii, 14–15].)

As for portents and prodigies, the play has no end of them. Chief of these, of course, is the prodigious storm that rages the night before Caesar is assassinated. A range of characters attests to the extremity of this event and to the extraordinary prodigies and portents with which it is attended. Casca reports to Cicero that not only has he never seen such a storm, the storm itself has been attended by any number of prodigies [I, iii, 5–28]. Casca's account is confirmed later by that of Calphurnia, who reports that 'A lioness hath whelped in the streets,/And graves have yawned and yielded up their dead./Fierce fiery warriors fight upon the clouds/In ranks and squadrons and right form of war,/Which drizzled blood upon the Capitol./The noise of battle hurtled in the air,/Horses did neigh, and dying men did groan,/And ghosts did shriek and squeal about the streets' [II, ii, 14–24].

Later in the play, Brutus is visited by Caesar's ghost, a sight that 'mak'st my blood cold, and my hair to stare' [IV, iii, 275–78]. Immediately before the battle of Philippi, on his birthday, Cassius reports what he now takes to be an omen to his intimate Messala. 'Two mighty eagles' which had accompanied their host from Sardis 'this morning are ... fled away and gone,/And in their steads do ravens, crows and kites/Fly o'er our heads and downward look on us/As we were sickly prey' [V, i, 79–86].

Bombarded by so many prodigious warnings of the dreadful events that are about to unfold, and of their own fates within them, the characters in the play are not only entirely unable to interpret these signs aright, they evince a wild variety of responses thereto. Cicero's remark, quoted above, that in such 'strange disposed time', 'men may construe things after their fashion/Clean from the purpose of the things themselves' [I, iii, 34–35], is a response to Casca's claim that far from being 'natural' events 'these prodigies' 'are portentious things' [I, iii, 28–32] in the face of which 'It is the part of men to fear and tremble/When the most mighty gods by tokens send/Such dreadful heralds to astonish us' [I, iii, 54–56].

Awe-inspiring portents to Casca, to Cassius these prodigies are just another occasion to display his constancy of mind, a crucial aspect of which is a decided absence of awe. Thus he tells Casca that 'I have walked about the streets,/Submitting me unto the perilous night', baring 'my bosom to the thunder-stone' and thus presenting 'myself/Even in the aim and very flash of it' [I, iii, 46–52]. Asked by Casca, 'but wherefore do you so much tempt the heavens?' [I, iii, 53], Cassius uses the question as the starting point for another rant about the way the unnatural preponderance of Caesar has turned Rome into a veritable 'monstrous state' [I, iii, 62–71]. For Cassius, then, the prodigies of the storm are not fit objects for wonder or fear; they do not presage horrors to come so much as prompt present action; the very action, in fact, which he is already bound and determined to take.

Brutus is even less alarmed than Cassius by the 'exhalations whizzing in the air' [II, i, 44]. Trapped between what he later calls 'the acting of a dreadful thing/And the first motion' [II, i, 63–64], deep in reverie about what must be done about Caesar, Brutus remains entirely unconcerned about the meaning of these prodigies, and merely uses the light shed by the lightning to read the anonymous missives sent to deceive him by Cassius and his accomplices.

As we have seen, Caesar affects a similar indifference to the light show of the previous evening. Glossed by Calphurnia as warnings to Caesar not to 'walk forth' that day, he takes them as 'predictions', but ones directed as much 'to the world in general as to Caesar' [II, ii, 8, 28–29]. Pressed by his wife with the claim that 'when beggars die there are no comets seen;/The heavens themselves blaze forth the death of princes' [II, ii, 30–31], Caesar replies with a standard assertion of the need for constancy of mind in the face of the unknowable determinations of fate. That, of course, is only Caesar's theoretical position. As we have seen, in practice he is a great deal more sensitive to the presence of political danger and to what omens and prodigies might have to tell him about his fate than his words imply. However, to the very end, the clash between his theory and his practice, between his drive, at all times, to perform his own virtue and his contrary impulse to peer into the future, to anticipate and avoid, rather than merely to ignore or confront, danger, prevents him from coming to anything like a settled resolution about what all these prodigies and prophecies might mean, and still less from heeding the warning that both they and Calphurnia's dream have provided for him.

For their part, until the very end, Brutus and Cassius follow Caesar's precepts and not his practice, by sustaining a position of settled indifference to such concerns. Even as Brutus is confronted by the spectre of Caesar's ghost, while he sweats in fear and his hair stands on end, he maintains an exemplary constancy of mind in the face of the 'monstrous apparition'. Unsure of what it is – his question 'is it some god, some angel or some devil?' remains, in the short run, unanswered – its claim that it is 'thy evil spirit Brutus' and that 'thou shalt see me at Philippi' elicits only the response 'why, I will see thee at Philippi then' [IV, iii, 275–84].

As we have seen, the play presents such an attitude of equanimity, the capacity to maintain a constancy of mind before the vicissitudes of fate, as central to Roman virtue. Here the attitude expressed by Brutus to Cassius on the eve of battle is something approaching normative. Brutus starts out by expressing a desire to know the outcome, but that, he knows, is a fond wish. 'It sufficeth that the day will end,/And then the end is known' [V, i, 122–25]. Facing an unknowable fate, the man of constant mind, knowing that death is certain, must be ready to embrace and face down any eventuality. The worst that can happen is death, and death is inevitable. Learning of Portia's suicide, Brutus observes that 'we must die, Messala:/With meditating that she must die once/I have the patience to endure it now.' While in that scene Cassius denies that he could emulate Brutus' superhuman self-control, elsewhere he produces a reasonable facsimile of it. Even as he interprets the 'ravens, crows and kites flying o'er our heads' as 'a canopy most fatal, under which/Our army lies, ready to give up the ghost', he also tells Messala that 'I believe it but partly,/For I am fresh of spirit and resolved/To meet all perils constantly' [V, I, 89–91].

In responding thus, both men are reacting according to the dictates of what Cassius describes to Brutus as 'your philosophy', a position according to which attention paid to the sorts of prodigies and prophecies staged in the play amounted to what Cassius contemptuously describes as 'superstition'. That claim occurs in a speech in which Caesar is said to have grown 'superstitious' only 'of late'. And even in his late, 'superstitious' phase, Caesar's responses to a series of prodigies and portents are constrained by his need to at least appear to be observing the dictates of Brutus and Cassius' 'philosophy'.

Clearly, Caesar's attitudes to such things are changing and in this he is not alone. Calphurnia enters, claiming that 'I never stood on ceremonies,/Yet now they fright me' [II, ii, 13–14]. Cassius, too, tells Messala that 'now I change my mind' and, departing from the Epicurean position he had previously espoused, 'partly credit things that do presage' [V, i, 76–78]. Of all the central figures in the play, it is the superlatively virtuous Brutus who is the last to come to such a change of heart. Only at the very end, when all is lost, does he admit that this outcome has been foretold, by 'the ghost of Caesar'; 'I know my hour is come' [V, v, 16–19]. Earlier, coming upon Cassius, slain by his own hand, Brutus had exclaimed 'O Julius Caesar, thou art mighty yet./Thy spirit walks abroad and turns our swords/In our own proper entrails' [V, iii, 94–96]. With his dying breath Brutus again acknowledges the hand of fate in his own end. 'Caesar, now be still./I killed not thee with half so good a will' [V, v, 51–52]. As he died by his own hand, Cassius, too, had conceded that 'Caesar, thou art revenged/Even with the sword that killed thee' [V, iii, 45–46].

The play then presents us with a variety of pagan Romans all of whom have been taught by the demands of Roman virtue and the dictates of 'philosophy' to regard any concern with prodigies, portents or prophecies as 'superstition'. They have also been taught to regard fate as unknowable and that the best way to meet it is an acceptance of the inevitability of death; an acceptance that is designed to lead not to fatalistic passivity but rather to an active pursuit of virtue and honour, safe in the knowledge that, if all else fails, one can choose death rather than dishonour or servitude and, in dying by one's own hand, cheat both tyranny and fate. That certainly is the view taken throughout by Brutus, Cassius and Caesar and in the end acted upon by both Brutus and Cassius. There is, then, a sense in which suicide represents the coping stone in the arch of the pagan philosophy attributed by the play to all its central characters. Certainly, there can be no doubt that within the republican 'philosophy' staged in the play, the deaths of both Brutus and Cassius are honourable. Coming upon the self-murdered Cassius, Brutus hails the nobility of his death, addressing him famously as 'the last of all the Romans' [V, iii, 99]. Antony delivers a similarly famous and definitive verdict over Brutus' corpse: 'this was the noblest Roman of them all' [V, v, 69].

And yet the play also shows us each of the central characters unlearning the lessons of (pagan) philosophy, of Roman virtue and republican honour; coming, in fact, to believe in what Calphurnia calls 'ceremonies' and what, at the end of the play, Cassius calls 'things that do presage' and nearer the beginning 'superstition'. And, of course, the play shows us that they are quite right to do so. After all, all the prophecies with which the play is studded come true. Caesar should have bewared the Ides of March; he does die under the daggers of his countrymen, as Calphurnia has foreseen; he should have looked out for Brutus, Cassius and the rest; subsequent to his death the Roman world is plunged into a bloody civil war, as Antony prophesies. The portents, too, prove the true harbingers of disaster that at least some of the characters take them to be: the prodigies of the night before Caesar's assassination have indeed 'blazed forth the death' of a prince; the crows and kites flocking above the republican army at Philippi do indeed mean what Cassius takes them to mean; the visitation of Caesar's ghost as Brutus' 'evil spirit' does indeed mean that his number is up. Having set out to slay 'the spirit of Caesar' [II, i, 166], Brutus and Cassius succumb to the revengeful attentions of that very spirit, killing themselves with the same swords with which they had cut Caesar down.

What, to the philosophy espoused by Brutus and Cassius, looked like 'superstition', is thus presented by the play as something else; something that any Elizabethan audience, inured to the structuring assumptions of innumerable tracts, sermons and indeed plays, would have identified as the operation of providence, to whose admonitory and punitive interventions into events it was anything but 'superstitious' to attend.[1] In at least some of the history plays analysed above, the operations of providence, embodied in the framing presence of prophecies, prodigies and portents, allows the audience an access to what the plays present as the patterning of events by providence that is far more complete and panoptical than anything available to any of the characters. Ceded, through the operation of such providence, something like a God's-eye view of the action, the audience can indulge in processes of judgement – moral, theological, political – that constitute inside their own heads what we might take to be the meta-argument of the play. Certainly they can see as 'providential' things that are ignored or misunderstood by the characters on stage. One thinks, in this case, of the consistent interplay between the different moral faults and foibles of Brutus and Cassius and of the repeated pattern whereby, disagreeing about what to do next, Brutus always wins the argument and always with disastrous results. Armed with the providential framework provided to them by the overall structure of the play, with its insistent pattern of portents and prophecies, the audience might well see this not only as a commentary on the contradictions between, say, the politics of honour and of faction, or even between the characters and moral qualities of Brutus and Cassius, but as an expression of a providential patterning of events, which uses the dominant characteristics (in Christian terms, the defining 'sins') of the central figures to frustrate their own purposes, bringing the conspirators to judgement and death at Philippi, even as the sins of Caesar and of Rome have been punished, in their turn, by their conspiracy and rebellion, and the civil war that ensues. Built into such a providential reading of the play would be the extraordinary blindness of several of the characters in the face of the signs and prophecies provided to them, which, if heeded, would have saved them from the fates visited upon them by play's end. Such failures to see things literally thrust in their faces by providence could themselves be seen as 'providential'. For here was providence using the sins and weaknesses of these men to bring them to punishments that their sins had deserved and that, however clear the warnings vouchsafed by heaven, their own (fallen) capacities had been entirely unable to perceive, let alone avert. Having been warned, and having ignored the warning, they had thus been rendered doubly culpable.

Such a reading of the play's action, would, of course, be an intensely Christian one, predicated on the existence of an omnipotent and immutably just and merciful God whose beneficent purposes could be seen working their way through the events of human history, in ways that not merely conferred meaning and coherence on those events but sent messages of admonition and exhortation about that meaning and coherence to all those with eyes to see. But the play, of course, is not about Christians, but about exponents of a pagan philosophy, which has, somewhere near its heart, notions of 'liberty' and 'justice', of 'nobility' and 'honour' entirely recognisable to a Christian audience as moral goods. The play also features a concern with the nature of the good death and with the need to square the purposes of humanity with a fate that no human can penetrate, paralleling quite closely the central concerns of many sixteenth-century Christians. But that 'philosophy' has no place for the omnipotent Christian God and no place, therefore, for providence as Christians constructed and applied it to their lives and times; no place, either, for the immortal Christian soul, nor for any concept of an afterlife in which salvation and damnation depend on some combination of the operations of divine grace and the conduct of the individual in this life.

None of the characters show the slightest regard for their fate in the next life. Insofar as it means anything to them, immortality is a function of immortal fame; something to be won by honourable service of the republic and the public performance of true honour and nobility, even in the face of death. Immediately after the murder of Caesar, Brutus and Cassius imagine their deed winning them fame down the centuries as it is played out in 'sport' upon the public stage. They shall be hailed, crows Cassius as 'The men who gave their country liberty' [III,i, 114–19]. It is, of course, one of the many ironies in which the play abounds that this very play is itself contributing to the process whereby such an immortal fame is conferred upon Caesar's killers. But, as the play shows, they have become famous not for having 'given their country liberty', which, after all, is something that they signally failed to do, but rather for giving their all in the service of what they took to be the general good and then meeting honourable deaths, when all was lost, at Philippi. That they die by their own hand only adds to the nobility of it all. For, under the right circumstances – and, as we have seen, the play makes it clear that these *are* the right circumstances – according to the Roman value system constructed by the play, and to the philosophy espoused by Brutus and Cassius, suicide is a noble and honourable response to the triumph of tyranny and the inexorable workings of what is always an inscrutable fate.

That, of course, was not a position open to orthodox Christians. And the play constructs its audience as such by enabling, even inducing, them to place the inherently Christian providential frame, afforded them by the prophecies, prodigies and structural symmetries of the plot, around the decidedly unchristian doings of the Roman, pagan and republican characters whose fates they are watching unfold on stage.

The heuristic act of applying Christian providentialism to the action of the play compounded the standard alienating or distancing effects produced by the God- or providence-eye view afforded to their audiences by many of the plays under discussion here. Put crudely, the audience could see more than the characters not merely because they were the audience, situated outside the action and thus able to see the overarching structures of the plot in ways that the characters simply could not, but also because they were Christians. The audience's application of their own (at least residually) Christian hermeneutic impulses to the providential signs that structure and comment upon so much of the action of this play would thus have accentuated the cultural gap that separated the pagan and republican Rome being staged in the play from the Christian and monarchical world of the audience.

The providentialism of the play reflects that of the murder pamphlet, the revenge tragedy.[2] and the history play. On the one hand, we could read the play as a murder narrative, with the cause of the assassination or murder being located both in Caesar's own sins, for which his violent death is a punishment, and in the sins of his murderers, sins which are shown being used to punish Caesar before leading the murderers themselves to judgement and perhaps to damnation. The tragic element here is provided by the very considerable virtues displayed both by Caesar and by at least some of his killers. Just as it was Caesar's palpable virtues and attainments that excited the envy and venom of the conspirators, so it was the virtues, as well as the sins, of at least some of the conspirators, that led them to the sinful act that rendered their own destruction certain.

But, of course, Caesar was not only a private man, and his murder was anything but a private, but rather an intensely public, and political, act. Accordingly, the providential judgements that his murder set in train were directed both at his murderers and at the entire Roman state, which, just as Antony had predicted in that mixture of a curse and a prophecy delivered in Act III scene i, is indeed plunged into popular insurrection, factional strife, civil war and the most spectacular form of political change; a change that replaces a republic not merely with the rule of Julius Caesar bearing the title of king but with the Roman Empire. Whatever one makes of that empire, or even of Augustus – and clearly there was a range of estimations available to any Elizabethan audience – the play makes it clear that, in the short run at least, things are going to get a good deal worse before they get better. If

Caesar appeared, at least to the conspirators, to be a tyrant, the rule of those ruthless power brokers, Antony and Octavius, seems certain to be considerably worse.

Taking the providential view which the play makes available to us, we might ask whether this outcome is a judgement and, if it is, upon what sins precisely is it being visited? A conventional answer would be that it is a judgement visited upon the sins of violent resistance, regicide and rebellion. But, as we have seen, to advance such an argument is immediately to raise the question of just what is being resisted in the play? Just what precisely is Caesar? Is he a prince at all? If he is a prince, is he a legitimate one? If Rome is still a republic, then Caesar's semi-regal power in the state, compounded by what Brutus calls his 'ambition' to become king, renders him not legitimate at all, but at best a usurper, indeed a traitor to the state bent on undermining the very principles of government that determine legitimacy in Rome. But if Caesar's rise to power has already changed Rome so that it is no longer really a republic, but in fact some kind of incipient monarchy, then Calphurnia's calling him a prince is a simple state-ment of fact and the third and fourth plebeian's proposals, made immediately after Caesar's murder, to 'let Brutus be Caesar' and to 'crown' Brutus [III, ii, 51–52] are not as ludicrous as they might at first seem. Indeed, they might be thought to betray greater insight into current political realities than the antique republicanism of Brutus. Certainly, in that case, Caesar would be a legitimate ruler, and killing him an act of treason. The question asked by the play is, therefore, a very precise one; whether – even in a polity in as much flux as Caesar's Rome, a polity in which questions of legitimacy and usurpation are entirely up for grabs – it is either lawful or sensible, just or prudent, to resort to violent means – conspiracy, assassination and rebellion – in order to preserve the public good and the constitutional status quo.

Putting the question in such a form might be thought to bias the issue in favour of an answer in the affirmative. But, in fact, the play seems to answer in the negative. That answer operates on a number of levels. Adopting the terms set by the analysis of earlier history plays, *Julius Caesar* combines the prudential political analysis, the political realism, of say *2* and *3 Henry VI* or of the *Henry IV* plays or even of *Henry V*, with the lurid providentialism of *Richard III*. At the level of secular political analysis, the play shows the difficulty of trying to control the course of political change or to arrest the progress of the sort of corruption that we see in *Julius Caesar* destroying the Roman republic. Despite their best intentions, the recourse of Brutus and Cassius to conspiracy and violence merely makes things worse; their best efforts to restore the republic only succeed, to adopt Antony's term, in sending 'mischief' abroad, subjecting both men and events to the deleteriously promiscuous influence of 'fortune'. In a state already rendered unstable by the process of political change, and now in situation newly destabilised by recourse to violence, a premium is put upon the capacity to mobilise and control the people. That in turn exposes and exacerbates the inherent tensions and contradictions operating between the politics of honour, legitimacy, popularity and faction. In other words, the desperate struggle for political advantage and power, set off by the initial recourse to conspiracy and violence, pits the principles (the politics of honour) that initially prompted, and were intended to legitimise, that recourse, against the corrupt and calculating means (the politics of popularity and of faction) necessary to win the resulting struggle for power. Hence the rebels' recourse to conspiracy and faction persistently undercuts their insistent claims to embody the causes of honour, liberty and true Romanitas, while their residual commitment to the politics of virtue fatally constrains and ultimately undermines the effectiveness of their practice of the politics of faction.[3] Thus, actions undertaken to restore a notionally stable *status quo ante* succeed only in making matters worse.

Viewed *sub specie aeternitatis*, from the perspective provided throughout the play by a series of archetypally providential warnings, prophecies and admonitions, such an outcome can be recast not only as the product of dynamics and contradictions inherent in the nature of this-worldly political manoeuvre, but also as the result of a providential plan, designed to use the sins of one group to punish those of another, to bring murderers and rebels to book while punishing the sins of the whole society with insurrection, civil war and tyranny. At both the providential and prudential levels of discourse, therefore, the play's answer to the question with which we started – whether violent resistance, even against a ruler whose legitimacy is as questionable as that of Julius Caesar, in a polity in as much flux as Caesarean Rome, is ever either justifiable or sensible – would seem to be a resounding no.

CHAPTER 23

Between *Henry V* and *Hamlet*

If we adopt the view of the political conjuncture of mid 1599 taken both by Essex and his intimates and by James VI, then we see a situation very like that conjured in the play, with issues of legitimacy, of loyalty and treason, freedom and tyranny, indeed with the future and form of the English commonwealth, very much at stake and up for grabs. The dilemma, the central question posed by the play, ran parallel to that confronting the earl of Essex and his supporters as they faced military failure in Ireland and political defeat at the hands of their enemies. For on one view, such a defeat was not just a private matter, part of the hurly-burly of court-centred politics, the struggle for office and influence under the crown, that characterised personal monarchy in almost any age. Rather the prospect of Essex's failure and disgrace brought with it the threat of fundamental political change; an ignoble peace with Spain, a diversion of the succession, a descent from free hereditary monarchy into something like tyranny.

The prospect of such change raised the question of the possibility of, indeed of the need for, 'faction' for the public good. The danger currently posed to the commonwealth, to the causes of 'honour' and of 'freedom', demanded the formation (in secret, but for the most public of purposes) of a group of men of honour, true nobility and virtue, united in their purpose to preserve the constitutional *status quo ante*, and thus the general good, from the processes of political change being visited on Rome by the ambition of Caesar and the corruption of the Romans themselves and on England by the triumph of Essex's enemies, the purblind tyranny of Elizabeth and the machinations of the Spanish.

Brutus is presented in the play as a figure of true nobility and unimpeachable honour, trapped in the 'phantasma', the 'hideous dream', that fills the space between 'the acting of a dreadful thing and the first motion' [II, i, 63–69]. This portrait of Brutus has a certain similarity to the situation of Essex, in Ireland. With events slipping away from him, with the queen, under the influence of his enemies, turning against him, and with those same enemies apparently about to triumph, we now know, the earl started to consider his options, which included the desperate expedient of open revolt. Twisting in the wind, subject to different pressures and advice, teetering on the edge of conspiracy and rebellion, appeals made both to his honour and his vanity, to his duty to the general good and to his friends, Brutus' situation has marked similarities to that of Essex.[1]

The 'faction' that gathers around Brutus is made up not only of men of honour but also of a series of malcontents and Machiavels, or rather it is made up of malcontents, like Ligarius, talking the language of honour, and of men of honour, like Brutus, reduced to acting and speaking like malcontents, using the language of faction, private interest and connection to recruit the likes of Ligarius to the cause. Cassius embodies these contradictions; we hear his envy of Caesar's greatness and his lack of favour at court – 'Caesar doth bear me hard' [I, ii, 312] – confirmed both out of his own and Caesar's mouth; we watch him appealing to Brutus' pride in order to seduce him into the plot; we observe him deluding Brutus through the manufacture of popular pressure; we learn of his corruption and greed; but we also watch him die nobly, at his own hand, for the cause of 'liberty'.

Brutus alone (almost) escapes such strictures. His very closeness to Caesar and the favour which Caesar bears towards him frees him from any suspicion that his animus against Caesar might be prompted by ignoble private considerations – by envy, frustrated ambition or revenge. Of course, if, with Antony, we define honour not in the public and 'republican' terms of devotion to the general good but in the more private and monarchical (?) terms of personal loyalty, Brutus' closeness to Caesar merely renders his betrayal of his friend and benefactor the more heinous. But on the subject of Brutus' honour even Antony relents, conceding, in virtually the last words of the play, that 'all the conspirators save only he/Did that they did in envy of great Caesar./He only, in a general honest thought/And common good to all, made one of them' [V, v, 70–73].

But, for all his hesitations on the brink, for all his elaborate concern with the dictates of 'honour', 'nobility' and 'the general' good, at the end of the day Brutus is, if not tricked, then 'seduced' (by Cassius certainly, but also perhaps in a certain sense by himself as well) into action. At this point, we might conceive of the relations between Cassius and Brutus as an encapsulation of the internal workings of the Essex faction. In the interactions of the two men we have a staging of debates and discussions, tensions and contradictions, that are contained and worked out not only within the counsels of the earl and his intimates but perhaps even within the earl's own head. On this view, the play can be seen as a staging of the internal contradictions and tensions of the Essexian project and ideological synthesis, as it faced its moment of crisis and of choice.

In order to make this claim it is not necessary to attribute to Shakespeare a positively preternatural knowledge of secret conversations taking place in far-away Ireland, but merely a conventionally Shakespearean capacity both imaginatively to inhabit and effectively to stage situations and dilemmas of which he had no direct knowledge or experience. We need only posit that in this play he was exercising those gifts in response to rumours from Ireland and from court, and on the basis of what has emerged from this book as a close and sustained engagement with both the organising political conundra of the Elizabethan *fin de siècle*, in general, and the ideological and cultural contradictions, both the possibilities and the dangers, inherent in the Essexian project, in particular.

In the play, but not yet in the world, Cassius seduces Brutus, or at least helps Brutus to seduce himself into conspiracy, assassination and rebellion. In effect 'bad Essex' seduces 'good Essex' and, of course, the consequences of that seduction are disastrous, not only for him and his fellows, but for the country that he and they are hoping to serve and save. Seeking to make things better, indeed to save the state, Brutus and the others succeed only in making things worse; opening the way for insurrection, civil war and for what the play strongly suggests will be the ruthless and tyrannical regime of Octavius and Antony and what the audience knows will be that most absolute of monarchies, the Roman empire.[2]

As we have seen, the vision here is much like that conjured in a series of Catholic tracts in which Robert Parsons and others claimed that when Elizabeth finally died, the unsettled succession bequeathed to England by the ruling clique of evil counsellors and Machiavels would lead inevitably to faction, civil strife and ultimately to a dynastic and religious civil war, at least as serious as the Wars of the Roses or the civil wars that had nearly torn apart the French monarchy, or indeed as those that ended the Roman republic. Thus, in *Julius Caesar* a commonly feared and fantasised outcome is shown to be the inevitable result of a decision to accede to the promptings of honour and of virtue and to (what, in the play, Cassius fraudulently presents as) the people's demand, to 'speak, strike, redress' [II, i, 47]. Here a version of the Roman past might be thought to be operating both as a commentary on the Elizabethan present and as a warning about the immediate future.

A trick – the restoration of unity and greatness to the realm through the combination of the politics of popularity, of honour and of legitimacy – that might just be pulled off within a stably monarchical polity by a superhero like Henry V, a political adept and man of genuine honour, a superbly trained Machiavel acting in the cause of returning legitimacy, virtue and order, proves here beyond the combined efforts even of Julius Caesar and Brutus. In the conditions of contested legitimacy, political change, popular insurrection and civil war, depicted in *Julius Caesar* and likely to be created in Elizabethan England if the succession crisis got any worse, as it surely would if even men of exemplary virtue and honour, like Brutus (or indeed Essex), succumbed to the siren song of faction, conspiracy and rebellion, all bets would be off, and tyranny, of one sort or another, would almost certainly be the outcome.

From, in *Henry V*, exploring and even celebrating the capacity of a great military hero, a master of all the political virtu(e)s, to shape events and, in some sense, refound his state, Shakespeare moved, in *Julius Caesar*, to warning against the extreme limitations placed on the capacity even of men of the highest virtue and prowess – a category within which both Caesar himself and his leading assassins all surely fall – to do any such thing. And yet there is nothing about the two positions to render them formally incompatible. For, if there is a sense in which Henry V is pictured refounding his state, he is also shown working entirely with the grain of monarchical legitimacy and the cause of dynastic right, trying to restore moral and political health to a polity the legitimacy of which is implicitly accepted by all as part of the natural order. That is true neither of Caesar nor of his assassins. For while Caesar is trying to change the very nature of the state from a republic to a monarchy, his assassins are trying to preserve a republican normality that the play reveals has long since ceased to pertain. In such a situation, in a polity in the throes of change, with no one sure either of where they stand or of what others intend, precipitate political action, however noble and 'conservative' in intention, is likely to unleash forces that no one can control and bring about outcomes – in the case in hand, the descent of the Roman world into anarchy and civil war and ultimately the conversion of the Roman state from a republic into an absolute imperial monarchy – that no one (not even Caesar) wants.

Applied to the situation of Essex what this means is that while his efforts ran with the grain of monarchical normality and of hereditary right, while he loyally fought the queen's wars against the foreigner, and cleared the way for the next successor, success was attainable – *if*, between them, he and James Stuart could emulate the self-control and political mastery displayed by that fantasy figure Henry V. If, however, convinced (with Brutus and Cassius) that his enemies were trying to change the state, bend the rules, and transform the polity, the earl allowed himself to take precipitate action, then all bets would be off.

On this view, the play represents, if not an active intervention into the immediate politics of the day, then an immediately pertinent comment thereon. And, as Gary Taylor has argued, the play contains Shakespeare's own heavily ironised reference to the role of the playwright or poet in politics. Not only do we have the scene in which the entirely innocent poet, Cinna, is mistaken for Cinna the conspirator and torn to pieces by the mob, we also have the even stranger one in which a nameless poet, hearing Brutus and Cassius at odds, forces his way into their tent to deliver an absurdly rhymed admonition to kiss and make up [IV, iii, 128–30]. In Plutarch it is the poet who ends the argument, but in Shakespeare's version his attempt to intervene ends only in derision and irrelevance summed up in Brutus' dismissive rhetorical question, 'What should the wars do with these jigging fools?' [133–35]. Poets and politics don't mix, it seems, with even the most well-meaning of poetic interventions provoking either the malice of the mob or the spleen of the good and the great.[3] On the other hand, of course, things might go better if people in power paid more attention to poets.

We need finally to turn to the Roman and pagan provenance of the play. The honour politics portrayed in *Henry V* had been largely monarchical, martial and chivalric. As a number of historians have shown, Essex sought to mobilise just such a version of aristocratic honour and military prowess in constructing a role for himself in the service of the queen and in presenting himself to the public as a leading servant of both queen and commonwealth.[4] But Essex and his circle were also known for their interest in other, classical sources for, and definitions of, honour, virtue and freedom. Men in the earl's circle, from Anthony and Francis Bacon to Henry Cuff, not to mention Sir Henry Savile, were engaged in the study of a range of classical, often late Roman republican and early imperial texts, seeking to construct from them politic histories both of the classical and of the English past, and to extract and epitomise models and apothegms with which they could interpret the politics of their own day and guide their own and their master's political choices and actions. A particular fascination here was exerted by the works of Tacitus, dealing, as they did, with the moment of transition from republican to imperial, and indeed to frankly tyrannical, rule under the Julio-Claudians, and with the acceptably stoic ways in which a variety of Romans had reacted to and interpreted these events. Tacitus, in fact, came to be viewed as the great guide to the ways of increasingly corrupt courts and to the study of polities mutating, as Fulke Greville later said of the late Elizabethan state, into 'a more precipitate absoluteness'.[5]

Heavily inflected by neo-Stoicism, the resulting set of concerns, or view of the world, was never restricted to the dictates of any one school of ancient philosophy, but represented rather a syncretic engagement with, and deployment of, a range of classical texts and authorities, many of them mediated through the compilations of classical wisdom and translations of ancient texts that a variety of scholars were producing, both in print and in manuscript, in England and on the continent, at precisely this time. Moreover as Paulina Kewes has recently argued, it would be a mistake to assume that Tacitean models were used only to counsel passivity and caution. As her analysis of Sir Henry Savile's activities in the early 1590s has shown, they could also be mobilised to argue for active intervention in the course of events.[6]

Such activities were not without a frisson of political danger. As we have seen, in 1599, John Hayward produced a heavily Tacitean history of Henry IV and dedicated it to the earl of Essex, whom he addressed as 'great indeed, both in present judgement and in future time'.[7] Unfortunately for Hayward, and for Essex, the book appeared at a highly charged moment in the earl's career and Hayward found himself in very hot water as a result, while the allegedly subversive contents of his book were used against the earl himself. Both *Julius Caesar* (and indeed *Henry V*) might be taken to be doing a version of the same thing, only with a great deal more subtlety and pointed indirection than poor

Hayward could muster. That is to say, the play was using a story about the Roman state at the actual moment of transition from republic to empire to address present concerns and conjunctures – while simultaneously commentating on the propriety and prudence of so doing.[8]

What the play shows us is the consequence of men of honour and virtue applying the dictates of the best wisdom that pagan philosophy and republican virtue have achieved to a situation of political change and incipiently monarchical rule. And, as we have seen, the results are disastrous, subject to the condemnatory comment, and ultimately to the punishment, of a supervening providence, the very existence of which the pagan philosophy espoused by even the most virtuous characters in the play either denies or is utterly unable to interpret.

We return here to the distancing effect wrought by the application, by the audience, of inherently Christian providential frames of interpretation to the doings of indubitably pagan characters. Viewed in their own pagan terms of reference, if not all of the actions, then certainly the ends of the likes of Brutus and Cassius are noble, as even Mark Antony acknowledges. But for an Elizabethan audience watching the action from the perspective provided by a Christian providence, and with an equally Christian notion of the immortal soul and of the afterlife, even the nobility of their deaths becomes seriously problematic. For not only are the conspirators' actions catastrophic in their wider political effects, they culminate in suicide, an act which, contrary to all Christian orthodoxy, the 'two noblest Romans of them all' clearly believe constitutes the vindication of a truly Roman constancy of mind before the exigencies of an unknowable fate and incipient tyranny. It is an attitude that prevents nearly all of the characters from taking seriously the providential and prophetic warnings in which the play abounds, before it is too late. To do so would be to show weakness, to reveal an inconstant, rather than a constant, mind; indeed, to take the woman's part.[9]

By killing themselves the likes of Brutus and Cassius clearly hope to vindicate their claims to virtue and thus to win the only immortality in which any of the characters in the play seems to be interested, an immortal fame, conferred on them by posterity for the nobility of their lives and deaths in the service of the state. But, as all Elizabethan Christians knew, this is not the sort of immortality that really matters. Born and formed in a pagan republic, before the advent of Christianity, and acting therefore according to a 'philosophy' framed without knowledge of Christian revelation, theirs is a form of virtue and a vision of immortality that, however admirable in itself, cannot apply to the Christian subjects of a Christian prince.

We have, then, a play that stages 'the noblest Romans of them all' following, to the best of their abilities, the dictates of the highest wisdom available to pagan Rome, ending in both personal and political disaster. If that is what following the dictates of Roman virtue, the promptings of the republican honour code and the principles of pagan 'philosophy' got you in a pagan, and at least still ostensibly republican, Rome, where might the decision to follow such principles in the Christian and monarchical context of Elizabethan England end? On one level, then, the play operates as a highly critical examination of the dangers of applying the (often inherently) republican and pagan values, currently being recovered from a range of classical texts and histories by a variety of scholars and politicians, directly to the conditions of a monarchical and Christian England. Of course, since Essex and his circle were known to be intently interested in bringing to bear on contemporary political and ethical questions the insights of the classical, and, in particular, of the Roman republican and early imperial, pasts, such a staging of the issue was not without direct contemporary relevance and reference.

For if the play can indeed be read as an examination of the dangers inherent in the particular political moment of the summer and autumn of 1599, and of the internal contradictions and temptations exposed by that moment within the Essexian project and synthesis, then the decisions reached by Brutus and Cassius, under the influence of the best wisdom of the ancients, and in emulation of the Roman virtue of their ancestors, become, in their turn, an awful warning to contemporaries not to repeat their mistakes, even as they sought to emulate their examples and virtue.

On this reading, the play compounds its central message about the unwisdom of violent insurrection and assassination, in a time of political change, with another equally salient warning about the further unwisdom of seeking to base political and ethical decision-making in a Christian monarchy on the principles, precepts and examples of pagan republicans. The play does this, or rather it forces its audience or readership to do it for themselves, by building into the very structure of the plot, prophecies, prodigies and providential coincidences and judgements of a sort that, in late Elizabethan England, positively demanded a Christian response from the reader or viewer.

In coming to that conclusion *Julius Caesar* presents us with a final irony, for, insofar as the play does take the form of a warning against the direct application of pagan classical sentiments and *sententiae* to contemporary political and ethical quandaries, it does so through the application of narrative templates, events and lessons, culled from the pagan and republican Roman past, to immediately contemporary concerns. The play, then, might be seen as an outstanding example of the very thing that it is warning against. Or rather we might take the play to be providing the exception that proves its own rule: an examination and application of the classical (pagan and republican) past to the (monarchical and Christian) English present of sufficient distance and subtlety to avoid the very pitfalls of which it warns; a positive example of how to do it, created even in the act of demonstrating the dreadful effects of doing it wrong.

For rather than promiscuously collecting and commonplacing a series of classical sententiae or axioms for 'use' and indiscriminately applying exempla and apothegms culled from the Roman and pagan past to the Christian and monarchical present, the play acts historically to set before its audience a set of ancient events in ways which enable them to compare and contrast the English, Christian and monarchical present with the Roman, pagan and republican past. At least the more alert members of the audience are thereby enabled to see through the claims to world-shaping and state-saving virtue, advanced in the play by the likes of Caesar and Brutus. By thus coming to a sense of why, in the past, even men as great as these had been doomed to fail, the play might be thought to be seeking to stop such tragic events repeating themselves in the present.

In the process, of course, the play transcends its own scepticism by providing a practical demonstration of how, through a properly sceptical and relativist approach, pagan and republican Roman history could and should be applied to present concerns; of how, in Shakespeare's hands, the dialectical and dialogical relationship between past and present, set up in the minds of the reader through the history play, could become a way to think about politics (and history) and bring the lessons of the past effectually to bear on the present in ways that transcended the hubris both of Shakespeare's (pagan and republican) constant Romans and of political groupings and actors of an altogether more contemporary provenance.

PART VIII

DISILLUSION: CHRISTIAN AND PAGAN STYLE

CHAPTER 24

Hamlet

In the period between Essex's return from Ireland and the immediate aftermath of his rebellion and execution, in *Hamlet*, Shakespeare wrote another play about a man trapped in a 'phantasma or hideous dream' located between the 'acting of a dreadful thing/And the first motion', a moment 'when the genius and mortal instruments/Are then in council, and the state of man,/Like to a little kingdom, suffers then/The nature of an insurrection' [II, i, 63–64]. The dilemma facing the central figure in both cases concerns resistance and conspiracy, assassination and rebellion. Is it either just or wise to resort to violent means to remove a usurper? In both plays the status of providential signs and prodigies, indeed the testimony of a ghost, are at stake. In both, questions of honour and of blood urge the central character towards action. In both, a central question confronting the hero is how to reconcile his drive towards action with the overarching dispositions of providence. Brutus confronts these questions as a member of a republic and as a pagan. For him fate is unknowable; the afterlife, and in particular the condition and fate of his soul, is never a question and suicide is always an option, indeed, in the last resort, the noblest way out of tyranny, dishonour and defeat.

There are, of course, a number of references back to *Caesar*, contained in *Hamlet*. Polonius famously observes that as a student 'I did enact Julius Caesar. I was killed i' th' Capitol' [III, ii, 102]. As Andrew Gurr points out, in performance that knowing reference would have added piquancy since it would have been Burbage in the role of Hamlet joking 'to Polonius about his taking the part of Julius Caesar and being murdered by himself as Brutus/Burbage'.[1] Regaled with stories of the 'portentous figure' of the ghost, Horatio recalls to Barnardo the prodigies to be seen in Rome, 'A little ere the mightiest Julius fell'. Then graves had opened 'and the sheeted dead/Did squeak and gibber in the Roman streets'. A variety of astronomical wonders – 'stars with trains of fire and dews of blood', various eclipses and 'disasters in the sun; and the moist star'– all served as 'the like precurse of fear'd events,/As harbingers preceding still the fates/And prologue to the omen coming on'. The like, he claimed, 'Have heaven and earth together demonstrated/Unto our climatures and countrymen' [I, i, 116–28]. These connections, both thematic and textual, between the two plays represent an important clue to their relationship both to one another and to the extraordinary series of events (stretching from Essex's departure to Ireland, through his return in disgrace, to his rebellion and death) against which they were written and performed and to which, I am arguing, they were, in part at least, addressed. It is to the pursuance of these themes and connections in *Hamlet* that we must now turn.

Hamlet is faced with a situation, that, viewed in one way, demands instant action, but that, when viewed in another, threatens disaster both to him and the state, if he acts precipitately. While Brutus must decide whether Caesar is a tyrant, Hamlet must decide whether Claudius is a murderer and a usurper. In that sense, both men confront inherently political situations. Both are visited by shades from the other side, that might also be devils, and must decide what to do about it. Both are concerned with the central question of whether, and in what circumstances, suicide represents a fitting or legitimate way out of their predicament. Both feel compelled to act through the demands of entirely secular, this-worldly, versions of 'honour'. Both use a fatalistic, indeed a positively stoic, acceptance of whatever fate dictates to enable them to act. Both are hailed at play's end as the epitome of nobility and valour.

But there are also very great differences between them. Unlike the pagan Romans in *Julius Caesar*, Hamlet enters the action encumbered or enabled – and the play, coming on as a revenge tragedy, does not initially resolve that interpretative choice – with a set of residually Christian assumptions and beliefs. Hamlet believes in an omnipotent Christian God, and accordingly also in the devil. He believes in the immortal soul and in an initially sketchily envisioned version of the Christian afterlife. While at one point he famously describes life after death as 'the undiscovered country, from whose bourn/No traveller returns', a place which 'puzzles the will' [Q2, III, i, 78–79; F, III, i, 79–80] from the outset his discourse prominently features both 'heaven', to which he fears at one point he might be about to consign Claudius, if he kills him at prayer, and 'the other place', 'hell', whence he fears the entity claiming to be the ghost of his father may have come [Q2, III, iii, 73–95; F, III, iii, 73–95]. Despite the avowedly Catholic context provided by the play's version of Denmark, whether Hamlet believes in purgatory is less clear, and by play's end tellingly irrelevant.[2] He also has something he calls a 'conscience' and agonises at some length about what it demands of him and whether it is 'honourable' to obey it. He also believes from the outset that, however tempting a way out of his increasingly unbearable situation, 'self-slaughter' is a sin, as he puts it 'against the canon' of 'the everlasting' [Q2, I, ii, 131–32; F, I, ii, 129–30]. None of these beliefs was available to the pagan characters in *Julius Caesar*.

Hamlet's situation is objectively no less 'political' than that confronted by Brutus and his fellow conspirators. As the dead king's son, and what Claudius describes as 'the most immediate to our throne' [Q2, I, ii, 109; F, I, ii, 107], if

Claudius really is the murderer and usurper described by the ghost, then the state is quite as 'out of joint' as Hamlet thinks it is and Hamlet himself surely has been 'born to set it right' [Q2, I, v, 186–87; I, v, 188–89].

On this basis, Hamlet might be thought to have a public, commonwealth-based, as well as a private, lineage-based, duty and justification to act against Claudius. In these circumstances private revenge could, perhaps should, double as legitimate resistance. And yet Hamlet never takes such a view of the matter. His mentions of his right to the throne are mere asides – Claudius, he observes at one point, has 'Popped in between th'election and my hopes [Q2, V, ii, 62–66; F, V, ii, 63–70] – and certainly do not amount to anything like a claim to any sort of public role in doing justice or saving the state from the rule of a usurper or a tyrant. This is doubly significant given the fact that, as Andras Kisery has pointed out, in Shakespeare's source, Belleforest's account of the revenge of Amleth, Amleth does indeed end by claiming that his status as the right heir renders his killing of Claudius an act of public, indeed of royal, justice.³ Shakespeare's Hamlet never gets close to voicing such sentiments. On the contrary, he takes a sedulously private view of his role as revenger and of the offences that he must punish.

Just as in *Julius Caesar*, there is much talk of honour and its promptings in *Hamlet*, but the sort of honour at stake is very differently constituted, deployed in very different ways and leads to different outcomes. As we have seen, in *Caesar*, the forms of honour talk that pervade the play are quintessentially public and political, because wholly civic and republican. They concern the obligation of the honourable man to vindicate his claims to virtue and nobility in the service of the general good. Insofar as notions of noble blood and lineage are in play they involve the duty to emulate or exceed the examples set by the noble deeds of one's ancestors, rather than any more private pursuit of the honour of any particular lineage.

Things could hardly be more different in *Hamlet*, where Hamlet's honour demands that he revenge the death of his father and what he describes as the dishonour – the 'whoring' – of his mother by Claudius. These sentiments are echoed by Laertes who proclaims, when confronted by the need to be revenged on Hamlet for the death of his father, Polonius, that 'that drop of blood that's calm proclaims me bastard,/Cries "Cuckold" to my father, brands the harlot/Even here between the chaste unsmirched brow/Of my true mother' [Q2, IV, v, 116–19; F, IV, i, 116–19].

Here, then, the demands of passion and revenge are identified with the honour of the household and lineage. Laertes' status as a true son of his father (rather than as a bastard) is made to depend on the passion he displays in seeking to revenge his father. Notions of sexual pollution and the dishonour of women serve as markers of the dishonour inherent in the failure to exact revenge, just as they had in Hamlet's earlier diatribes about his mother's lost honour and his need to wreak revenge on Claudius for that too. Laertes' wrongs admit of no other outcome than Hamlet's death, at Laertes own hand. 'And so have I a noble father lost,/A sister driven into desperate terms/Whose worth, if praises may go back again,/Stood challenger on mount of all the age/For her perfections. But my revenge will come' [Q2, IV, vii, 26–30; F, IV, iii, 26–30]. 'It warms the very sickness in my heart/That I shall live and tell him to his teeth/"Thus didst thou" ' [Q2, IV, vii, 54–56; F, IV, iii, 54–6].

Laertes is here using precisely the same language of honour, shame and revenge that Hamlet had earlier used in an attempt to force himself to act against Claudius. In the scene immediately following his first interview with the actors Hamlet introduces a fourth term, 'passion', which he proceeds to link integrally to 'honour' and 'revenge'. Having observed real tears in the eyes of an actor as he spoke his lines about the death of Hecuba, Hamlet compares the emotion betrayed by a mere player with his own lack of passion in the cause of his father. 'What's Hecuba to him, or he to her,/That he should weep for her? What would he do/Had he the motive and the cue for passion/That I have? He would drown the stage with tears,/And cleave the general ear with horrid speech,/Make mad the guilty and appal the free,/Confound the ignorant and amaze indeed/The very faculties of eyes and ears. Yet I,/A dull and muddy-mettled rascal, peak/Like John-a-dreams, unpregnant of my cause,/And can say nothing. No, not for a king,/Upon whose property and most dear life/A damned defeat was made.'

The initial argument here is about 'passion', the affective force that should move Hamlet to his revenge but hitherto has not. His failure so to do then prompts him to ask 'am I a coward?' an enquiry that prompts direct recourse to the binary opposition between honour and shame, around which the cult of the man of honour was organised. 'Who calls me villain? Breaks my pate across?/Plucks off my beard, and blows it in my face,/Tweaks me by the nose, gives me the lie i' th' throat/As deep as to the lungs? Who does me this?/Ha! Why, I should take it. For it cannot be/But I am pigeon-livered, and lack gall/To make oppression bitter, or ere this/I should have fatted all the region kites/With this slave's offal – a bloody, bawdy villain!' It is as though his failure to kill Claudius has revealed him to be such a coward that, given the lie by any Tom, Dick or Harry, Hamlet would simply turn the other cheek instead of responding with the instant reproof and revenge that should mark him off as a gentleman. There could scarcely be a clearer demonstration of the extent to which, in *Hamlet* in general and for Hamlet in particular, revenge is a matter of private honour and passion rather than of public justice and reason.

Hamlet's honour, his masculinity, his social identity as his father's son, what Polonius describes to Laertes as his 'self', is at stake here and, in failing to act, Hamlet has called all those things into question. This thought, combined with the mere mention of Claudius and his crime, does indeed move Hamlet to the sort of passionate outburst that he had so admired in the actor – 'Remorseless, treacherous, lecherous, kindless villain!/O vengeance!/Whoa!' – but that too now becomes a source of shame, as, instead of taking real revenge like a gentleman, he finds himself reduced to cursing and emoting like a woman, or a whore, or indeed an actor. 'What an ass am I! Ay, sure, this is most brave,/ That I, the son of a dear father murthered,/Prompted to my revenge by heaven and hell,/Must like a whore unpack my heart with words/And fall a-cursing like a very drab,/A scullion! Fie upon't, foh!' [II, ii, 495–522; F, II, ii, 553–82].

Later, at least in Q2, Hamlet tries to use the example of Fortinbras, who is about to risk his own life and those of thousands of troops in order to conquer from the Poles 'a little patch of ground that hath in it no profit but the name' [Q2, IV, iv, 17–18], in order again to force himself to act against Claudius on the grounds of 'honour'. The contrast between the martial virtue and valour, the true sense of honour, being displayed by Fortinbras and his own inaction provokes another outburst [Q2, IV, iv, 42–65]. Here again, we have recourse to 'honour' and another version of the brittle honour and shame culture against which, in that earlier soliloquy, Hamlet had measured his own performance in revenging his father's death. When a man's honour is engaged, the merest trifle becomes a just occasion for the most extreme and dangerous action. On this account, 'true greatness' is a function not of the inherent worth or virtue of the cause defended, or of the end pursued, but rather of the 'ambition' and 'spirit', the valour and mettle, being displayed and vindicated in pursuit of it.

The view of honour in play in these passages is inherently private and particular rather than general or public. It is intensely lineage-based, centred on the obligations owed by sons to their fathers, and dominated by the obliga-tion to revenge any slight offered to the standing of the lineage. It is thus no accident that central to Laertes' rage for revenge are questions of status, and in particular the absence of due respect for his father and his house. 'His means of death, his obscure funeral –/No trophy sword nor hatchment o'er his bones,/ No noble rite, nor formal ostentation –/Cry to be heard as 'twere from heaven to earth' [Q2, IV, v, 205–9; F, IV, i, 208–12]. The contrast with the notions of honour in play in Caesar could scarcely be more obvious.

The one thing that the ideals of honour operative in both plays have in common is their intensely secular, this-worldly character. For the Roman pagans, devoid of any notion of the immortal soul or the Christian afterlife, of an omniscient, perfectly just and perfectly merciful God, whose idea of provi-dence oscillates between the notions of fate and fortune, this was not a problem. For the Christian Danes in *Hamlet*, and indeed for the play's first Elizabethan audiences, it most indubitably was.

And, in fact, in *Hamlet* the linked notions of honour, passion and revenge feature predominantly in Hamlet's (unsuccessful) attempts to use these entirely secular values to force himself to act against Claudius. In so doing he is confronting what he describes as his own 'cowardice', which he equates with his rooted and recurring propensity to listen to the promptings of what he calls 'conscience'. He defines what he means by this word in the 'to be or not to be' soliloquy. There, starting out in a lucubration on the subject of suicide, which the play has already established is presenting itself to him with increasing urgency as one way out of his present intolerable circumstances, he reaches the famous conclusion 'thus conscience doth make cowards of us all'. What 'conscience' seems to mean here is attention to the likely consequences of this-worldly action in the next life. He then shifts the subject of his meditation away from suicide, observing 'And thus the native hue of resolution/Is sicklied o'er with the pale cast of thought,/And enterprises of great pitch and moment/With this regard their currents turn awry/And lose the name of action' [Q2, III, i, 83–87; F, III, I, 84–88].

Here, as throughout this speech, Hamlet's concerns are couched in general rather than in particular terms. It is a disquisition, as it were, on the human condition rather than on Hamlet's own circumstances, but it seems reasonable to assume that the 'enterprise of great pitch and moment' most likely to be on the audience's (and indeed on Hamlet's) mind at this juncture is his as yet unformulated purpose to kill Claudius. And the 'regard' that deprives such plans of 'the name of action' seems, again, to be concern for the consequences in the next life of actions undertaken in this. This, of course, recalls Hamlet's earlier disquisition on suicide in Act I, the general purport of which remarks was that it is 'noble' to be able to choose whether to live or die, whether to break divine law ('the canon of the everlasting') and risk thereby whatever the consequences of such actions might be in the next life. By the same token it is 'cowardice' to obsess about such things in a way that prevents the pursuit of 'enterprises of great pitch and moment', enterprises, that is, like Hamlet's purpose to revenge his father.

Stayed here by what we might want to call 'religious' considerations about the afterlife – what Hamlet calls considerations of 'conscience' and assimilates to cowardice – elsewhere, in other soliloquies, Hamlet invokes the entirely secular notions of honour, passion and revenge in what turns out to be a series of vain attempts to force himself to overcome the promptings of conscience and act with no concern for the consequences of his actions in the next life. Since they were pagans, such considerations could never have occurred even to the most virtuous and honourable of the Romans on display in *Caesar*, but they remained of pressing moment for the residually Christian Hamlet, who never succeeds in persuading himself simply to put aside the promptings of 'conscience'. In other words, with however much enthusiasm and passion he might talk to himself like an atheist, he continues (recalcitrantly) to act like a Christian.

Not, it must be said, like a good Christian, but like a Christian nevertheless; that is to say like someone for whom spiritual questions of the fate of the immortal soul in the next life remain of supervening importance. In the paroxysm of hyper-activity that envelops him after the play within a play has (correctly) convinced him of Claudius' guilt and (erroneously) convinced him of his own righteousness, Hamlet rushes off to confront his mother with the extent of her own sins. On the way he finds Claudius at prayer and notoriously refuses to dispatch him then and there because he is determined not to send Claudius to heaven rather than to hell.

As any number of commentators have pointed out, this is the nadir of Hamlet's spiritual fortunes, the moment when his consistently atheistical talk might seem to be about to consign him to hell.[4] But while his action in sparing Claudius is prompted by a desire to be revenged, that desire remains contained within, indeed fundamentally constrained by, his consuming obsession with issues of 'conscience' as he himself has defined them, that is to say, issues relating to the fate of souls in the next life, rather than merely with outcomes in this. And it is that impulse that saves him from the damning act of killing Claudius as he is in the throes of a final attempt to repent; an attempt that Hamlet's activities as theatrical impresario have, as it were despite Hamlet's worst intentions, provided for the king, but which his continued possession of the crown and wife for which he had killed old Hamlet, in the first place, prevents him from taking.

Thereafter Claudius plunges on down a chain of increasingly damnable sins and conspiracies in desperate search of security in this life, at the expense of salvation in the next. This confirms him as the ideal type of the reprobate soul; someone now unable to repent, despite his own certain knowledge that he must, if he is to be saved. In direct contrast, Hamlet pursues a very different trajectory, into the second half of the play. There he continues to commit sins, both inadvertent – his murder of Polonius – and deliberate – his carefully premeditated plan to send Rosencrantz and Guildenstern to their deaths in England. However, those sins now serve to call him to a sort of repentance and awaken in him a burgeoning sense of the real relation between his own floundering attempts to realise his destiny as a revenger and the overarching providence of God.

Thus his murder of Polonius elicits from him the crucial admission that 'For this same lord/I do repent, but heaven hath pleased it so,/To punish me with this, and this with me,/That I must be their scourge and minister./I will bestow him and will answer well/The death I gave him' [Q2, III, iv, 170–75; F, III, iv, 156–61]. Even as he acknowledges, for the first time, the role of providence in shaping his fate and receives his first intimations of the need to repent, the effects of Hamlet's frenetic activities in the previous scenes, in finally unmasking Claudius' guilt – again through the operation of conscience, albeit in this instance that of Claudius rather than of Hamlet – and attempting to bring his mother to a true acknowledgement of the facts of the matter and perhaps thereby even to a saving repentance, come back to haunt him.

This is inevitable, since his actions to this point have constituted a blasphemous attempt to usurp the prerogatives of God. Hamlet has been trying to decide the fate of sinful humanity in the next life, and, accordingly, his efforts have ended in disaster: with revenge unachieved; Claudius still on the throne; his mother confirmed in her conviction that Hamlet is 'mad' and thus left blissfully unaware both of Claudius' guilt and of her own desperately dangerous situation. As for Hamlet, having accidentally-on- purpose killed Polonius, he is now guilty of murder, and about to be packed off to seemingly certain death in England. In short, both his practical political and his spiritual condition seem desperate.

Hamlet is rescued from this predicament by a series of contingencies so bizarre and unlikely that the reigning conventions of pamphlet writing and theatre going, not to mention of sermonic commentary on both biblical and contemporary events, virtually demanded that they be regarded as the work of 'providence'. Of course, these same events could be organised under the rubric of 'fortune', with Hamlet's actions aboard ship attributed to his own capacity to seize the opportunity offered by fortune's tergiversations to the man of prudence or mettle. But that is precisely not how Hamlet chooses to view the matter. His comment that 'even in that was heaven ordinant' (Q2, V. ii. 48–50; F, V. ii. 48–50) imposes an aggressively providential interpretation on these events and in so doing looks back to his words spoken over Polonius' corpse and forward to his remark to Horatio in Act V that 'We defy augury. There is a special providence in the fall of a sparrow' [Q2, V, ii, 190–202; F, V, ii, 160–71]. (Perhaps tellingly, Q1 has 'there's a predestinate providence in the fall of a sparrow' [Q1, 17, 45–6].)[5]

Of course in *Julius Caesar* various pagan Romans had laid claim to a similar acceptance of the inevitability of death and the inscrutability of fate, and, as his paean to those, like Horatio, who can take 'Fortune's buffets and rewards' with 'equal thanks', who are not 'passion's slaves' but 'whose blood and judgement are so well co-meddled/That they are not a pipe for Fortune's finger/To sound what stop she please', implies [Q2, III, ii, 59–70; F, III, ii, 61–73], Hamlet himself can, at times, espouse what looks very like a Roman stoic attitude to life. But the likes of Brutus and Cassius had joined such notions with the belief that, in the last analysis, fate and tyranny could not only quite legitimately be cheated, but a sort of immortality could be achieved by means of what Hamlet terms 'self slaughter'. Hamlet's entirely Christian espousal of very similar sentiments on the subject of fate, redefined as providence, is now accompanied with aspirations to a very different sort of immortality. Thus, insofar as Hamlet does display many of the characteristics of the stoic in Act V, his emerges as a determinedly Christian stoicism.

This is Hamlet saved from adopting the expressly political means used in *Julius Caesar* by Brutus and his colleagues to save the state, and in *Hamlet* by

Laertes to pursue precisely the sort of revenge that Hamlet had spent most of the first half of the play (fruitlessly) exhorting himself to exact. The play makes it quite clear that the combination of conspiracy, appeal to the people and assassination put into practice by Brutus and his accomplices in *Julius Caesar*, and attempted by Laertes in *Hamlet*, was an option entirely open to Hamlet as well. Not only was he next in line to the throne, as Claudius explains to Laertes, Hamlet also enjoyed a great popular following, so great, in fact, that any move Claudius might have made against him would have been all too likely to have rebounded upon his own head [Q2, IV, vii, 10–25; F, IV, iii, 10–25]. Similarly, as an insider at court, protected, as Claudius again explains to Laertes, from the ire of the king by his mother's favour, all manner of conspiracy was available to him, as indeed his little plot with Horatio and the players showed rather well. Hamlet, however, had sedulously eschewed such means.

Unlike Hamlet, Laertes takes all these options as soon as they become available. Upon hearing that his father is dead, he returns to Denmark unannounced, uses his popular following and the rumours and suspicions surrounding his father's death to raise an insurrection, storm the palace and confront the king. This seals his fate, for the now frankly diabolic Claudius succeeds in doing to Laertes precisely what the ghost has failed to do to Hamlet; that is, tempt him into taking his revenge by the most dishonourable and damnable means possible. As P. K. Ayers observes, 'the murder-disguised-as-sporting-accident, originally proposed by Claudius, is treacherous enough', but 'Laertes' refinement with the poison' leads to the 'further reduction of his own status from warrior to duelist to assassin' and finally to that byword for cowardice and deceit, poisoner.[6]

Quite unlike Laertes, Hamlet had precisely not dared 'damnation', or consigned 'conscience and grace to the profoundest pit' [Q2, IV, v, 129–35; F, IV, I, 128–34] or vowed 'to cut his throat i' th' church', in order to 'be reveng'd/ Most throughly for my father' [Q2, IV, vii, 124; F, IV, iii, 99]. On the contrary, while he had tried to talk himself into action using precisely such terms, he had, in fact, chosen to *act* largely in the realm of conscience, and explicitly refused to kill Claudius, if not "i" the church', then certainly while at prayer. He had also utterly eschewed the politics of popularity and faction, conspiracy and assassination, to which precisely the same sentiments had led Laertes; a recourse that, in *Hamlet*, had fatal consequences for Laertes, just as it had, in *Julius Caesar*, not only for Brutus and the other conspirators, but also for the entire Roman state.

Sustained by what he initially took to be his own cowardly failure to suppress the promptings of conscience through the invocation of the aggressively secular discourses of honour, passion and revenge, Hamlet was then protected from the consequences of his folly, misapprehension and sin by the active intervention of providence, and finally by an emergent capacity to see the hand of providence working through events to shape his own role as both the scourge and minister of God. He thus enters the final scenes of the play no longer dependent on the say-so of the ghost, which has now completely slipped from view. It no longer matters whether the ghost was a devil, bent on luring Hamlet to damnation, for Hamlet now has reasons of his own to be revenged on Claudius, not to mention written evidence of the latter's malignity. He is no longer acting as his father's surrogate, animated by questions of honour and passion centred on the vindication of his lineage and his status as his father's son. He is now his own man; he, not his father, is now 'Hamlet the Dane'. And in that persona Hamlet can now fulfil, with a resolved conscience, his assigned role as an instrument of God's justice. As he asks Horatio, given Claudius' enormities, 'Is't not perfect conscience/To quit him with this arm? And is't not to be damned/To let this canker of our nature come/In further evil?' [Q2, V, ii, 62–66; F, V, ii, 63–70].[7]

Hamlet now feels free for the first time to plan the death of Claudius, something he implies he is about to do when he tells Horatio that although he knows that the time before news of the fate of Rosencrantz and Guildenstern arrives from England 'will be short. The interim is mine./And a man's life's no more than to say "one" ' [F, V, ii, 71–74]. But even now providence intervenes to save him from the role of political conspirator and/or premeditated murderer, that he has himself thus far avoided with such success. At this point, Hamlet once agains – just in case we haven't noticed – acknowledges the supervening sovereignty of divine providence, admitting to Horatio that 'if it be now, 'tis not to come; if it be not to come, it will be now. If it be not now, yet it will come. The readiness is all, since no man of aught he leaves knows what is't to leave betimes. Let be' (Q2, V, ii, 190–202; F, V, ii, 160–71). He is immediately plunged, entirely unknowing – indeed while intending to reconcile with Laertes – into the midst of the plot designed by Laertes and Claudius to destroy him. There, through a mixture of 'accident' – Gertrude drinking the poisoned cup – and the operation of 'conscience' – in this instance that of Laertes, who confesses to his and Claudius' malign intentions – Hamlet is literally forced into a series of entirely spontaneous reactions; reactions that effect precisely the sort of highly structured denouement that the conventions of revenge tragedy demanded and with which Shakespeare's other revenge tragedy, *Titus Andronicus* had concluded. But while in *Titus* that outcome is explicitly shown to have been the result of the careful plotting and co-ordinated action of the Andronici and the invading Goths, the very opposite is true in this play, where Hamlet acts on the spur of the moment. Were he not dying as he does the deed, one might almost say that he acts in self-defence. His mother is killed, but he has nothing to do with that. The man he kills has (albeit accidentally) just killed his mother and (rather more on purpose) murdered his father and in effect (with the poisoned sword he has placed in Laertes' hand for exactly that purpose) just killed him.

On the one hand, this is as close to killing no murder as it is possible to get. A tyrant might end up dead, but Hamlet is scarcely guilty of tyrannicide. On the other, Hamlet succeeds in inflicting on Claudius precisely the sort of death that he had wished for him when he had stopped himself from dispatching the king while at prayer. Claudius has indeed been killed in the midst of the most dreadful and damning sins, not drunk, swearing, or *in flagrante delicto*, but attempting to commit the most treacherous, premeditated murder it is possible to imagine. In his last words – 'Oh, yet defend me friends, I am but hurt' (Q2, V, ii, 308; F, V, ii, 278) – there is no trace of repentance, but rather a futile attempt to keep up appearances to the end.

Had Hamlet killed Claudius while he prayed he might not have sent the king to heaven, but he would almost certainly have consigned himself to the other place. Hamlet had avoided that fate, but only for the worst of reasons. But avoid it he had. Now he gets his wish, with, as it were, no blame attached, except, of course, that, by this point, it is no longer his wish or intention but rather providence's judgement. Thus has Hamlet been able to escape what Michael Neill terms the 'ironies that force the revenger to imitate the methods of the very adversary he seeks to destroy' even as he has also enacted them.[8] As Peter Ure puts it, Hamlet 'is able to achieve the act of revenge without ever really becoming a revenger', because providence, or the storyteller, has . . . abolished the role'.[9]

We are left then with providence's judgement upon the unrepentant Claudius rather than Hamlet's revenge upon his uncle. The moral and political effects of revenge, resistance and tyrannicide, of the doing of both private and public justice, have all been collapsed into one another and triumphantly achieved, and all without Hamlet having, self-consciously or purposefully, played any of those roles.

Moreover, the pile of bodies that is left littering the stage at the play's end enables the peaceful accession of a new prince, whose claims to legitimacy, based, as they are, on elements of hereditary right – Fortinbras' famous 'claims of memory' – and election, and the capacity providentially to reveal the real story of what has just happened as a miracle of God's justice visited upon usurpation, murder and tyranny, can be accepted by all. Unlike the arrival, in *Titus*, of Lucius with his army of Goths, that of Fortinbras, fresh from his campaigns in Poland, is completely accidental or at least entirely uncoordinated with events in Denmark, in general, and, in particular, with any political plotting or planning on Hamlet's part.

Thus has the state been saved and legitimacy and order restored without recourse to the civil war, the bloody political and moral chaos, into which Rome had been plunged by the assassination of Caesar. Viewed politically, and certainly in comparison with *Julius Caesar* and many another history play, *Hamlet* is thus a play with a positively happy ending.

Doubly so, if, at play's end, Hamlet is taken to be saved. After all, unlike in the sedulously pagan setting conjured in *Julius Caesar*, the issue of salvation, in the form of Hamlet's obsession with conscience, defined as concern with the fate visited upon souls in the next life consequent upon their conduct in this, has been a central motif or concern throughout the play. The central question of whether Hamlet can be revenged and still be saved has been added to, indeed, to some extent, has displaced, as the chief source of emotional energy and suspense, the conventional concern of the revenge tragedy with when and how revenge will be achieved. Here is the central hook upon which much of the audience's attention and anxiety has to this point been hung.

The fact that the sort of melancholy suffered by Hamlet in the early stages of the play was associated by contemporaries, on the one hand, with apostasy, religious despair and damnation, but also, on the other, with the sort of spiritual crisis that might well lead to conversion to true religion and thus to salvation, merely served to heighten the tension.[10] So too, did the ghost's intensely ambiguous status as either, in Hamlet's words, 'a spirit of health or goblin damned', bringing with it either 'airs from heaven or blasts from hell' [Q2 I, iv 40–41;F, I, iv, 19–20]. In addition, as Margreta de Grazia has argued, Hamlet's antic mode was associated with the traditional role of the vice, a character edged around with the demonic, who often ended the action being dragged off to hell by the devil himself.[11] Moreover, virtually everybody in an Elizabethan audience would have realised that it was quite possible to be the instrument and scourge of God and yet still to be damned. After all, the Bible and indeed many a contemporary sermon and pamphlet were replete with the tales of God punishing the sins of one group with the equally sinful acts of others, before consigning both to the fires of eternal judgement. All of which meant that, as again de Grazia has argued, the issue of Hamlet's salvation was front and centre for contemporary audiences in ways that it has most decidedly not been for more modern audiences and critics.[12]

A good part of the play's political meaning turns on this question. Famously the play, or rather Horatio, consigns Hamlet's soul to heaven, but by this point both Horatio and Fortinbras have reasons to say nice things about Hamlet, and the play leaves more than an element of ambiguity around the issue of Hamlet's salvation. While in Q1 Hamlet's final words – 'farewell Horatio, heaven receive my soul' [Q1, sc. xvii, 111] – do indeed seem to insist that, at the last, Hamlet's thoughts have turned to heaven and that he is therefore saved, his last words in Q2 and the Folio – 'the rest is silence' [Q2, V, ii, 342; F, V, ii, 312] – do not. Of course, they do not insist upon the opposite conclusion either, but leave the question open, for the audience to decide.

If the audience take Hamlet to be damned, then the play becomes merely a restatement – an intensely provocative and paradoxical restatement, it is true, but a restatement, nonetheless – of one of the central orthodoxies of late Elizabethan and Jacobean political theology. For if Hamlet is damned, the play is merely staging the inevitable consequence of usurpation and tyranny in revolt and regicide, while reminding us, through the fate of Hamlet, both in this world and the next, that the wages of those particular sins remain (both temporal and spiritual) death.

It is only if Hamlet is saved that the play becomes something rather more contentious, with the killer of a regnant prince being shown on stage ascending to a heavenly reward. Admittedly, even on this, the most optimistic view of the matter, the aperture opened by the play for 'resistance' is very narrow indeed. When Hamlet kills Claudius he is certain that he himself is dying. In this state, and for the first time in the play, there can be no chance that he could gain politically from the death of Claudius. About to pass from the world, he kills the king and then, with his dying breath, elects Fortinbras to the empty throne. Whatever else this is, it is as close to a politically selfless act as it is possible to get. Moreover, in marked contrast to, say, *Titus*, the play has gone out of its way to emphasise that the final denouement has been anything but planned by Hamlet. There has been faction and conspiracy aplenty, but all on the side of the revengees, Claudius and Laertes, and none on the side of the revenger, Hamlet, who has walked into a trap only to be rescued therefrom – pretty much completely if 'flights of angels' really have sung him 'to his rest' [Q2, V, ii, 343–44; F, V, ii, 314–15] – by the operation of providence.

In the transition from *Henry V* through *Julius Caesar* to *Hamlet* we have moved from a problematic centred on the capacity of the most virtuous men to shape events, indeed to save, even to refound, the state, through the self-conscious combination of the politics of popularity, honour and legitimacy, to a very different take on essentially the same question in *Hamlet*. *Henry V* had pictured a great man successfully combining those political modes to restore legitimacy to a state thrown into moral and political chaos by tyranny and usurpation. By contrast, *Caesar* had shown men of certainly as great, if not greater, intrinsic military and political virtu(e), that is to say Julius Caesar and Brutus, resoundingly fail to do the same to a Rome depicted in the throes of political and moral change, afflicted by a corruption and instability too great to yield to the state-founding efforts of even the greatest men.

Here different historical cases are being used to show how circumstances do indeed alter cases; to demonstrate how the lessons of the past, and the consequent attempts to emulate the achievements of men of even the greatest virtue, must yield to the particular circumstances in which those doing the applying find themselves and to which the examples and apothegms extracted from the study of history are to be applied. Get that wrong, misconstrue the circumstances, misapply the examples – and, as Cicero observes in *Julius Caesar*, there was always every chance that 'men may construe things, after their fashion,/ Clean from the purpose of the things themselves' [I, iii, 34–35] – and things could and would end in disaster, as they do in *Julius Caesar*.

I have argued above that in addition to these specific points about the politics of historiography, *Julius Caesar* was making a more specific comment upon the appropriateness of the direct application to Christian monarchies of *exempla* and *sententiae* extracted from pagan and republican sources. I have also argued that that case was further developed in *Hamlet*, in which a central figure with residually Christian impulses and beliefs found himself in a situation where the meaning and salience of those beliefs were put under enormous strain, but in which, by holding on to some basic Christian notions about 'conscience', the immortal soul, salvation and damnation, heaven and hell, and God's supervening providence – all of them quite unavailable to the pagan characters in *Julius Caesar* – that central figure was able to negotiate an interlocking set of both political and spiritual dilemmas, to dramatically different effect.

Indeed, he was able successfully to discharge his dual roles as God's minister and scourge without resort to any sort of political manoeuvre, ignoring the siren songs of honour, revenge and passion, on the one hand, and those of the politics of popularity and faction, of conspiracy and assassination, on the other. Thus enabled, Hamlet punishes otherwise secret sin, saves the state from tyranny and usurpation and creates conditions in which a ruler, whose legitimacy was acceptable to all, could restore order to the state. And on the most optimistic view of the play, he had been able to do all that while saving his own soul, into the bargain.

Essex – again

The period between the writing and first performance of *Henry V* and the writing and first performances of *Hamlet* encompassed the return from Ireland, in disgrace, of the earl of Essex, as well as his protracted period under deep suspicion and house arrest that culminated in his ill-fated rising and his consequent trial, condemnation and execution for treason. It is notoriously difficult to date the various versions of Hamlet precisely in relation either to one another or to events. There may well have been a version of a play by Shakespeare called *Hamlet* extant while Essex was still alive. But there are also some references in the texts that have come down to us to events that took place after his rebellion and execution in February 1601. The most we can say, then, is that the play was being written and revised through the period of Essex's final decline and fall and that it contains what may well be certain echoes and resonances of those events. I want now to try to read the play not merely in the context provided by but as a comment upon, or perhaps even as an intervention in, the events that followed on from Essex's return from Ireland in the autumn of 1599, when *Caesar* was being played as a new play at the Globe; events that culminated in the earl's execution for treason in 1601.

To begin, there are certain broad parallels between Hamlet and Essex after his return from Ireland. We have in Hamlet a figure deemed dangerous to the state, but too well connected, too well beloved by the queen and too popular with the people, to be destroyed at home. He is therefore sent abroad on official business to meet his fate there. But, seeing through the plot against him, he returns home unbidden and unannounced. That is exactly what many of Essex's supporters thought had happened to the earl in Ireland and if we pursue the parallel, then Hamlet back home from the pirate ship was in exactly the position enjoyed by Essex on his return from Ireland – under suspicion and surveillance, and subject to the malign, indeed the murderous, plots of his enemies.

Secondly we have Hamlet's madness. As Karin Coddon has pointed out, after his return from Ireland, during the time of his house arrest at York house and indeed subsequently, Essex 'suffered from what Timothy Bright would have called a "melancholie madnesse", replete with bouts of near-stupendous despair and religious mania'.[13] These were noted by contemporaries with alarm. John Harington reported after a visit to Essex that 'it resteth with me in opinion that ambition thwarted in its career, doth speedily lead on to madness: herein I am strengthened by what I learn in my Lord of Essex, who shifteth from sorrow and repentance to rage and rebellion so suddenly, as well proveth him devoid of good reason or right mind; in my last discourse, he uttered such strange designs that made me hasten forth, and leave his absence: thank heaven I am safe at home, and if I go in such troubles again, I deserve the gallows for a meddling fool: his speeches of the queen becometh no man who hath *mens sana in corpore sano*. He hath ill advisors, and much evil hath sprung from this source. The queen well knoweth how to humble the haughty spirit, the haughty spirit knoweth not how to yield, and the man's soul seemeth tossed to and fro, like the waves of a troubled sea'.[14] While he was in the custody of Lord Keeper Egerton, Essex's moods were closely monitored. In a letter to Henry Wotton, John Donne, then Egerton's secretary, described the earl's state of mind as a 'sickness'. While in some moods Essex evidently said the most outrageous things about the queen and his intentions towards her, in others he lamented his own sins loudly and called for the advice of divines. At one point, he consulted his old Cambridge tutor, John Overall, about his fears that he had grieviously offended God through his serial failure to keep the sabbath. On another occasion, he called upon his friend Southampton to 'repent', in a private letter that circulated in manuscript as a token of the earl's own repentance and personal piety.[15]

We have here a picture of the earl in the period after his return from Ireland as a man under suspicion and surveillance; a man known to be in a state of mental distress – 'sickness' – which caused him to oscillate between violent rage and threats and fits of religious melancholy and despair. The parallels between all this and Hamlet's state of mind and political circumstances are striking. Hamlet is certainly 'mad' and uses his madness to say some very threatening things about the king.[16] But Hamlet's 'madness' also takes the form of religious despair and melancholia. From the opening of Act II Hamlet is certainly under suspicion and surveillance. Of course, he is not, like Essex, under house arrest, although he is certainly threatened with confinement both by the king – 'I like him not, nor stands it safe with us/To let his madness range' [Q2, III, iii, 1–2; F, III, iii, 1–2] and by Rosencrantz – 'you do freely bar the door of your own liberty if you deny your griefs to your friend' [Q2, III, ii, 329–30; F, III, ii, 328–29]. If a version of the play was being written in the period before the rebellion, while Essex was confined in York House or subsequently plotting away in Essex House, then the parallels between what was being presented on stage and immediately current events could scarcely have been lost on a London audience. Under those circumstances what we are seeing in *Hamlet*, just like what we saw in *1 Henry VI*, would be the staging of events in the theatre even as they were still unfolding in the real world.

Indeed, in its final versions, the play might well be taken to advert to precisely this fact. After all, *Hamlet* also features the production of a play, with specially rewritten passages inserted into the text, commissioned by a major courtier for what are covert and potentially highly subversive purposes. Given the interest of the Essex circle in the drama – during the period of Essex's imprisonment in York House, two of his closest associates, the earl of Southampton and the earl of Rutland, were reported as passing 'away the time in London merely going to plays every day' – and as their willingness to use the theatre as a form of propaganda, a propensity that, on the argument being made here, dates back at least to 1*Henry VI*, this, in itself, is remarkable.

Of course, in the play, the players are entirely innocent of any involvement in Hamlet's conspiracy; they are presented as merely doing as a great man about the court asks them, unaware of his dangerously subversive intentions in so doing. Here it may be worth remarking that one of the crucial passages in the play that has been used to date it after the Essex rebellion concerns the actors. That is the reference to 'the little eyases', 'an eyrie of children' that 'are now the fashion, and so berattle the common stages – so they call them – that many wearing rapiers are afraid of goose-quills and dare scarce come hither' [F, II, ii, 337–42]. That passage is taken to be a reference to 'the Children of the Chapel who began to act at the Blackfriars at the end of 1600' and to the subsequent 'war of the theatres', a public slanging match between the company at the Blackfriars and 'the common stages', which took place in 1601, that is to say, well after Essex's revolt and execution.[17] This very precise, pointedly topical, reference, together with a cryptic claim a few lines earlier that 'their [the players'] inhibition' from playing in the city 'comes by the means of the late innovation' [Q2, II, ii, 295–96; F, II, ii, 330–31] – an aside which is often construed as itself an (in)direct reference to the Essex rebellion – characterise the play as a text that is speaking to a set of circumstances that post-date 'the late innovation'. These references are inserted just before the exchange, later in the same scene, in which Hamlet draws the first player aside to get him to agree not only to perform a play of Hamlet's choosing the next night but also to include in the performance 'a speech of some dozen or sixteen lines, which I would set down and insert in't' [II, ii, 530–36].

At a stroke these two passages do two things: they (re)date the play to the period after the revolt and they make it quite clear that, in the play at least, the players are entirely innocent of any involvement in Hamlet's subversive little ploy with the play within the play. Not only does Hamlet solicit their performance before the king, he chooses what play they should perform and personally doctors it to suit his own purposes. This is to insert into a play that now dates, or seems to date, from the period *after* the rebellion the excuses or explanations used by members of Shakespeare's company after the rebellion when they were called to account before the Council for having put on, at the behest of some of the Essex conspirators, a special performance of a play about the deposition of Richard II.

Finally, and perhaps most significantly, there is the close correlation between what Laertes is shown successfully pulling off in the play and what Essex and his followers tried and failed to do in London in February 1601. For Laertes is shown using his popularity with the people and their discontent with recent events to raise the crowd against the king and then, with their help, to burst past the king's guards – 'where is my Switzers? Guard the door' [Q2, IV, v, 97; F, IV, i, 96] – into the royal presence to demand a showdown with the king. And that, of course, was precisely what Essex had been contemplating doing in 1600 and had allegedly tried and failed to do in February 1601.

On this account, we can take the play to be an attempt to conjure up and comment upon the extraordinarily tense atmosphere in the months before the rebellion, with Essex first under house arrest and then holed up in Essex House, with rumours of rebellion and escape circling around him. In which case we can see the course adopted by Laertes in the play as a staging of one of the options before the earl. In the play, of course, Laertes' success in raising the city and storming the palace does him no good. He proves entirely unable to penetrate or see past 'the divinity' that continues to 'hedge' even a usurping murderer like Claudius (or indeed, on the views of at least some English Catholics, Queen Elizabeth herself) and quickly falls victim to Claudius' blandishments. His obsession with revenge and his addiction to the instrumental means of this-worldly politics prove his downfall as he falls into the treacherous court conspiracy that seals his fate. In the play, as we have seen, Laertes is the anti-Hamlet, but, on the current reading, Hamlet is the anti-Essex; the man whose triumph over the demands of honour and revenge, over the claims of lineage and political self-interest, and whose contempt for the politics of popular insurrection and court conspiracy, whose capacity, in the end and at the death, to trust in and wait upon providence preserves him from Laertes' (and Essex's) fate and in so doing saves both his own soul and the state from disaster. On this view, then, the play might be read as a fantasy happy ending to a story that in 1600–1 seemed to be in the process of ending very badly indeed.

In this version the central protagonist (Hamlet/Essex) does not (like Laertes/Essex) give in to the atheistic promptings of honour and passion, or to the desire for revenge (against his enemies, if not the queen herself); regards his current malaise not as a form of melancholy to be sloughed off or cured by action but as a genuine spiritual crisis, and as such as an opportunity to hear and heed the voice of conscience. Following his conscience, he avoids Laertes' resort to the politics of insurrection and conspiracy, a course of action that, as Laertes' example showed, could only end in disaster. Rather he waits on providence. As he does so, providence allows him the chance to revenge himself, while serving the causes of divine and human justice and ensuring the return of legitimate rule to the state.

On this account, *Hamlet* would indeed occupy a relation both to events and to Essex himself somewhat analogous to that ascribed above to *Henry V*, except, of course, that to offer comment, counsel and praise to Essex on his way to Ireland was a good deal less politically charged, indeed dangerous, an act than was continuing to comment on his affairs and fate after his return. As Leeds Barroll has argued, Essex and those around him were intensely interested not only in the drama but in other fictive and literary forms as modes of communication, indeed as forms of propaganda and even of political thought, not to say action.[18] After all, it was only because they believed in the power of their own image-making and that of their clients and associates, that the conspirators thought that they could raise the city against the court on that fateful day in February 1601. In Kevin Sharpe's resonant phrase, in the sort of cultural system operating between Essex and his circle, the popular stage and its audience, 'compliment' could also function as 'criticism' and both could work as forms of 'propaganda'.

In short, if the play, in anything like the forms in which it has come down to us, was written and performed before February 1601, then it is a remarkable staging of and commentary upon events even as those events were still playing themselves out. As such it joins the chorus of rumour and libel that attended the course of the earl's confinement; speculation so pervasive and perfervid that the regime staged two public demonstrations of his guilt to still it. The first in November 1599 arrayed all the central figures in the regime behind the claim that the expedition to Ireland had been the best-organised and most lavishly financed of all the queen's military campaigns, the failure of which lay entirely at the earl's door. The whole affair was staged at the end of legal term in Star

Chamber so that the assembled multitude could take versions of the official account back to their localities the better to convince the people that the earl had not been a victim of the malice and conspiracy of his enemies at court.

If that were not enough, there followed next June more formal proceedings against the earl; proceedings at which he was personally present and forced to acknowledge his fault and ask for pardon. Between those events the earl himself and those close to him spread rumours and leaked letters in which he presented himself to a variety of publics as a newly converted and repentant Christian, and a fit subject for the favour and forgiveness of his queen. On this account, then, the play can be read as a daring attempt to cash in on this rush of popular interest and rumour.

If it was written after the Essex rebellion, however, the play was a no less remarkable retrospective version of and commentary upon those events. Of course, what it meant in relation to Essex would change according to when it was played or read. Counsel, warning and wish-fulfilment before the event, afterwards, it would became commentary and moral critique, lament and renewed warning, not to Essex, of course, who was, after all, dead, but to others, about the dangers that, with Essex's adversaries triumphant and James VI still not safely ensconced on the English throne, still hovered around the commonwealth. Its meaning would, of course, shift once again after the peaceful accession of that other foreign claimant, arriving from the north, James VI and I. Of course, after the earl's movingly repentant death, and even more after James' accession, read or viewed in the right context or frame of mind, *Hamlet* might even become a complex form of apologia, the play taking its place alongside a range of posthumous ballads and libels that sought, after his execution, to rehabilitate and reconstruct the earl's reputation (while blackening that of his enemies).

The purpose of playing

It is not the least of its value to the current analysis that *Hamlet* itself contains an analysis of the 'purpose of playing', of the relation of the drama to its times, and an account of the ways in which mere playing could provide contemporaries with their surest guide to what was currently going on, in the real world. The play, in short, contains a contemporary account, as it were straight from the horse's mouth, of precisely the hermeneutic mechanisms, the interpretative back and forth, that this book claims were in operation in the relationship between these plays and at least some members of their first audiences. Or rather it provides an account of how a certain sort of playing – the sort on display in this play and others like it, rather than in any old plays – could provide an attentive audience member with that sort of insight and commentary.

Polonius famously describes the players as 'the best actors in the world, either for tragedy, comedy, history, pastoral, pastoral-comical, historical-pastoral, tragical-historical, tragical-comical-historical-pastoral, scene individable, or poem unlimited' [Q2, II, ii, 333–36; F, II, ii, 394–98]. There could scarcely be a clearer statement about the generic oddness of the play that the audience is watching nor a more obvious reference to the differences between it and the earlier version of *Hamlet* that had presumably primed their expectations of this one. The point is driven home by the extended speech of Pyrrhus given at Hamlet's request by the First Player, which is a parody of a quite different sort of play and, as such, entirely unlike anything else in *Hamlet*.[19]

Hamlet himself returns to that point in his instructions to the actors on how he wants his play to be acted. These are framed against a satiric account of how not to do it, which is itself almost certainly an equally satiric denunciation of a style of acting with which the audience was no doubt itself familiar and in which many of them would have seen the earlier Hamlet, or plays very like it, – *The Spanish Tragedy*, Shakespeare's own *Titus Andronicus*, any number of plays by Marlowe – bellowed out to considerable popular applause.

Hamlet denounces actors that 'neither having th'accent of Christians, nor the gait of Christian, pagan, nor man have so strutted and bellowed that I have thought some of Nature's journeymen had made men, and not made them well, they imitated humanity so abominably' [Q2, III, ii, 30–34; F, III, ii, 30–35]. 'O, it offends me to the soul to hear a robustious periweg-pated fellow tear a passion to tatters, to very rags, to split the ears of the groundlings, who for the most part are capable of nothing but inexplicable dumb-shows and noise' [Q2, III, ii, 8–12; F, III, ii, 8–12].

Against this negative image Hamlet proceeds to outline what he wants. 'Suit the action to the word, the word to the action, with this special observance, – that you o'erstep not the modesty of nature. For anything so o'erdone is from the purpose of playing whose end, both at the first and now, was and is to hold as 'twere the mirror up to Nature to show virtue her feature, Scorn her own image, and the very age and body of the time his form and pressure' [Q2, III, ii, 17–24; F, III, ii, 17–24]. The audience, then, has been put on notice that they are not getting the sort of play that the old *Hamlet*, and the style of acting in which that play would almost certainly have been played, might have led them to expect.

Rather, they are watching a new sort of play, being played in a very different style and one with a pressing contemporary purpose. After all, as Hamlet famously tells Polonius, the players are 'the abstract and brief chronicles of the time' [Q2, I, ii, 462–63; F, II, ii, 520], a time, identified at the close of Act I by Hamlet as being definitively 'out of joint'. If that did not get the audience's attention, alerting them (and us) to the play's 'purpose' in providing something like a pointed and direct commentary on 'the time' then surely nothing would.

As any number of commentators have observed, the seeming transparency of this (humanist) theory of, and justification for, theatrical representation is at complete variance with the complexity of the play's actual treatment, indeed performance, of performance and playing. After all, Hamlet enters the action decrying the falsity of 'playing'. The outward signs of his grief – 'my inky cloak' 'customary suits of black', all the 'forms, moods, shapes of grief' cannot, he tells his mother, 'denote me truly' precisely because 'they are actions that a man might play' [Q2, I, ii, 83–84; F, I, ii, 81–82]. Hamlet's grief is genuine, he famously claims, because he has 'that within which passes show'.

But the ease of that distinction between outward show – that which 'a man might play' – and inner truth or reality is then systematically broken down. From his meeting with the ghost onwards Hamlet is caught in a world of playing, where the need to tell the real from the merely performed is crucial both to his and the other characters' purposes and fate. His life and indeed his soul depend on his capacity to tell whether his uncle and the ghost are what they seem; and indeed whether he himself is sane or mad, suffering from a reality-distorting melancholy or from a reality-heightening religious despair. The extraordinarily dangerous knowledge which the ghost imparts to him puts him at odds with the entire social world, a world that immediately becomes a series of performances or pretences – with Claudius playing the role of a legitimate and virtuous ruler, Gertrude that of a loving mother and virtuous queen, Rosencrantz and Guildenstern that of Hamlet's friends and well-willers, even Ophelia that of of his doting lover.

If he is to survive, Hamlet must now navigate his way through, and penetrate to the truth or falsehood beneath, all of these performances. And he does so, at first, by himself playing a role, by putting on an 'antic-disposition', in effect by feigning madness. Except that, in allowing him to act out an inner mental and emotional torment, that madness is itself more than an act. Indeed, just as Timothy Bright had warned it might, his melancholy in itself becomes a temptation, something through which Hamlet himself must see, or get to the bottom of. For if his melancholy is more than an act, if it is a genuine malady, his conversations with the ghost are likely to have been a mere chimera, an illusion, very likely induced, not merely by his own affliction but also by the purposive interventions of Satan, designed to exploit that affliction and lead him to damnation. If, however, he is not 'mad', then the ghost both exists and is what it says it is. And if that is the case, he may need to take rather radical spiritual and political action.

Starting out positing a clear divide between that within which passes show and outward forms, moods and shapes, all of which a man might play, both in his relations with the outer, social and political worlds, the world of the court, but also in relation to his own inner life and consciousness, Hamlet ends up caught in a world of performance and appearance.

That the way out of this labyrinth is provided by theatrical performance is, of course, in itself remarkable. For in the performance of *The murder of Gonzago* the acting out of a fiction becomes the way to reach within to that which really does pass show, i.e. to that which cannot be disguised by any amount of outward performance: the operation of the conscience, in this case of the conscience of a murderer, Claudius. In the context of contemporary debates about the moral depravity of the theatre and its corrupting effects on its audience this represents an extraordinarily confident claim for the potency, the moral power, of theatrical representation. On this account, the theatre – the most self-consciously and overtly fictive set of illusions and performances imaginable – becomes the way in which Hamlet starts to see through the false surfaces, the mere appearances, the playing and performance, that characterise both the outer world of the court and indeed the inner world of his own consciousness.

In the crucial scene we are shown a play – *The murder of Gonzago* – being performed before an audience. But there is, of course, another play being performed here – the play that, when asked by Claudius the title of the performance they are watching, Hamlet terms 'the mousetrap'. In that play, Claudius is not a part of the audience but rather a part, indeed the central part, of the action, with Hamlet and Horatio providing the audience for the king's reaction to the play he is watching. Hamlet's jokey commentary on the action to the queen, to Ophelia and indeed to Claudius adverts to this aspect of the scene, inserting a very considerable element of threat into the action – a threat which reaches its height, of course, in his identification of the king-killer in the play, Lucianus, not as the king's brother but his nephew. For with that gloss the play becomes a reference not merely to Claudius' crime in killing a king, but also to his threatened or likely fate at the hands of his revenging nephew, Hamlet.

It is, of course, because all that is involved here is a mere play that Hamlet is able to raise the stakes and the pressure to this height even as he denies that there is 'any offence' in the argument of the play. 'No offence i'th'world. . . . Your majesty and we that have free souls – it touches us not. Let the galled jade wince, our withers are unwrung' [Q2, III, ii, 228–36; F, III, ii, 227–34].

All of which adverts to the relationship between a mere play – 'a knavish piece of work' [Q2, III, ii, 234; F, III, ii, 232] written 'in jest' – 'they do but jest. Poison in jest' [Q2, III, ii, 228; F, III, ii, 226] – and directly current events. On one view of the matter there can indeed be 'no offence in the world' in a play, precisely because plays are indeed 'knavish pieces of work', mere 'jests'. But as such they remain far from 'the purpose of playing' as Hamlet has outlined it earlier to the players. However, for those in the audience who can or do recognise either themselves or 'the time' in the action being played out on stage, their consciences as well as their attention may very well be engaged and the wider moral purposes of playing, as Hamlet has outlined them, might thereby be served. For, after all, there is a third play being staged here. Not only is *The murder of Gonzago* being watched by the court, not only are Hamlet and Horatio watching Claudius and the others watch that play in another play called *The mousetrap*, the audience ('we') are watching Hamlet watch Claudius in *The mousetrap* watching *The murder of Gonzago*, in yet another play called *Hamlet*.

What is being staged here is the play's own relation to its 'time', that is to say to the immediate political moment or conjuncture in which it was written and performed and to which it was very precisely addressed; a 'time' which on certain contemporary views was easily as out of joint as anything being acted out on stage. But at the very moment that the play is adverting most directly to that relation, it is simultaneously staging or articulating its own defence against giving 'offence' in that regard. Just as with Claudius and *The murder of Gonzago*, the relevant connections are not being made on stage at all but elsewhere, in the consciousness and the consciences of the audience. To those 'that have free souls' the play will remain just that, a play; in the estimation of many contemporaries, even of many avid theatre-going contemporaries, it will remain 'a knavish piece of work', a mere 'jest' and viewed thus there can indeed be 'no offence, no offence i' th'world', to be taken from it. But to others – in this far more like Hamlet, Horatio and Claudius than the other unknowing members of the audience for *The murder of Gonzago* – who do indeed recognise the parallels between what is being acted in front of them and the events through which they are living, that will not be the case. For them, at least, the moral purpose of playing will have been fulfilled.

Here is vindication not only of Hamlet's description of the players to Polonius as 'the abstract and brief chronicles of the time' but also of his later claim, made to Ophelia, that 'the players cannot keep counsel –they'll tell all' [Q2, II, ii, 462–63, III, ii, 134–35; F, II, ii, 520, III, ii,137–38]. On this reading, then, *Hamlet* contains within itself an account of the dynamics of theatrical performance, of the relationship of the theatre both to the times themselves and to its own audience's response to the staged version of the times with which it is confronting them. The resulting account is entirely congruent with, indeed more or less identical to, that underpinning the argument of this book. In short, it provides the heuristic principles underlying the current argument with immediately contemporary, indeed with immediately Shakespearean, warrant.

CHAPTER 25

The morning after the night before: *Troilus and Cressida* as retrospect

If, amongst other things, *Hamlet* can be read as an examination, both from the inside and the outside, of the political and the religious consequences of the implosion of the Essexian project, *Troilus and Cressida* can, in turn, be taken to be returning to that same topic, evoking and evaluating the political and moral wreckage left by the debacle of the Essex rebellion.

The manner of the earl's downfall – by turns, absurd, ignoble, ill-judged and, latterly, arguably traitorous – not merely dashed the hopes of those who had invested in a future remade by a combination of Essexian prowess, virtue and honour and Stuart legitimacy, it also rendered those hopes (viewed from the perspective provided by Essex's eventual failure and fate) at least as absurd and misguided (if not as ignoble and traitorous) as the earl's own conduct. In short, the greater the hopes invested in Essex, the greater the disillusion, self-disgust and despair likely to be occasioned by his failure and fall. And *Troilus and Cressida* is not a play in which such sentiments are in short supply.

The play returns to many of the central themes and topoi of the preceding plays; to the compatibility of the politics of honour, martial prowess, faction and popularity; to war itself as a source of honour, order and legitimacy; to the applicability of the language of the market to the political world, and that world's claims to be a source, perhaps, in this life, the ultimate source, of legitimacy and moral worth. In what follows I want to read *Troilus and Cressida* against *Henry V*, as a post-Essex commentary on the contemporary martial/political and, indeed, moral scene.

Both *Troilus and Cressida* and *Henry V* deal with the heroic matter of two wars, each, in its different way, integrally related to contemporary myths of Englishness. The relationship between Elizabethan English nationalism and what another play on the subject calls the 'the famous victories of Henry V' goes without saying. So too, given the traditional association between Troy and London (or Troynovant, as it was frequently called), and between the ancient Britons and the Trojans, does the relationship between almost any reading of the Trojan war and the situation of late sixteenth-century England.[1]

The wars in the midst of which both plays are set are justified (in part at least) through the discourses of martial honour and chivalry. Henry is shown brilliantly manipulating the norms of martial honour and indeed, in his wooing of the French princess, of (a studiedly non-courtly) courtly love, to achieve and legitimise his wider political purposes and ambitions and burnish his own image as a martial hero on the scale of Alexander the Great. Essex, too, had a habit of framing his martial adventures and service of the queen in heavily chivalric terms.

'Fluellenism' revisited

The comparison between Henry V and Alexander is famously made by the sometimes ludicrous and always antiquity-obsessed Fluellen. The terms upon which Fluellen's parallel between Harry of Monmouth and Alexander the Great are set are notoriously absurd; dependent, as they are, on the fact that a river runs through both Monmouth and Macedon. However, having started out ridiculous, the comparison gets serious, when, after he has discoursed on Alexander's most un-Henry-like passions, moods and drunken fits, in the course of one of which Alexander had killed his best friend, Clytus, Fluellen recalls that, in a very different, altogether more cold-blooded, spirit, Henry has killed his best friend, 'the fat knight with the great-belly doublet', 'Sir John Falstaff' [IV, vii, 22–50].

This passage has formed the basis of a full-scale denunciation of what has been called Fluellenism.[2] But even as it seems to render such identifications and parallels absurd, the passage works to incite the audience to continue to make them (thus anticipating many other such teasing disavowals and provocations to be written to the same effect by Ben Jonson). The effect is compounded by the fact that Fluellen is a character designed to remind the audience of that intensely Essexian figure Sir Roger Williams, whose funeral in 1595 Essex had turned into a public celebration of the martial and moral virtues that defined his cause. Not, of course, that the parallels are anything like exact, for, having evoked, in Fluellen, some of Williams' signature characteristics, Shakespeare then attributes to his character a slavish addiction to the ancient discipline of the wars diametrically opposed to the aggressively modernising stance taken by Williams himself on these questions. Fluellen, then, both is, and is not, Williams, the character being expressly designed both to evoke a set of distinctively Williams-and-Essex-centred themes and concerns, while simultaneously denying any such simple identification.[3]

The same function is fulfilled even more daringly in *Troilus and Cressida* by the passage in which Ulysses describes the play-acting caricatures, the crude parodies and impressions, of the leading Greek generals with which Patroclus is diverting Achilles during their period of withdrawal from the Greek war effort. There, 'like a strutting player', 'he pageants us', imitating even 'great Agamemnon' or the aged Nestor. 'And in this fashion all our abilities, gifts, natures, shapes/Severals and generals of grace exact,/Achievements, plots, orders, preventions,/Excitements to the field, or speech for truce,/Success or loss, what is or is not, serves/As stuff for these two to make paradoxes' [I, iii, 151–84]. We might think that herein the play is commenting upon its own procedures, inciting the audience to seek precisely such caricatures, such satiric vignettes and tableaux, embedded within the action of the play.

In *Troilus and Cressida* that invitation or, rather more accurately, that titillating tease, is compounded by the presence of Thersites, a foul-mouthed commentator on the follies and depravities of the great and the good. At one point Achilles tells his friend Patroclus, whom Thersites is in the process of glossing as a fool, that Thersites 'is a privileged man' [II, iii, 55], in effect licensed (like some of the playing companies themselves) by his status as a client or dependant of some of the most powerful members of the very elite he is deriding and guying. Of course, Thersites' is a dangerous game; but, beaten by Ajax, he finds another patron in Achilles, under whose protection (given, in part, to spite Ajax) he continues his scabrous commentary on the action of the play.

In passages like these the audience is being incited into (even as it is also being warned against) a search for Fluellen-like parallels and resonances. By openly adverting to the always fleeting and multivalent ways in which these plays set up and exploit, as well as undercut and deny, parallels with the wider political scene, such playful asides provide something of a warrant for the reading of the plays being essayed here. Indeed, on this account, we might even go further and claim that such passages – Fluellen's alternately absurd and serious comparisons between Alexander and Henry, the spoofs of leading political figures in the Greek camp performed by Thersites and Patroclus and indeed the play itself – provide something of a key to the typological conflation of various sorts of history being performed in these plays. Various histories (both recently vivid and distantly mythological) are conflated with the 'now' of performance and the world of immediately contemporary resonance and comment in and through which these plays operate. This is a direct evocation of the ways in which both this play and the others under discussion here could be simultaneously 'about' both 'history' and 'now', about the siege of Troy and contemporary politics.

Throughout *Henry V* the heroical aspects of Henry's career and victories are evoked and lauded in the most heightened language by a chorus. *Troilus and Cressida* starts, in heroic mode, with a similar scene-setting chorus. Thereafter, however, having got the Greek host to Troy and explained that the action of the play 'leaps o'er the vaunt and firstlings of these broils,/Beginning in the middle, starting thence away/To what may be digested in a play' [I, i, 27–29], the chorus is never seen again;[4] its place taken by the entirely scurrilous, low-life figure of that self-described bastard, Thersites, who, as Robert Weimann amongst others has noted, takes on many of the choric, commentating functions of the traditional Vice. Glossing V, ii, Weimann observes that 'at the primary level of mimesis – Cressida's dialogue with Diomedes – is seen and commented upon by Troilus, but the second level of acting – Troilus' dialogue with Ulysses . . . is seen and commented upon by Thersites . . . Although all three levels of acting are in turn watched by the spectators, the last is certainly closest to the audience in terms of speech, stage position, and the scope of the action he [Thersites] has seen.' 'Like . . . the vice figure before him', Weiman claims, 'Thersites is a provocateur of truth not a moral judge', or rather he is a moral judge whose entirely reductive moral judgements we are not meant (necessarily) to share. In this role, much like a chorus, he 'concludes scenes with marked frequency', providing 'sarcastic summary or evaluation of what has happened, spoken after the actors engaged in dialogue have left the stage'.[5]

On this basis, we might argue that while, in *Henry V*, the exalted language of the chorus is intended to invite the scepticism of the audience inciting them to contrast the inflated claims of the chorus with what is actually happening in the play, in *Troilus* the chorus-like commentary of Thersites works in the opposite direction; inviting, even daring, the audience to see through the inflated claims being made for themselves by the characters to the 'putrefied core' within. As Graham Bradshaw observes of the bizarre scene in which Hector kills an unidentified Greek knight soley to possess his gorgeous suit of armour, 'it is tempting to see this curious episode as a grisly, surreal *Gestalt*,' that 'vividly actualises that process of ruthless unpacking which the whole play so persistently enacts'.[6]

As in the English history plays, and in particular in *Henry V*, the play exploits the audience's knowledge of the outcome of this most famous of all wars. Thus, just as the audience knew that Hal would turn into Henry V and that Henry V would win at Agincourt, and that Julius Caesar would die under the knives of conspirators whose attempt to save the Roman republic would end in desperate failure, so everyone also knew that the Trojans were going to lose and that, as Troilus and Cressida claim, as they pledge undying fidelity the one to the other, they will indeed become bywords to successive generations; he for disappointed fidelity and love [III, 2, 177–78] and she for feminine duplicity and falsehood [III, 2, 191]. As Pandarus puts it, 'Let all constant men be Troiluses, all false women, Cressids, and all brokers-between panders!' [III, ii, 195–99].

Linda Charnes makes this aspect of the play central to her analysis. She argues that, in other history plays, when 'historical figures make unwitting references to their own historicity', this represents 'a strategy of irony that privileges the audience's metadramatic position'. But in this instance, given the very common identification of England and London with Troy, and given what happened to Troy at the end of a war not nearly as long as England's current struggle with Spain, what Charnes describes as the difficulty of fully embracing 'what is happening in the present moment when the future moment is already encoded as a past moment'[7] serves not so much to heighten the audience's sense of their own metadramatic omniscience as to sequester them within the same constrained and claustrophobic world as the characters themselves. The resulting sense of being trapped inside a story whose ending was only too familiar and which, despite the best efforts of the characters on stage, could not be averted, would thus have been rendered the more sinister and threatening.

The result of these ironies is a play whose 'generic inconsistencies'[8] were perfectly designed to set up and then frustrate the expectations of its audience. It offers, through its subject-matter, and through the presence, at the start, of a Henry-V-like chorus, the promise of the sort of epic-heroic performance (albeit here tinged with tragedy, rather than with triumphalism) contained in *Henry V*, only thereafter to provide something decidedly less exalted. Neither comic nor tragic, the play exists in the same sort of generically liminal space inhabited by *Hamlet*.

Market value

The play is about both martial and romantic honour; about the ethics and dynamics of what Thersites calls, in his own satirically reductive way, 'lechery and war'.

In addressing those topics the play activates the language of the market, using notions of value determined by the often duplicitous or self-interested relations between buyers and sellers to undercut the high-flown notions of inherent value and stable moral worth which characters on both sides of the conflict habitually (but also only intermittently, and often only when it suits their immediate political and rhetorical purposes)[9] use to legitimise their conduct and assert their claims to a supposedly undying fame and honour. As we have seen, the same move was made throughout the *Henry IV* plays but in *Troilus* it is arguably being deployed to even more devastating and corrosive effect.

In this play the language of the market is also applied to relations between the sexes and this leads, naturally and directly, to the language of both whoredom and of sexual disease. All of which calls into the most serious question any contest for honour or reputation played out in a war waged for the possession of women whose honour has been sullied by the very terms and course of the contest to possess them; a contest through which honour and shame are now being estimated and distributed. Market language also sullies the very notion of a fame or honour established through reputation; particularly when an emergent politics of popularity was threatening to render 'reputation', indeed 'honour' itself, dependent upon the whims of a variety of (more or less) 'popular' audiences.

However, this recurrent recourse to the language of the market and credit relations does not mean that the play is best conceived as, in any simple or direct sense, about 'the market', the perplexities of credit or indeed the 'cognitive burden' imposed by market relations on early modern English people.[10] Still less can the play's various paradoxes and antinomies be readily collapsed into what David J. Baker memorably describes as 'a grudge match between the Declining Aristocracy and the Rising Bourgoisie',[11] of the sort suggested by David Bevington and others.[12] There are, of course, no merchants in the play and the evaluative paradoxes and dilemmas that drive the action are to be found working themselves out not only amongst both the Greeks and the Trojans but also within the consciousness and language of all of the major characters. Thus, as Lars Engle observes, in this play even Achilles 'is curiously like a new man, even a self-made man ... The primordial aristocrats, models for the rest, here are full of commercial anxiety.'[13] This is an insight which applies just as well to the famous debate between Hector and Troilus about the pros and cons of returning Helen to the Greeks or of fighting on to the (bitter) end. Because of his notorious question 'what's aught but as 'tis valued?' [II, ii, 52], Troilus has been securely located by many critics under the sign of a market-oriented relativism. But he both replies with dismissive contempt to what he takes to be Hector's positively mercantile attempt literally to count the cost of keeping Helen –'fie, fie, my brother!/Weigh you the worth and honour of a king/So great as our dread father in a scale/Of common ounces?' [II, ii, 25–28] – and locates an ideal of honourable conduct in the sedulous keeping of contracts with merchants: 'we turn not back the silks unto the merchant/When we have soiled them' [II, ii, 69–70]. Similarly, for all his recourse to the supposedly objective criteria of natural law, Hector deploys the language of the marketplace with a will when, having tried to estimate the cost of the war in terms of lost Trojan lives, he concludes triumphantly that 'brother, she is not worth what she doth cost the keeping' [II, ii, 51–52]. As David J. Baker concludes, 'metaphors drawn from the code of the aristocrat and the lexicon of the merchant are both used here, but almost interchangeably. There is no suggestion that the one transcends or displaces the other.'[14]

   All this reflects the nature of what we might term late Elizabethan economic, political and cultural 'reality'. After all, the personal finances and credit of those serving the queen in the highest capacities were integrally tied to their perceived and actual standing in royal favour. Thus many noblemen like Leicester and Huntingdon, not to mention Essex, died deeply in debt, having virtually bankrupted themselves in the service of the crown. In Leicester's case he was so in debt to the queen that upon his death his lands were seized by the crown. The financial standing of such men was more often than not dependent on their capacity to raise money lent on the basis of their continuing favour with the queen. Absent that favour, the credit tended to dry up and the debts to be called in.[15] Moreover, as Lawrence Stone's work on the Cecils has shown, even those who made money from office did so in often precarious ways, their acquisition of landed estates and lavish building projects dependent on their capacity to raise huge loans from merchants anxious to make and keep friends in high places and willing to lend only on the presumption of continuing royal favour.[16] Although, unlike the Cecils, Essex was a noble of ancient lineage, he did not inherit a great landed estate from his father. According to Paul Hammer, his local power base 'did not compare with those of the great regional magnates such as the earls of Shrewsbury, Pembroke, Northumberland or Derby'. Indeed, Hammer refers, almost in passing, to his 'chronic finances'. Like his stepfather, Leicester, Essex spent a good of his own money on his (often military) service to the crown and his financial solvency was dependent both on his possession of the customs farm of the French wines, a concession once owned by his stepfather, Leicester, and his continuing capacity to raise loans based on his standing as the queen's favourite.[17] In disgrace after his return from Ireland, it was widely known that his future prospects hung on the queen's renewal of that farm. Thus on 10 October 1600, John Chamberlain told Dudley Carleton that he should not believe the various rumours of an incipient return to favour spread by the earl's supporters; 'till I see his licence for sweet wines renewed (that expired now at Michaelmas) or some other substantial favour answerable to it, I shall esteem words as wind and holy water of court'. Chamberlain wrote again on the 15th, reporting that 'the Earl of Essex keeps much in town, fed with hope that somewhat will follow, but the licence for sweet wines lies at anchor aloof and will not come in'.[18]

We have here, therefore, a political and economic scene in which the central figures in the regime, be they ancient nobles or (relatively) new men – Cecils, Dudleys, Hastings or Devereux – were all deeply implicated in a politico-economic system in which issues of credit, honour and reputation, of royal favour and economic viability, were integrally interconnected in ways that everyone – monarch and counsellor, courtier and nobleman, merchant and certainly the informed London public – understood implicitly. In short, neither in the world of the play nor in that of late Elizabethan politics was there any orderly ('feudal') before or any proto-capitalist, morally relativist, 'after' to be found locked in some death struggle for the future, but rather a conflictual 'now' defined, around the turn of the century, by war and the politics of court faction and popularity, of claims to pseudo-chivalric honour, military prowess, royal favour, (allegedly) immortal fame and good credit. The resulting tensions and anxieties were, of course, compounded by the prospect of the queen's death and the struggle over the succession and the new (Stuart?) regime that would ensue, thus potentially throwing all the fixed points of contact, favour and trust that underpinned the present distribution of power, prestige and credit into a potentially radically destabilising flux.[19] It is to characterise and critique, to interrogate, stage and ridicule, that political scene and moral universe (and its actual or potential consequences – we are talking about the siege of Troy, after all) that the language and concerns of the market are mobilised by the play.[20]

The case for war (and peace)

The play sets up a variety of parallels between its own narrative materials and contemporary situations and concerns. It is set in the midst of what has clearly become an interminable war; a war that has been going on for so long that its prosecution has become something of an end in itself. Certainly, when the original *casus belli* passes from the back to the front of the minds of the major protagonists they are unable to regard it with any great enthusiasm or zeal. This is shown most clearly on the Trojan side in a debate occasioned by the latest offer of terms by the Greeks. If the Trojans will hand over Helen, the Greeks will call it quits; 'all damage else –/As honour, loss of time, travail, expense,/ Wounds, friends, and what else dear that is consumed/In hot digestion of this cormorant war –/Shall be struck off" '[II, ii, 3–7]. Called upon to deliver his opinion of this offer, Hector argues that the Trojans should take it. As he points out, his own martial prowess secures him from any charge of fear of the Greeks, personal cowardice or the pursuit of private interest [II, ii, 8–17]. Seven years of war, Hector claims, have, or rather ought to have, cured the Trojans of any security bred in them by years of peace. Having seen what war costs and gained some sense of what war could do to their state, it behoved the Trojans to show circumspection, by prudently calculating the benefits and costs, the likely risks and outcomes, consequent upon continuing the war. And, on that basis, he advises that they should 'let Helen go'.

His first set of reasons for that advice concerns the self-evident discrepancy between the value of what they were fighting for, i.e. the person of Helen herself, and the costs in human lives that the war has already imposed upon them for keeping her. The two, he claims, were simply incommensurable [II, ii, 18–24]. To the wordy expostulations this suggestion elicits from Troilus, Hector summarises this part of his case: 'Brother, she is not worth what she doth cost/ The holding' [II, ii, 51].

This case is lent immediacy by Cassandra, who breaks into her brother's colloquy with a prophecy of doom [II, ii, 109–12]. Hitherto Hector has not mentioned the possibility of final defeat as an inducement to settlement, but such arguments represent a natural enough development of his acknowledge-ment of the need with, 'modest doubt', to search 'to the bottom of the worst' and he now endorses his sister's warnings. 'Now, youthful Troilus, do not these high strains/Of divination in our sister work/Some touches of remorse? Or is your blood/So madly hot that no discourse of reason,/Nor fear of bad success in a bad cause,/Can qualify the same?' [II, ii, 113–18].

The claim, slipped in towards the end of that speech, that they are in fact fighting in 'a bad cause' leads into Hector's other major argument for settle-ment: his acknowledgement that the Trojans are not fighting a just war. 'Nature craves/All dues to be rendered to their owners. Now,/What nearer debt to all humanity/Than wife is to the husband? . . . If Helen then be wife to Sparta's king,/As it is known she is, these moral laws/Of nature and of nations speak aloud/To have her back returned. Thus to persist/In doing wrong extenuates not wrong,/But makes it much more heavy' [II, ii, 173–88].

Hector's case for ending the war is thus based both on prudence and on right; on morality and on the calculation of likely outcomes and the consideration of past costs. Central to that case is his sense that the Trojans' position in fighting to keep Helen is against the laws of nature and of nations – a proposition backed up with a glancing reference to the authority of Aristotle – for it is precisely the injustice of the Trojans' cause that renders them the more likely to suffer the providential judgement prophesied with so much *Sturm und Drang* by Cassandra.

Hector's arguments on this score are opposed first by Troilus and then by Paris. Troilus' case for continuing the war is dominated by what he takes to be the demands of honour [II, ii, 25–32]. In reply to his brother's claim that Helen is not worth the lives and treasure expended and dangers inherent in trying to keep her, he claims that 'value' is a relative rather than an objective matter. 'What's aught but as 'tis valued?' [II, ii, 52]. To this radical relativism, Hector replies by claiming that 'value dwells not in particular will;/It holds its estimate and dignity/As well wherein 'tis precious of itself/As in the prizer. 'Tis mad idolatry/To make the service greater than the god;/And the will dotes that is inclinable/To what infectiously itself affects,/Without some image of th'affected merit' [II, ii, 53–60].

But Troilus will have none of this. On his account, Helen is worth keeping precisely because the Greeks want her back so much. Consequently, the struggle for her has become not so much a matter of the worth or otherwise of the thing or person being fought over, or indeed of the rightness of the initial cause, but rather of the respective worth or honour of the parties to the dispute. In short, the war has become an end in itself, something to be continued because it has been started and cannot be ended without the loss of the honour, prestige and face now invested, by both sides, in the struggle itself. 'It was thought meet/Paris should do some vengeance on the Greeks./Your breath of full consent bellied his sails' [II, ii, 72–74]. Paris, 'for an old aunt whom the Greeks held captive', had 'brought a Grecian queen, whose youth and freshness/Wrinkles Apollo's, and makes stale the morning./Why keep we her? The Grecians keep our aunt,/Is she worth keeping? Why, she is a pearl/Whose price hath launched above a thousand ships/And turned crowned kings to merchants' [II, ii, 77–83]. Theirs, Troilus claims, would be 'a theft most base/That we have stol'n what we do fear to keep!' [II, ii, 93–94].

At stake here is not merely the avoidance of baseness and the maintenance of honour, but the achievement of 'glory'. 'Were it not glory that we more affected/Than the performance of our heaving spleens,/I would not wish a drop of Trojan blood/Spent more in her defence. But, worthy Hector, she is a theme of honour and renown,/A spur to valiant and magnanimous deeds,/Whose present courage may beat down our foes/And fame in time to come canonise us' [II, ii, 195–202]. Thus Troilus concedes Hector's basic claim; based, as it is, on an act of 'theft', the war is 'unjust'. But in Troilus' view that is not the point; the original *casus belli*, no matter how unjust or dishonourable it may have been, can be made good, not merely justified but transformed into a point of honour, indeed into a source of 'glory', if enough effort is put into resisting the Greeks' counter-attack.

We have, then, on Hector's side, a theory of political action based on a careful calculation of risks and outcomes and on a theory of justice and value founded on natural order and natural law. His is a case based on 'reasons and fears'. On the other side, we have a radically relativist theory of action and of value, in which what matters is the defence of 'honour', the avoidance of all that is 'base' and the achievement of 'glory'. Such categories and claims have little or no direct connection with objective moral categories like justice but are rather to be established by the (successful) assertion of one's own claims to honour and of one's competitors' status as 'base'. 'Honour' and 'glory' are to be achieved (and 'baseness' avoided) by successfully competing with others in the struggle for the possession of objects whose value resides not so much in their inherent worth, as in how much they are prized by those competing for them. On this account, the fact that Helen is another's man's wife matters, not because it detracts from the justice of the Trojan cause, but because it increases the shame being heaped upon the Greeks by the Trojans' continued possession of her in the face of her former owner's best efforts to get her back. Similarly, the fact that Helen is objectively beautiful matters chiefly because it means that all men desire her and that therefore seizing her from the just possession of a rival represents a peculiarly sharp affront. What Paris concedes is the 'soil of her fair rape' can now be 'wiped off in honourable keeping of her', and that means the continued prosecution of the war, no matter what the costs or consequences. To give in now would, Paris asserts, be an act 'of base compulsion' [II, ii, 147–48, 153]. Having started, the Trojans must finish. To do anything else would be dishonourable.

Remarkably, having, to all appearances, 'won' the formal argument about whether to settle with the Greeks, at the end of these exchanges Hector simply gives in. To adopt the terminology used by Mark Kishlansky in his analysis of the political culture of early modern England, Hector is here practising 'consensus' as opposed to 'adversary' politics.[21] Or, as David J. Baker puts it, 'at issue for the Trojans is not whether a commodity's value is either intrinsic or subjective, but whether this value can and should be established and main-tained *individually* or *collectively*'. Thus Troilus accuses Hector, who has just denounced a view that grounds 'value' in the exercise of the 'particular will', of doing precisely that. Having at first endorsed the (collective) Trojan decision to seize and keep Helen, Hector is now reneging on that commitment for reasons of his own. Moreover, Troilus argues, private choices and agreements – whether mercantile bargains or marriages – become, once made, social facts and public commitments; agreements that the subsequent exercise of individual will or whim could not simply overturn, or at least not without the gravest of consequences for said individual's reputation or credit. Thus Troilus asks, if 'I take to-day a wife, and my election/Is led on in the conduct of my will,/My will enkindled by mine ears and eyes,/Two traded pilots 'twixt the dangerous shores/Of will and judgement. How may I avoid,/Although my will distaste what it elected,/The wife I chose?' [II, ii, 61–67].[22]

On this basis both Harry Berger Jr and David J.Baker go so far as to claim that 'the scene is focused less on Helen than on Hector's attempt to make Troilus work out more rationally the position he shares with him'.[23] It is, however, important not to get carried away. For what we have here is not a debate about the nature of 'value', still less one about the dynamics or demands of 'the market', upon which topics the two brothers do indeed share a good deal in common. Rather, the question they are arguing about is whether to end the war.[24] On that question Hector and Troilus are in fundamental disagreement and in the course of arguing the pros and cons they construe and then mix and match the various assumptions and modes of argument upon which they do agree in very different ways,[25] until, that is, Hector's shocking volte-face brings their debate to a sudden, jarring close.

But that does not mean we should agree with David J. Baker when he claims that Troilus simply 'wins the debate'.[26] After all, even as he falls in line with his brother's position, Hector tells us that, in his view, Troilus has done nothing of the sort. His stated opinions on the justice and prudence of the war are, Hector maintains, 'Hector's opinion/In this in way of truth', i.e. he was and remains in the right. On Hector's account, then, what the play shows us is not a debate (about 'value' or 'the market' or indeed about the war) being (substantively and definitively) won or lost, but rather Hector's assent being compelled and a previously constructed Trojan consensus being maintained. Troilus has not so much won a debate as compelled his brother's consent to a (collective) decision and a policy that he still believes to be both morally wrong and prudentially misguided. Troilus' victory has been rhetorical and, as it were, social, rather than substantive, and both Hector and the audience know it.

For at this point I think that the audience is not only intended to agree with Hector but also to be shocked and surprised by his capitulation; a response founded not merely on the powerfully conventional arguments and authorities that the play gives to Hector but also upon the audience's prior knowledge of the outcome of the siege of Troy; an outcome which Hector's strenuous efforts to come to a rounded 'image'[II, ii, 60] of the likely costs and consequences of the war have all but foretold. Hector's final concession/conclusion – 'I propend to

you/In resolution to keep Helen still;/For 'tis a cause that hath no mean depen-
dence/Upon our joint and several dignities' [II, ii, 189–93] – shows just how
much he has been compelled to go along to get along, preferring the collective
honour – the 'joint and several dignities' – of the Trojan leaders to what his own
earlier arguments, and the audience's prior knowledge, both reveal to be the
true interests of Troy. All of which puts Hector into an intensely equivocal, not
to say contradictory, relationship with a good many of his own stated beliefs
and perceptions. As we shall see, this is not the last time that Hector's involvement in the emotional and ideological logic driving the war causes him to act in
ways that are flatly contradictory to what we might term his best instincts and
impulses; that is to say, to the values inscribed in the general run of both his
statements and actions.

If, on Hector's view of the situation, the Greeks have the right of it, by this
point, that is not how it appears to at least some of the Greeks. When Diomedes,
is asked, by Paris 'who, in your thoughts, merits fair Helen most,/Myself or
Menelaus?' he replies, 'both alike'. Just like Hector, Diomedes sees the human
cost involved in the war as entirely incommensurate with what is ostensibly at
stake. 'For every false drop in her bawdy veins/A Greek's life hath sunk; for
every scruple/Of her contaminated carrion weight/A Trojan hath been slain.
Since she could speak,/She hath not given so many good words breath/As for
her Greeks and Trojans suffered death.' Through what appears to an instinctive
recourse to the double standard – Helen has, after all, been abducted by main
force – Diomedes evacuates his disgust at the situation on to the person of
Helen. On this view, given the nature of the *casus belli* and of the 'prize' to be
awarded to the winner, any notion of a just war is rendered absurd. Nor can
there be any 'honour' at stake in such a competition. As far as Diomedes is
concerned whoever is prepared to produce his 'inheritors' through such a
debased medium should be welcome to her. For Diomedes, then, Helen's
'soilure', her status as a fallen women, quite literally as a 'whore', caught (through,
of course, no fault of her own) between her husband and her captor, renders
her 'damaged goods' and any struggle for her favours not merely ludicrous but
equally demeaning, indeed dishonourable, to both sides to the dispute; sides
characterised by Thersites, with typical bluntness, as the 'cuckhold and the
cuckhold maker'. To the claim that 'you are too bitter to your countrywoman',
Diomedes replies bitterly that 'she's bitter to her country' [IV, i, 53–76].

Nor is this view of Helen as damaged goods and of both her husband and
her present possessor as actual or potential cuckolds limited to Diomedes and
Thersites. It pervades the language and basic assumptions of the Trojans themselves, with even the members of the central love triangle, and their intimates
and allies, unable to stop themselves making incessant (joking) reference to it.
Told that Paris has been wounded in battle, Troilus responds, 'Let Paris bleed.
'Tis but a scar to scorn;/Paris is gored with Menelaus' horn' [I, i, 107–8]. Later

Pandarus recounts an encounter between Paris, Troilus and Helen, in which Helen has been twitting Troilus with the paucity of hair upon his chin. 'Quoth she, "here's but two-and-fifty hairs on your chin, and one of them is white.' 'That white one is my father and all the rest are his sons,' Troilus had replied, only to be asked by Helen ' "which of these hairs is Paris, my husband?" ' "The forked one", quoth he; "pluck't out, and give it him" ' [I, ii, 152–60].

Here a certain sort of wit is being used both to advert to and to defuse the moral and emotional contradictions inherent in making the honour of Troy and the immortal fame of various Trojan heroes turn on the violent defence of an act of rape and the continuing practice of adultery. The resulting contradictions cannot, however, entirely be suppressed or elided even, perhaps particularly, in the discussion of the most serious matters of state. As Troilus, in debate with Hector, is praising Helen to the skies as 'a theme of honour and renown' [II, ii, 199] and a 'pearl' of 'inestimable' worth [II, ii, 81, 88], he uses arguments and language which unavoidably cast Helen (and at least potentially her defenders) in the most unflattering light. 'We turn not back the silks upon the merchant/When we have soiled them; nor the remainder viands/We do not throw in unrespective sieve/Because we now are full' [II, ii, 67–72]. David J. Baker's comment that it 'seems distasteful of him' to refer to Helen in such terms perhaps misses the point. His further claim that Troilus cannot be saying that Helen is 'irredeemably soiled' because 'he wants to keep her' seems just wrong. Troilus *is* saying, in the clearest possible terms, that Helen is irredeemably damaged goods *unless* the Trojans risk all to keep her, and that is the central moral paradox at the heart of the war and of the play.[27]

These very same issues are the subject of the same sort of uneasy mirth (and visceral disgust) amongst the Greeks. When Cressida is delivered up to the Greek camp in a prisoner swap for Antenor, she is kissed in turn by the leaders of the Greek cause. When it comes to Menelaus, he jokingly remarks that 'I had good argument for kissing once', only for Patroclus to nip in front of him with the claim that 'that's no argument for kissing now;/For thus popped Paris in his hardiment,/And parted thus you and your argument'. Cressida returns to the same sore point when Menelaus does claim his kiss. Offered three kisses for one, Cressida replies that 'you are an odd man; give even, or give none', only to be told in reply that 'every man is odd'. 'No, Paris is not, for you know 'tis true/ That you are odd, and he is even with you'. Unable to let the subject drop, Ulysses intervenes, claiming that that the battle of wits between Menelaus and Cressida is 'no match, your nail against his horn'. For all his levity of tone, however, Ulysses is not joking, commenting, at the first mention of Menelaus' status as a cuckold, 'O deadly gall and theme of all our scorns,/For which we lose our heads to gild his horns!' [IV, v, 20–53]. And underneath all this courtly wordplay runs the commentary of the insistently reductive and abusive Thersites for whom 'all the argument is a whore and a cuckold; a good quarrel to draw emulous factions and bleed to death with. Now the dry serpigo on the subject, and war and lechery confound all!' [II, iii, 68–72].

Neither is this sort of visceral disgust limited to Thersites. It is taken up not merely by Diomedes, but by Ulysses himself. In reply to Nestor's comment that Cressida is 'a woman of quick sense', Ulysses replies with brutal vehemence, denouncing her in precisely the same terms that Diomedes had used to demean Helen [IV, v, 55–64]. Just as Helen, taken by main force from the Greeks to Troy, is a whore, so, too, is Cressida, traded in the opposite direction, by the Trojans at the behest of Greeks, also 'a daughter of the game'. On this view of the situation, not only is Menelaus a cuckold, but Helen is a whore and Paris the paramour of a whore.

As Thersites' comments insistently imply, since the war is about or for Helen, the language of sexual insult and disgust employed, both in jest and in all seriousness, by both sides, serves to comment on the nature and justice of the war as well. We might, on this basis, take the visceral force of Ulysses' disgust at Cressida – who has, after all, merely given as good as she has got in the intensely sexualised welcome to the Greek camp that has just been visited on her, by, amongst others, Ulysses himself – as not only an involuntarily vehement (misogynist) expression of the double standard but also as an (equally misogynist and involuntary) evacuation on to an available female scapegoat of his own feelings of (self-)disgust and loathing about the war, a war, of course, that they are all now fighting to the (increasingly) bitter end.

But, of course, the action of the play 'confirms' Ulysses' estimation of Cressida's sexual and moral nature. For all her expressions of fidelity to Troilus, once shipped off to the Greeks, she swiftly allows herself to be seduced by none other than Diomedes, even giving him as a token the very same favour with which a distraught Troilus had entrusted her, as they parted in Troy. This, of course, is the same Diomedes who had derided Menelaus as a cuckold, Helen as a whore, and Paris, in effect, as her whoremaster. But now here he is paying earnest suit to a woman who, on his own account of the sexual honour system in terms of which the war is being fought, is equally 'soiled', by her previous sexual liaison with Troilus. The ironies and inversions embodied in Diomedes' conduct are paralleled by those being experienced by the watching Troilus, who is appalled by Cressida's faithlessness in succumbing to Diomedes' advances and affronted by Diomedes' conduct in seducing her. But this, of course, is the same Troilus who had defined honour, the honour for which the war is being fought, in terms of the possession and sexual enjoyment of a woman, Helen, who had herself first been seized, for political reasons, by main force and then seduced, and in terms of the assertion and defence of that possession against any and every Greek attempt to recover her. Arguably, Diomedes has behaved no worse (indeed rather better) towards Cressida than had Paris towards Helen, and Cressida herself has behaved no worse towards

Troilus and Diomedes than had Helen towards Menelaus and Paris. In the first instance, Troilus' account of the politics of honour had led him to insist that the Trojans should fight a war to the death to defend Paris and Helen. But now, with the tables turned by the logic of that very war, he feels both betrayed by Cressida and affronted by Diomedes.

In some ways, the result of this is the same as his earlier debate with Hector, in that Troilus emerges from both with a renewed commitment to the prosecution of the war, only now the 'honour' being asserted and defended is defined by a visceral anger and the war being embraced has accordingly become a ruthless pursuit of revenge. Not only that, but the logic of the same war that he had insisted, in debate with Hector, should be pursued for honour's sake, has led Troilus himself to acquiesce, without demur, in the surrender of Cressida to the Greeks. Of course, at one level, he had no choice. Antenor, the play makes clear, is regarded as central to the Trojan war effort; in military and political terms, his return is worth the surrender of any number of women (except, of course, Helen). As Paris, of all people, observes (accurately enough), 'there is no help./ The bitter disposition of the time/Will have it so' [IV, i, 49–51]. At the very least, such a conclusion represents the natural consequence of the logic underlying Troilus' own question, posed to Hector during their debate about the justice of the war: 'what's aught but as 'tis valued?' In this, both sexual and political, honour economy, women are the central mediums of exchange and tokens of value and Helen is valued (by, amongst others, Troilus himself) above the lives of thousands, indeed, above the certain survival of the Trojan state, while Cressida is valued only as a means to get back Antenor. On this account, Troilus gets to suffer the consequences of his own arguments and, in the process, to reveal the both moral and practical consequences of the wholesale abandonment of the objective criteria of justice and value and the prudential calculation of the right relation between ends and means to which, until the very end of their debate, Hector had been clinging, but which the exigencies of an unjust and total war has forced all of the characters, however seemingly 'virtuous', to abandon.

On this basis, it seems that on neither side is the war viewed as unequivocally just. In terms of natural law and justice, the Trojans are in the wrong and they can only avoid the logic of the argument that leads inexorably to that conclusion by discussing the crucial issues, not in the idiom of justice, of right and wrong, but of (sexual) honour and dishonour. But, once the *casus belli* is viewed in those terms – as the play makes clear it is by both sides – then it appears that neither side is in the right; or rather that, while the Greeks may formally have right on their side – as Hector insists, Helen is Menelaus' wife – the objects for which they are ostensibly fighting – Helen's virtue and Menelaus' and indeed Paris' honour – are all so fatally compromised as not to be worth the candle.

Faction and fraction

If the play takes a jaundiced view of the nature and justice of the *casus belli*, it also leaves us in no doubt that the moral and political effects of the war have been anything but positive. As we have seen, on the Trojan side, the war leads to the desertion of the cause of natural law and justice even by the 'virtuous' Hector and to the descent into the relativised politics of honour and reputation espoused, in theory and in practice, by Troilus and Paris (and indeed ultimately even by Hector himself). Behind that, of course, lurks the fate that everyone knows is awaiting the Trojans at war's end; a fate broadcast to both the characters on stage and the audience by what Troilus describes as 'the brain-sick raptures' of Cassandra [II, ii, 122]. But if we want a detailed account of the politically and morally deleterious, indeed disastrous, effects of the war, it is to the play's portrayal of the internal politics of the Greeks that we must turn.[28]

The first exchanges between Agamemnon and the other Greek generals establish that on their side the war is going badly. After seven years' siege, 'yet Troy walls stand'. And this fact has started to spread dissatisfaction and dissent through the ranks. The very leaders of the cause, Agamemnon laments, 'with cheeks abashed behold our works/And think them shames', when in fact their current difficulties are no more than tests imposed on them by the gods, setbacks and obstacles designed to test their mettle, and winnow 'the light away', leaving 'what hath mass or matter by itself' to lie 'rich in virtue and unmingled' [I, iii, 1–30].

Agamemnon, seconded by Nestor, is here trying to raise the morale of what is clearly a less than happy Greek camp. But the real nature of the troubles afflicting their enterprise only emerges in the next speech. This is delivered by Ulysses, according to whom the protracted experience of war has not enhanced the unity or determination of the Greeks but rather done the opposite. Where there should be agreement and order, there is now disagreement and faction. 'The specialty of rule hath been neglected;/And look how many Grecian tents do stand/Hollow upon this plain, so many hollow factions./When that the general is not like the hive/To whom the foragers shall all repair,/What honey is expected? Degree being vizarded,/Th'unworthiest shows as fairly in the mask.' [I, iii, 78–94].

Ulysses is articulating here the self-same image of order as somehow natural and organic, as hard-wired into the structure of reality, that had animated the archbishop of Canterbury's speech on the condition of England, at the moment that Henry V was contemplating his expedition into France.[29] Indeed, Ulysses actually starts his disquisition with the same (utterly conventional) image of the beehive that had provided the organising principle for Canterbury's speech. Where, however, Canterbury was producing a paean to the current condition of England, a condition which Henry's wars were designed to further and maintain, here Ulysses is about to embark on a lament upon the dire moral and political condition of the Greek camp, from which all such order, harmony, obedience and degree has been stripped by the war.

For it was an inevitable consequence of the naturalness that resided at the heart of his argument that when such natural order was disrupted or absent – 'take but degree away' – then all sorts of dreadful, unnatural, consequences naturally ensue – or, as Ulysses famously puts it, 'hark what discord follows'. 'Force should be right; or rather right and wrong,/ Between whose endless jar, justice resides,/ Should lose their names,/ Power into will, will into appetite;/ And appetite, an universal wolf,/ So doubly seconded with will and power,/ Must make perforce an universal prey/ And last eat up itself.' [I, iii, 94–124]. And such, Ulysses concludes, is indeed the condition in which the Greeks currently find themselves 'And 'tis this fever that keeps Troy on foot,/Not her own sinews. To end a tale of length,/Troy in our weakness lives, not in her strength' [I, iii, 129–37]. To this point Ulysses' has been a general, almost a metaphysical, account of disorder, disunity and disharmony. But he is proffering that general discussion only in order to make a far more precise point about the ways in which 'hollow faction' has indeed hollowed out the strength of the Greeks; the most immediate symptom of which condition being the withdrawal, in pique and pride, of Achilles, 'whom opinion crowns/The sinew and forehead of our host' [II, iii, 142–51].

From Achilles the disease of prideful faction has spread to Ajax, who 'keeps his tent like him,/Makes factious feasts like him, rails on our state of war,/Bold as an oracle, and sets Thersites –/A slave whose gall coins slanders like a mint –/ To match us in comparisons with dirt,/To weaken and discredit our exposure,/ How rank soever rounded in with danger' [I, iii, 188–96].

Together, Achilles and Ajax constitute a sort of soldiers' party, united in their contempt for the strategists, the policy-mongers and politicians, amongst the counsels of the Greeks. 'They tax our policy and call it cowardice,' Ulysses complains. 'Count wisdom as no member of the war,/Forestall prescience, and esteem no act/But that of hand. The still and mental parts,/That do contrive how many hands shall strike,/When fitness calls them on, and know by measure/Of their observant toil, the enemy's weight –/Why, this hath not a finger's dignity./They call this bed-work, mapp'ry, closet war;/So that the ram that batters down the wall,/For the great swinge and rudeness of his poise,/ They place before his hand that made the engine/Or those that with the fineness of their souls/By reason guide his execution' [I, iii, 197–210].

As for the policy wonks amongst the Greeks, they reciprocate by regarding the likes of Achilles and Ajax as brainless oafs, muscle men, to be manipulated and deployed to suit the higher, both political and military, purposes of the real brains behind the operation. Thus at one point Nestor observes that even Achilles 'were his brain as barren/As the banks of Libya – though Apollo knows,/'Tis dry enough' [I, iii, 328–30] would realise that it was him whom Hector was seeking to challenge to single combat. Elsewhere Ulysses refers simply and brutally to 'the dull brainless Ajax' [II, i, 382]. These verdicts are, of course, confirmed throughout the play by the scabrous commentary on the stupidity of both Ajax and Achilles maintained by their sometime client, Thersites.

The cure for this outbreak of factious disunity amongst the Greeks proffered by Ulysses and his companion Nestor is not however a stiff dose of discipline, the smack of firm government and a consequent return to 'normal'. Rather, they recommend a further round of (this time staged or manipulated) faction, a deliberate playing on the potential rifts and rivalries between Achilles and Ajax, designed to put them in their place and then to get them both back actively engaged in the general effort against Troy. Hector has just issued a challenge to single combat to any Greek daring enough to take it up. The assumption, on all sides, is that 'this challenge that the gallant Hector sends,/However it is spread in general name,/Relates in purpose only to Achilles' [I, iii, 322–24]. Achilles is, of course, still sulking in his tent and, on the face of it, this challenge from Hector seems the perfect opportunity to rouse him from his lethargy. That, certainly, is Nestor's opinion.

Ulysses, however, disagrees. Achilles 'already is too insolent' to be contained within the common effort and if he beats Hector his pride will swell still more. On the other hand, 'if he were foiled,/Why then we did our main opinion crush/In taint of our best man' [I, iii, 371–75]. Thus, rather than persuade, or even allow, Achilles to take up the challenge, the role of champion should be put up for lottery and Ajax allowed to win. Ajax should then be broadcast through the camp as 'the worthier man', which in itself should take Achilles down a peg or two. If Ajax 'come safe off,/We'll dress him up in voices' and continue the same undermining tactics on Achilles. 'If he fail,/Yet go we under our opinion still/That we have better men. But, hit or miss,/Our project's life this shape of sense assumes:/Ajax employed plucks down Achilles' plumes' [II, i, 382–87].

Thus, for all their publicly expressed horror at the onset and consequences of faction in the Greek camp, Ulysses and Nestor, the party of policy, of brain as opposed to that of brawn, have set about, not to heal the divisions afflicting the Greek host so much as to exacerbate and exploit them, in what they take to be their own and indeed the common interest.[30] The pride of Ajax and of Achilles is to be, if anything, increased and then used to play the one off against the other, because, as Nestor famously puts it, 'their fraction is more our wish than their faction.' [II, iii, 96–100].

What we are being shown here are the inner workings of 'faction' and 'policy' as, in a series of comical scenes, we watch the now absurdly vain Ajax being manipulated and paraded in front of Achilles. While Achilles refuses even to leave his tent to speak with the leaders of the Greek host, they build up Ajax, telling him he is a man of genuine parts and valour [II, iii 146–56, 174–75].

Having set up Ajax against Achilles and thus perfected their division of the soldiers' party, Ulysses and Nestor then turn their attention to Achilles, giving him the cold shoulder as they parade past his tent, scarcely acknowledging his greeting and studiously avoiding the subject of his continued refusal to fight. The rear of the procession is brought up by the lone figure of Ulysses, who approaches reading and proceeds, out of his text, to give Achilles a lecture on the real (intensely social and political) nature of martial honour and reputation and on the 'what have you done for me lately' dynamics of fame. 'No man is the lord of anything,/Though in and of him there be much consisting,/Till he communicate his parts to others;/Nor doth he of himself know them for aught/Till he behold them formed in th'applause/Where they're extended – who, like an arch, reverb'rate/The voice again, or, like a gate of steel/Fronting the sun, receives and renders back/His figure and his heat' [III, iii, 116–24]. On this view, there is no such thing as inherent worth or virtue; attributes, however glorious, exist, even to their possessor, only to the extent that he can see them being reflected back to him in the eyes and admiration of others. Here is an entirely affirmative answer to Troilus' question, posed to Hector, what's 'aught but as 'tis valued?'; an answer, be it noted, entirely at odds with the logic of the paean to order, harmony and degree with which Ulysses had started his address to the other Greek leaders.

Having rendered the ground rules of 'value' and of 'honour' crystal clear, Ulysses insinuates that his showdown with Hector, planned for the next day, is about to make the hitherto 'unknown Ajax' very highly valued indeed [III, iii, 131–42]. This relative neglect is but an inkling of what Achilles can expect in the future, Ulysses explains. The social nature of honour and fame being what they are, and Ajax's deeds, being but freshly done, cannot help but eclipse those of Achilles. 'All men', Ulysses explains, however transcendent their capacities, have rivals and 'what they do in present,/Though less than yours in past, must o'ertop yours … O, let not virtue seek/Remuneration for what it was;/For beauty, wit,/High birth, vigour of bone, desert in service,/Love, friendship, charity, are subjects all/To envious and calumniating Time … Then marvel not, thou great and complete man,/That all the Greeks begin to worship Ajax,/Since things in motion sooner catch the eye/Than what not stirs. The cry went once on thee,/And still it might, and yet it may again,/If thou would not entomb thyself alive/And case thy reputation in thy tent,/Whose glorious deeds but in these fields of late/Made emulous missions 'mongst the gods themselves/And drave great Mars to faction' [III, iii, 146–91].

Achilles, dim bulb though he is, gets the point immediately. It is what he calls 'his privacy' that has caused him to hide his light under a bushel of late and for that, he claims, 'I have strong reasons' [III, iii, 192–93]. At this point, Ulysses delivers the *coup de grâce*. ' 'Tis known, Achilles, that you are in love/With one of Priam's daughters.' To Achilles' shocked response, 'Ha? Known?' Ulysses replies with a paean to 'The providence that's in a watchful state'. 'There is a mystery – with whom relation/Durst never meddle – in the soul of state,/Which hath an operation more divine/Than breath or pen can give expression to./All the commerce that you have had with Troy/As perfectly is ours as yours, my lord;/And better would it fit Achilles much/To throw down Hector than Polyxena./But it must grieve young Pyrrhus now at home,/When Fame shall in our islands sound her trump/And all the Greekish girls shall tripping sing:/"Great Hector's sister did Achilles win,/But our great Ajax bravely beat down him"./ Farewell, my lord, I as your lover speak;/The fool slides o'er the ice that you should break' [III, iii, 192–217].

Ulysses and the faction of policy have, by this point, succeeded in getting inside the heads of the soldiers' party and their plans appear to be coming nicely to fruition. While Thersites entertains Achilles and Patroclus with his impression of the absurdly proud Ajax, parading up and down, preening himself before the next day's encounter with Hector, Achilles ponders his position. 'I see my reputation is at stake./My fame is shrewdly gored' [III, iii, 228–29]. It is a 'reputation' and a 'fame' that he fears can only be restored by killing Hector, which, of course, means breaking his previous promise to Polyxena to withdraw from active participation in the war.

By this point, the ironies of the play's insistent juxtaposition of the ethics and politics of the bedroom and of the battlefield have come together, almost in full circle. A war started to revenge an illicit affair between a Trojan man and a Greek woman is here being undermined by an equally illicit affair between a Greek man and a Trojan woman. The resulting clash between honour, defined in political or military terms, and in terms of fidelity in 'love', is here resolved not through an appeal to Achilles' better nature nor to his conscience, nor indeed to any objective criteria of virtue or justice, but rather through the manipulation of Achilles' concern for his 'reputation' or 'fame'. Viewed in terms of the tension between the politics of honour and of popularity, at least amongst the Greeks, the former has largely been collapsed into the latter, with honour being equated by both Ajax and Achilles (and indeed by Ulysses) with 'fame' or 'reputation', entities determined almost entirely by the inherently short-term, intensely fickle interactions of the would-be hero and his audience, or, to put it more abstractly, between virtue or prowess, on the one hand, and time and opinion, on the other. The link between fame and reputation and any notion of inherent moral worth, or stable ethical identity, has been, at the very least, seriously weakened, if not, in practice, destroyed.[31]

The only major figure in the play not entirely infected by these attitudes is Hector. As we have seen, during their discussion of the prudence and justice of the war, alone of the Trojan luminaries, he had retained a commitment to what we might term objectivist Aristotelian notions of virtue and inherent worth. In war, he retained a similar commitment to canons of justice, a commitment which ensured that his version of the 'honour' to be achieved on the field of battle retained at least some relation to wider ethical notions like justice or mercy. As Troilus, embittered by his loss of Cressida, prepares to wreak a terrible revenge, he rounds on Hector for his 'vice of mercy'. 'Let's leave that hermit Pity with our mothers,/And when we have our armours buckled on,/ The venomed vegeance ride upon our swords,/Spur them to ruthful work, rein them from ruth.' To which an appalled Hector can only respond 'Fie, savage, fie!' 'Hector, then 'tis wars', is Troilus' crushing reply [V, iii, 37–49].

Again, when confronted, not with his intended opponent, Achilles, but rather with Ajax, Hector relents. Ajax, it turns out, is Hector's 'father's sister's son' and accordingly Hector refuses a fight to the death with him [IV, v, 84–87]. Indeed, when, having made one pass at each other, the absurdly proud and glory-hungry Ajax wants to fight some more – 'I am not warm yet. Let us fight again' – Hector refuses. When even this magnanimous gesture provokes the claim from Ajax that 'I came to kill thee, cousin, and bear hence/A great addition earned in thy death', Hector responds with an even more vainglorious retort, only then to insist that 'The issue is embracement' [IV, v, 120–49].The audience is, I think, intended to agree with Aeneas' comment, made in acid tones to the envious Achilles, that 'in the extremity of great and little,/ Valour and pride excel themselves in Hector,/ The one almost as infinite as all,/ The other blank as nothing. Weigh him well,/ And that which looks like pride is courtesy' [IV, v, 74-83]. While this, of course, is not entirely true, for what looks like courtesy is also pride, Aeneas' remarks do point to an implicit contrast between Hector and that 'proud man', Achilles, a contrast confirmed by Achilles' outrageous conduct at his first meeting with his Trojan nemesis.

The politics of fame and the decay of honour

What is emerging here is a series of associations, comparisons and contrasts between Hector and Achilles. In many ways they are paired or twinned characters, obsessed with one another, they represent the epitome of martial prowess, the personification of the Greek and Trojan causes. But they are not the same. Indeed at times the play seems to present them as though they are polar opposites. Hector sustains a sense that 'honour', as he understands and acquires it, is an attribute, a social and moral quantity that remains integrally connected to and conditioned by other wider moral qualities and values. Unlike Achilles, Hector retains a position at the centre of the Trojan political system and honour culture. He is thus throughout presented as relatively secure in his own valour and repute. Thus, unlike Achilles, he does not become engaged in a ceaseless drive, at all costs, to augment and increase his own reserves of fame and reputation at the expense of others.

For Achilles, on the other hand, pride has ceased to be the product of what C.C. Barfoot has termed 'the ambience of evaluative salutation and emulative rivalry'[32] in which the heroes are supposed to live out their lives, and becomes instead an obsession with his own 'reputation' or 'fame', with how he appears in the eyes and accounts of others; something to be maximised and maintained at all costs. A creature or captive of his obsession with his own fame or reputation, he is thus left credulously vulnerable to the machinations and manipulations of Ulysses.

Thus isolated, with nothing to guide him other than his own drive for 'fame', Achilles has become a slave both to opinion and to passion. Alone of the characters in the play, Achilles has allowed the intense homosocial drives and emulous, narcissistic solidarities of the honour culture which defines him to develop into what the play implies is an openly homosexual attachment to Patroclus. By the same token, his refusal to fight is motivated by another sexual attachment, this one to Priam's daughter, Polyxena, that has caused him to down tools and withdraw into satiric retirement with Patroclus. It is a message from Hecuba and her daughter reminding Achilles of his oath to that effect that even now prevents him from acting on his vainglorious boasts to Hector made the night before during their meeting in the Greek camp.

By this point, all the careful planning and plotting of the party of policy lies in ruins, broken on the passions, indeed the passion-based treasons, of Achilles and the block-headed pride of Ajax. Thersites sums up the situation with typical relish and aplomb: 'the policy of those crafty swearing rascals – that stale old mouse-eaten dry cheese, Nestor, and that same dog-fox Ulysses – is proved not worth a blackberry. They set me up, in policy, that mongrel cur, Ajax, against that dog of as bad a kind, Achilles. And now is the cur Ajax prouder than the cur Achilles, and will not arm today, whereupon the Grecians begin to proclaim barbarism, and policy grows into an ill opinion' [V, iv, 8–16]. Indeed, Ulysses' plans appear to have produced exactly the opposite of their intended result, for it is Hector, not Achilles, who has been provoked into mighty deeds of arms by the, the public challenges and personal slights, both given and returned, the night before [V, v, 19–29].

What rescues the situation is not the policy of Ulysses but (again) the passion of Achilles. For during his ensuing killing spree Hector slays Patroclus and it is the resulting paroxysm of grief, rage and revenge that forces Achilles back into the fray. 'Great Achilles is arming, weeping, cursing, vowing vengeance. Patroclus' wounds have roused his drowsy blood,/Together with his mangled Myrmidons,/That noseless, handless, hacked and chipped, come to him,/Crying on Hector. Ajax hath lost a friend/And foams at mouth, and he is armed and at it,/Roaring for Troilus' [V, v, 30–37].

The contrast with Hector's entry into the day's battle could not be more stark. Where Achilles breaks an oath by fighting, Hector is driven into the field, against his own better judgement and the pleas of his family, by the need to keep one. For Hector takes the field against the desperate pleas of both his wife and sister that the omens are fatal and that he should stay at home that day. But Hector will have none of it; he is honour-bound by his oath, given in public, before the gods and to the Greeks, to fight that day. 'The gods have heard me swear.' 'Mine honour keeps the weather of my fate./Life every man holds dear, but the dear man/Holds honour far more precious-dear than life' [V, iii, 15, 26–28]. When Priam joins the women in entreating Hector to stay, Hector merely doubles down. 'I do stand engaged to many Greeks,/Even in the faith of valour, to appear/This morning to them.' 'I must not break my faith' [V, iii, 67–69, 71]. And so he goes to meet his doom, moved to the last by the prompt-ings of honour, or, in gendered terms, by the claims upon him of promises made in public to the other men who make up the honour community in and through which his own reputation has been constructed and maintained, rather than by the demands made upon him by the private emotions and ties that bind him to his wife, his sister and his father. It is a repeat of his earlier conduct in the debate with his brothers about the prudence and justice of the Trojan war effort, when, having won the argument in substantive terms of logic and morality, he had simply reversed himself to retain the good opinion of his brothers and maintain his 'dignity' and 'fame' as a man of 'honour'.

As the story dictates that he must and will, Achilles kills Hector. But in this version he does so in an entirely dishonourable way; a way which serves further to underline the contrast between the two characters' relation to 'honour'. For at the end of their first encounter, with Achilles winded and at Hector's mercy, Hector allows the Greek to recover. But Achilles is not grateful. 'I do disdain thy courtesy, proud Trojan./Be happy that my arms are out of use./My rest and negligence befriends thee now,/But thou anon shalt hear of me again;/Till when, go seek thy fortune.' To this Hector responds with extraordinary cour-tesy, given that he has just worsted Achilles in a fair fight: 'fare thee well./I would have been much more a fresher man,/Had I expected thee'. Clearly, for Hector this has been an affair of honour, a fair fight, a test of valour and prowess, that is to be continued [V, vi, 15–22]. Events prove that it is anything but that for Achilles, who is shown calling his Myrmidons to gather around him and 'when I have the bloody Hector found/Empale him with your weapons round about;/In fellest manner execute your arms' [V, vii, 4–6]. And sure enough, later, attended by his Myrmidons, Achilles does indeed find Hector alone and disarming after a long day in the field. To Hector's claim 'I am unarmed. Forgo this vantage, Greek', Achilles replies with an order to his followers. 'Strike, fellows, strike! This is the man I seek'. [V, ix, 9–10]. As Troilus had observed when reproving Hector for the merciful habits that regularly spared overmatched opponents, as he had just spared Achilles, ' 'tis war', or, in Achilles case, the passionate pursuit both of revenge and fame. For as his followers dispatch Hector, Achilles instructs them to proclaim that it is he, not they, who has killed Hector. 'On Myrmidons, and cry you all amain,/"Achilles hath the mighty Hector slain". 'Come, tie his body to my horse's tail;/Along the field I will the Trojan trail' [V, ix, 9–10, 13–14, 21–22.] Achilles' collapse of 'honour' into fame or reputation here reasserts itself; he may have pursued Hector wanting revenge, but now, having killed him, he wants to extract the last drop of 'honour', i.e. of 'fame', from the event.

As we have seen, Achilles finds and kills Hector when he is alone, vulnerable and unarmed. He is so, because he has just pursued and slaughtered an unknown Greek soldier to whose ornate armour he has taken a fancy. When the man refuses to yield but takes to his heels instead, Hector gives chase, making his motivation crystal clear in a crucial aside. 'Wilt thou not, beast, abide? Why then, fly on. I'll hunt thee for thy hide' [V, vi, 29–32]. Here, then, is no honourable display of prowess tempered with honour and mercy, but rather, to adopt Hector's own epithet, used to condemn Troilus' account of the true nature of warfare, a 'savage' pursuit of an enemy, who is to be hunted down like an animal, and all so that Hector can strip him of his elaborately wrought armour. Hector re-enters, dragging the now dead Greek. As he peels the spoils from the corpse, Hector remarks on the 'most putrefied core' that he finds within the 'goodly armour' that 'hath cost thy life'. [V, viii, 1–2]. As Eric Mallin has pointed out, the figure of the gorgeously clad Unknown Knight was a well known figure in the tiltyard performances of the Elizabethan court. On Mallin's account 'appearance in the lists as an Unknown Knight, speechless and gorgeously clad, betokened a special status. Not just anyone could be the Unknown. The role signified a courtier's distinctive position at a given tilt: he would enter in exquisite disguise to plead a specific grievance, or to announce extraordinary chivalric service to the queen.' The unknown knight is what Mallin calls a highly 'recogniseable Elizabethan image of chivalric privilege'[33] and Hector kills him for his armour.

It is, of course, not an accident that immediately after Hector has unchivalrously slaughtered this figure from the world of courtly chivalry, he is himself unceremoniously hunted down and killed by Achilles and his Myrmidons, who, with no thought of even the appearance of honourable or chivalrous conduct, slaughter Hector like a cornered animal, so that Achilles can appropriate and display both the slain Trojan's putrescent core and his 'goodly' outside. The core or corpse is dragged round the battlefield, the better publicly to demonstrate the addition to the (recently dimmed or dimming) legend of Achilles of the 'goodly' outside, that is to say, of the stock of fame and repute, the 'honour', accrued by 'the mighty Hector'.

These scenes recall the earlier debate between Hector, Paris and Troilus about the justice and prudence of the war. Then, having, to all intents and purposes, won the moral and prudential argument, Hector had suddenly changed his mind and embraced Troilus and Paris' vision of honour as something more or less devoid of moral content. Here, in the midst of battle, his eye

HOW SHAKESPEARE PUT POLITICS ON THE STAGE

caught by the chance of plunder, he dishonourably slaughters the figure of honour and is then slaughtered equally dishonourably himself. On this view, even someone as 'honourable' and 'virtuous' as Hector cannot remain immune from the tenor of the times, from the incessant and insistent demands of life in wartime. His persistent efforts to square the demands of virtue and honour, as he understands them, with the demands of total war are revealed as fatally flawed, indeed as illusory. Troilus' words at the end of their debate about the politics of pity come back here with renewed force: ' 'tis war'.

Bad Essex/good Essex

Let us turn now back to what we might take to be the play's most obvious or likely contemporary resonances. We start with the war itself. The play presents us with a war that has dragged on for years, with no likely end in view; with a war, in fact, that has been going on for so long that the participants have all but forgotten why it started. When they do pause to discuss its origins or causes, they have grave doubts about the justice, and, indeed, the prudence, of the whole enterprise, and can see no reason for continuing except that they are engaged and can find no 'honourable' way out. All this is surely likely, in 1602, to have struck a chord with contemporaries. The war with Spain, conducted in the Low Countries, in France, at sea and in Ireland, had been going on for nearly twenty years; peace was by now much talked about but by no means in view. With the conclusion of peace of Vervins between France and Spain, the only *casus belli* left standing was the protection of the Dutch, and, in certain circles, and indeed in many of the tracts advocating the conclusion of peace with Spain analysed by Dr Gajda, their revolt against Philip II was regarded as no more morally justifiable than the abduction of Helen of Troy was by Hector. At the turn of the sixteenth century, war-weariness, and concern about the impact of the war on the mores and politics of the country, were by no means unlikely sentiments upon which an account of the Trojan war, cast *in medias res*, might hope to play. Moreover, since it was with the Trojans that certain potent and widespread origin myths tended to equate or identify London and England, the outcome of this other unjust and imprudent war, with which everyone was heartily sick, seemed to point to an altogether unhappy conclusion for the English.

   Not that the play offered a stable view or equation of either side in the conflict with England (or, still less, with Spain). For one thing the depiction of the internal politics of the Greek camp was redolent of recent events in England. We have here, after all, a party of policy, led by a very old and rather dull man and a much quicker and altogether more effectively cunning, not to say Machiavellian, younger colleague; a man who, at times, speaks with the voice of an all seeing state; a state that almost knows more about the purposes and actions of many of its leading subjects and agents than they do themselves. Posed against this party of policy we have a party of rather stupid, but very proud and vain, soldiers. The soldiers despise the policy-mongers as weak and pointless, while the policy-mongers despise the soldiers as stupid, and attempt, by setting them against one another, to manipulate them for their own subtle, and even sinister, purposes. It is not hard to discern here glancing references to recent divisions within the English elite between the Cecils, *père et fils*, and Essex and his allies. For if in Nestor and Ulysses contemporaries might see references to Burghley and Robert Cecil, the parallels between Achilles and Essex are just as clear. Not only that, but the appeal to Achilles' vanity and insecurity, as, lurking in his tent, he refused to return to the field of battle, bore more than a slight resemblance to the ways in which an unwilling Essex had been induced to undertake what turned out to be his last, fatal command in Ireland. Similarly the relationship between Achilles and Patroclus was redolent of that between Essex and Southampton.

A good deal of ink has been spilt on the parallel between Achilles and Essex and the case is a strong one. The strongest literary evidence for such a connection comes, of course, from Chapman's translation of the *Iliad*, which he dedicated to Essex and in which dedication he explicitly compared the earl to Achilles.[34] Chapman had been trying to flatter the earl while he was alive, but Shakespeare was commenting upon his career after his catastrophic demise on the scaffold and many of the earl's less than positive characteristics, or rather negative versions of characteristics that, to his admirers, had (and could still) look like virtues, can be found in the character of Achilles. His obsession with his own military prowess and valour; his equal obsession with his fame and reputation; his brittle pride and unwillingness to brook any rivals; his tendency to respond to political difficulties or reverses by withdrawing from active involvement in affairs; his propensity to dally and intrigue with the enemy (as Essex allegedly had in Ireland with O'Neill); even the relative ease with which these propensities meant he could be manipulated by others, all these were readily paralleled in Essex's character and career.

But, as several commentators have argued, almost as good a case could be made for positive correlations, points of reference and resonance, linking Essex with Hector.[35] Like Hector, as Richard McCoy and Paul Hammer have both pointed out, Essex used the forms and claims of court chivalry and honour to frame and legitimise his career as a courtier, general, royal servant and favourite.[36] As Paul Hammer, in particular, has shown, Essex believed that the claims of virtue and honour, of noble autonomy and of the faithful defence of a royal mistress, could be reconciled in the service, and particularly in the military service, of crown and commonwealth. Like Hector, Essex was committed to squaring the demands of honour and of virtue and, of course, just like Hector, he discovered, to his cost, that, under current circumstances at least, it could not be done.[37]

The point, of course, is that we are not compelled to choose between or to refuse either set of associations.[38] After all, Hector and Achilles are bound together in the play; the one is the other's shadow or twin. From the outset, the fate of the one is fatally bound up with that of the other. They might, indeed, be taken as but the dark and light sides of the same character function. We might, therefore, on this account, regard Achilles as 'bad Essex', an epitome of all the earl's negative characteristics, of what his virtues turned into, as, under the pressure of circumstance and the machinations of his enemies, they became vices. Hector, on the other hand, fulfils two roles. Most obviously, flawed as he is, he is 'good Essex', an image of what the earl was like at his best, of what he aspired, and, at times, even managed, to be. But Hector also epitomises the moral contradictions and hypocrisies that rendered the Essexian attempt to square the demands of honour and of virtue, of personal devotion to the queen and service to the commonwealth, impossible. For, things being as they are, even Hector cannot always be Hector; ideal and reality cannot meet. The (both personally and collectively) tragic consequences of Hector's failure to follow through on the logic of his own arguments about the justice and necessity of ending the war and indeed of his entirely dishonourable slaughter of the unknown Greek for his armour, show this only too clearly. And so 'bad Essex' treacherously murders 'good Essex', in that very act sending his own residual claims to honour and virtue to the grave along with the body of his slain rival.

The use of twinned characters to personify different moral and political characteristics and to stage the interplay of those divergent propensities in the emergence or realisation of a third (Essexian) term has already been encountered, in 1 Henry IV, in the relations between Hal and Hotspur. That double portrait had also ended in a fight to the death, but the nature and outcome of the similarly fatal encounter between Achilles and Hector in Troilus and Cressida is the very opposite of what had happened in 1 Henry IV. Acknowledging throughout the honour and prowess of his rival, Hal had killed Hotspur, and then allowed Falstaff to claim the credit for the deed. Achilles, however, had had an unarmed and outnumbered Hector treacherously killed by others, in order then to lay an entirely false claim to the deed himself. While Hal's combat with his doppelgänger Hotspur had been central to the emergence of King Henry V out of the chrysalis of Prince Hal, the murder of Hector represents Achilles' final transition from the role of mythic hero, in which he had entered the action, to that of doomed coward, conferred on him at play's end by Troilus. We are being shown here the final transformation of honour, achieved on the field of battle, in the service of queen and country, into the ruthless pursuit, for their own sake and at all costs, of fame and popularity. Here is the final demonstration that, under the impact of total war and of factional political conflict, the politics of 'honour' and of 'popularity', the demands of 'honour' and of 'virtue', are neither synonymous nor compatible

Moreover, as both the good and bad aspects of Essex, that is to say, both Achilles and Hector, go off to meet their fate(s), the only purposes that are being served are those of the party of policy; that is to say, of Nestor and Ulysses. But even this outcome has not been wrought by their political cunning, but rather by Achilles' self-destructive, deviant and (if Thersites is to be believed) diseased, passion (for Patroclus). 'Essex', on this account, for all the machinations of his enemies and rivals, has brought his own (tragic-ish) downfall on himself. The result, however, is not limited to himself: Troy/England, too, is doomed. Here, perhaps, is the point where 'the history' and 'the tragedy' of 'Troilus and Cressida' meet.

But it is also worth remembering that, for all the intensity and conviction of his opening analysis of what it is that afflicts the Greek camp – a hollow(ing) faction, the spread of which he attributes, directly and entirely, to the diseased pride of Achilles – the only person in the play who has been shown indulging in self-consciously factious, Machiavellian manipulation, is none other than Ulysses – aided, of course, by Nestor, to whom the pricelessly factious line about their 'fraction' serving our purposes better than their 'faction' belongs. This raises the obvious question of whether one would ever buy a second-hand car from Robert Cecil (or indeed from Lord Burghley). Or, put more historically, it might be thought to advert to the gap between theory and practice, between ideal and reality, between the talk of good counsel and virtue in the service of the commonwealth and the queen, which was never far from Burghley's lips, and what appeared to his critics to be the self-serving, ruthless and perhaps even tyrannous nature of his actions and policies. Since the early 1570s a number of authors (most, but by no means all of them, Catholic — after all Burghley's critics included the likes of Spenser and Nashe)[39] had placed that yawning gap at or near the centre of their analyses of the Elizabethan regime as a conspiracy and a tyranny.

More generally, the play might be thought to conjure up a vision of a late Elizabethan world bedevilled by the politics of faction, on the one hand, and the politics of an increasingly spurious and contradictory honour, pride and popularity, on the other. Commenting upon the resulting mess, using the full range of (venereally) diseased metaphor, is the ubiquitous figure of Thersites. Whether or not Thersites is a caricature of John Marston, as a variety of scholars interested in the so-called 'war of the theatres' have argued, his presence in the play clearly refers to yet another well known aspect of the *fin-de-siècle* political and cultural scene – the vogue, both in the pamphlet press and on the popular stage, for scabrously satiric comment upon the doings of the political elite. In the play, at least, such comment is a part of the political struggles upon which the likes of Thersites are keeping up a supposedly independent commentary. For Thersites is, by turns, a creature of first Ajax and then of Achilles, in both roles a 'privileged' man, able to speak truth to power only so long as another (rival) source of power protects him. But that, arguably, is also what this play is (unsuccessfully as far as its subsequent performance history seems to imply) doing.

If we revert to the point at which we started, that is to say, to the vision of *Henry V*, we have, it must be admitted, come rather a long way. For in that play, the various impulses and drives of the contemporary political scene, the politics of honour and of popularity, had been united in one representatively royal figure, Henry V. War had been central to that unitive project. Dreadful though its immediate consequences may have been – ask the boys in the baggage train and the French prisoners taken at Agincourt about that – the medium- and long-term, moral and political, effects of war had been salutary. Internal division, subversion and faction had been suppressed; the foreigner repulsed, the nation united and purged under the rule of a virtuous and Christian prince, who was himself the master of a variety of political styles; able to slip, at a moment's notice, into whatever moral or rhetorical register best suited the attendant circumstances.

So much, then, for (Essexian) fantasy. With the earl's precipitate fall, there was nothing left of that project or prospect. War has now become the condition, not of unity and reformation, of virtue and social and moral health, but of conflict and contradiction, of corruption and disease. We move from the moral and discursive universe of the chorus of *Henry V*, and the start of *Troilus and Cressida*, to the reductively obscene (but far from inaccurate) commentary of Thersites. The different rhetorical and political modes that had been united in the person of Henry V now split apart, distributed amongst the divergent, indeed the antagonistic, personae not only of Achilles and Hector, but also of Ulysses.

What are being staged here are the cognitive and moral consequences of the fall of the earl of Essex for someone who, confronted by the very considerable contradictions and dangers of the later Elizabethan religious, political and cultural scene, had invested (rather too) heavily in a particular (Essexian and Stuart legitimist) vision of the immediate future as a means of coming to terms with and transcending the contradictions and dangers of the present. With the fall of the earl of Essex, there was now (for the moment) nowhere else to turn.

'War for a placket': the paradoxes of female rule – again

In the *Henry VI* plays and indeed in *Titus Andronicus* Shakespeare had serially conjured a political scene vitiated by an excess of female influence at the centre of power. But the history plays written since *Richard II* had dealt with a version of monarchical politics almost entirely devoid of female power or even influence. One crucial reason for this shift of emphasis had been the centrality of war to those plays and in particular to the role played by the aggressive conduct of war in the process whereby legitimacy might be regained, the nation united

and the commonwealth reformed. Of course, war, and the honour and legitimacy to be won in and through it, was quintessentially man's work and a politics dominated, and a commonwealth rebuilt, by war, is also a politics and a
commonwealth dominated by men. It is surely no accident that *Henry V* ends
with a foreign queen, bending, with comic incomprehension and pointlessly
stumbling protest, before the will of an English king, whose reign and status as
a true English, indeed incipiently British, monarch has been confirmed by the
miraculous victory at Agincourt. Here we might draw a comparison with the
Henry VI plays which were, in the persons of Joan of Arc, the duchess of
Gloucester and Queen Margaret, suffused with a female, often a foreign female,
influence, which was always malign and often associated with the dark forces
of witchcraft and (false) prophecy. There the effects of female power were
always bad; leading to the loss of legitimacy in division, sedition, and civil and
dynastic war. For legitimacy to return, politics had to be dominated again by
men, waging foreign wars. Again we have a war-dominated agenda, leading,
via Essex, to James Stuart; a fantasy of male power, of a politics dominated by
military men, providing a way out of the petticoat government of Elizabeth.

But in *Troilus*, a play written after the spectacular implosion of the Essexian
project, we are back to an entirely decentred, factionalised chaos, with an
absent female presence at its core. War is no longer, as it had been in *King John*
and *Henry V*, a source of national unity and legitimacy, a way to make up for a
previous politics of usurpation and tyranny by reconnecting the prince with
his people, driving out faction and sedition from the elite and reforming the
commonwealth. On the contrary, war is itself part of the problem, indeed in
many ways it is *the* problem, providing both the legitimising ground and material conditions for the descent into faction and the politics of fame and popularity, the lechery and war, that the play stages.

What remains is the haggard remnant of a politics of honour, organised
around the struggle for the possession and favour of women. In the debate
between Hector, Troilus and Paris about whether to end the war, Paris starts
out asserting the Trojans' duty to defend the honour and beauty of Helen
against all the world [II, ii, 199–202]. But by the end it has become clear not
only that the decision to continue to fight is a function of the need to defend
and assert the martial honour and prowess of Trojan men, but also that the
initial abduction of Helen had been a political, rather than an amatory, affair, a
form of revenge wreaked by the Trojans on the Greeks for former slights. And,
of course, Cressida's fate is determined solely by the demands of political expe-
dience and affairs of state.[40]

Helen and Cressida are portrayed as largely passive victims of the machinations and power plays of their various male 'suitors', captors and spouses, what
Mallin describes as 'the whims, lusts, negligence, or fury of courtiers'. For all
their seeming centrality to the plot, Helen appears only long enough to emerge

as an empty, vapid creature and disappears from view after Act III and, by the end, even Cressida has faded into the background.[41] Both women become complicit in their own fate only insofar as they use what resources of wit and physical attraction remain to them to invoke and manipulate, to their own advantage, the discourses of love and honour within which their male possessors' actions are framed and legitimised. Passed back and forth, they must make what they can of their situation, becoming, in the process, prime targets for the admiration and moral opprobrium, the desire and sexualised self-disgust, of the men.[42] Thus we find them being reviled as at best weak and faithless – as is Cressida by Troilus – and, at worst, simply as whores, as Helen is by Diomedes, and as both Helen and Cressida are by Ulysses. These estimations are, of course, echoed and amplified by the scabrous commentary on events maintained throughout by Thersites. The war, he claims, is being fought for 'a placket', hence the continuing connections between sexual desire, war and venereal disease – 'the Neapolitian bone-ache' – that Thersites obsessively recycles [II, iii, 16–19]. Significantly, it is after the scene in which both we and Troilus have observed the successful seduction of Cressida by Diomedes that Thersites provides perhaps his definitive verdict on proceedings: 'lechery, lechery; still wars and lechery; nothing else holds fashion. A burning devil take them!' [V, ii, 201–2].

The power dynamics (and gender politics) in play here are revealed in the scene between Troilus and Diomedes that precedes, indeed, prompts, Diomedes' later seduction of Cressida. Entrusting Cressida to Diomedes, who has been sent from the Greek camp to effect her exchange for Antenor, the heartbroken Troilus peremptorily instructs his Greek counterpart to look after her or else. Their exchange appears to start courteously enough – 'Entreat her fair and, by my soul, fair Greek,/If e'er thou stand at mercy of my sword,/Name Cressid, and thy life shall be as safe/As Priam is in Ilium' [IV, iv,112–15] – except that Troilus' remarks are based on the assumption of his superior martial prowess and organised around the intensely demeaning image of Diomedes begging Troilus for mercy on the field of battle.

This, of course, is a calculated slight, and Diomedes replies to it in kind by addressing not Troilus but Cressida. 'The lustre in your eye, heaven in your cheek,/Pleads your fair usage; and to Diomed/You shall be mistress and command him wholly' [IV, iv, 115–19]. Again, this seems courteous enough, but in fact it is another calculated insult; a remark designed to turn aside Troilus' implicit threat by paying court directly to Cressida, in terms which both remove Troilus from the equation and seem to threaten precisely the outcome – Cressida's seduction by a Greek – that most torments the Trojan prince. Troilus responds with a far more direct threat. 'Grecian, thou dost not use me courteously,/To shame the zeal of my petition to thee/In praising her. I tell thee, lord of Greece,/She is as far high-soaring o'er thy praises/As thou unworthy to be called her servant./I charge thee use her well, even for my

charge;/For, by the dreadful Pluto, if thou dost not,/Though the great bulk
Achilles be thy guard,/I'll cut thy throat' [IV, iv,120–28]. Diomedes, of course,
cannot react well to this and predictably enough he replies in kind. 'O, be not
moved prince Troilus./Let me be privileged by my place and message/To be a
speaker free. When I am hence,/I'll answer to my lust. And know you, lord,/I'll
nothing do on charge./To her own worth/She shall be prised; but that you say
"Be't so",/I'll speak it in my spirit and honour: "No" ' [IV, iv, 128–34].

On one reading, therefore, it is only Troilus' perfervid attempts to 'protect'
Cressida that arouse Diomedes' interest in her in the first place. Indeed, one
might argue that it was precisely because he has been instructed, in such
insulting terms, *not* to seduce Cressida, that the seduction of Cressida becomes
such a pressing point of honour for Diomedes. For in that one act he can subject
not only Cressida but, through her, Troilus, to his 'lust'; a term that encom-
passes both his free election, his right to do precisely what he pleases, when
he pleases, and a threat to act towards Cressida as his carnal desires prompt
him. In seducing and sexually possessing Cressida, Diomedes is thus violating
Troilus, an act to which the only proper response is violence, one act of physical
violation provoking another, in an honour-based cycle of violence, of assertion
and counter-assertion, to which, for all the protestations of undying love and
fidelity that attend the dealings between the sexes, the presence and possession
of the woman is almost incidental.

Linda Charnes' comment on Troilus' slighting aside that 'Paris is gor'd with
Menelaus horn' is of particular relevance here. 'Helen,' she observes, 'disappears entirely here, synedochised into the horn that "connects" Menelaus and
Paris in the bonds of "homosociality"'. The speech, Charnes claims, 'conjures an
image of sexual penetration not between Helen and Paris but between two
men, with Helen serving merely as the "horn" that both humiliates Menelaus
and penetrates Paris. Taking shape in Troilus' language of "heterosexuality" is
a fantasy of sadomasochistic homoeroticism', a fantasy that pervades the play's
account both of love and war.[43]

As the mutual obsession of Hector and Achilles implies, as the men compete
for fame and reputation the intensity of the resulting emulous competition can
lead to an obsession with the person and persona of the enemy/rival that is
disconcertingly like romantic love. Diomedes is pictured as having stalked
Aeneas around the battlefield for a week together, a pursuit which itself explains
the intensity of what Paris calls 'their despitful'st gentle greeting', their 'noblest
hateful love', when they finally do meet in time of truce. Achilles, desperate to
restore what he deems to be his wavering fame, becomes obsessed with his
Trojan equivalent, or doppelgänger, Hector. 'I have a woman's longing,/An
appetite that I am sick withal,/To see great Hector in his weeds of peace,/To talk
with him, and to behold his visage/Even to my full of view' [III, iii, 239–43].
For his part, Hector seems just as drawn to Achilles. Welcomed to the Greek

camp after his bout in the lists with Ajax, which of course he had intended to be a more fatal encounter with Achilles, he asks to be introduced 'to the worthiest', 'name by name', except, that is, for Achilles, whom he vows to pick out for himself. 'But for Achilles, mine own searching eyes/Shall find him by his large and portly size' [IV, v, 161–63].

The absent presence of women at the centre of the play reaches its logical end point, indeed its *reductio ad absurdum*, in Hector's challenge to the Greeks that 'he hath a lady wiser, fairer, truer,/Than ever Greek did compass in his arms' [I, iii, 275–76] and will meet in battle any Greek who cares to contradict him. This, of course, is mere pretence; behind it lies no concern with any woman, real or imaginary, but rather Hector's general concern to heighten his own claims to honour and prowess through combat with a man, and in partic-ular his (entirely reciprocated) obsession with his Greek counterpart, Achilles, to whom, as everyone knows, this seemingly general, woman-centred chal-lenge is, in fact, directed.

Thus, for all that the play centres on women, the problem it addresses is scarcely a surfeit of female influence but rather an absence of (male) monar-chical control; itself perhaps an inevitable product of female rule in time of war. Neither the Greek nor the Trojan polity is depicted as a straightforward monarchy. The Greek camp is composed of sixty-nine sovereign rulers. Their leader Agamemnon is merely *primus inter pares*. As the withdrawal of Achilles shows, he must rule by persuasion and deceit more than by royal command or fiat. To wage the war effectively he needs Achilles, and must bend and accom-modate to Achilles' moods and demands, rather than merely command his obedience. That position, of course, puts him at the disposal of the party of policy, who provide him with indirect means to gain ends that a more sover-eign ruler could achieve directly.

As for the Trojan side, while Priam is nominally king, the conduct of Trojan government is presented as thoroughly conciliar, conducted through open discussion amongst Priam's progeny and the other Trojan leaders. Priam's (like Hector's) voice is merely one against many and, as we have seen, at a crucial juncture he cannot even successfully command Hector not to take the field. For all his misgivings, in the end Priam must accede to his son's wishes, just as Hector had earlier felt compelled to give in to his brothers on the subject of ending the war. These failures or capitulations lead directly to Hector's death and, indeed, will lead to the destruction of Troy itself.

Again, there are obvious parallels to the ways in which English government was conducted under Elizabeth, particularly in time of war, when the queen became extraordinarily reliant on the service and expertise of military men and found the normal means of conciliar control over her servants extremely difficult to exert; a problem exacerbated not only by the disagreements and rivalries that often divided her military advisors and agents but also by Essex's energetic pursuit of his own version of the service of the crown, often against the express wishes, and even instructions, of the queen herself.

In the case of both Achilles and Hector, then, what is lacking, and what proves disastrous for both of them, is the absence of the smack of firm monarchical government. It is this that allows or enables the moral decline of Achilles and prompts the death of Hector. On this account, Essex is the victim not merely of the machinations of his enemies or indeed of the weaknesses of his own character – although the play does indeed show him to have been the victim of both – but also of the absence of that firm monarchical control that could alone have kept the politics of faction under control and kept Essex himself both honest and in line, as the faithful servant of queen and commonwealth that he always claimed and/or wanted to be. Thus, the problem here is not so much female rule, conceived as producing an excess of (corrupt or effeminating) female influence on the processes of government, so much as a lack of properly sovereign monarchical control; a lack or absence that might well be thought of, at least in late Tudor England, if not now, in post-Thatcher Britain, as the inevitable product of female rule.

The play concludes, as it started, *in medias res*, with two endings. First comes Troilus' doomed and desperate epic swearing of revenge on that 'great sized coward' Achilles [V, xi, 11–31]. This is followed by a mock requiem for panders, 'traitors and bawds', those 'brethren and sisters of the hold door trade', delivered by Pandarus, in direct address to an audience which, he is sure, contains more than its fair share of what he terms 'Winchester geese' from the neighbouring brothels of Southwark. [V, xi, 35–56].

As Harry Berger observes, if, throughout the play, Thersites has been continually saying ' "these men on stage are not heroes, but fools and knaves", Pandarus, turning towards the audience at play's end, adds "And so are you." '[44] This is a daring move that, just like the clown or the ruined monastery in *Titus Andronicus* or the chiming clock in *Julius Caesar*, serves to close, almost to nothing, the gap between ancient Troy and Elizabethan London, between the 'history' being performed on stage and the current experiences and realities of the audience. The passage thus directly adverts to, indeed acts out, what, on the current reading, all the plays I have been discussing here were doing. Pandarus ends by promising to 'bequeath' to the audience 'my diseases', that is to say, the venereal diseases of his 'aching bones'. The war and lechery, lechery and war of Thersites reaches across the centuries to create a transhistorical 'now' of war-torn disease, corruption and death, raising the question, if *Troilus and Cressida* is, as its various titles claim, both a tragedy and a history, just whose tragedy and history was it?

Conclusion

The history play and the post-reformation public sphere

The initial question that prompted this book was the role of public theatre, in general, and of the history play, in particular, in calling into being the various publics that made up the so-called 'post-reformation public sphere'.[1] In a previous book I argued that such publics were constituted by a series of pitches for support made by differently configured interest groups and factions, as they sought either to destabilise and displace or to perpetuate and shape the Elizabethan protestant state.[2] On one level, the drama as it has emerged in this book must be said to have had a secondary, indirect effect on 'the post-reformation public sphere'. For the forms of appeal and counter-appeal, the different modes of political communication, that have been seen as constitutive of the 'post-reformation public sphere' all predated, if not the public theatre itself, then certainly the history play. Not only that, but what was involved here were attempts to induce various groups and individuals to take one view of the current conjuncture as opposed to others, and on that basis, either now or in the future, to take certain forms of action, or exert certain forms of pressure on those in control of the levers of power.

While we might be dealing here with attempts to convince and persuade, the resulting pitches were anything but austerely rational in either their form or their content. Not exercises in dialectic but rather in rhetoric, they deployed all of the emotive appeals and the no-holds-barred tropes and tricks that, as Markku Peltonen has shown, came as second nature to all those trained in the norms and forms of classical rhetoric.[3] But however emotive their appeal, or slippery their modes of argument, these remained self-conscious attempts to persuade, to make a case, as often as not framed by the need to refute some pre-existing counter-argument, some rival view, if not of the world, then at least of the present conjuncture. As such, more often than not, such pitches claimed to base their arguments on certain shared sources of authority, knowledge or principle and launched appeals that at least affected to direct themselves as much to reason as to the emotions. Almost always, such attempts derived or sought to derive legitimation from some version either of the commonweal or of the cause of true religion. In short, they made cases, calling upon their audience or readership to choose between rival arguments, to make a judgement about what was true and what was false, and sometimes, at least, about what to do and what not to do, next.

As I have tried to argue elsewhere, in this period, this way of doing politics, and the modes of political communication and pitch-making that accompanied it, never became normative or even fully licit. Contemporaries habitually claimed to have recourse to such practices only in times of emergency, and to be doing so only in order to re-establish some version of normality, in which this mode of public pitch-making would have no place. On the contrary, 'normality' once achieved, order once restored, such behaviour was to be organised (once more) under the sign of sedition; something to be suppressed and punished, whenever and wherever it reared its ugly head. It was just that the exigencies of post-reformation politics, in general, and, in particular, the conflation of religious division with confessional conflict and dynastic uncertainty that made up the Elizabethan exclusion and succession crises, never allowed that sort of normality to be re-established. Thus, a politics of public pitch-making, designated by the opprobrious term of 'popularity' by those who disapproved of it, or at least of the use being made of it by their enemies or rivals of the moment, became a normal, albeit never a normative, feature of the political scene. Indeed, such moves and manoeuvres became a valuable and much used part of the toolbox of the public man or politician; as the discussion of popularity undertaken in *Richard II* and the *Henry IV* plays, analysed above, frankly acknowledged.

The role attributed here to the drama in relation to the politics of the day presupposes the existence of this mode of politicking and the emergence of certain sorts of adjudicating publics, with their voracious appetite for comment upon and insight into what was really going on in the contemporary political scene. And of course, by the late 1580s and 1590s all these preconditions were in place, certainly in London, but not only there. And thus, while the public theatre may not have initiated any of these developments, and been entirely incapable on its own of sustaining them, it most definitely sought to feed off, and in so doing to expand, the resulting 'post-reformation public sphere'. Not, of course, out of a principled desire to disseminate or increase political knowledge or to inculcate civic virtue, but rather because the spread of such attitudes and interests was likely to increase the appetite for a certain sort of play and thus redound to the considerable profit of those providing such plays to the viewing and reading publics.

On the face of it, one might think that that essentially parasitic, secondary role would be the extent of the public theatre's contribution to the development of the post-reformation public sphere. After all, plays were precisely not pamphlets or position papers. They neither made a case nor advanced or refuted arguments. As we have seen, the very terms of their existence prevented them from explicitly naming names, taking sides or attributing praise and blame to either specific persons or policies. Rather, than, like pamphlets or proclamations, trying to persuade or convince, to refute one view of the situation and replace it with another, plays, we might think, merely told stories, the resolutions of which represented, not successfully clinched arguments, but emotionally satisfying endings; moments of release, catharsis and vindication that satisfied, not the demands of rational argument, but rather those of narrative and emotional closure.

Admittedly, some plays aspired to the sort of argumentative or advocatory role usually played by pamphlets or position papers. Here perhaps the best example is *Gorboduc*. At its first performances, some scholars have argued, it was in effect urging the queen to settle the succession by marrying the earl of Leicester. When, in printed form (in 1565 and then again 1570) it was subsequently reinserted into the course of public debate, that was no longer a viable option. Now it took its part in campaigns, centred in parliament, to induce the queen to settle the succession or to do something about Mary Stuart. However, in all its several rescensions and contexts there can be no doubt that the play mounts both an emotional and a forensic case in favour of settling the succession, with the help of parliament, in the queen's own lifetime.

Very few of the plays under discussion in this book could be reduced to such precise take-home messages. Admittedly, played in a certain way, or viewed in a certain light, both *King John* and *Henry V* could operate as ra-ra exhortations to national unity behind, and xenophobic enthusiasm for, the war against the foreigner. Insofar as audience members bought into the equation of Henry with Essex made explicitly in certain versions of *Henry V*, they might have left the theatre with their enthusiasm not merely for the war but for the earl himself appropriately heightened.

As I have argued above, it might well have been the case that buying into the pro-war and pro-Essex message that *Henry V* undoubtedly contained, in effect, aligned you on the earl's side in the debate about peace and war currently being conducted in the public sphere described by circulating manuscript and rumour, so brilliantly evoked by Alex Gajda.[4] But firstly, for that to be the case, you would have had to know that that debate was going on, and there is no reason to believe that anything like all of the play's first audiences would have known any such thing. Moreover, being enlisted to that position by the play might be thought to be a very different experience from being persuaded into it by reading Essex's apology or some of the other pro-war tracts currently doing the rounds, which were making arguments and seeking rationally to persuade in ways that the play, certainly operating at the reductively propagandistic level at which many audience members might very well have experienced it, palpably was not.

Except that, as we have seen, *Henry V* was also a play that most definitely did operate at other than such reductively propagandistic levels of thought and feeling and any alert audience member who noticed that fact would almost immediately have become engaged in what one can only call an argument about the rights and wrongs of the war being staged in the play, and of Henry's reasons for deciding to fight it; arguments which, again, had much to say both about the present conjuncture in particular and indeed about the essentially prudential nature of monarchical politics, in general. Anyone engaging with the play at that level would thus have become engaged in an argument not only with the play but also with the times, indeed very likely with him- or herself, as the play forced them to weigh first one and then another view of the matter before coming to some final conclusion or resting place, or not. The same, of course, applied to that other nationalistic paean to the joys of foreigner-hating Englishness and denunciation of the spectre of foreign rule, *King John*. In both cases, of course, the stakes were raised, and the dialectical forces in operation considerably heightened, by the contrasts between Shakespeare's versions of these events and those staged in *The troublesome reign* and *The famous victories*, respectively.

The soundbite politics of emotional appeal and response, to, say, the call to national unity and martial enthusiasm in the face of the foreign threat, launched, in their different ways, by *1 Henry VI*, *King John* and *Henry V*, were quintessentially public, since they involved the evocation and public expression of collective emotions upon subjects of general interest and knowledge. However, since they involved altogether more controversial, and sometimes even forbidden, topics, the rather more complex arguments at work in those plays of necessity took place, not so much in public, as between the ears of individual audience members. On the one hand, then, nothing could be more public than the public stage, on which the intensely political actions of great heroes from the mythic past and great princes from the history of England or of Rome grappled with issues and dilemmas of the most obvious contemporary relevance and resonance, before audiences of thousands. But, on the other, these plays could only deal with such subjects in public in anything other than the most superficial way by leaving to the audience the really contentious, difficult and dangerous applications of the action on stage to contemporary concerns and events. Precisely because of their controversial, indeed illicit, character, while the ensuing discussions might initially have been prompted by the most public of public performances, the consequent processes of application and argument had to remain intensely private, trapped inside the heads of the individual members of the audience or at best expressed in private conversation with only the most trusted of interlocutors.

I say of individual audience members rather than of the audience more generally conceived because, while these plays located the particular pressure points, the crucial narrative, moral and political cruxes around which they were organised, with an almost forensic precision, they were also extremely careful never (definitively) to decide those crucial questions for the audience. Rather, as we have seen, over and over again, they moved to open themselves up to a variety of different applications and interpretations which were then left to the audience to decide. And that being the case it was inevitable that the members of the audience, which was, after all, composed of persons of very different opinions, presuppositions and religious identities, would resolve the questions posed to them by the play very differently.

Many, perhaps most, might not even have noticed what I have presented above as the crucial hints and signals that served to connect the play as acted with some really contentious contemporary issue, or more general moral or political or theological concern or crux. If, for instance, you missed the parallel between King John and Queen Elizabeth or between Arthur and Mary Stuart, set up in the early scenes of *King John*, you could take *King John* to be a stirring call to national unity against the foreigner, laced with a bit of papal legate bashing, and bastard-centred humour at the expense of the upper classes. Similarly, if, in 1592, you did not know that the court had recently been riven by rivalries between the likes of Raleigh and Essex, or that previous English military expeditions had been undermined not only by the personal squabbles of the commanders but also by more fundamental disagreements about what sort of war they were trying to fight, you might experience *1 Henry VI* as a similarly patriotic bit of foreigner and papist bashing, featuring the differently affecting deaths of an antique English hero (Talbot) and a positively demonic personification of popish disorder and misrule (Puzel). However, if you did know or notice those things, while the plays might not lose any of their basic, visceral anti-foreigner, pro-war animus, that basic take home message would emerge as the end product of an altogether different, more complex and controversial, chain of reasoning or internal argumentation.

But if something of that sort did happen, given the extremely sensitive, even dangerous nature of the issues being raised, that might very well not have led to an outbreak of public discussion of the rights and wrongs of the matter. Indeed, one might think that the last thing that was likely to eventuate from these sorts of transactions between play and audience was *public* discussion. On the contrary, the effects of such thought processes were very likely to be both individuating and privatising, rather than collective and public. When the plays most closely and controversially engaged the central issues of the day, and in so doing led their audiences to the edge, and beyond, of what they were supposed to think and say – when, that is, they were at their most contentiously 'political' – they were cutting against the unitive publicness which these plays also wanted to induce in their audiences, during the course of the action, but with peculiar intensity at play's end, when the whole point was to unite the audience in the intense experience of shared emotions, culminating in the collective expression of enthusiastic approbation of both the play and the performance. It was, and surely remains, the capacity of these plays to operate on these several levels, simultaneously, and with no diminution of the dramatic or emotional effectiveness of the performance as a whole, that gives them much of their abiding power and fascination.

Certainly, these plays fed off moments of collective emotion and catharsis, like that generated in *1 Henry VI* by the deaths of Talbot and Puzel, or by the justice-dealing carnage with which both *Titus Andronicus* and *Hamlet* end, or by the death of the quintessential tyrant Richard III and his replacement by that plaster saint, with-God-on-his-side, Richmond. But as we have seen, what these endings meant, politically, morally or theologically, would be a function of what individual audience members had made of the preceding action – I am even tempted to say, of the preceding argument – of the play. Thus, while the emotional response (of pleasure, pathos or catharsis) elicited from audience members at play's end might serve to integrate them into a quintessentially collective experience, their divergent sense of just what it was that had elicited that common catharsis or approbation might also serve to dissolve them again into a range of differently defined groups, if not into a mass of atomised individuals.

Pursued to extremes such an argument could lead us to posit as many interpretations of or responses to the play as there were audience members. But it has been the historicising purpose of this book, by setting the plays in a variety of directly contemporary discursive, ideological and political settings, simultaneously to heighten our sense of the various (political) meanings and interpretations that these plays could enable in or elicit from their audiences, while at the same time constraining the range and nature of those readings within the limits provided by those immediately contemporary concerns and contexts. Therein lay these plays' great contribution to the post-reformation public sphere and to the production of various adjudicating publics, intensely interested in how politics actually worked.

And it is this last that was surely the most abiding political effect of theplays under discussion here. For just like the Catholic tracts, nearly all of them both appealed to and heightened a popular interest in what politics was really like, in what was really going on under the carapace of cloying moral orthodoxy and high moral purpose provided by the official account of the doings of the good and the great. While the tracts had played on such fascinations and fears for partisan polemical and political purposes, the plays did so for commercial ones, seeking to maximise their appeal and reach but in so doing disseminating a particular way of looking at politics as something to be decoded; as a puzzle to be solved, involving different evaluations of the actions and intentions of particular political agents, the nature of the times and the interventions of either fortune or divine providence.

The result was what Noel Malcolm has described as 'a way of looking at political events that made them more open to discussion, since it both suggested that they needed to be deciphered and supplied some simple rules for their decipherment'. [5] Malcolm, of course, was talking about the black propaganda, the confessionally based stereotypes and conspiracy theories generated by the Thirty Years War in the 1620s and 1630s, but, as I have tried to show elsewhere, the education of various English publics in precisely this paranoid hermeneutic style had been going on, in the pamphlet press, and in various sorts of public performance, in texts produced, and performances choreographed, not only by the regime's Catholic critics but also by the regime itself, since at least the late 1560s, and, in the history plays and tragedies under discussion here, on the public stage, since at least the late 1580s. On this basis, therefore, the drama can surely added to the various media through which the 'post-reformation public sphere' was constituted, various publics were called into being, and certain ways of seeing and interpreting politics as process, disseminated.[6]

Indeed, as Andras Kisery has argued, by the very late sixteenth and early seventeenth centuries, a period he dubs rather memorably, 'Hamlet's moment', the resulting nexus of interests and capacities had become a key characteristic of a certain sort of self-consciously sophisticated observer of, and commentator upon, events, and a certain sort of play had come to be regarded as a prime source for the insights and apothegms, the memorisation, repetition and application of which had become a central attribute of this mode of self-presentation. Accordingly, when said plays were printed the relevant passages, the really crucial saws and *sententiae,* were marked off on the printed page as fodder for the commonplace book or the memory of the reader.[7]

Kisery tends to talk about this phenomenon in Bourdieusian terms of the search for certain sorts of social distinction or accomplishment, rather than of any very direct engagement with or interest in contemporary politics *per se.* In a similar vein Paul Yachnin talks of what he terms the 'populuxe' appeal of a theatre that offered its audience a faux familiarity with the concerns and styles of a court society and an elite politics in which they could never hope to participate or even view at first hand.[8] All of this is true enough, and there can be no doubt that these developments produced a social type so well known that by 1605–6 Ben Jonson could satirise it in the character of Sir Politic Would-be, a figure whom he clearly assumed his entire audience would instantly recognise and, under his instruction, ridicule.

However, I take these analyses to be too sedulously apolitical, too neatly separated off from the course of real political events and the ways in which increasing numbers of contemporaries actually perceived and interpreted those events. As the researches of various historians, most notably Noah Millstone are beginning to show, precisely the perceptual structures, the narrative expectations and tropes, inculcated and disseminated by, amongst a good many other things, the drama, were coming to shape the way political events were reported and discussed throughout the early seventeenth century. On the argument being made here, the plays offered their audiences a series of moral and narrative templates, plots in both the dramatic and conspiratorial sense of the word, in and through which to view and interpret the politics of the moment.[9] And once launched upon the world these templates could be used and used again, appropriated and applied to events and circumstances quite different to the ones that had called them into existence.[10] The plays provided for viewer and reader a training in a certain style of politique hermeneutics, a mode of political spectatorship and interpretation, and, under the right circumstances, even of political participation.

For there were political moments when more general perceptions of or opinions about what was really going on, about who were the real villains and who the real heroes of the piece, did count politically. And of course, the Elizabethan exclusion crisis, and indeed the so-called succession crisis that succeeded it, were precisely such moments, when it mattered supremely, or rather, if events took the wrong turn, it would matter supremely, if not what 'the people' *tout court*, then certainly what a very generously conceived notion of the political nation, not to mention almost the entire population of London, thought was *really* happening. For if the queen died or was killed with Mary Stuart still alive, or with the succession unsettled and political circumstances uncertain, it would matter a good deal which way the people jumped, just as it had when Edward VI died, and, in what Cliff Davies has called the only successful rebellion of the sixteenth century, Mary Tudor managed to rally support and frustrate Northumberland's attempt to divert the succession to Lady Jane Grey.

Moreover, we know that such considerations counted because, over a period of decades, not merely a small group of Catholic exiles, desperate to turn any eventuality into a crisis, but also central figures in the Elizabethan state, up to and including Lord Burghley and his kitchen cabinet, put a great deal of time and effort into selling one version or another of current political reality to promiscuously defined, socially heterogeneous, audiences, using the full range of contemporary media – that is to say, various sorts of print, rumour, circulating manuscript, performance, in the pulpit, in the courtroom, on the scaffold, at court and on the public stage – to do so.

If anything, these efforts became more frenzied in the 1590s when, with Mary Stuart dead, the now irredeemably unsettled succession combined with the advancing age of the queen to exercise a centripetal rather than a centrifugal influence on the politics of the court. In that situation the earl of Essex resorted or tried to resort, again and again, to the full range of public media, up to and including the public stage, to broadcast a particular view of the current conjuncture and of his own starring role within it.[11] By the end of the decade, the regime, now in the hands of Essex's enemies, was putting very considerable effort into broadcasting its own, very different, version of what was at stake in the current conjuncture and of the real nature of the earl's character and ambitions.

As a number of historians have pointed out, during the period from around 1598 until the immediate aftermath of the Essex rising such public case-making, and political commentary reached fever pitch. Some of this emanated directly from the circles around the earl – here one thinks of Essex's *Apology* and the various circulated manuscripts in which he justified his conduct or burnished his image during the final crisis, or indeed of the 'old play' about the deposition of Richard II staged on the eve of the rising by Shakespeare's company, the Lord Chamberlain's Men, at the behest of two of Essex's supporters. Some of these propagandistic efforts, like the hearings in Star Chamber or later at York House, through which the official version of Essex's conduct in Ireland were disseminated, or later his trial and execution themselves, emanated from the centre of the regime. But others were, as it were, spontaneously generated by third parties anxious to comment on or to profit from the buzz of interest and notoriety surrounding the earl and his fortunes. Here we should include the plethora of rumours and libels that attended the earl's departure for Ireland. On some accounts, it was the first flush of these libels that provided the real reason for the Bishops' Ban, which, Cyndia Clegg has plausibly argued, was intended by Whitgift to protect Essex from malign effects of the libels on his reputation in general and on his relations with the queen in particular. Here, too, we should include the printed version of the earl's *Apology*, the famous print glorifying him as the Lord's elected instrument, and, of course, Hayward's *History of Henry IV*, not to mention Shakespeare's play *Henry V*. Similarly spontaneous was the rush of libels that attended the earl's return from Ireland, many of which characterised him as the victim of the Machiavellian conspiracies of his enemies at court. So, too, were the London fasts for the earl's health that immediately preceded the rebellion, and the rush of variant manuscript accounts of his trial and execution, not to mention the contradictory libels and rumours, that followed it.

So worried was the regime by the popular response to the earl's fall that, as Arnold Hunt has shown, they put a great deal of time and effort into tuning the London pulpits, rushed into print William Barlowe's Paul's Cross sermon on the earl's fall and a full account of the his recent follies and iniquities penned by his erstwhile client and advisor Francis Bacon.[12]

This Essexian moment was also, of course, what Andras Kisery has termed 'Hamlet's moment', which not merely coincided with, but was arguably framed, and even produced, by the intense political crisis attendant upon the earl's fall and the equally intense public excitement about and interest in the manoeuvres that had brought the earl down. It thus seems slightly perverse to discuss the style of public engagement with politics, the mode of political spectatorship and interpretation engendered by this moment, exclusively in terms of the search for social or cultural distinction. Indeed, one might surmise that an attempt by contemporaries to organise such activities and interests under the sign of mere fashionable discourse and self-fashioning was a reaction against the real enough alarums and excursions that had produced that mental set during the previous decades; dangers that had just come to something like a head in the disastrous collapse of the Essex project.

However, that such modes of political interpretation did indeed come to be viewed in this way – and Kisery shows brilliantly just how and why they did – is in itself of the highest significance, since it shows them becoming normalised, readily recognisable features of the contemporary social, cultural and political scene. Yet even when viewed entirely in that light, they were not as devoid of directly political significance or salience as Kisery's, or still more Yachnin's, accounts would lead us to assume. For all that Jonson might have sought to ridicule and marginalise the cultural and political trends summed up in the figure of Sir Politic Would-be, in the right circumstances major political players continued to take the task of appealing to or moulding precisely this sort of self-consciously sophisticated and informed political public extremely seriously.

Sir Robert Cecil's death prompted the production and circulation of virulent libels, many of which returned, almost obsessively, to Cecil's alleged role in the destruction of Essex, as well as dwelling on his physical deformity, corruption, vast wealth, and equally voracious sex life. To prove his probity some of Cecil's erstwhile clients and admirers took the remarkable step of circulating in manuscript a series of hitherto entirely private memoranda in which Cecil had urged the king to reduce his extravagant expenditure, control corruption and reform the finances of the crown by cutting a deal with parliament. Again, then, we have libellous rumours of Machiavellian evil counsel and conspiracy at the very centre of power, now being countered by the release into the public domain of private documents, initially intended for the eyes of the king and his innermost circle only; documents which, in effect, shifted the blame for recent failures and scandals away from the evil counsellor figure – the deceased Cecil – and on to the king himself.[13] Shakespeare's last history play, *Henry VIII*, can be read as a response to that move, designed, in effect, to defend the king from such criticism, first by returning to the evil counsellor mode, concentrated in the play on the figure of Wolsey, and then by commenting favourably on the shift in the balance of power at court and in the ideological tone of the regime, created, in the play, by the king's decision to take the reins of power back into his own hands and rule through an ideologically split and factionally balanced court and council, and, in the present, by the political realignment consequent upon Cecil's death and the incipient marriage between the king's favourite the earl of Somerset and Frances Howard.

However, in the real world, things did not go as smoothly as Shakespeare and Fletcher envisaged. Instead, almost immediately after Shakespeare's play was performed, first the Essex divorce turned sour and then Somerset and Howard became caught up in the investigation into the murder of Somerset's former familiar and, on some accounts, his evil counsellor or *éminence grise*, Sir Thomas Overbury. Once the crime had come to light the resulting investigation and trials had, perforce, to take place before an adjudicating public opinion, armed with the now familiar tropes of popish conspiracy, evil counsel and court corruption as the most expeditious ways to make sense of what was being revealed to them. As Alastair Bellany has shown, what ensued was a struggle over the meaning of the Overbury affair conducted through the now usual range of media: rumour, circulating manuscript, print and, of course, in court and on the scaffold, public performance.

That in turn occasioned a debate within the regime about how best to handle the affair between two of the leading prosecutors in the Essex affair, Sir Edward Coke and Sir Francis Bacon. Coke wanted to go on the offensive, assimilating the murder to the familiar trope of popish conspiracy, and the equally familiar tale, told twice before, and regularly celebrated on the anniversaries of the Gowry conspiracy and the Gunpowder Plot, of a sinister conspiracy penetrated and punished by the prudence, sagacity and justice of King James himself. Yielding rather more to James' desire not to consign his former favourite and his wife to the scaffold – an outcome that Coke's method of dealing with the affair would have rendered all but inevitable – Bacon pushed a more equivocal strategy that James in the end adopted.[14]

But the whole affair again shows the salience of a certain style of public politics, of the need, at certain times of crisis, to cultivate and appeal to various political publics, some of whose attitudes and habits of mind had indeed been shaped by the politique heuristics of suspicion outlined by Kisery and Millstone and founded on the polemical back and forth of Elizabeth's reign; attitudes and habits of mind in the dissemination of which the public theatre had played a very considerable role.

But if we want a really serious demonstration of the continued salience of a public politics conducted in the now familiar terms of evil counsel, court corruption, foreign influence and popish (and now puritan) malignity and conspiracy, it is to the 1620s that we should turn. Many of the same elements that had produced the alarums and excursions of the 1590s – an increasingly fractious court politics; intensified religious disputes, in part prompted by disagreements over the nature of puritanism, and the extent of the puritan threat; war with the greatest (Catholic) power in Europe; the emergence of a controversial royal favourite determined to play the roles of soldier and statesman, to dominate the politics of the court, the distribution of royal patronage and the conduct of diplomacy and the fighting of the war; an economic crisis and trade depression compounded, this time, by plague and the costs of fighting the war, the nature of which became the topic of increasingly bitter debate – all these came back to haunt first the Jacobean and then the Caroline regime. Much of the resulting political debate harked back to different visions of Elizabeth's reign and of the Elizabethan war with Spain. The figure of Essex, as martial hero and royal favourite, bulked large here, with Essex's old client, Sir Anthony Wootton, even producing an extended comparison between Essex and Buckingham.

In the course of the ensuing political crisis it again mattered a great deal which narrative of contemporary politics, which conspiracy or series of conspiracy theories, you believed; who figured as the villains of the piece and who the heroes. As you might expect, the ensuing debates were (again) dominated by the tropes of evil counsel, court conspiracy and corruption, by the plots and manoeuvres of papists and foreign powers, and, this time around, not only of puritans, but also of dissident internal elements, *tribuni plebis*, as they were called, men allegedly intent on reducing the power of the crown and increasing the role in affairs of men, like themselves, who could mobilise a popular following. Indeed, the term 'popularity', so often thrown at Essex as some sort of insult, was now employed as a term both of art and of opprobrium to describe the activities of such men and of their 'popular' following.[15]

That such things mattered can again be confirmed by the simple fact that the central political actors in this drama, up to and including Charles I and the duke of Buckingham, not only thought in these terms – as Richard Cust has shown, the notion of 'popularity' and of a conspiracy of puritans and popular spirits to undermine his powers as king became a key interpretative category for the king – they also came to play the game of the public politics of popularity with a will.[16] Indeed, as Tom Cogswell has demonstrated, Buckingham emerged as something of a past master of the dark arts of popularity. His relation, given to the house of Lords in 1624, of his own conduct in Madrid some two years earlier dealt in the established coin of Spanish duplicity and malignity and featured himself in the heroic role of the man who had first seen through and then frustrated the machinations of the Spanish. Manuscript separate accounts of that speech circulated very widely, almost certainly at the duke's behest.[17] That same narrative was turned inside out and deployed against Buckingham by the earl of Bristol, who had featured in the duke's initial narrative in the role of Spanish dupe and evil counsellor, but who told a very different version of the same tale to the parliament of 1626, as it tried to impeach the duke.

Those impeachment proceedings were fuelled by a story in which the duke, and very possibly the then Prince Charles, had actually poisoned James I; a story that owed its origins to popish black propaganda written by Dr Eglisham and printed in Flanders.[18] Here were not only central features of the Overbury murder, undispelled by James' somewhat equivocal response thereto, coming back to haunt the house of Stuart, but also tropes and memes central to the libellous secret histories of Elizabeth's reign – after all, in *Leicester's commonwealth* Leicester himself had been presented not only as a notorious Machiavel, but as a poisoner and a potential killer of his queen – now dominating the proceedings of that cockpit of hot protestant indignation and zeal, the House of Commons.

Nor was the public theatre devoid of a role in all this. Despite the fact that the relationship of the stage to the crisis of the 1620s has not attracted anything like the scholarly attention it deserves, we do know, largely thanks to the work of Tom Cogswell, that in *The game at chess* what was essentially the view of the current conjunction espoused both by Thomas Scott and the duke of Buckingham – as set out in his relation of 1624 – was played out on the public stage, almost certainly with the connivance, if not at the behest, of the duke and prince Charles.[19] We also know that, at this, the crisis point of his political life, as he was attempting yet another relaunch of his career and rebranding of his persona, Buckingham turned to the public stage. Just days before his assassination, at his prompting and in his presence, a performance of Shakespeare's *Henry VIII* at the Globe attempted to turn the rhetoric of evil counsel and royal virtue in Buckingham's favour, one last time. Here was a recourse to theatrical means to achieve immediately political ends quite the equal of the far more famous occasion when a play about the deposition of Richard II was played at the behest of two of Essex's followers, on the eve of the Essex rebellion in 1601.

None of this makes any sense, indeed none of this could have happened, or, more precisely, these events could not and would not have taken the form that they did, without the very widespread presence of precisely the interpretative habits, satirised, at the time, by Jonson in *Volpone,* in the character of Sir Politic Would-be, and, some twenty years later, throughout *The staple of news* – a play which can, I think, usefully be read as a sort of dramatic riposte to *The game at chess.* More recently those same hermeneutic habits and reading practices have been described in some detail by Kevin Sharpe in his wonderful study of the reading and commonplacing habits of William Drake and are more broadly delineated in the brilliant work of Andras Kisery and Noah Millstone.[20] And so, even if the reading habits, the politique, conspiracy-centred, potentially paranoid, hermeneutic mode, outlined above, had indeed first been internalised as part of a completely apolitical search for social or cultural distinction, the fact that it had been so widely disseminated and deeply internalised, at least in part through the means provided by the public stage and the play book, had very serious consequences for the ways in which politics was both performed and consumed, particularly at moments of heightened excitement and tension, like those which attended the Essex divorce and the Overbury murder or which punctuated, indeed framed and fuelled, the extended political crisis of the 1620s.

Plays and politics

The conventional view of the theatre's involvement in such matters holds that the producers of plays were concerned solely to put bums on seats and, in so doing, to make a profit. If, on occasion, in order to do that they used their capacity to engage with current concerns and to stage in plain view what politics in a monarchical polity like Elizabethan England was really like, their purposes in so doing remained, we are told, primarily exploitative and commercial rather than, as it were, substantively political. These were not attempts to do politics, still less to affect political outcomes, so much as to exploit the engagement of their audiences with politics and hence with history, or, *pari passu*, with history and hence with politics, to their own (commercial) advantage.

Such an account, however, overlooks the origins of the history play in the repertoire of the Queen's Men and the decidedly political origins of the Queen's Men themselves. For, as we have seen, on McMillin and MacClean's account, the Queen's Men were set up by central elements of the Elizabethan regime for decidedly political purposes and, from the outset, both company and repertoire were designed to fulfil the directly propagandistic purposes of the regime. Again, as MacClean and Manley have shown, Lord Strange's Men were a company with a decidedly conservative and aggressively anti-puritan repertoire, notably distinct from that of the Queen's Men. The history play had a central role in these developments and again as McMillin and MacClean point out, throughout the 1590s Shakespeare set about systematically rewriting the history plays put on by the Queen's Men. His and his company's purposes in so doing may well have been primarily commercial; seeking to benefit from, and indeed to perpetuate, the popularity, not merely of a genre, but of specific plays, first established in the affections of theatrical audiences across the country by the pervasive influence of the Queen's Men. But since the activities of the Queen's Men had been from the first inherently political and since the history play was itself quintessentially, indeed inevitably, concerned with politics, to recast history plays first established in the public imagination by the Queen's Men was itself an inherently political act.

The plot thickens further when we remember that, as Manley and MacClean have suggested, the earliest history plays produced by Shakespeare, 2 and 3 *Henry VI*, and *Richard III*, not to mention *Titus Andronicus*, were all associated with, indeed arguably written for, Lord Strange's Men, a company whose patron, Sir Ferdinando Stanley, and whose repertoire represented a rather different, if not crypto-Catholic then certainly far more Catholic-friendly and virulently anti-puritan, strand of contemporary religio-political opinion than that broadcast by the Queen's Men.

As McMillin and MacClean explain, the Queen's Men had been founded at the height of the Elizabethan exclusion crisis, by figures – Leicester and Essex – central to Collinson's account of the monarchical republic of Elizabeth I. On Manley and MacClean's account, Shakespeare's plays, associated with Lord Strange's Men, were written after anxieties about the succession had ceased to be centred centripetally on the person of a single claimant, Mary Stuart – who was, after all, now dead – and were beginning to be concentrated, centrifugally, on the prospect of having to settle the succession in the midst of war with the greatest power in Europe, and in an atmosphere of considerably heightened religious tension and political conflict at home. The plays belonged, in short, to the period when the deaths of most of the leading figures of the Elizabethan regime, those founding fathers of the Queen's Men, Walsingham and Leicester amongst them, had created a certain amount of flux in the patronage politics surrounding the theatre, and a considerable amount of uncertainly, and therefore anxiety, about the precise composition and ideological timbre of the regime.

Indeed, 2 Henry VI staged a political conjuncture in which a regime characterised by the good government of a passing generation, epitomised in 2 Henry VI by the Lord Protector, Gloucester (and in the nearly contemporary Woodstock by an earlier holder of that same title) was being displaced by a group of younger aristocrats and counsellors whose corruption and factious ambition was threatening to destabilise the realm and, in 1 Henry VI, lose the war.

Moreover, of all the plays discussed in this book, those of the early 1590s, associated with Lord Strange's Men – that is to say, 2 and 3 Henry VI, Richard III and Titus Andronicus – were those that most intensively inhabit the world conjured by the Catholic tracts. As we have seen, the Henry VI plays evoke a world thrust into political and moral chaos by a contested succession; a terminally weak monarch, dominated by various species of evil counsel and an excess of female influence over the levers of monarchical power; a war with the greatest European power consequently disastrously mismanaged; and a realm plunged into civil dissension, popular revolt and civil war as a result. All these were, of course, central elements in the dystopian vision of the future with which the Catholic tracts – both The treatise of treasons and Leicester's commonwealth, which predated these plays by some years, and those compromising Cecil's commonwealth, which were being produced as, or just after, these plays were first written and performed – all predicted must and would follow should the queen die with the succession unsettled, as, by then, it seemed certain that she would. In Richard of Gloucester both the concluding sections of 3 Henry VI and Richard III featured an atheistical Machiavel actually doing what the Catholic tracts claimed that the likes of Leicester or the Cecils wanted to do; that is to say, by a policy of divide and rule, part the current monarch from her natural heirs, before assuming the throne for themselves. Just as both The treatise of treasons and Leicester's commonwealth had used the figure of Richard of Gloucester and his machinations to illustrate what was happening now and what might well happen next, if, that is, pre-emptive action were not immediately taken, so the play put a Leicester-like Machiavel on the stage and showed what would happen if he were allowed to work his evil way with an unsettled succession.

Where the tracts had centred on the vision of a monarch utterly subjugated to the evil counsel of a series of atheistical Machiavels, Shakespeare's plays figured the operation of evil counsel on Henry VI and Saturninus respectively through the adulterous love triangles linking Queen Margaret to Suffolk and

Tamora to Aaron the Moor. And in Aaron the Moor audiences were given a fully realised picture of what genuinely atheistical evil counsel looked like and, in the persecution and mutilation visited upon the Andronici, in general, and upon the quintessentially innocent Lavinia, in particular, a viscerally disgusting image of just what such an evil counsellor could accomplish given a suggestible (and tyrannical) enough monarch upon whom to work.

Save for her implicit (but complete) susceptibility to evil counsel, the Catholic evil counsellor tracts – or certainly those written in English rather than Latin – omitted virtually all mention of the queen. However, in Queen Margaret, Puzel and Tamora, these plays all featured a monstrous female figure, out of all male control, either aspiring to, or, for a time, enjoying, if not supreme power, then certainly dominant influence over those (as Elizabethan gender ideology would have it) inherently masculine preserves, the conduct of policy and the prosecution of war. This might be taken to register the visceral emotions and anxieties evoked by female rule; a fear and loathing attached directly to Elizabeth through the play with the figure of Astraea made in both *Titus Andronicus* and *1 Henry V* (where Puzel is described as Astraea's daughter).

In *Titus* the carefully choreographed injustice of the fates visited upon the Andronici in general, and on Lavinia and her 'martyred signs', in particular, might be thought to evoke what the Catholic tracts proclaimed was the frankly persecutory and tyrannical treatment meted out by the Elizabethan state to at least some of its Catholic subjects.[21] Through the opposition between the figures of Lavinia and Tamara, and through a series of classical allusions and images often used to praise Queen Elizabeth, these enormities were associated with the female rule of Gloriana. Again, through such violent, viscerally disgusting scenes as York being tormented by Margaret or Lavinia being taunted by a stone-faced Tamora and then violated and mutilated by her equally vicious sons, certain taboo subjects were being treated, if not quite subliminally, then certainly through the deployment of resonant (both verbal and visual) images and tableaux; images which might well enable in, or elicit from, the viewer (or indeed later from the reader) decidedly dangerous reactions or applications, for which, of course, the dramatist had no direct responsibility.

All these plays either end in, or start with, realms reduced to complete political and moral chaos. In both *Richard III* and *Titus*, the way out of that condition is presented as running through the direct experience of tyranny itself, out of the terrifying, but also in some sense purifying and unifying, effects of which a new regime could be constructed, through the linked means – clearly staged in both plays – of domestic conspiracy, foreign invasion and regicide. In *Titus* that outcome is brought about through the constitutional mechanisms provided by elective monarchy, and wrought by the political planning and fortitude of the Andronici, in alliance, of course, with the invading Goths. But in *Richard III* there is nothing elective about Richmond's rise to the throne and the means whereby he achieves it, and the means whereby Richard is removed, are wreathed in the prophetic and the providential. Richard's tyranny may clear away the scar tissue left by the Wars of the Roses and his deep dyed villainy unite a previously divided political elite against him, but his enormities also provide the audience with reason enough to accept the justice of his violent removal without examining too closely either the means – a combination of domestic conspiracy, foreign invasion and regicide – through which that removal has been achieved, or the strength of the hereditary claim to the throne enjoyed by his successor, Henry VII. But then again the identity of that successor as the present queen's grandfather might be thought to elide even more effectively the otherwise decidedly subversive nature of the events staged by the play. Or then again, it might not.

Alone of this group of relatively early plays (and particularly so, if it really was a prequel, written after 2 and 3 *Henry VI*), 1 *Henry VI* seems to offer a way out of the moral and political breakdown, the tyranny and dysfunction, evoked in both the other early histories and in *Titus*, that falls some way short of conspiracy, violent resistance and foreign invasion. As we have seen, it does so by suggesting how the spiral of decline, described in 2 and 3 *Henry VI*, might have been avoided in the first place. Or to put it another way, it suggests a means whereby, in future, disasters like the death of Talbot might be averted and victories over the foreign and popish other, of the sort figured in the unmasking, defeat and death of Puzel, might be rendered permanent rather than fleeting. And that is by suppressing the sort of personal rivalry, faction and disagreement that the play shows plaguing the counsels of the king and the conduct of the war, and uniting instead around a coherently aggressive prosecution of the war against the foreigner, well before the issue of the succession can add fuel to the fires of factional and personal rivalry and ambition – with the disastrous consequences staged in 2 and 3 *Henry VI* and prophesied in many of the Catholic tracts.

In this way, alone of the history plays written by Shakespeare and his collaborators before the closure of the theatres in 1593, 1 *Henry V1* looks forward towards the history plays, many of them rewrites of earlier versions from the repertoire of the Queen's Men, that Shakespeare produced after he became a member of the Lord Chamberlain's Men. These later plays increasingly left the conceptual universe of the Catholic tracts behind, in favour of what I have argued above was a distinctly Essexian agenda, organised around the national unity, and returning monarchical legitimacy, to be gained through a vigorous prosecution of war against a papalist, but by no means virulently popish, version of the foreign threat.

Insofar as the subsequent plays display any residual engagement with the Catholic tracts it was a largely negative one, with Shakespeare using his versions of the reigns of King John and Richard II definitively to reject Parsons' view, in the *Conference about the next succession,* that England was an elective monarchy, with a residual right, lodged in the commonwealth, to divert the succession, resist and even depose a peccant or tyrannical prince. Parsons had cited both John's reign and the deposition of Richard II in support of that view. In *Richard II* Shakespeare produced a version of Richard's deposition that directly contradicted Parsons' account of the same event. In *King John* he produced an account of that reign which explicitly ruled out of court any notion that the elections of both John and of the dauphin to the English throne were equally legitimate examples of the English commonwealth's power to divert the course of the succession as the dictates of the general good seemed to require, which had, of course, been Parsons' view of the matter. Similarly, where Parsons cited the transcendent excellence of the reigns of both Henry IV and Henry V to prove that God had providentially blessed the deposition of Richard II, Shakespeare produced a far darker and more equivocal account of Henry IV and a less than overtly providential one of his son, Henry V.

In both ideological and literary terms the crucial bridging text here was *King John.* In its picture of the illegitimacy and increasingly ineffectual tyranny of King John, the play ceded a great deal to the Catholic tracts, but its conclusion – embodied and voiced by the bastard – definitively refuted them. For the play pretty much directly exhorted its audiences to unite in the face of the foreign threat, no matter how undesirable, ineffectual or tainted with usurpation or regicide the current occupant of the throne might be. For only thus could the spectre of foreign rule be staved off and room be created for the return of legitimacy under the rule of a next successor whose hereditary right no one could reasonably challenge.

If, in its emphasis on war against the foreigner as the best source of national unity and monarchical legitimacy, *King John* looks back to *1 Henry VI,* it looks forward even more to *Henry V.* Similarly, in literary terms, the character of the bastard can be seen as a prototype for Hal in *1* and *2 Henry IV.* As we have seen, functions performed, or ethical or ideological quantities personified, in *King John,* by the bastard and Henry III – with the bastard providing a certain raw English virtue, loyalism and military spunk, and Henry III providing the crucial element of hereditary right – were combined in the *Henry IV* plays in the person of Hal.

In *King John* the various qualities necessary to return the realm to legitimate monarchical rule, after the tyranny and usurpation of King John, were provided, in effect, by the accident of (both legitimate and illegitimate) royal birth. The bastard's Richard Coeur de Lion derived political capacities are composed of martial prowess and his rather one-dimensionally full-throated reiteration of loyalty to the king and loathing of the foreigner as the ultimate political values. In *1 and 2 Henry IV,* while royal birth and its benefits are again a given, the qualities necessary to pull off what is essentially the same trick – the return of a society destabilised by a combination of tyranny and usurpation to something like 'normal' monarchical order – are shown to be both rather more complicated than any of the characteristics displayed by the bastard, and anything but innate. Rather they have to be self-consciously acquired and combined in just the right quantities if the job is to be done.

At stake is the precise nature or composition of the virtu(e) required to save the state. Hence, the central dilemma becomes how effectively to mix and match the politics of honour, martial prowess, popularity and monarchical legitimacy. I have argued above that this represents a recognisably Essexian agenda or problematic. Certainly, as Alex Gajda has shown, in the context of a war to the death with the overweening power and ambition of Spain and of a succession that remained, because of the queen's obstinacy, definitively unsettled, Essex and his inner circle viewed the earl as the saviour of the Elizabethan state, in the current reign, and of the principle of monarchical legitimacy, in the next. Amongst the earl's inner circle, while the supervening quality of the earl's virtue, and the honour of his ultimate purposes, were a given, the ideal combination of his various qualities and callings, as the bearer of ancient lineage, as a soldier, a statesman and a 'popular' politician, remained very much in question.[22]

Also in question was the religious composition of the earl's following and the religious implications of his agenda. Essex had a good many puritan clients and, as the leading defender of the protestant cause and patron of the puritans currently operating within the regime, enjoyed widespread support amongst the godly. But his circle also included a variety of Catholics, up to and including the renegade Jesuit Thomas Wright, and his view of the foreign threat posed to England, and indeed to 'Christendom', was a secular rather than a religious or heavily confessionalised one. That is to say, it was centred on the pride and ambition, the drive towards world domination, of the Hapsburg monarchy, rather than on the Antichristian nature of popery as a false religion. On this view, rather than the Spanish monarchy being the mere instrument of papal aspirations to universal monarchy, the pope was a catspaw of the king of Spain, one instrument amongst others, to be used to achieve world domination. Accordingly, Essex included in his circle loyalist Catholics willing to express their loyalty to the crown by actively resisting Hapsburg aggression. For Essex the important thing was not such men's religious beliefs but their political loyalties, and, in particular, their anti-Hapsburg credentials. For all the puritan godliness of many of his admirers, for Essex 'popery' was not an anti-religion so toxic, a nexus of spiritual error so demonically pervasive, as to damn all Catholics to hell and render any notion of Catholic loyalism an oxymoron.

On the contrary, Essex envisaged granting a version of 'liberty of conscience', indeed a form of 'toleration', to the right sort of Catholic, and saw the defence of the resulting conception of 'liberty of conscience' as a central plank in his ideological, as well as military, campaign against Hapsburg tyranny and aggression.

Of course, Essex's commitment to 'liberty of conscience' has to be seen within the context of his wider commitment to the maintenance of the protestant succession at all costs. On this view of the matter, toleration was something to be granted, to the right sort of Catholic, by monarchical authority lodged in safely protestant hands, in the context of a war being fought to the death against the leading Catholic power in Europe, as well, of course, as against his creature, the pope. But for many of Essex's Catholic supporters 'toleration' was but a stage on the road to the conversion of both the next successor, James VI, and, indeed, of the earl himself. In such a scenario 'liberty of conscience' would be a concession granted by Catholic authority only to the right sort of protestant, and under those circumstances puritans need not apply.[23]

There was, therefore, a series of tensions, if not contradictions, within the Essexian project itself and areas of disagreement and debate within the earl's inner circle, that concerned both the real nature or ends of that project and the best ways to realise those ends. And it is to those areas of tension, of actual and potential debate and disagreement, to which all of the histories that Shakespeare wrote after the closure of the theatres in 1593 consistently return.

In bringing 'history' to bear on those topics the plays replicate and play off another central feature of the Essex circle: the incessant combing of various histories, both ancient and more modern, for insights into the nature of the political process in general and of the current conjuncture in particular.[24]

To take the religious tensions first, Shakespeare's plays address these with his usual direct indirection. As we have seen, from 1 Henry VI, and with increasing intensity and insistence from King John through Henry V, the plays are organised around the need for national unity in the face of the foreign threat and for the most aggressive possible prosecution of the war in the main theatre of conflict on the continent. However, the enemy to be thus confronted is not conceived in anything like straightforwardly confessional terms. The elements of confessional insult that pervade 1 Henry VI, albeit largely emanating from the decidedly ambiguous figure of Puzel, are far less in evidence in King John and absent altogether from Henry V. Indeed, after 1 Henry VI, there is almost no trace of anti-popery as opposed to anti-papalism in these plays. Even if King John wears its anti-papal credentials on its sleeve, the enemy being confronted by the end of the play is neither popish nor papally backed, but simply foreign, in this case French. The same is true in spades of Henry V. When the relative, indeed, in Henry V, the absolute, absence of anti-popery is set against the rabid anti-puritanism to be found in many of these plays – for example, in the Cade scenes in 2 Henry VI, in that positively Leicestrian faux-godly Machiavel, Richard III and most notably in Falstaff, particularly in his original incarnation as Sir John Oldcastle – it would appear that something is being said about the contemporary religious scene, and the relative threats represented by popery and puritanism.

Admittedly by the late 1590s putting the boot into the puritans was neither a radical nor a risky gesture, but, given the central role ceded to the Lollards in John Foxe's account of the history of the true church in England as the legitimising precursors, indeed as the progenitors, of both the Elizabethan godly and of the post-reformation protestant national church, to recast the Lollard martyr, Oldcastle, as the fat hypocrite and coward, the crook and con man, Falstaff, was a remarkably daring and aggressive thing to do, since it amounted to a wholesale reversal of the conventional Foxeian account of the history of the true church in England. In Elizabeth's reign, the only people debunking Oldcastle and the Lollards in similarly explicit terms were Catholics like Harpsfield and later Robert Parsons. David Kastan is surely right to argue that just because Shakespeare took a similar line does not render him a Catholic, but it does, by the standards of the 1590s, if not those of the 1630s, make him a thoroughgoing, indeed really rather a radical and avant-garde, anti-puritan.

As Gary Taylor has argued, when we add *King John* to the equation, the Oldcastle affair emerges as the second time that Shakespeare's version of English history diverged fundamentally from that of John Foxe.[25] As the play *Sir John Oldcastle* shows, contemporaries were well aware of this fact, for that play reversed the polarities of Shakespeare's version, in effect equating Elizabethan puritans – albeit in this case, only moderate ones – if not with all Lollards, then certainly with godly loyalists like Oldcastle. This constituted a positive endorsement of the moderate puritans of Elizabethan England and a remarkably forthright condemnation of not only the popish persecutors of the Lollards but also (by implication at least) of the episcopal opponents and persecutors of the puritans. It also represented a comment upon just who the right recipients of any sort of toleration or liberty of conscience might be. In other words, it tilted the balance back in a decidedly moderate puritan direction, over against the decidedly anti-puritan (and perhaps even 'Catholic loyalist') tack, taken by Shakespeare. It also publicly defended one of Essex's most celebrated enemies against the assault on his ancestors that Lord Cobham clearly took the Henry IV plays to be,

There is much less indirection to be found in the plays' treatment of the central Essexian dilemma of the proper balance to be struck between the politics of honour and military glory, popularity, monarchical legitimism and political prudence or virtu. The *Henry IV* plays and *Henry V* take that issue head on; arguing that, while, just like Hotspur and Falstaff, the demands of honour and popularity cannot be allowed to predominate, having been put in their place, both were essential attributes for the successful politician. So, too, was the political cunning of that 'vile politician Bolingbroke', insofar as its workings could be masked by the operation of honour and popularity and harnessed to the cause of monarchical legitimacy and order. If, in the process, certain outward religious forms and claims had to be (if not duplicitously, then with every sign of self-conscious manipulation) enlisted to the cause of returning legitimacy, so be it. If the *Henry IV* plays show Prince Hal learning those lessons, *Henry V* shows King Henry practising the dark political arts, thus learnt, to triumphant, and, for all the duplicity and violence involved along the way, ultimately beneficent effect.

If, on one level, the result is a sort of fantasy happy ending for both the Essexian project and the Elizabethan succession crisis, the play represents a good deal more than an exercise in wishful thinking, agitprop and panegyric. For these plays also reveal themselves to be keenly aware of the actual or potential contradictions and dangers inherent in both the earl's personality and political style. The tensions within and between the politics of honour, of legitimacy and of popularity, that lie at the centre of the *Henry IV* plays and *Henry V,* the warnings against excessive pursuit of either the politics of honour and martial prowess, or of popularity, together with the various Essexian resonances and references attached to Hotspur, rather than to Hal, all betoken a sharp sense of the vulnerabilities and exorbitances that pervaded the various personae inhabited, and the sometimes contradictory propensities exhibited, by the earl. The result might well be read as a classic mixture of the criticism and compliment, the counsel and praise, that Kevin Sharpe has discerned in certain literary texts of the early Stuart period.[26]

As Paul Hammer has shown, Essex had long felt that he would have to save the queen, as it were, despite herself; pursuing policies that would protect the state and its monarch in the teeth of Elizabeth's rooted disinclination to do what Essex knew needed to be done, and in spite of the subtly undermining activities of various evil counsellors, all too eager to encourage the queen to do what she wanted, in the process lining their own pockets, furthering their own careers and doing the earl down at every opportunity.

After 1598, such feelings reached a crescendo, as the earl and others, including James VI himself, came to believe that those within the regime who were advocating peace with Spain might also be considering putting the succession itself on the table, in effect selling both the protestant cause and the cause of hereditary right down the river in return for peace with Spain, the preservation of their own careers and the destruction of their enemies. This, of course, considerably raised the stakes. In such desperate times, desperate measures were necessary, and it was that spirit of increasing desperation that pervaded the earl's circle, even as he debated long and hard whether to undertake the military expedition being prepared to suppress the Irish rebellion. Things only got worse once he got to Ireland and his campaign against Tyrone started to unravel. Essex became obsessed with the use to which his difficulties in Ireland were being put by his enemies at court, and famously, at one point, considered returning to England with an army of some three thousand men in order to confront his enemies and purge the court. Then, and after his unprompted return to what turned out to be permanent disgrace, there emerged, in the counsels surrounding the earl, moderate and radical tendencies. The likes of Henry Howard and Francis Bacon advised Essex to concentrate his efforts on winning back the favour of the queen. Others – at different points Southampton, Mountjoy and (allegedly) his secretary, Henry Cuff, who, after the event, had the distinction of being singled out for the starring role of evil counsellor (and scapegoat) in the official account of what had gone wrong with Essex – urged him to cut the Gordian knot of evil counsel now tightening around his throat with some sort of *coup de main*.

Shakespeare responded to the changed circumstances created by these political developments, and indeed by the Bishops' Ban of June 1599, by giving over English histories altogether and writing instead three history plays set in increasingly, both temporally and geographically, remote locales: the first, *Julius Caesar*, set in pagan and republican Rome; the second, *Hamlet*, in a version of dark age Denmark, that was remarkably reminiscent of post-reformation Europe; the third, *Troilus and Cressida*, in the midst of the siege of Troy. As I argued above, all three used the considerable licence conferred by their remoteness of setting to speak, with quite remarkable directness, given the charged circumstances, to current English circumstances and, in particular, to the dilemma and, latterly, to the fate of the earl of Essex.

Julius Caesar was written when there was still all to play for, and, as I have argued above, can usefully be twinned with *Henry V*, in that both plays consider the extent to which men of the highest virtu(e) can impose their will on events and shape the fate of nations. The former play takes a rather optimistic view of the matter, but in *Caesar* all the stress is on the necessity of fitting the action taken, and indeed the historical precedents and models guiding the action, to the nature of 'the times'. Violent interventions, based on an excessive estimation of one's own virtue and thus of one's capacity to shape events, and in this case to save or conserve a state far gone in corruption, and undergoing the throes of moral and political change, could only end in disaster, both for those taking the action and the state that they were trying to save. Moreover, definitions of political virtue and liberty, culled from pagan and republican sources, were simply inapplicable to the situation of the Christian subjects of a Christian prince.

Whether he knew it or not, and over the summer of 1599 he can have had no direct knowledge of what was happening in the intimate recesses of Essex's inner circle in Ireland, by taking this line, Shakespeare had aligned himself with those urging moderate courses on the earl in this, the climacteric point of his career.

Prudence and providence

In order to do so, Shakespeare had had recourse to the providential on a scale and level of intensity unheard of in these plays since *Richard III*. In that play the providential and the prophetic had operated, if not entirely to elide, then certainly simultaneously to occlude and legitimise the decidedly radical political action that had removed Richard from the throne and placed Richmond upon it. One might argue that something of the same was going on here, with a providential gloss or overlay serving to mask the essentially prudential, even Machiavellian, orientation of the play, which could easily be taken to be arguing that only when 'the times' were ripe; when the historical examples and exempla animating decision-making and action had been perfectly fitted to an accurate assessment of the current conjuncture; in short, only when the precise lineaments of the *occasio* presented by 'the times' to the wannabe saviour of the state had been ascertained, could action appropriate to the moment be framed, and a successful outcome attained.

But there is surely more going on here than that, for in *Caesar* the prophetic and the providential do not merely mask the real, prudential, even Machiavellian, argument of the play, they directly comment upon, and, to the play's first Christian audiences, if not to the pagan Roman characters in the play itself, roundly condemn, the radical political action that so signally fails to save the Roman state. In the process the play also reminds its audience that ultimately it was divine providence that shaped events and determined the fate of states, not the efforts of human political actors, however politically or personally virtuous they might be or think that they were. This moves the play into a decidedly different intellectual universe to that occupied by the history plays written since *Richard III*, which had almost uniformly concerned themselves with an essentially prudential, secular view of the political world, in which politics as performed (if not always as talked about) on stage was viewed as process, that is to say as the interaction between the intentions and actions of various political agents in pursuit of divergent, often mutually exclusive, interests and ends, the resolution to which was presented as the result of the sum total of those very interactions themselves. And providence was presented as having little or nothing to do with it.

The sole exception here is the speech by Carlisle in *Richard II*, but, as we have seen, that serves to project the supervening influence of providence forwards, on to events that, in history, have yet to happen, but which have already been staged in the *Henry VI* plays; plays in which providence had, in fact, played something of a peripheral, walk-on role, rather than providing the shaping force, the pervasive moral presence, pictured by Carlisle. Moreover, in the plays that Shakespeare actually wrote about the immediate aftermath of Richard II's deposition and death, events are pictured not so much as providential punishments visited upon the English for the collective sins of rebellion and regicide but rather as rationally explicable consequences of the disturbances to the political force field caused by Richard's tyranny and Henry's usurpation, and as such subject to the remedial action of properly informed and appropriately sagacious political actors.

We find explicitly providential readings of the situation coming out of the mouths of just two characters. The first is Henry himself, when sunk in the depths of despair, and he is immediately contradicted by the entirely secular, politique arguments of Warwick. In this scene, Henry is applying the logic of Carlisle's claim in *Richard II*, that the process of divine providential judgement is inexorable and inevitable and thus not at all susceptible to the efforts of fallen humanity to shape events in their own interests. But he is applying that logic, not to the distant events gestured at by Carlisle, which the audience, although not the characters in the play, know take place in Henry VI's reign. Rather he is applying that providential logic to events in his own reign, which, using an entirely different prophetic mode, Richard himself had predicted would see Henry and his supporters, the Percies, inevitably fall out over the spoils created by their collective sins of rebellion, regicide and usurpation. In seeking to reassure the king, and dispel his brooding sense that he is victim of a malign but inevitable fate, Warwick uses the logic of Richard's prophecy to undo the effects of Carlisle's. For there had, Warwick explains, been nothing prophetic about Richard's pronouncement. It had amounted to no more than a prediction, an exercise in political prognostication, a calling of the political shots. It therefore foretold outcomes that others, armed with precisely the same sorts of insights into the political process, precisely the same sense of the political probabilities, could avert or mitigate with relative ease.

2 Henry IV contains a scene in which we see different political agents make precisely similar prognostications about the likely behaviour of their adversaries. At Gaultree forest the rebels discuss the constraints under which the king is operating in order to judge the likelihood that his offer of a political settlement is genuine. They do so, as we have seen, in an entirely amoral evaluation of Henry's objective political situation and interests, and of course they get this particular prognostication entirely wrong. But only because the other side – the people whose interests, motives and behaviour they have been trying so minutely to parse and predict – are as aware as they are of the political force field in which they are operating. Aware that the weakness of the king's position will only be rendered the more apparent by any attempt to settle with the rebels, the king's party take violent and duplicitous action in order to avert precisely the position of political weakness that the rebels assume will constrain them to come to a settlement. In such scenes, then, these plays show us a variety of political agents practising the sort of prudential analysis of the political process that the plays themselves are conducting, or rather are enabling their audiences to conduct, on the basis of events being presented to them in the theatre or on the printed page.

If Henry IV is the first character we see mouthing such providential platitudes, the second is Archbishop Scroop. Where the layman Henry had been entirely sincere in his doom-laden construal of current events as an unavoidable providential judgement on his own past sins, the churchman Scroop is shown invoking providential arguments, about 'the blood of Richard, scrapp'd from Pomfret stones', entirely instrumentally. He does so in an attempt to drum up support for a rebellion the real causes of which the play goes out of its way to expose as contingently political, and, as such, subject to equally contingent political remediation.

In these plays, therefore, while intermittently gestured at, the topoi of providential control over human affairs and of ineluctable providential intervention as a punishment for past sin, get decidedly short shrift. If God's providential punishment of sin is operative in the *Henry IV* plays, it is so only on the individual level of Henry IV's increasing guilt, despair and perhaps even damnation, not on the collective, political level of the destruction of the entire Lancastrian political project. In *Henry V*, on the eve of Agincourt, Henry himself reverts to the notion that his enterprise might be doomed by the extent of his father's sins, but the outcome of the battle seems to prove definitively that that is not the case. Moreover, when, at the conclusion of *Henry V*, Shakespeare comes directly to address the relationship between the events being staged in *1 and 2 Henry IV* and *Henry V* and those of Henry VI's reign, he discusses those future outcomes (and past plays) under the rubric of human frailty – the divergent purposes and contradictory ambitions of those who will rule in Henry VI's name – and of historical contingency – the fact that his son will come to the throne 'in infant bands'. In this iteration, then, the ruin of the Lancastrian project is attributed to entirely contingent political factors rather than to the overarching, punitive intervention of providence foretold by Carlisle.

This is almost totally different from the relation between human political agency and the supervening authority of divine providence conjured in *Julius Caesar*, which, looking backwards, not only provides a stark contrast with the political world evoked in *Henry V*, but also, looking forward, in many ways anticipates the providence- and predestination-drenched world in which Hamlet subsists. For, as we have seen, *Hamlet* is a play about an intensely 'political' situation, that eschews any real discussion of politics as the pursuit, by secular, instrumental means, of outcomes limited to this world. On the contrary, the play is dominated by the concerns of 'conscience', defined (by Hamlet himself) as a virtual obsession with the consequences in the next life of actions taken in this. Hamlet converts his apparently political dilemma into a peculiarly intense exercise in the discernment of spirits, a soteriologically charged case of conscience, which he resolves by following, almost despite himself, the promptings of conscience, with at first disastrous results, from the consequences of which he is rescued, first, by the irruptive intervention of God's providence and then by his own emergently accepting sense of his status as the mere instrument of that providence. Only thus is he enabled, not to accept his (tragic) fate as a revenger, but rather to recognise and discharge his calling as the minister and scourge of God, and, at least on some readings of the end of the play, save his soul into the bargain.

Julius Caesar showed how pagan political agents, acting according to the dictates of republican virtue, could get things disastrously wrong, even in a pagan and republican Rome, let alone a Christian and monarchical England. *Hamlet* presents us with a Christian political agent, armed (at least initially) with only residually Christian notions about the immortality of the soul, the existence of heaven and hell, the reality of demonic, and therefore also of divine, intervention in the world. From these initial premises is born an obligation, indeed a determination, to follow the promptings of conscience, wherever they might lead and however much they might seem to contradict the demands of 'honour', 'passion' or 'virtue'. While *Julius Caesar* shows us both Caesar and his murderers getting things horribly wrong, *Hamlet* shows us its emergently Christian protagonist getting them (heroically) right. Viewed in terms of the Essex debacle the play might be taken as a mordant comment on how the earl might (or should) have acted had he been as concerned with the dictates of his conscience and the fate of his immortal soul as he had claimed to be immediately before his fatal decision to rebel, and as (by all accounts) he actually became, immediately before his execution.

Hamlet, of course, is followed by *Troilus and Cressida*. If we take *Hamlet* to be a relatively charitable judgement on the Essex fiasco, *Troilus* is the very opposite. It represents a bitterly illusionless, self-consciously mordant and cynical account of the moral and political wreckage left by the train crash of the Essex rebellion. Here is a world dominated by an interminable war without end, which no one on either side can justify, yet neither side seems able to conclude. We have a vision of the political world riven by faction; in which even men of the highest virtue or repute that this age can produce are so compromised by, so inextricably implicated in, the corruption and moral confusion that surrounds them that they are incapable of shaping events, even in ways they know to be both morally right and politically prudent. This is a world in which the highest ideals of order or value are articulated only to legitimise the basest of political manoeuvres; a world in which the demands of honour cannot be squared with those of the right and in which the demands of even a diminished, compromised honour must yield to the base imperatives of popularity.

We thus have three stages or phases in Shakespeare's writing of history plays. The first is located in the early 1590s, before the closure of the theatres in 1593, before the death of Sir Ferdinando Stanley, Lord Strange, the dissolution of Lord Strange's Men and the establishment of the virtual duopoly enjoyed after 1594 by the Lord Admiral's Men and the Lord Chamberlain's Men. During this phase, the plays written by Shakespeare and his collaborators move in much the same intellectual and thematic world as the Catholic pamphlets. Thereafter, once Shakespeare had made his patronage connection with the earl of Southampton and joined the Lord Chamberlain's Men, we have a distinctly Essexian phase, marked by a very different take on the current conjuncture and the English monarchical state from that laid out by Parsons' *Conference*. In the plays written after *Richard II* the central organising theme remains the same as that of the Henry VI plays; the nature of monarchical legitimacy; how such legitmacy might be lost and, once lost, how it might be reconstituted. Only now, within that problematic, from *King John* to *Henry V* there is a burgeoning concern with the tonic moral and political effects of a vigorous prosecution of war against the foreigner. That theme had first emerged in *1 Henry VI*, but in both *King John* and *Henry V* it moves to the front and centre of the analysis. The central, both historical and political, question emerged here as how far an individual, even of surpassing political gifts, could decisively shape events, and, more particularly, how such an individual might effectively combine the politics of honour and military prowess, of popularity, monarchical legitimacy, and latterly of faction, in order to restore legitimacy to a polity stripped thereof by a combination of usurpation and regicide, tyranny and misrule.

This middle period, organised, as it was, around a group of recognisably Essexian themes and concerns, came to an end as the Essex project imploded first in Ireland then, after the earl's return in his protracted disgrace and ultimate ruin, in England. The period produced the three plays with which this book ends – *Caesar*, *Hamlet* and *Troilus and Cressida*. Set in remote periods and locales, these eschewed English history altogether but used the very remoteness of their temporal and geographical settings to apply the history they were staging to contemporary events and concerns with a sustained intensity and an increasingly savage disillusion.

As we have seen, until it returns with full force in *Caesar* and *Hamlet*, in most of these plays, providence is in various forms of abeyance. For the most part, the English history plays of what has emerged here as Shakespeare's Essexian middle period – i.e. those written after 1594 and before 1599 – purveyed a secular view of politics as process, concentrated, as Blundeville had said the historian should concentrate, on delineating great deeds, and the role of the chief doers in shaping them. The result was something of a firewall between 'politics' and 'religion'.

'Religion' into 'politics' doesn't go

In none of these plays did Shakespeare have any time for bishops who play politics. One thinks here first of that quintessentially corrupt (popish, but, given the Whitgiftian associations evoked by his rivalry with the 'good duke' of Gloucester, not just popish) prelate, Cardinal Beaufort. But there is also Archbishop Scroop, who, in *2 Henry IV*, uses his reputation for personal piety to raise the people in support of the utterly secular and self-serving, if also self-protective, rebellion of the Percies, and the equally venal archbishop of Canterbury, whose all but incoherent justification of Henry V's French war is shown to be prompted by his desire to preserve the secular holdings of the clergy from the depredations of the Lollards and the crown. In fact, the only good bishop, indeed clergyman, to be found in all the plays under discussion here is the bishop of Carlisle in *Richard II* whose bona fides are proved by his loyalty to his prince. Carlisle prefers to tell prophetic truth to the newly establish power of the usurper Bolingbroke rather than, with the likes of the complacently providence-citing duke of York, go along to get along. Even Bolingbroke recognises the bishop's piety and accordingly he spares Carlisle from the harshest consequences of his later plotting against the new regime.

Of course, the pope was the archetypical proud, politicking prelate, and Shakespeare's antipathy to bishops who play politics perhaps reaches its apogee in the explicitly popish figures of Cardinal Beaufort – always appealing to Rome and using his papally conferred title as a cardinal for his own corrupt purposes – and of the papal legate, Pandulph, in *King John*. But Shakespeare's anti-prelatical propensity was redolent of more than an entirely conventional rejection of papalist clericalism. The plays under discussion here manifest a basic incompatibility between what we might term 'politics' and 'religion'; between the conduct of political life, the effective wielding of political power, even by relatively virtuous political actors – and, in these plays, relative virtue is all that the political life appears to allow – and the pursuit of salvation.

The ideal, of course, remains traditional enough; a self-animating and sustaining commonweal or social whole, a form of naturally hierarchical order, produced by the organic relationship between rulers and ruled, and sustained by the spontaneous discharge of the various social, political and moral roles and duties to which every member of the commonwealth has been called by God. These plays regularly genuflect before this traditional vision of order. It is a conceptual scheme that is shown animating Richard II's view of kingship. In the same play, it pervades the image of a properly governed commonwealth as a well kept garden. Both Ulysses' notion of order and degree and the archbishop of Canterbury's vision of the benign effects of the godly rule of Henry V also provide explicit, and much cited, statements of essentially the same view of how things could and indeed should be, when a legitimate ruler, whose legitimacy and right to rule is acknowledged by all, discharges the functions of his office with that combination of justice and mercy, of both the smack of firm government and the fatherly concern for the good of his subjects and realm, that are the distinguishing marks of the good ruler. In acting thus a monarch could truly fulfil his calling as God's vicegerent and thus truly mirror the benevolent rule of God over his creation. In a world like this there would be no contradiction between the conduct of rule in this life and the attainment of salvation in the next.

However, these plays never show us such a situation in action, still less perpetuating itself across the generations. Even in *Henry V*, which is the closest Shakespeare gets to staging the rule of a successful and virtuous prince, the various paeans to the effectiveness of Henry's rule, and the almost preternatural levels of order and harmony (allegedly) achieved by that rule, are consistently undercut, indeed, often as not, called into radical question. What that play in fact reveals is the extent of the sheer political effort, the multiple levels of persuasion and coercion, of duplicity, self-deception and self-projection, necessary to achieve order in a fallen world.

Indeed, these plays can be taken as a series of case studies of how, through various delinquent or tyrannous behaviours, legitimacy could be, or has been lost, and how, out of the moral and political chaos thus created, it might be restored again. And, of course, the things that these plays show destroying legitimacy and good government – monarchical weakness, an excess of female influence over the discharge of royal rule, unsuccessful foreign war, noble faction, usurpation, a dubious or contested right to rule, an unsettled or contested succession, various sorts of tyrannical misrule or monarchical exorbitance – are all of them drawn, not merely from history, but also from the realities of immediately contemporary politics in England and Scotland, France and the Low Countries.

And, in this context, it is worth noting that three of the four characters who voice the traditional vision of political and moral order – Richard II, Ulysses and the archbishop of Canterbury – have not only signally failed to live up to their own impeccably orthodox standards, they are in fact voicing these sentiments in order to further agendas that totally undercut the vision of order they appear to be embracing. Richard is attempting to justify his own disastrously tyrannical mode of kingship, and moreover doing so in a way, and at a time, when such speechifying is not only totally inappropriate, but likely to undermine the practical measures which alone might enable him to retain his crown and maintain 'order'. Ulysses is mouthing a moral and political orthodoxy that he is about to belie through his own self-consciously devious practice of the politics of faction and fraction, and the archbishop of Canterbury is hailing the glories of Henry's rule in order to encourage a war the justice of which is by no means clear, to protect the secular interests of the clerical estate. The only innocent party to give voice to such orthodox notions of order is the gardener in Richard II and he does so in terms which include rebellion, deposition and usurpation amongst the organically necessary means through which, when confronted by systematic misrule, true order might be restored to the commonweal.

If one were to generalise in theological terms about the situations staged in these plays, one might observe that, in a fallen world, the ideal of a natural hierarchical moral, social and political order, which is intermittently upheld for our admiration or lament will have always already been undermined by the human propensity to sin and, in particular, by the propensity of the good and the great to seek their particular private ends and interests rather than (and, therefore at the expense of) the common good. The result is that legitimacy – the claim and right to rule – is almost always, in some way, at stake and under contestation.

Moreover, as the extended deconstruction of the notion of legitimacy itself, undertaken in 2 and 3 *Henry VI,* shows, in practice 'legitimacy' was not only or even mainly a natural product of the ways in which the social and political order had been patterned by nature and by God, but always an achieved effect. Far from the natural consequence of the ordered progress of hereditary succession, legitimacy has continually to be produced and reproduced, using a range of not always compatible, or mutually reinforcing, claims. For, as young Arthur, Richard II and Henry VI all found to their cost, in the establishment of legitimacy stakes, simple questions of right might prove to be quite beside the point. As the fates of all three demonstrate, if the requisite political characteristics or skills were lacking, even the most apparently legitimate and secure prince in the world could come to grief.

In these plays, what we might term 'the legitimacy effect' has to be constructed out of a range of by no means always logically compatible factors, claims and arguments. Both *de jure* and *de facto* elements are always in play. And once constructed, legitimate rule has to be constantly asserted and enforced, experienced and performed, by both ruler and ruled, if monarchical normality is to be achieved and enjoyed. Shakespeare is, in short, an extraordinarily acute observer of the necessity (and the fragility) of the modes of representation and assertion required to sustain legitimacy in post-reformation England.[27]

In these plays, more often than not, in order to achieve or maintain some semblance of order in a fallen world, even the best of kings must have recourse to means and methods so deceitful, so formally unjust, so violent and ruthless, that, no matter how beneficent their political or moral effects might prove to be, they might well also call into the most serious question the personal salvation of the perpetrator. Here the means used even by Richmond, let alone by that 'vile politician' Bolingbroke, to remove the variously tyrannical King Richards confronting them, find parallels in the methods used by King John to establish and maintain himself in power and stave off the challenge of the French, and even in those adopted by that ultimate hero, Henry V, to affirm his (always already dubious or contestable) right to rule.

Consequently, of the kings staged in these plays, John dies in desperation, with no thought of repentance or salvation; the usurper Henry IV dies racked by guilt and tempted by despair. Even as he confronts death, his last words to his son have nothing of the spiritual or the repentant about them. His thoughts are not of heaven (nor even of hell) but entirely of this world. His advice to Hal is concerned solely with secular and political issues. His stated intention to go on crusade in order to expiate the crying sins sin of usurpation and regicide, with which *1 Henry IV* had opened, has now been transmuted into his advice to Hal that what he really needs to do is to start a war, any war, in order to cement his hold on power. To the end, Henry IV remains scarcely able to acknowledge, let alone properly to repent for, his own role in the events that led him to depose and kill his king and usurp the throne.

As for Henry's victim, Richard II, he shows no hint of repentance, no sense of his own sins, or even of the role that his own folly has played in bringing about his downfall. His last moments are spent in desperate and resentful ravings against his successor and in violent efforts at self-defence. At the end he expresses an absolute certainty about his own salvation that the audience – particularly an audience made up of Elizabethan Christians, whether protestant or Catholic – has no good reason to share. Richard's end might inspire pity but scarcely a secure sense that, as he claimed with such conviction, he was ascending, Christ-like, directly to heaven.

Finally, of course, there is Henry V. Unlike many of his monarchical predecessors in these plays we do not get to see Henry die or even approach death. Not only that, but *Henry V* is the only one of these plays that contains a picture of successful monarchical rule. Moreover, the play breaks off *in medias res* at the moment of Henry's greatest triumph. At one level, Henry is the epitome of the good prince, a ruler of surpassing virtue and prowess who brings unity and good government not only to England but also to an emergent Britain, by leading that nation to victory in a war against the greatest European power of the day. And yet, on another level, Henry is something of a Machiavel; his basic manoeuvre the prosecution of a war the justice of which the play goes out of its way to call into the most serious question. Henry is a master of a variety of different (and by no means always internally consistent or mutually compatible) claims to virtue and honour, which he displays, with perfect judgement and timing, to his own best advantage, as circumstances allow or demand.

However, Henry's ends are not private but public. While entirely beneficent in their effects – for the English certainly, if not for the French, they also have both spiritual and this-worldly costs, the nature of which, and his own responsibility for which, Henry never seems fully to understand, let alone to acknowledge or accept. The potentially decisive showdown with Williams and the other soldiers vindicates neither the morality of the king's position nor the justice of the war, but rather provides yet another occasion for Henry to display his intellectual and moral facility for turning a potentially disastrous slipping of the royal guard into yet another triumphant display of the transcendent otherness of kings.

Such selectively intense bouts of moral and spiritual obliquity were probably necessary if Henry was effectively to perform his both divinely allotted and self-chosen role as war leader, royal figurehead and national hero and thus return monarchical legitimacy to an England thrown into moral and political chaos by Richard II's tyranny and his father's rebellion, usurpation and regicide, but such moral blind spots and spiritual dead zones scarcely enhanced his chances of salvation.

For all of Henry's persistent God-talk, he never shows any sense of his own (arguably rather considerable) sins, nor any concern for his own salvation, and still less of even an incipient sense of the need for (personal) repentance. When he does address God, he does so in a thoroughly instrumental (and thus quintessentially 'popish') exchange, designed to bargain with the deity over the effects, on this-worldly outcomes, of the sins of others, which he then tries to offset with his own alms deeds. The play shows us that Henry understands what we might call the rhetoric of Christian and godly rule – he has the outward forms, the appropriately pious (but also decidedly popish) sentiments and emotions off pat – but what he does not quite get, and certainly has yet to make any time for, is the bit about sin, repentance and salvation. All of which recalls Hal's entirely self-conscious, meticulously staged, and therefore entirely insincere 'repentance' and/or 'conversion', depicted in the *Henry IV* plays.

As I argued above, the point of *Henry V* is not to make us choose, as all too many critics have tended to do, between two different visions of Henry, either as warrior hero and ideal Christian prince or as mealy-mouthed Machiavel, the consummate practitioner of all the ruses and deceits to which power is prone when seeking to maintain itself, but rather to show us that, contrary to conventional moral platitude, there is no necessary or real contradiction between the two. Henry is both, and in order to succeed in the former role, he has to be able to pull off the latter (and vice versa). For all his Falstaff-like, shape-changing opportunism, his capacity to turn any situation or exchange, however seemingly unpromising, to his advantage (vide the scene with Bates and Williams); for all his moral flexibility, his ability to shift the really hard moral choices and, as he appears to think, responsibilities, off on to others (the archbishop of Canterbury, the citizens of Harfleur, his own troops); for all his rhetorical skill, and his readiness, when the chips are down, to resort to ruthless violence, the play shows Henry not to be simply out for himself. He is not, in that sense, any sort of Machiavel, or rather, as A.D. Nuttall has observed, he is that ultimate paradox, a Machiavel for the common good; a prince willing to do all this, not just to win himself power and glory (although win power and glory for himself he most certainly does) but to restore unity and legitimacy to a polity from which they have been stripped by the combined actions and reactions of Richard II and his father. That in doing so he may commit sins that (unrepented) are likely to call his own salvation into the most serious question merely serves to highlight the extent of his self-sacrifice.

Given the gulf separating 'politics' from 'religion' in these plays, and the often corrupt, self-serving, and always entirely this-worldly calculations that are shown driving the political process, one might think that securing salvation in the next life, and power, order and security in this, were not merely two entirely distinct, but two entirely antipathetic ends. This impression might be thought to be compounded by the fact that of the kings on display in these plays, only Henry VI seems securely bound for heaven – something that makes him the exception that proves this particular rule; for Henry's saintliness is precisely that which renders him totally unfit for kingship and sends his kingdom to hell in a handbasket, even as his personal unworldliness and piety seem set to send him to the other place.

Henry VI apart, the only other royal political agent whom Shakespeare seems prepared to consign to heaven – and even in this case it is anything but a done deal – is Hamlet. And despite the fact that he is a prince of the blood and next successor to the throne, he takes a resolutely un-political view of his situation and eschews all the forms of political action – faction, conspiracy, a populist appeal to the multitude – that Laertes seizes with both hands and that in *Julius Caesar* even that most virtuous of men, Brutus, adopts to save the state, with fatal results in both cases.

Alone of the 'chief doers' depicted in these plays Hamlet remains throughout self-consciously preoccupied with the dictates of 'conscience' and in particular with the issue of salvation. Infinitely postponing the act of revenge, Hamlet does not delay but repeatedly takes frenetic, and desperately dangerous, action at the level of conscience, with seemingly disastrous consequences for himself and for Denmark; consequences from which he is rescued by the autonomous (and utterly underserved) intervention of divine providence. While the pagan protagonists of *Julius Caesar* are unable to perceive the shaping influence exerted by providence over events or to decode the repeated warnings and admonitions vouchsafed by providence to fallen humanity, in *Hamlet* we are shown a Christian political agent who is (ultimately and at the last) able to discern the supervening control exercised by divine providence over events and thus rightly to apprehend and embrace his own role as its instrument. But in order to do that he has had to remain acutely sensitive to the dictates of 'conscience', allowing them ultimately to drown out the (contrary) demands of 'honour' and 'passion'. This means refusing the role, not only of revenger, but still more of politician; roles that 'honour' and 'passion' (not to mention the narrative force fields of the revenge tragedy and the history play that *Hamlet* initially comes across as being) were insistently thrusting upon him. And, of course, this means eschewing the full range of political modes and manoeuvres adopted without a second thought by Laertes. These might well have enabled Hamlet to achieve the ostensibly honourable ends of revenge, not to mention the seizure of power and preservation of monarchical order, but only at the cost of his immortal soul. Indeed, one might argue that the play shows us that it was only by not pursuing those ends that he had been able to achieve all of them, and get to heaven.

And so, in the three history plays written during and after the final implosion of the Essexian project, the realms of politics and religion, of virtu and
virtue, which had been kept in tenuous contact the one with the other through
the fantasy figure of Hal/Henry V, finally split apart. The notion that a Christian
political actor of surpassing political and personal virtu(e), using the full range
of secular political analysis and action, might have been able to save both the
state and his own soul, having been definitively dispelled by the disastrous
failure of the Essex project, all that was left was a basic choice between a
Hamlet-style determination to follow the dictates of providence and conscience,
wherever they might lead and the sort of moral confusion and political failure
staged, the first time as tragedy, the second time as something rather more like
farce, in *Julius Caesar* and *Troilus and Cressida* respectively. In *Troilus*, set as it
is in pagan Asia Minor, providence plays no role, but, in the person of
Cassandra, prophecy certainly does, and, as a number of critics have argued,
the play places both the characters on stage and the audience in the midst of a
narrative the end of which everybody knows but from which no one can
escape. This is providentialism as a form of claustrophobic nightmare.

As we have seen, *Troilus* enables us to reconstruct what the world looked
like, in 1601, to someone who, in a whole series of plays, written throughout the
previous decade, had bought rather heavily into the Essex project. In so doing,
Shakespeare had got things spectacularly wrong and, having placed virtually all
his eggs in the basket of Essexian virtu and Jacobean legitimacy, he now looked
back, or rather perhaps allowed his audience to look back on the recent past and
to confront the immediate future, through the showily self-conscious, determinedly illusionless pessimism and bitter irony that pervades *Troilus and
Cressida*. But in so doing, at least at the level of practical political prognostication, he had got things spectacularly wrong again, for, as it turned out, it was the
removal of Essex from the scene that paved the way for the triumphantly unop-
posed and wholly peaceful accession of a new monarch and the successful
conclusion of the war with Spain. These resolutions were achieved by James VI
and I, at whose coronation Shakespeare marched, now clad in the royal livery
appropriate to a charter member of the newly renamed King's Men.

Of course, Shakespeare had scarcely been alone in his fascination with the
Essex phenomenon or in the assumption that Essex was the emerging man of
the age, someone whose military and political virtue was going to save the state
now and shape the next reign, in the near future. As an aspiring poet and dramatist, Shakespeare was on the edge of the court and in the midst of the court-
centred news networks and gossip circles of London. As someone with some
sort of patron–client relationship with Essex's intimate, the earl of Southampton,
Shakespeare had an entree of sorts into the circles around the earl. Indeed it
appears that Shakespeare was and remained decidedly connected in Essexian
circles. Not only did he name-check the earl in *Henry V*, at a moment of very

high political tension, in public performances at court of *The merry wives of Windsor*, he roasted Essex's enemy Lord Cobham, to whom central figures in the Essex circle came jokingly to refer as Sir John Falstaff. In addition, it was his company that was hired by two of the Essex conspirators to put on what was almost certainly one of his old plays, on the eve of what turned out to be the Essex rebellion. Shakespeare, then, had form as an Essex man.[28]

While not without its risks, until the very end, such commitments must have looked, and felt, much like a winning bet. After all, why, along with a host of his contemporaries, from London apprentices to kings, courtiers and intelligencers throughout Europe, should Shakespeare not have been fascinated by the Essex phenomenon? In plays about politics, why should he not have returned, over and over again, to the dominant topics, the major sources of fascination and anxiety, of the age; to the lineaments of the succession crisis with which the imminent prospect of the queen's death with the succession still unsettled threatened the realm; to the war currently raging against the greatest (Catholic) power in Europe; to the religious divisions and doubts, and indeed to the confessional conflicts, of the post-reformation, now so inextricably intertwined with the dynastic wars that were threatening to tear western Europe apart and plunge England into moral and political chaos. If along the way – at least at the level of practical political prognostication or commentary – he got a great deal, indeed virtually everything, wrong, all that proves is that it is not necessary to be politically correct, or at least correct about politics, to write plays that last.

Notes

Introduction and acknowledgements

1. While at the time this thought struck me with considerable force – leading me to think about this and other plays in ways that I had not previously considered – as with so much of what follows, it turned out to be anything but an original insight. As far as I can discover, the thought originated with Richard Simpson writing over a hundred years ago and has been picked up often since. See, for instance, Lily B. Campbell, *Shakespeare's histories: mirrors of Elizabethan policy* (San Marino, Ca., 1947), 142–43, and subsequently Howard Erskine Hill, *Poetry and the realm of politics, Shakespeare to Dryden* (Oxford, 1996), 64; Paola Pugliatti, *Shakespeare the historian* (Basingstoke, 1996), chapter 6. As for Troilus, as Robin Headlam Wells points out, 'it is a commonplace of earlier twentieth century criticism that in *Troilus and Cressida* Shakespeare was satirizing the England of Elizabeth's final years'. See his *Shakespeare on masculinity* (Cambridge, 2000), p. 51, fn. 55. See here Tucker Brook's, 'Shakespeare study in culture and anarchy', *Yale Review*, 17 (1928), pp. 571–77, 'I cannot help imagining that he is, however subconsciously, anatomizing the England of the dying Elizabeth: within the wall the febrile Essex type of decadent chivalry: without the strident go getters of the newer dispensation: Cecil/Ulysses and Ralegh/Diomed' (quote at p. 576) and James Savage, 'Troilus and Cressida and Elizabethan court factions', *University of Mississippi Studies in English*, 5 (1964), pp. 413–66.
2. See, variously, David Kastan, *A will to believe: Shakespeare and religion* (Oxford, 2014); Richard McCoy, *Faith in Shakespeare* (Oxford, 2013). The role of religion in Shakespeare's revenge tragedies is a topic to which I hope to return.

Part I

1. *A treatise of treasons* (1572), fol. 118r–v.
2. Ibid., fol. 120r.
3. Ibid., fol. 120r.
4. Ibid., fols. 120v–121v.
5. The references here are to Thomas Sampson and Thomas Norton, the former a leading puritan divine, and the latter a puritan client of William Cecil, on both of whom see the articles in *ODNB*. On Norton see the materials cited in n. 19 below.
6. D.C. Peck, ed., *Leicester's commonwealth: the copy of a letter written by a master of art of Cambridge (1584) and related documents* (Athens, 1985), p. 94.
7. Ibid., p. 99.
8. Ibid., pp. 177–78.
9. Ibid., pp. 135–36.
10. Ibid., pp. 131–32.
11. On Parsons' use of historical sources see Peter Holmes, 'The authorship and early reception of *A Conference about the Next Succession to the Crown of England*', *Historical Journal*, 23 (1980), pp. 415–29 and his *Resistance and compromise: the political thought of the Elizabethan Catholics* (Cambridge, 1982), pp. 221–3.
12. See Mortimer Levine, *The early Elizabethan succession question* (Stanford, 1966), pp. 168–70.
13. British Museum [BM], Egerton Mss 2836, fols. 42v.–43r.
14. Ibid. fols. 46r, 47r.
15. Ibid., fol. 47v.

16. Ibid. fols. 51r–v.
17. Ibid., fol. 51v.
18. Ibid., fols. 52v–53r.
19. Ibid., fols. 55r–v.
20. Ibid., fol. 53v.
21. Ibid., fol. 50v.
22. For Lucius see ibid., fols 49r–v, 50v; for Ferrex and Porrex see ibid., fols. 52r–v.
23. Ibid., fols. 45r–v.
24. Ibid., fol. 56v.
25. Ibid., fols. 65v–67r.
26. BL Stowe Mss 273, 'An answer to the discourse of John Leslie, bishop of Ross, intended to prove that the queen of Scots was entitled to the crown of England in preference to queen Elizabeth because the pope had deposed her and that her son was entitled to the crown of this realm after her decease'. Quote at fol. 20v.
27. Ibid., fol. 22v.
28. Ibid., fol. 24v.
29. Ibid., fol. 25r.
30. Ibid., fols. 25v–27r.
31. Ibid., fol. 29v.
32. Ibid., fols. 50r–51r.
33. There remained, of course, a considerable body of Catholic support for the Stuart claim. Indeed, differences over the succession ran through the centre of the so-called Archpriest controversy of the late 1590s. See P. Lake and M. Questier, 'Taking it to the street? The archpriest controversy and the succession', in Susan Doran and Paulina Kewes, eds, *Doubtful and dangerous: the question of succession in late Elizabethan England* (Manchester, 2014).
34. The oozlum bird is described by Wikipedia as 'a legendary creature found in Australian and British folk tales and legends. Some versions have it that, when startled, the bird will take off and fly around in ever-decreasing circles until it manages to fly up itself, disappearing completely, which adds to its rarity.' In my mother's generation the bird was an emblem for a sort of furious futility, a state which might lead someone, in a paroxysm of often entirely misdirected activity, to spin around and around in ever decreasing circles, before disappearing up his or her own rectum.
35. Wayne Rebhorn, 'The crisis of the aristocracy in *Julius Caesar*', *Renaissance Quarterly*, 43 (1990), pp. 75–111, quotation at p. 82. In making his central point Rebhorn cites the seminal article by Louis Montrose, ' "Shaping Fantasies": figurations of gender and power in Elizabethan culture', *Representations*, 1 (1983), pp. 61–94.
36. Erskine-Hill, *Poetry and the realm of politics: Shakespeare to Dryden*, 5. Part I of Erskine-Hill's book prefigures many of the central themes pursued below. Mention here should also be made of Marie Axton's *The queen's two bodies: drama and the Elizabethan succession* (London, 1977), to the example and insights of which this book is greatly indebted.
37. As Robin Headlam Wells observes, 'it is something of a paradox that materialist criticism, with its Foucault-inspired interest in the dynamics of power, should show less interest in the overt and well reported political conflicts of the period than in the more metaphysical question of how an emergent capitalist state acquires control over individuals by constructing them as seemingly autonomous subjects.' Headlam Wells, *Shakespeare on masculinity*, pp. 5–6.
38. Gary Taylor, 'Forms of opposition: Shakespeare and Middleton', *English Literary Renaissance*, 24 (1994), pp. 283–314, esp. pp. 310–11.
39. J.P. Sommerville, 'Richard Hooker, Hadrian Saravia, and the advent of the Divine Right of Kings', *History of Political Thought*, 4 (1983), pp. 229–45; Peter Lake, *Anglicans and puritans? Presbyterianism and Elizabethan conformist thought from Whitgift to Hooker* (London, 1988); John Guy, 'The Elizabethan establishment and the ecclesiastical polity', in J. Guy, ed., *The reign of Elizabeth I: court and culture in the last decade* (Cambridge, 1995), pp. 126–49; Ethan Shagan, 'The English Inquisition: constitutional conflict and ecclesiastical law in the 1590s', *Historical Journal*, 47 (2004), pp. 541–65.
40. On which see Anne McLaren, *Political culture in the reign of Elizabeth I: Queen and commonwealth 1558–1585* (Cambridge, 1999).
41. Patrick Collinson, 'The monarchial republic of Elizabeth I', first published in the *Bulletin of the John Rylands Library*, 68 (1987), pp. 394–424, then reprinted in his *Elizabethan Essays* (London, 1994), pp. 31–57, and his 'The Elizabethan exclusion crisis and the Elizabethan

polity' first published in the *Proceedings of the British Academy*, 84 (1994), pp. 51–92, and then reprinted in his *This England: essays on the English nation and commonwealth in the sixteenth century* (Manchester, 2011), pp. 61–97.

42. John Guy, *My heart is my own: the life of Mary Queen of Scots* (London, 2004); Stephen Alford, *The early Elizabethan polity: William Cecil and the British succession crisis, 1558–1569* (Cambridge, 1998); idem, *Burghley: William Cecil at the court of Elizabeth* (London, 2008).

43. Mortimer Levine, *The early Elizabethan succession question*; Susan Doran, *Monarchy and matrimony : the courtships of Elizabeth I* (London, 1996).

44. This paragraph draws very heavily on the seminal work of Simon Adams. See especially his essays, 'Faction, clientage and politics, 1550–1603', 'Eliza enthroned? The court and its politics' and 'The patronage of the crown in Elizabethan politics: the 1590s in perspective' all reprinted in his *Leicester and the court: essays on Elizabethan politics* (Manchester, 2002), pp. 13–67.

45. See the foundational revisionist scholarship of Michael Graves, much of it centred on the person of Thomas Norton, who had figured in Sir John Neale's parliamentary narrative as a leading member of 'the puritan choir' but emerged from Graves' scrutiny as a client of Burghley and what Graves termed a 'council man of business'. See Graves, *Thomas Norton: the Parliament man* (Oxford, 1994); idem, 'The common lawyers and the Privy Council's parliamentary men-of-business, 1584–1601', *Parliamentary History*, 8 (1989), pp. 189–215; idem, 'The management of the Elizabethan House of Commons : the council's men-of-business', *Parliamentary History*, 2 (1983), pp. 11–38; idem, 'Thomas Norton the parliament man: an Elizabethan MP, 1559–1581', *Historical Journal*, 23 (1980), pp. 17–35. As a crucial qualification of Graves' position see Patrick Collinson, 'Puritans, men of business and Elizabethan parliaments' in his *Elizabethan essays* (London, 1994); idem, 'Servants and citizens: Robert Beale and other Elizabethans' reprinted in his *This England*, pp. 98–121.

46. I summarise here the argument of Peter Lake, 'The politics of popularity and the public sphere: the "monarchical republic" of Elizabeth I defends itself', in P. Lake and S. Pincus, eds, *The politics of the public sphere in early modern England* (Manchester, 2007), pp. 59–94.

47. Collinson, 'Monarchical republic of Queen Elizabeth I' and 'The Elizabethan exclusion crisis'. Also see Helen Gardner, 'The historical approach to Hamlet' in J. Jump, ed., *Shakespeare: Hamlet, a casebook* (London, 1968), pp. 137–50.

48. Scottt McMillin and Sally-Beth MacClean, *The Queen's Men and their plays* (Cambridge, 1998), p. 67.

49. Ibid., pp. 57, 21.

50. Ibid., pp. 49, 59–60.

51. Ibid., p. 36.

52. Lawrence Manley and Sally-Beth MacClean, *Lord Strange's Men and their plays* (New Haven, 2014).

53. Cf. Craig Muldrew, *The economy of obligation* (Basingstoke, 1998).

54. Andrew Gurr, *The Shakespeare Company, 1594–1642* (Cambridge, 2004), chapter 1, 'The plan of 1594'.

55. McMillin and MacClean, *The Queen's Men*, pp. 50–1, 8.

56. Andrew Gurr, *The Shakespearean stage, 1574–1642* (Cambridge, 1992), pp. 212–13.

57. Andrew Gurr, *The Shakespeare Company*, p. 92.

58. I rehearse here the briefest possible outline of my 2011 Ford lectures, now published as *Bad Queen Bess? Libels, secret histories and the politics of publicity in the reign of Queen Elizabeth I* (Oxford, 2016).

59. John Guy, *The reign of Elizabeth I* (Cambridge, 1995); Susan Doran and Paulina Kewes, *Doubtful and dangerous: the question of succession in late Elizabethan England* (Manchester, 2014).

60. Paul Hammer, *The polarisation of Elizabethan politics: the political career of Robert Devereaux, 2nd Earl of Essex, 1585–1597* (Cambridge, 1999); Alex Gajda, *The earl of Essex and late Elizabethan political culture* (Oxford, 2012).

61. Gajda, *The earl of Essex*.

62. See Gajda, *The earl of Essex*, chapter 6.

63. Ibid.

64. Ibid.

65. Paul Hammer, 'The smiling crocodile: the earl of Essex and late-Elizabethan "popularity" ', in Lake and Pincus, eds, *Politics of the public sphere in early modern England* (Manchester, 2007), pp. 95–115. Idem, 'Myth making: politics, propaganda and the capture of Cadiz in 1596', *Historical Journal*, 40 (1997), pp. 621–42; 'Upstaging the Queen: the earl of Essex, Francis Bacon and the Accession Day celebrations of 1595', in D. Bevington, and D. Holbrook, eds, *Politics of the Stuart court masque* (Cambridge, 1998), pp. 41–66. For the wider background see Lake, *Bad Queen Bess?*

66. R.B. Wernham, *After the Armada* (Oxford, 1984).

67. J.H.M. Salmon, *The French religious wars in English political thought* (Oxford, 1959). For a detailed account of French anti-League tracts translated into English and printed in London see Lisa Parmelee, *Good newes from Fraunce: French anti-League propaganda in late Elizabethan England* (Rochester, 1996). In literary matters see Richard Hillman, *Shakespeare, Marlowe and the politics of France* (Basingstoke, 2002). It is worth remarking that the influence on the course of English Catholic thought and polemic of events in France is a central theme in Holmes, *Resistance and compromise* and in both the early and late work of John Bossy. See for instance his 'English Catholics and the French marriage, 1577–81', *Recusant History*, 5 (1959), pp. 2–16 and *Under the molehill: an Elizabethan spy story* (London, 2001). For a more extended account of the content of these tracts see Lake, *Good Queen Bess?* chapter 10.

68. The relations between pamphlets and play is the subject of important ongoing research by Alan Stewart.

69. Sharpe, *Selling*, part VI.

70. On this see David Kastan's seminal essay, ' "Proud Majesty Made a Subject": representing authority on the early modern stage', in his *Shakespeare after theory* (London and New York, 1999), pp. 109–27.

71. David Womersley, 'Sir Henry Savile's translation of Tacitus and the political interpretation of Elizabethan texts', *Review of English Studies*, 42 (1991), pp. 313–42.

72. Malcolm Smuts, 'Court-centered politics and the uses of Roman historians, c.1590–1630', in K. Sharpe and P. Lake, eds, *Culture and politics in early Stuart England* (London, 1994), pp. 21–43; 325–31. On the new humanism and reason of state see Richard Tuck, *Philosophy and government, 1572–1651* (Cambridge, 1993). On the tangled relations between the old Ciceronian, virtue-centred historiographies and the new politic ones see Blair Worden, 'Historians and poets', *Huntington Library Quarterly*, 68 (2005), pp. 71–93.

73. Fritz Levy, *Tudor Historical Thought* (Toronto, 2004), esp. chapters V and VII; Daniel Woolf, *The idea of history in early Stuart England: erudition, ideology, and 'The light of truth' from the accession of James I to the Civil War Place* (Toronto and London, 1990); for other readings of the chronicles see Annabel Patterson, *Reading Holinshed's Chronicles* (Chicago, 1994) and now for the best single discussion see David Womersley, *Divinity and state* (Oxford, 2010), which fills out the agenda bracingly set in his 'Against the teleology of technique' in *Huntington Library Quarterly*, 68 (2005), pp. 95–108. For by far the best account of Savile's Tacitean project now see Paulina Kewes, 'Henry Savile's Tacitus and the politics of Roman history in late Elizabethan England', *Huntington Library Quarterly*, 74 (20011), pp. 515–51. But this also needs to be read against the crucial remarks in Gajda, The *earl of Essex*, pp. 226–33.

74. On this genre see Anthony Grafton, *What was history?* (Cambridge, 2007); for an exemplary discussion of an influential English example of the genre from the 1620s see J.M.H. Salmon, 'Precept, example and truth: Degory Wheare and the *ars historica*', in Donald R. Kelley and David Harris Sachs, eds, *The historical imagination in early modern Britain* (Cambridge, 1997), pp. 11–36.

75. D.R. Woolf, *Idea of history*, pp. 10, 17.

76. F. Patrizzi, *Della historia diece dialoghi* (Venice, 1560) and a manuscript written by Aconcio while in the earl of Leicester's service, reproduced in *Huntington Library Quarterly*, 2 (1939–40), pp. 149–70.

77. John Blundeville, *The true order of writing and reading histories* (London, 1574), sigs. Fv–Fvii r, Aii, r.

78. For a magisterial discussion of which see Blair Worden, *The sound of virtue* (London and New Haven, 1996).

79. Ibid., quotation at p. 10.

80. Cathy Shrank, *Writing the nation in reformation England, 1530–1580* (Cambridge, 2004), *passim* but see esp. chapters 3, 4 and 5 on Thomas, Smith and Wilson respectively. Quotation

at pp. 110–11. Shrank's final chapter is, appropriately enough, on The *Shepheardes Calendar* and *The Old Arcadia*.

81. Winthrop S. Hudson, *The Cambridge connection and the Elizabethan settlement of 1559* (Durham, NC, 1980). Mary Partridge, 'Thomas Hoby's English translation of Castiglione's *Book of the Courtier*', *Historical Journal*, 50 (2007), pp. 769–86; idem, 'Lord Burghley and *Il Cortegiano*: Civil and martial models of courtliness in Elizabethan England', *Transactions of the Royal Historical Association*, 6th ser., 19 (2009), pp. 95–116. Also see Stephen Alford, *Kingship and politics in the reign of Edward VI* (Cambridge, 2002).

82. Worden, *Sound of virtue*, pp. 260, 255.

83. Woolf, *Idea of history*, p, 11.

84. Again I summarise the central argument of my *Bad Queen Bess?*

85. Blundeville, *True order*, sig. Ciii, r.

86. Ibid., sig. Aiv, v.

87. Ibid., sig. Cii, r.

88. Ibid., sig. Fii, v.

89. Ibid., sig. Diii, r.

90. Ibid., sigs. Biii, v–Biv, r.

91. Ibid., sig. Bii,v.

92. Ibid., sigs. Biv, v.–Bv, r.

93. Ibid., sigs. D, v.–Dii, r.

94. Ibid., sig. H, v.

95. Ibid., sigs. Hii, r–v.

96. Viewing the political uses of historical writing over what we might term the long seventeenth century, Paulina Kewes draws a broad contrast between the period before 1640 when historical writing was for the most part 'conceived as advice to princes or education of statesmen' and that between the 1640s to the 1670s when, as politics became more overtly polarised, more, as Mark Kishlansky might have put it, 'adversarial', that is to say, party-based and polemically bitter, 'topical uses of history became more explicit, crude and deliberately derogatory'. Then 'historical writings came to function as propaganda aimed at a mass market' and 'embodied drastic ideological divisions and disagreements'. The result was a 'rage for historical parallels' that reached its 'heyday between the 1640s and the 1670s'. While there is much to be said for this view, it elides the relation of the plays under discussion here both with contemporary politics and with the concerns of their first audiences. For all that they were often performed at court, the people being educated by these plays in the ways of the political world were not only or even primarily 'princes' and 'statesmen' but mass audiences in the London theatres and indeed sometimes in the provinces. While these plays did not 'function as propaganda aimed at a mass market' or 'embody drastic ideological divisions and disagreements' in anything like the same ways as works produced between the 1640s and 1670s, they did advert to some of the most sensitive political issues of the day and serve to educate their audiences in a certain way of viewing, if not doing, 'politics'. On this see Paulina Kewes, 'History and its uses: introduction', in a collection of essays on that subject published first as a special issue of *The Huntington Library Quarterly* (68, no. 1–2, 2005), pp. 1–31, esp. pp. 5–11) and later as a free-standing volume by California University Press. Also see the essay by Blair Worden in the same volume, 'Historians and poets', pp. 71–93.

97. See his ' "Politicians in show": the circulation of political knowledge in early seventeenth century political drama' (Columbia University Ph.D. dissertation, 2008), a reworked version of which is to be published by OUP in 2016 under the title *Hamlet's moment*. I am very grateful to Professor Kisery for permission to cite his work and for many discussions of these topics, to the study of which his book will represent a seminal contribution. Also see Zachary Lesser and Peter Stallybrass, 'The first literary *Hamlet* and the commonplacing of professional plays', *Shakespeare Quarterly*, 59 (2008), pp. 371–420. Blair Worden notes the commonplace book of the theatregoer Edward Pudsey in the Bodleian in which Pudsey 'extracted pithy statements from plays by Jonson and others and recorded them alongside quotations from the historical chronicles'. See his 'Historians and poets', quote at p. 88, n. 87.

98. Anthony Grafton and Lisa Jardine, ' "Studied for action": how Gabriel Harvey read his Livy', *Past and Present*, 129 (1990), pp. 30–78; Lisa Jardine and Bill Sherman, 'Pragmatic readers: knowledge transactions and scholarly services in late Elizabethan England', in Anthony Fletcher and Peter Roberts, eds, *Religion, culture and society in early modern Britain: essays in honour of Patrick Collinson* (Cambridge, 1994), pp. 102–24. This paragraph is deeply indebted to the work of Andras Kisery, which has informed a great deal of what follows.

99. Blundeville, *True order*, sigs. Eiv, r–v.
100. Sir Philip Sidney, *An apology for poetry (or The defence of poesy)*, ed. R. W. Marsden (Manchester, 2002), quotations at pp. 93, 83.
101. Fritz Levy, 'Hayward, Daniel, and the beginning of politic history in England', *Huntington Library Quarterly*, 50 (1987), pp. 1–34. Quotation at p. 5.
102. John Hayward, *The first part of the life and reign of King Henry IIII* (London, 1599), 'A.P. to the reader', sig. A4v. On this see Levy, 'Hayward, Daniel and the beginnings of politic history in England', p. 18.
103. On this see Paulina Kewes, 'History and its uses: introduction', pp. 1–31, esp. pp. 5–11. Also Blair Worden, 'Historians and poets', pp. 71–93.
104. As Phyllis Rackin puts it, in her *Stages of history* (Ithaca, 1990), p.139 : 'in the Boar's Head, the historical prince meets unhistorical characters who drink anachronistic cups of sack and wear anachronistic ruffs and peach-colored stockings. There is even a man called Pistol, a character whose very name is an anachronism and whose speech is stitched together from scraps of plays that were not written until the sixteenth century for a theatre that did not even exist at the time of Henry IV.'
105. Brian Walsh, *Shakespeare the Queen's Men and the Elizabethan performance of history* (Cambridge, 2009), p. 35. In the discussion summarised and applied to my purposes in these paragraphs, Walsh is, in many ways, revisiting territory initially explored by Phyllis Rackin in chapter 3, 'Anachronism and nostalgia', of her *Stages of History* (Ithaca,1990). Also see Jean-Christophe Mayer, 'The decline of the chronicle and Shakespeare's history plays', *Shakespeare Survey*, 63, *Shakespeare's English histories and their afterlives* (Cambridge, 2010), which, in its latter stages broaches similar themes to Walsh's work, but rather strangely does not engage with it.
106. Walsh, *Elizabethan performance of history*, p. 131.
107. Ibid., p. 53.
108. Ibid., p. 39.
109. Ibid., p. 154.
110. Ibid., p. 133.
111. This, of course, is the polarity around which Phyllis Rackin organised much of her analysis of 'Shakespeare's English chronicles'; see esp. chapter 2 ('Ideological conflict, alternative plots and the problem of historical causation') in her seminal *Stages of history*.
112. Martin Dzelzainis, 'Shakespeare and political thought', in David Scott Kastan, ed., *A companion to Shakespeare* (Oxford, 1999), pp. 100–16.
113. Walsh, *Elizabethan performance of history*, pp. 145–46.
114. Ibid., p. 148.
115. Ibid., p. 151.
116. Cited in Rackin, *Stages of history*, p. 112.
117. McMillin and MacClean, *The Queen's Men*, p. 161.
118. Ibid., pp. 165–66.
119. Walsh, *Elizabethan performance of history*, p. 170.
120. Ibid., p. 2.
121. Ibid., p. 19.
122. Walter Cohen, *Drama of a nation: public theater in Renaissance England and Spain* (Ithaca, 1985), p. 183.
123. Out of a huge literature see especially A.P. Rossiter, *Angel with horns: fifteen lectures on Shakespeare* (London, 1989) *passim* but especially chapter 3, 'Ambivalence: the dialectic of the histories' and Graham Bradshaw, *Shakespeare's skepticism* (Hassocks, 1987) and idem, *Misrepresentations: Shakespeare and the materialists* (Ithaca and London, 1993), *passim*, but especially p. 124, 'you write as though going round and round were the only good'. Also see Paola Pugliatti, *Shakespeare the historian* (Basingstoke, 1996), chapter 3, 'Perspectivism'.
124. As Graham Bradshaw observes, Shakespeare's purposive departures from his sources are 'more consistent with a wish to start, not to settle, debate'. Bradshaw, *Misrepresentations*, p. 32.
125. Annabel Patterson, *Censorship and interpretation: the condition of writing and reading in early modern England* (Madison, 1984), pp. 7, 18. 'Unlike other theories', Patterson writes, hers 'does not privilege either writer or reader, or eliminate either. It is hospitable to, indeed dependent upon, a belief in authorial intention; yet it is incapable of reduction to a positivist belief in meanings that authors can fix. Indeed, what this study of the hermeneutics of censorship shows happening over and over again is that authors who build ambiguity into their works have no control over what happens to them later.'

126. Richard Dutton, *Mastering the revels: the regulation and censorship of English Renaissance drama* (Iowa City, 1991), pp. 89, 85.

127. Deborah Shuger, *Censorship and cultural sensibility: the regulation of language in Tudor–Stuart England* (Philadelphia, 2006).

128. Dutton, *Mastering the revels*, p. 115.

129. Ibid., pp. 79, 80.

130. Ibid., p. 96.

131. Cf. Dutton's remark that 'we should be wary of crude analogies with Stalinist eastern Europe, where embarrassing historical figures comparable with More (like Trotsky) have been treated as villains or non-persons.' Ibid., p. 86.

132. The original reaction against the idea of a rigorous censorship system was in large part a response to the work of Christopher Hill, who emphasised the role of 'the censorship' in forcing underground the vast body of heterodox thought that he saw running through early modern England, 'from the Lollards to the Levellers', as he put it in a notorious article; a strand of thought the nature of which was revealed to the world in the efflorescence of radical thought and expression that the collapse of 'the censorship' in the 1640s enabled. Hill's account can be set against Nicholas Tyacke's concern with the ways in which the public expression of anti-Calvinist and proto-Arminian opinions was suppressed in the period before the 1620s. The work of Sheila Lambert was crucial in launching the reaction against the views of both Hill and Tyacke. See her 'The printers and the government, 1604–40' in R. Myers and M. Harris, eds, *Aspects of printing from 1600* (Oxford, 1987), pp. 1–29 and her 'Richard Montagu, Arminianism and censorship', *Past & Present*, 124 (1989), pp. 36–68. Also see her 'State control of the press in theory and practice: the role of the Stationers' Company before 1640' in Robin Myers and Michael Harris, eds, *Censorship and the control of print in England and France, 1600–1910* (Winchester: St Paul's Bibliographies, 1992), pp. 1–32. In literary matters a seminal early contribution was made by Blair Worden, 'Literature and political censorship in early modern England' in A.C. Duke and C.A. Tamse, eds, *Too mighty to be free: censorship and the press in Britain and the Netherlands* (Zutphen, 1987), pp. 45–62. These have been followed by a rush of more recent work. Of which see, for instance, Janet Clare, *'Art made tongue-tied by authority': Elizabethan and Jacobean dramatic censorship* (Manchester, 1990); Richard Dutton, *Mastering the revels*; Deborah Shuger, *Censorship and cultural sensibility*. On press censorship, Cyndia Clegg's masterful trilogy now dominates the field. See her *Press censorship in Elizabethan England* (Cambridge, 1997); *Press censorship in Jacobean England* (Cambridge, 2001); *Press censorship in Caroline England* (Cambridge, 2008). Also see what I take to be the best single treatment of the censorship of religious opinion, Anthony Milton's 'Licensing, censorship, and religious orthodoxy in early Stuart England', *Historical Journal*, 41 (1998), pp. 625–51.

133. Clare, *'Art made tongue-tied'*, p. 48.

134. For Dutton's discussion of Richard II see his *Mastering the revels*, pp. 117–27, quote at p. 125. For Clare's treatment of the same material, see her *'Art made tongue-tie'*, pp. 68–72.

135. See, for instance, Alex Walsham, ' "Domme "preachers"? : post-reformation English Catholicism and the culture of print', *Past & Present*, 168 (2000), pp. 72–123.

136. Peter Lake and Michael Questier, 'Puritans, papists, and the "public sphere" in early modern England: the Edmund Campion affair in context', *Journal of Modern History*, 72 (2000), pp. 587–627.

137. P. Lake, *Anglicans and puritans?*.

138. P. Collinson, *The Elizabethan puritan movement*, part 8.

139. Mortimer Levine, *The early Elizabethan succession question*.

140. J.E. Neale, 'Peter Wentworth', *English Historical Review*, 39 (1924), pp. 36–54, 175–205. Also see the article on Wentworth in ODNB.

141. Clare, *'Art made tongue-tied'*, pp. 72–76; Dutton, *Mastering the revels*, pp. 107–9.

142. In a paper on the early modern public sphere given at the Institute of Historical Research in July 2012.

143. See the discussions of *The Isle of Dogs* and *Sir Thomas More* in Dutton, *Mastering the revels*, pp. 107–9, 81–86, and Clare, *'Art made tongue-tied'*, pp. 51–58, 72–76. Interestingly, despite their proximity to the apprentice riots of the early 1590s, the no less incendiary Cade scenes in *2 Henry VI* seem to have escaped the attention of the censor, which can only call attention to the intensely situational, even episodic, workings of the 'system'.

144. See Peter Lake, 'Play it again, Solomon; the burning of Edward Elton's book and the "Calvinism" of James I, reconsidered', forthcoming.

145. We should note that when, as with the *Isle of Dogs* or later with the Bishops' Ban, circumstances did indeed dictate otherwise, the Master of the Revels was cut out of the action and the normal means of constraint and control were bypassed.
146. Cf. the remarks of McMillin and MacClean, *The Queen's Men*, pp. 13–14; 'the well-told story pits the crown against the city, with the crown attempting through its decisions to protect the theatre industry while gaining control over it, and we would suggest that the events listed above [concerning the foundation of the Queen's Men] do not "protect" the theatre industry as clearly as they place limits on its growth . . . When the privy council threatened the destruction of all play houses in 1597, apparently as a pretext for restricting the licensed companies and playhouses to two, the growing theatre industry of a generation before had been brought down to what most administrative minds would regard as a manageable size.'
147. Dutton, *Mastering the revels*, p. 126.
148. Thus Graham Bradshaw has made the interaction between a heterogeneous audience and the 'ambiguity' of the plays central to his critique of what he takes to be the 'neo Tillyardian habit of ironing out whatever conflicts with the critic's Authorized Version' through incessant recourse to a notion of 'the audience'. As he observes, 'Shakespeare belonged to that first generation of English dramatists whose livings depended on pleasing a mixed audience. He peopled his stage with Elizabethans who think and feel differently about different matters – like their counterparts in the audience, whose disagreements about matters large and small produced so many violent quarrels, litigation on the scale of a national epidemic and frequent fatalities.' Bradshaw, *Misrepresentations*, p. 32.
149. See Edward Burns' edition of *King Henry VI* (Arden Shakespeare, 3rd ser., London, 2000), pp. 1–9. Also see Lawrence Manley, 'Eagle and hound: the epitaph of Talbot and the date of *I Henry VI*' forthcoming. I should like to thank Professor Manley for allowing me to read this paper in advance of publication. The contrary position is adopted by, for instance, Michael Hattaway in his edition of the *1, 2 and 3 Henry VI* for the New Cambridge Shakespeare.
150. See Bate's edition of *Titus Andronicus* (Arden Shakespeare, 3rd ser., London, 1995), pp. 59–69.
151. The authorship is extensively discussed in Brian Vickers, *Shakespeare, co-author: a historical study of five collaborative plays* (Oxford, 2002), pp. 148–232. For Neill's comment see his article on 'Revenge tragedy' in Rebecca Bushnell, ed., quote at fn. 13.
152. James R. Siemon, ed., *King Richard III* (Arden Shakespeare, 3rd ser., London, 2009), pp. 44–51, quote at p. 46.
153. Manley and MacClean, *Lord Strange's Men*, pp. 106–7.
154. Brian Vickers, 'The troublesome reign, George Peele and the date of *King John*' in Brian Boyd, ed., *Words that count: essays on early modern authorship in honour of MacDonald P. Jackson* (Newark, 2004), pp. 78–116; Charles R. Forker, 'The troublesome reign, Richard II and the date of *King John*', *Shakespeare survey, 63, Shakespeare's English histories and their afterlives*, pp. 127–48, quote at p. 128; Beatrice Groves, 'Memory, composition, and the relationship of *King John* to *The Troublesome Raigne of King John*', *Comparative Drama*, 38 (2004), pp. 277–90.
155. See Professor Melchiori's edition of *The merry wives of Windsor* (Arden Shakespeare, 3rd ser., London, 2000), pp. 1–56.
156. David Bevington, ed., *Troilus and Cressida* (Arden Shakespeare, 3rd ser., London, 1998), pp. 6–11.
157. See for instance, Clare Asquith, *Shadowplay: the hidden belief and coded politics of William Shakespeare and his era* (New York, 2005).
158. See Lake, *Bad Queen Bess?*, chapters 3, 5, 14.
159. Gajda, 'Debating peace and war in late Elizabethan England', *Historical Journal*, 52 (2009), pp. 851–78.; idem, *The earl of Essex*, pp. 135–39, 183–88; Doran and Kewes, eds, 'Difficult and dangerous', passim.
160. Lake and Questier, 'Taking it to the street': P. Collinson, *Richard Bancroft and Elizabethan anti-puritanism* (Cambridge, 2013), chapter 10; P. Lake and M. Questier, 'The public politics of regime change: Thomas Digges, Robert Parsons and Sir Francis Hastings contest the religio-political arithmetic of the Elizabethan fin de siècle', forthcoming in the *Historical Journal*.
161. Gajda, *The earl of Essex*; Paul Hammer, 'The smiling crocodile: the earl of Essex and late Elizabethan "popularity" ', pp. 95, 115; Alex Gajda, 'Debating war and peace in late Elizabethan England' and idem, '*The State of Christendom* : history, political thought and the Essex circle', *Historical Research*, 81 (2008), pp. 423–46.
162. For an imaginative exercise in just such an experiment see Bradshaw, *Misrepresentations*, pp. 55–56, for an extended riff on the varied composition of the first audiences of *Henry V*.

Chapter 1: Losing legitimacy

1. Peter Lake, *Bad Queen Bess?*
2. On this see, for instance, Andrew Hadfield, 'The political significance of the first tetralogy', in John McDiarmid, ed., *The monarchical republic of early modern England* (Aldershot, 2007), pp. 49–63.
3. Edward Berry, *Patterns of decay: Shakespeare's early histories* (Charlottesville, 1975), pp. 36, 38.
4. In so doing as David Womersley has pointed out, Shakespeare goes considerably beyond, or rather very considerably improves upon, his sources in Holinshed and Hall: see Womersley, *Divinity and state*, pp. 239–42.
5. For a detailed (and perhaps overly determined) attempt to nail down the equivalence between Gloucester and Burghley see Chris Fitter, 'Emergent Shakespeare and the politics of protest: *2 Henry VI* in historical contexts', *English Literary History*, 72 (2005), pp. 129–58.
6. In his eagerness to identify Shakespeare as a radical opponent of the status quo, Fitter either does not notice or chooses to ignore the fact that the play leaves us in no doubt both of Gloucester's innocence of the charges brought against him and of the self-serving malice that lies behind those charges. The play is extremely critical of what it portrays as the almost entirely vicious propensities of an emergent establishment, built on the graves of old established counsellors like Gloucester, but it uses a somewhat idealised vision of the passing generation to make its case.
7. For the effects of this changing of the guard on religious policy see Patrick Collinson, *The Elizabethan puritan movement*, part 8, chapter 1. On the political atmosphere more generally and the feud between Essex and Raleigh, in particular, see Paul Hammer, *The polarization of Elizabethan politics*, pp. 64–70, 83–87. Also see Chris Fitter, *Radical Shakespeare* (Abingdon, 2011), pp. 108–9.

Chapter 2: Disorder dissected (i)

1. A resonant, and now famous, phrase coined by Natalie Davis in the title of chapter 5 of her *Society and culture in early modern France* (Stanford, 1975).
2. This aspect of the play has been much commented upon of late and what follows is deeply indebted to the seminal reading of the play in Jean Howard and Phyllis Rackin, *Engendering a nation* (London, 1997) chapters 6 and 7. Also see chapter 4 of Rackin, *Stages of history*, 'Patriarchal history and female subversion'.
3. See Martin Ingram, 'Ridings, rough music and the "reform of popular culture" in early modern England', *Past & Present*, 105 (1984), pp. 79–113; idem, 'Ridings, rough music, and mocking rhymes in early modern England', in Barry Reay, ed., *Popular culture in seventeenth-century England* (London, 1985), pp. 166–97; idem, ' "Scolding women cucked or washed": a crisis in gender relations in early modern England?' in Jennifer Kermode and Garthine Walker, eds, *Women, crime and the courts in early modern England* (London, 1994), pp. 48–80. For a different take see David Underdown, 'The taming of the scold: the enforcement of patriarchal authority in early modern England', in Anthony Fletcher and John; Stevenson, eds, *Order and disorder in early modern England* (Cambridge, 1985), pp. 116–36 and most recently Underdown's last article,"But the Shows of their Street": civic pageantry and charivari in a Somerset town', *Journal of British Studies*, 50 (2011), pp. 4–23.
4. Howard and Rackin, *Engendering a nation*, pp. 84–85.
5. Peter Lake, 'Deeds against nature: cheap print, Protestantism and murder in early Stuart England' K. Sharpe and P. Lake, eds, *Culture and politics in early Stuart England* (London, 1994), pp. 257–83, 361–7.
6. Emrys Jones, *The origins of Shakespeare* (Oxford, 1971), pp. 38–52; Beatrice Groves, *Texts and tradition: religion in Shakespeare, 1592-1604* (Oxford, 2007), pp. 42, 119–20; Donald Watson, *Shakespeare's early history plays: politics at play on the Elizabethan stage* (Basingstoke, 1990), p. 91. Watson makes the same point about the murder of Henry VI by Gloucester, ibid., p. 98.
7. As Dominique Goy-Blanquet observes, Shakespeare went considerably beyond his sources in putting together his picture of Margaret; 'just as in *2 Henry VI* he made her directly responsible for the murder of Gloucester, which in the sources she did no more than condone', so in 'York's mock coronation, Shakespeare borrows a molehill from Holinshed, a bloodied handkerchief from Kyd, and puts the whole blame on Margaret who, in the chronicle, was not

present at York's death'. Dominique Goy-Blanquet, *Shakespeare's early history plays: from chronicle to stage* (Oxford, 2003), p. 172. For an expansion of this point see Paola Pugliatti, ' "More than history can pattern": the Jack Cade rebellion in Shakespeare's *Henry VI, 2*, *Journal of Medieval and Renaissance Studies*, 22 (1992), pp. 451–78, pp. 459–61. 'What Shakespeare sees in Margaret as destructive ambition is described by Hall as courage and political virtue'.

8. For no apparent reason, Womersley identifies the 'fiend' at work here not as the devil but rather as 'Antichrist' (*Divinity and state*, p. 245). There seems to be no good reason for this identification, particularly since the diagnosis comes from the entirely orthodox (i.e. in late sixteenth-century terms, Catholic) Henry VI. Moreover, while the devil was widely believed to be active at the deathbed of many a Christian, so far as I am aware, 'Antichrist' was not. However, there is more at stake here than a certain looseness of thought or expression, for the point is crucial for Womersley's otherwise rather mysterious claim that 'the death of Winchester can be read as a lurid essay in the apocalypse'; which claim is, in turn, central to his attempt to read these plays as written within what he identifies as a determinedly, even an aggressively, Protestant 'mode of apocalypse' (ibid., p. 250); a mode that – whatever precisely he means by that phrase – seems to me to be almost entirely absent from both *2* and *3 Henry VI*, which are dominated, as Womersley himself observes elsewhere, by 'politique and Machiavelian elements'; elements which allowed Shakespeare 'to evoke the downward spiral into chronic political crisis which dominates', I would argue, not only *3* but also much of *2 Henry VI*. (See ibid., p. 259.)

9. As Pugliatti again points out, in Hall Beaufort is 'never connected with the plotting of Gloucester's death', which in turn is the grounds of the play's depiction of his desperate death, something at most hinted at in Hall. See Pugliatti, 'More than history can pattern', p. 461.

10. Watson, *Shakespeare's early history plays*, p. 98.

11. See Leah Marcus, *Puzzling Shakespeare* (Berkeley, 1988), chapter 2, 'Elizabeth', to which the following account is much indebted; although Marcus' attention is concentrated far more there on Joan of Arc as epitome of the evils of 'female dominance', she does make passing reference to Margaret's succeeding Joan 'as the reigning "disorderly woman" upon Joan's death'. See pp. 75, 89. Also see Katherine Eggert, *Showing like a queen* (Philadelphia, 2000), esp. chapter 3.

Chapter 3: Disorder dissected (ii)

1. See for instance Michael D. Bristol, *Carnival and theatre* (London, 1989), chapter 6, 'A complete exit from the present order of life'.

2. See, for instance François Laroque's remark that Cade's rebellion 'seems to herald the province of the land of Cockaigne' and his recognition in Cade of 'the vein of parodic eloquence that a Lord of Misrule would favour . . . a carnival king whose reign ushers in a world set upside down'. F. Laroque, *Shakespeare's festive world* (Cambridge, 1991) p. 251. On Cade's rebellion, utopia and what he terms 'the complex language of popular utopian memory' see Michael Bristol, *Carnival and theatre*, pp. 89–90. On the connections between festivity and revolt see Peter Burke, *Popular Culture in early modern Europe* (London, 1978), pp. 270–81. Also see Richard Wilson, 'A mingled yarn: Shakespeare and the cloth workers' in his *Will Power* (London, 1993), pp. 22–44.

3. C.L. Barber's observations that 'the scenes of the Jack Cade rebellion . . . are an astonishingly consistent expression of anarchy by clowning: the popular rising is presented throughout as a saturnalia, ignorantly undertaken in earnest' and that 'the village saturnalia of the Lord of Misrule's men was in its way a sort of rising; setting up a mock lord and demanding homage for him are playfully rebellious gestures, into which Dionysian feeling can flow' (*Shakespeare's festive comedies* (Princeton, 1959, pp. 13, 29)) do not perhaps do full justice to the serious political threat and intent of Cade, and, in certain moods at least, of his rebel followers.

4. Forthcoming in a volume of essays edited by Chris Fitter, to be published by OUP.

5. The quarto is reproduced in the Arden edition, 3rd series, edited by Ronald Knowles, pp. 376–497

6. Wilson, 'Shakespeare and the cloth workers'. While Wilson sees this as an attempt by the emergent theatre industry to distance itself from the taint of genuinely popular, plebeian festivity and disorder, to which certain elements in the city of London wanted to assimilate it, Chris Fitter sees what he identifies as the genuinely popular elements in these scenes as proof positive of a 'radical Shakespeare's' solidarity with the political agency of the people. See Chris Fitter, *Radical Shakespeare*, esp. chapters 2–5.

7. Laroque, *Shakespeare's festive world*, p. 252.

8. On this see Robert Hornback's seminal article, 'Staging puritanism in the early 1590s: the carnivalesque rebellious clown as anti-puritan stereotype', *Renaissance and reformation/ Renaissance et reforme*, 32 (2003), 31–67.

9. The N[ational] A[rchives], P[ublic] R[ecord] O[ffice], S.P. 12/ 239, fol. 123r.-124r, quote at fol. 123v.-124r., draft newsletter by Thomas Phelippes, 19 July 1591. The best account of the Hacket and Copinger affair and its connections with the mainstream puritan movement is now Michael Winship 'Puritans, politics, and lunacy: the Copinger–Hacket conspiracy as the apotheosis of Elizabethan Presbyterianism', *Sixteenth Century Journal*, 38 (2007), pp. 345–69. Also see Alexandra Walsham, ' "Frantick Hacket": prophecy, sorcery, insanity, and the Elizabethan puritan movement', *Historical Journal*, 41 (1998), pp. 27–66. On the anti-puritan uses to which this material was almost immediately put see Hornbeck 'Staging Puritanism in the Early 1590s', and P. Lake and M. Questier, *The Antichrist's lewd hat; puritans, papists and players in post reformation England* (London, 2002), chapter 13, esp. pp. 551–53. For the long-term association of puritanism with various sorts of 'popularity' see P. Lake, 'Puritanism, (monarchical) republicanism, and monarchy; or John Whitgift, antipuritanism, and the "invention" of popularity', *Journal of Medieval and Early Modern Studies*, 40 (2010) pp. 463–95.

10. Chris Fitter, *Radical Shakespeare*, chapter 3, 'Jack Cade, the Hacket rising, and Shakespeare's vision of popular rebellion', pp. 46–80. As we have seen, the play shows us Cade's plebeian followers displaying a healthy scepticism in the face of both his reformist and dynastic claims. On Fitter's account this leaves room for Shakespeare to retain an impeccably 'radical' appreciation for the political agency of the populace, when it was untainted by the class treason of demagogues like Cade. Be that as it may, the play's picture of Cade as a sort of Hacket-like puritan agitator, playing on both the susceptibilities of the people and the factious divisions and self-interest of the nobility to work his own ends, would scarcely have enhanced any sympathy with the people's cause that these scenes might have evoked in their first audiences.

11. P. Lake and Michael Questier, eds, *The Antichrist's lewd hat*, pp. 542–55.

12. Lake and Questier, *Lewd hat*, chapter 13 and Peter Lake, 'Conformist clericalism? Richard Bancroft's analysis of the socio-economic roots of presbyterianism', in William Sheils, William and Dianna Wood, eds, *The Church and wealth* (Studies in Church History, 24) (Oxford and New York, 1987), pp. 219–29.

13. P. Pugliatti, *Shakespeare the historian* (Basingstoke, 1996), p. 173.

14. Berry, *Patterns of decay*, p. 46.

Chapter 4: Hereditary 'right' and political legitimacy anatomised

1. Patrick Collinson, 'The monarchial republic of Elizabeth I', first published in the *Bulletin of the John Rylands Library*, 68 (1987), pp. 394–424 and then reprinted in his *Elizabethan Essays* (London, 1994), pp. 31–57; idem, 'The Elizabethan exclusion crisis and the Elizabethan polity', first published in the *Proceedings of the British Academy*, 84 (1994), pp. 51–92 and then reprinted in his *This England: essays on the English nation and commonwealth in the sixteenth century* (Manchester 2011), pp. 61–97.

2. BL Stowe Ms. 273, fols. 10v–11r; Bodleian Library, Carte Ms 105, fols. 22v–23r.

3. CUL Additional Ms. 9212, fols. 28v–29r.

4. As Womersley observes, the key term here is 'process', referring to 'the downward spiral into chronic political crisis' that forms the subjects of these two plays, and in particular of *Part 3*. For Womersley, this elicits what he terms 'an estrangement from the mode of apocalypse' – a mode that seems to me to be entirely absent from *2* and *3 Henry VI* – and the adoption of an altogether 'more naturalistic dramatic mode, in which politique and Machiavellian elements come steadily more to the fore'. Womersley, *Divinity and state*, p. 259.

5. As David Riggs has observed, 'the sundering of honour and politics is nowhere more apparent than in this play, where every attempt to invoke a political compromise is frustrated by the demand for personal revenge, until one finally arrives at the hollow pretense of "country's peace and brothers' loves" [V, vii, 36] that concludes the action'. David Riggs, *Shakespeare's heroical histories* (Cambridge, Mass., 1971), p. 132.

6. C. Kahn, *Man's estate: masculine identity in Shakespeare* (Berkeley, Calif., 1981), p. 85.

7. Howard and Rackin, *Engendering a nation*, pp. 91–93.

8. Berry, *Patterns of decay*, pp. 69, 73.

9. Ibid., p. 69.

10. Riggs, *Shakespeare's heroical histories*, p. 135.
11. As Naomi Conn Liebler puts it, 'we know before the play ends that Edward's reign is no more than . . . a kind of half-time interlude between the end of *3 Henry VI* and II, i, 40 of *Richard III.*' See her 'King of the hill: ritual and play in the shaping of *3 Henry VI*', in John Velz, ed., *Shakespeare's English histories: a quest for form and genre* (Binghamton, 1996), pp. 31–54, quote at p. 54.
12. I do not share Erskine-Hill's assessment of the debates conducted in these plays about genealogical right, i.e. I do not think that they unequivocally favour the Yorkist line. This is to take Henry's admission that 'my claim's weak' as though it were literally true; a final balanced judgement about the relative strengths and weaknesses of the Yorkist and Lancastrian claims, rather than reading it as a function of Henry's fatal weakness as king. Rather these plays establish that there are weaknesses in all the rival claims and that the right to rule cannot be established through purely jural means or arguments. In his *Divinity and state* Womersley follows Erskine-Hill's decidedly Yorkist line of interpretation, p. 247.

Chapter 5: How not to go there

1. See the materials listed in note 149 of the Introduction.
2. Womersley takes the fact that the play allows Mortimer to state a Yorkist version of dynastic right 'so plainly and unequivocally' to mean that Shakespeare can be read as simply endorsing what he terms the 'staunchly Yorkist' inflection of Foxe's version of late medieval English history. For Womersley this reinforces his claim that 'in *I Henry VI* Shakespeare dramatized Foxe's apocalyptic interpretation of Henry's reign as a period of intense, convulsive efforts against England by Antichrist'. Womerlsey, *Divinity and state*, pp. 246–47. On this basis he then claims that 'in the light of this explanation of the superior Yorkist claim to the throne, the practical defects of Henry's reign are strengthened from being mere instances of disadvantage to become instead the overt signs and tokens of a more fundamental wrong'. That claim is made on p. 247, but by p. 297 it has morphed into the altogether more comprehensive assertion that 'the sinful calamity' of the 'usurpation of the Lancastrians' was 'the political premise on which he [Shakespeare] had written the earlier plays'. There seems to me to be almost no textual warrant within those earlier plays for such a reading. It is thus surely no accident that this assertion is to be found not in Womersley's discussion of the *Henry VI* plays at all but rather in that of *Richard II*. Wormersley thus perpetuates a tendency endemic in a great deal of the criticism on these plays to read the *Henry VI* plays in terms of a providential framework set by *Richard II*. The more stringently chronological and contextual, i.e. historical, approach taken in this book renders such assumptions and procedures entirely out of court.
3. Cf. Gillian Woods, *Shakespeare's unreformed fictions* (Oxford, 2013), pp. 46–50.
4. Ibid., p. 53.
5. Ibid., pp. 55, 50.
6. Cf. P. Lake, 'The significance of the Elizabethan identification of the pope as Antichrist', *Journal of Ecclesiastical History* (1980), pp. 161–78.
7. L. Marcus, *Puzzling Shakespeare*, chapter 2, 'Elizabeth'.
8. Womersley flags the 'vigorous anti-Catholicism' which pervades the play, *Divinity and state*, pp. 241–44; noting that 'through Shakespeare's juxtaposition of events in France with events at home', *1 Henry VI* shows 'the English struggling with Antichrist on two fronts'. 'In *I Henry VI* Shakespeare dramatized Foxe's apocalyptic interpretation of Henry's reign as a period of intense, convulsive efforts against England by Antichrist; and he presented two Catholic and diabolicial figures, Winchester and Joan, as the joint spearheads threatening England in that crisis.' Quotes at pp. 244, 246. He does not, however, go on to note the close parallels between the situation staged in the play and events in the early 1590s when it was first written and staged or the puritan/anti-prelatical, as well as protestant/anti-papal resonances of this language and these scenes.
9. Woods, *Shakespeare's unreformed fictions*, pp. 50–51.
10. Paul Hammer, *The polarisation of Elizabethan politics*. For Essex's rivalry with Raleigh see pp. 64–68, 84–85. For the clash with Kildare see p. 90, n. 85. For Burghley's support of Essex over and during the Rouen campaign see pp. 102–5.
11. Hammer, *Polarisation*, pp. 106–7. For the news pamphlet see Paul Voss, *Elizabethan news pamphlets* (Pittsburgh, 2001), pp. 192–96.
12. Hammer *Polarisation*, p. 104.
13. Ibid., p. 111.

14. Sir Walter Raleigh, *A report of the truth of the fight about the Isles of Azores . . . betwixt the Revenge . . . and an Armada of the king of Spain* (London, 1591), sigs. Bv–B2r.
15. Ibid., sigs. B4r–Cv.
16. Ibid., sig. A3r.
17. Ibid., sigs. A3r–A4v.
18. Ibid., sig. C3r.
19. Ibid., sig. Dv.
20. Ibid., sig. D2r.
21. Ibid., sig. A4v.
22. Hammer, *Polarisation*, p. 116.
23. Ibid., pp. 115–18.
24. Ibid., p. 104.
25. Ibid., pp. 273, 288, 304.
26. Alexander Legatt, 'The death of John Talbot', in J. Velz, ed., *Shakespeare's English histories: a quest for genre and form* (Binghamton, 1996), pp. 11–30, quotation at p. 19.
27. Hammer, *Polarisation*, p. 288.
28. Ibid., pp. 116–17.

Chapter 6: *Richard III*

1. Donald Watson, *Shakespeare's early history plays*, pp. 110, 114, 119; Emrys Jones, *The origins of Shakespeare*, p. 195.
2. See Randall Martin, 'Catilines and Machiavels: reading resistance in *3 Henry VI*', in Richard Dutton, Alison Findlay and Richard Wilson, eds, *Theatre and religion: Lancastrian Shakespeare* (Manchester, 2003) pp. 105–15.
3. J. Howard and P. Rackin, *Engendering a nation*, p. 96.
4. John Danby, *Shakespeare's doctrine of nature* (London, 1949), p. 60.
5. Robert G. Hunter, *Shakespeare and the mystery of God's judgments* (Athens, 1976) p. 95.
6. Ibid., p. 91.
7. Womersley, *Divinity and state*, p. 259.
8. Malcolm Gaskill, *Crime and mentalities in early modern England* (Cambridge, 2000), pp. 227–34.
9. Ibid., pp. 219–20, 331–32, 233–34, 371–72.
10. Jones, *Origins*, p. 203.
11. On this see Harold Brooks, 'Richard III, unhistorical amplifications: the women's scenes and Seneca', *Modern Language Review*, 75 (1980), pp. 721–37.
12. Such practices are not without historical warrant or precedent. John Bossy notes the practice of having a mass for the dead said for a still-living enemy as a form of curse to hasten him or her on their way out of this world. Puritans too could allow themselves to pray for the death of their enemies, petitioning God that if he had no plans to bring their oppressors to repentance could he please remove them from the world sooner rather than later.
13. Brooks, '*Richard III*, the women's scenes and Seneca', p. 722.
14. Womersley, *Divinity and state*, p. 263.
15. Jones, *Origins*, p. 220.
16. Harry Berger Jr, *Making trifles of terrors: redistributing complicities in Shakespeare* (Stanford, 1997), p. 279.
17. For some pregnant remarks along these lines see Charles K. Cannon, ' "As in a theatre": *Hamlet* in the light of the doctrine of predestination', *Studies in English literature, 1500–1900*, 11 (1971), pp. 203–22.
18. Cf. Alison Thorne, ' "O, lawful let it be? That I have room . . . to curse awhile": voicing the nation's conscience in female complaint in *Richard III*, *King John* and *Henry VIII*', in Willy Maley and Margaret Trudeau-Clayton, eds, *This England, that Shakespeare* (Farnham, 2010), pp. 105–24.
19. Jones, *Origins*, p. 223.
20. Ibid., p. 231.
21. Womersley, *Divinity and state*, pp. 267, 262. Cf. Cannon's remarks that 'a rigorous, uncompromising view of predestination leads inevitably to the idea of a stage play' and that 'as the play presents the fiction of a character's acting for himself while actually following the script that has been set down for him' [in this instance by history and by Shakespeare], 'so life on earth presents the illusion of man's acting voluntarily while doing exactly what God

has predetermined before his life drama begins'. Cannon, 'Hamlet and predestination', quotations at pp. 220, 221.

22. As J.P. Brockbank has observed, the imagery of Richard hacking his way out of a thorny wood might be taken as a symbolic description of birth; see his 'The frame of disorder – Henry VI' in *Early Shakespeare* (Stratford-upon-Avon Studies, no. 3) London, 1961, pp. 97–98.

23. Robert G. Hunter, *Shakespeare and the mystery of God's judgments*, pp. 97, 78.

24. Ibid., pp. 98–99.

25. Barbara Hodgdon, *The end crowns all: closure and controversy in Shakespeare's history* (Princeton, 1991), p. 113. Also see Wilbur Sanders, *The dramatist and the received idea* (Cambridge, 1968), pp. 74–75. Quotation from *The true tragedy of Richard III*.

26. Cf. Jones, *Origins*, p. 205.

27. For this point see Moody Prior, *The drama of power: studies in Shakespeare's history plays* (Evanston, 1973), p. 137.

28. *The true tragedy of Richard III* (London, 1594), sig. I2r.

29. Hodgdon, *The end crowns all*, pp. 123, 124.

30. Pauline Croft, 'Libels, popular literacy and public opinion in early modern England', *Historical Research*, 68 (1995), pp. 266–85. Idem, 'The reputation of Robert Cecil', *History Today*, 43 (1993), pp. 41–47.

Chapter 7: Going Roman

1. T.J.B. Spencer, 'Shakespeare and the Elizabethan Romans', *Shakespeare Survey*, 10 (1957), pp. 27–38, quotes at p. 32.

2. Jonathan Bate, ed., *Titus Andronicus* (The Arden Shakespeare, London, 1995), p. 77.

3. Ibid., p. 21.

4. Lorna Hutson, 'Rethinking the "Spectacle of the Scaffold": juridical epistemologies and English revenge tragedy', *Representations*, 89 (2005), pp. 30–58.

5. On parallels between the play and the works of Southwell, see John Klause, 'Politics, heresy and martyrdom in Shakespeare's sonnet 124 and *Titus Andronicus*', in James Schiffer, ed., *Shakespeare's sonnets: critical essays* (New York, 1999), pp. 219–40.

6. See Nicholas Moschovakis, ' "Irreligious piety" and Christian history; persecution as pagan anachronism in *Titus Andronicus*', *Shakespeare Quarterly*, 53 (2002), 460–86.While I do not agree with all of his conclusions, the present reading of the play owes a great deal to this article. Andreas Hofele makes the association between the horrific violence portrayed in the play and the real events played out on the scaffold. He also makes an explicit link between the style of dehumanising violence found in the play and martyrdom, but the form of martyrdom he chooses to discuss is that of protestants, or rather proto-protestants – his main example is John Hus – by Catholics, as recounted by John Foxe. He makes no mention of the far more obvious and directly contemporary referent, the martyrdom of Catholics by the protestant Elizabethan regime, which, with its dismemberment and disembowelling of the victim's body and the subsequent boiling and public display of the resulting body parts, fits rather more closely both with the events staged and the imagery deployed in the play and with Hofele's concern with cannibalism as a way of figuring the dehumanising effects of extreme violence. See his *Stage, stake and scaffold* (Oxford, 2011), esp. chapter 4, 'Cannibal-Animal: figurations of the (in)human in Montaigne, Foxe and Shakespearean revenge tragedy'.

7. Eugene Waith, 'The metamorphosis of violence in *Titus Andronicus*', *Shakespeare Survey*, 10 (1957), pp. 39–49.

8. See the article on Walsingham in the *ODNB*.

9. The younger brother of Edward IV, Richard 'did put to death his two nephews . . . to wit king Edward V and his little brother, and made himself king, and, albeit he sinned grievously by taking upon him the crown in this wicked manner, yet, when his nephews were once dead, he might in reason seem to be lawful king, both in respect that he was the next male in blood, after his said brother, as also for that, by divers acts of parliament, both before and after the death of those infants, his title was authorised and made good, and yet no man will say (I think) but that he was lawfully also deposed again afterward by the commonwealth, which called out of France Henry Earl of Richmond to chastise him and to put him down. And took from him both life and kingdom in the field and was king himself after him, by the name of king Henry VII. And no man, I suppose, will say but that he was lawfully king also, which yet cannot be, except the other might lawfully be deposed'. Robert Parsons, *The conference about the next succession* (Antwerp, 1594/5), part I, p. 61.

Chapter 8: The Elizabethan resonances of the reign of King John

1. Michael Questier, *Catholicism and community in early modern England: politics, aristocratic patronage and religion, c. 1550–1640* (Cambridge, 2006).
2. Alex Gajda, *The earl of Essex*, pp. 135–40. For the claim that the appearance of the *Conference* disrupted the publication plans of the Essex circle at a crucial moment in 1595, see ibid. p. 139.
3. Beatrice Groves, 'Memory, composition and the relationship of *King John* to the *The troublesome reign of King John*', pp. 277–90.
4. John Leslie, *A defence of the honour of . . . Mary, Queen of Scotland, and Dowage . . . with a declaration as well of her right, title and interest in the crown of England* (London, 1569) with later editions printed in Liège in 1571, and Rheims in 1580 and 1584.
5. *A defence of the honour of the right high, mighty and noble Princess Mary Queen of Scotland and dowager of France with a declaration as well of her right, title & interest to the succession of the crown of England* (1569), fols. 52r, 63r–v, 77r–79r.
6. John Leslie *A treatise touching the right, title, and interest of the most excellent princess Mary, Queen of Scotland, and of the most noble king James, her graces son, to the succession of the crown of England* (Rouen, printed by G. L'Oyselet, 1584).
7. BL Stowe Mss 253, *An answer to a discourse of John Leslie*, fols. 22v–30r, quote at fol. 24r. Leslie's tract drew on, and in many ways summarised, earlier debates from the 1560s and in particular a nexus of arguments formulated by Edmund Plowden, for which see Marie Axton, *The queen's two bodies* and Mortimer Levine, *The early Elizabethan succession question*, esp. chapter 7, 'The rule against alien inheritance'; for Arthur see ibid., pp. 32, 102–4.
8. William Allen, *A true and modest defense of English Catholics*, in Robert M. Kingdom, ed., *The execution of justice in England* (Ithaca, NY, 1965), 168.
9. Ibid., pp. 244–45.
10. Ibid., p. 45.
11. *The two books of homilies appointed to be read in churches* (Oxford, 1859), pp. 593–94.
12. See Thomas Freeeman, 'John Bale's Book of Martyrs? The account of king John in Acts and Monuments', *Reformation*, 3 (1998), pp. 175–223.
13. Robert Parsons, *The conference about the next succession*, part I, p. 194.
14. Ibid., part II, pp. 87–90.
15. The first page numbers refer to Raphael Holinshed, *The chronicles of England from William the Conqueror . . . until the year 1577, faithfully gathered and compiled by Raphael Holinshed and continued from the year 1577 until the present year of grace 1585, newly amended and enlarged* (London, 1587), Vol. I. The page references in the squared bracket are to *Holinshed's Chronicles*, ed. Henry Ellis, 6 vols. (London, 1807–8), vol. 2. Thus, pp. 158–59 [p. 275].
16. Ibid., p. 158 [p. 274]
17. Ibid., p. 164 [pp. 284–85]
18. Ibid., 167 [p. 289]
19. Ibid., p. 164. [p. 286]
20. Ibid., pp. 191, 183, 'to appease this fury of the people not only policy but power was required'. [pp. 329–30]
21. Ibid., p. 175 [p. 304]
22. Ibid., pp. 177–78 [pp. 306–7]
23. Ibid., pp. 190–91 [pp. 329–30]
24. Ibid., p. 180 [p.311]
25. Ibid., p. 186 [p. 321]
26. Ibid., 190 [pp. 329–30]
27. Ibid., p. 192 [p. 336]
28. Ibid., p. 192 [p. 336]
29. Ibid., p. 180 [pp. 311–12]
30. Ibid., 191 [p. 330]
31. Ibid., p.186 [p. 322]
32. Ibid. [p. 300]
33. Ibid., p. 187 [p. 324]
34. Ibid., 192 [pp. 332–33]
35. Ibid., p. 196, 'it may seem that in some respects he was not greatly superstitious and yet not void of a religious zeal towards the maintenance of the clergy as by bountiful liberality bestowed in building of abbies and churches . . . it may partly appear.'

36. Ibid., p.192 [p.335]
37. Ibid., p. 168 [pp. 290–91]
38. Ibid., p. 192 [p. 332]

Chapter 9: The first time as polemic, the second time as play

1. I cite from the edition of *The troublesone reign* in Geofrey Bullough, *Narrative and dramataic sources of Shakespeare; later English history plays* (London, 1966), pp. 72–151.
2. On Wentworth see Sir John Neale, 'Peter Wentworth' *English Historical Review*, 39 (1924), pp. 36–54, 175–205 and the article in ODNB. See also Paulina Kewes, 'The Puritan, the Jesuit and the Jacobean succession', in Susan Doran and Paulina Kewes, eds, *Doubtful and dangerous: the question of the succession in late Elizabethan England* (Manchester, 2014), pp. 47–70.
3. Cf. Adrien Bonjour, 'The road to Swinstead Abbey: a study of the sense and structure of *King John*', *English Literary History*, 4 (1951), pp. 253–74; 'thus, if King John is considered as a usurper by Elinor and Faulconbridge – the two characters who are closest to him in blood and the stoutest supporters of his cause – it is clear that Shakespeare wanted his audience to realise that fact' (quotation at p. 257).
4. Robert Lane ' "The sequence of posterity": Shakespeare's *King John* and the succession controversy', *Studies in Philology*, 92 (1995), 460–81. Also see Mortimer Levine, *The early Elizabethan succession question*, esp. chapter 9 'The will of Henry VIII'.
5. Cf. David Womersley, *Divinity and state*, pp. 277–78; '*The Troublesome Raigne* goes to great lengths to present Philip as a noble character in whom distinguished birth is patent despite the obscurity of his circumstances', thus creating 'a picture of essential nobility asserting itself despite illegitimacy'.
6. Edward Gieskes, ' "He is but a bastard to the time": status and service in *The troublesome reign of King John* and Shakespeare's *King John*,' *ELH*, 65 (1998), pp. 779–98.
7. On this see Womersley, *Divinity and state*, pp. 278–79.
8. Gieskes, ' "He is but a bastard to the time": quotation at p. 787. Also see J.L. Calderwood, 'Commodity and honour *in King John*', in Eugene M. Wraith, ed., *Shakespeare the Histories: a collection of critical essays* (Englewood Cliffs, NJ, 1965), pp. 85–101.
9. Michael Mannheim, 'The four voices of the bastard', in Deborah Curren-Aquino, ed., *King John: new perspectives* (Newark, Del., 1989), pp. 126–35, quote at p. 129
10. Thus I think Womersley (*Divinity and state*, p. 274) goes a little too far when he describes the bastard as one who 'feels unthreatened by' the 'vulnerability', and 'untainted' by the 'corruption', of the time and is thus 'confident that he can surf on its turbulence to his own advantage'. At this point in the play, confidence is a quality that neither his speeches enunciate nor his actions enact. And later, of course, the mere pursuit of commodity does not characterise or explain his conduct.
11. Michael Neill, ' "In everything illegitimate": imagining the bastard in English Renaissance drama', in his *Putting history to the question: power, politics and society in English Renaissance drama* (New York, 2000), pp. 127–47, quote p. 144, quoting Joseph Candido, 'Blots, stains and adulteries: the impurities in *King John*', in Deborah Curren-Aquino, ed., *King John: new perspectives* (Newark, Del., 1989), pp. 114–25.
12. David Womersley, 'The politics of Shakespeare's *King John*', *The Review of English Studies*, 40 (1989) pp. 497–515, quotation at p. 502.
13. Jones, *The origins of Shakespeare*, pp. 242–44.
14. Bonjour, 'The road to Swinstead Abbey', pp. 258, 260; 'If John is a usurper "with no rights in the crown at all", it is obvious that Arthur, as the legitimate heir, is much more dangerous for him and, consequently, the temptation to do away with the boy – much stronger.' 'To Pandulph, that other and even greater master of the art of Commodity, such a course of action was inevitable: given the situation and character of John (which the Legate rightly estimates according to his own standards), the King was bound to act in this way.'
15. D. Womersley, 'The politics of Shakespeare's *King John*', p. 499.
16. On this see Womersley, *Divinity and state*, pp. 269–71.
17. As Dermot Cavanagh points out, here is King John articulating, in the most strident of terms, a distinctively post-reformation Tudor erastianism. D. Cavanagh, *Language and politics in the sixteenth century history play* (Basingstoke, 2003), pp. 82, 83.
18. See my *Bad Queen Bess?* pp. 200–6, 250–54.

19. *Holinshed's Chronicles*, ed. Henry Ellis, 6 vols. (London, 1807–8), vol. 2., p. 278.
20. For the bastard's status as a vice figure see David Womersley, 'The politics of Shakespeare's *King John*', esp. pp. 503–5. Also see Emrys Jones' remark that the bastard operates as a sort of 'folk hero' and a 'spectator surrogate', through whose responses 'the true meaning of the play is mediated to us'. Jones, *Origins of Shakespeare*, pp. 244, 252, 246. This seems to me to be more accurate as a description of the bastard in the first rather than the second half of the play. On this also see Womersley, *Divinity and state*, pp. 280–81, where he observes that the play's 'first audiences' 'would have seen a character from a recognizable dramatic tradition stepping outside that tradition and becoming something else under the pressure of circum- stances . . . The Bastard outgrows a form of character taken from the Morality play, just as he outgrows its politics, which are dominated by the twin axioms of order and royalism.'
21. Womersley, 'The politics of Shakespeare's *King John*', p. 505.
22. Robert Weimann, 'Mingling vice and "worthiness" in *King John*', *Shakespeare Studies*, 27 (1999), pp. 109–33, quote at p. 111, where Weimann observes that Faulconbridge is 'made faithfully to rehearse most of the attributes of the Vice, only to go beyond them. But in doing so, he reaches out, with a remarkable twist, for something new. He seeks to redeem the un- bridled energy of the valiant performer on behalf of his arduous task in the building of, historically speaking, an anachronistic image of the nation state.' Since it is so clearly, if not present in, then at least implied or, better yet, called into being, by the play, quite how or why the resultant image of 'the nation-state' is, 'historically speaking', 'anachronistic', must remain a mystery.
23. Michael Neill, ' "In everything illegitimate" ', p. 144. Also see Robert Jones, 'Truth in *King John*', *Studies in English Literature, 1500–1900*, 25 (1985), pp. 397–417, passim, see esp. p. 402.
24. Cf. Weimann, 'Mingling vice and "worthiness" '.
25. Womersley, 'Politics of Shakespeare's *King John*'. Now see idem, *Divinity and state*, pp. 276–77.
26. Robert Jones, 'Truth in *King John*', quote at p. 413, fn. 8. Also see Bonjour, 'The road to Swinstead Abbey', p. 269; 'The bastard here attains, on the spiritual and moral plain, the dignity of a great character . . . The Bastard is now the man in whom centres the interest and sympathy of the audience: although we may approve of the lords' indignation and side with them against John . . . as soon as it leads them to join their country's enemies, they forfeit our sympathy; whereas the Bastard, who showed as great a disapproval of the deed, not only preserves our sympathy but wins more by keeping true to the King, because he realizes that John, "for all his crimes and weakness, is the only possible rallying point in the hour of extreme national danger".' Michael Mannheim sees this choice, and the bastard's subsequent conduct, as an expression of a mature 'Machiavellianism' and his fiery speeches as a form of 'studied diction', as the bastard transforms 'his earlier verbal versatility into an art requisite for the new Machiavellian state'. See his 'The four voices of the bastard' in Deborah Curren- Aquino, ed., *King John: new perspectives* (Newark, Del., 1989), pp. 126–35, quote at p. 132. This seems to me to attribute a degree of calculation to the bastard for which the play provides no warrant. As does Womersley's account of essentially the same material, in which he avers that 'loyalty and patriotism are the answers he [the bastard] comes up with to the problem of how to live in a world dangerously stripped of absolutes' and that the bastard's decision 'implies that the political realm is one in which individuals can make rational choices without being bound to dogma'. This formulation seems to me subtly but crucially wrong, since we are precisely not shown the bastard making any sort of 'rational decision'. There is no sign of calculation, or even of ratiocination here but rather a visceral rallying to the defence of a deeply tainted English king and a deeply divided England currently threat- ened by foreign invasion and rule. Womersley, *Divinity and state*, pp. 280–81.
27. Calderwood, 'Commodity and honour in *King John*'.
28. David Kastan, ' "To set a form upon that Indigest": Shakespeare's fictions of history', *Comparative Drama*, 17 (1983), pp.1–15, quote at p. 9.
29. On the possibility of the bastard's taking the throne for himself see Calderwood, 'Commodity and honour in King John', p. 100; William Matchett, 'Richard's divided heritage in *King John*', *Essays in Criticism*, 12 (1962), 231–53. Not only, as Emrys Jones observes, is there 'nothing to support such a reading, which would run counter to everything we know of his character' [Jones, *Origins of Shakespeare*, p. 259], the bastard's status as a wholly fictional character made the notion of his seizing the throne in a history play quite out of the question. For this last point see Jones, 'Truth in *King John*', p. 416, fn. 10.

30. This calls into radical question Mannheim's reading of him as, in any straightforward sense, a Machiavel.
31. Jones, 'Truth in King John', p. 402.
32. James Calderwood has subjected the moral bona fides of the revolting English nobles to a searching examination and found them guilty of a barefaced hypocrisy and pursuit of their own commodity. See Calderwood, 'Commodity and honour in *King John*', esp. pp. 90–91. Again the play gives no real textual warrant for such suspicions, and, as Jones argues, provides us with no need to doubt the moral perplexity displayed by Salisbury even in the midst of his rebellion. See Jones, 'Truth in *King John*', p. 411.
33. For a different view which sees the bastard's decision-making and in particular 'the subjection' that he 'offers Henry' as 'not the unquestioning passive submission of the medieval subject, or the personal fealty of the chivalric knight' but rather 'the voluntary obedience of a citizen who actively participates in the public sphere' see Camille Slights, 'When is a bastard not a bastard? Character and conscience in *King John*', in Paul Yachnin and Jessica Slights, eds, *Shakespeare and character* (Basingstoke, 2009), pp. 214–31, quote at p. 229. This is a view for which there seems to be no warrant whatsoever in what remains the intensely monarchical political world conjured by the play which shows us that, in the face of the foreign threat, the bastard (and perhaps even the rebel peers) experience themselves as having no choice but to accept Henry as their king and that that acceptance is anything but 'passive'. (The resort here to the terms 'medieval' and 'chivalric', and the really rather odd use of the word 'passive' to describe political obligation under the sort of personal monarchy staged in the play seem to me both anachronistic and obfuscatory.) Having said that, while there is no evidence to suggest that the play is staging, within its version of John's reign, the operation of the sort of 'public sphere' envisaged by Slights, a case could be made that, by staging in plain sight, on the public stage, such a moment of dynastic and political crisis and by emphasising the political choice made by the bastard when he stuck to John's cause, the play might be thought to have been contributing to, fostering, and indeed exploiting, for its own commercial, as well as ideological, purposes, the operation of just such an arena for thinking and talking about politics in late Elizabethan England. In other words, it was making a pitch for a certain view of the current conjuncture in a world where other versions of that conjuncture were both actually and potentially in play. On all this also see Womersley 'Politics of Shakespeare's *King John*'. And now idem, *Divinity and state*, pp. 280–81.
34. See P. Lake, 'The significance of the Elizabethan identification of the pope as Antichrist', *Journal of Ecclesiastical History*, 31 (1980), pp. 161–78.
35. Kastan, ' "To set a form upon that Indigest" ', p. 14.
36. Cf. Maley, ' "And bloody England into England gone": empire, monarchy and nation in *King John*', in Willy Maley and Margaret Trudeau-Clayton (eds), *This England, that Shakespeare* (Farnham, 2010) pp. 49–61.
37. Jones, *Origins of Shakespeare*, p. 257.
38. As such it echoes closely the notions of 'Frenchness' being canvassed in the politique accounts of the situation in France, often written by avowedly Catholic authors, translated versions of which poured off the London presses in the 1580s and early 1590s. See Lake *Bad Queen Bess?*, chapter 10, esp. pp. 245–248.
39. As Robert Long has pointed out, the Stuarts were excluded from the English throne primarily by Henry VIII's will and by the claim that they were foreign born. Shakespeare's version of John's reign goes out of its way to challenge, if not to refute, both objections through John's willingness to overturn Sir Robert Faulconbridge's will and through the play's endorsement – delivered through the testimony of John's own mother and of the bastard – of the truth of Arthur's claim. See Long, 'Sequence of posterity', pp. 465–71.
40. See Womersley's brilliant remark that *King John* operates 'almost as a dramatic laboratory', designed to display 'the faultlines in customary attitudes and beliefs'. But, as Womersley observes, Shakespeare uses that laboratory not 'to produce fresh, unorthodox, insights at the level of doctrine'. There is nothing remarkable about the play's central contention that, in the face of the threat of foreign invasion and foreign rule, all should rally to the defence of the current monarchical incumbent. Its claim to the attention of both Elizabethan audiences and more recent commentators lies rather in its pitiless portrait of that incumbent as a usurper and an increasingly ineffectual tyrant and its invocation of the next successor as the ultimate guarantor of legitimacy and order. Thus, as Womersley concludes, it is in its 'recasting of the realm of politics . . . rather than in its mere doctrines', that the independence of *King John* lies'. See Womsersley, *Divinity and state*, pp. 273, 268, 280–81.
41. Paul Hammer, *The polarisation of Elizabethan politics*, pp. 117, 242–47.

Chapter 10: *Richard II*, or the rights and wrongs of resistance

1. Cyndia Clegg, ' "By the choise and inuitation of al the realme": *Richard II* and Elizabethan press censorship', *Shakespeare Quarterly*, pp.432–448

2. I thus find myself, for reasons that I hope will become clear below, entirely at odds with Deborah Shuger's claim that while other Elizabethan renditions of the reign concentrate on the details of 'Richard's misgovernment', in Shakespeare's account 'the question . . . is left hopelessly murky'. D. Shuger, 'Religion and honour in Richard II', in K. Graham and P. Collington, eds, *Shakespeare and religious change* (Basingstoke, 2009), pp. 40–41. On my reading, there is nothing murky about the delineation of Richard's tyranny in Shakespeare's version, although Shuger is quite right to observe that, unlike in the other contemporary accounts, the depiction of Richard's serial misgovernment is not the focus of Shakespeare's play. While A.P. Rossiter's claim that Shakespeare's *Richard II* would have been virtually unintelligible without the audience's prior knowledge of *Woodstock* may be somewhat over-stated, it is fair to say that the relatively lightly sketched details of Richard's mode of rule – for instance, the otherwise fleeting and rather opaque references to farming the realm – seem to rely on the fuller account provided by the earlier play. Indeed, Shakespeare may have been able to remain as deliberately vague about the details of Gloucester's murder as he was precisely because many of his audience would have been alerted by *Woodstock* to Richard's central role therein. Shakespeare's play can thus evoke the doubt surrounding Gloucester's death, using it to caste a pall of uncertainty and moral queasiness over the actions of all the characters in the play, safe in the knowledge that his audience 'knew', or had at least been (reliably?) informed by the earlier play, that Richard had indeed been up to his neck in the death of his uncle. See Rossiter, *Angel with horns: fifteen lectures on Shakespeare* (London, 1989), chapter 2, 'Richard II'. On the issue of the murder of Gloucester see A.L. French, 'Richard II and the Woodstock murder', *Shakespeare Quarterly*, 4 (1971), pp. 337–44.

3. Gerald Harriss, 'Medieval doctrines in the debates on supply, 1610–1629', in Kevin Sharpe, ed., *Faction and parliament: essays on early Stuart history* (Oxford, 1978), pp. 73–104.

4. Phyllis Rackin's claim (in her *Stages of history*, p. 122) that Shakespeare 'reconstructs' Richard 'as a bad ruler in almost every way that Elizabethan theory recognized'; 'he is luxurious and effeminate; he is a bad warrior and administrator; he imposes high and unfair taxes; he listens to flatterers, and he scorns Gaunt's good counsel', is thus something of an underesti-mate of what the play reveals to be Richard's serial and insurgent tyranny.

5. And, *pace* Berger's ingenious, but perhaps rather fanciful, reading, there is next to nothing in the text to suggest that father and son are not in fact collaborating in Hereford's challenge, delivered, via Mowbray, to the king, over Gloucester's death. Indeed, we might well construe their collective action as an attempt to mount such a challenge while (just) remaining within the bounds of deference to legitimate monarchical authority; just as we might construe Richard's council-backed interruption of the trial by combat as a brilliantly conceived and executed manoeuvre to disrupt that attempt, and thus to part father from son and de-fang the last vestiges of opposition to his rule. This, of course, is to privilege the play's political surface, a surface presented in performance to the play's first audiences, over against the latent meanings and tensions that Berger 'excavates' in and from the text. It is thus to prefer a political version of events that Berger's avowedly psychoanalytic reading tries to re-organise around a father/son dynamic. While such a dynamic is undoubtedly, indeed notoriously, present in the subsequent plays (conventionally taken to make up the so-called second 'Henriad'), its presence is by no means so obvious in *Richard II* itself. See Berger's 'Psychoanalysing the Shakespeare text: the first three scenes of the Henriad', in his *Making trifles of terrors*, pp. 148–67.

6. Berger, *Making trifles of errors*, p. 202, from the aptly titled essay '*Ars moriendi*, or, John of Gaunt and the practice of strategic dying'. Cf. Womersley's comment that 'Gaunt's deathbed reproaches to Richard have an under-tow of self-reproach, which reflect back critically on his compliance here (just as he also regrets his compliance over the banishment of his son, Bolingbroke)', Womersley, *Divinity and state*, p. 287.

7. See Dermot Cavanagh, 'The language of treason in Richard II', *Shakespeare Studies*, 27 (1999), pp. 134–60, esp. pp. 139–43.

8. A.D. Nuttall, *Shakespeare the thinker* (London and New Haven, 2007), p. 136.

9. Harry Berger Jr, *Making trifles of terrors*, p. 161.

10. Charles R. Forker, ed., *King Richard II* (Arden 3rd ser., London, 2002), pp. 58–59.

11. Cf. James Calderwood's remarks that Richard is practising a sort of kingly speech 'conceived of as sacramental and ontological, in which words are not proxies for things but part of the things themselves'. For Richard, ' "King" and "Richard" are not two words but one indissoluble name. The old metaphors linking kingly office and divine office are not analogical truths in Richard's imagination but anagogic ones, not metaphors but identities. The king is not *like*, he *is* the "deputy elected by the lord", "God's substitute", "the Lord's lieutenant" and so on.' See Calderwood, *Metadrama in Shakespeare's Henriad: Richard II to Henry V* (Berkeley, 1979), pp. 13, 17.

12. Nuttall, *Shakespeare the thinker*, p. 139. For the more conventional view of Richard as 'passive, naïve and impotent' throughout, see, for instance, Coppelia Kahn, *Man's estate*, pp. 66–68, quote at p. 66.

13. See Paul Gaudet, 'The "parasitical" counsellors in Shakespeare's *Richard II*: a problem in dramatic interpretation', *Shakespeare Quarterly*, 33 (1982), pp. 142–54, quotation at pp. 150–51.

14. Thus in *The dramatist and the received idea* (Cambridge, 1968), p. 193, Wilbur Sanders equates Bolingbroke with the principle of political 'necessity'.

15. See Cavanagh, 'The language of treason in Richard II', *Shakespeare Studies*, 27 (1999), pp. 143–54.

16. Ibid., p. 154.

17. Berger, *Making trifles of terrors*, p. 181.

18. Ibid., pp. 180–82.

19. Ibid., p. 169.

20. Here Deborah Shuger's verdict seems definitive. As she admits, 'the standard view of *Richard II* as narrating the passage from the sacral kingship of the middle ages to demystified realpolitik of modernity' has 'an impressive critical pedigree'. But it 'cannot be right because it makes no sense historically' since 'full blooded sacral monarchy is more a creature of the Tudor era' than of the late Middle Ages. Shuger, 'Religion and honour in Richard II', pp. 54–55. Also see David Womersley's verdict that in this play 'Shakespeare dramatized a particular form of monarchy in operation – a form of monarchy which the play's first audiences would have recognised as innovative, foreign to English legal custom, invasive of or insensitive to the rights of the subject, and Machiavellian to the extent that its priority is maintaining the state of the prince, irrespective of the broader needs of the common weal'. Womersley, *Divinity and state*, p. 288. On the other side of the argument see, for instance, Alvin Kernan, 'The Henriad: Shakespeare's major history plays', in Kernan, ed., *Modern Shakespeare criticism* (New York, 1970), pp. 245–75 and more recently Graham Holderness (*Shakespeare recycled: the making of historical drama*, Hertfordshire, 1992, p. 64) and Catherine Belsey, who sees both Gaunt and Richard as possessed by a nostalgia for a lost 'plenitude, for the unity of words and things, a desire for the simplicity and the certainty of a world which precedes the symbolic difference'. 'Making histories then and now: Shakespeare from Richard II to Henry V', in Francis Barker, Peter Hulme and Margaret Iverson, eds, *Uses of history: Marxism, postmodernism and the renaissance* (Manchester, 1991), pp. 24–46, esp. p. 44. Phyllis Rackin, in her *Stages of history*, identifies Richard as a quintessentially medieval figure and centres the play's appeal on the audience's 'nostalgic appetite for representations of an idealized feudal past'. On her account, 'Richard's deposition marks the loss of this idealized feudal world that formed the object of sixteenth century longing.' 'The medieval world . . . disappears with his deposition'. Quotations at pp. 117, 52. Thus, Phyllis Rackin and Jean Howard sum up what they term the opinion of 'many critics' by presenting *Richard II* as split 'between two models of royal authority', with Richard associated 'with a nostalgic image of mediaeval royalty, grounded in heredity and expressed in ceremonial ritual and Bullingbrook with the emergence of an authority achieved by personal performance and expressed in the politically motivated self-presentation of a modern ruler'. See P. Rackin and J. Howard, *Engendering a nation*, p. 142. It is by no means clear how the play can be construed as showing the serially theatrical Richard II to be innocent of 'politically motivated self-presentation' or the Bolingbroke who tries to stage-manage the deposition scene as blind to the value of 'ceremonial ritual' in establishing his legitimacy as king. Bolingbroke's efforts to use ritual to establish his own legitimacy may well fail, but then so (in the end) do Richard's. While Bolingbroke fails because he is a usurper, Richard fails because he has become widely acknowledged to be a tyrant, but then for Elizabethan audiences neither usurpation nor tyranny were distinctively 'medieval' concepts, but rather crucial categories for the evaluation of their current political circumstances in world a dominated, both at home and abroad,

by intensely personal monarchy. And England, of course, was a personal monarchy throughout what we have come to regard as the late medieval and the early modern periods. Wilbur Sanders takes a similar line, claiming that the play shows 'the old world order', characterised by what Gaunt calls 'Christian service and true chivalry', to be 'in its death-throes'. Of this there is no sign in the play. As Sanders himself admits, the chief spokesperson for what he wants to see as a quintessentially 'mediaeval' view of kingship is Richard and 'he has kept its husk in his notions of kingship but thrown away the kernel of Christian service' before the play starts. 'His commitment to the manipulative arts makes him fair game for the superior manipulator.' Given the emphasis placed by early modern monarchs of both confessional persuasions on their status as Christian rulers and defenders of true religion, and the almost equally strong tendency of their confessional opponents to see such claims as mere persiflage, ideological cover for the pursuit of political self-interest, this is not a situation likely to have struck any Elizabethan reader or spectator as peculiar either to the Middle Ages or indeed to any notion of a past radically different from the political present or near future. See Wilbur Sanders, *The dramatist and the received idea*, p. 192.

21. Nuttall, *Shakespeare the thinker*, pp. 141, 139.
22. Cyndia Clegg, 'Archival poetics and the politics of literature: Essex and Hayward revisited', *Studies in the Literary Imagination*, 32 (1999), pp. 115–32. But now see Jason Scott-Warren, 'Was Elizabeth I Richard III? The authenticity of Lambarde's "Conversation"? *Review of English Studies*, 64 (2013), pp. 208–30.
23. See Donna Hamilton's claim that the contemporary resonance of the different versions of kingship being canvassed in the play 'would seem to be incompatible with interpretations that consider the play to be about the passing of a period with a less modern kingship than that of the Renaissance, or interpretations that consider the play to be about the destruction of an era characterized by a kind and degree of order that could never be recreated'. On the contrary, she concludes, 'the dramatist saw in Richard's story an example of something that had happened once in England, and might happen again'. See her article 'The state of law in Richard II', *Shakespeare Quarterly*, 34 (1983), pp. 5–17, quotation at p. 16. Indeed it was as long ago as the 1870s that Richard Simpson pointed out the quite striking parallels between the picture drawn in the play of Richard's misgovernment as it slipped imperceptibly but palpably into tyranny, and the critique of the Elizabethan regime produced by Parsons and his associates in their tracts written in response to the proclamation of 1591.
24. Sanders cites the description of Mowbray's death as a moment when what he calls 'this vast geological change in cultural ideals comes suddenly into focus, and momentarily we pause, as on the summit on the last and highest ridge to survey the land we are leaving behind'. To which one can only reply that no we don't, since there is nothing antique or irrelevant about the play's use of the example of Mowbray's good death as a template against which to judge Richard's bad one. For, for all the popish forms it takes – and after all, even for the most stridently protestant of Elizabethans, Catholicism was scarcely a thing of the *past* – Mowbray's is a decisively pious and repentant end just as Richard's is not. *The dramatist and the received idea*, pp. 192–93.
25. As M.M. Reese observes, 'on a like occasion Henry VI sought forgiveness for his sins and a pardon for his murderer', whereas Richard 'dies in violence', promising 'never quenching fire' to his assassins and heaven to himself. See his *The cease of majesty* (London, 1961), p. 246.
26. Shuger, 'Religion and honour in Richard II', p. 51.

Chapter 11: Shakespeare and Parsons – again

1. It is usually assumed that this passage was censored from the printed version of the play but, as Jonathan Bate has argued, there is no reason to make that assumption. See Bate, *Soul of the age* (London, 2008), p. 257.
2. For a brilliant discussion of the politics of stage direction and speech prefixes in the various early modern and modern editions of the play see Emma Smith, '*Richard II*'s Yorkist editors', in *Shakespeare Survey*, 63, *Shakespeare's English histories and their afterlives* (Cambridge, 2010), pp. 37–448.
3. Berger, *Making trifles of terrors*, p. 169.
4. Barbara Hodgdon, *The end crowns all*, p. 133. Wilbur Sanders makes a similar point, remarking that the scene represents Richard's 'symbolic revenge' upon Bolingbroke since 'it makes him enact in public the deed which he has all but obscured from "the view of men" . . . he makes him seize the crown'. *The dramatist and the received idea*, p. 170. As Emma Smith observes, this means that the addition of the supposedly censored material actually makes

the scene not more transgressive but more orthodox, suggesting that 'only a king can "unking" a king and that the act of usurpation should be figured as a willed abdication rather than a unwilled conquest . . . When Richard is present in Act 4 Q4, he may give up his crown and scepter but he decisively seizes the stage and the audience, speaking 131 lines in contrast to Bullingbroke's eleven.' See her 'Richard II's Yorkist editors', quote at p. 40.

5. On this view, the revisionist account of Elizabethan parliamentary politics must be added to all the other aspects of 'modernity' that Shakespeare is so frequently taken to have prefigured.

6. A point made by Moody Prior, *The drama of power*, p. 152.

7. Berger, *Making terrors into trifles*, p. 177.

8. On Harry Berger Jr's estimate, 'Richard's performance of the discoronation rite and its sequel is a work of genius at both the political and psychological level. On the one hand he formally reenacts the self-deposition he has helped bring about, thereby publicly demonstrating his active relinquishment of the crown. On the other, he forces Bolingbroke to reenact his usurpation, thereby dramatizing the illegal seizure.' For Berger, 'the transfer of power is framed as a transfer of guilt'. Richard thus succeeds in promoting 'two very different kinds of danger: the external political danger of unending civil strife and the internal danger of unending guilt, the ineradicable sense of moral reprehensibility that can only be dealt with by displacing the inward war to more external inadequate wars – paternal, physical, civil, foreign.' On Berger's account, by play's end, 'Richard's stagy representation of himself as the hapless victim of the wicked usurper' has 'persuaded Bolingbroke and others to place the entire weight of guilt along with the discredited crown upon the usurper's head'. The result, he claims, is that 'the succession of kings in the Henriad is a genealogy of guilt', the 'increasing virulence' of which 'testifies' not only, as Berger puts it, 'to the abiding power of the murdered king, a power seriously under-estimated by the canonical view of Richard as a weak and politically inept ruler', but also to the abiding power of Richard's ideology, of his (and indeed Gaunt's) view of divinely ordained sacred kingship, of the subjects' supervening obligation to obey even the worst or most misguided of princes and of the entirely sinful nature and baleful (immediate and long term) consequences of resistance. Harry Berger Jr, *Imaginary audition: Shakespeare on page and stage* (Berkeley, 1989), p. 73.

9. Womersley, *Divinity and state*, p. 294.

10. Ibid.

11. The title of chapter 9 of *The dramatist and the received idea*, also see p. 193: 'though Bolingbroke stands condemned by the canons of equity laid down by his father, he is for the play, Necessity'.

12. Edward Berry, *Patterns of decay*, pp. 122, 119; in *The cease of majesty* M.M. Reese likewise notes (p. 285) that 'Faulconbridge is a link with the Prince Hal of the plays to come'.

13. John Danby, *Shakespeare's doctrine of nature*, pp. 77, 88.

14. Bonjour, 'The road to Swinstead Abbey', p. 270; 'John's career represents a falling curve, the Bastard's career a rising curve; and both curves, perfectly contrasted, are linked in a single pattern.'

15. Dermot Cavanagh, 'The language of treason in Richard II', which, in Cavanagh's words (fn. 21), identifies Gaunt's speech as 'a powerful constitutional statement of the necessity for a law-centred monarchy where it is the law from which the king's power derives and he is to rule according to it'. Such a view may be implicit in Gaunt's speech, but that view is never coherently or successfully articulated in the play as either the reason or even as the legitimation for Bolingbroke's rebellion or, still less, as the ideological underpinning of his regime. Cf. Donna Hamilton, 'The state of law in Richard II'.

16. Jonathan Bate, *Soul of the age*, pp. 270–71.

17. John J. Manning, ed., *The first and second parts of John Hayward's The life and raigne of king Henrie IIII*, Camden Society, 4th series, 42 (London, 1991), p. 61.

18. All of which prompts the thought that, if we read *Richard II* in this anti- or post-Parsonsian spirit, then, as Paul Hammer has recently argued, it makes that performance of *Richard II* on the eve of the 'Essex rebellion' – if, indeed, the play being performed was Shakespeare's – look much less like an incitement to rebellion and rather more like a cautionary meditation on the difficulty (if not the impossibility) of forcibly reforming a monarchical state without following Bolingbroke down a path that led inexorably from the removal of evil counsellors and the coercion of the prince to usurpation and regicide, thus sending both the state one was trying to save, and perhaps even one's own soul, to hell in a handbasket. Paul Hammer, 'Shakespeare's Richard II, the play of 7 February 1601 and the Essex rising', *Shakespeare Quarterly*, 59 (2008), pp. 1–35.

19. See Paul Hammer, 'Shakespeare's Richard II, the play of February 7, 1601, and the Essex rising', pp. 1–35; Blair Worden, 'Which play was performed at the Globe Theatre on February 7, 1601?', *London Review of Books*, 25/13 (2003), pp. 22–24. Now see the important discussion of these issues in Gajda, *The earl of Essex*, pp. 236–43.

Chapter 12: The loss of legitimacy and the politics of commodity dissected

1. This analysis is, of course, an entirely 'political' one, dominated by the lines of force, of interest and probability, operating in and through the relationships between the main parties. These had been set in motion by the deposition and murder of Richard II, in which acts all the major players were equally complicit, as anyone who had seen *Richard II* knew quite well. It was this political dynamic that Richard himself had outlined to Northumberland towards the end of *Richard II*. However, the same tensions and lines of force are susceptible to other forms of analysis and in his *Making trifles of terrors* Harry Berger Jr offers a largely psychological account of what is recognisably the same set of relationships and tensions. While, needless to say, the political reading offered here and the psychological reading offered by Berger are by no means mutually exclusive, the former would have been rather more obviously available to the play's first audiences than the latter, something which, for the purposes of the argument being pursued here – but *not*, it must be said, for any interpretation of the play outside of the determinedly historical focus being adopted in this book – might be thought to be a point of some significance.

2. Sandra Fischer, ' "He means to pay": value and metaphor in the Lancastrian tetralogy', *Shakespeare Quarterly*, 40 (1989), pp. 149–64. Also see Jesse Lander, ' "Crack'd Crowns" and counterfeit sovereigns: the crisis of value in *I Henry IV*', *Shakespeare Studies*, 30, 2002, pp. 137–61, and the remarks on this subject by David Kastan in his Arden edition of *I Henry IV*, pp. 62–69.

3. Cf. McAlindon's observation that 'the sickness which afflicts this body politic is loss of truth and wholeness, of loyalty and trust; that disease seems to touch every spoken word, infecting it with double meaning'. Tom McAlindon, *Shakespeare's Tudor history* (Aldershot, 2001), p. 116.

4. R. Ornstein, *A kingdom for a stage* (Cambridge, Mass., 1972), p. 144. Leggatt's comment that the 'thinking is that of the chivalric hero, but the words belong to the counting house' (*Shakespeare's political drama*, p. 94), is thus not quite right, since it considerably overestimates the ease with which 'the thinking' can be separated from 'the words'. That the one inflects the other in inextricable ways and that the result is an intense feeling of incongruity and even of contradiction is perhaps the point. As Racking points out, 'the "factor" image defines in advance Hal's victory over Hotspur in knightly combat as a repossession of the honor that rightly belongs to royalty, but it also compromises that honor by terms – "factor, "render-up", "engross", "strict account" and "reckoning" – that reduce the chivalric battle to a closely calculated financial transaction'. Racking, *Stages of history* (Ithaca, 1990), p. 78.

5. See McAlindon's remark that 'the problem of debt' is 'pervasive' in these plays; 'like all mortals, Falstaff owes God a death . . . and as with his other debts he will consider repayment only in the spirit of "anon, anon." But just as the snares and the fangs of the law eventually catch up with him, so too the laws of nature, dictating that the body decays in time, and that good health must be surrendered as the price of dissolute living, begin to assert themselves forcefully in the changed world of *Part 2*.' T. McAlindon, *Shakespeare's Tudor history*, p. 79.

6. Fischer, 'Value and metaphor', p. 163.

7. D. Kastan, 'The king hath many marching in his coats', in his *Shakespeare after theory* (London and New York, 1999), pp. 129–47.

8. Alan Dessen, *Shakespeare and the late moral plays* (Lincoln, Nebraska, 1986), pp. 81–82, cited in Fischer, ' "He means to pay" ', p. 161.

9. Fischer, 'Value and metaphor', p. 155, quoting Terence Hawkes, *Shakespeare's talking animals: language and drama in society* (London, 1973), p. 76

10. Cf. Craig Muldrew, *The economy of obligation* (Basingstoke, 1998).

11. Tom McAlindon, *Shakespeare's Tudor history*, pp. 28–34, 90, 157, quotation at p. 90; 'it can hardly be doubted that in 1597/8 Shakespeare was giving his audience a pointed, opening reminder that the political strife of late medieval England had much in common with the religio-political conflicts of the Tudor century – as well as a connecting link in the Percy family, uncrowned kings of the north.' Also see Lily B. Campbell, *Shakespeare's 'Histories': mirrors of Elizabethan policy*, pp. 229–35 (where she suggests that Shakespeare reworked his

sources deliberately to recall to his audience the events of 1569) and the verdict of Womersley, who remarks that 'the parallelism' being established here 'is not quite the same as one-for-one correspondence . . . As well as the rebellion of the Northern Earls of 1569, the extinguishing of the rebellion of the Percies at Gaultree Forest recalls the endgame of the Pilgrimage of Grace.' David Womersley, *Divinity and state*, pp. 323–28, quotation at p. 326.

12. On the Pilgrimage see T. McAlindon, *Shakespeare's Tudor history*, pp. 33–39, and 91, where he suggests that 'the elaborate treachery' with 'which the King's deputy suppresses the Archbishop's quasi-religious rebellion' 'recalls the collapse of the Pilgrimage of Grace'. Also see Womersley, *Divinity and state*, pp. 326–28.

13. Mervyn James, *English politics and the concept of honour, Past and Present Supplement 3*, 1978, eprinted in his *Society, politics and culture: studies in early modern England* (Cambridge, 1986),

14. See the perceptive discussion in McAlindon, *Shakespeare's Tudor history*, pp. 105–8, where he notes that 'John's conduct at Gaultree recalls Machiavelli's admiring comment on Castruccio Castracani, who was "ready to play false with the unfaithful, and willing to overcome by fraud those whom he desired to subdue, because he was wont to say that it was the victory that brought the glory, not the methods of achieving it"'. But while Prince John is presented not as 'a scheming tyrant or villainous intriguer, but rather a true Machiavellian prince, one who in the defence of the state unhesitatingly, and with no qualms of conscience whatsoever, engages in ruthless perfidy', Shakespeare also alters his sources to make that perfidy appear all the more clearly. 'This negative impression is powerfully reinforced by the elaborate hypocrisy with which the trick is invested . . . The crowning touch to the Prince's show of piety, his declaration that "God, and not we, hath safely fought today" (II, iv, 348) is a distancing, satiric irony that the author of the *Jew of Malta* would have commended.' Quotations at pp. 105, 106–7. For a contrary assessment which argues that, 'unlike us, the first audiences of *2 Henry VI* had no reason of principle to censure Prince John's conduct at Gaultree Forest', see Womersley's claim that because of 'their emphasis on the Bible and warning to the clergy not to involve themselves in secular matters', there are distinctively 'Protestant characteristics' in way the way that Shakespeare has the Lancastrians suppress the Percies' rebellion. See Womersley, *Divinity and state*, pp. 325–26, 328. There seems to be small enough basis for this claim, but if we were to take it seriously we would also have to admit that the play uses this resonance or association to produce a remarkably critical account of the relation between Lancastrian policy and Protestant principle, between what McAlindon quite rightly identifies as a (literally) Machiavellian pursuit of political advantage and the espousal of religious, indeed, on Womersley's account at least, of pointedly Protestant, principle.

15. See McAlindon, *Shakespeare's Tudor histories*, where at pp. 90–91 he lists a number of aspects of the play's staging of the late fifteenth century that in fact constitute 'a series of mutually supportive parallels between the troubles of the Tudor and Lancastrian dynasties'. Amongst these are 'the King's Tudor-style, anti-rebellion rhetoric at Shrewsbury', the 'conscription methods used by Sir John Falstaff and Justice Shallow' and the 'strongly Elizabethan character of Oldcastle/Falstaff's sanctimonious (Puritan) style' and, perhaps most importantly of all, 'the Henry–Mortimer relationship'. which, of course, he sees as recalling that between Queen Elizabeth and Mary Stuart. To all of which we should add the widely acknowledged fact that the tavern milieu, in which so much of the crucial action takes place, is of a determinedly and distinctively contemporary, i.e. Elizabethan, provenance. About 'history', then, the play is also about the 'now', not merely of performance, but of social and political actuality. On these issues of temporality see Brian Walsh, *Shakespeare, the Queen's Men, and Elizabethan performance of history* and the discussion (and appropriation) of his views in the Introduction.

16. If we take these plays as a retrospective comment upon the action of *Richard II*, it is worth observing that there is no trace here of any relief at having effected (or claim to be effecting) a return to an 'older', more 'conciliar', 'parliamentary' and even 'genuinely medieval', mode of kingship, of the sort imputed to Bolingbroke and his allies by Professor Womersley. The politics being staged here is an intensely monarchical and (early) modern one, as elsewhere in his argument Professor Womersley readily acknowledges. See David Womersley, *Divinity and state*, p. 285.

17. Berger, *Making trifles of terrors*, pp. 273–74.

18. Here again Harry Berger Jr's comments seem more than apposite; 'Henry lies uneasily and continues to do so to the end because he is always trying both to deceive himself and to resist

the attempt. What I find most poignant in this is the vivid process, the conflict, the discursive struggle, that couples the desire for moral legitimacy with despair at the futility of the desire. Time and again the speaker of Henry's language all but pronounces judgment on himself, and time and again he veers off to another bad-faith speech act that can only confirm the judgment.' 'Passing judgment on him' might well be 'redundant' for modern 'critics', as Berger observes, but, given the play's proximity to contemporary, i.e. Elizabethan, concerns and debates, it was surely a rather more urgent concern for the play's first audiences, who were also almost certainly rather more exercised by questions of soteriology and salvation than many modern critics or audiences have tended to be. See Berger, *Making trifles of terrors*, p. 250.

19. Cf. C.L. Barber's remark in *Shakespeare's festive comedies* (p. 218) that 'in these last scenes' Henry IV 'becomes ... almost a sacrificial figure, a king who sins for the sake of society, suffers for society in suffering for his sin, and carries his sin off into death'. Where Barber views Henry's status as a sacrificial victim for the sins and stability of the realm in, as it were, anthropological and symbolic terms, Harry Berger Jr casts the same matter in psychological ones, remarking that 'Henry seems motivated by a need to persuade himself that (1) Richard did not deserve to be king and that although (2) he – Henry – did not have the right to unking him, much less kill him, he nevertheless (3) heroically sacrificed his own chance for salvation and ran the risk of destroying his reputation for the good of his country'. Berger, *Making trifles of terrors*, p. 245.

Chapter 13: Learning to be a bastard

1. Robert Ornstein, *A kingdom for a stage*. Cf. Womersley's remark that Hal is displaying the 'necessary aloofness from his father of a son who is more deeply policied not only than he seems to be, but also than his father is.' David Womersley, *Divinity and state*, p. 318.
2. Beatrice Groves, *Texts and traditions*, pp. 132, 134.
3. E. Berry, *Patterns of decay*, p. 108.
4. Michael Davies, 'Falstaff's lateness: Calvinism and the protestant hero in Henry IV', *Review of English studies*, 56 (2005), pp. 351–78, esp. pp. 368–75 and, echoing Davies, Phebe Jensen, *Religion and revelry in Shakespeare's festive world* (Cambridge, 2008), pp. 191–92.
5. While there is absolutely nothing distinctively protestant about such a move, it undoubtedly both belongs to and evokes a world transformed by the complex interactions and transactions between the secular and the sacred consequent upon the reformation.
6. *The famous victories of Henry V*, scene vi, quotation at line 11, in Peter Corbin and Douglas Sedge, eds, *The Oldcastle controversy* (Manchester, 1991).
7. Davies, 'Falstaff's lateness', quotations at pp. 364–65.
8. For this point see Roy Battenhouse, '*Henry V* in the light of Erasmus', *Shakespeare Studies*, 17 (1985), pp. 77–88, p. 86 fn. 2, where Battenhouse points out that 'Henry has experienced no inward conversion or new faith, no miracle of the Holy Spirit such as John's gospel (chap. 3) [not to mention contemporary Elizabethan protestant norms] stipulates for a genuine Christian conversion.'
9. Even Henry's final speech to Falstaff, in which he takes on (again) the persona of Christ, seems far more like an attempt to say the right thing according to contemporary canons of theological orthodoxy and pastoral correctitude, and thus to display his own righteousness, than any very urgent attempt to save the old reprobate's soul; particularly when we remember, as we surely must, that it has only been the prince's patronage that has enabled Falstaff's rake's progress to be sustained throughout both plays. The 'lateness' here, if any 'lateness' there is, is surely at least as much Hal/Henry's as it is Falstaff's. See Davies, 'Falstaff's lateness', pp. 361, 367.
10. Davies, 'Falstaff's lateness', p. 364; Womersley, *Divinity and state*, p.310; also see Jensen, *Religion and revelry in Shakespeare's festive world*, pp. 191–92.
11. Unlike the pioneering work of Davies, Womersley and Grove, much of the most influential recent writing – a great deal of it new historicist or cultural materialist in its critical commitments – about these plays has been resolutely 'secular' in its concerns and frame of reference. A notable exception here is Jeffrey Knapp, who in a quite remarkable attempt to recuperate and ventriloquise Shakespeare's vision of what he terms 'theatrical ministry', states almost as a matter of fact that 'Shakespeare imagines the later plays of the cycle as vindicating his own claims to piety and religious purpose'. See his *Shakespeare's tribe* (Chicago, 2002), and *Shakespeare only* (Chicago, 2009), quotations at pp. 117, 113.

Chapter 14: Festive Falstaff

1. See, for instance, C.L. Barber, *Shakespeare's festive comedies*; Michael Bristol, *Carnival and theatre*; François Laroque. 'Shakespeare's "Battle of Carnival and Lent" ', in Ronald Knowles, ed., *Shakespeare and Carnival: after Bakhtin* (Basingstoke, 1998), pp. 83–96; Hugh Grady, 'Falstaff: subjectivity between the carnival and the aesthetic', *Modern Language Review*, 96 (2001), 609–23. Also Jensen, *Religion and revelry in Shakespeare's festive world*. But, as Grady and McAlindon, amongst a host of others, observe, the origins of Falstaff are diverse and complex; to quote Grady's own somewhat undifferentiated list, they can be found in 'the *miles gloriosus* and the Plautine parasite from Latin comedy; the comic vice of the late medieval moralities; the tradition of fools and folly from the Middle Ages and the related carnival tradition . . .; the *picaro* tradition and the related discourse on Elizabethan underground or rogue literature . . .; the Renaissance celebration of the body in Cervantes and Rabelais' (Grady, 'Falstaff', pp. 610–11 and McAlindon, *Shakespeare's Tudor histories*, p. 76.

2. Cf. Beatrice Groves, *Texts and traditions*, p. 131 and D. Womersley, *Divinity and state*, p. 320.

3. P. Collinson. 'Ecclesiastical vitriol: religious satire in the 1590s and the invention of puritanism', in J.A. Guy (ed.), *The reign of Elizabeth I: court and culture in the last decade* (Cambridge, 1995) pp. 150–70, and more generally on the anti-puritanism of the 1590s see P. Lake and M. Questier, *The Antichrist's lewd hat*, chapters 12 and 13.

4. Kristen Poole, *Radical religion from Shakespeare to Milton: figures of non-conformity in early modern England* (Cambridge, 2000), chapter 1. The present discussion is much indebted to Poole's analysis. Also see Robert Hornbeck's seminal article, 'Staging puritanism in the early 1590s: the carnivalesque rebellious clown as anti-puritan stereotype'. Also see David Scott Kastan, 'Killed with hard opinions: Oldcastle, Falstafff and the reformed text of *I Henry IV*', in L. Maguire and Thomas Berger, eds, *Textual formations and reformations* (Delaware, 1998), pp. 211–27.

5. To quote Kristen Poole on this point, 'the "prime church of the Ephesians" ', 'established according to the directives set out by St Paul', 'was often cited as a model for godly living'; 'the pre-Pauline Ephesians, on the other hand, were used as an example of those leading a wanton, ungodly lifestyle'. This latter form of the church of the Ephesians is usually taken to be what the page is referring to in his remarks to Hal, but this represents, as Poole remarks, 'a blanket refusal to consider the possibility of puritan overtones', overtones that, she points out, 'would have been glaringly obvious to an audience aware of both Falstaff's Lollard origins and his bacchanalian behavior on stage.' Poole, *Radical religion from Shakespeare to Milton*, pp. 203–4, n. 88.

6. Beatrice Grove, *Texts and traditions*, p. 132.

7. Michael Davies, 'Falstaff's lateness', esp. pp. 358–59.

8. On this see David Scott Kastan, 'Killed by hard opinions'. However, I agree with Paul Whitfield White that 'Kastan is mistaken . . . in arguing that late Elizabethans came to identify Oldcastle primarily with puritan radicals'. See White's 'Shakespeare and the Cobhams', in White and Suzanne Westfall, eds, *Shakespeare and theatrical patronage in early modern England* (Cambridge, 2002), p. 76, n. 20. As Gary Taylor points out, 'the controversy over whether Shakespeare intended to satirise the Cobhams has obscured the much more important fact that he portrayed a Protestant martyr as a jolly hypocite', and, one might add, as a sort of puritan, and in so doing adopted a version of Oldcastle's career far more commonly held by Catholics than by Elizabethan protestants. See Taylor's 'The fate of Falstaff', *Shakespeare Survey*, 38 (1985) pp. 85–100, quote at p. 98. The Foxeian account of the origins of the true church in England remained the predominant one in the 1590s. Far more was at stake in the maintenance of the 'Foxeian synthesis' of a vision 'of the church centred on the Christian prince and one centred on the godly community' than the fate of the puritan movement or the self-image of the puritan godly. (Kastan, 'Killed with hard opinions', p. 215, citing P. Lake, 'Presbyterianism, the idea of the national church and the argument from divine right', in M. Dowling and P. Lake, eds, *Protestantism and the national church in sixteenth century England* (London, 1987), pp. 193–224, quotation at p. 195.) Shakespeare's elision of Oldcastle/ Falstaff with a version of the Lollard and the puritan as subversives and hypocrites amounts to an exploitation of the predominant anti-puritan mood of the late 1590s in order to undercut versions of the English past absolutely central to the defence of the Elizabethan church against popery. This puts Shakespeare, if not on the side of the Catholics then certainly on that of the most avant-garde Hookerian conformists. See Peter Lake, *Anglicans and Puritans?, passim* but esp. chapter 4 and conclusion. Also see idem, 'The Anglican

moment? Hooker and the ideological watershed of the 1590s', in S. Platten, ed., *Anglicanism and the western Christian tradition* (Norwich, 2003), pp. 90–121.

9. See chapter 4, 'Perfect answers: religious inquisition, Falstaffian wit', in his *Shakespeare minus "theory"* (Aldershot, 2004).

10. See Taylor, 'Fate of Falstaff', p. 99, where he observes that 'in *King John* – as in *Part I* – Shakespeare tells the story of an early Protestant "martyr", whose life had been celebrated earlier in the century by both Bale and Foxe; but again, as in *Part I*, Shakespeare's account of this figure is not very flattering.'

11. See Lake and Questier, *Lewd Hat*, and P. Lake, 'Matthew Hutton: a puritan bishop?', *History* 69 (1979), pp. 182–204.

12. Thus C.L. Barber remarks of these plays, 'the dynamic relation of comedy and serious action is saturnalian rather than satiric, that the misrule works, through the whole dramatic rhythm, to consolidate rule'. Barber, *Shakespeare's festive comedies*, p. 205.

13. For discussions of the various political valences attributed to, or inherent in, the carnivalesque mode see Michael Bristol, *Carnival and theatre* and Graham Holderness, *Shakespeare's history* (Dublin, 1985), pp. 79–112. Barber too argues that the inversionary forms of carnival were not always devoid of subversive meaning or potential. Thus on the one hand he maintains that, 'when the forms for serious meaning are inevitable, received from accepted tradition, the comic reapplication of them need not be threatening', for then 'people . . . can afford to turn sanctities upside down, since they will surely come back right-side up'. But then he adds the rider that 'when traditions are in dispute, when individuals or groups are creating new forms and maintaining them against the world', 'it becomes necessary for those who "build the lofty rhyme" to be on guard against the "low".' This is an extraordinarily acute observation of obvious relevance to the subject of puritanism and the antipathy of the godly to all such forms of traditional festivity. See his *Shakespeare's festive comedy*, p. 83.

14. As C.L. Barber points out, Philip Stubbes denounced a variety of popular games involving lords of misrule 'just after denouncing the theatres', calling them ' "the other kind of plays, which you call Lords of Misrule" '. Barber, *Shakespeare's festive comedies*, p. 27. Not, of course, that all puritans were equally anti-theatrical or that all anti-theatrical writers were puritans, but even the non- or even (subsequently) anti-puritans amongst the opponents of the theatre (like Anthony Munday or Stephen Gosson) did have recourse to what we might term distinctively godly or puritan modes of argument when denouncing the theatre in print. See Lake and Questier, *Lewd hat*, chapter 11.

15. Peter Burke, *Popular Culture in early modern Europe* (London, 1978), pp. 270–81. Also see Richard Wilson, 'A mingled yarn: Shakespeare and the cloth workers', in his *Will Power* (London, 1993), pp. 22–44. Cf. C.L. Barber's observation that 'the village saturnalia of the Lord of Misrule's men was in its way a sort of rising': *Shakespeare's festive comedies*, p. 29 Also see François Laroque (Cambridge, 1991), p. 253.

16. Barber, *Shakespeare's festive comedies*, p. 14.

17. In Jesse Lander's view, this exchange introduces into the play for the first time a medium or means of exchange – the gift – that by its very nature goes beyond the narrow pursuit of commodity. In these gestures, James Calderwood claims that Hal 'transcends Hotspur's obsession with names and titles of honour' and 'in so doing he earns title to a far more impressive kingship than any of the pseudo-versions put before him throughout the play'. Calderwood, *Metatheatre*, p. 58. We might compare here Sherman Hawkins' claim that Hal's willingness 'to give back Hotspur's glories' on the field at Shrewsbury in *Part 1*, Act V, scene iv parallels his willingness to return the crown to his father in *Part 2*, Act 4, scene v and that the two gestures confirm his 'right to both'. Sherman Hawkins, 'Henry IV: the structural problem re visited', *Shakespeare Quarterly*, 33 (1982) pp. 278–301, quotation at p. 299.

18. Barber, *Shakespeare's festive comedy*, p. 215.

19. John Danby, *Shakespeare's doctrine of nature*, p. 84.

20. Gloating about Shallow's fate at his hands, Falstaff is, in fact, describing his own at the hands of Hal/Henry.

21. Calderwood, *Metadrama*, p. 95.

22. Ibid., p. 43.

23. A point emphasised by Calderwood, ibid., pp. 90–92.

24. Danby, *Shakespeare's doctrine of nature*, p. 92.

25. Barber, *Shakespeare's festive comedies*, p. 216.

26. For an account of these plays as a containing 'a brilliant image of reformation', see Womersley, *Divinity and state*, chapter 2, quotation at p. 315. See also Jensen, *Religion and revelry*, p. 191,

where she observes that Hal's 'pending personal "reformation" ' is identified with 'the epochal Reformation, for the time when "all the year were playing holidays" evokes a world of medieval Catholic revelry when, especially according to Protestant critiques, the calendar was littered with holy days'.

27. In her *Religion and revelry in Shakespeare's festive world*, Jensen stresses the attachment of festive culture to the traditional festivals of the unreformed, Catholic liturgical year and therefore the attachment of Elizabethan Catholics to those same festive observances. Puritans, too, tended to dismiss popular festive culture as offensively popish, but it is far from clear that, by the 1590s, only those we can meaningfully call Catholics either retained an attachment to those practices or resented puritan attempts to suppress them. Certainly there is no attempt in the *Henry IV* plays to code the festive world of Eastcheap or the Boar's Head as in any way 'Catholic'. It may, therefore, not be an accident, although it remains quite remarkable, that Jensen's book is devoid of any extended discussion of the *Henry IV* plays.

28. Unlike Professor Womersley, I do not see the resulting vision of monarchical order and power as avowedly or distinctively 'Protestant'. Its aggressive erastianism certainly ensures that is not in any recognisable sense of the word 'popish'. In that sense, it most definitely belongs to the post-reformation but it is not assertively protestant, still less, as Michael Davies and Phebe Jensen would have it, 'Calvinist'. (See Davies, 'Falstaff's lateness' and, following Davies' line of argument, Jensen, *Religion and revelry*, pp. 191–92.) What we have here, then, is precisely *not* 'a distinctive and recognizably Protestant account of Lancastrian kingship' (Womersley, *Divinity and state*, pp. 315, 323). Rather we have a version of Lancastrian kingship transposed into and addressed to recognisably post-reformation, late Elizabethan concerns and structures, in what I take to be, given the highly confessionalised context of the late 1590s, remarkably a-confessional ways. This, of course, is not to claim that the play eschews religious polemic of a rather virulent sort. On the contrary, as has been argued above, through its redescription of Oldcastle/Falstaff as an egregious hypocrite and evil counsellor, it indulges in a remarkably aggressive style of anti-puritanism, one at least potentially subversive of the dominant Foxeian account of the origins and nature of the true church in (and of) England. The result is that although the major religious divide in the play lies not between Protestants and Catholics but rather between puritans and non-puritans, the decidedly radical way in which that divide is characterised calls into question central areas of the mainstream protestant defence of the English church against Catholic allegations of innovation and schism. Given the dynamics of the late Elizabethan religious scene, that is an extremely significant, indeed, a strikingly bold, polemical and political choice. That none of this escaped the notice of contemporaries is shown by *The Oldcastle play*, analysed below. Remarkably, Womersley's discussion of Shakespeare's plays in *Divinity and state* is devoid of any mention, still less discussion, of the dynamics of puritanism or anti-puritanism; indeed the term 'puritan' only occurs fleetingly in his treatment of *2 If you know not me you know nobody*, at pp. 185–86. This means that he misses altogether these plays' most obvious and insistent engagement with immediately contemporary religious politics. The same cannot be said of another attempt to recuperate the religious world-view of these plays, that performed in two recent books by Jeffrey Knapp. Womersley's tendency to collapse puritanism into some sort of reformed mainstream, and thus to miss the aggressively anti-puritan edge of some of these plays, can usefully be compared and contrasted with Knapp's rendition of puritanism as a radically divisive, indeed thoroughly sectarian, phenomenon, inherently incompatible with a normatively inclusive, moderately protestant Hookerian Anglicanism or, as Knapp would put it, 'Erasmianism'; an ideological strand which Knapp sees as hegemonic both within the national church and amongst what he terms, with entirely unhelpful vagueness, 'theatre people'. (See Knapp's *Shakespeare's tribe*, Chicago, 2002, and his *Shakespeare only*, Chicago, 2009); for some mordant comments on Erasmianism as a suitably vague omnium-gatherum term under which modern commentators on the early modern past can organize various tendencies and opinions of which they approve see Noel Malcolm, 'Ecumenism and irenicism; the Wiles lectures, 1975' in Blair Worden, ed., *Hugh Trevor-Roper: the historian* (London, 2016), pp. 101–115, esp. p. 115. (Malcolm's comments are specific to Trevor-Roper, but, as Knapp's work shows, they also have a wider reach.) This enables Knapp (in this, just like Womersley) to elide (in Knapp's case by simply endorsing and thus naturalising) the radical anti-puritanism of these plays, which, I would argue, was sufficiently avant-garde to constitute something of an assault on the hegemonically reformed tenor of the late Elizabethan church and sufficiently uncompromising to call into real question the claims to irenicism and inclusiveness of those wielding such a virulent version of anti-puritanism as a polemical weapon.

As Knapp observes, 'opposition to sectarianism can seem sectarian itself' (*Shakespeare's tribe*, p. 51). But Knapp manages to avoid the logic of his own observation by simply accepting the characterisations of the godly produced by their enemies as sectarian and deviant, which makes about as much sense as taking the outpourings of the anti-theatrical pulpit and press either as objective reportage of what was going on in the theatres or as the voice of a monolithic 'puritanism'. Both Womersley's collapse of puritanism into a protestant mainstream, characterised by 'justified kingship' and 'reformation', and Knapp's faithful reproduction of the central elements of the extreme anti-puritanism of avant-garde conformity represent (different, indeed mutually exclusive) forms of 'Anglican' apologia. Both are based on the acceptance, as though they were simply true, of the polemically generated and ideologically constructed categories and claims of the post-reformation past. Modern scholars who, instead of subjecting to analysis and critique the assumptions and categories of the participants in the disputes they are ostensibly trying to understand, simply choose sides, are merely allowing some contemporaries to set the terms of their own analysis while consigning others to the dustbin of mere ideology. In so doing, they cannot help but replicate in their own work all of the exclusions and suppressions, the *parti pris* assertions and assumptions, the half-truths and exaggerations, that produced those inherently *parti pris* and polemical categories and claims in the first place. This is not to explain or imaginatively to inhabit the disputes and thought worlds of the past but merely to choose sides within and between them. It is a tendency all too common in both literary and historical studies. On the historical side of the equation, because the church of England had its origins in precisely this period and many of the current (bitterly contested) disagreements about the nature and ideological identity, the institutional and pastoral role, of that church have their roots in the disputes of the early modern (i.e. of the post-reformation) period, far too much of the recent literature on the religious history of that period has come to constitute a series of sotto voce, intra-Anglican, disputes about the nature of the Church of England, conducted under the guise of historical research and analysis. Thus a series of, as it were, private arguments, of interest only to the dwindling membership of the Anglican communion, threatens to dominate the historiography of early modern English religion; a subject of considerable interest and importance to anyone – Anglican or not, indeed Christian or not – concerned with the post-reformation period. Since the 1970s it has become a truth generally acknowledged – albeit not by Sir Keith Thomas – that 'religion' (broadly construed) must be of major concern to anyone interested in any aspect – political, cultural or social – of the history of early modern England. But that acknowledgement has been accompanied by a tendency to re-confessionalise the history of the post-reformation in what are almost entirely unhelpful ways. Put crudely, the history of early modern Christianity is too important to be left to the internal squabbles and parochial concerns of modern Christians, and particularly of modern Anglicans. The overt obtrusion of modern ideological concerns and agendas, most notably in the Marxist canon, has attracted the critical comment, indeed at times the rather shrill vituperation, of a whole range of scholars. It is time that the *parti pris*, almost entirely present minded, and thus thoroughly anachronistic, nature of much 'Anglican historiography' was subjected to a similar sort of (perhaps more measured) critical scrutiny by those scholars of the period fortunate enough not to be encumbered by such narrowly confessional, even sectarian, concerns. On the literary side, because of the very fine balance achieved in many of his plays between the various contending elements in immediately contemporary (i.e. Elizabethan and early Stuart) ideological dispute and reality-construction, and also because of the huge cultural capital now attached to his name and the exiguous, virtually non-existent, source base (outside of the plays themselves) for anything that Shakespeare himself thought or did, impersonating and appropriating 'Shakespeare' has become the perfect vehicle through which to perform this sort of intervention into a whole variety of (moral, political, religious and epistemological) disputes, both past and present. 'Shakespeare' here acts as a blank screen on to which can be projected values and positions dear to the heart of the observer, or, in a slightly more subtle version of the same syndrome, attitudes and positions of which the viewer virulently disapproves can be discovered in or recuperated from 'Shakespeare', so that, in the act of unmasking such positions in 'Shakespeare' the virtue of the commentator and the purity of his or her views, not to mention the subtlety and superiority of his or her method or sensibility, can be asserted or vindicated. At its most extreme, 'thinking with Shakespeare' can thus become an exercise from which anything that might have been written or indeed thought by Shakespeare (or his collaborators and contemporaries) disappears almost entirely, to be replaced by the present-minded concerns and insights of the person doing the 'thinking'. What we have here, in Knapp's and (to a lesser extent) even in Womersley's, positions, is, therefore, the simple reproduction of two diametrically opposed versions of Anglicanism, both of which seek to establish their claims to be both normal and normative by reproducing two very different images or versions of a puritan other. To adopt for a moment the language of the Anglican *via media*, for the modern scholarly observer these alternative positions represent something like the two 'extremes' which have to be avoided or rather transcended if the messy and contested middle ground, in which not merely 'puritan', but English protestant, identity *tout court* was being continually established and contested throughout the post-reformation period, is to be properly understood. In short, it seems to me impossible to get these issues straight without getting to grips with the subtle, complex and contested relationship of 'puritanism' and the reformed mainstream of English protestant thought. On all this see, variously, Patrick Collinson's, *Elizabethan puritan movement, Godly people* (London, 1983), *The religion of protestants* (Oxford, 1982) and *The birthpangs of Protestant England* (Basingstoke, 1988). Also see his essays 'Towards a broader understanding of the early dissenting tradition', in C. R. Cole and M. E. Moody, eds, *The Dissenting Tradition: essays for Leland H. Carlson* (Athens, OH, 1975) and 'Sects and the evolution of Puritanism' in Francis J. Bremer, ed., *Puritanism: transatlantic perspectives on a seventeenth-century Anglo-American faith* (Boston, Mass.: Massachusetts Historical Society, 1993). Also see Nicholas Tyacke, *Anti-Calvinists* (Oxford, 1987) and his *Aspects of English Protestantism, c.1530–1700* (Manchester, 2001); Kenneth Fincham, *Prelate as pastor* (Oxford, 1990); Fincham and Tyacke, *Altars restored: the changing face of English religious worship, 1547–c.1700* (Oxford, 2007) and Peter Lake, *Moderate puritans and the Elizabethan church* (Cambridge, 1982); idem, *Anglicans and puritans?*; idem, *The Boxmaker's revenge* (Manchester, 2002); idem, 'The Anglican moment? Hooker and the ideological watershed of the 1590s'; idem, 'Anti-Puritanism: the structure of a prejudice', in Kenneth Fincham and Peter Lake, eds, *Religious politics in post-Reformation England: essays in honour of Nicholas Tyacke* (Woodbridge, 2006), pp. 80–97. Anthony Milton, *Catholic and reformed* (Cambridge, 1994). For some preliminary remarks on the ideological work done by espousals of 'moderation' and the search for (and invocation of) the *via media* see P. Lake, 'The moderate and irenic case for religious war: Joseph Hall's *Via Media* in context', in Susan Amussen and Mark Kishlansky, eds, *Political culture and cultural politics in early modern England: essays presented to David Underdown* (Manchester, 1995), pp. 55–83 and 'Joseph Hall, Robert Skinner and the rhetoric of moderation at the early Stuart court', in Lori-Anne Ferrell and Peter McCullough, eds, *The English sermon revised* (Manchester, 2001), pp. 167–85. The discussion of this whole topic has now been raised to another level of coherence and ambition by Ethan Shagan, *The rule of moderation* (Cambridge, 2011).

29. As throughout Shakespeare's history plays, the efficacy of noble counsel, or, to adopt the somewhat anachronistic language of recent historical writing, the workings of 'the monarchical republic', are shown to be completely dependent upon the assertion of monarchical authority and the right exercise of royal will.

Chapter 15: *Henry V* and the fruits of legitimacy

1. For different readings of this passage against its various sources see Roy Battenhouse, '*Henry V* in the light of Erasmus', pp. 77–88; Andrew Gurr, '*Henry V* and the bees' commonwealth', *Shakespeare Survey*, 30 (1977), pp. 61–72. Now see Dermot Cavanagh's discussion of the resulting tensions and ambiguities, refracted through a discussion of the passage's Vergilian source in his 'Georgic sovereignty in Henry V', in *Shakespeare Survey*, 63, *Shakespeare's English histories and their afterlives* (Cambridge, 2010), pp. 114–26.

2. David Kastan, *Shakespeare and the shapes of time* (Hanover, NH, 1982), p. 59.

3. Howard and Rackin, *Engendering the nation*, pp. 168–69, citing Christopher Highley, 'Wales, Ireland and *I Henry IV*', in *Renaissance drama*, new ser., 21 (1990), 91–114.

4. T. Hawkes, 'Bryn Glas', in A. Loombia and Martin Orkin, eds, *Post-colonial Shakespeares* (London, 1998), 117–40.

5. As Battenhouse and Gurr both point out, the stakes implicit in the Alexander comparison are raised by the fact that, in the just war tradition founded by Augustine, Alexander stood out as the leading example of the proponent of unjustifiably aggressive wars of conquest. As Fluellen's comparison makes clear, Henry both was and was not like Alexander; like him in his military prowess, unlike him in his capacity to control his passions, and in his sublimation of his personal affections to the demands of state. Battenhouse, '*Henry V* in the light of Erasmus', pp. 82, 87, fn.10 and Gurr, 'Henry V and the bees' commonwealth'.

6. Moody Prior, *The drama of power*, pp. 324, 331. Although, as both Battenhouse, 'Henry V in the light of Erasmus' and Gurr, 'Henry V and the bees' commonwealth' point out, there is far from a perfect match between Erasmus' precepts about the true nature of the Christian prince and Henry's practice.

7. Robert Ornstein, *A kingdom for a stage*, pp. 183–84, and fn. 10.

8. Gurr, 'Henry V and the bees' commonwealth', p. 70, 'it is remarkable that the only actual combat on stage is Pistol's in IV, iv. Moreover that incident involves not fighting but bargaining for a ransom.'

9. Wayne Rebhorn, *The emperor of men's minds: literature and the Renaissance discourse of rhetoric* (Ithaca, 1995), p. 62

10. Gurr, 'Henry V and the bees' commonwealth', pp. 66–7, 'all the chroniclers attributed the victory to Henry's tactics, but not one gets a mention in the play apart from the killing of the prisoners, which has a special non-military significance. The work of raising morale is, in Shakespeare's presentation, Henry's essential contribution to the victory.'

11. G.K. Hunter, *English drama: the Age of Shakespeare, 1586–1642* (Oxford, 1997), p. 247.

12. Rebhorn, *Master of men's minds*, pp. 60, 63.

13. T. McAlindon, *Shakespeare minus 'theory'*, pp. 61–62. On the one hand, McAlindon's gloss on the speech – 'the idea that he would not try to prevent, or would in any way tolerate or condone, the "wildness" of infanticide and rape is wholly incompatible with his character as a leader whose rules demands execution even for the theft of a pax' – serves merely to illustrate the slightly absurd lengths to which his determination to defend his hero drives him. But, on the other, it also illustrates rather well the tensions and antinomies to which I am adverting.

14. See Gurr, 'Henry V and the bees' commonwealth', pp. 62, 68.

15. As Gurr notes, 'Elizabethan verdicts on the slaughter of prisoners were divided'. Gentillet condemned the practice outright and explicitly mentioned English conduct at Agincourt as he did so, while 'Gentillet's fellow lawyer Cornwallis' gave Henry a free pass on the basis of military expediency. But it remains the case that, of the available accounts of the incident, Shakespeare chose 'the least favourable version and underlined the choice with the uncomprehending muddle of Gower's interpretation of it'. Gurr, 'Henry V and the bees' commonwealth', pp. 68–69.

16. Susan Thorne attributes such tensions and potential contradictions to the need to 'find a way of negotiating the uncomfortable gap between an elitist tradition of martial valour and its popular reenactments'. In answer to which Henry (but also on her account Shakespeare, too) hits upon the solution of 'subsuming social demarcations in an ambiguously inclusive discourse of nationhood . . . Through such rhetorical sleights-of-hand, Henry contrives to suggest that all Englishmen, irrespective of class origins, are eligible to participate in his exalted "fellowship," provided their actions prove them worthy of it. The incipient contradictions in Henry's interpellation of the soldiers make his vision of a socially inclusive partnership . . . highly vulnerable to contestation.' See Alison Thorne, ' "Awake remembrance of those valiant dead": Henry V and the politics of the English history play', *Shakespeare Studies*, 30 (2002), pp. 162–87, quotation at p. 176.

17. Thorne, ' "Awake remembrance of these valiant dead" '; also see Joel Altman, ' "Vile participation": the amplification of violence in the theatre of Henry V', *Shakespeare Quarterly*, 42 (1991), pp. 1–32; Alan Sinfield and Jonathan Dollimore, 'History and ideology: the instance of Henry V', in John Drakakis, ed., *Alternative Shakespeares* (London, 1985), pp. 206–27.

18. Michael Goldman, *Shakespeare and the energies of drama* (Princeton University Press, 1972), pp. 59, 61, quoted in Lawrence Danson, 'Henry V: king, chorus and critics', *Shakespeare Quarterly*, 34 (1983), pp. 27–43, quotation at p. 30.

19. On this see Danson, 'Henry V: king, chorus and critics', quotations at pp. 30, 43.

20. On which see, for example, G.K. Hunter, *English drama, 1586–1642: the age of Shakespeare*, pp. 248–50.

21. Steven Marx, 'Shakespeare's pacifism', *Renaissance Quarterly*, 45 (1992), pp. 48–98, quote at p. 66.

22. In referring to these attempts to unite the audience Jeffrey Knapp goes from talking of 'eucharistic overtones' and 'Shakespeare's reformed hermeneutics' to asking whether 'Shakespeare preferred a theatrical to a clerical communion'. All this is an expression of what he terms Shakespeare's 'theatrical version of ministry', indeed of the sacramental and ministerial project of 'theatre people' as a whole. See his *Shakespeare's tribe, passim,* quotations at pp. 132, 133, 139 and from Knapp's *Shakespeare only,* p. 117. All of which seems to me to

represent the triumph of an entirely ahistorical liberal and/or Anglican sentimentality over both what is happening in the play and what the research of the last fifty or so years has revealed about the religious and political history of the 1590s, indeed of the post-reformation period *tout court.*

23. Leonard Barkan, 'Enlisting Harry Berger's imaginary forces', in Nina Levine and David Lee Miller, eds, *A touch more rare: Harry Berger Jr. and the arts of interpretation* (New York, 2009), p. 14.

24. See, in particular, Thorne, ' "Awake remembrance of these valiant dead" ' and Dollimore and Sinfield, 'History and ideology'.

25. Hugh Grady, *Shakespeare, Machiavelli and Montaigne: power and subjectivity from Richard II to Hamlet* (Oxford, 2002), p. 215; D. Kastan, *Shakespeare and the shapes of time* (Hanover, NH, 1982), p. 62.

26. Robert Ornstein, *A kingdom for a stage*, p. 182.

27. A.D. Nuttall, *Shakespeare the thinker*, p. 159.

28. Grady, *Shakespeare, Machiavelli and Montaigne*, p. 216.

29. D. Kastan, *Shakespeare and the shapes of time* (Hanover, NH, 1982), p. 62. As Kastan points out, the irony is only heightened if we remember that once 'the principle of "claiming from the female" [I, ii, 92] is affirmed', Henry's claim to the throne of England, let alone that of France, becomes subject to serious contest, 'for Mortimer's descent from Philippa (daughter of Lionel, duke of Clarence) has undeniable primacy in the line of Edward III from which both claims originate' (ibid., p. 62).

30. As David Kastan points out, the scene between the archbishop of Canterbury and the bishop of Ely can serve no other purpose than to call the moral imprimatur given to the king's war by the archbishop into the most radical question, ibid., pp. 60–61. For a superb close reading of these scenes see Bradshaw, *Misrepresentations*, pp. 47–56.

31. Bradley Greenberg, 'Sack drama', in Levine and Miller, eds, *A touch more rare*, p. 54.

32. Berger, *Making trifles of terrors*, p. 188.

33. Una Ellis-Fermor, *The frontiers of drama* (London, 1948), p. 47.

34. As P. K. Ayers observes in his brilliant article, ' "Fellows of infinite tongue": Henry V and the king's English' (*Studies in English Literature*, 34, 1994, pp. 253–77), 'there is little sense here of a humbled sinner seeking forgiveness, or an anguished soul release; Henry's prayer seems a curiously abject mixture of the pietistic and the self-serving . . . Once again Henry declines to accept much in the way of responsibility; the sin, he stresses was that of his father . . . The heart of his prayer is an implicit request that a past in which he played no part, and over which he can exercise no control, be erased from the record on which he is to be judged.' Quotation at pp. 262–63.

35. The verdict is Gary Taylor's, for which see Taylor, ed., *Henry V* (Oxford, 1984) p. 298. Also see the discussion in Greenblatt's famous essay 'Invisible bullets' in his *Shakespearean negotiations*. The key to the meaning of the speech is the phrase 'after all' which, of course, remains inherently ambiguous. Its most obvious meaning is that since Henry's repentance (for the sins of his ancestors) comes after both their seizure, and his own enjoyment of power, his repentance for their sins – he has made no mention of his own – must count for nothing. There is, of course, nothing inherently 'protestant' about such a recognition, since what is at stake is not the effect of Henry's almsdeeds on the souls of his departed ancestors, but rather on God's willingness to give him victory in tomorrow's battle. For what seems to me to be an entirely unlikely attempt to use this speech, together with Henry's alleged 'dissatisfaction with "ceremony"', in all its senses', to argue that Shakespeare was claiming 'Henry as a Protestant in respect of personal theological conviction' see Womersley, *Divinity and state*, p. 338. Also see, in a similar vein, Davies, 'Falstaff's lateness'.

36. For a different (and in my view somewhat sentimental) view of the 'practical joke involving disguise and false identity with his new favourites Fluellen and the bluff, honest Michael Williams' as providing a 'glimpse of that unfixed subjectivity which the young King had seemed to banish irrevocably (along with one of its principal signifiers, Falstaff) at the end of *2 Henry IV*', see Grady, *Shakespeare, Machiavelli and Montaigne*, p. 222.

37. Alison Oatland ' "Eat a leek": Welsh corrections, English conditions and British cultural communion', in Willy Maley and Margaret Tudeau-Calyton (eds), *This England, that Shakespeare* (Farnham, 2010), pp. 87–103, esp. pp. 96–101, quotation at p. 101.

38. P. K. Ayers, '. . . Henry V and the king's English', p. 274, n. 27.

39. L. Montrose, *The purpose of playing* (Chicago, 1996), p. 84.

40. Ayers, '. . . Henry V and the king's English', p. 260.

41. Bradshaw, *Misrepresentations*, pp. 84–85, citing Greenblatt, 'Invisible bullets' in his *Shakespearean negotiations*, p. 55.
42. Barber, *Shakespeare's festive comedies*, p. 207.
43. Prior, *The drama of power*, p. 327.
44. T. McAlindon, *Shakespeare minus 'theory'*, pp. 64, 84–85.
45. Bradshaw, *Misrepresentations*, pp. 7, 84–85.
46. Prior, *The drama of power*, p. 327.
47. E. Berry, *Patterns of decay*, p. 113. M. Prior, *The drama of power*, pp. 324, 330. Both are citing J.H. Walter, the editor of the Arden edition who demonstrated how closely Shakespeare based his Henry V on such models (of Christian kingship) in a point by point comparison between the qualities demanded by Erasmus and Chelidonius and 'Henry's principal characteristics as king.' J. H. Walter. ed., *Henry V* (London, 1954), pp. xv–xviii.
48. Una Ellis-Fermor, *The frontiers of drama*, pp. 45–46.
49. P.K. Ayers, '. . . Henry V and the king's English', p. 258. It is this, Ayers claims, in a brilliant insight, that best explains 'the cacophony of critical voices that surrounds the figure of Henry in all its guises.'
50. Some critics have presented Henry as occupying some moderate middle way, a *via media* constructed through a variety of contrasts between the moral extremes, the various rhetorical and political capacities and incapacities, exhibited by Falstaff, Hotspur and his father. Thus, McAlindon argues that 'in no other mature play of Shakespeare's is the mode of characterization so schematic as in *Henry IV*, where every device of language, staging and juxtaposition is mobilized in such a way as to locate Hal at a mean position between the destructive valour and impetuosity of Hotspur and the rationalized cowardice and dilatoriness of Falstaff. This particular form of schematism indicates how closely allied the play is to Erasmian ideas on timely action and the princely ideal.' McAlindon, *Shakespeare's Tudor histories*, p. 89. This seems to me considerably to overestimate the moral coherence of the various performances of royal virtue staged in *Henry V*.
51. Prior, *The drama of power*, p. 327.
52. Ibid., pp. 327, 331.
53. Robert Ornstein, *A kingdom for a stage*, p. 137.
54. T. McAlindon, *Shakespeare minus 'theory'*, p. 76. For similar sentiments, and a similarly downbeat verdict on the play's dramatic achievement, see Prior, *The drama of power*, p. 341.
55. Marie Axton, *The queen's two bodies*, pp. 97–115, esp. pp. 111–15.
56. C.L. Barber, *Shakespeare's festive comedies*, pp. 206–7, 219, 206; Ann Barton, *Essays, mainly Shakespearean* (Cambridge, 2006), chapter 10, 'The king disguised: Shakespeare's *Henry V* and the comical history'. For a plea to see the ' "magical ideas" ' of 'subplots' which he sees as rooted in what he terms a 'traditional dimension of popular acting' as 'profoundly integrated into the dramatic structure itself', see Robert Weimann, *Shakespeare and the popular tradition in the theatre* (Baltimore, Md., 1987), p. 242.
57. Cf. Prior's conclusion in his *The drama of power*, that 'the success of the hero of Agincourt, however, does not so much resolve' the questions raised by the previous plays 'about the demands of regal authority and the exercise of power', as 'evade them'. pp. 340–41.
58. John Danby, *Shakespeare's doctrine of nature*, pp. 89–91.
59. Nuttall, *Shakespeare the thinker*, pp. 151–52.
60. Barber, *Shakespeare's festive comedies*, p. 218. Steven Marx opines that the play might be thought to have arrived at a position not unlike that of a seventeenth-century French defender of Machiavelli, Louis Machon. Machon envisaged a situation in which 'the prince, imitating a divinity who put off his divinity in Christ in order to achieve the salvation of the world, puts off an ideal and otherworldly goodness in order to achieve the safety of the people, exchanging contemplative perfection for morally flawed actions . . . The idea that the king is an imitator of God . . . includes mimesis . . . of those modes of divine action that entail a lowering of the divine nature . . . "It is only a good prince who will hazard his own salvation to seek that of the subjects he governs." ' See Steven Marx, 'Holy war in Henry V', *Shakespeare Survey*, 48 (1995), pp. 85–97, quote at pp. 94–95. This means that, for kings, purgatory is a crucial doctrine. For, in a world in which the expiation of the sins of the dead by the living is no longer possible, the chances of salvation for even the best of princes looked slim. Such a world, and its fell consequences for even the most virtuous princely political actors is, of course, delineated in *Hamlet*. See S. Greenblatt, *Hamlet in Purgatory* (Princeton, 2001) Also see chapter 24 below. I hope to deal with the unforgivingly predestinarian structures of that play at length elsewhere.

61. Prior, *The drama of Power*, pp. 265, 340

62. D. Kastan, *Shakespeare and the shapes of time*, p. 73. *Pace* Greenblatt, 'hypocrisy' seems too blunt, and in many ways too self-serving, a term adequately to describe what is going on here.

63. Jeffrey Knapp's claim that 'throughout his history plays, Shakespeare regularly depicts the "purple testament of bleeding war" as a demonic inversion of Christianity', is backed up by three citations from *Henry V*, none of which make that point or anything like it. The passages cited are Epilogue, 9–14, 'Henry the Sixth, in infant bands crowned King/Of France and England, did this king succeed,/Whose state so many had the managing/That they lost France and made his England bleed,/Which oft our stage hath shown; and for their sake/In your fair minds let this acceptance take'; IV, i, 135–37, 'the King himself hath a heavy reckoning to make when all those legs and arms and heads chopped off in battle shall join together at the latter day and cry all "We died at such a place" and IV, viii, 120, 'Yes, Captain, but with this acknowledgement,/That God hath fought for us.' How Knapp expects his readers to get from these disparate passages to the conclusion for which they allegedly provide substantiation remains entirely unclear. *Henry V* certainly does not pull its punches about the horrors of war, but to claim, on the basis of 'evidence' like this, that it pictures war as 'demonic' or as a simple 'inversion of Christianity' does scant justice to the complexities of the play, and makes entirely unwarranted assumptions about just what this play's version of 'Christianity' amounts to. More generally, while it is true that the history plays certainly make the horrors of civil war (and to a lesser extent of war, in general) crystal clear, in *1 Henry VI*, *King John*, and even more in *Henry V*, the aggressive prosecution of war against the foreigner, in *King John* a war largely of self-defence, in *Henry V*, one of choice, is presented as the only source of national unity and monarchical (and even moral) legitimacy on offer. At stake here is the distinction (even, in a fallen world, the contradiction) between the demands of politics and religion, of true Christianity and effective monarchical rule. The resulting vision is tragic and is perhaps best regarded not so much as 'post-Christian', as post-reformation; certainly it reflects the realities of post-reformation religious division and confessional and dynastic conflict far more accurately than the entirely ahistorical style of 'Anglican moderation', the happy-clappy 'Erasmianism', imputed by Knapp not merely to 'Shakespeare' but to 'theatre people' in general. See Knapp's, *Shakespeare's tribe*, *passim*. The quotation cited above is from Kapp's *Shakespeare only*, pp. 116, 186, n. 35. For Knapp's critique of C.L. Barber and others for attributing a secularising, 'post-Christian' resonance or drift to Shakespeare in particular and to the Renaissance stage, more generally construed, see ibid., pp. 98–99, 110–11, 183 n. 4. Thus while one might agree with Knapp that Shakespeare may indeed have had a 'religious' as well as a political 'purpose in dramatizing Lancastrian realpolitik' (ibid. p. 99), it seems unlikely in the extreme that that 'purpose' bore any resemblance to that read into these plays by Professor Knapp.

64. Norman Rabkin, *Shakespeare and the problem of meaning* (Chicago, 1981), chapter 2, 'Either/or: responding to *Henry V*'.

65. For some sense of how how embattled the parties to the critical debates surrounding Henry's moral and exemplary status have become see T. McAlindon's lawyerly making of what he calls (quite unselfconsciously) 'the case for the Prince's defence' against a raft of critics ranging from Robert Ornstein to Stephen Greenblatt and encompassing A.C. Bradley, George Bernard Shaw and what McAlindon terms 'new historicists such as Phylis Rackin and David Kastan'. McAlindon, *Shakespeare's Tudor histories*, pp. 123–40, quote at 176. Also see chapter 3, 'War and peace in Henry V' in his *Shakespeare minus 'theory'*. McAlindon's position should be compared to the view advanced in Stephen Greenblatt's seminal essay 'Invisible bullets' to which chapter 2 of McAlindon's *Shakespeare minus theory*, 'Testing new historicism: "Invisible Bullets" reconsidered', is an extended response. McAlindon's bout with Greenblatt et al. is but a more recent version of previous engagements. Invoking a veritable rogues' gallery of 1950s malcontents and bounders, M.M. Reese denounced 'the hostile critics' as 'pacifists, republicans, anti-clericals, little Englanders, moralists, even as arbiters of etiquette' (*The cease of majesty*, p. 317). Moody Prior launched a systematic and far more subtle defence of the play from what he terms 'unsympathetic critics trying to find a consistent center for his [Hal/Henry's] character'. See Moody Prior, *The drama of power*, chapters 14 and 16, quote at p. 331. Unsurprisingly, McAlindon finds Prior's 'one of the plays most level-headed interpretations'. (*Shakespeare minus 'theory'*, p. 76.) As Graham Bradshaw puts it, essentially the same confrontation between pro- and anti-Henry interpretations was conducted, the first time around, during the 1950s, '60s and early '70s, in largely 'characterological' terms and then repeated, after, say, 1980 in stridently self-conscious 'ideological' ones. See his *Misrepresentations*,

pp. 3–8. Also see the mordant comment of Harry Berger Jr that 'harrying Harry with pietistic panache is currently considered a sign of liberal chic. And because the fifth Harry gets a very good press from other sectors, unlike his father, a tedious squabble has been going on between Harry-lovers and Harry-haters' (Berger, *Making trifles of terrors*, p. 250). The potential of the play to elicit such widely divergent interpretations, over a period of decades from critics with such different ideological commitments and critical approaches, might be taken to mean that the play allows ample textual warrant for all these views and that, to appropriate A.P. Rossiter, the resulting 'ambivalence' is central to its workings. These are issues not to be resolved one way or the other but rather retained and rendered central to our reading of the play. And the resulting tensions, the actual and potential contradictions and ambivalences, have wider implications for the ways contemporaries thought about kingship, political order and the relationship between 'politics' and 'religion' than Berger's exclusively psychological concentration on 'Harry's trouble with Harry' can reveal. Graham Bradshaw's comment that attempts finally to resolve such questions – and thus to decide issues left deliberately open by the play – serve 'to defeat those energies which make the play work' seems more than apposite. Bradshaw, *Misrepresentations*, p. 39. The approach adopted here is much indebted to Bradshaw's work.
66. M. Axton, *Queen's two bodies*, pp. 112–13, 'if Henry's claim to France was valid then so too is the Stuart claim to England'.
67. Alex Gajda, 'Debating peace and war in late Elizabethan England'.
68. Paul Hammer, 'The smiling crocodile; the Earl of Essex and late-Elizabethan "popularity" '.
69. For these see my *Bad Queen Bess*, esp. pp. 225–28, 277–81.
70. D. Bevington, *Tudor drama and politics* (Cambridge, Mass., 1968), p. 20, a remark made as part of a determined attempt to argue that Shakespeare's plays had nothing to do either with Essex or indeed with 'politics'.
71. Paul Hammer, *Polarisation of Elizabethan politics*, pp. 249–62 and idem, 'Myth-making: politics, propaganda and the capture of Cadiz in 1596'.
72. As Tom McAlindon puts it, in Hotspur's hands, 'the redemption of honour becomes an activity devoid of all moral value, a dangerous adventure which entails complete indifference to the lives of others and to the unity of the commonwealth'. T. McAlindon, *Shakespeare's Tudor histories*, p. 158.

Chapter 16: Contemporary readings: Oldcastle/Falstaff, Cobham/Essex

1. D. Womersley, *Divinity and state* p. 360. For Womersley's analysis for such purposes of *1 and 2 Robert Earl of Huntington* and *I Sir John Oldcastle*, see ibid., chapter 12.
2. G.K. Hunter, *English drama, 1586–1642: the age of Shakespeare*, pp. 240–41.
3. On this subject see, Alice-Lyle Scoufas, *Shakespeare's typological satire* (Athens, Ohio, 1979); Gary Taylor, 'The fortunes of Falstaff', *Shakespeare Survey*, 38 (1985), pp. 85–100; idem, 'Shakespeare, Richard James and the house of Cobham', *Review of English Studies*, 38 (1987), pp. 334–54; David Scott Kastan, 'Killed with hard opinions: Oldcastle, Falstaff, and the reformed text of *I Henry IV*', in L. Maguire and T. Berger, eds, *Textual formations and reformations*, pp. 211–27, now reprinted in Kastan's *Shakespeare after theory* (New York, 1999); Robert J. Fehrenbach, 'When Lord Cobham and Edmund Tilney "were at odds": Oldcastle, Falstaff and the date of I Henry IV', *Shakespeare Studies*, 17 (1986); E.A.J. Honigman, 'Sir John Olcastle: Shakespeare's martyr', in John W. Mahon and T. Pendleton, eds, *Fanned and winnowed opinions* (London, 1987), pp. 118–32; Peter Corbin and Douglas Sedge, eds, *The Oldcastle controversy* (Manchester, 1991), esp. pp. 9–12. By far the best and most balanced account is now to be found in Paul Whitfield White, 'Shakespeare and the Cobhams', in *Shakespeare and theatrical patronage in early modern England* (Cambridge, 2002), pp. 64–89, to which what follows is much indebted.
4. 'Biographical politics: Shakespeare, Jonson and the Oldcastle controversy', *Ben Jonson Journal*, 11 (2004), pp. 2–20, quote at p. 9.
5. On this aspect of the affair see White, 'Shakespeare and the Cobhams', pp. 85–86.
6. For a perhaps slightly strained argument that even that change retained an allusion to the doings of the Brookes, Lord Cobham, see Honigmann, 'Sir John Oldcastle: Shakespeare's martyr', pp. 128–29.
7. And this despite the fact that 'city comedy' was a genre yet to be invented and the play is not in fact set in the city but rather in the semi-rural and distinctly royal setting of Windsor.

8. As Peter Erickson observes, 'what Falstaff loses, Fenton recuperates. By providing a clear contrast with Falstaff's aristocratic imposture, Fenton enacts the rehabilitation and vindication of true aristocracy. Since Fenton reinstates aristocratic integrity, Falstaff becomes a parodic scapegoat who carries the burden of court corruption and is easily sacrificed to dispel resentment against it'; or, in the terms laid out by the current reading, Brook/Ford/Cobham's alter ego, Oldcastle/Falstaff has to be sacrificed in order to restore amicable relations and proper order at court. See Erickson, 'The Order of the Garter, the cult of Elizabeth, and class-gender tension in *The merry wives of Windsor*', in Jean. E. Howard and Marion F. O'Connor, eds, *Shakespeare reproduced* (New York and London, 1987), pp. 116–41, quotation at p. 124.

9. Erickson, 'The Order of the Garter', pp. 129, 130–31. 'The Queen's presence doubles the effect of female domination of the play and the impression of the Queen and the wives as strong women is further amplified because their power comes from a similar source – the culture-specific Elizabethan ideology of "political Petrarchism".' 'Like Elizabeth, the wives use love as a political device to shape, contain, and deny male desire; like the ageing queen in the 1590s, they engage in this activity as older women past "the holyday time of my beauty" (II, i, 1–2). The play reproduces and magnifies the pattern of provocation, deferral, prohibition, and frustration found in the cult of Elizabeth and the styles of courtship it activated.'

10. Paul Hammer, *The polarisation of Elizabethn politics*, pp. 297, 325–8, 381

11. As Erickson ('The Order of the Garter', p. 128) comments, 'as an endearing comic butt, Evans, the Welsh priest in *The merry wives of Windsor,* is given parallel treatment to Fluellen, Macmorris and Jamy in *Henry V*. Caius, the French doctor, is equivalent to the comic Dauphin in the history play.' All of which strongly implies that the play, as we now have it, must postdate *Henry V.*

12. See Professor Melchiori's edition of *The merry wives of Windsor* (3rd series of the Arden Shakespeare, London, 2000), Introduction, pp. 1–56.

13. Barkeley to Sir Robert Cecil, 19 April, 1600, from Essex House. Hatfield House, Cecil papers 78/76.

14. For the initial letter to the queen see Walter Bouchier, *Lives and letters of the Devereaux, earls of Essex* (London, 1853) 2 vols., vol. II, pp. 125–26. For the subsequent crawling apology see T[he] N[ational] A[rchives], P[ublic] R[ecord] O[ffice], S.P. 16/275, fol. 136r., Essex to the Queen, 4 October 1600.

15. N.E. McClure, ed., *The letters of John Chamberlain* (Philadelphia, 1939) 2 vols., vol. 1, p. 89, Chamberlain to Carleton, 10 October 1600.

16. T.N.A., P.R.O. S.P. 12/ 275, fol. 143r. John Chamberlain to Dudley Carleton, 10 October, 1600. *Letters of John Chamberlain,* vol. I, pp. 90–93].

17. See Kastan, 'Killed with hard opinions', p. 213, where he observes that 'no one has put forth any credible motive for the pragmatic Shakespeare to engage in such uncharacteristically imprudent behaviour', p. 213, and White, 'Shakespeare and the Cobhams', p. 86, where he similarly remarks that 'Shakespeare was too much of a pragmatist' to 'adopt any political or religious allegiance'. Since we only know that Shakespeare was such a 'pragmatist' because he did not take risks like these, there is more than a risk here of a perfectly circular argument whereby the established 'fact' of Shakespeare's 'pragmatism' is used to rule out of court any evidence that he might have behaved in ways which do not seem to us 'pragmatic' enough for Shakespeare. But what if, as he clearly did (more than once) over the Oldcastle fuss, Shakespeare did indeed take such risks? We are in danger of arriving here at a situation in which, when Shakespeare's behaviour does not accord with some pre-existing notion of his character, it must be either discounted or explained away.

18. Gary Taylor details other examples of Shakespeare knowingly playing on the fact that everyone knew that the fat knight was (still) Sir John Falstaff in 'The fortunes of Falstaff', p. 96.

Chapter 17: Oldcastle *redivivus*

1. I cite from the edition in Peter Corbin and Douglas Sedge, eds, *The Oldcastle controversy* (Manchester, 1991); for the date see p. 9.

2. W.J.D. Cargill-Thompson, 'Sir Francis Knolly's campaign against the *jure divino* theory of episcopacy', in C.R Cole and M.E. Moody, eds, *The dissenting tradition* (Athens, OH, 1975), pp. 39–77.

3. Richard McCabe, 'Elizabethan satire and the Bishops' Ban of 1599', *The Yearbook of English Studies*, 11 (1981), pp. 188–93, which reprints the text of the ban on p. 188, and stresses

throughout the political, rather than the moral, impulses underlying the ban. Now see idem, ' "Right puisante and terrible priests": the role of the Anglican Church in Elizabethan state censorship', in Andrew Hadfield, ed., *Literature and censorship in Renaissance England* (Basingstoke, 2001), pp. 75–94. Also see Cyndia Clegg, *Press censorship in Elizabethan England* (Cambridge, 1997), chapter 9.

4. I owe this point to Professor Heather James.

Chapter 18: The state we're in

1. A.D. Nuttall, *Shakespeare the thinker*, pp. 151–52, 165.
2. See Robert Miola, 'Julius Caesar and the tyrannicide debate', *Renaissance Quarterly*, 38 (1985), pp. 271–89.
3. For the claim that one of the central features of Shakespeare's discussion of Roman politics was the fact that they took place in carefully delineated pagan contexts see J.L. Simons, *Shakespeare's pagan world: the Roman tragedies* (Charlottesville, 1973).
4. I am referring here to the rise in interest in the England of the 1590s in both Stoic and neo-stoic philosophy and in Tacitean politic history. These represented particular developments of the more general tendency inherent within the humanist education of the Elizabethan elite to read classical texts for action; seeking to extract from a body of literary, philosophical and historical works, sententiae, maxims and exempla for emulation, that is to say for direct application to the moral and political cruxes and dilemmas of the present. On this, amongst a vast array of recent work on the vogue for neo-Stoicism, see Geoffrey Miles, *Shakespeare and the constant Romans* (Oxford, 1996). On Tacitean history see Malcolm Smuts, 'Court-centered politics and the uses of Roman historians, c.1590–1630', in K. Sharpe and P. Lake, eds, *Culture and politics in early Stuart England* (London, 1994), pp. 21–43; David Womersley, 'Sir Henry Savile's translation of Tacitus and the political interpretation of Elizabethan texts', *Review of English Studies*, 42 (1991), pp. 313–42. Now see the definitive account in Alex Gajda, *The earl of Essex*, chapter 6. For an important corrective to the conventional view and the best account of the contemporary political and ideological resonances of Sir Henry Savile's Taciteanism now see Paulina Kewes, 'Henry Savile's Tacitus and the politics of Roman history in late Elizabethan England', *Huntington Library Quarterly*, 74 (2011), pp. 515–51.
5. On the concept of neo-Roman notions of liberty and their prevalence in this period see Quentin Skinner, *Liberty before liberalism* (Cambridge, 1999).
6. See, for instance, Miola, 'Julius Caesar and the tyrannicide debate'; Irving Ribner, 'Political issues in *Julius Caesar*', *Journal of English and German Philology*, 56 (1957), pp. 10–22.

Chapter 19: The politics of honour (in a popular state)

1. See Vawter's '*Julius Caesar* : rupture in the bond', *Journal of English and Germanic Philology*, 72 (1973), pp. 311–28, quote p. 320.
2. Tom McAlindon sees this as a 'symbolic violation of her sexual identity'. Coppelia Kahn goes further, arguing that 'the site of Portia's wound, in her thigh, hints ambiguously at a genital wound – what psychoanalysis would take to be the wound of castration'. Thus, 'seeking to articulate symbolically the dominant masculine ideal of constancy, she also evokes ideals of femininity' and gestures towards the later act of self-harm with which she will end her own life. T. McAlindon, *Shakespeare's tragic cosmos* (Cambridge, 1991), p. 87; Kahn, *Roman Shakespeare*, p. 101.
3. Coppelia Kahn, *Roman Shakespeare*, p. 88.
4. Geoffrey Miles, *Shakespeare and the constant Romans*, p. 54.
5. As Miles observes, Caesar's speech 'combines the connotations of Seneca's two images of constancy: the rock and the God'. Caesar is, in short, claiming to be 'more than human', but while he thinks of himself as semi-divine, his own words reveal him to be something else altogether. 'Ice cold and stone hard, Caesar represents himself as the monstrous Stoic-stock of the anti-Stoic tradition'. Miles, *Constant Romans*, p. 134.
6. In his *The myth of Rome in Shakespeare and his contemporaries* (Cambridge, 2011) Warren Chernaik follows the general trend in recent criticism, which he describes as a 'tendency to treat Brutus with hostility, even disdain', speaking almost offhandedly of 'Brutus' habitual self-delusion' and describing this soliloquy as merely 'one of several instances of self-delusion

in Brutus'. Quotations at pp. 259, fn. 37, 83, 99. Andrew Hadfield goes even further, condemning the speech for not following the formal rules of rhetoric – what he terms 'the impure and eccentric nature of his argument' – even though, as he points out, Brutus' speech 'is not, of course, an oration as such' but a soliloquy. Andrew Hadfield, *Shakespeare and Republicanism* (Cambridge, 2005), pp. 180–81.

7. Anne Barton, '*Julius Caesar* and *Coriolanus*: Shakespeare's Roman world of words', in Philip Highfill, ed., *Shakespeare's craft* (Washington, 1982), pp. 24–47, quotation at pp. 43–4.
8. Gordon Ross Smith, 'Brutus, virtue and will', *Shakespeare Quarterly*, 10 (1959), pp. 367–79, quotations at pp. 373–74; Barton, '*Julius Caesar* and *Coriolanus*', p. 44.
9. Q.R.D. Skinner, *Liberty before liberalism*, pp. 45, 49.
10. For a brilliant interpretation of this scene in terms of the deployment of the figure of paradiastole see Quentin Skinner, 'Paradiastole: redistributing the virtues as vices', in Sylvia Adamson, Gavin Alexander and Katrin Ettenhuber, eds, *Renaissance figures of speech* (Cambridge, 2007), pp. 161–63. Ironically, in concluding that 'Brutus' victory is, however, a rhetorical one' and thus 'open to the danger that an orator adept at arguing in *utramque partem* may be capable of questioning and undermining his version of events', Skinner fails to notice that, in a genuinely republican (or perhaps, in his terms, "neo-Roman") moral and political universe, Brutus' victory would have been not merely rhetorical, but substantive, indeed, definitive. In revealing that Brutus' position is, in fact, contestable the play also acknowledges that Rome (and, perhaps, by implication, Elizabethan England) is, by this point, no longer, in any simple sense of the word, even a monarchical republic. In Skinner-world, as indeed in Shakespeare's world and perhaps even in the 'real' world, it would appear that 'rhetoric' wins out over 'republicanism' every time.
11. John Velz, 'Clemency, will and just cause in *Julius Caesar*', *Shakespeare Survey*, 22 (1969), pp. 109–18, quote at p. 112.
12. See the fine discussion of this speech by A.D. Nuttall, *Shakespeare the thinker*, pp. 180–83; Nuttall is here refining and defending the position adopted in his *A new mimesis* from the critique of Will Poole, ' "Unpointed words": Shakespearean syntax in action', *Cambridge Quarterly*, 32 (2003), pp. 27–48.
13. Thus Schanzer gets it precisely wrong when he asserts that 'Shakespeare's Brutus is by no means a doctrinaire republican' for whom 'Caesar's desire for the crown' does not 'in itself appear sufficient cause' to kill him. He is rather a doctrinaire republican with scruples; scruples which he tries to alleviate by certain *ad hominem* arguments against Caesar, arguments which he ends up dismissing in favour of the 'doctrinaire republican' position with which he started. For Brutus what is at stake *is* republican principle and thus for him the killing of Caesar is a wholly political act. See Ernest Schanzer, *The problem plays of Shakespeare* (New York, 1965), p. 55.
14. John Velz, 'Clemency, will and just cause in *Julius Caesar*', p. 111. 'Shakespeare portrays in him [Caesar] the kind of tyrant Seneca is concerned with in *De Clementia*. Seneca's tyrant acts *in voluptatem*, feeding the pleasure of his own will, without regard to just cause. Despite his protestations of constancy in the moments before his death, Caesar is a man of arbitrary and changeable will.'
15. John Velz '*Orator* and *imperator* in *Julius Caesar*'; style and the process of Roman history', *Shakespeare Studies*, 15 (1982), 55–75, quote at pp. 65–66; on rhetoric, its role and effects in the play, also see Gayle Greene, ' "The power of speech/to stir men's blood": the language of tragedy in Shakespeare's Julius Caesar', *Renaissance Drama* (Evanston, 1980), pp. 67–93 and Anne Barton, '*Julius Caesar* and *Coriolanus*: Shakespeare's Roman world of words', in Philip Highfill, ed., *Shakespeare's Craft* (Washington, 1982), pp. 24–47.
16. A point made forcibly by Hadfield, *Shakespeare and republicanism*, where he observes at p. 178 that 'the central feature of the republic at its height was rhetoric, the public art of persuasion, enabling listeners to weigh up evidence on either side of any argument and choose the right way forward'.
17. Velz, 'Orator and imperator in Julius Caesar', p. 112.
18. J.L. Simmons, *Shakespeare's pagan world* (Charlottesville, 1973), p. 99.
19. Wayne Rebhorn, 'The crisis of the aristocracy in *Julius Caesar*', pp. 78, 109.
20. Cf. J.L. Simmons' claim that 'Brutus' fear of the crown is, in John Palmer's words, "a pedantic horror of kingship".' See his *Shakespeare's pagan world*, p. 80.
21. C. Kahn, *Roman Shakespeare* (London, 1997), p. 88.
22. Miles, *Constant Romans*, p. 126. For the tensions within the Stoic ideal of constancy referred to here see ibid., chapters 2 and 3.

Chapter 20: Performing honour and the politics of popularity (in a popular state)

1. Miles, *Constant Romans*, pp. 136, 51–53, quote at p. 52.
2. J. Velz, 'The ancient world in Shakespeare; authenticity or anachronism? A retrospect', *Shakespeare Survey*, 31 (1982), pp. 1–12, quote at p. 10.
3. Miles, *Constant Romans*, p. 141.
4. Ibid., p. 140.
5. Ibid., chapter 4, 'Constancy and opinion; Renaissance neo-stoicism' and pp. 135–40.
6. Ibid., p. 139, where Miles speaks of 'the corruption of self-knowledge by "opinion". From now on, Brutus will, as Cassius wishes, have to be governed by "that opinion of [him]self/Which every noble Roman bears of [him]" '.
7. The binary choice between slavery and freedom, and the equivalence between those states and a Rome with Caesar alive and one with him dead, can only be characterised, in Schanzer's phrase, as 'quite unreal', or in Chernaik's as 'fallacious', if these basic republican premises are ignored. Thus 'Brutus' oratory' is not being used here to hide from the people fatal flaws or obvious gaps in his argument, but rather to exploit what he assumes are their basic commitments to his own version of republican principle in order to legitimise what would otherwise appear to be a savage and ungrateful act. Schanzer, *Problem plays*, p. 48; Chernaik, *Myth of Rome*, p. 83.
8. Chernaik, *Myth of Rome*, p. 83.
9. Gayle Greene quite accurately describes Brutus' speech as 'a brilliant piece of oratory', which emerges from her analysis as a rhetorically sophisticated attempt to win the support of the people, and as such a typical product of Roman republican culture. Gayle Green, ' "The power of speech/To stir men's blood" ', esp. pp. 82–85. Also see Schanzer, *The problem plays*, p.47; 'I cannot agree with commentators who speak of Brutus' oration as an example of political naïveté, of the scholar's inability to understand the common people or to present his case effectually. It seems to me, on the contrary, an extremely shrewd and highly effective piece of oratory.' The best analysis of the rhetorical workings of both Brutus' speech and Antony's response is now Quentin Skinner, *Forensic Shakespeare* (Oxford, 2014), pp. 110–17.
10. Velz, 'Orator and imperator in *Julius Caesar*', p. 56.
11. Sigurd Burckhardt, *Shakespearean meanings* (Princeton, 1968), pp. 8–9.
12. Greene, 'Language of tragedy in *Julius Caesar*', p. 87.
13. Ibid. p, 86.
14. Sigurd Burckhardt might be thought to be evoking much the same sense of dislocation and anachronism, albeit in relentlessly aesthetic or stylistic, rather than political and historical, terms, when he claims that if Cassius and Brutus are thought of 'as manifestly they think of themselves', that is, as 'plotters in the dramatic sense, men who have decided to author and produce a tragedy entitled "Julius Caesar"', then their moral and political choices can be seen as a function of an 'ideal of style', a preference for 'a tragedy of classical, almost Aristotelian, purity'. Burckhardt, *Shakespearean meanings* (Princeton, 1968), pp. 8–9.
15. Schanzer, *Problem plays*, p. 36.

Chapter 21: The politics of popularity and faction (in a popular state)

1. As Miles has shown, this is not the only meaning to be extracted from these densely compressed, ambiguous and finely balanced lines.
2. Alexander Leggatt, *Shakespeare's political drama* (London, 1988), p. 146.
3. Simmons, *Shakespeare's pagan world*, p. 101. 'Although Antony's oration is consciously directed to the emotions, he offers as much reason as Brutus, perhaps more. At least Antony cites specific actions and details for support, whereas Brutus' argument . . . fails to reckon with the facts.'
4. See, for instance, Ann Barton's censorious verdict on Brutus. 'The man who pretends, in Act IV, that he does not know about his wife's death, purely in order to impress Messala with the superhuman fortitude of the hero encountering pain, also tries to delude himself that the conspiracy is a kind of holy league.' Barton, 'Shakespeare's Roman world of words' p. 45.
5. Gordon Ross Smith, 'Brutus, virtue and will', *Shakespeare Quarterly*, 10 (1959), pp. 367–79.
6. Moody Prior, 'The search for a hero in *Julius Caesar*', *Renaissance Drama* (Evanston, 1969), pp. 81–101, quote at p. 94.
7. Kahn, *Roman Shakespeare*, p. 96. However, as the current account is designed to show, the contradictions involved here are not limited to those Kahn discerns operating 'between republican virtue and Roman emulation'.

8. Simmons, *Shakespeare's pagan world*, p. 104. Thus, *pace* Kahn and Rebhorn, it is not the case that the play reveals that the practice of 'emulation', the struggle to imitate and surpass the achievements and virtues both of one's ancestors and one's contemporaries, inevitably produces rivalries so unappeasable that they can only be ended either by civil war or the establishment of monarchical power. Rather, on the republican side, 'emulation', described by Rebhorn as 'an unstable combination of identification and rivalry, love and hate', has in fact served to confer a stable form of moral primacy and political leadership on Brutus, one quite unlike that claimed by and ceded to Caesar on the monarchical side of the argument. In that sense the play does delineate distinctly republican and monarchical forms of political authority, although, in the very particular moral and political circumstances staged by the play, it can hardly be said either to endorse the moral legitimacy or to underwrite the political efficacy of either. (See Kahn, *Roman Shakespeare*, pp. 216-17, 90 and Rebhorn, 'Crisis of the aristocracy', p. 77.)

9. Prior, 'The search for a hero in *Julius Caesar*'.

10. Gayle Greene, ' "The power of speech/To stir men's blood" ', pp. 70-71.

11. See, for instance, Rene Fortin, '*Julius Caesar*: an experiment in point of view', *Shakespeare Quarterly*, 19 (1968), pp. 341-47. '*Julius Caesar* becomes a richer play, more complex and more universal in its significance, if it is interpreted as an exploration of man's epistemological situation . . . Shakespeare, attuned to his times, seems to be dramatising the "new" skepticism about human reason that is set forth, for example, by Montaigne.' Quote at p. 346.

12. As McAlindon observes, 'one of the inevitable consequences of living in so changeful an environment is deep uncertainty'. T. McAlindon, *Shakespeare's tragic cosmos*, p. 95. As Miles puts the case, 'Rome itself is in a process of change from an old to a new order. The characters attempt to control this process, but we know in hindsight that their predictions are wrong and their actions tragically misguided; they move and act in darkness, unsure of anything.' Miles, *Constant Romans*, p. 128. McAlindon describes essentially the same predicament in more formal terms, when he sees the play structured, in part, by an antinomy between 'constancy' and 'change'. As he puts it, 'both Caesar and Brutus seek by their constancy to transcend change', and, we might add, to control events and shape the state. McAlindon, *Tragic cosmos*, p. 92.

13. In a famous passage Sigurd Burckhardt noted that much of the byplay about time – the uncertainty of the characters in the garden about what time it was and where the sun would rise – reflects their incapacity to judge the times in which they are living and therefore to know what timely political action might amount to. 'Brutus,' he concludes, 'is not guilty of treachery, nor of having embraced an inherently wrong political philosophy; he is guilty of an anachronism', an anachronism that, Burckhardt claims, Shakespeare signalled by having the clock strike at the very moment when Brutus has persuaded the conspirators to adopt his self-consciously antique and republican version of their conspiracy. 'The clock, striking as soon as he has irrevocably committed himself to the Old Style, signifies to us – though not to him – that time is now reckoned in a new, Caesarean style.' Burckhardt, *Shakespearean meanings*, pp. 5-9, quote at p. 9. On this account, Kahn and Rebhorn's tendency to see the play as a demonstration that the collapse of the republic and the rise of monarchy were inevitable products of the internal contradictions within the republican honour system and the rhetorical politics that fuelled that system underestimates the specificity of the play's historical setting and the centrality of issues of timing to its argument and structure.

Chapter 22: The politics of prodigy, prophecy and providence (in a pagan state)

1. On the ubiquity of providence in both the cheap print and indeed the mainstream theology of the day see Alexandra Walsham, *Providence in early modern England* (Oxford, 1999).

2. For a reading of the play as feeding off or assimilating itself to the revenge tragedy see Rabkin, *Shakespeare and the common understanding* (New York, 1967), pp. 114-19.

3. Norman Rabkin claims that Brutus' act of violence 'has automatically removed from history the feasibility of that high-minded governance to which he dedicates his life'. 'Because of his crime against the established order', Brutus has created a world in which 'success will go to the calculating'; in which 'one's chances for survival are in direct proportion to one's skill at seizing the main chance', and in which 'moral passion is of no value'. 'In the long range,' he concludes, 'both men [Brutus and Cassius] succumb to a historical process over which they have no control [but which, we might add, their own actions have, if not initiated, then very considerably intensified], while success goes . . . to the opportunist.' Rabkin, *Shakespeare and*

the common understanding, pp. 116, 118. Much is lost in the seeming transparency and seductive neutrality of the term 'established order' since the play has invested a great deal of time and energy into showing just how difficult it was in Caesar's Rome, and perhaps, by implication and application, in Elizabethan England as well, to discern just what 'the established order' was or meant and what the preservation of that 'order' demanded of its adherents. Moreover, the play has established that in Caesarean Rome, as perhaps in Elizabethan England, there is precious little room for 'high minded governance' of any sort. It is only by paying close attention to the specificities of the historical conjuncture being staged in the play, and indeed of the historical conjuncture during which the play was first written and staged, that the full resonance and subtlety of its discussion of these issues can be retrieved.

Chapter 23: Conclusion: between *Henry V* and *Hamlet*

1. Alex Gajda, *The earl of Essex,* pp. 35–37.
2. Here the play might be thought to anticipate and ventriloquise divisions that emerged within the Essex circle after his return from Ireland when, according to Alex Gajda, 'two factions had arisen around the earl during his political disgrace; one counselling action, the other "the course held by right noble Lord Harry [Howard]" which focused on the restoration of Essex's access through legitimate and pacific means.' Gajda, *The earl of Essex,* p. 60. Viewed in terms of that subsequent debate, the play might be thought to have anticipated the moderate and legitimist case.
3. On these incidents see Gary Taylor, 'Bardicide', in Tetsuo Kishi, Roger Pringle and Stanley Wells, *Shakespeare and cultural traditions* (Newark, 1992), pp. 333–49.
4. Richard McCoy, *The rites of knighthood: the literature and politics of Elizabethan chivalry* (Berkeley, 1989); Paul Hammer, '"Upstaging the Queen": the earl of Essex, Francis Bacon, and the Accession Day celebrations of 1595'; Gajda, *The earl of Essex.*
5. Gajda, The *earl of Essex,* pp. 46–52, 56–58, and chapter 6.
6. Malcolm Smuts, 'Court-centered politics and the uses of Roman historians, *c.*1590–1630'; J.M.H. Salmon, 'Seneca and Tacitus in Jacobean England' in Linda Levy Peck, ed., *The mental world of the Jacobean court* (Cambridge, 1991), pp. 169–88; 321–26; A.T. Bradford, 'Stuart absolutism and the utility of Tacitus,' *Huntington Library Quarterly,* 46 (1983), pp. 127–55. David Womersley, 'Sir Henry Savile's translation of Tacitus and the political interpretation of Elizabethan texts'. Fritz Levy, 'Hayward, Daniel, and the beginning of politic history in England'. Perhaps the best single study of Tacitean historiography in this period is now to be found in Paulina Kewes, 'Henry Savile's Tacitus and the politics of Roman history in late Elizabethan England'. Also see Gajda, *The earl of Essex.*
7. John J. Manning, ed., *The first and second parts of John Hayward's The life and raigne of king Henrie IIII,* Camden Society, 4th series, 42 (London, 1991), p. 61.
8. For the extent of Hayward's debt to Tacitus see Lisa Richardson, 'Sir John Hayward and early Stuart historiography' (University of Cambridge, Ph.D. dissertation, 1999).
9. Thus Coppelia Kahn has pointed out how 'Portia and Calphurnia worry and warn husbands who actually share at least some of their fears but who, once those fears are voiced by women, gain as it were an heroic warrant to override them and act in accordance with "masculine" virtue.' Kahn, *Roman Shakespeare,* p. 99.

Chapter 24: *Hamlet*

1. Andrew Gurr, *The Shakespeare Company,* p. 15.
2. Indeed as Anthony Low has pointed out, while Hamlet might have been transfixed by the appearance of his father's shade, the one thing this has not led him to do, or even to think of doing, is to pray for it. Aside from revenging him, Hamlet seems to think that there is nothing that he can do either to ameliorate his father's condition or alter his fate. 'Though the ghost plainly comes from Purgatory, and says so in terms as explicit as may be, short of an open declaration, neither Hamlet nor any of the younger Danes ever openly reveals that he has heard of such a place as Purgatory. As was the case with England, so in Hamlet's Denmark. Purgatory is not just abolished but effectively forgotten, as if it never were.' Anthony Low, 'Hamlet and the Ghost of Purgatory: intimations of killing the Father', *English Literary Renaissance,* 29 (1999), pp. 443–67, quote at p. 459.
3. Andras Kisery, *Hamlet's moment* (Oxford, 2016).

4. Thus in *The wheel of fire* (London, 1956), p. 36, G. Wilson Knight asks 'which then, at this moment in the play, is nearer the Kingdom of Heaven?' Robert G. Hunter, *Shakespeare and the mysteries of God's judgments*, p. 114; de Grazia, *Hamlet without Hamlet*, pp. 193–94.

5. In his *Hamlet and the acting of revenge* (Basingstoke, 1987) Peter Mercer consistently deploys the notions of 'fortune', 'chance' or 'fate' when discussing this aspect of the play. For instance, of Hamlet's refusal to kill Claudius at prayer, he observes 'that this moment of ironic frustration marks the beginning of the process whereby he [Shakespeare] employs, again and again, the chances of Fortune to rescue his hero from the annihilating necessities of revenge, to preserve him for some far more resonant end' (p. 216). Or again on p. 224, where he observes that 'as a revenger Hamlet was weighed down with the burden of an intolerable responsibility, but now, as the victim of another's plot he is free to engage with the chances of Fate'. Or again, at p. 237, he describes Hamlet's rescue by the pirate ship as 'this new movement of Fortune'. 'Shakespeare . . . makes the escape of his hero as fortuitous as possible. The pirate ship comes out of nowhere but his own desire, like a device in a romance. As we have noted already, chance in tragedy is usually fatal, not in the least obliging . . . But here chance brings a ship full of "thieves of mercy" from over the horizon to pluck the hero from his doom.' There is nothing innocent or inadvertent about Mercer's choice of key terms here; rather it underpins what remains, for all its acuity, the consistently 'secular' or a-religious tenor of his analysis. Not, of course, that an analysis of such events in terms of 'fortune' was unavailable to Shakespeare, to his protagonist, Hamlet, or indeed to the play's first audiences. It is just that the play itself does nothing to induce such a reading of events and Hamlet himself seems entirely free from any such hermeneutic tendency or temptation.

6. P.K. Ayers. 'Reading, writing and *Hamlet*', *Shakespeare Quarterly*, 44 (1993), pp. 423–39, quotation at p. 432.

7. See James Shapiro, *1599: a year in the life of William Shakespeare* (London, 2005), pp. 350–51.

8. Neill, 'Revenge tragedy', p. 336.

9. Peter Ure, *Elizabethan and Jacobean drama: critical essays*, ed. J.C. Maxwell (Liverpool, 1974), pp. 40, 42.

10. See Angus Gowland, *The worlds of renaissance melancholy* (Cambridge, 2006), pp. 175–76, and more generally Jeremy Schmidt, *Melancholy and the cure of the soul* (Basingstoke, 2007), chapter 3, 'Melancholy in Calvinist England'.

11. De Grazia, *Hamlet without Hamlet*, pp. 193–94.

12. Ibid.

13. Karin Coddon, ' "Suche Strange Desyns": madness, subjectivity and treason in *Hamlet* and Elizabethan culture', *Renaissance Drama*, n.s. vol. 20 (1989), pp. 51–75, quote at p. 51.

14. Ibid., p. 52.

15. Ibid., p. 55.

16. Cf. de Grazia, *Hamlet without Hamlet*, 'for Shakespeare's prince, the ruse of being *non compos mentis* does more than deflect suspicion. It gives Hamlet license to express equivocally what it would have been fatal to express directly: his resentment at having been defrauded of his imperial expectation' (p. 175). Also see Mercer's comments on Hamlet's behaviour after the murder of Polonius, 'he acts out all his witty brutality because it is safer to parade the dangerous irresponsibility of the mad man than to admit that he killed Polonius because he thought he was the King'. *Hamlet and the acting of revenge*, p. 227.

17. Ann Thompson and Neal Taylor, eds, *Hamlet, the texts of 1603 and 1623* (Arden, 3rd ser., London, 2006), p. 101, note on l. 271, p. 243, note on ll.328–60, p. 243, note on line 340.

18. Leeds Barroll, 'A new history for Shakespeare and his time', *Shakespeare Quarterly*, 39 (1988), pp. 441–64.

19. Shapiro, *1599*, pp. 325–26. 'It's one of the keys to understanding what makes Hamlet so distinctive: even as he paints over an earlier work of art, Shakespeare allows traces of what's been whitewashed to remain visible.'

Chapter 25: The morning after the night before

1. For the prevalence of the Brutus myth and its late sixteenth-century meaning see Matthew Greenfield, 'Fragments of nationalism in *Troilus and Cressida*', *Shakespeare Quarterly*, 51 (2000), pp. 181–200, esp. pp. 184–87.

2. Richard Levin, *New readings versus old plays* (Chicago, 1979), pp. 97–98 and esp. 209–29, Appendix, 'The figures of Fluellen'.

3. On Williams see the article in *ODNB*.

4. For comments on the contrast between the role of the chorus in *Henry V* and *Troilus and Cressida* see Harry Berger, Jr, '*Troilus and Cressida*: the observer as basilisk', *Comparative Drama*, pp. 122–36.

5. R. Weimann, *Shakespeare and the popular tradition in the theatre* (Baltimore, 1978), pp. 227, 228, 236.

6. G. Bradshaw, *Shakespeare's scepticism*, pp. 137–38.

7. Linda Charnes, ' "So unsecret to ourselves": notorious identity and the material subject in Shakespeare's *Troilus and Cressida*', *Shakespeare Quarterly*, 40 (1989), pp. 413–40, quotations at pp. 418, 419, 420.

8. The phrase is Charnes', ibid., p. 414.

9. See the brilliant article by David Norbrook, 'Rhetoric, ideology and the Elizabethan world picture', in Peter Mack, ed., *Renaissance rhetoric* (Basingstoke, 1994), pp. 140–64.

10. In this mode, David J. Baker even goes so far as to claim that 'Shakespeare and his company of merchant thespians' were attempting in this play to take 'one of the most anxiety-producing, deeply embedded problems in the contemporary marketplace and to stage it as entertainment'. See Baker, *On demand* (Stanford, 2010) p. 74.

11. Ibid., p. 79.

12. See p. 17 of Bevington's introduction to the new Arden edition of the play, where he asserts (as self-evident) the 'fact' that 'the decline of feudal aristocracy in the late sixteenth century was synchronous with an increase in bourgeois mercantalism. Clinging to an outmoded feudal ideology and to the orthodoxies of an unchanging social order based on order and degree, those who ruled medieval England found themselves displaced to an ever increasing extent by new wealth'. On this view the 'insistent commercial metaphors of *Troilus* . . . reflect unease in late Tudor England over social change' and insofar as the play does evoke or concern itself with Essexian echoes and themes it does so chiefly because 'Essex was the personification' of the 'beleaguered chivalry' of a declining feudal aristocracy. Thus can the clichés of a long-dead social history be invoked to underwrite a reading of this most political of plays that is largely devoid of either political context or analysis.

13. Lars Engle, *Shakespearean pragmatism: market of his time* (Chicago, 1993), pp. 155–56.

14. Baker, *On demand*, p. 84.

15. On this subject in general see Simon Adams, in his *Leicester and the court: essays on Elizabethan politics*. On Leicester see Adams' article in *ODNB*. On the disastrous impact of service to the crown on the both short- and long-term finances of the earls of Huntingdon see Claire Cross, *The puritan earl: the life of Henry Hastings, 3rd earl of Huntingdon, 1536–95* (London, 1966) and Tom Cogswell, *Home divisions: aristocracy, the state and provincial conflict* (Manchester, 1998).

16. On the Cecils and, in particular, Robert Cecil, see Lawrence Stone, 'The fruits of office', in F.J. Fisher, ed., *Essays in the economic and social history of Tudor and Stuart England, in honour of R.H. Tawney* (Cambridge, 1961) and at greater length in Stone's *Family and fortune: studies in aristocratic finance in the 16th and 17th centuries* (Oxford, 1979).

17. Paul Hammer, *The polarisation of Elizabethan politics*, pp. 277, 94, fn.110, 226–27.

18. T.N.A. P.R.O. S.P. 12/275, fol. 143r. Chamberlain to Carleton; N.E. McClure, ed., *The letters of John Chamberlain* (Philadelphia, 1939) 2 vols., vol. I, pp. 90–93.

19. Susan Doran and Paulina Kewes, eds, *Doubtful and dangerous*. Also see Gajda, *Earl of Essex*, chapters 1 and 3.

20. For two extensive accounts of the language of the market and of credit in the play, to which the preceding discussion is much indebted, see chapter 4 of David Baker's *On demand*, 'William Shakespeare's *Troilus and Cressida*: credit risks' and chapter 7 of Lars Engle's *Shakespearean pragmatism*, 'Always already on the market: the politics of evaluation in *Troilus and Cressida*'.

21. M. A. Kishlansky, 'The emergence of adversary politics in the Long Parliament', *Journal of Modern History*, 49 (1977), pp. 617–40; *Parliamentary Selection: social and political choice in early modern England* (Cambridge, 1986).

22. Baker's astute comment is thus that, in these exchanges, 'Hector and Troilus are claiming just the opposite of what they are usually said to be claiming'. Baker, *On demand*, p. 80.

23. Berger, '*Troilus and Cressida*: the observer as basilisk', p. 129. Baker echoes Berger almost word for word; 'as they argue further, it becomes clear that what we are witnessing is more Troilus' attempt to make Hector work out rationally the position he shares with him than the other way round.' Baker, *On demand*, p. 81.

24. And thus, insofar as David J. Baker is right that 'readers have been prone to insist . . . that this Trojan debate is really about a debate about markets and the sort of value they promote', such readers have been mistaken. Ibid., p. 79.

25. In short they are engaged in a process of rhetorical argument of the sort brilliantly explicated in the play by David Norbrook in his 'Rhetoric, ideology and the Elizabethan world picture'.

26. Baker, *On demand*, p. 84.

27. Ibid., p. 82. Harry Berger pushes these antinomies about as far as they will go, indeed perhaps slightly farther than the play itself pushes them, when he claims that for Troilus 'it is necessary to assert Helen's intrinsic worthlessness or irrelevance' since 'only in this way can the heroic imagination test its premises and set about finding the proper grounds of quarrel in a straw'. '*Troilus and Cressida*: the observer as basilisk', p. 129.

28. As Mallin observes, 'both Greek and Trojan camps recollect contemporary political acts and structures; both sides, and their transactions, establish compelling circuits of text and world. The Trojans in the play are coextensive with the Greeks in their referentiality; they simply evoke other aspects of a specifically Elizabethan dissolution. Troy differs in the heavier *ideological* freight of its representations' ('Emulous factions and the collapse of chivalry: *Troilus and Cressida*, *Representations*, 29 (1990), p. 145–179, quotation at p. 154).

29. Patricia Thomson, 'Rant and cant in *Troilus and Cressida*', *Essays and Studies* (London, England), 22 (1969), pp. 33–56.

30. As Gayle Greene observes, Ulysses' contradiction of his own stated principles here parallels almost exactly that of Hector: 'Ulysses preaches a philosophy of degree which he violates within the same scene, and which he later contradicts, when he advises Achilles that value is subjectively conferred; as, in the Trojan council scene, Hector argues to end the war, then immediately agrees to a position that makes a mockery of his own argument.' Gayle Greene, 'Language and value in Shakeseare's *Troilus and Cressida*', *Studies in English Literature, 1500–1900*, 21 (1981), 271–85, quotation at p. 280.

31. Alice Shalvi, ' "Honour" in *Troilus and Cressida*' in *Studies in English Literature, 1500–1900*, 5 (1965), pp. 282–302; Jean Gagen, 'Hector's honour', *Shakespeare Quarterly*, 19 (1968), pp. 129–37.

32. C.C. Barfoot, '*Troilus and Cressida*: "Praise us as we are tasted" ', *Shakespeare Quarterly*, 39 (1988), pp. 45–57, quotation at p. 49.

33. Mallin, 'Emulous factions', p. 168.

34. On this see for instance ibid., pp. 149–50.

35. Ibid., pp. 166–67; James Savage, '*Troilus and Cressida* and Elizabethan court factions', *University of Mississippi Studies in English*, 5 (1964), pp. 43–66.

36. McCoy, *Rites of knighthood*. Paul Hammer, '"Upstaging the Queen": the earl of Essex, Francis Bacon, and the Accession Day celebrations of 1595'.

37. Paul Hammer, *The polarisation of Elizabethan politics*.

38. Thus Mallin observes that 'neither Achilles nor Hector is a monochrome block of separable signification' and speaks of having to see 'the configuration of Hector–Essex in simultaneous, both/and relation to that of Achilles–Essex', if 'the complex unity of the Essex inscription' embedded in the play is to be successfully 'excavated' (Mallin, 'Emulous factions', pp. 167, 168).

39. See Bruce Danner, *Edmund Spenser's war on Lord Burghley* (Basingstoke, 2011) and forthcoming work on Thomas Nashe by Jenny Anderson. I should like to thank Jenny for many discussions on this and related points about Nashe.

40. Cf. Linda Charnes' remarks that 'the kidnapping and holding of Helen is important only insofar as it enables several kinds of "commerce" between Greek and Trojan men. Helen (and Cressida) are the conduits through which these men form crucial political and psychological connections with each other'. How Helen 'serves both as enabler of conflict and as enabler of erotic commerce reveals her central signifying power in the play. But this power is not hers to wield. Rather, it is available to the men in the play to use on a number of different fronts in their own relations to each other. The "transcendent" Helen is, in fact, the arbitrary signifier that confers "degree" or distinction on the possessor.' Charnes, 'Notorious identity', pp. 424, 426.

41. Mallin, 'Emulous factions', p. 169. On this basis, Mallin suggests that portrayed, as they are, 'as deeply flawed and wholly contingent upon external (strictly male) valuation and control', Helen and Cressida might well be read as 'caricatural antitypes' of Queen Elizabeth herself.

42. Cf. Gayle Greene, 'Shakespeare's Cressida: "a kind of self" ', in Carlyn Rith Swift Lenz, Gayle Greene and Carol Thomas Neely, eds, *The woman's part: feminist criticism of Shakespeare* (University of Illinois Press, 1983), pp. 133–49.
43. Ibid., pp. 425–26.
44. Berger, '*Troilus and Cressida*: the observer as basilisk', p. 131.

Conclusion

1. Peter Lake, 'The politics of popularity and the public sphere: The "monarchical republic" of Elizabeth I defends itself'.
2. Peter Lake, *Bad Queen Bess?*.
3. Markku Peltonen, *Rhetoric, politics and popularity in pre-revolutionary England* (Cambridge, 2013).
4. Alex Gajda, 'Debating war and peace in late Elizabethan England'.
5. Noel Malcolm, *Reason of state, propaganda and the thirty years war* (Oxford, 2007), p. 93.
6. Lake, *Bad Queen Bess?*
7. See Kisery, *Hamlet's moment*.
8. Anthony Dawson and Paul Yachnin, *The culture of playgoing in Shakespeare's England* (Cambridge, 2001), esp. chapter 2, 'The populuxe theatre'; Kisery, *Hamlet's moment*.
9. Ongoing and forthcoming research by Noah Millstone on the circulation of manuscript separates in the early Stuart period is about to transform our knowledge of how such mechanisms worked and how such habits of mind were disseminated. I should like to thank Noah for many discussions of this topic and for many insights that have informed my argument in this book.
10. Tom Cogswell and I have provided a worked example of how this might work from a slightly later period in a study of a particular performance of Shakespeare and Fletcher's *Henry VIII* in 1628. See T. Cogswell and P. Lake, 'Buckingham does the Globe: *Henry VIII* and the politics of popularity in the 1620s', *Shakespeare Quarterly*, 60 (2009), pp. 253–78. For a similar study of the way changing political circumstances might change the meaning of a play see P. Lake, 'Ben Jonson and the politics of "conversion": *Catiline* and the relocation of Roman (Catholic) virtue', *The Ben Jonson Journal*, 19 (2012), pp. 163–89.
11. Paul Hammer, 'The smiling crocodile: the earl of Essex and late-Elizabethan "popularity" '; Idem, 'Myth making: politics, propaganda and the capture of Cadiz in 1596'; 'Upstaging the Queen: the earl of Essex, Francis Bacon and the Accession Day celebrations of 1595'. For the wider back ground see Lake, *Bad Queen Bess?*
12. Gajda, *Earl of Essex*, pp. 45–46; Arnold Hunt, 'Tuning the pulpits: the religious context of the Essex revolt' in Lori-Ann Ferrell and Peter McCullough, eds, *The English sermon revised* (Manchester, 2000), pp. 86–114.
13. Pauline Croft, 'Libels, popular literacy and public opinion in early modern England', *Historical Research*, 68 (1995), pp. 266–85. Idem, 'A collection of several speeches and treatises of the late Lord Treasurer Cecil, and of several observations of the Lords of the Council given to King James concerning his estate and revenue in the years 1608, 1609 and 1610', *Camden Miscellany*, Camden 4th series, 34 (Camden Miscellany 29), (London, 1987), pp. 245–317.
14. Alastair Bellany, *The politics of court scandal in early modern England: news culture and the Overbury affair, 1603–1660* (Cambridge, 2002).
15. Richard Cust, 'The public man in late Tudor and early Stuart England', in P. Lake and S. Pincus, eds, *The politics of the public sphere in early modern England* (Manchester, 2007), pp. 116–43. Idem, ' "Patriots" and "popular spirits": narratives of conflict in early Stuart politics', in Nicholas Tyacke, ed., *The English revolution, c.1590–1720* (Manchester, 2007), pp. 43–61.
16. Richard Cust, 'Charles I and popularity', in Tom Cogswell, Richard Cust and Peter Lake, eds, *Politics, religion and popularity in early Stuart Britain* (Cambridge, 2002), pp. 235–58.
17. Tom Cogswell, 'The people's love: the duke of Buckingham and popularity', in Cogswell, Cust and Lake, eds, *Politics, religion and popularity in early Stuart Britain*, 211–34.
18. Tom Cogswell ' "The return of the Deade Alive": the earl of Bristol and Dr Eglisham in the parliament of 1626 and in Caroline political culture', *English Historical Review*, 128 (2013) pp. 535–70.
19. Thomas Cogswell, 'Thomas Middleton and the court, 1624: "A Game at Chess" in context', *Huntington Library Quarterly*, 47 (1984), pp. 273–88.
20. Kisery, *Hamlet's moment*. Noah Millstone, *Manuscript circulation and the invention of politics in early Stuart England* (Cambridge, 2016).

21. I draw here on the seminal work of Leah Marcus on *1 Henry VI* and of Heather James on *Titus Andronicus*. See Marcus, *Puzzling Shakespeare,* chapter 2, 'Elizabeth', and Heather James, *Shakespeare's Troy* (Cambridge, 1997), pp. 57–58, 79–84.
22. Gajda, *The earl of Essex.*
23. Ibid., chapter 3.
24. Ibid., chapter 6.
25. For this point see Gary Taylor's brilliant article, 'Forms of opposition: Shakespeare and Middleton'.
26. Kevin Sharpe, *Criticism and compliment: the politics of literature in the England of Charles I* (Cambridge, 1987).
27. In that sense they might be taken to confirm the overarching argument of Kevin Sharpe's magisterial trilogy on images of power, the first volume of which, *Selling the Tudor monarchy* (New Haven and London, 2009), has been a looming presence over the present argument.
28. The phrase is Jonathan Bate's, see the title of chapter 14 of his *Soul of the age.*

Index